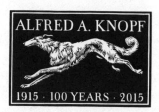

ALSO BY ZACHARY LEADER

Reading Blake's Songs
Writer's Block
Revision and Romantic Authorship
The Life of Kingsley Amis

EDITED BY ZACHARY LEADER
Romantic Period Writings, 1798–1832:
An Anthology
(with Ian Haywood)

The Letters of Kingsley Amis

On Modern British Fiction

Percy Bysshe Shelley: The Major Works
(with Michael O'Neill)

The Movement Reconsidered:
Essays on Larkin, Amis, Gunn, Davie,
and Their Contemporaries

The Life of Saul Bellow

The Life of
Saul Bellow

TO FAME AND FORTUNE,
1915–1964

Zachary Leader

ALFRED A. KNOPF New York
2015

THIS IS A BORZOI BOOK
PUBLISHED BY ALFRED A. KNOPF

Copyright © 2015 by Zachary Leader

All rights reserved. Published in the United States by Alfred A. Knopf,
a division of Penguin Random House LLC, New York,
and in Canada by Random House of Canada, a division
of Penguin Random House, Ltd., Toronto.

www.aaknopf.com

Knopf, Borzoi Books, and the colophon
are registered trademarks of Penguin Random House LLC.

Permissions acknowledgments can be found following the index.

Library of Congress Cataloging-in-Publication Data
Leader, Zachary, author.
The life of Saul Bellow : to fame and fortune, 1915–1964 /
by Zachary Leader.
pages cm
Includes bibliographical references and index.
ISBN 978-0-307-26883-9 (hardcover)—ISBN 978-1-101-87467-7 (eBook)
1. Bellow, Saul.   2. Novelists, American—20th century—Biography.
I. Title.
PS3503.E4488Z736 2015
813'.52—dc23
[B] 2014020092

Jacket photograph courtesy of the Saul Bellow Literary Estate
Jacket design by Carol Devine Carson

Manufactured in the United States of America
First Edition

To Alice

Contents

List of Illustrations

The Life of Saul Bellow

Introduction:
Bellow and Biography

Saul bellow was the most decorated writer in American history, the winner, among other awards, of the Nobel Prize for Literature, three National Book Awards, the Pulitzer Prize, the Formentor Prize, the American Academy of Arts and Letters Gold Medal for the Novel, and the titles Chevalier des Arts et des Lettres and Commandeur des Arts et des Lettres, awarded by the French Republic. At his death in 2005, as for much of his adult life, his standing in American literature could not have been higher.[1] On his deathbed, however, for a moment at least, none of this worldly acclaim mattered. As he slipped in and out of consciousness, Bellow opened his eyes, looked intently at his friend Eugene Goodheart, and asked: "Was I a man or was I a jerk?" "Jerk" is a Bellow word ("he always thought I was a jerk," Bellow has said of his father[2]); "man" here means "*mensch*," human being, someone to rely on, someone admirable, responsible, a person of character; being a *mensch* need have nothing to do with success, status, or wealth. What mattered at the end, Bellow's question implies, was the life he had led as a man.

The competing claims of life and art—the writer's "choice," according to Yeats—is a prominent theme in many biographies.[3] It was also a theme in Bellow's fiction, where it figures most obviously in his use of real-life episodes and characters, often only thinly disguised. In some novels and stories, people he knew, including friends and relations, were not only bound to see themselves depicted but they were meant to do so. "By the time I'm through with him," he is reported to have said of the model for Valentine Gersbach in *Herzog* (1964), "he'll be laughed right out of the literature business."[4] "I'll get you," he threatened his third wife, Susan, before he "loused her up" as the shrewish Denise in *Humboldt's Gift* (1975) ("I loved the way he loused up Sewell," comments Charlie Citrine, of Humboldt's depiction of a character based on R. P. Blackmur). "You've been a real Klondike," he told her; "I'll grind you to powder. Your name will be mud."[5] Bellow's fury in these instances (at the close friend who was cuckolding him, at the ex-wife he thought was bleeding him dry) was put to artistic use, though not without collateral damage. "My fictional life in a Bellow novel put me in the public domain," Susan Bellow wrote in an unpublished essay entitled "Mugging the Muse." "Not one of the outrageous questions over the years, however, asked about the dark heart of the matter. How does the prize winner's young and vulnerable son feel when asked in school if his mother is really so awful? Or when told by a buddy, who had the word from his mother, 'Don't read it. Your father did a number on your mom.'"[6] "I was horrified," writes one of the real-life models for Katrina Goliger, the mistress of Victor Wulpy, an unmistakable portrait of the art critic Harold Rosenberg, in the story "What Kind of a Day Did You Have?" On the eve of the story's appearance the real-life model was called by a friend who had read it and recognized her in Katrina: "I was dumbfounded . . . I never meant her to know." Bellow was Rosenberg's colleague and friend and was fully aware "that more than five years after Harold's death, May Rosenberg [his widow], and his daughter, Patia, were still very much alive. Not only were they still grieving—I was sure they were still furious enough with me about this."[7]

Bellow openly acknowledged the costs involved in such instances, to the user as well as the used. In *Humboldt's Gift*, Citrine, the Bellow-like protagonist, has made a fortune out of a play based on the character of his friend, the poet Von Humboldt Fleisher. "You took my personality and exploited it in writing your *Trenck*" (p. 338), protests Humboldt, a charge Citrine does not deny. Humboldt is himself based in large part on the poet Delmore Schwartz, whom Bellow met in the 1940s, when Schwartz worked at *Partisan Review*. By all accounts Schwartz was as brilliant and unstable a character as Humboldt is in Bellow's novel. Like Schwartz, Humboldt is manic-depressive, and in one of his manic moods, when he thinks Stevenson will defeat Eisenhower in the 1952 presidential election, he confides to Citrine that he expects to become a sort of cultural advisor in the new administration, in charge of sub-sidies and grants. In this, as in other respects, he recalls Falstaff ("the laws of England are at my commandment," Falstaff declares, when he wrongly thinks Henry IV dead), making Citrine a sort of Prince Hal, using and discarding Humboldt for a greater good ("art" rather than the state) or for ambition.[8]

This reading is bolstered by biographical fact: the Humboldt strand of the novel was born out of an incident in 1966 on a street in New York, when Bellow caught sight of the unhinged and impoverished Schwartz and hid from him (as Citrine hides from Humboldt in a similar scene in the novel). According to his friend Maggie Staats Simmons, who was with him at the time, Bellow was as distressed by his own behav-ior ("I know thee not, old man,"[9] says the newly elevated Henry) as by Schwartz's condition. When Schwartz passed by, Simmons told me, Bellow sat down with her and recounted what would become "pretty much the whole of the Humboldt part of *Humboldt's Gift*." The experi-ence was put to immediate use. Citrine's behavior as a writer is com-parable: "While I shed tears for my dead I was also patting down their graves with my shovel. For I did write biographies, and the deceased were my bread and butter. The deceased had earned my French decora-tion and got me into the White House" (p. 115). Those words report Denise's view, but elsewhere they are seconded by Citrine himself. "I did incorporate other people into myself and consume them. When they died I passionately mourned. I said I would continue their work and their lives. But wasn't it a fact that I added their strength to mine? Didn't I have an eye on them in the days of their vigor and glory?" (p. 282). The "gift" Humboldt gives Citrine, the literal gift, is a screen-play about a writer, Corcoran, whose "marvelous" book cannot be pub-lished because "it would hurt his wife and destroy his marriage." Yet "not to publish would kill him." "I have borrowed from you to create this Corcoran" (p. 338), Humboldt writes to Citrine.

BELLOW'S USE OF PEOPLE he knew, his responsibility toward them, the effect using them has on his character, figure as fictionalized top-ics throughout his writing, from *The Adventures of Augie March* (1953) (whose hero, "a Columbus of those near-at-hand," is nicknamed Bolingbroke, a user as ruthless and calculating as his son, Prince Hal) to *Ravelstein* (2000) (the fictional memoir of a figure as Falstaffian as

Humboldt). Augie is called "Bolingbroke" at the poker table: "I can't tell when you're bluffing because you always look so innocent. Nobody can really be as innocent as all that," a view Augie confirms: "My invention and special thing was simplicity. I wanted simplicity and denied complexity, and in this I was guileful and suppressed many patents in my secret heart."[10] Bolingbroke is comparably guileful. He may see his way to Richard's throne, as Hazlitt puts it, "afar off," but he bides his time, "only seizing it when he has it within reach, humble, crafty, bold, and aspiring."[11] These are accusations leveled at the writer-figures in Bellow's novels, among whom I would number Augie, the author, after all, of his adventures. It is not true, as Robert Penn Warren complained in an admiring review, that Augie "has no commitments"; the freedom he seeks is a writer's freedom, a detachment that allows him, as he puts it of the international circle that makes up his poker school, to learn "their language fast" (p. 802), even while they are boring him. When friends complain that he "couldn't be hurt enough by the fate of other people" (p. 899), Augie does not demur.[12] At times his charm recalls that of his creator, described by Philip Roth in an acknowledged fictional portrait as "like a moat so oceanic that you could not even see the great turreted and buttressed thing it had been dug to protect. You couldn't even find the drawbridge."[13]

The real-life model for Ravelstein, Allan Bloom, the author of *The Closing of the American Mind* (1987), had thought long and hard about the relation between Hal and Falstaff. Shortly before his death in 1992, he completed the final revision of *Love and Friendship* (1993), a collection of essays on Plato, Rousseau, four nineteenth-century novels, four Shakespeare plays, and "Two Strange Couples: Hal and Falstaff, Montaigne and La Boétie." In the dozen years before the book's publication, Bloom and Bellow, colleagues at the University of Chicago, "team-taught" all the works and authors it discusses, and Bellow had read and commented on the book in draft.[14] Two aspects of Bloom's treatment of the Hal-Falstaff relation stand out. The first is his depiction of Falstaff as a type of Socrates, a friend of the young and enemy not only of paternal authority but of convention and worldly accomplishment. Shakespeare describes Falstaff's death exactly as Plato describes Socrates's death, his body growing cold "from the feet up." Bloom himself, like Ravelstein, combined Socrates's refusal to be frightened of death with Falstaff's hedonism: "He will not change his life," writes Bloom of Falstaff, "for example his sexual behavior, in order to preserve it. He wishes to live as long as possible enjoying the real pleasures of food, drink, sex and wit."[15]

The second striking feature of Bloom's account of the Hal-Falstaff friendship is its implicit approval of Hal's rejection of Falstaff. Once he returns to the world of his father, Hal "succeeds, at least in his own lifetime, in bringing an end to the plague of civil war, establishing his own monarchy solidly, and expanding England's territory and influence. He has none of the defects of the other kings Shakespeare treats. His rule provides a textbook for future rulers."[16] These achievements derive in part from the skills or lessons Hal learns in Falstaff's company: "I'll so offend," he says, "to make offence a skill" (*King Henry IV, Part One*, I.ii.211–12). As Henry V, he rouses his men at Agincourt with a common touch imbibed at the Boar's Head. Calculation as well as self-disgust underlie the Prince's consorting with tapsters, so that "I can drink with any tinker in his own language." When the Dauphin mocks Henry V for his "wilder days," he does so, "not measuring what *use* we made of them" (*King Henry V*, I.ii.266–67). Bloom offers no criticism of Hal's use of others, his calculating watchfulness. Bloom approves this calculation.

Whether Bloom would have approved the use Bellow makes of him in *Ravelstein*, Bellow's last novel, has been a matter of dispute. To some, the novel's portrait is a betrayal; to others, it is as much what Bloom would have wanted, as Chick's portrait of Ravelstein is what Ravelstein wants. According to Bellow himself, the novel was, in effect, solicited by Bloom, just as Ravelstein solicits Chick to "do me as you did Keynes, but on a bigger scale. And also you were too kind to him. I don't want that. Be as hard on me as you like. You aren't the darling doll you seem to be."[17] In Chick's case, if this meant outing his subject, so be it: "unless the facts *were* known, no real life was possible"; "When he asked me to write a 'Life of Ravelstein,' it was up to me to interpret his wishes and to decide just to what extent I was freed by his death to respect the essentials. . . . I suppose he thought it wouldn't really matter because he'd be gone, and his posthumous reputation couldn't matter less" (pp. 59–60). What would matter was the end, the truthful portrait.[18]

In *Ravelstein* the form Chick's portrait takes is a memoir, a work of biography. Whether Chick is a novelist, like Bellow, isn't clear: he is a writer, a commercial success, has had books "on the low end" (p. 32) of the bestseller list; at one point, Ravelstein calls him an "artist"

(p. 84) but he is never called a novelist. In fact, none of Bellow's fictional surrogates is a novelist. The writers among them work in what Bellow thought of as lesser fields, often forms of what is now called "life-writing." There's Augie, there's Chick, there's Charlie Citrine, rich not just from *Trenck*, but from ghosting "people's personal memoirs" (p. 297) (in early versions, Charlie is, variously, a "hack biographer," "consultant to biographical dictionaries," editorial director of "American Biographical Archives").[19] In an unfinished novel, "Charm and Death," a thinly fictionalized portrait of Bellow's great friend, Isaac Rosenfeld, the protagonist quits graduate work at Columbia and lives "by reviewing, editing, translating, teaching in General Studies programs," but also by "writing commissioned biographies of pants-manufacturers and dealers in rare South American hides—lizard leather, crocodile. In the early days he would get five hundred dollars. He was fluent but the interviews, the study of materials took time." Bellow imagines the hassles and diplomatic necessities, as well as the limitations, of life-writing: "Widows and daughters (oedipal daughters) were sometimes difficult, often interesting, sometimes charming, but as time went on the work became less intriguing and less rewarding. Early freshness wore off, spiky neuroses, hard-core obstinacy, boastfulness, family pride were thrust out at him. . . . Still, people trusted him on the whole. He had no visible strategy with them. They liked his warmth. He was simple, good, or seemed to be so."[20] This passage recalls Joseph in *Dangling Man* (1944), Bellow's first novel: "About a year ago, I ambitiously began several essays, mainly biographical, on the philosophers of the Enlightenment. I was in the midst of one on Diderot when I stopped." Like Augie, Joseph is "amiable . . . well liked, [but] does not have what people call an 'open' look."[21] The most formidable of Bellow's life-writers is Artur Sammler, in *Mr. Sammler's Planet* (1970), who has long been at work on a memoir of H. G. Wells, described as his "lifework"; the most despicable is "stone-hearted" Willis Mosby, of "Mosby's Memoirs" (1968), whose recollections of life in Paris in the 1940s make use of the misfortunes of a friend for comic purposes.[22]

FOR BELLOW the novel is "the highest form of human expression yet attained," as worthy an end as kingship and crucial to the welfare of the state.[23] "To answer artistically," Bellow has written of Dostoyevsky, is to do full justice, to respect propositions and harmonies with which journalists and polemicists do not have to bother their heads. In the novel, Dostoyevsky cannot permit himself to yield to cruel, intemperate, and arbitrary personal judgements. The writer's convictions, perhaps fanatically held, must be tamed by truth.

The degree to which you challenge your own beliefs and expose them to destruction is a test of your worth as a novelist.[24]

As for why Bellow should feel impelled to greatness and to the heroic life, one answer might be social. There's a revealing paragraph in the story "Zetland: By a Character Witness" (1974) about the ambitions of young men like Bellow and his fellow high school intellectuals: "To be an intellectual was to be a parvenu. The business of these parvenus was to purge themselves of their first wild impulses and of their crazy baseness, to change themselves, to become disinterested. To love truth. To become great."[25] That Bellow sensed he could become great was another motive.

Hence, in part, his single-mindedness, his ruthlessness. "I became very obstinate at a certain point in my life," he told the Romanian novelist Norman Manea when he was eighty-four. "I knew what was necessary to remain a writer and I wasn't going to let anything interfere with it, not for my own sake so much as for the game itself as I felt it should be played." What might interfere were the demands of his life as a person, or of the lives of those around him. "In daily life," he told Manea, "I don't ask myself what is honorable and what is dishonorable but I do when I'm writing: I ask myself if it would be dishonorable to put the thing this way."[26] When Bellow's second wife, Sondra, nicknamed Sasha, complained of her depiction in *Herzog*, Bellow defended himself in similar terms, invoking Jack Ludwig's novel *Above Ground* (1968), which treats the central triangle of *Herzog* from the lover's point of view:

I made something of the abuses I suffered at your hands. As for the "humiliations" you speak of, I can match you easily. There is another book, isn't there. . . . It is monstrous to be touched by anything so horribly written. The worst thing about it, to a man who has been faithful to his art for thirty years, is the criminal vulgarity of the thing. I don't worry too much about my reputation, the "image" (I don't think you pay much attention to that, either) but I loathe being even peripherally involved with such shit. . . . But suppose the book had been good. . . . Can you see me demanding damages? I don't think you can.[27]

Perhaps the longest of Bellow's friendships was with David Peltz, who died in 2011 at ninety-six. Peltz was as remarkable in person as he was on the page, where Bellow thinly fictionalizes him as Woody Selbst in the story "A Silver Dish" (1978), George Swiebel in *Humboldt's Gift*, and George Samson in "Olduvai" or "Olduvai George," the novel Bellow abandoned in 1967 at Peltz's insistence. Bellow's editor at Viking, Denver Lindley, and his agent, Henry Volkening, were "crushed" when he gave in to Peltz's wishes (Peltz wanted the material Bellow drew on for a novel of his own). "This is electrically marvelous stuff," wrote Volkening, "the hell with . . . practical difficulties." "I would have suggested that you drop it for a while," wrote Lindley, "if these 50 pages had struck me as less than what they are: you at peak form."[28] Seven years after abandoning "Olduvai"—Peltz having failed to place his novel—Bellow wove one of its stories and its central character, now George Swiebel, into *Humboldt*. When an excerpt from the novel appeared in *Playboy*—the scene in which Cantabile threatens Citrine at the Russian Baths, based on a real-life episode Bellow had "given his word" he wouldn't use—Peltz was outraged. As Bellow knew, Peltz was saving the episode for his memoirs (the very memoirs he told me he was still at work on when I went to interview him in Chicago in 2008 when he was ninety-two). "I'm sorry you feel hurt," Bellow replied in a letter of July 14, 1974.

> Three years ago Bette [Howland] told you that I was writing about you. You were angry and forbid it. . . . What matters is that good things get written. . . . We've known each other forty-five years and told each other thousands and thousands of anecdotes. And now, on two bars suggested by one of your anecdotes, I blew a riff. . . . I created two characters and added the toilets and the Playboy Club and the fence and the skyscraper. What harm is there in that? Your facts are unharmed by my version. . . . Your facts, three or four of them, got me off the ground. You can't grudge me that and still be Dave Peltz.
>
> Now David, the nice old man who wants his collection of

memory-toys to play with in old age is not you. . . . The name of the game is Give All. You are welcome to all my facts. You know them, I give them to you. If you have the strength to pick them up, take them with my blessing. Touch them with your imagination and I will kiss your hands.

In the end, Peltz gave in: "Dear Saul, It's all right. When you find this note it'll be easier for you to call. I've been so adrift. In a sea of shit unexpressed. Thinking every undeveloped happening will accrue into a spiritual bank account. But time like inflation is thinning it all out. You are right in this matter. And I will let be. See you soon, Love, David." Later, in a 1980 interview with D. J. R. Bruckner, Peltz recounted an exchange with Nelson Algren about the anecdote. Speaking of Bellow, Algren declared: "He's a goddamn fool if he doesn't use it. Who do you think you are? You're part of his environment and he has the right to use his environment." As Peltz told Bruckner: "And he was right."[29]

The phrases I want to highlight here are: "What matters is that good things get written" and "You are welcome to all my facts. . . . If you have the strength to pick them up, take them with my blessing. Touch them with your imagination." By "good things" Bellow means good fictional things; facts are mere starting points, nothing unless they are touched by imagination, brought alive by what Wordsworth called "the visionary gleam" (Wordsworth is often invoked in the pages that follow). For Bellow, "the fact is a wire through which one sends a current. The voltage of that current is determined by the writer's own belief as to what matters, by his own caring or not-caring, by passionate choice. It is not *in news* that it matters whether a man lives or dies. The mattering or not mattering is not a product of facts, but of judgment, of caring."[30] Richard Stern, a novelist friend, "couldn't write about me," Bellow told Mark Harris, also a novelist, "because as a writer he couldn't *subordinate* himself to me"; nor, presumably, could he subordinate himself to mere fact. I see this comment, which Harris records in *Saul Bellow: Drumlin Woodchuck* (1980), his biographical study of Bellow, as meant to put Harris off, and as a put-down.[31] "I'm a bird not an ornithologist," Bellow liked to say. Because he wrote so close to life, he always needed, his fifth wife, Janis, told me, a real-life face or character to get him off the ground, and because so many of his works—for example, all the stories in the collection *Him with His Foot in His Mouth* (1984)—take the form of fictional portraits, frequently of identifiable models, he was often ready to distance his works from life-writing, and to denigrate life-writing, as unworthy of the pain or betrayal it involved, not being art.

What makes Bellow a bird not an ornithologist is his ability to transform facts or experiences into great literature, thus changing them. This view of art as new creation is often invoked as a defense against accusations of slander or defamation. Art can be viewed in other ways; for example, as imitation or mimesis, the oldest of aesthetic aims and pleasures. Mimesis, too, involves touching experiences or facts with the imagination. Bellow was a famed noticer and his novels and stories are packed with things perfectly seen. In *Herzog*, the novel that made him rich and famous, Moses Herzog, in sweltering Manhattan, comes in sight of a building being demolished:

> At the corner he paused to watch the work of the wrecking crew. The great metal ball swung at the walls, passed easily through brick, and entered the rooms, the lazy weight browsing on kitchens and parlors. Everything it touched wavered and burst, spilled down. There rose a white tranquil cloud of plaster dust. The afternoon was ending, and in the widening area of demolition was a fire, fed by the wreckage (p. 593).[32]

The pleasure afforded by this passage is of recognition or recollection: "that's just how it is" or "just how it would be," rather than "I'd never seen or thought of it like that," more mirror than lamp. Or take a second example, from an episode in the aquarium in Chicago, which Herzog visits with his daughter June:

> "*There* is the turtle!" June shouted. The thing rose from the depths of the tank in its horny breastplate, the beaked head lazy, the eyes with aeons of indifference, the flippers slowly striving, pushing at the glass, the great scales pinkish yellow or, on the back, bearing beautiful lines, black curved plates mimicking the surface tension of water. It trailed a fuzz of parasitic green (p. 701).

Imitation is not the only source of pleasure or art in this passage. The slow, ineffectual striving of the turtle's flipper is lent poignancy by subjective coloring, the helplessness of Herzog's own striving, just as the lazy weight of the wrecking ball gains resonance from Herzog's breakdown, his sense of having been pounded. Both moments serve larger narrative and thematic purposes, those of design or unity, aesthetic values different from imitation. But the core pleasure is mimetic, the product of a thing brought perfectly to life. So rich with mimetic pleasures is Bellow's writing that when he creates a character who resembles an identifiable person, the temptation is to believe that character is the person perfectly captured, as accurate or artful an imitation as the descriptions of wrecking ball or turtle.

One such character in *Herzog* is Sandor Himmelstein, a choleric lawyer. Himmelstein is a "large dwarf" with a misshapen body and "a proud, sharp, handsome face." Here he is in the morning, working himself into a rage over the mess left by his daughters the night before:

> Herzog heard a cry from Sandor at the kitchen sink. "Look at this crap! Not a pot—not a dish—there isn't a spoon that's clean. It stinks of garbage. It's just a sewer here!" The old dog, obese and bald, escaped in fear, claws rapping on the tiles—clickclick, click-click. "Spendthrift bitches!" he shouted at the women of his house. "Frigging lice! All they're good for is to wag their asses at the dress shops and play gidgy in the bushes. Then they come home, and gorge cake and leave plates smeared with chocolate in the sink. That's what gives them the pimples."
>
> "Easy, Sandor."
>
> "Do I ask for much? The old veteran runs up and down City Hall, from courtroom to courtroom—out to Twenty-sixth and California. For them! Do they care if I have to suck up to all kinds of pricks to get a little business?" Sandor began to rake out the sink. He threw eggshells and orange rinds into the corner beside the garbage pail—coffee grounds. He worked himself into a rage and began to smash dishes and glassware. His long fingers, like those of a hunchback, gripped the plates soiled with icing. Without losing beauty of gesture—amazing!—he shattered them on the wall. He knocked over the dish drainer and the soap powder, and then he wept with anger. And also at himself, that he should have such emotions. His open mouth and jutting teeth! The long hairs streamed from his disfigured breast (p. 505).

In 1961, while *Herzog* was still a work in progress, Bellow sent an extract from the manuscript to *Esquire*.[33] Himmelstein, then called

Carlos, featured prominently in the excerpt. As soon as he sent it off, Bellow began to worry. "I had frightful nightmares," he wrote to Susan Glassman, not yet Susan Bellow, in a letter of April 24, 1961: "I dreamt that Carlos was suing. He's such a hornet, how would he not? And then I awoke and the prospect was even worse. It panicked me. And I've involved *Esquire*. Of course, I don't really think he'd do anything, it would make him look like a real idiot. He can't afford it professionally. Still. You know. It's dreadful not to be able to write about real matters; it turns all this into real child's play while industry and politics do as they like, drive us into the [bomb] shelters, make our lives foolish horrors and disfigure the whole world. Anyway, some of the facts have been fiddled with to place the scene in Chicago." There would be more fiddling. In a later, undated letter to Susan, Bellow reports that "at the last minute I changed Carlos to a crippled war veteran, a hero of Omaha Beach. For the book itself I'll have to consult long with Viking lawyers. Hate to lose Carlos *comme il est*."

Carlos *comme il est* was a lawyer named Jonas Schwartz, a tiny man with a misshapen body. He did not sue, but he was not pleased. He had been Bellow's friend, had tried to represent both Bellow and his second wife in their divorce, and when forced to take sides chose the wife, while professing continued loyalty to Bellow. Himmelstein has that same history with Herzog and Herzog's second wife, Mady. In a letter of December 6, 1975, the lawyer Bellow employed after Schwartz, John Goetz, recalled "my last meeting with our distinguished antagonist Jonas Schwartz, in a crowded elevator, shortly after *Herzog* came out. He gave me his characteristically friendly glare, and shouted. 'Have you seen Saul's book?' Without waiting for a reply, he went on, red-faced, doing his best to jump up and down: 'I'm in it! And he makes me a son of a bitch! ME, Jonas Schwartz, a son of a bitch!'" Goetz and Schwartz were not the only witnesses from this period for whom "making something" of Schwartz, putting a current through the wire of fact, meant capturing something real about him, bringing him alive, as well as turning him into a brilliant comic grotesque, a figure out of Dickens. I am not saying that Himmelstein is Schwartz, who was no doubt a more complicated, certainly a more serious, person than his fictional alter ego (he was, among other things, a prominent civil rights attorney who had argued before the Supreme Court). But his temperament, appearance, and situation were similar to those of Himmelstein and that was enough to lead others to see him as "a son of a bitch," especially since that's how Bellow, who saw things so clearly, might have viewed him. For James Wood, faced with instances like these, "an awkward but undeniable utilitarianism must be in play: the number of people hurt by Bellow is probably no more than can be counted on two hands, yet he has delighted and consoled and altered the lives of thousands of readers."[34] Though opinions will differ about the morality of this calculation, that Bellow accepted it is something worth knowing about him, as a man and as an artist.

BELLOW'S LIFE AWAY from the desk was rich in incident, with ample evidence of affection, warmth, generosity, and loyalty, but there are times when his nonwriting life does not show him in an honorable light, especially when it interferes with or impedes the work. To some writers, the prospect of biography poses no threat. "I remain completely indifferent to how people think about me," V. S. Naipaul, another Nobel Prize winner, has written, "because I was serving this thing called literature." The access Naipaul granted his authorized biographer, Patrick French, results in a book of astonishing frankness, in which the most intimate and damaging revelations come from Naipaul himself.[35] Bellow was not like that: he acknowledged the human costs of his service to literature. In *Mr. Sammler's Planet*, when the hero's good-hearted but dim daughter steals a manuscript she thinks of vital use to her father's book, she does so out of the conviction that he'd "pay any price" to serve creation: "A creative person wouldn't stop at anything. For the creative there are no crimes. And aren't you a creative person?" (p. 163). This is neither Sammler's view nor Bellow's, though both knew full well why it might be thought so. Writing came first, but it was not everything. In this, Bellow was like Benn Crader, the botanist-hero of *More Die of Heartbreak* (1987), a world-renowned figure. "Uncle didn't *have* to get into this," his nephew, Kenneth, the novel's narrator, tells us, speaking of Benn's impending marriage. "He had his science. The trouble was that he was ambitious. Asked too much. The happiness of a recluse wasn't enough for him, nor were his telepathic powers with plants."[36] What Bellow was ambitious about was love. "The one thing I don't regret is having fallen in love often," he said in an interview toward the end of his life. "What was I trying to prove, that I wasn't a beast, that I had a heart after all, instead of a dried-out, soured nut in an old nutshell?"[37] Although not always a *mensch*, the man he wished to be, he was no jerk, a term more easily applied to Naipaul as he presents himself in public and in interviews.

This attitude explains some of Bellow's unease with his own biographers, as well as with those who saw his writing as biographical or autobiographical. He did not like the prospect of biography, partly for reasons that might apply to all persons passionate about their work. "The greater your achievements," the narrator of *More Die of Heartbreak* tells us, "the less satisfactory your personal and domestic life will be. . . . The personal facts often are base. The scientist who didn't recognize his own son, the student waiting on tables, has set up housekeeping with one of his male graduate students. Never mind his sexual preferences (one of the blessings of the new indifference), but the private life is almost always a bouquet of sores with a garnish of trivialities or downright trash" (p. 31). When I began work on this biography in 2007, one of the first people I interviewed, Monroe Engel, Bellow's initial editor at Viking, told me that I had one great advantage over my predecessors: Bellow was no longer alive. Bellow's previous biographers or would-be biographers—Ruth Miller, Mark Harris, James Atlas— had all been able to ask him questions about his life and work. I owe much to what he told them, as to the interviews they recorded with those of his friends and acquaintances who died before I came on the scene. Bellow was wary with all three biographers, sometimes helpful, especially at first, sometimes prickly, often evasive. The wariness colored or shaped what they wrote, obviously in the case of Harris, where it became pretty much his book's subject. After initially, if fitfully, helping Atlas, Bellow withdrew and turned against him, helping to produce the note of resentment some have heard in Atlas's book, on which he labored for almost a dozen years, reading reams of manuscripts and correspondence, conducting hundreds of interviews.[38] I encountered Bellow only once, at a garden party in Cambridge, Massachusetts, in the summer of 1972. He had come to Harvard to be awarded an honorary degree (along with the British politician Roy Jenkins and the economist Paul Samuelson, among others). It was a hot afternoon and some of the men at the party were wearing shorts and Hawaiian shirts. Bellow wore a brown silk suit and what I assumed was a Borsolino hat. Standing in front of a table surrounded by admirers, he looked bored or stern, certainly not cheerful. I was a graduate student in English and a fan of his writing so I joined the circle and listened for a while. I remember nothing of what he said.

Bellow was fifty-seven in June 1972, when Harvard awarded him that honorary degree. Three days earlier he had received an honorary degree from Yale. His most recent book, *Mr. Sammler's Planet*, had, the previous year, won his third National Book Award. As I now know, he had plenty of reasons not to be cheerful that afternoon. The story of his life is long and complicated. He would continue writing, publishing, and teaching for another thirty or so years, well into his eighties. He was a gregarious man, quick to laugh, very funny, often charming, by no means always forbidding. Despite his grudge bearing, he had a wide acquaintance and made efforts to keep in touch with old friends. He liked to go out and do things and meet people after his morning stint at the desk. In 1970, when he was probably the most acclaimed novelist in America, he took on the job of chair of the Committee on Social Thought at the University of Chicago. He served on numerous boards and fellowship committees, exercising significant power in the literary world, helping certain writers and intellectuals he approved of to find agents, editors, publishers, fellowships, and teaching jobs, thwarting the hopes of those he disapproved of or disagreed with, always excepting the genuinely talented.[39] He was a restless man as well as a gregarious one and traveled widely, one of several reasons why, though he valued family, he found family life difficult. He loved and neglected his three sons, each from a different mother. A fourth child, Naomi Rose, was born when he was eighty-four, to his fifth wife, Janis. Handsome and flirtatious, he had a number of serious affairs, as well as many shorter ones. He took a keen interest in his wider family, in nieces, nephews, cousins, aunts, uncles, many of whom appear as characters in his stories and novels. He was often embroiled in public controversy, over foreign affairs, race, religion, education, social policy, the state of the culture, the fate of the novel. He read deeply in a range of fields and literatures, and for over thirty years spent several afternoons a week discussing works of literature, philosophy, and social and political theory with graduate students and colleagues at the University of Chicago. Gore Vidal called him "the only American intellectual who read books."[40] He also, of course, knew and relished the culture of the streets, disconcerting visiting intellectuals such as Lionel Trilling and Hannah Arendt with anti-glamour tours of Chicago, including the roughest of skid row bars, neighboring slums, a coal yard where he once worked.

BELLOW'S FULL LIFE ACCOUNTS FOR the length of this biography, to be followed by a second volume covering his last forty years. Long biographies are often deplored, especially by reviewers. In 1960, Bellow's friend Richard Ellmann won the National Book Award for Nonfiction for his biography of James Joyce. At the awards ceremony Ellmann defended the book's length on several grounds. "If an individual life is described too leanly," he declared, "we grow anxious, we suspect distortion, we wonder if the essences are really there." These essences grow out of particulars, many of them social: "We want to see the personality of the subject as a series of concomitant relations with other people. Longing for his total embodiment, we are dissatisfied if we are shown merely or principally his private self." Moreover, "if we want to see the social self, we do not want to see it only in its formal stances." This view is buttressed by Samuel Johnson, who thought the domestic life best suited to display a subject's "prudence and virtue"; today, Ellmann thought, readers want also to know a subject in less flattering lights, "when they are exhibiting bad temper, fear, or boredom."[41] I share Ellmann's assumptions about what literary biography ought to do or be. Unsurprisingly, I take issue with the view that biography is invariably lowering, or that the motives of biographers are invariably base. What Ellmann leaves out in his defense of long biographies, oddly given his strengths as a critic, is discussion of the writing. The detailed attention given to Bellow's writing in this biography will show or remind readers how rich and deep it is, and how pleasurable.

FINALLY, a word about names. I have made the decision to refer to Bellow's girlfriends, of whom there were many, by their first names, because this is the way he referred to and thought of them, because their last names often changed, and because to refer to them by last names sounds anachronistic. The matter of names irritated Bellow when raised by biographers (though no writer, Dickens excepted, was better at them). Bellow had a sister named Zelda who became Zenka then Jenka then Jane. Maury and Sam, his elder brothers, changed their surnames from Bellow to Bellows. Maury had been Moishe, Sam had been Schmuel. Bellow himself had been Schloimo or Schloimke, then Solomon, then Saul. Why these changes, I asked Bellow's middle son, Adam, a question he himself had asked his father. Bellow told him a story. There once was a Polish Jew named Max Pisher who moved to Germany and changed his name to Mauritz Wasserstahl. Then he moved to France and became Maurice de La Fontaine. This story explains the Bellow family's changes of first names, but what of last names? Daniel Bellow, Bellow's youngest son, thinks the change to "Bellows" might have had something to do with the brothers not wanting to be thought Italian (when introduced or when the name was spoken). Atlas says Sam and Maury were "modeling themselves after Charlie Bellows, a well-known Chicago criminal lawyer who had once been the Bellows' neighbor,"[42] an explanation that fits the Pisher story. Spellings were also unfixed. In a letter of December 19, 1972, Maury signs off: "Your loving brother, Morris or Maurice. Take your choice." (He is Maury in what follows, as in many letters and documents.) There are similar changes or instabilities in the names of a number of Bellow's childhood friends and acquaintances. Such refashioning and uncertainty are part of immigrant experience, of the negotiating of old and new worlds or "systems," to use a Bellow term. Understanding Bellow's inheritance from immigrant experience is crucial to understanding both the man and the writer. So we begin in Russia, before he was born.

I

Russia/Abraham

A STORY IS TOLD in the Bellow family about a moment of violence in the life of Abraham Bellow, the novelist's father. In the summer of 1923, in Montreal, Abraham was in trouble. Deep in debt, with a wife and four children to feed, he had failed in a succession of jobs: as farmer, baker, dry goods salesman, jobber, manufacturer, junk dealer, marriage broker, insurance broker. Now he was a bootlegger on a small scale, pursued by agents of the revenue (in part because he was too poor to pay bribes). He and his partner, determined to make a killing, borrowed money to rent a truck, loaded the truck with crates of bootleg whiskey, and at nightfall headed for the border. Their plan was to sell to rumrunners up from New York, serious criminals. They never made it to the border. They were hijacked on the road, everything was taken, the liquor, the truck. When Abraham tried to resist, he was beaten, tossed in a ditch, and left to find his way back home on foot.

The whole family knew of the planned sale, even eight-year-old Saul, who helped to paste fake labels on the whiskey bottles. When morning came and Abraham had not returned, Saul's oldest brother, fifteen-year-old Maury, was sent to find him. He ran to the partner's place of work and waited. Eventually, he saw a figure in the distance, running "like the demons of hell were following him." It was his father, in torn clothes, bloody, in tears. Reaching out to him, the boy said, "Pa, Pa! What's wrong?" In the version of the story told by Maury's son, "then my grandfather just beat the shit out of my father."[1]

To explain this moment one must know something of Abraham's history. He was born in Russia in 1881, the first son of Berel and

Shulamith Belo (from the Russian *byelo* or *bely* meaning "white"). Berel was remembered by his children and grandchildren as a man of great learning and fierce temper. He was a traveling salesman for a wholesale grocer.[2] He had red in his beard, "like all the men in our family," drove a hard bargain, and was alleged to have been one of only seven men behind the Pale of Settlement, the area of czarist Russia to which most Jews were restricted, to know the Talmud by heart, a story of dubious authority told also of the narrator's grandfather in *Humboldt's Gift* (1975), where the number of such men is ten not seven.[3] In "Memoirs of a Bootlegger's Son," a thinly fictionalized autobiographical novel begun and abandoned by Bellow (after 172 typed pages) in the first half of the 1950s, around the time of *The Adventures of Augie March* (1953), the Berel figure is described as "a famous Chassid." Hasidism, a movement of pietistic enthusiasm among Orthodox Jews, particularly poor Jews from Eastern Europe, was associated with dance, song, storytelling, mysticism, and scholarship. In the novel, when the Abraham character, Jacob Lurie or "Pa," has a drink, a rare occurrence, he is said to "lay his head on one shoulder and snap his fingers and dance a few Chassidic steps."[4] Abraham's mother was the daughter of a flax merchant from Druya, the town where Abraham was born, on the border of Belarus and Latvia.

Druya was a small town, a shtetl rather than a village.[5] Abraham went to cheder or Hebrew school in Druya, where he learned his alphabet ("Aleph, an ox. Beth, a house") and how to read the prayer book and the Bible. Once the alphabet was mastered, "without further waste of time, the book was opened and you read *Bereshith boro Elohim*—the old story. God created heaven and earth" (p. 20). For boys who were willing and talented, yeshiva followed, where one studied the Torah (the Pentateuch or Five Books of Moses) and Talmud (rabbinical and other commentary and disputation concerning Jewish laws, customs, ethics, history). Abraham was sent away to yeshiva at a very young age.[6] There he froze and starved, was infected with lice, and was soon back home. The family moved around, at some point settling in Dvinsk (Daugavpils), the nearest big town, thirty-six miles west of Druya.[7] In the "Memoirs" manuscript, Abraham's fictional alter-ego, Jacob Lurie, is said to have been at yeshiva till he was eighteen (p. 2), though Bellow later has him brag that "at thirteen I was a young man. At fifteen I earned a living. At seventeen I had my own business in Kremenchug [in central Ukraine]" (p. 6). It has also been said that Abraham pursued rabbinical studies in Vilnius (Vilna), "the Jerusalem of Lithuania."[8] He was vain of his knowledge of the Talmud and disdainful of fellow Jews who had not attained some level of yeshiva education. One of his granddaughters remembers him dismissing the Jewish learning of an acquaintance with a Yiddish phrase, *lernen ken er vi di vant*, "his learning is as flat and featureless as a wall." She also remembers him conversing knowledgeably on Talmudic matters with her maternal grandfather, an ordained rabbi.[9]

Abraham was not one for the life of learning. He was restless, a traveler, "a good raconteur,"[10] quick to anger, very loving one minute, very angry the next. In a 1990 interview Bellow described him as "violent, strong, authoritarian. He seemed to us as children an angel of strength, beauty, and punishment. His affections were strong, too. He was a passionate person." Though neither a big man nor especially muscular, he was hot-blooded or *ungehapteh* (Yiddish), fighting with everyone. Bellow admired his father's bravery. "He was a very feisty man, enviably I think. . . . He was just willing to fight." In an undated letter to Irving Halperin, a professor of humanities at San Francisco State University, Bellow described his father as "a furious man, whirling with impatience. . . . a heavyweight tyrant following the example of Grandpa Bellow."[11] The oldest son, Maury, bore the brunt of Abraham's hot temper, which he inherited, and Maury's son, Joel, is understandably tough on his grandfather. "He liked tumult, he liked to cause a lot of hell." He was "unmannerly, undisciplined, a troublemaker." What Joel remembers hearing of Abraham's time at yeshiva is a story about mixing pepper in the rabbi's snuff.[12] He also remembers his grandfather having fistfights in the street, into his sixties, after he'd become a prosperous Chicago businessman. If the old man was crossed, "he'd go at it physically." There was a fistfight over the next door neighbor's wife, with whom he was carrying on. He was hot-blooded in several senses. "I suspected he had his adventures," Bellow told an interviewer, "must have had." ("It's an exceptionally smart man who isn't marked forever by the sexual theories he hears from his father," declares the narrator of Bellow's story "A Silver Dish." Bellow, of course, was an exceptionally smart man.[13]) "He was a dude," Joel concludes of Abraham, "Very important. Very important to all the boys. A tough guy. Tough emotionally? I don't think so."

Like Maury, Bellow was beaten by his father, but he was loved by him, and loved back. In the novella *A Theft* (1989), the narrator, Ithiel Regler, describes watching a television program about child abuse:

> Most of what they showed was normal punishment in my time. So today I could be a child-abuse case and my father might have been arrested as a child-beater. When he was in a rage he was transformed—he was like moonshine from the hills compared to store-bought booze. The kids, all of us, were slammed two-handed, from both sides simultaneously, and without mercy. So? Forty years later I have to watch a TV show to see that I, too, was abused. Only, I loved my late father. Beating was only an incident, a single item between us. I still love him. Now, to tell you what this signifies: I can't apply the going terms to my case without damage to reality. My father beat me passionately. When he did it, I hated him like poison and murder. I also loved him with a passion, and I'll *never* think myself an abused child.[14]

This was Bellow's own attitude to his father, whose capacity for love and affection he recalls as vividly as his impatience and rage. The sixteen-year-old narrator of "Memoirs of a Bootlegger's Son," Joshua Lurie, is the oldest child in the family. Like Maury, he is fat and most frequently in the line of fire. "I never could do much to please my father" is the novel's first sentence. The middle son, Willie, is asthmatic, quiet, like the middle Bellow son, Sam. Willie keeps a low profile, gliding in the firstborn's slipstream. The youngest, Ben Zion, is described as watchful, intelligent beyond his years, dreamy, his father's favorite. He is seven when the novel opens and is called Bentchka, as Bellow was called Schloimke in his family, an endearing diminutive of Schloimo, Yiddish for Solomon. When Joshua doubts his father's love, it is the mother who reassures him: "Loves you? He loves all his children. Only his troubles are sometimes too much for him. You must understand that" (p. 8). When she describes how his father kissed Joshua's head the day he was born, as he kissed the heads of all his newborn infants, Joshua feels the kiss "in my scalp, under my hair and even in the mouth, the palate" (p. 7). When she upbraids the father for berating Joshua, "Pa would end up by being astonished that she should think he didn't care for me. 'Why,' he'd say. 'I love all my children. My children are everything to me'" (p. 7).

Though learned in Jewish lore, Abraham was not particularly Orthodox. It was his wife who was Orthodox. He had been disaffected, Bellow said, as a *Yeshiva Bocher*, a young Talmudic scholar. Religious practices were "an impediment . . . He didn't turn his back on them but neither did he recommend them to his children." What religion impeded, Abraham thought, was business, which has no time for finer or ineffable feeling, for beauty, wonder, love. In business, one has to be sharp, alert, self-interested: "You must be sure that you get the better end of the deal, that you don't get the dirty end of the stick."[15] This seems to have been Berel's view as well as Abraham's. Before Bellow's parents married, his mother's wealthy brothers agreed to pay a dowry of 10,000 rubles. When the money was not immediately forthcoming, Berel threatened to call off the wedding. The brothers paid up. Abraham could be comparably hard, an apostle of self-interest. At his grandson Joel's Bar Mitzvah, Joel's father, Maury, by now extremely wealthy, invited a number of non-Jewish friends and business acquaintances. Abraham was well aware they'd been invited. After the grandson's reading, Abraham stood up to give a speech. He had advice to bestow, as well as congratulations: if ever Joel was in a position to do a favor for someone, and had a choice between doing it for a Jew or a non-Jew, "he should remember where he came from and do it for a Jew." Maury and his wife stood up and left the room.

Abraham was smart as well as feisty, with a fine head for figures and a sharp tongue. His movements were compact and precise, he was handsome, well dressed, a dude ("Papa was, he still is, such a dude," declares the narrator of Bellow's 1987 novel, *More Die of Heartbreak*, "and I resemble him, inevitably"; "I've noticed," says Ravelstein to Chick, in *Ravelstein* [2000], "that since your marriage your dress standards have dropped. You once were something of a dude"[16]). Like Berel, Abraham went into business, though little is known of his early years. In *Herzog* (1964), the narrator's father has an education almost identical to Abraham's. After yeshiva he enters into business: "He shaved. Became a modern European. He worked in Kremenchug for an Aunt as a young man" (p. 565), like "Pa" in "Memoirs of a Bootlegger's Son," who moved to Kremenchug at thirteen, ran his own business at seventeen. How closely Abraham's immediate post-yeshiva years resembled those of his fictional alter egos is impossible to say. What is known is that in 1905, at the age of twenty-four, he had done well enough to marry Lescha (from Elisheva, the Hebrew form of Elizabeth) Gordin, a pretty girl from a family wealthier than his own, one affiliated with a rival strand of Judaism. Lescha's father was *Misnagid*, anti-mystical, anti-Hasidic, suspicious of religious enthusiasm. In a letter of May 25, 1984, to an Israeli correspondent, Hanna Shoshana Friedman, Bellow reflected on the more tolerant relations between strains of Orthodoxy at the turn of the century: "Post-Holocaust Judaism is markedly different, and when Herzog's parents were married it was possible for a *shadchen* [marriage broker] to arrange a match between an orphan girl whose father had been a *mishnagid* and a lively young man from the Yeshiva whose father, although a Hassid, did not turn up his nose at a substantial dowry."[17]

Lescha Gordin was no orphan, though whether her father, Moses (Moishe, Movsha), was alive in 1905 is unclear.[18] He was no longer alive three years later, when Maury (also Moishe, Movsha) was born, since Jews do not name sons after living relations. What is known of Moses Gordin is that he was born sometime in the 1840s and that his wife, Sara, born four years later, outlived him, at some point moving in with her sister, Rachel,[19] and her family, first in Dagda, a small town some twenty-six miles northeast of Druya, then in Riga. According to her death certificate, Lescha was born in Dagda "about 1883" (she knew neither her birthday nor the year of her birth); Russian records suggest an earlier date, either 1877 or 1879.[20] The number of Lescha's brothers and sisters is also uncertain. Bellow and his sister, Jane, thought their mother one of twelve siblings, but only seven are named in official records, and no one in the family remembers the names of all twelve.[21] The records also complicate family lore in respect to Moses, thought by some members of the family to have been a rabbi in Vitebsk. He may have been at one time, but in police files from Vitebsk, compiled in 1889, he is listed as a merchant, and the only reliable census from the period, taken in 1897, lists him as the owner of a bakery specializing in Russian bagels or *baranki*. According to family testimony, the bakery and other businesses were managed by relatives—grown children, in-laws—while Moses devoted his time to serious study. Family testimony also records that at one point Moses rented a large and profitable farm, with at least eighty milking cows plus other livestock, which, again, he did not himself manage. As Bellow puts it, studious Moses "never did a day's work in his life, except the very hardest."[22] In 1897, the family was living in Lipushki, a small village twenty-five miles north of Dagda. The house the family lived in is described as built of wood and covered by hay.[23]

By 1905, the year of Lescha's wedding, the family was back in Dagda, living in state. In addition to owning a bakery, they ran the local post office, employed servants and a governess, and had a dacha in the countryside. Two of Lescha's brothers contributed significantly to the family's wealth: Nota or Notka (later Nahum) and Rafael (later Robert). These brothers figure prominently in the early life of Abraham. Notka was born in 1872, Rafael in 1876. In 1891, at fifteen, Rafael ran away to South Africa, made a fortune in diamonds, and became Robert. Family legend has it that he returned to Dagda in time for Lescha's wedding because he'd had a dream that his father was dying. When he returned, he brought or bought a gold necklace for his mother and helped with Lescha's dowry and the cost of the wedding. "He was a very good boy," Bellow told an interviewer, "except for running away from home."[24] Notka also contributed money to the family. The 1897 census lists him as twenty-five years old and on reserve military service in the Russian army. According to the youngest of his eight sons, Notka had all his teeth knocked out by Moses expressly to render him unfit for active duty. By 1905 Notka was living in St. Petersburg, outside the Pale of Settlement, and had become Nahum. What made the move possible was his marriage to a "Czar Nicholas widow," whose husband's rank and death in service allowed her certain privileges. Chief among these privileges, as far as Nahum was concerned, was the right to continue living in St. Petersburg with a new husband who lacked papers of residence. In St. Petersburg, Nahum owned property, a six-story house, a twelve-bedroom apartment, and three kosher restaurants in or around Nevsky Prospect, the city's grand boulevard, several streets north of its Jewish district.[25] He also traveled widely, living for periods in London, where he had commercial interests, and Germany, where he became involved in the furniture business, eventually importing German furniture to St. Petersburg. After the widow's death, he married a much younger woman. He had four sons from each marriage. The youngest son from the second marriage knew nothing of the first family, including of the fate of his half brothers.

The wedding of Lescha and Abraham was attended by Abraham's nephew Louis Dworkin, but all that is remembered of his accounts of it is the wrangle over the dowry.[26] In "Memoirs of a Bootlegger's Son," the Lurie wedding is held in the woods and said to have lasted a week, with daily banquets and music. Eminent rabbis came, twelve of them, "each more wonderful than the one before" (p. 18). Abraham told his granddaughter Lesha Bellows Greengus (named after her grandmother, whose name is spelled "Lescha" throughout this chapter, as in at least one official document) that after the wedding the bride's brothers helped him to purchase a "license" (forged) to live and work in St. Petersburg. There, from 1905 to 1913, the new family prospered. Three children were born in quick succession: Zelda (later Jane) in 1907, Moishe (Maurice, then Maury) in 1908, and Schmuel (Samuel) in 1911. Shloime/Shloimke (later Solomon, then Saul) was born in 1915, after the family had fled to Canada. Abraham set up business as a self-employed "produce-broker" (Bellow's term), presumably the occupation he pursued behind the Pale. Nahum, with his restaurant connections, may have helped him do so. "In Petersburg," writes Bellow in the "Memoirs," Pa Lurie "had made a handsome living. He dealt in produce and traveled widely. He was the largest importer of Egyptian onions and Spanish fruit" (p. 35), as well as in Turkish figs.[27] His business took him everywhere in Russia. Here is his fictional alter ego, Lurie, greeting guests from the Old Country:

> They never came from a place so remote that he hadn't been there. "I've covered Russia from end to end," he'd say. "I know your town very well. It's twenty miles from Tula. I visited the wonder Rabbi there. The richest Jew in your town was Kolya Warshavsky. He owned a mill and three stores. Also, he was a forest merchant. He had two sons, Abraham and Yonah." "Itzhak was the younger son, not Yonah," the wondering visitor might correct him. But Pa was always near enough; his memory was prodigious and he wowed everyone. "But how do you know all this, Mister Lurie?" people would say. "Oh," answered Pa, "I know Russia as well as my own house" (p. 68).

Ruth Miller, a student of Bellow's in Chicago in the late 1930s, recalls meeting Abraham and being grilled by him, much to his son's irritation and embarrassment: "Who was my father? My grandfather? Where did they come from? What was the name of the town in Lithuania? What did my father do for a living? What business were my uncles in? When did they come to America? How old were they when they came? Do I know the name of the ship?"[28]

Abraham's intensity—recalling Bellow's descriptions of his father as "whirling with impatience," "furious," "passionate"—derived in part from his experiences in Russia. The long history of Russian anti-Semitism is marked by periods of exceptional virulence. One such period began with the assassination of Czar Alexander II in 1881, the year Abraham was born. Alexander's twenty-six-year reign was relatively tolerant of the Jews. Disraeli called him "the most benevolent prince that ever ruled in Russia."[29] The reign of his successor, Alexander III, began with a wave of pogroms, as agents of the state spread rumors associating Jews with the assassination. The hated reactionary Konstantin Pobedonostsev (1827–1907), chief procurator of the Holy Synod and a fanatical anti-Semite, was put in charge of the government. He blocked all measures to improve the conditions of the Jews and initiated new measures to worsen them. The 1882 May Laws called for the forced removal of Jews from villages to towns and hamlets. As most Jews worked as shopkeepers, small merchants, publicans, artisans, and moneylenders—there was virtually no Jewish peasantry or nobility—the effect of the laws, especially within the crowded towns and hamlets of the Pale, was increased joblessness. According to the historian Salo Baron, "It has been estimated that in many communities up to 40 per cent of the entire Jewish population consisted of families of so-called *luftmenshen*, that is, persons without any particular skills, capital, or specific occupations."[30]

The movements of Lescha Gordin's family, from shtetl, to village, to town, were likely a product, either direct or indirect, of discrimination. Nahum Gordin's missing teeth certainly were. Nahum was born in 1872. From 1827 to 1874, Jews who were drafted into the army, some as young as twelve, were subject to a twenty-five-year compulsory tour of duty. After this barbaric length of service was reduced, they were still systematically disadvantaged, even in reward for loyal conduct. The aim of such treatment was to force Jewish soldiers to convert to Russian orthodoxy. "The chief benefit to be derived from the drafting of Jews," wrote Czar Nicholas I in a confidential memo, "is the certainty that it will move them most effectively to change their religion."[31] If Nahum Gordin avoided active duty in the army by losing his teeth, his father did so by losing his name. Official records confirm the story Bellow was told about Moses Gordin's name: that it was originally Imenitov. What Bellow seems not to have known (no one in his immediate family ever heard him speak of it) is that Imenitov is not a Jewish name. According to genealogical records compiled by relatives from Russia and Israel, Moses's father, Nota Imenitov, was the son of a graf or count, the largest landowner in Rezekne, in Latvia. He was not Jewish. At some point, so the story goes, Nota fell in love with a Jewish girl from Rezekne.[32] The girl's father, unmoved by his prospective son-in-law's titled family, wealth, and threats, would only consent to their marriage if Nota converted, which he did. Nota's father, the graf, promptly disinherited him. To support themselves, the couple went into business, running an inn, which seems to have prospered. "Educated and quick of mind" is how Nota is described in a memoir by his great-grandson, Moshe Gordin.

The Imenitovs, Nota and his wife, Selda, had three sons: Popa, Moshe, and Wulf. To avoid being conscripted into the army, Moshe, the middle son, was adopted by a family named Gordin, which had no sons. Being adopted in this way was usually a financial transaction, a common practice of Jews in Moses's situation. As the sole Gordin son, Moses could not by law be conscripted.[33] When Moses himself became a father, however, he was either unable or unwilling to arrange a similar adoption for Nahum, or to find and hire a substitute, something the conscription laws also permitted. Substitutes were inevitably the children of the very poor and socially outcast, families desperate for money. The number of recruits conscripted from each community was higher for Jews than non-Jews, and what one historian calls "the macabre job of selecting recruits" was left to the Jewish communities themselves, exacerbating divisions of religious practice (Hasidim vs. Mitnagdim), kinship, and class.[34]

That Nahum and his brothers, like Abraham, went into business rather than the professions may also be attributed to anti-Jewish discrimination. The May Laws restricted educational opportunities for Jews in several ways. A *numerus clausus* or quota system was established limiting to 10 percent the number of Jewish students allowed to attend secondary schools inside the Pale, to 5 percent outside it, and to 3 percent in St. Petersburg and Moscow. The effect of the law was severely to limit the number of Jews capable of competing for an already limited number of places in universities and professional schools. In "The Story of My Dovecote" (1925), the first of two childhood sketches dedicated to Maxim Gorky, Isaac Babel thinly fictionalizes his experiences in 1904 as a ten-year-old Jewish schoolboy in the Odessa province. This was the year Babel was to take entrance exams for Russian secondary school and the *numerus clausus* for his school "was harsh, only five per cent"[35] (even though Odessa was inside the Pale). When Babel received top marks in his class, the wealthy parent of a classmate, also a Jew, bribed the teacher to reduce his marks. The wealthy child got the place. A year later, like the boy in the story, Babel tried again and this time there was no interference. In the story, to celebrate the fictional son's triumph, his father threw a party, inviting all his friends:

> grain-dealers, estate brokers, and itinerant salesmen who sold agricultural machines in our region. These itinerant salesmen sold machines to everyone. Both muzhiks [peasants] and landowners were afraid of them, as they could not get rid of them without buying something. Of all Jews, the itinerant salesmen are the most worldly and cheerful. At our feast they sang drawn-out Hasidic songs made up of only three words, but with many funny intonations. . . . Old Lieberman, who taught me Hebrew and the Torah, also came to our house that evening. . . . He drank more Bessarabian wine than he should have . . . and he called out a toast in my honor in Hebrew. In this toast the old man congratulated my parents, and said that by passing this examination I had won a victory over all my foes, I had won a victory over the fat-cheeked Russian boys and the sons of our roughneck rich. Thus in ancient times had David, King of the Jews, won a victory over Goliath, and just as I had triumphed over Goliath, so too would our people, through its sheer power of mind, triumph over the foes that surround us, eager for our blood (p. 605).[36]

A month into the new school year, a pogrom broke out in Odessa and the boy's beloved granduncle (referred to as "Grandpa"), a fishmonger, was murdered by rioting townsfolk: "Two perches had been shoved into Grandpa—one into his fly, the other into his mouth—and although Grandpa was dead, one of the perches was still alive and quivering" (p. 610).[37] A pigeon the boy had purchased that morning for his prized dovecote was grabbed from him by a local Russian peddler, a cripple in a wheelchair ("the boys from our street bought cigarettes from him, the children liked him" [p. 607]). With the pigeon still in his hand, the cripple, frustrated at being unable to join in the looting, knocked the boy to the ground. The pigeon was crushed against the boy's temple, its innards "trickling down the side of my face" (p. 609). "Their seed must be stamped out," cried the cripple's wife, "I cannot abide their seed and their stinking men!" (p. 609). The tale ends with the boy reunited with his parents, hiding from the pogrom.

The Odessa pogrom was one of hundreds to occur throughout Russia in 1905, the year Abraham and Lescha married and moved, with forged papers, to St. Petersburg (as Babel himself did in 1916). What sparked the pogroms was a massacre in St. Petersburg. On January 22, 1905, later known in Russia as "Bloody Sunday," troops guarding the Winter Palace opened fire on a huge procession of demonstrators intent on delivering an antigovernment petition to Alexander III's successor, Nicholas II (who reigned from 1894 to 1917). Hundreds of demonstrators were killed (figures range from two hundred to a thousand). Thus began the so-called 1905 Russian Revolution, a year of political unrest resulting in the execution of 14,000 people and the imprisonment of 75,000.[38] The government identified the Jews as leaders of the unrest, as some were, and fomented anti-Jewish feeling throughout the empire, tacitly supporting "patriotic" demonstrators such as those Babel describes running amok in "The Story of My Dovecote."

In the period the Belos lived in St. Petersburg, according to Kenneth Trachtenberg, the narrator of Bellow's late novel *More Die of Heartbreak* (Kenneth's specialism is "Czarist culture in its final phase"), the city was "a mixture of barbarism and worn out humanist culture" (p. 179). Its atmosphere is brilliantly evoked by Andrei Bely in his novel *Petersburg* (1916), described by Vladimir Nabokov as one of the four great masterpieces of twentieth-century prose (the others are Joyce's *Ulysses*, Kafka's *Metamorphosis*, and "the first half of Proust's fairy tale *In Search of Lost Time*").[39] Bely's novel swarms with conspirators, terrorists, suspected terrorists, police informers, and double agents. It opens in 1905 and closes in 1913, the exact years the Belos lived in the city. Its central characters, aside from the variously personified city itself (with its living statues, louring mists and clouds, and ominously expanding spheres, presaging explosion) are Apollon Apollonovich, an obvious figure of the hated Pobedonostsev (also of Tolstoy's Alexei Karenin), and his son, Nikolai, a character straight out of Dostoyevsky. Nikolai, a student of philosophy, has become entangled in a terrorist plot to blow up a high government official: his father (as Kenneth puts it, "he didn't really want to be a parricide. An apparent ethical logic drew him on. But by and by it . . . crumbled away" [p. 179]).[40] Nikolai's chief contact among the plotters is an impoverished radical named Alexander Ivanovich Dudkin, who, like many a radical or suspected radical, is resident in the city on forged papers. Several scenes involving Dudkin are set in restaurants on or around Nevsky Prospect. Almost all the characters in the novel are frightened of something: discovery, betrayal, disorder, assassination. As a consequence, their movements and reactions are extreme, immoderate. In their translation of *Petersburg*, Robert A. Maguire and John E. Malmstad offer an explanatory note for the sentence "Apollon Apollonovich opened the door to his office." It reads: "This is one of the rare instances in the novel when a door is simply opened. As in Dostoyevsky, they usually fly or swing open (or shut) with some violence."[41]

Neither Abraham nor Lescha Belo was a radical nor much interested in politics, but their circumstances were, inevitably, anxiety-inducing (in "Memoirs of a Bootlegger's Son," Pa Lurie is described as "nervous as a fox" [p. 13]). In later years, Bellow remembers his mother talking of "how wonderful it was in the Heim [homeland, Old Country] for them. Well, it was not the Heim for them."[42] Though the family was affluent, their prosperity was founded on deception. The official Jewish population of St. Petersburg in the period the family lived there was not more than 2 percent, though the unofficial or illegal population was much higher (in 1878, the city governor thought the number of illegal Jewish residents "considerably greater" than the legal population). According to Benjamin Nathans, a historian of late-nineteenth-century Russian Jewry, illegal residents like the Belos

> were often referred to as living *na dvorianskikh pravakh* (with a courier's rights), where *dvorianskii* alluded both to aristocrats (*dvoriane*) and the apartment house courtyard superintendents (*dvorniki*) whom it was necessary to bribe in order to preserve the fiction. Similarly, a Jew who bribed a doorman (*shveitsar*) was known as *shveitsarskii poddany*, a triple pun signifying "a subject of Switzerland," "a subject of the doorman," and—to Yiddish ears—"a sweating subject."[43]

For eight years the Belos lived *na dvorianskikh pravakh*. There were servants, coachmen, fine linens, a dacha (in *Herzog* and "Memoirs of a Bootlegger's Son," the dacha is located in nearby Finland). Louis Dworkin's wife, Rose, remembered the gloves Lescha brought with her to Chicago (from St. Petersburg via Montreal): they were "bejeweled and very fancy" and with other fine items left the impression that "there had to be money there." "That was a golden time for my mother," Bellow told an interviewer, of the St. Petersburg years, "that was when she was a young bride and there was plenty of money, and they were living in the Capital, and they went to Café Chantants and so forth and so on."[44] It was in Petersburg that she began to be called Liza instead of Lescha, and in Petersburg that she first read Tolstoy in Russian, and Abraham all of Pushkin, Lermontov, Chekhov, Turgenev, and Dostoyevsky, as well as Tolstoy (or so he claimed). Between 1869 and 1910, Nathans reports, "the declared native language of nearly half the city's Jews shifted from Yiddish to Russian, at nearly identical rates for men and women."[45]

Yet fears of betrayal or discovery remained, and were eventually realized. Sometime in 1912 or 1913 Abraham's illegal residence was made known to the authorities. Perhaps he was informed on, or failed to pay a bribe, or was late with a bribe, or was implicated by forgers or their intermediaries? Perhaps he himself was charged with supplying false papers? In later years, Abraham would take out a tattered copy of a journal article detailing his arrest, conviction, and subsequent escape to Canada. Bellow describes the article as written in the Russian alphabet on green newsprint. Joel Bellows, his nephew, remembers seeing the article, as does Bellow's niece, Lesha Bellows Greengus. According to Joel, it contained a photograph of Abraham in the top right-hand corner, and a headline reading: "A Jew Escapes." The article has disappeared and attempts to find it among Bellow's papers at the University of Chicago or in newspaper archives in Russia have proved fruitless. Only four documents have surfaced of potential relevance to Abraham's case, two from the Russian-language Jewish periodical *New Dawn*, and two from the Russian-language newspaper *Early Morning*. They concern a group of Jews arrested for forging papers for illegal residency, and for possessing such papers. The second of the *New Dawn* articles, published on March 21, 1913, reports that the Jews who received the forged papers were declared innocent and released from custody, not having known the documents were forged. Those who supplied the documents, however, were sentenced to two years' imprisonment. Their names were Kurkovskz, Isakovich, and Belousov. Belousov might be Belo or Belous. The dates of the case accord with family history, as does the length of sentence. But the initials given for Belousov in the *Early Morning* articles are "H.L." not "A.B." (for "Abraham Berelovich"), and the trial took place in Moscow.[46] In the end, all that can be said for certain of Abraham's arrest and imprisonment is what is said of Pa Lurie in "Memoirs of a Bootlegger's Son": "Pobedonostyev's police had arrested Pa and Pa had escaped from them" (p. 12).

What would it have mattered, though, if one could prove that Abraham Belo was Belousov, a seller or supplier of illegal papers as well as a purchaser? Would that make one think differently of him, or make him more of a criminal? "The big criminal!" Abraham's son, Sam Bellows, is remembered as saying, when the tattered article was brought out and read to grandchildren ("in the spirit of 'look where we came from, look how fortunate we are'"): "All he wanted to do was to make a living." A Jew who wanted to make a living in Russia in 1905, certainly a good living, would be unlikely to get anywhere if he obeyed the law. To obey it thirty-five years later would get him killed, as it did many of Abraham's and Lescha's relatives who remained behind in the Pale.[47] The literature of Jewish "criminality" in St. Petersburg makes just this point, in novels, stories, and poems by or about Jews whose illegal residence and employment in the capital are their only or initial crimes.[48] That an ambitious and energetic illegal resident such as Abraham might get involved in supplying forged papers or bribing officials is neither improbable nor, it could be argued, especially blameworthy, except insofar as it exposed him and his family to greater risk.

This background—of systematic discrimination and forced, some would say victimless, crime—underlay not only Abraham's and his family's subsequent attitudes to the law, but Bellow's fascination with those who lived outside it. In *The Ghost Writer* (1979), Philip Roth's fictional alter ego, Nathan Zuckerman, identifies Bellow's fictional alter ego, Felix Abravanel, as "a New World cousin" of Isaac Babel, by which he means the Isaac Babel of the Benya Krik stories, about the Jewish mobster-king of Odessa: "the gloating, the gangsters, all those gigantic types. It isn't that he throws in his sympathy with the brutes—it isn't that in Babel, either. It's their awe of them. Even when they're appalled, they're in awe. Deep reflective Jews a little lovesick at the sound of all that un-Talmudic bone crunching. Sensitive Jewish sages, as Babel says, dying to climb trees. . . . It's Babel's fascination with big-time Jews, with conscienceless Cossacks, with everybody who has it his own way."[49]

Not having it one's own way was the reality for Abraham, in Montreal as in Russia, and it had its effect on all the members of the family, even after their various successes in Chicago. In "Memoirs of a Boot-legger's Son," Pa explains to Joshua why he became a bootlegger:

> Driven to the wall. No alternative, Yehoshua my boy. You see what *die Mama* and I have gone through to keep coats on your backs and shoes on your feet and bring you up as Jews and not as enemies of Jews.
>
> When Pa spoke such things in his whisper, wide-eyed, he bent his knees—his body sank a little, he swayed it sidewards towards his knees as he had done when he told Bentchka that he didn't have a penny in his purse. It was a way of poor Jews and had humor and despair. Out of bitterest feeling Pa pressed his shoulders upward and spread his fingers wide and gave a hiss of laughter and talked to himself like a buffoon by his own name. ". . . Ah, Yankov, Yankov, you poor fool and eternal pauper / There's nothing in your till and nothing in your hopper." . . . He behaved like a painted man on the stage in the role of a poor Jew. Yet he did it to throw himself free of the creature of misery (pp. 97–98).

The mature Saul Bellow was anything but powerless, was a man who seemed from the outside to have "had it his own way" more than most. But that is not how it felt to him, often enough for friends, relations, and colleagues to remark on it. "Somehow, under deep layers, the old irremovable feeling lurks that I am a born slightee," Bellow writes to his friend Melvin Tumin on April 21, 1948, in a letter announcing that he has just won a Guggenheim Fellowship. According to his nephew Joel, a characteristic gesture of Uncle Saul's, as characteristic as the sideways tilt with which he'd watch the world, or the way he'd throw back his head in laughter, was a gesture very like Pa Lurie's. With arms bent at the elbow, shoulders raised, palms up, he'd act out or ask: "What's a man to do?" Which is to say, I'm powerless, the situation is out of my control, it cannot be helped. This gesture is familiar in Jewish litera-ture, particularly from Eastern European writers in Yiddish, such as Sholom Aleichem, a great favorite of Abraham Belo's and an author his son later translated. In the introduction to his 1963 anthology, *Great Jewish Short Stories*, Bellow describes the outlook of these writers: "We must make what we can of our condition with the means available. We must accept the mixture as we find it—the impurity of it, the tragedy of it, the hope of it."[50] Something of this attitude is retained, I am suggesting, even by Jews who defy state authority, as did Abraham Belo in Russia in the early 1900s, or cultural authority, as did Saul Bellow in America in the early 1950s.

In Abraham's case, though, in St. Petersburg in 1913, the result of defiance was prison, or would have been, had it not been for his escape. Bellow seems never directly to have said how his father managed this escape, either in interview or to family members, for all his interest in stories of *di heym* (*die Heimat* in German), the sorts of stories Abraham often told. "What I especially remembered of those Sunday afternoons," Lesha Greengus reports, "was that these folks would spend hours retelling their stories from the past, which included terrible suffering and loss." She remembers the tattered article but no details of Abraham's escape from his prison sentence, nor does she remember anyone asking for details, "though if anyone would, [Saul] certainly would have."[51] The "Memoirs" manuscript offers little help in this regard: "Then Pa was seized by the police for illegal residence. My uncles got him out of prison, and we escaped to Canada" (p. 35). In *Herzog*, the article on green newsprint is alluded to, but almost nothing is said about the escape: "Father Herzog sometimes unfolded it and read aloud to the entire family, translating the proceedings against Ilyona Ivakovitch Gerzog. He never served his sentence. He got away. Because he was nervy, hasty, obstinate, rebellious" (p. 554).

In *The Bellarosa Connection*, published in 1989, twenty-five years after *Herzog*, Bellow offers a story in some respects like Abraham's. At the heart of the novella is a miraculous escape. Harry Fonstein, a Jew living in fascist Rome under false papers, is caught by the authorities: "A police check was run, my papers were fishy, and that's why I was arrested."[52] One night a stranger comes to Fonstein's cell as he awaits deportation by the SS: "The message from this Italianer was: 'Tomorrow night, same time, your door will be open. Go out in the corridor. Keep turning left. And nobody will stop you. A person will be waiting in a car, and he'll take you to the train for Genoa.'" Fonstein asks who has arranged his rescue and is told "Billy Rose" (the Broadway producer, gossip columnist, sidekick of gangsters, of whom Fonstein has never heard). Rose (née Rosenberg) is running an underground operation helping European Jews to escape from Italy in World War II ("He must've seen Leslie Howard in *The Scarlet Pimpernel*" [p. 40]). The next night, "the guard didn't lock my door after supper, and when the corridor was empty I came out." The escape itself is described in detail:

So I opened every door, walked upstairs, downstairs, and when I got to the street there was a car waiting and people leaning on it, speaking in normal voices. When I came up, the driver pushed me in the back and drove me to the Trastevere station. He gave me new identity papers. He said nobody would be looking for me, because my whole police file had been stolen. There was a hat and coat for me in the rear seat, and he gave me the name of a hotel in Genoa, by the waterfront. That's where I was contacted. I had a passage on a Swedish ship to Lisbon (p. 41).[53]

In a fascinating account of the genesis of *The Bellarosa Connection*, Bellow's wife Janis tells of a dinner they were given at the home of Vermont neighbors in May 1988. At the end of the dinner the host told a story about a friend and colleague who had been a European refugee in the early 1940s in fascist Italy. This was the seed or spark from which the novella sprang. The host's colleague had been imprisoned in Rome, but had managed to write to Billy Rose on the advice of a friend; Rose had Italian contacts who organized an escape; the friend ended up in Cuba, from which he eventually made his way to the United States. The host's recounting of the escape was detailed, though Janis was distracted at the dinner and cannot be sure how much of it Bellow reproduced in the novella, how much he added or altered. Almost as soon as he began work on the story the next day, however, it was "no longer about [the host's] friend."[54] The ingredients Bellow wove into *The Bellarosa Connection* were various. Janis identifies them as "event, accident, memory, and thought—what he had read, what we had discussed, and the contents of his dreams." In the writing, they became new: "When pieces of life begin to find their way into the work, there is always something magical about the manner in which they are lifted from the recent—or distant—past or the here and now, and then kneaded and shaped and subtly transformed into narrative. . . . To watch these details working their way into or out of the novella is nothing like the cutting and pasting of actual events. Biographers, beware: Saul wields a wand, not scissors" (p. ix).

The idea that Abraham's escape from prison in St. Petersburg is one of the ingredients "kneaded and shaped" into *The Bellarosa Connection* is suggested partly by the intensity and particularity with which Fonstein's escape is imagined, partly by the story's fictional frame. The unnamed narrator of the novella hears the full story of the escape at a Sunday family gathering, in the presence of his "keen-eyed" father (p. 37). The father "had a passion for refugee stories," had heard this one many times, and had himself told the narrator about it before Fonstein does. The narrator in turn will hear it many times on many Sundays, "in episodes, like a Hollywood serial." There are similarities in background between narrator and author, both earning their living through memory (the narrator runs something called the Mnemosyne Institute, "as profitable as it was unpronounceable," says his father, with the "comic bewilderment" Bellow's own father sometimes adopted when speaking of his son's profession[55]), and it is tempting to believe that the escape owes something to Abraham. Behind this belief lie several prior assumptions: that the phrase "escapes" from the remembered headline "A Jew Escapes" means "escapes from prison," as opposed to "escapes from sentencing, or serving a sentence"; that the phrase "got him out of prison" from "My uncles got him out of prison, and we escaped to Canada," from "Memoirs of a Bootlegger's Son," means "broke him out of prison," as opposed to, say, "put up bail (which he skipped, escaping to Canada)."[56] In the absence of police records (destroyed by fire in 1917), one can only surmise. Janis Bellow says: "The Bellarosa account didn't borrow from family adventure."[57] If she's right, then the particulars of Abraham's escape from prison (in whichever sense one takes the phrase) remain oddly unimagined in Bellow's writing, as well as oddly unrecalled in interview, personal reminiscence, and correspondence.

The Atlantic crossing, the last episode of the family's removal to the New World, is lost to memory, too. What is known is that the Bellows departed from Southampton on the *Ascania*, a ship of the Cunard Line, and arrived in Halifax, Nova Scotia, on December 26, 1913. The *Ascania* was built in 1911 and carried two hundred first-class passengers and 1,500 third-class passengers. Three details of the actual crossing survive, from the recollections of Bellow's sister, Jane: that her brother Sam, two at the time, was the sole member of the family not to suffer from seasickness; that he jumped from bunk to bunk in high spirits; and that the children were ordered to call Abraham uncle not father, as he was traveling under false papers. In the ship's manifest, directly below the names of Lescha and the children, the name "Rafael Gordin" appears, the original of Robert Gordin, Lescha's brother from South Africa. "Rafael" is listed as twenty-nine years old (Abraham's age in 1913); his place of birth, like that of Lescha and the children, is listed as "Russia"; his "race or people," like theirs, as "Hebrew"; and his occupation as "Labourer."[58] Abraham was indebted to Robert for lending him his name as well as his money.

"SOMEBODY OUGHT TO DO a monograph on the Jewish responses to the various lands of their exile," declares Kenneth Trachtenberg in *More Die of Heartbreak*. "Russia was peculiarly nasty, but Jews nevertheless were strongly drawn to the Russians" (p. 17). This claim was certainly true of Kenneth's creator. Bellow was proud of his Russian heritage, in literature, even in politics (at least for a while), and in temperament. In high school, he and his bookish circle dubbed themselves the Russian Literary Society. "We were so *Russian* as adolescents," he told Stanley Elkin, writing of himself and Isaac Rosenfeld in a letter of March 12, 1992. "As an adolescent I read an unusual number of Russian novels," he told an interviewer. "I felt it was the Heimat, you know." "The children of immigrants in my Chicago high school . . . believed that they were also somehow Russian," he writes in an essay of 1993, "and while they studied their *Macbeth* and Milton's *L'Allegro*, they read Tolstoy and Dostoyevsky as well and went on inevitably to Lenin's *State and Revolution* and the pamphlets of Trotsky."[59] As an undergraduate at the University of Chicago, Rosenfeld rented an "apartment" (in fact, a whitewashed coal cellar) on Woodlawn Avenue in Hyde Park. Its virtues, in addition to how little it cost, are described by Bellow in "Zetland: By a Character Witness" (1974): "It was bohemian, it was European. Best of all, it was Russian! The landlord, Perchik, said that he had been game-beater for Grand Duke Cyril. Abandoned in Kamchatka when the Japanese War began, he trudged back across Siberia. With him Zet had Russian conversations."[60]

The influence of Russian literature on Bellow's writing is clear. Dostoyevsky is the spirit presiding over his first two novels (along with a daunting "Flaubertian standard"), and he remains a presence throughout his career. V. S. Pritchett identifies Dostoyevsky's influence in the "sense of looseness, timelessness and space" in Bellow's novels and stories,[61] the room they find for historical and philosophical depth, for ideas and theories. It is there also in the comic depiction— more pronounced in Bellow than in Dostoyevsky, but Dostoyevskian nonetheless—of the fictional spokesmen of these ideas and theories, even those who are most dangerous or pathological. Tolstoy's influence is more diffuse, a matter of balance or objectivity, as in Bellow's attraction to, and intimate knowledge of, the worlds he deplores and seeks to rise above, worlds of sensual glamour, social complexity, and material power. Tolstoy also offers Bellow a model of the writer's life and method. "I carry numerous projects with me in endless gestation," he writes to a correspondent in 1980. "Now and then I am happily delivered of one of them. This, come to think of it, is the method preferred above all by Tolstoy." "Pretty soon I'll be unassailable," he jokes to Herbert Gold, the novelist, "and I can write philosophy like Tolstoy,"[62] a remark made in the handsome, ramshackle, dachalike house in rural New York Bellow purchased in 1956, a little Yasnaya Polyana. Here Bellow lived briefly with his second wife, Sondra Tschacbasov, known as Sasha.[63]

In politics, the Russian influence also played a part. "You have to understand the Jews of my generation, whose parents were usually born in Russia," explains Bellow's sometimes friend Alfred Kazin ("Avrahm Gedolyevitch Kazin" in the correspondence, to Bellow's "Saulchick"). For these Jews "czarism was hell" and the Russian Revolution "would give them for the first time some kind of freedom."[64] Kazin was Bellow's exact contemporary, born five days before him (on June 5, 1915). In *A Walker in the City* (1951), the first volume of Kazin's autobiographical "New Yorker Trilogy," he re-creates the vision of socialism he held as an adolescent: "one long Friday night around the samovar and the cut-glass laden with nuts and fruits, all of us singing *Tsuzamen, tsuzamen, ale tsuzamen!* Then the heroes of the Russian novel—our kind of people—would walk the world—and I—still wearing a circle-necked Russian blouse *à la Tolstoy*—would live forever with those I loved in that beautiful Russian country of the mind."[65] In more sober terms, in a letter of November 5, 1990, to a correspondent from behind the Iron Curtain, Bellow explains "the great power of 1917 over us":

Among intellectuals the Revolution was the most prestigious event of the century and Lenin had an enormous influence: Lenin the thinker and Lenin as a most desirable human type, the chief representative of a *modern* intellect and an example of how intellectuals might obtain political power. . . . We—and I am thinking of Jewish adolescents in Chicago in the Thirties—we drew the line at Stalin and by the time the war began we understood how wrong we had been about 1917. Marxism Leninism fell away completely during and after World War II. From that time the Soviet Union represented despotism in its most boring form. But I needn't go on in this vein. I'm sure it's all quite clear to you. Old hat. I've told you all this to make clear to you how peculiarly *Russian* the young Jews of my generation were.[66]

Abraham saw "1917" very differently, as did Bellow's grandfather, judging by suggestions from the fiction. When the revolution began, Berel Belo was in his eighties and still energetic. He traveled from Dvinsk, where he was living, to St. Petersburg (then called Petrograd), when and why is not remembered, and at one point took refuge in the Winter Palace.[67] We have no details of his adventures there, though Grandpa Herzog also ends up in the Winter Palace, where he is depicted as a combination of pious scholar and business shark, like Berel:

> With the instinct of a Herzog for the grand thing, he took refuge in the Winter Palace in 1918 (the Bolsheviks allowed it for a while). The old man wrote long letters in Hebrew. He had lost his precious books in the upheaval. Study was impossible now. In the Winter Palace you had to walk up and down all day to find a *minyan* [the quorum of ten Jewish males required for public prayer and other religious obligations]. Of course there was hunger, too. Later, he predicted that the Revolution would fail and tried to acquire Czarist currency, to become a millionaire under the restored Romanoffs (p. 555).

Abraham shared Father Herzog's skepticism about the revolution. "When I brought people home," Bellow recounts, "especially people who had been to the Soviet Union, young Americans who had done some kind of work there, he gave them a hard time. 'You don't know Russia. You don't know what's happening there.' And he was right. But I felt ashamed that he should be such a reactionary."[68]

Bellow did not feel ashamed of his father's open expression of emotion, a quality he thought of as Russian as well as Jewish. "The Jews valued Russian emotionalism very much," he told the same interviewer, "as long as the emotionalism didn't turn into murder, as often happened." In a 1961 profile of Nikita Khrushchev, he locates the Soviet premier's power and appeal in just this emotionalism: "we praise the gray dignity of our [Western] soft-spoken leaders, but in our hearts we are suckers for passionate outbursts."[69] "Russian in his rage" is how Zetland's father is described (p. 249); for the Russian scholar Kenneth Trachtenberg, "there is a special Russian asset, which is the belief that Russia is the homeland of the deeper and sincerer emotions. Dostoyevsky among others promoted this reputation for unlimited passion" (p. 91).[70] At the start of Bellow's career, Dostoyevsky was his idol and "American" reticence his enemy. *Dangling Man* (1944), his first novel, opens with a challenge to "hard-boileddom . . . an American inheritance": "Do you have feelings? There are correct and incorrect ways of indicating them. Do you have an inner life? It is nobody's business but your own. Do you have emotions? Strangle them. To a degree, everyone obeys this code. . . . If you have difficulties, grapple with them silently, goes one of their commandments. To hell with that! I intend to talk about mine."[71]

Another aspect of Bellow's Russian inheritance is the incongruity or unpredictability of the emotions expressed, as well as their intensity and openness. The volte-face or unexpected turn, from benevolence to cruelty, and back, is a stock feature of Russian life and letters. It is crucial to the power of the scene that opens this chapter, when Abraham "whales on Maury" (as the oldest of Bellow's three sons, Greg, puts it). Unanticipated, disproportionate reactions such as Abraham's even have a name in Russian, *proizvol*, "of which no closer translation than 'arbitrariness' suggests itself."[72] Dostoyevsky's novels are full of these reactions, as are Babel's stories. Both authors are drawn to the sorts of characters who produce them, notably *faux bonhommes* or malign buffoons, of whom Fyodor Karamazov is the best-known example (Bellow likens Khrushchev to him).[73] In *The Victim* (1947), Bellow's second novel, we get a version of the type, in the figure of Kirby Allbee, an anti-Semite who torments the novel's central character, Asa Leventhal, a Jewish subeditor on a trade magazine. Allbee is based in part on Father Karamazov-like figures in two Dostoyevsky stories, "The Eternal Husband" and "The Double." Though of WASP heritage, he's a Russian type, volatile, querulous, "slightly jeering, slightly presumptious," yet with "no hint of amusement" in his eyes.[74] The mocking self-pity of Allbee and other such figures connects them to Yiddish as well as Dostoyevskian prototypes, to the *schlemiel* of Jewish folk humor and the stories of Sholom Aleichem. According to Bellow's friend, Ruth Wisse, professor of Yiddish at Harvard, the *schlemiel* is "the Jew as he is defined by the anti-Semite, but reinterpreted by God's appointee."[75] "It was clear that the man was no fool," says Leventhal, whom Allbee blames for his troubles, "but what was the use of not being a fool if you acted like this" (p. 200). In *The Victim*, the anti-Semitic doppelgänger, appropriately, recalls a Jewish type (the novel's title applies to Allbee as well as Leventhal, the result of what Bellow describes as "a perverse kind of favoritism toward outsiders and strictness with the beloved children—which originates, I think, with my father"[76]). Allbee's faux humility and faux good humor are like those of Pavel Pavlovitch in "The Eternal Husband," Golyadkin's double in "The Double," and Father Karamazov, but they are also like those of Pa Lurie, capering in self-parody, "to throw himself free of the creature of misery." The Russian type and the Yiddish type fold together.

Abraham was a difficult father for Bellow to deal with not only because of his Russian Jewish background, but because he was an immigrant. "Yes, I had a tyrannical father," Bellow wrote to Irving Halperin. "Russian-Jewish fathers were naturally tyrannical. But they knew, as their children did not, how very different from the Russian life of their own boyhood our lives in America were. . . . Our lives seemed to them a paradise which we had done nothing to deserve." While fathers like Abraham strained to negotiate a foreign land in a foreign language, they watched their children do so with comparative ease. They also found themselves forced to rely on their children, to interpret, explain, translate. "The great loss was the loss of language," writes Bernard Malamud, who also had a Russian Jewish immigrant father. "You have some subtle thought and it comes out like a piece of broken bottle."[77] The injured pride of such fathers was particularly expressed in front of their sons, or when sons resisted, something their new surroundings seemed to encourage. As Bellow continues in the letter to Halperin: "Our fathers lacked the support of a tyrannical society, and we were not in awe of their authority. Sensing this, they turned up the heat. But without an authoritarian society to support them, they seemed quite weak, alas, and their storming did not impress us."

Sons with fathers like Abraham often developed a prickly, combative manner. Philip Roth invokes this manner and the background that produced it when explaining his wariness of Bellow, with whom he did not become close until the late 1980s, almost thirty years after they'd first met. To Roth, born in 1933, Bellow's generation of Jewish writers and intellectuals, men like Kazin, Philip Rahv, and Lionel Abel, "a formidable bunch," seemed difficult and unwelcoming. But then "these are almost all guys who had really tough times with their immigrant fathers. And even when they didn't have a tough time with an immigrant father, they had an immigrant father." Roth remembers Kazin arguing with him, wagging a finger under his nose and saying: "You don't understand a word I say. You don't even understand when I say you don't understand." Irving Howe, author of *World of Our Fathers* (1976), also had a Russian Jewish immigrant father. On the day his father died, Howe stood by his hospital bed, feeling "almost nothing," staring "at the shrunken body of the man who would never again greet me with an ironic rebuke." Earlier, on the way to the hospital, his father "still had enough strength to argue against my proposal that we hire a private nurse. He didn't need one. And what could a nurse do, make him young again? His eyes glinted as he said this, waiting to see if I would record his last stab at paternal irony. . . . I hired a private nurse and, to no one's surprise, my father accepted her without protest. His obligation had been to argue against hiring her, mine to hire her."[78]

Roth stresses the differences as well as the similarities between the Jewish American writers and intellectuals of Bellow's generation. "Saul was unlike any of the others, and none of them resembled him, but they shared certain characteristics." The differences extended to relations with fathers. Though all had difficult immigrant fathers, these fathers were difficult in different ways. Though their sons all argued with them (Greg Bellow remembers "terrible screaming fights" between his father and grandfather), and could be argumentative and prickly in turn, what they felt for them differed. When Howe's father's died, "close to the end he told my son that finally I had been a good son. He did not say a loving son." Howe implicitly accepts the truth of this judgment when he adds that "he, perhaps not such a good father, had been a loving one, always ready, after his opening sarcasm, to accept my foolishness and chaos."[79] Abraham Bellow was a loving father if not a good one, while his son was a loving son. The fathers in Bellow's fiction are almost all difficult or deficient; the ones modeled on Abraham are also loving.

These reflections may help to explain Bellow's fictional versions of Abraham, more particularly his versions of Abraham's return from the hijacking, which omit Maury's beating. In "Memoirs of a Bootlegger's Son," when Joshua is sent to find his father, he discovers him already at the workplace: "I ran in panting and said, frightened, 'Pa, Pa!' and Pa said, 'It's all right, my son,' and put his hand on me to quiet me. 'Don't be frightened, Joshua'" (p. 140). In *Herzog*, the father is met not in the workplace, but at home, by the whole family. He enters the kitchen bloody, bruised, his clothes torn: "'Sarah!' he said. 'Children!' He showed his cut face. He spread his arms so we could see his tatters, and the white of his body under them. Then he turned his pockets inside out—empty. As he did this, he began to cry, and the children standing about him all cried" (p. 564). Leaving out the violent encounter with Maury can be seen as the act of a good son, a loving son, an American son. There are also narrative grounds for the omission. The scene is recalled by a narrator like Bentchka or Schloimke; Moses Herzog is the youngest son not the oldest, and has been least subject to the father's violence ("I was the child and plaything of everyone and I was spared the harsher aspects of family life," Bellow recalled of his upbringing[80]). The scene is narrated from the point of view of a child not an adolescent, with a childlike vision of the father and the world.

This childlike vision was particularly powerful for Bellow; it never left him, and was cultivated. Like Victor Wulpy in the story "What Kind of a Day Did You Have?," Bellow believed that "genius *must* be the recovery of the powers of childhood by an act of the creative *will*." As a child, Bellow saw his father in biblical terms: "My childhood lay under the radiance (or gloom) of the archaic family, the family of which God is the ultimate father and your own father is the representative of divinity." He saw the Bible, moreover, in familial terms: "[the Pentateuch] was not a fairy tale. It was a holy book, in Hebrew, and you knew that it had to be true, because it said God created the world—and here was the world. Here's the proof. Right outside the window was your proof." The biblical Abraham, the father of his people, and Abraham Bellow were somehow the same: "It was impossible for a child of eight to make all the necessary distinctions, and I didn't even try to make any distinctions. . . . I felt very cozy with God, the primal parent, and by the time I was up to the Patriarchs (I was five or six years old), I felt they were very much like members of my family. I couldn't readily distinguish between a parent and the heroic ancestors—Abraham, Isaac, and Jacob, and the sons of Jacob, especially Joseph."[81] This is the way Victor Wulpy as a child remembers thinking of the Old Testament. In 1912, in his basement cheder on the Lower East Side,

The street, the stained pavement, was also like a page of Hebrew text, something you might translate if you knew how. Jacob lay dreaming of a ladder which rose into heaven. *V'hinei malachi elohim*—behold the angels of God going up and down. This had caused Victor no surprise. What age was he, about six? It was not a dream to him.

Jacob was dreaming, while Victor was awake, reading. There was no "Long ago." It was all now. The cellar classroom had a narrow window at sidewalk level, just enough to permit a restricted upward glance showing fire escapes under snow, the gold shop sign of the Chinese laundry hanging under the ironwork, and angels climbing up and down (p. 321).[82]

Some part of the child's reverence for the father lived on in Bellow, as it does in his characters. In the incident recounted in the story "Something to Remember Me By" (1990), which ends with a paternal clout to the head ("My father rose from his chair and hurried toward me. His fist was ready"), the narrator is a high school senior, hence seventeen or eighteen not six, but he's a younger not an older son, no Maury. He still thinks of his father's "blind, Old Testament rage" not "as cruelty but as archaic right everlasting."[83] The adults in Bellow's fiction, or some of them, share as well as inculcate this childlike view. In *The Adventures of Augie March*, the child Augie spends summers with his mother's cousin, a woman of "great size and terrific energy of constitution." Her excesses of emotion—"Cousin Anna wept enough for everybody and plastered me with kisses at the door of her house, seeing me dog-dumb with the heartbreak of leaving home"—were "untamed by thoughts." She observed every Jewish holiday, including the new moons, prayed with fervor, "her eyes dilated and determined," and had "her own ideas of time and place, so that Heaven and eternity were not too far" (p. 401). Cousin Anna thought it a duty to teach Augie about the Bible:

> It was a queer account I got from her of the Creation and Fall, the building of Babel, the Flood, the visit of the Angels to Lot, the punishment of his wife and the lewdness of his daughters, in a spout of Hebrew, Yiddish, and English, powered by piety and anger, little flowers and bloody fires supplied from her own memory and fancy. . . . She was directing me out of her deep chest to the great eternal things (p. 412).

Bellow the child, instructed like Augie, saw the world as did the child Moses Herzog. When Father Herzog, beaten and ashamed, begins to cry, and his children begin to cry, Moses is overpowered: "It was more than I could bear that anyone should lay violent hands on him—a father, a sacred being, a king. Yes, he was a king to us. My heart was suffocated by this horror. I thought I would die of it. Whom did I ever love as I loved them" (p. 564).

Bellow's decision to leave Maury's beating out of published versions of Abraham's return owes something to feelings like these—feelings inherited from Abraham himself. When news came from Russia of Berel Belo's death, Bellow remembered, Abraham "burst into tears then took a razor and cut his vest," as Jewish custom demands.[84] In "Memoirs," Pa Lurie's father writes letters to his son in Canada after the October Revolution. Like Father Herzog, Father Lurie has taken refuge in the Winter Palace in St. Petersburg, the "Tsarskoe Seloe." In elegant Hebrew he complains of the absence of a synagogue, how cold it is in the palace, how people are being shot in the streets. "Shall I ever again see the faces of my children?" he asks. Pa Lurie's voice sticks as he reads the question and he has to leave the room. This scene appears in *Herzog* in almost exactly these words, and ends with the father leaving the room (p. 555). In "Memoirs," though, Bellow has the narrator, the oldest son, reflect on the father's reaction: "When something like this happened, I was much moved, like the rest. But I knew I was a sucker. I spoke to my heart and said that it was a sucker. I knew that before long I would run afoul of Pa, and he would forget that after all I was a son, too, and would lay into me. In a burst of temper, he could slap you with both hands before you had a chance to cover your face. He was power-fully fast. When the color of anger came into it, his face was powerfully clear" (p. 14). There are narrative grounds for omission of this passage in *Herzog*. The scene is narrated from the point of view of nine-year-old Moses, like nine-year-old Bentchka.

Grandpa Belo was not the only member of the family to suffer after the revolution. Lescha's brothers, the family's benefactors, lost everything. In 1919 the Bolsheviks came in search of Nahum Gordin to confiscate his property. According to his son, they entered Nahum's buildings, slashed open the beds, and smashed the furniture in search of gold and jewels. Nahum hid in the attic above one of his restaurants, caught pneumonia, and died in May 1919.[85] All his properties were confiscated, though his widow and children were allowed to rent two rooms of the twelve-bedroom apartment they had once owned, with use of a now communal bathroom. In these rooms the widow lived with her four sons and brother-in-law, Robert, who had also lost his prop-erty, and was drinking heavily.[86] When news reached Lescha in Canada of her brother Nahum's death, she was inconsolable. Here is how Ma

Lurie reacts in "Memoirs": "On the day she received the news of Aaron's death, when she had been doing a Monday wash, she sat sobbing by the tub. Except to mourn, Jews were forbidden to sit on the floor. She hung over the tub, and her arms in gray sleeves, trailed in the water." Joshua reaches down to lift her up and feels the beating of her heart, "racing, furious, sick and swift" (p. 33). This scene appears in *Herzog*, in much the same words, and, again, what follows in "Memoirs" is cut. As soon as Joshua lifts his weeping mother, Pa Lurie rages at her, beside himself with suspicion that she has been sending money to her brothers and mother. "When he flew into a rage, he forgot himself altogether, and lost his sense of shame" (p. 32).

In a letter of June 14, 1955, to Leslie Fiedler, while at work on and still pleased with "Memoirs" ("a handsome new book, which is so far highly satisfactory"), Bellow describes himself as "creep[ing] near the deepest secrets of my life." In later years, he is said to have thought "Memoirs" too sentimental to publish. But the novel could also be thought of as too tough to publish, unflinching, unforgiving. From this perspective, suppressing the manuscript was the act of a pious and loving son. After 1964, there was also a practical impediment, since a number of characters and key episodes from the manuscript had appeared in *Herzog*, reworked from the younger son's perspective. These reworkings suggest the complexity and intensity of Bellow's feelings for his father. One element of Abraham's life, however, has only been hinted at here: the shame produced by the series of humiliating failures in Canada that preceded his bootlegging. These failures belong to the chapter that follows, though they obviously played a part in his violence toward Maury after the hijacking. They shaped and shadowed Abraham, and Bellow's feelings toward him, even after the family rose to prosperity in the Chicago years. As the adult Moses Herzog puts it: "I am still a slave to Papa's pain" (p. 566).

In a letter of October 19, 1953, after the publication and great success of *The Adventures of Augie March* and while still at work on "Memoirs," Bellow reassured his friend Sam Freifeld, who had had a difficult conversation with Abraham:

> I don't know what anyone can do about my father except to change his character and that lies within the power of no one. Therefore, whatever you said, you said on your own account or in the name of justice, but practical effect I think there should be none. Myself, I have tried to hold no grudge and I had already answered his letter

before yours arrived. I see no reason why I should not be faithful to whatever was, in the past, venerable in my father and I do the best to make allowances for the rest. I wouldn't be uneasy about this at all if I were you. It's just like my father to begin to be generous long after the rest of the world has begun. He's impressed by my new fame and even more by the sales of the book and so now he feels uneasy and wants, too late, to go on record as a good parent. I try to make him feel there is plenty of time.

It is not clear which letter Bellow is referring to here. The only one to survive around this date was written on September 23, 1953. In it Abraham sends money for further copies of *Augie*, tells Bellow he is feeling all right, though just out of the hospital after suffering a slight heart attack, praises the success of the book, and reports that everyone else in the family is fine. The letter ends: "Wright me. A Ledder. Still I am The Head of all of U." It is signed: "Pa A. Bellow."[87]

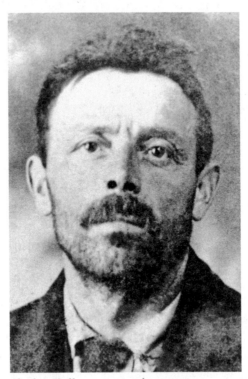

Abraham Bellow, passport photo, 1913

SB's maternal grandfather, Moses Gordin, shortly before his death, c. 1905 (private collection)

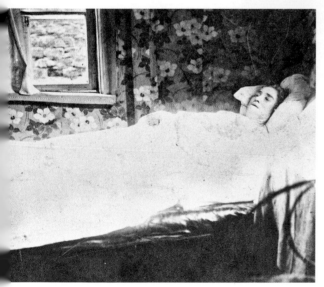

SB's paternal grandmother, Shulamith Belo, on her deathbed. There are no surviving photos of Berel Belo, SB's paternal grandfather. (private collection)

SB's maternal grandmother, Sara Gordin (private collection)

Houses in the Jewish
district, Druya (courtesy
of Alexander Feigmanis)

Jewish cemetery,
Druya (courtesy of
Alexander Feigmanis)

SB's father, Abraham Bellow (far right), produce broker,
St. Petersburg, c. 1907 (private collection)

SB's favorite portrait of his
mother, Liza Bellow
(private collection)

Lachine Canal,
Canada (courtesy
of Alice Leader)

130 Eighth Street, Lachine,
Canada. SB was born in the
ground-floor apartment.
(courtesy of Alice Leader)

Rue Napoleon, at the crossing
with rue St. Dominique, in
the Jewish district of Montreal,
with Mount Royal in the
distance. SB and family lived
at 1092 St. Dominique. "What
was wrong with Napoleon
Street? thought Herzog.
All he ever wanted was there."
(courtesy of Alice Leader)

The Bellow family, Montreal,
c. 1920; from left to right: SB,
Liza, Jane, Abraham, Maury,
Sam (private collection)

Royal Victoria Hospital, Mount Royal, where SB spent "four to five" months in 1923, aged eight (Alice Leader)

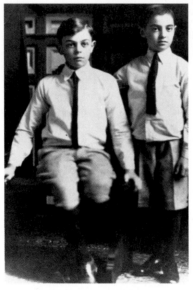

Sam and SB, c. 1924 (private collection)

SB and sister Jane (private collection)

SB's first home in Chicago, 2629 West Augusta Street, in Humboldt Park, 2014 (courtesy of John Hellmuth)

Sam Freifeld, SB's friend, early twenties (private collection)

(*left*) David Peltz, SB's friend, late teens (courtesy of Kathy Peltz Rivera)

Ethel and wheelchair-bound Ben Freifeld, the model for Einhorn in *The Adventures of Augie March*, "the first superior man I knew," 2160 Division Street, Chicago, early 1940s (courtesy of Judith Freifeld Ward)

Sydney J. Harris. "Skinny Sydney with his wild ways, his tics and rages, ran the show." (courtesy of Lindsay Harris)

Oscar Tarcov at sixteen, 1935
(courtesy of Nathan Tarcov)

SB at fourteen,
summer 1929

Isaac Rosenfeld (second from right, top row) at thirteen with his afternoon
Yiddish class. A year later he would be addressing the Tuley Debating Club
on Schopenhauer. (courtesy of Daniel Rosenfeld)

The wedding of Maury and Marge Bellows, 1934. Fourth from left, standing, Sam Bellows; then SB; then sister Jane; SB's stepmother, Fanny Bellow; Maury; and Abraham Bellow. Marge, the bride, is seated between her parents. (private collection)

Maury Bellows. "For me, the overpowering brother." (courtesy of Joel Bellows)

(*above*) Sam Bellows. "A mild person, clever and thoughtful . . . American in hatching deals and multiplying bank accounts." (private collection)

The University of Chicago, with the trees of the Midway in the foreground; Harper Library and the social science offices, including those of the Committee on Social Thought, to the left and behind; and the Loop skyscrapers in the distance

SB in 1957, revisiting Goff House
(1326 E. 57th Street), where he roomed as
an undergraduate (courtesy of the University
of Chicago Photographic Archive, Special
Collections Research Center, University of
Chicago Library; photo by Morton Shapiro)

Melville J. Herskovits, professor of
anthropology, Northwestern University,
early 1930s (Northwestern University
Archives)

Northwestern University, Evanston, Illinois, with its leafy, lakeside campus
ten miles north of the Loop, mid-1930s (Northwestern University Archives)

2

Canada / Liza

THE *ASCANIA* DOCKED AT Halifax, Nova Scotia, in December 1913, the day after Christmas. Abraham's sister, Rosa (originally Raisa) Gameroff, and her husband, Max (Mikhail), were present to meet the new arrivals. Max had come first to the New World, summoning Rosa and their four children from Dvinsk in 1908, after he'd found work as a laborer on the Canadian Pacific Railroad. Rosa, born in 1876, five years before Abraham, was followed by two other Belo siblings, a younger brother and sister: Willie (Elya Velvel), married to Jenny; then Annie (Channah), married to Max Cohen. Willie and Jenny eloped and came to Canada partly for political reasons, fearing persecution for having joined the Bund, the Jewish socialist organization. Berel Belo so disapproved of Willie's youthful politics that he apprenticed him to a brushmaker. "The Bellows did not work with their hands," Saul Bellow explains, "they were not tradespeople, and to apprentice Willie to a brushmaker was meant to be especially humiliating and punitive because he would be working with hog bristles." In Canada, Willie found work as a grocer, though later, after moving to Brownsville in Brooklyn, New York, he returned to brushmaking. Bellow "loved him dearly. He was a very feeling, cheerful, generous humorist, without much power of self-expression." Max Cohen, Annie's husband, owned a small dry goods store in Canada, and would eventually move to Augusta, Georgia, "selling schmattes [cheap clothing] on the instalment plan to black field hands." Bellow described him as "a cheerful, engaging, hand-to-mouth ganef [thief]."[1]

The three Belo siblings and their families lived in Lachine, Quebec, a quiet working-class town, previously a village, about nine miles southwest of Montreal (since 2002 an incorporated borough of the city). Lachine's most prominent feature is the Lachine Canal, on the St. Lawrence River. The canal affords passage to and from the North Atlantic and the Great Lakes, bypassing the dangerous Lachine Rapids; the kept waters of its locks and reaches border the town, distancing and softening what Bellow describes as the river's "platinum rush."[2] When the Bellows arrived in 1913, factories and warehouses lined much of the canal and the river beyond, for stretches blocking them from sight. The town's inhabitants, immigrant laborers from Russia, Ukraine, Greece, Scandinavia, Sicily, Poland, Italy, and Hungary, were further cut off by close-packed stucco and brick bungalows and two-flats.[3] The major employers along the canal were the French Canadian Dominion Bridge Company, the Dominion Textile cotton mills, Canada Malting, Brights Wine, lured to the town by access to water for hydraulic power, industrial processes, easy shipping. By 1909 the number of immigrant Jews in Lachine had grown sufficiently to found a small synagogue, the Beth Israel on Ninth Avenue, on the east side of the town. In an article of October 1, 1909, in the *Canadian Jewish Times* announcing the synagogue's opening, its congregation was described as made up largely "of artisans and mechanics in one or other of the large industrial establishments surrounding the town." By 1917, a second synagogue had opened, Tiferes Israel, on Sixth Avenue. The house the Bellows were taken to by the Gameroffs, the house where Bellow was born, was at 130 Eighth Avenue, described by him as "in a Jewish enclave,"[4] though one also containing families named Davis, Miller, and Dunsimore. The house was one block from the shops and businesses of Notre Dame Street, the town's main thoroughfare, and between the two synagogues.

When Rob Rexler, the narrator of "By the St. Lawrence" (1995), Bellow's last published story, returns to Lachine, after more than seventy years away, he finds it much changed. In 1984, Bellow, too, returned to Lachine, after a comparable absence, to attend a ceremony renaming the town's library in his honor. The house Rexler describes as his birthplace, "on Seventh Avenue or on Eighth," was like Bellow's birthplace, a modest brick two-flat. The Gameroffs lived above the Bellows, in a slightly larger apartment, with a bigger stove. Uncle Willie had his fruit store nearby, on Notre Dame Street, where Bellow remembers him "flipping open brown bags with a smart crack."[5] As a child, Rexler felt "hemmed in" on his street; seventy years later most of its houses have gone, replaced by vacant lots, though his own house survives, as does Bellow's today. From its narrow front yard Rexler can see "the wide river surface—it had been there all the while, beyond the bakeries and sausage shops, kitchens and bedrooms" (p. 2).

The river is a potent symbol in "By the St. Lawrence," a source of the sublime. For Bellow the child, however, the canal was what mattered. Only minutes from the house, its soothing presence recalls Wordsworth, a lifelong influence on Bellow's writing, on the River Derwent, which flowed past the garden of his birthplace, composing his thoughts "to more than infant softness."[6] Also prominent in Bellow's Lachine memories was tiny Monk Park, Monkey Park to the Bellow children, an island of banked earth, maple trees, a level expanse of grass, and benches. Here Bellow was taken by his mother or brothers and sister, or the young Native American nurse who tended him as an infant. Entrance to the park is at Seventh Avenue, across a simple iron footbridge. In Bellow's day, barges moved slowly through the nearby locks; the Caughnawaga Indian reservation was visible downstream on the far bank of the river.[7] Bellow remembers his nurse chewing his meat for him before putting it into his mouth, a detail that recalls Artur Sammler in childhood, covering his mouth, when he coughed, "with the servant's hand, to avoid getting germs on his own hand" (p. 49). The nurse is one of several affectionate female protectors to figure among Bellow's earliest memories: Mrs. Dettner, from the neighborhood candy store on St. Louis Street, giving him molasses candy and buttoning his rompers; Mrs. Mancuso, the Italian landlady, kissing him till he was "dizzy"; his mother, "mute with love," bundling him in woolens and setting him down in the snow with a small black stove shovel. Lachine was "paradise," he told the audience at the library's renaming. "I never found it again."[8]

The Gameroffs played a crucial and complex role in the life of the Bellow family. Bellow himself adored them, his parents were much in their debt, but there was friction and bad feeling between Rosa and Abraham and Liza. In 1905, when the Bellows moved to St. Petersburg, Max Gameroff was a conscript in the Russo-Japanese War (1904–5). In "By the St. Lawrence," he is fictionalized as Uncle Mikhel, who is said to have deserted the Russian army after Japan's victory, somehow reached western Canada, then labored for years for the Canadian Pacific Railroad (p. 7). In "The Old System" (1968), Uncle Braun has a similar history, stolen from his young family "to eat maggoty pork" in a despised "goy" war, escaping through Manchuria when the war was lost, arriving in Vancouver on a Swedish ship, laying track for years (p. 92). The same figure appears as Uncle Yaffe in *Herzog* and Uncle Jomin in "Memoirs of a Bootlegger's Son," where in both he is also said to have served in the Caucasus: "*A finsternish!* [a darkness] . . . too cold for dogs."[9] In all his fictional incarnations, Uncle Max is described as short, powerful, with a tight or close beard, and feeling brown eyes (in "By the St. Lawrence," each of these eyes has "a golden flake on it like the scale of a smoked fish" [p. 7]). Intelligent, mild, with "a grim humor about him" (the phrase is from "Memoirs," p. 46), like all the Gameroffs he was also salty and satirical. Bellow remembers him with his sons, up on the back porch of the Eighth Avenue apartment, reading aloud the matrimonial advertisements from the Yiddish papers: "Young widow, well endowed, looking for a husband."[10] Uncle Braun entertains his family in similar fashion in "The Old System": "all but Tina, the obese sister, took part in this satirical Sunday pleasure" (p. 94).

After leaving the railroad, Uncle Max started a business buying and selling scrap metal out of his yard; he also worked as a carpenter and sold used furniture. In *Herzog*, Bellow describes Uncle Yaffe stooped over piles of old plumbing and electrical fixtures, tires, rusted metal, junk of all sorts: "Without straightening his back he could pitch pieces of scrap where they belonged—iron here, zinc there, copper left, lead right, and Babbit metal by the shed" (p. 559). When World War I broke out, scrap metal was much in demand, for shipyards and the Western Front. The fortunes of the Gameroffs thrived in the years the Bellows lived below them. "Moneywise, they were among the first families," we learn of their fictional equivalents in "Memoirs." "They lived simply and they were known as hard dealers. In the synagogue, they rated very high and had seats against the eastern wall, the best because closest to Jerusalem" (p. 48).

Rosa Gameroff was the power in the family and a figure of fascination to Bellow. Tough, irascible, grudging, she was "at war with everyone" (words from *Herzog*, p. 558, but applicable to her fictionalization in "Memoirs" and the stories). "When she said something about you," we learn of Aunt Julia, the Rosa character in "Memoirs," "you were criticized to the heart. It was merciless, for she was a harsh judge of character. . . . She uttered the most damaging and shrewd remarks conceivable, a sort of poetry of criticism, fault-finding and abuse"; Aunt Julia had "a great genius with words"; in the women's section of the

Lachine synagogue, she prayed and read from the Hebrew "as well as any man" (pp. 46, 48). When she learns that Pa Lurie has become a bootlegger, her scorn has nothing to do with the profession's illegality. What she scorns is her brother's deluded belief that he could succeed at it. "Can a gipsy build an iron bridge? Can a bear make pancakes?" (p. 133). "Why should anyone comfort you," she asks after the hijacking. "Here are people who are playing for high stakes. Ships and factories, do you hear? Fortunes of money, whole distilleries. And you come creeping along with your six tins of whiskey and your cockroach partner in his Model T" (p. 145).

In all versions, the Rosa figure has a thin face, pinched nose ("to cut through mercy like a cotton thread" ["The Old System," p. 93]), high and alarming color (a product of hypertension), "cruelly" thick legs, "wildly overdeveloped" buttocks ("so that walking must have been a torment") ("By the St. Lawrence," p. 8), and an enormous bosom. Both Joshua from "Memoirs" and Moses from *Herzog* spot a large bankroll tucked in this bosom, rent money from tenants. It was Rosa not Max who invested in real estate, buying up vacant lots at the edge of town, then small buildings, trudging painfully from property to property. In "By the St. Lawrence," the Rosa figure is Aunt Rozzy, with "the fiery face of a hanging judge," "wicked to everyone. Except, perhaps, little Rexler" (p. 8). In "The Old System," she is Aunt Rose, described as "the original dura mater—the primal hard mother," a woman who takes pleasure in her hardness, "hardness of reckoning, hardness of tactics, hardness of dealing and of speech" (p. 93). When upbraided for a comparable hardness, Aunt Julia attacks: "Weakness makes me sick. It turns my stomach. When the rest of the world turns kind then I'll be kind, too, but not until. I hate fools" (p. 146).

Rosa Gameroff's initial impression of her newly arrived relatives was not favorable, or so the fiction suggests. "I can still see you getting off the train at Halifax," comments Aunt Zipporah to Father Herzog, "all dressed up among the greeners. *Gott meiner!* Ostrich feathers, the gloves" (p. 559).[11] It was the family's pride, "the caste madness of *yichus* [family status or prestige]" (p. 558), that offended Aunt Zipporah. She had been irritated by it from the start, back *in der Heim*. In "Memoirs of a Bootlegger's Son," the extravagance of the Lurie wedding, and of Ma Lurie's rich brothers, puts Aunt Julia's nose out of joint: "Aunt Julia and Aunt Taube [the Annie figure] felt Ma's people to be too proud. Ma's wedding had been overly grand for them" (p. 18). In *Herzog*, Aunt Zipporah complains of the extravagance of St. Petersburg: "You got used to putting on style . . . with servants and coachmen." Though marvelously biting to her brother, much of Zipporah's criticism is aimed at his wife. The Liza figure is seen as snobbish in her delicacy and refinement, also in her ambition for her children, the wrong wife for a husband without steady work. In the Bellow family, it was Liza who insisted that daughter Jane have piano lessons, at $3 a month. The Herzog daughter, Helen, also has piano lessons, but as Aunt Zipporah points out, she is no musician. Helen "plays to move the family," an indulgence, like Ma Herzog's mooning over the lost life *in der Heim*, instead of working. "Everyone must work. Not suffer your whole life long from a fall. Why must your children go to the conservatory, the Baron de Hirsch school, and all those special frills? Let them go to work, like mine" (p. 559). Similarly, while Father Herzog lived comfortably in St. Petersburg, thanks to Ma Herzog's brothers, and escaped to Canada, again thanks to the brothers, Zipporah's husband came alone and unaided to the New World, after freezing in the Caucasus. Only until he'd found steady work and saved enough money did he send for the family: "But you—you want *alle sieben glicken* [all seven lucky things]. You travel in style, with ostrich feathers. You're an *edel-mensch* [refined]. Get your hands dirty? Not you." These words are from Zipporah's answer to a request for a loan. "If I started to give, and indulged your bad habits," she continues, "it would be endless. It's not my fault you're a pauper here" (p. 561).

Saul Bellow was born on June 10, 1915. He was delivered, according to family legend, by a French Canadian doctor who had to be fetched from a saloon and "was quite drunk when he arrived." The narrator of "The Old System" is delivered by an Anglo Canadian version of this doctor, "faltering, drunken Jones, who practiced among Jewish immigrants before those immigrants had educated their own doctors." The first thing Jones does is to tie Mother Braun's hands to the bedposts, "a custom of the times" (p. 93). Once delivered, the infant Braun is washed, covered with a mosquito netting, and laid at the foot of his mother's bed.[12] In an undated letter, probably written in the early 1980s, Bellow's sister, Jane, seven in 1915, remembers coming home from school and finding "a beautiful white bundle with an angelic face covered with white cheesecloth lying at the foot of Ma's bed. I was happy with the arrival of a new baby, yet disappointed because I so much wanted a sister! I felt a sense of responsibility for you while you were growing up and kept a watchful eye. . . . Ma was tired and busy with her chores and I had to help out."[13] Maury, the elder of Bellow's two brothers, was seven at the time of the birth; Sam, the middle brother, was four.[14] In "Memoirs," Joshua, the Maury figure, describes his baby brother, Ben Zion or Bentchka, as having been delivered "after great trouble." When Joshua is allowed into the room to see the baby, his father is also present: "This is a clear vision in me, of the white infant, the iron bedstead, white bed cover, Ma holding the child to her side while Pa's moustaches gently touched its head. Ma's dark eyes in this warm room seemed to see what they had longed to see" (p. 7).

Bellow's earliest memories went "back to the age of two" and when checked with his sister proved "quite accurate."[15] In his speech at the Lachine library he described these memories as "vigorous and . . . in bright colors." From infancy, perception was for Bellow "a consuming appetite," an active process, no wise passiveness. The world was "grasped . . . tightly with my senses, and perhaps just as energetically with intuitions." Among specific memories, he mentions the banter between passing bargemen and the people alongside; he recites the first verse of a bargemen's song: "The cook she's nam was Rosie, she came from Mo'real. And was chamber maid on a lumber barge in the Grand Lachine Canal." The wonders of Lachine included a Native American policeman named John, from the Caughnawaga reservation, a huge man said to be capable of "driving a spike into a fence with the palm of his hand"; a man named Isvolsky "who owned a famous goat"; an older gentleman "who had invented a perpetual-motion machine powered by springs." But everything was a wonder to the infant Bellow. "Looking back, I think I had a kind of infinite excitement going through me," Bellow said, speaking of his sense of the world at two or three, "of being a part of this, of having appeared on this earth. I always had this feeling . . . that this is a most important thing, and delicious, ravishing, and nothing happened that was not of deepest meaning for you—a green plush sofa falling apart, or sawdust coming out of the sofa, or the carpet that it fell on, the embers dropping through the grates. . . . Everything is yours, really. There's nothing around that you don't possess."[16] For Bellow the child, as for Wordsworth the child, "every common sight / To me did seem / Apparelled in celestial light." As he puts it in the "Chicago Book," an unpublished, unfinished work of nonfiction, much mined for *The Dean's December* (1982), "I grew up convinced of the Wordsworthian linkage of 'a life and a soul, to every mode of being.'"[17]

Part of what strengthened the infant Bellow's sense of the world as his possession, a delicious and important place, was the closed-off existence of the immigrant family, of the immigrant mother especially:

> The sense that you got from your parents and from your uncles and your aunts and their families, cousins, etc., was that you had been brought by stormy seas and cast up on this shore and that you clung to each other and that your mother was the source of all human connectedness. And that what happened to the family, and what happened to her children, was of the utmost importance. Nothing more important. So that when you fell down the stairs and got a big bump on your head . . . her crying aloud and solicitude made you feel that you were—it never even entered your mind that you were anything but—cherished, and so you returned the feeling, of course. And I think it had something to do with the sense of being helpless aliens.[18]

In *The Adventures of Augie March*, as soon as Augie's family disintegrates, "common sights" cease to shine: "The house was changed also for us; dinkier, darker, smaller, once shiny and venerated things losing their attraction and richness and importance. Tin showed, cracks, black spots where enamel was hit off, threadbarer, design scuffed out of the center of the rug, all the glamour, lacquer, massiveness, florescence, wiped out" (p. 448). That the adult Bellow returned so frequently in his writing to childhood scenes, and held his extended Lachine family so dear, derived in part from a sense that he owed to them both his extraordinary powers of observation, powers he sought to draw on and keep alive, in Victor Wulpy's words, "by an act of the creative *will*."

These powers were visionary as well as empirical. In "Memoirs of a Bootlegger's Son," the infant Bentchka is repeatedly described as watchful, a quality unexpectedly linked with dreaminess: "Bentchka had a habit of drooping his head and dreaming at things with one eye" (p. 42). The preposition "at" in the phrase "dreaming at" suggests that the looseness of dream, or dreaminess, is somehow part of the act of perception. A much later passage is similarly unexpected in its mix of mental processes: "Bentchka listened and smiled in his dreamy, analytical way. His face was like satin, and he looked at things from the left side, with a slightly turned head" (p. 132). The faculties described here are in part sensory, in part something deeper. "Analytical" suggests a conscious process, but in an interview Bellow says his infant observation "wasn't entirely voluntary. It wasn't based on ideas. It was the given." When challenged by his interviewer to explain how "the physicality of someone or something" wasn't an idea, he replies: "The abstraction came later. Actual life was always first."[19] By "analytical," then, Bellow means something like "imaginative," which fits with "dreamy." The surface, "actual life," is in itself a source of fascination, but it is also the way to meaning, to what it is Bentchka is "dreaming at." Moses Herzog reflects on "the family look, the eyes, those eye-lights" (p. 650), moving from surface to something inward, from or through "eyes" to "eye-lights," a movement Bentchka seems also to be making in observation, which is partly why he is called "watchful and intelligent beyond his years" (p. 99). Bellow depicts him—an imagined version of his infant self, perhaps even a recalled version—sitting in his crib in winter looking through its bars "at the sparrows as they ruffled on the wires and on the glass clusters of the telephone poles and dropped down to peck in the horse-churned, sleigh-tracked snow. You could leave him alone; he'd amuse himself for hours" (p. 49). This sort of looking, through what Chick in *Ravelstein* calls "metaphysical lenses" (p. 98), recalls Hazlitt on the adult Wordsworth, marked by "a severe, worn pressure of thought about his temples, a fire in his eyes . . . as if he saw something in objects more than the actual appearance."[20]

Much of Bellow's intense looking, from infancy onward, was at bodies, faces, ways of moving. "When I was a very small child," he told his friend Keith Botsford, it wasn't what people said, "so much as the look of them and their gestures, that spoke to me. That is, a nose was also a speaking member, and so were a pair of eyes. And so was the way your hair grew and the set of your ears, the condition of your teeth, the emanations of the body. All of that. Of which I seemed to have a natural grasp." Bellow believed, "all my life," that the person, or something in the person, was inseparable from his or her appearance. "If a man or woman looked a certain way then it meant something to me, about their characters."[21] In "Memoirs," for example, on the eve of the hijacking, the skin around Pa Lurie's eyes, and the way he holds himself, tell us everything we need to know about his situation, his state of mind, even his fate: "Something appeared to have got him by the back of the neck and the head and twisted them forward so that he could not recover his normal posture. It was painful to see. The skin was tightened at his eyes so that his eyes would sometimes suggest those of an animal picked up by the scruff of the neck" (pp. 134–35). In "By the St. Lawrence," Uncle

Mikhel's fortitude, shrewdness, and solidity find expression not in what he says but in his body and bearing:

> Though his hands were palsied, Uncle Mikhel could weed and tie knots. His head, too, made involuntary movements but his eyes looked at you steadily, wide open. His face was tightly held by the close black beard. He said almost nothing. You heard the crisping of his beard against the collar oftener than his voice. He stared, you expected him to say something; instead he went on staring with an involuntary wag of the head (p. 7).

The perfectly weighted pauses in this last sentence, the unerring punctuation, vivify what is seen. Similarly, in "By the St. Lawrence," when cousin Ezra, one of the sons of the Uncle Max figure, has business thoughts, his solemnity is enacted in the writing: "He brought his white teeth together and a sort of gravity came over him" (p. 4).

Often Bellow describes parts of the face or body rarely noticed or seen as expressive, or expressive in the ways Bellow describes. In *Seize the Day* (1956), when the conman Tamkin's face grows resolute, "on either side of his mouth odd bulges formed under his mustache" (p. 65), a characteristically close and idiosyncratic observation (idiosyncratic because resolve is conventionally located in the set of the jaw). Elsewhere, Tamkin is described as "pigeon-toed, a sign perhaps that he was devious or had much to hide" (p. 52), which works once one recalls the posture of shy or guilty children. On other occasions, Bellow's descriptions of bodily appearances and processes are harder to understand. In *The Adventures of Augie March*, Clarence Ruber is described as having "a slow, shiny Assyrian fringe on his head" (p. 560). "Shiny" and "Assyrian" are clear, but why "slow"? In *Humboldt's Gift*, an old girlfriend is identified by "the neat short teeth, the winsome gums, the single dimple in the left cheek" (p. 290). The odd phrase here is "winsome gums" (because pink, young, healthy, presumably). Given the descriptive riches of Bellow's fiction, how much he notices, one is reluctant to question such details, especially when what is mystifying is immediately preceded by what is striking or right (the girlfriend's "neat short teeth"). A similar juxtaposition, also from *Humboldt's Gift*, occurs in the description of the gangster Cantabile: "His mouth was wide, with an emotional underlip in which there was the hint of an early struggle to be thought full grown. His large feet and dark eyes also hinted that he aspired to some ideal, and that his partial attainment or non-attainment of the ideal was a violent grief to him" (p. 88). The expressive properties of "large feet" in this passage are occult, a product of what Chick, from *Ravelstein*, calls "private metaphysics," "a way to communicate certain 'incommunicables'" (p. 95). They testify to Bellow's faith in his perceptual powers, even when the meanings they yield cannot be defended in rational or adult terms. This faith derives from what are for the child comparably inexplicable "first epistemological impressions" (Chick's phrase, p. 96). Although the most sophisticated and learned of men, the adult Bellow described himself in an interview as "clinging to the discovery of the world that occurred when I was very young," a discovery experienced in something like "a state of intoxication." "How can anybody possibly say he understands this [world] with his intellect," he continued. "You understand this with your instincts and with your heart and with your passions."[22]

Another way of clinging to the child's sense of the world is to surround oneself with larger-than-life characters. The narrators and central figures of Bellow's novels share this propensity. "It would be against my rule of truthfulness," confesses Kenneth Trachtenberg in *More Die of Heartbreak*, "to conceal the fact that I am fond of preposterous people" (p. 209). "I loved the way you would carry on," Albert Corde tells Dewey Spangler in *The Dean's December* (1982). "You were extravagant. You'd holler and bawl at your poor mother, and call her a whore. . . . It gave me terrific pleasure. I never saw anything like it."[23] "I had a weakness for characters like Cantabile," confesses Charlie Citrine, "demonstrative exuberant impulsive destructive and wrongheaded" (p. 171) (which also explains his attraction to the wild-man poet Von Humboldt Fleisher). All the novels contain characters who balloon into Dickensian or Balzacian monstrosity, to the amusement or wondering dismay of their narrators. Here is eight-year-old Moses Herzog attending cheder in the cellar of a local synagogue:

> The pages of the Pentateuch smelled of mildew, the boys' sweaters were damp. The rabbi, short-bearded, his soft big nose violently pitted with black, scolding them. "You, Rozavitch, you slacker. What does it say here about Potiphar's wife, *V'tispesayu b'vigdi . . .* 'And she took hold of . . . '"
>   "Of what? *Beged.*"
>   "*Beged.* A coat.

"A garment, you little thief. *Mamzer* [Bastard]! I'm sorry for your father. Some heir he's got! Some *Kaddish* [son]! Ham and pork you'll be eating, before his body is in the grave. And you, Herzog, with those behemoth eyes—*V'yaizov bigdo b'yodo?*"

"And he left it in her hands."

"Left what?"

"*Bigdo*, the garment."

"You watch your step, Herzog, Moses. Your mother thinks you'll be a great *lamden*—a rabbi. But I know you, how lazy you are. Mothers' hearts are broken by *mamzeirim* like you! Eh! Do I know you, Herzog? Through and through" (p. 548).

Whether the rabbi here derives from a real-life prototype, as does Bentchka's teacher, gentle Reb Shika, modeled on a man Bellow describes in interview in terms identical to those used for the fictional Shika, is unknown. But Von Humboldt Fleisher does, as does Dewey Spangler, as does Aunt Zipporah (Rozzy/Rosa/Julia). "Saul was no monster," Philip Roth warned me, "but he loved monsters, and you're going to have to interview them." Some of the people Bellow loved could well be described as monstrous, others were larger-than-life in endearing or admirable rather than alarming ways. In *To Jerusalem and Back* (1976), Bellow depicts the city's mayor, Teddy Kollek, as "a furiously active man. . . . A hurtling, not a philosophical soul": "His nose is straight, short, thick, and commanding; his color is ruddy; his reddish hair falls forward when he goes into action. Balzac would have taken to the mayor. . . . But no category will hold a phenomenon of such force" (p. 86).[24] Part of what Bellow enjoyed about Kollek, according to Kollek's son, Amos, was "the way my father knew how to manipulate people, including himself [Bellow, that is], hooking them into doing something for the city." Amos remembers the smile on Bellow's face as he watched Kollek work him. "Everyone serves his ends," Bellow writes of the mayor, approvingly, "and no one seems harmed by such serving" (p. 86). Bellow's enjoyment of Kollek and other larger-than-life figures can be explained as typical of novelists, always on the lookout for characters, and as admiration for a species of energy and unselfconsciousness available to him only vicariously (in this view, Bellow is like Charlie Citrine, who describes himself as "a nicely composed person, [who] had had Humboldt expressing himself wildly on my behalf, satisfying some of my longings" [p. 107]). Neither view is incompatible with the one expressed here, that for Bellow the vividness of real-life Dickensian or Balzacian types not only re-creates something of "first epistemological impressions" but allows him to observe from the position of the child.

In later life, Bellow speculated on the dangers as well as the creative benefits of such a position. In an undated notebook entry, from the mid-1960s, he jotted down a series of remarks related to the intensity of early experience:

> Unwillingness, reluctance to recognize the reality of the present moment because of attachment to something in childhood.
>
> Therefore a brother rather than a father to the children.
>
> And the great fatigue of a struggle of fifty years. Feel it in my arms, in my very *fists*.
>
> Locate the Old System with passion—not so other things.
>
> Maggie [Simmons, a girlfriend] is part of this. Has the purity of earliest connections.
>
> Miraculous to have accomplished so much in the world while in such bondage.
>
> But they heard my childish voice—and their own childhood in it.
>
> Nadine [Nimier, another girlfriend] said *T'es un bébé*.

Here, fidelity to the past is "bondage" as well as creative boon; the past alone is located "with passion"; what is "pure" is what is found in what is "earliest." In the late novella *The Actual* (1997), the narrator, Harry Trellman, "after forty years of thinking it over," describes his feelings for his high school love, Amy Wustrin, as "an actual affinity," explaining that "other women might remind me of you, but there was only one actual Amy" (pp. 100–101). Amy is "actual" because she came into Harry's life at the moment of erotic awakening, when his capacity to feel was most intense. In an interview, Bellow also attributes the strength of his Judaism to early attachments: "That's where the great power of it comes from. It doesn't come from the fact that I studied the *Talmud* or anything of that sort. I never belonged to an orthodox congregation. It simply comes from the fact that at a most susceptible time of my life I was wholly Jewish. That's a gift, a piece of good fortune with which one doesn't quarrel. It is what exists in feeling that matters."[25] How much of a "bondage" attachments like these were for Bellow, how true it was that they rendered him "unwilling" or "reluctant" to "recognize the reality of the present," will be discussed (like the notebook entry) in later chapters. That Bellow himself sometimes saw them as such, though, is clear. Nor was he alone in doing so. "He can't form permanent attachments," Marvin Gameroff, grandson of Rosa and Max, said of Bellow, whom he loved and admired. "His fidelity is to his past."[26]

The great drama of that past, in the Lachine and Montreal years, was Abraham Bellow's struggle to support his family. In "Memoirs of a Bootlegger's Son," Pa Lurie's situation broadly parallels Abraham's, though there are differences. The Bellows arrived in Canada with money smuggled out of Russia. Much of this money was quickly spent on land purchased in Valleyfield, Quebec, some forty miles southwest of Lachine, not far from the Gameroffs' summer house in Huntingdon, along the Chateauguay River. Abraham seems to have intended at first to farm the land. Bellow's account of why the venture failed comes in an interview: "They were out in the bush somewhere and the wolves howled at night. There weren't enough Jews for a minyan, a congregation, very disturbing and the kids kept getting lost in the woods. My mother complained, so we moved back into Lachine."[27] In "Memoirs," much the same account is given. Though Ma Lurie, like Liza, was "not a city woman by upbringing," it is she who objects most clearly to life in the country: "It was plain enough. No synagogues, no rabbis, no kosher food, no music teachers, no neighbors, no young men for Zelda [Jane's Russian name]. It would be good for the health of the younger children, that was true, but she wasn't going to have us grow into cowherds, no finer feelings, no learning" (p. 43). The major difference between fictional and real-life accounts is that in real life the land seems not only to have been purchased but the family actually lived on it for a period, or so Bellow says in the same interview. In "Memoirs" the Luries merely scout out the farm: "It was an excursion" (p. 43), one that occurs after the family moves from Lachine to Montreal. In reality, the episode took place earlier: "so we moved back into Lachine where my father was temporarily employed as a baker."

More precisely, as the driver of a bakery wagon. Bellow remembers this job "very well because I was often on the seat with him" (this was when he was three).[28] In "Memoirs," Pa Lurie invests the remainder of the money he had brought from Russia in a partnership with three other men who owned a bakery. He then falls out with them, as they were "quarrelsome and rough . . . swore obscenely and held Pa for a dude." The partners' view of Pa was not groundless, since "the misery of his sudden fall [from St. Petersburg affluence] was too hard to hide," as was his distaste for the job his partners gave him, that of harnessing a horse and driving the bakery wagon. "He had never before harnessed a horse. Over there, only coachmen and teamsters knew how to harness. Pa had to learn to do it by lantern light in the cold Canadian nights, with freezing hands." The partners were unsympathetic, in the manner of Aunt Rosa: "Why should it be so terrible to have become one of them?" There were physical fights and finally "Ma insisted" and Pa "gave up the partnership" (p. 35). Had he not withdrawn, he agreed, he'd either have killed one of his partners or been killed by one of them.

Of the other aborted professions listed in "Memoirs"—junk dealer, marriage broker, shop owner, manufacturer—the one that came closest to success was manufacturer. Pa Lurie goes into business with Aunt Taube's husband, Uncle Asher. They set out to manufacture burlap bags or sacks, Uncle Asher having somehow obtained an order for munitions bags during the war. A loft is rented and some machines, two women are hired to sew the bags, but the first order is deemed not up to specification and canceled. "When this happened there was a big family quarrel. Everyone got into it." Aunt Taube, like Aunt Julia, wore the pants in her family, and haughtily criticizes Pa Lurie. Ma Lurie takes exception to her criticisms, which she calls ungrateful. It was Pa Lurie, when flush in St. Petersburg, who had loaned Asher and Taube the money not only to get married but to come to America. For his part, Pa Lurie blames Asher for the failure: "He tried to save money on the material. That was why we lost the contract" (p. 39).

What is known of the real-life story differs in several respects from Bellow's fictional version. A possible model for Asher was Max Cohen, husband of Annie, Abraham's younger sister, though those of their surviving offspring I have talked to recall no stories of the failed venture.[29] Joel Bellows heard of it "from my father, from Sam, from Saul." As he tells it, Abraham went into business with a "ne'er-do-well" cousin: "Just as Grandpa was not suited to a life of crime, this cousin was not suited to making a living by any honest means." Somehow the partners got a contract with the Canadian Pacific Railroad to provide burlap sacks for coal. For a while the business did well. Then they cheated on materials, not double-stitching, or doubling-over the seams, or lining the sacks. The sacks began to break. "It was a disaster. Grandpa had to move into Montreal." Why exactly Abraham had to move to Montreal is not explained. Perhaps he was fleeing creditors? Perhaps hard words were exchanged, as in "Memoirs," and he or Liza or both wished to get away from their Bellow relations? This was one of a number of instances in the family's history in which business ventures caused tensions and ruptures between relations. Though it is unclear from Joel's account which of the partners was most at fault, the episode reinforced a widespread belief in the family that Abraham was not, for all his devotion to business, very good at it.[30]

The move to Montreal took place when Bellow was three, sometime before November 11, 1918, Armistice Day, which he remembered "because there was a tremendous noise. All the kids were standing on the front steps. We were all outside yelling, though I didn't know why exactly."[31] The apartment the family found was at 1092 St. Dominique Street, in the heart of Montreal's Jewish neighborhood.[32] St. Dominique Street is two blocks east of St. Lawrence Boulevard, or Boulevard St.-Laurent, known as the "Main." The Bellows lived in a second-floor apartment in a row of unprepossessing two-flats. The apartment consisted of four bedrooms, a water closet down the hall, a kitchen, and a parlor, which contained a piano for Jane and an imitation oak sideboard, on which stood the family samovar and candlesticks from St. Petersburg.[33] At the rear, behind the kitchen (in *Herzog* the kitchen is described as primitive, sunless, cavelike), was the coal bin and a small annex used as a sort of shed. The back staircase, "with its dried cat shit," led down to a tiny backyard (in "Memoirs" the backyard is too small for a grown person to walk in).[34] The three boys shared one room, Jane had another, the parents a third, and there was a room for a boarder to help with the rent. The rent for a comparable six-room cold-water flat on the same block was $15 a month.[35] Napoleon Street, only five blocks long, was just to the north, Roy Street was just to the south. The closest synagogue, also on the second floor of a two-flat, was at the corner of Napoleon and St. Dominique. Two blocks north of Napoleon, straight up St. Dominique, was an open-air market on Rachel Street. Here the Bellows' drunken boarder, Daitch (Ravitch in *Herzog*), worked at a fruit stall. To the west of the Main, and parallel to it, was St. Urbain Street, where the novelist Mordecai Richler and the poet Irving Layton (né Izzie Lazaroff, Bellow's exact contemporary) grew up. Richler writes of St. Urbain Street as the center of Montreal's Jewish ghetto: "Where Duddy Kravitz sprung from the boys grew up dirty and sad, spiky also, like grass beside the railroad tracks. He might have been born in

Lodz."[36] But St. Urbain Street was a step up from St. Dominique Street. According to Bellow's neighbor and childhood playmate Willie Greenberg, who lived at 1088 St. Dominique, the great hope was "to get out of the ghetto and move to St. Urbain or Esplanade."[37]

Joseph, the protagonist of Bellow's first novel, *Dangling Man*, grew up on St. Dominique Street, which he describes as "in a slum between a market and a hospital [the Montreal General Hospital, on Dorchester Street, now Boulevard René-Lévesque]."[38] From stairs and windows Joseph watched the life of the street and what he saw "remained so clear to me that I sometimes think it is the only place where I was ever allowed to encounter reality" (pp. 60–61). A similar claim is made by Moses Herzog on behalf of Napoleon Street: "rotten, toylike, crazy and filthy, riddled, flogged with harsh weather. . . . Here was a wider range of human feelings than he had ever again been able to find. . . . What was wrong with Napoleon Street? thought Herzog. All he ever wanted was there" (p. 557). The Jewish Main was an unlikely paradise, a place of high-density tenements, gloomy yards, stale, pungent cellars and stores, small clothing factories and workshops (by 1921 the garment trade, centered on the Main, employed fully one quarter of all workers in the city),[39] kosher butchers, barrels of herring, pickle barrels (a dipper of pickle brine cost 3 cents ["Memoirs," p. 103]), "syphon" or seltzer men, pushcarts selling shoes, pots, clothing, bagels on a string. According to Irving Layton, "for a poet nothing could have been better. Nothing. Raw, vulgar, dynamic and dramatic. . . . Sometimes I'm sorry for my children who lived in the suburbs and never had anything like this."[40] The harshness or ugliness was part of the poetry—the snow "spoiled and rotten with manure and litter, dead rats, dogs" (*Herzog*, p. 556), fog rising "from the yawning river," the "rancid sugar smell" of the local grocery, its "terrible dust of nutrition" ("Memoirs," pp. 118, 4).

Everything was out in the open, not only at home, where cramped quarters meant no privacy, but in the street. In *Dangling Man*, Joseph remembers as a child looking into a curtainless room near the market and seeing "a man rearing over someone on a bed" (p. 61). Joshua Lurie sees something similar in "Memoirs," while walking with Pa Lurie to synagogue on a clear summer's evening: a man approaches a bed by an open window, lies on top of a woman, whose ribbed cotton top barely covers her large belly, and "their black eyes turn and together meet those of the father and the son" (p. 11). Death was in the open as well. During the great flu epidemic of 1918–19, Bellow and his brother Sam used to sit in the front window watching the funeral processions: "I can remember the *corbillard* [hearse], the bands, the funeral marches, and the *cortege* with its black horses."[41] The son of the Bellows' landlady died in the epidemic; Bellow remembered seeing the white face of the dead boy, surrounded by flowers.[42] Herzog, too, "had seen everything." On Napoleon Street "he was spattered forever with things that bled or stank. . . . He remembered chicken slaughtering . . . those fiery squawks when the hens were dragged from the lath coops, the shit and sawdust and heat and fowl-musk, and the birds tossed when their throats were cut to bleed to death head down in tin racks, their claws going, going, working, working on the metal shield. Yes, that was on Roy Street."[43]

As in Lachine, not all the Bellows' neighbors were Jewish. An English family named Saunders lived across the street. The father was a cabinetmaker and Bellow spent much time in his basement shop; Herbert Lionel Saunders, the son, known as Davey, who would become a distinguished physicist, was a playmate. A pair of French Canadian old maids lived in a neat little house set back from the street, with a choke-berry bush in the front yard, from which Bellow and Willie Greenberg stole berries. Catholic girls marched to school in twos, escorted by nuns. Highlanders in kilts strolled from barracks on Pine Street, one block south of Roy. "The only trouble we kids ever had," according to Willie Greenberg, was from a French Canadian beat cop.[44] But Bellow remembers French Canadian schoolboys shouting obscenities and insults: "I soon understood that I was a Zhwiff—a muzhi (maudit) Zhwiff at that."[45] There were also Chinese in the neighborhood, running laundries and other small businesses. As a child, Bellow was struck by the resemblance of his first Hebrew teacher, Reb Shika Stein, to a Chinese. Reb Stein was small, and his yarmulke reminded Bellow of the skullcaps worn by Chinese men.[46] Non-Jews, though, were very much in the minority. From 1880 onward, and particularly after 1900, Yiddish-speaking Jews from Russia flooded into Montreal. By 1905 Yiddish was the third most spoken language in the city, after English and French, and Jews made up its largest immigrant community. The Main was safe, shtetl-like, but also, as Bellow puts it, "surrounded by the others, by the goyim."[47]

The Montreal goyim were divided geographically: to the west of the Main, they were mostly Anglophone, to the east, mostly Francophone. The cultural and linguistic duality of the nation as a whole helped the Bellow family retain its Yiddish roots, as Michael Greenstein, a Canadian critic, puts it, "somewhat longer" than if they had immigrated directly to the United States.[48] Growing up in a Canadian rather than an American shtetl, Bellow felt less need to conform to New World ways, which may partly explain the ease with which he later accepted or acknowledged his mixed cultural heritage. As he told the audience at the Lachine library,

> I never felt it necessary to sacrifice one identification for another. I've never had to say that I was not a Canadian. I never had to say that I was not Jewish. I never had to say I was not an American. I took all of these things for granted and in me you see a sort of virtuoso act of integration of all these diverse elements and I feel no particular conflict. I never felt any special discomfort over any of these elements. I've taken them all for granted because they are part of my history. I think a human being has to be faithful to his unique history. If that history is mixed, scrambled, anomalous, difficult for any outsider less exotic to put together for himself, that's not my fault. . . . I was faithful to what I was. I lived that way and I tried to write that way.

For Bellow, such faithfulness was a form of piety, which he thought of in Santayana's terms, as "reverence for the source of one's being."[49] Piety in this sense could also be said to underlie Bellow's mixed language or style. At home, he spoke to his parents in Yiddish. They spoke to each other and to the older children in Yiddish or Russian. At school he spoke English. In the street he spoke English or French. And from the age of three he studied Hebrew. As a young child, "I didn't know what language I was speaking and I didn't understand if there was any distinction among these various languages." Linguistic multiplicity "was a common thing in Europe—it was much less common in the United States where everybody had one ambition: to become an American as quickly as possible and to speak English. We didn't have that. We were in Canada."[50]

Bellow wrote little about his schooling in Canada, and rarely spoke of it in interviews. At five he balked at attending kindergarten, then bitterly regretted not going, "because all the kids were at school and I was alone in the street."[51] At six he entered the Devonshire School on St. Cuthbert Street, just west of the Main, a Protestant Board School where pupils sang "God Save the King" and recited the Lord's Prayer (in 1923, the Prince of Wales visited Montreal, and Maury and Saul went to see him as he passed in parade, waving his gloves at the crowd).[52] At seven Bellow attended the Strathearn School on Jeanne-Mance Street, a new school, with bright classrooms and large windows, and only a short walk from home, perhaps fifteen minutes.[53] Here, too, the education was English and Protestant, with British schoolbooks, and a drummer in a Boy Scout uniform marching pupils to school. The route from St. Dominique to Jeanne-Mance passed a synagogue on Milton Street, where Bellow attended cheder (at some point, Abraham seems to have decided that Reb Shika was too soft, the reason Pa Lurie gives for removing Joshua from the fictional Shika in "Memoirs"). When classes were out at the Strathearn School, at three in the afternoon, Bellow and his schoolmates ran to Milton Street. In "Memoirs," the boys tumble into the cheder, quarreling, conspiring, punching one another, chewing sunflower seeds, choking the inkwells with the husks. The rabbi—whiskered, hatted, scowling, the rabbi who calls Bentchka a *mamzer*—"pummels" them into silence (p. 22).

When free of rabbis and school, Bellow and his friends collected and traded treasures: empty cigarette boxes (Nizams, Honeysuckles, Sweet Caporal), chocolate wrappers (crimson and gold, brown and silver), acorns and chestnuts (from Mount Royal, Montreal's largest park). Bellow was obsessed with Indians as a child, read many westerns, and practiced stalking through the park like an Indian scout, careful not to crack twigs. In "Memoirs," his fictional alter ego, Bentchka, "always playing with things he found in the gutter," makes a bow and arrows out of the ribs of a discarded umbrella, firing them into empty chicken coops stacked in the yard (p. 74). Although not allowed a dog, the Bellows had cats. In "Memoirs," the Luries' cats "belonged to Bentchka" (p. 57) (the adult Bellow also had cats). On Sunday mornings, the boarder, Daitch, would take Bellow, or one of his brothers, to the *schwitz* or steam bath (a block away, at the corner of Napoleon and Colonial, and still in operation). He also gave the boys presents and taught them to play chess. When it was too cold for Bellow to go outside, he helped his mother in the kitchen and listened to her stories. It was not until he was eight, in his last year in Montreal, that he became a reader, nor does he seem to have written stories as a child. According to Willie Greenberg, however, he had a reputation as a talker or teller of tall tales, a chip off the old block. "*Oy, is dos kind a bluffer!*" Greenberg remembered his mother saying, an exclamation translated in the *Montreal Gazette* as "Is this kid a bullshitter!"

In the absence of radio, the family provided its own entertainments. Jane played the piano. Abraham read aloud from the stories of Sholom Aleichem (the year Bellow was born, Aleichem visited Montreal and gave a reading at the Princess Theatre, southwest of the Main). Abraham also, like Max Gameroff, read aloud from the Yiddish papers, not only from *Der Forvertz* (*The Forward*), with its popular "*Bintl Briv*" or "mail bundle" column, but from *Der Kanader Adler* (*The Canada Eagle*), founded in 1907.[54] When Aunt Zipporah visits the Luries in *Herzog* she brings a present of one fresh egg, "wrapped in a piece of Yiddish newspaper (*Der Kanader Adler*)" (p. 564). From the *Eagle*, the Bellows learned the basics of Montreal political life; they also read items of national and foreign news, particularly concerning the key cities of European Jewry, such as Paris, St. Petersburg, and Rome. The *Eagle* was left-leaning. It campaigned for workers' rights and raised funds for worthy causes, including the philanthropic Baron de Hirsch Institute (where Jane took piano lessons, like those deplored by Aunt Zipporah) (p. 599). The *Eagle* also ran humorous pieces and a range of tabloid attractions. The wife of Pa Lurie's bootlegging partner was a great reader of the Yiddish press: "She would take the Yiddish papers, lock the door and read the serial romances, the *Bintel Brief* and the murder trials" (p. 105).[55]

Nature figured in young Bellow's life not only on visits to Mount Royal, but in summers with his Gameroff cousins, both in Lachine and in their cottage in Huntingdon. The whole Bellow family sometimes visited for short periods in Huntingdon, staying in what Bellow describes as a "shack" on the Gameroff property.[56] Several of Bellow's stories draw on episodes and settings from these summers. In "By the St. Lawrence," Rexler recounts an experience in his seventh or eighth summer when running errands with Cousin Albert. Though the story is mostly set in Lachine, it is a summery Lachine, with fragrant tomato plants, shaded periwinkle, sunlight shining through June leaves. In "The Old System," the Quebec countryside becomes the Mohawk Valley in upstate New York, a landscape dominated by the Mohawk River, remembered as "powerful and dark, an easy, level force" (more like the Chateauguay than the St. Lawrence). Braun, the story's narrator, also recalls a huge sycamore tree by the river, "like a complicated event, with much splitting and thick chalky extensions" (p. 92).

Here and elsewhere in his fiction, Bellow is a close and knowledgeable observer of nature. Though he was the great novelist of urban America, his attraction to the countryside was lifelong and powerful: early in his career, in the 1950s and early 1960s, he owned a house in the Hudson Valley; in the 1970s he began spending summers in Vermont, and eventually he built a house there. Part of the appeal of both locations was their resemblance to the Quebec countryside of his youth.[57] Bellow was also a frequent summer visitor to Aspen, Colorado, bought land there, and for some time intended to build a house on his property.

The appeal of Bellow's Lachine and Huntingdon summers owed much to his Gameroff cousins, Shmuel David, Meyer, Louis, and Lena. These cousins were older, the boys strong, handsome, playful, and affectionate.[58] The oldest, Shmuel David, was fifteen years Bellow's senior, more an uncle than a cousin. He is in part the model for Isaac Braun, the hero of "The Old System." Cousin Isaac was "born to be a man, in the direct Old Testament sense" (p. 92). He was also an *homme à femmes*[59] ("'I fought on many fronts,' Cousin Isaac said, meaning women's bellies" ["The Old System," p.102]). "They were all sexy people," recalls Rexler of his Lachine cousins, identical in number, age, and birth order to Bellow's real-life cousins and to the fictional Braun cousins. In "The Old System," seven-year-old Samuel is initiated into the mysteries of sex by Cousin Tina, as Bellow was at roughly the same age by cousin Lena (thirteen at the time).[60] Tina is sullen and stout, with "smoky black harsh hair"; as she lifts her dress and petticoat, her belly and thighs swell before Samuel, and the little boy experiences "agonies of incapacity and pleasure." Excited and frightened in equal measure, "Braun felt too small and frail for this ecstasy" (pp. 94, 95). The association of large women with sexual excitement recurs in Bellow's fiction. In "What Kind of a Day Did You Have?," Katrina Goliger, Victor Wulpy's mistress, is described as "the full woman, perhaps the fat woman, woman-smelling" (p. 335), and her sexuality revivifies. In *The Bellarosa Connection*, the heroine, Sorella, is so big "she made you look twice at a doorway. When she came to it, she filled the space like a freighter in a canal lock" (p. 60). Sorella is courageous, clever, formidable. She's also attractive, with neat ankles, small feet, and a pleasant feminine voice. "She set her lady self before him, massively," the narrator tells us. "The more I think of Sorella," he later admits, "the more charm she has for me" (p. 68).

Months after the episode with Lena, young Bellow's life altered dramatically. In the winter of 1923, when he was eight, he suffered an attack of appendicitis. After an emergency appendectomy at the Royal Victoria Hospital on Mount Royal, he developed serious infections, including peritonitis. He got these infections either because the appendix had burst, or begun to burst, or because the operation was ineptly performed (the chief surgeon at the Royal Vic, Sir Henry Gray, was "credited with killing more American soldiers than the Germans did," according to Bellow's brother Sam),[61] or simply because infections can occur whenever one operates, especially in an age before the availability of antibiotics. In addition to the peritonitis, Bellow developed pneumonia. There were more operations, four abdominal operations, and Bellow remembers drifting in and out of consciousness (he was anaesthetized with ether, dripped onto a gauze mask over his mouth and nose). When recuperating from these operations, "my belly was haggled open—it was draining. I stank" (in the unfinished story "Here and Gone," eight-year-old Imminitov's wound is drained by a doctor carrying a big syringe, the sort used for basting in the kitchen; in the unfinished novel "Charm and Death," the protagonist recalls an identical wound at an identical age, drained by a "tube into his open belly secured by a diaper pin").[62] For a while the doctors feared that Bellow had contracted tuberculosis (this is what Charlie Citrine is hospitalized with in *Humboldt's Gift*, also at eight). "I was very sick, close to death," Bellow told an interviewer, nor was he the only boy close to death in Ward H, the small boys' ward. "Occasionally one of the kids would die and then the stretcher would be brought in and in the morning there was an empty bed." The boys knew what an empty bed meant, "although nobody talked about it" (partly because the distance between beds prevented discussion). When boys disappeared at night, "you had to make your own record of them." Bellow knew his condition was perilous; on occasion he was well enough to climb out of bed and read his chart: "it was very unpromising."[63]

Bellow spent "four to five" months on Ward H, where it was hospital policy to allow child-patients only a single visit a week, from a single visitor. These visits were meant to be short; there were no chairs in the ward.[64] Bellow's parents took turns visiting, in a winter he remembered as especially harsh, with "heavy snows, fantastic icicles at the windows, streetcars frosted over" (in *Herzog*, which briefly fictionalizes the hospital stay, the icicles are described as "like the teeth of fish, clear drops burning at their tips" [p. 439]). Bellow had never before been separated from his family, never been in a situation where "you can't call out in the night for anybody, because nobody is going to come." "I loved new experiences," he said, "but even for me, it was a little much."[65] What his time in hospital taught him was that he was on his own: "I had nobody to depend on but myself, so I began to make all kinds of arrangements for myself," including arrangements involving his parents. There were "things you couldn't tell the parents. You protected them in a way."[66] Chief among these things was the anti-Semitism of the nurses, especially pronounced at Christmas, a holiday Bellow remembered his mother mocking (the hospital made a fuss at Christmas, with a tree in the ward and a gift stocking at the foot of each bed).[67] Bellow also remembers keeping quiet about meals ("eating diced pork on a tin plate. Horrible food!").[68] When a nurse said to him, "You don't have napkins on St. Dominique Street," he said nothing to the nurse or to his parents, "though I knew we had napkins."[69] "You were a little Jewish kid and they kept reminding you of it," he recalled, "which would make me very angry. I was mad enough to kill. But I was also very puny. I was eight years old and I weighed forty pounds or something like that."[70]

It was in hospital that Bellow became a reader, "read everything I could get my hands on," not only his hospital chart, but the funny papers, stacked beside the patients' beds: Katzenjammer Kids, Barney Google, Boob McNutt, Happy Hooligan, Slim Jim, Mutt and Jeff. He also read *Raggedy Ann, Black Beauty, Uncle Tom's Cabin*. His most important reading, though, was kept from his parents. "There was nobody to talk to except the ladies from the Bible Society, the Christian ladies we used to call them, with copies of the New Testament" (elsewhere, "a New Testament for children").[71] He and the ladies would read passages aloud, and when they went away he read the whole book himself. The Gospel stories in particular "were a real shocker, because I didn't have any idea about all this other side of things." He'd heard of Jesus, but only "marginal information, unfriendly (why should it have been friendly?)."[72] He was shocked when Jesus died, never having read a story in which the hero died. "I was nuts about the guy," the adult Bellow recalled to a friend[73]; "I was moved out of myself by Jesus," he wrote in a letter of June 22, 1991, to the biblical scholar Stephen Mitchell, "by 'suffer the little children to come unto me,' by the lilies of the valley . . . by his deeds and his words." That Jesus was a Jew "counted heavily" in his favor. At the same time, "I would never have joined the enemies of the Jews as supporters of Jesus. That would have been impossible."

The charge that the Jews crucified Jesus troubled the eight-year-old. "I thought the Jews should really not have done that," he remembers thinking. He was also worried about being blamed: "How could it be my fault? I am in the hospital." As he concluded at the time, "I didn't have it all quite straight."[74]

Bellow was most concerned to protect his mother. In "Here and Gone" the mother of eight-year-old Imminitov brings vanilla ice cream. It is too frozen to get a spoon in, so cold has the journey been from home. The mother is remembered turning her face to the side as she looks at Imminitov, slightly favoring her left eye, a trait her son inherits (p. 17). She stands by the bed and says very little, certainly in comparison to the boy's father on his visits. In "Memoirs of a Bootlegger's Son," it is Joshua, the Maury figure, who is hospitalized. Joshua is a bold, forward boy, as was Maury, and Ma Lurie cautions him "to remember that we were poor and that we were Jews from St. Dominique street and therefore must not provoke anyone" (p. 77). When Ma Lurie enters Ward H in her felt galoshes, she has a handkerchief pressed to her mouth, "for she suffered with her teeth in the cold" (p. 79). Hospital visits take place in the afternoon. When they end and the day begins to darken, dinner trolleys clatter in the corridors; at such moments, even brave Joshua feels like giving in to tears.

It is the mother Bellow associates with tears, with fearfulness, with religious piety. Liza's male ideal was her father, a man of great learning and piety. Her hope was that all her sons would become *lamdonim* (rabbis or scholars), though Bellow, the youngest, "was born to it—you could see" (words Ma Lurie applies to Bentchka in "Memoirs," p. 81). Bellow was *moi kresavitz*, my beauty, the favorite, for several years the only child at home, too young for school. On St. Dominique Street, Liza's life, trailed by the watchful child, was one of continuous washing, cooking, cleaning, mending, dreaming. "I often wonder about my mother," Bellow told an interviewer, "how she lived under those circumstances."[75] In *Herzog*, the "withdrawn" side of Moses's mother's face is described as "melancholy," "dreaming," as if she were always "seeing the Old World," the lost St. Petersburg world of servants and fine linen and dachas. Moses's six-year-old daughter, Junie, has a comparably withdrawn expression: "the bit of melancholy in her beauty—that was his mother . . . pensive, slightly averting her face as she considered the life about her" (p. 676). This life was not only materially impoverished and arduous but confined. Bellow's father was out in the world, speaking

English, however imperfectly. The children were at school or playing in the street with friends. Liza was at home, never learned to speak much English, never learned to read it at all. When she went out, it was mostly with family, to visit relatives. A great treat for Liza was a movie matinee on the weekend. Bellow sometimes accompanied her and remembered a low rumbling in the theater, that of dozens of child translators, himself included, whispering in Yiddish to their mothers.[76]

In Bellow's fiction, there are hard mothers and soft mothers, Rosa types and Liza types, though no two characters possess identical traits, and some combine the traits of both (as does Artur Sammler's mother, who is haughty, lacking in compassion, an enthusiast of Schopenhauer, after whom Artur is named, and indulgent, spoiling her son with croissants and hot chocolate). Soft mothers in the Liza mold are, variously, melancholy, pious, sensitive, sickly, dreamy, superstitious, unworldly, weak in mind, and passionately devoted to family. In *Dangling Man*, Joseph's dead mother is mentioned only twice. In the first instance, Joseph is four and his mother refuses to cut his curls; Aunt Dina, "a self-willed woman," defies her sister and takes him herself to the barber. When they return, the mother is given an envelope with Joseph's curls, and begins to cry (p. 53). In the second instance, Joseph recalls the night his mother died. The nurse calls out to the family and "from all parts of the house we came running." Moments before her death, Joseph notices that "her lips seemed to move crookedly in a last effort to speak or kiss" (p. 83). In *The Victim*, Leventhal's "unfortunate" mother is mentioned only once. What he remembers of her, he tells us, is her "abstracted look," which might also be a look of madness, though "he had only his father's word for it that she died insane" (p. 185). Tommy Wilhelm's mother in *Seize the Day* dies in the winter of 1934 or 1932 (he and his father argue about the date), a year before or after Liza Bellow died. What he owes her is "sensitive feelings, a soft heart, a brooding nature, a tendency to be confused under pressure" (p. 21). In *Henderson the Rain King* (1959) we learn a good deal about Henderson's distinguished father. What we learn about his mother is that she wrote poetry, was treated badly by the father, and was dead by the time Henderson was sixteen.[77] In *Herzog*, the hero's mother, as we have seen, shares many traits with Bellow's mother. What she dreams of on Napoleon Street, in addition to St. Petersburg finery, is her lost family: "her father the famous *Misnagid*, her tragic mother, her brothers living and dead" (p. 555). Why her mother is tragic is not explained, as if motherhood itself were sufficient explanation. It is on Napoleon Street that Ma Herzog's hair turns gray, her teeth fall out, and "her very fingernails wrinkled. Her hands smelled of the sink" (p. 556).[78] Ma Herzog, like Tommy's mother, like Albert Corde's mother in *The Dean's December*, like Louis's mother in "Something to Remember Me By," like Bellow's mother, dies when the son is an adolescent.[79]

In *Humboldt's Gift*, Charlie Citrine reflects on the legacy of the mother-son bond. Though Bellow had little time for psychoanalytic explanation, Charlie sees the "intense way of caring" he and his mother shared as creating problems for him in later life:

> I never lost this intense way of caring—no, that isn't so. I'm afraid the truth is that I did lose it. Yes, sure I lost it. But I still required it. That's always been the problem. I required it and apparently I also promised it. To women, I mean. For women I had this utopian emotional love aura and made them feel I was a cherishing man. Sure, I'd cherish them in the way they all dreamed of being cherished (p. 293).

This way is characterized by Charlie's first serious girlfriend, his first love, without rebuttal, as "phoney." The mother is not being blamed here—the fault is Charlie's, for projecting an intensity he knows he does not feel, and for requiring and arousing the genuine article in women. The mother-son bond affects all subsequent relations, but for Charlie there was nothing of *Hamlet* or *Oedipus* in it, no erotic component, an absence psychoanalysis would attribute to repression. The relevant model is Romantic, that of the child's oneness with the mother, then with Mother Nature or the outer world (after the mother's early death, in the case both of Wordsworth and Bellow), followed by an inevitable fall into separation or adulthood.[80]

That the Liza figure's qualities were to Bellow strengths as well as weaknesses—values—is seen most clearly in *The Adventures of Augie March*. Rebecca March ("Mama") is at sea in Chicago, meek, nervous, simpleminded. Her eyesight is failing, she has very few teeth left, her hands are rough and reddened from domestic drudgery. She has three sons and no husband (her husband deserted the family). The sons are Simon, the oldest, Augie, the middle child, and Georgie, who is "mind-crippled" (p. 440). "Simon and I were her miracles or accidents," Augie tells us. "Georgie was her own true work in which she returned to her fate after blessed and undeserved success" (p. 389). The family is run by Grandma Lausch, a Rosa figure, to whom Mama, guilty over her failure as a wife, surrenders her powers, partly in penance, partly out of incapacity.[81] "Against the old lady's authority she didn't dare to introduce her feelings," says Augie, "but when she took me into the kitchen to put a compress on me she nearsightedly pored over my scratches, whispering and sighing to me, while Georgie tottered around behind her" (p. 395). Ma's soft sighs and whispers counter the Machiavellian hardness of Grandma Lausch, all "guile, malice, and command" (p. 387) (Grandma Lausch has feelings, but keeps them tightly controlled). It is Grandma's aim, Augie says, "to wise us up": "the trustful, loving, and simple surrounded by the cunning-hearted and tough, a fighting nature of birds and worms, and a desperate mankind without feelings" (p. 391). Grandma Lausch has the wisdom to negotiate hard Chicago, hard America. Mama, in contrast, possesses a wisdom "without any work of mind, of which she was incapable" (p. 443), and Georgie does, too. This wisdom is "the oldest knowledge, older than the Euphrates, older than the Ganges," "something full of comment on the life of all of us" (p. 438). Ma and Georgie cannot take care of themselves, but they "do with [the] soul." Like Wordsworth's "Idiot Boy," Johnny Foy, Georgie has the look of "a seraph" (p. 441), "a far traveller" (p. 445). The wisdom he and Mama transmit, a matter of love and feeling, lies beyond the material realm.

Liza's wisdom, Bellow suggests in an interview, was like that of Mama March, but Liza was not Mama. Mama March could never read Tolstoy, Liza's favorite novelist (in *Augie*, it is Grandma Lausch who reads Tolstoy). Nor was Liza as passive or downtrodden as Mama March. Bellow borrows real-life qualities and oppositions in drawing his characters, then exaggerates them to meet dramatic or fictional ends; his characters, he explained, have more "esprit" (or less, as in the case of Mama March) than their real-life prototypes.[82] Liza Bellow's life in Canada, and later in Chicago, was hard; she was dependent, dreamy, and melancholy, but unlike Mama March she could put her foot down, as she did over the farm in Valleyfield. The character who comes closest to Liza in Bellow's fiction is Ma Lurie in "Memoirs of a Bootlegger's Son," itself the most autobiographical of Bellow's fictions. Ma Lurie is often a steadying influence on Pa Lurie. When despairing, Pa calls himself a *bettler* (beggar), a dirty, half-mad figure, the sort frequently encountered "in the yellowish streets of Jewish Montreal." Ma Lurie answers soothingly, smilingly: "Not yet, by any means" (p. 40). Later in the manuscript, we are told that Pa "had conversations by the hour with Ma, in their bedroom. She gave him comfort" (p. 134). After the Luries set up as marriage brokers, as did the Bellows, Ma takes almost as big a part in entertaining and interviewing as Pa: "Pa put on more of an exhibition. There was more of poetry in Ma's way. Ma's way was sober; Pa's was likely to be striking" (p. 66). Ma tells a prospective couple about a movie she has seen: "'Oh, it is *harzreisend*,' said Ma. It was the greatest compliment Ma could give a movie to say it had torn her heart" (p. 67). When Pa is away from home, Ma talks to Zelda and Joshua, the two eldest children, about schemes to raise money for a shop of some kind (p. 130). She even delivers the occasional bottle of bootleg whiskey: "it was hard for her . . . she was not shy but she had her own sort of ladylike ways. There was no place for these now" (p. 104). It is Ma who nerves Pa up to approach Aunt Julia for a loan: "You have to do it. They can give you the money, and Jomin doesn't have a bad heart" (p. 49). When Aunt Julia visits on another occasion, there is a violent quarrel: Ma calls her "a black spider," Julia curses her, and Ma bursts into tears (p. 73). When Julia refuses Pa the loan and denounces weakness, Ma cries: "And I hate wickedness." After this exchange the two women "stared at each other in wild agitation" (p. 146).

The sequence of events that leads in "Memoirs" to Pa Lurie's flight to Chicago begins with his arrest for bootlegging. A lawyer with influence is found, one used to dealing with immigrants in trouble. There is the matter of bail, which Ma sets out to raise, but the manuscript breaks off before we learn if she succeeds. In its last scene, Ma and Joshua walk up the Main, having just left the lawyer. It is Indian summer (at which point the narrator, Joshua, interjects, "I simply can't help it, it was," stressing the scene's documentary truth). Ma is depicted as tired, dressed in heavy clothing: "Her cheeks were drawn in, making you aware of bone, and teeth and eyes. The pulses were beating strongly in her throat, where a blue vein was stretched" (p. 171). With difficulty, throatily, Ma declares: "We won't stay here in Canada any more. I refuse. We fell in here. We have to climb out and leave. If we don't, it will be the same thing again and again. This time I have decided, and Pa will do as I say for a change. We will go to the States." Pa has a favorite cousin in Minneapolis, one Ma had known and liked *in der Heim*. This cousin owns a bakery and will employ Pa. Ma also has relatives in St. Paul and Minneapolis. But Ma has another reason to remove the family from Montreal: "Your father's sisters have no respect for me. I can't struggle against them any more. They even made fun of me when I was carrying Ben Zion. I am not going to spend my life under that Julia. She wants to devour me. She lives off my miseries. . . . Your father will obey me for a change" (p. 172).

Nothing like this scene is recounted by Bellow in interview. But then he offered very few specifics about the removal from Canada to Chicago, where a real-life cousin, Louis Dworkin, owned a bakery. "My father left for Chicago in the winter of 1924," Bellow told Keith Botsford. "It was nearly summer when I rejoined the family [from the hospital]. I didn't go back to school. That same summer, my mother brought the children to Chicago."[83] Both Abraham's entry to the United States in winter and the family's entry in summer, on the Fourth of July, were illegal.[84] Bellow was nine and still very much under the influence and

Liza and the children, Lachine, 1918

protection of his mother, "clinging to affection and the family,"[85] clinging also to the mother's faith. "My mother was very religious and I grew
up in a religious family, the religious feeling was very strong in me
when I was young and it persisted." In Chicago, however, Liza's influence would come under threat, in "a great struggle between the street
and the home."[86] In Chicago, when away at school or playing with
friends, Bellow recounts, "I had to be shrewd and a good manager and
a wiseacre and a smartass and all the rest of it. In my family, of course,
my mother wasn't at all like that, but the rest of the family made haste
to acquire the necessary smarts." Bellow's father and brothers deplored
Bellow's "dreamy side," an inheritance from Liza, and mocked it. But
this side, he came increasingly to feel, was crucial to his achievement as
a writer. Like memories of his childhood in Canada and of his mother,
it was something "I've always tried to protect."[87]

3

Chicago / Maury

LATE IN 1923, Abraham Bellow wired his cousin Louis Dworkin to say he was on his way to Chicago. Cousin Louis, a tall, energetic man, fifteen years younger than Abraham, met him at the station and brought him to the home of his sister, Flora Baron. Flora and her husband, Isidor, a newspaper distributor, lived in a small brick bungalow on Hamlin Avenue in the Humboldt Park area of northwest Chicago, a neighborhood of Poles, Swedes, and Jews from Russia and Eastern Europe. Louis and Flora both came from Druya. They were related to Abraham on his mother's side (Bellow's paternal grandmother was their aunt). Flora, a member of the Bund, came first, fleeing political persecution, or the fear of persecution; Cousin Louis followed in 1912, to avoid the draft. The first leg of Louis's lone journey, at sixteen, was to Dvinsk, by horse and buggy; there he spent a night with Bellow's grandparents, Berel and Shulamith. The next morning he set off for St. Petersburg to board a ship bound for England; from Goole, in East Yorkshire, where the ship disembarked, he traveled to Liverpool, boarded a ship for New York, from where he traveled by train to Chicago, arriving with a piece of paper on which was written Flora and Isidor's address.[1]

Cousin Louis and the Barons were generous to the Bellows, helping family as they'd been helped in turn. When Louis arrived in Chicago in 1912, he had been offered a job by one of Isidor's cousins, Meyer Teitelbaum, owner of the Imperial Baking Company, located at 1012 North Marshfield Avenue near Augusta Boulevard. Louis's first job at the bakery was cleaning pans, at $6 a week. Then he drove a horse and buggy, delivering orders. The bakery was small, little more than an oven and a garage for the buggy. Louis worked hard, saved his money, and soon learned all aspects of the business (in Druya, his father, Abraham Dworkin, had been a miller). Within three years of his arrival he married Rose Fasman, "a warm, dark, blue-eyed woman,"[2] in Bellow's words, to whom he had been introduced by Flora. Rose was a shrewd businesswoman. In 1919, partly at her urging, Louis purchased the bakery from Teitelbaum. He and Rose, who did the books, were joined in 1922 by Jack Dworkin, Louis's younger brother, newly arrived from Druya. Louis, Rose, and Jack formed a corporation, expanded the bakery's production and product line, and moved farther west to larger premises, at 1011 North Damen Avenue (previously Robey Street, in the neighborhood now known as Wicker Park). That the expansion and the move were partly financed by a relative of Rose's helps to explain her equal partnership in the corporation: each of the partners, Louis, Jack, and Rose, owned a third. "She was not one of your grannies," Bellow writes of Riva, a Rose-like character in "Cousins" (1974), "she had been a businesswoman." Riva, in her eighties in "Cousins," is too old to drive, but she "overruled everybody and would not give up her Chrysler."[3] Rose Dworkin, in her twenties, was the first woman Bellow ever saw behind the wheel of a car, which she drove "more effectively and certainly more safely than Cousin Louie himself."[4]

Abraham, at forty-three, was put to work in the bakery by Cousin Louis, on the night shift. From twilight to dawn he worked, stacking "boxes"—large, awkward wooden trays—onto wagons, harnessing horses, lugging sacks of flour and sugar, barrels of jelly, tubs of shortening, learning to ferment rye bread dough in long troughs (the bakery's "Imperial Famous Rye Bread"), stoking the ovens with scrap lumber and mill edgings, the bark still visible, easing loaves in and out of the ovens with fourteen-foot wooden spatulas or peels. At the end of the night shift, Abraham returned to sleep on a folding cot in the Barons' kitchen. (Cousin Jack, who also lodged with the Barons, had the second of the bungalow's two bedrooms; there were four rooms in total in the house.) The bakers Abraham worked alongside during the day were Poles. The delivery wagons were driven by Jews. In the second of his Jefferson Lectures in the Humanities, an honorary lecture series established in 1972 by the National Endowment for the Humanities, Bellow recalls hearing how Petrush, the watchman, who had lost a finger in one of the machines, "slept drunk on the flour sacks, and the rats hopped over his feet."⁵ "Everyone was dusted with flour," Bellow writes in the "Chicago Book." "Boots and overalls were clotted with dough. The bakers worked in undershirts, big-muscled men and very white-skinned, scooping the loaves up with quivering long-handled peels and pummelling at the kneading-vats, slapping down the unbaked loaves loudly."⁶ Bellow was fascinated by the bakery and its workings, memories of which find their way into unexpected passages of the fiction. Well-born Eugene Henderson, for example, from *Henderson the Rain King*, remembers tormenting the local miller during boyhood summers in the Adirondacks. He would run into the mill with a stick, club the flour sacks until he was "almost choking with the white powder," then rush out through the dust as the miller yelled and cursed. This memory returns to Henderson in Africa, sparked by a magical pink light that appears on the side of his white hut, its color identical to that "on the floury side of the mill as the water dropped in the wheel."⁷

At the Imperial Bakery, Abraham worked, in Bellow's words, "with angry efficiency." From the start, as in the past, he had trouble accepting the role of employee: "He did not consider himself a worker, but he was not an owner either. He was somehow between management and labor. It would have been temperamentally impossible for him to refrain from sharing the managerial overview. He thought of inventories, bills, orders."⁸ It is a tribute to the good nature of the Dworkins, and to their sense of family, that they never quarreled seriously with Abraham, and that when he left the bakery to start up a business of his own, one that drew on contacts made through it, there were no hard feelings. Louis's daughter, Vivien Missner, remembers her father and Abraham as "very close cousins," constantly consulting in Yiddish, joking and laughing. Vivien's description of her father as "very warm and gregarious . . . charitable, caring" was seconded by Bellow and other members of the family. As befitted a younger cousin, Louis deferred to Abraham and his reputed business success in St. Petersburg, and cousin Jack was also respectful. Bellow remembers Jack as "obstreperous, a big, shrewd, good-natured, rowdy man who handled the wooden boxes as if they were tin cafeteria trays."⁹ In *The Adventures of Augie March*, Jack can be seen in the character "Five Properties," Anna Coblin's "immense" brother, while Anna and her husband, Hyman, are modeled on the Barons. Five Properties is a fabulous grotesque, "long armed and humped," with a head growing directly off a "thick band of muscle as original as a bole on his back," hair "tender and greenish brown" (picking up the tree imagery of "bole"), eyes "completely green, clear, estimating, primitive, and sardonic," and "an Eskimo smile of primitive simplicity . . . kidding, gleeful, and unfrank." Here is Five Properties at work:

> He was the life of the quiet little lard-smelly Polish groceries that were his stops, punching it out or grappling in fun with the owners, head to head, or swearing in Italian at the Italians, "*Fungoo!*" and measuring off a chunk of stiff arm at them. He gave himself an awful lot of delight. And he was very shrewd, his sister said. It wasn't so long ago he had done a small part in the ruin of empires, driving wagons of Russian and German corpses to burial on Polish farms; and now he had money in the bank, he had stock in the dairy, and he had picked up in the Yiddish theater the fat swagger of the suitor everybody hated: "Five prope'ties. Plente money."[10]

Jack Dworkin took no offense at the Five Properties character, unlike another purported real-life model, an uncle of Bellow's boyhood friend Sam Freifeld. This uncle thought the character defamatory, threatened to sue Bellow, and Freifeld, an attorney, had to dissuade him. Though only a few of the outraged uncle's qualities were those of Five Properties, and his family was quite unlike the Coblins, the two had enough in common, as Freifeld's daughter, Judith, puts it, "that that was the story." The "plente money" part certainly fit, as did the Coblins' generosity. Freifeld's uncle made a fortune in the hotel business, his son made even more money, and in 2007 the family donated $35 million to the University of Chicago.

It took Abraham six months to earn enough money to bring Liza and the children to Chicago. The family was smuggled across the border by bootlegging associates. When their train arrived at the Harrison Street station (in some accounts the Dearborn Street station) on the Fourth of July 1924, Abraham and Cousin Louis were there to meet it.[11] The journey had been hot and uncomfortable. The family came by coach, sitting up the whole night. Because of the heat, the windows were open and cinders and soot from the locomotive blew into the carriage and over the passengers; the dark green mohair of the seats bristled the children's legs.[12] Most memorable of Bellow's impressions upon arrival was the appearance of his father, whom he had longed to see: Abraham had shaved off his mustache and the bareness of his upper lip "was a shock to me."[13] After greetings and embraces, the St. Petersburg trunk was retrieved from the baggage car—with its samovar, thick-handled silver, taffeta petticoats, old family photographs and locks of hair, the treasures Liza refused to part with—and the family climbed into Louis's Dodge touring car. Bellow was now, he thought, having recently turned nine, too old to be dandled on his father's knee, a matter only of partial regret, since the disappearance of Abraham's "cigarette-saturated" mustache "made another man of him, temporarily."[14] The route to the Barons, where the family was to stay, followed the trolley lines up Milwaukee Avenue to the city's northwest side. As it was the Fourth of July, the air was full of the smell of gunpowder from World War I veterans shooting off rifles brought home from France, and from powder caps ("sonofaguns") taped to the trolley tracks by children and set off by passing streetcars.

At the Barons', the living room furniture had been pushed to the side and the floor swept. It was on the floor that the Bellows were to sleep. Flora welcomed the family with deep feeling and a meal of "smoked Great Lakes whitefish."[15] "Cousin Flora was like her brother," Bellow recalled, "large, handsomely expressive, much moved by our coming. The table was set for us, the beds were ready. She and her round, bald, smiling husband Baron with his blinking tic—these large people gave us tacit assurances that we had come to a place where human qualities were what they were elsewhere."[16] In "Cousins," Bellow uses Flora Baron as a model for Shana Metzger, "a person of great force . . . a wide woman, a kind of human blast furnace" (p. 200). In *Augie March*, she becomes Anna Coblin, as memorable as her brother. Anna's "great size and terrific energy of constitution . . . produced all kinds of excesses. Even physical ones: moles, blebs, hairs, bumps in her forehead, huge concentration in her neck" (like her brother's "thick band of muscle as original as a bole"). What immediately identified Anna as modeled on Flora, according to relatives, was her "spiralling reddish hair" (Louis Dworkin's hair, a crested Iroquois or Mohican stripe, was also red, as is Shana Metzger's in "Cousins"). Anna's hair, an index of her energy, sprang "with no negligible beauty and definiteness from her scalp, tangling as it widened up and out, cut ducktail fashion in the back and scrawled out high above her ears" (p. 399).[17]

With so many relatives crowded into the Barons' small bungalow—five adults, including cousin Jack, and five children, including the Barons' daughter, Rose—housekeeping was difficult, as it was at the Coblins'. "The filth of the house," writes Bellow in *Augie*, "and particularly of

the kitchen, was stupendous. Nevertheless, swollen and fire-eyed, slow
on her feet, shouting incomprehensibly on the telephone, and her face
as if lit by that gorgeous hair which finally advanced her into royalty,
[Anna] somehow kept up with her duties" (pp. 401–2). Chief among
these duties was the provision of meals. These meals were "of amazing character altogether and of huge quantity. . . . Bowls of macaroni
without salt or pepper or butter or sauce, brain stews and lung stews,
calves'-foot jelly with bits of calves' hair and sliced egg, cold pickled
fish, crumb-stuffed tripes, canned corn chowder, and big bottles of
orange pop. All this went down well with Five Properties, who spread
the butter on his bread with his fingers" (p. 405). Bellow plays up the
crudity of the Coblins for comic effect, but the prevailing emotion in
these passages is affection. In "Cousins," Ijah Brodsky, the story's narrator, explains his attraction to Shana Metzger and her family: "It may
be that persons of her type have become extinct in America. She made
an immense impression on me. We were fond of each other, and I went
to the Metzgers' because I was at home there, and also to see and hear
primordial family life" (pp. 200–201).

After they had spent some weeks with the Barons, Cousin Rose,
Louis's wife, found the Bellows a place of their own. This was the
top-floor apartment in a brick two-flat at 2629 West Augusta Street,
between Rockwell and Washtenaw, near the southeast corner of
Humboldt Park. The apartment was two streets away from Lafayette
Elementary School, which Bellow attended, and six from the Imperial Bakery. Originally German, the neighborhood was now mostly
Polish, intermixed with Scandinavians, Ukrainians, and Jews (African
Americans were a rarity in Humboldt Park, though Bellow had a black
schoolfriend, Milton Littlejohn); the Bellows' landlord, a Polish laborer
named Lusczowiak, lived in the apartment below. Augusta Street was
unpaved, with horses and few cars. It was lined with bungalows and
brick two-flats, three-flats, and six-flats. The clumsily constructed
back porches of the flats looked out onto ill-kempt yards and alleyways
dotted with crabgrass, ragweed, and burdock.[18] The sidewalks in front
were broad ("land was cheap, and the government was liberal with it"),[19]
at least in comparison with those of St. Dominique Street in Montreal,
and the front yards and steps well tended. After work, house-proud
Polish workers—locksmiths, electricians, factory employees—clipped
hedges and cut grass, planted geraniums in old washtubs (Chicago
geraniums seemed to Bellow "to have been cranked up from the soil"),[20]

and pointed the brickwork on their buildings, which they then covered "with many layers of waxy red, chocolate or green paint."[21] There were a few shops on Augusta Street ("Novison the cobbler, Brown the dry-goods man, Raskin the Grocer"),[22] but street life proper began on Division Street, the neighborhood's main east–west artery, four blocks north of Augusta, where there were many Jewish retail stores.[23]

The Jewish community in Humboldt Park had a distinct character. In 1931, seven years after the Bellows arrived in Chicago, the number of Jews in the city was close to 300,000. Roughly a third of this number lived in Lawndale, just below Humboldt Park (many having moved there from Maxwell Street, to the east, a shtetl-like neighborhood increasingly populated by African Americans, the site of a famous open-air market). The Jewish population of Humboldt Park was a third the size of that of Lawndale and a quarter the size of the population of Humboldt Park as a whole. It was less Orthodox than the Lawndale population and less insular. Of Lawndale's sixty synagogues, fifty-eight were Orthodox. Humboldt Park, in contrast, contained Reform and Conservative Jews, had a reputation for promoting Yiddish culture, and attracted political and religious radicals, many of whom held forth from soapboxes on Division Street. The Division Street soapbox orators, Bellow writes, included "revivalists, vegetarians, pacifists, Zionists, followers of Henry George, Karl Marx or Bakunin."[24] Often they spilled over into the park itself, where "tailors and pressers read their Yiddish poems to each other."[25] On Division Street men carrying office typewriters or "uprights" could be hired, for 25 cents, to write letters to family and friends in the Old Country.[26] Ceshinsky's bookstore was "where the Polish-Russian-Yiddish intelligentsia" gathered to gossip and declaim ("They wore pince-nez. They smoked with curious gestures").[27] In front of the neighborhood Walgreen's drugstore at Division and California, barrels of used books were sold, for 25, 19, or 12 cents. In junior high school, Bellow found a copy of Schopenhauer's *The World as Will and Idea* in the 19-cent barrel.[28] Among the places to eat on Division Street was the Tolstoy Vegetarian Restaurant, with a large photograph of the novelist in its front window. Other Division Street landmarks were the Russian Baths, at the corner of Wolcott Avenue, and a constellation of movie houses: the Harmony, the Biltmore, the Crown, the Crystal. To get into the movies as a boy, Bellow and his friends refunded empty pop bottles, at a penny each, or retrieved tennis balls on the park courts, at 10 cents an hour. Bellow also dug for coins among the cushions and springs of the parlor sofa, where his exhausted father sometimes stretched out for a rest.

The major social division in Humboldt Park was between the streets to the east and west of the park. West was better, more affluent, and it took several years for the Bellows to move there. The Augusta Street apartment found by cousin Rose, in which they lived for two years, consisted of five rooms: three bedrooms, a parlor, and a kitchen, dominated by a large iron-and-nickel cooker. As Abraham earned only $25 a week, to support a family of six, it was all they could afford. Abraham would come home in the morning in time to have breakfast with the children before they went off to school. After they left, he would hang his floured work clothes in the bathroom and sleep all day. "If we made noise and woke him," recalls Bellow, "he sprang from bed like a tiger. He went white, he went red most abruptly. His rages transformed him extraordinarily."[29] The three boys shared the bedroom at the back of the apartment, off the kitchen, Jane shared a bedroom with her parents (mostly her mother, given Abraham's work schedule), and the third bedroom, the best, fronting Augusta Street, was rented to a "roomer," Ezra Davis, a punch press operator the Bellows had known in Montreal. (When the roomer left, the bedroom became Jane's, a sore point with the three boys, who continued to share.) Ezra Davis's dream was to be an opera singer. In the autobiographical essay "A Matter of the Soul" (1975), Bellow gives him the pseudonym Jeremiah, and describes him as "this gentle, hopeless man, my particular friend" (as the boarder Daitch had been his particular friend in Montreal). Davis took singing lessons with Alexander Nakutin in the Fine Arts Building in Chicago and gave impromptu concerts in the Bellows' kitchen. "He rose on his toes, his octagonal glasses sweated," writes Bellow, "talentless and fervent, he made his friends smile."[30] At the end of *Humboldt's Gift*, with a characteristic rush of plot, the lodger, Menasha Klinger, helps to bring the novel to a providential close. Menasha, like Davis, came to Chicago in the 1920s to study singing, supporting himself as a punch press operator, and Charlie Citrine was his favorite: "I could talk to him when he was only nine or ten, and he was my only friend" (p. 322). Menasha's simple goodness and appearance out of nowhere are like something from Dickens. Charlie calls his appearance "dreamlike." But as Menasha reminds him, "When you turn into a personage, Char-

lie, it's much less of a coincidence than you think" (p. 22), a private reference, perhaps, to a fan letter Davis sent Bellow on January 30, 1964,
praising *Augie*—the first contact the two men had had in thirty years.

WHAT FIRST STRUCK nine-year-old Bellow about his new surroundings were the gaps or spaces between buildings, "which gave me a sense
of an unreasonable kind of emptiness." He often played in empty lots
as a boy in Chicago, "on the cinders, broken glass and flattened bottle-
tops."[31] Montreal for him, the Montreal of the Main, had been "tightly
packed," "closebacked"; Chicago was "more open, more spacious, more
empty . . . mysteriously empty despite the humanity in it, a steppe, a
prairie," with "street after street without variety, eight blocks to the
mile, sector after sector, framed in that colossal and mysterious emptiness." This emptiness spread far beyond the city, and was later seen by
Bellow as formative.[32] Among his papers in the Regenstein is a photo-
copy of Rebecca West's introduction to a selection of Carl Sandburg's
poems. Bellow has underlined several passages, beginning with a discussion of the "curious loquacity" of Chicagoans, and moving on to the
city's unique geographical attributes. Given the Bellow family's Russian background, and Bellow's debt to Russian writing, he was bound to
be struck by the following passage, one of the first he underlines:

> Chicago, like Leningrad, like Moscow, is a high spot [this is figura-
> tive, Chicago has no hills], to use its own idiom, on the monotony of
> great plains, a catchment area of vitality that rejoices extravagantly
> in its preservation because elsewhere in this region it might have
> trickled away from its source and been swallowed up in the vastness
> of the earth.

One consequence of the threat of being swallowed up is a quality of
vehemence and significance common, West writes, to both Chicagoans
and Russians. As she puts it in another underlined passage: "a man who
is self-conscious will emphasize his actions so that his self can the better
come to a conclusion regarding them, and since he is desirous that his
self shall be able to draw some meaning from them he will be careful to
put much meaning into them."[33] "You needed the good," writes Bellow.
"Refused to be cheated of it, dug for it under paved streets and in vacant
lots as it were and inevitably imagined it where it was not."[34]

You needed the beautiful, too. Unpaved Augusta Street was not beautiful, nor were the streets surrounding it. Humboldt Park, however, was, with its rose gardens and lagoon. On hot summer nights, whole families, including Bellow's, would sleep out of doors there. Also beautiful was Lake Michigan, but the lake played little part in the lives of immigrants from the northwest side. As Isaac Rosenfeld, a boyhood friend and fellow writer, puts it, the Chicago of Humboldt Park was "dry-docked." "You did not enter into imaginative relations with it," writes Bellow of the lake. "Venetian or Neapolitan possibilities never entered your mind. You lived inland in a kind of unconscious austerity or penance."[35] Trips to the lake in summer, to escape the heat, proved to be of sociological rather than aesthetic interest. The North Avenue streetcar stopped at Clark Street, five blocks short of the lake, and the Division Street line stopped at Wells, another five blocks inland (to ride the Division Street trolley cost 3 cents, "a thrilling ride, too, because at that time . . . the streetcar would dive under the Chicago River and you came up inside the Loop"[36]). To get to the water from Wells Street involved a walk through the Gold Coast, "the seat of wealth and high style between Clark Street and the lakefront."[37] Laden with towels, lunch baskets, brown paper bags, and bottles of soda, beach-bound immigrants glimpsed the rich "in classy restaurants cutting fabulous steaks." To hurry the crowds across Lake Shore Drive, a policeman "now and then gave you a hard prod in the ribs." Otherwise, the Gold Coast "suffered these slum hordes with quiet hostility." Once at the water, the beauty of the lake was obscured by standing crowds. Rebecca West thought the beaches were jammed because there was no room to swim. "They stood in crowds," Bellow writes, "because many of them were unable to swim."[38]

As for the city's flora and fauna, in *Herzog* Bellow writes of "certain flowers, peculiar to Chicago, crude, waxy things like red and purple crayon bits, in a special class of false-looking natural objects" (p. 661). The commonest Chicago tree, the cottonwood, he describes as "loutish-looking," "graceless" (in *Herzog* he calls it "shabby").[39] Matter per se seemed to have "a special Chicago character, as though its molecules were coarser, cruder, without Eastern or European delicacy, the soil more lumpy, the weeds and grasses clumsier."[40] Even the atmosphere was coarse: "no air but Chicago's was ever so oddly dark at midday."[41] "There was not much beauty to look at," Bellow writes, recalling his first impressions of the city, "unless you had the gift of deeper perception." Chicago refined this gift in Bellow, making him a "connoisseur of the near-nothing." He could even find beauty in the cottonwood. In spring, he writes of the tree, it produces "soft curling red catkins which fall on the pavement and are wonderfully fragrant underfoot"; later it releases "fluffy floating seeds which hover and slide in the slow currents of late spring."[42] He recalls sitting in back rooms—perhaps the back bedroom on Augusta Street—on winter afternoons looking out "at the first hardened snow and the dragging smoke which rises with difficulty in zero weather,"[43] a perception as "deep" as that of Wordsworth in "Tintern Abbey," in which the smoke of vagrants, seen from high above the Wye Valley, rises "in silence, from among the trees."

It was the street that impressed, particularly now that Bellow felt more grown up. He was determined, after his experiences in the hospital, to be out in the world, active, no longer weak or sickly.[44] Neither home nor Lafayette Elementary School nor the basement cheder in the synagogue at Rockwell and Augusta nor Sunday School at the Jewish People's Institute in Lawndale could keep him from the street. "The books spoke one language and the streets another," and both appealed. Street language was "rough cheerful energetic clanging largely good-natured Philistine irresistible" and American. "The children wanted the streets," Bellow writes in the "Chicago Book," "they were passionate Americans, they talked baseball, prizefights, speakeasies, graft, jazz, crap games, gang wars." Part of this passion derived from the high spirits of the 1920s: no foreign wars, "a public made good-natured by prosperity, the Philistine booboisie engrossed in cranking its flivvers [like the Ford Model T], playing golf in knickers, and mixing bathtub gin. Juvenile, circus-parade Chicago suited children immensely, especially the children of immigrants." Especially the children of Jewish immigrants. It was the Jews who threw themselves into American life most fully (the word Bellow uses is "hysterically," citing the "eagle screams of Al Jolson and the Yankee Doodle prancing of George M. Cohan").[45] The Poles sent their children to parochial school; there were few Polish pupils at Lafayette Elementary or the succeeding schools Bellow attended ("although we played with them, we played 'Piggy Move Up,' a ball game").[46] Bellow went from school to cheder every weekday, studying the Talmud from three to five, learning to write Yiddish in Hebrew characters. He retained his mother's deep religious sense, her "dreaming" side. But once he was old enough to choose, "the power of street life made itself felt,"[47] as it did, in different ways, for his brothers and sister, and his father. Only Liza, cut off by language, domestic duties, and gathering ill health, remained untouched by its appeal. "A few blocks from the house she was lost," recalled Bellow. "In those days, every drugstore had an electric mortar-and-pestle on the sign, you know, the pharmacist's pestle and mortar. Whenever she saw one from the streetcar, she would say, 'we're here!' No Mom, we're not home; it's just another drugstore."[48]

Assimilation was harder for Abraham than for his children, but from the start he was pro-American. "At the table, he would tell us, This really *is* the land of opportunity; you're free to do whatever you like, within the law."[49] Such views, Bellow thought, were encouraged by the Yiddish papers, "which were very helpful to the immigrant Jews— to explain things and acquaint them with the history of the U.S." Abraham would surprise Bellow with facts about the American Constitution, the founding of the colonies, the religious tolerance of Roger Williams of Rhode Island, all gleaned from *Der Forvertz*.[50] What also encouraged assimilation, Bellow came to realize, was the abstract, propositional character of American identity. Phrases like "conceived in liberty" and "dedicated to the proposition that," from Abraham Lincoln's "Gettysburg Address" point to a nation born of intellectual choices. "To be an American," writes Bellow in the second of his Jefferson Lectures, "was neither a territorial nor a linguistic phenomenon but a concept—a set of ideas, really."[51] "Being an American always had been something of an abstract project," declares Ijah Brodsky, the narrator of "Cousins." "You came as an immigrant. You were offered a most reasonable proposition and you said yes to it" (p. 231). Experience, however, the reality of daily life in America, is what mattered most. "You were safe, as Jews had never been in Europe," Bellow explained in an interview. "Here you could realize all the secular ambitions of the Jew, to be rich, to be happy, to be safe, and that was never real for European Jewry. At least that was how it appeared to Jews of the older generation, to Jews of my father's generation."[52]

This sense of safety applied as much, or almost as much, to illegal immigrants as to legal ones. "My father could never get over it. He would say, 'Look, I carry no papers. I can do whatever I please. I can go wherever I like. There is no one to deny me my rights of citizenship. If there were any attempts to undermine my rights of citizenship, it would become a scandal. The country would never stand for a thing like that. So I go around without papers, without passports, without identification, and it's perfectly alright."[53] That Abraham was not, in fact, a citizen, did nothing to temper the pride he took in America's protection of his rights. In Bellow's story "A Silver Dish" (1978), the protagonist's father, like Bellow's father, is an illegal immigrant: "He became an American, and America never knew it. He voted without papers, he drove without a licence, he paid no taxes, he cut every corner."[54] Abraham voted without papers, but he paid his taxes, never learned to drive, and cut fewer corners than the father in "A Silver Dish." He liked voting because, as Bellow puts it, "he'd pull the Roosevelt lever and Roosevelt would be the President" (in later years, results were less automatic). "'I always loved to vote,'" he told Bellow, "with a real kind of sentimental reverence." As for paying taxes, "he'd say, 'Well it's almost April 15th' and 'I don't mind giving, I don't mind paying my taxes in a country like this.'"[55] These sentiments were common among Jewish immigrants of Abraham's generation. Bellow tells of going to see a friend from school, Joey Sugarman, who lived on Division Street. It was election time and from the convention hall the radio was broadcasting the roll call of states: "Joey's father, a big, bearded Orthodox Jew, a *shochet*, or ritual slaughterer, was calling out the names of states in alphabetical order, singing them out like a cantor, just ahead of the radio: 'Maine, Maryland, Massachusetts.' Very red in the face, very fond of his citizenship."[56]

Abraham felt guilty about his illegal residence, but accepted its necessity. After all, Chicago accepted Al Capone and Big Bill Thompson, the mayor, who was in Capone's pocket. "Information about corruption, if you had grown up in Chicago, was easy to accept," says Charlie Citrine in *Humboldt's Gift*, "it harmonized with one's Chicago view of society" (p. 99). This view derived in part from the local press, the "verbal swagger" of which both echoed and inspired the street (good government reformers were labeled "goo goos" by the Chicago papers).[57] But it also derived from political reality. Thompson was mayor from 1915 to 1923, and was reelected in 1927, when Bellow was twelve. That year, for 25 cents, Bellow stuffed mailboxes for a precinct captain in his ward, the Twenty-sixth, "a party man [who] belonged to the machine." He also happily accepted free tickets to the Riverview Amusement Park on Western Avenue, courtesy of City Hall. In Thompson's second term, which lasted until 1931, "even schoolchildren understood that the real power in the city was divided between the Johnny Torrio–Al Capone organization to the south, and Dion O'Banion and Bugs Moran's North Side bootleggers. Racketeers, gangs were in charge." A similar understanding or acceptance—knowing, street-smart—extended to national politics. Under President Harding, scandals proliferated. As Chicagoans saw it, in Bellow's words, "this was the tempo of the decade. Prohibition led to racketeering, and racketeering produced a popular belief that everyone was on the take."[58] According to the street, "there were always two sets of facts, two languages, two codes—there was the *beau ideal* and there was the hustle."[59]

To help out with money in the early years in Chicago, the older Bellow boys took on after-school jobs. For the same reason, immediately after finishing high school, Jane became a stenographer, working in offices. Sam and Maury were "what we used to call hustlers. They sold papers in the streets, peddled chocolate bars on the commuter trains."[60] Maury worked for a while at the American Express Company, as a "baggage-smasher," loading trunks and suitcases on trucks.[61] When old enough, Saul also took on after-school jobs, but was no great shakes as a hustler, certainly in comparison with his brothers. The excited idealism of his youth, an extension of his childhood sense of wonder and belonging, "made it easy for practical people to pick your pockets as soon as there was something in them worth stealing."[62] In *The Adventures of Augie March*, Augie's older brother, Simon, tries to instruct him, as does Grandma Lausch, in the ways of the street. Simon works at newsstands and Grandma Lausch pesters him to get Augie a job at the stand in the La Salle Street station. She urges Simon to offer his boss a bribe ("Believe me, he's waiting for you to offer him one" [p. 420]). When Augie finally gets the job, his customers shortchange him and he's fired. "They throw the money down and grab a paper; you can't leave the stand to shag them," Augie complains. Simon's contemptuous reply is: "You couldn't get that money out of somebody else's change, could you?" (p. 421). Even before Augie goes out to work, he's enlisted in scams. Grandma Lausch coaches him on how to hoodwink Mr. Lubin, the caseworker. Then she coaches him on how to hustle the opticians at the dispensary, to obtain cheap spectacles for Mother March. In like manner, Bellow was instructed to shortchange the dentist, not by Maury, but by their mother. When one of his teeth went bad she accompanied Bellow to have it pulled, waiting outside. She said, "After he pulls it give him this fifty-cent piece. Say it's all you've got."[63] Liza was the least street of the Bellows, but was hardly naive or timorous. When she and Abraham went over household bills, deciding "whether to pay the landlord first or the grocer or the coal bill,"[64]

Bellow was enlisted to add up the figures. It was a way of checking on his progress in arithmetic, but it also introduced him to the calculating and corner cutting needed to support the family.

Calculating, corner cutting, hustling, petty illegality—this element of street life entered the Bellow household through the very heating system. In Prohibition Era Chicago, the Slav population brewed its own beer (in Polish, *piva*) which invariably exceeded the 0.5 percent limit imposed by the Volstead Act. In winter, beer fumes from the landlord's ground-floor apartment mingled with the heat rising from the single furnace vent in the Bellows' parlor. On Division Street, local hardware stores openly displayed equipment for home brewing. Fraudsters and confidence men as well as radicals and crackpot theorists mounted Division Street soapboxes, some of them as celebrated as the city's gangsters. In 1956, three years after the publication of *Augie*, Bellow published a portrait of Chicago's "Yellow Kid" Weil, "one of the greatest confidence men of his day." The Kid was famous for having made and lost $8 million in his lifetime, and for claiming never to have cheated an honest man, "only rascals."[65] After a big score, he bragged to Bellow, he would rent an entire floor of the Edgewater Beach Hotel (now demolished) "and fill it with naked hookers."[66] He was also a thinker and a reader: "His favorite authors seem to be Nietzsche and Herbert Spencer."[67] Some criminals, "the baser sort," disapproved of the Kid: "In their view, you should sneak up on people to pick their pockets, or break and enter to burglarize their houses, but to look them in the eyes, gain their confidence, that is impure." Bellow depicts the Kid in his eighties, "spruce and firm-footed, with his beard and wind-curled hat . . . the living figure of tradition in the city."[68] The other living figure of tradition in the city—the gangster or racketeer—rarely bothered locals in the street. Baby Face Nelson was born and raised in the Humboldt Park area, at 942–44 North California Avenue. John Dillinger's gang hid out in an apartment at 1740 Humboldt Boulevard, from which Dillinger often strolled to and through the park, entering from the northwest corner, at North and Kedzie. The Circus Gang, a subsidiary of the Capone Syndicate, had headquarters at 1857 North Avenue, at the eastern edge of Humboldt Park. From here, on February 14, 1929, the killers in the St. Valentine's Day Massacre set out for North Clark Street, where the massacre took place. Bellow was thirteen at the time.

FROM HIS FIRST DAYS in Chicago, North Avenue was a key destination for Bellow, almost as alluring as Division Street. Near the intersection with Rockwell Street were Scandinavian shops and fraternal lodges, a tiny movie house specializing in Hoot Gibson and Yakima Canutt westerns, the Anarchist Forum was nearby at the corner of Evergreen Avenue and California, the Daughters of Zion Charity Day nursery and the Association House ("the Sosh"), a settlement house, also at 2150 West North Avenue, where Bellow and his friends played basketball and hung out. Most important was the Humboldt Park Branch of the Chicago Public Library (in the choice between Hebrew school and poolroom or playground, Bellow told an interviewer, "the playground won out—together with the public library"[69]). Bellow became a user of the library, which was about half a mile from his home on Augusta Street, at the age of nine, already "a confirmed reader."[70] He describes trips to the library in winter, in zero-degree weather, books in hand, feeling as if his toes "had been guillotined." Inside, the library was "pleasantly rank," the pages of its buckram-bound books, stained "by soup or cocoa or tears" were often "fiercely annotated." Among the library's habitués were autodidacts, loafers, compulsives ("memorizing long poems, historical documents or statistical tables").[71] From the Anarchist Forum came Tolstoyan vegetarians, Swedenborgians, single taxers. Bellow's initial borrowings were "all sorts of self-improvement, self-development, books," a legacy of his lengthy stay in the hospital and consequent determination not "to remain weak and be coddled." The same motive partly drew him to boys' books, with their clean-cut heroes (he mentions Frank Merriwell and Dink Stover of Yale, and Nick Carter, detective). Frontier and adventure novels also appealed, as in the fiction of Rafael Sabatini, Jack London, and James Fenimore Cooper (a favorite of his brother Maury), with their "pioneers . . . independent men. Going into the wilderness with your ax and gun (and your smarts). Very important."[72]

The breadth and maturity of Bellow's early reading in Chicago is sometimes hard to credit. Ezra Davis, the singing roomer, remembers coming in from work to see him at the kitchen table reading *War and Peace* and *The Possessed*. If this was the kitchen table at Augusta Street, Bellow was ten at most. In another account, Bellow is said to have gone through all the books in the children's section of the library by nine and graduated to the adult section, "where he began with Gogol's *Dead Souls*."[73] He read the stories of Maupassant and O. Henry, Romain Rolland's *Jean-Christophe*, *The Wizard of Oz*, *The Decameron*, Upton Sinclair's *The Jungle*, the *Encyclopedia Americana* (bought for the March brothers by Grandma Lausch in *Augie*), as well as a coverless prose translation of *The Iliad*, which he found in a closet shelf in the Barons' bungalow. He also read Chicago newspapers, following the Leopold and Loeb case when it broke in 1924, and two years later the Dempsey-Tunney fight and Charlie Chaplin's *Gold Rush* ("It was up to me to find ways to reconcile the Trojan War with Prohibition, major-league baseball, and the Old Country as my mother remembered it").[74] "I read everything I could lay my hands on," he recalled in an interview, "brought home armloads of books . . . all kinds of books. It was hit or miss. I'd finish one at four o'clock and start another at five o'clock."[75] According to Ruth Miller, by nine Bellow was writing stories in imitation of O. Henry and Jack London and "by ten, he knew he wanted to be a writer."[76] Bellow speaks of his earliest writing, "in grade school," as imitating "things that stirred me greatly," often things from popular magazines or bestsellers (he cites the wilderness adventure stories of James Oliver Curwood).[77] But he dated his ambition to become a writer to later years, sometimes to high school, sometimes to college.[78] According to a childhood sweetheart, Esther Robbins, who met him when they were "twelve or thirteen," Bellow's writing ambitions, like her acting ambitions, were clear early on. She recalls the following exchange from junior high school days "as though it were yesterday": "'When you're a famous actress, Es, will you remember me?'" Bellow asked. "And I answered, with all the prophetic wisdom of childhood, 'You will be a famous author, Saul, long before I become an actress.' I must have been psychic, although it was easy to recognize his potential, even at that age."[79] Robbins also remembers spending "many a pleasant evening together in the Chicago public library on North Avenue," though "after we entered Tuley High, Saul and I went our separate ways."

Bellow spent two years at Lafayette Elementary School, entering in the third grade ("I was a little behind because of my half-year in the hospital").[80] Then he transferred for a year to the Columbus School, presumably because of the family's move to the first of two apartments on Cortez Avenue, one street north of Augusta. This apartment, at

2226 Cortez, was on the ground floor of a three-flat just east of Oakley Boulevard (hence three blocks east of the old Augusta Street apartment). Cortez was a quieter street than Augusta, the three-flat had a sun porch in front, a garden in the back, better furniture (bought from the departing tenants), and a pay telephone in the kitchen. Columbus Elementary School was closer to the new apartment than was Lafayette. A year later, in 1927, Bellow enrolled in Sabin Junior High School, where he was to stay for three years, before entering Tuley High School on September 3, 1930, at fifteen. The only elementary school records that survive for him are a Registration Card and a Progress Report from Lafayette. The Registration Card lists his age, the names of his parents (Liza is wrongly "Lillian"), date and place of birth, date of entry to school, and date of leaving school; the Progress Report contains entries for year and grade of instruction, but nothing under the headings "Mentality," "Interest," "Industry," "Scholarship," "Special Aptitudes," and "Conduct." There are no Chicago public school transcripts or reports for Bellow's single year at Columbus or the three at Sabin Junior High. All Bellow records of Lafayette School in his writing or in interviews is lining up in the playground by twos "in the stinging wind," marching in the corridors, sitting stiffly at his desk during roll call, "hands clasped on the top of the desk or folded behind one's back—the two fundamental disciplinary positions,"[81] and being baffled by baseball (when a ground ball was hit past him, one of the boys said, "You looked at that ball as if it was an object of idle curiosity").[82] He remembered the teachers at Lafayette as mostly unmarried women, exceptions being Mrs. Davis, who, in a rare departure from classroom business said of Charles Lindbergh, "I do hope, from my heart, that he is as good a young man as he is brave, and will never disappoint us," and Mrs. Cox, "a long gaunt woman in her fifties," who spoke of Tennyson and Longfellow. In the "Chicago Book," Bellow quotes Santayana on such teachers: "sensitive, faithful and feeble; their influence helps to establish that separation which is so characteristic of America between things intellectual, which remain wrapped in a feminine veil, and, as it were, under glass, and the rough business and passions of life."[83]

Of the education Bellow received at Sabin, he records that "'Americanism' was very strong, and there was a core program of literary patriotism."[84] "Our schoolteachers, when I was a boy in Chicago, were something like missionaries," he writes in "The Distracted Public," a lecture he gave in Oxford on May 10, 1990. "They earnestly tried to convert or to civilize their pupils, the children of immigrants from every European country. To civilize was to Americanize us all."[85] For many pupils, Bellow included, these teachers were the first "real" Americans ("that is to say, American Americans . . . whose fathers fought in the Spanish-American War, or Civil War") they'd ever met. That such teachers thought "we were *of right* Americans" was a special encouragement ("of course, the true social facts were very different," Bellow adds. "You learned those later").[86] Mrs. Jenkins, who taught eighth-grade history and drama, was Bellow's favorite, "a wonderful old woman" whose father had been in Andersonville prison camp during the Civil War. Mrs. Jenkins recounted her father's stories to her pupils, leading Bellow to "read a lot about the Civil War, Grant's memoirs and Sherman's as well." As for literary works, "when you read Melville or Mark Twain or Fenimore Cooper, you were greatly excited . . . and you thought—well, you know, I too am on patrol in the wilderness, or I too am floating down the Mississippi. You identify yourself so thoroughly with these things as a child, that later you're surprised when anyone tries to pry you away from them, or question your authenticity, your *right* to these things, as was later to happen. . . . I didn't really begin to learn about these things until I went to High School." In literary terms, by 1930, the year he entered Tuley, Bellow "was an American entirely. I read the *American Mercury*, the novels of Edith Wharton, Sinclair Lewis, and Sherwood Anderson."[87]

In addition to Americanizing its pupils, a "family of man" or universalist dimension marked Bellow's early schooling, another welcome encouragement to pupils whose parents were foreign-born. In "Cousins," Ijah Brodsky, the narrator, recalls his geography lessons in the Chicago public schools of the mid-1920s:

> We were issued a series of booklets: "Our Little Japanese Cousins," "Our Little Moroccan Cousins," "Our Little Russian Cousins," "Our Little Spanish Cousins." I read all these gentle descriptions about little Ivan and tiny Conchita, and my eager heart opened to them. Why, we were close, we were one under it all. . . . We were not guineas, dagos, krauts; we were cousins. It was a splendid conception, and those of us who opened our excited hearts to the world union of cousins were happy, as I was, to give our candy pennies to a fund for the rebuilding of Tokyo after the earthquake of the

twenties. After Pearl Harbor, we were obliged to bomb the hell out
of the place (p. 238).

The "eager heart" of the child Ijah (whose adult vision of cousinhood,
as this passage suggests, narrows radically) is like the "state of excitement" of the child Bellow, a state that made it easy to pick his pockets.[88]

To his fellow students, Bellow was remembered as controlled and
knowing in class.[89] Esther Robbins describes the first time she set eyes
on him, in Mr. Boehm's science lesson: "We must have been twelve or
thirteen. . . . He was a very handsome boy, with a thoughtful, analytical
and often brooding expression and a somewhat sardonic smile that gave
him an air of superiority." When Mr. Boehm catches Bellow having
copied from another pupil's notebook and threatens to punish him, "in
spite of the threat Saul was adamant in his refusal to 'tell' and I was so
impressed I wrote him a note telling him how wonderful I thought he
was." They became sweethearts. "We went to parties together where
we played spin the bottle, went on hikes in the Forest Preserves, bird-
watching and catching bugs and butterflies which he helped me mount."
At Sabin, they were involved in dramatic readings for school clubs. In
Miss Herzer's English class Bellow played Petruchio to Esther's Kate
in *The Taming of the Shrew*. In Mrs. Jenkins's drama class they had parts
in an adaptation of Booth Tarkington's *Penrod and Sam*, and performed
to a paying audience in the school auditorium. Both excelled in English
and journalism, vying for honors, arguing a good deal, often heatedly.
At Christmas, when made to sing carols, they composed their own
"ethnic" versions[90]; in summer, they spent long evenings talking on the
front steps of Esther's building. Upon graduation they were designated
"The Boy and Girl Most Likely to Succeed." As Esther saw it, what
drove them was a desire "to be American in every sense of the word."

Though Bellow often visited Esther's home she was never invited
to 2226 Cortez Avenue or to the third-floor apartment at 2200 Cortez,
where the family lived until 1930. "In all the time we spent together,"
she writes, "he rarely spoke of his family." She suspected he might have
been ashamed of his parents' foreign accents and ways. Esther's parents
had come to America at an early age and were more Americanized than
the parents of most of her friends. When she discovered, from reading *To Jerusalem and Back*, that Bellow wore the traditional "tzitzes"
or "fringes" under his shirt until he was six, she thought he might also

have been embarrassed by his family's religious Orthodoxy.[91] Although in later years Bellow had no difficulty acknowledging all aspects of his background, the adolescent Bellow seemed to act at times as though he did. Esther recounts a moment one summer at the Oak Street Beach, the packed beach Rebecca West writes about,[92] when Bellow suddenly leapt up saying, "Quick, there's my aunt! Let's run!" As they grabbed their things, all the money from Bellow's pockets fell into the sand and was lost. They had to walk home, giving Esther blisters for a week. Was Bellow ashamed to be seen with a girl by his aunt, or was he ashamed of the aunt, or of the girl herself (though Esther was a nice Jewish girl, "certainly presentable enough, with a trim little figure that did credit to a bathing suit")? "We were so terribly insecure," she concludes, "and so very sensitive." The anxieties of Bellow's parents may also have figured in this context. "Of course they were all very suspicious of my outside contacts," he recalls of his family, "afraid these were all alienating influences." Abraham might subject Esther to a grilling about her background, the sort he gave Ruth Miller. Finally, there was the matter of his mother's health. Not long after the family arrived in Chicago, Liza was diagnosed with breast cancer and had a mastectomy. "So that was the main drama of family life," Bellow recalls, "and my father was frantic and didn't have time to bring up the children himself, and he wouldn't have known how to do it anyway. So what happened was we had a dying mother, as we discovered after a few years in Chicago."[93]

BELLOW THOUGHT LONG and hard about the anxieties of immigrant Americans and their children. "The distortions they suffered in Americanizing themselves," he recounts in interview, "also charged them with a certain energy." It was this energy "that built the great cities" (in addition to making Esther Robbins the girl most likely to succeed). The cost was assimilative anxiety, perhaps expressed in Bellow's reluctance, or seeming reluctance, to introduce Esther to his family, or her insecure, or seemingly insecure, speculation about its sources. "Though everybody wanted to be an American," Bellow agrees, "everybody's secret was that he hadn't succeeded in becoming one."[94] This is a theme in several Bellow stories. In "Cousins," there is Cousin Mendy, who "had a peculiar relish for being an American of his time." Mendy is "a complete American, as formal, as total in his fashion as a work of art" (p. 228). "He was a man-and-boy Midwesterner, living out of a

W. C. Fields script. And yet in the eyes under that snap-brim fedora there had always been a mixture of Jewish lights, and in his sixties he was visibly more Jewish. And, as I have said, the American model he had adopted was now utterly obsolete" (p. 230).[95] The Jack Dworkin character in "Cousins" is "mountainous" Cousin Shimon, with huge hands and a "hump of strength" like Five Properties' "bole." Cousin Shimon "cares nothing for the seersucker jacket that covers his bulging back. He bought it, he owns it, but by the way he wears it he turns it against itself. It becomes some sort of anti-American joke" (p. 220). The Americanized narrator, Ijah, makes this observation, which is partly admiring, even though Cousin Shimon doesn't like him.

In a 1974 commencement address at Brandeis, Bellow talked of the pain involved in assimilation ("I find it hard to think of anyone who underwent the process with joy"). Those who were lucky enough to escape this pain were either oblivious or indifferent, like the Cousin Shimon character, or clueless, lacking imitative talents. "I remember a cousin," Bellow told the students, "Arkady from the old country who declared that his new name was now, and henceforth, Lake Erie. A most poetic name, he thought." When someone set him straight, Arkady "simply became 'Archie' and made no further effort to prove himself a real American."[96] In the story "Him with His Foot in His Mouth" (1982), the narrator-protagonist, Herschel Shawmut, cannot stop himself from making hurtful remarks, wisecracks, jokes. The remarks are uncontrollable, like seizures or hysterical symptoms, and Shawmut is "as astonished by them as anybody else." Most of the wounding remarks he utters, Bellow himself had uttered, he admitted in an interview, and the story offers a wide and brilliant survey of their possible origins. One such origin, reductive but not wholly dismissed, is offered by Shawmut's supposed friend, Eddie Walish, who eggs him on when a wisecrack is approaching but is "careful not to be incriminated as an accessory." According to Walish, "I had raised myself by painful efforts from immigrant origins to a middle-class level but that I avenged myself for the torments and falsifications of my healthy instincts, deformities imposed on me by this adaptation to respectability."[97] Shawmut identifies Walish's interpretation as the sort of "clever, intricate analysis" popular in the Greenwich Village of the time, but he also admits that "it was hard for me to acquire decent manners, not because I was naturally rude but because I felt the strain of my position." He then offers a perfect example, because so coarse, of assimilative anxiety, of doomed and distorting effort: "Of course I overdid things and wiped myself twice where people of better breeding only wiped once. But no such program of betterment could hold me for long" (p. 378).

ESTHER ROBBINS WAS NOT Bellow's first childhood love. In elementary school, he developed a crush on Rosalyn Tureck, born a year before him. Tureck, at nine, was a promising musician, had made a professional debut, and would go on to become an acclaimed pianist and harpsichordist, particularly as an interpreter of Bach. Bellow remembers her as flirtatious, lively (like Esther), and out of his league, though in later years, after both were famous, they corresponded warmly. In "Cousins," the character of Virgie Dunton, Ijah's childhood love, is a harpist, who has had a long and successful career, like Tureck, and Ijah is smitten with her from the start. "Whenever possible, I attended her concerts; I walked in her neighborhood in hopes of running into her, imagined that I saw her in department stores" (p. 233). Ijah's wife, Sable (Isabel), mocks his childhood mooning. Whether Liza Bellow knew of her son's mooning over Tureck, the son does not say. Liza had musical as well as rabbinical ambitions for her children. If Bellow was not to be a great *lamden*, he might be a great violinist, like Jascha Heifetz, Mischa Mischakoff, of the Chicago Symphony, or Toscha Seidel. Hence the weekly violin lessons he went to in the Fine Arts Building on South Michigan Boulevard, a long trolley ride away. There Bellow was taught by Grisha Borushek, "a stout gloomy man from Odessa seeking a prodigy."[98]

Bellow had some talent as a child violinist, enjoyed playing, and at twelve had performed Bohm's "Moto Perpetuo" in a student recital at Kimball Hall. But he was no prodigy, no Rosalyn Tureck, and when he made mistakes, the peevish Borushek, impatient for the next Heifetz or Menuhin, "would snatch the bow and whip my bottom with it." Bellow forgave him ("obviously I lacked the gifts he was looking for"), was grateful for the instruction, and until middle age "sought out opportunities to play with other amateur musicians, in duets and trios." He was also grateful to his musical sister, Jane, "a perfect metronome (metrognome) of a pianist,"[99] for introducing him to Mozart. The family now owned a radio and on Saturday afternoons there were live broadcasts from the New York Philharmonic.[100] Through such means, as he explained in a speech of December 5, 1991, delivered on the occasion of the Mozart Bicentennial, "although I was not trained in a conservatory, I absorbed a considerable amount of music, and while I preferred books to instruments, there were odd corners of my existence reserved for Handel, Mozart, Pergolesi, etc."[101] In music periods at Sabin, the teacher wound up the gramophone and played "Chaliapin singing the 'Song of the Flea' or Galli-Curci the 'Bell Song' from *Lakmé* or Caruso or Tito Schipa or Madame Schumann-Heink."

The emotions these recordings elicited were anatomized by Bellow in a speech he gave in 1974 to open a conference of Verdi scholars. Chief among them was a sense that classical music, like all high art, was irrelevant: "tough or sensitive, we somehow grasped the tacit Chicago assumption that this was a rough place, a city of labor and business, gangs and corrupt politics, ball games and prizefights. . . . This was a place where matter ruled, a place where stone was value and value stone. If you were drawn towards a higher life—and you might well be, even in the city of stockyards, steel and gangsters—you had to make your own way toward it."[102] The "prodigious power" of the city, Bellow realized early on, "lay in things and the methods by which things were produced. What Chicago gave to the world was goods—a standard of living sufficient for millions."[103] No American city in the 1920s was a bigger manufacturer. When not making goods, the city made money moving and trading them, as market and transportation hub.[104] "Chicago," Bellow writes in the "Chicago Book," "is for me one of the terms that expresses the depth of our penetration into the physical world."[105]

Much the same lesson was gained from Bellow's experiences as an unpaid usher at the Auditorium Theatre, one of the city's great cultural institutions. It owed its existence to business moguls, principally Ferdinand Peck, a real estate tycoon and philanthropist, but also, among others, George Pullman, of railroad fame, Marshall Field, the department store magnate, and Martin Ryerson, the lumber and property tycoon, whose intentions were to build the world's largest, grandest, most expensive theater, a rival to the Metropolitan Opera House in New York City. The firm of Dankmar Adler and Louis Sullivan was engaged to design and build the auditorium, which was finished in 1889. Frank Lloyd Wright described it as the "greatest room for music and opera in the world." Until 1929, it was the home of the Civic Opera, and Bellow recalls attending performances by the Ballet Russe de Monte Carlo and the San Carlo Opera, probably while still in junior high school.[106] The wealthy audience members Bellow ushered to their seats, especially the men, were often reluctant or inattentive spectators. "In Chicago the normal male despised this female sickliness," he writes in the first of the Jefferson Lectures, "the phony singing dagos wearing rompers and carrying knives. . . . I know those attitudes well. As a student usher at the same Auditorium Theater during the annual visits of the San Carlo Opera Company, I struggled with my own vulgarity."[107] Chicago may have "earned the right to be considered the center of American materialism—the classical center," but for Bellow its cultural pretensions "aren't very significant." He associates them with boosterism: "The rich, growing more boorish and ignorant with every decade, put up money for museums, orchestras, opera companies, art associations, arty clubs and so on,"[108] but such expenditures, concessions to culture, "were not and never would be the main thing."[109]

THE KEY FIGURE IN Bellow's "Americanization" was his brother Maury. When Bellow enrolled in Lafayette Elementary as a third grader, Maury enrolled as a senior at Tuley High School. Almost immediately, he "made a beeline for the Loop,"[110] the city center. In the 1920s, the Loop was as lively at night as it was during the day, a "hustling, brawling place of small shops, busy crowds, cooking odors,"[111] quite unlike the Loop today, all office buildings and gleaming skyscrapers. Jazz musicians hung out on Randolph Street, prizefighters at Trafton's Gym, there were huge billiard halls, like Bensinger's, where crack pool players and hustlers vied, and vaudeville houses, where stars like Jimmy Durante or Sophie Tucker performed. After graduating from Tuley, Maury enrolled in a Loop law school "for city boys from the immigrant neighborhoods."[112] To pay his tuition, he found work with an Italian lawyer named Roland V. Libonati, a member of the Illinois House of Representatives from 1928 to 1942 (later a state senator, then a United States congressman). Maury worked in Libonati's office answering calls, complaints, and letters; then he became Libonati's bagman, "a collector of tribute, graft-dollars from Chicagoans who needed things done." Libonati was an advisor and lawyer for Al Capone, and a lifelong friend ("I liked him, because he respected me"). As a legislator, he was associated with the syndicate-backed West Side Bloc, which opposed or circumvented anticrime bills for over forty years, from Prohibition onward. Maury collected money for Libonati in a little Gladstone bag, skimming off a portion for himself, half of which he gave to his mother ("before branching out into haberdashery and women").[113] "He never got caught and that's lucky," Bellow told Philip Roth in their interview, "because they would have broken his hands." In the story "Something to Remember Me By," set in 1933, the narrator's elder brother, Albert, is described as "a night-school law student clerking for Rowland, the racketeer congressman. He was Rowland's bagman, and Rowland hired him not to read law but to make collections. . . . Toward me, Albert was scornful. He said, 'You don't understand fuck-all. You never will.'"[114]

Maury eventually obtained a law degree, but he never practiced (his illegal status may have prevented him from taking the bar examination). He quickly established himself as what Bellow calls "a businessman and a blowhard."[115] He wore loud, expensive clothes (Albert wears a derby, "called, in those days, a Baltimore heater . . . and a camel's-hair topcoat, and pointed, mafiosi shoes" [p. 424]). His manner was brash, full of "Loop know-how," boastful, often about influential friends, including syndicate friends, but also about how much he knew, "all sorts of outrageous knowledge—political, financial, erotic. He was very proud of his extraordinary group of connections, his cynicism, his insiderhood."[116] At home, Maury set his face against family sentiment and religion. He was "full of contempt" for kashruth (dietary laws) and Jewish observance.[117] He was "for total Americanization": "from the first he would say to me when we arrived from Canada, 'Enough of this old crap about being Jewish' and so forth." In the Bellow family, "there was a great deal of affection floating around very freely," and Maury "wanted to get rid of it immediately because it enslaved [him] to my father's will."[118] To a lesser extent, Bellow thought this was true also of Sam, the middle brother, "but the rest of us enjoyed this affection and kindness."[119] Maury was not without feelings for his family, but he was against their open expression. In *Herzog*, Moses's rich older brother, Alexander, or Shura, has similar feelings, and similar attitudes toward those feelings. The adult Shura is described as Moses's "handsome stout white-haired brother, in his priceless suit, vicuña coat, Italian hat, his million-dollar shave and rosy manicured fingers with big rings." A figure of "princely hauteur," he "knew everyone, paid off everyone, and despised everyone." Moses calls him a disciple of Thomas Hobbes in his contempt for universal concerns—the concerns that bedevil Moses. What softens his contempt for Moses is "family feeling." Also, "it amused Shura that his brother Moses should be so fond of him" (p. 494).[120]

Lesha Greengus, Sam's daughter, remembers Maury as "the most volatile" of the brothers, more volatile even than Abraham. But she also remembers him as capable of being "very charming." Mark Rotblatt, Maury's grandson, remembers him as "ruthless, tough, could cut you and just turn his back and walk away, but also there was a level of deep emotion." "He freezes when he's offended," Bellow writes of Maury in a letter postmarked January 9, 1962, to his third wife, Susan, "and if you think *I'm* vulnerable, I recommend you study him." Maury's daughter, Lynn Rotblatt, Mark's mother, spent much of her life fruitlessly seeking his approval; she called her father and his cronies "the Animals." As a schoolboy, Bellow was dazzled by Maury: "his histrionics had a dramatic influence on our feelings, and the fact that he was physically impressive—big and stout, aggressive, clever—simply added to the effect."[121] It was Maury who introduced Bellow "to the idea of chasing women, drinking, being wild at parties." Maury read books, read voraciously, but didn't want anyone knowing that he did, "liked to be thought of as a tough guy and a non-reader."[122] When Maury visited Bellow's apartment in later years, especially in company, "he'd pour it on. He'd take a book off the shelf and he'd say, 'Who's this guy Prowst you keep reading? Who's this Prowst?' I'd say 'Oh he's some Jew or other.'"[123]

Maury began drawing away from the family almost as soon as they arrived in Chicago. As Bellow remembers it, "being older, he had a more urgent sense of the need to Americanize himself, to repudiate the family. . . . He was old enough to go his own way."[124] Vivien Missner, Louis Dworkin's daughter, recalls very little of him, except that he was distant, standoffish, "not particularly impressed by my father, one way or another," and often absent from family gatherings.[125] With his own family he was ruthless. After a business dispute with Lynn and her husband, Leonard Rotblatt, Maury cut the family off completely. Mark, their son, first met his grandfather when he was fourteen, at his father's funeral. "He walked in, he was very much the distinguished elder gentleman. He had on this camel hair jacket, very dapper, with the silk scarf, very elegant." After the breakup of his first marriage, Maury moved to Florida, visiting Chicago mostly for business reasons. "Maury would blow into town," Greg Bellow remembers, "he'd be like a house on fire, he was just on the go all the time, constantly wheeling and dealing, constantly putting deals and people together. . . . He loved to abuse waiters, I saw him do it. He loved to lord it over people." Greg moved to California after college and remembers Maury showing up for a Super Bowl (Miami was playing) "with a claque of friends. He must have brought twenty people with him, and they were all, fundamentally, deferring to him and he was the star of the show. He loved it." Maury had a son out of wedlock, but never saw him. On June 17, 1980, in a letter to the son, Dean Borok, Bellow tried to warn him not to expect much from his father. Borok had written to Bellow after reading *The Adventures of Augie March*, which he thought contained a thinly fictionalized account of his birth: "He sees none of us—brothers, sister, or his two children by his first marriage, nor their children—neither does he telephone or write. He had no need of us. He has no past, no history. . . . He probably has some money—he thought of little else all his life."

Bellow's fascination with Maury can be gauged by the number of Maury figures in his fiction. In addition to Shura in *Herzog* and Albert in "Something to Remember Me By," there's Simon in *The Adventures of Augie March*, Philip in "Him with His Foot in His Mouth," and Julius (Ulick) in *Humboldt's Gift*.[126] Each of these characters is the narrator's older brother. Each is stout, rich, flashily dressed, self-assured, and boastful. In *Humboldt's Gift*, Julius is a real estate operator in Corpus Christi, Texas (after leaving Chicago, Maury was a real estate operator in Florida, then bought an estate in Thomasville, Georgia, for his second wife, where she raised horses). "I loved my stout and now elderly brother," declares Charlie Citrine. "Perhaps he loved me too. In principle he was not in favor of strong family bonds. Possibly he saw brotherly love as an opening for exploitation" (a possibility in real life that was to lead to problems between Maury and Bellow). Charlie is prepared to take some blame for Julius's distance. "My feelings for him," he admits, "were vivid, almost hysterically intense, and I could not blame him for trying to resist them. He wished to be a man entirely of today, and he had forgotten or tried to forget the past" (p. 239). Charlie's girlfriend, Renata, can't understand why he's so crazy about Julius: "Let me recall a few of the things you told me about him. When you were a kid playing with toys on the floor he would step on your fingers. He rubbed your eyes with pepper. He hit you on the head with a bat. When you were an adolescent he burned your collection of Marx and Lenin pamphlets. He had fist fights with everyone, even a colored maid" (p. 346).

Julius makes his first fortune, his Chicago fortune, as did Maury, "somewhere between business and politics . . . connected with the underworld although without being a part of it" (Jimmy Hoffa was a guest at the wedding of Maury's daughter, Lynn, in 1956). When divorce wipes Julius's fortune out, as it did Maury's, he moves to Texas, starts a second family, and makes a second fortune in property. "It was impossible to think of him without his wealth. It was necessary for him to be in the money, to have dozens of suits and hundreds of pairs of shoes, shirts beyond inventory" (p. 346). According to his son, Joel, Maury owned 300 suits and 100 pairs of shoes, would return from trips to Europe with great laundry baskets full of "perfumes and watches and clocks and shoes and dishes and glassware. . . . And people would come over—Saul and Sam and Nina [Sam's wife] and their kids—and my father would hand these things out; it was like the King of France." One summer in the 1940s, when Sam and his family and Abraham and his second wife were on holiday in Oconomowoc, Wisconsin, Maury hired a small plane to come visit for the day. When he left, he had the pilot buzz the resort, which thrilled Abraham.[127] In *Humboldt's Gift*, Julius, like Maury, plays the anti-intellectual, but Charlie knows that he often "shut himself up in his office with a box of white raisins and read Arnold Toynbee and R. H. Tawney, or Cecil Roth and Salo Baron on Jewish history. When any of this reading cropped up in conversation he made sure to mispronounce the key words" (p. 379). Why Charlie wanted to be an intellectual was beyond Julius, but if he had to be one, "why couldn't you be the tough type, a Herman Kahn or a Milton Friedman, one of those aggressive guys you read in *The Wall Street Journal*?" In disgust, Julius adds: "Pa should have slapped you around the way he did me" (p. 374).

All his life, Maury was "a fattie" (son Joel's phrase). In *Humboldt's Gift*, Julius's appetite is compulsive. On the day before open heart surgery (Maury's surgery was a quadruple bypass), while entertaining potential backers for a large real estate deal, Julius begins eating. At a fish place he buys smoked shrimp and smoked marlin for his wife, pulling off pieces of the marlin "before the fish was removed from the scale." By the time he returns home, he's eaten it all. He then stops at the fruit stall to buy persimmons: "The fish had been eaten. We sat with him under a tree sucking at the breast-sized, flame-colored fruit. The juice spurted over his sport shirt, and seeing that it now had to go to the cleaner anyway he wiped his fingers on it as well." After viewing the property, Julius suggests that the party get a drink "and something to eat." At a Mexican restaurant, he devours a plate of chicken breasts with bitter chocolate mole sauce. When Charlie can't finish his, Julius does: "He took my plate. He ordered pecan pie à la mode, and then a cup of Mexican chocolate" (p. 387). Back home Julius and Charlie sit in the garden. Charlie is exhausted, but "arrogant, haggard" Julius is full of financing schemes and architect's plans. While talking, he "reached gloomily into one of his trees and picked handfuls of fruit. . . . He stood plucking and eating, spitting out stones and skins, his gaze fixed beyond me" (p. 388). John Updike wrote a largely unfavorable review of *Humboldt's Gift* when it appeared in 1975, which upset Bellow. Fifteen years later, in the fourth of his Rabbit books, *Rabbit at Rest* (1990), he gives Nitrostat-popping Rabbit Angstrom a comparably junky and compulsive appetite, for similarly, if more explicitly, representative reasons. "It's a typically American heart," Rabbit's doctor tells him, "full of crud." Heartless, too, servicing a paunch "that in itself must weigh as much as a starving Ethiopian child." Julius, like Maury, like Updike's Rabbit, identifies wholly with American materialism.[128] He's more heartless than Rabbit, but less heartless than Maury, judging at least from the testimony of Maury's children and grandchildren, who are not as forgiving as Bellow.

In Bellow's fiction, this sort of greed and aggression often go with something poignant. In *The Adventures of Augie March*, Simon is as monstrous as Julius. Like Maury, he marries a woman with money and political clout. This woman, Charlotte Magnus, proves an excellent businesswoman, as did Maury's first wife, Marge Yudkoff (Maury would cut the deals, according to Greg Bellow, and Marge would see that they worked: "they made a very good team"). When the family got together on Sundays and discussion turned to business, Marge was the only woman to take part. But the business powerhouse from Marge's side of the family was her mother, Fanny Yudkoff, who founded a string of shoe shops, then small department stores. Grandma Yudkoff's affection for Maury meant that he was never at a loss for risk capital. It was her money that helped the Bellowses buy the first of their hotels, the Sherry, on the corner of South Shore Drive and 53rd Street.[129] Simon's Charlotte, like Maury's Marge, is heavy and plain, though she's shrewd, tough, and clearly mad for Simon, as Marge was for Maury. Simon argues with her a lot, but also likes her.[130]

How Simon treats women we learn first in a scene at the North Avenue beach, where he makes "bullish approaches" to ones he finds attractive, "his eyes big and red." When a girl bends over "to choose a plum from her lunch bag . . . he'd start to blare like brass and he'd

hit me on the arm and say to me, 'Look at the spread on that broad.'"
Then he'd get "violent and lustful" and make a brute charge. Yet "the
girls were not always frightened of him; he had a smell of power, he was
handsome" (p. 648). Simon's brute appeal, and the manners or tone of
the world he moves in, are memorably evoked in the scene in which
he brings Augie home for dinner. Though Charlotte joins them, her
mother, Mrs. Magnus, has been temporarily banned from Simon's sight
for wearing cheap dresses. At the end of the meal, Augie makes Charlotte bring Mrs. Magnus in for cherries and coffee:

> Simon worked himself into a rage at Mrs. Magnus in her brown
> dress. He tried to read the paper and cut her—he hadn't said a word
> when she came in—but finally he said, and I could see the devil in
> him now. "Well, you lousy old miser, I see you still buy your clothes
> off the janitor's wife."
>
> "Let her alone," said Charlotte sharply.
>
> But suddenly Simon threw himself across the table, spilling
> the cherries and overturning coffee cups. He grabbed his mother-
> in-law's dress at the collar, thrust in his hand, and tore the cloth
> down to the waist. She screamed. There were her giant soft breasts
> wrapped in the pink band. What a great astonishment it was, all of
> a sudden to see them! She panted and covered the top nudity with
> her hands and turned away. However, her cries were also cries of
> laughter. How she loved Simon! He knew it too.
>
> "Hide, hide!" he said, laughing.
>
> "You crazy fool," cried Charlotte. She ran away on her high
> heels to bring her mother a coat and came back laughing also. They
> were downright proud, I guess.
>
> Simon wrote out a check and gave it to Mrs. Magnus. "Here," he
> said, "buy yourself something and don't come here looking like the
> scrubwoman." He went and kissed her on the braids, and she took
> his head and gave his kisses back two for one and with tremendous
> humor (pp. 872–73).

Maury was like this. "He took up with a succession of shiksas," Bellow
recalls, "but he didn't drop the Jewish women altogether. He was quite a
collector of ladies."[131] Looking out the window of his Gold Coast apartment, Maury's grandson, Mark Rotblatt, points to a building where "all
my grandfather's contemporaries, all of them very wealthy older Jewish

men, had their mistresses." The building is ugly: "the one building on the Gold Coast that was cheap." It was also convenient: "You could keep your mistress and you could go visit her when you tell your wife you're going out for a paper or a cigar or something." There Maury kept the woman who would become his second wife. He and his friends called it the *nafke* building, from the Yiddish word for "whore." In this context, as Mark explains, it means "whore-pig" or "sex-pig."

Before Simon checks out the women at the North Avenue beach, he goes for a swim. It is here, very briefly but clearly, that Bellow registers the price Simon pays for the life he has chosen, for the person he has made himself. When Simon dives into the water off the point, Augie worries that he does so "with a thought of never coming back to the surface alive, as if he went to take a blind taste of the benefits of staying down. He came up haggard and with a slack gasp of his mouth and rough blood in his face. I knew it made a strong appeal to him to go down and not come up again" (p. 647). Earlier, Augie sees suicidal impulses in "the way [Simon] drove and the way he leaped forward in arguments, hit him who would; he kept a tire tool under the driver's seat for his weapon in traffic arguments, and he cursed everybody in the street, running through lights and scattering pedestrians" (p. 640).[132] Julius Citrine is subject to similar impulses. When Charlie goes to Europe, Julius asks him to purchase a marine painting for him. Charlie spends hours in antique shops and art galleries in Madrid in search of the sort of painting his brother wants: "But in all the blue and green, foam and sun, calm and storm, there was always a rock, a sail, a funnel and Julius wasn't having any of that." As Charlie puts it, "nobody cared to paint the pure element, the inhuman water, the middle of the ocean, the formless deep, the world-enfolding sea" (p. 410). Philip Roth remembers Maury searching for this painting in London, when he met him with Bellow. In *Humboldt's Gift*, Bellow has Charlie speculate on the attraction of such a painting, which he partly attributes to Julius's recent heart operation: "Maybe he had had it with the ever-alert practical American soul. In six decades he had spotted all the rackets, smelled all the rats, and he was tired of being the absolute and sick master and boss of the inner self. What did a seascape devoid of landmarks signify? Didn't it signify elemental liberty, release from the daily way and the horror of tension?" (pp. 410–11). Charlie briefly considers going to the Prado, finding a painter to paint an empty seascape, paying him $2,000, and then, as a sort of tribute to Julius, charging him $5,000.

Such saving vulnerabilities evoke no real-life echoes in Maury's children and grandchildren. They are as tough on Maury as he seems to have been on them. After he hit or was verbally abusive to his children, Joel remembers, Maury "would, indeed, feel badly about it, but there was nothing compensatory, there was no offset." His attitude was: "'You had it coming.' . . . And when it was over, it was over. 'What was it we were talking about before I hit you?'" This quickness both to anger and to release from anger, Joel also ascribed to Bellow, as did Bellow himself. The crucial difference was one of degree, between nasty or angry remarks, on the one hand, and physical abuse and rage, on the other. For Joel, Maury was like Abraham, when Abraham beat Maury after the hijacking. Bellow never suffered Maury's level of abuse. "This is so repetitious," Joel says of Maury's beating after the hijacking. "When my father would come home and I'd run to meet him, I never knew whether he was going to hug or kiss me or whether he was just going to start slapping me." Joel's sister, Lynn, he claims, had it worse: "he'd kick her, slap her, push her, verbally abuse her. . . . My sister, she was just a stationary target, I mean she didn't have a chance." Bellow knew of Maury's behavior, had himself, to a much lesser degree, been subject to it in childhood, and wrote about it, but he never lost the love and admiration he felt for his older brother, the brother who lifted him onto his shoulders to see the Prince of Wales pass by. "No matter what Maury did," Bellow's oldest son, Greg, recalls, "Saul would always forgive him." "The instant I saw him I loved him again," declares Augie of Simon, after Simon had, in effect, abandoned him. "I couldn't help it. It came over me. I wanted to be brothers again" (p. 865).

Bellow's attitude to Maury, who was to die in 1985, was like his attitude to American materialism, against which he set his face, but to which he was powerfully drawn.[133] It also relates to his attitude to money. As we will see later, Bellow valued money, valued having it more than spending it, though he never valued it enough to know much about it or to put himself out to make any. Something of his attitude is revealed in the story "Him with His Foot in His Mouth," in which the narrator, Herschel Shawmut, gets involved in a deal with his older brother, Philip, a businessman. Philip is rich, fat, aggressive, and located now in Texas. When he learns that Shawmut, a musicologist, has earned serious money by writing a college textbook for introductory classes in music appreciation, he's both impressed and affronted (according to Mark Rotblatt, when Maury learned that Bellow had won the Nobel Prize, he was affronted, which is why he never considered accepting Bellow's invitation to attend the ceremony, as did Bellow's sister, Jane, and brother Sam: "How dare Saul win the Nobel Prize" was how Mark reconstructs Maury's thinking, "when *I'm* really the smart one, *I'm* the one").[134] In Bellow's story, older brother Philip asks Shawmut what he's going to do with his money, whether he's going to invest it, how he's going to protect himself against taxes and inflation. "His interest in my finances excited me," confesses Shawmut. "For once he spoke seriously to me, and this turned my head." Similar feelings seem to have played a part in Bellow's several business ventures with Maury, also with other relatives, as speculator, investor, developer. *"Vu bin ikh?"* ("Where am I in this?") Bellow would ask when the brothers talked of possible deals. His eagerness expressed a wish to count in his siblings' eyes, or to be counted among them, as well as to make money. For Lesha Greengus, "Where am I in this?" became a Bellow catch-phrase, like "What's a man to do?" and the gesture that went with it. In "Him with His Foot in His Mouth," Shawmut admires his brother for reasons he can explain only as "a *given*, a lifelong feeling, a mystery" (p. 395). To Philip, Shawmut's fondness for him is "contemptible in an adult male," a reaction Shawmut sees as "American." "He abominated these reminiscences of mine," Shawmut reports, "for he was thoroughly Americanized" (p. 395).

In the unedited transcript of one of Bellow's interviews with Philip Roth, dated December 2, 1999, Maury enters the conversation in connection with *The Adventures of Augie March*. For Roth, as for others, *Augie* is the first of Bellow's novels to give voice to "the language you spoke and the stuff you heard, the American argot that you heard on the street." In a discussion of the novel's reception, Bellow mentions Lionel Trilling, a crucial early supporter of his writing, remembered here as "dead against" *Augie*. After Bellow showed him the novel's first hundred or so pages, Trilling's reaction was: "It's very curious, it's very interesting but somehow it's wrong." This reaction Bellow calls "the academic view." Roth then asks Bellow if he thinks Trilling was "blind to the American?" by which he means the American language, the language of the American street. Bellow answers that Trilling "didn't have much feeling for it." As the interview progresses, "Trilling" becomes shorthand not so much for "the academic view" as for the New York view, in particular that of the *Partisan Review* crowd. For Roth, this crowd "didn't have much feeling for America as a subject . . . for the lives of the people in the city houses as a subject" (a judgment that will be considered more closely in later chapters). Nor, Roth adds, did Trilling have much understanding of Bellow's sense of himself as a Jew. According to Roth, "there was a way of being a Jew and that was Trilling's way, but this [Bellow's way] was a strange way because it was both a way out and a way in. Because it wasn't just that you were finding a way out of being a Jew; you were finding a way as a writer into being a Jew without doing what Malamud did." Bellow admired Malamud, who was a friend, but in the exchange with Roth he characterizes Malamud's "way" as "shtetl stick adapted to the U.S.A." "That's right," Roth pitches in, "with all the sentimental baggage that comes with it." In *Augie March*, Roth continues,

> you plugged into Jewish aggression and Jews as businessmen and the Howes of the world [he means Irving Howe] always identified the Jewish success in America with what was in fact the Jewish failure: socialism. The Jewish success in America is obvious, it's business. You don't have to be a genius to figure that out but when he writes his big book on Jews in America [*World of Our Fathers*] he doesn't mention business. It's all about the unions, it's all about socialism, and it's all about the whole Europeanized side of Jewishness, the pushcarts, and so on. But the real thing the Jews did in America, their great, their real genius and success, was in business, and that drives him crazy, he doesn't want to hear about it. But that's what's at the heart of your book, which is the small-time lawyers, the owners of the middle-sized businesses, the conniving and cheating. You were not ashamed of Jewish aggression because you saw it as American aggression. . . . It was Chicago aggression.

"My eldest brother was a lesson to me in this respect," Bellow answers. When Roth asks: "Was he an American lesson for you?" Bellow answers: "Yes." Roth's conclusion is: "So you were lucky the overpowering brother was the totally American brother. . . . So he overpowered you and made you write *Augie March*. You were your brother's creature." Roth is speaking very freely here, the transcript is unrevised, and Bellow withdraws slightly, pointing out that Maury "didn't like [*Augie*] when I wrote it." Roth then interrupts Bellow, partly, it seems, to correct any impression he may have given that Bellow was passive in the making of the novel: "You spin out of his American—this is an oversimplification—But if you think of your father's Roger Williams [that is, Abraham's interest in American history] and your brother's exploitative nature and big aggressive being, you're the next. . . . You spin off of that into that America." "That's right," Bellow answers: "I just spin off both of them." "And the spin they gave you," Roth concludes, "is much greater than the impact of these guys in New York talking their European talk. . . . The father and the brother were in you." Later in the interview, Roth corrects or refines his sense of Bellow's America, "because really the passion in the book is for Chicago. . . . Really Chicago is your America." To which Bellow replies, "That's true." The discussion of Maury's role in the making of *Augie*, of Maury as Chicagoan, and of Chicago as America, ends with the following exchange:

> ROTH: So your brother's spirit—your brother is the household deity of *Augie March*.
> BELLOW: In a way.
> ROTH: You can give him credit now, Saul.

Lynn, Marge, Maury, and Joel

BELLOW: Yeah. Poor Maurice, he's gone. . . .

ROTH: What did he make of—You told me he didn't like *Augie March*. What did he say to you?

BELLOW: Well, he was just concerned with the image of himself as it came through. He didn't give a damn about anything else. Of course, he pretended to be far more vulgar than he was.[135]

In the edited version of this exchange, the version printed in *The New Yorker*, only Bellow speaks, incorporating Roth's words and attributing to Maury a wider and more generous sense of the book's achievement— out of brotherly love, or family feeling, or need:

> For me, the overpowering brother was the totally American brother. He overpowered me and in a sense he led me to write *The Adventures of Augie March*. He didn't like the book when he read it, but he granted that I had in my cockeyed way done something significant and it was necessary that he should figure in the book. He was aggressive and I recognized in him the day-to-day genius of the U.S.A.[136]

4

Tuley

IT WAS LIZA who in 1928 prodded Abraham to leave the Imperial Bakery and start his own business. If he stayed, she argued, he would always be an employee. She also provided crucial capital, from what in Yiddish is called a *knippl*, the money a wife saves out of household funds (in "Memoirs of a Bootlegger's Son," Pa Lurie accuses Ma Lurie of saving in this way for her brothers in Russia). The business Abraham started supplied bakeries like Imperial with wood chips to fuel their ovens. He found premises in the railroad district of the city. A cousin of Liza's, Lazer Bailen, originally from Dagda, was briefly enlisted as partner.[1] Abraham traveled to lumberyards in Michigan and Wisconsin, arranged deals to buy wood scraps and rejected pieces of wood, then had them shipped in freight cars to Chicago. Once in Chicago, the wood was trucked all over the city. For a man with only rudimentary English, who was used to conducting business in Yiddish, making such arrangements cannot have been easy, even with contacts gained through cousin Louis (according to Sam's children, Lesha Greengus and Shael Bellows, while still at Imperial, Abraham began gathering the names and addresses of wood salesmen who dealt with Chicago bakeries).[2] For the adolescent Bellow, the new business was an eye-opener: "Before I knew it I was in the railroad district . . . which very few kids of my background ever got close to. And we knew all the Jewish bakeries in Chicago. That was a great privilege for me."[3]

The business was a modest success, a first for Abraham in the New World, and the Bellows began to enjoy a degree of prosperity. In 1931 they moved to an apartment on the west side of Humboldt Park, at 3340

Le Moyne Street, just below North Avenue,[4] where rents were higher, and people ran their own businesses. To escape the boiling summers, Liza and the children stayed on a farm in Benton Harbor, Michigan, with Abraham joining them at weekends (Benton Harbor is where Augie meets the Fenchal sisters, Esther and Thea, in Chapter 8 of *The Adventures of Augie March*). Then the nature of the business changed. Gas ovens were brought in by the bakeries, for which coal was needed, not wood. Abraham found himself, as Bellow puts it, in "another non-Jewish business," one he "never in his wildest imagination dreamed about." In 1931 new premises were found for what became the Carroll Coal Company, on West Carroll Street, southeast of Humboldt Park. These premises—a coal yard and rudimentary office—were surrounded by what Bellow describes as "a sort of slum, semi-industrial neighborhood where there was light industry and there were poultry markets, wholesale markets all around, along with railroad people coming in." The coal yard Simon leases in *Augie* is similarly located: "the first rains made a marsh of the whole place. It had to be drained. The first coal was unloaded in the wet. The office itself was a shack; the scale needed expensive repairs" (p. 640). Across the way "was a stockyards siding, dusty animals bawling in the waiting cars, putting red muzzles to the slats; truck wheels sucked through the melting tar [it is high summer], the coal split and tarnished on the piles" (p. 642). Two years later, in 1933, property was rented from the Chicago and Eastern Illinois Railroad at 1800 West Carroll Avenue near Wood Street, a block west of the company's original premises. The advantage of the new site was that it added a spur track and overhead facility for unloading the coal directly.

The neighborhood around Carroll Coal was tough: "fighting and guns were common; the unions were present, and there was a lot of strife."[5] While in high school, Bellow worked some weekends at Carroll Coal, mostly on the scales (in *Augie*, "that long, brass, black-graduated beam where I weighed" [p. 699]). When there was nothing to weigh, he'd sit in his father's office and read. He recalls one occasion when he was interrupted by a raid on the brothel (a "Negro whorehouse" in *Herzog* [p. 652]) across the street, probably for nonpayment of protection money. From the window of the office, he could see the police tossing beds, bedding, and furniture onto the sidewalk. When he had work, it was routine: first he'd weigh trucks when they were empty, then he'd weigh them when they were loaded, billing their owners for the coal bought. The business started out with three used trucks, eventually acquiring as many as fifteen. Outside contractors also brought in trucks, between ten and thirty, depending on the weather.[6] During the Depression, some of these trucks, including those owned by the company, would drive up and down the street selling coal by the bag (rather than by the ton) for domestic heating and cooking. Bellow's friend David Peltz remembers carrying the company's white canvas bags (presumably stronger than those Abraham manufactured in Montreal) up icy back staircases in winter. On one occasion in *Augie*, Simon sends Augie out with his yard manager, Happy Kellerman, to drum up business. They find coal-and-ice dealers in local taverns, or in their sheds, or "by the church, by the funeral home, or on a moving job" (p. 644). As Augie watches, Happy cons the dealers "with specious technical information about BTU's [a standard measurement of heat] and ash percentages," enticing them "by undercut prices and the pick of the coal" (p. 645). Happy is terrified when driving in the neighborhood: "His fear in the Bohunk streets was that he would run over a kid and a crowd would tear him to pieces in its rage" (p. 644). Simon also sends Augie into Chinatown to pass out handbills advertising coke, "which the laundry Chinese favored above other fuel" (p. 645). As Bellow recalled, Carroll Coal "brought me into the slums in a way I never had access to before."[7]

Both Maury and Sam were involved with the coal company from the start. It was they who ordered the glistening Pocahontas coal from West Virginia; it was they who paid the bills and organized sales; who arranged for the coal to be packed in bags and trucked; who found new customers. Because of Abraham's immigrant English, and the fact that he couldn't drive, he depended more and more on his sons. Sam's daughter, Lesha, explains: "He couldn't make calls on current customers. He couldn't make cold calls on potential new customers. He couldn't go to the bank for loans. He couldn't negotiate the purchase and sale of real estate. He couldn't deal with the lawyers, judges and politicians." In *Augie*, Bellow makes much of Simon's handling of these tasks: "Simon was wised up as to how to do things politically—to be in a position to bid on municipal business—and he saw wardheelers and was kissing-cousins with the police; he took up with lieutenants and captains, with lawyers, with real-estate men, with gamblers and bookies, the important ones who owned legitimate businesses on the side and had property. During the chauffeurs' and hikers' strike he had squad cars to protect his two trucks from strikers who were dumping coal in the streets" (p. 645). At one point during a strike, Augie is dispatched by Simon to the police to let them know when a load is setting out from the yard. At another, he is sent to the morgue to identify an employee, a coal shoveler, "shot with our pay envelope empty in his shirt pocket." Augie recognizes the employee: "his black body rigid, as if he died in a fit of royal temper, making fists" (p. 669).

Abraham remained the nominal head of Carroll Coal, but what he mostly did was keep the books and watch over the scales used to weigh the coal. Business decisions, particularly those involving investment and expansion, were made by Sam and Maury, often after having to meet or overcome Abraham's objections. Some months before the move to 1800 West Carroll Street, and before marrying Marge, Maury left the business, tired of arguing with his father. In 1933, with money from Marge's family, he started a coal company of his own, Capitol Coal, later Bellows Coal, a move Abraham and Sam seem to have accepted (there was no break in relations, at least none reported by Bellow, or recalled by his nephews and nieces). "Both businesses were so small," Maury's son, Joel, explains, "and the retail coal business was then so huge, that they could easily survive without knowingly competing."[8] With Maury gone, Sam alone guided Carroll's growth (it was he who negotiated with the CE & I Railroad for new premises), patiently answering, quietly circumventing his father's worries, principally about real estate deals and the investment of company profits. "*Far mir iz genug. Di altitshke est*," Abraham would say: "For me it's enough. The old lady is eating." Sam had begun working for his father in the wood business (while Maury was in law school) and continued working with him at Carroll Coal for a further twenty years, until Abraham's death in 1955. Sam married in 1935 and moved from the family home to an apartment near Lincoln Park, but two years later he and his wife returned to Humboldt Park to an apartment on Kedzie and Division, within walking distance of his father. Every workday morning at 5:30, Abraham would ring the doorbell of Sam's apartment to go with him to the office. On Saturdays, they went to shul together. Sam was the brother who stayed at home and built the family business. According to Greg Bellow, speaking also of his maternal aunt, Catherine Goshkin, "the lore was, there was a designated child, designated by the family, to take care of the parent, and that was Sam's role. My father always would say, you see the way Catherine takes care of Sonia [her mother, Greg's maternal grandmother]? Well, it was implied that Sam was the one who stayed at home and his charge was to make sure Grandpa was okay."

It was a charge Sam complied with dutifully, just as he dutifully set out to make a fortune in business. But making a fortune in business was not his original ambition, as it had been for Maury. After graduating from Tuley High School in 1929, Sam attended Crane Junior College, as would Bellow. Crane, the first junior college in the United States, offered an abbreviated liberal arts program for $5 a semester. After a year, Sam applied to Northwestern University Medical School, to which he was accepted. However, the tuition fee at Northwestern was $250 a year, and when he asked his father for help, Abraham turned him down: the money was needed to buy a car for the business, and Sam was needed as a driver.[9] Sam then went to Northwestern itself to inquire about financial aid. He was turned down. Some fifty years later, in 1983, after his granddaughter, Rachel Greengus (later Schultz), had been accepted into medical school at the University of Cincinnati, Sam set up an education trust to pay for her tuition. The granddaughter had for many years spoken of her wish to become a doctor, but only at this point did she learn of her grandfather's thwarted ambitions. "Zayde [Grandpa] was a very modest and private man," she explains. "The private side of him did not need to be reminded of his early life when a lack of money meant unfulfilled dreams." That he set up the trust, amounting to some $100,000, suggested to the granddaughter how deeply he felt this early disappointment.[10] According to Lesha Greengus, Rachel's mother, Sam sometimes talked wistfully about the medical careers of friends but "never uttered a word of complaint."

Keeping quiet about one's feelings, keeping one's cards close to one's chest, keeping in the background: these were characteristics of Sam. "Everybody in the family had a family title except Sam," Bellow said of his brother at a speech celebrating Sam's sixtieth birthday. "Sam had no handle . . . but he was dear to us just the same."[11] Elsewhere, Bellow described Sam as "a mild person, clever and thoughtful," "a clean man; a real stand-up man."[12] In a letter of July 16, 1985, Bellow's friend Israeli novelist John Auerbach recalls first meeting Sam: "He came late because of a minor traffic accident, and I remember how cool and composed he was and how unconcerned about his damaged Cadillac—he was joking and in a good mood and [I] admired and envied the quietness and cool temper of this man." In *Herzog*, Moses's middle brother, Will, is similarly cool: "substantial, shrewd, quiet. . . . In a family of passionately expressive people like Father Herzog and Aunt Zipporah Will had developed a quieter, observant, reticent style" (p. 725). It was the style of an anti-Maury. According to Greg Bellow, Sam was "as smart and worldly as Saul or Maury, but didn't flout conventionality" (to Bellow, although Maury was the "American" brother, Sam was "certainly American in hatching deals and multiplying bank accounts").[13] In addition, as Greg puts it, he was "very sweet and kind, a nice guy, he had social graces."

When most under Maury's influence, but at other times as well, Bellow saw Sam's "niceness" as weakness: "My two brothers were very different," he said in an interview. "One of them was just contemptuous and the other was frightened to make a move on his own. The bold one married a non-Jew [Maury's second wife, Joyce] and the timid one married a Rabbi's daughter, so his house was super kosher. I became conscious that my oldest brother was doing me good. That is to say, he couldn't Americanize himself fast enough; the middle brother just hung back."[14] Hanging back was not what the adolescent Bellow needed or could manage. Later in life, though, he presents Sam-like qualities as admirable. Toward the end of *Herzog*, when Moses is most frantic, his middle brother, Will, comes to his aid. Moses has had a traffic accident and has been arrested. There's a pistol in the car (to shoot his adulterous wife, Madeleine, and her lover, Gersbach), he hasn't money to post bail, and he looks terrible, as if in the midst of a breakdown (in fact, he's about to emerge from one). Moses advises his brother not to go by appearances:

"What were you doing with that gun?"

"You know I'm no more capable of firing it at someone than Papa was. You took his watch chain, didn't you? I remembered those old rubles in his drawer and then I took the revolver too. I shouldn't have. At least I ought to have emptied it. It was just one of those dumb impulses. Let's forget it."

"All right," said Will. "I don't mean to embarrass you. That's not the point."

"I know what it is," Herzog said. "You're worried." He had to lower his voice to control it. "I love you too, Will."

"Yes, I know that."

"But I haven't behaved very sensibly. From your standpoint. . . . Well, from any reasonable standpoint. I brought Madeleine to your office so you could see her before I married her. I could tell you didn't approve. I didn't approve of her myself. And she didn't approve of me."

"Why did you marry her?"

"God ties all kinds of loose ends together. Who knows why! [. . .] And then I put all that money into the house in Ludeyville. That was simply crazy."

"Perhaps not," said Will. "It is real estate, after all. Have you tried to sell it?" Will had great faith in real estate (p. 726).

Moses turns down Will's invitation to have dinner at his home, complaining that he looks a mess, "as if I'd just arrived in this country. . . . Just as we arrived from Canada. . . . On the Michigan Central. God, we were filthy with the soot" (p. 727). Will does not respond. Like the eldest Herzog brother, Shura, he has no time for reminiscences. In this, Will is not only like Maury but like Sam, described by Lesha as "not one to dwell on the past." After the exchange about real estate, a paragraph describes Will: "He was an engineer and technologist, a contractor and builder; a balanced, reasonable person, he was pained to see Moses in such a state. His lined face was hot, uneasy; he took a handkerchief from the inner pocket of his well-tailored suit and pressed it to his forehead, his cheeks, under the large Herzog eyes." Sam was not an engineer, but he was technically minded and good with figures. Lesha remembers him quickly adding up an entire page of numbers in his head without a pencil. At the police station, Will persuades Moses to visit a doctor; Moses is "not entirely surprised . . . to learn that he had a broken rib" (p. 727). While Moses and the doctor banter, Will "faintly" smiles, arms folded, Moses notes, "somewhat like Father Herzog . . . [with] a bit of the old man's elegance." Will has as little interest in this banter as in reminiscence: "He had no time for such stuff . . . running a big business. . . . He mixes grout to pump into these new high-risers all over town. He has to be political, and deal, and wangle and pay off and figure tax angles. All that Papa was inept in but dreamed he was born to do. Will is a quiet man of duty and routine, has his money, position, influence, and is just as glad to be rid of his private or 'personal' side" (p. 728). With such qualities, Sam built Carroll Coal, always the core family business, into a profitable company, and with associated real estate and development deals, became a millionaire and a pillar of the Jewish community in Chicago.[15]

Sam's wife, Nina, the daughter of Rabbi Moses Wolf Kahn, of the Orthodox Tifereth Zion congregation at Wolcott and Division, helped to steer her husband to Jewish Orthodoxy. But so, too, did Liza. As Lesha puts it, "My father must have seen in my mother and her family the religious ideals that were so vital to his dying mother." The courtship began in South Haven, Michigan, "a miniature Catskills *borscht* belt,"[16] in the summer of 1932, when both the Bellow and Kahn families were vacationing at the same kosher resort, Yashenovsky's. Bellow's earliest surviving letter, to a girlfriend from Tuley, Yetta Barshevsky, was written one night from the resort, while "my brother next door snores softly, insistently" (the brother was most likely Sam). Sam and Nina's courtship was complicated by Liza's illness and the fact that the Kahns had already picked out someone, a rabbi, for their daughter to marry. From 1932 to 1935, while Sam worked for his father, the couple continued to see each other, with little contact between the families. They finally married on May 20, 1935, a little over two years after Liza's death, and a year after Abraham's remarriage. When the families got together to celebrate religious holidays, Abraham and Rabbi Kahn would discourse on Talmudic matters, and Bellow would spar with them both. The discussions were always in Yiddish. As Lesha remembers, Rabbi Kahn would quote from the Bible and Bellow would quote from Shakespeare.[17]

Bellow fought fiercely against pressure from his father and brothers to go into business. What he wrote about businessmen was often deeply unflattering and very funny, especially when discussing culture. In an October 1972 speech at the Chicago Public Library, he reported the following remark from a Chicago building contractor: 'My wife made me go to see the Sistine Ceiling when we were in Rome and I want to tell you [he said from the corner of his mouth] it was a lot of crap.' For a connoisseur of Chicago business gorillas, there is a certain charm in this, but you have to grow up here to savor and appreciate it."[18] His feelings about businessmen, however, were not wholly negative: business shrewdness is given its due in the fiction (as in the depiction of Sigmund Adelsky in *The Actual*, loosely modeled on the Chicago billionaire A. N. Pritzker), as is business toughness (even in a character as appalling as Harold Vilitzer in *More Die of Heartbreak*).[19] Toward Orthodox Jewry he was often hostile, and he sometimes spoke of his brother Sam as imprisoned in the world he'd chosen. "I was brought up in an

Orthodox household," he wrote to Herman Wouk in a letter of May 21, 2000, "and I came to consider orthodoxy intolerable. One of my brothers married into a rabbinic family which expected him (as a *proster yid*) to provide financial support for the brothers-in-law and dowries for the sister." A *proster yid* is a common, ill-mannered, unlearned Jew. Bellow's use of the term reflects his family's sense that the Kahns regarded themselves as better than the Bellows, proper Jews in several senses. The Old World expectations of Sam's in-laws, the letter suggests, were viewed by Bellow through New World eyes. Though Saul and Maury were divided over business, "we were united in our disapproval of brother Sam and his formal orthodoxy."[20]

In "The Old System," however, discussed in Chapter 2, Bellow enters sympathetically into the mind of a hero who is both an Orthodox Jew and a shrewd and daring businessman. Isaac Braun, eldest son of hard Aunt Rose and steady Uncle Braun, makes a fortune after World War II by financing and building shopping centers and cheap housing developments. Isaac built "with benevolence," but "was stingy with land, he built too densely" ("all such places," the story's narrator pronounces, "are ugly").[21] Isaac is in dispute with his sister, Tina. He won't cut her and their two brothers into his deals, "where the tax advantages were greatest. The big depreciation allowances, which she understood as legally sanctioned graft. She had her money in savings accounts at a disgraceful two and a half per cent, taxed at the full rate." The reason Isaac won't do business with Tina and their brothers is that they abandoned him at a crucial moment in his career, "a desperate moment, when the law had to be broken." Bellow imagines this moment with all the suspense of Harry Fonstein's escape from prison in *The Bellarosa Connection*. Isaac gains inside information about the relocation of the Robbstown Country Club, for WASPs only, where he and his brother, Mutt, used to caddie as boys in the 1920s. For $100,000, "the entire amount to be given under the table," the head of the club's board of directors, Ilkington, "a long, austere man with a marbled face. Cornell 1910 or so. Cold but plain. And in Isaac's opinion, fair," undertakes to persuade the club's board to accept Isaac's bid for the property. Once the property is developed into a shopping center, the deal will be worth $500,000 apiece to the Brauns. Isaac will do all the contracting himself. He has a friend on the zoning board who will "clear everything for five grand" (p. 98). Although he put the deal together, and undertakes to do the actual building, if each of the Brauns contributes $25,000, they will be equal partners. On the morning of the day Isaac is to deliver the money to Ilkington, they renege:

> "How do you know Ilkington can be trusted?"
> "I think he can."
> "*You* think. He could take the money and say he never heard of you in all his life."
> "Yes, he might. But we talked that over. We have to gamble"
> (p. 99).

They refuse. At this point in the story, Bellow recounts Isaac's business history, which is close to that of Shmuel David Gameroff, the eldest son of Rose and Max Gameroff (as Chapter 2 suggests, Isaac's family is partly based on the Gameroff family). "Cousin Isaac had put his stake together penny by penny, old style, starting with rags and bottles as a boy; then fire-salvaged goods; then used cars; then learning the building trades. Earth moving, foundations, concrete, sewage, wiring, roofing, heating systems. He got his money the hard way" (p. 100). Instead of letting the deal collapse, Isaac goes directly to the bank and borrows $75,000 at full interest. This he gives to Ilkington in his parlor, with its "pork-pale colors of gentility." Bellow imagines the courage Isaac's gamble involves, how alien he finds the territory he has entered:

> Ilkington did not touch Isaac's briefcase. He did not intend, evidently, to count the bills, or even to look. He offered Isaac a martini. Isaac, not a drinker, drank the clear gin. At noon. Like something distilled in outer space. Having no color. He sat there sturdily but felt lost—lost to his people, his family, lost to God, lost in the void of America. Ilkington drank a shaker of cocktails, gentlemanly, stony, like a high slab of something generically human, but with few human traits familiar to Isaac. At the door he did not say he would keep his word. He simply shook hands with Isaac, saw him to the car. Isaac drove home and sat in the den of his bungalow. Two whole days. Then on Monday, Ilkington phoned to say that the Robbstown directors had decided to accept his offer for the property. A pause. Then Ilkington added that no written instrument could replace trust and decency between gentlemen (p. 101).

Isaac becomes a millionaire, leader of the congregation at the synagogue, appointed to state commissions, but lives an increasingly traditional or Orthodox life, "an ample old-fashioned respectable domestic life on an Eastern European model completely destroyed in 1939 by Hitler and Stalin" (p. 104). Tina is scornful: "He reads the Tehillim [Book of Psalms] aloud in his air-conditioned Caddy when there's a long freight train at the crossing. That crook! He'd pick God's pocket" (p. 98). The more successful and Orthodox he becomes, the more, ironically, Isaac feels the pull of American business reserve, a counterweight to American business daring: "what you showed, among these people, you showed with silence. Of which, it seemed to Isaac, he was now beginning to appreciate the wisdom. The native, different wisdom of Gentiles, who had much to say but refrained" (p. 109). He could never, for instance, discuss Tina with these people: "they would never discuss a thing. Silent impressions would have to do. Incommunicable diversities, kindly but silent contact. The more they had in their heads, the less people seemed to know how to tell it" (p. 110).

This way of behaving is just the opposite of what the story presents as "the Old System," the Jewish way of intense and voluble family feeling, of the open expression of anger and love. The Jewish way, the narrator admits, is easily exploited (as in the "circus of feelings" [p. 116] orchestrated by Tina in the story, or Moses Herzog's "potato love"), but intense feeling, weeping from the heart, also offers "an intimation of understanding. A promise that mankind might—*might*, mind you—eventually, through its gift which might—*might* again!—be a divine gift, comprehend why it lived. Why life, why death" (p. 116). The story closes on a sublime or cosmic note balanced between affirmation and pessimism. About its central figure, however, it is largely idealizing. For all Tina's scorn—of Isaac's "Orthodox cringe"—he retains a dignity rooted in Jewish tradition. This dignity is seen in the Yiddish he speaks, "unusually thick in Slavic and Hebrew expressions. Instead of 'important people, leading citizens,' he said '*Anshe ha-ir*,' Men of the City. He, too, kept the Psalms near. As active, worldly Jews for centuries had done" (pp. 97–98). Only once does the narrator distance himself from Isaac's piety, when he imagines him thinking "the world had done for him exactly what he demanded. . . . That meant his reading of life was metaphysically true. Or that the Old Testament, the Talmud, and Polish Ashkenazi Orthodoxy were irresistible" (pp. 101–2). The next paragraph begins: "But that wouldn't altogether do."

Sam Bellows was not Isaac Braun. Sam was a small man, unlike Isaac, the shortest of the Bellow brothers, dapper, witty, quiet but not solemn. Inside the home, he was a traditional father and husband; outside it he was reserved with women, a little frightened of them, at least according to his granddaughter Judith and Bellow himself.[22] Isaac is the Braun brother who boasts of having "fought on many fronts," a joke Sam would appreciate but not have made about himself. Isaac has sexual magnetism: "upstate women said he gave out the positive male energy they were beginning to miss in men. He had it. It was in the manner with which he picked up a fork at the table, the way he poured from a bottle" (p. 101). "Saul made you think that he was big," remembers Vivien Missner, who was fond of both brothers. "Sam didn't have that." Similarly, though Sam was *frum* (pious, Orthodox), he was neither as austere nor as removed as Isaac, who "belonged to no societies, never played cards, never spent an evening drinking, never went to Florida, never went to Europe, never went to see the State of Israel" (p. 104). Sam did all of these things. He not only visited the state of Israel, but purchased a large apartment in Jerusalem, where the family often stayed.

What connects the real man, Sam, and the fictional character, Isaac, in addition to business acumen and Jewish Orthodoxy, is *tsuris* (trouble, worry) with family. Abraham was not the only figure in the Bellow family Sam had to placate over business. In addition to helping his in-laws by including them in real estate and other ventures, and doing deals with Maury (which were sometimes rocky), he helped both Saul himself, who several times invested with him, and Jane, their sister, whose character was in some ways like that of Tina in the story. Physically, Jane was not at all like Tina: Jane was pretty, neat, concerned with appearances. She was also vain, the pampered only daughter in a patriarchal family. "As the Jews would say, she was the princess of the family," Bellow told an interviewer,[23] the one with her own room, the one with piano lessons, the one used to getting her way. In the summer of 1929, after her mother had been diagnosed with breast cancer, Jane married Charlie Kauffman, a dentist. There was a civil ceremony on 20 August, but because Liza was too ill to attend, a religious ceremony was also held at home.[24] Liza wanted security and respectability for her children. At the time of the wedding, Maury was studying law, Sam was at Crane Junior College preparing for medical school, and Jane had found a professional man to marry (only Saul was a source of worry, without practical interests or ambitions). Partly so Jane could take care of her mother, the newlyweds lived at home, only moving into a place of their own after Liza's death in 1933.

Jane was ambitious for status and money and like Tina had a strong will. "Nobody could sway Tina," we learn in "The Old System," "she had consulted her own will, kept her own counsel for so long, that she could accept no other guidance. Anyone who listened to others seemed to her weak" (p. 97). "She had a totalitarian air. . . . Her aim must have been majesty. Based on what? She had no great thoughts. She built on her own nature. On a primordial idea, hugely blown up. . . . Her eyes had an affronted expression; sometimes a look of sulphur; a clever look, also a malicious look—they had all the looks, even the look of kindness that came from Uncle Braun" (p. 103). According to Lesha, "that entire section where Saul describes Tina is the way he would talk about Jane." Tina's great concern in the story is money; Jane "was always scheming about money. Her usual object was my father who was in business with his father; of course my grandfather played into her crazinesss as well. He was forever threatening to change his will depending on who was in his good graces at any particular time."[25] Lesha has sympathy for Jane: "She was just as interested in doing deals as the boys were. She suffered for being a woman in that family." That Lesha's own mother, Nina, a tiny woman, but a powerhouse, was so active in Chicago's Orthodox Jewish community, in women's organizations and clubs, charities and educational foundations, may partly be explained by Sam's refusal to allow her to work. He also discouraged her from learning to drive. In "The Old System," Isaac's wife "was obliged to forget how to drive. She was a docile, darling woman, and she was in the kitchen baking sponge cake and chopping liver" (p. 104). Nina Bellows was neither docile nor, in Bellow's eyes, particularly darling, though as her granddaughter, Rachel Schultz, points out, sponge cake and chopped liver were among her "signature" dishes.[26]

Jane's husband, Charlie, was "a broad blocky man,"[27] easygoing, without professional ambition. He began his practice around the time of the marriage in a second-floor walk-up on Argyle Street in the North Side uptown district, a mixed neighborhood of Scandinavians, Jews, Irish, and Germans. The practice consisted of a waiting room, reached by a dark corridor that smelled of Charlie's cigars, a tiny lab, little more than a closet, where he made dentures, and a room with a dentist's chair where the dentures were fitted. The practice stayed in this location for forty-four years, until Charlie's death in 1974. Here is how Bellow describes him in the unpublished "Chicago Book": "Times changed but not the techniques he had learned at the Loyola School of Dentistry. Nor his relaxed ways. He locked the office and went out to the track. He played cards after hours with the pharmacist below, and professional pals from the street, Dr. Leef and Dr. Soloway. He liked plain food, broad jokes, did not care to follow new developments in dentistry. His wife, my sister Jane, was impressed by the affectations of the high-powered dental gentry downtown who talked about the courses they were giving and the papers they read at conventions. Charlie paid them no mind." While at Tuley, Bellow had an after-school job delivering wreaths for a florist, sometimes in Charlie's neighborhood, at 50 cents an afternoon, as does seventeen-year-old Louie in the story "Something to Remember Me By." Louie's story is set in February 1933, the year and month Liza dies, which makes him Bellow's age. His brother-in-law is a dentist like Charlie, looks like Charlie, has Charlie's character and history, and an office identical to Charlie's in a building where Charlie's building is located. This building is where Louie is robbed of his money and his clothes by a prostitute (in exactly the manner described in the autobiography of the prostitute Chicago May, a book read "often" by the Mexican book thief, Padilla, a friend of Augie March's from Crane Junior College).[28] Given the neighborhood, Louie's misfortune is unsurprising. In the "Chicago Book" Bellow describes it as "known for its handbooks, hookers, and clip joints,"[29] hardly a location to please Jane, who was keen on refinement ("refined, that was the highest thing you could say about somebody," Greg Bellow remembers of her) and respectability. "My sister wants him to open a Loop office," Louie explains, "but that would be too much of a strain. I guess he's for inertia."[30]

Isaac's difficulties with Tina recall Sam's with Jane. Maury and Bellow distanced themselves from Jane's complaints (in Tina's words, "Does he remember his brothers when there is a deal going?" "Does he give his only sister a chance to come in?" [p. 98]). Maury, according to Rachel Schultz, "couldn't be bothered with her; his ego was as big as hers."[31] Bellow was outwardly respectful, humored her, and tried not to get involved. This was Sam's way as well, but it was harder for him to ignore her. They were in each other's world. When the Bellows moved to Le Moyne Street, at the beginning of the Depression, they were all in each other's world, everyone living at home. Liza was ill with cancer and often bedridden, or resting on the sofa in the parlor. Jane and Charlie lived in Jane's room (presumably Charlie helped with the rent). The three brothers still shared a room. Every morning Sam and Maury set off for work with Abraham, whom Bellow described as "frantic" with worry over Liza. Sam went dutifully, his hopes of medical school dashed, Maury impatiently, eager to be his own boss. Around this time, according to Atlas, Sam and Maury added the "s" to their surname, "as part of their Americanization—and to get some distance from their father."[32] Despite the modest success of Carroll Coal, business remained a struggle and a worry. All the Bellow men—Jane, too—were tough, quick-witted, and sharp-tongued, given to Yiddish sarcasm and invective. Lesha Greengus attributes the harshness of their language— harsher to outsiders, perhaps, than to the Bellows themselves—in part to Yiddish, a view Bellow, whose Yiddish was *edel* or refined, would endorse. Speaking of his father as stern patriarch, he recalled him also as humorist,

> a great joker and kidder and very sharp sometimes, in a nasty way, getting at you, in Yiddish, which is a language . . . which someone once described as two-thirds invective. . . . No matter what you said you could easily turn it around and it would be the reverse. If your mother called you an angel it meant you were a devil. If she said your hands were clean, it meant that your hands were filthy. If your nose was running you were complimented on your well-wiped nose. So everything was turned around, comically, and sometimes quite relentlessly; we wouldn't spare each other in those days.[33]

Thus Bellow's family life in the early 1930s: crowded, tense, loving, fractious. In comparable circumstances, Louie, in "Something to Remember Me By," describes himself as "secretive about my family life. The truth is that I didn't want to talk about my mother. Besides, I had no language as yet for the oddity of my peculiar interests" (p. 414).

BELLOW'S PECULIAR INTERESTS—peculiar in the eyes of his family—were formed in the years at Tuley, from September 3, 1930, to January 26, 1933.[34] Tuley was founded in 1892 as Northwest Division

High School. In 1906 it was renamed Murray F. Tuley High School, after Judge Murray F. Tuley (1827–1905), a Cook County judge, the "Nestor" of the Chicago bench, and author of the state of Illinois's Act of Incorporation of Cities.[35] Ten years before Bellow entered the school, it had been extensively expanded and modernized, with new classrooms, laboratories, gymnasiums, a swimming pool, shop rooms, and a large assembly hall seating 1,500. It had a reputation as one of the most modern and academic high schools in the city, and its pupils, for the most part, came from immigrant families. Bellow described his classmates as "the children of bakers, tailors, peddlers, insurance agents, pressers, cutters, grocers, the sons of families on relief."[36] The education he received was sound but undemanding: "You knew something of American history. And by the time you got out of high school, no one had to tell you who Socrates was."[37] The older Tuley English teachers, drawn "from the State universities, from Illinois, Michigan, Wisconsin," were "innocent fogies . . . who actually loved Shakespeare and Milton and Edmund Burke and Shelley."[38] Bellow was grateful to them for being made to memorize passages from Wordsworth, Keats, Shakespeare, Milton (writing in 1972, he imagines that "a majority of [today's] high school students would probably identify 'Lycidas' as a sexual perversion, a hard drug or a mafia leader").[39] He mentions no inspirational teachers or courses. On July 9, 1984, in response to a request for information about his education from William J. Bennett, chairman of the National Endowment for the Humanities, Bellow recalls being assigned Plutarch and Holinshed to read alongside *Julius Caesar* and *Macbeth*. As his English classes advanced through the centuries, Dickens, George Eliot, Macaulay, "and a great many nineteenth century poets" were assigned. Elsewhere, he singles out Wordsworth as a lasting influence: "'The World Is Too Much with Us' may, for all I know, have been my introduction to the subject of distraction. . . . Nor did I miss his point about emotion recollected in tranquillity—or his emphasis on the supreme importance of a state of attention or aesthetic concentration that would put the world of profit and loss in its place." Coleridge's "Rime of the Ancient Mariner," another classroom text, also struck deep: "when I think of the power of a tale-teller to obtain attention, I remember that glittering eye."[40] Lessons in English composition provoked mixed feelings: "We, the sons of immigrants, were taught to write grammatically. Knowing the rules filled you with pride. I deeply felt the constraints of 'correct' English. It wasn't always easy, but we kept at it conscientiously, and in my twenties I published two decently written books." Then correctness became inhibiting, "the wrong track."[41]

In his sophomore year, Bellow read *The Merchant of Venice*, which "went pretty deep." Of the way it was taught, he mentions only the absence of "apologetics" or "an idea of defamation," which he found "very liberating." "Everything was out in the open in those days," he recalled. "Nobody was immune. Not Jews, not Italians, not Greeks, not Germans, not Blacks. . . . It was a far more open society than before ethnic protectionism began."[42] When a high school student wrote to him in 1992 asking why he should study Latin, Bellow replied that he was grateful for the three years he'd spent studying the language. His teacher, Mrs. Klinsik, the sister of a famous vaudeville comedian, used to decorate the walls of the classroom with Latin mottos (*Dum spiro spero, Est avis in dextra melior quam quattuor extra*), never allowed her students to read any texts, and constantly drilled them on conjugations and declensions. As a consequence, he still remembered his nouns and verbs, could "now and then" amuse himself by translating Latin texts, and was able to identify the Latin roots of English words.[43] He reports almost nothing of the other subjects he studied: Spanish, General Science, Mathematics, Civil and Social Studies (including Economics and Common Law), European History, U.S. History, Drawing, Music, Physical Education, Boys' Shop, and Dramatics.[44] He was not, according to official records, an outstanding student. Even in his best subjects (English, European History, U.S. History, Civics, and Social Studies), he earned twice as many "G" (Good) marks as "E" (Excellent) ones. Only in Physical Education do "E" marks predominate (Bellow played basketball and tennis, and was a good distance runner, lettering on the track team).[45] After three years at Tuley, his class rank was 97 out of 254,[46] a number that accords with accounts from his classmates and from Bellow himself. According to Dave Schwab, who worked on the school paper: "He seldom spoke out. . . . I doubt whether anyone could have detected anything special about him." According to Arthur Wineberg, his exact contemporary at Tuley, Bellow graduated without "any of the top honors." Wineberg remembers him in class as "intense," "determined," and "very quiet." When he did speak, though, "he always had something important to say," especially about literature.[47]

"Unwilling to study, I was bookish nevertheless," recalls Louie in "Something to Remember Me By" (p. 414). Where Bellow shone was outside class, among a circle of precocious and ambitious students, several of whom became lifelong friends, all of whom figure in Bellow's reminiscences, some in his fiction, thinly disguised. In this circle, "there was a certain amount of defiance on the level of ideas," but no disobedience. When the debate club got together, "Miss Johnson or whoever said 'What are we going to talk about today?' and the kids would shout 'Revolution, Radicalism, Religion, Race, any of those Rs.'"[48] In a letter of reference of February 22, 1979, for his nephew Mark Rotblatt, whose grades had suffered from the death of his father, Bellow recalls how "it took me some years to recover from my mother's death at about the same age, and my own record was quite poor. I managed before too long to pull myself together. I have considerable feeling for Mark on this account. I know what it is to be stupefied by mourning." Bellow is talking here of his first year of college, but throughout his three years at Tuley his mother's illness weighed on the family. Performance in school was low on his parents' list of concerns. As Abraham saw it, formal education was a luxury given economic uncertainty; to Liza, it was largely incomprehensible. Though both parents read nineteenth-century Russian novels, and Abraham knew something of American history, they rarely inquired about Bellow's intellectual or literary interests: "For one thing there wasn't time enough for the parents to listen, or interest enough, because they were so busy. . . . So each child in the family went his own way at an early age and my way happened to be American History, American Literature, English Literature especially."[49] Even if they'd wanted to intervene— to monitor homework or free time—they'd not have succeeded. Aside from insisting on after-school jobs, "the parents didn't try to control us too much," recalls Sidney Passin, the younger brother of Bellow's friend Herb Passin, "because they wouldn't be able to. We were all American kids and they were Old World." The Depression, too, paradoxically, helped free Bellow to pursue his interests. In a world of Hooverville slums, soup lines, foreclosures and evictions, jockeying for grades, to get ahead, for a career, seemed pointless.[50]

So Bellow read and read. On the streetcar heading to Saturday jobs, either at Carroll Coal or Goldblatt's department store on 47th and Ashland, where he worked in the shoe department, or the Sunset Ridge Golf Course in Winnetka, he was never without a book, either a pocket-sized Modern Library volume (Flaubert, Swinburne, Oscar Wilde, Nietzsche), or one of the 5-cent blue books published in Kansas by Haldeman-Julius (stories by Maupassant, "little essays on Darwin and on agnosticism, if not atheism").[51] Louie in "Something to Remember Me By" also reads on streetcars: "Reading shut out the sights. In fact there *were* no sights." In addition, Louie remembers reading late at night, in the kitchen, "in deep silence, snowdrifts under the windows, and below, the janitor's shovel rasping on the cement and clanging on the furnace door. I read banned books circulated by my classmates, political pamphlets, read 'Prufrock' and 'Mauberley.' I also studied arcane books, too far out to discuss with anyone" (p. 416). The writers Bellow most frequently recalls, aside from those assigned in class, fall into three broad categories: twentieth-century American novelists; nineteenth-century European, including Russian, novelists and philosophers; and political theorists, mostly Marxist. Of European novelists, he singles out Balzac, Zola, and Dostoyevsky.[52] Of American novelists, the names that recur are Theodore Dreiser, "whom I admired most,"[53] Sherwood Anderson, Sinclair Lewis, and John Dos Passos (among American poets he most frequently mentions Whitman). What linked the American authors and acted as a special encouragement for the young Bellow was that they "resisted the material weight of American society," a weight that pressed upon him directly through his father and brothers. Dreiser in particular proved "what was not immediately obvious—that the life lived in great manufacturing, shipping, and banking centers, with their slaughter stink, their great slums, prisons, hospitals, and schools, was also a human life." That Dreiser, Anderson, and Lewis had lived in Chicago, meant that "here, too, right here, the raw materials of literature were present. . . . Sister Carrie and the Spoon River Anthology [of Edgar Lee Masters] proved it."[54]

Dreiser's attraction for Bellow had several sources. Dreiser's social theorizing—about materialism, desire, consumer culture, American manners—appealed to the adolescent intellectual. "The true meaning of money yet remains to be popularly explained and comprehended," begins Chapter 7 of *Sister Carrie* (1900).[55] "For all the liberal analysis of Spencer and our modern naturalistic philosophers, we have but an infantile perception of morals," Dreiser announces at the beginning of Chapter 10 (p. 87). When drinking with his cronies, George Hurstwood, who makes Carrie his mistress, tells droll stories, the sort that compose "the major portion of the conversation among American men under such circumstances" (p. 266). Hurstwood's more substantial counterpart in *Jennie Gerhardt* (1911), the other Dreiser novel Bellow

especially admired, is Lester Kane. Kane has a powerful intellect but
acts foolishly. Dreiser explains: "We live in an age in which the impact
of materialized forces is well-nigh irresistible; the spiritual nature is
overwhelmed by the shock." After several paragraphs in this vein, Dreiser concludes that Kane "was a product of a combination of elements—
religious, commercial, social—modified by the overruling, circum-
ambient atmosphere of liberty in our national life which is productive
of almost uncounted freedoms of thought and action."[56] Passages like
these combine with what H. L. Mencken, another early influence on
Bellow, calls Dreiser's "inexorable particularity," a quality Bellow, with
his faith in the revelatory power of detail, approves. "Everything fasci-
nates him," Bellow says of Dreiser, "factories, horsecars, hotel lobbies,
a machine which makes keys, a hardware warehouse, luxury shops, fast
women, plausible salesmen, exponents of social Darwinism and other
bookish ninnies, sturdy railroad men. He's drunk with all this, thinks
The Windy City the most marvelous thing that ever happened. When
I read him I am inclined to think so, too."[57] Bellow praises Dreiser
most warmly, however, for his depth of feeling. Beyond the "clumsy,
cumbersome" theorizing and "many familiar 'art' gestures, borrowed
from the art-fashions of his day, and even from the slick magazines,"
lies a profound respect for his characters. In *Jennie Gerhardt*, "the delicacy with which Jenny allows Lester Kane to pursue his conventional
life while she herself lives unrecognized with her illegitimate daughter,
the depth of her understanding, and the depth of her sympathy and of
her truthfulness impress me. She is not a sentimental figure. She has a
natural sort of honor."[58]

Bellow's interest in philosophy is variously traced. In 1995, in a talk
at the University of Chicago, he recalled being "an enthusiastic Sha-
vian" in high school. "Shaw had put me on to Ibsen," he explained,
"from Ibsen I passed to Strindberg, and from Strindberg I got into
Nietzsche."[59] Mencken may also have led Bellow to Nietzsche, as he
led him to *Sister Carrie* and *Jennie Gerhardt* ("the best American novel I
have ever read, with the lonesome but Himalayan exception of *Huckleberry Finn*").[60] Bellow read Mencken in *The American Mercury* in the
1920s and described his *Selected Prejudices* (1927) as one of "the going
things in 1930, when I was fifteen years old."[61] Mencken's attacks on
"booboisie" America, Bellow recalled, "found [their] largest public
among schoolboys like me or village atheists and campus radicals."[62]
In 1907 Mencken published *The Philosophy of Friedrich Nietzsche*, the

first book on Nietzsche to appear in English, and in 1920 he translated Nietzsche's *The Anti-Christ* (1888). Despite Nietzsche's explicit criticisms of Herbert Spencer and Darwin, in Mencken's eyes he was a social Darwinist, as were Dreiser and other early Bellow influences, Upton Sinclair, Jack London, H. G. Wells. How much of Nietzsche Bellow understood or approved as a schoolboy is hard to tell. He closely followed the Leopold and Loeb case in the papers, and would have read the attacks on Nietzsche by Clarence Darrow, Loeb's lawyer. In notes to Philip Roth, he talks of Leopold and Loeb in Darrow's terms, as having had their heads turned "by the Nietzschean ideas they wildly misunderstood," and in *Herzog*, he lets Moses express qualified admiration for Nietzsche (in comparison, at least, to the distaste he feels for Nietzsche's followers),[63] though Moses does so as an adult, a professor of intellectual history.

Mencken saw in Nietzsche confirmation of his long-held belief that life was a struggle to which some people were well suited by birth and others were not, a view the adolescent Bellow might have accepted when voiced by Mencken, or when Mencken claimed it for Nietzsche. When voiced by Oswald Spengler, however, also an important early influence, it was disturbing. "Smart Jewish schoolboys were poring over Spengler at night," Bellow recalls (see the adolescent Moses Herzog, "struggling and drowning in the oceanic visions of that sinister kraut" [p. 652]).[64] Bellow kept his copy of Spengler's *The Decline of the West* (1918) on the mantelpiece at Le Moyne Street, where it was seen by a stout man who came periodically to collect 25 cents from his mother for an insurance policy. "He would carry a heavy ledger under his arm and engage me in deep conversation about Spengler, he had great interest. And also the Polish barber in the neighborhood was a Spenglerian."[65] Spengler's view that the great civilizations of the West were "Faustian" but that Jews were "Magians," naturally at odds with Faustians, was hard for young Bellow to take. "When I read this I was deeply wounded," he recalls. "I envied the Faustians, and I cursed my luck because I had prepared myself to be part of a civilization, one of whose prominent interpreters told me that I was by heredity disqualified."[66] Reading Spengler had much the same effect on the adolescent Herzog, making him "sick with rage" (p. 652). In later years, Bellow would associate Spengler with Henry Adams and T. S. Eliot's *The Idea of a Christian Society* (1939), which made him more American, since "I knew there would be no place for me as a Jew in that sort of civilization. Therefore all the greater was my enthusiasm for embracing the American democracy with all its crudities, which nevertheless granted me an equality which I felt was mine by right. I wasn't going to be ruled off the grounds by those WASP hotshots."[67]

The other philosopher to influence the adolescent Bellow was Arthur Schopenhauer. Nietzsche's first and most accessible book, *The Birth of Tragedy* (1872), begins with a quotation from Schopenhauer's *The World as Will and Idea* (1818), in which reality is likened to "a stormy sea that, unbounded in all directions, raises and drops mountainous waves, howling . . . a world of torments."[68] For Schopenhauer, only the veil of Maya—"mere appearance," "illusion," in particular the illusion of individual identity—makes this reality bearable. In *The Birth of Tragedy*, however, Nietzsche identifies a way of experiencing Schopenhauer's reality more directly than through illusion or appearance: through Dionysian art, Greek tragedy. As Moses Herzog puts it in his letter to "Dear Herr Nietzsche," the Dionysian is to be commended for allowing us to face the howling storm, "to endure the sight of the Terrible, the Questionable . . . to witness Decomposition, Hideousness, Evil . . . to live with the void" (p. 740). In a later novel, *Mr. Sammler's Planet* (1970), Schopenhauer figures more directly. Artur Sammler, named after Schopenhauer, has survived the Holocaust and knows all about reality as "Decomposition, Hideousness, Evil." He, too, has read Schopenhauer—at sixteen, like Bellow—as well as Nietzsche, but has little faith in the claims of the Dionysian, at least in the "debased" form the Dionysian takes in the 1960s. Nor has he anything to say for Schopenhauer's related view that the sex organs are the seat of the Will, "the single narrow door to the truth."[69] For Schopenhauer, in Sammler's words, Will is "the cosmic force . . . which drives all things. A blinding power. The inner creative fury of the world. What we see are only its manifestations. Like Hindu philosophy—Maya, the veil of appearances that hangs over all human experience."[70] At a controversial moment in the novel, a black pickpocket whom the elderly Sammler has spotted at work, and who knows he's been spotted, corners him in the lobby of his building, shoves him up against a wall, and exposes himself, in an attempt to frighten, silence, assert dominance. When reflecting on the incident, Sammler invokes Schopenhauer: "He [the pickpocket] took out the instrument of the Will. He drew aside not the veil of Maya itself but one of its forehangings [his unzipped trousers] and showed

Sammler his metaphysical warrant" (pp. 172–73). From veil of Maya to unzipped trousers; the idea of the sex organ as metaphysical warrant is treated with defeated contempt by Sammler, whose reaction the narrator is here recording. "Humankind lives mainly on perverted ideas," Herzog writes in his letter to Dear Herr Nietzsche, "any philosopher who wants to keep his contact with mankind should pervert his own system in advance to see how it will really look a few decades after adoption" (p. 741).

All Bellow says of his initial reaction to *The World as Will and Idea* is that "as a high-school junior" (hence at sixteen) he "tried to read [it]. I think I grasped it fairly well." He also mentions passing along his copy, the copy he bought for 19 cents from a barrel outside Walgreen's, to his friend Sydney J. Harris, and that Harris covered its margins with "mad scribbles."[71] The Tuley "expert" on Schopenhauer (also on Kant, Hume, Rousseau, Voltaire, Dewey, et al.) was the youngest and most gifted of Bellow's friends, Isaac Rosenfeld. In a brief obituary in *Partisan Review*, published in 1956, shortly after Rosenfeld's death at thirty-eight, Bellow describes him addressing the Tuley Debating Club as a fourteen-year-old freshman: "I hold the gavel. Isaac rises and asks for the floor. He has a round face, somewhat pale, glasses, and his light hair is combed back with earnestness and maturity. He is wearing short pants. His subject is *The World as Will and Idea*, and he speaks with perfect authority. He is very serious. He has read Schopenhauer."[72] Neither from this memoir, nor its fictional counterpart, the story "Zetland: By a Character Witness," nor from "Charm and Death," the unpublished novel that is the story's source, can one tell how much Schopenhauer fourteen-year-old Rosenfeld or his gavel-wielding friend understood. A lot, one imagines. In the story, the Rosenfeld character, "still wearing knickers . . . was invited by neighborhood study groups to speak on the élan vital, on the differences between Kant and Hegel." The narrator describes him as "professorial, Germanic, the wunderkind."[73] Rosenfeld himself left a possible account of his understanding in *Passage from Home* (1946), his only novel, whose hero, Bernard, is in several ways like his creator. Bernard recalls being fourteen "when I had first begun to read books that were well above my head":

What exaltation that had been! I remember how I had read *First Principles* [Herbert Spencer] all of a fall and winter, had gone over each page several times and copied whole sections in a notebook to force what sense and meaning I could out of a heavy text. I had also read Schopenhauer and Nietzsche and had gone about for days in a great wild excitement, feeling there was light in me, strength and courage, an infinite capacity and hunger to understand life.[74]

From the time Rosenfeld entered Tuley in September 1932, he was the star of Bellow's intellectual circle. Rosenfeld's precocity owed much to his father, as difficult a man as Abraham Bellow, though differently difficult. Rosenfeld's mother, Miriam, died in the flu epidemic of 1918, when he was not yet two, and his father married twice more. When Bellow met Isaac in 1932, relations between Rosenfeld's father and stepmother, the third wife, were terrible, with many fights and threats of leaving, mostly on the father's part. The family lived in a spacious apartment on Spaulding Avenue, just east of Humboldt Park, a few blocks from the Bellow apartment on Le Moyne. Rosenfeld's grandparents lived in the apartment below and his two maiden aunts, his father's sisters, in the apartment above. The aunts worked as "practical" or home nurses, often for dying patients (like the dying Liza Bellow); they thought of themselves as surrogate mothers to Rosenfeld, to whom they were fiercely devoted. According to his biographer, Steven J. Zipperstein, Rosenfeld found this devotion "intrusive . . . more an extension of their own hunger to be loved than an expression of their feelings for him. Nowhere, not even in the bath tub, could he escape them."[75] Rosenfeld's father was also intrusive in his demands and expectations. Unlike Abraham Bellow, Sam Rosenfeld spoke good English and had long held a steady job, as a buyer of dairy products for Stop and Shop, an enormous retail food store on Wabash Avenue in the Loop.[76] Zipperstein describes him as "a closed man, easily bruised, with a vast capacity for recollecting hurts and slights."[77] In "Zetland," Bellow describes the father's fictional alter ego, Max Zetland, as "surly," "bullheaded," "built like a fullback, with a black cleft in the chin and a long mouth. You would wear yourself out to win this mouth from its permanent expression of disapproval" (p. 242). Zetland's father and aunts "read Russian novels, Yiddish poetry, and were mad about culture"; it was the father who pushed Zetland to be "a junior Immanuel Kant" (p. 241). In his spare time, Rosenfeld's father visited Ceshinsky's on Division Street, "at home" as Bellow puts it, "among the Jewish writers who polished their aphorisms at the back of the bookstore."[78] That some people were smarter or fitter to survive than others, Sam Rosenfeld knew in his bones, without recourse to Mencken, Nietzsche, or Spengler. When Zetland senior rides the El to work each morning, he barely registers the little bungalows below, where "Poles, Swedes, micks, spics, Greeks, and niggers lived out their foolish dramas of drunkenness, gambling, rape, bastardy, syphilis, and roaring death." Nor has he more time for the WASP overclass, judging "with furious Jewish snobbery the laxity and brainlessness of the golf-playing goy" (p. 243). When Rosenfeld's father met Bellow in 1933, his disapproval was immediate: "To me he had every objection imaginable—I was a senior, just about to get my diploma. Isaac was just ending his freshman year. I was a lightweight, leading Isaac astray and the 'old guy'—in his early forties—was determined to get rid of me. He was downright about it. He said, 'You're not in Isaac's class.'"[79]

Rosenfeld did his best to become the wunderkind his father required, "a winning number in the Jewish-father sweepstakes."[80] That he *was* a wunderkind helped. But the effort left him a "rigid . . . nervous, fastidious boy,"[81] and was to have dire consequences in later life. At Tuley, part of his "oddity," as Bellow saw it, was the seeming equanimity with which he accepted the identity imposed upon him, with attendant social disadvantages. Pale, bespectacled, stocky but sickly, an obvious non-fighter, oblivious to baseball, street-corner games, the newspaper life of the nation (prizefights, gangsters, scandal), and almost all low-cultural pursuits, Isaac failed, as Bellow puts it, "to be an American." That he seems not to have been bullied—"a merciful impossibility"[82]—was partly a product of sweetness of character, a quality attested to by several Tuley contemporaries. In "Zetland," the adolescent hero is described as "loving, virtually Franciscan, a simpleton for God's sake, easy to cheat. An ingenu" (p. 246). The real-life Zetland had what Bellow calls "ingenuous charm," which he illustrates in the way Rosenfeld told wisecracks, "often preceded by [a] pale-blue glance. He began, he paused, a sort of mild slyness formed about his lips, and then he said something devastating."[83] Zipperstein recounts an example of sly ingenuous charm, apparently at the age of two. During a visit from one of his father's friends, infant Isaac was making noise and his father yelled at him. "Isaac turned to his father and said, in a mixture of Yiddish and English, '*fun a bissel tummel* [from a little bit of noise] the world comes an end.'"[84]

In the post-Tuley years, Rosenfeld gave voice to what he saw as the costs of his upbringing. As the adolescent Bernard puts it in *Passage from Home*, "Everything I did marked me as his son. My whole life was an acknowledgement and a denial" (p. 53). "I was a very serious young man," writes Rosenfeld in an autobiographical story, "The World on the Ceiling" (1956), "interested only in philosophy and politics, with a way of wrinkling my face in thought which I had copied from a portrait of Hegel. I had no girlfriends, no frivolities; I had a *Weltanschauung*. This pleased my father, but he kept his pleasure to himself."[85] Of Zetland's father, Bellow has the son say,

> "He wanted me to be John Stuart Mill. . . . Or some shrunken little Irzkowitz of a prodigy—Greek and calculus at the age of eight, damn him!" Zet believed he had been cheated of his childhood, robbed of the angelic birthright. He believed all that old stuff about the sufferings of childhood, the lost paradise, the crucifixion of innocence. Why was he sickly, why was he myopic, why did he have a greenish color? Why, grim old Zet wanted him to be all marrow, no bone. He caged him in reprehending punitive silence, he demanded that he dazzle the world. And he never—but never— approved of anything (pp. 244–45).

According to Zipperstein, Rosenfeld "was certain that he had never experienced the pleasurable abandon nor the wholeness that he associated with childhood,"[86] gifts Bellow was absolutely certain of, carried with him through life, and drew on repeatedly as a writer. This difference between the friends played a part in their later rivalry and estrangement. In some respects, the relationship resembled that of Wordsworth and Coleridge, with Rosenfeld the Coleridge figure: brilliant, wildly precocious, damaged, burdened by abstraction, then by an exaggerated embrace of feeling. What Wordsworth drew from Coleridge, particularly in the early years of their friendship, Bellow drew from Rosenfeld: intellectual stimulation, philosophical ballast, qualities he would seek out later in life from figures in some ways similar. In looking back on the gradual dissolution of their friendship in the 1940s, Bellow takes a lot of the blame. "I loved him," he recalls in the foreword to a collection of Rosenfeld's writings, "but we were rivals, and I was peculiarly touchy, vulnerable, hard to deal with—at times, as I can see now, insufferable— and not always a constant friend."[87] In the Tuley years, however, when

Rosenfeld was widely perceived as Bellow's intellectual superior, there were relatively few such tensions.

The other key member of Bellow's social group, certainly in intellectual terms, was Oscar Tarcov, whose parents, like Bellow's and Rosenfeld's, were Russian Jewish immigrants. Tarcov's father dealt in carpets and was often away from home on business. He had escaped the Ukraine in 1905, accused of killing a Cossack during the pogroms of that year. His wife, Manya, is remembered by her grandson, the political philosopher Nathan Tarcov, as "illiterate in three languages" (Russian, English, Yiddish), a description originating from his father. Oscar Tarcov grew up in a large family. When Bellow knew him in the Tuley years, it consisted of his parents, sister Ruth, who was a year younger than Oscar, sister Jeanne, who died of TB in 1940, and two much older sisters, Anita and Florence, and their husbands. By 1933, there were ten people in the Tarcov apartment on Le Moyne Street.[88] Oscar's intellectual interests were literary, philosophical, and political, though as with Bellow and Rosenfeld, politics were secondary (in Nathan Tarcov's words, "what literary and intellectual people were supposed to do"). Tarcov graduated from Tuley in 1935, two years after Bellow, a year ahead of Rosenfeld. Then he attended the University of Chicago, where he studied anthropology with Robert Redfield (Rosenfeld would study philosophy). At the end of the 1930s, Tarcov went to New York to become a writer, returned to Chicago, went to graduate school for a year at the University of Illinois at Urbana-Champaign, went to New York again, returned, got married, and two years after that, in 1943, had a child, Nathan's sister, Miriam. To support his family he eventually took a job with the Anti-Defamation League, writing at night. He would publish his first and only novel, *Bravo, My Monster* (1953), nine years after Bellow's first novel, *Dangling Man*, and seven years after Rosenfeld's *Passage from Home*.

Bravo, My Monster is spare and horrific, a parable of the Holocaust, and its debt to Kafka, remarked on in admiring reviews, is clear: the monster is a man, a "maniac," neither named nor described in any detail; his unnamed victim, the novel's narrator, lets him into the apartment; the monster's motives, the origins of his malice, are unspecified; the puzzling and ingenious punishments he inflicts are unrelenting; the victim's cries and calls are not heard, no one comes to his rescue or to inquire of his whereabouts; the city he lives in is unnamed; step by step, as the victim fears will happen but cannot bring himself to believe, the monster tortures him to death. The novel ends with an italicized envoi: "This phantasy is dedicated to those who, like the victim of this tale, answered their doorbell and on the threshold met evil in the likeness of man." The poet and critic Allen Tate called *Bravo, My Monster* "a brilliant, highly original exploration of a realm of experience opened up by Franz Kafka." Bellow, too, associated Kafka with the Holocaust, calling *The Metamorphosis*, "the most impressive story that I know of in that line."[89] In a brief review of the novel in *Saturday Review* (October 31, 1953), Bellow declared that "Mr. Tarcov has learned from Poe and from Kafka how to cut us off from the normal world at one stroke. This does not mean that he is to be thought of as a brilliant imitator. He has his own understanding of this mystery and is a writer of no small independence and of very considerable literary talent."[90]

TARCOV, LIKE ROSENFELD, died young, at forty-five of a heart attack. His first heart attack occurred in 1958 at thirty-nine. After a lengthy recuperation, he quit his job with the Anti-Defamation League and determined to devote his life to writing. In the five years that remained to him, he produced stories and dramatic pieces, and at his death a play had been optioned, though it was never produced. The dramatic pieces, mostly one-act plays, were produced off-Broadway, several by the Herbert Berghof Group (with which Bellow later had dealings). The first was a realistic family drama, but the later pieces were lighter, more abstract, with surrealist elements reminiscent of Ionesco. The stories appeared in *The Reconstructionist*, *The Antioch Review*, *The New Mexico Quarterly Review*, and *Chicago* magazine, and often take the form of fables. Though, in Nathan Tarcov's words, "warmer, more humane, more Jewish, more humorous" than Kafka's stories, they are Kafkaesque in form: abstract, spare, symbolic. The influence of Kafka was a point of connection between Tarcov and Rosenfeld, one that was to distinguish their writing from Bellow's, certainly in the post-Tuley years. In 1944, two years before *Passage from Home* was published, Rosenfeld won the first *Partisan Review*–Dial Press novelette award for a Kafkaesque novella, "The Colony." When *Passage from Home* appeared it was praised by the sociologist Daniel Bell in a review entitled "A Parable of Alienation," as a retelling of the story of the prodigal son. Irving Howe also praised the novel for its parable-like qualities: its spareness, focus on the internal rather than the external, and consequent openness to symbolic identifications.[91] In a review essay of 1947 in *The New Leader* entitled "Kafka and His Critics," Rosenfeld both championed Kafka for his symbolic richness and chided critics for the "partial" character of their readings, "which are mistaken in thinking themselves mutually exclusive." For Rosenfeld, "there is no other writer whose subject matter . . . is so broad, or whose symbols, whatever their partial explanation, are so closely articulated in a statement that embraces and gives the quality of so much of modern experience."[92] Kafka's influence on Rosenfeld was to prove inhibiting. In Zipperstein's words, Rosenfeld "more than embraced Kafka, aiming to make himself into his prime, contemporary disciple."[93] His stories grew increasingly spare, laboring under a burden of symbolic correspondences. "When I read his fiction," Alfred Kazin recalled, "I could see the theoretician standing apart from the writer of fiction and waiting to comment on the action that had been impatiently sketched in. . . . Isaac, even as a novelist, was more interested in ideas than in manners."[94]

At Tuley, Kafka was much in the air, and Bellow was influenced by him early in his writing career, as unpublished works from the late 1930s and early 1940s, and *Dangling Man*, his first novel, suggest. In recalling these years, however, Bellow rarely mentions Kafka, and when he does it is with misgivings. In the interview in which he talks so eloquently of his childhood faith in close observation ("The abstraction came later. Actual life was always first"), Bellow mentions having read Kafka on Balzac. Kafka couldn't bear Balzac's novels because they "contained too many characters. He's asked, aren't you interested in characters? And he says, No, I'm only interested in symbols. And I could see that as a source of dramatic power. Especially when I was growing up, I found that a 'personality' could also be constructed of something artificial. Something of conceptual origin. On the other hand, the number of types and roles were really limited: they soon became tiresome because they were derivative." Elsewhere, Bellow associates Kafka with Joyce, whom he greatly admired, and Gertude Stein, as key figures from the 1920s who "took the novel into an impossible blind alley."[95]

Though fascinated by theories and concepts, Bellow drew strength and meaning as a novelist from particulars, the streaks of the tulip. When assessing each other's writings, this difference contributed to tensions between the friends. There were differences also in their sense of writing as vocation or mission. Bellow's single-mindedness was clear to all his Tuley friends. As David Peltz puts it (in words quoted in note 89 in Chapter 3), "he was focused, he was dedicated to becoming what he was, from the beginning. I mean, he never veered." To Bellow's thinking, both Rosenfeld and Tarcov veered: Rosenfeld was too scattered, too unstable for such single-mindedness, and in the post-Tuley years, as Bellow wrote to George Sarant, Rosenfeld's son, "his liberation degenerated into personal anarchy."[96] Tarcov, Bellow implies, was too responsible, too much the *mensch*. When Tarcov died, Bellow wrote a moving letter of consolation to Nathan: "I hope that you will find— perhaps you have found—such friends as I had on Le Moyne St. in 1933. Not in order to 'replace' your father, you never will, but to be the sort of human being he was, one who knows the value of another man. He invested his life in relationships."[97] As with Rosenfeld, Bellow takes the blame for tensions in the friendship with Tarcov. In the letter he writes: "Oscar and I had an unbroken friendship for thirty years, and since I was sometimes hasty and bad-tempered it was due to him that there were no breaks."

Bellow, Tarcov, and Rosenfeld formed a triumvirate. Sam Freifeld, the richest of Bellow's Tuley friends, was slightly apart. Freifeld's family was a model for the Einhorns in *The Adventures of Augie March* ("personages *like* them appear in *Augie March*," Bellow wrote to Freifeld on July 12, 1950, though "someone else is in your place").[98] In the copy of the novel Bellow gave to Freifeld, the inscription reads: "To Sam, the historian of the Einhorn family." Sam's father, Ben, described by Bellow in the same letter as "too rich to be held by oblivion," ran an insurance business, Freifeld and Son, located at 2610 West Division Street; the "Son" was Ben, the business having been founded by his father, Harry, who came to Chicago from what is now Romania. Harry Freifeld's nickname, as in *Augie*, was "the Commissioner," and according to his granddaughter, Judith Freifeld Ward, who never met him, but heard many stories of him from her father, he was "very flamboyant . . . a bit of a con man and an operator as well." The Commissioner made money through property and development deals, often highly leveraged, as well as through insurance, mostly on the northwest side, and his son made more money again, which he managed to hold on to through the early years of the Depression. Sam grew up in affluence, in a large apartment in a forty-unit apartment building owned by the family. The Freifelds had a maid and a fancy automobile (in *Augie*, the "big red Blackhawk-Stutz" [p. 452]). They also owned a pool hall, where Sam and his friends often hung out. In the 1983 essay "In the Days of Mr. Roosevelt," Bellow recalls how his "boyhood friend Fish" (Freifeld) "who was allowed to help himself to a quarter from the cash register in his father's poolroom, occasionally treated me to a hotdog and a stein of Hires root beer on Randolph Street."[99] Though wheelchair-bound, unable to use his legs, and with limited use of his arms, dapper Ben Freifeld had great style, "pizzazz" in his granddaughter Judith's phrase; he could dominate a room, and Sam had something of his father's largeness of personality. In a biographical sketch, Rosenfeld praised the youthful Sam Freifeld for "his energy, high esteem of himself, inviting all to share in his being." Judith's sister, Susan Freifeld, describes their father as "a very vivid personality, loved to hold forth and tell stories. . . . A great talker." "He's in danger of losing his great gift of life," writes Bellow of Freifeld (for reasons unspecified) in a letter of 1947 to a mutual friend, Melvin Tumin, "I hate to see it happen to Sam who was so full and so overfull."[100]

Full of himself as well as of life, Freifeld could be pompous, could talk through his hat, often about books of which he'd read only the first chapters. Sid Passin remembers being taken under Freifeld's wing for a short time: "he 'taught me about life' . . . taught me how to drink. First he taught me how to smoke. Sam had his own private pipe tobacco and he had thirty-three different kinds." Freifeld's ebullience kept him at the center of the group, but so, too, did his relative wealth, like that of Charlie Citrine's boyhood friend, later lawyer (as Freifeld would become Bellow's lawyer), Alec Szathmar in *Humboldt's Gift*, "not big-rich, only neighborhood-rich" (p. 202). David Peltz, a close friend of Bellow's, but more distantly acquainted with Tarcov and Rosenfeld, remembers that Freifeld "always managed to have more money than anybody else. Sam had the library, the records, and the record-player, and his mother made the hamburgers, and we used to meet there and talk sex and philosophy and Marxism and Freud." Peltz remembers Freifeld as Citrine remembers Szathmar, who "in boyhood had had bikes and chemistry sets and BB guns and fencing foils and tennis rackets and boxing gloves and skates and ukuleles" (p. 202). Peltz worked for the Freifelds, carrying Ben Freifeld on his back like a sack of Carroll coal (down the front stairs, into the car, off to the movies or the beach), which is how Augie carries William Einhorn. He remembers Freifeld in the Tuley years as generous but also "an arrogant ass with his opinions." Bellow, too, had mixed feelings about Freifeld, as does Charlie Citrine about

Szathmar, whose "warm brown eyes" are described as both "full of love and friendship" and "not especially honest" (pp. 203–4). Szathmar's plush office contains framed portraits of his father and grandfather, reminding Charlie "of old days on the West Side." Charlie's feeling toward Szathmar "was after all family feeling" (p. 204), even though he could see through Szathmar's sense of their respective characters: "In Szathmar's breast there was a large true virile heart whereas I had no heart at all, only a sort of chicken giblet—that was how he saw things. He pictured himself as a person of heroic vitality, mature, wise, pagan, Tritonesque. But his real thoughts were all of getting on top, of intromission and all the dirty tricks that he called sexual freedom" (p. 205). When Szathmar memorizes "Prufrock" in college, he does so "as one of his assets," to get girls. Citrine feels bad about noticing such defects in his friend: "to atone I let him go on denouncing me" (p. 205). His last word on Szathmar, toward the end of the novel, is that "Szathmar is a good fellow in his own way. From time to time I speak harshly of Szathmar, but I really love him, you know" (p. 441).

These words are from a novel published in 1975, at which point Bellow and Freifeld were barely speaking. By 1982 and the publication of *The Dean's December*, animosities had hardened (as we shall see, there were wrangles over money and lawyer's advice, accusations on both sides of being used). Albert Corde's lawyer is, literally, family: his cousin, Maxie Detillion. In high school, Maxie shared Corde's and Dewey Spangler's literary interests: "He said he did, anyway. A showman even then, Maxie used to recite 'The Ballad of Reading Gaol.' . . . Dewey Spangler had made wicked fun of him. 'Fat-ass lowbrow . . . gross and dainty . . . Arse Poetica'—these were some of the cracks he used to make. But later Dewey turned tolerant. . . . Corde's opinion had followed the reverse pattern" (p. 67). By 1997, in *The Actual*, Bellow gives his heroine, Amy Wustrin, a gross and familiar-sounding husband, Jay Wustrin: "a stout man, dancing, he swung his broad backside, but his feet were very agile" (p. 32). In his school days, according to Amy, Jay would memorize bits of poetry to recite, "when he was putting the make on girls. After we were married, I looked up all his source books. The passages were underlined, and just from Chapter One. He never read an entire book in his whole life" (p. 55). In the Tuley years, such defects were viewed, for the most part, affectionately.

Bellow's feelings about Sydney J. Harris were more rivalrous. In "I Got a Scheme!," he describes Harris as "my closest friend, in early adolescence."[101] Harris lived east of the park, on Iowa Street, just east of Robey (now Damen), only blocks from where the Bellows once lived on Cortez. He, too, went to Columbus Elementary School and Sabin Junior High, although Bellow was two years older and believes they only met in "1929, perhaps 1930," at the Association House. Here, in addition to playing basketball, they started a little newspaper. "I was the editor of it," Harris remembered, "and Saul was the assistant editor." "We worked on that paper for most of one year," Bellow wrote in a memorial speech given shortly after Harris's death in December 1986, "doing the whole thing from scratch, even making up the dummy and taking it to the printer."[102] At Tuley, Harris was also editor of the school paper, *The Tuley Review*, "the only freshman who had ever been the editor," and Bellow was a staff writer, a pattern that, as Harris put it, "repeated itself a few years later, when in 1937 I started a magazine called *The Beacon*," on which Bellow worked briefly as literary editor. Bellow seems to have been happy to let Harris take the lead in these ventures. Harris was obsessed with newspapers and worked on them all his life. He left Tuley without graduating, became a copyboy "on the old Hearst newspaper when I was fifteen," worked on the *Chicago Daily News* and the *Chicago Sun-Times*, and for thirty years wrote a column entitled *Strictly Personal*, which was syndicated throughout the United States and Canada.

Looking back on the friendship, Harris claimed that he "knew at once that Saul had an imaginative capacity that I never had. I have no imaginative abilities. I never have tried to write a short story in my life, much less a novel." This assertion is untrue. At Tuley, Harris wrote stories, a novel, even poetry, and was as ready as Bellow to discuss Huysmans, Verlaine, Baudelaire, "all that stuff." As Bellow puts it in the memorial speech, "we didn't shrink from Schopenhauer's *The World as Will and Idea*, we didn't shrink from Spengler's *Decline of the West*. We were willing to try our hand at everything." When Bellow and Harris were together in the Tuley years, Mencken was the presiding spirit: "we were devoted to the *American Mercury* and our mouths were full of Menckenian profanities and irreverences." The two friends spent whole evenings walking each other back and forth across Humboldt Park, between their two houses, "talking up a storm but especially about literature and about how bad everything was and about our prospects as writers." In later life, much to Harris's embarrassment, Bellow would recite from memory passages from his friend's adolescent poems. In the memorial speech, he offered the opening lines of "Rebellion": "I rebel against this living hell / This form of mockery sublime." He recalled arguing with Harris until two in the morning, then pooling their pennies (Bellow's "daily allowance" while in high school was 10 cents)[103] to share a nickel hot dog "at a joint called MGM" ("Many Good Mouthfuls"). For the nickel one got the hot dog, "plus potato chips, plus lettuce and tomatoes, plus all the pickle, relish, mustard and so on you could load into [the bun]" (p. 5). The subjects the two friends debated were literary, intellectual, and political; they also talked about girls, whom they chased "indiscriminately on Division Street and in the corridors of Tuley High School" (p. 8). In retrospect, Harris was struck by how little Bellow had to say about the supposed master themes of his fiction, Jewishness and Chicago. "We looked toward the East all the time," he recalled, "and we would have thought it very provincial to be concerned about the city very much. And as far as the Jewishness was concerned, that was a complete blank. That was just something not discussed or talked about." Rosenfeld was the one in the group, according to Harris, who was concerned with Jewishness.

Bellow spent a lot of time at the Harris apartment during his high school years, and often slept over, partly to escape tensions at home. Harris's father was a Russian Jewish immigrant, his mother English, from London. In the memorial speech, Bellow remembers Harris's father as "a charming man," with an original, quirky sense of humor; his mother was also charming and funny. Harris was an only child and Bellow was amazed at the way he was allowed to speak to his parents: "Skinny Sydney with his wild ways, his tics and his rages ran the show— he lied, he threatened and he stormed, he played the genius and the dictator." Partly this behavior was "theater," the rages put on, but Bellow was still shocked by his friend's language: "Get back to the kitchen you old Cockney bitch," he remembers Harris shouting when his mother entered the parlor where he and Bellow were at work, "How dare you interrupt?" To which the mother, angry, but also performing, would answer, "Yer no child of mine. . . . They switched yer on me in hospital." Had Bellow tried such language at home, his mother "wouldn't have let me get away with it, and my father would have knocked me down."[104] On other occasions, Mrs. Harris would enter the parlor and recite "very well" passages from Shakespeare's history plays, which she'd had to memorize at school in London. Bellow remembers the relations between Harris and his mother as having "a very liberating effect on me, especially hearing him swear at his mother from time to time was extremely uplifting." Though "kindred spirits," they "fought all the time and we swore profanely . . . and Sydney could be very abrasive and I was abrasive with him."[105]

What Mrs. Harris interrupted when she entered her parlor were writing sessions. "We wrote at opposite ends of the big table, on yellow second sheets from the Woolworth ten-cent store. At this square borax table, its surface protected by a carpet-like cover, we wrote stories, poems, essays, dialogues, political fantasies, essays on Marxism—on subjects we didn't really know too much about."[106] They also criticized each other's work, "unsparingly and often cruelly and there was a great deal of yelling back and forth." Harris impressed Bellow by having a typewriter, a tiny one he borrowed from his cousin, and by knowing that you were meant to provide future editors with a word count.[107] One of the pieces they worked on together was a novel called "Herbert Sanders."[108] In interviews, Bellow described this novel as a joint venture, but in the memorial speech he attributes it to Harris alone: "Then about 1931, it must have been, Sydney wrote a book. I think he was then sixteen years old." Bellow remembered "Herbert Sanders" "very well, it was a combination of automatic writing and all kinds of . . . surrealistic insights. It was a very free-wheeling work." The introduction Bellow wrote to accompany the novel was "at least as long" as the work itself. When both novel and introduction were finished the two authors were determined to see it in print. "On a street corner on a very cold day in February," they flipped a coin to see which of them would take the manuscript to New York to find a publisher. Harris won the toss and immediately set off with the manuscript. "He tucked it under his sweater on the spot. He started thumbing his way down Division Street and then he was gone." Bellow is unsure about dates in the memorial speech. He says Harris wrote the book "about 1931," which means the February trip to New York must have taken place in 1932. At this date Harris, who was born on September 14, 1917, was fourteen and Bellow sixteen ("I think I was sixteen at the time," Bellow writes in the speech. "Sydney was about a year my junior"). Amazingly, Harris not only reached New York but managed to meet John Dos Passos, who invited him to stay in his apartment on Riverside Drive. He also managed to contact Pascal "Pat" Covici, who had come to New York from Chicago, where he had run a successful publishing company and bookstore, the haunt of Sherwood Anderson, Ben Hecht, Theodore

Dreiser, Edgar Lee Masters, and other Chicago writers. In New York, Covici joined forces with Donald Friede, publishing works by Wyndham Lewis, Clifford Odets, and Nathanael West, among others. Two years after Harris's trip to New York, Covici-Friede signed John Steinbeck, and twenty or so years later, after Covici moved to Viking, he became Bellow's editor, shortly after publication of *The Adventures of Augie March*.

Though he refused to publish "Herbert Sanders" and "wouldn't spare so much as a glance at my Hemingway [i.e., Hemingwayesque] introduction," Covici was impressed with fourteen-year-old Harris, offering him a contract to write a novel about revolutionary high school students in Chicago. Meanwhile, back in Humboldt Park, Harris's parents were distraught, having been given no warning about the trip and few details about where Sydney had gone. Mrs. Harris called Bellow repeatedly "for information which I, of course, wasn't about to give"; then she came to the Bellow apartment to make her case to Bellow's parents. In "I Got a Scheme!," Bellow remembers the interview taking place "in my mother's sickroom." Still he refused to say anything: "I was very sorry for Sydney's mother, who was in tears, but there was nothing I could do without violating the code. So I said—no, I know nothing." Maury got involved at this point and "was very threatening." He insisted that Saul be questioned at police headquarters. Bellow remembered the streetcar ride to 11th and State Street, "Sydney's mother weeping, my bossy brother determined to tag me hard and teach me a lesson." At the station, Bellow underwent interrogation in the Missing Persons Bureau, "but I still didn't talk. I tried to convey to Mrs. Harris that her boy was all right. There wasn't something that had gone wrong. I wanted her to know that he had gotten to New York safely but we had taken an oath so I couldn't do anything." To Roth, Bellow explained: "Adolescents in those days were bound by gangland rules. You didn't rat on a buddy." After the Missing Persons Bureau, Bellow "felt that I could tough it out with the best of them." On the journey home, Maury lit into him, and as soon as they got back to the apartment he broke open the single locked drawer of Bellow's dresser and discovered all Harris's letters, with their excited accounts of his journey, of John Dos Passos, of the contract with Covici.

In *The Dean's December*, Albert Corde's friend from boyhood, the journalist Dewey Spangler, is given something of Harris's background and character (also something of Richard Rovere's background and character), including a fictional equivalent of the whole "Herbert Sanders" episode (the novel he and Corde cowrite is titled "Death on the El"). When Corde's dresser drawer was forced open by "Uncle Harold," who lived upstairs, he "called everyone together and read Dewey's letters to the gathered family. Corde's mother was then dying." Among the letters Dewey writes to Corde from New York is one that says "The reader at Harcourt loves my part of the book, but says that you should go into the hotel business with your dad" (p. 241). In "I Got a Scheme!," Bellow recalls a similarly hurtful passage, and something of his family's reaction: "In the judgment of the publishing illuminati I would do well to enter my father's business. Only my mother grieved for me. Everybody else was delighted to see me go down in flames." When Harris returned to Tuley, he did so in triumph: on a Greyhound bus in the memorial speech version of the episode, on a train in the version to Roth, "with a hundred bucks in his pocket [two hundred in the Roth version] and a signed contract from Covici." As Bellow puts it in "I Got a Scheme!," "Famous and rich, [he] was far too busy now to write a book for Covici. He soon became the leg-man for Milton Mayer who covered Chicago for *P.M.*, the New York paper founded by Marshall Field. Eventually, Sydney became a *Chicago Daily News* columnist who specialized in the education of adolescents."

Bellow's Tuley pals had a reputation, one they cultivated. According to Harris, they saw themselves in opposition to what he called the "Ra Ra boys, who, of course, got all the pretty girls." They ran the Scribblers' Club and the Debating Club and the *Tuley Review*; they invented names for their circle: the Division Street Movement, the Russian Literary Society. Harris wrote a poem about the group, making fun of its rivalries and pretensions. To the dismay of his friends it was published by Harriet Monroe in *Poetry* magazine in December 1935. Harris was eighteen when the poem appeared, though he claimed he wrote it when he was sixteen. It was called "I Come to Bury Caesar" and subtitled "Being a litany, an anecdote, and an adolescent assertion of bravado." Nicely self-reflexive, the poem traces the reaction of a circle much like Bellow's to the news that one of their number, Farefield, has had a poem accepted by *Poetry* magazine.

> *. . . Farefield, with an expression*
> *Not quite like anything I had ever seen before,*
> *Turned to us and casually said,*

"I've just been accepted by Poetry,*"*
Eliot laughed, and Isaac turned quite red,
And I smiled stiffly, clearing the burned
Charcoal fumes from my dolichocephalic head.

Farefield's poem is called "Heil, Hamlet," and Harris, or the speaker of his poem, thinks it "quite possible" *Poetry* accepted it only because "Harriet" was "out of town" ("But all the same I could have died"). His friends put a brave face on ("Isaac had regained his poise, / And sneered sedately at the boys"), as Farefield preens ("Smoothing the sleek / Black curls back of his left ear"), but Farefield gets it in the end:

The dinner, of course, was a fiasco
Even Lasco, (the incorrigible showman)
Sensed that the scene was definitely extra-Roman.
For Caesar-Farefield lay inert upon the floor,
And Brutus-I knelt down to tie an errant lace,
And Casca-Isaac's face
Was a study in anthropology;
And Pound and Eliot, intending no malice,
In delicate rages delicately tore
Their respective pages
From dear Harriet's . . .
Intellectual
But highly ineffectual
Anthology . . .

Ambition should be made of much
Sterner stuff.

Q.E.D.

"Lasco" is Louie Lasco, closer to Bellow and Peltz than the others, and only loosely part of the group. In an interview, Harris called his poem "a little parody" and claimed it was "all about Saul," though Bellow is hard to identify as any one character. "Pound and Eliot" might be Tarcov and Bellow, for no reason other than that Isaac, presumably, is Rosenfeld, "I" is Harris himself, and "Farefield" is Freifeld, whose one claim to intellectual fame at Tuley, at least according to Sidney Passin, is that he wrote a poem called "Heil, Hitler," "before others were writing" (though Passin may be confusing Freifeld with Farefield, or with Harris).[109] What is clear is the general character of the group, of all such groups, like the Auden circle at Repton, with its youthful posturing ("Eliot stretched in a chintz-covered chair, / While Pound sat around / Sipping a sloe gin fizz"), ambition, and art worship.

IN ADDITION TO intellectual rivalry among Bellow and his friends, there was rivalry over girls, and in this respect Bellow, the best-looking member of the circle, and the oldest, was the acknowledged champion. The girls in question seem not to have shared the boys' intellectual or literary interests, at least none are reported to have done so, though they were often political. Chief among the political girls was Yetta Barshevsky, a year above Bellow, though born in 1915, the class orator at her June 1932 graduation ceremony. Barshevsky was slight, high-voiced, and good-looking. George Reedy, a fellow Tuley graduate, later press secretary to Lyndon Johnson, recalled her as "one of the most beautiful . . . women I have ever seen and her beauty was accompanied by one of the finest minds I have ever encountered. To top it off, there was not the slightest case of arrogance that would be common in almost anyone else with such endowments."[110] To Bellow, in a three-page speech, "In Memory of Yetta Barshevsky," delivered at her memorial on September 22, 1996, Yetta "always seemed to me to have a significant sort of Jewish beauty." She was also "fearless and formidable." Before the graduation ceremony, she submitted her speech as class orator to be vetted by the school authorities, who approved; then she gave a wholly different and more radical speech. According to Bellow, "the immigrant parents at the graduation ceremonies were delighted with Yetta's oration": she used words like "penury" and "mitigate," which of itself impressed them, as it impressed Bellow ("I knew 'mitigate' only from books. I had never heard it spoken"), and she used them in the service of a fiery pledge: "'We will do right by you,' was what she was telling them. 'We will give you mitigation.'"

Yetta Barshevsky lived on Spaulding Avenue, just north of Division Street, around the corner from 3340 Le Moyne Street, and Bellow was "a frequent visitor" at her home. She played a part in his political education, earnestly lecturing him on Leninism and Trotskyism as they walked home across Humboldt Park after school, or sat talking on the steps of the Humboldt Park boathouse or in its Rose Garden. Bellow had a crush on her, but she was already engaged to Nate Gould (né Goldstein), also a political radical, recently graduated, whom she would marry (as she would marry Max Shachtman, the Trotskyist leader, after her marriage to Gould ended).[111] Whether Barshevsky gave Bellow much encouragement romantically is unclear. The wildly self-conscious letter he wrote to her from South Haven, Michigan, on May 28, 1932, shortly before his seventeenth birthday, mixes poetic hyperbole ("I am thinking, thinking Yetta, drifting with night, with infinity, and all my thoughts are of you") with ironic deflation ("I hate melodrama. The only thing I hate more than melodrama and spinach is myself. You think perhaps I am insane? I am"). Bellow threatens jokily that "I the young idealist will lay his woes and his heart at Pearl's feet" (Pearl was Oscar Tarcov's girlfriend). If Pearl won't have him he'll "go home and write heart-rending poetry and play the violin."[112]

Bellow's great love in the Tuley years was Eleanor Fox, but their relationship was stormy, partly because he was playing around, partly because she was playing around to get back at him. Eleanor lived on Kedzie Avenue, on the western edge of the park, just a few blocks from the Bellow apartment on Le Moyne. As she explains, "Saul, Isaac Rosenfeld, all those guys lived on our side of the park. So we all had to cross every day to go to school, to come back from school. . . . They would all come to my house. My mother was a very gregarious lady, so they lived at my house, all those guys did. My mother would feed them and keep them and treat them so well." Eleanor, a beauty, entertained the guys but "had a separate thing" with Bellow, which, of course, the guys envied. So they "snitched" on him when he met other girls, either in the park or in one of the "English basements" which served as places of assignation. According to David Peltz, English basements, some-times "Polish basements," were cheap ground-floor apartments that could be rented for as little as $5 a month. A group of boys would pool their money for rent, furnish the place with a sofa or some chairs from the Salvation Army, and use it as a clubhouse, often with a jokey name ("The Humboldt Park Athletic Association" is a name Peltz remem-bers). Here they also arranged meetings with girls, though any sex they engaged in was mostly petting ("We didn't have sex in high school," Peltz told Atlas, "that all happened later. We talked about it, but we didn't do it).[113] Fred Glotzer, another Tuley friend, remembers freezing on the pavement in front of one such basement, waiting for Bellow to raise the blind and give the all-clear.

If the girl he was with wasn't Eleanor, Eleanor would soon hear of her. "The women would tell me a little," Eleanor remembered, but it was the boys who were "all on my side." When Eleanor herself snuck off with another boy, "because [Bellow] was sneaking," his pals quickly let him know: "They *loved* telling him I had other dates, you see, and that would infuriate him." Once Bellow hitchhiked out to Eleanor's summer house in Michigan City, Indiana, arriving unannounced, saw her wearing the fraternity pin of an older boy, the son of a prominent Chicago politician, and ripped it off, tearing her dress. "I mean, the fury this guy would go into." David Peltz recalls a comparable episode when Bellow discovered that Eleanor had written him a love letter, accompanied by a crushed flower. Bellow "came running up the steps to my bedroom," Peltz recalls, "and he saw the letter and he said, 'Me she sends weeds; you flowers.' Then he took the letter and he ran out of the house." In a letter of July 24, 1994, to Louis Echeles, another Tuley acquaintance, later a prominent criminal attorney, Bellow recalled giving his track team letter to Eleanor: "she sewed it on her sweater. But whatever pleasure there was to be got out of her she gave to somebody else."

Eleanor remembers Bellow as critical and superior "but charming as all hell: he could have anybody he wanted." "He sure had something I cared about," she recalls, "otherwise I wouldn't have gone out with him all those years." Bellow's male friends also felt this something. To Eleanor, "it was sort of like a sexual thing, almost. He was the best-looking one of the bunch. He was the best-dressed, not expensive, necessarily." The passion Bellow felt for Eleanor in high school he vividly memorializes in his fiction. "In my highly emotional adolescence," Charlie Citrine recalls, "I had loved Naomi Lutz [Naomi was one of Eleanor's given names]. I believe she was the most beautiful and perfect young girl I have ever seen, I adored her, and love brought out my deepest peculiarities." When he was sixteen, Charlie continues, "I had my own little Lake Country, the park, where I wandered with my Modern Library Plato, Wordsworth, Swinburne, and *Un Coeur Simple*. Even in winter Naomi petted behind the Rose Garden with me. Among the frozen twigs I made myself warm inside her raccoon coat. There was a delicious mixture of coon skin and maiden fragrance. We breathed frost and kissed" (p. 76). Another version of Eleanor is Louie's girlfriend,

Stephanie, in "Something to Remember Me By," with whom he necked in the park "in the dead black night . . . my hands under her raccoon coat, under her sweater, under her skirt, adolescents kissing without restraint. . . . She opened the musky coat to me to have me closer" (p. 415). Amy Wustrin, in *The Actual*, Harry Trellman's adolescent love, is also remembered for her raccoon coat, her distinctive swaying walk, and a sexual appeal that made subsequent women mere approximations. When Harry sees her again after many years apart he wonders "whether she would wear a raccoon coat if I were to buy one for her" (p. 103).

Eleanor Fox's father was a respectable podiatrist, like Naomi Schultz's father, with a practice on Randolph Street in the Loop, and wealthy theatrical clients. He didn't like Bellow and Bellow didn't like him. Her mother, however, thought Bellow charming. Shortly after graduating from Tuley, Bellow asked Eleanor to marry him ("He didn't want to leave me with all these guys, these people who were always at my house"). She turned him down, saying she wanted to finish high school and become a teacher (she became a high school principal, unlike Naomi Lutz, who only becomes a crossing guard). After she graduated, he tried again: "He went to my mother, who adored him, and said I want to get married to your daughter. She said, 'Oh, wonderful! You're going to get married!'" But again Eleanor refused: "I said I wouldn't marry him for anything. How do I know he isn't going to have five wives?—which is exactly what happened." Also, Bellow was quick to the boil, combustible, like his father. ("You were a violent kid," Naomi tells Charlie. "You almost choked me to death because I went to a dance with some basketball player. And once, in the garage, you put a rope on your neck and threatened to hang yourself if you didn't get your way" [p. 291].) Then there was Bellow's talk, which often confused Eleanor, and the sharpness of his tongue. Eleanor was a good student, but no intellectual. She wrote a style column for *The Tuley Review* and arranged lunches and fashion shows for high school girls at Marshall Field's department store, a job that made her "the most popular lady in the school." Adolescent Bellow looked down on these activities, as he looked down on her father (because he was a podiatrist, she says; because he was a "pretentious" podiatrist, the fiction suggests, furious if called "Mister" not "Doctor").[114] Bellow gave her books to read, saying "this will do you more good than Marshall Field." They'd go to the movies and he'd sneer: "very few of them, none of them, were at his level—Hollywood, you know." He'd take her to Trotskyist meetings:

"Terrible." "He was educating me all the time," she recalls, much as Naomi recalls being educated by Citrine in *Humboldt's Gift*. "You were thrilling," the adult Naomi tells him, "but I never knew where you were at with your Swinburne and your Baudelaire and Oscar Wilde and Karl Marx" (p. 291). Charlie's defense is Bellow's: "Those were intoxicating books and I was in the thick of beauty and wild about goodness and thought and poetry and love. Wasn't that merely adolescence?" Naomi smiles and answers "I don't really think so," then quotes her father's opinion: "your whole family were a bunch of greenhorns and aliens, too damn emotional, the whole bunch of you" (p. 292).

In 1994, after the publication of her book on Bellow, Ruth Miller received a letter from Norman Dolnick, a Tuley classmate of Bellow's (a basketball player in high school, as it happens, though Bellow did not know this). Dolnick relayed some of Eleanor's objections both to the Naomi Lutz character in *Humboldt's Gift* and to Miller's identification of the character with Bellow's third wife, Susan Glassman. In the letter he also reveals that, urged on by Sydney Harris, he had a fling with Eleanor: "In a vengeful turn, he introduced me to Eleanor, as he said, to take her away from Saul. It was a delightful assignment. Eleanor has many charms so I was a beneficiary. Eleanor later told me she had tired of Saul's need to dominate. My more casual manner was easier to take."[115] Bellow was sent a copy of the letter and wrote to Dolnick on October 10, to say that he'd never known "you were one of her lucky favorites" or that Harris had urged him to seduce Eleanor. As for his own behavior: "I can't actually say what I was like at seventeen—mixed up, unable to absorb the shock of my mother's death and the breaking up of the family. I must have been a bit frantic, and Eleanor apparently saw this as a 'need to dominate.'" Later he admits that he was "explosive now and then—she seemed to me—no, she really was—a beauty, and I loved her. More, perhaps, than any of my lucky rivals." He describes Eleanor as "quite clear about the life she wanted: a house in Evanston, a convertible, a charge account at Field's, membership in the country club. A boy preparing to write stories and novels could never satisfy wants like those. And she'd never have put up with my many, many failures." When Dolnick showed Eleanor what Bellow had written, she expressed amusement "that you and Norm are rehashing events that took place sixty years ago" (a line Bellow himself took in his letter). She hadn't been upset by *Humboldt's Gift*, though she objected to his characterization of the life she wanted: "You are wrong in saying I needed materialistic satisfaction. At that time I wanted gentle love, and kind treatment and trust." What she remembers is that "you were *mean*, and volatile. I recognized your genius, great emotional need and capacity to love. I was unable to cope." Had she married him at an early age, "I would have been one of your five wives." She is sorry if he "felt mistreated or that I didn't care—I probably loved you more than any other man in my life but it was not to be."

Eleanor Fox was not the only person troubled by Bellow's volatility: "My mother, who was unfamiliar with America and didn't really know how things worked here, was frightened by my excess. I was a bohemian and a left-winger and all of these serious, unusual things and she was worried. She was dying and wouldn't be here to take care of me." Bellow knew of his mother's worry at first hand, but also from the testimony of "a girlfriend in high school whose mother was my mother's seamstress." His mother would "unburden herself to the seamstress whom she liked very much. Then the word would get back to me by way of the girl. I really looked very bad in those days. I looked like a lost cause."[116] As his mother's health deteriorated, her anxiety about Bellow was fed by Abraham, who "was often heard to say that I *had* been a clever child," but was now "succumbing to American emptiness and *narishkeit* [foolishnesss]."[117] Soon, however, Liza's dying subsumed all other worries. In a tiny spiral notebook in the Regenstein, undated, Bellow recalled that "my mother towards the last had the look of a woman waking from an ill-omened dream—whose happiness (happiness within misery, family happiness unaffected, really, by poverty) was now to end in death. Her face became dark. Good nature ended. She often looked sullen, like a sleeper roused from his siesta by a loud noise on the roof. Her face was dark. The look was calm, but withdrawn." Liza had been ill with breast cancer for years and was often heavily sedated. At her death, on February 28, 1933, at ten at night, the family fell apart. In *Herzog*, Bellow presents a powerful fictional account of her last weeks. Late in "a frightful January, streets coated with steely ice," Moses sits at the kitchen table in a rage, reading Spengler, his heart "infected with ambition, and the bacteria of vengeance." From her sickroom, his mother sees light under the door and walks the length of the house to the kitchen.

> Her hair had to be cut during her illness, and this made those eyes hard to recognize. Or no, the shortness of her hair merely made their message simpler: *My son, this is death.*

I chose not to read this text.

"I saw the light," she said. "What are you doing up so late?" But the dying, for themselves, have given up hours. She only pitied me, her orphan, understood I was a gesture-maker, ambitious, a fool; thought I would need my eyesight and my strength on a certain day of reckoning.

A few days afterward, when she had lost the power to speak, she was still trying to comfort Moses. Just as when he knew she was breathless from trudging with his sled in Montreal but would not get up. He came into her room when she was dying, holding his school books, and began to say something to her. But she lifted up her hands and showed him her fingernails. They were blue. As he stared, she slowly began to nod her head up and down as if to say, "That's right, Moses, I am dying now." He sat by the bed. Presently she began to stroke his hand. She did this as well as she could; her fingers had lost their flexibility. Under the nails they seemed to him to be turning already into the blue loam of graves. She had begun to change into earth! (pp. 652–53).

Eleanor Fox at eighteen

Politics/Anthropology

I N THE SPRING of 1934, just a year after Liza Bellow's death, Abraham married Fannie Gebler, a widow who lived in the neighborhood. It is Jewish custom for widows or widowers to wait a year before remarrying. Fannie came from Galicia, had no children, and brought with her a sum of money, between $7,500 and $10,000, which she gave to Abraham for his business. She was kind to Abraham's children, who remembered her fondly. From photographs taken at Maury and Marge's wedding she looks a handsome woman, like Father Herzog's second wife, the Widow Kaplinsky, who "had been a stunning girl" and in her sixties "had thick handsome strong brows and a heavy braid of animal brown" (p. 664). In her eighties, when we encounter her in *Herzog*, the Widow Kaplinsky is slow but shrewd, careful with fraught Moses. Moses remembers Father Herzog complaining toward the end of his life that "he had brought his iron to a cold forge. *A kalte kuzhnya, Moshe. Kein fire.* Divorce was impossible because he owed her too much money" (p. 667). According to Joel Bellows, Abraham complained in similar terms about Fannie Gebler, though Joel also recalls being told that Fannie "took great pride in the fact that Abraham wanted to have sex the night he died, and she had to turn him down" (Abraham died in 1955, at seventy-four). Soon after the marriage, Jane and Charlie moved to their own apartment in Rogers Park, Sam and Nina married and moved to an apartment in Lincoln Park, and Maury and Marge married and moved to an apartment on the South Side. A month before Liza's death, Bellow enrolled as a student at Crane Junior College in the Loop, where he stayed until the beginning of the next academic year.

At some point in 1935, probably in the autumn, Abraham and Fannie moved from Le Moyne Street to a one-bedroom apartment at 3434 Evergreen Avenue, a few blocks away.

Bellow tried to hide his distress at Liza's illness and death. "It was a very shattering experience for him when she died," David Peltz remembered, "he couldn't talk much about it, but he did talk about it"[1]—to Peltz, not to Eleanor Fox, who remembered "very little reaction," by which she means very little talk, for she also sensed "something lonely" about him, an impression shared by Fred Glotzer, who recalled Bellow at the same time as "kind of a lonely guy who needed approval from his friends." This was the period in which Bellow slept nights at the Harris apartment. "I was turned loose—freed, in a sense: free, but also stunned."[2] Albert Corde's family in *The Dean's December* is very different from Bellow's, having money and connections, but the illness and death of Corde's mother suggest the last days of Liza Bellow, as Corde's feelings suggest those reported by Bellow himself. "I was grieving so hard," Corde recalls to Dewey Spangler, "just back from the cemetery. It was one of those winter days of cast-iron gloom, nothing but gray ice" (p. 233).

Bellow was not alone in moving from Tuley to Crane. Yetta Barshevsky was already there, as was Nate Gould; Arthur Wineberg entered at the same time as Bellow. Crane was founded in 1911, after Jane Addams, John Dewey, and other influential progressives lobbied the city to provide higher education for the poor. It offered an abbreviated baccalaureate program, modeled on the first two years of a four-year undergraduate degree.[3] Its first students (thirty-two in 1911) were mostly immigrants from the near West Side. By 1931, it had a student body of more than three thousand. In *The Adventures of Augie March*, Bellow describes this student body as made up of "children of immigrants from all parts, coming up from Hell's Kitchen, Little Sicily, the Black Belt, the mass of Polonia, the Jewish streets of Humboldt Park." During the early years of the Depression, Crane was both overcrowded and underfunded (in Augie's words, "they filled the factory-length corridors and giant classrooms with every human character and germ" [p. 524]), and for periods its teachers went unpaid, the fate of other municipal workers in 1930s Chicago, including police and firemen. Bellow's English teacher at Crane, Miss Ferguson, remembered one protest in which unpaid teachers pushed their way into the mayor's office "and chased him round his desk."[4] This mayor, Anton "Pushcart

Tony" Cermak, was forced by the deepening crisis to go cap-in-hand to FDR, whose nomination as Democratic candidate for president he had tried to block in 1932. The president-elect was in Florida, recovering from a difficult campaign, and on February 15, (two weeks before Liza Bellow's death) an attempt was made to assassinate him at an outdoor speech at which Cermak was present. Roosevelt was unhurt but Cermak and four others were shot, and nineteen days later, on March 6, 1933, the mayor died of his wounds. As the funding crisis intensified over the spring and summer, Cermak's successor, Mayor Edward Kelly, was forced to sack 1,400 teachers, shorten the workweek, and close Crane. Chicago's most progressive educational institution, "the people's college," was shut down two months after the opening of the city's much touted World's Fair, "A Century of Progress." There were mass protests against the closure and cuts, including a meeting of over thirty thousand at the Chicago Stadium on July 21. Students and teachers, supported by prominent allies such as Clarence Darrow, as well as an increasingly radicalized union movement, marched together "to save educational opportunity for working people." Embarrassed and alarmed by the public outcry, Mayor Kelly was forced not only to authorize the reopening of Crane in 1934, but to add two new sites, one in the heart of the Lawndale district on the northwest side. By this date, Bellow had enrolled in the University of Chicago. His half year at Crane had been marked as much by political unrest over the funding crisis as by coursework (English 101, Spanish, Math, English History), and he reports very little of what he learned (except to say that Miss Ferguson of English 101 was keen on rules of composition, which she sang out in class to the tune of Handel's "Hallelujah Chorus").[5] Augie March, a more easygoing type than Bellow, contrasted the work he did at Crane with that of his fellow students:

> demon-brained physicists, historians bred under pushcarts, and many hard-grain poor boys who were going to starve and work themselves bitterly eight years or so to become doctors, engineers, scholars, and experts. I had no special eagerness of this kind and never had been led to think I should have, nor gave myself anxious cares about being revealed a profession. I didn't feel moved to take it seriously. Nevertheless I turned in a fairly good performance in French and History. In things like Botany, my drawings were cockeyed and smudgy and I was behind the class (p. 526).

BELLOW'S INVOLVEMENT IN politics in the 1930s began at Tuley and continued throughout his college years, first at Crane, then at the University of Chicago, Northwestern University, and the University of Wisconsin. His rich friend Sam Freifeld helped to introduce him to political theory and commentary, generously lending him influential journals and texts. "What he wanted from them," Bellow recalls in "In the Days of Mr. Roosevelt," an article published in December 1983 in *Esquire*, "was no more than a few quick impressions—he was no scholar—and after he had read a few pages he passed the magazines and pamphlets on to me. Through him I became familiar with Karl Marx and V. I. Lenin; also with Marie Stopes, Havelock Ellis, V. F. Calverton, Max Eastman, and Edmund Wilson."[6] Bellow mentions reading Marx's *Value, Price and Profit* (1898) in the office of Carroll Coal; he also mentions reading Lenin's *The State and Revolution* (1917) and Leon Trotsky's pamphlets, singling out "Germany: The Key to the International Situation" (1931), in which Trotsky argues, in Bellow's words, that "Stalin's errors had brought Hitler to power"[7] (principally by identifying the Social Democrats as a greater threat to Germany than the Nazis). Bellow's skills as a public speaker were tested at Tuley in the debating club, where local and national issues, as well as works of political theory (*The Communist Manifesto* on one occasion) were debated. "My oratory has not improved since I debated the chain-store issue at Tuley," Bellow wrote to Nate Gould, in a letter of February 1, 1967. Outside school there were debates on soapboxes and in the halls and clubs around Division Street. Bellow singles out those at what he calls "the forum," a church hall on California Avenue, where the arguments of "socialists, communists and anarchists attracted a fair number of people." Such arguments were "the beginning of my radical education."[8] David Peltz's uncle, David Bronstein, ran a similar forum on Friday nights at his mission house, the Peniel Community Center ("Peniel" is Hebrew for "face of God") on Washtenaw and Crystal, just off California and Division. Bronstein, a convert to Christianity, had married Peltz's father's sister, who also converted. The forum he ran discussed political as well as religious issues, which is only partly why the Tuley crowd attended. "He'd have a huge audience," Peltz explains, "because cocoa was served and coffee was served and donuts at the end, and anyone could say what they wanted." After an appeal from Bronstein or his wife or a guest speaker to accept Jesus, "the Stalinists got up and they made speeches and the Trotskyites got up and they made their speeches and the Norman Thomas supporters gave their speeches." Peltz remembers Freifeld and Herb Passin speaking at Peniel, though never Bellow.[9]

"In high school I was a socialist," Bellow told an interviewer. "In college (1933) I was a Trotskyist." What made Bellow a Trotskyist, he claims, was reading Trotsky's *History of the Russian Revolution* (1932), "even though most of it was party-line."[10] Trotsky's *History* attacks Stalin's personal dictatorship and intolerance of criticism, the parasitic Soviet state bureaucracy, the doctrine of socialism in one country (as opposed to world or permanent revolution), and what Leszek Kolakowski calls "the forgeries of Stalinist historiography."[11] It also defends Bolshevism as a political system, arguing that the Soviet Union, for all its defects, remained a worker's state, because it owned the means of production. In 1932, Bellow and his friends (minus Sydney Harris, who "never became a Marxist. . . . We kind of split because I was looked upon as a betrayer of the cause"[12]) were prepared to accept this defense. "We belonged to the movement," Bellow continues, "we were faithful to Leninism and could expound its historical lessons and describe Stalin's crimes."[13] The Tuley Trotskyists could talk the talk—of "surplus value," "rate of profit," "the fetishism of commodities," "hegemony" (much invoked by Freifeld), what Marx "really" meant, whether FDR's reforms "were saving the country for capitalism, only the capitalists were too stupid to understand this."[14] Presumably they also pondered what Irving Kristol, speaking of his fellow Trotskyists at City College in New York, called "the overwhelming question that haunted us, namely whether there was something in Marxism and Leninism that led to Stalinism? To what degree was there a connection? This was the question that all along bothered us, that was a prelude to our future politics."[15]

Trotsky's appeal to the Tuley circle, as to the Trotskyists at City College, had several sources. That he was Jewish played a part, as did his reputation as an intellectual. The "vanguard fighters" of the October Revolution, especially Lenin and Trotsky, whose names Bellow first heard "in the high chair while eating my mashed potatoes," were thinkers and theorists as well as men of action. Trotsky had been president of the Military Revolutionary Committee in the October Revolution, the creator and first commander of the Red Army, the Soviet Union's first commissar of foreign affairs, Lenin's right-hand man. He also "read

French novels at the front while defeating Deniken,"[16] wrote literary criticism as well as political theory, was a friend of André Breton and Diego Rivera, and was first championed in America by Max Eastman, editor of *The Masses*, a socialist periodical mixing art and politics. In 1935, Trotsky declared that "politics and literature constitute in essence the contents of my personal life."[17] Trotsky's embrace of cosmopolitanism, his outsider status, his exile and persecution, also contributed to his appeal. As Bellow puts it, "we were, of course, the Outs; the Stalinists were the Ins. We alone in the U.S.A. knew what a bad lot they were."[18] Though greatly outnumbered by the Stalinists, the Trotskyists embraced their minority status, thought of themselves as smarter and more cultured than the Stalinists. "The Stalinists were middlebrow," remembered Irving Howe, at City College with Kristol, Nathan Glazer, and Daniel Bell. "The Trotskyists were highbrow, because they thought in the kind of terms that you had when *Partisan Review* started coming out [in 1934], the union of two avant gardes, a political avant garde and a cultural avant garde. We prided ourselves on reading Joyce and Thomas Mann and Proust, maybe not completely, but at least dipping in, whereas they were reading palookas like Howard Fast."[19] Prominent figures in the American Trotskyist movement were professors of philosophy, like James Burnham and Sidney Hook, witty and brilliant polemicists, like Max Shachtman, mixing, in Howe's phrase, "intellectual rigor and destructive quarrelsomeness."[20] To Burnham, *The History of the Russian Revolution* was distinguished by Trotsky's style, which "cannot be separated from his view of history." Trotskyists, in other words, cared about language and writing. "My closest friends and I were not . . . activists," Bellow recalls, "we were writers. . . . Through 'revolutionary politics' [the quotation marks are knowing, retrospective] we met the demands of the times for action. But what really mattered was the vital personal nourishment we took from Dostoyevsky or Herman Melville, from Dreiser and John Dos Passos and Faulkner."[21] In this admission, Bellow again resembles Wordsworth, who at a comparable age, and in a comparable period, that of the French Revolution, "skimmed, and sometimes read / With care the master pamphlets of the day" (Paine, Burke, Godwin), toured revolutionary Paris, at one point pocketing a stone from the Bastille, but did so "affecting more emotion than I felt," less moved by revolutionary sites than by a work of art, "the painted Magdalene of Le Brun, / A beauty exquisitely wrought."[22] Like Joseph in *Dangling Man*, who cites Plato, like young Wordsworth,

Bellow ultimately regarded politics "as an inferior activity." As Joseph admits, "I never enjoyed being a revolutionary." "No? Didn't you hate anyone?" "I hated, but I didn't enjoy" (pp. 100–101).

Abraham Bellow was scornful of his son's politics. When Bellow brought political friends home, Abraham gave them a hard time. One such friend was Albert Glotzer, Fred Glotzer's younger brother. Glotzer's Russian immigrant parents had been members of the Bund, and Albert recalls being taken as a child to socialist debates on Division Street at the Old Style Inn, opposite the entrance to Humboldt Park. At eight he was selling socialist literature on Division Street. At fifteen, in 1923, he joined the American Communist Party, founded in Chicago in 1919, quickly rising to prominence in its youth section. He then joined a Trotskyist faction of the party. By 1928 Trotskyism was a state crime in the Soviet Union and Glotzer's faction was expelled before the end of the year; in May 1929, its members formed a rival party, the Communist League of America (CLA), headquartered in New York.[23] Glotzer, at twenty, was named to the new party's National Committee, and two years later was sent to Europe on a fact-finding mission. Here he met with French and British Trotskyists before traveling to Turkey to meet with the exiled Trotsky himself. Glotzer spent six weeks with Trotsky, discussing the activities of the CLA and helping him with his correspondence (including letters to H. L. Mencken and Upton Sinclair). After returning to the United States, Glotzer met up with Trotsky two more times: in France in 1934 and then in 1937 at the Dewey Commission hearings in Mexico, where he acted as court reporter. Bellow saw a good deal of Glotzer after his return to Chicago in the mid-1930s, often with Glotzer's brother, Fred, or at political meetings.[24]

The Chicago Trotskyists were fierce factionalists, but their fierceness was mostly verbal or intellectual rather than physical. Stalinist fierceness was often physical. In an interview, Sydney Harris mocked the internecine wars and splits of the Trotskyists ("they wandered off into the fifth and sixth dimensions with Lovestoneites and Shachtmanites"),[25] but preferred their politics to those of the Stalinists. "In those days the Stalinists were a terribly brutal lot. They were like thugs. They'd go up and down Division Street and North Avenue and they'd break up the Socialist Party meetings, and they were really real hoodlums." Zita Samson (later Cogan), who lived on the corner of Kedzie and Le Moyne, near Eleanor Fox, and was a lifelong friend of Bellow's, remembered being visited at Tuley by "a party of three fellow travelers telling me I should stop seeing Bellow," because Bellow and his friends "were anti-Stalinist." Dropping or cutting politically incorrect friends or acquaintances was a matter of principle to many Communists; it was also party policy. The sociologist Seymour Martin Lipset, another City College Trotskyist, explains: "As far as the Communists were concerned the Trotskyists were not only traitors, they were fascists. They had a policy that no Communists were supposed to talk to a Trotskyist or debate them. They *could* talk to socialists"[26] (even though in Germany, according to Stalin, socialists were more dangerous than fascists). Sacrificing the personal to the political was a frequent theme in fiction of and about left politics in the period, as was the ineffectuality of Trotskyist types. In Lionel Trilling's *The Middle of the Journey* (1947), set in the mid-1930s, just after the Moscow Trials, the central character, John Laskell, a Trotskyist-sounding liberal ("we pretty much limit ourselves to ideas—and ideals. When we act, if we can call it action, it's only in a peripheral way"), describes the faces of more politically engaged friends: "both had that brooding blind look that is given by men to the abstractions they admire, in the belief that a lack of personal being is the mark of all great and admirable things."[27]

In *Dangling Man*, Joseph is enraged when a past party acquaintance refuses to speak to him. Revisiting an old hangout, "where, at almost any hour of the afternoon or evening, you could hear discussions of socialism, psychopathology, or the fate of European man," Joseph spots Jimmy Burns, whom he's barely seen "since the days when we had been Comrade Joe and Comrade Jim" (p. 20). In those days, Joseph recalls, Burns had a large-scale map of Chicago in his room, with pins in it: "he was preparing a guide for street-fighting, the day of the insurrection" (p. 23). Burns cuts Joseph: "he looked through me in the way which is, I suppose, officially prescribed for 'renegades'" (p. 20). Joseph, however, won't ignore Burns's slight, for reasons he details:

> Forbid one man to talk to another, forbid him to communicate with someone else, and you've forbidden him to think, because, as a great many writers will tell you, thought is a kind of communication. And his party doesn't want him to think, but to follow its discipline. So there you are. Because it's supposed to be a revolutionary party. That's what's offending me. When a man obeys an order like that he's helping to abolish freedom and begin tyranny (p. 21).

Joseph forces Burns to acknowledge him, which Burns does curtly, reluctantly. Joseph has made a scene, he explains to a companion, because "I haven't forgotten that I believed they were devoted to the service of some grand flapdoodle, the Race, *le genre humain*. Oh, yes, they were! By the time I got out, I realized that any hospital nurse did more with one bedpan for *le genre humain* than they did with their entire organization. It's odd to think that there was a time when to hear that would have filled me with horror" (p. 22).

That Trotskyists did little practical good was a charge leveled at Bellow and his friends from the left as well as the right. David Peltz was no Stalinist, no Communist of any sort, but he approved certain activities of the Stalinists. Always the most physically active and practical of Bellow's friends, as well as the most street, he saw the local Stalinists as engaged in the community, unlike the Trotskyists: "They [the Stalinists] formed a group, when people were being dispossessed, were being evicted from their apartments. Their furniture would be moved in the street, to the sidewalks, by sheriffs. There were a group of us—Bellow never belonged to that group, none of them [he means the Trotskyists] did. I joined in order to move the furniture back into the house after the sheriffs left. This was a band of people formed by the Communists. I was not a Communist but I engaged in the moving." That Bellow himself suspected the practical irrelevance of his politics is suggested by a letter of January 30, 1995, to Glotzer. "When Banowitz's bakers went on strike," he writes, of an incident in the early 1930s, "they chanted while picketing '6 cents! Union bread!—and Hands off China!' I was standing next to Banowitz whom I knew because my father sold him scrap for wood for the ovens and he said to me '6 cents, union bread maybe I could do it but what could I do about China?'" Bellow was also conscious of the dangers of toeing the line. "Every ideology at that age," he recalled of the 1930s, "presented itself to me as an orthodoxy; and there was something about radical orthodoxy that resembled [religious] orthodoxy in that it was enforced by people who insisted rigidly on the legitimacy of their political position. After all, being a Trotskyite was in a way like being a Jew. Although Trotsky denied that he was a Jew."[28] Political engagement threatened what Bellow believed one of his strengths as a writer: truth to particulars, truth through particulars, however complicating.

Bellow's view of Franklin Roosevelt illustrates this strength. To both Trotskyists and Stalinists, Roosevelt, for all his support from working people and the foreign-born ("it was bliss to hear FDR say that in this country we were all of us aliens"),[29] was an agent of capitalism; that was the line, even during the Popular Front (1934–39), in which Stalinists supported broad alliances on the left, adopting, in Bellow's words, a "temperate and apparently conciliatory" rhetoric. Bellow himself had few illusions about FDR, who was "no crusader, no enemy of entrenched privilege, 'no tribune of the people,'" and no intellectual. Though "a not ungrateful beneficiary"[30] of Roosevelt's policies, Bellow liked them "less and less as time went by." But even when most radical, early in his college years, he gave Roosevelt his due, acknowledging his appeal as politician and leader. This appeal, Bellow suggests, was a matter of touch or feel. Here is how "In the Days of Mr. Roosevelt" ends. Bellow describes being an undergraduate at the University of Chicago, "fully armored in skepticism, for Roosevelt was very smooth and one couldn't be careful enough. But under the armor I was nonetheless vulnerable." At nine o'clock one summer evening, Bellow walks east along the Chicago Midway, listening to Roosevelt's broadcast on the radios of parked cars:

> You could follow without missing a single word as you strolled by. You felt joined to these unknown drivers, men and women smoking their cigarettes in silence, not so much considering the President's words as affirming the rightness of his tone and taking assurance from it. You had some sense of the weight of troubles that made them so attentive, and of the ponderable fact, the one common element (Roosevelt), on which so many unknowns could agree. Just as memorable to me, perhaps, was to learn how long clover flowers could hold their color in the dusk.[31]

ONE OF THE PLACES Bellow might have been going that evening was the World's Fair, which was still open in the summer of 1933. The fair was located on the South Side of the city, in a narrow strip of shore along Lake Michigan, between 39th and 12th Streets. There David Peltz had a job pulling a rickshaw, while being pestered for whores by boozy tourists, and for boozy tourists by whores. Bellow's friendship with Peltz was the longest of his life, but was not always easy. Peltz was born a month after Bellow, on July 9, 1915; when they first met, walking home from Tuley in 1930 at the start of the school year, Peltz lived on Robey Street, a block or two from Cortez. He had four sisters, three younger and one older. His mother, like her sister, was a convert to Christianity, and his father was wild, an operator. Peltz was street from the start, of necessity. In 1925 his father escaped bankruptcy by fleeing Baltimore for Chicago. Previously he'd fled Europe, scabbing in a seaman's strike and jumping ship in New York. Escaping to Chicago did little for the Peltz family fortunes. After Peltz's first and only year at Tuley High School, his father couldn't pay the rent and the family moved apartments. This was pretty much the end of Peltz's formal education, though he kept up his Tuley friendships. He took on various jobs: helping in his father's pants-making shop (a "cut, make and trim" shop); lugging coal for Bellow's family; tending to Ben Freifeld; caddie-ing in summers in Winnetka.

Like Morris Selbst in Bellow's story "A Silver Dish" (1978), Peltz's father was "elemental," "digestive, circulatory, sexual," and strong, as was Peltz himself.[32] "Most of my life I was in superb physical condition," Peltz declared to me in an interview in 2008 when he was ninety-two. Yet he also admitted to "a lot of medical events." Here is a flavor of his talk: "I've had tumors excised, radiated. I've had one of the most dangerous tumors known, called the Merkle cell carcinoma. I have a tumor on my prostate. When your PSA reaches five, people get the prostate taken out. Well mine is 340 and I said, 'When I'm *sick*, I'll do something about it.' The doctors don't understand it." Bellow makes much of these sorts of medical miracles and of his friend's vitality in *Humboldt's Gift*. A character very much like Peltz, George Swiebel, teaches Charlie Citrine to cure neck pain by standing on his head, a technique Peltz learned in real life from a ballerina and one Bellow employed into his seventies. Other Swiebel remedies, originally Peltz remedies, are more extreme:

> Immediately after his gall-bladder operation [George] got out of bed and did fifty push-ups. . . . From this exertion, he got peritoni-tis and for two days we thought he was dying. But ailments seemed to inspire him, and he had his own cures for everything. Recently he told me, "I woke up day before yesterday and found a lump under my arm."
> "Did you go to the doctor?"
> "No. I tied it with dental floss. I tied it tight, tight, tight . . . "
> "What happened?"

"Yesterday when I examined it, it had swelled up to the size of an egg. Still I didn't call the doctor. To hell with that! I took more dental floss and tied it tight, tight, even tighter. And now it's cured, it's gone. You want to see?" (pp. 50–51).

Bellow draws on Peltz and his adventures not only in *Humboldt's Gift* and "A Silver Dish," where his name is Woody Selbst (Billy Seltzer in draft), but also in several unpublished works: "The Closer," a story about aluminum siding salesmen in Los Angeles (Peltz's job after failing as a Hollywood screenwriter, the start of what became a lucrative career as a contractor), and "Olduvai George," an unfinished novel the first fifty pages of which exist in draft.

From the beginning of their friendship Peltz offered Bellow advice about emotional as well as physical problems, including about his love life. He also kept Bellow informed, as George Swiebel keeps Charlie Citrine informed, "about criminals, whores, racing, the rackets, narcotics, politics, and Syndicate operations" (p. 41). It was Peltz who introduced Bellow to the Russian Baths on Division Street. And it was Peltz who was threatened there with a baseball bat, having stopped payment on a gambling debt, as does Charlie Citrine in *Humboldt's Gift*. The real-life debt was incurred at a poker game in the 1950s at Nelson Algren's apartment on Wabansia Street, in one of the city's Polish districts. Peltz met Algren in the WPA (Works Progress Administration), when he was writing for the Federal Theatre Project: "He was my kind of guy. We drank together. We went to the track together." Studs Terkel was in the game, as was William Friedkin, who would go on to direct *The French Connection* and *The Exorcist*. Algren thought the big winner, a guy who owned currency exchanges, was flashing cards to his associate, "Big Injun," employed to collect on bad checks. "They played out of each other's pockets," Algren told Peltz. "I want you to stop your check." Algren then left town on a freighter to China. As was mentioned in the introduction to this book, when the *Humboldt's Gift* version of the story was excerpted in *Playboy*, Peltz was outraged. He was saving it for a novel of his own, and Bellow had "given his word" that he wouldn't use it. It took Peltz a long time to forgive his friend, or to say he forgave him.

Peltz's initial attraction to Bellow derived from Bellow's knowledge of books. At sixteen, Peltz "fell into" *War and Peace*, discussing it with Bellow on long, exhilarating evenings in Humboldt Park; then he "went into" *Crime and Punishment*. Peltz loved Bellow but is hard on him; Bellow, through the character of George Swiebel, is hard back about Dave, but also loving:

> George with his brown, humanly comprehensive eyes is not stupid except when he proclaims his ideas. He does this loudly, fiercely. And then I only grin at him because I know how kindly he is. He takes care of his old parents, of his sisters, of his ex-wife and their grown children. He denounces eggheads, but he really loves culture. He spends whole days trying to read difficult books, knocking himself out. Not with great success. And when I introduce him to intellectuals . . . he shouts and baits them and talks dirty, his face gets red (p. 61).

Peltz's warmth and vigor, clear from adolescence and still obvious at ninety-five, combined with a streak of crudeness, as in the following description of how and when he and other boys of his era first had sex:

> In those days losing one's virginity had enormous male status. Almost all of my generation lied about it. The earlier you lost it the greater the status. My fear of entrapment brought on a late encounter at the age of eighteen for the cost of a dollar with a neighborhood hooker who was loving and who sandwiched my penis in the cleavage of her breasts almost blowing the top of my head off. Lasco [a Tuley friend] paid for it, needing support for his first encounter, with money pilfered from his mother's purse. Saul never discussed his feelings about sexuality only the dropping of some names. I don't have the slightest notion as to when he lost it.[33]

For Bellow as a "connoisseur of Chicago street talk," Peltz was a great resource. Nor is his language always coarse; sometimes it is lyrical, as when describing the *shvitz-bod* (steam bath), with its furnace rocks "molten white and red." In the Russian Baths, Peltz says, "you go to hell to get purified." Then you have a *plaitsa* (rubdown), "with eucalyptus leaves and pin oak leaves tied together into a brush, dunked in a bucket of soap and water, and lathered over the body." Though Charlie Citrine cannot always count on George Swiebel getting on with his intellectual friends, he often introduces him to them, as Bellow introduced Peltz to colleagues from the University of Chicago. When Hannah Arendt, who, in Bellow's words, thought her "peculiar gift in this life [was] to be the representative of German High Culture," came to Chicago, it was Peltz he chose to show her around.[34] Mischief may have played its part in the introduction, but Bellow may also have wanted to expose Arendt to something of the vitality of Chicago street life, which Peltz both knew and embodied. Peltz declined, nervous of Arendt and touchy about being presented as "a Chicago character." But Bellow valued Peltz, as he valued the street, and was careful to acknowledge his attraction to both. In an interview in 1980, when asked to describe his life in the 1930s, he begins with his reading, then his intellectual friends, then his knowledge of Chicago street types, including "the low-life . . . the tough guys . . . the boys training to be hoodlums"—neither Peltz nor Lasco, but people they knew, people Maury knew, people who tickled Bellow and whom he watched closely. "One of my baseball pals at Tuley High School," he told the interviewer, "became chief executioner for the Chicago mob when he grew up. Dave Yaris. Dead now so I can mention his name. We had no idea. He had a violent temper. A *very* violent temper. I never saw anybody's face turn as red as his, when he was frustrated, when somebody blocked him in the middle of a shot on the basketball court. He was transformed. He had this strange murderous seizure. But, of course, he soon recovered and went on with the game. . . . It was useful to him in his career later."[35]

BELLOW ENROLLED IN the University of Chicago on October 3, 1933, at eighteen.[36] His father "very unwillingly" agreed to pay the tuition fee of $300 a year ($100 for each of the year's three quarters, Autumn, Winter, and Spring). As Bellow explains:

> I was not doing a pre-med course, like so many of my high school classmates. Nor did I study chemistry. Nor law. Nor economics. My father couldn't readily explain to his friends just what I was doing at the university, and perhaps he resented the embarrassment I caused him. Most of my classmates knew exactly what they were here for; they plugged away at their biochemistry. Even the mathematicians thoroughly understood that it was wrong to dream away three hundred dollars in tuition at a time when the banks were tottering. Serious energetic students understood what sacrifices their families were making. Their outlook was practical.[37]

To support himself, Bellow took on Saturday jobs, at Woolworth's, at the windowshade section of Goldblatt's department store (previously he'd worked in the shoe section), and "other little jobs, anything I could get. I stuffed mailboxes for politicians when there was an election." These jobs earned him $3 a week, not quite enough for El fares and lunches at the Commons. There was no question of a scholarship: "I was mentally not steady enough,"[38] partly because he was still mourning Liza's death, perhaps also because of the strain of defying his father and brothers. Bellow was now open about his ambitions, always carrying a briefcase full of his stories and manuscripts: "In college I behaved as though my career was to be a writer, and that guided me. Not a career as a teacher or any other professional activity but as a writer."[39] On transferring to Northwestern University in 1935, Bellow was asked to fill out an admissions form. In answer to a question about "your reasons for desiring a college education, your reasons for entering the school which you have checked [Liberal Arts], and your reasons for believing you will be successful," he wrote: "I am pursuing a course which has dominated my life for ten years."[40] When teased or doubted in pursuit of this course, he bristled. As he told an interviewer: "I didn't feel like being intimidated by anybody. It got my dander up."[41]

Bellow was detached as a college student, partly for these reasons, partly because of the undergraduate program at the University of Chicago, which had been revised in 1930–31 by Robert M. Hutchins, its recently appointed president. Hutchins was thirty in 1929 when he came to the university. He was inaugurated as president just after the stock market crashed. A witty and attractive figure (to the sociologist Edward Shils, "the most handsome man I have ever seen"),[42] Hutchins was also forceful and impatient in pursuit of his goals. At the beginning of the Depression, the number of graduate and professional students at the University of Chicago numbered four times that of the undergraduates; from its inception in 1892, the university favored research. The radical restructuring Hutchins introduced, stressed compulsory year-long interdisciplinary courses.[43] The four-year degree Bellow embarked on as a freshman was divided into two parts: a "College" component, with required General Courses in the first two years, followed by more specialized or advanced courses offered to juniors and seniors by the departments. Students moved out of the college by passing examinations, and Hutchins made much of the fact that these examinations could be taken or retaken whenever a student wished, regardless of

course credits or attendance. The idea behind the College component, which Hutchins tried and failed to extend over all four years,
was to tailor undergraduate training to undergraduate needs. Before
Hutchins, many courses offered to undergraduates, only 2 percent of
whom would go on to do academic research, focused on the collection and description of data, rather than on a discussion of the ends to
which this data should be put. To Hutchins, and what Bellow called
Hutchins's "whippers-in,"[44] the philosopher-administrators Mortimer
Adler and Richard McKeon, metaphysics and the great books of Western culture offered the best way of fostering such discussion. Philosophy was preferred to empirical, fact-based disciplines partly in response
to the great crises of the period. As Hutchins and his followers saw it,
economics, sociology and political science, particular strengths of the
university, had done little to predict or prevent the Great Depression
and the rise of fascism in Europe. What was needed, they argued, was
the development of "intellectual virtues," the sort that would help students to determine for themselves what were just or proper codes of
conduct, laws, and social arrangements.[45]

In his first year, Bellow was required to take four courses each quarter: two yearlong General Courses (Biological Sciences and Social Sciences), a yearlong English course (Introduction to the Study of Poetry
in the Autumn, Introduction to the Study of Drama in the Winter, and
Shakespeare in the Spring), and a year of elementary French.[46] In the
second year, which he did not complete, he took three more yearlong
General Courses (Humanities, Physical Sciences, and Social Sciences
II), plus a single elective each quarter (Bellow chose an introductory
anthropology course in the Autumn and an introductory economics
course in the Winter, and withdrew from the university in the Spring).
As at Tuley, his marks were mediocre, exclusively Bs and Cs in his
examinations, mostly S (Satisfactory) in course reports.[47]

Though an uninspired student, Bellow approved "the spirit of
Hutchins in which the place was saturated," in particular the intoxicating illusion the General Courses offered that "if you met all the
requirements, you would graduate knowing everything there was to
know about the physical sciences, the biological sciences, humanities, and the social sciences. . . . There was a kind of crazy, cockeyed
arrogance in all this, which really appealed to young Jews from the
West Side." What did not appeal was the anonymity of large lecture
classes, with as many as four hundred students marching into large

lecture halls: "I got tired of this anonymity. I wanted a chance to distinguish myself. You took a comprehensive examination, and even if you got a good mark, you were still answering multiple-choice questions, you weren't being asked to write essays. I was in shallow waters here."[48] Among the lecturers Bellow remembers hearing were Professors Ferdinand Schevill, the American historian, Norman MacLean, from the English Department, and Thornton Wilder, a visiting professor brought in especially by Hutchins, who had been a classmate of his at Oberlin College. Bellow remembered Wilder as "very excitable, a pacer, and a very demonstrative orator." He was "the first real writer I'd had any contact with" ("real," here, meaning "of quality," "contact" meaning being part of a large lecture audience). "It was really lovely to listen to him," Bellow told an interviewer, "though I didn't know what the hell he was talking about. Really, it was beyond me." Gertrude Stein also lectured in the College when Bellow was there. Her lectures, too, were beyond him: "I didn't understand word two. Word one I may have understood, but by the time I got to the second, it was just no go."[49]

What Bellow did understand, in English lectures at least, often bored him. "It was just no go. I wasn't interested in English prosody and I didn't care about a caesura, and I didn't care about Venus Urania, as in Shelley's poetry."[50] He also didn't care for the way some lecturers "had eyes only for the glorious classical past, dismissing the contemporary. Only greatness need apply. Local boys and girls, swarming in the foreground, were ephemerists; high-and-mighty professors admitted no connection between James T. Farrell [author of the *Studs Lonigan* trilogy] and Sophocles."[51] In the Social Sciences, much of what Bellow was asked to read was "dreadful pedestrian stuff in political science and sociology." He was required to read Plato and Aristotle, "so I read Plato and Aristotle, and I enjoyed Plato a great deal and Aristotle was a little rougher for me" (Aristotle was "the going thing on campus," which counted against him. "I would naturally resist that"). In Winter Quarter 1935, he took Economics 201, a nonstarter: "I spent the whole term reading George Bernard Shaw. . . . I couldn't help it. I didn't crack a book." Speaking in general of his undergraduate experience at Chicago, Bellow concludes: "I was always just a little bit to the side, from whatever was going on. I would do it, but I didn't feel I was a part of it."[52] In a letter of June 3, 1984, to the widow of the social scientist Ithiel de Sola Pool, a contemporary of Bellow's at Chicago, he describes how different they were as students: "He *studied* his Aristotle and Sorel.

I merely read them. He was absorbed in his teachers. I only watched those teachers from my own angle." Among University of Chicago teachers, Bellow mentions Nathan Leites, an instructor in political science. Bellow "adored" Leites—though Leites teased him by calling him a *romancier*, "which was just a cut above *rentier*, another category with a jeer in it"—but "for his eccentricities, not his learning." In the letter to Pool's widow, he recalls the way Leites walked down 57th Street, "very fast while reading some thick foreign book, not slowing his pace while crossing busy Woodlawn Ave." In a letter of June 29, 1987, to the historian Roberta Wohlstetter, after reading of Leites's death in *The New York Times*, Bellow again writes affectionately of his oddity: "there was something in him I appreciated—an unwarmable coldness that he himself deplored." Bellow's angle is that of the novelist rather than the student. What he remembers of Professor Scott, of the English Department, is the tailcoat he wore to proctor final examinations, "making fun of the old-fashioned academic formality of his own youth." What he remembers of Mortimer Adler, who lectured on Aristotle, was that there was something absurd about him: "I had only to look at him, even as an undergraduate, to see that he had nothing useful to offer on the conduct of life. He lectured on Prudence, or Magnanimity. It was—well, tomfoolery."[53] "I was a very contrary undergraduate" is how Bellow describes himself in his 1976 Nobel Lecture. Though Walter Blair, who taught Bellow on both the Shakespeare and introductory poetry courses, claimed he thought him "outstanding" (in discussion sections, presumably), the marks he gave him on his course were "Satisfactory." What especially struck Blair was Bellow's manner: he didn't seem "a damned bit intimidated."[54]

This manner was deceptive. When not in class, Bellow spent "more hours than I could afford" playing pool on the second floor of Mandel Hall, where lectures for the General Courses were held. A would-be pool shark, he tried and failed to master the technique of reverse-English, and "my conscience grew more swollen and painful with every failure."[55] Nor was he completely comfortable with the role of bohemian *romancier*. In an undated notebook in the Regenstein, probably from the mid-1970s, later drawn on in the first of the 1977 Jefferson Lectures, Bellow offers an account of "the furnished rooms in which I lived" when a student in Hyde Park in the 1930s, including in boardinghouses on Kenwood Avenue and 57th Street, at the eastern edge of campus, and at Ellis Avenue and 56th Street, on the western edge:

the rooms were silent as a rule—abandoned by life and purpose—
that was what you felt. They were characteristically musty and sour,
the wallpaper paste had dried and sifted down in powder. . . . Wood-
boring insects were inside gnawing for years in a chair leg, making
a trail of fecal dust, cockroaches in the toilet, mice everywhere,
traces of innumerable roomers who smoked and ate and copulated
or were ill, or grieved or lost themselves in books. To be thoroughly
bohemian was best here and to accept your condition, your style of
life cheerfully, driving your cart and your plough over the bones
of the dead. As a bohemian you had strength, you stood for something, you took an attitude towards work or towards property. But if
you were not a bohemian at heart you might be depressed, you were
certain to suffer. The first day in one of these rooms was always
harrowing. I unpacked my books. They had the power to exorcise
fear and strangeness, or should have had it. I turned the large green
blotter to its clean side, if it had one, and arranged my manuscripts.[56]

In 1934, in the Spring Quarter of his freshman year, Bellow shared
the room on Ellis Avenue with an unnamed friend from Tuley.[57] The
room looked out over what was then the Home for Incurables and Bellow was fascinated by the ingenious wheelchairs, arm-propelled and
foot-propelled, passing outside: "I was absorbed by these contraptions
more than by the texts I should have been studying." When his roommate told him about the fate of an aunt, Dora Kaplan, the woman who
shot Lenin early in the 1920s, Bellow suspected that "knowing me to
be something of a Marxist," he "was warning me to sober up and stick
to my books."[58] As such instances suggest, Bellow was sensitive to concerns about the course he had set himself, at some level sharing them.
Nor was he impervious to the humiliations of poverty, the sort Joseph
resentfully records in *Dangling Man*, inflicted both by circumstances
("your condition, your style of life") and belittling relatives.

"I unpacked my books": for protection, reassurance. When threatened by guilt—for wasting time, while the family sacrificed to meet
university fees—books preserved a "delicious freedom." Instead of feeling guilty, "you could have wonderful discussions about remorse, drawing on Freud or on the class morality denounced by Marx and Engels.
You could talk of Balzac's ungrateful children on the make in Paris, of
Dostoyevsky's Raskolnikov, the student with the ax, or of the queer
bad boys of André Gide." "I *did* stick to books," Bellow recalls, "but

those were not the books connected with the courses I was taking."[59] More likely, they were books he'd heard of in the lounge in Wieboldt Hall, where a group of Modern Language students gathered, "rather interesting young men."[60] Among these young men Bellow mentions Paul Goodman, recently graduated from City College in New York, at work on a PhD in English, soon to become a prominent writer and public intellectual; Edouard Roditi, a twenty-three-year-old under-graduate, previously at Balliol College, Oxford, a French-born Ameri-can whose poems and translations had already appeared in *transition* and T. S. Eliot's *Criterion*; William Barrett, who started graduate work at City College at fifteen, received his PhD from Columbia at twenty-two, and was teaching at Chicago at twenty-three. When Isaac Rosen-feld arrived at the university in 1936, he befriended this group. Later, Harold Kaplan, studying French on a scholarship, would join in their discussions. All the Wieboldt Hall men went on to have distinguished careers in New York or further afield. When Rosenfeld moved to New York in 1942, with a small stipend to do graduate work in philosophy at NYU, or Bellow came to visit, which he frequently did from the late 1930s onward, the contacts they'd made at Wieboldt Hall helped to smooth their way, particularly among writers and editors at *Partisan Review*.[61]

The young men in Wieboldt Hall argued over André Gide, Proust, Joyce, T. S. Eliot, and Hemingway, none of whose writings, Bellow recalled, appeared in the College curriculum. "There were no courses of that sort offered on campus that *I* was eligible for. If you knew a lot of French you could read Proust in the French Department. I didn't know that much." In the university library and reading room, however, there were shelves of contemporary literary magazines: *transition*, *The Dial*, *The Little Review*, *The Times Literary Supplement*. The look of the uni-versity also helped. As Bellow puts it, "these modern books and authors were certified or accredited *physically* by the Quadrangles themselves, by the gothic gables and ornaments of the campus." The surrounding city, though not unliterary, was literary in ways too local or provincial for "Roditi and company." The Stockyards were nearby and everyone had read *The Jungle*, but Upton Sinclair was not discussed (nor, pre-sumably, were Theodore Dreiser or Sherwood Anderson). "We were concerned with modern civilization in its entirety, as seen by Freud, as described by Marx, Lenin, and Sorel, as presented by Cocteau, or sent up by the Surrealists and the postwar Dadaists."[62] These concerns were unique less in their intellectual seriousness than in their avant-garde and European character; everyone at the university was intellectually serious. As Rosenfeld puts it in "Life in Chicago," an article published in 1957 in *Commentary*, students at the University of Chicago, especially in the 1930s, "made up a fairly uniform body. Football was out, and with it went the usual rah-rah accessories of collegiate and fraternity life. Raccoon coats, pennants, beanies, megaphones and sloganized flivvers may have flourished in the twenties; but the thirties and forties . . . were lean and studious years, with students forming a self-conscious intellectual elite, newly introduced to Aristotle, Aquinas, and a revolutionary college program which gave great advantages to the bright and more industrious."[63]

In the summer of 1934, at the end of his freshman year, Bellow went on a road trip with Herb Passin, still a student at Marshall High School, an adventure like that of Harris's 1932 trip to New York to sell "Herbert Sanders." The two boys hopped a freight train heading for Canada. Bellow had just turned nineteen, Passin was seventeen, but had already bummed around on boxcars with Nelson Algren. They set off with $3 between them. In South Bend, Indiana, their train passed a Studebaker plant where the workers were on strike, yelling and cheering from the rooftops and the open windows. "We shouted and joked with them, rolling at about five miles an hour in summer warmth through the fresh June weeds." "It was very dangerous, very rough," Passin recalled, with armed police patrolling the rail yards and hardened and ragged hobos crowding into the boxcars.[64] In Detroit they were arrested on false charges and kept in jail overnight. At Canada, they were turned away at the border, lacking papers. Here they split up: Passin headed to New York City, Bellow sneaked into Canada at Niagara Falls. Once past the border, he headed straight for the Gameroffs in Lachine and Montreal, where he stayed a few weeks visiting with his cousins and aunts and uncles. After wiring Maury for money, he rode home by bus. Maury made him repay his fare by working as weighmaster at his coal yard, until he fired him for reading on the job. A version of this episode appears in Chapter 9 of *The Adventures of Augie March*, in which Augie is variously chased by police, molested by a hobo, and awed by the passing landscape, "the jointed spine of the train racing and swerving, the steels, rusts, bloodlike paints extended space after space in the sky, and then other existence, space after space" (p. 577).

Politics figured in Bellow's life at the University of Chicago rather as they had at Tuley. He went to meetings of the Spartacist Youth League, a Trotskyist organization, partly to meet girls; handed out leaflets; denounced the Stalinists of the YCL (Young Communist League), who dominated the American Student Union; and debated with liberals and socialists at meetings of the Young People's Socialist League (YPSL), defending the Trotskyist line. When he transferred to Northwestern University in September 1935, he became more active politically, perhaps because the administration and student body at Northwestern were conservative, certainly in comparison to staff and students at the University of Chicago. While at Northwestern, he wrote for *Soapbox*, published by the University of Chicago Socialist Club (Rosenfeld, Tarcov, and Reedy were among its editors), helped to found a comparable Socialist Club at his own university (Northwestern was predictably "shocked at the idea of radical politics on campus"),[65] and joined up with Sydney Harris in 1937 as associate editor of *The Beacon*, subtitled "Chicago's Liberal Magazine," writing political articles and book reviews and arguing with Harris in favor of a more radical line for the paper. At some point in 1936, according to an undated letter to Irving Halperin, he considered joining the Loyalists in Spain until he discovered "that I couldn't go anywhere because I had no papers." To get these papers, he learned, would involve "a good deal of legal work," which he couldn't afford. Abraham professed himself "perfectly willing that I should fight in Spain, but then he knew that I had no way of getting out of the country."[66] It was also at Northwestern, in his senior year, that Bellow took a job as a union organizer for the CIO (Congress of Industrial Organizations), presumably through Trotskyist contacts. "This was more than I could resist," he recalled in a letter of August 9, 1994, to Alvin Edelman: "My task was to sign up dishwashers and chambermaids for elections under the provisions of the Wagner Labor Relations Act. I was poaching on AF of L [American Federation of Labor] territory and the hoodlums of the hotels and restaurants local were chasing me around the city with intent to do physical harm. Thus my straight-A average was disfigured by a 'C' in a required course."[67] This episode in Bellow's life is fictionalized in Chapter 13 of *The Adventures of Augie March*, where there is little to choose from between corrupt bosses and corrupt union officials and where Augie barely escapes a vicious beating. "I just didn't have the calling to be a union man or in politics," he concludes. "It wasn't what I was meant to be" (p. 739).

BELLOW'S ABRUPT WITHDRAWAL from the University of Chicago in the spring of 1935 came about as the result of an accident at Carroll Coal. "For years we all worked to pay it off," Bellow recalled in an interview of February 9, 1970, in *Time* magazine, his only published reference to the accident. According to James Atlas, a truck driver was killed when unloading a shipment of coal, the company's insurance policy had lapsed, Bellow's brother Sam having forgotten to renew it, and Abraham was forced to pay costs, which meant he couldn't come up with Bellow's university fees. Because money was now especially tight in the family, Bellow was enlisted to work on the scales at Carroll Coal. Maury's son, Joel Bellows, remembers hearing a different version of the accident, both from Bellow and from Maury: one of Carroll Coal's trucks ran over a little boy, and the lack of insurance was Abraham's fault, the result of a conscious decision not to renew the policy. For Joel, invariably hard on his grandfather, the "feature event" in the story was Abraham's reaction: "he takes to his bed because of this thing and lays in bed for days, crying, weeping, trying to work through so that he was not the perp, the one responsible for what happened." By June, Bellow had found the money to attend summer school at the University of Wisconsin at Madison, where he took three English courses, earning two As and a B. That autumn he returned to Chicago and enrolled as a junior at Northwestern. "I suppose I wanted attention" is how he explained the decision not to return to the University of Chicago.[68]

The attention Bellow received at Northwestern had several sources: he was Jewish, unlike 95 percent of the student population (26 percent of the student population at the University of Chicago was Jewish),[69] he was politically radical, and he was an aspiring writer. That he was very smart and good-looking, "though shy and introverted," according to Helen Jaffe, a fellow student, also attracted notice.[70] Northwestern was founded by Methodists in 1851, almost four decades before the University of Chicago. Evanston, the North Shore suburban town where it is located, is ten miles from downtown Chicago, and nothing at all like Hyde Park or Humboldt Park. Its main street, Sheridan Road, winds through the university's pretty lakeside campus, past spacious Victorian and turn-of-the-century mansions with wide manicured lawns. Staid, affluent, and overwhelmingly Republican, Evanston is where attractive but not so bright Katrina Goliger lives, rich mistress of Victor Wulpy in "What Kind of a Day Did You Have?" It is also the home of rich Mrs. Skogland in "A Silver Dish," where it is described by Bellow as "High Episcopal Christian Science Women's Temperance Evanston" (p. 24). In *Augie March*, Mr. and Mrs. Renling live in Evanston, where they own an upmarket sporting goods store, selling hunting, shooting, yachting, and tennis equipment to "country-club sports and university students" (p. 531). The first question Mr. Renling asks Augie when interviewing him for a job is: "*Jehudim?*" Augie answers: "Yes. I guess." To which Renling replies: "Well, out there on the North Shore they don't like Jews." Then, "brimming frostily with a smile," he adds, "they like hardly anybody" (p. 530). Augie gets the job, is decked out in handsome tweeds, and succumbs to the allure of WASP style: "It was social enthusiasm that moved in me, smartness, clotheshorseyness. The way a pair of tight Argyle socks showed in the crossing of legs, a match to the bow tie settled on a Princeton collar, took me in the heart with enormous power and hunger. I was given over to it" (p. 535). Bellow's clothes at Northwestern, many from Marshall Field, were more formal than those of his fellow students, but they didn't fit, being hand-me-downs from Maury.[71]

Bellow began his first year at Northwestern commuting from Hyde Park, then from his father and Fannie's one-bedroom apartment at 3434 Evergreen Street.[72] Eventually he moved into a room in a boardinghouse on Gaffield Place, a quiet street just blocks from the center of campus. In university records, under "Activities," for junior year he lists "*Daily* [for *The Daily Northwestern*] reporter," though he wrote only occasionally for the paper,[73] and for senior year, "A.S.U." (for American Student Union). Under "Rebates," for junior year he lists "Odd Jobs," averaging ten hours per week, amounting to $100 for the year; for senior year "Ss Ptime" (Sales Part-time), averaging eight hours per week, amounting to $80. In a pseudonymous profile of the university published in the December 1936 issue of *Soapbox*, Bellow disparages his fellow students as bound "for bond houses, insurance companies, Dad's business, storm troops; and perhaps a few for the breadlines. Only food for the suburbs, first nights, bridge clubs, Daughters of the Eastern Star [affiliated to the Masons], writers of new Red Networks."[74] *Red Network, A Who's Who and Handbook of Radicalism for Patriots* (1934) was the work of Mrs. Elizabeth Dilling, an Evanston resident and virulent anti-Communist. According to Mrs. Dilling, Marxism and "Jewry" were synonymous, and the president of Northwestern, Walter Dill Scott, was "on the payrolls of Moscow." The ludicrousness of President Scott as Communist is Bellow's starting point in the *Soapbox* article, entitled "This Is the Way We Go to School." The only reason Scott seems liberal ("Red" to Mrs. Dilling) is that he has nothing radical to resist: "Whenever any objector arises, the inmates of the Greek Houses, the cheerers, the swaggerlads, the boys who put things over, attend to his complaints. . . . Anyone who rashly aspires, in the first bloom of optimism, to raise his voice against the food, the social order, the Republican Party, or God is quickly overhung intellectually and morally by the thick, inert, dispiriting fog that the North Shore brews. Evanston, the home of Northwestern, is not only intellectually flatchested, but holds it a virtue."

Bellow stood out. Being in a minority appealed, made his radicalism more meaningful; his intellectual ambition was noticed and approved by his professors.[75] In the *Soapbox* piece, Bellow declared that "on the whole the faculty is quite hopeless," "the students do not require fine teachers; the university does not require students who require fine teachers." In reality, as he knew from experience, Northwestern had a number of fine teachers, professors of distinction. By the time he wrote the *Soapbox* piece he had established good relations with several of them, both in the English Department and in the Department of Sociology and Anthropology, where he also found a small pocket of fellow radicals. The most important of the literature teachers were Edward B. Hungerford and John T. Frederick, both of whom taught courses in writing. Hungerford, a Shakespeare scholar, "confessed he couldn't handle me," Bellow later recalled, but they remained lifelong friends; he was, Bellow remembered, "a loveable man who did me a great deal of good."[76] Frederick, a novelist as well as a scholar, whose courses mostly ran in the journalism school, never taught Bellow in a class, but took an interest in his fiction, at least once meeting him in a restaurant in downtown Evanston to discuss it. In the autumn of 1938, after Bellow left the university, Frederick got him a job with the WPA, at the Illinois Branch of the Federal Writers' Project. Bellow also got on well with Moody Prior, whose Elizabethan drama course he took. Northwestern did not have the prestige of the University of Chicago—its academic rank was solid rather than outstanding—but Bellow thrived there. In his first or junior year, he took eight English courses, plus French and Geology. In his senior year he took five courses in Anthropology, one in Zoology, and three in History. In all but one of his courses in

English and Anthropology he received A grades, the exception being a first semester English course, for which he received a B. His marks in History and French were As and Bs. His only Cs were in Zoology and Geology.

And he was writing stories. According to Helen Jaffe, these were mostly character sketches, "generally plotless." Only one of them has survived, his first to be published and the earliest example we have of his fiction (there is no manuscript material from his university or high school years). "The Hell It Can't!," a story of 1,300 words, appeared in *The Daily Northwestern* on February 19, 1936, having been awarded third prize in a "Campus in Print" contest from the previous semester (John T. Frederick was one of the contest's three faculty judges). The story takes its title from the Sinclair Lewis novel *It Can't Happen Here*, published on October 21, 1935. At the end of the second chapter of the novel the following exchange occurs, involving Mr. Falck, the Episcopal reverend in a small Vermont town, Doremus Jessup, editor-proprietor of the town's newspaper, and several local businessmen much exercised by "Jew Communists and Jew financiers plotting together to control the country": "'Didn't Hitler save Germany from the Red Plague of Marxism? I got cousins there. I *know*!'" "'Hm,' said Doremus, as often Doremus did say it. 'Cure the evils of Democracy by the evils of Fascism! Funny therapeutics.'" This exchange prompts the wealthiest of the businessmen to say that it "might be a good thing to have a strong man in the saddle, but—it just can't happen here in America." The chapter ends: "And it seemed to Doremus that the softly moving lips of the Reverend Mr. Falck were framing, 'The hell it can't!'"[77]

Bellow's story takes place in America, but a largely unspecified America (a mention of the Chicago Cubs is the sole clue to its setting). The absence of particulars is Kafkaesque, as is the utter helplessness of its protagonist, Henry Howland, in the face of state-sanctioned lawlessness. The style is spare, with little verbal flourish. America is at war in Europe and Henry has somehow evaded conscription. The story begins when he is discovered, awakened in the middle of the night, marched through town by thuggish citizen-vigilantes, and brought to "a low room with a narrow brown-boarded ceiling." Here his captors beat him "steadily, grimly, taking turns." Henry insists he is no coward, which makes his refusal to go to war a matter of principle, though the principle in question is never identified. All we know of the war itself is that it is happening in Europe. The story ends with Henry inspecting his wounds, "the tenuous red tracks" of a whipping. The last sentence reads: "He was five blocks from home," and the message is "the hell it can't!" A state that behaves as this one does, allowing resisters to be beaten with impunity, whipping its citizens literally, also figuratively, into a patriotic or nationalist frenzy like that of the rioting townsfolk in Babel's "The Story of My Dovecote" ("shop windows and walls plastered with signs . . . FIGHT. DON'T BE AN ENEMY AT HOME"), is as bad as the states it opposes, a view easier to credit when the crimes and provocations of the enemy are unspecified. At the date the story was written, Germany was steadily rearming, Hitler having repudiated the disarmament clauses of the Versailles Treaty and introduced conscription in March 1935, the anti-Jewish Nuremberg Laws had been announced in September of the same year, and Mussolini had invaded Ethiopia in October. As the poet Delmore Schwartz, soon to become Bellow's friend, put it, looking back on these years, "the slow, loud, ticking imminence of a new war" shadowed everything.[78] The implicit line Bellow's story takes on this new war is Trotsky's, that there is little to choose from between the two sides. "A modern war between the great powers does not signify a conflict between democracy and fascism," Trotsky wrote in his June 1934 manifesto, "War and the Fourth International," "but a struggle of two imperialisms for the redivision of the world."[79] The story's acceptance of this view is easier to credit in 1936, even in 1944, when its influence is felt in *Dangling Man*, than it would be when the full scale of Nazi atrocities was clear, though Bellow himself admits "we knew what happened to the Jews in Europe: we knew and we didn't know. Somehow it didn't come through."[80]

It was not just Trotskyists, of course, who resisted the coming war. Many liberals, as well as pacifists and old-line isolationists did so, as did Norman Thomas, the spokesman for American socialism. Bellow was not alone at Northwestern in his antiwar views, or on other issues. The closest of his friends at the university was Julian Behrstock, literary editor of *The Daily Northwestern*. Behrstock came from a similar Chicago background to Bellow's, went on to have a distinguished career at UNESCO in Paris, and remained Bellow's friend and correspondent throughout his life. He was political at the university, active in the ASU, as was his older brother, Arthur, a graduate student in English. As an undergraduate, Arthur, too, had also been literary editor of *The Daily Northwestern*. Before returning as a graduate student in 1936, when Bellow and Julian were seniors, he traveled to the Soviet Union, taking a job as a reporter on the *Moscow Daily News*. Neither Behrstock brother, according to Julian, was a Communist, though both were subsequently pursued by investigative bodies, Arthur by Senator James Eastland's Internal Security Subcommittee, Julian by Joseph McCarthy and the House Un-American Activities Committee.[81]

Bellow was a friend of both Behrstocks and is likely to have known, or known about, their close friend, Jack Harris (né Herscovitz), an anthropology major at Northwestern who went on to Columbia University to do graduate work in 1935. In the war, Harris was a secret agent with the OSS (Office of Strategic Services), precursor to the CIA.[82] Like the Behrstocks, he was pursued by anti-Communist investigators. In 1952 he was called to testify before Senator Pat McCarran of the Internal Security Subcommittee. He repeatedly invoked the Fifth Amendment, the constitutional guarantee against self-incrimination, as had the Behrstocks, to protect friends and associates.[83] As early as 1943, Harris was under investigation by J. Edgar Hoover, and the first of his three FBI files, dated July 27, 1943, sheds interesting light on political attitudes at Northwestern in Bellow's undergraduate years.[84] According to the testimony of Professor Bergen Evans of the English Department, Harris "was a close friend of JULIAN and ARTHUR BEHRSTOCK, Jewish students, who attended Northwestern University. EVANS stated that JULIAN BEHRSTOCK was a leader of the American Student Union, an organization that flourished on the campus of Northwestern University during the early 1930's. . . . He described this organization as being made up of a group of students, who were of a poor class, some of whom were 'crackpots,' and all of whom did not have a chance of getting anywhere socially with the social click [*sic*] on the campus. He said the group used to delight in doing things that would shock the townspeople of Evanston, as well as the Chicago Tribune." Though Harris "never at any time said anything to EVANS in any way indicating any affiliation with the Communist Party," and though Evans "stated that he personally did not understand exactly what a Communist was," he (Evans) "personally believed that of all the individuals he ever knew, he felt that HARRIS would be the most likely one to be a Communist."

Evans's account of the "crackpot" nature of the Behrstocks and the American Student Union doubtless owed something to a campus-wide dispute in Bellow's senior year, one Bellow reported on, involving Julian Behrstock and Northwestern's Department of Naval Science and Tactics (established in 1919 to protect Lake Michigan from invasion). The department had banned Navy students from participating in what it called "communistic discussion," principally a war symposium. In March 1937, Julian Behrstock, at the time editorial chairman of *The Daily Northwestern*, wrote an article criticizing the ban. When ordered to retract the article and print a statement vindicating the Navy, Behrstock resigned, as did the entire editorial board. Bellow wrote about the episode in an article in the very first issue of *The Beacon*, published in April 1937. Though listed on the magazine's masthead as "S. G. Bellow," the article appeared under his *Soapbox* pseudonym, John Paul (an attack on the anti–New Deal journalist Westbrook Pegler in the same issue was written by "Herbert Sanders," the hero of Harris's novel). The article was entitled "Northwestern Is a Prison" and is full of undergraduate indignation. After the editorial board of the *Daily* resigned, what Bellow calls "an intrepid but small band of professors voted to declare Navy credits invalid in the Liberal Arts school." Their motion was defeated, but the administration, fearing that the conflict "would become a matter of national interest," capitulated, admitting that Behrstock "had every right to protest against censorship." The article ends with a smack at Northwestern. "There is no doubt," Bellow writes, "that the university intends to keep a careful eye on him. He is too close to the campus radicals. He began his term with an abortive campaign for Norman Thomas; abortive because the University would have none of it." Now, the article concludes, Behrstock "has another chance. More properly speaking, he is paroled. For Northwestern is in this respect an intellectual prison."

The Beacon was short-lived, lasting less than a year. Its raison d'être is explained in "A Declaration of Policy," a leader immediately preceding Bellow's article. In it the editors describe the magazine as "a response to the thousands of people in Chicago and the middle-west who until now have had no medium for the expression of their liberal and progressive activities." *The Beacon* "will give a voice and an audience to such activities," including those of "student groups, labor unions, liberal organizations, church groups working for peace." It belongs to no faction: "The Communists may call us 'Trotskyites'; the Socialists may call us 'Stalinites'; Mr. Hearst will look at the cover and call us 'reds.' We are none of these." Harris described the monthly as "like the *Nation* or the *New Republic*," in form as well as content, with a first half devoted to politics and commentary, and a second half to books and the arts. He found financial backers for the magazine and persuaded well-known public figures to write for it, including Norman Thomas, James T. Farrell, and Paul Douglas (later senator of Illinois).[85] Other contributors included Isaac Rosenfeld and Arthur Behrstock. *The Beacon* folded when it lost its funding. As Harris explains, "in '38 there was a very hard bump, which meant nothing to people like us who were on salaries but a couple of men who were supporting the magazine got very nervous. . . . They pulled their horns in and the magazine just folded."

Bellow had already left, quitting *The Beacon* in the autumn of 1937, perhaps for political reasons, perhaps because he was no longer in Chicago, having enrolled as a graduate student in anthropology at the University of Wisconsin at Madison. A political motive is suggested by an undated letter he wrote to James T. Farrell earlier in 1937, presumably in his capacity as literary editor. Bellow had not yet met Farrell, but admired his writing, defending the novel *A World I Never Made* in a review in the same April 1937 issue as "Northwestern Is a Prison" (the review appeared under the byline "Saul Gordon Bellow").[86] Farrell was to become an influential supporter of Bellow, as well as an influence on his writing. For some time Bellow had been pestering Al Glotzer to arrange an introduction. In his 1937 letter, he asks Farrell if he thinks *The Beacon* serves a useful function. If the answer is yes, "I for my part will undertake a long narrative of the whole venture and try to explain my position on it." He then distances himself from Harris, whom he describes as "a shrewd, opportunistic bastard." Bellow hopes to move Harris to the left by "load[ing] the magazine with Bolshevik writers of national reputation," the sort too celebrated for Harris to reject. For Harris, the magazine's fortunes take precedence over politics. Though the Stalinists "pronounced the magazine anathema," the Popular Front strategy of broad alliances meant that as "the liberals swarm around us . . . so do Broder's [*sic*] minions flock to the liberals" (Earl Browder was chairman of the Communist Party). A number of organizations affiliated with, or infiltrated by, Communist Party members, have asked for advertising space, "which Harris freely, even prodigally gives." Bellow suspects he may one day give space to openly Stalinist organizations: "Harris thinks nothing of assassinating a scruple or knifing a principle if thereby he can profit."

IN HIS TESTIMONY to the FBI, Bergen Evans admits that he did not know Jack Harris well, recommending that the agency speak to Melville J. Herskovits, professor of anthropology at Northwestern, under whom Harris had studied. Harris had listed Herskovits as a referee in his application for a position with the OSS. In the FBI report, Herskovits is described as "sponsor for the National Federation for Constitutional Liberties, the North American Committee to Aid Spanish Democracy, and the American League Against War and Fascism, all of which are reported to be Communist Front organizations." "In view of this fact," it concludes, "Professor HERSKOVITS was not interviewed." Of all Bellow's university teachers, Herskovits (1895–1963) was the most influential, both in his field and with Bellow himself. Like Bellow, he came from Jewish immigrant parents. His father, described by his biographer as "a clothing merchant," came from Hungary, his mother from Germany.[87] The family was middle-class and Herskovits grew up in medium-size towns and cities in the Midwest, most with relatively small Jewish populations. Though his parents sent him to Hebrew school and he briefly considered studying for the rabbinate, the family celebrated Christian as well as Jewish holidays. From the start, questions of difference and identity—cultural, social, national, racial—preoccupied Herskovits, precisely the questions that drew him, as they were to draw Bellow, to anthropology.

Herskovits received his undergraduate degree from the University of Chicago. He then moved to New York for graduate study, first at the New School for Social Research, then at Columbia. Both professionally and personally, he was on the left. As a social scientist, he opposed biological determinism, laissez-faire economic theory, and hierarchies of race, gender, and culture. In politics, he was briefly a member of the IWW (Industrial Workers of the World), writing in defense of union activism and attacking the "staunch, unerring stupidity" of the Republican Party.[88] Bellow may first have encountered him in the pages of Mencken's *American Mercury*, where he wrote articles mocking a range of middle-class pieties. At Columbia, Herskovits studied under Franz Boas, at the suggestion of two of his New School professors, Thorstein Veblen and Alexander Goldenweiser. Like Herskovits and other pioneers of modern anthropology, including Emile Durkheim, Lucien Lévy-Bruhl, Marcel Mauss, Edward Sapir, and Robert Lowie, Boas was Jewish. Chief among the prevailing notions and practices of traditional or nineteenth-century anthropology Boas questioned were the supposed interdependence of race, language, and culture, the evolution and ranking of races ("a race is commonly described as the lower," Boas wrote, "the more fundamentally it differs from our own"),[89] and the "scientific" basis of racial superiority, in particular that provided by "anthropometry," a subfield of physical anthropology that distinguished between races by measuring visible traits or "phenotypes" (for example, skull or brain shape and size). According to Herskovits's biographer, Jerry Gershenhorn, three factors influenced Boas's attacks on mainstream anthropology: "his liberal philosophy, his strict attachment to scientific accuracy, and, perhaps most important, his Jewish identity," factors that also underlay his identification with the plight of African Americans.[90]

After lecturing in anthropology at Columbia (where Zora Neale Hurston was one of his assistants) and at Howard University, in Washington, D.C., Herskovits moved to Northwestern in 1927 as the sole anthropologist in the Department of Sociology. He was one of only two professors at the university of Jewish background (the other was an economic historian, William Jaffe). Like Bellow, Herskovits thrived at Northwestern, staying there for the rest of his career. In 1929 he convinced the university to rename the Sociology Department the Department of Sociology and Anthropology, but it was not until 1938, a year after Bellow left Northwestern, that a separate Department of Anthropology was established at the university, with Herskovits as its chair. Herskovits's book *The American Negro: A Study in Racial Crossing* (1928) established him as an authority not just on the relations between African culture and African American culture, but on the interrelation of cultures in general, a new field of study in anthropology. In addition, he was seen by many American anthropologists, as one recent authority puts it, as "the founder of African studies in this country."[91] Among the courses Bellow took in anthropology as a senior were "The Races of Man," "Primitive Social Organization," and "Primitive Art" (he skipped "Primitive Economics"). At the time, Herskovits was at work on *The Myth of the Negro Past* (1941), a pioneering text in African American studies. The myth exposed by the book was that the "Negro" had no past. Through patient field study in the mid-1930s in the West African kingdom of Dahomey, Herskovits exposed this myth, revealing the cultural continuity of black Africans and black Americans.[92]

Herskovits was a charismatic lecturer and a conscientious teacher and mentor, adept at finding his students scholarships and places in graduate school. In an interview in 2008, Jack Harris remembered him as "very generous and kind," though also possessed of "a tremendous ego. . . . I did not think less of him for it."[93] Herskovits could be demanding and possessive, and his "close attention to the work of his students was viewed by some as meddling paternalism."[94] His relations with Bellow were friendly, though with moments of irritation on both sides.[95] Bellow's settled ambition was to write, but he had also to consider ways of supporting himself (or to postpone having to support himself). One such way was to go to graduate school. When he approached the chairman of the Northwestern English Department, William Frank Bryan, a specialist in Old and Middle English, about doing graduate work in English, he was told: "You've got a very good record, but I wouldn't recommend that you study English. You weren't born to it." Getting a job, being accepted by the students, would be difficult. Perhaps he should consider anthropology. Bellow described this moment as "one of my earlier significant encounters with this view that because I was not born to an English-speaking family I had no business in that line of work. I was told that. So I accepted a fellowship in anthropology at the University of Wisconsin." As Bellow told an interviewer, Bryan "did me a great favor. My secret reaction was 'Well, the hell with you,' as I walked out."[96] The encounter produced a lifelong antipathy, mild but real, to English Departments and English Department types, including Jewish English Department types.[97]

It was Herskovits who arranged the fellowship at Wisconsin.[98] In a letter of reference, he described Bellow as hoping to make "a study of acculturation among the French Canadians whom he knows intimately, having lived the earlier years of his life in a French Canadian town." Wisconsin was the perfect place for such a study: "I don't know where he could be better prepared." Herskovits was fulsome in praise of Bellow in his references: he was "a first rate student," "unusually mature in his approach to problems which require originality of attack," a writer of "unusual ability"; in addition, he was "a pleasant person. He seems to make friends readily and to hold them."[99] Wisconsin had several advantages. It was close to Chicago, now the site of serious romantic as well as family ties, as we shall see; Isaac Rosenfeld would be there as a junior transfer student from the University of Chicago (whether he or Bellow applied first, or whether they applied together, is unremembered), and Herskovits's old teacher, Alexander Goldenweiser, late of the New

School, was to be visiting professor of anthropology for 1937–38. Bellow and Rosenfeld may have roomed together for a period at Wisconsin, at 112 South Mills Street, a twenty-minute walk south from campus.[100] In letters to Oscar Tarcov, Bellow reported on his studies and on how he and Rosenfeld were getting on. Tarcov was himself considering studying anthropology and Bellow was encouraging, in a letter postmarked October 2, 1937: "It's a hell of a lot better than the English department. And if you are not going to train yourself in a money-making technique you could choose no better field. It is the liveliest, by far, of all the social sciences." Bellow calls anthropology "the best discipline, the one that will aid you most," by which he means as a writer. Its only drawbacks are "prehistory and physical anthropology and parts of descriptive anthropology. . . . Necessary implements, the tools of social philosophy. With a little effort and application you can brush them out of the way. Moreover, if you are good at rationalizing, you can find certain charms in even the tools."

In the same letter, Bellow offers an account of his Chicago leave-taking. "There was an awful blowout before I left," he reports; Abraham "started giving me a Polonius," in the process damning "all the things I stood for, which was the equivalent of damning me also." Arthur Behrstock was visiting, "and no sooner did the old man discover Art had been in Russia than he withered him with arguments and with insults." Once Behrstock left, Bellow "blew up," telling Abraham what he thought of his advice, vowing "to live as I saw fit." This speech he delivered "without faltering, and I didn't do it in subdued terms. . . . The coalbins resounded with my shouts and imprecations, till the old man as a defense measure decided that he was needed somewhere and swam off into the gloom." Money was involved in the argument. Bellow declared "that if he didn't want to give me his measly allowance in Madison, I would as lief stay in Chicago"; there he would get a job, marry, "and live independent of the family forever more." According to Bellow's brother Sam, Abraham was "heartbroken because I have not written to him. Did he expect a manifesto of love after such a clash?" Sam encouraged Bellow to get in touch, which Bellow says he will do. "But what have I to say to him [Abraham]. . . . To him I am a perverse child growing into manhood with no prospects of bourgeois ambitions, utterly unequipped to meet the world (he is wrong, not unequipped but unwilling)." Then the letter calms down and Bellow describes his family as "good folk, when they are not neurotic." "What, after all, can we expect," he asks Tarcov. "Such conflicts must come if we are to honestly follow out the concepts we learn or teach ourselves."

BELLOW'S INITIAL IMPRESSIONS of Wisconsin were positive. The classes he mentions in the letter to Tarcov are a seminar in advanced social psychology "with the great Kimball Young" (a sociologist, the grandson of Brigham Young), with readings from Durkheim, Baldwin, Cooley, Dewey, Mead, Thomas, and others (according to the university course catalogue); a philosophy class "with friend Vivas, about whom Isaac will be delighted to write you" (this was "Philosophy of the Arts," taught by Eliseo Vivas); a course in European prehistory (taught by Charlotte Gower, an assistant professor); and a course on classical economists ("Smith, Ricardo, Mill and their contemporaries").[101] The only course not mentioned was "Anthropological Problems," taught by Goldenweiser, an introduction to "current anthropological literature and methods." Goldenweiser, Bellow's advisor, especially impressed: "Even Isaac is completely won by the man. A perfect cosmopolite, a perfect intellect. He knows as much Picasso as he does Tshimshian religion, he knows Mozart as well as Bastian, and Thomism as well as Polynesia. You ought to see the books that line his shelves. Next to Kroeber stands Sidney Hook, and Lenin, and of course many of Trotsky's pamphlets. . . . He is a piano virtuoso, an esthetician, a Bolshevik, a deeply cultured man." When Tarcov suggested a visit to Madison, Bellow, in a letter postmarked November 8, 1937, encouraged him to come during the week; on a weekend, "you will have no opportunity to see our pets perform" (he means Goldenweiser and Vivas). Goldenweiser was a big drinker and bon vivant and enjoyed entertaining students (according to Atlas, he had come to Wisconsin after being dismissed from Columbia "for various sexual misdemeanors").[102] In a letter of May 31, 1989, to T. Douglas Price, himself a professor of anthropology at Wisconsin, Bellow recalled "many a drunken party with Goldenweiser, Charlotte Gower, [Morris] Swadesh, the linguist (we shared three small rooms in the house of a railroader's widow), and Eliseo Vivas, the philosopher, and Isaac Rosenfeld, one of Vivas's students." Tarcov was not the only Chicago friend to visit. Ithiel Pool came through town "on one of his political trips (4th International business)," bunking in Bellow's room.[103] Money was tight at Wisconsin and Bellow applied for an NYA (National Youth Administration) part-time job, as an assistant either to Swadesh, who had a research appointment in the department, or to Charlotte Gower, who was at work on a study of New Glarus, a Wisconsin village that retained many of the customs of its Swiss namesake.[104]

The first months at Wisconsin went well. Rosenfeld arrived a few weeks before Bellow and found a room near campus, at 1314 St. James Court, though he seems not to have stayed there long (by September 19 he was writing to Tarcov from 11 North Mills Street, nearby). "There is a loveliness, wistfulness here," Rosenfeld reported in the letter. Later, on September 25, he writes that "we are not antagonizing each other—or, considering his [Bellow's] far more gentle nervous organization, let me say that I am not antagonizing him." "The first days of the term were warm and hazy," Bellow remembered. "We went canoeing on Lake Mendota. I capsized the canoe—Isaac luckily was still on the dock and helped me up the wooden ladder." Back inside Rosenfeld's room, Bellow wrapped himself in a towel, "and we began to talk." It was Indian summer, "beautiful and somnolent," and the room was "filled with sunlight." What the two friends talked about was neither philosophy nor anthropology but literature. "We went from Shakespeare to Dickens to Kafka, from Tolstoy to Isaac Babel, from Balzac to Proust to Malraux. We were big on Theodore Dreiser, Hemingway, Dos Passos, Thomas Wolfe and Faulkner. Delmore Schwartz's 'In Dreams Begin Responsibilities' [published in 1937 in *Partisan Review*] I considered then to be a masterpiece."[105]

The two friends were never to be closer, happy, as Steven Zipperstein puts it, to be "outside the reach, finally, of both parental homes."[106] They wrote poems and playlets together, traded jokes and literary schemes and ambitions. "Saul and I have batted the old surrealist ball around quite a bit," wrote Rosenfeld to Tarcov. In this period, perhaps on a visit from Tarcov, the friends worked on his surrealist play "Twin Bananas," which they later performed in the lobby of the Harper Library at the University of Chicago.[107] The finest of their joint productions, variously dated, was a Yiddish parody of T. S. Eliot's "The Love Song of J. Alfred Prufrock." Rosenfeld was enormously proud of the parody, as is clear from an article he wrote in the first issue of *The Beacon*, the one that contained Bellow's article "Northwestern Is a Prison." "The Precocious Student at the University of Chicago" was written by Rosenfeld under his own name, but uses pseudonyms for the students it describes. In Harper Corridor, "a Trotskyite is holding the Y.C.L. at bay," an "accredited clever girl" sits smoking on a bench, while poets "stand about letting themselves be admired." One of these poets "bespectacled and dull-faced, with loosely hanging clothes (he was fat at one time) has translated T. S. Eliot into Yiddish. He quotes his translations twice a day and pretends that he feels he is making a fool of himself so that people (who have already memorized his translations) will have to beg him to quote." This poet has a friend named Raskolnikov (Bellow, presumably, given his love of Dostoyevsky and his volatility) who is "also a surrealist" and has written a poem "about a comma spreading mustard on its sides."

The Prufrock parody is funny as well as clever and has been extravagantly praised by poets and Yiddishists alike. It was known by word of mouth and only published in 1996, in an article by Ruth Wisse, professor of Yiddish at Harvard and Bellow's friend.[108] When asked in 1999 to name the finest poem published by an American in the twentieth century, Robert Pinsky, U.S. poet laureate, listed the Prufrock parody first, wrongly crediting it to Bellow alone (Bellow always acknowledged that Rosenfeld was the prime author).[109] Wisse is almost as extravagant as Pinsky. In *The Modern Jewish Canon: A Journey Through Language and Culture* (2000), she says of the poem: "If asked at what point American Jewish letters gave notice of its independence from Anglo-American Modernism, I would cite the day Isaac Rosenfeld, with the help of Saul Bellow, composed the Yiddish parody of 'The Love Song of J. Alfred Prufrock.' T. S. Eliot was the giant who could not be ignored. The giant had charged the Jews with corrupting his culture. What better way to credit him as a poet and discredit him as an anti-Semite than by Yiddishing the poet who so feared the Yid?"[110] The parody's best-known couplet is the original's best-known couplet: "I grow old, I grow old, / I shall wear my trousers rolled," which becomes *"Ikh ver alt, ikh ver alt / Un der pupik vert mir kalt"* ("I grow old, I grow old / And my belly-button grows cold"). Eliot's "In the room the women come and go / Talking of Michelangelo" becomes *"In tsimer ve di vaybere senen / Redt men fun Karl Marx un Lenin"* ("In the room where the wives are / Speaking of Karl Marx and Lenin"). The parody's title is *"Der shir hashirim fun Mendl Pumshtok,"* "The Song of Songs of Mendl Pumshtok." Pumshtok's song is more down to earth, more bodily, than Prufrock's: not "Do I dare to eat a peach?" but *"Meg ikh oyfesen a floym?,"*

"May I eat a prune?" Throughout, Eliot's fear of physicality is mocked. In Zipperstein's words, the poem "is packed with wet socks and dirty bedding; its women are 'wives,' not the desiccated seductresses of Eliot's imagination." Zipperstein connects the poem to the Yiddish stage, with its "long, odd, gloriously sectarian tradition of translations (of Shakespeare and other canonic works, most famously *King Lear*) that announced themselves as 'translations and improvements.'" Bellow and Rosenfeld knew this tradition as well as they knew Eliot and Pound, and though the parody pokes fun, it is serious. Through it, Zipperstein argues, the authors "denounced their own exclusion as Jews from the English canon . . . and sought to underscore what they could bring to English if only it opened itself to them."[111]

Bellow and Rosenfeld worked hard in their courses at Wisconsin, at least at the beginning. Vivas thought them "the two best students in the class."[112] In a letter to Tarcov postmarked September 29, Bellow reported that Rosenfeld was "a serious scholar now, and if he doesn't break down into his characteristic monadic delivery he'll be a gent of substance when the year is out. He reads earnestly and constantly. He is suddenly grave, and for the past week he has given no sign of surrealism." Rosenfeld was comparably upbeat, in a letter of his own to Tarcov: "We are together most of the time. . . . He peppers me with anthropological references, and I counter with casuistries, nice logical buts and ifs and whereases. If neither of us is driven to the wall he will say—'All right—granted! So where is the argument?' By this trick of admission the argument is usually forgotten. The trick always works."[113] Bellow's letters say nothing of the political scene at Madison, but Rosenfeld describes it in the letter postmarked September 19. "So far we have met only Stalinists," he writes to Tarcov, "who are confused, New Yorkers, nice, snooty people. Know nothing, never heard of Trotskyism. I am posing as a liberal, biding my time." As for girls, Rosenfeld adds, "the Movement, I must confess, offers the richest possibilities. The Stalinists here, judging from the ones I have met, are a bunch of impotent flirts." Bellow encouraged the younger Rosenfeld in this area, as in others. With "you gone," Rosenfeld writes to Tarcov on September 25, after the latter's visit to Madison, Bellow "has devoted his paternal solicitude to me, as next in line in the rank of his juniors, and edifies me endlessly with advice, example and apothegm. Most recently, fathering me, he said 'Gentle Isaac, alas, you are all marrow and no bone.' By way of setting the improving example, he has been all bone, these last few days. All in order to help me overcome my pitiful marrowness. He has even begun taking off weight by way of bringing out the bone!"

Bellow's reading at Wisconsin—anthropological, philosophical, sociological—served his writing, as ballast, corroboration. In *To Jerusalem and Back* (1976), he recalls reading David Wight Prall for Vivas's course Philosophy of the Arts and being struck by Prall's notion of "aesthetic surfaces": "Prall was speaking of ordinary life and common experiences, of a cup of coffee or the folds of a curtain, a bucket under the rain pipe: 'Lingering, loving contemplation' of flavors, colors, shapes, fragrances,'" a contemplation Bellow valued and drew on as a writer. Later in *To Jerusalem and Back*, Bellow recalls a question that absorbed him "when I was a graduate student in anthropology." It involved "bands of Eskimos who were reported to have chosen to starve rather than eat foods that were abundant but under taboo. How much, I asked myself, did people yield to culture or to their lifelong preoccupations, and at what point would their animal need to survive break through the restraints of custom and belief?"[114] The immediate context here is Israel's survival; in 1937 it was Bellow's survival as a writer, in defiance of his family and of material considerations.

The left politics of many anthropologists in the 1930s was part of what drew Bellow to study the subject. At the heart of anthropology, he told Keith Botsford, was "a very democratic idea. Everybody is entitled to equal time. They have their culture and we have ours, and we should not get carried away by our ethnocentrism."[115] For an outsider in particular, it was encouraging to learn that "what was right among the African Masai was wrong with the Eskimos." Later, Bellow came to see this teaching as "a treacherous doctrine—morality should be made of sterner stuff. But in my youth my head was turned by the study of erratic—or goofy—customs. In my early twenties I was a cultural relativist."[116] The appeal of erratic or goofy customs persisted for Bellow, even as an antirelativist, and can be seen especially in *Henderson the Rain King*, a novel set in Africa written by an author who had not yet been there. The customs Bellow devises for the fictional Wariri and Arnewi tribes, partly drawn from the anthropological texts he studied at Northwestern and Wisconsin, are what make his fictional Africa so magical and funny (the book was composed, Bellow told a journalist, "during a time of great personal difficulty. The worse things got for me personally the more amusing I began to think the whole thing was").[117] They also connect to the novel's main themes. Henderson, its protagonist, is in despair when he leaves home, lacking or having neglected dimensions of life—mystical, bodily—that he hopes to find in Africa. Anthropology, Bellow thought, illuminates these dimensions by studying cultures in which they are especially prominent or visible. Unfortunately, most anthropologists, even the "very best" (Bellow cites Malinowski and Radcliffe-Brown), describe them reductively. "I soon realized," Bellow told Botsford, "simply because you read Malinowski and Company didn't mean that you knew the Trobriand Islanders. What you knew was the version of an educated civilized European." Bellow detected "a kind of buried arrogance in the whole idea of the anthropologist: in the idea that because the Trobrianders are simpler, their depths can be sounded. Thoroughly. With simple peoples we can nail down the meaning of life."[118] Such arrogance is possible only if one misses out or undervalues the mystical dimension of life, reducing its "meaning" to an idea or theory.

Bellow's story "Cousins" (1975) attributes the prominence of Jews in anthropology to an affinity with this mystical dimension, despite the "educated civilized European" (that is, reductive) nature of their attempts to describe the cultures in which it figures. According to the story's narrator, Ijah Brodsky, who first becomes acquainted with anthropological studies in Madison, Wisconsin, "rooming with my cousin Ezekiel on the wrong side of the tracks" (Ezekiel is lecturing on primitive languages at the university), Jewish anthropologists "may have believed they were demystifiers, that science was their motive and that their ultimate aim was to increase universalism," but they were wrong to do so.

> A truer explanation is the nearness of ghettos to the sphere of Rev-
> elation, an easy move for the mind from rotting streets and rancid
> dishes, a direct ascent into transcendence. This of course was the
> situation of Eastern Jews. The Western ones were prancing and
> preening like learned Germans. And were Polish and Russian Jews
> (in disgrace with civilized judgment, afflicted with tuberculosis and
> diseased eyes) so far from the imagination of savage practices? They
> didn't have to make a Symbolist decision to derange their senses;
> they were born that way. Exotics going out to do science upon exot-
> ics. And then it all came out in Rabbinic-Germanic or Cartesian-
> Talmudic forms (p. 213).

In the case of anthropology's treatment of the bodily or sexual dimension, the attraction was chiefly political. "Radicalism was implied by the study of anthropology," Bellow recalled, "especially sexual radicalism—the study of the sexual life of savages was gratifying to radicals. It indicated that human life was much broader than the present." The broadness of sexual habits and mores in the cultures studied "gave young Jews a greater sense of freedom from the surrounding restrictions. They were seeking immunity from Anglo-Saxon custom: being accepted or rejected by a society of Christian gentlemen."[119] For Bellow, anthropology's attitudes toward the body and sexuality folded into those of Freudian and other psychologies, including the theories of Wilhelm Reich, as important to *Henderson* as those of the anthropologists.

LIKE IJAH BRODSKY, Bellow read and pondered anthropological and ethnographic studies throughout his life. In *Henderson*, he returns, as he would in *To Jerusalem and Back*, to the question of food and cultural taboos, drawing on Herskovits's *The Cattle Complex in East Africa* (1926). Like the tribes studied by Herskovits, Bellow's fictional Arnewi risk starvation because of their extreme reluctance to kill their cattle for food. Elsewhere, Bellow gives the Arnewi more than fifty terms for the various shapes of the horns of their cattle, which recalls the twenty-eight words used for "cattle" by the East African tribes in Herskovits's book. These and other resemblances are identified by Eusebio L. Rodrigues in "Bellow's Africa," a study of the novel's sources. Rodrigues also identifies Arnewi traits borrowed from the writings of the Reverend John Roscoe (1861–1932), who led the Mackie Ethnological expedition in Central Africa, particularly in *The Soul of Central Africa* (1922) and *The Banyankole* (1923). For Wariri traits and customs, he points to Frederick E. Forbes's two-volume study, *Dahomey and the Dahomans* (1851), Tor Irstam's *The King of Ganda* (1944), and Sir Richard Burton's *A Mission to Gelele, King of Dahomey* (1864) and *First Footsteps in East Africa* (1856) (the source of "Joxi," the Wariri's form of "trample massage"). Rodrigues also points out that Bellow has Henderson mention Burton, disparagingly, in a letter to his wife. Rodrigues is at pains to demonstrate the originality of *Henderson* as well as its indebtedness, providing ample evidence of "Bellow's genius for transmuting bare facts into vivid dramatic event."[120] But Bellow was open about his sources. "During the Depression I wasn't having much luck with the sorority girls," he told a

Montreal reporter, "so I spent two years in library stacks reading missionary accounts of life in Africa. After a while it all melted into a glowing lump and became Henderson the Rain King. . . . Herskovits, my old professor at Northwestern, had his nose put out of joint by it. . . . He claimed it was a serious subject that I was making light of, but other specialists have told me it was an accurate account."[121]

Bellow's interest in "primitive" cultures started well before college. For example, in a letter of December 10, 1988, to Professor Ronald Rompkey, a Canadian English professor and the biographer of Sir Wilfred Grenfell, he suggests a much earlier ethnographic source for *Henderson* than those identified by Rodrigues. Grenfell (1865–1940) was a medical missionary to the aboriginal peoples and other inhabitants of Newfoundland and Labrador. Rompkey had written to Bellow to inquire about him in connection with *Henderson*. "In boyhood, two books by Sir Wilfred Grenfell deeply influenced me," Bellow replied, "one was *A Labrador Doctor* [1919] and the other a stirring narrative called *Adrift on an Iceflow* [*Adrift on an Ice-Pan* (1909)]." Bellow then suggested tentative connections between Eugene Henderson and Grenfell: "Henderson had a great appetite for free spirits (for other free spirits, I should perhaps say). Besides, Sir Wilfred was a self-sacrificing physician and you will remember that on his return from Africa Henderson meant to enter medical school." At the end of the novel, Bellow might have added, Henderson's plane stops in Newfoundland to refuel. The hero is let out onto a "frozen ground of almost eternal winter, drawing breaths so deep they shook me, pure happiness, while the cold smote me from all sides." He begins to gallop around "the shining and riveted body of the plane, behind the fuel trucks. Dark faces were looking from within. The great, beautiful propellers were still, all four of them." In the novel's last sentence, Bellow describes him "running—leaping, leaping, pounding, and tingling over the pure white lining of the gray Arctic silence" (p. 413).

Fifteen or so years after *Henderson*, in "Cousins," Bellow again drew directly on anthropological and ethnographic sources. The story opens with Ijah "playing hooky" from work with two "huge faded green books, dating from the beginning of this century." These books contain reports "of the Jessup Expedition, published by the American Museum of Natural History. Siberian ethnography. Fascinating. I was beguiled of my griefs (considerable griefs) by these monographs. Two tribes, the Koryak and the Chukchee, as described by Jochelson and

Bo[r]goras, absorbed me totally." The Jessup North Pacific Expedition (1897–1902) was directed by Franz Boas. Its aim was to study the relationships between tribes on either side of the Bering Strait. Waldemar Jochelson and Waldemar Borgoras were Russian Jews and political radicals. While exiled in Siberia they acted as field-workers on the expedition, examining the tribes on the Russian side of the strait, and writing a number of expedition reports. Ijah, a wealthy lawyer, shuts himself away in his fancy Loop office and is transported to Siberia by these reports, with their descriptions of customs and beliefs as erratic, goofy, and mystical as those of the Wariri, the Arnewi, or the ghetto Jews of Russia and Eastern Europe (Jochelson's and Borgoras's people). Here is how Ijah describes his reading:

> About this arctic desert, purified by frosts as severe as fire, I read for my relief as if I were reading the Bible. In winter darkness, even within a Siberian settlement you might be lost if the wind blew you down, for the speed of the snow was such as to bury you before you could recover your feet. If you tied up your dogs you would find them sometimes smothered when you dug them out in the morning. In this dark land you entered the house by a ladder inside the chimney. As the snows rose, the dogs climbed up to smell what was cooking. They fought for places at the chimney tops and sometimes fell into the cauldron. There were photographs of dogs crucified, a common form of sacrifice. The powers of darkness surrounded you. A Chukchee informant told Bo[r]goras that there were invisible enemies who beset human beings from all sides, demanding spirits whose mouths were always gaping. The people cringed and gave ransom, buying protection from these raving ghosts (pp. 210–11).

"Cousins" raises questions of kinship on several levels, including those Bellow was introduced to as a student of anthropology. "The important works by people like Malinowski," he told an interviewer in 1980, "were not only studies of Trobriand Islanders." In reading these works, "you felt that you were really onto something much bigger than a study of savages—besides there were so many savages in Chicago it was only realistic to turn your attention to anthropology."[122] The story rejects naive universalism, while also rejecting Enlightenment presumptions of superiority. Ijah advises bankers on foreign loans, governments on the rescheduling of debts, speaks at the Council on Foreign

Relations. What absorbs him, however, is "spiritual investigation," a search for "real being under the debris of modern ideas." This search he conducts by reading works of ethnography and anthropology, "in a magical trance, if you like, or with a lucidity altogether different from the lucidity of *approved* types of knowledge" (p. 221).

From the mid-1980s until his death in 2005, Bellow worked intermittently on a novel titled "All Marbles Still Accounted For." By 1994 he had written 294 pages of the work and on August 9 informed Rebecca Sinkler of *The New York Times* that "my aim is to wrap up 'Marbles' (the title of the book I have sworn to deliver to Viking Press) no later than January." According to Janis Bellow, he would have finished the novel had a near-fatal illness, other projects, and suddenly diminishing powers, not intervened. "Marbles" takes its protagonist to New Guinea, about which Bellow read widely. Much of this reading was recommended to him by the controversial American medical researcher and physician D. Carleton Gajdusek, whom Bellow met in 1976, when he and Gajdusek were awarded Nobel Prizes. Gajdusek's prize, which he shared with Baruch S. Blumberg, was in Physiology or Medicine. It derived from the study of kuru, a disease widespread in the 1950s and 1960s among the South Fore people of New Guinea. Gajdusek lived among the Fore, studied their cultures, and performed autopsies on kuru victims. These autopsies led him to the conclusion that the disease was spread by the practice of funerary cannibalism. Gajdusek provided Bellow with copies of his journals, containing photographs as well as descriptions of Fore customs, and with a four-page list of periodical articles and books on South Pacific tribes. Among Bellow's papers in the Regenstein are reprints of a number of these articles, as well as bound copies of the journals.

IF BELLOW'S INTEREST IN anthropology was lifelong, his interest in a career as an anthropologist was short-lived. As Indian summer faded, the demands and pressures of the autumn term crowded around him. By December 7 he had moved closer to campus. He was now at 1314 St. James Place, near Rosenfeld, at 11 North Mills Street. It is not clear how they were getting on. In the December 7 letter, in exasperation, or mock exasperation, Bellow calls Rosenfeld "intolerable," obsessed with a paper "on the Absolute as conceived by Josiah Royce." If the paper pleases his professor, Rosenfeld "will stay. If not he will return."

Rosenfeld himself was pleased: "I wrote a paper this week-end on Royce," he tells Tarcov in a letter postmarked December 9, "wherein I disembowelled him thoroughly, clean as a whitefish, and disposed of Absolute Idealism to such satisfaction, that I hesitate now, to subscribe to the best of all possible tenets: metaphysics is nonsense." The paper was composed in a period of "happy, suppressed existence . . . hearing neither bird-call, flesh-call, telephone-call." Bellow, too, was furiously writing papers at this period, or furiously not writing them: "I have several on my hands, more than I should perhaps have undertaken. The result is, of course, that I bear more than my normal load of fretting. I know I waste more time fuming and bustling than I spend in work. But I can't break the habit." He completed only one of his courses, Goldenweiser's, for which he got an A. Bellow gave several reasons for his decision to leave graduate school and return to Chicago: "My interest in anthropology began to run out when I was told I had to take archaeology courses, physical anthropology courses, and linguistics courses. I didn't want to get into *that*. I didn't see the point of it. I didn't mind measuring people's skulls for a bit, but I didn't want to fool with bones for a year. I left at Christmas to come back to Chicago." Elsewhere, he attributed his impatience with anthropology to the magnetic pull of fiction: "Every time I worked on my thesis it turned out to be a story." This was the view also of Goldenweiser, who thought him too much of a literary stylist to be an anthropologist. "It was a nice way of easing me out of the field,"[123] Bellow thought. But Goldenweiser, himself "more literary than anthropological," identified a key incompatibility between Bellow and "the field." The trouble with anthropologists, Bellow acknowledged, was that they weren't writers. Hence the reductive nature of their attempts to describe the mystical dimension, also the feel of primitive cultures. "You knew when you met these scholars that they would never understand what they had been seeing in the field. To me they were suspect in part because they had no literary abilities. They wrote books but they were not real writers. They were deficient in trained sensibilities. They brought what they called 'science' to human matters; matters of human judgment, but their 'science' could never replace a trained sensibility." This sensibility, Bellow continues, "was what I acquired without even knowing it."[124]

In the letter of December 7 to Tarcov, Bellow announces that he will be back in Chicago on December 17. Nothing is said about quitting graduate study. Bellow may only have decided not to return to Madison after he left. Romantic motives, as well as intellectual ones, underlay the decision. In an earlier letter to Tarcov, postmarked October 13, Bellow says he cannot accept anthropology "wholly," not only because he's a writer, but because "just now I am deeply in love, and I think I shall continue in love, because it is my salvation." The person he was in love with would become his wife. In returning to Chicago to stay, he was committing himself not just to a life of writing but to life with her.

6

Anita/Dangling

THE GIRL'S NAME WAS Anita Goshkin and Bellow met her in Hyde Park in the summer of 1936, before the start of his senior year at Northwestern. By the spring of 1937 they were engaged. Anita had been at the University of Chicago only a year, having transferred from the University of Illinois at Urbana-Champaign, as a junior (shortly after the death of her father, which suggests the move may have been motivated by family or financial considerations). The "grimy" sociology books she carried at their first meeting were for a summer course at the university. She was six months older than Bellow, born on December 12, 1914, and like him lived on the North Side, in Ravenswood, a modest suburb of small courtyard apartment buildings. Bellow told his son Greg that he'd had his eye on Anita for some time, before gathering the courage to speak to her. Her cousin and childhood playmate, Beebee Schenk (later de Regniers), was a friend of Bellow's, and may have told him to look out for her.[1] On their first date, they went swimming in Lake Michigan off the Point, a Hyde Park landmark. In *Herzog*, Bellow fictionalizes the moment they met. Moses sees Daisy, who will become his first wife, under the El at 51st Street. Pretty and fresh in appearance, with large "slant green" eyes, she wears a simple seersucker dress and small white shoes. Her "golden but lustreless" hair is held in place by a barrette and her legs are bare. Moses sees the square-cut neck of her dress as expressive of character: "stability, symmetry, order, containment were Daisy's strength." Her "laundered purity" also strikes him, as does her coolness and regular features, those of "a conventional Jewish woman." As Moses stands behind her on the El platform, a "fragrance of summer apples" rises from her bare neck and shoulders (pp. 542–43).[2]

This fragrance is also expressive, for Daisy is a country girl of sorts, raised near Zanesville, Ohio. Anita came from a similar background, in Lafayette, Indiana, not exactly the country, but not Chicago either. Her parents, like Bellow's, were Russian immigrants. Her father, Morris, arrived from the Crimea after the pogroms of 1905, settling in Lafayette for the same reason the Bellows settled first in Lachine then in Chicago: because he had relatives there. He worked as a milkman, then opened an ice cream parlor. What Greg Bellow remembers hearing of his maternal grandfather is that he was "quiet, kind and gentle." It was Sonia, Morris's wife, a forceful, opinionated, modern woman, a suffragette in Russia, who ruled the roost, encouraging her daughters to be independent and insisting that they go to college.[3]

Like Bellow, Anita was the only member of her family to be born in the New World. A late arrival, she was much doted on. She had two brothers, Jack (also known as J.J.) and Max, seventeen and ten years older, and two sisters, Catherine and Ida, sixteen and fourteen years older. The sisters became librarians, earned higher degrees in library science, traveled in Europe, were lovers of high culture, and never married. When they retired, they moved to New York, living together in an apartment close to Lincoln Center, to be near the ballet. Of the brothers, Jack, the eldest, had an affair in college with a non-Jewish girl. When she got pregnant, he married her. According to Greg, Anita's mother was so scandalized by these events, "that, basically, she forced Jack to divorce . . . and move back in." Jack's son, Jack Jr., was raised out of state by his mother and on rare visits to Lafayette "was kept on the back porch, incommunicado." When the Goshkins moved to Chicago and the son visited, his father "checked into a hotel." Anita's other brother, Max, a machinist, also lived at home, well into his forties.

Anita was political at college. When Greg was a student at Chicago, "with great pride" she pointed out to him the spot in the lobby of the Social Sciences building where she had once sold a hundred copies of *Soapbox* in an hour. She attended political meetings and regularly spoke at them. She went to Gary, Indiana, to organize steelworkers, was arrested, and spent a night in jail, along with Bellow's friend Oscar Tarcov. Her interest in politics was practical; she had little patience for theoretical or doctrinal dispute. The two-year MA program she entered in March 1937 in Chicago's School of Social Service Administration involved fieldwork at the Michael Reese Hospital, one of the oldest and largest teaching hospitals in Chicago. There Anita met Bruno Bettelheim, who later remarked to Greg on his mother's beauty. Anita finished the first year of the course but not the second, which required that she write a dissertation. She could not write, or thought she could not write, a conclusion she'd been led to as an undergraduate. "My father told me he wrote most of her term papers," Greg recalls. After abandoning her MA in 1939 she got a job at the Chicago Relief Administration giving out welfare checks. By this date she and Bellow had been married over a year.

That Bellow had been contemplating marriage for some time is clear from his letter to Tarcov of October 2, 1937, but the actual decision seems to have been made on the spur of the moment. Among Anita's friends at the University of Illinois was Cora DeBoer, a psychology student. Cora was a pretty blond girl from a comfortable middle-class family; her father, a first-generation Dutch immigrant, was a successful Chicago physician, her mother belonged to the DAR (Daughters of the American Revolution), as did Cora herself. After graduate work in psychology, Cora went on to a career as a counselor, both in the Chicago school system and in private practice. Through Anita and Bellow, she met Bellow's friend, Herb Passin, a student of anthropology at the University of Chicago (where he would get his master's degree in August 1941).[4] Herb and Cora fell in love and sometime after Bellow's return to Chicago from Madison for the Christmas holidays, the two couples hatched a plan to elope in a double wedding. On December 31 they climbed into Cora's 1934 Ford and drove to Indiana, where it was possible to obtain a marriage licence without having to take the required blood test (for venereal disease); that the test took days to process and they were unwilling to wait is what suggests that the plan was hastily conceived. In Michigan City, sixty miles south of Chicago, they found a justice of the peace, lied about being Indiana residents, and were married that afternoon. Then they drove back to Chicago, celebrating over dinner at a Japanese restaurant on the near North Side, the only place they could find open.[5]

When the newlyweds told their parents what they had done, neither the Goshkins nor the DeBoers seem to have objected, or to have objected much. Anita's mother immediately took the couple into her home; the Passins' only child, Tom, "never heard that Cora's parents had any trouble with Herb being Jewish. If they did, it didn't last long."[6]

Herb's parents, however, minded a great deal that Cora was not Jewish and Bellow's father was also upset ("I had defied him by getting married," Bellow told Roth[7]), not because he disapproved of Anita, but because he thought Bellow could not support himself, let alone a wife or family. As Lesha Greengus, Sam Bellows's daughter, puts it, the family liked Anita, but "everybody worried about Saul making a living. That is what my grandfather worried about. This was a constant conversation and a genuine and loving worry between my father and grandfather." Maury, too, worried about how Bellow would support himself, while also sneering at his poverty. In *The Adventures of Augie March*, Simon, Augie's Maury-like brother, urges him to marry Lucy Magnus, his wife's sister; to marry for money, in other words, as *he* had done. When Augie delays and demurs, "things became more tough for me at the yard" (p. 668).

The family home Bellow entered into in the New Year was a crowded one. In addition to Sonia, there was Jack, now forty, Catherine, thirty-eight, Ida, thirty-five, and Max, thirty-three. Bellow briefly took a job working for Maury (as Augie does for Simon), but was soon fired for absenteeism. He was determined to become a novelist, and to their credit, Anita and her family were ready to give him a chance to do so. As Bellow puts it in "Starting Out in Chicago" (1974), his "affectionate loyal and pretty wife insisted that he must be given a chance to write something."[8] So each morning, after Anita and her siblings boarded the Lawrence Avenue streetcar or the Ravenswood El to go to work or study, Bellow retreated to a bridge table in a back bedroom and wrote. The table faced "three cement steps" and "the brick gloom of a passageway." The only other person at home was Sonia, his mother-in-law. At half past twelve, they had lunch together. "The cooking was good. We ate together in the kitchen. The meal was followed by an interval of stone. My mother-in-law took a nap. I went into the street. Ravenswood was utterly empty." For amusement he would wander over to the bridge on Lawrence Avenue and look at the Drainage Canal. Then he'd walk back home, "to the pages of bad manuscript, and the silent dinner of soup and stew and strudel, after which you and your wife, washing dishes, enjoyed the first agreeable hours of the day." It was Anita's family who paid both for her graduate study and for Bellow's freedom to write, supplemented by handouts, often grudging, from the Bellows.[9]

What agitated Bellow at this time was less what he was writing, about which we know nothing ("I am glad to say I can't remember what

I was writing in Ravenswood," he says in "Starting Out in Chicago." "It must have been terrible"), than the isolation writing entailed. "I had to learn that by cutting myself off from American life in order to perform an alien task, I risked cutting myself off from everything that could nourish me." American life was indifferent rather than hostile: "it simply lacked interest in your sort of game."[10] As Bellow puts it in the first of the Jefferson Lectures, though, "no doubt, it was courageous to assert that a world without art was unacceptable," he didn't feel courageous. Writing of himself at twenty-two, he recalls that he felt at sea: "it was no more than the simple truth that the hero of art was himself unstable, stubborn, nervous, ignorant, that he could not bear routine or accept an existence he had not made for himself."[11] In addition, "the problem of those you loved was very keen. They didn't know what you were up to. You yourself didn't have a confident grasp of it."[12] This problem is the subject of Bellow's first published story (in *Partisan Review*, May–June 1941), "9 a.m. without Work," the first of "Two Morning Monologues." Set in the 1930s, it is narrated by Mandelbaum, a recent college graduate, unemployed, waiting to be called into the Army, a "hero of art" like his creator and no less "unstable, stubborn, nervous" ("ignorant," too, though bookish, reading Walter Scott and Malraux). Mandelbaum tries but cannot find a job, has difficulty "disposing of the day" (like Joseph in *Dangling Man*). His father, Jacob, pushes him out of the house each morning to search for work, puts embarrassing advertisements in the newspaper on his behalf, and can't understand why he's still unemployed. "So and so's son is working for so much and so much. A dumbbell. . . . It seems simple to him. And he never tires. 'You're a teacher, aren't you? Five years in college. The best. Alright, you can't get a teacher's job? . . . So get another job for a while'" (p. 231). Elsewhere: "'A good boy, a smart boy, American, as good as anybody else—but he hasn't got a job.' One. Two: 'Look at the money I spent on him'" (p. 230).

In looking back at this period, Bellow focuses on Sonia, his mother-in-law, and Jack. Sonia kept a tidy house. One felt her "strength of will in all things. The very plants, the ashtrays, the pedestals, the doilies, the chairs, revealed her mastery. Each object had its military place." The effect of this mastery was "to paralyze the spirit"; "the house had a tone which had to be resisted." Some afternoons Bellow drove Sonia to the cemetery in Jack's Hudson (Jack was a successful Loop lawyer, once even arguing a case before the Supreme Court). There she tended her husband's grave, pulling weeds with her "trembling, but somehow powerful, spotty hand."[13] As several of Bellow's fictions suggest, Sonia's influence on Anita was strong. In "Far Out," an unpublished novel he was at work on in the late 1970s, a Sonia-like character figures prominently. "Far Out" exists in a typed manuscript of a hundred pages, seen by Bellow's agent and by his publisher. Set in the early 1950s, it concerns Peter Vallis, a hero in several ways like his creator, whose wife, Nettie (née Maslow), resembles Anita. Peter and Nettie meet as Moses and Daisy meet, under the El at 51st Street.[14] They live in Manhattan in an apartment on West End Avenue, where Bellow and Anita briefly lived at the same period. Their marriage is in trouble, as was the Bellow marriage in the early 1950s. In Nettie's ordering of the apartment, Vallis senses "a kind of preventive magic in the choice and deployment of every object." This magic, he is convinced, Nettie learned "from her old mother, techniques of control direct from the master but without the old woman's confidence." Among the apartment's unpleasing objects is a rectangular fish tank holding two goldfish. "Life in a gallon of water." In the highly organized kitchen, Nettie pins a row of brown envelopes labeled "Food, Maid, Travel, Tobacco, Entertainment, Allowance" (p. 59).

Vallis accepts Nettie's arrangements as he accepts the plain dinners she cooks him. "He took his pocket money from its envelope without complaint." Nettie is "a most beautiful woman and a good one" and Vallis benefits from her orderly domestic regime even as he chafes under it. He also sees himself as part of its cause.

> He understood the difficulty. He knew also that if she was opinionated about the Consumer's Union, or instalment buying or child psychology or socialism he was in part responsible. The moves he made were unsettling, mysterious, radical. You saw in the household the sympathetic magic by which she hoped [to] hold tight. If he *would* make, unmake, remake himself he could not fault her for the elaborate rigid forms her beauty had been taking, the tightness of the belts she wore, the squaw impassivity with which she smoked, the heavy roll of fair hair with which she surrounded her head, like Bach or Handel in court wig. Clearly he was responsible, insofar as she could not guess what was going on in her husband's head. Her only recourse was to be wifely as wife was understood in Canton, Ohio. She could not rule by decree like her mother (p. 60).

Vallis's description of himself in this passage recalls Joseph in *Dangling Man*, as volatile as a character from Dostoyevsky. Joseph's wife, Iva, is reduced to tears by his impulsiveness, quickness to anger and to take offense, and by the force of his personality ("I had dominated her for years," [p. 69]). Joseph sees Iva's virtues and insists that he loves her, "yet she is as far as ever from what I once desired to make her. I am afraid she has no capacity for that," by which he means no capacity for "worth-while ideas" (p. 111). Vallis has similarly mixed feelings about Nettie, "who could spend whole decades trying to figure out what would satisfy him, what he wanted. He was so theoretical, notional, cultural, so fluent, came at her from so many sides, produced so many arguments that he made her feel—he strengthened her secret judgment on herself—that she was a slow, stupid woman, and sullen" (p. 73).

In the October 1937 letter to Tarcov, Bellow declared himself "deeply in love" with Anita and for some years seems to have remained so, but there were problems in the marriage from the start. These problems bewildered Anita, and Bellow left no clear account of them in interviews or written reminiscences. In the fiction, however, some suggestive patterns emerge. In *Seize the Day* (1956), Tommy Wilhelm, a very different character from Joseph and Vallis, describes the failure of his first marriage: "I just couldn't live with Margaret. I wanted to stick it out, but I was getting very sick. She was one way and I was another. She wouldn't be like me, so I tried to be like her, and I couldn't do it" (p. 42). As Vallis watches Nettie, he senses fear beneath her composure. To live with this fear, to live with Nettie, was to be "housebroken to evil" (p. 62). (Like Bellow in the early 1950s, Vallis is much influenced by Wilhelm Reich's notions of sickness and evil, in particular of the deforming fear of death.) When Vallis contemplates leaving Nettie, or lies to her about his feelings or what he's up to, his heart aches and he suspects he might be crazy, "one of the heavily *justified* lunatics" (p. 73). Yet the fact is, she cannot be like him, and he cannot be like her.

"I HAD A DISCIPLINE to learn at the bedroom table," writes Bellow of his time in Ravenswood. As he strove to make himself a writer, he paid close attention to his brother-in-law Jack, a determined self-fashioner, "dark, grim, kindly and reserved."[15] Jack's project was to become the "complete American, as formal, as total in his fashion as a work of art," words that describe Cousin Mendy, his fictional alter ego in "Cousins."[16] In "Starting Out in Chicago," Bellow describes Jack as "a Republican, member of the American Legion, a golfer, a bowler; he drove his conservative car conservatively, took the *Saturday Evening Post*, wore a Herbert Hoover starched collar, trousers short in the ankle, and a hard straw hat in summer. He spoke in a pure Hoosier twang, not like a Booth Tarkington gentleman but like a real Tippecanoe dirt farmer."[17] Mendy has most of these traits, plus others described by his cousin Ijah Brodsky as "the idiocies and even the pains of his Protestant models, misfortunes like the estrangements of husbands and wives, sexual self-punishment. He would get drunk in the Loop and arrive swacked on the commuter trains" (p. 230). Mendy's self-fashioning is doomed. "In the eyes under that snap-brim fedora there had always been a mixture of Jewish lights, and in his sixties he was visibly more Jewish" (p. 230). So, too, Jack: "All this Americanism was imposed on an exquisitely oriental face, dark with curved nose and Turkish cheekbones." In the act of making themselves, both Mendy and Jack become vulnerable, calling to mind Cousin Arkady, from the Old Country, who decided his new name was now and henceforth "Lake Erie." Cousin Arkady appears in both the fictional "Cousins" and the nonfictional "Starting Out in Chicago" at exactly this point, after describing the ultimate failures of Mendy and Jack. "As I was making a writer of myself," Bellow writes of Jack, "this exotic man was transforming his dark oriental traits and becoming an American from Indiana." In "Starting Out in Chicago," Bellow sees himself with comparable irony. In Ravenswood his aim was "to enjoy my high thought and to perfect myself in the symbolic discipline of high art. I can't help feeling that I overdid it."[18]

The Ravenswood period lasted less than a year. Once Anita quit graduate school and began work for the Chicago Relief Administration, earning $25 a week, she and Bellow moved away from the Goshkins' to a place of their own in Hyde Park, where they rented a second-floor apartment in a courtyard building on the corner of Harper Avenue and 57th Street, near the lake and half a dozen blocks from the quadrangles of the university. The apartment consisted of a large front room, with windows overlooking the courtyard, a tiny kitchen, and down a short hall a small bathroom and a small bedroom. The front room was furnished sparsely, with a couch, a desk, a large bookcase, and a card table placed between the windows. Anita left the apartment each morning for work and Bellow sat at the card table and wrote, as he had in Ravenswood. He also attended classes at the university, failing to complete

"Introduction to Linguistics" in Winter Quarter, also "Economic History of the Middle Ages" in Summer Quarter (though he did manage a C in a course on Mayan and Aztec cultures taught by A. R. Radcliffe-Brown, the English social anthropologist). Shortly after the move to Hyde Park, Bellow came down with pneumonia and every afternoon during his illness, Irving Janis, an undergraduate friend, later an eminent psychologist (originator of the term "groupthink"), "read to me by the hour, recognizing that I needed to be read to, just then."[19] Bellow depicts himself in this period as isolated, under pressure, as much from himself as from others, but at times he stresses how little money was needed to survive in the Depression: "I suppose it cost about $1,200 to be poor in those days. . . . Everybody was doing it, all my friends were doing it."[20]

Bellow found several part-time jobs after moving to Hyde Park. The first was teaching twice a week at the Pestalozzi-Froebel Teachers College, for aspiring primary schoolteachers, mostly young Jewish girls from immigrant families or Midwestern farm girls. The college was located in the Fine Arts Building on South Michigan Avenue (where he'd taken violin lessons with Grisha Borushek), convenient to the Chicago Public Library at Randolph Street, the Crerar Library, and the Art Institute. Among Bellow's pupils was sixteen-year-old Ruth Miller, later to become a friend and the first of his biographers. Miller took "English Composition" with Bellow (who taught "Anthropology, English, anything; I was a troubleshooter"[21]) and kept the reading list for his course, which started with *Crime and Punishment*, then *Madame Bovary*; *A Portrait of the Artist as a Young Man*; *Sons and Lovers*; *Chrome Yellow*; *Winesburg, Ohio*; *Sister Carrie*; *Manhattan Transfer*; and *A Farewell to Arms*. Bellow's teaching method was to read aloud one or two of his pupils' weekly essays and then "tell us what he thought, not of our essays but of the book and its author."[22] When Ruth Miller went to his office to discuss her work, he would read from his own writing by way of example, usually from one of the novel manuscripts he carried about with him. Bellow thought highly of Miller and invited her to visit him in Hyde Park, which she did with a friend (Miller is the source of the description of the 57th Street apartment). The girls had never been to Hyde Park, and after a tour of the Midway and the university ("This is where you should be"), Bellow brought them back for tea with Anita. In her biography, Miller remembers that Bellow was proud of the apartment. What she remembers of Anita is the dirndl skirt and peasant blouse she wore, and the strudel she served, made by Sonia. When Miller mentioned that her aunt also made strudel, but without nuts, Anita was very firm: "No, no, that's not possible. There have to be nuts."

The Bellows were proud of the freedom their apartment represented. An odd moment in the visit occurred when first Anita, then Bellow, took their tea bags out of their cups and whirled them over their heads, laughing and shouting. "'I always wanted to do this,'" Miller remembers Anita saying, as the tea bag splattered "walls, windows, curtains, rug, couch, easy chair, the desk, and the books."[23] Miller and her friend were gratifyingly startled, especially when invited to join in. As Bellow wrote of himself at this period, "he was as powerfully attached to silliness and squalor as to grandeur."[24] "He was always being talked about in our household as a bohemian," Joel Bellows, Maury's son, remembers, "he and Anita, sitting on the floor with their friends in the dark, listening to classical music. Can you imagine! In *our* family." On a visit to a later apartment, on Kimbark Avenue, near 52nd Street, Joel remembers, "we took some of my father's old clothes, monogrammed shirts. They opened the door, it was a formal visit. . . . I had been primed by my parents: they were poor people, don't ask for anything, don't bother them for anything. And my father came into the room, big handful of shirts, and he threw them on the floor, and it was a matter of lording it over him. I identified with my uncle."

In addition to teaching, Bellow found work in the autumn of 1938 with the Illinois Federal Writers' Project, part of Roosevelt's WPA. The Chicago office of the Illinois Writers' Project was a loft on East Erie Street, just north of the Loop, and its state director was John T. Frederick, whom Bellow had known at Northwestern. To be certified for relief, Bellow had to confirm that he was unemployed and had tried and failed to find work (according to Atlas, he was interviewed for a job at Hearst newspapers, where an executive with a nose "like a double Alaskan strawberry" claimed he had no aptitude for writing[25]). Fellow writers from the Chicago office included Richard Wright, at work on *Native Son*; Isaac Rosenfeld, who was turned down for a job at Chicago's *Yiddish Courier*; Nelson Algren, a friend of David Peltz's (also employed by the WPA, at the Federal Theatre Project); and Jack Conroy, like Algren, a published novelist, also editor of the left-wing periodicals *Rebel Poet*, *The Anvil*, and *The New Anvil*. Algren did not get on with Bellow: "He [Algren] disapproved of my politics and I didn't care for his so we exchanged more hard looks than we did words."[26] As Bellow saw it, Algren and Conroy paraded their proletarian roots. In "Writers, Intellectuals, Politics, Mainly Reminiscence" (1993), he describes the personal style of the two men, "our stars," as "dated," though their Popular Front politics were still very much alive. To experience these politics today, he adds, "you need do no more than mention Whittaker Chambers or Alger Hiss or J. Robert Oppenheimer or the Rosenbergs at a dinner table."[27]

Writers' Project employees were of two sorts: the writers themselves, who were on relief (and made up 90 percent of the staff), and the editors and administrators, who were on a salary. The editors and administrators came to the office every day; the writers came once a week, to report on the research tasks or "fieldwork" they'd been set by their editors. Bellow's editor, a geographer named Nathan Morris, had been at Tuley two years before him. He received his undergraduate degree from the University of Chicago in 1935, the year the Federal Writers' Project was launched. As the major task of the Chicago branch of the project was to compile a state guidebook, eventually published in 1939 as *Illinois: A Descriptive and Historical Guide*, Morris's knowledge of geography was an asset.[28] Bellow was initially assigned to compile statistics about newspaper and magazine publishing (one of Rosenfeld's assignments was to research pigeon racing), for Part 1 of the *Guide*, "The General Background" (Parts 2 and 3 are "Cities and Towns" and "Tours"). Bellow mostly conducted this research at the Newberry Library, across the street from the soapbox orators of Washington Square Park, known locally as Bughouse Square, to whom he'd listen on lunch breaks. The work bored him. When Frederick, "a very decent and imaginative man,"[29] discovered Bellow was bored, he set him to work writing biographical profiles of "Midwestern" writers (elsewhere "Illinois" writers or "American" writers).[30] "None of them," Bellow suspected, "were ever meant to be used," nor, mistakenly, did he think they'd survived. Had they survived, Bellow told an interviewer, "I'd be distressed. I was only 22 years old and I knew nothing."[31] Bellow was paid $24 a week at the Writers' Project ("I never had it so good"), but the main benefit of working for the WPA, which he always praised, was that "I was able to justify the idea that I was a writer."[32]

THE BELLOWS' SOCIAL CIRCLE in the late 1930s and early 1940s was close. Chief among their Hyde Park friends were Rosenfeld, working on an MA in philosophy at the University of Chicago (awarded in August 1941) and living in a grim, cramped attic apartment ("essentially, in perpetual darkness," a state he found congenial); Oscar Tarcov; his sister Ruth, who would marry Herb Passin's brother, Sid, move with him to New York, and eventually find work at *The New Republic*; the Schenks, Beebee and her husband, Peter; and the boys from Wieboldt Hall, especially Harold "Kappy" Kaplan, whose wife, Celia, had been close to Anita at the University of Illinois (Anita found Celia a job in Chicago as a social worker).[33] Tarcov married Edith Hamberg in 1942, having been introduced to her by Bellow. "My mother was working in a bookstore downtown," Nathan Tarcov explains, "and Saul walked in one day and said, 'Want to come to a party tonight in Hyde Park?'" She said yes, and when she arrived "met my father and rather rapidly fell in love and got married." Edith had been in the country for only a year or so, having escaped Germany in 1939 (before coming to Chicago at twenty-one, she spent a year in England). In Germany, she had been an active Zionist, in early adolescence joining a small youth movement called the Werkleute inspired in part by Martin Buber's teachings. An American relative arranged for her to settle in Chicago. Her parents, German Jews from Hanover, affluent, cultured, patriotic (her father had been awarded an Iron Cross First Class for bravery at Verdun), had stayed on too late to survive. Within a year of the marriage, the Tarcovs' first child, Miriam, was born.

Bellow's relations with these friends were often fractious. The effort required to overcome his family's disapproval and incomprehension, to get into print and establish his identity as a writer, made him combative ("he had his dukes up all the time," in Harold Kaplan's words), resentful of slights, real or imagined.[34] Nowhere is this touchiness clearer than in his correspondence with Tarcov, the mildest of his close friends. Tarcov was a junior when Bellow returned to Chicago from Madison in December 1937. Like Bellow, he was determined to be a writer. After taking his degree in the summer of 1939, he worked briefly as a bartender in a rough area west of Hyde Park, then moved for several months to New York (where all true writers lived), before returning to the Midwest at the beginning of 1940 and enrolling as a graduate student in anthropology at the University of Illinois at Urbana-Champaign. He lasted a year in graduate school before returning to New York, but by the end of 1941 he was back in Chicago. "It was complicated," Nathan explains, of the movements of his father, Bellow, and Rosenfeld in the late 1930s and early 1940s: "Oscar, Isaac and Saul went to New York at different times. It was almost like they took turns. . . . There was a sense that [New York] was the center of the world. There was the fear that the others would go to New York and you would be left behind in Chicago."[35]

Soon after Tarcov left Chicago for New York, Bellow wrote to him about their friendship.[36] "You are perfectly right," he admits in an undated letter (probably written in October 1939), "we should have had a talking out before you went away. But to be perfectly frank too, I didn't care, at the time that you left, to talk to you. I was neither angry nor disgusted, but disaffected," as he was also with Herb Passin, for falling under the influence of his Christian-pacifist father-in-law, "the terrible Doctor." In a later letter, postmarked December 5, Bellow attributes his disaffection to "the condition our circle was in." "You and Isaac and a few others were gummed into a very disagreeable relationship," he complains, "but there was very little friendship in it actually and more jealousy, covert rage, detestation and in fact a need to use one's friends as one should use one's enemies." As a consequence, Bellow "was shot into the Freifeld camp." In response to "a lot of disagreeable buffoonery" on Tarcov's and Rosenfeld's part, "of course immediately I became a boor." Only toward the end of the letter do Bellow's complaints subside, or seem to subside. "In the last five months or so," he admits, "there has been time for the harder feelings to fall away and be replaced by some of my affection for you. I hate like all hell to have you estranged for the worst of all possible reasons; attempt at honest analysis."

Later letters to Tarcov describe tensions in the Bellow marriage. "A good deal of what you say about Anita I couldn't dream of denying," Bellow concedes in an undated letter, probably from early 1940. "I have had a great deal of trouble lately over her and several times in the last two months we have been on the verge of separating." Their quarrels are "not out of trivial things but out of the fact that in numerous ways we are disagreeable to each other;" "the principal reasons for marriage have no existence any longer." Bellow is determined, though, not to give up on the marriage, "because I don't want another failure added to an already long list." A similar determination underlies his persistence with "Ruben Whitfield," a novel he hoped to have finished by the spring, but now finds "painful and sometimes even obnoxious." This is Bellow's only reference to "Ruben Whitfield," unless it became "The Very Dark Trees," a completed novel that was accepted for publication in 1942, but of which no trace survives. The trouble with "Ruben Whitfield," Bellow confesses to Tarcov, is that its subject requires "a much better developed writer and a more fully developed individual. It wasn't really my project. My views and interests changed so often in the course of the writing that every month I wanted to go back and do the whole thing over in a new way." Some parts of the manuscript were revised as many as four times and the resulting inconsistencies are "so transparent and fatuous that I want to abandon it. But I am going to finish it." He had been a writer for two years and had published nothing.

A third and related problem raised in the letter to Tarcov concerns politics. "This idea of 'finish it' is present," Bellow tells Tarcov, "not only in 'Ruben' and in my marriage but also in the movement." The split in the Socialist Workers Party occasioned by the Hitler-Stalin Pact and the Soviet invasion of Finland left many party members, Bellow included, disillusioned. Trotsky's defense of the pact, as was seen in the previous chapter, was supported by the majority faction in the party, led by James P. Cannon. The minority faction, led by Max Shachtman and James Burnham, and supported by Bellow's friend Al Glotzer, denounced the pact, declaring the Soviet Union an imperialist aggressor and an enemy to socialism. "I was alienated before the factional fight," Bellow writes to Tarcov, "but now the whole affair has become nauseous." If the minority capitulates, "I am finished." Rosenfeld has already quit the party, Bellow tells Tarcov, and Bellow himself is on the verge of doing so. But he will wait till the party convention in April 1940 before making his final decision. "It's a goddamn crime that at the time that the war is on us the only revolutionary party in the country falls to pieces. We'll be crushed too, I think."[37] When the Cannonite faction prevailed in April, Burnham, Shachtman, and Glotzer left the party, along with 40 percent of its membership, Bellow and Tarcov included.

As Bellow's worries mounted—over the novel, the marriage, politics, the gathering war—he received an unexpected stroke of good fortune. Almost eight years after his mother's death, an insurance policy she had taken out in his name came due. Perhaps she put it in his name out of worry over his dreaming propensities, perhaps out of favoritism (though according to Lesha Greengus, Maury was the favorite, as is Shawmut's businessman brother, "fat-assed Philip the evildoer," in "Him with His Foot in His Mouth"[38]). Each week Liza had paid a quarter into the policy, collected by the bookish insurance agent Bellow remembered coming to the apartment on Le Moyne Street, "forever trying to engage me in conversation about the books he saw in my mother's kitchen. He was extremely keen to discuss 'The Decline of the West.'" The policy had now matured into the sum of $500. When news of the windfall reached Bellow's family, Abraham immediately asked for the money, "all five hundred bucks of it. He needed it badly, but I refused to part with it."[39] Instead, Bellow decided with Anita to use the money to travel to Mexico. As early as the letter to Tarcov of December 5, he was alluding to the trip, which he thought would take place in February. They did not, in fact, set off until June. Bellow explained their decision in his interview with Philip Roth:

> It was essential that we should go. Europe was out of the question since the Germans had just overrun Paris. Deprived of Paris, I simply had to go to Mexico. Looking back, I see more agony than boldness in this decision. I was, as kids were to say later, making a statement. I had spent most of my life in weary, stale, flat, and unprofitable Chicago and I needed barbarism, color, glamour, and risk.[40]

Bellow gave notice at Pestalozzi-Froebel, recommending Tarcov as a replacement; Anita quit her job; then she and Bellow set about "get[ting] rid of all encumbrances: furniture, lease, et al." In early June, instead of traveling directly to Mexico, they took a Greyhound bus to New York, arriving on the day Paris fell to the Germans, June 14, 1940. In New York, they visited friends from Chicago (several of the boys from Wieboldt Hall, and Al Glotzer, who had contacts with Trotsky and his protectors in Mexico). They also visited Bellow's Uncle Willie, whom grandfather Berel had punished by apprenticing him to a brushmaker. "Unemployed, and brooding his life away in Brownsville," Uncle Willie was affectionate to his nephew, but had a family to feed: "I ought to have shared the five hundred bucks with him." The visit chilled Bellow: "Uncle Willie in Brownsville illustrated what might happen to a Bellow who rebelled [in Willie's case by joining the Bund against his father's wishes]. He would be humiliatingly shot down." Much easier was the visit to Uncle Max in Augusta, Georgia, where Anita and Bellow stopped briefly before continuing on to New Orleans. Uncle Max, the cheerful "ganef" mentioned in Chapter 2, sold cheap clothing on installment to black field hands. As for New Orleans, all Bellow recalled to Roth was that he and Anita "[hung] around the Latin Quarter pointlessly for a few days before traveling on to Mexico City."[41]

THEY ARRIVED IN Mexico City on June 24, and stayed in the country for three months, as long as the $500, now $450, lasted, "passing from marvel to marvel and from amazement to amazement. . . . I was in a state of giddiness and rapture."[42] Under the influence of the travel essays in D. H. Lawrence's *Mornings in Mexico* (1927), which Bellow read on the bus journey south, he and Anita checked into the Hotel Monte Carlo (the hotel San Remo in Lawrence's 1926 novel, *The Plumed Serpent*), in the city's *centro histórico*, where Lawrence and his wife Frieda had stayed. The hotel turned out to be frequented by prostitutes; it was very busy at night but deserted during the day. Toward the end of the month the Bellows were joined by the Passins. Herb Passin had received a grant from the University of Chicago, where as an undergraduate he had been taught by the anthropologist Robert Redfield. The grant was to do fieldwork in the northern province of Chihuahua with the Tarahumara Indians, the subject of his proposed PhD dissertation.[43] Herb and Cora spent the summer with the Bellows touring Mexico, before Herb's fieldwork began in the autumn.

From Mexico City the two couples headed first to Cuernavaca, to the south, then to Pátzcuaro, in the state of Michoacán, then to Taxco, where they stayed for some weeks, and where relations between Bellow and Anita were especially difficult. At one point, according to Atlas, Bellow went off for a week with another woman.[44] Anita then had a very public retaliatory affair and after furious recriminations went off alone to Acapulco. In the interview with Roth, Bellow describes this episode circumspectly: "My mood was investigative. I wanted to see firsthand what the characters I was spending my time with [in Taxco] were up to. I sent my wife away to Acapulco—then a beach with a few huts. My strong desire was to go it alone. It never occurred to me that it might be a danger to Anita to be shipped off."[45]

Eleven years after the trip to Mexico, Bellow published a story in *Harper's Bazaar* entitled "By the Rock Wall" (April 1951), which may shed light on this episode. "Willard," the protagonist, recalls a moment, fifteen years earlier, when he and his wife, married only a year, went to Italy for "a delayed honeymoon." After two weeks in Rome, Willard decides he wants to go to Siena by himself for a week. "Why can't I come with you?" the wife asks. His answer is: "Well, I would like to go somewhere alone. We've been together for months now. Sometimes I feel I'd like to visit a place alone." The narrator explains what Willard was feeling: "She had to be with him, had to be an encumbrance, he had to order for her, explain things for her in the hotels because she was too timid to try to speak Italian; he felt he could not see things for her putting herself between. It was miserable of her to fear being alone for a week." All this was true, but as Willard also knows, his wife thought he was "getting rid of her so that he could chase women" (something he had done in the past). He encourages her to go off alone herself, to Amalfi (not a bad equivalent to Acapulco in 1940). The wife is terrified, but once she gets to Amalfi, she has an affair, presumably in retaliation. This affair she denies to Willard, though American friends knew of it. In the story's present, fifteen years later, the wife finally admits to the affair, encouraged by a conversation Willard has initiated, full of confessions of his own. The next morning Willard is furious. "What did you do that to me for?" To which she answers, "What did you leave me for? What did you expect?"

Bellow's description of the Acapulco episode occurs in a paragraph that begins: "I had been brought up to worry, but the worry seems not to have taken." Of the ingredients Bellow sought in Mexico—"barbarism, color, glamour, and risk"—the last was especially important, because it was connected to freedom, not just from external impediments but from internalized ones, the sort that made him fear a fate like Uncle Willie's (the sort handed down through generations of Old Country experience, immigrant experience, Jewish experience). "Everybody has his own pattern for liberation," Bellow told Roth of the time in Mexico, "and my own liberation took the form of an escape from anxiety." In Mexico there were "no uncles, no family bonds," also, he discovered to his delight, no worries, or fewer worries: "I never gave a thought to what would happen after my money had run out"; "I have to say also that I very rarely gave my father a thought"; "I discovered a talent for doing things in a headlong style."[46]

This talent led Bellow to Daniel P. Mannix, and to the eagle Mannix trained to hunt iguanas in the mountains around Taxco. Bellow met

Mannix through the Australian pulp fiction writer Jack Champion, part of a circle of expatriate writers, artists, jewelers (Taxco is famed for its silver), and bohemians, who hung out in a cantina in town called Paco's. Mannix was an author, a journalist, a photographer, an outdoorsman, an animal and bird trainer, and a side-show performer (sword swallowing, fire eating). Well-born and good-looking, from a Main Line family in Philadelphia, he came to Taxco in 1940 on honeymoon with his wife, Jule, rented a villa on the edge of town, and each morning set out from the villa to train Aguila ("eagle" in Spanish), an American bald eagle he had brought with him to Mexico. When Aguila was not in the mountains ripping lizards and iguanas apart, he perched in a bathroom in the villa, on a water tank just below the ceiling. According to Mannix, Bellow visited the villa only once and they did not talk together "for more than a few minutes." According to Bellow, in the interview with Roth, "seven mornings a week I was out with Mannix." Bellow's memories of these outings—or his borrowings from published accounts by Mannix—underlay the most memorable and bizarre episode in the Mexican section of *The Adventures of Augie March* (in Chapters 15 to 17), when Thea Fenchel, Augie's fierce girlfriend, persuades him to accompany her to Mexico to train the eagle Caligula. A condensed version of this episode was excerpted as a story entitled "The Eagle" in *Harper's Bazaar* in its February 1953 issue, and when Mannix read it, he threatened to sue. In Bellow's words, "Mannix demanded billing in his own name and Viking Press advised me to give him a footnote."[47]

What fascinated Bellow about Aguila, "a creature of boundless freedom and power," was that so magnificent a predator, "a death-dealing life force," could be made "to obey his trainer like any lesser creature."[48] Augie is comparably fascinated with Caligula. He watches spellbound as the eagle "ride[s] like an Attila's horseman through the air"; yet he hates the kill, "to see the little lizards hit and squirt blood, and their tiny fine innards of painted delicacy come out under Caligula's talons while he glared and opened his beak" (pp. 782, 781). When one of these lizards nips Caligula, the bird retreats, infuriating Thea. For Thea, "fierce nature shouldn't be like that" (p. 782), fierce nature is pure, while the human world is full of fearfulness and deceit. Caligula's "humanity" (i.e., fear and fallibility) is thus "hard to take" (p. 790). Like other "reality instructors" in the novel, Thea preaches hardness, what Grandma Lausch calls "a fighting nature of birds and worms" (p. 391).[49] "You stinking coward! You crow!" (p. 789), Thea later shrieks at the bird. How can Caligula fight iguanas "if a little nip does this to him?" (p. 782). When Augie describes the iguanas, one sees her point:

> These beasts were as fast and bold as anything I had ever seen, and they would jump anywhere and from any height, with a pure writhe of their sides, like fish. They had great muscles, like fish, and their flying was monstrously beautiful. I was astonished that they didn't dash themselves into pellets, like slugs of quicksilver, but when they smashed down they continued without any pause to run. They were faster than the wild pigs (p. 788).

To fight and vanquish such beasts, Augie implies, is, on the one hand, a task worthy of an eagle, emblem of heroic nobility, emblem also of Mexico and the United States; the image of Caligula ripping at the painted delicacy of the smaller lizard's innards, on the other hand, suits his Roman name.[50]

In the mountains with Mannix and Aguila, Bellow recalls, "the sun shone so dramatically, so explicitly, you were never allowed to forget death."[51] Death and sunlight are twinned in the Mexican settings of Bellow's fiction, as they are in Mexican or Aztec mythology. As Augie travels through Monterrey, all the objects he sees, "trees, bushes, stones," are "as explicit as glare and the spice of that heat could make them" (p. 768). Prominent among these objects are "corpses of dogs, rats, horses, asses, by the road. . . . Which is all to emphasize how openly death is received everywhere" (p. 771). "Where they [the giant iguanas] hung out," Augie tells us, "the light was very hot" (p. 778); "it was glorious how he [Caligula] would mount away high and seem to sit up there, really as if over fires of atmosphere" (p. 770). Later Augie talks of Mexico's "broadcast or exposing versus discreet light." What this light exposes, in addition to death or violence, is illusion. "What I want of the contrast of broadcast or exposing versus discreet light is to suggest what the claims are, or the illusions, the discreeter seems to allow" (p. 779). The sorts of illusions Augie has in mind are those Thea brings with her to Mexico, of pure or perfect being, of pure or perfect love. During his time with her, Augie finds a book in the villa which he reads throughout the Mexican episode, an anthology of utopias, including "Campanella's *City of the Sun*, More's *Utopia*, Machiavelli's *Discourses* and *The Prince*, as well as long selections from St. Simon, Comte, Marx and Engels" (p. 791).

When Caligula backs off after being nipped, as if "humanized" by pain, Augie grins. "'Why, if you're hurt, what do you expect?'" he asks Thea, "humanizing again." "Don't you grin about it," Thea cries. "I'm not," he replies, "it's the sun making me squint" (p. 782); the sun that exposes all. In the story "Mosby's Memoirs" (1968), Willard Mosby, on a Guggenheim grant, sits in a villa above Oaxaca writing his memoirs (Bellow wrote the story on a visit to Oaxaca in March 1967): "Stone-hearted Mosby, making fun of flesh and blood."[52] In his way, Mosby has been as fierce a reality instructor as Thea. But Mexico unsettles him. As he gazes below to the town, "bougainvillea pour[s] down the hillside, and the hummingbirds [are] spinning." He feels "ill with all this whirling, these colors, fragrances, ready to topple on him." It is death he senses in the exposing light: "Behind the green and red of Nature, dull black seemed to be thickly laid like mirror backing." His "fine blue eyes," in addition to being "direct, intelligent, disbelieving," are "light-pained" (p. 355). Only at the end of the story, when he finds himself in the tomb of a temple in Mitla, a work of perfect mathematical calculation, does he seek the light. Inside the tomb, he cannot breathe: "His heart was paralyzed. His lungs would not draw. . . . I cannot catch my breath! To be shut in here! To be dead here. . . . *Dead*—dead. Stooping, he looked for daylight. Yes, it was there. The light was there. The grace of life still there. Or, if not grace, air" (p. 373).

Stone-hearted Mosby has made a tomb of himself: "His doom was to live life to the end as Mosby" (p. 372). As his memoirs make clear, he has been inhuman in his treatment of others. In Mitla, the Zapotecs who built the temples practiced human sacrifice, "under Aztec influence" (p. 373) (Aztec sacrifice is mentioned in *Augie* as well [p. 771]). In the Aztec foundation myth, which Bellow would have known from Radcliffe-Brown's course on Mayan and Aztec cultures, the promised land, a wished-for place of purity and perfection, is signaled by the sudden appearance of an eagle perched on an *opuntia* or cactus growing out of a rock. In a modern version of the myth, depicted in the coat of arms of Mexico, there is the added symbol of a snake being killed by the eagle. This snake is sometimes depicted with a ring of feathers around its neck, which makes it look like an iguana (as well as the Aztec god Quetzalcoatl, Lawrence's "Plumed Serpent"). The iguanas in *Augie* are described as "really huge, with great frills or sails—those ancient membranes. The odor here was snaky, and we seemed in the age of snakes. . . . As I pointed [one] out we saw the Elizabethan top of him scoot away" (p. 788). Bellow weaves allusions to Aztec and later Mexican mythology into the Mexican chapters of *Augie*. These allusions, like Mexican light, reveal the cruelty and impossibility of Thea's and Mosby's dreams of perfection and invulnerability.[53]

Like Mosby's villa above Oaxaca, the villa the Bellows and the Passins rented while in Taxco was on a hill overlooking the town. It was owned by a Japanese painter, Tamiji Kitagawa, and came with a maid, who served breakfast on the terrace. In *Mornings in Mexico*, Lawrence writes of sitting outside on a patio at Christmas, in bright sunshine, "looking at a bit of sky and trees, then looking down at the page of his exercise book."[54] When not out with Mannix and Aguila, Bellow, too, according to Herb Passin, spent his mornings writing (not all that successfully: "I was groping"[55]). In the afternoons, he learned to ride, as Augie does. After a siesta, he and Anita used to stroll down into the town, eventually winding up at Paco's. Here Bellow drank and played cards with the pulp writers and artists who were its habitués, and whom, in the interview with Philip Roth, he describes as "low company." His attitude toward the crowd at Paco's seems to have been like Augie's attitude toward the crowd at "Hilario's," and his opinion of the pulp writers Wiley Moulton and Iggy Blaikie. It is at the poker table that we learn why Moulton calls Augie "Bolingbroke," questioning his air of innocence.

As was suggested in this book's introduction, Shakespeare's Bolingbroke becomes Henry IV partly through guile and simplicity, or feigned simplicity. When he defies royal banishment in *Richard II*, he says he has returned simply to "lay my claim / To my inheritance" (II. iii.134–35). His son is comparably guileful, hanging out at the Boar's Head while also hanging back. For Bellow, hanging back was habitual, a writerly detachment, but in addition his time in Mexico helped him to see that he would never be as bohemian as the crowd at Paco's. Although Herb Passin recalls that "we'd get so drunk we had to crawl up the hill,"[56] Bellow was never a great drinker. Nor would he ever settle for the lowered ambitions of the pulp writer. He learned the language but he remained apart. "It's certainly true that you have to lead a double life, maybe a quadruple life for that matter," Bellow admits in his conversation with Norman Manea, a fellow novelist. "I know perfectly well that that's the case because I experience it every day, just as you do."[57]

Among the people Bellow met at Paco's were Joseph Hilton Smyth, the publisher of *The Saturday Review of Literature*, and his girlfriend, an African American cabaret singer named Hazel Scott. The cadaverous Smyth was the author of pulp novels (*I, Mobster; To Nowhere and Return*), who in 1938 emerged from bohemian obscurity in Greenwich Village to purchase two venerable American magazines, *The Living Age* and *North America Review*. He then bought a third, *Current History*, plus a large interest in *Saturday Review*. The source of Smyth's wealth remained mysterious until 1942, when the FBI arrested him, along with two associates, and accused him of spying for the Japanese. Smyth pled guilty, confessing that he had received $125,000 over the previous four years for serving as a Japanese agent.[58] When Bellow met him in Taxco in the summer of 1940, he was flush, accompanied by the beautiful, light-skinned Scott, already a star on radio and in the clubs of New York. Born in Trinidad and Tobago, Scott trained at Juilliard, was mentored by Art Tatum and Teddy Wilson, performed as pianist and singer with Count Basie, starred on Broadway, played twice at Carnegie Hall, and later married the African American pastor and politician Adam Clayton Powell Jr. An outspoken critic of racial injustice, later of McCarthyism, she was often accused of having Communist sympathies. When Bellow met her with Smyth she had just turned twenty.

Smyth and Scott are the likely inspiration for the interracial couple in a novel Bellow worked on in 1940 entitled "Acatla," the name he gives to the Taxco-like setting of the Mexican scenes in *Augie* (taken, perhaps, from the town of Acatlán, in Puebla, a state to the southeast of Taxco). "Acatla," the earliest surviving Bellow manuscript, consists of 66 pages, in three fragments, from a work of at least 106 pages. It describes the consequences of an interracial couple, the Hobarts (an assumed name, they're not married), booking into a hotel in Acatla. The hotel, Las Palmas, is managed by Scinatti, "of Piedmontese heritage" (p. 26), and when some American guests complain about the presence of the interracial couple, Scinatti decides, "from a business standpoint" (p. 21), that the couple will have to go. After all, "I can't tell them [the protesting Americans] what to like. It is not for me to tell them" (p. 45). Later Scinatti argues that "one man cannot change everything. . . . You will not change anything. I will not change anything" (p. 48). When two young students, one a political radical, protest at the decision, Scinatti remains firm. Another guest in the hotel recognizes Mrs. Hobart as Emma Paulas, whom he used to see "in New York at the Kangaroo Club" (p. 29). Among the bigoted American residents at the hotel are the

Alexanders, like something out of Lawrence ("He stood tensely on the stirrups as if determined to overmaster his horse, to make it submit to his will" [p. 53]). The first and longest fragment ends with the Hobarts ejected from Las Palmas. The second much shorter fragment, titled "Chapter III," consists of little more than preliminaries to an account of Hobart by a character named Bartell. "There have been times when I would have paid to be unable to remember a single thing about Richard Hobart" (p. 77), Bartell begins, sounding like Marlow in *Heart of Darkness*, or John Dowell in Ford Madox Ford's *The Good Soldier*, at which point the fragment breaks off. The third fragment, "Earl Huner," is comparably brief and teasing. A character named Jacoby begins telling the early history of Hobart and his brother, Jay, who were involved in a failed scam of some sort in Europe. And again the fragment breaks off.

The writing in "Acatla," a third person narrative, is controlled, polished, nothing more. Rare moments of life occur in description, as when a character feeds a doe and feels "the humid, massy softness of the creature's muzzle" (p. 40), or when Mrs. Hobart breakfasts in the hotel with "the trained composure of a person who had mastered the secret of imperturbable privacy under the public stare" (p. 32). It is the content of "Acatla" rather than its style that is noteworthy, in particular its preoccupation with racial injustice, the subject of "The Very Dark Trees," the novel Bellow would finish the following year. Bellow's interest in race was fostered by his studies not only at Northwestern but at the University of Chicago, which had a tradition of research into "Negro-White relations." Passin, too, was interested in race. Redfield, his teacher at the University of Chicago, was an authority on the subject, and immediately before coming to Mexico, Passin had worked on a University of Chicago excavation project at Kincaid, Illinois, a poor farming region in the center of the state in the Ohio River Valley. The WPA employed impoverished black and white farmers from the area to do the digging at the site, and Passin became interested in the racial makeup of the community, as well as in the ethnological peculiarities of the region. In addition to their work on the excavation site, he and a fellow graduate student, Robert Bennett, with the encouragement of Redfield, decided to interview the diggers at Kincaid about a range of issues, including their attitudes to race.[59] In Taxco, therefore, when Bellow talked of or read from a work in progress, something he did throughout his life, he would have found in Passin an informed and interested listener.

The most memorable of Bellow's adventures in Mexico occurred late in the trip. Through Al Glotzer and a European woman Bellow had met in Taxco, an interview with Trotsky was arranged for Bellow and Herb Passin, for the morning of August 20. The meeting was to take place at Trotsky's villa at 19 Avenida Viena in Coyoacán, now a district of Mexico City, at that time a village just to the south. "One of my reasons for going to Mexico," Bellow told Norman Manea, "was to have some conversation with Trotsky." When he and Passin arrived at Avenida Viena, they noticed "an unusual amount of excitement."

> We asked for Trotsky and they said who are you, and we said we were newspapermen. They said Trotsky's in the hospital. So we went to the hospital and asked to see Trotsky and they opened the door and said, he's in there, so we went in and there was Trotsky. He had just died. He had been assassinated that morning. He was covered in blood and bloody bandages and his white beard was full of blood.[60]

In fact, Trotsky did not die until the evening of August 21, after an operation, and more than twenty-four hours after the attack. The assassin was a mysterious Soviet agent, Ramón Mercader, who had infiltrated Trotsky's inner circle.[61] Trotsky was in his study reading, when Mercader, standing behind him, took an alpine axe from beneath the raincoat he was carrying and smashed it into the back of the Old Man's head. The blow penetrated seven centimeters into the skull. Trotsky screamed and struggled with the assassin; bodyguards rushed in and would have beaten Mercader to death had Trotsky not stopped them.

In "Writers, Intellectuals, Politics: Mainly Reminiscence" (1993), Bellow gives a slightly different and more detailed account of his and Passin's visit to the scene than the one he gave to Manea:

> It was on the morning of our appointment that he was struck down. Arriving in Mexico City, we were met by the headlines. When we went to his villa we must have been taken for foreign journalists, and we were directed to the hospital. The emergency room was in disorder. We had only to ask for Trotsky. A door into a small side room was opened for us, and there we saw him. He had just died. A cone of bloody bandages was on his head. His cheeks, his nose, his

beard, his throat, were streaked with blood and with dried irides-
cent trickles of iodine.[62]

According to Passin, in an interview with Atlas, the meeting with
Trotsky was arranged for August 21 not 20. News of the attack on
the previous day reached them when they arrived in the city and they
immediately hurried not to the hospital but to the morgue, on Calle
de Tacuba. It was in front of the morgue that the police waved them
through the gathered crowds. "They went up a flight of stairs, Passin
recalled, 'and there, by God, was Trotsky.' The open coffin was surrounded by a crowd of photographers on ladders."[63]

Bellow drew on this episode both in *Augie* and in "The Mexican
General," the second of his fictional contributions to *Partisan Review*,
published as the lead item in the May–June 1942 issue.[64] The story grew
in part out of the visit to Coyoacán, in part out of a visit to Janitzio,
the main island in Lake Pátzcuaro, in the state of Michoacán. In an undated
postcard to Al Glotzer, Bellow described Janitzio as "the wildest place
I have ever seen . . . el presidente's private reserve—muy primitive you
know, with pigs underfoot." It was here that he encountered the model
for the general, "a police official I met in Pátzcuaro accompanied by
two ladies"[65] (according to Atlas, the general was Colonel Leandro A.
Sánchez Salazar, *jefe* [chief], the title given to the general in the story,
of the Mexican secret police, later, with Julián Gorkin, coauthor of
Murder in Mexico: The Assassination of Leon Trotsky [1950]).[66] The story's
setting is the tourist town of Pátzcuaro, and the general is accompanied by three ladies, his "nieces," with whom he is on intimate terms.
He has come to Pátzcuaro to recuperate from the stress of managing
the scenes surrounding the assassination of Trotsky (the *viejo* or "the
old Russo"). "It didn't all happen in Coyoacán," the general's lieutenant, Citron, explains, "it merely began there: the rest took place at the
Cruz Verde hospital and at the mortician's at Tacuba 4 and elsewhere"
(p. 244). The general has political ambitions and parades his authority
at the murder scene, the hospital, and the morgue, allowing photographers and journalists inside ("'But no noise,' he said. 'Please respect
the presence of the Señora [Trotsky's wife, Natalia Sedova]'" [p. 247]),
making statements, inserting himself into photographs, showing up at
ceremonies and memorials, always in uniform, "always next to the old
woman" (p. 250).

No one in the story is equal to the occasion of the great man's death. Citron's job is to watch the sobbing assassin: "I have seen better behaved murderers than that one. I felt sorry for the *viejo*. He deserved a more manly antagonist" (p. 245). The general has little sense of the importance of Trotsky: "he could feel no more than his own part of it. He knew nothing at all about the rest, the two old people and the murderer and what it meant to have an enemy at the other side of the world at whom you could never strike back" (p. 248).[67] Citron, a thoughtful man, "a man of superior education" (p. 180), is depressed by the distance between the event's importance and his experience of it, "a lack of fitness that throws suspicion on everything and makes us sure there must have been precisely such vanities and blunders in the greatest Passions. Although it would be cheap to discredit them for that" (p. 249). He feels "carried along" by events, distressed by and vaguely complicit in the vulgarity over which the general presides. In this, he is like his creator. Before Bellow decided to meet Trotsky, he worried over his motives. "I thought, how could I go see the great man and take up his time by discussing theoretical questions that he understood a thousand times better than I, especially since he invented the theory himself. I couldn't possibly have argued with him."[68] Though "always a little reluctant to push myself on people," he nonetheless decides to go, for reasons he lamely justifies: "Finally, I thought, I have an introduction now to him, and I am in Mexico, and will take the bus and make an appointment." The funeral, which he attended with Passin, was "the usual Trotskyite oratory."[69]

In Chapter 20 of *Augie*, Bellow sends his hero, heartbroken over the failed love affair with Thea, to Coyoacán, where a Trotskyist friend from Chicago, Hooker Frazer, is part of the Old Man's inner circle. Augie arrives sometime after an earlier assassination attempt of May 1940 (the Mexican painter and Stalinist David Siqueiros was one of its leaders), and Frazer tries to enlist him as a bodyguard. The plan is for Trotsky to take off his beard and mustache, cut his hair, and travel incognito through the country as a tourist. To do this, Frazer explains, "he's going to need a nephew from the States" (p. 858). Though "rescue and peril" attract Augie, he is wary of being "sucked into another one of those great currents where I can't be myself" (p. 858). In the end, he agrees on the plan, but is relieved when the Old Man vetoes it. What persuades him is proximity to greatness. He was "flattered by the chance to be with this giant historical personality, speeding around the mountains" (p. 859). Something similar seems to have motivated

Bellow, both in attempting to see Trotsky and in attending his funeral. After the funeral, he and Passin returned to Acapulco where they met Anita and Cora and stayed some days at the Excelsior Hotel, high above the bay. There they swam, sunbathed, and watched local boys dive for coins from the rocky cliff. Passin then went off to his fieldwork with the Tarahumara Indians and the Bellows and Cora climbed into her Ford, the car they had eloped in, and headed back to Chicago. The only thing the Passins' son, Tom, remembers hearing of the Mexico trip was that his mother fearlessly negotiated the mountain roads on the journey home.

ONCE BACK IN Hyde Park, the Bellows rented an apartment at 5235 Kimbark Avenue, one street closer to the campus than Kenwood Avenue. Anita returned to social work and Bellow resumed teaching at Pestalozzi-Froebel (among the courses he taught were Anthropology I and American Minority Groups[70]). The war and the draft figure prominently in his correspondence. In a letter postmarked December 9, 1940, Bellow writes to Tarcov with news of his draft number: 282, which means that even "with every possible deferment I can't hope to stay out of uniform longer than a year. . . . At best I can only make class 2 [deferred from the draft because of occupational status]." Bellow professes not to be fussed by this news: "I was surprised that I personally was getting away with it so long. . . . It's a rather heavy-footed irony that I who hate so much and fear so much anything of a 'kill' or 'crush' connection should be drawn into army service so quickly."

In a letter to Tarcov of January 21, 1941, Bellow is silent about the draft, and apologizes for not being able to repay a loan. He needs money for a trip to Windsor, Ontario, the southernmost city in Canada, for reasons he does not specify. The purpose of the trip is revealed in a "Petition for Naturalization" issued by the Department of Justice on June 2, 1943. According to the petition, Bellow entered the United States on January 31, 1941, from Windsor, arriving at Detroit and seeking naturalization under Section 311 of the Nationality Act of 1940. In a subsequent letter to Tarcov, of February 8, Bellow writes: "I'm completely legalized now and there is no danger for me as long as aliens are not touched, and even then it is safe to suppose that Canadians will have relative immunity when they start filling the camps (for I believe there will be camps). So far indications are that since I am a non-citizen I am not draftable and, while I don't feel exactly comfortable and secure, it is reasonably permissible for me to make some plans for next year." The reference to "camps" recalls "The Hell They Can't!" and suggests a continuing Trotskyist doubt about the war, in spite of Bellow's opposition to Trotsky's views on other political issues.[71]

Bellow's attitude to the war was reinforced by *Partisan Review*, which as he told Keith Botsford in his interview, "had considerable influence with me." People he admired at the time, such as Dwight Macdonald and Clement Greenberg, "kept saying, 'Don't kid yourself, this is just another imperialist war. Don't be seduced by propaganda as people were in World War I.'"[72] The formal position *PR* took on the war was no position at all, or no single position. In "A Statement," published at the front of the issue of January–February 1942, the first to appear after Pearl Harbor, the editors (Clement Greenberg, Dwight Macdonald, George L. K. Morris, William Phillips, and Philip Rahv) agreed to disagree. "No two editors," they admitted, "hold the same position on all major issues. The actual outbreak of hostilities has not altered this line-up. It is clear, therefore, that *Partisan Review* can have no editorial line on the war. Its editors will continue to express themselves on the issue as individuals." If readers find the views expressed by individual editors "radical" ("in the literal sense of 'going to the roots'") so be it: "No intelligent decisions can be made without a full consideration of alternatives." Behind this staunch endorsement of freedom of expression, it has been suggested, lies an element of calculation, especially after the cooperation of Allied forces with Stalin, from 1941 when the Nazis invaded the Soviet Union, to the end of the war in 1945. As Hugh Wilford puts it in *The New York Intellectuals: From Vanguard to Institution* (1995), "even Macdonald recognised the need for editorial self-restraint lest the government crack down on *PR* as an anti-war publication." But opinion was genuinely divided, as it was with Bellow. Though "sobered up" by the fall of France, as earlier by the Nazi attacks on Jews in Warsaw in 1939, "I was still in the grip of leftwing ideology."[73]

There were also temperamental and career reasons for Bellow's ambivalence about the war, in addition to his hatred and fear of "kill" and "crush." When "Two Morning Monologues" was published in the May–June 1941 issue of *PR*, Bellow was only twenty-five, proud to be appearing in the same pages as T. S. Eliot, Randall Jarrell, Allen Tate, James Burnham, Clement Greenberg, and Dwight Macdonald. Earlier that spring, Philip Rahv and his wife had come out to Chicago, accompanied by William Barrett. Rahv was introduced to Bellow by Barrett and was impressed, as he was with Harold Kaplan, characterizing them both as "the Delmore Schwartz type: brilliant and yet at the same time methodical and responsible."[74] "Two Morning Monologues," however, was the sole fiction Bellow had published in five and a half years[75]—despite spending the last three and a half of those years as a full-time writer, or almost a full-time writer, taking on only part-time work, dependent for financial support on his wife and on handouts from his family. Since his marriage, Bellow's stories had been rejected not only by well-known publications such as *The Saturday Evening Post* and *The Kenyon Review*, but by obscure periodicals, most recently, *Accent*, published out of the University of Illinois at Urbana-Champaign.[76] Had *PR* not accepted the monologues, and later "The Mexican General," he told Norman Manea, "I don't know what I would have done. . . . I would have been very deeply discouraged." Yet he was not proud of the stories ("I thought I could do better"),[77] a characteristic reaction, evidence of confidence in his powers. Though he might doubt his ability to support a writing life, Bellow rarely doubted his potential as a writer. His extreme sensitivity to criticism in these years—throughout his life, some would say—had less to do with authorial anxiety than with wanting his due. As William Barrett, late of Wieboldt Hall, put it, the "chip" Bellow carried on his shoulder in the 1940s was "of self-confidence."[78]

BELLOW'S FAITH IN his powers is illustrated by the fate of "The Very Dark Trees," the novel he was at work on for most of 1941. What we know of the plot of this novel comes primarily, via Atlas, from Nathan Gould, who remembers it as Kafkaesque, a fable about "an enlightened southerner," a teacher at a Midwestern university, who suddenly, on the way home from class, turns black. Once home, his wife doesn't recognize him, then locks him in the basement so as not to alarm the neighbors. Gould remembered the novel as funny. He also remembered that Bellow's friends referred to it as "White No More." On February 23, 1942, Bellow sent a draft of the novel to William Roth, editor in chief of the Colt Press, who had written to him a year earlier after reading the "Two Morning Monologues." Except for a reworked opening chapter, the manuscript was a first draft, two hundred pages long, between sixty and seventy thousand words, and Bellow was sending it, he explained in a covering note, "at Rahv's insistence." The Colt Press was a small outfit in San Francisco, but had published books by Edmund Wilson and Henry Miller, as well as the first novel of Paul Goodman, also late of Wieboldt Hall. In his cover note, Bellow announced that "the Army is hot on my heels and I should like to have the fate of the book decided before I leave." For reasons he does not specify, he was no longer immune from the draft.[79]

After hearing nothing from Roth for six weeks, Bellow wrote a second letter, on April 2: "The Army has just notified me that I will be inducted on June 15 [a date that allowed him to finish his term's teaching at Pestalozzi-Froebel]. . . . Please let me know how I stand at your earliest opportunity" (in a P.S. he asks Roth if he's interested in "novelettes": "I have several which I am very eager to publish"). The next day a letter from Roth arrived (his and Bellow's letters crossed in the mail). Roth liked the novel, would publish it in November, and Bellow would receive an advance of $150 on date of publication. Bellow wrote back the same day "bowled over" by the news and agreeing to the terms. He had two and a half months to get the novel ready for publication and enough money from teaching not to need an advance right away. The next letter he wrote to Roth, on June 24, was less upbeat: "After rushing like the devil to get through in time, I was turned back temporarily at the induction center on a technicality." He would not now be inducted until mid-July, but as he'd given up his teaching job he faced debts and "an incomeless month unless you can see your way clear to advancing me something." Roth's answer, which we know about from Bellow's answer back, was worse than a refusal: he himself had been drafted, into the Office of War Information, was about to be shipped to Alaska, and was suspending all Colt's publishing plans for the duration of the war. He enclosed a check for $50, offering more money if Bellow needed it. Bellow's undated response was stoical and sympathetic. Though "terribly hard hit by the bad news," he thanked Roth for the $50, which he would have returned "if I did not need it so badly, having gotten myself in debt." As for the manuscript: "If you don't think you can find someone to take it I should like you to send it back so that I can offer it to a few more publishers before the war snuffs out all my chances."

Before Roth accepted "The Very Dark Trees" it had been turned down by James Laughlin of New Directions, who had seen only six or seven chapters. Laughlin later turned down Bellow's suggestion, in a letter of April 2, 1942, about "novelettes" ("Since you publish a poem of the month why not also a novelette of the month? . . . I have several sixteen to twenty thousand word stories. They are not *New Directions* in your sense of it. But then I think originality is a better criterion than bizarre form"). After Roth closed down Colt, the manuscript was sent to the Vanguard Press, which had published Nelson Algren's first novel and James T. Farrell's *Studs Lonigan* trilogy. Vanguard started life in 1926 as a charitable foundation, underwritten by the American Fund for Public Service, better known as the Garland Fund (named after the radical philanthropist Charles Garland). Its first publications were cheap editions of the works of Marx, Engels, and Lenin, on the model of the Haldeman-Julius classics Bellow read as an adolescent. In 1932 Vanguard was purchased by James Henle, a journalist who had worked as an editor at *McCall's*, and who aimed to preserve the imprint's left-wing character while also making a profit. He received four reader's reports on "The Very Dark Trees." The first described the novel as "an extraordinary tour de force"; the second, from Evelyn Shrifte, who would become president of Vanguard in 1952, found it impressive but puzzling (she wanted Henle to read it to tell her not only what he thought of it commercially but "what you think [the] author is trying to say"); the third felt it didn't come off, especially toward the end, where "the story of the negro witnessing the Trotsky episode is just too fantastic, and seems to be stuck in the book"; and the fourth "didn't take to [it] at all," illiterately complaining that its analysis of race "could have been done without the miracle hoi-polloi" (also that "the narrator, in spite of his symbolical tragedy, is singularly unattractive"). Vanguard turned the novel down, but Henle was impressed with Bellow, and asked to see future works.[80]

Bellow was as little satisfied with "The Very Dark Trees" as he had been with the *Partisan Review* stories. After Roth was forced to abandon publishing plans, Bellow informed him that "Rahv wrote in Macdonald's name that he would undertake to peddle the novel for me." In the same undated letter, Bellow explained that "I feel I am miles and centuries away from *The Very Dark Trees*—whole developmental heights. Oh, I still feel it deserves publication, in fact since I will never have time to finish any of the long things I have started I am determined it *must* be published, for it is to give me the right (in the postwar period, if we have one) to continue as a writer. But in a sense it is business, not literature. I am taking your word and am working over a novelette which is, well, fifty times better than the novel." As the letter suggests, part of Bellow's ambivalence about the war was its likely effect on his writing:

it would prevent him from finishing long works and thus from having "the right . . . to continue as a writer." Publishing "The Very Dark Trees" mattered for the same reason, a "business" reason. Soon after receiving Roth's acceptance letter at the beginning of April, Bellow provided *PR* with a contributor's note for the May–June 1942 issue, which opens with "The Mexican General" (followed by contributions from Kafka, James T. Farrell, Lionel Trilling, and Christopher Isherwood, among others): "Saul Bellow, a young Chicago writer, is now in the Army. Colt Press is bringing out his first novel, *The Very Dark Trees.*" By the time the issue appeared, Bellow was neither in the army nor was Colt bringing out his novel. Sometime after the rejection from the Vanguard Press toward the end of the year (one of the Vanguard reports is dated November 6, 1942), Bellow destroyed what seems to have been the sole manuscript of "The Very Dark Trees," tossing it down an incinerator chute. "When I picked it up and read it through I got cold feet," he recalled. "I thought it just wasn't good enough. And I destroyed the manuscript. I thought—not this—I don't want this albatross hung around my neck. I just threw it into the furnace."[81]

The immolation was partly a product of changing circumstances. In the intervening months, "business" worries had receded, as "literature," in the form of what was probably an expanded version of the "novelette," looked the business.[82] Early in June 1943, some six months after Vanguard's rejection of "The Very Dark Trees," Bellow was at work on the final revision of a novel with the Dostoyevskian title, "Notes of a Dangling Man," the first chapter of which had been accepted by *PR* (it would appear under this title in the issue of September–October 1943).[83] When Bellow finished the revisions he sent the novel off to Henle at Vanguard. According to a memo of June 27, Vanguard had all but promised to publish a book of short stories by Bellow "next year." "I think we should do everything possible to keep Mr. Bellow happy," reads a penciled note on the memo, "he is a writer of distinction and we shd. feel proud to publish his book." On July 7 Bellow received a telegram from Henle reading: "AM DEEPLY IMPRESSED BY DANGLING MAN BUT WANT TO GET ANOTHER OPINION." On July 21 the novel was accepted. Henle offered a $200 advance, half upon signing. Seven months later it was published under the shortened title *Dangling Man.*

By this date, on the strength of the stories in *PR*, Bellow had acquired an agent. "His name is Max Lieber," Bellow wrote in a letter of October 1942 to Melvin Tumin, a friend from the University of Wisconsin, now doing fieldwork in Guatemala (for a PhD in anthropology at North-western, under Herskovits).[84] Lieber's office is "a cold, dim cell on Fifth Avenue near 44th Street." Though a Communist—Whittaker Chambers's closest friend "after the Alger Hisses"[85]—his primary interest, Bellow reports in another undated letter to Tumin, is profit. "'Balzac wrote for money,' he says. 'Oh, don't sneer. So did Shakespeare and so did Beethoven. And you'll either come around or remain obscure. We'll see whether you sneer when you're forty.' I assured him it was an ineradicable trait and that I would sneer till eighty if I lived that long." Lieber had well-known clients, "such talents as Erskine Caldwell and Albert Halper, etc.," and "now that we have each other I may start appearing in print a little more often, providing, of course, that I have the leisure and power to write in the Army."[86] On February 24, 1943, as Bellow polished *Dangling Man*, Lieber offered a story titled "Juif" to Whit Burnett, editor of *Story* magazine. In a penciled note to Lieber's letter, either Burnett or someone else at *Story* described its subject: "Anti-semitism in a children's tb ward in Canada."[87] The story was rejected. "Juif" was the seed for "Memoirs of a Bootlegger's Son," parts of which, including Joshua Lurie's stay in the children's ward at the Royal Vic, would find their way into *Herzog* and *Humboldt's Gift*.

Though Bellow was right about "The Very Dark Trees" (that he could "continue as a writer" without it), even work he valued, "literature," involved compromise. Another Bellow story from this period, "The Car," was offered to *Partisan Review* and rejected, for reasons relayed to Bellow by Macdonald. Bellow's response to this rejection makes clear the difficulties he was having fitting himself to the literary tastes of his audience, in the first instance, the magazine's editors and readers.[88] These tastes were European and modernist and "The Car" failed to meet them in part because of what Macdonald called its "centerless facility which destroys the form by excess elaboration." Bellow was prepared to admit weaknesses in his writing (partly attributable, he felt, to his circumstances), but not exactly the weaknesses specified by Macdonald.

> It is not because I write too easily that I sometimes fail. I would be more successful, perhaps, if I did write with more careless dash. But what I find heartbreakingly difficult in these times is fathoming the reader's imagination. If he and I were both of a piece, it would not

be so hard. But as it is I am ringed around with uncertainties and I often fail to pull myself together properly, banishing distraction and anxiety. And so I find myself perpetually asking, "How far shall I take this character? Have I made such and such a point clear? Will the actions of X be understood? Shall I destroy a subtlety by hammering it?" etc.[89]

In both *Dangling Man* and *The Victim*, his second novel, Bellow was, he later explained, "establishing my credentials, proving that a young man from Chicago had a right to claim the world's attention, so I was restrained, controlled, demonstrating that I could write 'good.'"[90] As the response to Macdonald suggests, though, writing "good" was a strain, not only because Bellow was unsure of his audience, but because in seeking to meet its needs he felt he was losing touch with himself. The initial rush of composition—twenty thousand words in two weeks, he told Tumin—was followed, as so often in his career, by a period of torturous development and polish. In this period, he both pursued and resented what he called "letter-perfect" writing, a "Flaubertian standard." "Not a bad standard, to be sure," he admitted, but restricting: "because of the circumstances of my life and because of my upbringing in Chicago as a son of immigrants. I could not, with such an instrument as I developed in the first two books, express a variety of things I knew intimately."[91]

Evidence of resentment and resistance is found on the very first page of *Dangling Man*, a novel made up of the journal entries of Joseph, among the least controlled of Bellow's protagonists. In the following passage, quoted in part in Chapter 1 in connection with Russian openness of expression, Joseph takes aim:

Do you have feelings? There are correct and incorrect ways of indicating them. Do you have an inner life? It is nobody's business but your own. Do you have emotions? Strangle them. To a degree, everyone obeys this code. And it does admit a limited kind of candor, a closedmouth straightforwardness. But on the truest candor it has an inhibitory effect. Most serious matters are closed to the hardboiled. They are unpracticed in introspection, and therefore badly equipped to deal with opponents whom they cannot shoot like big game or outdo in daring.

If you have difficulties, grapple with them silently, goes one
of their commandments. To hell with that! I intend to talk about
mine, and if I had as many mouths as Siva has arms and kept going
all the time, I still could not do myself justice.

Hemingway is the main target here, but behind him lies an army of
the unfazed, with Flaubert at its head. Joseph is anything but unfazed,
but that hardly makes him unique, certainly to readers of *PR*. He's a
figure out of European fiction, from Dostoyevsky, as we've seen, from
Kafka, as the absence of a surname suggests, from Rilke, whose *Notebooks of Malte Laurids Brigge* (1910), "really hypnotized and turned [me]
on. . . . Seemed to turn on a channel for me."[92] When Harold Kaplan
was lent a copy of the first chapter of *Dangling Man* by Clement Greenberg, he pronounced it "very finished and professional," but also "rather
conventional."[93] In resisting prevailing tastes, Joseph reflects them,
which makes him like his creator.

IN THE LETTER TO Macdonald about "The Car," Bellow calls *Dangling
Man* "a semi-autobiographical novel," and Joseph is like his creator in
a number of ways. He's handsome and knows it, having been "brought
up to think myself handsome" (p. 52). His eyes, "rather too full, a little
prominent, in fact," are guarded, even forbidding, as if "keeping intact
and free from encumbrance a sense of his own being, its importance"
(p. 16). He's quick to anger, often puts his foot in his mouth ("I couldn't
help myself," he explains, after an unfortunate remark, "I was suddenly
in a state of mind that required directness for its satisfaction" [p. 12]),
and he has "a mad fear of being slighted or scorned, an exacerbated
'honor'" (p. 107). His circumstances are also like Bellow's. Joseph has
waited seven months to be drafted when the novel opens. Four months
later, still dangling, he volunteers, on the novel's last page. During this
period, everyone tries to set him straight. His brother, Amos, a mixture
of Sam and Maury, wants him to go to officer training, so he won't
be ordered about. "I'm used to that," he replies (p. 44). Amos advises
him to marry money and can't "accept the fact that it is possible for
a member of his family to live on so little" (p. 41). Joseph grew up
on St. Dominique Street, with a Montreal childhood like Bellow's (the
photograph of his maternal grandfather is that of Bellow's maternal
grandfather, Moshe Gordin[94]). His politics, like his draft status, resem-

ble Bellow's: "as between their imperialism and ours, if a full choice were possible, I would take ours" (p. 59). For some years, he has lived in cheap apartments and rooming houses near the university, including one on Dorchester Avenue, where Bellow lived in 1944–45. His in-laws "live on the Northwest Side, a dreary hour's ride on the El" (p. 10). Iva, his wife, whom he loves but cheats on and neglects, is pretty, patient, sympathetic, and "as far as ever from what I once desired to make her" (except in their quarrels, which give her a "brave, shaky, new defiance" [p. 70]). His circle of friends, a putative "colony of the spirit" (p. 26), is scattered by war and the lure of New York, its occasional gatherings tense with external as well as internal pressures.

These resemblances were clear to Bellow's family and friends ("absolutely, no question about it," according to Sam's daughter, Lesha); less clear was Bellow's relation to Joseph's state of mind at the novel's end, an important question given Bellow's later distance from what many reviewers thought of as the novel's representative pessimism ("I can't read a page of it without feeling embarrassed," Bellow told an interviewer in 1963, "the ideas in it are the ideas of a very young man"[95]). As was mentioned in the introduction to this book, before dangling, Joseph had worked on "several essays, mainly biographical, on the philosophers of the Enlightenment. I was in the midst of one on Diderot when I stopped" (p. 5). He had also "made a study of the early ascetics, and, earlier, of Romanticism and the child prodigy" (pp. 17–18). Joseph's intellectual background is like that of Moses Herzog, who succumbs to a sense of the failure or impossibility of Romantic—though not exclusively Romantic—notions of brotherhood or common humanity, greatness of purpose, honesty, agency, "pure freedom" (p. 112). In Herzog's case, in a time of personal crisis, the result is breakdown; in Joseph's case, in a time of world crisis, the result is resignation, bolstered by disillusion, or freedom from illusion, of the sort voiced by many of the contributors to *Partisan Review*, or by the writers and thinkers they wrote about and valued, not just Dostoyevsky and Kafka, but Nietzsche, Sartre, Camus, and Flaubert. "I am no longer to be held accountable for myself," Joseph declares in the novel's last words, written on his last day of civilian life:

I am grateful for that. I am in other hands, relieved of self-determination, freedom cancelled.

Hurray for regular hours!

And for supervision of the spirit!
Long live regimentation!

When chided by a friend, the writer and sociologist David T. Bazelon, about the novel's dispiriting conclusion, Bellow defended it, in a letter of March 22, 1944, as "ironic": "I don't advise others to follow the *Dangling Man* into regimentation. I don't encourage surrender. I'm speaking of wretchedness and saying that no man by his own effort finds his way out of it. To some extent the artist does. But the moral man, the citizen, doesn't. He can't." That the artist "to some extent" finds his way out is a Flaubertian notion. In the 1960 essay "The Sealed Treasure," Bellow writes of Flaubert's belief that "the writer by means of imagery and style must supply the human qualities that the exterior world lacked. . . . The important humanity of the novel must be the writer's own." This view Bellow sees more widely in modern or modernist fiction: if "the insistent aesthetic purpose in novelists like Flaubert and Henry James and Virginia Woolf and James Joyce is tyrannical at times," crowding out other forms of purpose, "we are greatly compensated with poetry and insight, but it often seems as though the writer were deprived of all power except the power to see and to despair."[96] In *Dangling Man*, views like these are voiced by Joseph's friend John Pearl, a painter who supports himself by working in an advertising firm. "The real world," Pearl writes, "is the world of art and of thought. There is only one worth-while sort of work, that of the imagination" (p. 64). When in despair about modernity, Joseph agrees: "In spite of the calamity, the lies and the moral buggery, the odium, the detritus of wrong and sorrow dropped on every heart," an artist like Pearl "can keep a measure of cleanliness and freedom" (p. 65).

Joseph is no artist, but Bellow describes him, in an undated letter to Tumin, as a man who strives "with all his heart" to resist the pressures of modernity. That he succumbs to them in the end is "because his age *requires* it."[97] Joseph writes of being "harried, pushed, badgered," not only by external forces but by "the world internalized": "It wants me to stop living this way [i.e., in pursuit of "pure freedom"]. It's prodding me to the point where I shall no longer care what happens to me" (p. 120). In another letter to Tumin, Bellow offers a nonliterary source for Joseph's sense of his situation:

Passin is back, and I was never more glad to see him. We were together on Monday. To talk to him made me realize how badly my thinking had been going. I tried to discuss Erich Fromm's *Escape from Freedom.* The book had impressed me greatly and affected me emotionally. I believed it, swallowed it and could find no words to explain or arguments to defend it. Lack of steady contact with people is beginning to have a deleterious effect on me.

I don't know if you have read the book. Its thesis is that freedom has proved too burdensome to modern man. Historically it has been hard-won through revolution and martyrdom and against nature, inward and outward. Its premium has been a more highly perceptive and dignified race of men. Its shortcoming loneliness and anxiety. Man's lot in a civilized world is to be lonely unless he can reunite himself with it on a higher level, that is on a level where he continues to be free. Now you can see why it had such appeal. It suddenly became clear that I was eager to go into the army from weariness. I too wanted submission, like any Stuttgart grocer. For a while I was ashamed of myself, until it came to me that autonomy is a peacetime luxury and when one doesn't know whether to plan one month, two months or three weeks ahead freedom of choice narrows down to the way one fixes one's hair or to the way one words his prayers. I think you will find your Indians more self-determined.[98]

It is hard to make out from this letter what in the end Bellow thinks of Fromm's ideas. He begins by being impressed and persuaded by them; then finds he can't explain or defend them properly to Passin. When he says he was ashamed to find himself submitting "like any Stuttgart grocer," until he realized that autonomy was impossible in wartime, one cannot tell if he still believes this, or if he now believes he was wrong to believe it. When he says a "lack of steady contact with people" (like Passin) has had "a deleterious effect" on his thinking, does he mean "because it allowed me to take Fromm seriously"? One cannot tell, as one cannot wholly or confidently accept the conclusion of *Dangling Man* as ironic. Ironic on Bellow's part but not Joseph's? Or on Joseph's as well? "I think it will have to end with questions not answers," Bellow rightly predicts in the letter to Tumin.[99] In a letter of March 25, 1944, to Alfred Kazin, Bellow begins with familiar misgivings about the novel, which he calls "not what it should be, not what I can write." Nevertheless, "the idea—the impossibility of working out one's own destiny freely in such a world—is a genuine one." By "such a world" does Bellow mean this specific world, of impending war and induction, or the world of Fromm's "modern man," the world also of fashionable European or modernist pessimism? The latter, Philip Rahv would have said, given his praise of the novel as instrumental in "the Europeanization of American literature";[100] the former, Edmund Wilson implied in *The New Yorker*, praising the novel as "one of the most honest pieces of testimony on the psychology of a whole generation who have grown up during the depression and the war."[101]

The reviews in general seconded Wilson's view that Bellow had captured the mood of a generation. In the words of Kenneth Fearing, from the *The New York Times Book Review, Dangling Man* portrayed "what must seem to many others an uncannily accurate delineation of themselves." Delmore Schwartz, in a review in the Summer 1944 issue of *Partisan Review* entitled "A Man in His Time," began by declaring: "Here, for the first time I think, the experience of a new generation has been seized." This experience Schwartz describes as a series of disillusions: first with faith; then with democratic capitalism (under the influence of Marxism); then with Marxism. "In what seems to be utter desolation," Joseph is forced "stage by stage, to even greater stages of disillusion."[102] Of the negative reviews, the one that most upset Bellow was Diana Trilling's in *The Nation*. "Mr. Bellow is talented and clever and he writes with control and precision," she conceded, but "I find myself deeply opposed to novels of sterility—or, rather, to small novels of sterility." "Yes, Dangling Man is bitter," Bellow allowed, in an indignant letter to James Henle protesting the review, "but the book is square and honest. It is probably not great, but it is not 'small.' As for the accusation that my physical world lacks dimensions [Trilling called it "nondimensional"], that is just nonsense; she hasn't read the book if she says that." Bellow rightly dismisses this last accusation. Though the novel's Chicago feeds Joseph's sense of fallen modernity, its wintry landscape is vividly evoked, with snow "wreathing back and forth over the street" (p. 104), streetcars "rocking on [their] trucks from side to side and nicking sparks from the waving cable" (p. 75), cheap rooming houses in which one breathes "the staleness of cabbage and bacon and of the dust sifting behind the wallpaper" (p. 74). Inside these rooming houses, according to Delmore Schwartz, the lives lived, like the furnishings, are familiar:

Here are the typical objects of a generation's sensibility: the phonograph records, the studio couch, the reproductions of Van Gogh, the cafeteria; and the typical relationships: the small intellectual circle which gradually breaks up, the easy and meaningless love affairs, the marriage which is neither important nor necessary, the party which ends in hysterical outbreaks of sickness of heart, the gulf separating this generation from the previous one and the family life from which it came.

When Mel Tumin counseled Bellow to forget the Trilling review, "Bellow flew into a rage and ordered him to leave the table. They didn't speak to each other for almost a year."[103]

As Bellow's literary career took off, his draft and citizenship status began to clarify. On June 29, 1943, as part of the naturalization process, Tumin and Oscar Tarcov signed sworn affidavits of witness that Bellow was "in every way qualified to be admitted as a citizen of the United States." Five weeks later, on August 3, 1943, "Saul Gordon Bellow" was issued a Certificate of Naturalization and became a United States citizen. The certificate describes Bellow as "formerly of British nationality," twenty-eight, with fair complexion, brown eyes, black hair, five foot, eight and a half inches tall, 165 pounds. In the letter to Dwight Macdonald, written at roughly the same period, "nearing the end of *Notes of a Dangling Man*," Bellow declares that "as a IA, [I] cannot go back to teaching" (this is also when he complains that the uncertainty of his draft status makes it "impossible to make the best use of one's capacities"). The summer of 1943 was eventful in other ways. Anita became pregnant with Greg, who was born on April 16, 1944, a month after publication of *Dangling Man*. The birth was difficult, involving an emergency cesarean. Both mother and infant nearly died and Greg spent the first five days of his life in an oxygen tent. Bellow stayed up all night at the hospital waiting for his son to be delivered, kept company by Irving Kristol, recently arrived from New York to be with his wife, Gertrude Himmelfarb, a graduate student at the university. Kristol remembers walking around the hospital with the expectant father "for at least two hours." After the birth, Bellow went to Beebee Schenk's to deliver the news and to eat a breakfast of a dozen fried eggs. In the summer, he was called up for a physical, and once more deferred, having been diagnosed with an inguinal hernia. "Immediately I went into the hospital to have surgery," he recalled to Botsford, but "the operation was not successful."[104] It took many months for Bellow to recover, and he spent weeks in constant pain.

Then it was back to waiting. Earlier, in an undated letter of 1942 to Mel Tumin, he had claimed to be looking forward to being drafted, out of exasperation:

> The organization which has sent you so many hundreds of miles away to study aborigines [in Guatemala] might more profitably have engaged you at home. Goosing-relationships between the wives of siblings have fewer mysteries than the operation of a single draft board. In two months my status has changed three times and so far as I can tell will change again within the next two weeks or so. Is it any wonder that I *longed* to be called? Is it strange to prefer no future to an uncertain one? *Juge en toi-même.*

He also had "more serious" reasons for longing to be called:

> I find the prospect of enjoying the benefits of a peace without having contributed to the peace (of whatever sort; I am hoping for the

SB and Anita, 1937

best) intensely disagreeable. I realize that as an artist I have the principled right to claim exemption. It would be just, but in all conscience I could not plead for it. Besides it would be foolish, don't you think so? Like filing an appeal to be released from an epidemic on the grounds that someone should live to record it. No. You remember the advice of the old German in *Lord Jim*—"In the destructive element immerse."

It took him three years to act, because "I was writing."[105] By April 1945, however, though still writing, he had had enough, like Joseph, and enlisted. He joined the Merchant Marine and was assigned to the Atlantic District Headquarters of the United States Maritime Service in Sheepshead Bay, Brooklyn. The war in Europe was coming to an end, VE Day less than a month away; the war in the Pacific was still on, the atom bomb had not yet been dropped. One other consideration underlay Bellow's decision. As he recalled to Botsford, by 1945 he had "recognized Hitler for 'what he was.' I knew most of the story, and not only did I feel that my Jewish Marxist friends were wrong in theory, but I was horrified by the positions they—we—had taken. That was the end of that. And I felt that I should do something in the war."[106]

7

New York

W HEN ANITA BECAME PREGNANT in late summer 1943, she and Bellow were on the verge of leaving Chicago for New York. They had given up their apartment at 5532 Kenwood Avenue and were living in a rooming house nearby, the Huppeler house, at 5524 Kenwood, where they had lived for some months in early 1941. The Huppeler house was a popular residence for graduate students in the early 1940s, several of whom were ex-Trotskyists known to the Bellows. Mrs. Huppeler, the owner, was a tiny white-haired old lady who lived in the building and guarded it "like a dragon."[1] Gertrude Himmelfarb, who had come to the University of Chicago in 1943 on an *Encyclopaedia Britannica* fellowship, was already in residence when the Bellows moved in. She remembers Mrs. Huppeler as "very alert," with "red eyes," "the scariest little thing, we were all in awe of her." Himmelfarb's husband, Irving Kristol, was in the Army for most of the time the Bellows lived in the Huppeler house (serving in the infantry from 1941 to 1945). Gertrude Jaeger, another graduate student, later an eminent sociologist, also roomed in the house. Her husband, Philip Selznick, was a figure of some fame on the left, leader of the Trotskyist faction known as Shermanites ("Sherman" was Selznick's party alias); he, too, became an eminent sociologist, an authority on law and sociology, and, like Kristol, was mostly away in the Army from 1943 to 1946. Another political couple from the Huppeler house were Bess and Martin Diamond. Martin Diamond preceded Bellow into the Merchant Marine, serving from 1943–45. An ardent socialist and stump orator, he, too, like the Kristols, later turned to the right. After the war he studied political philosophy with Leo Strauss at Chicago, eventually becoming a professor of political theory at Claremont College and a leading Straussian.

"Intermittently the husbands would be there," Himmelfarb remembers, "until they had to go off to the war." Bellow did not go off to the war until after he and Anita had left the Huppeler house. They had moved into an apartment at 5400 Dorchester Avenue, next to what Daniel Bell, who would take it over in 1945, called "a sort of student complex" (now demolished). Among the new apartment's attractions, Bellow wrote, was "a wonder of a bath in which I can lie at full length."[2] Bellow's presence in Chicago was intermittent because of his many trips to New York from the later 1930s onward. That the Bellows could afford the Dorchester Avenue apartment was partly the result of "a whopper of a job,"[3] one that fed Bellow's passion for ideas and books. The job was to work in the editorial department of *Encyclopaedia Britannica* on a project initiated by Mortimer Adler and promoted by Robert Hutchins, who was chairman of the Board of Editors of the *Encyclopaedia*, as well as president of the University of Chicago: a two-volume index or *Syntopicon* (Adler's coinage, meaning "a collection of topics") of the major ideas contained within the fifty-two volumes of the Hutchins and Adler series Great Books of the Western World. This series comprised 431 works by seventy-one different authors, to be prefaced by three introductory volumes: *The Great Conversation*, a rationale or defense of the "Great Books" concept and of liberal education in general, written by Hutchins, and the two-volume *Syntopicon*. It took ten years and close to $2 million to complete the project, which was published in 1952.[4]

Bellow's work on the *Syntopicon* began toward the end of the summer of 1943, on the heels of his failure to secure a job at the Committee on Social Thought. The Committee (also "Social Thought") was a small interdisciplinary faculty at the University of Chicago founded in 1941 by the historian John U. Nef, the economist Frank Knight, the anthropologist Robert Redfield, and Hutchins. Its aim was to break down the barriers between intellectual fields or disciplines, principally literature, philosophy, religion, art, politics, and society. In the early 1960s, it became Bellow's academic home for almost thirty years. "Nothing less than this job could keep me in Chicago," Bellow wrote to his publisher, James Henle, in 1943, about the possibility of joining the Committee.[5] Nothing except the *Syntopicon* job, a kindred enterprise. Bellow's duties on the *Syntopicon* were partly managerial, to oversee the work of readers (a hundred altogether, split into teams), meeting with them, or some of them, twice a week. The readers were responsible for specified "Great Books," noting the appearance within them of one or other of 102 "Great Ideas" Adler and an earlier team of assistants had come up with as keys to Western literature and thought. These ideas were divided into as many as fifteen subtopics, for which citations and cross references were noted. The resulting two-volume work was arranged alphabetically, from "Angels" to "Love" (Volume 1) and "Man" to "World" (Volume 2). Adler and his team included topics such as "Art," "Truth," "Courage," "Law," and "Theology," while rejecting, for reasons hard to discern, "Belief," "Authority," "Friendship," "Intuition," and "Utopia." The aim of the *Syntopicon*, in Adler's words, was to overcome a key problem of knowledge, that "different authors say the same thing in different ways, or use the same words to say quite different things."[6] Among the topics Bellow oversaw as editor were "Happiness," "War," "Statesmanship," and "The Good." The works and authors he himself indexed were Plutarch and Tacitus, Plato's *Republic*, Aristotle's *Nicomachean Ethics*, Hobbes's *Leviathan*, Herodotus, and Thucydides.[7] The *Syntopicon* offices were in the basement of the Social Sciences building, bordering the Midway. Bellow's pay was $2 an hour. Himmelfarb, who later became an intellectual historian, was also employed by *Encyclopaedia Britannica* as part of her fellowship. "I remember they sent me a whole set of the *Encyclopaedia* and then I would have tear sheets of the articles I was supposed to review. . . . I was a first-year graduate student . . . actually editing articles on Robespierre and I know not what." For Himmelfarb as for Bellow, such work was intellectually engaging, as was Hyde Park itself. Irving Kristol tells a story of his first visit there, in the early 1940s: "I came from New York where the only college discussions had been on Marxist themes. I walked into the drugstore on the corner of 57th Street and Kimbark and there was a group of four people sitting . . . passionately discussing something by Plato. It never happened in City College. I never saw such a thing. . . . I was so impressed." To New Yorkers, Himmelfarb recalls, "Chicago was a kind of intellectual center. Harvard, Yale, they were all very prestigious universities, but if you wanted to be an intellectual, Chicago was the place to be."

Bellow wanted to be an intellectual, but he wanted to be a writer as well. Hence in part the pull of New York, for reasons of "business" as well as "literature" (his distinction from the undated letter to Philip

Roth about "The Very Dark Trees," quoted in Chapter 6). "I came to New York toward the end of the thirties," he says in "Writers, Intellectuals, Politics: Mainly Reminiscence" (1993), by which he means on short visits, like the one he and Anita made in the summer of 1940 before going to Mexico.[8] Charlie Citrine of *Humboldt's Gift* makes his first visit to New York in 1938, riding the Greyhound bus from Madison, taking "the Scranton route" in a trip of "about fifty hours" (p. 55). These visits increased for Bellow after the autumn of 1942, when Isaac Rosenfeld was given a small stipend to study in the graduate program in philosophy at NYU, in the department of Sidney Hook and James Burnham. Rosenfeld was newly married, to Vasiliki Sarantakis, whom he'd met two years earlier, while both were students at the University of Chicago. Vasiliki was lively and attractive, a great tonic to Rosenfeld, boosting his confidence as a writer and a man. Within months of arriving in New York, Rosenfeld was writing to Tarcov with news that he'd sold a short story and a poem to *The New Republic* ("I wish something of Saul's had appeared too").[9] Vasiliki found work at the magazine, as secretary to Alfred Kazin, its literary editor. It was at this point that Bellow began to visit the city more frequently, traveling on his own because Anita could not leave her job at Michael Reese Hospital. Bellow stayed with the Rosenfelds on his visits, first in their cramped ground-floor apartment on the Upper West Side, on 76th Street near Riverside Drive (two and a half rooms, bathtub in the kitchen, bugs, dirty clothes and dishes everywhere), then at 85 Barrow Street in Greenwich Village (no less cramped and squalid), to which they moved in 1943. If there were such a magazine as *Bad Housekeeping*, Bellow has Zetland, the Rosenfeld character, say, in several of the unpublished manuscripts devoted to him, then Lottie, his wife, would be its editor.[10]

Rosenfeld lasted only a year as a philosophy student, much of which he spent writing stories, poems, and reviews for *Partisan Review, Commentary*, and *The New Republic*. These reviews were sharp, learned, and bold. Soon after leaving NYU, he wrote a *New Republic* article attacking the work of his teacher, Sidney Hook, the most influential Marxist theorist in the country and a ferocious polemicist, "with a street-brawler's willingness to jump into a fray at the slightest provocation."[11] In 1944, as mentioned in Chapter 4, Rosenfeld won the first *Partisan Review*–Dial Press novelette award for "The Colony," a Kafkaesque fable. The award brought $1,000 and Rosenfeld was seen as a "golden boy" (a phrase used of him by Irving Howe), "*shoyne boychick*" (its Yiddish equivalent, used

by David T. Bazelon, a friend from Chicago).[12] Rosenfeld was generous with his contacts among New York literary circles. When Bazelon
arrived in New York from Chicago in 1943, Rosenfeld, in the words of
his biographer, "introduced him to nearly everyone he knew of intellectual importance." Being with Rosenfeld, as Bazelon put it, 'you could
take your life seriously, any part of it you wanted, and he would really
help—he really wanted to help.'"[13]

Bellow needed no help in taking his life seriously, but he clearly
benefited from Rosenfeld's introductions. Among the first of these was
to Kazin, who writes about meeting Bellow in his memoir *New York
Jew* (1978). Kazin was Bellow's exact contemporary, only five days his
senior, but had been writing for *The New Republic* for almost a decade,
from the age of nineteen. He became the magazine's literary editor at
twenty-seven, succeeding Malcolm Cowley and Edmund Wilson, and
published his first book, *On Native Grounds* (1942), a study of American literature from the 1880s to the present. Lionel Trilling, writing
in *The Nation*, called it "quite the best and most complete treatment
we have of an arduous and difficult subject."[14] Kazin's first impression of Bellow, who had published almost nothing at this point, was
that "he carried around with him a sense of his destiny as a novelist
that excited almost everyone around him. Bellow was the first writer
of my generation . . . who talked of Lawrence and Joyce, Hemingway
and Fitzgerald, not as books in the library but as fellow operators in
the same business." Kazin was an operator himself, in the New York
intellectual scene, combative and rivalrous. Yet Bellow's confidence
impressed rather than antagonized him: "He was putting himself up as
a contender. Although he was friendly, unpretentious and funny, he was
ambitious and dedicated in a style I had never seen in an urban Jewish
intellectual. He expected the world to come to him."

Bellow impressed Kazin in other ways. He could make someone see
"the most microscopic event in the street" and think it worth seeing
"because *he* happened to be seeing it." He thought up "very funny jokes,
puns and double-entendres," laughing through them "fast, with hearty
pleasure at things so well said." His voice, when telling stories, was one
of "careful public clarity,"[15] yet he never talked for effect: "His defini-
tions, epigrams, were of a formal plainness that went right to the point
and stopped. . . . There was not the slightest verbal inflation in anything he said." Almost as impressive to Kazin was the range of Bellow's
observations, extending well beyond "topics generally exhausted by

ideology or neglected by intellectuals too fine to consider them."[16] Bellow's attention to details of physiognomy and appearance was as striking in life as on the page: "he liked to estimate other people's physical capacity, the thickness of their skins, the strength in their hands, the force in their chests." Though "a nimble adept of the University of Chicago style, full of the Great Books and jokes from Aristophanes," he was also an unembarrassed Yiddishist, a proud Yiddishist, as well as an aficionado of "big-city low life": "Saul was the first Jewish writer I met who seemed as clever about every side of life as a businessman. He was in touch."[17]

That Bellow seemed at ease with his Jewishness—that Jewishness seemed the source of his ease—also impressed Kazin. "He was proud in a laconic way," Kazin writes, "like an old Jew who feels himself closer to God than anybody else." When challenged, however, Bellow "could be as openly vulnerable as anyone I ever met. Then he would nail with quiet ferocity someone who had astonished him by offering the mildest criticism." To Kazin, Bellow was "a man chosen by talent, like those Jewish virtuosos—Heifetz, Rubenstein, Milstein, Horowitz."[18] These descriptions were recorded thirty-five years after Kazin and Bellow first met, and may well be colored by a sense of the later man. When he read *New York Jew*, Bellow could not recognize himself. "I didn't have an air of success," he protested. "I felt as weak in the knees as everyone else. I didn't know what the hell I was doing."[19] Though a similar retrospective projection may distort the accounts of other witnesses, they are largely admiring, particularly of Bellow's self-possession and reserve. "Very strong-willed and shrewd in the arts of self-conservation" is how Irving Howe remembers him.[20] Though "civilized and gentle" in manner, in William Barrett's phrase, "the chip of self-confidence was there on the shoulder just the same."[21] To William Phillips, of *Partisan Review*, Bellow's "strong sense of being set apart" was clear from the start. Though subject to "episodes of suspicion, when he questioned someone's loyalty or attitude towards his work" ("I bite people's heads off when they cross me," he tells Tumin in an undated letter of 1942), his manner was "self-assured, almost relaxed. . . . Saul was extremely sweet and gentle, and, when he felt at home, extraordinarily charming. Even his egocentricity added to his charms." Phillips recalls Bellow as "extremely handsome, with soft, large eyes and long lashes, giving focus to a soft, quizzical look that was not entirely lost on women,"[22] an impression women corroborated. In *Common Soldiers: A Self-Portrait and Other Portraits* (1979), the bohemian artist Janet Richards describes him in 1942 as "irresistible, rather small and slight but strong, with curly black hair and large black eyes that missed nothing. They were ironic and sweet and not so much intellectual in impression as shrewd."[23] In *Poets in Their Youth: A Memoir* (1982), Eileen Simpson, John Berryman's first wife, recalls that it was "generally agreed" among the women in her circle that Bellow "was 'a dish.'"[24] Ann Birstein, Alfred Kazin's second wife, describes him as "stunning, the ultimate beautiful young Jewish intellectual incarnate."[25] After seeing the author photograph on the jacket of *Dangling Man*, an executive from MGM offered to make him a movie star, playing what Bellow called "the guy 'who loses the girl to the George Raft type or Errol Flynn type.'"[26] In Kazin's words, Bellow had "the conscious good looks of the coming celebrity."[27]

IN ADDITION TO TRYING to place novels and stories on his visits to New York, Bellow sought money from foundations. In 1943, while working on the *Syntopicon*, he applied for a Guggenheim Fellowship. Kazin and James Henle of Vanguard wrote on his behalf, along with James Farrell. In a brief statement of accomplishments, Bellow admitted that he'd had little success until he began publishing in *Partisan Review* three years earlier, at the age of twenty-five. His first novel, *Dangling Man*, would not appear until 1944, and he was then at work on a novel about "a middle-class individual" named Victor Holben. The theme of this novel was "the meaning of those capacities by which man at his best is distinguished: love, generosity and genius." (No traces of it have survived, nor does *The Victim*, which Bellow soon began, fit its description.) He was turned down, like many first-time Guggenheim applicants, especially fiction writers who had not yet published a book. Two years later, bolstered by additional references from Edmund Wilson and Eliseo Vivas, he applied again, after *Dangling Man* had appeared to mostly good reviews. In this second application, nothing was said of Victor Holben. *The Victim* was announced as Bellow's next novel, contracted to be published by Vanguard. Again he was turned down.[28]

Through connections with literary journalists and publishers in New York, Bellow picked up reviewing and other paid assignments. According to Atlas, Robert Van Gelder, the editor of *The New York Times Book Review*, commissioned him to review a range of books, which Bellow then sold on (he also had an affair with Van Gelder's assistant,

Marjorie "Midge" Farber, who later identified herself as the model for Thea Fenchel).[29] Victor Weybright, of Penguin Books, employed him to read for the imprint's first list. He was interviewed for staff jobs at *Time* magazine and *The New Yorker*. Through *Partisan Review* he met foreign writers and editors. In a letter of September 11, 1942, Harold Kaplan writes to Mel Tumin about a day he and Bellow spent with the art critic Clement Greenberg, an editor at *PR*, and "his gal, Jean Connolly, wife of Cyril Connolly." The day was not a success. "Bellow, catastrophically, paid no attention to the two English women who had been summoned largely for his benefit (and theirs to be sure)." Bellow later recalled that Greenberg thought it "important [for a young writer] to come under the influence of an older woman. She would prepare him for the world, teach him about sex, cure him of brashness—she would civilize you, French-style."[30] On this occasion, Greenberg lectured the two young men "paternally, on how European women expect little attentions and how lucky we were to meet people like that at our age and what the hell was wrong with us." What was wrong with Bellow was that he had expected to meet the writer Eleanor Clark, who was "reputed to be very lovely and very fatal" (they eventually met in the offices of *PR*, only becoming good friends after Clark married Robert Penn Warren).[31] When Kaplan discovered the name of one of the Englishwomen he and Bellow had ignored, "a rather handsome middle-aged citizenness in red hair, cigarette-holder and slacks," he was much chagrined: "she was *the* Allanah Harper, former editor of *Echanges* [the French quarterly, which she founded], friend of Virginia Woolf, Valéry, Gide, Joyce, Eliot and Cocteau and on and on. I wept bitter tears."[32]

Bellow's interview for the job at *Time* was a disaster. The editor in charge of personnel, Dana Tasker, had been favorably impressed with Bellow, leading him to believe that he would be hired. "It seems agreed that I will get a job," he wrote to Freifeld on June 12, 1943. "The question before the editors is whether I should write domestic or foreign stuff. I may do Art or Religion. (They like to put you in a field you know nothing about.) Or Education. I'm not sure. All novices start at 75 and after three months go to $100—formerly my average monthly earnings." A job at the magazine, Bellow told Freifeld, would give him "more money than I ever had in my life and I won't know what to do with it." The letter closes with an invitation to Freifeld's wife, Rochelle, and daughter, Judy, "to stay with us [in New York, when he gets the job]," while Freifeld is away from home, serving in Army intelligence.

Through James Agee, the film critic at *Time*, a meeting was arranged between Bellow and Whittaker Chambers, the former Soviet spy, who edited the books and arts pages of the magazine. When Bellow entered his office, Chambers was sitting in a wingback chair facing away from him. Chambers asked him what he thought was Wordsworth's best poem and Bellow replied by asking what Wordsworth had to do with his getting a job in journalism. When Chambers persisted, Bellow named "Ode: Intimations of Immorality." For Chambers, the only Wordsworth poem that mattered was *The Excursion* (in Byron's words, "writ in a manner which is my aversion"), a work anti-Romantic in both style and content, thus acceptable to the conservative Chambers, who had become a ferocious anti-Communist. There was no job for Bellow, Chambers announced. On his way out, Bellow was approached by a man in the office, a disgruntled employee, who shook his hand, and told him it was his "lucky day." Tasker felt bad for Bellow, and through his friend Ik Shuman, an editor at *The New Yorker*, got Bellow an interview at the magazine, again with no result.[33]

Bellow frequently told the story of his meeting with Whittaker Chambers, often altering details. In one version, he is given a job writing film reviews, but it lasts only a day. Here is the account he gave in a 1975 television interview in Britain, reprinted in *The Listener*:

> I was fired at the end of the day by Whittaker Chambers. I came into Chambers' office, and he took one look at me. He was obviously determined to get rid of me and he said: "Do you know who Wordsworth was?" I said: "Yes." He said, "I want to know what sort of poet he was." I said: "Well, he was a romantic poet. But I don't see what that has to do with reviewing moving pictures." He said: "Never mind that, there's no room for you in this organisation, you're fired." My friends told me: "Chambers hates the romantic Wordsworth—he cares only for *The Excursion*, he adores *The Excursion*, which is not a romantic poem." So I lost my job.[34]

A similar account was offered by Bellow in a later interview, in which the firing took place on his second not his first day in the job.[35]

Bellow fictionalized the episode in *The Victim*, published five years later. In the novel, Asa is interviewed by the editor of *Dill's Weekly*, a Chambers-like bull of a man named Rudiger, who keeps him waiting for an hour, has his back to him when he enters, is red-faced as well as red-haired, and cuts him off as soon as he begins to speak with the words "No vacancies, no vacancies here. We're filled. Go somewhere else." Leventhal answers back, a heated exchange follows, creating "an atmosphere of infliction and injury from which neither could withdraw" (p. 177). After the interview, Leventhal worries that "Someone like that can make trouble for me"; Rudiger might "have me black-listed" (p. 179), a possibility Harkavy, Leventhal's friend, makes light of, before going on to caution Leventhal against paranoid suspicion:

> "There isn't a thing he can do to you. Whatever you do, don't get ideas like that into your head. He can't persecute you. Now be careful. You have that tendency, boy, do you know that? He got what was coming to him and he can't do anything. Maybe that Allabee, what-do-you-call-him, put him up to it, wanted to play you a dirty trick. You know how it goes: 'There's a fellow bothering me. Do me a favour and give him the works when he comes around.' So he does it. Well, he fouled his own nest. You follow me, boy? He fouled his own nest. So by now he realizes it was his own fault and he had it coming. How do you know it wasn't rimmed?"
>
> "You really think they did? I don't know. And I didn't bother that Allbee. I only asked him once."
>
> "Maybe he didn't put him up to it. But he might have. It's a possibility. Something like that happened to another friend of mine— Fabin. You know him. They gave him the works, and it was a put-up job. Only he didn't talk back the way you did. He just let them fling it at him. No, you did right and you haven't got a thing to worry about."
>
> Nevertheless, Leventhal was not reassured (pp. 179–80).

Allbee is the Dostoyevskian double who haunts Leventhal throughout the novel, partly because he thinks Leventhal deliberately lost him his job. "You were sore at something I said about Jews. . . . You wanted to get even" (p. 170). Just as Leventhal suspects that Allbee and Rudiger set him up, so Allbee thinks Leventhal set him up: "You went in and deliberately insulted Rudiger, put on some act with him, called him filthy names, deliberately insulted him to get me in bad. Rudiger is hot blooded and he turned on me for it. You knew he would. It was calculated. It worked" (p. 169). After Allbee was fired, "I couldn't get a job" (p. 203); hence his present deplorable state: drunk, dishev-

eled, broke, alone. Allbee is from an old New England family, once
had money (through his wife, now deceased), and deplores New York,
where "it's really as if the children of Caliban were running everything.
You go down in the subway and Caliban gives you two nickels for your
dime. You go home and he has a candy store in the street where you
were born. The old breeds are out. The streets are named after them.
But what are they themselves? Just remnants . . . last week I saw a book
about Thoreau and Emerson by a man named Lipschitz" (p. 259).

Bellow seems to have entertained similar suspicions about the interview with Chambers. In a letter of April 10, 1982 to Eileen Simpson,
he congratulates her on *Poets in Their Youth.* In the memoir Simpson
recounts a comparably disastrous interview Berryman had with Chambers, one also arranged by James Agee. Bellow comments: "I suspect
that Agee was aware that he was sending hopeless cases to Chambers who baited and dismissed them. Did these two have an arrangement? Funny that John and I should never have discussed this. Agee
was saintly, and Chambers prophetic and both did the work of Henry
Luce . . . John and I missed that one. Perhaps he would have disagreed
with me, as he did about [Edmund] Wilson and, in some degree, [Allen]
Tate. But we needn't go into that here." What Bellow and Berryman
disagreed about in respect to Wilson and Tate is not specified. Though
Wilson, like Agee, professed himself hostile, in print and in person, to
the genteel and the established, Bellow seems to have suspected him, as
he did Tate, of harboring Allbee-like attitudes toward Jews and other
Calibans, immigrant types displacing "the old breeds" (who have streets
named after them, as in Tate's and Agee's Old South or Wilson's East
Coast or Princeton). Agee was not Allbee, but like him he was well-
born, expensively educated (Phillips Exeter, Harvard), a womanizer,
and a hard drinker ("everyone drank heavily," William Phillips recalls,
"but Agee was in the top ten; perhaps he was an alcoholic").[36] He and
Chambers were close friends, shared an office at *Time,* and reviewed
books together; Sam Tanenhaus, Chambers's biographer, describes
them as "confidants, an oddly compatible pair."[37] Hence Bellow's suspicions about Agee in the letter to Simpson, which suggest a source for
Leventhal's suspicions about Allbee. They also mirror Allbee's suspicions about Leventhal. In other words, Bellow knew the suspicions of
his characters from the inside. In his writing, however, he distanced
himself from them, alert to their consequences: born of prejudice, they

bred prejudice, in victim as well as bigot, another way Leventhal and Allbee are doubles.[38]

AT THE CENTER of Bellow's early experiences in New York were the writers and editors at *Partisan Review*. In his foreword to a 1996 anthology of fiction from the magazine, he makes clear what it meant to him in the 1930s and 1940s. In comparison to "the *Southern*, the *Hudson*, the *Kenyon*," *Partisan Review* offered "what we longed for,"

> deep relevance, contemporary high culture, left-wing politics, avant-garde painting, Freudian mining of the unconscious or Marxist views of past and future revolutions. In *Partisan Review* you could read George Orwell, André Gide, Ignazio Silone—during the Civil War in Spain, I remember, *Partisan Review* printed a curious piece by Picasso, "The Dreams and Lies of President Franco." These were *Partisan Review*'s European heavyweights. On our own side of the Atlantic *Partisan Review*'s contributors included Edmund Wilson, Sidney Hook, James Burnham, Paul Goodman, Lionel Trilling, Clement Greenberg, James Agee, and Harold Rosenberg.[39]

The magazine was founded in 1934 by Philip Rahv and William Phillips, under the auspices of the Communist-controlled John Reed Club of New York (located at 430 Sixth Avenue between 10th and 11th Streets), which is where the two editors first met.[40] Neither editor had any money, and the magazine would never have gotten off the ground without the assistance of established Communist writers like Mike Gold, author of *Jews Without Money* (1930), Joseph Freeman, the editor of *New Masses*, and John Strachey, the British Marxist, who agreed to give a talk organized by the editors (its subject was dialectical materialism), which raised what Phillips describes as "the unbelievable sum of eight hundred dollars, enough to run a little magazine for a year on a collapsed economy."[41]

From the beginning, *PR* mixed politics and culture. Although initially it supported the party's call for a conspicuously proletarian literature, it warned against narrow or mechanical applications of Marxist doctrine, as when *New Masses* writers worried "whether Proust should be read after the Revolution and why there seemed to be no simple proletarians in the novels of André Malraux."[42] In an editorial in its third issue (June–July 1934), Rahv and Phillips warned that "zeal to steep literature overnight in the program of Communism results in . . . sloganized and inorganic writing." What the editors sought was a Marxist aesthetic compatible with modernist and other formal innovations, an objective that brought them into increasing conflict with official Communist literary policy. Larger political pressures also came into play, eventually precipitating a break. In 1935, the party introduced its Popular Front or People's Front strategy, a threat to the openly anti-capitalist and pro-Soviet John Reed Clubs. A directive went out to dissolve the clubs and back more broadly liberal groups (the American Writers' Congress, the League of American Writers), a move that effectively eliminated much of *PR*'s support. After a short-lived merger with Jack Conroy's *Anvil* (short-lived, according to Phillips, because Conroy "was too populist and anti-intellectual"[43]), in December 1936 publication of the magazine was suspended entirely.

The loss of party support was for Rahv and Phillips both a blow and an opportunity. If new money could be found, they would relaunch *PR* as an independent magazine, no longer muting or masking criticism of party policy, political as well as literary.[44] It was F. W. Dupee, the literary editor of *New Masses*, who helped find the money. Like Rahv and Phillips, Dupee was disillusioned with Communist literary politics and in search of a less rigid, less bureaucratic journalistic home. He introduced the *PR* editors to a Yale classmate, Dwight Macdonald, a writer for Henry Luce at *Fortune*, but leaning "in the direction of the Communist party." The daylong argument in which Rahv and Phillips battered Macdonald for this leaning, led him to join the effort to revive *PR*. "I still have a picture of Rahv and myself backing Macdonald up against a wall," Phillips writes, "knocking down his arguments, firing unanswerable questions without giving him time to answer, and constantly outshouting him."[45] Macdonald and Dupee introduced Rahv and Phillips to a third Yale classmate, George L. K. Morris, a wealthy art critic and abstract painter. With Morris's financial backing, *PR* was relaunched in December 1937, with editorial offices located in Macdonald's apartment, and an editorial board consisting of Rahv, Phillips, Dupee, Macdonald, Morris, and one other friend of Dupee and Macdonald, Mary McCarthy, who was described by William Barrett as "the one woman whom the circle could not intimidate in any way."[46] When

Bellow met McCarthy he thought her "beautiful in a sort of enamelled way," "a little unnatural," "charming," and "very snappish. I was a little too timid for that sort of thing."[47] Phillips characterized the new board of *PR* as "remarkably aggressive and varied."[48]

Bellow's attitude to the *PR* circle was complicated. As Barrett puts it, "he needed to observe the New York intellectuals, to be stimulated by them, and learn from them what he wanted—that was his job as a writer, and Bellow was a full-time writer. But he moved always at the edge of the circle."[49] "I wouldn't belong to anything," Bellow told Botsford. "I was never institutionally connected with any of these people. I was the cat who walked by himself."[50] His wariness was partly ideological, partly personal. "Our program is the program of Marxism," the editors declared in an opening statement in 1937 in the first relaunched issue, "which in general means being for the revolutionary overthrow of capitalist society, for a workers' government, and for international socialism." In the 1930s and early 1940s, Bellow still endorsed this program, or at least gave it lip service. The magazine's attitude to literature was another matter, revered contributors notwithstanding. "Marxism in culture," Rahv and Phillips declared in that 1937 statement, "is first of all an instrument of analysis and evaluation" (p. 4). In "Writers, Intellectuals, Politics: Mainly Reminiscence," Bellow offers an anecdote illustrating the reductive consequences of this view. In *PR* circles, "small distinction was made between an intellectual and a writer. The culture heroes who mattered were those who had ideas. Sidney Hook, in many respects a sensible man, once said to me that Faulkner was an excellent writer whose books would be greatly improved by dynamic ideas. 'I'd be glad to give him some,' he said. 'It would make a tremendous difference. Do you know him?'"[51] In an interview with Botsford, Bellow recalls overhearing a conversation between Rahv and Phillips in 1942 in the magazine's Astor Place offices: "Rahv enters and asks Phillips, 'Has anything for the next number come in?' Phillips says, 'None of the important stuff,'" meaning political, critical, academic contributions.[52] For Bellow, the important stuff was fiction, poetry, drama.

The confrontational style of the *PR* crowd, which amused Bellow in small doses, also helped to keep him at a distance. Philip Rahv set the tone. He was born Ivan Greenberg in the Russian Ukraine, did not come to the United States until he was fourteen, after stays in Austria and Palestine, and made no attempt to lose his Russian accent. "He carried his 'Russianness' like a flag of pride," Irving Howe recalls. "It meant being comprehensive, definitive, theoretical, overwhelming."[53] Rahv was self-taught, never graduated from high school; the New York Public Library was his alma mater. Here he gathered the materials of a formidable education. In the early years of the Depression, when not in the library, he stood in breadlines and slept on park benches, eventually finding work as a Hebrew teacher. Hebrew was one of his six languages: the others were Russian, German, Yiddish, French, and English. "Rahv" (meaning "rabbi") was his party name, and soon began appearing over reviews in the *Daily Worker* and *New Masses*. These reviews were hard in several senses, and domineering, like their author. "One person took to himself the preponderant power in shaping the magazine," recalls William Barrett, "and that was Philip Rahv. He did so by sheer self-assertion; by the power and force, and at times the sheer rudeness of his personality."[54] When charged by Clement Greenberg with denigrating friends and colleagues behind their backs, often to persons in positions of power (publishers, editors, heads of foundations), Rahv answered: "Everybody does it." When told "but not like you," and pressed to explain his behavior, he tried again: "I suppose it's just analytic exuberance" (a phrase Delmore Schwartz characterized as "Philip Rahv's euphemism for putting a knife in your back").[55] Irving Howe remembers that whenever he met Rahv "he would propose that I write something to 'smash them.' Always there was a 'them,' from Stalinists to New Critics."[56]

Social life in *PR* circles could also be daunting. "An evening at the Rahvs," recalled the writer and critic Elizabeth Hardwick of parties at their West Tenth Street town house, "was to enter a ring of bullies, each one bullying the other."[57] Rosenfeld described a gathering at the Rahvs' as "like throwing darts."[58] Parties at the Phillipses' were no less intimidating, according to Irving Kristol:

> I got a plate of food, and there was a couch, and so I walked over and sat down in the middle of the couch, not knowing who was going to join me, and not really much caring. Well, what happened was, Mary McCarthy sat down on one side of me, Hannah Arendt sat down on the other side of me, and then Diana Trilling pulled up a chair and sat facing me. And I was a prisoner, I couldn't get out. And they then had a long hour-and-a-half discussion on Freud, in which they were all disagreeing. I don't remember what the dispute was.

All I know is that I sat there quiet and terror-stricken. And my wife was across the room giggling endlessly.[59]

"These people didn't know how to behave," Diana Trilling recalled. "Intellectuals knew how to think but they didn't know how to behave," especially in respect to women. "Those parties were absolutely horrible if you weren't on the make, sexually," she continues, "if you were neither a name nor sexually available, you should have stayed home, because it was just a misery . . . . The wife of William Phillips, Edna Phillips, and the wife of Philip Rahv, Nathalie Rahv, both told me after I got to be friends with them in later years that they had had to take several stiff drinks before every one of those parties in order to get through them, they were so miserable."[60]

William Phillips was a less domineering figure than Rahv, though dealing with him could be tricky. Born in Brooklyn into a family of poor Russian Jewish immigrants (his father changed the family name from Litvinsky), he attended City College, did graduate work in philosophy at NYU and Columbia, but was put off an academic career because of difficulties or inhibitions in writing, a not uncommon experience for editors. In his memoir, *Intellectual Follies*, Lionel Abel describes Phillips as "more boyish than Rahv, mischievous, catty even, quite witty, and with a gift for subtlety. . . . It was Rahv who took the initiative in almost all serious matters, and William who made the jokes at Rahv's expense."[61] Aiding Phillips in these jokes was Delmore Schwartz, who joined the *PR* circle in 1937, the year the magazine published "In Dreams Begin Responsibilities," the story that made his literary reputation. To give a flavor of *PR* banter, here is William Barrett, an unoffical staff writer at the time, on an editorial meeting in which "the subject—or target" was Alfred Kazin. Phillips complained that Kazin "insists so much on his sincerity when talking to me, that he makes me feel insincere." Rahv then recalled Diana Trilling's characterization of Kazin as "the starry-eyed opportunist," and Schwartz quoted Mary McCarthy wondering aloud why "when Alfred had been in Italy they didn't press all the olive oil out of him." *PR* was publishing pages from Kazin's "Italian Journal" and when someone asked "Why an Italian Journal?" Schwartz answered "Well, Goethe wrote an Italian Journal, and Alfred decided he would do one too."[62]

Hostility to Kazin was partly a matter of style—Kazin was too earnest and intense—partly a product of his association with the rival *New*

Republic, with whom *PR* had been at loggerheads politically (for its support of party causes and of the Soviet Union). Kazin was among the closest of the new friends Bellow made in New York, and himself no shrinking violet. "I was raised in a school of toughness," he records in a journal entry of 1942, "and I've always lived militantly, thinking hard, working my life out hard." "My aggressiveness has been terrible," reads another entry; "all my life I have lived like a bullet going through walls: I have thought only of my own progress." Kazin stuttered badly in his youth and "attained a tyrannical fluency so that I might never be found gaping and gapping." When ill and tense, "ready to pick a fight," he reminds himself in another entry, to "lay off, comfort yourself with every possible comfort; *stop mauling yourself*." In later years, happy in bucolic Amherst, "I look for trouble, I long for discord." In discussing fellow New York intellectuals in his journals, Kazin is as biting as his detractors: "I felt his own clumsiness, ruggedness, harshness" (of Clement Greenberg); "Always proving a point at the expense of others—always winning the little victory—always the provincial little Jewish boy putting his foot on the conquered antagonist" (of Sidney Hook); "that fatal particle of vulgarity . . . which gets between everything he says like sand" (of Irving Howe); "like hawks, waiting to pounce . . . what tenseness because of the control, the politesse, the civilizing and hold in leash of so much passion" (of faculty at the New School).[63] To some, Irving Howe for instance, rudeness was seen as both Jewish and a matter of principle: "Rudeness was not only the weapon of cultural underdogs, but also a sign that intellectual Jews had become sufficiently self-assured to stop playing by gentile rules. At the least, this rudeness was to be preferred to the frigid 'civility' with which English intellectuals cloak their murderous impulses, or the politeness that in American academic life could mask a cold indifference."[64]

Kazin's treatment of women was no different from that of the men Diana Trilling describes. Ex-wives are not always reliable about their ex-husbands, but here is Ann Birstein, the third of Kazin's four wives, in her autobiography, *What I Saw at the Fair* (2003), recalling their first meeting. Birstein was twenty-three and had just published her first novel. Kazin was thirty-five and a power in literary-intellectual circles. He entered the room talking very fast, immediately patronized his host, who took umbrage; then the two men embarked on an argument that lasted over an hour. During this argument, Kazin barely acknowledged Birstein, the only other guest. "He was scary," she recalls. At the end of the argument, he turned to her with a brief glance and said: "Nice legs." Shown a copy of her book by their hostess, he asked: "Is that that first novel that was panned in *Commentary*?" At dinner, Kazin ignored her, although she was sitting opposite him. So absorbed in argument was he that at one point she felt impelled to lean across the table to prevent him from dipping his jacket into the spaghetti sauce, a courtesy he noted without thanking. Later he pocketed her packet of cigarettes. When she timidly asked him for one, he said: "Why don't you buy your own?" When she told him they were her own, he replied: "Possessive, aren't you?" (a joke presumably).[65] The roughness of Kazin's manners was noted by others as well, including those of equal or greater literary standing. At a *PR* party, Kazin walked up to Lionel Trilling and asked him: "When are you going to dissociate yourself from that wife of yours?" (he meant politically). Diana Trilling was standing behind her husband and only just managed, "perhaps mistakenly," as she puts it in her autobiography, to restrain his lifted fist.[66]

Bellow loved anecdotes like these and put several of them in his stories. In "Him with His Foot in His Mouth," he delights in a put-down originally uttered by the art critic Harold Rosenberg, perhaps the closest of the new friends he made in New York. Herschel Shawmut, the story's narrator, who is prone to spasms of rudeness and aggression, recounts meeting "the late Kippenberg, prince of musicologists" at a conference. The night before Shawmut is to speak, he invites himself over to Kippenberg's room to give the great man a preview of his paper. Kippenberg resembles Rosenberg physically, being "a huge man" (Bellow called Rosenberg "the only man I know who fills a telephone booth from top to bottom"),[67] crippled (he walks with two sticks), with eyebrows "like caterpillars from the Tree of Knowledge." As Shawmut reads from his talk, Kippenberg begins to nod. "I said, 'I'm afraid I'm putting you to sleep, Professor.' 'No, no—on the contrary, you're keeping me awake,' he said. That, and at my expense, was genius, and it was a privilege to have provoked it. . . . I would have gone around the world for such a put-down."[68]

In "What Kind of a Day Did You Have?" (1984), Rosenberg, who died in 1978 at seventy-two, is clearly the model for Victor Wulpy, a seventy-year-old intellectual who, like many in the *PR* circle, had "so much to say that he overwhelmed everybody who approached him."[69] Victor's mistress, Katrina, no longer talks to him of the children's book she is writing, since it makes him "cross-eyed with good-humored boredom" (p. 291). "Kingly," "withering," several cuts above what he called ("when he got going") "the animal human average," or, to quote Wyndham Lewis, a favorite author, "the dark equivocal crowd saturated with falsity" (pp. 306, 324), Victor's concern is ideas, his respect is "reserved for people who lived out their *idea*" (p. 306). He was "not the type to be interested in personality troubles. Insofar as they were nothing but personal, he cared for nobody's troubles. That included his own" (p. 305). Though capable of political naïveté (as during the May 1968 French student crisis, "when he agreed with Sartre that we were on the verge of an inspiring and true revolution" [p. 333]), for the most part his ideas, his living for ideas, even his manners, are treated with respect. That his behavior can seem comical at times, in its indifference to feeling or convention, makes him like Socrates in the *Symposium*, admirable yet not quite human. Nowhere is this Socratic mixture of qualities clearer than in Victor's demeanor when facing death. He and Katrina are aboard a small private plane flying from Detroit to Chicago in a violent snowstorm:

> As was his custom, he sketched out a summary. It included Katrina and took the widest possible overview. They were in a Cessna because he had accepted a lecture invitation, a trip not strictly necessary and which (for himself he took it calmly) might be fatal. For Katrina it was even less than necessary. For her he was sorry. She was here because of him. But then it came home to him that he didn't understand a life so different from his own. Why did anybody want to live such a life as she lived? I know why I did mine. Why does she do hers? It was a wicked question, even put comically, for it had its tinge of comedy. But when he had put the question he felt exposed, without any notice at all, to a kind of painful judgment. Supposedly, his life had had real scale, it produced genuine ideas, and these had caused significant intellectual and artistic innovations. All of that was serious. Katrina? Not serious. Divorcing, and then pursuing a prominent figure—the pursuit of passion, high pleasure? Such old stuff—*not* serious! Nevertheless, they were together now, both leaning far over in the banking plane; same destiny for them both (p. 348).

As Victor thinks about Katrina, he seeks to explain her hold over him. Though composed, like Socrates, in the face of death, unlike

Socrates he's also in thrall to Eros. A flurry of images of Katrina "both commonplace and magical" flit through his head; as he drives toward their meaning, toward the "idea" of Katrina's "sexual drawing power," the Cessna begins to tumble, its metal sides crackling "as if the rivets were going to pop like old-time collar buttons." Katrina then interrupts, like Alcibiades:

> "Now listen, Victor. If it's death any minute, if we're going to end in the water . . . I'm going to ask you to tell me something."
> "Don't start that, Katrina."
> "It's very simple. I just want you to say it . . . "
> "Come off it, Katrina. With so much to think about, at a time like this, you ask me *that*? Love?" Temper made his voice fifelike again. His mouth expanded, the mustache widening also. He was about to speak even more violently.
> She cut him off. "Don't be awful with me now, Victor. If we're going to crash, why shouldn't you say it? . . . " (p. 349).

She should know why, Victor having recently lent her Céline's *Journey to the End of the Night*, in which the adventurer Robinson refuses to tell his mistress that he loves her and she shoots him dead ("He couldn't say 'I love you,'" realizes Katrina, a Tinkertoy heavy thinker, "it would have been *mauvaise foi*").[70] Victor ponders: "Atheists accept extreme unction. The wife urges, and the dying man nods. Why not?" Then the plane levels off. "They had found smoother air again and were sailing more calmly" (p. 350). The fancy Chicago executives who sent the Cessna, send a limo, "all power and luxury"; Victor makes it to his lecture and Katrina is dropped off at her home in Evanston. As he exits the car, he squeezes Katrina's fingers and she wishes him luck: "Not to worry. I'm on top of this," he tells her, pressing ahead. At a memorial for Rosenberg, Bellow remembered his friend saying: "I've heard of old age, and sickness, and death, but as far as I'm concerned those are merely rumors," a remark uttered when "he was visibly not well, not young . . . he refused to be affected by the contemplation of mortality."[71] Katrina, in contrast, feels "a clawing at her heart and innards— pity for the man, which he didn't feel for himself" (p. 351).

Bellow admires Victor, as he admired Rosenberg, not only for his energy and bravery, but for his honesty, a quality most clearly illustrated in Victor's case by the serious thought he gives to Katrina. "As a subject for thought, [Katrina] was the least trivial of all. Of all that might be omitted in thinking, the worst was to omit your own being. You had lost, then" (p. 349). Katrina, or her appeal, has become part of Victor's being, and he can't figure out how; that is, he cannot reduce her/it to an "idea." Admirable to keep trying, but as the story implies, mental effort takes you only so far. "I dislike making statements about a literary development that depends on the imagination and will have no real existence until imagination has brought it forth," Bellow writes in a letter to Rosenberg, defending literature over criticism. "*Herzog* may change the picture, my arguments in *Encounter*, never."[72]

Rosenberg could be tough and overbearing, like others in the *PR* circle. In "Writers, Intellectuals, Politics: Mainly Reminiscence," Bellow describes him as "extraordinarily fluent, persuasive, domineering, subtle and sharp."[73] "It did not distress him," Bellow writes elsewhere, "to think harshly about basic errors, and if he liked you he could say devastating things. . . . It was assumed that you were intelligent enough to think them over. For me, this was salutary—objectivity-building."[74] A similar toughness—objective, comic, unsparing—marks Bellow's account, in a conversation with Norman Manea, of "What Kind of a Day Did You Have?":

> Here is the woman throwing herself away on this super-intellectual who has a certain amount of charm, has a real wit, and even has a solid character despite the fact that he's talking so much all his life. He's a great talker, but he hasn't talked himself into inanity. So he can still respond to her. He knows perfectly well what she's talking about. She wants to use this crisis to force him to say I love you, and he's thinking: What female madness is this, what a time to bring it up, we're facing the end! And still I think there's an amount of admiration for her, for her nerve, her chutzpah, her determination to make her pitch at the last moment.
>
> It's very complex. The whole thing is very complex. For instance, why should he grudge her? They're both going to die. He might as well humor her. So she might well say. So you ask. . . . Well, what good is it if you're getting him to say I Love You under duress? That won't do either. . . . Yes, he's this sort of high-class intellectual, but as I say, it hasn't destroyed his humanity entirely, if I may put it that way. . . . And there's no coming between a Jew and his jokes—a sort

of permanent love of paradox and funny occasions, even if it costs you. So he's indignant that she should be using death to intimidate him at the very last moment—because it may be that they're never going to end this flight in safety. Anyhow, the whole passage gives me *naches* [Yiddish: proud joy].[75]

As this passage suggests, affinity as well as amusement and admiration played its part in Bellow's attraction to Victor and his real-life model. Though careful to keep a distance from the *Partisan Review* crowd, his intelligence could be like theirs, hard, mocking, dismissive.

BELLOW FIRST ENCOUNTERED Rosenberg in the pages of *Partisan Review* (though he may have come across his name while working on the Illinois volume of the Writers' Project American Guides series, of which Rosenberg was national director).[76] In the Jefferson Lectures, he writes of sitting on a bench in Jackson Park in 1940, reading Rosenberg's essay "On the Fall of Paris" (in the issue of November–December 1940). At the time, Bellow was feeling particularly isolated, at odds with family and community, yet he also felt "intimately connected with the vital needs of them all." The "all" in question, he acknowledged, were wholly ignorant of those needs, and would consider him "very curious indeed" if they knew what he thought they were. He, in turn, considered the needs of family and community to be curious, as he considered anyone "living without the higher motives of which I was so wildly, perhaps ridiculously, proud" (an admission that recalls Victor Wulpy's incomprehension of "such a life as [Katrina] lived"). In his youthful idealism, the sentences from Rosenberg's essay that most struck Bellow were these: "In all his acts ... contemporary man seems narrow and poor. Yet there are moments when he seems to leap towards the marvellous in ways more varied and whole-hearted than any of the generations of the past." Bellow was himself "narrow and poor" at twenty-five, but "I would, for the sake of us all," he remembers vowing, try "to leap towards the marvelous."[77]

In 1940, such a leap might take a young man to New York. Though Paris had fallen, what it stood for might be revived. "The School of Paris," according to Rosenberg, was distinguished by its internationalism; it was "world-wide and world-timed and pertinent everywhere," epitomizing "the Modern in literature, painting, architecture, drama, design." In this "magnanimous milieu," artists of all nationalities "discovered in themselves what was most alive in the communities from which they had come." Rosenberg's vision of "a creative communion sweeping across all boundaries" was certain to appeal to Bellow, who knew what it was like to feel disadvantaged by his background, unsure of a place in the culture of his nation. Paris released artists from all such restrictions, "from national folklore, national politics, national career . . . from the family and the corporate taste," thus freeing them to find value in local attachments.[78]

In the concluding paragraph of "The Fall of Paris," Rosenberg declares that, though Paris, or what it stands for, may rise again, "no one can predict which city or nation will be the center of this new phase."[79] To an ambitious writer from Chicago, New York was as good a place as any. Not only did it draw artists and intellectuals from all over the United States, but from the mid-1930s onward it sheltered an unprecedented influx of European artists and intellectuals, including prominent contributors to PR. For Bellow, PR itself was a virtual Paris: Rahv and Phillips "thrilled us by importing the finest European writers and familiarizing the American literary public with them. Where else would you find Malraux, Silone, Koestler and company but in *Partisan Review*?"[80] On returning to the city from war duty, Kazin was in no doubt as to its cultural centrality: "New York was triumphant, glossy, more disorderly than ever, but more 'artistic,' the capital of the world, of the old European intellect, of action painting, action feeling, action totally liberated, personal, and explosive."[81]

Action painting was Rosenberg's coinage. In Lionel Abel's words, "Harold addressed himself to making clear that no alternative to, or ideological therapy for, our condition of homelessness has yet been found, and until something of that order is discovered, our only valid works of art, our only valid actions, must continue to express a certain distance from things, from others, even from ourselves." As Rosenberg himself put it, "At a certain moment, the canvas began to appear to one American painter after another as an area in which to act—rather than as a space in which to reproduce, redesign, analyze or 'express' as object, actual or imagined. What was to go on the canvas was not a picture but an event."[82] For William Phillips, this definition of the new painting "was a remarkably suggestive characterization of the spirit animating the artistic community at the time,"[83] a spirit captured in

SB and Anita (private collection)

Edith and Oscar Tarcov (courtesy of Miriam Tarcov)

Cora and Herb Passin
(courtesy of Jean Passin)

Vasiliki and Isaac Rosenfeld
(courtesy of Daniel Rosenfeld)

SB and Mel Tumin, Evanston, 1942 (courtesy of Sylvia Tumin)

(*left*) SB, Anita, and Harold ("Kappy") Kaplan, New York, 1940 (private collection)

(*above*) Trotsky assassinated, Mexico City, 1940 (courtesy of Corbis Images)

Daniel P. and Jule Mannix and their American bald eagle, Aguila, the model for Caligula in *Augie March*, Mexico, 1940 (courtesy of Getty Images; photo by J. R. Eyerman/ LIFE Picture Collection)

SB and Anita, Mexico, 1940 (private collection)

Lionel and Diana Trilling in Riverside
Park, near Columbia University, 1942
(courtesy of James Trilling)

Alfred Kazin, New York, 1946 (Magnum
Images; photo by Henri Cartier-Bresson)

(*left*) Heinrich Blücher and Hannah
Arendt, 1960 (courtesy of Corbis Images;
photo by Fred Stein)

New York intellectuals: (standing) Lionel Abel; (seated, left
to right) Bowden Broadwater (husband of Mary McCarthy),
Elizabeth Hardwick, Miriam Chiaromonte, Nicola
Chiaromonte, Mary McCarthy, John Berryman; (at bottom,
from left) Dwight Macdonald, the actor Kevin McCarthy
(brother of Mary McCarthy) (courtesy of Archives and Special
Collections, Vassar College Libraries)

David Bazelon, SB's friend from Greenwich Village days (courtesy of University of Delaware Library, Newark, Delaware)

Clement Greenberg (on the right) and Barnett Newman (on the left) at the Cedar Tavern in Greenwich Village, 1959 (Getty Images; photo by Fred W. McDarrah)

Harold Rosenberg (courtesy of University of Chicago Photographic Archive, Special Collections Research Center, University of Chicago Library)

Arthur Lidov (courtesy of Alexandra Lidov)

(*left*) Mitzi and Herb McClosky, c. 1943 (courtesy of Mildred McClosky)

(*left*) SB and Greg (seven weeks old), August 25, 1944 (private collection)

SB in Spain, 1947 (private collection)

(*left*) Eleanor Clark, Robert Penn Warren, and their infant daughter, Rosanna Warren, 1954 (courtesy of Corbis Images; photo by Sylvia Salmi)

Max Kampelman (in the middle, black curly hair and glasses), SB's lodger in Minneapolis. A conscientious objector, he is pictured with Civilian Public Service (CPS) workers, a year or so before volunteering for the Minnesota Starvation Project in the mid-1940s. (courtesy of the American Friends Service Committee)

The Bellow home at 58 Orlin Avenue, Prospect Park, Minneapolis, shared with lodgers Max Kampelman, Bart Leiper, and Ed McGehee (courtesy of Alice Leader)

Diarmuid Russell and Henry Volkening, SB's agents (from Michael Kreyling, *Agent/ Author*, Farrar, Straus and Giroux, 1991)

Monroe Engel, SB's editor at Viking, late 1950s (courtesy of Harvard University Archives; photo by Bill Tobey)

Sidney Hook, 1949, the year he reported for *Partisan Review* on the International Day of Resistance to Dictatorship and War, in Paris (courtesy of Corbis; photo by Sylvia Salmi)

(*above*) 24 rue Marbeuf, site of the Bellows' first Paris apartment (courtesy of Alice Leader)

The cafés of Saint-Germain, 1946, five minutes from SB's writing room at the Hôtel de l'Académie on rue des Saints-Pères, the first street to the west (or left here) of Café de Flore (Getty Images, 1946)

Harold "Kappy" Kaplan, in his apartment at 132 boulevard du Montparnasse, 1940s (courtesy of Leslie Kaplan)

Paolo Milano

SB in Salzburg, 1950
(private collection)

Schloss Leopoldskron, Salzburg,
Austria, home of the Salzburg
Seminar in American Studies
("a Marshall Plan of the Mind"),
where SB taught in 1950 and 1952
(courtesy of Getty Images;
photo by Angelika Korschlager)

SB, Anita, and
Greg in Rome, 1950
(private collection)

Kazin's typically overheated formulation: "action painting, action feeling, action totally liberated, personal, and explosive."

Rosenberg's great critical rival, Clement Greenberg, shared this sense of the new painting's explosiveness. What marks it off from the other arts, he writes in the essay "'American-Type' Painting" (*Partisan Review*, Spring 1955), is that it "continues to create scandal when little new in literature or music does."[84] *PR*'s support of literary modernism was hardly daring; by the early 1940s, T. S. Eliot and Joyce were as much heroes of the academy as of the avant garde. What was daring was aligning this support with Marxist theory. Rosenberg's "new phase" would come, Greenberg argued, from the visual arts, which, more thoroughly than literature, sought meaning outside subject matter or representation. For Greenberg, the new painting found meaning in "pure form" rather than "action" or "event." "Abstract expressionism," the name Greenberg gave to the new painting, was seen as an endpoint of modernism, in the visual arts at least, what painting must inevitably become given the conditions of capitalism. Modernist painting, Greenberg argues in "Towards a Newer Laocoön" (*Partisan Review*, July–August 1940), began with Courbet, whose pictures were marked by a "new flatness" and "an equally new attention to every inch of the canvas, regardless of its relation to the 'centres of interest.'" With impressionism, "painting becomes more an exercise in color vibrations than representation of nature." Manet, similarly, "saw the problems of painting as first and foremost problems of the medium, and he called the spectator's attention to this" (p. 302). Finally, cubist painting sought "the destruction of realistic pictorial space, and with it, that of the object" (p. 308). With cubism, painting was brought "to the point of the pure abstraction, but it remained with a few exceptions, for the Dutch, Germans, English and Americans to realize it. It is in their hands that abstract purism has been consolidated into a school, dogma and credo" (p. 309)—a school located in the studios and taverns of Greenwich Village, where Franz Kline, Willem de Kooning, Jackson Pollock, and others lived and socialized; a credo or dogma formulated in the pages of *Partisan Review*, where Rosenberg and Greenberg addressed readers and editors whose primary interests were literary and political. Soon, in William Barrett's words, the abstract expressionists and/or action painters were seen as "the first American artists to have created a truly international style, and with their arrival, it was claimed, the center of art had now definitely passed from Paris to New York."[85]

Bellow's relations with Greenberg were problematic. Early in his time in New York they were close. In the foreword to the *PR* fiction anthology, he describes himself as "very briefly a protégé." Greenberg's high seriousness impressed him, though eventually it put him off, as his Marxism did. He had, Bellow explains, "no illusions about Stalin. Stalin was loathed; Lenin was idolized. Lenin was hard, strict, pure and stern—merciless as a revolutionist must be when he takes power. Clem was himself strict, doctrinaire, pure and hard and believed that he was doing in art what Ilyitch had done in politics."[86] This belief derived from Greenberg's defense or account of abstract expressionism along determinist lines. "I have offered no other explanation for the present superiority of abstract art than its historical justification," he writes at the end of "Towards a Newer Laocoön," "what I have written has turned out to be an historical apology for abstract art" (p. 310). In both the "Laocoön" and an earlier *PR* essay, "Avant-garde and Kitsch" (Fall 1939), inspired in part by Macdonald's film criticism, and edited by Macdonald, Greenberg laid out what the art historian T. J. Clark calls "a theory and history of culture since 1850—since, shall we say, Courbet and Baudelaire."[87] This date coincides with the thought of Marx. "It was no accident," Greenberg writes in "Avant-garde and Kitsch," "that the birth of the avant-garde coincided chronologically—and geographically, too—with the first development of scientific revolutionary thought in Europe" (p. 49). That the movement Greenberg describes was away from representation also played a part in the dissolution of the friendship with Bellow, perhaps even more so than Greenberg's rigidity and dogmatism, or his claim for the "scientific" nature of his theories or their service to the proletariat. In Bellow's words,

> Clem planted his flag and claimed the "abstract" in the name of revolution. He gave historical reasons for this and told us that without a correct view of history our efforts would be barren.
>
> There was no room for the likes of me in this historical picture. I was obviously stuck between kitsch and avant-garde owing to my concern with persons and with the external world. Because of my unwillingness to yield to historical necessities I was struck from Clem's list of the elect.

Greenberg figures prominently in the foreword to the *PR* anthology, from which this passage is taken, because "for some years I had thought of him as the soul of the magazine." Now, Bellow believes, he was mistaken, not only because Greenberg "could not associate himself with any group. No editorial board could ever be pure enough to suit him" (Greenberg resigned from *PR*'s board, as did Macdonald, in 1943, Macdonald to start *politics*, Greenberg to become art critic of *The Nation*); more important, the magazine itself was "eclectic, willing to be heterogeneous, open to new talent in every form," cohesive only in that its editors "knew real writing when they saw it"—which is the sort of thing one says at the end of such a foreword, but also something Bellow believed.[88]

THOUGH AVANT-GARDE IN their sympathies, few of the writers and editors of *Partisan Review* could be called bohemian. Bellow's experience of bohemian life in Greenwich Village came mostly through Rosenfeld and Vasiliki and their friends. Rosenfeld's circle included *Partisan Review* writers and NYU and Columbia academics; there was as much talk of Marx, modernism, and Freud in the Rosenfeld parlor as at the Rahvs' or the Phillipses'. But the manners of Rosenfeld's circle were different, hipper, more cynical, not much bothered about getting things written or done, or making it. In "An Exalted Madness," the shortest of the "Zetland" manuscripts ("Charm and Death" is the longest), the circle is described as "a group of bohemians, college graduates carrying on their education without much discipline in an extended adolescence." In this circle, the writers who mattered were Kierkegaard, D. H. Lawrence, and Baudelaire, the Baudelaire who believed "that human beings are made equal through sin and shame, each man knowing in his heart of hearts how weak, hypocritical, corrupt and ignoble he is" (p. 4). Such knowledge, the narrator thinks, licenses wickedness, which "becomes the basis of fraternal feeling" among Zetland's friends. The narrator, however, is "a brand-new Ph.D., and an Assistant Professor at Princeton." Zetland's friends think him uncool. "The prominent intellectuals I met in the Village considered me a goose," he recalls, "known in the Village only as a friend of the Zetlands" (p. 5).

Like Rosenfeld, Zetland is only in part bohemian. When Bellow challenged Rosenfeld about his behavior in the Village years, his friend was quick to defend himself. In an undated journal entry from the early 1940s he recalls "how after making a thorough fool of myself, I am asked (by Saul?), 'Why do you have to be such a fool?' I flare up; I cry it is better to be a fool than not a fool, to dare ridicule." A later journal entry sketches out the "climactic scene" of a story Rosenfeld is considering writing set in the Village: "A seder, which soon degenerates into a cocktail party. The Haggadah is burlesqued, no one can read, no one understand. The host (I?), who has made an effort to reform, to fly right, live straight . . . also succumbs to the degeneration. They light up tea; a fight (Calder [Willingham, the writer]?); he [the host, "I?"] makes a play for the chick, leaves with her when the guests leave. Comes home very late. His wife is up. . . . She says very calmly she is going to leave him the next day. No tears. The children are still up. They are amused by everything."[89] In "Charm and Death," Zetland is caught up in Village ways in just this fashion, while seeking to resist them:

> He was a family-man; that was not bohemian. But he was a bohemian also, in his manner, in his easy way with money, in the hours he kept. But the Village had an orthodoxy of its own, Modernist orthodoxy. He didn't accept that fully either. He had his standards (from adolescence, A. Z. Crocker said). These went back to Plato, to Tolstoi. He applied them to himself and to his own writing. It was a high-principled ragged life and until he was thirty or so he was as he seemed (p. 46).

The Rosenfelds, like the Zetlands, kept open house. While Vasiliki went to work, Rosenfeld spent the day writing or working or walking the dog, the unattractive, constipated Smokey ("Zet put her in the bath-tub and gave her an enema. A terrible, necessary, comical event" [p. 49]).[90] People dropped by all the time, but especially on Friday and Saturday nights. Among those frequently found at 85 Barrow Street were David Bazelon, from Chicago, who introduced Rosenfeld to his friend Calder Willingham; Ray Rosenthal, an editor and translator; the beat writer Milton Klonsky; the brothers Herb and Willy Poster (né Bernstein), well-known Village characters; Alfred Kazin, who stayed for a period in the Rosenfeld apartment, after breaking up with his first wife; Manny Farber, a painter and film critic; his wife, Janet Richards; Farber's psychoanalyst brother, Leslie; Leslie's wife, Midge, with whom Bellow was having an affair; James Agee; and the poet Weldon Kees, who lived on the Lower East Side, on St. Mark's Place, in an apartment below that of Harold Rosenberg and his wife. In another "Zetland" manuscript, the narrator describes his friend's circle as made up of "painters, musicians, economists from the New School, academic philosophers, self made intellectuals, surrealists, off beat journalists, original girls, stockbrokers, even, whose university education had given them a taste for conversation they couldn't satisfy on Wall Street."[91] A Wall Street type like one of these stockbrokers is found in "An Exalted Madness." The narrator is stopped by an executive who says: "'Oh, you're Donald Rich, Zetland's pal from Chicago. Wasn't he something—a blood-bank. When I was low, I'd go to Bleecker Street [for Barrow Street in all the manuscripts], that *hegdisch*, for a transfusion.' A good word, *hegdisch*: it refers literally to the destruction of the temple, but more familiarly it is reserved for domestic squalor" (p. 2).[92]

The most bohemian of Rosenfeld's friends were Herb and Willy Poster. According to Janet Richards, Herb Poster had been a child prodigy at the University of Michigan, in line for a career as an academic philosopher. When the brothers inherited money—from their father's property dealings in Brownsville, Brooklyn—Herb dropped out. Though he continued to think about philosophy, mostly at night with the aid of gin and dope ("tea" in the argot of the day), he did so to no demonstrable end. His brother, Willy, a close friend of Richards's, was more outgoing, though only marginally more productive (writing the occasional article for *Commentary* and other publications). Both brothers spent a lot of time pursuing women ("they kept a special cash fund to pay for abortions," according to Rosenfeld's biographer, Steven Zipperstein; according to Kazin, they shared girlfriends and organized "public orgies").[93] Occasionally, late in the afternoon, Willy would bring Richards, who saw nothing of the rumored orgies, to the Hudson Street apartment the brothers shared. "Willy had to push Herb out of his nest of blankets," Richards writes. "He would emerge silent, rumpled, strange in the extreme, but friendly. He would eat something extraordinary, like an Eskimo Pie or a couple of walnuts, wander around and then retire to the bedroom for his breakfast joint. Willy retired with him."[94]

Neither Willy nor Herb ever talked of the source of their income or of their father, who named them Herbert Spencer Bernstein and William Shakespeare Bernstein, though every Sunday they took the subway to Brownsville to visit their mother, whom they adored. As Richards puts it, Willy, in contrast to Herb, was "extremely sociable . . . a committed gadabout, seeking in the streets and his friends' flats entertainment, while others worked at their disgusting jobs or toiled over their typewriters and easels."⁹⁵ The Posters' attitude toward work was shared by others in Rosenfeld's circle. When this attitude was held by writers, it was bound to irritate Bellow, given his fierce dedication to writing. In a letter to Bazelon of April 10, 1949, Bellow writes from Paris of Milton Klonsky, who was depressed. "I was a little low myself when he arrived, but in the Empyrean by comparison; hence no company for him. Besides, I was working. Do I say 'besides'? That was the ray that blights, for Milton."⁹⁶

In the "Zetland" and "Charm and Death" manuscripts, the Posters become Arlo Hahn and his brother, Waldo. When Zetland needs to borrow money from Arlo, arriving at his apartment "well supplied with suggestions from Russian literature" (Dostoyevsky seeking a loan from Turgenev at Baden, "the prophet gambler in one of his creepy phases, confessing perversion and vice"), Arlo is quick to spot his sources: "A reader himself, he would say: Don't overdo this Dostoyevsky stuff— all this spleen-swallowing, sneaking Jesus, love-hate routine" ("Charm and Death," p. 51). Then he'd give Zetland the money. Though Arlo despises conventional morality, he is generous and not without family feeling. "For a person who agreed verbatim with Marx and Engels on the bourgeois family and sex relations, it was curious how he doted on his cranky mother, his screwy brother Waldo" ("Charm and Death," p. 25). To outsiders or the unhip, the Posters could be snide and superior. "Willy & Herb, schmuck-baiters" begins an undated entry in Rosenfeld's journals.⁹⁷ Wallace Markfield, who fictionalizes Rosenfeld and his circle in the novel *To an Early Grave* (1964) (later a 1968 film by Sidney Lumet, *Bye Bye Braverman*), has them taunt the novel's narrator for his respectable job and new suit. "*A m'chyah* . . . Look at the quality, look at the tailoring. How nice it hangs."⁹⁸ Despite their affluence, the Hahns despise appearances, or affect to despise them, living in worse squalor than the Zetlands, "in bleaker filth than anyone, on carpetless boards, grimy folding canvas chairs . . . pullchain toilet never washed" ("Charm and Death," p. 51).

The other prominent bohemian from the "Zetland" manuscripts is A. Z. Crocker (in one manuscript "Al Dinborg"), "a Marxian with a detailed interest in finance and bourgeois politics" ("Charm and Death," p. 22). Crocker is modeled, in part, on David Bazelon, who moved from writing to finance to law. He, too, has money, compensation for an accident (railroad in "Charm and Death," traffic in "Zetland"), in which he lost an arm, as had his model, who lost his arm at the age of seven. Crocker is smart, unillusioned, as much of a womanizer as the Hahns (in his journals, Rosenfeld alludes to "our famous phrase about 'marriage as a base of operations'"[99]), and if anything tougher on Zetland's "innocence" than they are. Bazelon shared this toughness, which he partly attributed to the loss of his arm: "This [the accident] stimulated my mind ahead of time, or out of sequence, and this led almost immediately, I think, to two different but simultaneous distortions of emphasis: (1) I sought too much outside my own physical being for compensatory jurisdiction (control in fact and by right) of my own body; and (2) I became both internally and externally imperialist as to the jurisdiction of the mind—my own and others."[100] The narrator of "Charm and Death" hates the cynical "imperialist" character of these friends of Zetland—hates the friends themselves, for contributing to Zet's ruination—but gives their account of him its due:

> A. Z. Crocker and Arlo Hahn were advanced intellectuals, Modernists. They held a tough point of view. Zetland saw them clearly enough. He was not about to follow their example, not about to surrender the soul-beliefs and love-beliefs, but part of their harshness was realistic. One must stop faking. Acknowledge lack of feeling and be free from false feeling at least. Live in the shadow side of what used to be the soul. Be the dead man that in reality you are. Be dead to the old tyranny of the Good and step away from the metaphysical police of Moses and Mt. Sinai (p. 52).

Crocker's assault on Zetland's beliefs is discharged "like an electrified iron mass through the trifling sociability of Village parties and encounters" (p. 21). He wants Zet to write porn, "Lots of good guys do," partly for money, partly because "it was precisely the task of talent to dismantle itself, degrade itself as harshly as possible so as to elude exploitation and not to fool itself into collaboration with the social order" (p. 22). Here is Crocker on "enthusiasm," a particular bugbear to Village bohemians: "He's got that visionary, *enthusiastic* pastrami-fat gleam in his eye, the poor prick! Listen to him when he gets going about Transcendentalism. He gets that saleable glow. How do you think he got the job at *Fortune?*" (p. 23).[101] In the "Zetland" manuscript, Zet is criticized by a Francophile Village type who complains, "*Il nous fait la morale!*" (p. 40). In "Zetland and Quine," another "Zetland" manuscript, which combines elements of "Charm and Death" with "Far

Out," Zetland is accused by "opinion in the Village" of "lacking the iron of Modernism, in either Nietzschean or Leninist hardness" (p. 9). Throughout the "Zetland" manuscripts, the protagonist is too high-minded for his bohemian circle, clinging to his standards "in spite of all, even when he felt like chopping up everyone with an axe and hanging himself from the frontroom ceiling" (p. 50). For *Partisan Review* types, in contrast, he is lightweight, unserious, a disappointment after the initial wunderkind or *shoyne boychick* phase:

> Occasionally he published a bright essay, and wrote an unusually good style, but he got above himself now and then, tried to be serious beyond his means. The leading German and Italian refugee intellectuals didn't think much of him. His culture was patched together, American style, no Greek and Latin; he was neither a native American Wildman nor a cultivated Wasp. The leading German bluestocking [Hannah Arendt comes to mind] dismissed him. It may have gotten back to her that he said she resembled George Arliss in the role of Disraeli. But if it didn't it was sufficient that he had misbehaved at one of her evenings and he wasn't asked uptown again to eat *Dobuschtorte* and to hear the lady speak of Heidegger or the Mass Society. In such circles, Xinnie [the Vasiliki figure] of course had no standing at all. She was only the pretty Macedonian woman married to that Ostjude Village character from Chicago. Such snubs put Zetland in a rage. . . . He swore he'd get this arrogant Krautess or that Dago litterateur who patronized him ("Zetland," pp. 43–44).

For all Bellow's wariness of the *Partisan Review* crowd, he was closer to its view of Rosenfeld than to the views of bohemians like the Posters. He despised the flip sarcasms of Village types, their abyss mongering and self-absorption, their sloth, their sneering at bourgeois careerists, himself included.[102] Above all he despised them for the effect he thought they had on Rosenfeld. "Village life, as he interpreted it," Bellow wrote to Rosenfeld's son, George Sarant, in a letter of September 9, 1990, "was his undoing. I don't entirely blame the village, but his liberation degenerated into personal anarchy." "He did not follow the fat gods," Bellow wrote of Rosenfeld after his death. "I think he liked the miserable failures in the Village better than the miserable successes Uptown, but I believe he had not understood that the failures had not failed enough but were fairly well satisfied with the mild form of social revolt which their incomplete ruin represented."[103]

These accounts of Rosenfeld and his circle came decades after the 1940s. The "Zetland" manuscripts are from the 1970s and their disapproval of Village bohemianism may not accurately reflect Bellow's feelings at the time, or so the correspondence suggests. In letters of 1948 and 1949 to David Bazelon, for example, Bellow writes as a friend of long standing, offering advice, helping Bazelon to find work, inviting him to visit (in Minneapolis, in Paris). Though he objects to some of Bazelon's views, characterizing them as Village orthodoxy, he does so without rancor. In a letter of January 5, 1948, he defends *The Victim* against Bazelon's strictures: "I do think that Village sensibility has peculiar dangers. In the Village where so much desire is fixed on so few ends, and those constantly narrowing ends, there is a gain in intensity and a leak and loss in the respect of solidity. The Village is too unfriendly to the common, much too Gnostic. Besides, the novelist labors in character, not in psychology, which is easier and swifter. . . . The Villagers are poetic theorists in psychology and consider a vision of character naive when it fails to satisfy their hunger for extremes." The judgment recalls Bellow's letter to Harold Rosenberg on the greater capacity of *Herzog* to change the world than any essay in *Encounter*. The letter ends "Love," as does a letter of May 27, 1948, which makes the same point in respect to anthropology, which, Bellow tells Bazelon, "doesn't consider people at full depth. Anti-poetic, therefore basically unfaithful. Mere botanizing."

Only at the end of 1949, on December 3, does Bellow's friendly tone change, when he answers what he calls a "horrible and wolfish" letter from Bazelon (about a woman who had hurt Bazelon and with whom Bellow was on friendly terms). Bellow reacts angrily to the letter, characterizing Bazelon in terms that recall A. Z. Crocker and the Hahns. "Though I have often put up with your thinking me so," Bellow writes, "I am not stupid. . . . Had our friendship rested, childishly, on 'literary loyalty' we'd have been through long before this. You must think me an idiot if you believe I haven't known for years what attitude you took toward it" (his work, that is). Two days later, Bellow writes to Tarcov about Bazelon's "hideous letter" and its naive assumption that he hadn't known "what opinion his Hudson Street friends had of my writing." From this moment on, the correspondence falls away, as does the friendship.[104] What the correspondence makes clear is that in the 1940s, though Bellow saw in Rosenfeld and his friends what the narrators of the "Zetland" manuscripts saw (the narratives are retrospective, hence "saw"), he was closer and more sympathetic to them, certainly to Bazelon, than the manuscripts suggest. This is particularly true in respect to a prominent plot strand in the manuscripts not yet discussed: their accounts of Zetland's interest in the theories of Wilhelm Reich and in Reichian therapy. Bellow's depiction of Reichian theory and therapy is devastating in the "Zetland" manuscripts (as it is in "Far Out," where they also figure prominently), but in the late 1940s he himself was drawn to both. By 1951, he admitted to Norman Manea, he had "turned into a follower of Wilhelm Reich."[105]

IN 1945, when Bellow enlisted in the Merchant Marine, he was assigned to the Atlantic District Headquarters of the U.S. Maritime Service in Sheepshead Bay, Brooklyn. He chose the Merchant Marine for several reasons: the recruiters had assured him he'd have plenty of time to write once training was over, certainly more than he'd have in other service branches (as Daniel Bell put it, "the merchant marine was an easier life," with fewer "rigidities" than the navy or army); he knew he'd be stationed in New York, at least initially; and, as both Bell and Harold Kaplan suggested, there was a tradition of Trotskyists and ex-Trotskyists joining the Merchant Marine. Bell explains this last reason: "It was partly that you weren't participating in an imperialist war. It was also—a curious thing—that the insurance was always handed over to the Party [in the case of unmarried men, who made up the majority of enlistees, the Party was named as beneficiary], a great potential source of income both for the Communist Party and the Trotskyist branch." Great because insurance for the Merchant Marine was especially high, given the danger of wartime voyages: 733 American cargo ships were lost in waters off enemy shores during World War II; crew members died at a rate of one out of twenty-six.[106] One final reason for choosing the Merchant Marine was offered by Bellow himself: "the war in Europe was then coming to an end,"[107] effectively removing the principal drawback to the service: its extreme danger. In *The Adventures of Augie March*, Augie, too, becomes a merchant mariner. Although he shares Bellow's political leanings and something of his history, he says he joined the service because of a recent hernia operation (like the one

Bellow had in the summer of 1944), which meant "I still wasn't accept-able to the Army or the Navy" (p. 914).

When the war in Europe ended, on May 8, 1945, VE Day, Bellow was still in boot camp in Brooklyn. In June, he was sent to Baltimore for three weeks of "boat drills, brine, heavy meals, sun, hell-raising."[108] On the Chesapeake Bay, trainee merchant mariners practiced raising and lowering lifeboats, rowing, firefighting drills, abandon-ship drills. In *Augie* they are described as "rambunctious, mauling and horsing around, prodding with boat hooks, goosing and carrying on, screaming about female genitals." Rowing went on for "hours and hours" across the curling waters of the Chesapeake Bay, likened to "a huge bed of endive." On Saturdays, the trainees were allowed into Baltimore, "where the tramps of the port were waiting on Clap Hill, and the denominations with printed verses" (p. 919). After Chesapeake Bay, Augie and his fellow trainees are returned to Sheepshead Bay, where he studies book-keeping and ship's medicine before embarking on the ill-fated Atlan-tic voyage that leaves him stuck in a lifeboat with a deranged ship's carpenter, Basteshaw. Bellow, by contrast, was returned to Sheepshead Bay to be put to work for the Maritime Commission, living in bar-racks within easy reach of Manhattan, staying for weekends with David Bazelon in the Village. During this period, on August 6, the atomic bomb was dropped on Hiroshima. Three days later a second bomb was dropped on Nagasaki. On August 15 the Japanese surrendered, signing the instruments of surrender on September 2, officially ending the war. Less than two weeks later, on September 15, Bellow was released to inactive service. He had been a merchant mariner for less than six months.

Now began a year of much movement in Bellow's life. At the end of September, two weeks after his release, he returned to Hyde Park, to Anita and Greg (who was known as Herschel in the family, "a fine old Yiddish name").[109] Bellow was determined that the family leave Chicago. The plan, he wrote to Sam Freifeld, was to "move East" and "make my way Rosenfeld-style, as a free lance."[110] Chicago, he wrote to James Farrell on September 15, the day of his discharge from active service, "grows more like Siberia all the time." He was now in the midst of "one of my annual drives to get out," which in the past followed the same pattern: "I come in, petition the Czar to free me from ban-ishment, he refuses and I get into the Pacemaker [the Chicago–New

York train] with the other condemned and return." For whatever reason (because the *Britannica* job, to which he could return, would finish on January 1, because he and Anita were tired of lengthy separations and he missed his son as well as wife), this time the drive to get out worked. The Czar (Anita?) acceded to a move East.

Toward the end of September, Bellow returned to New York to find a place for the family to live. In the Atlas biography, Anita and Greg accompany him, the whole family arriving "on the doorstep of Arthur and Victoria Lidov"[111] at the end of September. Arthur Lidov, a painter and illustrator, had graduated from the University of Chicago with a degree in sociology in 1936, overlapping with Bellow. After nine months in Palestine, he returned to the university to do graduate work in art history. He also worked for the Chicago WPA art project on murals and sculpture commissions, and showed his paintings at Art Institute select exhibitions. He, too, moved to New York in 1945, immediately after marrying Victoria, less than a year before the Bellows. According to Lidov's second wife, Alexandra, recounting "what I heard from my husband," Bellow and Lidov had not known each other in Chicago, meeting for the first time in New York, when Afred Kazin introduced them one afternoon.[112] Kazin's biographer, Richard M. Cook, says it was Bellow who introduced Kazin to Lidov.[113] In any event, at some point the three men met at 91 Pineapple Street, in Brooklyn Heights, an old run-down family house on the edge of Fulton Street, where the Lidovs rented a fifth-floor studio apartment, which they later sublet to Kazin. According to Kazin, the building smelled of "burned out pasta and indecipherable Greek salad," but the studio had a fine view of the Brooklyn Bridge.[114]

Around about the time Bellow and Lidov met, Lidov's career as a commercial artist illustrating feature articles for magazines and designing covers for *Fortune* had begun to take off, and he and Victoria moved from Pineapple Street to a house in upstate New York, in Patterson, rented from the heiress wife of his agent. Bellow himself was in search of a place in roughly the Patterson area, not inconveniently far from Manhattan but not in suburbia, and "on an impulse," according to Atlas,[115] Lidov invited the Bellows to use his house as a base while searching for a place of their own (whether Lidov's wife, Victoria, with whom he was soon to separate, was consulted is unclear). This is when Kazin, having separated from *his* wife, Natasha ("Asya") sublet the Pineapple Street studio, where he was to stay until 1952.[116] Bellow then returned to Chicago, he and Anita packed up the apartment at 5400 Dorchester Avenue (which Daniel Bell and his wife were to move into, Bell having been recruited to teach sociology at the university by the economist Maynard Krueger[117]), and Maury and Marge agreed to store their furniture and belongings at the grand Lake Shore Drive hotel they now owned, managed, and lived in, the Shoreland, today a University of Chicago dormitory. On October 3 Bellow sent "fraternal greetings" to Bazelon "from the Old Sod," reporting his "triumphal" homecoming: "Whatever I do or fail to do I have the blessings of love and happiness in marriage. I don't have to ask whether the world is real or whether it is food enough for me; I can ask no greater blessing for myself or anyone dear to me." "We are not staying in Chicago," he then adds. "As soon as we hear from the Lidovs we move." They heard within the week. "We had an easy trip," Anita reported in a postcard to the Tarcovs, on October 10, 1945, "and are fairly well settled here."

Anita's initial impression of the Patterson area and the Lidovs' place was positive. "It's a swell house on a hill—with simply beautiful grounds—it's like living in the middle of a Park." During the time the Bellows lived with the Lidovs—between four to six weeks, Lidov told Alexandra—relations between the two families were mostly good. No complaints survive about household expenses or crying babies or the Lidovs' two cats and dog. There was not, however, much contact between the couples: Bellow was writing hard, deep into *The Victim*, or reading, for reviews or for publishers, or house hunting. He worked in the living room, while Lidov worked in the attic, painting flat out "sixteen hours a day, seven days a week." Lidov rarely saw Anita and the baby, there were no joint meals, few leisurely conversations, except for during the very occasional train rides the two men took together into Manhattan (Bellow took the train into the city once a week, Lidov only rarely, so busy was he with deadlines). "It is a long way to New York," Anita wrote to the Tarcovs, "1½ hours by fast train—2 hours by slow, and most of them are slow. It's an all-day affair when you do go in."

Arthur Lidov was a generous man, with a big personality. In *New York Jew*, Kazin writes of his "sweet pomposity." In his *Journals*, always more caustic, he calls him a "pompous jerk," "an inordinate man in every sense." Kazin praises Lidov for looking after his dying brother-in-law (Kazin's, that is), notwithstanding accompanying "officiousness and blather."[118] Lidov was serious about his art, including his commercial art, which he thought capable of depth and meaning, no mere advertising. Part of what kept him at his easel, painting continuously, was the decision to work in egg tempera, not an illustrator's medium. He was also a master carpenter, constructing handsome bookshelves in the Pineapple Street studio and subsequent dwellings, and an inventor of sorts, holding a patent for a spoke-less bicycle wheel meant to be impervious to flats, developing a new technique for bas-relief. Only after Lidov left Patterson, relocating in a converted brownstone on the Upper West Side, did he and Bellow became close. In 1951 Bellow wrote part of *Augie* in a small side room off Lidov's main studio. During this period, Lidov painted Bellow's portrait (two preparatory drawings for the portrait were purchased by the National Portrait Gallery in Washington, D.C.), perhaps while Bellow was creating the character of Basteshaw, the ship's carpenter, in *Augie*, a late addition to the manuscript.[119] "Did you recognize the man in the lifeboat?" Bellow asked Kazin. "He was astonished, outraged that I hadn't seen the exact resemblance. 'It's your landlord.'"[120] Basteshaw is "built like a horse. . . . His poise was that of a human fortress, and you could never catch him off balance" (p. 951); much of his conversation was medical and scientific (Lidov became a specialist in medical and scientific illustration); Basteshaw was full of theories, convinced of his genius. When stuck in the lifeboat with Augie, Bastsehaw does not want to be rescued: he wants to be interned by the Spanish so that he can continue his experiments in biochemistry (with Augie as his assistant, he hopes to "understand the birth of life and be in on the profoundest secrets" [p. 963]). Not surprisingly, Augie thinks he's mad. "The fellow was really out of his mind," Augie declares after their rescue. "But even then, in anger, I thought, what if he really was a genius too" (p. 965).

AFTER A MONTH OR SO of looking, the Bellows found a house in the town of Holmes in Dutchess County, ten miles from Patterson. By November 17, 1945, the family was well enough ensconced to issue invitations for Thanksgiving (Bazelon's invitation advised him to catch a train from Grand Central Station and to dress warmly). The house represented a big change for the Bellows: it had eight rooms and they could entertain (because of the number of Thanksgiving guests, Bellow warned Bazelon, there was likely to be "a shortage of overnight space"). Almost as soon as the family moved in, however, Anita and Greg were forced to return to Chicago where Anita's brother Jack was dying of cancer. On January 12, 1946, Bellow wrote to Henle describing himself as "holding down this eight-room house, a servitor to the pipes and heaters." On January 15, he complained to Bazelon that he'd been "alone for a week" and invited him to come out to the house: "You can have one room to sleep in and another to work in. We have something *resembling* heat. We can gadabout in the car. I can promise you everything but swimming and women."[121] Bellow's manner here masks anxieties about money, especially now that Anita wasn't working (she did not work for the first five years of Greg's life). In addition to reviewing (unsigned pieces for *The New York Times Book Review*, *The Nation*, and *The New Republic*), and selling the review copies on for one third the retail price, he was forced to take on editorial work, helping, as was previously mentioned, to choose titles for the first list of Penguin paperbacks to be published in the United States. The "three or four page" reports he wrote for his Penguin bosses, Victor Weybright and Eunice Frost, the latter "dove-like and forbearing," were not especially remunerative: "I was paid five dollars for every work of fiction, and ten dollars for non-fiction books. I read them most attentively and carried a sack of books up and down the Harlem Valley. Of course, I preferred the non-fiction because it was easier to scan quickly and didn't really hold my interest as deeply as a novel did."[122] Eventually, after Anita's and Greg's return from Chicago, it became impossible to meet the family's expenses; in June 1946 the Bellows were forced back into "exile," returning to Anita's mother's apartment in Ravenswood. Yet Bellow described himself at this period, in a letter to Henle, his publisher, as "in a high state of excitement": the novel was going well. Shortly after they arrived in Ravenswood, moreover, the family was offered a free apartment in New York for the summer from Leo Spiegel, a psychiatrist friend of Lidov's, The apartment was at 622 West 113th Street and the Bellows took it. Here they stayed for several months until Bellow at last found more permanent employment, as an instructor in the newly founded Humanities Division of the Department of General Studies at the University of Minnesota.

HOW BELLOW GOT the post at Minnesota, and how he got on there, begins the next chapter. In the fall of 1946, while teaching, he put *The Victim* through a final revision. On January 7, Henle was sent a "first draft." His less than rhapsodic response on February 3 elicited a wounded and wounding letter from Bellow. This letter Henle answered indignantly, defending Vanguard against Bellow's complaints about lack of promotion for *Dangling Man*. On March 15, Bellow wrote a more conciliatory letter, though still upset by Henle's lack of enthusiasm for the new novel. He was madly revising, he announced, "living on Benzedrine tablets." By the end of the summer proofs arrived and the novel was published on November 6, 1947, at the beginning of Bellow's second year at Minnesota. What it takes from New York, the use it makes of the city, is clear from the opening paragraph:

> On some nights New York is as hot as Bangkok. The whole continent seems to have moved from its place and slid nearer the equator, the bitter gray Atlantic to have become green and tropical, and the people, thronging the streets, barbaric fellahin among the stupendous monuments of their mystery, the lights of which, a dazing profusion, climb upward endlessly into the heat of the sky (p. 145).

Two epigraphs precede this paragraph: one from "The Tale of the Trader and the Jinni," in Sir Richard Burton's *Thousand and One Nights*, a second from Thomas De Quincey's *Confessions of an English Opium Eater*. The first introduces a rich merchant, oppressive heat, and a cruelly arbitrary, or arbitrary-seeming, misfortune, of a sort soon to be visited on the novel's protagonist; the second, from a section of the *Confessions* entitled "The Pains of Opium," is part of a recurring laudanum-induced nightmare, that of a rocking ocean "paved with innumerable faces, upturned to the heavens; faces, imploring, wrathful, despairing; faces that surged upwards by thousands, by myriads, by generations." These faces are "oriental," arising, it has been suggested, from subconscious colonial guilt or anxiety on De Quincey's part, as well as from the Eastern origins of opium.[123] Together the epigraphs suggest qualities picked up in the opening paragraph and woven throughout the novel. To begin with, urban heat, heavy, burdening, suffocating: at dawn "the factories were beginning to smolder and faced massively, India red, brown, into the sun" (p. 171); at dusk "still a redness in the sky, like the flame at the back of a vast baker's oven" (p. 159); at night "a new tide of heat . . . thickening the air, sinking grass and bushes under its weight" (pp. 229–30). This heat suggests the East or Orient— "surely the sun was no hotter in any Singapore or Surabaya" (p. 183)— as does the light of the city, very different from the "broadcast light" of Mexico. The "long lines of lamps" outside the "defile" of Leventhal's street give off a sickly yellowish glow (p. 371), like the "yellowish hot tinge" (p. 361) of Allbee's bloodshot eyes, "the yellowish-green water" on the journey to Staten Island, and the light that washes over the towers on the shore, like "the yellow revealed in the slit of the eye of a wild animal, say a lion, something inhuman that didn't care about anything human and yet was implanted in every human being too, one speck of it, and formed one part of him that responded to the heat and the glare, exhausting as these were" (p. 183).[124]

The heat of the city, a jungle heat as well as an oriental heat, is dazing. So are the city's thronging crowds and crashing noises. For Allbee, New York is all pushing Calibans; Leventhal, similarly, is oppressed by the city's "overwhelming human closeness and thickness . . . innumerable millions, crossing, touching, pressing" (p. 290). Then there's the racket: "the swirling traffic too loud, too swift" (p. 226); "the tumultuous swoop of the Third Avenue train rising above the continuous, tidal noise of the street" (pp. 363–64); "the concussion of the train" (p. 338). Images of flood and drowning ("What was that story he had once read about Hell cracking open on account of the rage of the god of the sea, and all the souls, crammed together, looking out?" [p. 290]) evoke Schopenhauer's vision of reality, quoted in Chapter 4: "a stormy sea that, unbounded in all directions, raises and drops mountainous waves, howling . . . a world of torments." In such a world, the self, or its agent, the *principium individuationis*, is the frailest of boats. A comparably dark vision of New York is offered in *Mr. Sammler's Planet*, which explicitly cites Schopenhauer. In *Seize the Day*, as in *The Victim*, Schopenhauer is unmentioned, but the world of New York is no less the world as described in *The World as Will and Idea*: "And the great crowd, the inexhaustible current of millions of every race and kind pouring out, pressing round, of every age, of every genius, possessors of every human secret, antique and future, in every face the refinement of one particular motive or essence— *I labor, I spend, I strive, I design, I love, I cling, I uphold, I give away, I envy, I long, I die, I hide, I want.*" What sounds here in each voice is Schopenhauer's "Will," "the cosmic force . . . which drives all things," the inner manifestation or dimension of the outer storm, "the inner creative fury of the world" (p. 96).[125]

This fury sounds in Bellow's Chicago as well as in his New York, but Chicago has enticements and excitements, and exhilarating power, even in *Dangling Man*. New York in Bellow's fiction, certainly in *The*

Victim, is almost unrelievedly grim (even on a morning the heat lifts, Leventhal witnesses a scene of crazy violence outside his window, leaving him feeling "he really did not know what went on about him, what strange things, savage things" [p. 219]). The intellectual ferment that drew Bellow to *Partisan Review* and the Village in the early 1940s, for example, survives here only as aggression and amorality: in the interview with Rudiger, Bellow's version of the interview with Chambers, with its "atmosphere of infliction and injury from which neither could withdraw" (p. 177); in Allbee's jeering despair, reminiscent not only of Rosenfeld's Village friends, quoting Baudelaire and Dostoyevsky, but of the anti-Semitic Céline. Here is Allbee on Leventhal's "Jewish" belief that "there's no evil in life itself": "It's a Jewish point of view. You'll find it all over the Bible. God doesn't make mistakes. . . . But I'll tell you something. We do get it in the neck for nothing and suffer for nothing, and there's no denying that evil is as real as sunshine." Leventhal's Jewish righteousness is an ignoble, bourgeois fantasy:

The editorial board of the "new" Partisan Review, *circa 1937. Clockwise from upper left: George L. K. Morris, Philip Rahv, Dwight Macdonald, William Phillips, and F. W. Dupee.*

You people take care of yourselves before everything. You keep
your spirit under lock and key. That's the way you're brought up.
You make it your business assistant, and it's safe and tame and never
leads you toward anything risky. Nothing dangerous and nothing
glorious. Nothing ever tempts you to dissolve yourself. What for?
What's in it? No percentage (p. 260).

"Dissolve yourself," Allbee means, in the void, Schopenhauer's howling
storm. For all its surface attractions, the promise New York seemed to
hold out to Bellow, the esteem it held him in, in his fiction it is seen as
overwhelming, a threat to the self.[126] Hence, in life, the distance he kept
from it, even when in its midst.

8

Minneapolis

B ELLOW'S TULEY FRIEND Sam Freifeld helped him get the job at Minnesota. Freifeld entered the Army in the autumn of 1943 after working in his father's insurance business and studying at the John Marshall Law School at night. When he finished basic training he was assigned to the Office of the Provost Marshal General, in charge of law enforcement issues, where his duties were to investigate major felonies, murder, rape, robbery. In 1944 he was sent for CID (Criminal Investigation Division) training in Fort Custer, Michigan, followed in 1945 by six months further training at the CID German Language and Criminal Law School, at the University of Minnesota.[1] While at Minnesota, Freifeld met and befriended a bright, energetic assistant professor in political science named Herbert McClosky. McClosky was born in 1916, a year after Bellow, and grew up in the slums of Newark, New Jersey, the son of a Polish Russian immigrant named Michalovsky or Maglusky ("McClosky" was the flippant or hasty invention of an Ellis Island official). At the University of Newark (now Rutgers University–Newark), McClosky majored in political science, moving in 1940 to the University of Minnesota for graduate work. Exempted from military service on medical grounds, he was appointed assistant professor of political science early in 1946, teaching courses in political science and in the university's Humanities Program.

Early in his career at Minnesota, McClosky gravitated toward a cluster of influential social psychologists teaching on the Minneapolis campus, among them Paul Meehl, chair of the Department of Psychology, a key figure in developing the Minnesota Multiphasic Personality

Inventory, later a president of the American Psychological Association. Meehl became McClosky's close friend at the university, and was respected by Bellow. A therapist as well as a psychologist, he treated Bellow as a patient for a brief period in 1958.[2] Meehl helped McClosky to win a grant from the Social Sciences Research Council to pursue training in social psychology, psychometrics, and survey research, and from the mid-1950s on the two friends pioneered the application of social science techniques (empirical, behaviorist) to the study of politics, designing and applying elaborate surveys to determine voter preferences and beliefs. This approach, according to the political scientist Philip Siegelman, inaugurated a revolution in American social science, one that divided the field for at least thirty years. McClosky's literary friends, Bellow included, disapproved of the turn his research had taken, and his wife, Mitzi McClosky, remembers strenuous arguments between the two men, "like a fast moving tennis match." Both could be "ruthless in attack, but they weren't [ruthless] with each other."[3] Over specific political policies, parties, and personalities, at least in the 1940s, the two friends were more compatible, though Bellow had less faith or interest in politics than McClosky. By the mid-1940s McClosky, like Bellow, had turned against Trotskyism. He became a friend and supporter of Hubert Humphrey, a doctoral candidate in political science at Minnesota who had left graduate work in 1943 to run for mayor of Minneapolis (a post he held from 1945 to 1948). McClosky was part of the brain trust Humphrey assembled to combat local government corruption, racism, and anti-Semitism (in 1946, the year Bellow arrived, Carey McWilliams, editor of *The Nation*, described Minnesota as "the capital of anti-Semitism in America").[4] McClosky also helped Humphrey to create the Democratic-Farmer-Labor Party (DFL), and to fight off Communist attempts to take over the new party.

The connection between McClosky and Freifeld came about through Mel Tumin. While a freshman at the University of Newark, McClosky met and became friends with Tumin, a fellow undergraduate and Newark native. Before Tumin transferred to Wisconsin, where he met Bellow and Rosenfeld through his roommate, Leslie Fiedler, a Newark friend,[5] he introduced McClosky to the girl who would become his wife, Mildred Gurkin, known as Mitzi. After graduating from Wisconsin, Tumin went to Northwestern to do a PhD in anthropology with Herskovits. There he met a number of Bellow's friends, including Sam Freifeld. When the Freifelds arrived at Minnesota for Sam to begin

CID training, they looked up the McCloskys at Tumin's urging. In 1945, McClosky was interviewed for a job at the University of Chicago, and Freifeld urged him to contact the Bellows in Hyde Park. McClosky had never met Bellow but had read *Dangling Man* at Tumin's suggestion and admired it. Freifeld assured him that the Bellows would welcome a houseguest. "Sam was a fixer," Mitzi McClosky remembers, "he said don't worry about it. I'll tell him you're coming, he'll put you up," which he did, in a room with nine-month-old Greg. Though McClosky didn't get the Chicago job, the trip was worth it: he and Bellow "hit it off from the beginning"; Anita was "very generous, as always . . . very open and welcoming to Saul's friends," and McClosky found himself staying longer than he'd intended. When Bellow came to Minneapolis to visit the Freifelds, he spent an afternoon with the McCloskys. He was as impressive as he'd been in Chicago. In Mitzi's words, "Herb just fell in love with him, and after that it was total unconditional love and admiration."

Philip Siegelman, a colleague and friend, describes McClosky as "very tough, very aggressive. He was a street kid from the slums of Newark." Though an intellectual with "a tremendous appetite for reading," he was "not at all a conventional academic." Short, wiry, pugnacious, with "an aggressive and gleeful glint in his eye," McClosky prized intelligence and strength of mind, and "didn't take any shit in any way, had no tolerance for nonsense or equivocation." As Mitzi puts it: "intellectually, he liked to travel first class, and boy was that [Bellow's mind] first class." "He prided himself on knowing the top novelists and one of the top psychologists and he had this pantheon of heroes, and once you were in . . . he was extraordinarily loyal," remembers Siegelman's wife, Ellen, a graduate student at the time. From the start, McClosky was Bellow's advocate at the university. "Herb was a fierce friend and a great appreciator," Mitzi explains, "and he could protect Saul. He had that part of him, Saul felt safe with him." He was "one of Saul's life managers." "Saul formed very special friendships with men who were forceful," she continues, "who would kind of take control." Freifeld was one of the earliest of such men, helping with business affairs, car insurance, storage, what his daughter Susan calls "the most mundane tasks" ("My Dad was just so proud to be his boyhood friend. So proud of his accomplishments"). "Cancel the policy, please, as of the 25th," Bellow writes to Freifeld in November 1946, in a warm, newsy letter, "and send me the bill, or better yet bring it in. Kiss Rochelle for me, whom I prize above all women." After he passed the bar in the mid-1950s, Freifeld became for a period Bellow's unofficial lawyer.

When Mitzi first met Bellow, she was struck not only by his intelligence but by the way he presented himself. He wore a suit: "he was dressed very differently from the campus crowd." At their second meeting, when the McCloskys visited the house in Dutchess County, Bellow was alone, Anita having returned to Chicago with Greg to be with her dying brother. This time he appeared in "a green velvet corduroy shirt and a cap." She remembers him as "very proud that he kept the place neat." When the McCloskys learned that the Bellows could no longer afford the Dutchess County house and had to return to Chicago, Herb set out to bring Bellow to Minneapolis: "He steered the whole thing through," Mitzi remembers, "for Saul it was a miracle." The "thing" was an instructorship in the Humanities program at the University of Minnesota. The program was part of the university's Department of General Studies (later the Department of Interdisciplinary Studies), created only a year before Bellow's arrival. It was modeled on general education and contemporary civilization programs at Harvard, Columbia, and Chicago, and had practical as well as pedagogical aims, principally that of meeting an anticipated increase in enrollment after the war. The large interdisciplinary courses offered in the Humanities program were devised by two distinguished faculty members, Alburey Castell (philosophy) and Joseph Warren Beach (English), assisted by interested younger faculty, among them Herb McClosky.[6] The comparable Social Sciences program was headed by Arthur Naftalin, chair of Political Science, who years later would succeed Humphrey as mayor of Minneapolis. Among Naftalin's assistants were the historian and social theorist Benjamin Nelson, who became a friend of Bellow's (also a model for the scholar-theorist Egbert Shapiro in *Herzog*), and Andreas Papandreou, the economist, later the Greek prime minister. Bellow was in several ways a good fit for the Humanities program: he had been an undergraduate at Hutchins's University of Chicago, taught widely at Pestalozzi-Froebel ("Anthropology, English, anything"), and worked on the *Syntopicon*. But he had no higher degree or scholarly publications.

The appointment seems to have been arranged very late (too late for Bellow to be listed in the projected General Studies Budget for 1946), perhaps facilitated by the influx of returning veterans. Undergraduate enrollment at the University of Minnesota jumped from 12,000 in 1945 to 27,000 in 1946.[7] Some 18,000 of these new students were ex-GIs, beneficiaries of the Servicemen's Readjustment Act of 1944, the GI Bill. Returning servicemen were offered $500 for tuition, free textbooks, and a living allowance of $50 a month if single or $75 a month if married. The huge new student body meant more housing as well as more faculty, much of it arranged, like Bellow's appointment, at the last minute. Barracks-style housing was constructed in the football stadium, existing dorms were "double-decked," and a University Village was set up on the St. Paul campus (the University has campuses in each of the Twin Cities of Minneapolis–St. Paul), consisting of a row of trailers, Quonset huts, and metal barracks originally owned by the federal government. The Quonset hut section of the village was set aside for nonresident and foreign graduate students. By 1950 it accommodated 674 families. It is here that the Bellows ended up when they arrived at the university in September 1946. "The hut is of presswood and paper," Bellow wrote to David Bazelon on November 22, 1946. "If it were of stone it would resemble a cave and I a caveman. Since it is the aforementioned material it is more like a barrel and my affinity is to Diogenes." "We're in a kind of paper-walled hutch that looks like something wasps make," Bellow wrote to Robert Penn Warren. "I know that rabbits live in hutches, but this isn't a hive either. But hutch or hive it has no running water and no dividing wall or partition."[8] Real rabbits were the Bellows' neighbors, scurrying across the grassy areas between the huts. Each hut was equipped with a sleeper-sofa, a two- or three-burner hot plate, and a small bathroom, but no shower. Showers were taken in a central bathroom across Como Avenue, on the southern end of the St. Paul campus, where there were also facilities for laundry. Heating was provided by a small kerosene stove. Bellow was so cold in the hut he feared he would develop arthritis.

The Bellows lived in University Village through December. Abraham paid them a visit that autumn and was appalled to find members of his family living in such conditions. The McCloskys put him up, but because they did not keep kosher, he took nothing but black coffee in their house (Abraham "did not eat out," according to his granddaughter Lesha Bellows Greengus[9]). Yet he loved "talking for hours about Saul's foolish choice of working for such a small salary when he could have joined him in the coal business." A distant relation from the Old Country, Wolf Kissin, lived in Minneapolis, and Abraham looked him up; he and Kissin had been to cheder together in Druya, and Kissin was a rabbi (so he could eat with the Kissin family). Over coffee at the

McCloskys', Abraham kept up what Herb McClosky described as "a threnody of complaint." "He was heartbroken," McClosky told Atlas. "He really thought Saul was a failure."[10] How father and son got on during the visit is not recorded, nor is it known if Bellow asked his father for money. Asking for money humiliated Bellow and provoked fierce fights, the screaming arguments recalled by Greg. In *Herzog*, Moses describes the time Father Herzog threatened to shoot him when asked to underwrite a loan. With such requests, the father "lost his temper every time, and when he wanted to shoot me it was because he could no longer bear the sight of me, that look of mine, the look of conceit or proud trouble. The elite look. I don't blame him, thought Moses. . . . His heart ached angrily because of me. And Papa was not like some old men who become blunted toward their own death. No, his despair was keen and continual. And Herzog again was pierced with pain for his father" (p. 667).

Bellow was capable of such a look. Mitzi McClosky remembers him as frequently proud and defensive in this period, especially in company. His instructorship had to be approved by the English Department, which was responsible for half his $2,500 salary. Joseph Warren Beach, cofounder of the Humanities Program, was also chair of the English Department, and when McClosky set out to bring Bellow to Minnesota, the first thing he did was to loan Beach a copy of *Dangling Man*. "I have this friend who I think is incredible," Mitzi recalls Herb telling Beach, "and I'd like you to read his book." A couple of weeks later, Beach met McClosky in the bookstore and said: "Very interesting, your friend. He has a wonderful Jewish mind." McClosky realized immediately that Beach did not know he was Jewish ("it hadn't come up"). "He has a wonderful mind," he replied. Beach saw the look on McClosky's face and when he called him later, according to Mitzi, "Herb was fuming. Beach said, 'I know you were upset, but I don't know why you were so upset.' But he did know, Herb thought, it was on his mind." "To his credit," Mitzi continues, "I think Beach was appalled at what he said when he saw the look on Herb's face; he apologized profusely, but it was the way he saw [the book], what he thought."

Bellow was not the first Jew to be employed by the English Department at Minnesota. The Miltonist Arnold Stein was a member of the department from 1940 to 1942 and Leonard Unger was hired as an assistant professor in 1945, the year before Bellow's arrival. Unger was born into a Yiddish-speaking family in Corona, New York, and brought up in Nashville, Tennessee, where he was educated at Vanderbilt University, home to the Fugitive and Southern Agrarian writers. Among these writers were John Crowe Ransom, Allen Tate, Cleanth Brooks, Andrew Lytle, Donald Davidson, and Robert Penn Warren, all of them at one time teachers or students at Vanderbilt. Ransom, Brooks, and Warren were founding fathers of the New Criticism, by the late 1940s the dominant literary theory or methodology in American English departments. When Warren came to Minnesota in 1942 from Louisiana State University, he had already published two novels, two books of poetry, and two works of literary criticism, one a key text of the New Criticism, *Understanding Poetry* (1939), coauthored with Cleanth Brooks. That Unger had studied with Warren at LSU played a part in his hiring. Unger and Bellow soon became friends, chatting in Yiddish ("unashamedly" says Atlas[11]) in the corridors of the English Department. "Leonard and I have sized each other up as people from the same layer of the upper air (or lower depths; whichever you like)," Bellow wrote to Warren, with whom he also got on well.[12]

It was Warren, ten years Bellow's senior, who helped to smooth his way with the WASP grandees of the department, not just Beach but Samuel Holt Monk, Huntington Brown, E. E. Stoll, and Henry Nash Smith, distinguished scholars all. The extent to which these figures looked down on Jews and nonscholars, as Bellow suspected, is difficult to determine. Mitzi McClosky, who knew them as a graduate student in English, a faculty wife, and a friend of Bellow's (later of John Berryman and Isaac Rosenfeld, who were also to teach in the English Department), recalls a certain "scorn for new writers." The grandees were "good in their field," she acknowledges, but "fuddy-duddies." She also speaks of "a very strong prejudice in the universities and the English departments: we were supposed to be very upper class, British even." Siegelman concurs: Beach, Monk, Brown, et al. "were all Englishmen. They were like English dons." Though Leonard Unger got on well with his senior colleagues, he "conceded" that some of them "weren't above 'unwitting' anti-Semitism," as in Beach's remark about Bellow's "wonderful Jewish mind." Atlas describes Bellow as "intimidated by these 'well-bred WASPs,' with their charming, acidic condescension, their moneyed airs, and their 'Emersonian, gaunt New England' looks" (presumably Bellow is the source of these quotes).[13] "We went to parties," Mitzi McClosky remembers, and Bellow "was always bristling after he got the job, always bristling with imagined insults and possible insults."

Yet Beach was good to Bellow. At Warren's urging, he got him both a raise and a chance to teach literature courses as well as composition courses. After Bellow complained to Warren about having to mark freshman composition papers, Beach turned up to one of his classes unannounced: "I was terrified out of my wits, but I got through it somehow."[14] Shortly afterward, he advanced Bellow from the rank of instructor to assistant professor, raising his salary by a thousand dollars. Nor could Beach be called narrowly academic. He helped to found the interdisciplinary Humanities Program, wrote books on James, Hardy, Meredith, contemporary American fiction, Auden's revisions, and eighteenth-century English poetry. He also wrote poetry, publishing his second volume two years before Bellow arrived. Educated at Harvard, where he later taught, and patrician in appearance (Warren described him as "a grand old gent"), a hiker, swimmer, tennis player, and enthusiastic dancer at parties, Beach could be warm and open in his friendships.[15] Bellow was never an intimate, but he got on with Beach. With Alburey Castell, cofounder of the Humanities Program, in Mitzi's words, "Saul actually became close." He also had good relations with the eighteenth-century scholar Samuel Holt Monk, successor to Beach as chair of English, and author of an influential book on the sublime. "Sam Monk is wonderful," he reported to Warren in a letter of November 17, 1947, "as you probably know" (to Bazelon, in an undated letter from autumn 1948, he called Monk "a very decent, generous and intelligent guy"). Mitzi took a graduate course in nineteenth-century poetry with Monk and describes him as "richer and fuller in person than some of the others . . . and he was warm." Henry Nash Smith, a Texan with graduate degrees from Harvard's pioneering American Civilization program, founder of the myth and symbol school of the interpretation of American literature, helped to establish American Studies at Minnesota, another interdisciplinary program. In 1949, Leo Marx, also from the Harvard program, joined the English Department, mostly to work with Smith in American Studies. Marx was Jewish and Smith had taught him in 1945–46 at Harvard as a visiting professor.

Other factors aside from ethnicity and scholarly narrowness played a part in Bellow's wariness of English Department types. Senior faculty at Minnesota lived comfortably, often in what Warren's biographer, Joseph Blotner, calls "English cottage-style houses."[16] The Minneapolis suburbs are rich in parks and lakes, with excellent facilities for swimming, riding, picnicking. The professors socialized together: Warren and Brown were lakeside neighbors, often walking the paths along Lake Calhoun or Lake of the Isles; Beach's wife, Dagmar, and Warren's wife, Cinina, shared confidences and early afternoon drinks. The Bellows lived in a Quonset hut. "Mpls. is the middle bourgeois kingdom," Bellow wrote to Bazelon on November 12, 1946, "it is fat, it shines, it gleams by day and smells of low pleasures by night." "There were several worlds," Mitzi McClosky reports. "Ours was one where he was very comfortable. We had a lot of displaced Easterners and people that Saul could easily mix with. But then there was the English Department." Bellow left no record of English Department colleagues snubbing him or treating him discourteously, "but Saul always felt like he was on display, not paranoid, because he was justified in knowing those feelings were there." Parties were particularly difficult. "The Beaches had a lot of social life," Mitzi recalls, "and I remember one day we went to a picnic that the Beaches provided and all the time Saul was just so fearful of insult and feeling out of place. I just remember the look on Saul's face, the nostrils would quiver, the lips would quiver. He was like a sensitive race horse ready to bolt." These were the months when Bellow was at work on the last chapters of *The Victim*, delivered on January 7, 1947.[17] The gathering paranoia and prejudice in the novel may have been exacerbated by comparable feelings in Bellow, or they may have helped to produce those feelings.

BELLOW'S PREOCCUPATION WITH anti-Semitism in the mid-1940s was theoretical as well as personal or historical. It was also shared by the intellectual world that mattered most to him. In the spring of 1946, his friend Harold Kaplan, "Kappy" to all who knew him, edited a special issue of *Partisan Review* entitled "New French Writing." Kaplan had served in North Africa during the war, and after VE Day was seconded to the American embassy in Paris, where he was to stay for many years. He had written his doctoral dissertation at the University of Chicago on Proust, spoke fluent French, and had published stories and articles in *PR* in addition to its most recent "Letter from Paris." The "New French Writing" issue contained contributions from Camus, Sartre, Malraux, Valéry, and Genet, among others, and reviews of and about French writers (by William Barrett, Delmore Schwartz, and Clement Greenberg). Camus's contribution was "Two Chapters from 'The Myth of Sisyphus,'" Sartre's was "Portrait of an Anti-Semite," an English translation of the first half of *Réflexions sur la question juive* (1946), published in English in 1948 as *Anti-Semite and Jew*. Sartre's contribution provoked much debate in intellectual circles, as did further installments that appeared in *Commentary* the following year, with influential responses from Sidney Hook and Bellow's friend Harold Rosenberg.[18] Lionel Abel describes the Sartre essay as "more talked about than any other intellectual effort of the period."[19] "I shared immediately in the excitement," Irving Howe recalls of the debate it sparked, "it was tremendously stimulating."[20] What helped to make "Portrait of an Anti-Semite" so controversial, according to Howe, was the "pungent detail which is Sartre's specialty." In illustrating the prevalence of anti-Semitism in France, Sartre offers a scattering of remarks and acts attributed to unnamed acquaintances. These include the talentless young actor "who asserted that the Jews kept him from having a career in the theatre by always giving him servile jobs"; the classmate at the lycée who lost his scholarship to a Jew ("You're not going to try to make me believe that that fellow whose father came from Krakow or Lemberg understood one of Ronsard's poems or one of Virgil's ecologues better than I"); the fishmonger who denounced competitors as Jews, a fact they were hiding, thus exposing them to deportation to the camps; the woman who took a Polish Jew as a lover, but only let him caress her breasts and shoulders. "She got enormous pleasure," Sartre explains, "from the fact that he was respectful and submissive and also from the fact that she divined his violently frustrated and humiliated desire."[21]

In a letter of July 15, 1983, to the composer George Rochberg, Bellow picks up on a point implicit in Sartre's anecdote about the anti-Semitic woman. "Not long ago," Bellow writes, "I was reading a chapter from the memoirs of a goofy old pal of mine, Lionel Abel. He writes that he went to the movies with his mother in 1946, and in the newsreel they were shown the corpses of Jews rotted and falling apart as the bulldozers pushed them towards excavated pits. Abel's mother said, 'We Jews will never survive the disgrace of this.' To be victimized in this manner brought the Jews into disgrace. Others have no use for people who have been victimized to such a degree, and they have no use for themselves." Before the newsreels and firsthand accounts, what happened to the Jews in Europe, Bellow elsewhere recalls, "remained the Jewish Question instead of the horror it should have been."[22] As Hook put it, in his review of *Anti-Semite and Jew* in *Partisan Review* (May 1949), the truth of the Holocaust changed everything: "That they died was one blow;

how they died another; the way the rest of the world reacted to the news a third" (p. 465). Bellow was never one to turn the other cheek, but in 1946 he was especially vigilant, powered by a visceral sense of the disgrace, the humiliation, of the blows Hook enumerates. The vigilance had its dangers. In *The Victim* they are seen most vividly in a passage describing Leventhal's father:

> *Ruf mir Yoshke, ruf mir Moshke,*
> *Aber gib mir die groschke*
> "Call me Ikey, call me Moe, but give me the dough. What's it to me if you despise me? What do you think equality with you means to me? What do you have that I care about except the *groschen?*" That was his father's view. But not his. He rejected it and recoiled from it. Anyway, his father had lived poor and died poor, that stern, proud old fool with his savage looks, to whom nothing mattered save his advantage and to be freed by money from the power of his enemies. And who were the enemies? The world, everyone. They were imaginary (p. 232).

Bellow, like Leventhal, was determined to call out his enemies, but he also wanted to avoid paranoia, with its resulting alienation. Father Leventhal's "view" is clearly self-defeating. At the same time, Bellow writes this view with relish, as in the relish he brings to Father Zetland's "furious Jewish snobbery."[23]

IN DECEMBER, after Bellow's promotion and raise, the family was able to move to a modest shingle house at 2225 Hillside Avenue in St. Paul. They stayed here for less than a year, the owner having put the house on the market in May. Greg was now two, the age at which Bellow taught him to point first to his ass, then to his elbow, declaring him "Smarter than most Harvard graduates." Earlier, he'd taught him to eat herring. In his "Biographic Sketch" of his mother, Greg paints the first year in Minnesota as a harmonious time. "Saul and Anita were seen as a team—two stars much equal and admired—though Saul shone above all." Drawing on recollections from his mother and friends of his parents, he describes Bellow as "very considerate and respectful with Anita at home and in public. He took a role in household duties and came home to play with me while Anita made dinner." Mitzi McClosky recalls, "No matter what, around 4pm Saul would get up and say 'I've got to go home and play with my kid.'"[24] Mitzi describes the Anita of these years as steady and straightforward: "always herself . . . very solid. She wasn't afraid of anyone, I don't think, and she would just be herself." At social occasions Anita usually talked with the women, "and a lot of times she just didn't go [because of Greg]." But when present, "she held her own, she was a very truth-telling person. What she thought, she said, and she said it clearly and bravely." She was "a formidable woman." This is an impression shared by Max Kampelman, who boarded with the Bellows the following year: "She was a wonderful wife, in my judgment, she balanced him. She needled him, little digs to him, but a wonderful person." The digs were teasing not cruel: "Anita was tolerant of him, it seems to me"; "Saul was not an easy person."

In 1955 Bellow published a story in *The New Yorker* that reveals something of his ambivalence about marriage and fatherhood. By this date the marriage to Anita was over. Gregory was eleven. The story, "A Father-to-Be," concerns a man quite unlike Bellow, in circumstances quite different from Bellow's. Rogin, a thirty-one-year-old research chemist on his way to supper at his fiancée's apartment, is burdened with responsibilities: the fiancée has debts and bills that he's helping to pay, he's putting his younger brother through college, his mother's annuity doesn't cover her expenses. Joan, the fiancée, is beautiful, well educated, happy, and "aristocratic in attitude": "She didn't worry about money. She had a marvelous character, always cheerful."[25] At Christmas, Joan buys Rogin "a velvet smoking jacket with frog fasteners, a beautiful pipe and a pouch. . . . Before she was through she had spent five hundred dollars of Rogin's money" (p. 144). Neither Anita nor the woman Bellow left her for, the woman he was involved with when writing "A Father-to-Be," was like this woman. It is the larger feelings in the story that are revealing.

On the subway to Joan's apartment, Rogin takes note of a young man sitting next to him:

> This was a man whom he had never in his life seen before but with whom he now suddenly felt linked through all existence. He was middle-aged, sturdy, with clear skin and blue eyes. His hands were clean, well formed, but Rogin did not approve of them. The coat he wore was a fairly expensive blue check such as Rogin would never have chosen for himself. . . . There are all kinds of dandies, not all of

them are the flaunting kind; some are dandies of respectability, and Rogin's fellow passenger was one of these. His straight-nosed profile was handsome, yet he had betrayed his gift, for he was flat-looking. But in his flat way he seemed to warn people that he wanted no difficulties with them, he wanted nothing to do with them (p. 150).

The "gift" the young man betrays, his good looks, he chooses to mute or flatten, as he does his clothing, which is blandly conservative and expensive; he "seemed to draw about himself a circle of privilege, notifying all others to mind their own business" (p. 150). What most upsets Rogin about the young man's appearance, however, is its familiarity:

> His clear skin and blue eyes, his straight and purely Roman nose—
> even the way he sat—all strongly suggested one person to Rogin:
> Joan. He tried to escape the comparison but it couldn't be helped.
> This man not only looked like Joan's father, whom Rogin detested;
> he looked like Joan herself. Forty years hence, a son of hers, pro-
> vided she had one, might be like this. A son of hers? Of such a
> son, he himself, Rogin, would be the father. Lacking in dominant
> traits as compared with Joan, his heritage would not appear. Prob-
> ably the children would resemble her. Yes, think forty years ahead,
> and a man like this, who sat by him knee to knee in the hurtling car
> among their fellow creatures, unconscious participants in a sort of
> great carnival of transit—such a man would carry forward what had
> been Rogin (pp. 150–51).

This vision frightens and moves Rogin, "the pity of it almost made him burst into tears" (p. 151). He thinks of the effort required to negotiate a life and the tricks life plays on one: "The whole thing was so unjust. To suffer, to labor, to toil . . . only to become the father of a fourth-rate man of the world like this, so flat-looking with his ordinary, clean, rosy, uninteresting, self-satisfied, fundamentally bourgeois face. What a curse to have a dull son! A son like this, who could never understand his father. They had absolutely nothing, but nothing, in common, he and this neat, chubby, blue-eyed man" (p. 151). Rogin considers the wider implications of having such a son: "personal aims were nothing, illusion. The life force occupied each of us in turn in its progress towards its own fulfillment, trampling on our individual humanity, using us for its own ends like mere dinosaurs or bees" (p. 152). So exercised does Rogin become by these thoughts that he arrives at Joan's apartment determined to break off the engagement. For a woman, he thinks, being used like this by biology is "inevitable": "But did it have to be inevitable for him? Well, then, Rogin, you fool, don't be a damned instrument. Get out of the way!"; "I won't be used, he declared to himself. I have my own right to exist. Joan had better watch out" (p. 152).

Rogin arrives at the apartment dusted with snow, having walked from the subway. Joan greets him with a kiss and a smile, wearing an expensive housecoat that "suited her very well" (p. 153). After fetching a towel to dry the melting snow from his head, she insists on washing his matted hair. "Full of his troubled emotions," Rogin rehearses the things he plans to say to her: "Do you think I was born to be taken advantage of and sacrificed? Do you think I'm just a natural resource, like a coal mine, or oil well, or fishery, or the like? Remember, that I'm a man is no reason I should be loaded down." In the bathroom, Joan makes Rogin take off his shirt, then brings a stool in from the kitchen. She sits him down against the cool enamel of the basin as "the green, hot, radiant water reflecting the glass and the tile, and the sweet, cool, fragrant shampoo poured on his head." This is how the story ends:

> "You have the healthiest-looking scalp," she said. "It's all pink."
>
> He answered, "Well, it should be white. There must be something wrong with me."
>
> "But there's absolutely nothing wrong with you," she said, and pressed against him from behind, surrounding him, pouring the water gently over him until it seemed to him that the water came from within him, it was the warm fluid of his own secret loving spirit overflowing into the sink, green and foaming, and the words he had rehearsed he forgot, and his anger at his son-to-be disappeared altogether, and he sighed, and said to her from the water-filled hollow of the sink, "You always have such wonderful ideas, Joan. You know? You have a kind of instinct, a regular gift" (pp. 154–55).

Rogin's anxieties—his fears of an impersonal life force "trampling on our individual humanity"—are washed away by a loving, motherly woman: "She began to kiss him, saying, 'Oh, my baby. You're covered with snow. Why didn't you wear your hat? It's all over its little head'—her favorite third-person endearment" (pp. 152–53). Such women appear elsewhere in Bellow's fiction. In *Herzog*, Ramona Donsell soothes frantic Moses, easing off his shoes, cooking him shrimp Arnaud, putting black lace panties on under her dress. Ramona promises Moses "comprehensive happiness" (p. 603), will lead him from "wild internal disorder" (p. 619), "hatred and fanatical infighting," to married bliss, family bliss, for "she senses that I am for the family . . . I am a family type" (p. 616). Moses *is* a family type, loves his brothers and parents, loves his children, Marco and little Junie, when he thinks of them; like Rogin, he has a "secret loving spirit." He also values domestic order: "clean shirts, ironed handkerchiefs, heels on his shoes" (p. 620). Ramona provides these services and more, like sexy Joan, who presses her body against Rogin's back as she washes his hair. Renata Koffritz, in *Humboldt's Gift*, is even sexier, a wild child of the 1960s, but Renata, too, is keen on marriage and family. George Swiebel, the David Peltz character in *Humboldt*, approves of Renata: "She's a good cook. She's lively. She has plants and knick-knacks and the lights are on and the kitchen is steaming and goy music plays" (p. 190). Charlie Citrine concurs, though what he most loves is Renata's "cheerfulness" (p. 342). Yet for Charlie, for Moses, and, one suspects, for Rogin, the "comprehensive happiness" offered by such women is not enough. As Naomi Lutz, Charlie's first love, puts it: "Do you think they're really going to give you the kind of help and comfort you're looking for? . . . It's like an instinct with women. . . . You communicate to them what you have to have and right away they tell you they've got exactly what you need, although they never even heard of it until just now. They're not even necessarily lying. They just have an instinct that they can supply everything that a man can ask for, and they're ready to take on any size or shape or type of man. That's what they're like. . . . Then you award the contract. Of course nobody can deliver and everybody gets sore as hell" (p. 296). What Charlie wants, and Renata can't deliver, is what Moses and Rogin want: a sense, to quote from one of Moses's letters, "that life may complete itself in significant pattern. Some incomprehensible way. Before death. Not irrationally but incomprehensibly fulfilled" (p. 724).

Rogin's imagined dull son signals the indifference of the life force to "significant pattern" (or "personal aims," "individual humanity"). To the extent that women are in tune with the life force—embody it, are driven by it, identify with it—they share this indifference, finding their men mystifying. Bellow sees comedy as well as pathos in this situation, sometimes siding with the women, by depicting their men as childish, whiny, impossible; sometimes siding with the men, to whom the women are variously stolid, limited, endearingly vulnerable.[26] The situation the men put the women in is unfair. Bellow's male characters seek them out because they promise order, stability, certainty, the pleasures of wife, lover, homemaker, and mother combined. The closest of these women to Anita is Daisy in *Herzog*, "an utterly steady, reliable woman, responsible to the point of grimness." As we have seen, Moses blames himself for her increasing rigidity and stolidity: "By my irregularity and turbulence of spirit I brought out the very worst in Daisy. *I* caused the seams of her stockings to be so straight, and the buttons to be buttoned symmetrically. *I* was behind those rigid curtains and underneath the square carpets. Roast breast of veal every Sunday with bread stuffing like clay was due to *my* disorders, my huge involvement—huge but evidently formless—in the history of thought." Daisy does not scoff at this involvement—"She took Moses' word for it that he was seriously occupied"—but she does not understand it, respecting it as "a wife's duty" (p. 543) rather than a human duty. Anita was proud of Bellow's fiction, made material sacrifices for it, for the "significant pattern" it represented to him and to his readers. Nor was the order or meaning she sought in life merely domestic or personal. She sought it in her work as well, and she worked all her life (excepting Greg's first five years), as an administrator in hospitals, with health providers, welfare agencies. She sought it also in politics, to which she remained committed, as Bellow grew increasingly disenchanted.

What makes "A Father-to-Be" memorable is its willingness to enlist our sympathy for a father who subordinates paternal love to "higher values," despising the son he imagines. Dr. Adler in *Seize the Day* despises Tommy Wilhelm, his son, but is himself despicable. Elsewhere in Bellow's fiction, love or care of children, not always one's own children, is itself the higher value. In the final pages of *Henderson the Rain King* and *Humboldt's Gift*, recovery or growth is signaled by protection of a child (the orphaned Persian boy Henderson cares for on the flight back to the United States, the son Renata leaves with Charlie at the Ritz in Madrid). In *The Victim*, Leventhal's concern for his nephews is wholly admirable: "He traveled two hours in order to spend ten minutes in Mickey's [hospital] room" (p. 269); "he would go to any lengths" (p. 356) to save Philip, Micky's older brother. In *Herzog*, Moses's return to sanity is set in motion by episodes involving the welfare of Junie, his daughter, but his deficiencies as a parent are also emphasized, a product in part of concern for the survival of "his heritage" (Rogin's term, a preoccupation also of Joseph in *Dangling Man*, whose obnoxious niece, Etta, "must be aware of the resemblance she bears to me" [p. 42][27]). In Moses's outings with Marco, the child of his marriage to Daisy, both father and son are awkward and bored. Moses prepares for these outings by memorizing facts and stories to entertain the boy, otherwise "the time passed heavily" (p. 519). Marco tries his best to look interested: "The child would not reject his well-meant gift. There was love in that, thought Herzog. . . . These children and I love one another. But what can I give them? Marco would look at him with clear eyes, his pale child's face, the Herzog face, freckled, his hair crew-cut, by his own choice, and somewhat alien. He had his Grandmother Herzog's mouth." Moses measures Marco for Herzog traits, seeking out his heritage in his son. "Well, okay, kid, I've got to go back to Philadelphia now," he tells him, though "he felt, on the contrary, nothing necessary about this return to Philadelphia" (p. 520).

IN A LETTER of May 13, 1947, Bellow told Henle that he did not know if his contract at Minnesota would be renewed. By mid-June, all was well. Not only had the renewal come through, but Bellow was invited by Russell Cooper, associate dean of SLA (Science, Literature, and the Arts), to accompany a group of students traveling to Spain for the summer. It was just what Bellow needed, he wrote to David Bazelon, "a marvellous break." "Henle'll probably kill me for skipping out without reading proof of The Victim, but I can't pass up the opportunity to take a paid trip, just as I couldn't pass up the opportunity Britannica offered me of a paid education."[28] Bellow had been working flat out to finish *The Victim*, he wrote to Henle, living, as was quoted previously, "on benzedrine tablets"; to Mitzi McClosky he complained of feeling "old and worn down." He had been impossible to live with for months, Anita complained to the McCloskys, irritable, inaccessible. When Herb said something like "Don't worry, it's what you get with genius," Anita replied, "Genius, shmenius, his father's the same way."

The McCloskys heard complaints from both sides. Those from Bellow they heard on board ship, for they, too, were taking a student group to Europe, to England not Spain. There were, in fact, three groups of students traveling to Europe, one to Spain, one to England, one to France. Each group was accompanied by a faculty advisor nominated by the students. When the students chose Herb McClosky for the England trip, he suggested Bellow for the Spain trip, or seconded a student suggestion that Bellow be chosen, probably from Robert Johnson, who had taken one of Bellow's Humanities courses and was a great admirer. Johnson was among the oldest of the student leaders who devised the study abroad program, one of the first in the United States (today arranging exchanges to more than seventy-five countries). The name he and his fellow students chose for the program reflected their idealism: Student Project for Amity Among Nations (SPAN). Its aims, as described in publicity material, are to "satisfy [a] growing curiosity about the world outside the United States and simultaneously make a contribution to a better world."[29] The program was funded by local businesses and had an academic component, which had to be approved by the university. Students were required to devise a project, supervised by a faculty member, for which they received course credit. Bellow's duties were to meet with his students once a week in a café in Madrid to discuss their projects. There were ten of them, six men and four women. Some of the male students, like Johnson, were not much younger than Bellow; as he recalled to Barbara Probst Solomon in a letter of September 26, 1997, they "had no need of my guidance." The female students "did need my guidance, but never asked for it. There was only one pregnancy."

This was Bellow's first trip to Europe. It would have been Anita's first trip, too, but shortly before departure the faculty advisors were informed that the ship, the *Marine Jumper*, a converted cargo vessel, would not be safe for small children. Anita was forced to stay behind with Greg, an arrangement she may have welcomed, given Bellow's recent irritability, or so Mitzi suspected. Once the ship set sail, on June 21, Anita and Greg went off to Wisconsin for a two-week holiday, described in a letter of July 23, 1947, to Evelyn Shrifte of Vanguard as "at a Kosher resort with my in-laws—it wasn't as bad as I thought it would be." Mother and son returned to Chicago rather than Minneapolis after the holiday, living with the Goshkins. "I shall be staying here till Saul comes back," she wrote again to Shrifte. "I don't see much point in staying in Minneapolis alone for the rest of the summer." In Chicago, Anita spent her days looking after Greg, visiting friends from Hyde Park, and dealing with Bellow's correspondence. A publication date for the novel had to be set. The galleys of *The Victim* were missing the opening quotation from *The Arabian Nights*, she reported to Shrifte in the letter of July 23. "I know Saul would be very much upset if this was not in the book."

The crossing took nine nights and was rough, both uncomfortable and tedious. Passengers slept in narrow bunks, twelve to a room, women and men segregated. Bellow was seasick for the first few days, though fine by the time the ship docked at Le Havre.[30] From the dock the three groups traveled to Paris, where the Spanish group stayed for a week (the McCloskys and the English students went directly to London). Bellow was put up by the Kaplans and the students stayed at a hotel on the Left Bank. The train trip to Madrid took two days and began inauspiciously. "One of his students was left on the platform in Paris," Anita reported in the July 23 letter to Shrifte, "two others left their luggage in the station and so on. He is having his troubles. He sounds rather lonely and depressed." The journey itself was hard. For two nights Bellow got no sleep; the crowded compartment was filthy. In the "Spanish Letter" Bellow wrote for *Partisan Review* (February 15, 1948), he begins with the last link of this journey, on the express train from Irun, a Basque town on the Spain-France border, to Madrid. A Spanish gentleman suddenly engages Bellow in conversation, "not casually, by design, preventing me from looking at the ships in the silver, coal-streaked evening water" (p. 181). The man has "measuring, aggressive, melancholy eyes" and speaks to Bellow in minute detail about hydroelectric power, on the grounds that "we were American and therefore interested in mechanical subjects," the first of several ignorant assumptions about Americans Bellow records. The man comes from a military family, is a Franco supporter, has fought in Russia and Poland "against the Reds," and is now in the police. He makes the Irun–Madrid journey three times a week. "Tired of his conversation and of humoring him," Bellow "refused to respond, and at last he was silent" (p. 183). On the station platform in Madrid, he sees the man taking careful note of the name on the side of his group's hotel bus. When Bellow catches his eye, he looks away. "Presumably he had to know where I was staying in Madrid to complete his report" (p. 184). The opening sentence of the "Spanish Letter" reads: "The police come first to your notice in Spain, taking precedence over the people, the streets, and the landscape" (p. 181).

ON THE *Marine Jumper*, Bellow met a passenger named Francisco García Lorca, a handsome, dapper professor of Spanish Literature at

Columbia, the younger brother, editor, and translator of the poet Fede-
rico García Lorca, who had been shot and killed by anti-Republican
forces in 1936, shortly after the outbreak of the Spanish Civil War.
According to Atlas, the brother provided Bellow with an introduction to a circle of Madrid intellectuals and writers "that gathered in a
café near Bellow's pension in the Puerta del Sol; its members included
the Basque novelist Pío Baroja y Nessi, the literary journalist Ernesto
[J]iménez Caballero, and various members of the anti-Franco underground."[31] In an interview with Keith Botsford, Bellow described what
sounds like this circle as "a *tertulia* [a salon, usually held in a public
place rather than a home] in the café near my pension, which was in the
middle of Puerta del Sol. I had a letter to some people—Germans, who
had been journalists during the Civil War. They received me and introduced me to people like Jiménez [sic] Caballero, a fascist and a literary
man in the Cortes, with whom I had a few dinners."[32]

It is not clear from the Botsford interview whether "people like
Jiménez Caballero" (Pío Baroja, for example, himself a sort of fascist, or
fascist precursor) were part of the Puerta del Sol *tertulia* or belonged to
a separate circle, the one described by Atlas, which numbered "various
members of the anti-Franco underground." It seems strange that members of the anti-Franco underground should be meeting at Puerta del
Sol, a square in the heart of the city's historical district, for in 1947 the
most prominent building in Puerta del Sol housed the Dirección General de Seguridad, Franco's security police. "The broad face of Seguridad," Bellow writes in the "Spanish Letter," "dominates the Puerta del
Sol with barred and darkened windows" (p. 184). It was also strange
that fascists and members of the anti-Franco underground should be
members of the same circle. But Giménez Caballero was an unusual
supporter of Franco, being both anti-Nazi and philo-Semitic, and if
Pío Baroja was a fascist, he was a fascist much admired by John Dos
Passos and Hemingway. These complications, together with the simple
fact of being in Europe, with so much new to take in and assimilate,
checked or softened Bellow's quickness to take offense. He was storing
up impressions, holding his cards close to his chest, as in Taxco. That
Spain was impoverished, defeated, unthreatening, helped him to do so.
"The place was still shot up," he recalled to Botsford. "Madrid itself was
like a throwback to a much earlier time. The streetcars, for instance,
were strictly Toonerville trolleys."[33]

Bellow's dinners with Giménez Caballero must have taken place at Horcher, an elegant wood-paneled restaurant with views over the Retiro, the city's largest park. Horcher is a German restaurant, something of a Madrid institution. It was a favorite meeting place of German journalists and soon became a Bellow hangout. At Horcher he got to know "quite a few Fascists as well as the Papal Nuncio. And I had a lady friend who had been employed by the Nazi embassy. Very charming German lady and still quite young" (no doubt the "blonde, buxom girl" Atlas says Bellow had an affair with while in the city, "the secretary of the head of the Spanish secret police"). Horcher was also where Bellow met the son of the Prussian chancellor Bernhard von Bülow. "Since when does a kid from Chicago get to meet a papal nuncio?" Bellow recalled asking himself. Or have dinner at the "Nunciatura." At this dinner, one of the nuncio's assistants, an Italian, told him, "these Spaniards were not Europeans—*son moros*, they are Moors. They don't really belong to the European community." The German lady was similarly dismissive, claiming the Spanish "had no real feelings. . . . They really are heartless." For Pío Baroja, in contrast, it was Germans who were heartless, though, as he told Bellow, "at first I could not believe that they were burning their captives in ovens" ("Spanish Letter," p. 194). "Madrid in 1947 was a great eye-opener for me," Bellow told Botsford. "I met a great many Spaniards; it was my first prolonged contact with Europeans and the European intellectual."[34]

The interest these intellectuals took in Bellow, he claimed, was mostly a product of his being an American. "People were curious. They hadn't seen many Americans. Spain had been completely sealed off for years . . . even a trifling instructor from Minnesota was eagerly taken up by them."[35] Spanish attitudes to America were at once superior and envious. "All these discussions of national character were occasions of resentment," Bellow writes in the "Spanish Letter," "and the resentment was particularly strong when it was the American character that was discussed." Hence comments like: "America is still looking for a soul; our soul is very old"; or talk of "American emptiness," "unhistorical Americans who live only in the future" (p. 194). Yet everyone craved "American good things—Buicks, nylons, Parker 51 pens, and cigarettes" (p. 185). In the penultimate paragraph of the "Spanish Letter," Bellow describes an encounter with the proprietor of a station restaurant in Bobadilla, a railway junction between Málaga and Granada. The restaurant was busy yet the proprietor "behaved toward me with iron *dignidad*." Why? Because he "recognized me as an American, one of the new lords of the earth, a new Roman, full of the pride of machines and dollars, passing casually through the junction where it was his fate to remain rotting to death." In the final paragraph of the "Spanish Letter," the proprietor's dignity is paired with that of a resident of Bellow's pension, a "comandante" who had served with Franco in Morocco. "The comandante," Bellow writes, "is, after all, the tyrant's friend, and the tyrant, too, believes in organization and is trying to trade his way into the new imperium" (p. 195).

Despite observations like these, Bellow relished his summer in Spain. "I felt I was returning to some kind of ancestral homeland. I felt that I was among people very much like myself, and I even had notions that in an earlier incarnation I might have been in the Mediterranean. I was absolutely charmed by it, by everything."[36] Domestic familiarities were especially striking: "people had Tolstoyan-style households, with a feudal servant class. Even their gestures, the way they smoked, reminded me of my father. And the heavy white table linen was like the table linen my parents had." Spain energized Bellow, even the heat energized him. A summer storm in Madrid—*"una tormenta"* to madrileños—"begins with a plunge, falling with the heaviness of drops of mercury. In ten minutes it is over; ten minutes more, and it has dried" ("Spanish Letter," p. 187) (the only green grass Bellow saw in Madrid, he writes, was in front of the Prado). In the outlying slum districts along the Manzanares River, he was struck by the *gente humilde* (the humble) "choking the streets and bridges and lying on blankets on the dusty banks under the scanty acacias. It is like a vision of the first moments of resurrection, seeing those families lying in the smothering dust and milling in the roads." He watches a father lead his infant daughter, a toddler, down to the dirty green water: "She has soiled herself, and he washes her with a certain embittered tenderness while she clings screaming to his lanky, hairy legs" (p. 188). The residents of Bellow's pension are observed with equal closeness, beginning with Juanita, the landlady. Juanita is on terms of "obvious intimacy" with the one important resident of the pension, an admiral stationed in the ministry, which Bellow knows because he has seen her enter the admiral's room without knocking. What he notices about the pension's other residents, respectable middle-class types, is how difficult it is for them to maintain bourgeois standards. Without *enchufes* (contacts, influence, from *enchufe*, Spanish for electric socket) the inevitable drop in class is "measureless" (p. 187).

In August, Bellow "took my Minnesota show on the road," visiting Segovia, Granada, Córdoba, Málaga, and Ronda. Anita was alarmed when she received a letter from Bellow saying he was going to Granada and Cádiz. "On Monday night there was a terrible explosion in which hundreds of people were killed and thousands injured," she wrote to Shrifte on August 21. "Now maybe he never even got to Cádiz but maybe he did. I go on thinking he is all right as we are fortunate people and I am hoping our luck will hold out this time." Before the trip south, Bellow traveled with an acquaintance from the American embassy to Alcalá de Henares, birthplace of Cervantes. There he attended a political trial of tramway workers accused of distributing *Mundo Obrero*, a Communist newspaper. The trial, held in a courtroom lined with soldiers and presided over by army officers, was a travesty. "The doctrines of 1789 are for us like the morals of Christianity," a Spanish acquaintance told Bellow, "pieties. We are not strong enough to enjoy the Rights of Man" ("Spanish Letter," p. 193). Resistance to Franco was now confined to "isolated mountain districts in the north and in Andalusia" ("Spanish Letter," p. 190). On the trip south, Bellow spent much time with his student Robert Johnson, who had become a friend as well as a follower. A native Minnesotan (like 90 percent of the university student body in 1946), Johnson was funny, easygoing, and smart. "It's a hard lot, in America, to be born in the blonde and decent Midwest," Bellow wrote to him on February 13, 1950, "but you've stood up to it beautifully and I love you for it." Bellow inscribed Johnson's copy of *The Victim*: "To the Sancho Panza of our Spanish travels." "Saul tilted at windmills and I came along," Johnson explained, describing himself as "a goy with a *Yiddisher kopf* [a Jewish head]."[37] During the last weeks of Bellow's stay in Madrid, he and Johnson sublet an apartment in Plaza de la Independencia, on the northwest corner of the Retiro, and when the summer was over, Johnson joined Bellow and the McCloskys on a ten-day holiday in Paris.

In Bellow's story "The Gonzaga Manuscripts" (1954), set in Madrid, Alcalá de Henares, and Segovia, the central character, an ardent young Midwesterner, is much like Johnson. Clarence Feiler, a graduate of the University of Minnesota, is described as having a small blond beard, blue eyes, and "a rosy beard-lengthened face," like Johnson's face, according to Mitzi McClosky. Feiler studied Spanish at the university, as did Johnson, and develops a passion for the verse of Manuel Gonzaga, "one of the most original of modern Spanish poets, and in the class of Juan Ramón Jiménez, Lorca, and Machado."[38] In California, where Feiler now lives, and where Johnson moved after college, he hears from a Spanish Republican refugee about lost Gonzaga manuscripts containing more than a hundred poems. The manuscripts are reputed to be somewhere in Madrid, which Feiler first visited as a student at Minnesota, and he sets out to find them, powered by a desire "to do a decent and necessary thing, namely, bring the testimony of a great man before the world" (p. 114). Feiler is self-consciously anti-religious, another Johnson trait, and the intensity of his commitment to Gonzaga is "Romantic" in Wyndham Lewis's sense, a species of "spilt religion" (to Atlas, Johnson described himself as a "'pagan' who claimed the only commandment he'd never broken was the one that forbade worshiping a graven image"[39]). Feiler travels to Madrid and takes a room in a pension with views overlooking the Retiro. Pension La Granja is within easy walking distance of the Puerta del Sol, "with its crowd of pleasure-seekers, beggars, curb-haunters, wealthy women, soldiers, cops, lottery-ticket and fountain-pen peddlers, and priests, humble door-openers, chair-menders, and musicians" (p. 124). Here Feiler finds the same attitudes to America that Bellow and Johnson encountered. "I hope you won't mind if I tell a story about Americans and the size of things in Spain," begins Gonzaga's literary executor, a suave member of the Cortés, "with his irony and his fine Spanish manners" (p. 125). "Have you come to study something?" asks Feiler's landlady, "there's a great deal here to interest people from a country as new as yours" (p. 115). At dinner with the executor, Feiler sits next to "an Italian Monsignore" (from the Nunciatura, presumably) and "a German gentleman." When asked "Was American really a sort of English," Feiler replies, "I've seen people cry in it and so forth, just as elsewhere." The executor makes it clear that he thinks Feiler incapable of comprehending Gonzaga's poems, and in response Feiler feels an "ugly hatred" grow and knot in his breast: "He wanted to hit him, to strangle him, to trample him, to pick him up and hurl him at the wall" (pp. 127–28). When asked, yet again, why Gonzaga interests him so much, he replies: "Why shouldn't I be interested in him? You may someday be interested in an American poet" (p. 134).

IN THEIR TEN DAYS in Paris, Bellow, the McCloskys, and Johnson spent a good deal of time walking along the Seine, going in and out of bookstores. They visited the Jeu de Paume, ate hamburgers and drank milkshakes at the American Legion Center (a special treat for the McCloskys after three months of English food), and studied passersby. They also spent time with the Kaplans. Mitzi and Kappy had gone to Weequahic High School together in Newark, though he was a grade ahead of her. She remembers him as president of the school's "French Academy" and a force in student politics. By his own admission, Kappy was a fervent assimilationist. "From the beginning, I was absolutely determined to be a good American, WASP in style." In Paris, he became more French than the French, like Kenneth Trachtenberg's father, Rudi, in *More Die of Heartbreak*, a figure of "amiable superiority" (p. 3). Though Mitzi remembers Bellow as "clearly impressed" with Paris, Kappy found him wary and suspicious. "Bellow thought I was a patsy for a lot of things," Kappy explains. "You had to be fiercely yourself and independent. He became madder and madder at me because I became more and more French. He thought I let them walk all over me." What Kappy remembers from Bellow's visit in 1947 is that he was "very pissed off with the Spanish," in particular with Spanish intellectuals. "Who do they think they are? They haven't done anything worthwhile in the arts since the sixteenth century." Bellow and Kappy had known each other for almost ten years, first through their wives, then as Wieboldt Hall habitués. They were friends but Bellow was not easy with Kappy, partly because of Kappy's Francophilia, partly because he was a rival of sorts. Kappy was tall, handsome, charming, as attractive to women as Bellow (like Rudi Trachtenberg, he was "biologically very successful" [p. 10]). He was also a talented writer, perhaps the most talented of Bellow's early writer friends, Rosenfeld included. At the beginning of the 1950s, he published two novels with Harper and Brothers, *The Plenipotentiaries* (1950) and *The Spirit and the Bride* (1951), about sophisticated expatriates in Paris. "A remarkably gay and witty book and often very wise" is how Lionel Trilling described *The Plenipotentiaries*.[40]

In addition to being a rival, Kappy was a disappointment, since writing, as both he and Bellow came to recognize, was not a vocation for him. If Kappy made Bellow uncomfortable, his wife, Celia, put him at his ease, in part because she was an excellent Yiddishist, always a plus in Bellow's book. When Kappy decided in 1954 to make a career in the foreign service, he told a French interviewer, "my wife was strongly against it. She thought I should follow a literary trade, become a novelist like our friend Saul Bellow."[41] Bellow's complex attitude to Kappy is revealed in a letter of April 21, 1948, to Mel Tumin. Tumin had complained about Kappy, and Bellow reports that both Herb McClosky and Isaac Rosenfeld had expressed "a like complaint." The trouble, Bellow explains, is that "Kappy has made himself after his own image, has chosen to be the Parisian Kaplan and has put behind him the part of his history that doesn't fit the image." The desire "to free himself from the definition other men give him" Bellow associates with "the Nietzschean 'Grand Style,'" and is not of itself to be condemned.

> Why should he be the Kaplan his mother bore and Newark stamped when he has the power to be the Kaplan of his choice? You have felt that, I have, Passin has. Only some of us have had the sense to realize that the man we bring forth has no richness compared with the man who really exists, thickened, fed and fattened by *all* the facts about him, all of his history. Besides, the image can never be *reyn* [pure, in Yiddish] and it is especially impure when money and power are part of its outfit.

This last point alludes to the privileged diplomatic circles Kappy had begun moving in, tempting him from a richer, truer self: "Kappy is an official. In justice to him, however, it must be said that it would be hard to resist exploiting such great gifts, it would be hard for anyone." Presumably the gifts here are money and power. The next sentence, however, suggests that they may be Kappy's gifts as a writer, which he is betraying: "It's the best, the strongest, the most talented whose lives miscarry in this way. I deeply hope, for Kappy that he recovers before the damage to his power to feel goes any further."

BELLOW'S SPIRITS WERE LOW on the ship home. "He was really quite sober and thoughtful," Mitzi McClosky recalls, weighed down by worries about his marriage and *The Victim*. He had put off looking at galleys and now had to face them. The job bored and dismayed him: "I want to throw them in the ocean," he told the McCloskys. The worries he expressed about his marriage were of several sorts. He felt constrained, crowded in the marriage; Anita "kept him on a short leash"; he had married too young, had not had the adventures he needed. "I'm too old," he complained to Mitzi. "I'm a young man but I'm old." "He felt he was aging in the bourgeois family life that he had enjoyed. . . . Saul had a real thing about aging." His ambivalence—wanting stability, solidity, not wanting it—Anita would not understand: "She had a strong set of values and they were very formed and not too negotiable," recalls Mitzi. "I don't think she had the tolerance for ambiguity that Saul did." He could not communicate to her what he was after or how the order she provided and he enjoyed also impeded his search for freedom. Freedom from what? Fidelity? Domestic responsibility? He owed Anita a lot, he acknowledged. It was she who had made it possible for him to write *Dangling Man*: "Anita worked, he stayed home and wrote. She arranged the marriage, everything, she took care of him. She was a force, formidable, and he thought she was beautiful. . . . But that didn't mean he didn't see other women. He always did." Partly Mitzi sees Bellow's behavior as typical of the times. "Have you seen *Mad Men*? Then I need not say more. . . . Men did not feel they were manly unless every attractive woman wanted to sleep with them." In Bellow's case, frequently, "women came after Saul. He hardly ever went after a woman. It was a question of accepting." (This is not an impression others have corroborated, as Mitzi realizes: "I'm not saying some women won't say otherwise.") At the same time, "Saul gave me some of the first lectures I heard on the beauty of monogamy. . . . He was a proponent of monogamy."

Those lectures occurred in the first months of the friendship between the Bellows and the McCloskys. Bellow talked of how he and Anita had worked through their early difficulties, how they'd come to an agreement. "The way they worked it through," he told Mitzi, "was that Anita wouldn't stand for it, and if he did [go off with someone else], *she* would. She was going to be his equal and she held him to that. Whatever he did, she would never have given him permission to be free." Bellow accepted those terms, Mitzi thought, while also being incapable of living up to them. He was torn: "It [promiscuity, adultery] was not a happy thing entirely for Saul," as it was for other men of his acquaintance. "He was uncomfortable." What was clear to Mitzi on the voyage home was that Bellow's sense of "being locked in, of his own volition," was coming to the fore.

In this state, Bellow embarked on a shipboard affair. When he, Johnson, and the McCloskys boarded the *Marine Tiger* at Le Havre, they noticed a group of students, not Minnesota students, talking animatedly on deck. Among them, Mitzi remembers, was "a very lovely, petite brunette, in jeans, with a red kerchief jauntily arranged around her head. She was very attractive, because of the animation in her face, very cute looking." She was nineteen, a student at the University of Wisconsin, and Mitzi never saw her again on the journey home, nor did Bellow once mention her on board ship. That spring, however, he approached the McCloskys with a request: would they put the woman up for a night, as she was coming to Minneapolis. "He didn't say much about it, he was extremely private about it, but what he did say was: 'I have to let her know that Anita and I are *not* going to separate.'" The girl's name was Betty and Mitzi guesses that Bellow had led her to believe, as he had himself begun to believe, that his marriage was over. "Whatever relationship they had," Mitzi thinks, "it was not an ordinary one, because Saul did speak freely to us about other women. He might have thought that she was eligible for more than an affair." When Betty arrived, she was "very reserved and contained." Bellow came to pick her up for the afternoon and later that day, shortly after returning, she left for Wisconsin ("broken-hearted," Mitzi assumes). The McCloskys never saw her again, although they heard that she went on to become an academic, a professor of English, Mitzi thinks. In later years, Bellow went to some lengths to protect her identity.

The reunion with Anita took place on September 23, the day Bellow's ship docked in New York. The omens were not good. Nothing survives of their correspondence over the summer (except snippets of news in Anita's letters to Vanguard), but it can't have been reassuring, given the state Bellow had worked himself into on the voyage home. In the event, the meeting was not at all what he expected. Anita was not resentful. She had enjoyed the summer. She, too, had needed a break. Her time in Chicago, she told Mitzi, had been fun, full of visits to friends, with lots of swimming for Greg. She had slimmed down, had a tan, looked "absolutely gorgeous," "ten years younger." Bellow's doubts and fears washed away, like Rogin's in "A Father-to-Be." "When he got back, we had a honeymoon," Anita confided to Mitzi. She and Bellow spent a week in New York seeing friends, consulting with publishers, and eating. Bellow had lost "about twenty pounds" while abroad, as well as developing what he thought was an ulcer. In an attempt to gain back some of the weight he went on an eating binge in New York. "No doubt there was an ideological reason for eating so much," he suggested, in a letter of October 5 to Robert Penn Warren. "We may not be strong in Phoenician ruins but we *do* have steamed clams." Having overdone the clams, he was now "living on milk and eggs, principally." The family returned to Minneapolis three days after the start of the quarter, moving into a large old house at 58 Orlin Avenue in Prospect Park, a suburb full of professors, but with, in Philip Siegelman's words, "an overlay of intellectuals who were learning how not to be Huntington Brown and how not to be Samuel Monk."[42] In 1950, the McCloskys would move to Prospect Park as well, to 70 Orlin Avenue, a few doors away from the Bellows' old house.

The Bellows could only just afford the Orlin Avenue house. To meet expenses they took in lodgers. There were two extra bedrooms, one was rented by Ed McGehee, a Southerner and a poet, a friend of Robert Penn Warren's, the other by Max Kampelman, an instructor and graduate student in political science. After a time, McGehee asked the Bellows if they would like a third lodger. His name was Bart Leiper,[43] and McGehee said that he and Leiper could share a room. The arrangement meant more money for the Bellows and they agreed to it. "Saul thought two roommates unremarkable at the time," Greg writes, "but later realized they were gay."[44] "They [the Bellows] didn't treat them as a couple," Mitzi remembers, "nor did they come out as a couple." For a while, McGehee and Bellow were close, making plans for an anthology to be entitled "*Spanish Travelers* or something like that . . . from Casanova to Roger Fry. Random House has already expressed interest in this."[45] The other lodger, Max Kampelman, was a conscientious objector under Section 4(e) of the Selective Service Act, permitting alternative "work of national importance under civilian direction." Kampelman came to Minneapolis in 1944 after volunteering for the Minnesota Starvation Experiment, a clinical study directed by a noted public health professor, Ancel Keys, under the auspices of the University of Minnesota Medical School, the Selective Service System, and the Civilian Public Service. The aim of the study was to determine the effects, physiological and psychological, of severe starvation, and to test and devise rehabilitation regimens and strategies. Kampelman, with whom Bellow became close at this time, was the only Jew among the thirty-six volunteers and at the end of the experiment resembled a concentration camp victim. "I went from 160 pounds to slightly more than 100 pounds." Yet he suffered the least psychological damage of any of the volunteers, a fact he attributes to the courses he was allowed to take at the time. When the war broke out, Kampelman was two courses short of receiving his NYU law degree. By completing the courses at Minnesota he not only earned his degree, but managed to think about other things aside from food. He then took courses in political science, got to know Herbert McClosky, was invited to stay on at Minnesota as an instructor in political science and to pursue graduate studies, and through McClosky learned that the Bellows had a room to rent. "I don't even remember how much rent I paid. We developed a warm friendship. It was not landlord/tenant."

Kampelman remembers lots of talks with Bellow about politics. They were both anti-Soviet, though Bellow was slightly to the left of Kampelman. Kampelman's opposition to the war, despite being based on pacifist rather than Trotskyist grounds, "helped our relationship as far as Saul and Anita were concerned." He, too, like McClosky, became an advisor to Hubert Humphrey, in the campaign "to recapture the Party [in Minnesota] from the Communists." When Humphrey became a senator in 1949, Kampelman moved to Washington as one of his legislative assistants. In later years, he practiced law at the influential Washington firm of Fried, Frank, Harris, Shriver & Jacobson, and headed diplomatic missions for both Jimmy Carter and Ronald Reagan, negotiating with the Soviet Union over nuclear and space arms. Kampelman recalls being teased by Bellow in their talks on Orlin Avenue: "There was a little dig once in a while, towards me, towards Herbie. You know, he wasn't going to do what we were doing. We were cooperating with the establishment. . . . It was always with a smile . . . a kind of intellectual digging, probing." Kampelman differed from Bellow, and McClosky, in being actively engaged with the Jewish community and Jewish organizations. Bellow and McClosky never hid their identity as Jews: McClosky was fully involved in the Humphrey administration's efforts to combat anti-Semitism (in 1946 Kampelman was shocked to discover that Jews in Minnesota could not join the Automobile Club) and when *The Victim* came out on November 6, 1947, it was praised by *Time* as "the year's most intelligent study of the Jew in U.S. society."[46] For Kampelman, however, they were "not active, not identified. . . . I mean on campus there was a Jewish organization. I identified myself with them, not Herbie," nor Bellow, for whom such identification was restricting, such organizations bourgeois, too respectable.

The Bellows did a lot of entertaining at 58 Orlin Avenue. Through the McCloskys they made friends with political science faculty, graduate students, Humphrey aides and acolytes. Mitzi remembers Bellow playing music at gatherings at the house; on Wednesday nights he regularly played duets with a political science graduate student named John

Sandstrom (Bellow on the recorder, Sandstrom on the violin).[47] Though money was tight, Anita "would always have some cake and some coffee for people," with friends often staying for dinner. The lodgers were treated as part of the family. Bellow's friends had to be careful not to be too admiring. On the one hand, Mitzi remembers, "he hated people who fawned on him"; on the other hand, he "had to feel . . . that they somehow saw that he was special." "I always felt the fragility of his ego," says Mitzi. The people who interested Bellow were surprising to her. Though he didn't suffer fools, he did suffer oddballs. "He really loved strange people," Mitzi recalls, people with "something unusual" about them, people who were larger than life. The McCloskys entertained frequently, often on Saturday nights (Kampelman remembers baby-sitting for Greg on such evenings). Before the move to Prospect Park, they lived in a second-floor apartment in a large Victorian house at 701 University Avenue South, near the campus. Often, late in the evening, after official dinners and receptions, Mayor Humphrey would show up, alone or with an entourage. Though no oddball, he was hardly ordinary. Siegelman, an admirer, describes him as "a machine of volubility and good will. Remembering everybody's name . . . incredible animal vitality" (like Teddy Kollek, another politician to whom Bellow was drawn). "I liked Hubert Humphrey a lot," Bellow recalled to Norman Manea. "I knew him when he was Mayor of Minneapolis, when I was a young instructor at the University of Minnesota. He was very intelligent, amiable, good-natured, warm-hearted, a real prairie Democrat, friend of the people and so on. He wasn't faking it. He was really like that, and he was a charming person, always, to be with, and he didn't have any airs, not even when he was vice president."[48] In 1964 Bellow seriously contemplated writing a book about Humphrey, "taking for my model Liebling's job on Earl Long." The problem was that "I like the man too well to do him any injury but I don't want to paint the conventional oil picture either." When Johnson picked Humphrey as vice president, Bellow's enthusiasm for the project cooled. As he recalled in a letter of November 23, 1983, to Carl Soberg, "I came to see him when he was Vice President and he was willing to have me follow him about. Seeing that LBJ kept him on so short a tether, and anticipating no pleasure from junkets to Michigan to crown Cherry Queens I dropped the whole matter. There was no point in writing about poor Hubert's misery as Vice President. He was LBJ's captive."

In his second year at Minnesota, Bellow was asked to take over

Robert Penn Warren's creative writing seminar. Warren had won a Guggenheim and was in New York consulting on a stage adaptation of *All the King's Men* (1946), winner of the Pulitzer Prize for Fiction. Bellow was also scheduled to teach Humanities I (Voltaire, Paine, Goethe, Rousseau, Burke, Tolstoy et al.), as in the previous year, but was run-down from the push to finish *The Victim* and the summer's exertions and anxieties. After he failed to shake persistent illness, on doctor's orders his autumn teaching was restricted to a single course, Warren's seminar. In Winter and Spring quarters he would return to a full load of three quarters, teaching Humanities and composition courses as well as the seminar. In the letter to Warren of October 5 he reports on the students in the seminar. One student in particular has caught his eye. "I agree with you that he may turn out tremendously good or a tremendous bust," Bellow writes to Warren. "Just now I believe he feels his desire to become a writer may be a dishonorable desire, treason to his savagery and his anger. I think he still has very much a bum's view of the settled, established, comfortable and fat, and looks at us all with grim, undergroundling eyes, hectic, hungry, resentful and somewhat pathetic. Vulcanically proud, too. I think he may be a very fine writer if he doesn't resist the idea of organization as part of the comfortable and fat." This student draws Bellow not only because he's talented, but because he's torn in ways Bellow was torn: between "organization," both away from the desk (the ordered family life Anita offered) and at it (the "Flaubertian standard"), and an "undergroundling" view, in which "savagery and anger" are seen as "gift," "heritage," part of his "individual humanity." "His feet went into that shrimp little dance of his," Bellow reports to Warren of the student, "he began to look pinched. . . . 'I'm not interested in being a great novelist. *You* be the great novelist.' *Und so weiter.* I finally got him to stop this by a kind of cold cautery." In a letter to Warren of November 17, Bellow reports of another student that "the seminar has produced one complete schizophrenic already. Perfectly clinical. He writes well, too." Unfortunately what this second student writes is surrealist and "the sun of surrealism is set." As for the efforts of the other students, "the rest you know: novel of political corruption, dream utopias, etc." Bellow here is clued in, canny, "organized," while also drawn to extremity, anger, oddity. Siegelman remembers him as "a reluctant teacher," Herb McClosky as "a clock-watcher," reluctant to lose writing time, especially when deadlines loomed. Atlas quotes the recollection of a former student, Douglas

LaRue Smith, on Bellow's approach: "Just look on me as your friendly barber. I'll lather you, but you have to shave yourself," which seems a good way of describing a writing teacher's role (Atlas quotes it to show that Bellow "wasn't one to nurture talent"[49]). Not all would-be writers can write, no matter how much nurturing they receive.

The letter of October 5 to Warren came with a request. Bellow was again applying for a Guggenheim Fellowship. It was his third attempt. The other referees were Edmund Wilson, Alfred Kazin, and Eliseo Vivas, all of whom had written for him in the past.[50] In the application, Bellow gives a fuller account of his plans than in previous years. He outlines several works, a novel and two "novelles" (later "novelettes"), none of which was written, though formal and thematic features of the works he outlines figure in later writing. The novel was tentatively titled "A Young Eccentric." Its protagonist "has two outstanding characteristics. First, it is temperamentally necessary for him to create excitement and complications about himself. Secondly, he cannot bear to succeed but must always, after incredible stratagems, *almost* succeed." This syndrome he explains at the end of the description: "My conception of the protagonist of this comedy is that he resists definition; he cannot endure to be committed, to see an end to his possibilities, and in this he is thoroughly modern and thoroughly American," like Augie March. Then there's the nature of the young eccentric's adventures: hectic, oddball, picaresque, like Augie's or Henderson's: "He gives what amounts to a lecture at a gathering on 'Themes in History' and at the same time tries to promote a scheme for buying coffee *fincas* in Guatemala." (Tumin had conducted his research in Guatemala.) The eccentric's erotic entanglements are also hectic: he "makes advances to other men's wives, proposes marriage to several girls at the same time . . . after courting [a] young woman for several months, he asks her younger sister to marry him." In addition to the novel, Bellow briefly describes the "novelles." The first, based on the life of Croesus, "as we know it from the anecdotes of Herodotus and Xenophon," considers the idea of greatness. Bellow quotes de Tocqueville, a lifelong influence, who describes this idea as unacceptable in democratic societies. In keeping with the novelle's theme, Bellow thinks big: "We have experienced in the last two centuries a considerable devaluation of man; the scope of the mind has, through science, been immensely extended while that of the personality has shrunk. That is what I would like to take up in *Croesus*." As he says earlier in the proposal: "I am interested in considering a condition of mind in which the idea of greatness is acceptable."

"Croesus" never materialized, but over the next few years William Einhorn, from *Augie March*, did. Einhorn was Bellow's tribute to Sam Freifeld's father, Ben, a figure "too rich to be held by oblivion." For Augie, Einhorn, a Humboldt Park property magnate, is "the first superior man" he'd ever met, a modern-day Caesar, Machiavelli, and Ulysses. "I'm not kidding when I enter Einhorn in this eminent list," Augie declares.

> It was him that I knew, and what I understand of them in him. Unless you want to say that we're at the dwarf end of all times and mere children whose only share in grandeur is like a boy's share in fairy-tale kings, beings of a different kind from times better and stronger than ours. But if we're comparing men and men, not men and children or men and demigods, which is just what would please Caesar among us teeming democrats, and if we don't have any special wish to abdicate into some different, lower form of existence out of shame for our defects before the golden faces of these and other old-time men, then I have the right to praise Einhorn and not care about smiles of derogation from those who think the race no longer has in any important degree the traits we honor in these fabulous names (p. 449).

Nothing in the plans Bellow outlines in his Guggenheim application, nothing in anything he'd written before *Augie*, sounds like this; the voice of the novel is a later creation. But democratic or American greatness is a theme throughout his writing and his life ("*You* be the great novelist"), as are the forces that would deny or derogate greatness. These include not just "science" but "specialization," as in the mockery and the pressure Augie faces for refusing to be tied down, displaced versions of the mockery and the pressure Bellow faced from his father and brothers for refusing to settle into a profession or business, persisting as a writer. "Specialization was leaving the likes of me behind," Augie explains. "I didn't know spot-welding, I didn't know traffic management, I couldn't remove an appendix, or anything like that" (p. 876). A similar refusal to specialize or be tied down, in addition to WASP prejudice, real or perceived, explains Bellow's attraction to Humanities programs and the Committee on Social Thought; to all literature, not just English literature; to big ideas, great works of philosophy, history, anthropology, sociology. In describing the second proposed novelle, as yet untitled, Bellow labels the forces opposing greatness and freedom "the theology of 'this world.'" He says very little about the novelle, since "I have already begun to write it and do not, for that reason, want to describe it further." Its themes survive in later work, of course, notably in the teachings of Grandma Lausch in *Augie*, "one of those Machiavellis of small street and neighborhood" (p. 384). The original title of *Augie* was to be "Life Among the Machiavellians," that is, life among what in the Guggenheim application Bellow calls "The Children of Darkness," an allusion to Luke 16:8: "The children of this world are in their generation wiser than the children of light."

The Victim was published on November 6, 1947, and well received by the critics. In the *Nation*, Diana Trilling, who had irritated Bellow by calling *Dangling Man* "small," judged it "hard to match in recent fiction, for brilliance, skill and originality" (the review made Bellow regret his "roughness" with her husband in a recent essay on novelists and critics in *The New Leader*).[51] The reviews in the daily *New York Times* and in *Time* (the remark in *Time* about its being "the year's most intelligent study of the Jew in U.S. society" came from an end-of-year roundup) were largely positive, though like the other reviews "singularly stupid" (Bellow's judgment in a letter to Henle), "incredibly vulgar" (in a letter to Bazelon of December 1, 1947). Bellow was clear about the novel's strengths as well as its limitations: "*The Victim* where it is successful," he writes on December 18, 1948, to the novelist J. F. Powers, a friend, "is a powerful book. I take my due for it. There aren't many recent books that come close to it and I can't take seriously any opinion that doesn't begin by acknowledging that. There you have it. I'm not modest." When Bellow's father saw the reviews, he was unimpressed: "The fact that I was a celebrity last week made no difference to him. . . . He doesn't read my reviews, only looks at them." Bellow was in Chicago for Thanksgiving, and Abraham offered to make him "a mine superintendent at ten thousand. . . . A mine's a mine, but *Time* is a mere striving with wind." The only reviewer Bellow exempts from criticism in the Bazelon letter is Elizabeth Hardwick, whose notice appeared in *Partisan Review*. He was glad she "didn't take the axe to me. She's very formidable."[52] Hardwick's review, from a "Fiction Chronicle" in the issue of January–February 1948, leaves *The Victim* till last, after discussion of novels by Dreiser (*The Stoic*, in which "the writing . . . is worse than ever"), Sartre's *The Reprieve* ("an achievement of some sort . . . [if] vague and rather superficial"), and Erskine Caldwell's *The Sure Hand of God* (the work of an author with "no real interest in his subjects . . . frantic, bewildered, obviously disoriented as a writer"). Bellow, in contrast, is fiction's great hope. His new novel is distinguished by its "thorough and exquisite honesty" and "many levels of meaning," levels "contained in the situation in which the characters find themselves and not in the surrounding rhetoric." On the basis of *Dangling Man* and *The Victim*, Hardwick declares, "it would be hard to think of any young writer who has a better chance than Bellow to become the redeeming novelist of his period."

But *The Victim* did not sell. After three months it had sold 2,257 copies, only about seven hundred more than *Dangling Man*, despite the fact that Henle had written in November to say he had secured an advance sale of 2,300 (also despite the novel's eliciting inquiries from both Hollywood and Broadway). Bellow was upset. "I hardly know what to say," he wrote to Henle on February 9, 1948, "after two years of wringing to pay bills and fighting for scraps of time in which to do my writing. Have I nothing to look forward to but two years of the same sort and a sale of barely two thousand for the next novel I write? And can it be worth your while to continue publishing books which sell only two thousand copies? I don't understand this at all; I feel black and bitter about it, merely."[53] In an unsent letter to Henle, he elaborates on his disappointment: "This year I have been ill and teaching leaves me no energy for writing. I had hoped that I would be able to ask for a year's leave but I shall have nothing to live on if I do, and I see next year and the next and the one after that fribbled away at the university. My grievance is a legitimate one, I think."[54] What prompted Bellow to put these grievances on paper, though he stopped short of sending them, was a note he'd received from Henle saying that "he expected the progressive Book Club to have *The Victim* as its March choice." This news depressed Bellow, since the book's cost for members would be seventy-five cents: "It seems to me that this is tantamount to remaindering the book and getting shut of it" (in the event, a thousand copies were sold by the club, earning Bellow $750). Why, moreover, couldn't anyone find the book in bookstores? "Friends and acquaintances in various parts of the country who had seen reviews of *The Victim* and tried to buy it,"

Bellow continues, were "told by local booksellers that they had never heard of it. . . . The University of Chicago bookstore and Woolworth's didn't even know I had published a book. As a Chicagoan and a Hyde Parker, I feel hurt by this."[55]

These unsent complaints survive as extracts in a letter to Henry Volkening, Bellow's agent since 1944. Volkening had not been involved in the deals Bellow made with Vanguard, nor had Bellow's previous agent, Maxim Lieber. When the Hollywood inquiry came in, Bellow forwarded it to Volkening without telling Henle. Henle and Volkening got along (after publication of *Dangling Man*, Henle recommended Volkening as a good agent for Bellow's stories), but Bellow thought it best to wrangle over sales of *The Victim* himself. "[Henle] would probably prefer dealing with me," Bellow explained to Volkening. "[James T.] Farrell has never had an agent and Farrell, it seems, has established the pattern for the ideal connection of publisher with author."[56] Volkening approved this strategy and cautioned Bellow to tone down his complaints, which he did ("I answered him, more mildly than the first time," reads a letter of February 18), but still Henle responded defensively. "He said that in the long run I couldn't miss (but how long is long?) and that Farrell and every other serious writer in America had the same bad row to weed." Bellow remained unpersuaded, answering that "Farrell's books started to come out during the Depression and that these are fat years." There was something "fundamentally wrong" with Vanguard, he concluded in the letter to Volkening. It was simply "too small an organization to push a book to the retailers."[57] To push this book in particular, he elsewhere suggests. "The fact is," he declares to Volkening, in the letter received on January 9, 1948, that "Henle did not care much about The Victim and was inclined to treat it as a Jewish book. . . . His first letter on receiving the mss. simply flabbergasted me. I sat down, shaken, to write an exegesis. His tastes and sympathies are with the Farrell and Calder Willingham sort of novel and not with my sort." Relations between the two men did not improve. "Henle and I haven't unlocked horns yet," Bellow writes to Volkening in a later, undated letter. "He wants to make peace but he's nettled and, pacifying though his letters are on the whole, he can't resist slipping in one more provocation. And hell, I have nothing to lose by speaking my mind."[58] To Bazelon, Bellow writes of having "sent Henle raging mad letters, but he holds he isn't to blame."[59]

Bellow wanted to get out of his contract with Vanguard, which had rights to his next two books. He also wanted to get out of teaching for the coming year ("three years of teaching straight is more than flesh and blood can endure"). The aims were related. To finance a year without teaching he would need a much bigger advance than Vanguard could offer. If he won the Guggenheim he might just survive on the $2,500 stipend, but he had been turned down twice and wasn't sanguine about his chances. When Bellow asked Henle if he had "a right to devote all my time to writing," Henle's answer, as reported to Volkening, was that "I had indeed. No more. Other publishers have offered me the opportunity. One wanted to give me enough money for a year."[60] Shortly after receiving Henle's reply, Bellow made up his mind to change publishers. Then he won the Guggenheim. Henle wrote to congratulate him, and as Bellow told Frank Taylor of Random House, one of the publishers pursuing him (Random House was Warren's publisher, and Taylor had visited Bellow's creative writing seminar in Minneapolis, searching for new authors), "you simply can't answer a letter of congratulation with a sharp appeal for release."[61] On April 23, however, three weeks after the Guggenheim announcement, Bellow wrote to Henle asking to be let out of his contract. Six days later, Henle agreed, in a letter Bellow described to Volkening as "quite bitter." Henle's response ends: "you may take this letter as Vanguard's formal assent to your placing your succeeding—I hope the pun is justified—works elsewhere." Bellow's decision was spurred by preceding Henle communications reported to Volkening: "last week a royalty statement arrived from Vanguard and I learned that as of the first of January I still owed $170 on my original advance of $750 for The Victim"; "I still owe him money," he complained to Volkening, "and doesn't he seem pleased in his letter." In the letter congratulating Bellow on the Guggenheim, Henle had offered a $1,200 advance on a new novel: "The Fellowship, Henle understood, would not be enough and he was offering me this money because Vanguard also desired that I should devote myself exclusively to writing. This last phrase was taken from a letter I had sent Henle quite some time before I knew anything of the Guggenheim. No particular note had been taken of it by him then."[62]

Volkening played no part in the break with Vanguard, had counseled restraint, and Bellow apologized to him for the reproaches he was sure would come his way from Henle. "None of this was your doing. . . . I apologize in advance for any bad feeling between you that I may cause."[63] But there was none. Volkening was a hard man to dislike, charming, honest, and devoted both to literature and to his authors; he remained Bellow's agent until his death in 1972. He was thirteen years older than Bellow, born in 1902. His background was German— his grandfather had served in the German army in World War I—and he grew up in Yorkville, the German section of Manhattan. According to Harriet Wasserman, who was hired by him as an assistant in 1960, Volkening had been teased in school for his German background and "was haunted for the rest of his life" by the anti-Semitic treatment received by a classmate at Princeton (whether he joined in this treatment is unclear from Wasserman's account, though she says "he wished he could redo and make amends").[64] After Princeton, Volkening went to Fordham Law School and worked in real estate, which he did not enjoy. He was literary and managed to get a post teaching English literature at night school at New York University. There in 1927 he befriended a fellow instructor, "a huge, black-haired man at a desk nearby," the novelist Thomas Wolfe, about whom he wrote a long profile in 1939.[65] It was Wolfe who introduced Volkening to Maxwell Perkins, who was his editor at Scribner's, midwife to *Look Homeward, Angel*, the enormous novel Wolfe was working on at the time, and Perkins who told Volkening he ought to consider becoming an agent (after first telling him that he had no editorial openings at Scribner's). Some weeks later, Diarmuid Russell, a young editor recently fired from G. P. Putnam's Sons, came to see Perkins, and was given the same advice, along with Volkening's name. In May 1940, after several meetings, the two young men decided to go into business together, forming Russell and Volkening Literary Representatives, each putting up a stake of $5,000. Russell's title in the new business was president, Volkening's treasurer.

Diarmuid Russell would have been consulted by Volkening over Bellow's contracts and manuscripts, certainly in the early years of the agency. He was born in Dublin in 1902, the son of the Irish poet and visionary AE (George William Russell). A tall, handsome man, an outdoorsman, he immigrated to the United States in 1929 after working in the editorial offices of the Dublin periodical *The Irish Statesman*, edited by his father and his father's good friend William Butler Yeats ("Uncle Bill"). After a spell in Chicago, working in the book department of Marshall Field, he returned to New York in 1935 to take up an editorial position at Putnam, where he was unhappy about the firm's treatment of its authors. Almost as soon as Russell and Volkening opened for business, Russell had secured its first author, Eudora Welty. Welty was "Diarmuid's" author, as was Bernard Malamud, signed four years later; Bellow was "Henry's," as was Ralph Ellison, acquired in 1943. But within house, certainly in this period, the divisions were not strict. "I know I should have written to you earlier," Russell wrote to Welty on October 8, 1940, "but I had to wait till Henry and John [Slocum, secretary to the firm] had read the book too. . . . Henry thinks it is going to be taken and will sell well."[66] Malamud came to Russell through Volkening, whose first client was a Manhattan high school English teacher named Michael Seide, author of a collection of stories entitled *The Common Thread*. Seide recommended Volkening to Malamud, a teaching colleague previously represented by Maxim Lieber, Bellow's old agent. When Malamud called, Russell happened to answer the phone and thus became his agent. Seide never published another book, although Volkening stuck with him. Both agents were unshakably loyal to their authors and determined to represent only writers of quality. Their list was small and distinguished. Thomas Wolfe eventually joined it, as did Wright Morris, Peter Taylor, J. F. Powers, May Sarton, A. J. Liebling, Barbara Tuchman, and Anne Tyler.

Henry Volkening was a city type, one of several ways in which he was unlike Diarmuid Russell (another was in height; Volkening was short). He wrote frequent, newsy letters to authors and editors, full of gossip, shrewd advice, and praise. When his authors came to New York he took them for lengthy "drunches" at the Century Association, a club with a distinguished literary history, located on West 43rd Street. Volkening liked to drink and the "Drenchery" served supersized martinis and other cocktails, with second portions in little silver jugs. Authors were advised that they need not keep up, and Bellow often took the precaution of eating before lunch to survive the drinks. Yet Volkening was a careful businessman, kept the firm's records (in pencil, without benefit of an adding machine), and advised on a range of issues, personal and financial as well as literary. Bellow liked and counted on him, and judging by correspondence there were almost no spats or accusatory moments in their lengthy association. The association began inauspiciously, however, before publication of *Dangling Man*. After reading one of Bellow's stories in *PR*, Volkening wrote asking to see other work. Bellow sent him a story entitled "On the Platform," now lost, which was "curtly dismissed." A few weeks later, after *Dangling Man* came out, Volkening wrote again, asking to see something else, if Bellow could "forgive the wham we gave the short story." Bellow sent something that wasn't whammed and Volkening became his agent, though it was only after the break with Vanguard that Volkening felt free to represent Bellow the novelist.[67] "The way's open and we can begin to consider proposals," Bellow wrote after receiving Henle's letter of release.[68] These proposals, it turned out, were for a quite different novel from the one Bellow described in the Guggenheim application. The new novel, already in the works, was to be titled "The Crab and the Butterfly."

Volkening's advice was that Bellow should pitch the novel either to George Joel at the Dial Press or Harold Guinzburg at Viking. There was also Frank Taylor, of Random House, to consider, with whom Bellow had been in correspondence, and whose boss, Bennett Cerf, had also written.[69] On May 13, Bellow wrote to Bazelon to say that he would be in New York "on Monday Tuesday and Wednesday to do some sharp trading." He arrived on the Pacemaker on Monday morning, in time to have lunch with Volkening "and spend a few hours plotting." At Viking he met with a young editor, Monroe Engel, to whom he'd been recommended by a mutual friend (Engel is not sure, but thinks the friend might have been Isaac Rosenfeld). Engel, himself a writer, had come to Viking from Reynal and Hitchcock, where in his first week an unsolicited manuscript crossed his desk entitled "Under the Volcano" by Malcolm Lowry. It had been turned down by "quite a few" publishing houses but Engel rated it, as did his fellow editors, when he brought it to their attention. It was a good way to begin a publishing career. Engel knew all about Bellow, not just from the mutual friend but from Bellow's novels and stories: "'The Mexican General' in *Partisan Review* was important in giving publishers a sense that Saul Bellow was a coming man," he recalled. "I had no doubt whatsoever that I wanted us to give him a contract, which we did, and I remember the advance was $3,000, which was then considered very generous"—it was more than double what Henle had offered.

Engel's first impressions of Bellow were that he was "confident, already rather witty," but also realistic about his situation. "He knew that he was not a commercial success and didn't know what a larger publishing house would do." When Engel's wife, Brenda, first met Bellow it was at the Rosenfelds' apartment on Barrow Street. "Isaac was telling stories and they seemed to me just superb and when Saul jumped in and started telling a story I thought to myself how can he interrupt, who is he? He told a wonderful story, very funny. . . . It surprised me that he had the confidence." On May 23, Bellow signed a contract with

Viking, which would remain his publisher for the next thirty years. "It reads wonderfully," he wrote to Volkening on the same day. "I hope my novel reads half as well." On July 5, 1948, he wrote to Frank Taylor in response to a letter whose tone relieved him "more than I can say." He had been tempted by Random House, took to Albert Erskine, Taylor's colleague, "no less than to Monroe Engel. Believe me, there was *absolutely* nothing personal about the reasons for my choice." These reasons are vague in the letter, something about "an unlaid prejudice having to do with large houses and small." Bellow was sorry "to have had—how to say it without presumption!—to disappoint. . . . But, on the scene, in New York, I found things so working themselves out as to convince me that I had no other alternative. It was all like radar acting on my intuitions."[70]

The origins of the newly contracted novel are clouded. That it was an expanded version of a "novelle" or "novelette" is clear. "Just at present I'm working on a novelette called *The Crab and the Butterfly* which maybe *Partisan* will publish. Rahv has an idea that something should be done for the novella and has written to say that he plans to run one a year—in imitation of *Horizon*."[71] The work promised Rahv was to derive from neither of the two novelettes Bellow described in his Guggenheim application, but from a third, at the time titled "Who Breathes Overhead" (from Schiller: "Who breathes overhead in the rose-tinted light may be glad"), described in a letter to Bazelon of January 5, 1948.[72] Henle had agreed to publish a volume of stories after *The Victim*. Sometime before Bellow broke with Vanguard, he mentioned to Volkening in an undated letter that he had "a collection of three novelettes," as well as some shorter works, actual short stories. Perhaps, Bellow speculated in a letter of December 7, 1947, to Volkening, Henle might actually "prefer to publish a novelette singly, as a *very* short novel. Originally my last novel [*The Victim*] was to have run about forty thousand words; it somehow got out of hand." This tendency for works to get out of hand, short stories becoming novelettes (or novelles or novellas), then novels, was lifelong. In the same letter, as well as in another undated letter, Bellow mentions that he had promised Rahv and *Partisan Review* "first crack at" one such novelette, unnamed. "It's now about 25,000 words and not yet done. . . . Another novelette, Children of Light and Children of Darkness is finished but wants rewriting."[73] In a letter dated simply December 1947, Bellow writes to Volkening that the story he had promised Rahv, as early as the summer of 1947, was tentatively titled "Amor Fati" (soon to become "Who Breathes Overhead"). It was the sort of story "no other magazine would touch . . . I'm convinced because of the title, plus a certain freedom of expression." The title comes from Nietzsche, *Ecce Homo*, section 10: "My formula for greatness in a human being is *amor fati*: that one wants nothing to be different. . . . Not merely bear what is necessary, still less conceal it . . . but *love* it."[74]

All that survives of "The Crab and the Butterfly" is a chapter published in the November–December 1950 issue of *Partisan Review* entitled "The Trip to Galena." The setting of this chapter is a hospital room in Chicago (the trip to Galena is recounted). There are two characters in the present of the story, both invalids: Weyl, who talks, and Scampi, who listens. Scampi is in the hospital with a broken wrist. He is not Weyl's roommate. Weyl's roommate, Mr. Charney, is only referred to in the story; he is seriously ill, just barely "holding his own," and Weyl has "put up [a] battle" over him of an unspecified nature.[75] In his interview with Philip Roth, Bellow described "The Crab and the Butterfly" as about "two men in a hospital room, one dying, the other trying to keep him from surrendering to death."[76] Of these two, "The Trip to Galena" gives us only Weyl, who ponders the possibility of a noble life, a life of greatness, but cannot decide whether our "original nature is murderous" or "there's something redeemable in the original thing" (p. 788), an opposition that suggests the contrast implied in "Who Breathes Overhead" between those "down below" and those who "breathe overhead in the rose-tinted light," though it may also suggest the opposition of "Children of Light and Children of Darkness." In the letter to Tumin, Bellow explains the title: "The crab is human tenaciousness to life, the butterfly is the gift of existence which the crab stalks. The crab cannot leap or chase but stands with open claws [like Grandma Lausch?] while the creature flaps over him." How or if this opposition is embodied in the two roommates is unclear. Is Weyl the butterfly or the crab? Or is he drawn or torn by qualities or propensities associated with both creatures, as suggested at moments in "A Trip to Galena"? One cannot tell. On March 8, 1948, Bellow wrote to Bazelon that "since October I've done nothing but a novelette of about thirty thousand words—a dazzlingly white elephant, too short for a book and too long for a magazine." A month later Bellow decided it would become his next novel, and Viking not *Partisan Review* or Random House would publish it.

WITH A $3,000 ADVANCE in hand, $2,500 from the Guggenheim, and a year's leave of absence from Minnesota, Bellow pondered his options for the coming year. In the March 8 letter to Bazelon, after he'd gotten leave but before the Guggenheim or the Viking contract, he laid out several possibilities: "We wanted to go to Europe, but the putsch in Czechoslovakia [backed by the Soviet Union] makes the war seem too close and the next long night (the final?) about to start. We thought of going to New Mexico but they test atom bombs there. Let me not breathe neutrons. Or the West Indies. Have you any ideas?" For a while there was a plan to live in Guatemala (where Tumin had been researching), then in the country outside New York, but on June 4, 1948, Bellow wrote to Henry Moe, of the Guggenheim Foundation, that "the house we had been promised in New York had fallen through." The plan now was to live in France, "as we have received an invitation from friends in Paris to join them and have been assured of living-quarters by them." These friends were the Kaplans: Kappy had written to say that "it would cost about 5 grand to live in Paris for a year," and with the Guggenheim and the Viking contract they could afford it. Anita was keener on Paris than Bellow; she "has a severer travel bug and won't be happy till she's crossed the Atlantic," he told Frank Taylor of Random House in the letter of July 5, 1948, whereas "I'd still prefer a Jamaica-like place." To Mel Tumin, Bellow worried, in an undated letter, that France or Italy would be "too exciting and disturbing," a hindrance to his writing: "I came back last fall exhausted and sick and for three months was good for nothing." He wanted to stay put, "settle for good. . . . I'm weary of milling around, living in a different house each year." There were also disturbing memories from the Mexico trip: "Anita did so badly in Mexico with the language; she was terrified and clung with all her weight to me; I couldn't tolerate that. The results, though I haven't said so before—perhaps didn't really understand—were disastrous. Nearly fatal. But she promises to behave differently in France."[77]

On June 30, the Bellows moved out of 58 Orlin Avenue, staying with the McCloskys at 701 University Avenue South till July 20. They would be in Chicago with Anita's family from July 20 till August 20, then on to New York and Paris. In the letter of July 5 to Taylor, Bellow was still trying to book passage to Le Havre. On September 15, after several weeks in Manhattan, he, Anita, and Greg set sail for Europe on the *De*

Grasse, a ship of the French Line. Before leaving New York, according to Atlas, Bellow had a clandestine meeting with Betty, the Wisconsin student from the previous summer. Atlas quotes from a letter Bellow wrote to Betty while abroad. She had written to him care of American Express under an assumed name—"M. Bacalao, Spanish for *codfish*. (Bellow had in mind a line of García Lorca's: *'Ya te veo, bacalao, dunque nienes disfragado'*—'Now I see you, codfish, under your disguise')."[78] Betty still entertained hopes, which, from the evidence of the letter Atlas quotes, Bellow understood but sought to discourage. "Though I've always kept clear of promises and commitments," there was "a kind of chemistry in the soul" between them, "where hopes are in the mixture." "I feel it isn't good enough to be 'legally' fair," he admits, not where "the most complex and subtle things happen." Hence "my writ-

SB and Herbert McClosky on the Marine Tiger,
September 1947

ing now . . . because I neither forgot you nor want to be forgotten—but remembered *en quelque sorte*." "It was a typical letter from a married man to a girlfriend," Atlas writes, "gently equivocating but with the clear signal that the relationship had no future."[79] It might also have been simply sincere.

9

Paris

"I SEEM TO BE UNABLE TO accustom myself to ships," Bellow wrote to Henry Volkening on September 27, 1948, shortly after the *De Grasse* docked at Le Havre. "A very light sea made me sick the second day out and it wasn't till we were nearly on the other side before the feeling left me." The voyage took nearly two weeks and among the passengers were "about a hundred Southern college girls practicing their French on stewards and deckhands."[1] Once on land, life was calmer, "save for the robberies we've been subjected to. Prices are doubled as soon as [one] opens one's mouth, [as] though one were to have two heads and a beret on each." Bellow and Anita and Greg settled into an apartment at 24 rue Marbeuf, in the Eighth Arrondissement. It was owned by "an old English gentleman who used to race automobiles and who still writes articles for the racing magazines in London." The gentleman's name was Pope and at the turn of the century he "had broken all racing car records between Nice and the English Channel." Bellow was struck by his clothes, in particular "a dull mulberry colored lounge suit which made him look as if he had been laid out for burial but had risen from the coffin to complete unfinished business."[2] Pope with his rapacious French wife were off to Cannes for the winter, to write a book using the typewriter Bellow had brought over from New York "for a bribe" ("a new Remington portable typewriter, which the landlady absolutely demanded as a gift").[3] The period of rental, he wrote on October 20 to Henry Allen Moe, secretary of the Guggenheim Foundation, was uncertain, anywhere from two months to seven, "though the coal strike will induce [the Popes] to remain, I think."

Five days later, Bellow was reporting to Monroe Engel that "I've already been at work for two weeks," interrupted only by "the occasional fusillade of French under the window or at the back of the house." The window in question was in Mr. Pope's study, which Bellow had taken over. So solitary was his life in those first few weeks that he might have been in Minneapolis, "except that Minneapolis houses are much better heated." Once the threatened strikes took effect, there would be no heating at all; already "three million tons of coal were lost and everyone expects cuts in electric power and gas. In some parts of the city the electric *coupures* have already started and Paris pitch black is no place for us."

What Bellow called the "encapsulated" nature of his early days in Paris was partly willed.[4] "You have to draw in from the beauty of the place to accomplish anything," he wrote to Volkening on October 25. "And then the beauty is very much complicated by the terror of the strikes and the rattle of scrapping that many people fear may turn into a booming civil war." Janet Flanner, of *The New Yorker*, was one of these people, reporting in a journal entry of October 5 that France's condition was "dangerous," its strength "flowing away" in "choleric politics," "falling money," "strikes in French mines, banks, government services."[5] Conditions were better for Americans in France than for the French. The summer of 1948, Flanner predicted, would see "the biggest influx of American tourists since the great season of 1929." These tourists would be treated—by the state if not its citizens—"as shiploads of precious metal."[6] Dollars were much in demand (the Popes insisted that the Bellows pay their rent in dollars); tourists, even tourists without automobiles, were entitled to unlimited gasoline coupons, which could then be sold on the black market to the French, whose gas was rationed. Bellow complained of being cheated, yet was able to rent a room to write in, in a modest Left Bank hotel, for a dollar a day. The Bellows were relatively well off in Paris. They had $5,000 to live on, combining the Guggenheim grant and the Viking advance for "The Crab and the Butterfly," and the rate of exchange was 550 to one.[7] They ran a car, employed a full-time maid (called a *bonne à tout faire*), and after Anita found work, a Danish au pair named Lilian Bodnia. They even kept a dog, a French poodle named Malou, later taken over by the Kaplans. In December, according to a letter of January 2, 1949, to Volkening, the family had enjoyed "a very pleasant holiday on the Riviera, at Nice and San Remo."

One drawback to living in Paris was having to deal with the French, beginning with Mme Pope, the landlady. Upon their arrival, she presented the Bellows with a detailed *inventaire*: "An amazing document! A catalogue of every object in the house, from the Chippendale chair to the meanest cup, fully and marvellously described." When at last the list had been gone through, ending in the kitchen with "three lousy tin spoons," and the landlady departed, Bellow "turned a somersault over the Chippendale chair and landed thunderously on the floor. This lightened my heart for a time."[8] The apartment was cluttered, "a gilded cage"[9]; the building "fussy"[10]; the neighborhood too far from what Bellow came to think of as "my Paris," "between the boulevard du Montparnasse and the Seine."[11] Four-year-old Greg was a threat to Madame's *objets*; he needed room to run around. At the end of April or early in May, with the imminent return of the Popes, the family moved, at which point Mme Pope took them to court. One of her *objets* had been broken. Atlas recounts the proceedings, as remembered by Bellow: "*Sortez les mains de vos poches,*" the magistrate ordered: "*Ce n'est pas Amérique.*"[12] Found guilty of damaging property, Bellow was ordered to pay compensation, though when the Popes failed to produce receipts, the money was refunded. The family had lived at 24 rue Marbeuf for almost eight months, though after the December holiday on the Riviera, Bellow had absented himself for a further six weeks, spending January in Rome, looking for somewhere to live ("next April we'll move there together," he explained in a letter to Volkening of December 17), and simply getting away from home, because "I want to get off and think through a novel, or novels, for there are several in my mind."[13] Shortly after returning to Paris, he rented the room to write in, at the Hôtel de l'Académie on rue des Saints-Pères, just above boulevard Saint-Germain; the study at rue Marbeuf depressed him.[14] At the end of *The Adventures of Augie March*, Augie finds himself in an apartment very like 24 rue Marbeuf, on rue François-Ier, which crosses Marbeuf near the Champs-Elysées: "I'd pass days trying to get used to this moldy though fancied-up apartment, somewhat obstinate, seeing that it was now my place. But there was no getting anywhere with the carpets and chairs, the lamps that looked as if grown on Coney Island, cat-house pictures, alabaster owls with electric eyes, books of Ouida and Marie Corelli in leather binding, smelling like spit" (pp. 975–76).

It was Kappy who found the Bellows the rue Marbeuf apartment, assuring them that, though not cheap, it was worth the money. Kappy and Celia lived on the Left Bank, like almost everyone Bellow knew or wanted to know, in an eighth-floor apartment at 132 boulevard du Montparnasse, directly above Matisse's studio. The vast living room of the apartment, also once an artist's studio, was perfect for parties, and became, if not quite a salon, then what Kappy called "an unofficial American cultural center."[15] After long years of occupation and war, he recalled, "now suddenly there was this cheery place with balconies overlooking the city and this sense that everything was *open*" (the view stretched all the way to Sacré-Coeur in Montmartre).[16] Among the guests the Kaplans entertained at boulevard du Montparnasse were Albert Camus, Maurice Merleau-Ponty, Raymond Queneau, Raymond Aron, Georges Bataille, David Rousset, Emmanuel Levinas, Louis Guilloux, Jacques Lacan, Miles Davis, Arthur Koestler, Cyril Connolly, Stephen Spender, Alberto Moravia, Ignazio Silone, Norman Mailer, Czeslaw Milosz, Richard Wright, James Baldwin, James Jones, Irwin Shaw, Theodore White, Saul Steinberg, Truman Capote, James T. Farrell, Mary McCarthy, Lionel Abel, Herbert Gold, Joseph Frank, and Nicola Chiaromonte. Jean-Paul Sartre and Simone de Beauvoir stayed away, angry at William Barrett's negative review of *Being and Nothingness* in the "New French Writing" issue of *Partisan Review*, which they'd helped to assemble. Sartre refused to accept Kappy's protestations that he'd had nothing to do with Barrett's review, hadn't been consulted about it or seen it in advance. Soon Beauvoir was spreading rumors that Kappy was a CIA agent.[17]

When the Bellows moved to Paris in September 1948, Kappy was employed by the United States Information Service (USIS) as an unofficial press and cultural attaché at the embassy. He had arrived four years earlier, on the heels of General Leclerc's liberation of the city in August 1944. Previously he'd been stationed in North Africa in a unit broadcasting Allied propaganda to France, which had grown out of a comparable unit in New York, headed by the French journalist Pierre Lazareff, later editor of *France-Soir*. The New York unit was small (about ten people), secret, and sponsored by General Eisenhower under the auspices of the army's Psychological Warfare Branch. Kappy was assigned to it partly on the recommendation of his professors at the University of Chicago, Robert Vigneron and René Etiemble, both on leave from the Ecole Normale Supérieure.[18] The North African unit was headed by Pierre Schaeffer, a composer, journalist, and broadcaster. Kappy was the only member never to have been to France. His colleagues—writers, artists, newspapermen—mocked his academic French, which helped to perfect it, and provided many contacts. Among New York colleagues, he mentions André Breton, who presented the broadcasts, and Simon Michael Bessie, who was to become his publisher at Harper Brothers. When Kappy arrived in Paris, he was detached to the United States embassy, helping to set up its consulate on the rue Saint-Florentin. He found the Montparnasse apartment "by luck"; when he moved in, there was a German uniform hanging in the closet. Within a year, he was joined by Celia and three-year-old Leslie (their daughter, named after Leslie Fiedler, a close friend since high school). One of Kappy's jobs at the embassy, in addition to advising the ambassador, was to organize tours for new colleagues or visiting writers, politicians, and intellectuals (Senator Fulbright, Richard McKeon, Sidney Hook, who was scandalized when taken to the *Bal Nègre*). He also encouraged students from the *grandes écoles* to study in the United States. In the late 1940s, he recalled, "the great schools came under heavy Communist influence, if not control" and the hope was that "simply by getting acquainted with our country, they [the students] would become more favorably disposed toward it. It was perhaps an illusion!"[19]

Despite temperamental and other differences, Kappy and Bellow shared important interests. In "A Minor Scandal," his "Paris Letter" for the December 1947 issue of *Partisan Review*, Kappy criticizes both Sartre (elsewhere called "a generous man, but incredibly stupid about politics"[20]) and the opinions of French intellectuals, mockingly identified by the writer and polymath Boris Vian as "Simone de Merlartre, Sarleau de Pontrevoir, Merloir de Beauvartre, etc." The minor scandal of the title involved "my friend Patrick" (the poet and art critic Patrick Waldberg, whom Kappy met in North Africa). At a party given by Claude-Edmonde Magny, a "*femme de lettres*," Waldberg threw a glass of Armagnac in the face of Curzio Malaparte, the Italian novelist, prisoner of war, and onetime fascist sympathizer. Kappy had no use for Malaparte and the "characteristically slick and abject" way he "jerked facile tears" over the victims of the camps. "We live in our history, not above it," Kappy writes at the end of the "Paris Letter," "and we finally choose between drinking our armagnac or throwing it into someone's face" (pp. 492, 505). Kappy's anger came from a year reading "books, brochures, and articles about concentration camps" (p. 493). The most impressive of the books he read were by David Rousset, a survivor of

Buchenwald. Rousset records the horrors of the camps but also looks beyond or behind them, showing that "even in such hells as Dora and Matthausen, social groupings were formed, the struggle for power took place between Poles and Germans, for example, or between the political and the common-law prisoners" (p. 494). Kappy was particularly struck by Rousset's account of collaboration among the inmates, without which Buchenwald could not have functioned: "the S.S. were far too few to staff any but the top posts of the bureaucracy" (p. 499). Chief among collaborators were the German Communists and because Rousset had been a Trotskyist and could speak "the Marxist language," he learned their story. By the time of his capture in 1944, the Communists were "virtually in complete control of the camp . . . after a long, costly, bloody struggle against the common-law criminals, who had ruled the camps from their inception until the outbreak of total war" (pp. 499–500).

Rousset's first book, *L'Univers concentrationnaire* (1946), ends on what Kappy calls a "note of strength." This note Bellow was bound to have heard, just at the time he was at work on "Who Breathes Overhead," the germ of "The Crab and the Butterfly" (first mentioned in a letter to Bazelon of January 5, 1948, a month after the appearance of Kappy's "Paris Letter"). Rousset finds in the camps, in Kappy's translation of the book's final sentences, the "dynamic realization of the power and the beauty of the fact of living, in itself, brutal, entirely devoid of all superstructures, of living even through the worst collapses, or the gravest retreats. A sensual freshness of joy constructed on the completest knowledge of the ruins and, in consequence, a hardening in action, a stubbornness in decisions, in short a deeper and more intensely creative health" (p. 501).[21] The moral complexities of this "health" recall Bellow's idea for "The Crab and the Butterfly," quoted in the previous chapter, in which the crab is "human tenaciousness to life" and the butterfly "the gift of existence which the crab stalks." In the "Paris Letter," "human tenaciousness to life" is admirable when associated with Rousset, despicable when associated with Malaparte, and both when associated with the kapos of Buchenwald, who in "saving from physical destruction a larger percentage of Communists," created a population of survivors who "can only function today as the docile instruments of another police-power in Germany, namely the N.K.V.D." (p. 501).[22]

FROM THE START, Bellow granted Paris its architectural beauty, but he had little to say in favor of its weather, the Parisian *grisaille* or gloom. "Depressed and sunk in spirit," he writes of himself in this period, "I dwelt among Madame's works of art that cold winter. The city lay under perpetual fog, and the smoke could not rise and flowed in the streets in brown and gray currents. An unnatural smell emanated from the Seine."[23] This passage comes from "The French as Dostoyevsky Saw Them" (1955), the foreword Bellow wrote to Dostoyevsky's *Winter Notes on Summer Impressions* (1863), published in French under the title *Le Bourgeois de Paris*. Bellow came across the book on the stand of a *bouquiniste* near the Châtelet, and immediately took to it, "unable to suppress certain utterances of satisfaction and agreement." Dostoyevsky's jaundiced view of Parisians was his view; "the French in 1862 were not substantially different from those of 1948."[24] Nor were Bellow and Dostoyevsky alone in their view: "*Gay* Paris? Gay, my foot! Mere advertising. Paris is one of the grimmest cities in the world. I do not ask you to take my word for it. Go to Balzac and Stendhal, to Zola, to Strindberg—to Paris itself." In 1948, Bellow admits, he "was a poor visitor and, by any standard, an inferior tourist."[25] He attributes these deficiencies to defensiveness, a background like Dostoyevsky's: "I, too, was a foreigner and a barbarian from a vast and backward land" (that is, he was treated as such). In explaining the indifference and inaccessibility of French Parisians, he "often" reminded himself that "old cultures are impermeable and exclusive—none more so than the French." It was naive of him to "expect these people to take you to their hearts and into their homes. They have other and more important things to think about. Food, for one."[26] Nevertheless, the behavior of the French offended him, as he had been offended in the summer of 1947 by the similar behavior of the Spanish.

France aroused Dostoyevsky's "profoundest hatred." Bellow's antipathy was milder, and not a product of disillusion. "There is not a nation anywhere that does not contradict its highest principles in daily practice," he writes in "The French as Dostoyevsky Saw Them," "but the French contradiction was in his eyes the very worst because France presumed to offer the world political and intellectual instruction and leadership." In his youth, Dostoyevsky suffered exile for his faith in those presumptions, as a participant in the "Petrashevsky 'conspiracy,'" inspired by the writings of "Saint-Simon, Fourier, and Sébastien Cabet among others."[27] Bellow had no such faith, not after reading Harold Rosenberg's "The Fall of Paris."[28] Nor, he claims, was he susceptible to the glamour of the city's prewar past. "I was not going to sit at the feet of Gertrude Stein. I had no notions of the Ritz bar. I would not be boxing with Ezra Pound, as Hemingway had done, or writing in bistros while waiters brought oysters and wine. In simple truth, the Jazz Age Paris of American legend held no charms for me." He was equally immune to the allure of Henry James's Paris, citing James's *The American Scene* (1907), with its descriptions of the "unnatural squawking" of Lower East Side Jews in New York: "You wouldn't expect a relative of those barbarous East Siders to be drawn to the world of Madame de Vionnet, which had, in any case, vanished."[29] Only an odd undated letter to Volkening, written early in 1949, suggests a susceptibility to the Paris of American legend. In it Bellow describes running into F. Scott Fitzgerald, "your old college pal and fellow Princetonian," at the Casino in Montreux. He writes that he and Fitzgerald hadn't seen each other since a bibulous lunch in Paris, which had ended "at ten that night at the Ritz bar." Bellow says he was involved with a woman Fitzgerald knew, and after detailing his difficulties with this woman, who was pursuing him, he tells Volkening of a recent visit from his English publisher ("a very fine fellow—he took me out and I met some of the celebrities—Mr. Michael Arlen, and some of the Left Bank people"), then of a trip to Provence, then of a subsequent meeting with Fitzgerald in Geneva, where they talked of Zelda's recent committal to an asylum.

The letter is pure fantasy, a satire; Fitzgerald had been dead for nearly a decade. The wish fulfillment it plays on is that of what Janet Flanner calls "the tourist intelligentsia."[30] The wish Bellow wanted fulfilled in Paris was less fanciful: that the city would prove a place where art and ideas mattered (even if no longer a place to "leap towards the marvelous," in Rosenberg's phrase). "In politics continental Europe was infantile—horrifying," certainly in comparison to America or American democracy. What America lacked, however, "was the capacity to enjoy intellectual pleasures as though they were sensual pleasures. This was what Europe offered, or was said to offer."[31] But intellectual pleasures proved hard for Bellow to find in his Paris years. "I did keep up with French ideas," he recalls in "Writers, Intellectuals, Politics: Mainly Reminiscence," "read Sartre in *Les Temps Modernes* and Camus in *Combat*. I also took in an occasional lecture at the Collège de Philosophie."[32] At the bar of the Pont Royal, haunt of Sartre and Beauvoir, he met Richard Wright, the author of *Native Son* (1940). Wright, who knew both Kappy and Bellow, arrived in Paris in 1946 and was "immediately welcomed" by the existentialists, who "soon had him reading Husserl" (a figure "I ignorantly held in great respect").[33] Wright, however, was an exception; most Americans, Bellow believed, were "hated" by the existentialists, as by the French in general.

One source of this hatred was political. On April 30, 1949, at the suggestion of David Rousset, its chief initiator, an International Day of Resistance to Dictatorship and War was held in Paris, a response to a Communist-inspired World Congress of Peace, scheduled for April 1949, also in Paris. Rousset was on the Executive Committee of the Rassemblement Démocratique Révolutionanaire (RDR), a group of left-leaning writers and critics, among them Jean-Paul Sartre. Invitations to the event were issued jointly under the name of the Executive Committee and the editorial staff of the breakaway left-wing daily newspaper *Franc-Tireur*. Sidney Hook, implacably anti-Communist, attended the proceedings and reported on them in the July 1949 issue of *Partisan Review*.[34] He pronounced the level of political sophistication of the twelve thousand or so delegates—from England, the United States, Holland, Belgium, Italy, Western Germany, Spain, and France—"incredibly low . . . in tone, expression, and content" (p. 726). He deplored the "obsessive fear among avowed non-Communists in France, particularly in French literary and intellectual circles, to challenge in any fundamental way the Soviet myth. Ignorance of conditions in the Soviet Union was matched only by ignorance of conditions in the United States" (p. 724). Hook was appalled that the organizers "refused to invite men like Koestler, Burnham, and Raymond Aron" (p. 724). Most speakers were openly critical of the Atlantic Pact, pleading for neutrality between the two blocs, "as if the liberties of Western Europe were threatened equally by the Soviet Union and the United States. . . . One got the impression that they believed that the Atlantic Pact was imposed upon the governments of Western Europe in the same way as Vishinsky [*sic*] set up a government in Rumania. In a statement read to the Sorbonne audience, Sartre, Merleau-Ponty, and Wright made an explicit equation between the terroristic annexations of the Soviet Union in the East and the Atlantic Pact in the West, condemning both 'equally and for the same reason'" (p. 727). When questioned as to the nature of American imperialism, "no coherent or consistent account could be elicited. It was hard to separate opposition to chewing gum, Coca-Cola, the *Reader's Digest* (bestselling periodical in France) from condemnation of segregation, the monopoly of the atom bomb, and the 'colonization' of Europe achieved by the Machiavellian device of sending bread and machinery to rebuild Europe" (p. 728).[35]

Bellow attended the conference and described it, in a letter of May 19, 1949, to J. F. Powers, as "an awful fiasco. Hook and James Farrell upheld the Marshall Plan and the Atlantic Pact. They couldn't have made themselves less popular, for that reason. The Pact is death, as far as the French left is concerned." He shared Hook's scorn for the equation of American and Soviet systems, as well as Hook's sense that for French intellectuals and their American admirers "it costs nothing—there are absolutely no risks—in denouncing American culture and foreign policy," whereas criticizing the Soviet Union was considered daring, even dangerous, given France's proximity to "Soviet outposts in Europe" (p. 732). Bellow "strongly suspected," he told Botsford in an interview, that Sartre and the French intellectuals who published in *Les Temps Modernes* "expected the West to fall to communism and they would be advantageously placed when this happened." "Why was it they were unable to criticize the Russians in 1956? To behave as they did, you had to be attracted by more than doctrine. You had to have some idea of possible advantages."[36] "The sad fact is," Hook concludes in his "Report on the International Day Against Dictatorship and War," "that at present the fears of France are deeper than its hopes and courage" (p. 732). What is needed, he suggests, is what Kappy provides, in person and through his work: contact with patriotic Americans who are politically and culturally sophisticated and willing to admit to and protest against injustices in the United States: "The informational re-education of the French public seems to me to be the most fundamental as well as the most pressing task of American democratic policy in France" (p. 731). This idea lay behind Hook's involvement a year later in the CIA-funded Congress for Cultural Freedom, which sought to spread "informational re-education" throughout Europe.[37] Looking back on the period, in "Writers, Intellectuals, Politics: Mainly Reminiscence," Bellow declared that "activists like Hook made a difference. Their contribution to victory in the cold war can't be measured but must be acknowledged. . . . I give Hook full marks for the wars he fought and admire him."[38]

BELLOW'S PERIPHERAL CONNECTIONS with the task of "informational re-education" began early. In New York, in March 1948, he had attended a meeting, as did Kappy, who was visiting at the time, of the newly formed and short-lived Europe-America Groups (EAG). The aim of the EAG was to provide support to European intellectuals "in the face of the extreme polarity of Soviet and American power." Stalinism was identified as "the main enemy in Europe today," but American capitalism was also attacked, for "the social and economic and racial iniquities this system perpetuates."[39] The purpose of the March meeting was to discuss money, the proceeds from recent fundraising activities, to be used to facilitate travel and contacts between French, German, Italian, and Spanish intellectuals. The money would also go to purchase and distribute a "'Standard' Book Bundle," a list of recommended titles: Arthur Koestler's *Darkness at Noon*, Erich Fromm's *Escape from Freedom*, Robert and Helen Lynd's *Middletown*, Carlo Levi's *Christ Stopped at Eboli*, Ignazio Silone's *Bread and Wine*, William Faulkner's *Light in August*, *The Partisan Reader: Ten Years of Partisan Review, 1934–1944: An Anthology*, and Bellow's *The Victim*. From the start, the EAG was riven by factions. Bellow and Kappy had been brought to the meeting to support what Mary McCarthy called "the Sidney Hook gang" ("the purists," in her novel *The Oasis*), for whom neutralist positions and "outreach" (to pro-Soviet or hard-left organizations) were considered naive if not actually treasonous. That "gang" included the *PR* editors, Meyer Schapiro, Saul Steinberg and Nicolas Nabokov, as well as Hook, and was opposed by a group spearheaded by Dwight and Mary Macdonald, Mary McCarthy, and Nicola Chiaromonte, the Italian critic and journalist. Whether Bellow knew he had been invited to the meeting to support a particular faction is unclear. Also unclear is how seriously he weighed the potential dangers from the right, the sort stressed by Chiaromonte and Dwight Macdonald and minimized by "the purists": Franco in Spain, the Christian Democrats in Italy, antidemocratic elements among the Gaullists in France. What is clear is that under the direct influence of French anti-Americanism, particularly from the non-Communist left, Bellow moved to the right.

In analyzing this anti-Americanism, Bellow stressed the role played by guilt and national pride. In his "Report," Hook expresses surprise at how little criticism of the Marshall Plan there was at the International

Day. "When I asked for an explanation of this one Frenchman dryly remarked that they had all put on some weight as a result of it. More significant was the admission many were prepared to make in private but not in public that the Marshall Plan had saved France from the Communists and De Gaullists" (p. 727). Two weeks before the International Day, in an entry of April 15, 1949, Janet Flanner offered support for this view in her journal. The Marshall Plan's European Recovery Program was now a year old; in celebration, the French minister of finance and economic affairs, Maurice Petsche, "thanked the Americans for the millions of tons of coal that have kept the wheels of French industry turning; the cotton that the French mills weave two days out of three; the wheat that has lately supplied a quarter of the French bread; and the gasoline on which French trucks roll one day out of two. 'All this merchandise,' he said with emotion, 'has been given us gratis by the American government.'"[40] To French patriots, such indebtedness was shaming. Also shaming was French conduct during the war, in particular the conduct of the French Communists and their sympathizers, what Hook calls "the eloquent and, if properly construed, damning fact that the Soviet Union and the Communists everywhere had actively collaborated with the Nazis, that the French Communists had sabotaged the French war effort until Hitler took the initiative against Stalin." What made protesting against this history difficult was "the bad conscience of most Frenchmen and the seeming futility of raking up the past" (p. 731). Hook was undeterred: "Despite the myths and legends that sprang up after the liberation, there was not much of a resistance movement to the Nazis in France. In 1940 when the war seemed irretrievably lost, almost the entire population collaborated in some form or other with the Vichy government and passively accepted the occupation" (p. 730).

This was Bellow's view. "Bad conscience," he told Philip Roth, underlay French anti-Americanism:

Not only had they been overrun by the Germans in three weeks, but they had collaborated. Vichy had made them cynical. They pretended that there was a vast underground throughout the war, but the fact seemed to be that they had spent the war years scrounging for food in the countryside. And these fuckers were also patriots. La France had been humiliated and it was all the fault of their liberators, the Brits and the G.I.s.[41]

When patronized and subjected to ignorant prejudice about America, Bellow thought of the conduct of the French during the war. On July 16 and 17, 1942, a mere six years prior to his arrival in Paris, 13,152 Jews were rounded up in the Vélodrome d'Hiver, just south of the Eiffel Tower, and sent to concentration camps. Of the 42,000 Jews in France who were deported to the camps, only 811 returned. This figure came from an article of July 22, 2012, in the *Guardian* reporting on a speech given by François Hollande at the site of the Vélodrome. Not one German soldier was mobilized for the roundup, known to the French as the Vél d'Hiv Rafle. The entire operation, the article reports, was conducted by French police "said to have worked with an enthusiasm that surprised the German occupiers who had commanded them."[42] Hook mentions in his "Report" that the evening session of the International Day was held in the Vélodrome d'Hiver, but says nothing—may not have known—of its connection to the Rafle.

WHAT BELLOW SAW AS the nihilism of modern French literature and thought, of existentialism in particular, he linked to atrocities like that of the Vél d'Hiv Rafle. The Paris years forged the link. While conceding the thinness of American culture, "I was aware also of a seldom-mentioned force visible in Europe itself to anyone who had eyes—the force of a nihilism that had destroyed most of its cities and millions of lives in a war of six long years. I could not easily accept the plausible sets: America, the thinning of the life impulses; Europe, the cultivation of the subtler senses still valued, still going on."[43] This awareness helped to sink "The Crab and the Butterfly." Bellow had arrived in the city with "several hundred pages of manuscript." The grimness of those pages deepened in the Parisian *grisaille*. "I was terribly downcast," Bellow recalled to Roth. "Thinking my gloomy thoughts beside the medicinal Seine and getting no relief from the great monuments of Paris, I sometimes wondered whether I shouldn't be thinking about a different course of life. Maybe I should apprentice myself to an undertaker."[44] Even "The Trip to Galena," a chapter of "The Crab and the Butterfly" he approved of, explains why he might feel this way. Weyl, the character meant to make the case for life in the novel, has a peculiar way of going about it. What he recounts of his past makes him sound a familiar type: alienated, ruthlessly honest or "authentic," violent, more like Joseph in *Dangling Man* than Leventhal in *The Victim*. Weyl's sister, Fanny, though of similar temperament, chooses, like Simon in *The Adventures of Augie March*, to marry into money and respectability, urging her brother to do so as well. Where Augie is tempted, Weyl is adamant: good faith outweighs not just material but moral considerations: "I'd take up anything I thought feeling had stayed in. If in the right things, okay. If not, I wouldn't have stopped at grave-robbing" (p. 782). Yet nothing moves him. "I was bored," he confesses, "but because I'm energetic, energetically bored, melancholy. And if there's anything I hate, it's that romantic Hamlet-melancholy. I despise it. I despise it in myself" (p. 791). Speaking of himself in the third person, Weyl declares: "If he can't keep himself going a little under the angels, he ought to be a nihilist" (p. 792).

But Weyl already is a nihilist or has been one. He recounts a senseless act of violence committed as a soldier in Rome at the end of the war. Unprovoked and perfectly sober, Weyl smashes a whiskey bottle over the head of a man he'd stopped to ask for directions. "What was the reason?" asks Scampi; Weyl replies:

> I haven't found out. Maybe it was my personal act of war. Or an idea that a man is bound to do everything in his lifetime. . . . Yes, it must have been my act of war, since I was there, to do something lousy and hateful on my own, and did it spontaneously, a piece of violence in my personal quality. Since I was on the ride of the world, to ride the hateful thing through. All right, I joined; I became a member. I signed up with the blacks, if you like. It doesn't make any difference, does it? (p. 793).[45]

The echoes here are of Camus's Meursault in *The Outsider* or Gide's Lafcadio in *The Caves of the Vatican*, even of Céline's Robinson in *Journey to the End of the Night*, a book Bellow read and admired in his early twenties. In Paris, Bellow read Céline's *Les Beaux Draps*, appalled by its virulent anti-Semitism. "By putting a hand to my neck," he told Alice Kaplan in a letter of August 9, 1991, "I can still feel the hackles those fine sheets raised." Though "a superb writer," Céline was "nihilism plus," "impossible" as a human being. In an interview with Bellow, Norman Manea recalls reading somewhere "that in the first period in Paris, after the war, you were speaking about Céline and Sartre in the same way" (he has in mind the first Botsford interview, in which Sartre's essay on Frantz Fanon is described by Bellow as "trying to do on the left what Céline had done on the right—Kill! Kill! Kill!").[46] "In Paris," Bellow replies, "I had friends with whom these were the subjects that were discussed, not only Céline and Sartre but all of those European ideas and subjects." Céline's Paris "was still there" in the late 1940s, he writes elsewhere, "more *there* than Sainte-Chapelle or the Louvre."[47] In "The Trip to Galena," Céline's presence is evoked by Weyl's belief that "the ride of the world" is inevitably "hateful," or that to live life fully is "to ride the hateful thing through," as if journeying "to the end of the night." In Paris, more strongly than ever, Bellow came to see this view as wrong, both morally and in fact. The ride could be exhilarating, funny (though not in Céline's way), even heroic, an idea hard to square with a protagonist like Weyl. For Bellow, "lousy and hateful" acts, no matter how "spontaneous" or invested with "personal quality," remain lousy and hateful. As the critic Daniel Fuchs puts it: "Weyl is an instance of the negativism he resists. He lacks the liberating tone and that tone would come only with the creation of Augie March."[48] Though in "The Crab and the Butterfly" Bellow made use of a currently fashionable negativism, "there was something in me perhaps of a Jewish origin which had nothing to do with nihilism, I was terribly downcast and writing about a hospital room, and coaxing a dying man to assert himself and claim his share of life."[49] Being stuck with Weyl was like suffering a debilitating disease.

IN LATER YEARS, Bellow's view of the French and of Paris mellowed. In "My Paris" (1983), written for *The New York Times Magazine*, he recounts several warm memories of the city from the late 1940s, mainly of the Left Bank, to which the family moved in late April or early May 1949, when "the old auto-racer and his wife came back from the Côte d'Azur."[50] On the Left Bank there were cheap bistros, small bookstores, "dusty old shops in which you might lose yourself for a few hours," stationers who carried "notebooks with excellent paper," an umbrella merchant with "sheaves of umbrellas and canes with parakeet heads and barking dogs in silver." It was enjoyable "wandering about, sitting in cafés, walking beside the liniment-green, rot-smelling Seine." At such times Bellow could feel, as the French put it, "*aux anges* in Paris." But there was no question of the city molding or "finishing" him: "I was already an American, and I was also a Jew. I had an American outlook, superadded to a Jewish consciousness. France would have to take me as

I was."[51] As he wrote to Sam Freifeld in a postcard of May 28, 1949, not long after moving to the new neighborhood: "we're here still and not Frenchified"; he himself was "more stubbornly barbarian than ever."

According to Laure Reichek, the French wife of Bellow's painter friend Jesse Reichek, the new apartment the Bellows moved to at 24 rue de Verneuil in the Seventh Arrondissement, was "warm, comfortable, full of old French furniture." It was five minutes from Bellow's writing room in the Hôtel de l'Académie on rue des Saints-Pères, and a further five minutes from the cafés of Saint-Germain: Deux Magots, Flore, and Le Rouquet, Bellow's favorite, at the corner of Saints-Pères and Saint-Germain.[52] Bellow's routine in Paris was to write until late afternoon, lunching in his room on sandwiches put up for him at home by the *bonne à tout faire* and carried to work by him in his briefcase. Then, as he explains in a letter of December 5, 1949, to Oscar Tarcov, "I go home, shave, play with the kid a while, go out along the Seine, read in a café, etc." Two afternoons a week Bellow and Reichek would meet at Le Rouquet to play casino, speak Yiddish, drink cocoa, and discuss art and culture, discussions remembered affectionately by Bellow as lectures from Reichek "on Giedion's *Mechanization Takes Command* and on the Bauhaus" (Reichek had been a student of Moholy-Nagy in Chicago).[53] Saint-Germain in the late 1940s, as Janet Flanner describes it, sounds a little like it is today. In a journal entry of June 23, 1948, she likens the area to "a campus for the American collegiate set. The Café de Flore serves as a drugstore for pretty upstate girls in unbecoming blue denim pants and their Middle Western dates, most of whom are growing hasty Beaux-Arts beards." The bar at the Pont Royal, "which used to be full of French Existentialists," is now full of American tourists "often arguing about Existentialism."[54] A year later Bellow echoes her description in a letter to Bazelon of July 10, 1949: "You're lucky not to be in the big tidal crowd that washes the stones of St. Germain des Prés. The French complain that they can't hear French in the Quarter any more. The Americans complain of the same thing. The 'old residents' are sore about the influx, and everybody is ungrateful." In the same letter he lists the New York intellectuals who have been through: "Milano [Paolo, a friend from Greenwich Village and *Partisan Review* circles, the dedicatee of *The Victim*] arrived two weeks ago. Now, Will Barrett is here. Uncle Clem [Greenberg] and Phillips are expected soon, so we're not out of touch with the old country. I'll never be a real expatriate because I'm always glad to see them."

Most of Bellow's friends in the Paris years were American. After serving in the war, Jesse Reichek arrived in 1947 from Ann Arbor, where he'd briefly taught first-year design. He came to Paris to paint, but in order to qualify for the GI Bill he enrolled in the Ecole des Beaux-Arts. When he discovered that he would be required to attend classes five days a week, he transferred to the Académie Julian, in the rue du Dragon, which was happy to take his money and leave him alone to paint. Reichek met Bellow through another painter, Charlie Marx, described by Laure Reichek as "the only New York Jew in the group who had money." Marx and his wife, Caroline (née French, from the pharmaceutical company, Smith, Kline, and French), lived in a spacious two-bedroom apartment at 33 rue Vaneau, where the Bellows would eventually live.[55] In a letter of December 5, 1949, to Oscar Tarcov, Bellow blamed his lack of French acquaintances on the fact that "you have to make an enormous effort to justify yourself to the French and prove that you're not a barbarian at best and a pain in the ass at worst." In the unpublished story "Nothing Succeeds," set in Paris in 1948, the narrator describes the French as "irritable, rancorous, tremendously susceptible to boredom, tremendously equipped for bickering, infighting, vexation and spleen."

> *Oh! C'est marrant, agaçant, emmerdant. Il a du front, du toupet. Il me rase, il me casse les pieds.* . . . As pleasantly as I knew how I asked a man on the Champs Elysées to direct me to the rue de Berri. He said with a terrific smile that he hadn't the slightest idea where it was. Actually it was about fifty feet ahead, the next street up. . . . Where was the rue de Berri? He said smiling, in a perfect rapture of nastiness and capturing a splendid opportunity "Je n'ai aucune idée!" But this was typical, and it was real.[56]

Rue Vaneau, five or so streets southwest of rue de Verneuil, had a distinguished literary and intellectual pedigree. Karl Marx had lived at number 38, Ernest Renan at number 29, Antoine de Saint-Exupéry at number 24. When the Bellows lived at number 33, a large apartment building, André Gide lived nearby, at 1 bis rue Vaneau, where Camus had briefly lived; Eduardo Paolozzi, the Scottish sculptor, and Nicola Chiaromonte also had apartments in number 33.[57] Bellow got to know the street while still at rue de Verneuil; sometime toward the end of 1949 he gave up his writing room at the Hôtel de l'Académie and rented a room at number 33.[58] The building was owned by the French wife of a Swedish sea captain, Janine Lemelle, a "jolly" woman who not only liked Americans but was a decent landlady. That she once owned a bookshop ("hers was a literary house") was also in her favor, as was the fact that she brought Bellow coffee twice a day. At some point, Bellow struck up a deal with her, agreeing to install a gas hot-water heater in her kitchen in exchange for two months' rent: "It gave her great joy to play with the faucet and set off a burst of gorgeous flames. Neighbors came in to congratulate her. Paris was then in what Mumford called the Paleotechnic Age."[59] Among the congratulating neighbors were two American painters, Margaret Stark and Jane Eakin, who also rented rooms from Madame Lemelle and who became friends with Bellow. Other artists Bellow met, again mostly American, belonged to a set centered on Jean Hélion, a French painter long resident in the United States, and his wife, Pegeen Guggenheim, also a painter, the daughter of Peggy Guggenheim. Ulrich "Jimmy" Ernst, another painter, the son of Max Ernst and Pegeen Guggenheim's stepbrother, was connected to the Hélion set. Laure Reichek remembers meeting Richard Wright and the choreographer Merce Cunningham at parties at the Hélions', which were less grand than Kappy's parties in Montparnasse. "Kappy was upscale," recalls Laure. "I remember seeing on the grand piano a spray of roses in a crystal vase. Who can afford a whole branch or spray of roses, something you buy in a fancy flower shop?" Bellow was on the periphery of the Hélion circle but Laure remembers him engaged in animated discussions with her husband and other painters on such topics as "the function of art in the modern world, the limits, if any, to artistic subject matter."

Nicola Chiaromonte became a good friend of Bellow's in this period. They had known each other in New York, through both *Partisan Review* and the Europe-America Groups. Chiaromonte was ten years older than Bellow, a man of great charm and warmth, though as William Phillips puts it, "given to periods of silence especially with talkative people—a trait that reinforced the role of saint assigned to him by many of his friends."[60] This role William Barrett, Phillips's coeditor at *PR*, explains: Chiaromonte "had lived through, or actually fought in, all the major conflicts of the time about which most of the intellectuals in New York had only argued."[61] In 1934, he left Rome for Paris, where he was briefly associated with anarchist movements; two years later he flew with André Malraux's Republican squadron, becoming the model for the character Scali, an art-historian-turned-bomber, in Malraux's novel *Man's Hope* (1937). After fleeing occupied France for Algeria, where he befriended Albert Camus, Chiaromonte came in 1941 to New York, where he met his second wife, Miriam, and supported himself by writing not only for *PR* but for *The New Republic*, *Atlantic Monthly*, and Dwight Macdonald's *politics*. After the war, in 1947, he returned to Italy, where he wrote theater criticism for the liberal weekly *Il Mondo*. When Bellow visited Rome in February 1949 to get away from rue Marbeuf, he looked Chiaromonte up.[62] Later that year, Chiaromonte returned to Paris to live, writing the "Paris Letter" for the February 1950 issue of *Partisan Review*.

In addition to living in the same apartment building as Chiaromonte, Bellow saw him at parties at the Kaplans', in the cafés of Saint-Germain, and on visits to the Russian-born Italian writer and political philosopher Andrea Caffi, who occupied rooms below Bellow's room in the Hôtel de l'Académie. It was Chiaromonte who brought Caffi to Paris from Toulouse, where he had been active in the French resistance. Chiaromonte was the courier for monies from the Europe-America Groups, and it was these monies that in 1948 helped to pay for Caffi's relocation to Paris and subsequent rent and expenses. Caffi interested Bellow because he so thoroughly fitted the image of the European intellectual émigré. Born in 1887 in St. Petersburg to Italian parents, he was trained as a historian (in Berlin, with Georg Simmel), was fluent in several languages, an accomplished Greek scholar, devoted to books and learning. Caffi had formal manners, loved conversation (with men, he disliked women), and passed most of the day "in bed drinking coffee and writing learned notes to himself." What money he earned came from work as a reader for Gallimard and from articles for Dwight Macdonald's *politics*, written under the signature "European." "He was tall but frail," Bellow recalled, with "an immense head of hair, and a small nervous laugh, but he was a serious man."[63] To Lionel Abel, "Caffi represented, and tried in his own way to re-establish, the kind of atmosphere that may have prevailed in the circles of atheists and libertines in the seventeenth century, and the salons of the *philosophes* in the eighteenth."[64] "Caffi was the guru," said Kappy, speaking of the older man's relationship with Abel and other disciples. "For a year," Abel wrote, he saw Caffi at the Hôtel de l'Académie, "almost every day at lunch and dinner."[65] Bellow took Caffi seriously. "I listened to Mr. Caffi when he described America as the new Rome," he told Roth. "I was deferential and respectful, aware that he was trying to do good, to raise my mental level. He did as much for his Italian disciples—his helpers. They brewed his coffee and moth-proofed his winter clothes."[66] Much of Caffi's talk was political or historical. His bête noire was what he saw as the nineteenth-century notion that genius was unsociable or even antisocial. He spoke and wrote eloquently of the miseries of life in Russia under the Stalinists. In 1917, as an Italian journalist in St. Petersburg, he spent much of his salary feeding starving children.[67] Abel recounts how the Italian poet Ungaretti came to visit Caffi at the Hôtel de l'Académie with Italy's ambassador to France. Ungaretti's mission was "to ask Caffi's forgiveness for the poet's support of Mussolini under fascism."[68] Kappy—known to Caffi as "Ka-Plan Marshall"—was no disciple, but he, too, was a frequent visitor. Soon after Bellow began work on *Augie* he gave Caffi pages to read. "He's a real writer," Abel remembers Caffi saying, pleased to find the young American novelist free of what, speaking of Joyce, he called "the hubris of modernism."[69] "When one of his visitors said that I did not seem to be getting what an American should get out of Paris," Bellow recalled, "M. Caffi wisely replied that it was only natural that I should be thinking of America most of the time."[70]

IT WAS DURING the Paris years that Bellow paid his first visit to England. In the autumn of 1949, William Phillips came to Paris on a Rockefeller grant, accompanied by his wife, Edna. The Phillipses saw a lot of the Bellows that autumn, and just before Christmas they and Bellow traveled to London together. Anita's work, as well as the needs of five-year-old Greg, kept her in Paris, where she had a job at the American Jewish Joint Distribution Committee (JDC), a relocation agency for European refugees. At first she worked in its child care department, visiting orphanages, "trying to teach the directors what we do in America . . . [though] I never even saw an orphanage in America" (Greg remembers accompanying her to work one day and visiting an orphanage, a place with "long, bleak, frightening corridors"). After six months she was "promoted to the medical dept . . . conducting a survey of the chronically sick in France—who are receiving aid from J.D.C. It brings me into contact with all the Jewish clinics in Paris."[71] Greg, meanwhile, enrolled for a second year of kindergarten, to avoid a French elementary school, though he remembers being "completely bilingual and able to entertain adults by imitating Americans trying to speak French."[72] In a letter to the McCloskys, the source of her quotes about the JDC, Anita writes of Greg that he "goes to school in the morning and I am home for lunch"; that he adores the Danish girl who takes care of him; and that Anita feels guilty about being away during the week and spends "all Saturday and Sunday with him—as a result I have no time for myself." This is as close as she comes in the correspondence to complaining about her circumstances, about missing trips or being stuck at home.

Arriving with the Phillipses in London on December 16, Bellow planned to stay for "five or six days."[73] Shortly thereafter, Cyril Connolly, editor of *Horizon* and a *PR* contributor, threw a party for them. "The room was filled with bright talk," Phillips remembered, "which the English appeared to have invented, and the overall effect was a spirited cadence in a language that was both familiar and foreign." Phillips felt "like the mythologized American primitive abroad."[74] Some months earlier, in the May 1949 issue of *PR*, the one in which Bellow's monologue "A Sermon by Dr. Pep" appeared, Connolly's "London Letter" gave some indication of what Bellow might expect. "Let us suppose," writes Connolly, "that a young novelist, we will call him Harold Bisbee, whose first novel so perfectly shaded off the social boundary between the Far and Middle West, has collected enough prize money to visit his London and Paris publishers" (p. 523). What will greet him at the party his English publisher throws for him? "As he looks round the crowded cocktail party, hugging a thimble of something warm and sweet with a recoil like nail polish remover, he will certainly observe four facts about English writers. They are not young, they are not rich, they are even positively shabby; on the other hand they seem kind and they look distinguished, and their publishers look hardly more prosperous and hardly less distinguished than they do" (p. 525). Connolly ranks the writers likely to be present: "the Sitwells are generally in the country but Mr. Eliot will probably be there, accompanied by Mr. John Hayward. . . . Towering over the rest are Mr. Stephen Spender and Mr. John Lehmann, two eagle heads in whose expression amiability struggles with discrimination. . . . About nine inches below them come the rank and file, Mr. Roger Senhouse, Mr. Raymond Mortimer, Mr. V. S. Pritchett, Miss Rose Macaulay, Miss Elizabeth Bowen, Quennell, Pryce-Jones, Connolly, we are all there" (p. 525). If he is lucky, young Mr. Bisbee will meet an English girl "struck by something poetical in his fading youth." She will take him to bed "'*sauter pour mieux reculer*,' as is the English way, and after talking about frigidity there for an hour and a half she tells him about her former lovers, and bursts into tears" (p. 526).

What Bellow reported about Connolly's party and the party thrown for him by his English publisher, John Lehmann, is that he was either patronized or cut by the people he met, and that everyone seemed to be homosexual or drunk or both.[75] "I wish I had stayed in a temperance hotel with the temperate," he wrote in an undated letter to Robert Hivnor. "Although I don't judge the inverted with harshness, still it is rather difficult to go to London thinking of Dickens and Hardy, to say nothing of Milton and Marx, and land in the midst of fairies. My publisher is one; all the guests at his cocktail party were ones; all the *Horizon* people, with the single exception of a man who apparently suffered from satyriasis, likewise at their cocktail party. This single exception was chasing Sonia Brownell Orwell. . . . It was confounding. Modern life is too much for me."[76] Bellow had not met Lehmann before; when the publisher visited Paris in September, he was out of town and Lehmann had to make do with the "inverts" Gide and Truman Capote, who had just published his first novel, *Other Voices, Other Rooms*.[77] Though Bellow didn't think much of London literary life, he liked London: "There was a fire in the Covent Garden basement, carol-singing in Trafalgar Square led by a spontaneous girl who stood on the base of a statue."[78] He records no patronizing anti-Americanisms, though William Phillips writes of being greeted by Geoffrey Gorer, whom he had never met before, with the words: "You have destroyed the monuments of Europe" (by which Gorer meant they had been marred by American GIs carving their initials or names or slogans on them). Phillips answered, as Bellow might have done, that American GIs "kept Europe out of concentration camps."[79]

IN PARIS, Bellow's American friends were mostly writers and intellectuals. He became especially close with Herbert Gold, an ambitious young novelist from Cleveland, Ohio, who was nine years his junior. Gold came to Paris in 1949 on a Fulbright Scholarship, on the eve of finishing his first novel, *Birth of a Hero* (1951). His wife, Edith, was also on a Fulbright, to study literature at the Sorbonne. Gold remembers Bellow in 1949 as "already a figure." In a 2008 memoir, he calls him, along with Richard Wright, "the most esteemed American writer in residence during my three years there, 1949–1951." Bellow was "destined to be America's new great novelist," an impression supported by his "confident and graceful lounging, on view especially at the café Le Rouquet near Saint-Germain-des-Prés." The younger writers in Paris—Gold names James Baldwin, Evan Connell, Terry Southern, Otto Friedrich, George Plimpton, and Max Steele—looked on admiringly: "We would-bees on our G.I. Bill money, our Fulbright money, our selling our clothes, cigarettes, and dollars on the black market, saw him as an Old Master in his early thirties. He had climbed the heights while some of us were still peddling hashish to gullible Frenchmen under the chic American name 'marijuana,' or serving as gigolos to existentialist millionaires, or worst of all, cadging handouts from family grinds back home."[80]

Bellow was generous to Gold and other young writers: with money ("he would always pick up the checks"), introductions, invitations to parties; he introduced Gold to Jean Hélion, the Reicheks ("Laure was young, beautiful"), Kappy, whose novel, *The Plenipotentiaries*, he recommended (Gold "didn't like [it] very much," though Kappy himself was "clever and charming and funny"). Most important, Bellow read Gold's novel in manuscript and praised it, not only to Gold but to Monroe Engel, who bought it for Viking. "Thanks to his generosity," Gold writes, "I became a published writer."[81] Gold's devotion to Bellow was noted by others in their circle. "He was like an acolyte," remembers Eileen Geist, American translator of Louis Guilloux, a French novelist long admired by Bellow: "He knelt at Saul's feet literally." Geist recalls sniggering with James Baldwin over what they saw as Gold's fawning; she also remembers Gold approaching them and saying: "I don't think the two of you like me very much," to which Baldwin replied: "Not particularly." What Gold remembers of Geist is that she and her husband, Stanley, gave good parties. "We used to be invited to the Geists a lot. They would come over. We're having Jean Genet, Saul Bellow, someone at Gallimard. We're having them for dinner. Come and have a drink." Years later Eileen told him: "If we'd known you were going to be important, we would have invited you to dinner more often." What Gold remembers of James Baldwin, who was a twenty-five-year-old unpublished novelist at the time, is that "Saul was a little sarcastic about him."[82] American literary Paris, in other words, was not unlike literary New York. Yet it is the mildness of Bellow's sarcasm Gold emphasizes: "He was hard on a dead writer like Henry James. He was hard on academic writers and critics, like Trilling. But on someone like Mary McCarthy he'd just be negligently sarcastic. I didn't see him as vicious at all. In fact, when I was being hard on the late Sinclair Lewis he disciplined me, called me to order, and actually I learned to appreciate that."[83]

Eileen and Stanley Geist, at whose apartment the Bellows were given dinner as well as drinks, moved to Paris in 1949, the same year as the Golds, renting an apartment diagonally across from the one the Bellows rented on the rue de Verneuil. Stanley Geist had been a Junior Fellow at Harvard and came to Paris on the GI Bill to write. The Geists had some money ("Our families gave us nice checks on birthdays"). Eileen worked for the Marshall Plan, the Paris office of which she remembers as "like a college campus, like the Ivy League. You had a princess—a French princess—who was the receptionist, filing. She'd gone to Bryn Mawr." Eileen was outgoing and sociable, Stanley was quiet and reserved, especially about his writing. "He was a writer who wrote," says Eileen, "but you never saw anything he wrote, except introductions and prefaces." Bellow trusted Stanley's literary taste, sent him pages, and was gratified when he praised them. "Even Mary McCarthy would show her stuff to Stanley," Eileen remembers. "She, too, trusted his judgment." What Laure Reichek remembers about parties at the Geists' is that they were crowded and racy, with lots of flirting. Being young (eighteen in 1949) and French, she was also struck by the confidence and affluence of the expatriate crowd: "Those people had good clothes. Those people could afford the best things." Kappy's wit and charm impressed her, as did his French; Eileen, a translator, called Kappy's French "perfect," "amazing." The Americans Laure met in Paris "had no inferiority complex about being unsophisticated"; their easy confidence seemed to say: "We're so powerful; after all, we liberated you."

Laure and Eileen speak fondly of Bellow in these years as sharp, attractive, full of "hilarious" jokes and stories. But they also remember him as dangerous with women. "Once I saw him with a woman," Eileen remembers, "I knew that the last thing a woman with a brain should do is have something serious with Saul Bellow." Not so much because he was promiscuous (in Kappy's phrase, "already famous for being extraordinarily busy with ladies"), as because "he was the kind of man who thought he could change women. If they weren't the way he wanted them, he could make them the way he wanted. And he couldn't.

I mean, who can? You don't." What Laure remembers of Bellow at parties is that "he would turn on the charm the minute a woman walked into the room; he expected every woman to fall flat on her back . . . and a lot of women did" (in Kappy's words: "if a woman caught his attention, you'd have a lot of trouble getting it back"). Because Laure was living with Reichek, Bellow "didn't try it on me except maybe once or twice. He couldn't help it." She attributes this behavior to "insecurity plus discontent in one's own sexual life," a view she calls "an assumption but also an observation, looking at other couples." When asked if Bellow was more of a womanizer than other men in their circle, she replied: "Yes." As for Anita, who was often at these parties, Laure remembers her as "a nice person" but "plain," though "she could have [looked good], if she thought that was important." She also remembers Anita as "not flirtatious at all." Eileen Geist concurs: "I found Anita rather boring . . . but she was very nice . . . kind of a social worker type. I don't mean that pejoratively." Anita *was* a social worker, one whose days were spent helping concentration camp survivors and orphaned children. She wanted quiet, stability. In Greg's words, she "was tired of the moving from here to there," at one point so upset with all the changes "that she simply sat down on the baggage in some train station or wharf. Saul recalled, 'I had to move the luggage and your mother'"; she could count twenty-two addresses in the fifteen years of her marriage to Bellow.[84] Her mood must also have been affected, according to Mitzi McClosky, by Bellow's refusal to give her another child, because he knew the marriage would not last. This knowledge he would not or could not bring himself to communicate to Anita, nor could he face it himself, though it was clear to all their friends.

KAPPY'S FICTION, which Bellow admired, sheds light on the sexual mores of the expatriate community during the Paris years, as well as on Franco-American relations in general. *The Plenipotentiaries* is set in Paris in 1947 and centers around a young American couple: Patricia, who works for the American Graves Registration Command, lectures on the Marshall Plan, and is mixed up in a shadowy political conspiracy; and Tony, her fiancé, recently demobilized in North Africa, who comes to Paris to study painting with Pierre Tarski, "the only new painter in the world."[85] Patricia is a New Woman, politically earnest; Kappy has described her in an interview as "the sort of liberal internationalist I was, very much a liberal, not a neoconservative, welcoming the fact that the United States had been cast in this role [as world power], which made me in my twenties an important figure in the Embassy here." Tony is earnest intellectually, pestering everyone with deep questions "about the metaphysics of Picasso, and the philosophy of *L'Etre et Néant*" (p. 4). The novel's narrator, P. W. Strauss, a much older American, is at work on a novel titled *The Plenipotentiaries*, part political thriller, part comedy of manners, like the work he narrates (the novel has several such self-reflexive touches).[86] In the nonthriller part, Pat and Tony become romantically involved with Tarski and his wife, Marie. The Tarskis love each other but have a "French" attitude to marriage: Pierre seduces Pat and Marie seduces Tony, occasioning much damaging and instructive reflection on the part of the young Americans.

Tony and Pat are the "plenipotentiaries" of the novel's title, because that is how they are treated by the French. "Will you please tell me," André Gide asks Tony, after Tony has climbed six flights of stairs to the Great Man's apartment (presumably at 1 bis rue Vaneau), "when you propose to allow the General [de Gaulle, that is] to come to Algiers?" "Like everyone else," the narrator explains, Gide "was giving Tony full powers, appointing him envoy extraordinary and plenipotentiary. We are all ambassadors" (p. 82).[87] Kappy may not have been a literal government agent, as Beauvoir suspected, but French attitudes, his fiction implies, make him a figurative one, like all Americans in Europe. "We're nothing but pretexts," Pat tells Tony, speaking of their relation to the Tarskis. "Don't you see? They batten on us in some monstrous way! They use us, or rather they use some myth we inspire, god only knows what! Youth, vitality, America—it's more gruesome than you think!" (p. 214). Contact with France endangers what the novel suggests is genuinely American about Tony and Pat, "a desire to be 'right.'" Tony explains, speaking of Americans in general: "We push forth on our odyssey with our eyes fixed on principle, for we have not yet learned how many winds there are and how powerless we shall be in the currents. When we begin to realize, the principle becomes subtler and more endearing—and that is the onset of irony." Picking up the figure of the double agent or plenipotentiary, he adds: "our mission becomes a mystery—and that, too, is the onset of irony. . . . The world's order has frontiers and rivers, passports and regulations, territorial disputes and strained relations! The double agent acquires a sense of humor!" (p. 206).

The complications of *The Plenipotentiaries* recall James's *The Ambassadors*. In Kappy's second novel, *The Spirit and the Bride* (1951), Jamesian echoes give way to Sartrean ones, the sort Bellow drew on (along with those of Dostoyevsky, Schopenhauer, and Nietzsche) in his first two novels, the sort he was to reject decisively in the Paris years. In an interview, Kappy described *The Spirit and the Bride* as "too ideological," written under the influence of "Heidegger through Sartre and Lacan." The difference between the two novels is seen in their endings. *The Plenipotentiaries* ends as *Dangling Man* does, with the issues it raises unresolved.[88] At the end of *The Spirit and the Bride*, the protagonist, John Clifford, unlike the protagonists of *The Plenipotentiaries*, or Weyl in "The Trip to Galena," seems actually to have found what he, like Rimbaud, seeks: "*La vraie vie*," "real life" (p. 127). A familiar modernist/existential descent into the void leads to breakthrough rather than breakdown. Rimbaud went off to North Africa in search of "*La vraie vie*"; Clifford seeks it in the North African underbelly of Paris, in glamorized violence and extremity. At the end of the night, literally, he is reborn, a new Adam.

> He walked up to the Place Maubert in search of a taxi. When a cat darted across the narrow street, he said to himself, gravely: *Animal I name thee cat.* The sun was already high and bright, which meant a hot day for Intra-European Payments. And there was a taxi, as Clifford saw it: *I name thee taxi.* A pity this was not Sunday, he thought wearily, as he got into the car. God rested on the seventh day (p. 245).

French thought offers a way through in the novel, perhaps because Kappy is American; for Bellow it leads to nihilism, perhaps for the same reason. The effect it has on relations between the sexes is dismaying. Clifford's marriage is described at the beginning of *The Spirit and the Bride* as lifeless. He and his wife "lived undramatically together, rather dully, in an aura of tenderness, minor irritations and boredom" (p. 8). Whether the marriage will revive after Clifford's breakthrough is left unclear.[89] In *The Plenipotentiaries*, the Tarski marriage, though not loveless, is open, which means "authentic"; as a consequence, it causes pain. Though truthful it could not be called happy. Contact with French culture splits Patricia and Tony. As for Kappy himself, French in this respect as in others (judging by his own testimony, that of his friends, and that of his unpublished autobiography), though he "adored" his wife, he was almost as "busy with ladies" as Bellow. "For some reason," he writes in the autobiography, "practically all the younger French men we knew (e.g. Camus, Merleau-Ponty, Sartre, René Leibowitz, Pierre Schaeffer, et *j'en passe!*) were inveterate Don Juans."[90] He and Celia "grew up together, we were children together. We were really in the Platonic sense one person." But under the influence of "four years away, North Africa, and the sort of prevailing ideology among us," he began having affairs. The prevailing ideology "was very stupid but very commonly accepted"; especially stupid was "the fact that you were supposed to tell all this, you had to be frank about it, that excused everything, which of course it didn't, it excused nothing. So to the insult was added the injury of this openness, to the point where the women felt obliged to do the same thing" (as Marie Tarski does in *The Plenipotentiaries*). "They would sort of force themselves to have affairs, sometimes they were inclined that way. I felt that way about my wife." The existentialist overlay to all this truth telling was clear: it was "exactly what Sartre meant when he said the world is divided, in a gross way, between the *salauds* [bastards] and the authentic people who were open about everything. . . . They all bought the whole business. . . . The most brilliant of that generation, they were all terrible philanderers. Camus behaved absolutely outrageously."

The most serious of Bellow's infidelities in the Paris years came toward the end of his stay and was short-lived. At a party at Kappy's he was introduced to Nadine Raoul-Duval. Nadine, who was twenty-three in 1950, came from a prominent French Protestant family. She had been unhappily married to Jean-Annet d'Astier de la Vigerie, a fighter pilot and hero of the resistance, himself the scion of a prominent French Catholic family. When Bellow met her, Nadine was recovering from an affair with Pierre Schaeffer (under whom Kappy had served in North Africa), having previously had a brief fling with Kappy himself (brief because Kappy, she told Atlas, was "*très marié*"[91]). Though miserable about the end of the affair with Schaeffer, she "came to my house and fell into Saul's arms" ("*Et lui?*" she adds of Bellow, in response to Kappy's quote). To Kappy, Nadine was "a smashing young lady, very dashing . . . a sort of smart-talking, very witty character who knew everybody and everything in Paris"; Eileen Geist remembers her as "beautiful and racy. . . . You just couldn't help but like her." At the time she and Bellow met, Nadine was working at *Rapports: France–Etats Unis*, a job she needed, having a small child and little income. The aim of *Rapports* was to provide what Sidney Hook called "informational re-education": to counter French misconceptions about life in the United States, the Marshall Plan, international affairs, and American culture.[92] According to Atlas, the affair with Bellow was serious enough for him to suggest to Nadine that they run off together to Africa. "He was very insistent," Atlas quotes Nadine as saying, "and so attractive that I was strongly tempted to go," though in a letter to me she insisted there was never any question of her doing so (*"J'étais une maman très normale!"*). Even had she been childless, she would not have gone.[93] As she told Kappy, when Bellow spent the night after fights with Anita, they had "a very good relationship, we make love wonderfully." In the morning, however, "feeling he should be only basking in me and thinking what he's going to do with me," she would wake to the sound of "tap, tap, tap, on the typewriter." Bellow was downstairs at work on *Augie*: "He'd never stop writing." Four years later she married the French novelist Roger Nimier.

Anita found out about the affair and was furious. Not only with Bellow but with the Kaplans. "She was outraged by all this," Kappy remembers. "She had put him through the lean times. 'I did all this. He owes me something.' Well, that's the wrong tack to take with Saul. He would not stand for that for one minute." Anita blamed the Kaplans for the affair, accusing Celia, wrongly Celia claimed, of knowing about it; Kappy himself claimed to be "busy at the Embassy" at the time, "terribly overworked," and not to have paid much attention to what was going on between Bellow and Nadine. Herbert and Edith Gold were privy to the aftermath of the affair, accompanying Bellow, who "needed to get away," on a long car journey to Spain.[94] According to Gold, Bellow "wailed and wept as we drove. He was also funny and full of curiosity about himself and knew the map." Gold's account of the trip, from his memoir, presents Bellow as miserable, furious, and wholly alert throughout, with "an almost metabolic perspicacity." By the time they reached Banyuls-sur-Mer, near the Spanish border, where they would part, Bellow's "unnerving claim for attention to his marital agonies" had exhausted the Golds: "His need was exclusive, unflagging, draining." They left him at the hotel and sat down outside under an umbrella, dreading "the meal we were about to have with him before [he] drove on into Spain." Then they saw Bellow emerge from the hotel:

He was bounding towards us with a boyish grin, hair slicked down after his shower, eyes bright and skin fresh, chipper and restored. We were drained by the sufferings he seemed to shed. He was ready for a glass of wine and a good meal of the local fish stew, and his nose was twitching as he approved of the girls on their high wooden clogs in the town square of Banyuls-sur-Mer.[95]

In a letter to Oscar Tarcov, Bellow offered a quite different account of this trip. According to him, it was Gold who talked nonstop: "He went on for a thousand kilometers about his early days, his Papa, and his Mama and his favorite games and his school activities" ("I was trying to entertain him," Gold later explained). Edith Gold's memory of the trip, as recounted to Atlas, was that "they *both* talked: 'He [Bellow] was in great spirits. We had a lot of fun.'" She remembered hearing nothing of Bellow's difficulties with Anita, only that he said he "'had to get away.'"[96] In an interview, Gold recounted the substance of Bellow's complaints about Anita, interspersed with comments of his own: "Partly that she was jealous and she had reason to be jealous, and he was just utterly bored with her. She was not literary. She was not particularly attractive, at least to me. . . . He was having a lot of affairs, he was available. . . . He married too young." Later in the interview Gold described Bellow as "very negligent, he was very impatient of her." What Bellow needed, he admitted to Gold, was to break with Anita, but he couldn't. All that is reported of the rest of Bellow's trip comes from his letter to Gold of December 16, 1997:

> I share your recollections of our trip to Banyuls. Can it be that I was then driving my own car? Or was it your car? I ask because at Banyuls I hitched a ride to Barcelona from a . . . big-hearted businessman although he didn't say what his business was. What he did say rubbing his chin was *j'ai la barbe serrée.* He took me to a cabaret in Barcelona with several exciting women. And I ate a fine dinner of seafood—to the horror of my ancestors, probably. All these nasty little creatures scraped up from the sea-mud. Next I took a ferry to the offshore islands where I chased after a lovely American woman. I'm sorry to say that this resulted in a fiasco at the moment of embrace. I am tempted to believe that Anita sent me off under some hex. Anyway, I made my way back chastened. But what really bothers me is that I can't remember where I left my car.[97]

In an undated letter to the McCloskys, written around the time of this trip, Bellow sheds indirect light on his feelings about Anita and his marriage. His subject is academic life, to which he was reluctantly contemplating a return: "I haven't been able to resist safety, and I haven't been able to rest in it." Were he to return to Minnesota, "the greatest charm of it would be living with you and Mitzi once more. But I know that I'll jump again; that I couldn't permanently stay. Because I understand that the best of me has formed in the jumps."

BELLOW MIGHT WELL BE talking of his writing here as well as his marriage, and of the decisive jump he made some months before the letter, the jump that found him his voice as a novelist. In the spring of 1949, as he was walking to his writing room, "deep in the dumps," his eye was caught by the municipal workers cleaning the Paris streets.[98] Each morning the street cleaners "opened the hydrants a bit and let water run along the curbs."[99] Bellow often told the story of what happened next, but its fullest and most finished form is found in the interview with Philip Roth:

> Well, there was a touch of sun in the water that strangely cheered me. I suppose a psychiatrist would say that this was some kind of hydrotherapy—the flowing water freeing me from the caked burden of depression that had formed on my soul. But it wasn't so much the water flow as the sunny iridescence. . . . I remember saying to myself, "Well, why not take a short break and have at least as much freedom of movement as this running water." My first thought was that I must get rid of the hospital novel—it was poisoning my life. And next I recognized that this was not what being a novelist was supposed to have meant. This bitterness of mine was intolerable, it was disgraceful, a symptom of slavery. I think I've always been inclined to accept the depressions that overtook me and I felt just now that I had allowed myself to be dominated by the atmosphere of misery or surliness, that I had agreed somehow to be shut in or bottled up. I seem then to have gone back to childhood in my thoughts and remembered a pal of mine whose surname was August—a handsome, freewheeling kid who used to yell out when we were playing checkers, "I got a scheme!"

At Joel Bellows's Bar Mitzvah, 1952. Standing, left to right: Shael and Lescha Bellows, Lynn Bellows, Marge and Maury Bellows, Jane Bellow, Sam and Nina Bellows, Joel Bellows; seated, Abraham and Fanny Bellow.

Group photo at Yaddo, 1953: (standing) SB center, Milton Klonsky to his left; (seated) Josephine Herbst (third from right), Paolo Milano (fourth from right) (courtesy of the Corporation of Yaddo)

Theodore Roethke (courtesy of Corbis Images/ Bettmann)

Bernard Malamud, 1957. "It did Corvallis [Oregon State University] great credit to have imported such an exotic. . . . We were cats of the same breed." (courtesy of Corbis Images/David Lees)

(*left*) Delmore Schwartz, center, in full flow at the White Horse Tavern, 1959 (courtesy of Getty Images, Fred W. McDarrah)

(*above*) Irving Howe, 1961. "I resented being categorized as rational: it seemed to foreclose possibilities of glamour." (courtesy of Robert D. Farber University Archives and Special Collections Department, Brandeis University)

(*above*) John Berryman, 1966. "Clean shaven then [1952], he seemed off on some other planet, and looked like a bright young corporation executive in his business suit, necktie, and glasses" (Leon Edel). (courtesy of Corbis Images/Bettmann)

Irving Kristol and Norman Podhoretz, London, 1954, in the offices of *Encounter* (courtesy of David A. Bell; photo by Daniel Bell)

Chanler Chapman, the model for
Eugene Henderson, at Sylvania
Farms, Barrytown, Dutchess
County, New York (courtesy of
Historic Red Hook)

Fanny and Ralph Ellison, c. 1960 (courtesy of
Library of Congress, Prints and Photographs Division,
from the Ralph Ellison Papers)

SB, Greg Bellow, and Jesse Reichek at Tivoli,
Dutchess County, New York, 1957
(private collection)

Ted Hoffman and
Greg Bellow, Tivoli,
1957 (private collection)

Gore Vidal on the
porch of Edgewater,
his Greek revival
mansion on the
Hudson, Barrytown,
Dutchess County
(courtesy of Getty
Images; photo by
Leonard McComb for
LIFE magazine)

Pyramid Lake Guest Ranch,
an hour's drive northeast of
Reno, Nevada (courtesy of Special
Collections Department, University
of Nevada, Reno)

Joan and Harry Drackert,
proprietors of the Pyramid
Lake Guest Ranch (courtesy of
Special Collections Department,
University of Nevada, Reno)

Pascal ("Pat") Covici,
SB's editor at Viking
(courtesy of Joan Covici)

Richard Stern, novelist and
professor of English, University
of Chicago (courtesy of *The Chicago
Maroon*)

SB, guest lecturer in Richard Stern's creative writing class, presumably in the presence of Philip Roth, though Roth is not visible in the photo, 1957 (courtesy of University of Chicago Photographic Archive, Special Collections Research Center, University of Chicago Library; photo by Morton Shapiro)

Philip Roth, Martha's Vineyard (courtesy of Ann Mudge Backer)

Sasha, SB, and Adam, Tivoli, c. 1957 (courtesy of Sasha Bellow)

SB and Adam, Chicago, 1957 (private collection)

Paul Meehl, professor of
psychology, University of
Minnesota, therapist and friend,
1966 (courtesy of University of
Minnesota Archives, University
of Minnesota–Twin Cities)

3139 East Calhoun Parkway, Minneapolis,
the last home shared by SB and Sasha
(courtesy of Alice Leader)

Ralph Ross, chair of humanities,
University of Minnesota, 1961
(courtesy of University of Minnesota
Archives, University of Minnesota–
Twin Cities)

Greg Bellow and Joseph Warren Beach,
Minneapolis (private collection)

Bette Howland, c. 1956
(courtesy of Jacob Howland)

Rosette Lamont, professor of French, a model for
Ramona Donsell in *Herzog* (private collection)

Susan Glassman Bellow
(courtesy of Daniel Bellow)

SB and Susan, Martha's Vineyard, 1964
(courtesy of Daniel Bellow)

On the beach in Puerto Rico:
Penny and Tom McMahon,
Keith Botsford, and SB, 1961
(courtesy of Keith Botsford)

John U. Nef, founding chair
of the Committee on Social
Thought, University of
Chicago (courtesy of University
of Chicago Photographic Archive,
Special Collections Research
Center, University of Chicago
Library)

Edward Shils, professor of sociology, a friend
and colleague at the Committee on Social
Thought (courtesy of *The Chicago Maroon*)

SB, 1964 (courtesy of
Lebrecht Photo Library;
photo by Jeff Lowenthal)

Bellow decided immediately to write the imagined life of this pal and his family, last seen in the 1920s. The decision "came on me in a tremendous jump. Subject and language appeared at the same moment. The language was immediately present—I can't say how it happened, but I was suddenly enriched with words and phrases. The gloom went out of me and I found myself with magical suddenness writing a first paragraph." This suddenness he figures in the language of the inaugurating experience: "It rushed out of me. I was turned on like a hydrant in summer."[100]

There is a parallel here as before with the experience of Wordsworth. A comment of Robert Penn Warren's, quoted by Bellow, explains the connection. Warren liked writing in foreign countries, "where the language is not your own and you are forced into yourself in a special way."[101] In the winter of 1799, Coleridge persuaded Wordsworth and his sister, Dorothy, to accompany him on a trip to Germany, nominally for work purposes: in Wordsworth's case to collect materials for a long philosophical poem. Coleridge spoke German but Wordsworth did not. Depressed and isolated, Wordsworth suddenly found himself writing verse about his childhood, one passage after another. Incidents from his boyhood flooded back to him, crowding out crabbed and influence-inhibited false or abandoned starts, in which "either still I find / Some imperfection in the chosen theme, / Or see of absolute accomplishment / Much wanting, so much wanting, in myself" (*The Prelude*, 1.263–66). What set in motion Wordsworth's sudden burst of creativity was a memory of himself at four, bathing in the River Derwent at Cockermouth, or standing alone, "A naked savage in the thunder shower," an image resembling Bellow's vision of "freewheeling" Charlie August yelling "I got a scheme!"[102] When he writes about this creative breakthrough in *The Prelude*, Wordsworth, like Bellow, describes the inaugurating experience as coming from outside himself: a literal "sweet breath of heaven / Was blowing on my body, [I] felt within / A correspondent breeze, that gently moved / With quickening virtue" (1.34–37). What unites Bellow's memory of Charlie August and Wordsworth's "naked savage" is a sense of being at home in the world, untrammeled: "In Paris, where [*Augie*] was being written," Bellow recalls, "it was Charlie (Augie) who resisted influence and control. Childish and fresh he sat at the checkerboard and shouted 'I got a scheme!' I, the writer, might be hampered, depressed. Charlie,

however, was immune." Bellow in Paris was less isolated than Wordsworth in Germany, knew plenty of people, had good French, but when
he later asked himself "whether I was at that time forced into myself in
a special way . . . I am able to answer in the affirmative."[103] "The Crab
and the Butterfly" was put aside and Bellow began to write at speed
what became *The Adventures of Augie March.* In an undated letter to
Volkening, written shortly after he'd begun work on the new book, he
says that though he hopes to have a first draft of "The Crab and the
Butterfly" in June, "progress has been slowed, for various reasons, one
of them being that I have been unable to hold back from *The Life of
Augie March,* a very good thing indeed."

In subsequent letters, enthusiasm increases. On June 10 Bellow
writes to Volkening to say that the first draft of "The Crab and the
Butterfly" is "almost done," and that "*From the Life of Augie March* is
the best thing I've ever written. The first is a book such as I might have
done two, three or five years ago—a good book but nothing transcen-
dent. This is why I've had the notion that it would be better to publish
Augie first." As such passages suggest, whatever Bellow's frustrations
away from the desk—with French condescension, with Anita, with the
European left—from the spring of 1949, when alone in his room at the
Hôtel de l'Académie or later at rue Vaneau, he was flying; and "home"
was Humboldt Park, Hyde Park, at dinner with the Coblins, at the
beach with Einhorn. Although Volkening cautioned him against telling
Viking that he was at work on a new and different novel, by October 24
Bellow was confessing to Monroe Engel that he had "dived into something else," on which he was working "faster than I've ever been able to
work before. I do one fairly long chapter a week, and I expect to have
the length of a book in first draft by Christmas." In the same letter, he
announces that *Partisan Review* is to publish the first chapter of the new
novel in its November issue.

The decision to lay aside "The Crab and the Butterfly" was exhilarating; by the autumn, the consequences of having done so began to
surface. If Volkening worried that Bellow was risking relations with
Viking (Engel was alarmed at first, though "impressed" with the chapter in *PR*),[104] Bellow worried that he was risking his chance of another
Guggenheim (a renewal, something then possible). His worries were
well founded: the evidence suggests that he was turned down for a
renewal because he hadn't finished the novel he said he would finish.[105]
Bellow's sense of himself as author meant there were emotional con-

sequences to laying the novel aside. On October 21, some weeks after returning from Spain, he wrote to Herb and Mitzi McClosky describing his feelings. He says nothing about his relations with Anita or other women; what he talks about is having given up on "The Crab and the Butterfly": "It was dismaying to falter when I had so much pride in going a steady pace—*at least*! You can see that I have been rattled, not to say wounded, in Europe. The whole thing is hard to give an account of, but I've had a whole breastful of ashes, not merely the Ash Wednesday sign on the forehead of Milano when he read the last chapter of the book I abandoned, say[ing] it was *maudite* [horrible]. . . . He was right, it is *maudite*." To Monroe Engel, in the previously quoted letter of October 24, 1949, Bellow describes his agitated state. After reading over "The Crab and the Butterfly," he concluded that the level of the writing "had to be raised"; if not, the book would have to be "scrapped": "I was in a state. . . . All my cherished pride in being a steady performer took a belly-whop."

Engel associated Bellow's unhappiness about giving up "The Crab and the Butterfly" with his unhappiness about his marriage. In an interview, he recalled Anita as "a very nice woman, a very capable woman and a good mother to Greg," but the world she and Bellow grew up in "was not going to be his world and I think the switch when he went from that book he abandoned to *Augie March* was part of the same thing. . . . He started travelling in a much faster world. He became less and less interested in her." At the time of the trip to Spain, Bellow may also have been anxious about *Augie* itself, for all its coming in floods ("All I had to do was be there with buckets to catch it").[106] In a letter to Bazelon of September 7, he declares: "I'm *learning now* to write. The cost is awful, in health and, possibly, sanity. . . . I'm planning to drive South alone; perhaps to Barcelona to think things over while I soak in the Mediterranean."

Once in Spain, Bellow experienced the familiar symptoms he'd experienced late in the summer of 1947 when he was stressed. When he returned from Spain they were alleviated in ways that also recalled the earlier summer: "I couldn't get any food down. I had too much heart pressure and I lost weight. I can't explain it. As soon as I returned to France I was able to eat. It seems to me, as I write, that the feelings were like those of being in love. Quite weird." In love with *Augie*? With Nadine or some other girl? Bellow's symptoms suggest ambivalence, about abandoning "The Crab and the Butterfly," about his marriage.

As in 1947, he may have feared Anita's anger and the fate of his family; not just whether the marriage would survive, but if it did, where they all would be living and on what. Presumably Anita forgave him when he returned. Very few of her letters from the Paris years survive, and those that do contain little in the way of personal revelation. In a letter of November 13 to the Tarcovs she announces matter-of-factly that "Saul has been working very hard. . . . The first chapter of his new novel is in the November P.R. I've just read chapters 2 and 3 and it's terrific. Best work he has ever done. He put away the novel he was working on last year—he was not satisfied with it. He went to Barcelona for two weeks to freshen up and get away from us for awhile. We were in Paris all summer." An undated letter to the McCloskys, written sometime early in 1950, is similarly matter-of-fact:

> Our plans for the next few months are as follows—Saul is going to Salzburg to teach at the American University then in April Greg and I are going to meet him and drive down to Italy for May–June and July and then back to Paris in August and to U.S. on Aug 29th. I've not been out of France since we've been here—I went to Nice last year—and I want to see a little of Europe before I leave—that's why we are planning a tour. Saul went to England for Christmas and to Spain in October. Now he's staying close to home as he wants to finish Augie March by spring. I don't see how he can—it's half done now and really wonderful—the best thing he has written yet.

Nothing in the correspondence suggests that Anita had doubts about the marriage. As for Bellow, though Spain was no help to his digestion, it seems temporarily to have calmed his anxieties. On December 5, in a letter to Oscar Tarcov he writes as if at ease with his circumstances. "Speaking generally, I'm in an enviable position," he admits. "I'm in France, extremely comfortable, comfortably employed, and want for nothing except some extremely necessary things which nearly everyone else lacks too. . . . When I come back from seeing Spanish cities or speak with deportees and survivors, I know there's nothing in my private existence that justifies complaint, or melancholy for myself." After quoting Genet, he declares: "Frankly, I'm sick and tired of all that kind of melancholy and boredom. France has given me a bellyful of it."

BELLOW'S SALZBURG JOB WAS in a program designed to provide "informational re-education." The Salzburg Seminar in American Studies, as it was formally known, was held annually at the Schloss Leopoldskron, in a southern district of the city. The seminar was founded in 1947 by three Harvard men: Clemens Heller, a history graduate student originally from Austria, the son of Sigmund Freud's publisher[107]; a senior named Richard Campbell; and a young English graduate instructor named Scott Elledge. The seminar's aim was to encourage intellectual exchange between American and European intellectuals and students; it was sometimes referred to as a "Marshall Plan of the Mind."[108] Though Harvard University declined to fund the seminar, the Harvard Student Council raised money for it, and solicited private donations. Schloss Leopoldskron, an eighteenth-century rococo palace, had an interesting history. Originally the home of the archbishop of Salzburg, it passed through various hands in the nineteenth century, including those of King Ludwig I of Bavaria. After a period of dilapidation, it was bought and renovated in 1918 by Max Reinhardt, the theater director and impresario, cofounder of the Salzburg Festival. In 1938, Reinhardt, a Jew, was forced to flee Austria, and the Nazis confiscated the property. When at the end of the war ownership reverted to Reinhardt's widow, she allowed the founders of the seminar to use it for their sessions, an arrangement brokered through Austrian relations of Heller. The first seminar was held in the summer of 1947 and included among its instructors Margaret Mead, Alfred Kazin, F. O. Matthiessen, and the economists Wassily Leontief and Walt Rostow.

Ted Hoffman, the seminar's program director in 1950, figured prominently in Bellow's life in the following years. He was born in Brooklyn in 1922, studied with Trilling and Mark Van Doren at Columbia, and in 1946 took a job with MGM in its Foreign Title division. In the fall of 1947 Hoffman met and fell in love with Lynn Baker, a recent Radcliffe graduate. Baker had been awarded a scholarship to study at the Sorbonne and as luck would have it Hoffman's MGM job involved a project in Paris, to make a series of educational shorts from old newsreels. When the project was completed, a Harvard friend of Baker's, Kingsley Ervin, who knew and worked with Clemens Heller, asked her and Hoffman if they'd help run the winter program at the Schloss.[109]

Lynn cannot remember how she and Hoffman met Bellow, perhaps through Ervin, or another Harvard friend, John McCormick, a graduate student in comparative literature, who also worked with Heller (and was a friend of Delmore Schwartz's), or one of Bellow's colleagues at Minnesota, either the theater scholar and critic Eric Bentley or Henry Nash Smith, who taught at the seminar in 1949. It was McCormick who invited Bellow to come to Salzburg in April 1950. A second invitation, for the winter of 1951, was issued by Hoffman after the Bellows had returned to the States.[110]

Bellow enjoyed his month in Salzburg, "in which there was less work than other things."[111] Though scheduled to deliver lectures, he wrote to Hoffman to say that he felt discussions were "more effective, and I've had considerable experience at Minnesota whipping them up, even in large classes." The topic Bellow chose for these discussions was "American Fiction from Dreiser to the Present," and the texts assigned were e. e. cummings's *The Enormous Room*, Dreiser's *Jennie Gerhardt*, Anderson's *Winesburg, Ohio*, Faulkner's "The Bear," and "perhaps also Fitzgerald's *Babylon Revisited* and *The Last Tycoon*" (the inspiration, perhaps, of the joke letter to Volkening about meeting Fitzgerald in Montreux and Geneva). If pressed, Bellow wrote to Hoffman, he would add Hemingway's *The Sun Also Rises* to the syllabus, though "he's discussed to tatters."[112] When not in class or writing, Bellow went sightseeing in Vienna as well as Salzburg. In Vienna "the Russians were still in occupation. . . . I was fascinated, of course, I went to see the monuments . . . I didn't like Vienna much." In the pages of his memoir, *New York Jew*, devoted to the Salzburg seminar, Alfred Kazin describes the Austrians as "the most enthusiastic Nazis in German-speaking Europe." Just "down the road" from Schloss Leopoldskron was Camp Riedenberg, a transient camp for Jewish displaced persons, which Kazin visited. The city's elaborate cultural offerings unsettled him, especially those involving Jewish musicians, as when Yehudi Menuhin performed at the music festival "under the good German Furtwängler, who had led the Berlin Philharmonic all through the Hitler period."[113] Bellow's correspondence has little to say of such matters, nor do they figure in later accounts. He says nothing of the many GIs in Salzburg, headquarters of the American military in Austria. Of the students he taught—Scandinavians, Sicilians, Viennese—he speaks fondly, describing them as "overjoyed and enthusiastic," having "a hell of a good time"[114] Kazin also liked his Salzburg students, describing them in ways that recall "The Gonzaga Manscripts" and Kappy's fiction: "The European students watched the American lecturers with awe. They were the audience, and we in Europe were the main event, absorbed in ourselves, in the rich, overplentiful runaway society whose every last detail we discussed with such hypnotized relevance to ourselves. In this war-torn year of 1947, the Europeans could not help becoming aware that they were simply out of it. We *were* the main event. We were America."[115]

FROM SALZBURG, the Bellows traveled on May 2 to Venice, then on to Florence, arriving in Rome in mid-May. There they saw much of Paolo Milano, with whom Bellow was close in these years. Milano was a decade older than Bellow. He was Jewish, born and educated in Rome, but in 1939, a year after Mussolini's adoption of the *Manifesto della raza* (Manifesto of Race), he left Italy for France. When France was occupied, he fled to New York, arriving in the United States in 1940, a year before Chiaromonte. Fluent in French, German, Spanish, English, and Italian, Milano soon found work at the New School and then as professor of Romance Languages at Queens College, CUNY. He also began writing for *Partisan Review* and *The New York Times Book Review*. Although living in Rome in the summer of 1950, he did not return permanently until 1955, when he became chief literary critic for *L'Espresso*. Bellow valued Milano for his critical acumen, urbanity, and wide knowledge of European books and writers. It was Milano who introduced Bellow to Ignazio Silone, Elsa Morante, and Alberto Moravia. He also, Bellow later declared, introduced him to Rome, the January 1949 visit notwithstanding. Bellow was a reluctant sightseer. In a letter of May 22, 1950, to Volkening, he admits to being "already weary of touring and admiring. I can't abide passing through a place and visiting all the monuments as listed. Also the kid has put his ban on churches and won't enter another one. He's now seen St. Peter's, the biggest of them all, and feels he understands the principle." In a letter of June 18 to Robert Hivnor, however, Bellow writes: "This time I *saw* Rome, Paolo Milano leading." He was also, of course, writing. Every morning, for the six weeks he was in the city, he sat and wrote at an outdoor table at the Casina Valadier in the Borghese Gardens, overlooking the city from Pincian Hill. Wholly absorbed in Augie's adventures, "I happily filled several student notebooks and smoked cigars and drank coffee, unaware of the close Roman heat as long as I did not move about. A waiter later told me that the poet

D'Annunzio had enjoyed working in this same place. . . . Latterly, reading Goethe's 'Conversations with Eckermann,' I learned that the great poet composed one of his tragedies in the Borghese Gardens."[116]

In addition to guiding the Bellows around Rome, Milano recommended that they visit Positano, a picturesque fishing village near Sorrento on the gulf of Salerno, described by Bellow in a letter of July 15 to Engel as "four thousand feet of mountain descending to the Gulf in a width of about eight hundred yards." Bellow spent three pleasurable and productive weeks there, staying at the Pensione Vittoria, at a rate negotiated by Milano ("At American prices we couldn't have afforded it").[117] His morning routine at Positano was little different from that at Rome, according to the Hivnor letter: "write from eight in the morning, swim at noon; and then that lethal lunch which I'm too hungry to turn away; at three, when I'm supposed to read Hegel, my lids are coming down." "By rising early to beat the heat," he wrote to Engel, "I've written a long lot of *Augie March*; at four hundred pages it's nothing like finished. It may be again as long." A week before arriving in Positano, on June 15, Bellow wrote to Volkening about an invitation he'd received to travel to Berlin to attend "a conference of the most lofty anti-Stalinists." This was the conference out of which grew the Congress for Cultural Freedom. Bellow seriously considered going, worried that "five lotus eating weeks [in Positano] would not agree with me." His decision to stay was a wise one, given how much he got done. He even managed a rare poem, "Spring Ode," which owes as much to the inaugurating "Augie" moment as to the beauties of the Amalfi coast. It opens with a cleansing that recalls the Paris streets: "Thunder brings the end of winter, / Rinsing the yellow snow from the gutter."[118]

The route the Bellows took to Paris was lazy and circuitous. They left Positano on July 20, briefly went back to Rome, then traveled to Siena, Florence, Turin, and Grenoble, returning to 33 rue Vaneau on August 1. A month later they set sail for New York, arriving on September 4, Labor Day. Anita and Greg traveled directly to Chicago; Bellow followed a few days later. In Chicago, he visited friends and family, returning early in October to New York to find a place for them all to live, a plan arrived at after months of fruitless inquiry and speculation, mostly about university positions. Over those months, Richard Ellmann tried to get Bellow a Briggs-Copeland Fellowship at Harvard; the McCloskys lobbied for him at Minnesota; Henry Volkening sounded out Princeton ("I put Princeton last," Bellow wrote to him, undiplomatically. "I think there'd be too much chicken shit in it. My uninformed opinion!"[119]). Bellow also asked Volkening, in an undated letter, to inquire about teaching night courses at NYU. In addition, he asked him "to thank Trilling for his troubles in my behalf" (Trilling had written to Henry Moe in support of a renewal of Bellow's Guggenheim). On March 27, Bellow wrote to Robert Penn Warren to ask if he knew anyone at the New School "who could throw a little evening work my way." Meanwhile, he was waiting to hear from Bennington, Bard, Sarah Lawrence, and Queens College. On March 26, 1950, he wrote to Monroe Engel asking him to inquire of Harold Guinzburg, the owner of Viking, about apartments in the New York area (as Bellow explained in the undated letter to Volkening, "Mr. Guinzburg of Viking has real-estate in Queens and perhaps a flat for me"). If no full-time university post materialized, Bellow told Engel, he'd have to "piece out an income by teaching, reviewing, etcetera. That can't be done anywhere but in New York." Engel suggested Bellow contact Isaac Rosenfeld, at this point teaching in the Humanities Program at NYU. When Bellow did, Rosenfeld responded with "a remarkably cold note, asking me to explain why I had asked his consent to apply at NYU and at the same time had my agent approach Ross [Ralph Ross, head of the Humanities Program]. I 'had my agent' do no such thing, and I wonder why Isaac is so battlesome about it."[120] He would find out soon enough, for Ross offered him a one-year part-time job in the same program as Rosenfeld.

When Bellow returned to New York from Chicago to search out a place to live, he stayed with the Lidovs, now in a spacious apartment/studio on the Upper West Side, at 44 West 95th Street. Here Bellow kept up his writing routine, working on *Augie* each morning in a small room off Lidov's studio. Eventually, Harold Guinzburg came up with an acceptable four-room apartment in Forest Hills, Queens, and Bellow returned to Chicago in October to retrieve the family furniture from storage and help in the move east. The address of the new apartment, in a plain redbrick building, was 6608 102nd Street, a few blocks from Queens Boulevard. Herbert Gold described the building as "sad and awful and tractlike . . . a real comedown."[121] Bellow would not be there most days, having rented a room for writing in Greenwich Village, on MacDougal Alley, near Washington Square ("In those days you could rent one for three or four dollars a week").[122] That winter they were all hit by illness: "First there was a virus, and then the grippe," he wrote to the McCloskys on January 30, 1951. "I had a bad case of the latter, aggravated by a penicillin reaction. I'm only one day out of bed—flat for nearly a week, and during the breather between semesters, too, when I had planned to do so much. And then I've been forbidden to smoke, too. Permanently; I can never again have a pipe or a cigar; not even a cigarette." Soon after settling in Queens, Anita got a job at the branch of Planned Parenthood in Far Rockaway, running a birth control clinic ("another job close to her heart," in Greg's words).[123] Greg, finally out of kindergarten, was enrolled for "a few miserable weeks" in the local public school, then moved to the private Queens School, recommended by Paolo Milano and his wife. The Queens School, according to Greg, was "progressive": teachers were called by their first names, it admitted African American students (the sons of Jackie Robinson and Roy Campanella), and "no one taught me to read or write." For Anita, its chief attribute, or what would prove its chief attribute, was that it offered after-school day care: "allowing her to work after Saul moved out."

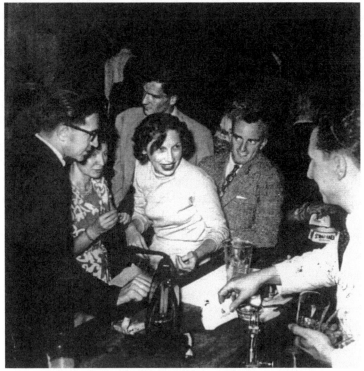

In a Paris boîte, *Kappy Kaplan on the left wearing glasses, Celia Kaplan in the center in a white sweater*

10

Princeton/Delmore

I N THE FINAL TWO YEARS he spent writing *The Adventures of Augie March*, Bellow drew heavily on recent experience, especially his time in Paris and in the Merchant Marine. While at work in the small side room off Arthur Lidov's Manhattan studio, he took the character of Basteshaw, the ship's carpenter Augie finds himself marooned with in the novel's penultimate chapter, from Lidov. In March 1950 Bellow sent Monroe Engel the first 100,000 words of the novel. Engel replied a month later with praise but also concern about control, design, shape. Bellow responded on April 30 reminding Engel that what he'd been sent was "raw mass" which hadn't yet been read over consecutively. Bellow was buoyed by what he'd written, also by how much of it there was: "the abundance gives me confidence, and wherever that and the life, the feeling of the book, are connected there'll be no pruning." Though he'd "never had such a mass to knead and shape," he had "an instinctive sense of what the finished thing will be." He even had an image for the book's shape:

> a widening spiral that begins in the parish, ghetto, slum and spreads into the greater world, and there Augie comes to the fore because of the multiplication of people around him and the greater difficulty of experience. In childhood one naturally lives as an observer. And it may be that Augie doesn't sufficiently come forward at first; but in my eyes, the general plan of the book—its length—justified this. I have a further part in mind for almost all the characters introduced. . . . Another two hundred pages and the design will be

almost entirely visible; and there will be *still* more—the second part will be again as long, with sections on the war and the life of a black-marketeer in Europe and a final, tragic one on the life of the greatest Machiavellian of them all, Augie's brother Simon.

It was Bellow's plan, he told Volkening in a letter of March 26, "to have the first large part of *Augie March* (about 120,000 words) published as the contracted novel." He thought this first half "could stand by itself," and was anxious to reveal his plans for a second half of equal length. "I could never put over this half as the whole, saying nothing about the rest. If Viking wants to wait for the whole quarter of a million words, perhaps it will extend my subsidy for another six months."

Augie's brother, Simon, makes his final appearance in the novel, the one Bellow calls "tragic," after the Mexico chapters, in scenes set in Chicago and Paris. Simon is in a jam much like the jam Maury was facing when Bellow was at work on this chapter. After release from the Merchant Marine, Augie returns briefly to Chicago. Simon is now "making real dough. . . . When he told me how the money poured in he always laughed, as if astonished himself" (p. 909). With the dough comes a mistress, Renée, "a blond doll. . . . A *zaftige* piece too, in a mink stole," whom Simon tells Augie he loves. They met in a nightclub in Detroit and "she left her husband the same night we met" (p. 908). Simon sets Renée up in a fancy apartment and sees her every day. Augie wonders about Simon's wife, Charlotte, whom he married for money and whose family helped finance his businesses. "I didn't think it would be so hard for you to understand how this is," Simon replies. "This has nothing to do with Charlotte. I don't tell Charlotte what to do. Let her go and do the same" (p. 910). Like other mistresses in Bellow's fiction, Renée is vulnerable, her sexy persona only partly fits: "she looked immature, but maybe that means that she didn't bear this gold freight with the fullest confidence" (p. 910). Nervous with Augie, Renée professes undying love for Simon. "As this may have been true," Augie writes, "it was kind of a pity that she had to throw suspicion on it by extra effort" (p. 911).

Simon is greedy, wanting both Renée and Charlotte. "I want no trouble out of you about her," he tells Renée. "I respect her. I'll never leave her under any circumstances. In her way she's as close to me as anybody in the world." As Augie puts it, "he was romantic about Charlotte too" (p. 912). Everything Simon buys Charlotte he buys Renée. He sends Renée to Charlotte's doctor, "the best doctor" (p. 913). When he and Charlotte go to Florida on vacation, Renée arrives a day or two later, put up by Simon in "as swanky a hotel" (p. 916). The money Renée costs is not the problem, the problem is logistical, requiring "constant thought and arrangement-making." Logistics poison Simon's life: "Poor Simon! I pitied him. I pitied my brother" (p. 916). Charlotte puts up with Simon's affair for a while, then demands that he end it. When he confronts Renée she screams at him and threatens him with lawyers, and when Charlotte turns up at Simon's lawyer's office, Renée curses her. Both Charlotte and Simon slap Renée ("You should have heard what she was saying," Simon tells Augie. "You would have done the same" [p. 917]), then they all burst into tears. Only when Simon offers Renée a large sum of money does she agree to go off to California. Four months later she returns saying she is pregnant and Simon calls her a crook over the phone. After a silence, she hangs up, which alarms Simon. At the hotel where she's staying, he discovers that she has tried to kill herself, and is four months pregnant. Augie learns all this from Simon in Chapter 22. Four chapters later, in the novel's final pages, Augie asks: "Did she have a kid?" "No, no," Simon answers, "it was just a bluff. There wasn't any kid" (p. 989).

But there was a kid. Charlotte takes Augie aside and explains. They are in Paris, where Augie now lives. Charlotte and Simon have come for a visit, staying at the Hôtel de Crillon.

> Simon's trouble with Renée had been all over the Chicago papers, and she took it for granted that I had read about it. . . . Renée had sued him and made a scandal. She claimed she had a child by him. She might have accused three other men, said Charlotte, and Charlotte knew what she was talking about you can be sure; she was a well-informed woman. If the case hadn't been thrown out of court right away she was ready with plenty of evidence. "I'd have given her a case!" she said. "The little whore!" (p. 989).

Simon's story was Maury's story: Charlotte, a "solid and suspecting woman in her early thirties, handsome, immovable in her opinions" (p. 988), was, as we've seen, modeled on Marge, Maury's wife; Renée was modeled on Maury's mistress, Marcia Borok, known as Marcie. A child was born to Marcie in 1947, a son she named Dean. When approached by this son, Maury rejected him brutally ("The last time I saw my old man," Dean wrote to Bellow, "he gave me fifty bucks and told me to get lost").[1] After the scandal, Bellow and the rest of the family heard nothing of Marcie, until the son read *The Adventures of Augie March* in 1980 and realized that it contained a version of his own birth. He then wrote to Bellow, who was moved by his letter, as was Bellow's brother Sam when Bellow showed it to him. The letter, which does not survive, was written from Montreal, where Dean had gone to avoid the draft. Bellow's reply, in a letter of June 17, 1980, is addressed to "Mr. Borok." It was partially quoted in Chapter 3. In it he offers sympathy and a warning of sorts (about Maury's character and how little his son should expect from him). After apologies for delay, Bellow admits that he and Sam found it difficult to picture the life led by their newly discovered nephew:

> But that's hardly strange when you think that we have no clear picture of our eldest brother's life, either. He sees none of us—brothers, sister, or his two children [by now Maury and Marge had split and he was living in Thomasville, Georgia, with his second wife, Joyce]—neither does he telephone or write. He had no need of us. He has no past, no history. . . . I tell you all this to warn you about the genes you seem so proud of. If you've inherited them (it's possible you have) many of them will have to be subdued or lived down. I myself have had some hard going with them.

Dean Borok had, indeed, inherited the family genes, judging by his looks and by the letters he wrote to Bellow over the next twenty-five years. These letters are increasingly vituperative, funny, and threatening, described by Borok himself as of "unbelievable venom and bitterness."[2] Why, Borok complains, hasn't the Bellow family—"a bunch of insignificant, petit bourgeois assholes"[3]—done anything to help him? Has his uncle not recognized his talent? Why is his life so lonely and hard? "You *never* looked this good," he writes in 1992, in a letter containing snapshots, one of himself posing in a tux, another in a Speedo. Earlier, on November 24, 1990, he sent a snapshot of himself as a ghoul, with blood running from his mouth and a large knife in his hand. "I have got it *all over you*. Eat your heart out, you rube! In terms of talent I have got it all over you." The 1992 letter ends "Eat my dust" (other letters end "Either pay me now or pay me later, you cocksucker," "Ambiguously yours," and "Love"). The letters were sent to Bellow c/o the Committee on Social Thought, on one occasion along with a box

of pornographic films, sex toys, and photographs of Borok performing sex acts with women (in Montreal he owned a leather shop called
Dean's Boutique de Cuir, specializing in S&M; later in New York he
worked as a designer of leather handbags, trained in martial arts, and
performed as a stand-up comedian, as he'd done in Montreal). Bellow,
understandably on guard, stopped writing after the initial response, but
kept Borok's letters, for legal reasons, perhaps, or to make use of in a
novel. Their anger is powerful, at times frightening, and often wittily
expressed.

Bellow knew about Marcie and Maury before he left for Paris in September 1948. Oscar Tarcov wrote to him about the subsequent scandal.
In a letter to Tarcov of June 26, 1950, Bellow laments Maury's sins
"tumbling from the closet. I knew something about them, of course,
but wasn't abreast of them all and hadn't heard about the suit till you
wrote me of it. I'd like to know more. It moves me to think of my father
in this, and of the kids." Joel Bellows, Maury's son, remembers meeting
Marcie. On Saturdays, Maury would take Joel to the Covenant Club at
10 Dearborn Street (a thinly fictionalized version of the club appears in
Chapter 21 of *Augie*, in a scene of memorable boorishness on Simon's
part). "We were walking out," Joel recalls, and "I heard this voice saying
'Maury' . . . and there was this woman, red-haired, who began to make
a fuss over me. He could not wait to get away from her. We got into
the car and he said: 'Son, you just cannot tell your mother about this.
It wasn't my fault. She came up to me on the street, blah, blah, blah.'"
Several years later, "we're down at the new Saxony Hotel [in Miami, a
hotel part-owned by Maury and Marge]. We have adjoining rooms. My
sister and I in one room, my parents in another room. 'We gotta have a
conversation . . . . There's going to be a newspaper story that comes out
and we all have to pretend that nothing happened.'" *The Miami News*
printed the story on December 30, 1949, under the headline "Blonde
Serves Club Owner as Father of Her Children." Marcie was identified
as "a twenty-year-old blonde nightclub entertainer" with two children,
a two-year-old and a seven-month-old. Maury, she claimed, was the
father of them both.[4] She followed him to Miami because he'd agreed to
adopt them, though when she arrived he backed out of the agreement.
So she served him with a subpoena, granted by one judge, overturned
the next day by another. On the night of December 30, Joel remembers,
"we walked into the dining room of the Saxony Hotel and they had
these strolling violinists and everything, and we walked in, there was

always this big buzz, two hundred, two hundred fifty, three hundred people sitting there having dinner . . . and we walked in and there was silence, silence. We just walked in as if nothing had happened."[5]

When *Augie* came out in 1953, Maury was angry to discover that the novel contained a version of the Marcie affair. He and Bellow stopped talking for a period, though Joel does not believe it was as long as five years, as has been claimed.[6] "Saul wasn't that important to my father," Joel declares, flatly, woundingly (Joel loved his uncle but his feelings are complicated by a history of legal and business disputes). Why Bellow included the episode, risking Maury's displeasure, can be explained thematically. Simon was "the greatest Machiavellian of them all" and the novel rejects Machiavellianism, with its limiting "realism" about human possibility, happiness, freedom. In Paris, Charlotte explains to Augie the origins of the affair with Renée: "If he didn't have such an abnormal idea about being happy in the first place it wouldn't have happened. Who told him he had any business to expect all that? What right has anybody? There is no such right." Augie hates talk like this, won't have it. "How much of this did Simon have to hear? If she didn't stop she'd turn him into stone. He'd have turned into stone long ago if it hadn't been for these Renées. What are you supposed to do, lay down your life? That's what she wanted from him and what she meant by 'right.'" Simon is ashamed of the scandal the affair brings, "stony with shame," wants to keep the whole thing quiet, but what, Augie asks, do Simon's sins amount to? "All they were about was his mismanaged effort to live. To live and not die. And this was what he had to be ashamed of" (pp. 991–92). These words also had a personal meaning for they were written in the midst of Bellow's break with Anita.

At the end of the fictional account of Maury's affair, Augie declares: "I love my brother very much. I never meet him again without the utmost love filling me up. He has it too, though we both seem to fight it" (p. 991). In the letter to Dean Borok, Bellow offers advice, a present of sorts. Borok's initial letter seems to have included an account of his sufferings, what elsewhere, in a letter of October 15, 1996, he calls the story of "a child left to the elements and continually kicked in the teeth by a rich and influential family." Bellow advises his nephew to write this story, "if you can find the right way to do it. . . . To get rid of it, as it were. In writing it successfully, you will forgive everyone in the process. Yes, all those who sinned against you will be forgiven. (That's what I would call a successful effort to get one's life down on paper.)"

Maury may have been angry with Bellow for fictionalizing the affair with Marcie, but Simon is depicted as suffering and he is pitied. Augie forgives him his sins, including his sins as a brother, seeing them, as he sees his own sins, as attempts to be free.

THAT THE FORM OF freedom the novel emphasizes at the end is sexual—as if it held the key to other forms of liberation—is a product not only of Bellow's own unhappiness in his marriage but of the New York milieu to which he returned in 1950. Had he stayed in Paris, to be further provoked by the French left, the political material that he cut in draft might have been retained ("I had to throw away about two hundred pages at the end," Bellow wrote to Robert Penn Warren on November 27, 1952, "and re-write them"). That material concerns Hooker Frazer, the graduate assistant in political science whom Augie meets in Chapter 11 and who turns up again in Mexico with Trotsky in Chapter 20 and then, briefly, in Paris in the final chapters. Had the Frazer material been kept, the liberation emphasized at the novel's end would have more likely been from dogma, the cult of "hardness," or the belief in politics as panacea. In the discarded pages Augie joins Frazer's political movement, the Committee for a Reconstituted Europe (CRE), funded by the millionaire Robey (a more serious figure in draft than the one Augie meets in Chapter 21 of the finished version). Frazer gets Augie to read political theory: the Greeks, Rousseau, Burke's *Reflections on the Revolution in France*, John Stuart Mill.[7] In the course of discussing this material, Frazer criticizes liberals for their lack of "hardness." He calls the concentration camps a sign of serious intention as well as hateful. At this point Augie snaps, already disillusioned by his experiences working for CRE in Spain (experiences later made use of by Bellow in "The Gonzaga Manuscripts"). What is now clear to Augie is that "the Germans were destroying the subject itself of politics." He will have nothing more to do with Frazer and CRE.

Daniel Fuchs thinks Bellow cut this material from the final version of *Augie* because it was too serious, both for the novel as a whole and for its hero. Augie's response to Frazer "sounds more like Artur Sammler on Hannah Arendt than it does Augie March of the final version."[8] But the cut may also reflect new thinking on Bellow's part. By ending with Simon's shame, the novel emphasizes the power of internalized social constraints rather than political ones, a power Bellow calls "tragic" in the letter to Volkening. Augie alludes to this power in his initial description of Renée. In her role as mistress, Renée presents herself in the line of "*femmes galantes*, courts of love, Aquitaines, infantas, Medicis, courtesans, wild ladies." That she only partly succeeds in doing so comes as no surprise to Augie: "You may think that for this all you have to do is surrender to instinct. As if that were so easy!" (p. 911). The difficulty of surrendering to instinct, of overcoming inhibition, is not a major theme in *Augie*, though it became a central preoccupation in the novels that followed. In *Augie* external impediments, material needs and values, predominate. In New York, however, where the political material was discarded and the final chapters rewritten, it was the internal obstacles to life and freedom that mattered most to Bellow, money worries notwithstanding.

These obstacles also predominated in the lives of Bellow's friends. The late 1940s and 1950s were for Isaac Rosenfeld "the most painful in his life."[9] His literary star was fading, his fiction was stalled, his personal life was a mess. Steven Zipperstein, Rosenfeld's biographer, summarizes the journal entries for these years: "Among his more persistent themes was his fear of homosexuality. He connected it to his aggression towards men, his jealousy, his incessant womanizing. This fear meshed with periods of dark depression. He fell ill with maladies that seemed psychosomatic, suffering flus and fevers that were often accompanied by frustratingly long periods of listlessness."[10] Bellow was Rosenfeld's colleague at NYU from 1950 to 1952 and a frequent object of his envy and aggression. "I'm jealous of him," Rosenfeld wrote in an undated letter of 1950 to Tarcov, "and I think he is of me; I'm ready to admit it, but I don't think he is. . . . He's poured everything into his work, which seems to be all he lives for. He's really very sad and the 'literary figure' and the self consciousness don't hide it."[11] According to Zipperstein, Rosenfeld felt burdened "by Bellow's sense of him as having failed literature; he spoke of Bellow with anger and disappointment, something akin to the hurt of a failed lover."[12] Bellow speaks of Rosenfeld in comparable terms. "As to Isaac," he wrote to Tarcov on March 26, 1952, "you know how I've always felt about him. But . . . this past year, I changed considerably toward him, tired of being envied and grudged every bit of success or imagined success. I finally became angry. Making every allowance possible, his bad luck and difficult life, my own vanity and conceit, I still resent his not too well hidden hope that I fall on my face."

Before Bellow got to this point, he made several attempts to rekindle the friendship. The most important of these attempts was to take seriously Rosenfeld's enthusiasm for the theories of Wilhelm Reich. As he explained in the interview with Norman Manea: "Some of the most extreme eccentrics in Greenwich Village were doing it [Reichian therapy] at the time, including a very close friend of mine, Isaac Rosenfeld, whom I loved dearly. I did almost everything he did, or he did what I did."[13] To Atlas, Bellow downplayed his Reichianism: "I enjoyed it as a game then being played . . . I didn't want to lose Isaac when all that was happening. So I went through the analysis, too, just to stay close." To Philip Roth, he said he undertook the therapy "because [Rosenfeld] insisted that I had to have this done, since he was doing it. About three years. Once or twice a week. . . . And it was a link between Isaac and me. I felt that I could not let him go through this without going through it myself so that I would know what was happening to him." The evidence, however, suggests other motives for Bellow's involvement, motives connected both to the wider application of Reichian theory and to personal difficulties on Bellow's part, including difficulties of a sexual nature.[14]

The appeal of Reichian theory was widespread and fascinating. Reich, whose parents were Jewish, arrived in New York in 1939 at the age of forty-two, only days before the outbreak of war. In Vienna and then Berlin, he had gained a reputation as an apostle of sexual liberation. Such liberation, he claimed, would cure mental illness; it would also defeat fascism. In *The Function of the Orgasm* (1927), a book well known in the 1940s in Greenwich Village (it was translated into English in 1943), Reich declared that "there is only one thing wrong with neurotic patients, *the lack of full and repeated sexual satisfaction*"[15] (his italics). This satisfaction was to be attained through the right kind of orgasm, sometimes referred to as "total orgasm." Soon after arriving in the United States, Reich invented a device he called an "orgone energy accumulator," a five-feet-high wooden box or cabinet, lined with metal and insulated with steel wool. This box, he claimed, could improve a person's orgasms, increasing the body's capacity to absorb what he called "orgone energy," a mysterious life force circulating in the atmosphere in the form of waves or currents or rays. The orgone box trapped orgone energy ("How the energy penetrates the metal, we do not know," he conceded).[16] By sitting naked in the box, a patient "accumulated" this energy in concentrated form, in the process dissolving social and cultural constraints, known as "character armor."[17] Reich claimed that one could feel "sexual excitation" when absorbing orgone energy. He also claimed that the orgone box was effective in treating cancer, radiation sickness, and minor physical ailments such as varicose veins and psoriasis. When cures to these ailments failed to material-ize, Reich blamed atomic energy, everywhere feared at the time, which he said "aggravated" the orgone energy.[18] Reich was convinced of the scientific basis of his theories. He lobbied the Atomic Energy Commis-sion at Oak Ridge, Tennessee, to test the orgone box as a possible cure for radiation sickness. He even persuaded Albert Einstein to investigate the box. It took Einstein two weeks to dismiss Reich's theories.[19]

Yet the theories thrived, particularly among intellectual and bohe-mian types who were disillusioned with politics. Paul Goodman praised Reich in an influential article entitled "The Political Meaning of Some Recent Revisions of Freud," published in July 1945 in Dwight Macdon-ald's *politics*, a month before the bomb was dropped on Hiroshima. Erich Fromm's *Escape from Freedom* (1941), which influenced Bellow's *Dan-gling Man*, borrowed liberally from Reich, without acknowledgment. By 1947 Reich's Orgone Institute Press was selling four to five hundred copies of his books a week. Orgone boxes were used by Norman Mailer, J. D. Salinger, Allen Ginsberg, Jack Kerouac, and William Burroughs. Christopher Turner, in *Adventures in the Orgasmatron: Wilhelm Reich and the Invention of Sex* (2011), quotes Alfred Kazin: "Everybody of my generation had his orgone box, his search for fulfillment. There was, God knows, no break with convention, there was just a freeing of one-self from all those parental attachments and thou shalt nots." Turner also quotes Philip Rieff in *The Triumph of the Therapeutic* (1961): "The artists and the writers who followed Reich were, like him, defeated men of the left; for the defeated who, nevertheless, retained their pride of alienation, Reich's brave announcements of the end of politics turned failure into a kind of victory." James Baldwin, looking back on the late 1940s and 1950s, offers a related account of Reich's influence, in an essay entitled "The New Lost Generation" (1961):

> the discovery of the orgasm—or, rather, of the orgone box—seems the least mad of the formulas that came to hand. It seemed to me ... that people turned from the formula of the world being made better through politics to the idea of the world being made better through psychic and sexual health like sinners coming down

the aisle at a revival meeting. And I doubted that their conversion was any more to be trusted than that. The converts, indeed, moved in a certain euphoric aura of well-being, which would not last. . . . There are no formulas for the improvement of the private, or any other, life—certainly not the formula of more and better orgasms. (Who decides?) The people I had been raised among had orgasms all the time, and still chopped each other with razors on Saturday nights.[20]

Bellow suspected that Rosenfeld was drawn to Reichianism by anxieties about his sexuality. "He was haunted . . . by an obscure sense of physical difficulty or deficiency, a biological torment or disagreement with his own flesh."[21] Rosenfeld was later to admit this openly. As he told Mitzi McClosky, in Zipperstein's paraphrase, "never had he managed to satisfy Vasiliki sexually and she openly acknowledged that this was the case."[22] Atlas quotes an unnamed acquaintance on Rosenfeld's therapy: "He goes to Queens for fucking lessons."[23] That related anxieties troubled Bellow in this period is suggested by his failure with the "lovely American lady" in Barcelona, a result of "fiasco at the moment of embrace" (a failure implicitly attributed to guilt: "Anita sent me off under some hex"). For both men, Reichian therapy also promised an end to more general anxieties. According to the writer and critic Ted Solotaroff, therapy helped Rosenfeld "struggle against the pettiness and defensiveness and prevarications of the ego for the larger claims and possibilities of existence," claims and possibilities "of one's instinctual life."[24] Bellow pursued the instinctual life warily. Rosenfeld pursued it recklessly, though self-consciously. "Isaac could be serious while clowning," Bellow recalled in a letter of August 11, 1990, to George Demetriou, a lapsed Reichian who had written to ask about Rosenfeld's therapy. "He half-laughed at himself while he declared that he was a fully orthodox Reichian." So committed was Rosenfeld to Reich's theories of sexual experimentation that he urged his four-year-old son, George, to touch the little girls he played with in Washington Square Park, to put his hand down their panties.[25] He tested the beneficial powers of his orgone box by growing tomatoes inside it to improve their taste. He put his neighbors' sick pets inside his box (he put his cat inside it to cure it of diarrhea, to disastrous effect). Friends with headaches were encouraged to wear a "shooter," an absurd apparatus invented by Reich consisting of what Bellow described as a "tin crown" with an inverted funnel attached. A rubber hose issued from the spout of the funnel and connected to a small orgone box, enabling the shooter "to focus rays on colds, scratches, and cuts."²⁶ Reich invaded Rosenfeld's work and his relationships. His book reviews, in Mark Shechner's words, "appropriated Reich's bioenergetics dualisms to gauge imaginative success: organism versus mechanism, potency versus rigidity, flow versus blockage, release versus restraint."²⁷ At NYU, Rosenfeld turned his literature classes into seminars on Reich's theories. He talked about sex to everyone he met, took many lovers, and encouraged Vasiliki, his wife, to do likewise, to the detriment of their marriage ("It was," recalls Monroe Engel, "very puzzling, because the night they announced they were going to split, they couldn't take their hands off each other"). At one point, Vasiliki admitted to Mitzi McClosky, she was even "naughty with Saul."²⁸

Some months after Bellow's return to New York in 1950, he installed an orgone box in the apartment in Queens. Though Reich encouraged followers to purchase boxes through authorized agents, Bellow got his from Herb Passin's brother, Sidney, a carpenter and set designer in New York, who built one for Rosenfeld as well (Kazin describes Rosenfeld's box as like "a cardboard closet or stage telephone booth" standing "in the midst of an enormous confusion of bedclothes, review copies, manuscripts, children, and the many people who went in and out of the room. . . . Belligerently sitting inside his orgone box, daring philistines to laugh, Isaac nevertheless looked lost"²⁹). Soon after installing his box, Bellow began Reichian therapy. "For two years," he told Manea, "I had this nude therapy on the couch, being my animal self. Which was a ridiculous thing for me to have done. . . . What attracted me was that it was the mind-body idea, that it wasn't just my mind but my body that made me what I was."³⁰ From childhood Bellow had believed facial and bodily features, gestures, and movements were indicative of character, a belief he never lost. The belief he lost—only entertained seriously in these years—was in the curative power of untrammeled instinct. In the interview with Manea, he recalls what initially attracted him to Reich's ideas and what he soon came to see as their dangers:

The Freudians were only interested in the mind to the neglect of the body and the theory of this analysis was that your neuroses took some physical form, some muscular form. So if you wanted to know who you were and what you were going through and all the rest of it, then you had to take off every scrap of clothing until you became familiar with the physical expression of your neurotic characteristics. A lot of foolery, but at the time it held a lot of appeal for me. I don't know why it did. I know it was very destructive. . . . It had a very bad effect on me. First you learn to give in to your temper and then you find you can't control it. So there were some bad scenes on subway platforms, when people would challenge me and I was ready to fight at any minute. Absolute nonsense. I'm lucky I wasn't killed.

Rosenfeld's therapist, Richard G. Singer, practiced on the Lower East Side.[31] Bellow's therapist, Chester Raphael, practiced in Queens, in Forest Hills, near Bellow's apartment and Reich's first American residence, where he set up the Orgone Energy Laboratory in his basement.[32] Raphael and Singer had been pupils of Reich and both were MDs. Bellow began therapy with Raphael early in 1951, two years after Rosenfeld began with Singer. In a letter of August 11, 1990, to Demetriou, who had also been a patient of Raphael's, Bellow confessed that he had long tried to write about his therapy: "Chester and his room have been going round and round in my head for decades now. I can't say that I came away empty-handed." What he came away with were some eight hundred pages of unpublished manuscript. These pages comprise draft material for two unfinished attempts at a "Zetland" novel, "Charm and Death" and "Zetland and Quine," and the unfinished "Far Out," discussed in Chapters 4, 6, and 7. In the "Zetland" novels the patient in therapy is Zetland himself, a character based on Rosenfeld; in "Far Out" he is Peter Vallis, whose character and situation resemble Bellow's. All three novels are set in the early 1950s, and all three depict a therapist named Dr. Edmund Sapir. The manuscripts are undated but were mostly composed in the 1970s, twenty or so years after Bellow's sessions with Dr. Raphael.[33]

"Far Out" begins by reflecting on the postwar period, a time when "the world seemed to pause and breathe awhile" and "here and there" people "took it on themselves to diagnose the dreadful trouble and find remedies for it—generous people, often very thoughtful, often greatly deluded, but intent nevertheless on doing the right thing, the thing that would deliver us. . . . " The ellipsis here is Bellow's; it ends the novel's first paragraph. What follows is an eighteen-page account of a therapy session, versions of which appear also in the two "Zetland" manuscripts. As Peter Vallis journeys on the subway to Dr. Sapir he tries not to prepare himself: "Anxious trying was part of his problem. What was needed was that he should be entirely and naturally *himself*. There was your challenge" (p. 1). Vallis takes off all his clothes and lies down on the plastic couch "still warm from the body of the large girl who preceded him." Dr. Sapir sits beside him on a low chair. In Reichian therapy, talking alone is inadequate. "The methods were violent, the treatment was harrowing. And the breaking out was sexual because the locking in was sexual." The therapist is trained to uncover "character-neuroses . . . physically expressed in muscular tensions." These tensions are revealed "in your posture, your face, your eyes, your breathing, your voice, your sexual performance. Everything about you, what you liked or disliked, whether you were open or disguised, true or phony depended on the degree to which you were armored. Hence nakedness" (p. 2). Vallis knows the theory behind the therapy, has "studied the major books, Dr. Reich's *Character Analysis* and *The Function of the Orgasm*, and mastered the underlying principles" (p. 5). Reichian therapy involves "taking great risks, gambling with his sanity. . . . So he was not toying." "To go back to the base, the creature of flesh and blood, and make another start, biologically" is its aim; to succeed is possible only if "you were not used up, if your instincts were still by some miracle alive after so much starvation and abuse" (p. 6).

Dr. Sapir's office and consulting rooms are in the basement of his house, a nondescript brick villa in a street of nondescript brick villas (a style Vallis describes as "Mick Tudor"). The consulting room is "windowless, insulated, soundproof," so that "you could rant, curse, sob, scream, kick or pound with your fists" (p. 5). Sapir's manner impresses Vallis, being "always earnest . . . medical and correct" (p. 7). When he speaks doctrine or theory, however, he becomes "a True Believer and a jargon-grinder." Vallis takes only what he thinks he needs: "the vital aura, the large alert eye, the incredible strength and rootedness of the out-twisting hair. No secret filth. No Mask" (p. 8). His own mask is hard to unfix, hence his discomfort on the couch:

> Immediately he was not himself. He was artificial. That was the paradox. Nudity produced a crisis. Heart pounding, dimming sensations in the head, muscles stiffening, genital shrinking, shortness of breath, sweating, distraction. Gripped by intense anxiety he lay on the couch and waited. Here a common man would be superior,

more master of his natural self. Any animal, cat, dog, could lie calmly breathing. When Vallis took his small son to the zoo, there was the tiger in luxurious heavy rest, fully, calmly, drawing breath (p. 9).

"Heavy" is good, what Keats called "a fine isolated verisimilitude." It recalls Dahfu, king of the Wariri, in *Henderson the Rain King* (1959), "sumptuously" at rest (p. 241).[34] Henderson's faith in Dahfu's methods of instruction (he's being readied to succeed Dahfu) is unillusioned, like Vallis's faith in Dr. Sapir's method. That Dahfu's teachings are "Reichian" has frequently been noted:

> For his sake I accepted the discipline of being like a lion. Yes, I thought, I believed I could change; I was willing to overcome my old self; yes, to do that a man had to adopt some new standard; he must even force himself into a part; maybe he must deceive himself a while, until it begins to take; his own hand paints again on that much-painted veil. I would never make a lion, I knew that; but I might pick up a small grain here and there in the attempt (p. 373).[35]

In *Henderson the Rain King*, Dahfu's "therapy" is physically life-threatening: he insists on Henderson entering the den of Atti, a lioness. Vallis's therapy in "Far Out" is threatening psychologically. "You don't look well, Mr. Vallis," Sapir begins. Vallis admits to feeling mean, cramped, knotted, out of control. Sapir surveys him again: "I see a sullen, closed-up, vindictive looking man." When Vallis tries to explain, Sapir cuts him off. "Are we going to have a conversation of general interest? I've noticed how helpful you are. You supply the other person with the words he's looking for, and you finish sentences for him. You want to please, and be civil" (p. 11). The interruption annoys Vallis, which was its aim. Sapir now describes Vallis as "stung, glaring. It comes into your eyes but the rest of you is indifferent. . . . You feel nasty and venomous but you don't know how to discharge the venom." Vallis claims he is merely trying, reasonably, to consider what Sapir says. Sapir returns to the attack: "Reasonable to swallow venom? It's cowardly and dead. You're afraid to burst out. You appease me." He then describes the naked Vallis as looking like a pig: "you are quite a fellow in your suit and tie, but here, lying on your back, you look self-indulgent, overfed, without tone, porky. You lie there like a pig. How do you feel about giving such an impression?" As Vallis lies "naked and at a disadvantage" (p. 13), Sapir asks: "Is that how you lie in bed with your wife?"

> "Why don't you shut up?"
> "Why don't you tell me to."
> "Well, shut up. You're a sadistic man, a bastard."
> "Well, don't choke on it, get it out."
> "You're a shit, Sapir."
> "You don't like me much."
> "Fucking right, I don't. You're a sadist and a nasty shit."
> "Tell me, then."
> "I will. I'd like to see you dead. I could kill you myself."
> "Yes, but you're afraid of it. Why can't I hear it with some real fire, and why can't you put some voice into it?"
> Vallis cried out wildly, suddenly, "Aaaaaah!" He split his dry lip.
> "Come on, you're stifling it. I want to hear the full voice."
> "Haaaah! Aaaaa! AaaaaH!"
> "Open the throat up. You're not getting there. I want your voice to reach your feelings. Real, for once" (p. 14).

Sapir notices a purple blotch on Vallis's chest: "You're congested there" (p. 15) (the word "congested" figures prominently in descriptions of Tommy Wilhelm and Eugene Henderson, the heroes of the two novels after *Augie March*). "Then as Vallis began to think how to reorganize himself (reorganize *what?*) the Doctor said, 'Are you beginning to see how it is with you?' Vallis was beginning to see" (p. 16).

If therapy served only personal ends for Vallis, "it wouldn't be worth the bother." Like his creator, he seeks the widest possible understanding or context for his condition, "in continual pursuit of the highest frame of reference" (p. 53). Why is he the way he is? Because of his past, his family, his marriage, but also because "essential elements were gone from civilized life, and the rest going fast. The moral nature become so flabby it accepts murder. . . . In short, right and wrong are dying. Each human being an object in a universe of objects, clearly outlined by false definition, shrunken in affect, living in mysterious monstrous cities that are culturally desert and wild" (p. 17).[36] There is a parallel here with Wordsworth, who, like Vallis, denied that his return to nature, literally to the countryside after residence in France and London during the early years of the French Revolution, was a withdrawal from politics. For Wordsworth, no humane or workable politics was possible unless it was grounded in nature or human nature, much contested terms in late-eighteenth-century political polemic. Vallis, too, seeks a return to nature or the natural, through therapy, which he sees as a way of facing or understanding rather than evading recent horrors, more horrific even than the horrors of the French Revolution and Terror. For Vallis, no move against evil "could be made by a cold mind, however good its understanding. Those who believed they were thinking were only brooding about their sexual defeat. To think you had to recover potency. Your thinking now was poisoned from beneath" (p. 17).

The therapy session at the beginning of "Far Out" concludes with Sapir asking: "And how is it with your wife, Mr. Vallis?" which prompts the thought: "Oh, what a sad subject that was!" (p. 18). In a later chapter, Vallis, an academic, is quizzed by his mentor, Liston Huff, a professor of politics at Princeton, with whom he is collaborating on a book provisionally titled "A Political History of Modern Europe." Professor Huff is an extreme rationalist, has "a cold mind" (he's like Willis Mosby of "Mosby's Memoirs," who is also from Princeton). He understands the underlying rationale of Reichian therapy: modern man must return to nature, access to nature is sexual, the sexuality of modern man is blocked. What he leaves out, Vallis suggests, is what being blocked feels like, by which Vallis partly means, what marriage to Nettie, a character much like Anita, feels like: "It's not a matter of seeing stars when you have an orgasm, but rather getting nothing but disappointment from the embrace, only bitterness and ashes in your mouth. That's where the funk is, absolute crippling funk, hysterical dread, emptiness and panic." Earlier Vallis tells Huff: "I start with this state of funk. The creature as a creature sees it can't do what's demanded of it, is at the end of its tether" (pp. 86–87).[37]

GIVEN A COMPARABLE STATE of funk, Bellow was quick to accept an invitation from Ted Hoffman to return to Salzburg at the beginning of 1952, this time to deliver public lectures as well as to conduct seminars. On December 17, 1951, he set sail for Paris, spending the week between Christmas and the New Year with the Kaplans. The subject Bellow chose to lecture and conduct seminars on in Salzburg was "The American Novel from Hawthorne to the Present," with discussion not just of major American novels but of D. H. Lawrence's *Studies in Classic American Literature* (1923), William Carlos Williams's *Life Along the Passaic River* (1938), Walt Whitman's *Specimen Days* (1892), and the essays of Henry James (on Zola, Flaubert, and Maupassant). Bellow was not always an inspired or inspiring public speaker. At Salzburg, he sometimes read passages from *Augie March* instead of lecturing. John McCormick remembers him laughing delightedly while reading an episode from Augie's adventures in Mexico: "He was having a wonderful time . . . better than the rest of us."[38] Bellow was aware of his deficiencies at the podium. In unpublished manuscript material titled "Don Juan's Marriage" and "A Lover from America," attempts at what in 1953 Bellow described as "a novelette to be titled 'A Lecturer in Vienna,'"[39] the Don Juan of the title is a handsome expatriate from Minnesota named Bernage (in various manuscripts, Herman, Julian, and Ralph). In 1948 Bernage comes to Vienna with a much delivered lecture on "The American Character."[40] This lecture bores him and on the train from Paris he decides to talk instead on "Individuality in America." As a speaker, Bernage's "best was not always too good," partly because he spent little time on his lectures. In Vienna, "as usual, he was unprepared" (pp. 20–21, "A Lover from America"). "Prolific in ideas but not strong in organization" is how Bernage describes himself (p. 18). As he neither possesses nor especially values the qualities that make for good public speaking ("a clear head and a simplicity of motive"), he finds lectures "always a struggle and an ordeal." In a café in Vienna he jots down notes for "Individuality in America." These notes raise themes central to *Augie March*:

> "Individuality in America—further remarks," he began. "The pursuit of happiness, correctly interpreted, does not signify chase. Not as 'hunting bears.'" . . . "Meaning more like this: broadest instincts of creation, productivity, harmony, love and so forth, are capable of fulfillment. No guarantees against pain by Founding Fathers, but submission to pain not required. Concept of sin rejected. 'Pursuit' may be interpreted as 'Right to hope.' Many a downfall, yes. But hope returns" (p. 28, "Don Juan's Marriage").

When Bellow arrived at Schloss Leopoldskron on this second visit, McCormick was struck by his luggage: a single suitcase and "the largest typewriter I've ever seen in my life."[41] Bellow had come to write. Each morning, after a breakfast of porridge and coffee left at his door at 7:45, he worked on *Augie*. Lectures and seminars were in the afternoon, and in the evening there were concerts and social events. "I begin to love hotel rooms," he reported in a letter of January 25, 1952, to Robert Hivnor, who was taking over his courses at NYU. "Or these baroque rooms at the Schloss. Wonderful painted furniture, Bavarian flowers, etc. But they won't let me stay." If Bellow's rooms were like the poet Karl Shapiro's, which were on the same floor, they consisted of a small sitting room and an adjoining bedroom, with a view of the lake below and of high snowy mountains, one of which housed Hitler's Berghof, his Berchtesgaden mountain residence. As on his previous visit, Bellow was impressed by the students. To Volkening in an undated letter he pronounced Salzburg "good for my nerves" (though "I've paid a price daily in the classroom"). Once out of the classroom, as one student put it, Bellow "was at his best when just talking with a few people." There were writers and aspiring writers among the students: the British novelist William Sansom, several years older than Bellow, had already published a novel and a collection of short stories; Pearse Hutchinson, an Irish poet living in Geneva, especially impressed Bellow, who recommended him in an undated letter to Katie Carver, an editorial assistant at *Partisan Review*, later Bellow's editor at Viking. Bellow also got on well with the other lecturers. Shapiro, editor of *Poetry*, became a lifelong friend. In *Reports of My Death* (1990), volume two of *Poet: An Autobiography in Three Parts* (1988–90), Shapiro claimed that two female students at Salzburg had fallen for Bellow, and that one "might have spent a night with him."[42] This possibility was reported to the administration by a drama professor named N. Bryllion Fagin, who was promptly ostracized by the other lecturers.

Bernage is more Byron's Don Juan than Mozart's. In "Don Juan's Marriage," he intends to return to Paris after his lectures to marry "Françoise"; in "A Lover from America," he's already married to her. On the train from Salzburg to Vienna, in both manuscripts, he finds himself engaged in conversation with an Austrian girl who makes an obvious pass at him. This pass he reluctantly responds to: "it saddened him that habit, or conditioning so betrayed him, and yet he felt an extremely full, hot, delightful streaming and pulsating sensation, and there could be nothing wrong with that in itself" (p. 5). In Vienna he encounters Adelaide, "a girl he had met in Nice." "It might not be right for him to see Adelaide in his present state of feelings about Françoise, but there could be no harm in it provided they had an understanding." The satire here recalls Donna Julia in Canto 1 of Byron's poem: "Yet still she must have thought there was no harm, / Or else 'twere easy to withdraw her waist. / But then the situation had its charm, / And then—God knows what next—I can't go on" (stanza 15). Later, Bernage describes Adelaide as warm, boisterous, but also demanding, in a way that recalls Bellow's difficulties with "the lovely American lady" in Barcelona. "She was critical of him the first time; he made it up to her later. . . . He had only spent a few nights with her in Nice but that was enough" (pp. 12–13).

ON FEBRUARY 1, 1952, the day before he was to sail back to New York from France, Bellow wrote to Volkening instructing him to stop forwarding his mail to Forest Hills: "I have some sad things to tell you of Forest Hills . . . probably none that will surprise you." On March 18 he wrote to the McCloskys from 17 Minetta Street, off Washington Square, an apartment he found through his friend Lillian Blumberg McCall.[43] "As you can see from the above address, things are not going terribly well. Nor yet desperately unwell." Two days later he wrote again, explaining more fully: "I don't know how serious 17 Minetta St. is; I'm in the process of finding out. In November when I moved here I considered myself divorced. Now I simply consider myself calm." Bellow had spent little more than a year with Anita and Greg in Forest Hills, a year that included the trip to Salzburg and a summer during which he mostly stayed in Greenwich Village while they were at the seashore near Patchogue, Long Island ("I have to teach. I have to work on my book," he explained to Tarcov in an undated letter of 1951, "and I have some matters to work out alone"). He seems also to have given up his writing room on MacDougal Alley, taking over a cold-water flat on Hudson Street from Rosenfeld, in a shabby building known in the Village as the Casbah.[44]

Bad news on the domestic front mixed with brighter professional news. For several years a steady stream of stories and reviews—in *Commentary, The Hudson Review, Penguin New Writing, Harper's Bazaar, The New Leader, The New York Times Book Review,* and *Partisan Review*—helped to spread Bellow's name in the literary world. A play based on *The Victim* was produced off-Broadway at the President's Theater and described as "not uninteresting" by Brooks Atkinson in

The New York Times (the reviewer for *Billboard* was comparably muted in his praise, pronouncing the play "definitely not a commercial product for Broadway").[45] Less mixed good news arrived on February 27: the National Institute of Arts and Letters awarded Bellow a $1,000 grant "in recognition of your creative work in literature" (the judges were W. H. Auden, Van Wyck Brooks, Malcolm Cowley, John Hersey, and Mark Van Doren). On March 17, Elizabeth Ames, of Yaddo, the retreat for artists in Saratoga Springs, New York, replied enthusiastically to Bellow's inquiry about a stay. Since "the members of the committee are familiar with your work," she wrote, it would not be necessary to call on referees; she herself had admired his writing "for a long time."[46] One afternoon when Bellow was in Monroe Engel's office at Viking, the receptionist announced that Marianne Moore was outside; as Engel recalls, "so I walked out into the waiting room with Saul and I said, 'Miss Moore, this is Mr. Bellow,' and she said, 'Saul Bellow?' and I said 'Yes,' and she said "I like your stuff,' and he was flabbergasted and said, 'Well, I like your stuff, too.'"

The news about *Augie* was also good. In the letter of March 18, 1952, to the McCloskys, Bellow reported that the novel was "nearly done" and that the publishers had advanced him more money ($500 in January, "so I have no $ worries this summer"). At nine hundred pages, however, it would need to be cut, especially as Viking had finally decided to publish the book in one volume not two. In December an extract from *Augie* appeared in the Christmas issue of *The New Yorker*.[47] That same December, at a dinner given by John Marshall of the Rocke-feller Foundation, Lionel and Diana Trilling described Bellow as the most talented novelist of his generation (Marshall had previously turned Bellow down for a grant, after others at the Rockefeller had encouraged him); Lionel Trilling thought Bellow "virtually certain" to produce four or five significant novels over the next ten years.[48] On March 3, 1953, *The New Yorker* sought to secure Bellow as a regular writer, send-ing a $100 check "in consideration of your entering into a 'first reading' agreement," one involving "all fiction, humor, reminiscence, and casual essays" (for which accepted pieces would receive a higher than normal fee). As for the job at NYU, though it paid little (just over $2,000 after taxes), it left Bellow's days free. Meanwhile other universities came call-ing. In early April Bellow accepted a six-week post as "Visiting Writer" at Reed College in Portland, the University of Oregon in Eugene, and the University of Washington in Seattle. NYU was "miffed" when told of the acceptance, refusing to allow Hivnor to take over Bellow's classes again; to make them up, Bellow would have to cut short visits to Chicago and Minneapolis en route.

The trip out west was successful but tiring. As Bellow wrote to Volkening on April 19 from Portland, "they have me talking all day and drinking at night. At four AM they bring me home, at eight one [i.e., of his academic hosts] [is] on the phone. They get their money's worth. I sure as hell will need those five weeks at Yaddo." In Seattle Bellow met a client of Russell and Volkening, the poet Mary Barnard, a protégée of sorts of Ezra Pound. He found her a "very dim, smooth, sloping, scattered-snow type. Echoes that take their time coming back." Theodore Roethke, at the University of Washington, a bear of a man, was more voluble, especially when making the rounds of Seattle bars with Dylan Thomas, also visiting at the time. "Roethke I adored," Bellow recalled in a letter of November 9, 1972, to Barnett Singer, a young Canadian historian; Dylan Thomas, who would be dead within the year, "I admired and pitied. I couldn't keep up with them, though, for I'm not a real drinking man" (also because early each morning he was at work on *Augie*, both at the Hotel Meany in Seattle and the motel in Portland where he was put up by Reed). In Portland, Bellow had a brief affair with Alice Adams, an aspiring author, twenty-six at the time. Adams was to become a well-regarded novelist and a regular *New Yorker* contributor and Bellow supported her throughout her career. When she published her first novel, *Careless Love* (1966), he wrote on February 23 offering both praise and criticism. "It gave me a good deal of pleasure," he writes, though its concerns were narrow, about "women who live completely in relationships. . . . The woman who ends the trend will be gratefully remembered." He also admits to reading "as though the woman had been you." "It made me think of Oregon and that drunken night when you told me that I came on compulsively as a *heymish* [cozy, unpretentious] type." Adams was not the only woman to succumb to Bellow's *heymish* charms. While he was away, his Minetta Street neighbor Lillian Blumberg McCall collected his mail: "and soon my living room began to fill up with stacks of perfumed letters on expensive note paper. I could tell from the postmarks when he was getting farther from New York and when he was on his way back" (p. 113).

The most important of the literary contacts Bellow made on this first trip west was with another aspiring novelist, Bernard Malamud. In 1952 Malamud was an instructor at Oregon State in Corvallis, a land grant college that became Oregon State University in 1961, the year he took up a teaching post at Bennington. A year older than Bellow, Malamud had not yet published his first novel, *The Natural*. They met at a reading Bellow gave at the University of Oregon, got on well, and when *The Natural* was published, Bellow praised it warmly in a letter of July 28, 1952: "Every page shows the mind and touch of a real writer. The signs are unmistakeable." When Malamud died in 1986, Bellow recalled their first meeting. What struck him at the time were Malamud's "expressive eyes" and the oddity of finding so obvious a New York type in inland Oregon: "It did Corvallis great credit to have imported such an exotic. He was not an exotic to me. We were cats of the same breed."[49] The two novelists remained friends and were often linked in the public imagination. Bellow joked that Malamud, Bellow, and Roth were the Hart, Schaffner, and Marx of the American novel.[50] Had it not been for *Augie*, he might have seen a great deal of Malamud in the 1950s. In an undated letter to the McCloskys, he explains: "The U of Oregon offered me an associate professorship and a lot of money but I couldn't have set aside *Augie March*."

SOMETIME AFTER Bellow's return to New York in May 1952 he received a job offer from Princeton, "last" among prospective employers in the undated letter to Volkening quoted in the previous chapter. The offer came via Delmore Schwartz, who had recently been appointed to take over the university's creative writing program for the academic year 1952–53. R. P. Blackmur, who ran the program, had been awarded a grant from the Rockefeller Foundation to lecture in the Middle East.[51] Blackmur was a friend of Schwartz's and recommended him as his replacement; Schwartz in turn recommended Bellow as his assistant. Schwartz had been angling for a job at Princeton for several years. On learning of Blackmur's leave, he suggested John Berryman as a replacement. If Berryman wasn't available, however, "you might do worse," he wrote, than hiring "one of the children of Israel."[52] Berryman was on a Guggenheim, hence not available, Blackmur took the hint, and Schwartz got the job, at a salary of $5,000; Bellow's job, an instructorship, paid $4,200, and was agreed over lunch at Lahiere's, a French restaurant and Princeton institution (it figures, thinly disguised, in J. D. Salinger's 1955 story "Franny"). At the lunch, Blackmur talked almost exclusively to Schwartz; both were big talkers and big drinkers. Bellow was a big noticer ("saw your old pal Blackmur at Yale," he wrote to John Berryman in a letter postmarked November 23, 1960. "He drops lighted cigarettes in the furniture and slowly searches for them. This made good sport for the sober watchers. I was one"). At parties, according to the English writer Al Alvarez, Blackmur served whiskey "in tumblers big enough to wash your hands in."[53] Bellow didn't much like Blackmur, who could be nasty when drunk. In *Humboldt's Gift*, he fictionalizes him as Professor Martin Sewall, head of creative writing at Princeton. Sewell is an old friend of Von Humboldt Fleisher's, a character closely modeled on Schwartz, though also drawing on aspects of Rosenfeld and Berryman. Sewell appoints Humboldt as his replacement, and Humboldt suggests Charlie Citrine as his assistant. The three men meet for lunch at "the French restaurant" in Princeton, for Charlie to be vetted by Sewell. But Sewell "had little to say to me . . . I was an apprentice and a bit player and Sewell had treated me like one." This treatment, Citrine confesses, "made me sore. But such vexations always filled me with energy as well." Here is Citrine's initial description of Sewell: "a muttering subtle drunken backward-leaning hollow-faced man" (pp. 35–36).[54]

Once Blackmur gave the okay, Bellow's appointment had to be approved by the English Department, which tended to look down on creative types. Blackmur himself, though formidably learned, was not a scholar, had no university degree, not even a high school diploma. When appointed in 1946 as Resident Fellow in Creative Writing, he was already a literary celebrity, as both poet and critic, which counted against him; that he kept the department at arm's length also counted against him. In 1951 he was made a full professor, though unusually for professors of his day he was never offered a chair. When Bellow's appointment came before the department, it was vetted by the acting chairman, Robert R. Cawley, a Miltonist. It sailed through. Cawley talked to Robert Penn Warren, now at Yale, who assured him that Bellow "did excellent work at Minnesota"; he also interviewed "several other people, mostly students, who worked under Bellow at NYU. All reports were excellent." In person, Bellow impressed. "He has the right experience, is of the right age, and has the right prestige of publication to be a sound influence on the students here."[55]

Bellow's few recollections of teaching at Princeton are flat and unmemorable, perhaps defensive. "I met my classes and taught my pupils," he told Botsford. "Some of them seemed likeable. I wasn't over-whelmed by the Ivy League. I was curious about it. I had heard of these ivy-college compounds for class and privilege. I didn't assume a posture of slum-bound disaffection." To another interviewer, Robert Gutwil-lig, he remarked that "it was the first time I was socially inferior to my students. But that was good too" (though in what way, Bellow did not say).⁵⁶ The life that mattered for him at Princeton, as elsewhere, was at his desk, cutting and polishing *Augie*. "This week," he wrote the McCloskys in a letter postmarked September 10, 1952, "I turn the cap shut on *Augie* in his pickling mason jar and am ready to play peek-a-boo again with the universe." On November 10, however, writ-ing to Volkening, he still had five chapters to go: "Thus the Liberation comes this month" (it wasn't till January 7, 1953, in a letter to Warren, that he announced "*Augie's* finished, thank God").

The universe of Princeton which he was about to play peek-a-boo with, mostly at parties, was especially starry. Schwartz himself was a star, a fiery meteorite burning itself to bits. John Berryman, at Prince-ton on a Guggenheim, would soon shine forth with "Homage to Mis-tress Bradstreet," published in *Partisan Review* in 1953, "the poem of his generation," according to Robert Fitzgerald.⁵⁷ Edmund Wilson, a sort of Hesperus, and his wife, Elena, had taken a house in town for half the year ("an unchallenged eminence," Bellow called him, though also "a bit like Mr. Magoo . . . [not] literally short-sighted, but he had eyes only for what was useful in his projects. He also had the same gruff Magoo strained way of speaking. Partly colloquial, partly highbrow").⁵⁸ Wilson was in Princeton to deliver the Christian Gauss Seminars in Criticism, begun by Blackmur in 1949 (there were four sets of Gauss Seminars that year, each consisting of six weekly lectures followed by an hour's discussion). Paul Tillich delivered the opening set of lectures (in October–November) on "Love, Power, and Justice"; Wilson's lectures (in December–January) became *Patriotic Gore: Studies in the Litera-ture of the American Civil War* (1962); Leon Edel's lectures (February–March) were on narrative subjectivity in fiction, particularly in modern "stream of consciousness" novels; and Irving Howe (April–May) lec-tured on the political novel. The audiences for the Gauss lectures were small and select; attendance was by invitation only, issued by Blackmur. Those at Edel's lectures included Robert Fitzgerald, who helped admin-ister the sessions in Blackmur's absence; Bellow; Berryman; Schwartz;

Schwartz's wife, Elizabeth Pollet; Erich Kahler, the historian; R. W. B. Lewis, a resident fellow at Princeton;[59] and the year's other lecturers, Wilson, Howe, and Fitzgerald. Edel's recollections of the audience begin with Berryman:

> Clean shaven then, he seemed off on some other planet, and looked like a bright young corporation executive in his business suit, necktie, and glasses. Saul Bellow was working on his *Augie March*—short, slim, with his quick wit that bounced and bounded as if he were playing a fast game of tennis. Delmore Schwartz's interventions with tangential questions nearly always seemed a fireworks display. It was a high-powered group.[60]

Other literary visitors to Princeton in the academic year 1952–53 included Randall Jarrell, who had taught there the previous year, and Allen Tate and his wife, the novelist Caroline Gordon. Tate had taught at NYU with Bellow, and he and Gordon often came to Princeton to visit their daughter, Nancy, and her husband, Percy Wood, a wealthy psychiatrist. At a Christmas party at the Wilsons', when Wood extended his hand to Theodore Roethke, who was visiting over the holidays, Roethke knocked him to the floor. Someone had told him Wood ran a residential care center for patients with psychological problems and Roethke thought he had come to commit him. He had been committed before and was frantic not to be so again.[61] Arthur Koestler was a less frantic visitor. He and his wife, Mamaine Paget, had recently moved to nearby New Hope, Pennsylvania (to the excitement of Wilson, who'd been in love with Mamaine in 1945 in England). Bellow knew Koestler from Paris, where, with five-year-old Greg, he once encountered him on the Boulevard Saint-Germain. Koestler said: "Ah? You're married? Is this your *child*? And you've come to *Paris*?" He was teasing, but only partly. "To be Modern, you see," Bellow explained to Botsford, "meant to be detached from tradition and traditional sentiments, from national politics and, of course, from the family."[62] Also on the Princeton scene was Ralph Ellison, whose first novel, *Invisible Man*, had just won the National Book Award, and who "came down regularly to attend our parties." Bellow not only wrote a glowing review of *Invisible Man* in *Commentary*, but was on the committee that chose it for the National Book Award over Hemingway's *The Old Man and the Sea* and Steinbeck's *East of Eden*. He and Ellison were soon to become close friends and housemates.[63]

In addition to these starry figures, Princeton was the home or place of work of several old friends, including William Arrowsmith, Monroe and Brenda Engel, and Mel and Sylvia Tumin. Bellow had known Arrowsmith in Minnesota, when Arrowsmith was a GI studying Japanese. At Princeton he was at work on a PhD in classics. "I was very happy in his company," Bellow recalled to Botsford.[64] As for the Engels, they were around Princeton because Monroe had given up his job at Viking to write and to study for a PhD in the English Department (Pat Covici, a more senior editor at Viking, was now looking after Bellow, as he looked after John Steinbeck, Arthur Miller, and Malcolm Cowley). To Monroe Engel, who had been an undergraduate at Princeton, the local literati constituted "a real scene . . . not without its sillinesses and its troubles, but offering a lot of amiable talking, drinking, and other amusements, and occasionally some pretty aggressive moments of education."[65] One such moment involved Mel Tumin, now a professor of sociology at Princeton. Bellow had known Tumin since graduate school in Wisconsin; they had been friends for more than fifteen years. Then Tumin read *Augie* in proof, sometime in the spring or summer of 1953. "Mel was not crazy about it," Sylvia Tumin recalled, "and with Saul if you weren't crazy about it that really soured the friendship, for a long time." To the McCloskys, Bellow complained of Tumin's reaction: "too much sociological and literary analysis, I suppose, crippled him, as they do many others in reading." From 1953 onward, according to Sylvia, Bellow only "now and then" kept in touch. Though the friendship revived in the 1960s, it never recovered its intimacy.

Others who undervalued *Augie* received similar treatment. When John Lehmann, Bellow's British publisher, read the first six hundred pages of the manuscript, his focus was mostly on problems of length. Bellow exploded in a letter of July 10, 1951.

> Damn, what a letter! It surpasses anything I've ever seen. Not a word about the quality of the novel. If you can find nothing better to say upon reading *Augie March* than that you all "think very highly" of me, I don't think I want you to publish it at all. I'm not selling you a commodity. Your attitude infuriates me. Either you are entirely lacking in taste and judgement or you are being terribly prudent about the advance. Well, permit me to make it clear once and for all that it doesn't make a damn bit of difference to me whether you publish the novel or not. You have read two-thirds

of it, and I refuse absolutely to send you another page. Return the manuscript to Viking if you don't want to take the book.

Bellow

When Lehmann wrote back in protest, Bellow softened somewhat, while insisting on the special character and value of the novel. Writing on July 19, with Lehmann's letter in front of him, he passionately and without embarrassment forwarded his own and *Augie*'s claims:

> I know you haven't seen anything like my book among recent novels. I've been reviewing them; I know what they are. They're for the most part phoney, or empty-hearted, banal and bungling. I should have thought it would do something to you to see *Augie*. By your own admission you had almost finished reading the manuscript, and yet you had nothing to say about it. You were cool; businesslike, merely; you were terribly patronizing and you put me in a rage. In London you had made me feel—or tried to make me feel—that you had done me an immense favor in publishing my novels. I will *not* be made to feel that about *Augie March*. It damned well isn't necessary.

The letter ends with Bellow admitting the difficulties caused by the novel's length: "but I don't want to hear about the difficulties exclusively. As to your being treated as a salesman, I think you're under a misapprehension. It wouldn't have made any difference to me what a salesman thinks of my book."

It is possible to see the influence of Wilhelm Reich at work in these letters. In the letter of July 19, immediately after denouncing Lehmann, Bellow writes: "I think that, having blown my top, I have, for the most part, cleared the air." So sudden a mood change recalls the therapy session in "Far Out," as does Bellow's assumption that with catharsis all is forgiven. He was hardly alone in this assumption. "In recent years I have unwittingly given offense," Bellow wrote to George Demetriou on April 5, 1990. "In my day, however, hardly anybody was ostracized for speaking his mind." From the start, however, Bellow was *soupe au lait* ("the type that comes down as fast as he boils up" [Augie's self-description, p. 441]). His volatility, like the "mad fear of being slighted and scorned" felt by Joseph in *Dangling Man*, was an inheritance from his father and his family ("a people of tantrums," to use Joseph's phrase) (p. 107). It was a tendency exacerbated by early struggles against father and family, by the restrictions of his background, by prejudice, and by his immediate circumstances in the early 1950s (the protracted dissolution of his marriage, guilt over his son, worries about money). Over and above these factors, however, stood a perfectly defensible conviction that *Augie March* was a work of power and originality. He was damned if he would let pass any slighting or lesser valuation.

BELLOW'S SENSE OF his importance as a writer, of the importance of writing itself, and of the suffering it entails, was fed at Princeton by those to whom he was closest, beginning with Delmore Schwartz. Schwartz's doomed charisma, as *Humboldt's Gift* memorably attests, fascinated and moved Bellow, and was clear early on. When William Phillips first met Schwartz, shortly after *Partisan Review* published "In Dreams Begin Responsibilities" (1937), he "felt immediately . . . in the presence of a strange and possessed being, endowed with some extraordinary nervous and intellectual energy. . . . He was always moving, twitching, talking, intense and excited, his eyes looking for your response to him. Yet he was affable and friendly, almost ingratiating, with a kind of clumsy and persistent charm."[66] "In Dreams Begin Responsibilities" was written when Schwartz was twenty-two. When William Barrett read it, he was taken aback by how good it was and how mature: "here was something completely formed and wonderfully perfect."[67] The dust jacket to Schwartz's fourth book, *The World Is a Wedding* (1948), a collection of stories, bore praise from Wallace Stevens, William Carlos Williams, Hannah Arendt, John Crowe Ransom, and Mark Van Doren.

Blackmur had known Schwartz in Cambridge in the 1930s, when Schwartz was a graduate student at Harvard and Blackmur a freelance critic and poet. In 1949, shortly after Blackmur arrived at Princeton, he invited Schwartz to give one of the first Gauss Seminars (Schwartz spoke on T. S. Eliot, who had himself been "much impressed" by "In Dreams Begin Responsibilities"[68]). Schwartz was teaching creative writing at Harvard and in the summer of 1950 was invited to teach at the Kenyon College School of Letters, with William Empson, Robert Lowell, L. C. Knights, Kenneth Burke, and Allen Tate. He returned to Kenyon the following summer, where his students included Richard Howard, John Hollander, and Hilton Kramer. He himself, however, was blocked. *The World Is a Wedding* had been his first book in five years, and included stories long in print, among them "In Dreams Begin Responsibilities." He could not finish the novel or any of the stories he was working on, producing dozens of unfinished drafts. Though in 1950 he published a volume of poems, "by 1952 he was confessing to John Berryman that he hadn't written a line of verse in years."[69] He quarreled with Philip Rahv and broke with William Barrett. He attacked his great booster Allen Tate (for awarding the 1949 Bollingen Prize to Ezra Pound, a decision Bellow also deplored). Chief among Schwartz's many grievances was the failure of his writing to make any money. When *Time* magazine praised *The World Is a Wedding*, according to James Atlas, in his biography of Schwartz, Schwartz calculated that "even if only 10 percent of *Time*'s three million readers read the review, and only 10 percent of those purchased the book, he would sell 30,000 copies."[70] Only 3,500 copies had been printed, but "two years later less than half the edition had been sold."[71] That serious writers went unrewarded in America, despite their heroic struggle against what he saw, in Atlas's phrase, as "the seductions of mass culture and middle-brow culture,"[72] became an obsession with Schwartz. As his own power to write receded, he devoted more and more time to fantastical schemes to secure literary funding, sinecures, influence, for himself in the first instance but for others as well, including Bellow.

In early December 1951 Schwartz and his wife, the novelist Elizabeth Pollet, moved from New York to a dilapidated three-bedroom farmhouse in rural New Jersey, a few miles from the village of Baptistown. The aim of the move was to lead a quiet writing life, away from the distractions of literary society. But at the time Schwartz was neither quiet nor capable of writing anything but letters. As Atlas puts it, "once they settled in, he became as harried as ever."[73] Schwartz had borrowed money to buy the farm and a used car, and to cover expenses Elizabeth had to find a job in Princeton. James Laughlin of New Directions, Schwartz's publisher, advanced him $1,000 toward the farm and went on to help in other ways, prompted in part by the many manic letters Schwartz sent him. Here's a representative passage from a letter of January 19, 1952, written before the job at Princeton materialized:

> My life at present consists of an imitation of all the difficulties encountered by Laurel & Hardy, Abbott & Costello, Hercules, John Berryman, and anyone who was ever drafted into the army. I must rise at 5:30, drive 33 miles with Elizabeth to Princeton's

Art Museum where she is employed, waste my diminishing life and day gassing away with the literati all day while my wife works for our food, gasoline, and kerosene, lunch lavishly at Princeton's most expensive restaurant at my own or my wife's expense since the installed literati won't eat anywhere else and think it rude of me not to go with them, etc. At 5, I drive Elizabeth back to our country estate and when we get home after driving over unfamiliar country roads in the dark I am so enervated and exasperated and exacerbated by all that occurred that I get good and drunk which makes me feel untroubled by the fact that the pump has broken down every other day, the windshield wiper on the car does not work, there is no heater in the car, and I am not in all truth a native country boy.[74]

In addition to getting good and drunk, Schwartz took drugs, both barbiturates and amphetamines, as he had for many years. By the time of the Princeton job, he had developed such a tolerance for amphetamines that on some days he needed twenty Dexedrine pills just to counter the barbiturates. To quote Atlas again: "hyperactivity and compulsive talking were not simply character traits, as Delmore's memoirists have supposed, but symptoms at least in part induced by his dependence on Dexedrine. Moreover, the notorious paranoia that dominated his last years was aggravated—and could even have been induced—by amphetamines. His violent rages and suspiciousness conform to patterns of what is known as amphetamine psychosis."[75] The effect of drugs and alcohol on Schwartz's appearance was marked. Eileen Simpson, Berryman's wife, recalls seeing him for the first time after several years rushing to catch a train at Princeton Junction: "The little running steps propelling him forward in jerky starts and stops were slower now that he had put on weight. The head was as noble as ever, and the shy smile of greeting as engaging, but the hangover he said he was suffering from (a quotidian affliction now) only partly accounted for the puffiness in his cheeks, his mottled complexion and, most disturbing of all, a haunted look in his darting over-alert eyes that I had never seen before."[76]

That Blackmur could hand over his fiefdom at Princeton to a man in such a state, and that the Princeton English Department approved the appointment, is variously explained. Schwartz could be brilliantly funny and smart. In Irving Howe's words, "he was still a wonderful talker, a first-rate literary intelligence—the sort who can light up the work of a poet or novelist with a single quick phrase." He could also be gentle and tactful when dealing with young writers, as Howe knew from personal experience. As a literary mover and shaker, he had influence, for all his instability, boasting, again as Howe recalls, of "holding down five jobs without working at any of them."[77] In the summer before Bellow came to Princeton, Schwartz had become what Atlas calls "an impresario of journals and committees."[78] Laughlin invited him to serve as a "confidential literary consultant" to *Perspectives U.S.A.*, a Cold War periodical funded by the Ford Foundation. His salary as a consultant was $100 a month. Laughlin also invited him to serve as guest editor of a future issue, with a budget of $2,500. Later in 1952, he upped the salary to $550 a month, recommending Schwartz as consultant to "Intercultural Publications," the Ford Foundation subsidiary set up to oversee its Cold War publications. At some point Schwartz received a further $220 a month to serve as consultant to *Diogenes*, a journal published in four languages by the International Council for Philosophy and Humanistic Studies, and funded by UNESCO. One day a week Schwartz hurried to Princeton Junction to catch a train to the city, as on the occasion Eileen Simpson recounts. There he'd rush from the cramped *Partisan Review* offices in Astor Place to the Hotel Pierre on the Upper East Side, home to *Perspectives*. It was not true that he did no work at these jobs: in addition to weekly visits, he sent out a stream of long advisory letters. Counseling foundations and editors and moneymen about articles and authors fed Schwartz's hunger for wealth and power.

Schwartz was hardly alone in his instability: Romantic notions of the poet as tortured genius were in vogue in America. "Ted was not in his right mind," Eileen Simpson wrote of Roethke. "Cal [Lowell] in Salzburg, had gone clear out of his again. Delmore had changed so heartbreakingly one could no longer use the word 'crazy' in the old innocent way when talking about him."[79] John Berryman was the least stable of the lot. To Leslie Fiedler, "they were all Stradivarius violins . . . and at any moment a string could snap."[80] Simpson quotes Wordsworth's "Resolution and Independence," from which she drew the title of *Poets in Their Youth: A Memoir* (1982), on her years with Berryman: "We poets in our youth begin in gladness / But thereof come in the end despondency and madness" (lines 48–49). She might also have quoted earlier lines: "As high as we have mounted in delight / In our dejection do we sink as low" (24–25). Or in our rage: "Where the rage comes from I don't altogether understand," Berryman wrote to his mother in a letter of April 12, 1953: "I think it may be an unavoidable concomitant of a certain kind of intolerably painful, exalted creation. Any artist not a saint, that is, who loves humanity as much, while torturing himself as much, as I did during parts of the composition of the poem . . . may be bound to take it out on humanity."[81] For Schwartz, the extremes suffered in creation were in the service of mankind, offering "deliverance" or "redemption" from a debased modernity, what Wordsworth calls "a state of almost savage torpor." Hence his conviction that poetic suffering was a product as much of neglect as of heightened sensitivity, poets being, in Shelley's phrase, "unacknowledged legislators of the world."[82] In "The Vocation of the Poet in the Modern World," an essay published by Karl Shapiro in the July 1951 issue of *Poetry*, Schwartz exhorts the poet to "dedicate himself to poetry, although no one else seems likely to read what he writes; and he must be indestructible as a poet until he is destroyed as a human being."[83] Irving Howe recalls being dismayed by such notions. Schwartz and Berryman made him feel "deplorably, even amusingly, sane: if they wrestled with chaos, I surrendered to coherence. . . . I resented being categorized as rational: it seemed to foreclose possibilities of glamour." As Howe saw it, "Berryman, Schwartz, and Bellow formed a haughty young aristocracy of letters, devoted to the stress of their temperaments, bound together by a fraternity of troubles."[84] These troubles were what art demanded of the artist. Bellow had his share of troubles but his life was nothing like as unstable or tormented as those of Schwartz or Berryman. Yet Howe is right to see all three writers as "devoted to the stress of their temperaments." "Not anything I'm terribly proud of" is how Bellow recalled his Reichian therapy when interviewed by Philip Roth, "but you could not keep your respect for yourself if you had not faced the ultimate rigors."[85]

BELLOW'S TROUBLES CAME to a head over Christmas. In the late spring and summer of 1952, sometime after he returned from the trip west, relations with Anita briefly improved. While at Yaddo in June (for two weeks not five) he instructed Volkening's secretary "to go back one address on her list and send my mail to 6608 102nd St. Forest Hills. Wish me luck at that address. I'll do all I can to make it permanent, and hope it is where happiness means to lead me." In the September 10 letter about turning the cap shut on *Augie*, he reported to the McCloskys that "all the Bellows live and flourish." The letter to Volkening on

November 10, however, ends disquietingly: "You know what makes everything happen? Love, Henry. You ought to know that by now. Only Love is married to Hate, isn't it? You know, a new mythology ought to go good. Ambivalence is their little daughter who lives on the shores of the Superego, etc." By the end of the year the little daughter had disappeared. On December 28, just out of the hospital, having been laid up over Christmas with viral pneumonia, Bellow wrote to Sam Freifeld that "the situation is bad. Her rigid unlovingness has driven me out—that and nothing else. I've done my best to stay and often I've felt that either going or staying threatened me with death. So I tried to choose the braver and at least less ignominious death."[86] To Robert Hivnor, now teaching in Portland, he wrote that he was "trying to make life tranquil and not think of my family, of the last chapter of *Augie* which needs redoing, of various assignments, of money, of education or of love." In an attempt to discuss less painful subjects, he writes of Bart Leiper, who has turned up as an editor at Bantam Books. "He seems fine," Bellow reports, adding "if only he didn't gossip about me to Anita!—but here I go again." When the breakup finally came, Greg Bellow recalls, "my mother was shattered." Though it "had been coming for years," Anita "hoped, in vain, that the marriage would not end."[87] Sometime in this period, Anita's seventy-nine-year-old mother, Sonia, alarmed at her daughter's unhappiness, took the train east to try to sort things out. It was too late: Bellow had left for good. He and Anita had been married for almost eighteen years. They were both thirty-seven and Greg was eight.[88]

In Princeton, Bellow boarded in the spare room of a large ground-floor apartment belonging to an associate professor of English named Thomas Riggs III. According to Eileen Simpson, it was this room Roethke took over "for a week or so" at Christmas when Bellow was in the hospital with pneumonia, and to which he was hustled back after knocking down Percy Wood. The address of the apartment was 12 Princeton Avenue, minutes from the campus; Bellow's room was furnished with a cot and towering bookcases. Blackmur also had an apartment in the house, as did R. W. B. Lewis, who lived across the hall; the Berrymans lived around the corner at 120 Prospect Avenue, directly opposite Mel and Sylvia Tumin. Early in the term, until the final break with Anita, Bellow lived with Riggs only on teaching days; there was also a period when he was nomadic, moving between Riggs's place, the Schwartzes' farm, and friends in the Village. When eventually he moved in full-time, he and Riggs became close friends. "He was a heavy drinker—multiple personal defeats, a despairing character. He died in the next year—the year following—when I was no longer at Princeton. I was laid low by his death—by the circumstances of his life."[89]

Bellow made several attempts to depict a Riggs-like character in his fiction. Riggs is the model for Kit Quine in "Zetland and Quine," with whom Zetland boards, and for Christopher Rood in "Far Out," with whom Vallis boards. Both Quine and Rood teach in the Princeton English Department, both drink too much, suffer from failed marriages, are shaky and depressed. According to local gossip, Rood, in "Far Out," "married an angel who gave him the works"; he also had "a very bad war . . . was finally sent back from Italy on a Section Eight," much to the distress of his stern father, who "served with distinction in 1917" (p. 43). Rood is Old Princeton, WASP in manner, though his family background is Catholic. Riggs, too, was Old Princeton; his father, Thomas Riggs Jr., studied engineering at Princeton and, like Rood's father, "had been on Pershing's staff, and later was Governor General of something or other—Alaska, perhaps" (Riggs's father was governor of the Alaska Territory, appointed by Woodrow Wilson). Like several WASP characters in Bellow's fiction (Ilkington, for example, in "The Old System," who enters into a property deal with Isaac Braun), Rood is reserved, especially about his feelings, "could never in the world tell Vallis what his trouble was. Or anyone" (p. 55). He has a sister, Claudine, a "flaming hardnosed woman" (she served in the Marine Corps during the war) who seems to have inherited their father's character, "but with the accident of a single chromosome. Unsex me here!" (p. 60). The sister looks after their aged mother, who drives her mad; she wants her brother to take over the mother's care. In "Zetland and Quine," Kit's mother lives "about a block up the way" and his sister tells him: "If you can put up your Jew chum, you can take mother off my hands" (p. 30). Riggs, too, had a difficult elderly mother who lived in Princeton and was looked after by his sister, Elizabeth, as also by helpers, one of whom, a young Irish girl, recalled her over twenty years later, in a letter of March 1, 1976: "I didn't like the lady (most people didn't) and I didn't stay with her too long."[90] The helper remembered playing Scrabble and Snap with Riggs and Bellow. In "Far Out," Sally Flavin, also Irish, looks after Rood's mother, and occasionally drops by after dinner to play Hearts or Old Maid with Vallis and Rood. "She shuffled the deck with pre-nubile innocence and told Irish anecdotes with the Irish turn of phrase which pleased Vallis, and Rood even more [Rood teaches Synge and Yeats at Princeton]. She was the blessed pure-in-heart, to them" (p. 35).

Zetland rooms with Quine two days a week. He thinks Quine needs therapy—but then he thinks everybody needs therapy. In "upperclass professorial gentile Princeton," Zetland decides, "repression itself was repressed. Here genteel America pronounced itself guilty of failure and sentenced itself to boredom in these roomy, fusty, fine, gloomy houses." Zetland is impressed by the trees in Princeton. Unlike the cottonwoods of Chicago, the "monumental Princetonian elms . . . rose beautifully over the streets and made a second interior of the street, under yellow and rust leaves." The light they filter into Quine's apartment is yellow. In late afternoon, "he and Quine sat with drinks in this yellow light" (p. 17). Zetland tells Quine about Dr. Sapir and Reichian theory and finds he can "talk more freely to Quine than to the intellectuals in the Village" (p. 32). One night he hears Quine sobbing in his sleep, and from that night no longer suspects him of "overdoing" his unspoken suffering. The sobs are "nightmare cries, yelps, soft yelps . . . sometimes doglike and sometimes resembled the weeping of a young girl" (p. 26). In "Far Out," Vallis and Rood are comparably close; Vallis makes clear the difficulties in his life, particularly in his marriage:

> He must give up the settled life he had laid out for himself. Funda-mental mistakes had been made. . . . Vallis had become accustomed to Nettie's good order, but a kind of heaviness went with it which had to be resisted. Getting away from her was no bad thing, but Vallis was uneasy about the boy. Nettie invariably told him that Harry asked for him. She had reasons of her own for doing that (p. 24).

Rood, too, sobs in his sleep and Vallis describes these sobs as an "appall-ing self-betrayal, this *other* voice." In both manuscripts, the appearance of the Riggs character is conveyed in deft touches. Quine's eyes "bulged slightly from his thin gentle face. He shaved carelessly. There were specks of dried blood on his chin and tufts of whisker on his throat" (p. 42); Rood, too, has "crusty scratches on his face, and his chin and jaw were burry, bristled" (p. 51). Both Quine and Rood are bald; as Rood sobs in his sleep, Vallis notes "the red vulnerable head sweating, too frightened even to turn" (p. 49).

Nothing is said in either manuscript about parties, though Riggs, according to Bellow, loved giving them. In the Botsford interview, he describes these parties as "open-house . . . in the old-fashioned Greenwich Village style. People in large numbers tramped in and out, noisily eating and drinking and smoking, looking for useful contacts, gabbing, putting on the make. . . . Edmund Wilson was absolutely delighted with this Village revival; he adored Riggs's parties."[91] The parties were for the Princeton literati, plus an occasional promising graduate student. Robert Keeley, one such student, later United States ambassador to Greece, among other countries, describes the parties as racy. His girlfriend, soon to be his wife, came along and was pursued by both Bellow and Berryman. The best known of the parties at 12 Princeton Avenue was given just before Christmas by Bellow rather than Riggs, to celebrate the publication of the excerpt from *Augie* in *The New Yorker*.[92] Eileen Simpson remembers arriving at the party with Berryman, after a more typical Princeton gathering, "where there had been a lighted tree, milk punch and carol singing." The music that greeted them at 12 Princeton Avenue "was the growl of a saxophone," the atmosphere was raucous and charged: "We entered a dimly lit smoke-filled room where people were standing around with no-nonsense whiskey and gin drinks in their hands." Bellow approached them "with an open-mouthed smile which made one smile in reflex. He seemed to be the only person present who was in a genial mood." Argument was everywhere: "ripostes whizzed back and forth like tracer bullets through the murky atmosphere."[93]

At some point during the party Schwartz walked into the kitchen to see Elizabeth, his wife, reach into the jacket pocket of Ralph Ellison for a match. Ellison was a handsome man. Both Schwartz and Elizabeth had been drinking, Schwartz heavily. In what Simpson calls "a frenzy of jealousy," Schwartz grabbed Elizabeth's wrist and yanked her out of the kitchen into a back room. Neither Simpson nor Berryman had been in the kitchen, but when they walked past the back room Berryman saw Schwartz "bearing down on" Elizabeth and rushed forward to stop him. Simpson then rushed forward to stop Berryman: "'Don't you see?' John shouted, throwing off my hand, 'He's going to hurt her.' . . . John's shout alerted others. Elizabeth escaped. Delmore was subdued."[94] In Bellow's fictional version of this episode, there is no such rescue. Citrine, unlike Simpson, is witness to the original offending act:

I was present in the kitchen when Kathleen made a serious mistake. Holding her drink and an unlit cigarette she reached into a man's pocket for a match. He was not a stranger, we knew him well, his name was Eubanks, and he was a Negro composer. His wife was standing near him. Kathleen was beginning to recover her spirits and was slightly drunk herself. But just as she was getting the matches out of Eubanks's pocket Humboldt came in. I saw him coming. First he stopped breathing. Then he clutched Kathleen with sensational violence. He twisted her arm behind her back and ran her out of the kitchen into the yard. A thing of this sort was not unusual at a Littlewood party, and others decided not to notice, but Demmie and I hurried to the window. Humboldt punched Kathleen in the belly, doubling her up. Then he pulled her by the hair into the Buick. As there was a car behind him he couldn't back out. He wheeled over the lawn and off the sidewalk, hacking off the muffler on the curb. I saw it there next morning like the case of a super-insect, flaky with rust, and a pipe coming out of it (pp. 143–44).

What Brenda Engel remembers of the party is that Schwartz slapped Elizabeth and Ellison exclaimed "*Delmore!*" According to another witness, Schwartz "stormed off, literally dragging her along, handbag, shoes, cigarettes, hairpins flying."

THIS OTHER WITNESS WAS Bellow's new girlfriend, Sondra Tschacbasov; the party was her introduction to his Princeton world. Sondra, at various times also Saundra (the name on her 1931 birth certificate), Sandra, or Alexandra (or Sasha, the name Bellow mostly called her, and the one to be used here), was young, twenty-one, very pretty, very confident in manner.[95] They'd met at the offices of *Partisan Review* where she worked as a secretary, neither happily nor successfully. The meeting was sometime in the autumn of 1952. She'd gotten the job at the end of the summer after graduation from Bennington. One of her professors, Francis Golffing, a poet, translator, and *PR* contributor, recommended her; she was interviewed by Katie Carver, the magazine's editorial assistant, and by Philip Rahv, who gave her the job "only because he thought I was pretty." At the time, as she openly admits, she couldn't type, spell, decipher proofreading symbols, or take dictation, "but I was a Bennington girl . . . and that had a certain cachet in those days. In general, it meant you were savvy, sophisticated and up to the mark on all things modern in art, dance, theater, literature, and sex" (p. 57).

One office task Sasha was equal to was answering the telephone. When Bellow called and asked for Philip Rahv, the following dialogue ensued, as reconstructed in her unpublished memoir, "What's in a Name?"

> "And who are you?" he asked, "I don't recognize your voice—you must be someone new."
> He had an easy flirtatious style and I responded in kind.
> "I am, and why should it matter"? I asked.
> "Well I know all the girls who work at *Partisan Review*" (p. 65).

When Sasha told him her last name was Tschacbasov, spelling it out, he pronounced himself "enchanted" and said he'd soon be down "to see its owner." They met, he telephoned her the next night, then took her out for dinner, "but I said 'no' that night, when he took me back to the Ansonia" (the handsome Upper West Side apartment building where she lived, the setting for *Seize the Day*). Bellow persisted in the weeks that followed and though Sasha remembers him as "boyishly charming, attentive, flattering and seductive," she continued to say no. When he invited her to the party at 12 Princeton Avenue and to spend the weekend with him ("staying at the Princeton Inn—alone"[96]), she had still not slept with him.

The party was on a Friday, a workday for Sasha, and she arrived late. Though she knew very few people there, she was bolstered "by the knowledge that I was wearing my best (and only) black dress, hair up, a lot of makeup, and an enormous Maltese silver cross." Her exotic appearance was enhanced by the cigarettes she smoked, gold-tipped black Sobranies ("I had given up on the pipe—although it attracted men, all they did was talk to each other about tobacco") (p. 66). What struck Sasha right away about the party was how many more men there were than women. Of the few people she knew, the first to approach her was R. W. B. Lewis, who had taught her Melville at Bennington. "Already flushed with drink," Lewis asked her "point blank if I was sleeping with Saul yet, because they were all placing bets." It was "tough," she recalls in the memoir, to see a person she looked up to "turn out to be a buffoon." When Lewis went on drunkenly to say that at Bennington he'd seen "a glimmer" of what she would become, "it was clear he wasn't talking about my intellectual development . . . I never forgave him." Then Delmore Schwartz appeared, a friendly face familiar from weekly visits to *Partisan Revew*. He immediately told her that Rahv and Phillips "disapproved of Saul dating the 'help.'" By eight o'clock John Berryman was on the floor drunkenly reciting from the unfinished "Homage to Mistress Bradstreet," "while holding my shoe-less foot and calling me 'Miss Beauteous Sondra.' I had no idea who he was and even less of what he was saying." "In retrospect," she adds, "it is amazing how many of them were alcoholics" (pp. 66–67).

The women Sasha met at the party are remembered no more warmly. Schwartz's wife "was drinking heavily and unapproachable." Brenda Engel "was sober and unapproachable." "There was no way I could be friends with these women," Sasha realized. "I was not a wife, I was too young, clearly inexperienced, and too attractive to the men, and a lot of women found [Bellow] attractive, as well, and were annoyed to find me in place" (p. 67). She was not wrong in sensing the women's hostility. Sylvia Tumin remembers their first meeting: "Saul came up—we were living in the next block—with this very young woman; obviously he'd already left Anita, and she comes and she's wearing this huge cross. I mean it was huge. All right [said resignedly], 'Not Sandra, *Sondra*.' I guess I'd just had my first son, so he brought her up to the apartment. We chatted." Brenda Engel's sympathies were with Anita: "I thought she was getting a very raw deal. I thought she was a very worth-while person, a very loyal person. . . . That's about the same time Isaac [Rosenfeld] left Vasiliki." Ann Birstein, Alfred Kazin's wife, didn't like Sasha at all: "She had big breasts and wore a big cross that hung down between them. Obviously, the combination did something for Saul." She remembers Sasha saying "stupid" things, for example that "she could have had her choice between Saul Bellow and Philip Rahv" (no choice at all to Birstein, Rahv being "a gravel-voiced gorilla"). When-ever the date of some recent historical event was mentioned, Sasha would ask: "'How old was I then?' and we would have to marvel at how young she was. Actually she was only two years younger than I, which didn't stop her making statements to me beginning with the phrase, 'For people of *my* generation.'"[97] Lillian Blumberg McCall, Bellow's friend from Minetta Street, found Sasha "extremely pretty" but also "utterly baffling and selfish, and self-absorbed." Part of what made her baffling was her "incredible sex appeal. The very thought of her made

Philip Rahv drool. . . . Other men I knew were wiped out by Sash who seemed to always be thumbing her nose at life. It was an attractive quality of insouciance and irreverence."[98]

Sasha was "not often at ease" among Bellow's circle, unsurprisingly. "I was still a college kid sitting in with a bunch of professors." She was "Saul's girl" and mostly ignored in conversation. "If I thought I was under the radar in Princeton," she recalls, after meeting Mary McCarthy and Hannah Arendt in New York, "these ladies never took notice of me at all" (p. 70), treatment she both understood and resented. What she had going for her "in the eyes of some" (mostly men, one imagines) was "the way I put myself together, the personal style." She had been raised "in the world of artists and performers" and knew how to present herself: "I had a 'look,' and Saul was hot for the Russian mystique." None of his friends expected the relationship to last: "it was a fairly commonplace thing to sleep with one of your students or a recently graduated editorial assistant." That Bellow continued to find her interesting, Sasha writes in the memoir, ought to have suggested to his friends that she was intelligent and articulate, "however, no one actually elicited an opinion from me about anything." Meanwhile, she was falling in love with Bellow. "He was energetic and unflagging in his pursuit of me. That was flattering and, ultimately, successful." She knew that he was married, that he had married young, and that he no longer lived with his wife. Though he sometimes talked of marrying her, "he had no real plans to divorce that I could see. Nor did I particularly care at the time" (p. 69).

The quality that most drew Sasha to Bellow, in addition to his persistence, was his attitude toward his work, an attitude that seemed to her to contradict Romantic and bohemian stereotypes, distinguishing him not only from Schwartz, Berryman, and Rosenfeld, but from the artists she had grown up with, in particular her painter father. "What was most seductive," she writes, "was the very workmanlike way he viewed himself in his craft. He was a writer, not an Artist. He 'went to work' so to speak, like it was a regular job, and he was obviously serious, committed, and as long as I lived with him (and forever after, as far as I knew) he followed the same daily routine consistently. You could set your watch by him—an early breakfast, work in his study, emerge for lunch (with a book—not his), and then edit the morning's work" (pp. 71–72). The strictness of this routine is partly what had put off Nadine Raoul-Duval in Paris. Sasha thought it admirable, also intriguing. She saw Bellow as "part middle-class Jewish business man" (with an office at home), "part contemplative, scholarly rabbi" (with words as his religion). "What a relief from my whirling dervish of a parent, all untrammelled passions and unbridled habits and desires!" (p. 72).

THOUGH OTHERS CORROBORATE Sasha's account of Bellow's daily routine, they recall the act of writing for him as strenuous, at times frenzied. In a letter of December 31, 1981, Bellow himself writes of composing *The Dean's December* "in a kind of fit." In 1964, speaking of *Henderson the Rain King*, he tells the interviewer: "I wrote it in a kind of frenzy."[99] He would head to his study with a towel around his neck, like a boxer, emerging with it soaked in perspiration from the effort of concentration.[100] He liked to write with Mozart blaring.[101] When asked in a questionnaire on the composing process if he worked out his plots in advance, or made charts, or began by writing out biographies of his characters, or used file cards, he replied "No" to each question.[102] "Do you begin at the beginning?" asked the interviewer in 1964. "I always begin at the beginning," he replied. "My ambition is to start with an outline but my feelings are generally too chaotic and formless. I get full of excitement which prevents foresight and planning."[103] He thought of *Augie* as a letting loose, a letting free, water sluicing down Paris streets (though when Sasha first knew him much of his time at the desk was spent pruning, polishing, proofing). His approach to writing was both Romantic and bourgeois, as was his facility or fecundity. "You're not like John Berryman," Bellow's friend Richard Stern wrote to him in an undated letter from the mid-1960s: "You don't dive for these pearls—they just come to you. The oyster breaking your nose as it snaps open. But then you bring pearls up. So few even know what a pearl is." Bellow was rarely blocked or anxious about drying up; though often depressed and despondent, it was not because he'd "begun in gladness," in a Wordsworthian blessed infancy (recall little Bentschke in "Memoirs of a Bootlegger's Son"); gladness did not of itself or "thereof" bring despondency, let alone the madness of a Berryman or a Schwartz. Though Bellow's gifts of perception and expression came to him naturally, they had to be properly attended to, by which is meant not just that they had to be ordered or shaped, but that he had to be in a position to receive them, concentrating, undistracted. First the oyster snaps open for him, as Stern puts it, "then you bring pearls up"; the spontaneous overflow is recollected in tranquillity. What Mozart teaches us, Bellow has written, is not simply that "there are things which must be done. Easily or not at all" (an allusion to Keats's "If poetry comes not as naturally as the Leaves to the tree it had better not come at all"), but that "concentration without effort is the heart of the thing."[104]

Sasha's sense of Bellow as businessman is hard to square with notions of the writer as outsider. Was Howe right to group him with Schwartz and Berryman, neither of whom was likely to be thought of as businesslike?[105] In "The Distracted Public," a Romanes Lecture delivered at Oxford University on May 10, 1990, in a passage partly quoted in Chapter 4, Bellow identifies with the Romantic view. In school in Chicago, memorization figured prominently, particularly in English classes:

> I memorized many of Wordsworth's poems. "The World Is Too Much with Us" may, for all I know, have been my introduction to the subject of distraction, for Wordsworth's warning not to lay waste our powers by getting and spending was not lost on me (although I had so little to spend). Nor did I miss his point about emotion recollected in tranquillity—or his emphasis on the supreme importance of a state of attention or aesthetic concentration that would put the world of profit and loss in its place.[106]

The world of profit and loss impinged more directly on Bellow than on Wordsworth. Putting it "in its place" meant putting it below what in the lecture he calls "human essences,"[107] but it also meant putting it center stage, to convey its power to attract and distract. As Philip Roth explains, speaking of *Humboldt's Gift*, in a passage quoted in Chapter 3: "business . . . that's what's at the heart of your book, which is the small-time lawyers, the owners of the middle-sized businesses, the conniving and cheating. You were not ashamed of Jewish aggression because you saw it as American aggression."

America was to be criticized, but it was also to be defended, especially in the face of European condescension. Here is Bellow's response to another questionnaire, sent in 1976 by the German writer Heike Douriné: "Nothing would please me more than answering the list of questions you recently sent me but I am unfortunately so occupied that it is impossible for me to give myself this pleasure," a sentence that might almost have been written by the enraging Frenchman in "Nothing to Declare" (smiling as he claimed not to know the location of the rue de Berri). "I will say this, however, there is much to criticize in America, of course. I, myself, am something of an expert in this line and it is as an expert that I tell you that most European criticism of American culture is itself terribly banal." In "An Interview with Myself," published in 1975 in the *New Review*, Bellow recalls entering the Restaurant Voltaire in Paris with the novelist Louis Guilloux. The waiter addressed Guilloux as "Maître," which left Bellow unable to decide "whether to envy him or to laugh up my sleeve." Later he says, "in America we have no Maîtres, no literary world, no literary public" (an odd assertion coming from what was then America's most respected novelist, who must, at least once, have been comparably greeted by an American waiter, a Chicago waiter). "Many of us read, many love literature," Bellow continues, "but the traditions and institutions of literary culture are lacking. I do not say that this is bad. I only state it as a fact that ours is not a society that interests itself in such things."[108] In the late 1940s and early 1950s, Bellow was especially skeptical about European traditions and institutions, as in "The Gonzaga Manuscripts" or his accounts of postwar Paris. Even in the Guilloux anecdote, which leaves him not knowing what to feel, he calls the waiter "smarmy."

FROM ITS OPENING WORDS and Mark Twain title, to its closing reference to Christopher Columbus, *The Adventures of Augie March* trumpets the strength and vitality of American culture. This is partly because it was inspired by firsthand experience of Europe—of its exhaustion, political naïveté, ignorance of America, and recent horrors. That Bellow was not alone among American writers and intellectuals in expressing patriotic sentiments played an important part in the reception of *Augie*. In the May–June 1952 issue of *Partisan Review*, the editors ran the first part of a three-part symposium on the topic "Our Country and Our Culture." Over successive issues twenty-four contributors addressed the topic, for the most part agreeing with the "Editorial Statement" that opened the symposium.[109] This statement was written by William Phillips and Delmore Schwartz, a collaboration Schwartz engineered "because he wanted to avoid what he thought was Rahv's clumsy and ostentatious style."[110] The editors began by announcing the "apparent fact" that American intellectuals "now regard America and its institutions in a new way," as no longer "hostile to art" (p. 283). To bolster this apparent fact supporting quotations were provided, stretching from 1879 to 1947. "We are the disinherited of art!" is the first quotation, from Henry James, "the soil of American perception is a poor, little, barren, artificial deposit." Ezra Pound, writing in 1917, begins: "O helpless few in my country / O remnant enslaved! / Artists broken against her, / Astray, lost in the villages, / Mistrusted, spoken against." The quotations from Van Wyck Brooks and John Dos Passos, written in 1918 and 1937, respectively, are comparably discouraging. With Edmund Wilson, however, writing in 1947, all is changed:

> My optimistic opinion is that the United States at the present time is politically more advanced than any other part of the world. . . . We have seen in the last fifty years a revival of the democratic creativeness which presided at the birth of the Republic and flourished up through the Civil War. This began to assert itself strongly during the first two decades of this century, was stimulated by the Depression that followed the blowing-up of the Stock Market, and culminated in the New Deal. It was accompanied by a remarkable renascence of American arts and letters.

According to Phillips and Schwartz, the renascence Wilson identifies has come about for two reasons. The first recalls Harold Rosenberg's 1940 *Partisan Review* essay "On the Fall of Paris":

> For more than a hundred years, America was culturally dependent on Europe; now Europe is economically dependent upon America. And America is no longer the raw and unformed land of promise from which men of superior gifts like James, Santayana, and Eliot departed, seeking in Europe what they found lacking in America. Europe is no longer regarded as a sanctuary; it no longer assures that rich experience of culture which inspired and justified a criticism of American life. The wheel has come full circle and now America has become the protector of Western civilization, at least in a military and economic sense.

The second reason for the renascence Wilson identifies is more concisely stated: "there is a recognition that the kind of democracy which exists in America has an intrinsic and positive value: it is not merely a capitalist myth but a reality which must be defended against Russian totalitarianism" (p. 284).

The optimism of the editors is not without qualification. To begin with, "American economic and political institutions have not suddenly become ideally beneficent." There is also the problem of mass culture, which makes the serious artist "feel that he is still outside looking in" (p. 284). The concept of mass culture was popularized in America in the 1940s and 1950s by Dwight Macdonald, in influential essays published in *politics* and *Diogenes* (the quarterly for which Schwartz acted as consultant).[111] But the authority the editors quote is Ortega y Gasset, for whom the mass "crushes beneath it everything that is different, everything that is excellent, individual, qualified and select. Anybody who is not like everybody, who does not think like everybody, runs the risk of being eliminated" (p. 285). The mass figures prominently in Schwartz's contribution to the symposium, which brings its third and final installment to a close. For Schwartz, the writer or artist must remain an outsider, although the term he now uses is "non-conformist."[112] The "chief prevailing fashion" today is "the will to conformism," founded on "the startling discovery that the middle class is not entirely depraved, that liberalism does not provide the answer to all social questions, and that a state of perpetual revolution in literature and art is neither an end in itself nor the chief purpose of either literature or revolution" (p. 595). The sole point of connection between Schwartz and the prevailing fashion is his acceptance that "only America can any longer guarantee the survival of that critical non-conformism without which the very term intellectual—and the reality of the intelligence—is meaningless." In the past, the nonconformist, whether writer, artist, or intellectual, had a choice "between exile in Europe, which was a kind of non-conformism, and the attitude exemplified in America in every period and in a variety of ways from Emerson to Mencken. Now that there is no longer a choice, the tradition and the vitality of critical non-conformism is more important than ever" (p. 597).

In such a way Schwartz squared his Romantic view of the poet with current trends, freeing himself to accept various jobs for the Ford Foundation and to allow his name to appear on the masthead of the Committee for Cultural Freedom.[113] According to William Barrett, the other associate editor at *Partisan Review*, Schwartz had little choice, given the direction the magazine was taking. In the summer of 1952, Barrett was invited to lead an International Seminar at Harvard, nominally directed by Professor William Y. Elliot, but in fact managed by a young graduate student named Henry Kissinger. The aim of the seminar was "to give a certain number of chosen foreign intellectuals a more adequate picture of American cultural life. Above all, it was to show that there could be an opposition to Communism from the Left, that American attitudes were not summed up in McCarthyism, and that there were in fact American intellectuals of the Left who were vigorously anti-Communist." Barrett got the job because *"Partisan Review* was now publicly recognized as the leading magazine expressing this point of view, and I was hired to lead the Seminar as a representative editor."[114]

Bellow is very funny about Schwartz's dealings with foundation big-wigs and the panjandrums of the Cultural Cold War, particularly in connection with his campaign to become a permanent member of the Princeton English Department. The campaign began with Schwartz cajoling Bellow into serving as emissary to Carlos Baker, now the English Department chairman. Bellow was to suggest to Baker that if the department agreed to give Schwartz tenure, the Ford Foundation would underwrite a chair for him. He was also to stress Schwartz's work as a consultant to the foundation and his relationship with James Laughlin, who oversaw many foundation-sponsored literary enterprises. These points Bellow duly made, presenting them, as instructed, as his own. Then Schwartz wrote to Laughlin, asking for his help. "Since one of the purposes of the Ford Foundation is to *spend* rather than to *make* money, I can't imagine that there would be any objection on the Foundation's part or any difficulty for you whatever."[115] Laughlin agreed to help, by which he meant writing on Schwartz's behalf. Schwartz took this agreement as a guarantee that the foundation would come up with the money. When, to Bellow's astonishment, the Princeton English Department agreed to offer Schwartz a tenured post, Schwartz turned his attention directly to the foundation, writing letters to Robert Hutchins, late of the University of Chicago, now the foundation's associate director. He also telephoned Hutchins in Pasadena, offering to come out to talk with him. Hutchins was not encouraging. Eventually he turned Schwartz down and the scheme collapsed. In *Humboldt's Gift*, Humboldt receives a comparable rejection on the day of Citrine's Princeton party.

The Hutchins figure in *Humboldt's Gift* is Wilmoore Longstaff of the Belisha Foundation. Bellow has him say yes to Humboldt, a decision later overturned by the Belisha trustees. He also has Humboldt actually meet Longstaff, whereas Schwartz never met Hutchins. Unauthorized, Humboldt steps into Longstaff's private elevator and pushes the button to his penthouse office. When confronted by Longstaff's secretary, he admits he has no appointment, "but he *was* Von Humboldt Fleisher, the name was enough. Longstaff had him shown in." The Belisha Foundation is richer than the Rockefeller or Ford Foundations and Longstaff has "hundreds of millions to spend on science and scholarship, on the arts, and on social improvement" (p. 136). Citrine imagines Humboldt in Longstaff's office, "swooning with wickedness and ingenuity, swollen with manic energy, with spots before his eyes and maculations of the heart" (p. 137). When Longstaff approves Humboldt's scheme for a chair at Princeton, Humboldt rushes by cab to visit a certain Ginnie in the Village, a Bennington graduate to whom Citrine's girlfriend has introduced him:

> He pounded on her door and said, "It's Von Humboldt Fleisher. I have to see you." Stepping into the vestibule, he propositioned her immediately. Ginnie said, "He chased me around the apartment and it was a scream. But I was worried about the puppies underfoot." Her dachshund had just had a litter. Ginnie locked herself in the bathroom. Humboldt shouted, "You don't know what you're missing. I'm a poet. I have a big cock." And Ginnie told Demmie, "I was laughing so hard I couldn't have done it anyway."
>
> When I asked Humboldt about this incident he said, "I felt I had to celebrate, and I understood these Bennington girls were for poets" (p. 138).

Sasha's Bennington roommate, Anita Maximilian, the daughter of a wealthy Manhattan furrier, was taking classes at the New School at the time this scene is set. She lived in a lower Fifth Avenue apartment near the *Partisan Review* offices, and Sasha was a frequent visitor. Maximilian described the apartment to Atlas as "like *Partisan Review* headquarters. . . . I'd come out of the shower and there would be Paolo Milano . . . or John Berryman or Saul."[116] According to Sasha, Maximilian had affairs with the poets Louis Simpson and John Berryman, and had "a perfectly undisciplined dachshund called Schatzie" (p. 80).

———

BELLOW WAS FREQUENTLY called upon, from *Augie* onward, to advise foundations, sit on boards and committees, and interact with corporate types. In "What Kind of a Day Did You Have?" he makes clear the excitements and enticements of such a role, its fat fees, private jets, and executive audiences ("bankers, economists, former presidential advisers" [p. 288]). Many years after the collapse of Humboldt's scheme to become a Princeton professor, Citrine finds himself in a helicopter with Wilmoore Longstaff, as handsome a figure as Robert Hutchins: "like a movie-star, like a five-star general, like Machiavelli's Prince, like Aristotle's great-souled man." All his life, Longstaff "had fought technocracy and plutocracy with the classics. He forced some of the most powerful people in the country to discuss Plato and Hobbes. He made airline presidents, chairmen, governors of the Stock Exchange perform *Antigone* in boardrooms. Truth, however, is truth, and Longstaff was in many respects first rate. He was a distinguished educator, he was even noble" (p. 137). Bellow moved in and out of the world of such men,

Sondra "Sasha" Tschacbasov, early 1950s

and was rewarded by them with fellowships, trusteeships. He became a figure of influence in literary and intellectual circles. As he grew in eminence, he was swamped with requests: for references, publishers, agents, fellowships, jobs in academe, writing assignments. These requests he answered conscientiously, while steadily producing novels and stories, bringing up pearls. He lived the life Schwartz dreamed of, while staying true to his gifts of perception and expression (about foundation heads as well as failed poets). In *Augie March*, the work that launched him on this life, he makes the case for his country and its culture, without ignoring its faults. In no respect is this case stronger than in the novel's language, a language Bellow rightly saw as new and wholly American.

11

Augie/Bard/Sasha

BELLOW KNEW THAT he was doing something new with *The Adventures of Augie March*. What he discovered with *Augie*, he told Philip Roth, was "that I could write whatever I wished, and that what I wished was to get into words the appearance of a gallery of personalities—characters like Grandma Lausch or Einhorn the fertile cripple, or Augie March himself. Years of notation ended in the discovery of a language that made everything available."[1] One of the "great pleasures" of this language, he elsewhere recalled, "was in having the ideas taken away from me, as it were, by the characters"[2] (an admission echoed in a letter of February 15, 1961, to the writer Louis Gallo: "When I got the idea for *Augie March*—or rather when I discovered that one could free oneself"). The language of the novel overrides ideas and conventions of style. Martin Amis, Bellow's great champion, calls its style one "that loves and embraces awkwardness, spurning elegance as a false lead, words tumbling and rattling together in the order *they* choose." Among the examples Amis approvingly cites are "glittering his teeth and hungry," "try out what of human you can live with," "a flat-footed, in gym shoes, pug-nosed woman," constructions that vivify the thing described or the describer or both.[3]

The language of *Augie* had been pressing on Bellow for several years, as evidenced by the 1949 monologues "A Sermon by Dr. Pep," published in May in *Partisan Review*, and "The Thoughts of Sergeant George Flavin," published by John Lehmann in *Penguin New Writing 38*. "Dr. Pep" is based on the orators Bellow listened to in 1938–39 in Chicago's Washington Square Park, known locally as Bughouse Square.

Bellow was working at the Newberry Library at the time, across the street from the square, conducting research for the Federal Writers' Project. Dr. Pep preaches vitality, Augie's great quality; unlike Augie, however, he's cracked, monomaniacal. After a long winter in the Newberry among nuns, antiquarians, and "young girls getting up assignments for Teachers' College [perhaps the Pestalozzi-Froebel Teachers College, where Bellow taught at the time]—pale, hot-faced young girls whose laps were never meant for notebooks" (p. 455), Pep is ready to deliver his sermon: "on disease and health, and true and false nourishment, out of my readings in Galen and Hippocrates." What sets the sermon going is the nearby smell of "White-Castle hamburger-onions" (p. 456). High/low juxtapositions like these, of hamburgers and Hippocrates, are the monologue's meat and drink. The sermon begins with "the question of why the creature is ground up—not only in hamburger but in its allies chopped steak and Salisbury steak, and other euphemisms of the menu as well, and in croquettes and hash" (p. 458). "Bad conscience" results from such grinding, "a reality is subtracted along the way and something spoiling creeps in" (p. 458). Other cultures do a better job of acknowledging these subtractions: "the wild Melanesian and the Kalahari dwarf are in a better state than we. The Mithraic communion of bread and wine and the totem animal masks of the cult, almost all we have left, are hidden in a little trimming of St. Peter's. The White Tower ketchup bottle is not enough of a symbol of the sacrifice of life" (p. 459).

That way of talking is unlike anything in *The Victim* or *Dangling Man*, but it is close to the way Augie talks. Pep's observations and coinages also recall *Augie*, as in the tame cat "eating her way wag-headed into a mackerel with her nice needles" (p. 459) or the "bedoldrummed" Greek fleet at Aulis (p. 461). Augie's descriptive phrases, often hyphenated, are comparably striking: "Aeneas-stirred Mediterranean" (p. 944), "a coal-sucking Vesuvius of chaos" (p. 582), "a tremendous Canada of light." (p. 577). "Notations" like the "wag-headed" way Pep's cat eats appear on every page (in a letter of November 28, 1953, Bernard Malamud praises Bellow's ability in *Augie* "to call all things by some name"). Sitting up naked in bed in Mexico, Augie and Thea look out their hotel window and see the manager's tiny father "mouse around in the enormous flowers." His two little granddaughters appear in the garden "like white birthday cake" (p. 780). The girlfriend of Guillaume, the "dog-coiffeur" and trainer, is "a great work of ripple-assed luxury"

(p. 597). In the old folks' home where Grandma Lausch ends up, the inhabitants have "rashy, vessel-busted hands" (p. 491). Augie in the pool hall listens to "frying jazz and the buzz of baseball broadcasts" (p. 473). Augie's vitality is different from Pep's: Pep's is vatic, manic, Augie's resilient, picaresque; both are comic. Pep is small in stature ("not the star-browed Apollo measuring one noble foot of space between the eyes") but large in spirit, like Whitman: "I partake of everything in my own flesh; I strum on Venusberg and float in the swamp. I do a one-leg schottische along Clark Street and buff the friendly public with my belly" (p. 459).

Sergeant Flavin lacks Pep's erudition but makes up for it in street smarts. On his way to a "Retreat for Catholic Men of the Chicago Police Force," he can think of better ways to pass a gloomy February weekend—"not that I'm disrespectful."[4] The police officer who comes to a religious retreat straight from brawls and knifings and fights in pool rooms needs time to adjust: "you won't float him out of that on sweet smoke and tinging bells so easy" (p. 48). The retreat, Flavin tells us, is not far from the Sunset Ridge golf course near Wilmette, where, like Bellow, he used to caddie; also nearby is the Garden of Allah, where the boxer Tony Canzoreri used to train. "There was plenty of sporting money around in those days," Flavin recalls, "and those big handsome women, they'd throb you up with a look as if they put their hand on you" (p. 49). Sergeant Flavin admires priests (he could be a character in James T. Farrell's *Studs Lonigan* trilogy): "There's nobody smarter. They know the wildness of the world and how it has to be stood off and what the state of things is and what our line of work is like and with who. You can't loose or bind, as they say, without strong hands and studying knots. That's the old wisdom that's held the world steady two thousand years and will be with it to the last shake, you can give odds" (p. 51). "Give odds," "with who," "throb you up," "float him out"; these are the locutions or notations forcing their way into Bellow's prose in the late 1940s, along with everything else he knew and read.

In November 1949 Bellow published a third monologue, "Dora," in *Harper's Bazaar* (where Pearl Kazin, Alfred's sister, worked). A forty-five-year-old spinster, Dora is neither street nor erudite. Orphaned early in life, with no close family connections, she lives in a rooming house in Manhattan. Dora is pleasant enough, but keeps to herself. She is devoted to her work as a dressmaker, at which she excels. Her language is plain, neither *Augie*-like nor Flaubertian, though the story she tells implicitly affirms Bellow's motives in adopting the *Augie* style. One night the man next door, "a typical-looking individual you hardly ever notice" (p. 190), has a stroke; Dora hears him drop "with his whole weight" (p. 198). Entering his room, she finds him naked on the floor, unconscious. She has never spoken to this man, though they knew each other by sight. No one knows much about him, the police have no one to notify. The man's nakedness leads Dora to focus on him for the first time, really to see him. "There is a difference between one and another. Making garments, you get to realize that. It sinks in in the most peculiar ways, by the hips and bosom of one person and the shape of another, that the difference between this one and that one is a very important thing, almost like a sign from God" (pp. 198–99). Later she thinks: "if you don't care about the differences one thing might as well be another, meat candy and candy meat. It might as well be the trunk falling as the man falling" (p. 199). She begins to visit the man in hospital, where he remains unconscious. The episode leaves her "shaken out of myself" (p. 199), by which she means, out of her closed-off self.

"Dora" connects with *Augie* and "A Sermon by Dr. Pep" in stressing the integrity of individuals, the importance of particulars of character and appearance (often identical for Bellow), and the deforming influence of social construction or categorization. In *Augie March*, this theme is reinforced by allusions to Chicago as Babel. "On warm days I went up to the roof and had a look at the city," Augie recalls. "Around was Chicago. In its repetition it exhausted your imagination of details and units, more units than the cells of the brain and bricks of Babel" (p. 906). The desire to reach heaven by material means (bricks) or human reason (brain cells) is hubris and the nemesis it begets is not only a confusion of tongues, the inability to understand one another or to connect, but a tendency to see people as units, indistinguishable bricks or cells. Augie, in defiance, is "one of a humanity that can't be numbered" (p. 745), can't be ground up, which is partly why he resists or evades the many "reality-instructors" he faces: Grandma Lausch, Einhorn, Mrs. Renling, Simon, Thea Fenchel, Manny Padilla, Clem Tambow. In discussing the origins of *Augie* with Philip Roth, Bellow recalls his experiences in Mexico: "The challenge was to emerge intact from these would-be dominators. To extract the secret of their powers from them while eluding their control became my singular interest."[5] In a letter of November 1953 to Edith Tarcov, Bellow admits to feeling "that the world asks an undue degree of control over us. At any rate, I am constitutionally unable to accept so much control and have passed this inability along to Augie."

A fourth and final pre-*Augie* monologue, the "Address by Gooley MacDowell to the Hasbeens Club of Chicago," was published in the summer of 1951 in *The Hudson Review*. Gooley is like Dr. Pep, a breathless autodidact (Atlas calls him "an early incarnation of Herzog"[6]). Though ideas have long been Gooley's province, his address concerns the inadequacy of "intelligence connected to human advancement" (p. 223). In school "I sprung my elbow waving to answer questions" (p. 223); more recently "I've been starting to reconsider to what end I hoped to be so smart" (p. 222). The "Hasbeens Club," friends from the reading room of the Crerar Library on Randolph Street, "our homespun Bodleian," "will want to know why I have it in for thought, suddenly" (p. 224). Gooley's answer is that thought obstructs: "as you get better by the correction of intellect you may lose your nature" and cease to experience "feelings of being that go beyond and beyond all I ever knew of thought" (pp. 226, 227). Learning also obstructs: "What a load you can buy for a buck, in anthologies, out of Augustine, Pascal, Aristotle, Nicholas of Cusa, super-brain Goethe, and it's a confusion for us" (p. 226). Gooley's advice is like Wordsworth's in "The Tables Turned": "quit your books." As the Wordsworth speaker, "William," tells his friend "Matthew": "Books! 'tis a dull and endless strife," "Our meddling intellect / Misshapes the beauteous forms of things." What is needed, William says, is "spontaneous wisdom breathed by health," "a heart that watches and receives." This advice is like Whitman's advice in "Song of Myself": "loafe" ("I loafe and invite my soul, / I lean and loafe at my ease observing a spear of summer grass"). For ideas men like Gooley, however, or Pep or Augie or Bellow, loafing is labor; the search for a true self or soul, "a furthest creature that wears various lives or forms as a garment, and the life of thought one of the greatest of these" (p. 227), is, in Augie's words, "hard, hard work, excavation and digging, mining, moling through tunnels, heaving, pushing, moving rock, working, working, working, working, working, panting, hauling, hoisting. And none of this work is seen from the outside. It's internally done" (p. 979).

IN THE MONTH that "Dora" appeared, *Partisan Review* published "From the Life of Augie March," an early version of the novel's opening chapter. The British novelist Adam Thirlwell makes much of the differences between 1949 and 1953 versions. That the opening paragraph of the 1949 version is twice as long as that of the 1953 version leads him to argue that "free-style . . . is a consciously edited style."[7] (though the Chicago chapters of the novel show least evidence of revision[8]). Thirlwell cites the memoirs of the Duc de Saint-Simon as an influence on the finished work, on the strength of a single reference made to him by a man Augie meets in New York, a descendant (his name is Alain de Niveau and he turns up in Paris at the end of the novel [p. 980]). Saint-Simon's prose style, Thirlwell writes, "was not courtly: it was not stylish. Instead, it allowed itself contradiction, periphrasis, precision. It was a style based on an impacted note form, a concentrate of information and imagined information whose source was malice, was gossip." A striking passage from the *Memoirs* describing Madame de Maintenon, Louis XIV's second wife, is compared with Bellow's "great sharp packed description" of Grandma Lausch.[9] That Bellow himself never mentions Saint-Simon as a source, either in correspondence or interviews, never names him as an influence, does not trouble Thirlwell. The larger point, about the worked nature of the style, however, is a good one (as long as "worked" is distinguished from "smoothed" or "regularized"). Robert Penn Warren, in a *New Republic* review of the novel (November 2, 1953), makes a related point when he claims that Bellow's "long self-discipline in the more obviously rigorous method [the Flaubertian standard] made it possible for Bellow now to score a triumph in the apparent formlessness of the autobiographical-picaresque novel." Warren draws a parallel with "the really good writers of free verse," all of whom began "by practice in formal metrics."

The European writers Bellow does mention as influences—he names no Russian novelists—are Joyce, Fielding, and the nineteenth-century masters Scott, Balzac, and Dickens. As he explains in an undated response to a letter of November 28, 1953, from Bernard Malamud, "I took a position in writing this book. I declared against what you call the constructivist approach. A novel, like a letter, should be loose, cover much ground, run swiftly, take risk of mortality and decay. I backed away from Flaubert in the direction of Walter Scott, Balzac, and Dickens. Having brought off the method as well as I could, I must now pay the price. You let the errors come" (a comment that recalls Randall Jarrell's definition of the novel: "a prose narrative of some length that has something wrong with it"[10]). That *Augie* is a "loose baggy monster,"[11]

Henry James's term, is as clear as its "rebellion against small-public art" ("My real desire was to reach 'everybody'"[12]); less clear is its connection to the Joyce of *Finnegans Wake*. Bellow explains: "I took what I was writing as a project with its own rules. You know, towards the end of his life, Joyce was writing sentences of a very curious kind. They contained a challenge to the world. It's a question of how to provoke new responses and get rid of some of the old stuff that people thought they wanted. Anyhow, it was a wonderful game, I think. That was the way I saw I was doing and I think Joyce in his way was up to the same thing."[13]

If late Joyce inspired Bellow as a maker of curious or challenging sentences, Fielding inspired him as a narrator. During the writing of *Augie*, Bellow told Daniel Fuchs, he read *Joseph Andrews* (its full title is *The History of the Adventures of Joseph Andrews and of His Friend Mr. Abraham Adams*) "off and on."[14] Like Augie, Joseph is a good-natured and buoyant hero of low station whose adventures are couched in heroic terms. In *Joseph Andrews* these terms are mocking; in *Augie* they are ultimately serious. Clem Tambow makes fun of Augie's "nobility syndrome. . . . You want there should be Man, with capital M" (p. 879), but Bellow does not. Here is Augie on Einhorn, "the first superior man I knew": "I'd ask myself, 'What would Caesar suffer in this case? What would Machiavelli advise or Ulysses do? What would Einhorn think?' I'm not kidding when I enter Einhorn in this eminent list. It was him that I knew, and what I understood of them in him" (p. 449).[15] *Joseph Andrews* proceeds episodically, like *Don Quixote*, an acknowledged influence. The narrative is loose, a model for the looseness of *Augie*. In both *Augie* and *Joseph Andrews*, episodes and characters appeal first because of their intrinsic qualities. As Robert Penn Warren puts it of the incidents in *Augie*, "awareness of their place in the overall pattern dawns late on us," exactly the reverse, he claims, of the way incidents are presented in Bellow's earlier novels.[16] In *Augie*, moreover, respect for the integrity of characters and episodes (what Warren calls Bellow's "fine old relish of character for character's sake") is thematically appropriate. Toward the end of the novel, however, the limitations of the picaresque or episodic form surface. Augie tires of adventuring. What he now seeks, in addition to freedom and love, is "use," what Lionel Trilling, in a brief review of the novel in *The Griffin*, calls a "function" as opposed to a "fate," terms drawn from the novel itself. This change in Augie's outlook suggests development or maturity, qualities the picaresque is ill-suited to portray. In Paris with Stella, an early example of the Bellovian floozy, Augie hatches a scheme to run "an academy and foster-home . . . [a] private green place like one of those Walden or Innisfree wattle jobs under the kind sun, surrounded by velvet woods and bright gardens and Elysium lawns sown with Lincoln Park grass seed" (p. 970) (what exactly Stella will do in this paradise is hard to see). This fantasy collapses at the news that Stella is unfaithful to Augie. But was it ever seriously entertained? Augie has always held to the belief that "a man's character is his fate" (p. 906); his problem has been to find and stick to that character, the "axial lines" he strives "to have my existence on," free from "noise and grates, distortion, chatter, distraction, effort, superfluity" (pp. 901, 902). That others have little time for such striving, see it as hopelessly old-fashioned, he knows full well:

> Guys may very likely think, Why hell! What's this talk about fates? And will feel it all comes to me from another day, and a mistaken day, when there were fewer people in the world and there was more room between them so that they grew not like wild grass but like trees in a park, well set apart and developing year by year in the rosy light. Now instead of such comparison you think, Let's see it instead not even as the grass but as a band of particles [like the cells or bricks of Babel], a universal shawl of them, and these particles may have functions but certainly lack fates. And there's even an attitude of mind which finds it almost disgusting to be a person and not a function. Nevertheless I stand by my idea of a fate. For which a function is a substitution of a deeper despair (p. 971).

In the novel's final paragraph, a second use or function is hinted at when Augie declares himself "a sort of Columbus of those near-at-hand" (like Bellow, author of the novel just read). To some readers, including several reviewers, this declaration, like the earlier dream of an Elysian foster home, appears out of nowhere. Both schemes serve values Augie holds dear throughout the book: loving memories of Mama and "mind-crippled" Georgie, Augie's brother, underlie the foster home idea; similarly loving memories motivate Augie's "near-at-hand" discoveries, principally the novel's "gallery of personalities." "People *will* feel exposed, ridiculed, no matter how you deal with them," Bellow wrote in a letter of November 30, 1953, to Sam Freifeld, whose father was the model for Einhorn: "They can't think that perhaps it was my aim to love not shame them," a comment recalling Bellow's advice to

Dean Borok, that in writing a successful account of his life "you will forgive everyone in the process. Yes, all those who sinned against you will be forgiven."[17] That the functions Augie comes up with at the end of the novel are consistent with his values, however, does not explain why he comes up with them when he does. Norman Podhoretz, reviewing the novel in *Commentary* (October 1953), sees little sign of development in Augie. Though he "goes through everything, he undergoes nothing. He doesn't change in the course of the novel; he doesn't even learn, for all his great show of having learned. He merely resists the apparent lessons of his experience."[18]

Trilling's remarks about "function," in an otherwise admiring review, disturbed Bellow. "As Mr. Bellow defines him," Trilling writes, "a person has a fate rather than a function, and powers of enjoyment and of love rather than achievement," a distinction Trilling thinks false, since "without function it is very difficult to be a person and to have a fate."[19] "People have accused me of asociality," Bellow writes in the November 1953 letter to Edith Tarcov. "Trilling asserts that Augie is 'wrong' i.e. unprincipled." This assertion Bellow denies, while also suggesting the deforming capacities of "sociality" or function: "Squeezed into 'functions' in which all higher capacities die of disuse, we are considered unprincipled if we comment on the situation by so much as a laugh. Can Augie be anything but, in his mild way, an outlaw? Only, instead of being outside, as a Cain or Ishmael are outside, his desire is to be an Augie" (or a Huck, resisting the culture that would "civilize" him). To Trilling himself, on October 11, 1953, Bellow wrote of Augie as representative, in the line of American or Emersonian individualism, certainly, but also as a man of his age: "I was constantly thinking of some of the best young men I have known. Some of the very finest and best intentioned, best endowed, found nothing better to do with themselves than Augie. The majority, whether as chasers, bigamists, forgers and worse, lacked his innocent singleness of purpose. They had reached the place where they fixedly doubted that Society had any use for their abilities." Nor was Bellow prepared to accept that the values Augie stood out for were in any way impediments to function: "To love another, genuinely to love, is the inception of a function, I wished to say," though he admitted that the position he was defending had not been consciously adopted. "On the whole," he declared at the end of the letter, "I was fairly free of deliberate intentions."

To Leslie Fiedler, in a letter of October 25, 1953, he complained of having to discuss the novel in such terms: "Though I was always of the opinion that people were hard to give pleasure to, it was nonetheless a shock to see how many suffered from low seriousness—my new favorite description of the 'earnestness' of deep readers. What makes people so sober? We've sunk a great depth if the funnyman also finds it necessary to be a prophet. I have my own share of low seriousness, of course, but I think of it as a curse." To Bernard Malamud he complained of people missing "the fun of the book. They suffer from culture-gravity. They say 'picaresque' and don't laugh. The baseball people landing on your *Natural* with both feet are in the same league."[20] Trilling replied to Bellow in a letter of November 4, 1953. "You mustn't ignore the doctrinal intention of your book—I mean its cultural, characterological, moral point, whether or not it was consciously made. . . . I think that the difference between us in our view of what is implied [about function versus fate] makes a sounding cultural fact, which we ought to prize and keep ringing." The only lightness in Trilling's letter occurs at the end, where he expresses "great pleasure from seeing Augie on the best-seller list so regularly," though this "no longer means what it used to, alas."

IN THE MONOLOGUES as in *Augie*, not all the risks Bellow takes pay off. On the level of the sentence, colloquialism at times veers into incoherence. Here is Gooley on the Hasbeen charter: "While as to being dry on the chaos waves by the management and steering of wit, haven't we taken care of that in our charter, declaring nobody can trust knowing the angles to obtain salvation?" (pp. 226–27). There are a number of sentences like this in *Augie*; they are the price Bellow pays for a prevailing brilliance. The new style was liberating, he later confessed, but "I was incapable at the time of controlling it and it ran away from me." "Looking back," he elsewhere explains, "I think I took off too many [restraints], and went too far. . . . I had just increased my freedom, and like any emancipated plebeian I abused it at once."[21] When asked what the novel was about, he would sometimes answer, "it's *about* two hundred pages too long."[22] In mitigation, he could cite American as well as Joycean precedents: not just what Roth calls "the engorged sentences of Melville and Faulkner,"[23] but the excesses and irregularities of American naturalism, of Theodore Dreiser, Sherwood Anderson, James T. Farrell, and John Dos Passos, staples of the courses and lectures Bellow offered while at work on *Augie*. Dreiser's influence has already been discussed. While admitting the inelegance of his style, Bellow praised him for "depth of feeling," "profound respect for his characters," and the range of his interests. "He was fascinated with everything," Bellow remarked, an observation that recalls Malamud on Bellow's ability "to call all things by some name."[24] Dreiser, like Five Properties, like Bellow himself, was "hipped on superabundance" (*Augie*, p. 406).

The influence of Anderson, Farrell, and Dos Passos is clear from the profiles Bellow wrote of them for the Federal Writers' Project.[25] Anderson's life as well as his work inspired Bellow. "About 1910, the successful president of a flourishing paint company, he walked abruptly out of his office and never returned. . . . Now he set out to repudiate and undo those years." Bellow quotes Anderson's explanation: "I must quit my buying and selling, the overwhelming feeling of uncleanliness. I was in my whole nature a taleteller. The taleteller cannot bother with buying and selling. To do so will destroy him" (p. 4). After seven novels, Anderson had still not properly expressed his "whole nature," or as Bellow puts it, he had "still not become too adroit a novelist" (p. 7). Anderson himself said of his early novels, "they were not really mine."[26] In the linked stories of *Winesburg, Ohio*, however, Anderson "looses himself from the restrictions of the novel and does wholeheartedly the work he is really fitted for. He no longer blunders or struggles among ideas with incomplete mastery, and for the first time he can be read without irksome reservations" (p. 9). Irksome awkwardnesses, however, remain, as Anderson himself admitted. In "An Apology for Crudity," published in *The Dial* (November 8, 1917), he declared that the "true novelist is a man gone a little mad with the life of his times. . . . If he be at all sensitive to the life about him, and that life be crude, the figure that emerges will be crude and will crudely express itself. . . . We shall, I am sure, have much crude, blundering American writing before the gift of beauty and subtlety in prose shall honestly belong to us."[27]

In discussing *Winesburg, Ohio*, Bellow says less about the crudity of Anderson's writing than about its strangeness. "Anderson's characters in Winesburg," he declares, "are far from being real. They need not be entirely so; they need only be credible. And so, to the point of credibility he exaggerates them" (p. 10), which is what Bellow does with the characters in *Augie* and in the monologues. Anderson's characters are often oddly learned, like Bellow's characters, mixing high culture and low. Bellow quotes Joe Welling, the Standard Oil agent in Winesburg, clearly a reader of Heraclitus. Joe stops young George Willard in front of the Winesburg feed store:

> "You carry a little pad of paper in your pocket, don't you? I knew you did. Well, you set this down. I thought of it the other day. Let's take decay. Now what is decay? It's fire. It burns up wood and other things. You never thought of that? Of course not. This sidewalk here and this feed store, the trees down the street—they're all on fire. They're burning up. Decay, you see, is always going on. It don't stop. Water and paint can't stop it. If a thing is iron, then what? It rusts, you see. That's fire too. The world is on fire."[28]

George Willard, to whom everyone speaks, resembles Augie in several respects. "He is groping about trying to find himself," his mother explains. "Within him there is a secret something that is striving to grow" (p. 25). This "secret something," like the "whole nature" Anderson sought to realize in becoming a writer, is an equivalent to Augie's "axial lines." In the last tale in *Winesburg*, George leaves for the city. Here are the final words of the book: "when he aroused himself and again looked out of the car window, the town of Winesburg had disappeared and his life there had become but a background on which to paint the dreams of his manhood" (p. 230). The implicit identification of hero and author recalls the ending of *Augie*. Augie, too, will "paint" or recount his discoveries, as "a sort of Columbus of those near-at-hand."[29]

The language of James Farrell, another influence, is if anything cruder than Dreiser's and Anderson's, but then so are his characters. He writes, as Bellow puts it, "about things he knows absolutely," the corners and prairies of South Chicago; his fiction "is undisguisedly autobiographical" (p. 1). Farrell, too, was inspired by Anderson. "If the inner life of a boy in an Ohio country town of the nineteenth century was meaningful," Farrell declares in "A Note on Sherwood Anderson," "then perhaps my own feelings and emotions and the feelings and emotions of those with whom I had grown up were important. . . . I thought of writing a novel about my own boyhood, about the neighborhood in which I had grown up." This neighborhood "possessed something of the character of a small town,"[30] as did Bellow's Humboldt Park. Augie's settings, however, range widely, lending variety and dynamism to his adventures; Farrell's characters in *Studs Lonigan* stay put, which is partly why his fiction, even at its best, "moves slowly . . . carries super-fluities" (p. 5).

For dynamism and variety, the Chicago novelist—or Chicago-born novelist—who comes closest to the Bellow of *Augie*, as several reviewers remarked, is John Dos Passos, the subject of the last of the profiles Bellow wrote for the Writers' Project. The Dos Passos profile also begins by relating the life to the writing. Dos Passos is described as "travelling constantly—the Near East, Russia, Italy, Turkey, the Balkans. Something of this constant moving finds its way into his writing, making it fluid, rapid—country, people, lives are seen from express trains, portholes, fast cars" (p. 7). In *Manhattan Transfer* (1925), where Dos Passos's style "makes its first full appearance," the characters "appear to live under an impossible electric pressure. . . . It is bewildering, this pressure of lives and courses, but it catches as nothing else can the thick, beating, composite life of the city itself" (p. 7) (the pressure under which Farrell's characters labor, though also impossible, is wearing rather than electric). Hence the compacted language of *Manhattan Transfer*, an obvious influence on the language of *Augie*, though nothing like as subtly deployed. Bellow singles out "the typographical running together of words: 'nilegreen,' 'redbrick,' 'but in pit-blackness something inside clangs like a fire engine,'" the way Dos Passos "combines, welds, pushes forward like an engine himself. His raciness and daring are more than simply experimental. He is not merely an 'experimental novelist.' He is a stirring writer. Skyscrapers, smoke, machines are new things; they call for a new language" (p. 9).

Dos Passos may also be a source for Bellow's view of Chicago as Babel. In the Writers' Project profile, Bellow quotes the beginning of Chapter 2 of *Manhattan Transfer*, entitled "Metropolis": "There were Babylon and Nineveh, they were built of brick. Athens was gold marble columns. Rome was held up on broad arches of rubble. In Constantinople the minarets flame like Great Candles round the Golden Horn. Steel, glass, tile, concrete will be the materials of the skyscraper" (p. 8). Bellow's Chicago is as electric as Dos Passos's Manhattan, but when Augie looks out at it from Simon's apartment he is dismayed. In "Looking for Mr. Green" (*Commentary*, March 1951), the most powerful of the stories Bellow published pre-*Augie* (the only one he reprinted in 2001 in his *Collected Stories*), Chicago as Babel terrifies. Set in the Depression, the story concerns an ex-student of the classics, George Grebe, whose job is to deliver relief checks to the South Side, "in the

Negro district,"[31] an all but impossible task. Everywhere Grebe inquires he meets incomprehension and obfuscation; nothing he encounters is stable or familiar. "Nobody would get to know even a tenth of what went on among these people" (p. 184), says a white store owner who lives among them. Grebe's supervisor is an educated man but he's also a lawyer, and money, he claims, is the ground of all appearance: "I'll tell you, as a man of culture, that even though nothing looks to be real, and everything stands for something else, and that thing for another thing, and that thing for a still further one—there ain't any comparison between twenty-five and thirty-seven dollars a week, regardless of the last reality. Don't you think that was clear to your Greeks? They were a thoughtful people, but they didn't part with their slaves" (p. 181). The language of real things and last realities, the language of Plato, recurs in the story, with the black slum standing for a world not so much of matter as of flux, instability. The store owner who warns Grebe about the impossibility of his task works himself into a fury: "It was a long speech, deepening with every word in its fantasy and passion . . . a huge, hugging, despairing knot, a human wheel of heads, legs, bellies, arms, rolling through his shop" (p. 184). Though written at the time of *Augie March*, "Looking for Mr. Green" points beyond it, to *Mr. Sammler's Planet* (1970) and *The Dean's December* (1982).

THAT AUGIE IS JEWISH and speaks an English in which Yiddish inflections, constructions, and expressions are heard, is part of what makes him a Columbus. In recounting his adventures, he discovers an American speech largely absent from high culture.[32] The guardians of this culture, Bellow told Philip Roth, were "our own WASP establishment, represented mainly by Harvard-trained professors." "These guys infuriated him," Roth later commented. "It may well have been the precious gift of an appropriate fury that launched him into beginning his third book not with the words 'I am a Jew, the son of immigrants,' but rather by warranting that son of Jewish immigrants who is Augie March to break the ice with Harvard-trained professors (as well as everybody else) by flatly decreeing, without apology or hyphenation, 'I am an American, Chicago born.'" Roth calls Augie's decree "precisely the bold stroke required to abolish anyone's doubts about the American credentials of an immigrant son like Saul Bellow." At the end of the novel when Augie says "Look at me, going everywhere!" Roth describes him as "going where his pedigreed betters wouldn't have believed he had any right to go with the American language."[33]

The influence of Yiddish on *Augie March* is more than a matter of phrases or of familiar character types. In "Laughter in the Ghetto," a review of Sholom Aleichem's last novel, *The Adventures of Mottel, the Cantor's Son* (*Saturday Review*, May 30, 1953), Bellow notes how "the most ordinary Yiddish conversation is full of the grandest historical, mythological and religious allusions. The Creation, the Fall, the Flood, Egypt, Alexander, Titus, Napoleon, the Rothschilds, the sages, the Laws may get into the discussion of an egg, a clothes-line, or a pair of pants. This manner of living on terms with all times and all greatness contributed, because of the powerlessness of the Chosen, to the ghetto's sense of the ridiculous." It seems likely also to have contributed to Bellow's depiction of Einhorn as Caesar. Then there's the hardness or harshness of Yiddish. "You may have heard charming, appealing, sentimental things about Yiddish," Herschel Shawmut writes in "Him with His Foot in His Mouth," "but Yiddish is a *hard* language, Miss Rose. Yiddish is severe and bears down without mercy. Yes, it is often delicate, lovely, but it can be explosive as well. 'A face like a slop jar,' 'a face like a bucket of swill.' (pig connotations give special force to Yiddish epithets.) If there is a demiurge who inspires me to speak wildly, he may have been attracted to me by this violent unsparing language."[34] The force or bite of Bellow's depictions of street types and Machiavels owes something to the example of Yiddish, as does the freedom with which he mixes idioms. Irving Howe and Eliezer Greenberg describe Yiddish as "always in rapid process of growth and dissolution . . . a language drenched in idiom, and therefore a resourceful term in a dialectic or tension in which the thesis was Hebrew and the synthesis a blend of speech so persistently complex and ironic—really a kind of 'underground' speech—as to qualify severely the very values it was dedicated to defend." Yiddish stories are comparably mixed, drawing simultaneously on a Hebrew base and the fiction of Europe. They are high/low, traditional/modern, solemn/jocular, moving "from the Hasidic wonder tales and the grotesque fiction of Gogol; from the comic legends about Hershel Ostropoler, a kind of Jewish Till Eulenspiegel, and the fiction of Chekhov; from folk stories about the Rothschilds and the world-view of Cervantes."

These quotations are from *A Treasury of Yiddish Stories* (1953), published by Viking, the first of six such editorial collaborations between

Howe and Greenberg.[35] Among the stories collected in the *Treasury* is Isaac Bashevis Singer's "Gimpel the Fool," translated by Bellow. In *A Margin of Hope*, Howe explains how the translation came about (in the year he and Bellow were at Princeton): "Bellow had a pretty good command of Yiddish, but not quite enough to do the story on his own. So we sat him down before a typewriter in Lazer's apartment on East Nineteenth Street. Lazer read out the Yiddish sentence by sentence, Saul occasionally asked about refinements of meaning, and I watched in a state of high enchantment. Three or four hours, and it was done. Saul took another half hour to go over the translation and then, excited, read aloud the version that has since become famous. It was a feat of virtuosity and we drank a schnapps to celebrate." Howe sent the story to Rahv and Phillips, who published it in the May–June 1953 issue of *Partisan Review*. At the time, Singer was known to readers of the Yiddish press but to relatively few *Partisan Review* readers. "Hey, where'd you find him?" Rahv asked Howe.[36] The story made Singer's name. In a letter of July 12, 1995, to Janet Hadda, Singer's biographer, Bellow explained what he felt he'd brought to it and learned from it: "what was perhaps lacking in my own work back in the early 50s was a full and satisfactory immersion in the Eastern European Jewish subject matter; what was necessary in translating Gimpel was a rich and complex English style. Singer had the one, I had the other." The translation worked because the story was so good and because Bellow valued it—this was no "shtetl kitsch"—but also because, disclaimers notwithstanding, Bellow had a feel for the shtetl, through the Orthodox and authoritarian components of his own upbringing in Montreal and Humboldt Park.

On a more local level, the level of the phrase or sentence, Bellow was well-suited to translation from the Yiddish. According to Howe and Greenberg, "parts of speech enjoy a fluidity in Yiddish that is almost impossible to render in English. In one story that the editors translated, a goose is described as having *beryed* herself towards a food pail. The word *beryed* is a noun referring to a super-efficient, even fanatical housewife. . . . The author, by twisting *berye* into a verb that describes the busy movements of a goose, has brought to the sentence an aura of suggestiveness that may be said to give the natural environment a distinctive Jewish shade. The best equivalent we could find was 'bustle,' but it was hardly very brilliant."[37] Bellow might have done better, judging by coinages such as "bedoldrummed," which are "Yiddish" in the freedom with which they reconfigure fixed or usually fixed parts of speech in English. The language Bellow gives Gimpel is idiomatic ("so I made tracks," "I never want to start up with them"), delicate ("I saw the new-born child's face and loved it as soon as I saw it—immediately—each tiny bone"), and direct ("She ate and became fat and handsome").[38]

THOUGH BELLOW WAS ADAMANT in resisting the label of Jewish American writer, he was perfectly aware that his Jewishness would play a part in the reception of *Augie March*. The reviews in general were strong. Trilling's admiring notice in *The Griffin* and Warren's review in *The New Republic* were followed by a rave from Delmore Schwartz in *Partisan Review*, in which he declared *Augie* a greater novel than *The Adventures of Huckleberry Finn*.[39] *The New York Times Book Review* gave *Augie* a front-page review, by Robert Gorham Davis, a professor of English at Smith College. It also ran an interview with Bellow by Harvey Breit, the editor.[40] Davis, like Warren, praised Bellow for the richness and variety of his character drawing, and for not being afraid "to seem more interested in life than in art." He also compared *Augie* favorably to Dos Passos's *U.S.A.* (for its "enormous range of discriminating reporting"). Breit begins the interview with Bellow by describing him as "fanning out" from "the tough, tight literary magazines" and "the severer literary critics" to "broader and brighter domains," what Bellow, after Wyndham Lewis, called a "big-public" readership. Later, on December 13, the *New York Times Book Review* published John Berryman's "A Note on *Augie*," which discusses Bellow's debts to and differences from Dreiser, while suggesting that the American naturalist he most resembles is Stephen Crane. On the one hand, though Bellow rarely mentions Crane (and only then to see him as an ancestor of Hemingway, a quite different sort of writer), his style, like Crane's, is "powerful," "singular," and "salutary." On the other hand, in being "inclusive and tidal" it "clearly belong[s] on the Dreiser side."

Two other strong reviews are worth noting. In *The Saturday Review*, which ran a full-page drawing of Bellow on its front cover, and a sidebar interview, Harvey Curtis Webster, a professor of English at the University of Louisville, compared the experience of reading *Augie* to that of reading *Ulysses* when it first came out in 1922.[41] In the *New York Post*, Harvey Swados called *Augie* "very possibly the most significant and remarkable novel to have been published in the United States in the past decade."[42] The commercial reception of the novel was also gratifying.

Sales were boosted by several prepublication deals. *The Griffin*, where Trilling's notice appeared, was a publication of the Readers' Subscription, a high-end book club he, W. H. Auden, and Jacques Barzun had founded; *Augie* was a featured selection. The Book-of-the-Month Club selected *Augie* as an alternate. In December Bellow received a check for $2,000 from Viking, as an additional advance against earnings. Henry Volkening, meanwhile, was forwarding offers from foreign publishers.[43] Early in the New Year, *Augie* won the National Book Award for Fiction, and on January 31 the *Times Book Review* published Bellow's "How I Wrote Augie March's Story."

AMONG THE FEW less favorable notices, two stuck out. In *The New Yorker*, the novelist Anthony West, son of H. G. Wells and Rebecca West, wrote a symbol-mongering review that Bellow thought "disgraceful," so much so that on September 25 he wrote to Katherine White, the magazine's fiction editor, to complain.[44] White, who had not read the novel, forwarded Bellow's letter to the magazine's editor, William Shawn, recently appointed successor to Harold Ross. When Shawn received Bellow's letter, according to White in a letter of October 13, "he immediately got hold of the book and read it. . . . Mr. Shawn agrees with you that Anthony West was flatly wrong in his statements about the symbolism." Though *The New Yorker* had no letters page, Shawn agreed to break precedent and publish a response from Bellow, provided "it was written as a calm correction, not as a general and heated attack on the critic." The response would appear "under our usual heading 'Department of Correction.'" At the end of the letter relaying Shawn's decision, White added: "How seriously we take this mistake you can judge by the fact that this is the first time in the history of the magazine—if my memory is correct—that we've asked an author to write a reply to a book review." In the end, Bellow decided against replying, partly because he was satisfied "that Mr. Shawn agrees with me that I have been done an injustice," partly because he couldn't be bothered: so "vast, involved and peculiar" was the confusion of West's review, he declared in a letter to White on October 27, "that I don't feel brave enough or capable enough to deal with it. There are some misunderstandings that simply weaken you when you contemplate their complexity."[45]

The second distressing notice *Augie* received was the Norman Podhoretz review in *Commentary* ("The Language of Life," October 1953), behind which Bellow saw conspiracy rather than confusion. Podhoretz was twenty-three in 1953, recently returned from Cambridge, where he had studied with F. R. Leavis. Although a rising young man in New York literary circles, he was not yet well known. He was given the assignment to review *Augie* by Robert Warshow, an editor at the magazine, "because almost every other possible reviewer they could think of was either a friend of Bellow or had read the novel in manuscript and praised it privately to him." Bellow was a contributor to *Commentary* and, as Podhoretz puts it in his memoir, *Making It* (1967), "the staff admired him and was entirely in sympathy with what they took him to be trying to do in this new book. . . . But they did not want to 'set up' a review, and they had chosen me as a disinterested party." Podhoretz had read *The Victim*, which impressed him, knew Bellow was the "White Hope" of what he calls "the family" (i.e., the New York literati), but had never met him. He set about his task conscientiously, reading *Dangling Man* and rereading *The Victim*, "before going on to *Augie*, which I had every expectation of admiring. But to my dismay, the further I got into it, the less I liked it: it seemed forced, strained, shrill, and finally even tiresome." As a student of Leavis, Podhoretz told me in an interview, "I had very stern ideas about what a good novel is and this wasn't a good novel." Podhoretz was frightened by his own reactions, since he'd been told by Warshow that Lionel Trilling, his teacher and mentor as an undergraduate at Columbia, thought the novel extraordinary; Trilling, he knew from experience, "was far from promiscuous in distributing praise." In addition, "everyone else I respected was reportedly overwhelmed." *Making It* is very frank in detailing Podhoretz's ambitions. In the case of *Augie*, however, "try as I may and aware as I am of how hungry I was for attention, I can unearth no such motive in the piece I eventually wrote. . . . The most powerful impulse I remember having, in fact, was to fake the review or not write it at all, for I was in terror of the scorn that might be heaped upon me for making a mistaken judgment."[46]

The review was far from wholly negative. In its penultimate paragraph Podhoretz calls *Augie* "an impressive *tour de force*, impressive enough to earn the right to be criticized as a criticism of life." The last sentences of the review read: "Mr. Bellow has the very genuine distinction of giving us a sense of what a real American idiom might look like. It is no disgrace to have failed in a pioneer attempt." Podhoretz's grounds for criticizing *Augie* derive partly from the previously quoted passage about Augie's lack of development, partly from a reviewer's sense that there was something willed in its high spirits: "the book is almost bursting at the seams in its effort to be exuberant." Even in passages Podhoretz quotes approvingly, "the strain is apparent." Bellow admitted similar flaws in later years.[47] Where the review seems perverse is in its claim that "we are more aware of the words than the objects, of Mr. Bellow than of the world." Awareness of Mr. Bellow and his words no more prevents most readers from finding Grandma Lausch or Five Properties or Einhorn or Caligula (the eagle) memorable than awareness of Dickens and his words prevents readers from finding Magwitch or Micawber or Betsey Trotwood or Bull's-Eye (Bill Sikes's vicious dog) memorable, though as a 1950s Leavisite, Podhoretz would probably have been stern about Dickens as well. One is always aware of the writing in *Augie*, but the novel is also full of things, places, thoughts, characters, "objects" not only perfectly captured but present "for themselves," as both Penn Warren and Robert Gorham Davis suggested. In a later essay, "The Adventures of Saul Bellow, 1953–1959" (1964), Podhoretz drops that particular objection, confining his criticisms to the novel's picaresque form and the forced nature of its exuberance. (When I interviewed him in 2008, however, he returned to the criticism of Bellow's intrusive presence, confessing that "not a single character in his novels has ever come truly alive for me; they just all seem to me marionettes, puppets, figures through which to manipulate arguments.") In the 1964 essay, Podhoretz offers an explanation for what he sees as the forced quality of the novel's high spirits. Though Bellow is praised for being the first writer of the postwar period to give expression in a novel "to a new phase of American cultural history," one marked by "an exhilarating new impulse to celebrate the virtues of the American system and of American life in general" (as in the *Partisan Review* symposium "Our Country and Its Culture"), unfortunately, "like the ethos of which it was the most remarkable reflection, *Augie* was largely the product not of a state of being already achieved, but rather of an effort on Bellow's part to act as though he'd already achieved it. As a test case of the buoyant attitudes of the period, in other words, *Augie* fails."[48]

Podhoretz's review infuriated Bellow and turned its author into a figure of controversy. In *Making It*, Podhoretz claims that "everyone at *Commentary* was much impressed with the piece," even those, like Warshow, who admired both Bellow and the novel. Bellow then orchestrated "a campaign to discredit me." Warshow had sent Bellow a copy of the review in advance of publication, "with a dissenting and mollifying covering letter." Bellow was unmollified. In a two-page single-spaced reply, which he copied "to a dozen or more people," Bellow protested the charge of false spontaneity, mocked "your young Mr. P." with his fancy Cambridge and Columbia education, and dismissed Warshow's proffered dissent. Trilling, Bellow decided, had been behind the review. In Podhoretz's words, Bellow suspected that "Trilling had for some dark purpose been completely insincere in his own glowing review of *Augie March* . . . then, in collusion with the editors of *Commentary*, he had put me up to writing a piece which represented what they all really thought about *Augie* but were afraid to come out and say. Not only did Bellow apparently believe this fantasy; he actually persuaded many of his friends that it was true." There was, however, "some foundation" in Bellow's suspicions, Podhoretz admits: "the family actually felt some-what less enthusiastic about *Augie* than his famous touchiness, and their genuine desire to see one of their own make it as an important American novelist, had bullied them into pretending to feel."[49]

Although there is no evidence that Trilling himself did any conspir-ing, "there might have been a grain of truth," according to James Atlas, in Bellow's belief that he'd been targeted. In an interview with Atlas, Clement Greenberg, an editor at *Commentary* at the time, admitted that "we told Podhoretz not to like it," while Podhoretz described himself to Atlas as "the designated hit man."[50] In *Ex-Friends* (1999), a second memoir, Podhoretz writes of having "the misfortune shortly after the piece had appeared to run into John Berryman, who was one of Bellow's most ardent boosters. Staggering drunkenly over to me at a party in the apartment of William Phillips, he snarled: 'We'll get you for that review if it takes ten years.'" Bellow and Podhoretz were not to meet "until many years later (by which point he had still not forgiven me, and never really would)."[51] Though Bellow later wrote for Podhoretz at *Commentary*, corresponding with him about articles and potential articles, and once shared a platform with him in Washington, D.C., at a meeting to mobilize support for Soviet Jewry (at which his whispered insults about Alfred Kazin, who was also present and whom he'd turned against, brought them closer), he never abandoned his suspicions. In a letter of August 18, 1991, to Florence Rubenfeld, Clement Greenberg's biographer, he recalled the episode: "Norman was Lionel's protégé and Norman had tried to do me in. He says as much in his autobiography.

It did seem that Lionel was playing a double game since he had praised the very same book extravagantly. He and I had a sharp exchange about this." In 1999, as mentioned in Chapter 3, Bellow told Philip Roth that Trilling had been "dead against" *Augie*; at the same time he recalls Trilling's reaction to reading the first hundred pages: "It's very curious, it's very interesting, but somehow it's wrong." If this recollection is accurate, it may have played some part in suspicions about the sincerity of the *Griffin* review. Bellow was eighty-four at the time of the interview with Roth, however, and it may be that he is recalling the review itself, with its complaints about function versus fate.

Alfred Kazin shared Bellow's distrust of Trilling. In his memoir, *New York Jew*, "*the* barrier" between himself and Trilling is said to be the latter's fondness for the words "scarcely," "modulated," and "our educated classes." "The extent of Mr. Bellow's success in these pages," writes Trilling in the *Griffin* review, quoted by Kazin, "may be judged from the familiarity of the matter upon which he exercises his talents." Bellow, Kazin suggests, could never get over Trilling's "nerveless compromised accents," a tone that owed much to a reverence for Henry James, and was shared by other Jewish literary intellectuals and professors of English in the 1950s, notably Philip Rahv and Leon Edel, James's biographer and editor.[52] That Bellow was at this time as much a rebel against what might be called the "Jamesian standard" as the "Flaubertian standard" is clear from the famous opening sentence of *Augie March*, with its proud patriotic declaration—about James's great subject, "the whole American question."[53] The sentence is itself anti-Jamesian in its directness. Also anti-Jamesian is its Pep-like mix of registers: vernacular ("free-style" "go at"), biblical ("knock" is from "Ask and it shall be given you; seek, and ye shall find; knock and it shall be opened unto you," Matthew 7:7). At the end of the opening paragraph, after a reference to Heraclitus, Augie tells us that "there isn't any way to disguise the nature of the knocks by acoustical work on the door or gloving the knuckles." The knock is a knock: crude, hard, loud. The knock this novel is, is also jangling, jarring. The opening recalls a moment in James's *The American Scene*, referred to by Bellow several times and alluded to in Chapter 9, in discussion of Bellow's immunity to the Paris of James's Madame de Vionnet. Returning to New York, after long absence in Europe, James is taken by friends to the Lower East Side of Manhattan, a setting marked by "the hard glitter of Israel." The Café Royal, with its many Yiddish-speaking authors and performers, is described by James as "one of the torture-rooms of the living idiom." "Who can tell," he asks, "in any conditions, what the genius of Israel may, or may not, be 'up to.'" The quotation marks around "up to" suggest two unequally offensive meanings: "good enough for" or "equal to," which is merely patronizing, and "conniving."[54] Leon Edel's discussion of this passage is couched in—Kazin would say compromised by—the nerveless accents of a Trilling or a James: "His view of the Jews in the mass had always been distant; he had repeated the clichés by which their national distinctness was marked in the English novels."[55]

Augie March was published in the same year as the first volume of Edel's five-volume biography of Henry James. As it happens, Edel was one of the judges of the 1954 National Book Award for Fiction (for novels published in 1953), along with Mary McCarthy, Arthur Mizener, Gerald Sykes, and David Dempsey. When the judges declared *Augie March* the winner, they also, unusually, declared their decision unanimous, a measure undertaken to counter rumors, spread by McCarthy, that Edel had argued against Bellow. These rumors Edel denied, explaining that at a first meeting of the judges McCarthy had been so convinced that the prize should go to Bellow that she declared there was no reason for them to meet again. The other judges disagreed, and as Edel puts it, "Mary construed our procedural discussion as hostility to Saul's book." Bellow believed McCarthy's account, being as suspicious of Edel as of Trilling, seeing the standards of both not only as compromised but as a threat to his freedom as a novelist. When next he met Edel, he cut him (the Bellow version of turning the other cheek).[56] He never cut Trilling, but many years later, when Trilling came to Chicago to give a talk, he invited him out for a drink at a very rough bar, a location Diana Trilling describes as "a gathering place of drunks and deadbeats. . . . What other explanation of Bellow's choice could there be than the wish to test Lionel's ability to handle himself in such surroundings?"[57] It is hard not to see Bellow's behavior here as payback or punishment—for what he saw as collusion with the enemy. Bellow had to fight to become an author and thought himself in competition with those who doubted his claims. When Sam Freifeld implied, or seemed to imply, that Bellow had been presumptuous in criticizing T. S. Eliot's play *The Confidential Clerk*, he replied as follows, in a letter postmarked May 23, 1954: "Do you mean that he's a mighty Niagara and I a mere squirt? Possibly. But someone has to stand up for Jews and democrats, and when better champions are lacking, squirts must do what they can."

Bellow was not alone in this position, in being determined to fight his corner. In a journal entry of November 28, 1954, Kazin writes of opening his copy of the fortieth anniversary issue of *The New Republic* and discovering that the editors "hadn't included a *single* piece by me or mention," an omission that leaves him "furious with myself for not being *militant* enough, 'like Saul' say in fighting against the creepiness and conformity of the present."[58] Schwartz, too, thought of himself as embattled, but could joke about the cause, as in a letter of December 10, 1954: "It does seem as if the New-York-International style is winning out. A leading review in the London Times Lit. Supl. (of a biography of Gladstone) begins 'What a sorry mishmash . . . etc.'" The letter ends: "Call me Mishmash."

VIKING DID WELL by *Augie March*, spurred on in part by Lynn Hoffman, whose job as a reader for the press Bellow helped her to obtain (the Hoffmans had returned to the States in 1951, Ted to get an MA in English at Columbia, where he'd been taught as an undergraduate by Mark Van Doren and Lionel Trilling, Lynn to the job at Viking). Lynn was determined to see that *Augie* was not outshone by Steinbeck's *East of Eden*, "a vastly inferior book" which she remembers being presented to sales representatives "in a florid mahogany box carved by the master himself."[59] The launch party Viking gave for *Augie* was a grand affair, the occasion of what Sasha calls "my finest social moment." In a black dress, hair tucked into a large black fox hat, with a matching fox muff (courtesy of Maximilian furs), "I stood with Saul in the receiving line as people congratulated him. Ah, the look on William Phillips's face! 'It was never my idea, you know,' he whispered to me as he shook hands. Rahv said nothing."[60] Bellow was excited at the party but exhausted, having just begun a new job at Bard College, a small liberal arts college in Annandale-on-Hudson in Dutchess County, a job Ted Hoffman helped him to get. After finishing his MA at Columbia, Ted turned to the theater, a passion he'd developed in Paris and Salzburg, partly under the influence of Bellow's old Minnesota colleague Eric Bentley, now teaching at Columbia and writing theater criticism for *The New Republic*. During this period, according to Lynn Hoffman, "Ted became a sort of Consigliori to Saul," in the line of Sam Freifeld and Herb McClosky. That spring Hoffman had been appointed head of drama at Bard and when he learned of a vacancy in the Division of

Languages and Literature, recommended Bellow.[61] The chair of the division, the poet Ted Weiss, approved the recommendation and on June 6 Bellow received an official letter from the president of the college, James H. Case, offering a one-year appointment at a salary of $4,500. Bellow was pleased to take the job for several reasons: he could pretty much teach what he wanted ("Studies in American Literature, English 201," Hawthorne, Melville, Dreiser, Dos Passos), the attractive country setting would compensate for low pay, and "I could entertain my little boy there—take him out of the city, keep him with me on holidays and long weekends. Much nicer than dragging him around to museums and zoos in New York. Nothing is more killing. To the divorced, the zoo can be a Via Crucis."[62]

Bard College was quite unlike the places Bellow had previously taught. It was founded in 1860 as St. Stephen's College, "a pre-theological school with high educational standards and an emphasis on the classics."[63] In 1928 St. Stephen's affiliated with Columbia University. By 1933 it had begun to adopt progressive educational practices, and in 1935 it changed its name to Bard College. During the war, under the guidance of a dean, later president, from Bennington College, Bard "continued its pioneering efforts in the field of educational experiment." By 1944, it retained only the loosest of ties with the Episcopal Church, and when it began to admit women as well as men it severed its connection with Columbia. President Case was appointed in 1950 and a year later Blithewood, a beautiful Hudson River estate, was gifted to the college. It added 825 acres to the "old" campus and gave Bard wide frontage on the Hudson River. In 1953, when Bellow arrived, the ratio of staff to students was one to seven. The average size of any teaching group was less than ten students, and full-time faculty were asked to devote at least six hours a week to individual counseling and instruction, in addition to six hours devoted to group instruction.[64] It was, Bellow wrote on September 22 to Simon Michael Bessie, Kappy's publisher, the "roughest" teaching job he'd ever had: "Progressive for the students, reactionary for the enslaved teachers." "Never have I worked so hard at teaching," he wrote to Edith Tarcov in a Thanksgiving Day letter. "Small colleges demand infinitely more of you, and it is a thankless and poorly paid labor. On Fridays I generally have to go to New York to have my teeth—preserved: they are in that stage. And when I have finished running around the City and have returned from my visit to Forest Hills I reach Barrytown on Sunday in a state of exhaustion."

Bellow found the students at Bard bright, bohemian in style, and demanding, "terribly earnest in every sense of the term."[65] Bard was "like Greenwich-Village-in-the-Pines," he later recalled; or, as Sasha put it, "Bennington with boys."[66] Mary McCarthy, who taught at Bard in 1945, when it had only eighty students, and subsequently at Sarah Lawrence, another progressive college, wrote a novel, *The Groves of Academe* (1952), set in a college "quite a bit like Bard," with recognizable fictional portraits of several faculty members still in place when Bellow arrived. The male students at the novel's Jocelyn College are divided into a "beer-and-convertible crowd—the ex-bootleggers' and racketeers' sons, movie-agents' sons, the heavy-walleted incorrigible sons of advertising geniuses who had been advised to try Jocelyn as a last resort" and "an unusual number of child prodigies, mathematical wizards of fourteen, as well as . . . cripples of various sorts" (mental as well as physical). The female students, in contrast, are mostly pretty and healthy, "with the usual desires and values, daughters of commercial artists, commercial writers, radio-singers, insurance-salesmen, dermatologists, girls who had failed to get into Smith or nearby Swarthmore . . . narcissistic, indolent girls wanting a good time and not choosy, girls who sculpted or did ceramics of animals, or fashion-drawing, hard-driving, liverish girls, older than the rest, on scholarships." "Unlike most advanced young women," McCarthy writes of a young idealistic member of the literature department at Jocelyn, "she dressed quietly, without tendentiousness—no ballet-slippers, bangles, dirndls, flowers in the hair."[67]

In *A Trip into Town* (1961), a novel by Michael Rubin, who had been a student at Bard when Bellow was there, Suki Goodman, one of McCarthy's "advanced young women," falls for Leon Kossof, a newly arrived professor, author of the recently published *The Fortunes of Shlomo O'Brien*, about a hero "trying by turns to identify himself with one 'meaningful' cause after another, and then to escape all his influences." Kossof's novel, which is described as a "picaresque saga," traces its hero's fortunes "the length and breadth of the Western Hemisphere." It makes its author famous. Suki goes after Kossof not only because he's a literary celebrity but also because "he's *gorgeous*." To the narrator, Kossof seems "a prototype of confidence and strength, a definition of poise and purpose. . . . This was a very successful man, an author at the peak of his creative powers, the darling of literary cocktail parties, a book club selection." Hence the crowd he attracts at his first lecture: "at least a dozen girls were there. . . . Oddly enough, they were all very pretty."[68] Kossof has a tendency to wander in lectures, barely mentioning the text, and attendance soon dwindles, though the loyal followers who stay with him hear brilliant lectures on Dostoyevsky. When away from the lectern, on walks with the narrator, he "tended to turn gloomy. He rarely talked intimately about himself . . . but dealt in broad generalizations, as though his personal problems were indicative of the state of the world." When Kossof breaks off with Suki, it is to marry the woman he's been living with throughout the affair. "Let me be frank," he confesses to Suki, "and tell you outright that you flattered me. . . . What veteran would not take advantage when offered a lovely young lady?" At the same time, "I also flattered *you*. I am a fairy tale for you. What young girl does not want to sleep with an 'artist' at least once in her life." Though Suki is "dear" to him, Kossof is "deeply in love with Hannah. . . . It was still always my bond to Hannah that touched my imagination."[69] There is clearly something of Bellow in the character of Kossof. Sasha asks in her memoir: "Were there other women at this time? Apparently, if what I read and heard later was true, but it never occurred to me to think so at the time or for some time to come" (p. 82).

If the style of the students at Bard was bohemian, the style of the faculty was conservative or Ivy League. "Castaways from ships that had foundered en route to Harvard or characters who had fallen from grace at Yale" is how Bellow described his colleagues, "still refining the airs they had acquired in the great Ivy League centers."[70] On visits over the summer, Bellow and Sasha had met some of the faculty. Both were particularly fond of the Weisses (Ted's wife, Renée, was the sister of one of Sasha's freshman roommates at Bennington). Bellow's colleagues in the Division of Languages and Literature were eight in number[71]: Keith Botsford, a twenty-six-year-old writer, educated at Yale and the University of Iowa, was, like Bellow, a new appointment (this was his first full-time job); Irma Brandeis, a Dante scholar, the muse of Eugenio Montale, was ten years older than Bellow and the most senior member of the staff; the poet Anthony Hecht, eight years younger than Bellow, came via Bard itself, where he'd been an undergraduate, but also Kenyon College, Columbia, and the University of Iowa, where he'd taught in the Writers' Workshop; Andrews Wanning, a poet and literary scholar (Choate, Yale, Cambridge), was a seventeenth-century specialist; the Swiss-German Willie Frauenfelder ("a nice, gentle man," according to Botsford) taught languages; Warren Carrier, cofounding editor, with Weiss, of the *Quarterly Review of Literature*, taught writing; and Texan novelist William Humphrey, no Bellow favorite, taught American literature. Jack Ludwig, from Winnipeg, another aspiring writer, a self-professed "Joycean," came to Bard via both UCLA, where he'd recently received his PhD, and a brief teaching stint at Williams College.

A week or so after Bellow received his appointment letter from President Case, he took the train from Grand Central Station to Rhinebeck, a picturesque journey up the Hudson, past wide vistas and grand estates, several of which are described by Henry James and Edith Wharton. There he was met by the Hoffmans, already in situ. Ted Hoffman, like McClosky at Minnesota, was happy to smooth Bellow's way, directing him to the registrar, introducing him to Bard faculty, helping him to find a place to stay. The weekend before Fall Semester, Sasha remembers, there was a lawn party for the faculty followed by a cocktail party at the home of Felix Hirsch, who had come to Bard from Germany, where he had been political editor of the *Berliner Tageblatt*. Sasha was particularly struck by Jack Ludwig, though "not in the least for any romantic reason." She had arrived for the weekend without party clothes, felt ill-dressed and ill at ease, and then "this very round faced, fat guy, wearing a hideous checked jacket that even a bookie might have rejected, gave me a joyful, humorous smile and I responded gratefully" (p. 74). Ludwig also made a strong impression on Botsford, who remembers seeing him at a party for new faculty "in Chanler Chapman's tatty big farmhouse, roomy and reeking of drink." Botsford arrived there straight from New York City. That morning, he'd gone early to Bloomingdale's book department to purchase a copy of *Augie March*. By the time his train arrived at Rhinebeck, Augie was in Mexico (an episode "I didn't believe"). At the party, Botsford spotted Bellow immediately; he was now famous thanks to reviews of *Augie* and accompanying profiles and portraits:

> He stood against a wall with a glass in one hand which he held before him protectively. What I took in first was his visibility: academic smart, but always as I remember him with a little gaud about him: in this case a bright foulard in his pocket. I kept looking. Of course I wanted my turn with him; Augie bubbled in my mind. His hair was still dark, way up on the temples; his lips were fleshy, his

mouth generous, part of the *animal ridens*, a joke behind good teeth. But the eyes got me. . . . They were oblique, as at an angle to each other; the right eye was wary, like a permanent Id, the left gobbled up detail. It was with his left eye that he suddenly saw me.

. . . There was an obstacle between us: a bulky Winnipeg hockey body, a heft arm leaning against the wall, a mass of hair that bristled, resilient and thick, hair by hair, and a flow of Yiddish, of back-slapping laughter. This was Jack Ludwig, also newly arrived at Bard, with its prey. And yes, I knew that then. I was watching a rape, an attempted possession. Jack backed off. "I need a drink," he said and away he lurched: audible still, a very needy man. Saul said, "Thank God you rescued me from that butcher boy Yiddish! Let's go get some fresh air."[72]

If Botsford is right about the party venue, Bellow was, in effect, at home, having rented an apartment above the carriage house (tractors, boats, cars) on the grounds of Sylvania Farms, Chanler Chapman's estate in Barrytown, just south of Annandale. Chapman came from grandee stock, not that he looked it. He was a descendant of the Astors as well as the Chanlers; his first wife, Olivia, was a grandniece of Henry James; his father was John Jay Chapman, described by Gore Vidal as "easily the most original of American essayists." A local "character," Chapman affected a backwoods gruffness and slovenliness; he also possessed what Vidal describes as "an eerie and entirely unjustified self-assurance" ("eerie" is a Vidal staple, as in Richard Nixon's "eerie but touching propensity to fuck up").[73] Chapman called his estate the "Piggery," stomped around in muddy boots and overalls, but also enjoyed showing off his father's library. He published a monthly broadsheet entitled *The Barrytown Explorer*, which printed his poems. The apartment Bellow rented from him had charm, but in Sasha's words was "as bare as it could be. No toilet, even" (p. 75). Everything, toilet included, had to be purchased, mostly from local yard sales. Initially, in the early autumn, Bellow and Sasha made do with a mattress, a Mexican blanket, a rickety wooden table, four kitchen chairs, and an assortment of mismatched pots, pans, and kitchenware. Then it got cold. By November Bellow was freezing: the wind blew in from the Hudson, there was barely any heating, and Chapman refused to supply wood for the furnace. Bellow accused him of trying to freeze him out; he accused Bellow of being cold because he was a writer and didn't move around enough.[74] There were other tensions. "He complained that the drain didn't work and that the place smelled," Chapman recalled. "He was right, of course, because the whole place stank."[75] According to Winthrop ("Winty") Aldrich, Chapman's cousin, Bellow claimed that Chapman shot his cat.[76]

At the end of December, Bellow cleared out, with Chapman protesting that he owed him rent. From December onward, from Monday through Thursday, Bellow stayed in a spare room in the Hoffmans' house, a former rectory just below the Bard campus (described by Lynn Hoffman as "damp and wormy").[77] On weekends, when Lynn returned from her job at Viking, Bellow stayed in Manhattan in an apartment he'd rented at 333 Riverside Drive, near the Broadway apartment Pearl Kazin sublet from her brother Alfred. Pearl had left *Harper's Bazaar* and was now working at *The New Yorker*. She needed someone to help with the rent, and because Sasha and Saul could not "cohabit" (for legal reasons, given divorce proceedings), Sasha moved in. Sasha liked Pearl: "I found her to be bright, good-hearted, the first one of the women I met through Saul who didn't either ignore me, feel competitive, or just merely tolerate me" (p. 81). Bellow's apartment was small and spare, though if one stood on the toilet one could just glimpse the Hudson. It was near Sasha, however, and at some point its Upper West Side location became an object of close scrutiny for Bellow, and the setting of his next published novel, *Seize the Day*.

Bellow and Hoffman got on well during the week, sharing household chores and working quietly on lectures and classes and on their own writing. Bellow had good relations with most of his colleagues, especially the younger ones. "He was a handsome, very gentle fellow," recalled Robert Koblitz, a professor of government, "extremely sensitive to people . . . very well liked." Another colleague, William Wilson, remembered him as "extremely affable. . . . Curious about the world and interested in all sorts of things."[78] Outside the Division of Languages and Literature, Bellow admired Heinrich Blücher, Hannah Arendt's husband (Arendt herself rarely appeared on campus). Blücher, a poet and philosopher, had been brought to Bard in 1952 by President Case to devise the college's "Common Course" (a general humanities or "Great Books" course). To Alfred Kazin, in a letter of January 7, 1954, Bellow described Blücher as "*good*. . . . Maybe you could arrange to work with Heinrich. That would make Bard worth your while." (Kazin was inquiring about teaching at the college.) The only colleague Bellow had difficulties with was the Texan novelist Bill Humphrey, described by Botsford as talented but with "a small-town narrowness of vision, a Calvinist streak." These difficulties came to a head, according to Sasha, in a fierce argument over Melville, although she records neither the cause of the argument nor the sides taken (p. 80).

In addition to Bard faculty, a handful of outside writers and intellectuals lived in the area. Prominent among these figures, and a bridge to the old "river families," was Gore Vidal, who in 1950 bought Edgewater, a grand Greek Revival house in Barrytown. The house was built in 1820 and once lived in by Chanler Chapman's illustrious father (to buy it cost Vidal $6,000 plus a $10,000 mortgage). The political journalist Richard Rovere was part of Vidal's circle, as was F. W. (Fred) Dupee, who taught at Columbia during the week, and had an apartment in New York on the Upper West Side near the apartment Bellow rented. Both the Roveres and the Dupees lived in Rhinebeck, the Dupees and their two children in a handsome old house called Wildercliff. It was Dupee who introduced Mary McCarthy to the Bard campus (and was the model for Howard Furness in *The Groves of Academe*). Rovere was described by Bellow as "the only genuine democrat in this literary set"[79]; Dupee, in contrast, was much taken by the river grandees, especially by Margaret Aldrich, a relation of Chanler Chapman, who had known Henry James. "Fred's obsession with these characters," Vidal writes, "was more than balanced by Saul Bellow's loathing for them."[80] When taxed with arrogance by Keith Botsford, speaking many years later of their time at Bard, Bellow thought immediately of the grandees: "I made a point of speaking down to people (the nobs) who believed that I should look up to them. My lack of humility was aggravated by the rejections I met or expected to meet. Those confrontations were a part of my education."[81] Vidal, though a nob of sorts, was an intellectual rather than a social snob; he not only admired Bellow's writing but liked his company. In addition to calling Bellow "the only intellectual who read books," as mentioned in the Introduction, Vidal thought him "very funny, and we both saw the world from a satiric point of view." Bellow's hostility to the grandees, Chapman in particular, was entertaining to Vidal: "The rows between thick-skinned master and mutinous serf gave us all joy." Vidal also remembers an evening at Edgewater to which the Dupees brought Lionel and Diana Trilling. "The Trillings follow me into the Green Room. Merrily, Saul greets Lionel. 'Still peddling the same old horseshit, Lionel?'"[82]

GIVEN THE SPLIT with Anita, the push to finish *Augie*, and anxieties about its reception, Bellow was not always the easiest of companions in this period, at least for those closest to him. Anthony Hecht remembers gracious and friendly Saturday night dinner parties at the carriage house in Barrytown: "Saul and Sondra entertained wonderfully," he told Atlas. Bellow was "very genial, open, accessible, full of fun."[83] Sasha's memories were more mixed. She had never run a household, having grown up in hotels "where they changed the sheets for you every day." She didn't know how to cook. She had never lived with a man. She found life with Bellow exciting but testing. In New York, on weekends, there were glamorous dinners and parties with celebrities: Lillian Hellman, Arthur Miller, John Steinbeck (at a party given by Pat Covici for Alberto Moravia). At Bard, Sasha learned how to set up a household and "soon got the hang of it in the kitchen and began to enjoy the challenge" (p. 77). Bellow was loving but he was also critical. She remembers his anger when she returned to Barrytown from Manhattan with two champagne glasses from Baccarat to celebrate "our making a home together." He had given her money to buy household items and thought she'd used it for the champagne glasses. When she unwrapped the glasses, he was furious. "He flared his nostrils at me and thrust out his lower lip and accused me of being 'extravagant,' 'spoiled,' 'thoughtless'" (pp. 75–76). She began to cry, explaining that she'd used her own money to purchase the glasses. Bellow apologized but accusations of extravagance persisted, in part a product of anxieties about the impending divorce and payment of alimony. "He complained about money all the time," Vidal recalled in an interview, convinced that "no matter what happens there isn't going to be any."[84] In her memoir, Sasha defends herself against accusations of extravagance, while quoting a friend who once said of her: "She would give you her last dime, even if she only had a nickel" (p. 76). There were also accusations and arguments about sex ("you expect too much," Bellow told her), accompanied by Bellow's insistence that Sasha see a Reichian therapist, "both to fix me up, and to help me understand him (his words, not mine)." Reichian therapy mystified Sasha, particularly when her therapist discouraged her from using an orgone box ("I had heard scary but intriguing things about it"), advice that annoyed Bellow: "Why did I not need it and he did?" (p. 82).

Bellow's suspicions about Sasha's truthfulness were especially hurtful in respect to her painful stories of her upbringing. At the heart of these stories stood her father, the painter Nahum Tschacbasov, who had even more names than his daughter. He was born Nahum Lichter in Baku, Russia. When his family moved to Chicago in 1905 after the pogroms, he was seven or eight. There he was known, variously, as Nathan Richter, H. H. Richter, Hanathan Richter, Nate Lichter, and Nathan Lichterman. "The way I heard it," she writes, "the original family name was Georgian, something like Cherbachev or Shebashoff" (p. 3). It was her paternal grandfather who first changed the name, buying a forged German passport in the name of Lichterman to get out of Russia. "Tschacbasov," an approximation of the Russian original, was the name Sasha's father adopted in Paris, where he moved the family the year after she was born, determined to become a painter (he thought the new name would look impressive on canvas). In Chicago, he had been a businessman, though of what sort is not clear. Sasha believes he made a fortune in the 1920s and 1930s as an "efficiency expert," the term then for management consultant, under the name Hanathan Richter. Always a big spender, his fortunes fluctuated wildly. Sasha's mother, Esther, his second wife, had been his secretary. In Sasha's memoir, she is described as "a shy, studious, sweet-natured girl" (p. 9), valedictorian at Tuley High School (some half dozen years before Bellow attended). She married Sasha's father in 1929, when she was nineteen or twenty. When Sasha was born, in the Michael Reese Hospital (where Anita Bellow once worked), the family lived at the Edgewater Gulf Hotel, a "swanky address in Chicago at the time." To celebrate, her father went out and bought a yacht, which he named the *Sondra*. After her mother's death, an uncle offered Sasha an alternative explanation both for the move to Paris and for the family's change of name: "My father had been a well-known con man in Chicago and had fled when things got hot" (p. 10). He may also have fled to avoid paying child support for the children of his first marriage, whom he abandoned after their mother died and custody was awarded to her parents.

In France, Tschacbasov ("Nate" to his wife, "Chuck" to his friends) studied with Adolph Gottlieb and Fernand Léger and began to have exhibitions. When he returned to the States it was to Brooklyn Heights rather than Chicago, to a brownstone on Pineapple Street, the first of the family's "many transient dwellings around the boroughs" (p. 21) (where Alfred Kazin and Arthur Lidov later lived). Here he established a reputation in artistic circles as a painter and political activist. "My parents were definitely Communists," Sasha writes, "not that they ever joined anything officially" (p. 21). "Chuck" was a volatile figure, and among gallery dealers gained a reputation for being hard to handle. Sasha describes him as "a man of enormous energy . . . difficult to head off when he set his mind to something" (p. 8), "a dark and dominating presence, often erupting without warning, a demon, really, clever and wicked." He had a Svengali-like manner, "a practiced, seductive air, with a challenging edge towards women that some found irresistible." In the early years in New York, "before he went over the edge completely," he had good relations with other artists, including the Soyer brothers, Milton Avery, William Gropper, David Burliuk, and Philip Evergood (p. 23). In 1935 his paintings appeared in a show at the Gallery Secession with those of Mark Rothko, Adolph Gottlieb, and other modernist and expressionist painters who formed a group called "The Ten." Though he eventually broke with this group, he retained the support of a loyal coterie, including the lawyer-collector Sam Goldberg, who also entered Bellow's life in this period, quite independently. Tschacbasov was single-minded and obsessive as a painter (by one estimate he produced more than seven thousand canvases) and resolutely bohemian in his habits. Eventually, after yet another move ("I think I can count 12 moves in New York alone between 1935 and 1942" [p. 28]), it was thought best to give Sasha a more settled environment. In 1940, at the age of nine, she was enrolled in the Manumit School (from the Latin "manumission," freedom from bondage), a progressive Quaker and socialist school located near Pawling, New York, about an hour from the city. Sasha adored the school: "I don't ever recall being homesick" (p. 31).[85] When, after several years, money difficulties forced the Tschacbasovs to move to Oklahoma, where relatives promised work, and they had to withdraw Sasha from the school, she was devastated.

In the main body of her memoir, Sasha skips the years between twelve and twenty. Only in a postscript, probably written two years later, does she describe them, beginning with a paragraph recounting how difficult they were to write about and how much she has repressed. The second paragraph begins: "Here's what I definitely know: my father began to come to my bed in the night either in Oklahoma or just after our return to New York" (p. 122). She was twelve. By the time she started high school, when the family was back in New York living in the Chelsea Hotel, "there was no way I could keep him from me if I was alone with him" (p. 125).[86] He told her that what they were doing "was not really wrong, it was bourgeois to think so, look at ancient Egypt, and furthermore, it was my fault, I had been provocative (at eleven or twelve?). And I had better keep quiet or there would be real trouble, my mother would never believe me, guaranteed. He said he would give me the weekly allowance I had been asking for. . . . The bargain was clear: keep very quiet, let it happen, get the money. I learned to negotiate like a fishwife" (p. 126). The abuse continued through high school and was accompanied by threats. Only in 1955, shortly before she and Bellow married, did Sasha tell her mother what had happened. This was when her parents were separated for a time, over her father's affairs with other women. Sasha's mother listened to her daughter's tale of abuse in teary silence but "just couldn't accept it" (p. 123). Later that day she called Tschacbasov, who denied everything. "'He says you are a pathological liar. I don't know what to believe.' It was the first time I heard that phrase, but not the last. I was stunned. We never spoke of it again" (p. 123). Her mother then returned to her father, who "was brutal to her, demanding she renounce me utterly. . . . She just couldn't do it, any more than she could accept my truth fully" (p. 124).[87]

Could Sasha have resisted? "It seems now that I should have been able to, but at the time I saw him as all-powerful, looming, frightening, and yet in some way hard to explain, there was some guilty pleasure mixed in with the disgust and horror." She coped with these feelings by burying them: "I was good at pretending. . . . I perfected passivity, was later to be famously aloof with men, ruthlessly suppressing my sexual instincts. . . . I was a mess" (p. 127). One of the reasons she went to Bennington, she suggests, was that it was "unencumbered by male students" (p. 129). She had only a single brief romance while in high school and "had not been willing to think about men in that way, not one time, for the entire next five years" (p. 69). "It isn't that I was timid," she said in an interview, "I was passive." "Men would just really have to come in and get me and I tended not to notice a lot of it because I didn't want to." When Bellow first met her in 1952, she was "a *demi-vierge*" (p. 69), sharing an apartment with one of her father's students. This student her mother had introduced her to, not knowing that Tschacbasov was sleeping with her. Tschacbasov was often at the apartment—the girls were now in the Ansonia—and when Sasha found out what was going on, she moved out, to live at 25 Fifth Avenue with Anita Maximilian, recently separated from her husband.

In the months before the move, shortly after beginning work at *Partisan Review*, Sasha "seriously began to think about Catholicism," an interest she had developed at Bennington while studying medieval history with Franklin Ford. She contacted the Society for the Propagation of the Faith, where Bishop Sheen, "the first 'televangelist,'"[88] gave weekly instruction to small groups. Bishop Sheen was "mesmerizing and dynamic. . . . Handsome, too." Sasha "quickly caught his particular attention. Soon enough I was his spiritual daughter, his 'dushka' as he began to call me . . . he described it as a Russian word for Soul." At chaste weekly dinners, Sasha and the bishop "talked cozily of Thomas Aquinas, Thomas Merton and, marvellous bonus, he even knew of a number of the 'little' literary magazines. And, at times he slipped me a little extra spending money. Finally, a good father! Money without favors." In December 1952, Bishop Sheen baptized Sasha at St. Patrick's Cathedral, giving her a new name, Maria Kristina. "That Bishop certainly knew how to win me over—give me an exotic name, a beautiful antique rosary (his baptismal gift), a chaste embrace, and I was sold on the whole thing" (p. 64). When *Partisan Review* let Sasha go, Bishop Sheen offered her a job editing the Catholic magazine *World Mission*.

In wooing Sasha, Bellow had two fathers to overcome. At some point in the wooing, he enlisted the help of Ted Hoffman, a lapsed Catholic, a tactic Hoffman described as "a fool's errand."[89] What worked was Bellow's persistence: he and Sasha spoke on the phone "for hours"; his trips to the city from Princeton grew more frequent. That Bellow seemed to take Sasha's Catholicism seriously was crucial: "He was fascinated by my conversion, my yearning for the spiritual experience" (though she also admits "maybe it was mostly about sex or the chase and he just wanted to get me into the feathers") (p. 68). Dealing with Tschacbasov, the literal father, was easier. In May 1953, at a party at the Ansonia to celebrate Sasha's twenty-second birthday, Bellow met her parents for the first time, along with members of her father's entourage. There was dancing at the party and Tschacbasov danced with Sasha "too much, too close, smirking at Saul; I was stiff and miserable, couldn't get out of his grip without a scene." Later Tschacbasov baited Bellow, calling James Joyce "too baroque," T. S. Eliot "a fag writer," *Augie March* "too rococo" (he had read a few pages of the novel in one of the magazine excerpts). Bellow responded "very smoothly," with cutting sarcasm, "and Chuck left in a fury, my mother running after him." Several days later, Tschacbasov told Sasha that Bellow was too old for her and that she should consider going out with the brother of her roommate (whom he had propositioned at the Chelsea Hotel, she later learned) (p. 68). Bellow's cool besting of Tschacbasov made Sasha "feel safe . . . he was an anchor, a haven, a North Star." She was a damsel in distress, he a knight in shining armor.

When at last she consented to go to bed with Bellow, shortly after Bellow read her "the better part" of *Augie*, which she found "dazzling," Sasha assumed a second identity: "Now it was sex, sin and literature. An irresistible brew. I was hiding from the Bishop as well as my father, and at the same time enjoying the public role as Saul's girl" (p. 72). (She was also hiding, for legal reasons, the fact that she and Bellow were mostly living together.) As she got to know him better, Bellow, too, seemed to change: she saw how needy he was, for praise, reassurance; what she calls his "melancholic, suspicious, furious" side emerged.[90] Sasha wanted Bellow "to continue his role as my rescuer, but this fantasy was starting to crumble." In the memoir, she recalls an angry outburst in which Bellow called her whole history into question. "Maybe being with a young girl was beginning to feel like a lot of work, perhaps he was too exhausted from his own worries to listen willingly to my stories of growing up at the Chelsea. So he really shocked me one day when he lashed out, saying that he wasn't sure he entirely believed any of it" (p. 82). Sasha's tendency to fantasize fed such suspicions. While at Bennington, she was mortified when it was discovered that Tschacbasov was not her birth name. "At nineteen, I was attempting to live up to or, at least with, this grand (counterfeit) Russian name by embellishing family history to suggest, if not actually promote, a romantic image of Russian emigres fleeing the Revolution. How humiliating was the predictable response from my roommate and her mother to the unveiling of the Richter name" (p. 2).[91]

OVER THE COURSE of his year at Bard, Bellow began to spend more and more time with Jack Ludwig, described by Vidal as "Iago in permanent pursuit of an Othello." Anthony Hecht made a similar comparison: "There was something very malevolent about Jack. . . . He took an Iago-like pleasure in double-crossing someone who didn't know he was being double-crossed."[92] "Iago is a bit strong," Phil Siegelman protested. "He was rotten to the core but he wasn't Iago." By the end of the year, Botsford was closer to Ludwig than to Bellow. He often had dinner with Ludwig and his wife, Leya, and daughter, Susie, in their tiny apartment. Frequently when Botsford came for dinner Jack was away, at other times he'd stay for a while, then "slope off noisily. He had to see Saul, to work at the office, to see a student. I felt it, but didn't say so to Leya, as a kind of sexual urgency" (*Fragments*, p. 24). Atlas quotes a Bard student named Elsa, perhaps the Elsa whom Bellow had been sleeping with, or so Ludwig told Sasha, perhaps also "the other chick in the chickenyard," in Ralph Ellison's phrase, a girl pursued by both Ludwig and Bellow: "There was something very lacking in Jack. . . . He wanted to *be* Saul Bellow."[93] This remark recalls what Moses Herzog hears about Valentine Gersbach, the Ludwig character in *Herzog*: "People say that Gersbach imitates me—my walk, my expressions. He's a second Herzog" (p. 608). Botsford sums up Ludwig's relation to Bellow like this: "Young man, head stuffed with knowledge and responsibilities, takes up a new job and finds himself faced with The Real Thing, the man he always wanted to be" (p. 6).[94]

To Alfred Kazin, who was fond of Ludwig "in a sort of way," "Jack was not to be believed. . . . Nothing fazes him, nothing intervenes, in the unremitting drama of his self-advancement. . . . Only none of it is real. He reminds me of the actor-manager of some provincial repertory theatre, forever beating down the creditors. . . . He looks into one's eyes, burrows his image into one's consciousness. 'Look at me! See how positive, how manly, how electric and alive!'"[95] To Greg Bellow, looking back, Ludwig was a familiar type: "My father would surround himself with people like that all the time, who were conflating reality and artistic notions. I didn't think twice about it because everybody did that. Some were people of great talent, other people thought themselves people of great talent."[96] Botsford, whom Greg identifies as another of this type, makes much of Ludwig's disability, "a visible blemish, a damaged foot, that kept him from play and a proper childhood." This "blemish" became "a weapon in his armory; you weren't allowed to feel sorry for him because he wasn't sorry for himself. He had conquered all that bad stuff and was on the rise and he took you over—as he had tried to do with Saul, the night of Chanler Chapman's party" (p. 4).[97] Greg Bellow agrees: "In my view, Saul's connection to Jack resided in the man's tolerance for suffering, his capacity to absorb feelings, and his ability to appear sympathetic to Saul's constant complaining. Jack suffered palpably every day. One leg was shorter than the other, and he walked with a pronounced limp. Worse, he suffered from a joint disease that flared up painfully and forced him to remain in bed until it subsided. Jack's palpable suffering in silence made a deep impression on my father."[98] Other factors, in addition to Ludwig's stoicism and sympathy, figured in Bellow's attraction to him. As Botsford points out, Ludwig was both "a provincial youth" and "Jewish where there were not many Jews and none quite like him" (p. 4). During walks in the woods, Ludwig sometimes joined Bellow in performing Reichian exercises. As Anthony Hecht told Atlas: "He would take Jack with him and they would both roar."[99] Ludwig became a confidant and was soon dispensing advice on Bellow's sex life.

Ludwig's sympathy for Bellow was accompanied by outright flattery. According to Hecht, "Saul was always a sucker for flattery, and Jack would lay it on with a trowel."[100] Joseph Frank and his wife, Marguerite, known as Giguitte, remembered Ludwig as sycophantic in the extreme, but then much about Ludwig was extreme. He had a loud basso voice, a hearty laugh, thick black hair, heavy black eyebrows, a strong, square jaw. "He had a powerful presence," Phil Siegelman recalls, "a great gift of the gab, a willingness to engage." Botsford describes him as having "a stature, a sheer physicality, that suggests coal-mining or combine harvesting, anything requiring brawn and that peculiar explosive intensity that so marked his loves (of great writers) and his disapprovals of what wasn't *echt*, that didn't conform to his ebullient sense of what counted in life" (p. 4). When Ludwig arrived at Bard he had written almost nothing, his only book being an anthology entitled *Stories, British and American*, coedited with Richard Poirier, a lifelong friend. His self-assurance, however, was as eerie as Chanler Chapman's. In *Herzog*, when at last the scales fall from Moses's eyes, he sees Gersbach's confidence, his readiness to answer all questions, for what it is: "the infallible sign of stupidity. Did Valentine Gersbach ever admit ignorance of any matter? He was a regular Goethe. He finished all your sentences, rephrased all your thoughts, explained everything" (p. 572). "With pinochle players he plays pinochle, with rabbis it's Martin Buber, with the Hyde Park Madrigal Society he sings madrigals" (p. 635). Herzog's lawyer, Simkin, partly modeled on Sam Goldberg, takes issue with this interpretation:

"Well," said Simkin, "he's nothing but a psychopath on the make, boastful and exhibitionistic. A bit clinical, maybe, except that he's a recognizable Jewish type. One of those noisy crooks with a booming voice. What kind of car does this promoter poet drive?"

"A Lincoln Continental."

"Heh, heh" (p. 635).

Ludwig was a popular teacher, if not always a conscientious one, according to Phil Siegelman, who remembers him boasting "about never having to prepare for classes." With students, he could be embarrassingly familiar. Ted Hoffman recalls him loudly advising passing Bard students "on the best kind of condoms."[101] In such stories Ludwig resembles Gersbach, "that loud, flamboyant, ass-clutching brute" (p. 518). Other witnesses, especially from later years, paint a different picture. At Minnesota, where he taught after Bard, he was very popular with students. When his contract was not renewed in 1961 after three years as a temporary lecturer, three hundred students signed a petition on his behalf, and dozens of newspaper articles and letters to the editor were written by parents and faculty as well as students in protest against the decision.[102] After Minnesota Ludwig went to Stony Brook, at the time the State University College on Long Island, where he was also popular with students. The writer Carolyn McGrath, who was taught by him in the early 1980s, remembers him as "one of the finest teacher I had in college." Far from answering or explaining everything, he was "utterly Socratic, he would pose a question, let the class deliberate it, but withhold his own opinion. . . . He once asked a class, 'Which is the more modern author: Joyce or Pynchon?' Everyone else answered 'Pynchon.' I answered 'Joyce,' but Ludwig didn't tip as to his opinion. I'm still pondering the question, which is as it should be." In his dealings with McGrath outside of class he was "always a gentleman, always respectful," nor did she ever hear other students complain about him.[103] "Jack could be boorish and overweening," concludes Botsford, "but he was also a friend and, if not prodded, far from being stupid or unpleasant."[104]

BELLOW'S PROBLEMS WITH Anita tormented him while he was at Bard. When he left her, she went into a depression. Writing to her mother, she admitted that the marriage was over, but she refused to grant Bellow a divorce.[105] In a letter of February 21, 1954, to the Tarcovs, however, she suggests that it was Bellow who was holding things back. "Saul was supposed to go out to Reno around Christmas but delayed so long that he couldn't. He is supposed to go this summer but I doubt if he will. I don't think he wants a divorce it is more convenient for him this way." Anita was a more reserved correspondent than Bellow and her upbeat accounts are sometimes oddly phrased.[106] She writes of having "run around dating a lot" in the fall, but that "I really wasn't happy doing it—so I quit." Her current "happiness and good spirits" come "from within" rather than being "dependent on someone else." "Too often I am so happy to be alone and uninvolved." "*Too* often"? Conflicting emotions sound also in the sentences that follow:

> Not to have to worry if someone else is depressed, hungry or sick is a real pleasure. Then I begin to feel guilty for feeling so good and wonder if I don't ever want to get married again. Then I quit worrying about it and enjoy my good feelings. I get up every morning feeling happy—what else can one ask from life?

Sometime after receiving this letter, Edith Tarcov wrote to Bellow about Anita. After filling him in about Oscar's heart trouble, a "constant anxiety," she describes Anita much as Anita describes herself. She begins by hoping that "matters between you . . . are settled now." Then she writes of recently seeing Anita: "she seemed so willing to be sensible . . . she as a whole seems fine, much freer than I ever saw her, much gayer and more direct. That terrible obsession, of feeling constantly as your inferior, admiring you and resenting it too, that has hold of her these many years, has left her. But by some other things she expressed most vividly and heart-breakingly how hard it was for her, not to love you anymore."

Meetings with Bellow accomplished little. Something of their difficulty can perhaps be seen in Bellow's depiction of the meetings between Tommy Wilhelm and his wife, Margaret, in *Seize the Day*. Having walked out on Margaret and their children, Tommy wants a divorce. He has a much younger girlfriend, Olive, a Catholic, whom he wishes to marry. Tommy claims Margaret is resisting; she claims "he did not really want a divorce; he was afraid of it." When he asks Margaret "Don't you want to marry again?" she answers "No." "She went out with other men, but took his money. She lived in order to punish him" (p. 79). Margaret has Anita's good looks, her hair "cut with strict fixity above her pretty, decisive face" (p. 94). Her voice fits Bellow's description of Anita's character, being "measured and unbending, remorselessly unbending" (p. 93). Hearing Margaret's voice awakens in Tommy "a kind of hungry longing, not for Margaret but for the peace he had once known" (p. 93). Margaret prides herself "on being fair-minded" (p. 94), but in arguments over money, over having to chase Tommy for money, she is hard, vindictive: "she brooded a great deal and now she could not forbear to punish him and make him feel pains like those she had to undergo" (p. 95). Arguments between Bellow and Anita seem to have been no less charged and intractable. It was agreed that Bellow could see Greg every other weekend and for a month in the summer; otherwise, nothing was settled. In addition to the issue of divorce there were arguments about child support. At one point, Anita, strapped for cash, appealed to Abraham for money to buy a winter coat. Greg suspects that "she intended to make Saul look bad, but crying poverty did not endear her to the Bellows."[107] For years Anita had been the main breadwinner in the family. Now that *Augie March* was a success, she felt that she had a right to expect something in return, or at least not to have to fight Bellow over money for Greg. But Bellow worried about his capacity to produce another windfall. As he wrote to Oscar Tarcov, in an undated letter of April 1954, he was "in the ridiculous term people have reported, an avant garde writer," but one "with a slick writer's requirements." What guarantee was there that such an author could make a living at writing? "For one year it may be possible, and after that—who knows?" Bellow was also reluctant to hand over the first real money he'd made through his writing to the person he thought of as blocking his freedom. Although his correspondence in this period shows flashes of feeling for Anita, it makes her out as unreasonable about money. "Still being sheared of my earnings by my dear wife of the former incarnation," Bellow writes to Sam Freifeld on April 25, 1954; "I am being stripped," he writes to John Berryman in an undated letter of the same month, "Anita B. has not let up in her campaign to get me crucified." Greg describes Bellow as behaving spitefully in this period. After custodial visits, "it was rare that he left without taking a piece of fruit from the fridge, fruit for which he felt he was paying, and putting a few books under his arm. And he needled Anita." He could also be possessive. When Lillian Blumberg McCall invited both Bellows to a party in Greenwich Village, and a man flirted with Anita, "Saul got so upset that the two men got into a fight in the street."[108]

The Wrecker, a one-act play Bellow published in 1954 in *New World Writing*, a paperback literary anthology, reflects these feelings.[109] The play was published about the time Bellow wrote a theater chronicle for *Partisan Review* (May–June 1954) and it marks the beginning of a decade-long intermittent interest in playwriting, which resulted in several productions both on and off Broadway.[110] It concerns a married couple, Albert and Sarah, whose building is to be demolished and turned into a school. Like all the building's inhabitants, the couple has been offered a thousand dollars to vacate their apartment early. Albert, however, is determined to tear down the apartment himself, their home for fifteen years (in effect, the length of the Bellow marriage). "Think what you could do with a thousand dollars," Albert's mother-in-law tells his wife. "You could get a new coat" (p. 195). Unheeding, Albert sets about his task with comic gusto. "I feel like Samson in the Temple of Gaza," he cries, carrying a hammer on one hip, a hatchet on the other, and holding a crowbar. "Take cover, ye Philistines, your oppression is ended. . . . Though you took my hair and put out my eyes and bound me in your mill your walls are doomed" (p. 198). Sarah is hurt and bewildered by such talk. "I didn't know you hated it so" (p. 199). When her mother attacks Albert, however, she leaps to his defense: "I know what he's been through" (p. 201). As Albert wrenches the top off the mantelpiece, Sarah's knickknacks scatter to the floor. "Oh, my things!" she cries. "The sea-shells! The little jug from Vermont! The little cups!" (p. 202). When asked if he has suffered in every room in the apartment, even the bedroom, Albert is momentarily taken aback: "No more than the others, probably" (p. 203). He invites Sarah to join him in the wrecking: "Didn't it ever make you want to yell? Didn't you ever feel here that you were in a cage?" She refuses. "I papered and painted these walls myself, and washed the floors and the woodwork" (p. 204). Albert's response is pure Wilhelm Reich: "Sometimes you ought to give in to your violent feelings. It's great to be angry. Anger is beautiful. It gives you a sense of honor. It brings back your self-respect" (p. 205).

Matters come to a head over the bedroom. Sarah accuses Albert of not loving her. "Of course I love you," he replies (p. 205). She puts her foot down: "if you wreck the bedroom, you'll be moving into the new apartment by yourself" (p. 207). Again Albert presses her to join him in the wrecking. When she continues to resist, he accuses her of being "far too rigid—far, far. You have to learn to be more flexible. It's a practical matter. For the sake of your health. . . . Let's wipe out some of the falsehood. Let's admit what our souls tell us is true and stop denying it" (p. 208). Only after Albert injures himself in the course of smashing his way to health, does Sarah agree to join in. As he watches her first delicate blows, a stage direction tells us, he "doesn't look happy"

(p. 210). He's not sure he likes Sarah as wrecker ("On you it doesn't look so good"), especially when she suggests they start on the bedroom together. "Is it really," he asks, "I mean from your standpoint—such a good idea?" "You don't want to wreck it?" she asks, before declaring: "I do, now when I think of some of the things that happened, all of a sudden I want to express what I never dared." Albert asks what she's trying to tell him. "What is there to tell? Do I have to draw pictures?" It is Sarah not Albert who now says "maybe the best way to preserve the marriage is to destroy the home." In the last line of the play, Albert replies mildly: "It may well be." This line is followed by the stage direction: "CURTAIN (After which, a thunderous crash)" (pp. 210–11). It is the husband who wrecks the marriage. He is, however, no Samson, being weak, wavering, insecure.

There are connections here with "By the Rock Wall," the story Bellow published in *Harper's Bazaar* in 1951, discussed in Chapter 6. In this story, which contains a fictionalized version of the retaliatory affair Anita had in Mexico after Bellow went off with another woman, the protagonist's insistence upon honesty almost wrecks his marriage. Neither Albert nor Willard, the husband in "By the Rock Wall," can handle the truth, despite their supposed devotion to it. Nor, judging by his behavior during the wrangles over divorce, could Bellow the man. Bellow the author, however, could see unfairness, insensitivity, and comic selfishness in his protagonists, while approving their determination to live freely and honestly. In life, Bellow was often harsh and unforgiving with those who blocked him, even while acknowledging their claims or feelings. In a letter to Freifeld of May 23, 1954, he begins with accusations about Anita and money, then moves on to larger complaints: "She always *took* far more than she gave. I don't reproach her with anything; her nature is her own reproach. I am genuinely sorry for her but I can feel more compassion as an ex-husband."

AT THE END of the teaching year, Bellow finally felt he had enough money to devote himself for a period wholly to writing, complaints about being "sheared" by Anita notwithstanding. He resigned from Bard in June and discouraged feelers from the universities of Iowa and Minnesota. To Ted Weiss, who had been on leave in Oxford, he summed up his time at Bard: "Since I had to be there, I ended by rejoicing in the experience. It was quite something. . . . I'd have made some compromise and stayed if I was a stronger character. But you've got to have stability *somewhere* to survive this *pays de merveilles*, cloud-cuckoo, monkey-on-the-back, *avant-garde* booby cosmos, and I'm afraid I just don't have it—grit, gumption, spunk, stick-to-itiveness, values founded on rock." There had been much to enjoy in the year: "the sight of a skinny, pallid little boy arriving in a chauffeur-driven Cadillac," "excellent" conversations, walks, violin duets with Emil Hauser, who taught music at the college and was once first violinist in the Budapest String Quartet. "But I couldn't survive meetings and in the end stopped attending. And if I had to choose between trichinosis and talking for an hour with F. Hirsch I'd—you know! Where's that raw pork? And Case [the college president]—an Ivy League *schlimazel* [loser]!" The colleagues he would miss were Jack Ludwig, Ted Hoffman, Heinrich Blücher, and Andrews Wanning. Weiss had asked if Bellow would be coming to Europe and Bellow answered that he wouldn't: "My son can't do without my help this year.—It is also somewhat the other way around. But he's starting at another school; I'm beginning another book." These were also the reasons he would be living in New York in the coming year, a place, he told the McCloskys, he "despised": "I stay because of Greg. But, also, I am writing a book and can't undergo a dislocation now."[111] In his memoir, Greg confirms the impression created by such passages: of his father's importance to him and of his importance to his father. He writes of looking forward to Bellow's weekend visits, of trips to MoMA and the Metropolitan Museum of Art, of lunches at the Eighth Street Delicatessen, double or triple features of W. C. Fields and Mae West or the Marx Brothers ("Saul and I knew every quip by heart and laughed until our sides hurt. For years my father used humor to jolly me out of the bad mood that always overtook me when it was time to say goodbye"). He describes Bellow as "the parent who understood me best"; after he left the family, "I felt like a deep-sea diver cut off from my oxygen." He also says of this period: "I do not remember either parent criticizing the other."[112]

In the summer of 1954, Bellow rented a cottage near Slough Pond in Wellfleet, a fishing village at the far end of Cape Cod. He and Greg would spend the month of July there. Before the trip, Greg lobbied hard with both parents for a dog, on the grounds that "If I got a dog, I'd never be sad."[113] Anita agreed on condition that Bellow did the housebreaking. Greg was then given a puppy from the litter of Anita Maximilian's dachshund, Schatzie. It was Bellow who named the puppy Lizzie, after

Elizabeth Barrett Browning (both dog and poet had sad eyes). Lizzie accompanied father and son for the month on the Cape, also for several days prior to the month, when Bellow lectured at the Bread Loaf School of English in Vermont.[114] On July 7, Bellow wrote to the school's director, Reginald Cook, to say that son, dog, and father had arrived safely at Slough Pond, finding the cottage "in a setting of pines, ticks and sun. Nevertheless we made ourselves comfortable and are happy." Soon they were regulars on the beach at Wellfleet, "La Plage des Intellectuels," where among the visitors that summer were Alfred Kazin and his second wife, Ann Birstein; Mary McCarthy and her third husband, Bowden Broadwater; Arthur Schlesinger Jr.; and Harvard English professors Harry Levin and Daniel Aaron. The beauty of the place—long white sand beaches, high dunes, freshwater lakes—washed the city away; the socializing brought it straight back. Of gatherings at Wellfleet, Alfred Kazin writes: "Upon the beach they sat, discoursing, and loud was the sound of battle, louder than the waves."[115] On August 10, Mary McCarthy reported to Hannah Arendt that Kazin "was here and cutting me dead, quite unjustly, since I don't like him. On the other hand, I don't dislike him so *totally*. Saul Bellow was here too, with son and dog, not very friendly either."[116]

Sasha came up from New York on weekends only. For the most part, Bellow was in sole charge of Greg, which meant that Greg, ten that summer, was on his own in the mornings. On weekend visits Bellow would take a morning off writing, on monthlong visits he wrote every day. Once the morning stint was over, afternoons were mostly spent at the beach, swimming, playing, chatting. In the evenings, there were cocktail parties, as interminable for Greg as the mornings. Ann Birstein was struck by how attentive a father Bellow was at Wellfleet, and how handy he was with domestic chores. She recalls him watching with disapproval as she ironed one of Kazin's shirts. When she asked if he thought he could do it better, "he whipped expertly through several of Alfred's shirts, long-sleeved ones too, having learned how from being the youngest child and following his mother around as she did the housework."[117] Both father and son needed this time together for emotional or personal reasons, but fathering in general may have mattered to Bellow because of what he was writing, a novel that grew in part out of a conspicuous absence from *Augie March*. In the interview he gave to Harvey Breit in *The New York Times Book Review*, Bellow described his father as "a fascinating character." When Breit asked him if his father appeared in *Augie*, Bellow said "No, I've saved him." The novel he saved him for was the one he was writing that summer, "Memoirs of a Boot-legger's Son," much quoted in the opening chapters of this book. In a letter of December 7, 1954, to John Berryman, Bellow describes the novel as "a handsome new book, which is so far highly satisfactory." He then gives it the jokey title "Memoirs of a Bootlegger's Son, or The Song of the Oedipus Complex."

In his application for a second Guggenheim Fellowship, Bellow described "Memoirs" as being about "the fortunes of an immigrant and his eldest son; I follow their lives for forty years, from Canada to the States, and describe the efforts of the father to make a fortune and those of the son to remain a son. In the end, it is the old father, per-haps, who has become the American?" At the very end of the summer of 1953, shortly before the publication of *Augie*, Bellow took Greg with him to visit Lachine, a bonding trip that was also a research trip: the two purposes went together, as did Bellow's fathering and his reflec-tions on fathering, both on Abraham's fathering and his own (when he and Greg got to Lachine, Bellow told Bernard Kalb in *Saturday Review*, he was dismayed to find "the street pretty much monopolized by a supermarket"). Why Bellow gave up on "Memoirs of a Bootlegger's Son," which in its most finished form consists of 172 typed pages and contains many powerful and moving passages, is not clear. Atlas, as was mentioned in Chapter 1, says he thought it too sentimental, presumably repeating what Bellow told him.[118] In the letter to Berryman immedi-ately after the "Song of Oedipus" subtitle, Bellow writes: "I don't worry about that either. Do you know, though, as I creep near the deepest secrets of my life, I drop off like a lotos-eater. I am being extremely lazy." This passage can be read in two ways. On the one hand, it can be said to support the view Atlas offers, as if Bellow sensed something easy or escapist about the novel. To be immersed in the earliest experiences of childhood was for him like being in lotos-land, pleasurably drugged (earlier in the letter he says "I'm growing so lazy, John, it appals me. I don't even worry. My anxieties are like old dogs. They no longer run after rabbits. They only dream and whine, asleep"). The lotos-land glow that suffuses "Memoirs," according to this line, is like Moses Her-zog's "potato love," a sentimentality he deplores.[119] In such a reading, the phrase "I drop off like a lotos-eater" might suggest not only "I fall asleep" but "I grow slack or 'lazy' as a writer," as in "even Homer nods." On the other hand, the passage might suggest that Bellow abandoned the novel because of its closeness to forbidden material ("the deepest secrets of my life"), even though he implies this is not the case ("that" in the phrase "I don't worry about that either" must refer to the Oedipus Complex), a reading supported by Bellow's reply to a letter from Berryman of April 8, in which he complains of finding correspondence difficult because "my heart is lazy, and I am tired. Also, I am loath to say what I think." In addition to these admittedly fine-spun readings, practical or down-to-earth considerations may also figure. The manuscript breaks off at the point when the Lurie family departs for the United States. How, in what is to follow, was Bellow to avoid repeating material from *Augie* (his mother's isolation, relations between the Lurie brothers, especially between Joshua, the Maury figure, and "Bentchka," the Bellow figure, urban life during the Depression)? There was also Bellow's family to consider. "Memoirs" was drawn more closely from life than anything Bellow ever wrote. Though loving about Pa Lurie, it is also highly critical. Abraham might not read it, but if he learned of its contents, as he learned of *Augie*'s contents, he would not be pleased.

Abraham's health was poor at this time; he had heart trouble. His granddaughter Lesha remembers him as "a big smoker . . . always hacking." In the September 23 letter of congratulations he wrote to Bellow about *Augie*, he mentions having recently been in the hospital for observation: "The X-rays come—and very good with the exception the[y] find I had a slight heart attack. Still I hope to be good for the next ten years." In the year before he died, from the spring of 1954 onward, he complained of ill health. On February 7, 1955, he wrote from the Waverly Hotel in Hot Springs, Arkansas, that "Two weeks we improved a little. Stil we no so well. We are not anymore young—I am 75. Also aunte [Fannie, his second wife] is not more a spring chicken." On March 17, 1955, he went in for a complete checkup at the Edgewater Hospital in Chicago, where he was found to have had a slight coronary thrombosis, hardening of the arteries, and an enlarged heart. Though comfortably off, living in retirement on the North Side with Fannie, a shrewd, even-tempered woman, in a modest house at 6135 North Rockwell Street (described with uncanny precision in *Herzog*),[120] active at the local synagogue (its president, for a time), visited dutifully every Sunday by children and grandchildren, he remained difficult and quarrelsome. Like Father Herzog, he got "stormier and more hot-headed and fractious as he aged" (p. 633). According to Greg, "Abraham found financial threats the best way to reassert his waning authority." He frequently announced changes in his will when displeased with one or other of his children. As Greg describes it,

> He would go so far as to call his lawyer, often in the middle of the night. . . . Morrie tired of this routine early on and turned up his nose at his share to emphasize its paltry size, but Abraham's mercurial threats had serious consequences for Sam, Jane, and Saul, whose fragile finances made him particularly vulnerable. My father would rush back to Chicago to learn about the new will. By the time the family had assembled at Grandpa's insistence to hear of the new asset division, he and the offending child had patched things up and the crisis would blow over until Abraham pulled the same stunt again and the whole scene was repeated.[121]

These episodes took place during the period when Bellow was at work on "Memoirs of a Bootlegger's Son." He was also at work on "Memoirs" when Abraham died, on May 2, 1955, of a heart attack. The death shattered Bellow. "When my father died I was for a long time *sunk*," he wrote to Mark Harris, author of *Saul Bellow: Drumlin Woodchuck* (1980). Ruth Miller came to pay a condolence call at Bellow's apartment at 333 Riverside Drive and "when Saul opened the door, he was weeping."[122] At the funeral in Chicago, he wept so conspicuously that he embarrassed Maury, who told him not to "carry on like an immigrant." Maury had business friends there "and he was ashamed of all this open emotionalism," an inheritance from Abraham.[123] As Bellow wrote to Martin Amis on March 13, 1996, on the occasion of Amis's father's death: "Of course you *are* your father, and he is you. I have often felt this about my own father. . . . I'm obviously very like him: out of breath with impatience—and then a long inhalation of affection." At some point in the year before Abraham's death, Bellow put "Memoirs" aside and began work on the story that would become *Seize the Day* (originally titled "Here and Now—Here and Now," after also considering "One of Those Days" and "Carpe Diem"). *Seize the Day* was published in the 1956 summer issue of *Partisan Review* (*The New Yorker* passed on it because of its length), a little over a year after Abraham's death. It is as concerned with fathers and father-son relations as the unfinished "Memoirs," but is much tougher in its depiction of both. Tommy Wilhelm, the son, is at times repellently weak ("In him we see the failures of 'feeling'"[124]); his father, Dr. Adler, is repellently hard, as autocratic as Pa Lurie but with none of his redeeming features. How, readers have wondered, did Bellow move from *The Adventures of Augie March* to *Seize the Day*, works so different in mood, register, and form? The answer is he didn't. *Seize the Day* grows out of "Memoirs of a Bootlegger's Son," a work written during a period of intense preoccupation both with Abraham at the end of his life and immediately afterward, and with Greg following the family's dissolution. As Bellow wrote to Leslie Fiedler, explaining the effect of the separation on Greg, "I doubt that he will suffer as much from our divorce as I suffered from my parents' 'good' family life. I love Gregory and I know how to make him feel my love. He is injured, but not really seriously injured and his position also has its advantages." Hence Bellow's refusal of an invitation from Fiedler to visit Montana: "I couldn't arrange to have Gregory travel

Keith Botsford, SB, Irma Brandeis, Anthony Hecht, Willie Frauenfelder, Warren Carrier, Jack Ludwig, Andrews Wanning, Bill Humphrey

from his summer camp all by himself, and the time we spend together in summer is too important. It is the only time during which I live with the kid, and we both look forward to it."[125] In a letter of May 23, 1953, to Freifeld, he reports that he almost bought a house in Sag Harbor, on Long Island: "I need a place of my own very, very badly. I am nearly ready to *sit* and be Columbus's chronicler not one of his crew. It would do Gregory good, too, he loves to be with me, and it makes him happy to come to me in a settled place." Yet after a month of full-time single parenting—a month in which he also wrote every day, "for a living" as well as posterity—he confessed to Robert Hivnor, in an undated letter of August 1954, that "I am completely worn out from acting as G's tutor, governess, cook and baseball buddy, and can't wait to get back to New York."

12

Pyramid Lake

IN LATE MARCH 1955, a little more than a month before Abraham's death, Bellow received word from Henry Moe that he had been awarded a second Guggenheim Fellowship. When Moe asked for his estimated income for the coming year, Bellow answered on March 29 "about $3,000," adding that "as you will perhaps recall, I have two dependents" and that "there may be other money coming in but I can't be sure of it." Bellow's intention was to spend at least half the fellowship year in Rome, though in other correspondence he mentions spending time in Spain as well. He estimates travel expenses at "about $500," living expenses at "about $3000," and clerical and other smaller expenses at "about $300." Given these figures, he asks the foundation "to consider my request for a Fellowship grant of $3800. This should enable me to finish my novel now in progress."

Bellow never made it to Rome. He went to Nevada instead to secure the divorce he was unable to obtain, or obtain on what he felt were acceptable terms, in New York. "I see no reason to pay tribute in order to remain in New York," he explained to Henry Volkening. "I prefer the horse to the subway."[1] On June 3 he wrote to Sherry Mangan, the author and editor, then living in Málaga, to say that he hoped to get out of Manhattan soon, but that "before I (or we) come to Spain, a short stay in Nevada is required of me, divorce laws being of a near-Spanish backwardness. So we should be arriving in Europe in February of 1956." In Nevada Bellow could obtain an uncontested divorce in six weeks, the shortest residency requirement in the country. To obtain a unilateral decree took three months, during which time he was meant not to leave the state. On the eve of the six-week deadline, negotiations with Anita remained deadlocked; Sam Goldberg, Bellow's lawyer, had nothing positive to report. As Bellow wrote on November 5 to Ruth Miller, his old pupil, "unless Anita is converted I shall have to be here a good while longer; and if she's on some Road to Damascus it's odd she hasn't reached it yet. . . . I don't expect her to stop persecuting me." He was not the sort to accept what he saw as persecution without hitting back. "She's in for a bit of a shock herself," he added in the letter to Miller, a remark explained in a letter to Freifeld, written the same day: "Anita should soon be served with my complaint. I *love* that."

Bellow's plan after obtaining the divorce was to remain with Sasha but to stay single. "I have no intention of bouncing from divorce into marriage," he wrote to Volkening on October 19, after a month in Nevada. "When I have lived for a year or so freed from my burden and still feel as I do about Sondra we will begin to think about marrying." What he felt about Sondra (Sasha was still something of a private name, not yet adopted widely or consistently or by Sasha herself) is suggested in correspondence. "Sasha is infinitely more happy than she's been in her life, I think," he writes in the undated letter to Berryman in which he talks of Anita's "campaign to get me crucified." "A poor book by Arnold Bennett I read this a.m.—*Lillian*—had one good thing in it. A young girl requires making. A man makes her into a woman. Whither then? I hope she'll become my wife, but it is a great thing to have waked someone into life, and Sasha is a very considerable human being." There was, the letter suggests, an element of fantasy in Bellow's as well as Sasha's sense of their relationship, a Pygmalion element in Bellow's case. Though there were tensions and arguments between them, they were a couple, and for the most part Bellow's friends, certainly his men friends, approved (not that they were likely to have said so if they didn't). "You seemed very happy with Sandra and she with you," wrote Isaac Rosenfeld on May 25, 1955. "It is important that you learn to have fun," wrote Sam Freifeld on June 3. "I think Sandra can do a good job if you will let her. . . . You know that if anybody is capable of giving you happiness, she is. She has my unqualified affection."

After a second summer at the Cape with Greg, during which, at Pat Covici's suggestion, he set to work expanding *Seize the Day* from thirty to forty thousand words, and before journeying to Nevada, Bellow accepted a well-paid assignment from *Holiday* magazine to write an article about Illinois. When he handed the article in, it was rejected, confirming his fears about writing for a living. "The editors told me to write the piece in my own way," he complained to Sam Goldberg in an undated letter from Nevada, "and then were appalled by my long discussion of boredom in the Midwest. They wanted me to cheer things up a little, like a true native son. But I couldn't do that." The article, "Illinois Journey," was eventually accepted in a shortened form almost two years after completion, appearing in the issue of September 22, 1957.

What is immediately clear from "Illinois Journey" is how engaged Bellow was by the assignment, for all his stress on the boredom of the state. It offered him a way out: of New York, where he had been living for almost a year and which he'd come to abhor, and of himself and his problems. When he writes of the monotony of driving through the state it is the landscape, the thing seen, that preoccupies him. Here is the article's opening paragraph:

> The roads are wide, hard, perfect, sometimes of a shallow depth in the far distance but so nearly level as to make you feel that the earth really is flat. From east and west, travelers dart across these prairies into the huge horizons and through cornfields that go on forever: giant skies, giant clouds, an eternal nearly featureless sameness. You find it hard to travel slowly. The endless miles pressed flat by the ancient glacier seduce you into speeding. As the car eats into the distances, you begin gradually to feel that you are riding upon the floor of the continent, the very bottom of it, low and flat, and an impatient spirit of movement, of overtaking and urgency, passes into your heart.[2]

In describing the people he meets on his journey, so unlike the people at Bard or in New York literary circles, he neither sneers nor patronizes, even when he finds what they do or say odd or comical. In Nauvoo, in the northwestern part of the state, the Mormons built a city and erected a temple in 1839. When the prophet Joseph Smith was murdered in neighboring Carthage in 1844, his followers fled Nauvoo, leaving many vacant homes and businesses. Gradually, a steady stream of believers began to return, refurbishing its buildings, putting up historical markers, opening views onto the Mississippi.

> Nauvoo today is filled, it seemed to me, with Mormon missionaries who double as tourist guides. When I came for information I was

embraced, literally, by an elderly man; he was extremely brotherly, hearty and familiar. His gray eyes were sharp, though his skin was brown and wrinkled. His gestures were wide, ample, virile, and Western, and he clapped me on the back, as we sat talking, and gripped me by the leg. As any man in his right mind naturally wants to be saved, I listened attentively, but less to his doctrines perhaps than to his Western tones, wondering how different he could really be from other Americans of the same type (p. 200).

Bellow measures the places he visits in Illinois against their moments of influence. If the article has a theme it is the inexorable progress of American materialism. Almost a hundred years ago, Galena (the setting in part of "A Trip to Galena," the only surviving portion of Bellow's abandoned novel "The Crab and the Butterfly," *Augie*'s immediate predecessor) was a center of commerce, as were other small towns Bellow visits, such as Cairo (pronounced "Cayro") and Shawneetown. Galena is now "a remote place beside a shrunken river," bypassed by the railroads. Ulysses S. Grant lived in Galena and his house has been turned into a museum, "but it is a museum within a museum, for the town itself is one of the antiquities of Illinois, and it has a forsaken, tottering look" (p. 198). In Shawneetown, Bellow is told a story about bygone days, when "representatives from a little northern community called Chicago once approached the bankers of opulent Shawneetown for a loan and how they were turned down because Chicago was too remote a village to bother with. 'Well, look at us now,' my informant said to me" (p. 201).

THE CAR BELLOW USED for the Illinois journey was the one he used to drive out west to Nevada, an old Chevrolet. He did not travel alone. Sasha came along on the trip, not to stay with him in Reno, but to be driven to California, to Malibu, to be the guest of a friend, Sand (Suzanne) House, now married to a Hollywood executive named James Higson, a producer of the popular television game show *Queen for a Day*. After Sasha quit working for Bishop Sheen's *World Mission*, she found a job writing press releases for a small public relations firm. The job bored her and when she lost it, as Bellow wrote to Kazin on June 29, 1955, it was "to great delight. First she was affronted, and then it made her, as it should have done, happy." In addition to being without a job, she was soon to be without a place to live; the Kazins were returning to New York from Massachusetts (Alfred had been teaching at Smith College) and needed their apartment back. At this point it was proposed that Sasha help Bellow and Delmore Schwartz with a publishing project Schwartz had wangled for them at Viking. The project was to produce an anthology entitled "What the Great Novelists Say About Writing the Novel" to be used as a textbook. By July 1955, the manuscript was six months overdue and Pat Covici wrote to ask when it would be submitted (this question Schwartz evaded, while procuring an advance for another project, the "Portable Heine").[3] Sasha, the editors decided, was just the person to hunt down passages for the anthology. While Bellow settled in Nevada and got his divorce decree, she would work at the library at UCLA. Since she had no money, Bellow agreed to pay her expenses. Though the anthology was never completed, the job was real enough, and Sasha had the requisite literary skills, or so Schwartz seems to have thought. "Please tell Sasha that I've read her review," he wrote to Bellow on December 19, 1954, "and would be delighted to have her write my reviews for me at the usual rates."

To Sasha the drive west was among the best times she and Bellow had together, "a wonderful carefree trip . . . once we got past the endless cornfields of Nebraska, with spectacular drives through the Badlands (where the car broke down) and Yosemite, talking, laughing, and snuggling in at night in rustic motels." As she put it in an interview: "we'd have a lot of hot sex at night and then get into the car in the morning."[4] The motels were mostly little cabins with kitchenettes. They'd stop in the late afternoon, buy groceries, and Sasha would cook dinner, leaving something for the next day's lunch. At Mount Rushmore, "I remember trying to slice a pot roast in the car with his penknife on a winding road past those enormous presidential stone faces" (p. 84). Bellow did all the driving. Although Sasha had driven in college, she had no driver's license. (Bellow liked to drive and liked cars, and when he could afford them, bought good ones.) After a few days in Malibu with Sasha and the Higsons, he left for Nevada, arriving in Reno on September 27. Shortly afterward, as arranged, Sasha rented a room in Westwood, just off the UCLA campus, buried herself in the library during the week, and spent weekends at the Higsons' beach house on Malibu Colony Road. She remembers that Bellow called her "nearly every night" (p. 85).

When Bellow got to Nevada he stayed initially at the Pyramid Lake Guest Ranch, a dude ranch about an hour northeast of Reno. The ranch, on the southwestern shore of the lake, was owned by Harry Drackert, a former rodeo champ, and his wife, Joan, a prizewinning trapshooter. The Drackerts were among a dozen or so guesthouse operators in the Reno area catering to wealthy out-of-state residents waiting for divorce. The Thoroughbred and quarter horses Harry raised at the ranch, for both racing and ranch use, grazed untethered by the lakeside. A. J. Liebling stayed at the Pyramid Lake Guest Ranch in 1949 when seeking his divorce, returned to the area frequently, and wrote several *New Yorker* articles about the lake and his experiences there. He described the guesthouse business as "a cash crop in the summer," involving peculiar requirements for its cowboy proprietors, some amatory, others less demanding (for example, "the daily corvée of bringing a detail of the women in to shop [in Reno] and have their hair done").[5] When Bellow arrived, most of the summer residents had gone, and there were few new guests in the months to follow (the Drackerts were to close the business the following year). Writing to Volkening a day after arrival, all Bellow says of the place is that it's windy—"this wind I'm sitting in threatens to carry me and my thin paper over the next mountain"—and that he plans to stay only until he finds an apartment to rent. But he stayed several weeks, leaving because it was too expensive to stay.

The place he moved to, he wrote to Volkening on October 19, was a one-room "cabin or shack, decent and pleasant in its way, but its isolation is beyond anything you've ever seen. I thought it would be better to live like this for a while and study my soul, and I still think it is the wise course for me. I have even begun to work again, after weeks of idleness. But there are times when I must, and literally do, howl." The shack was thirty miles from Reno on the edge of a Paiute Indian reservation, surrounded by low copper-colored mountains and overlooking Pyramid Lake. The American explorer John Charles Frémont named the lake after the most striking of the bizarre rock formations jutting from its changeable blue expanse: a six-hundred-foot-high tufa-encrusted pyramid near the eastern shore (tufa is a chalky sediment produced by a chemical reaction to algae). The lake was beautiful but otherworldly, like the surrounding landscape, which often appeared in science fiction movies set in outer space.[6] One-sixth saline, it was home to strange fish, described by Arthur Miller (who is soon to enter the story) as "whiskery and forbidding, of an unevolved kind found only here, it was said, and in a lake in India."[7] These strange fish, the unevolved cui-ui, were discussed in Liebling's *New Yorker* articles, titled "The Lake of the Cui-ui

Eaters"; the species was two million years old. Less ancient but impressive in their own way were the lake's enormous cutthroat trout, named for the red gill slashes just behind their heads.

Bellow's shack, built out of old railroad ties, belonged to Margaret "Peggy" Marsh, the owner of a neighboring pink house. Electricity for both residences was provided by a Model T Ford engine; the place was silent except for the twice daily whistle and clack of a long freight train passing nearby. The air at Pyramid Lake was exceptionally clear. A rattlesnake-infested island a mile distant looked a hundred yards away. To make a phone call Bellow had to walk half a mile down a dirt road to a phone booth on the main highway, "a road travelled by perhaps three vehicles a day and none at night." Once a week he would drive into Reno to buy groceries, do laundry, visit the library, have a meal out, or go to a movie. The drive in and out of Reno was featureless, all sand and sagebrush, but as Miller notes, "out on the desert, far from the vehicle track, there were sometimes signs of life underground . . . a pair of shorts hung out on a stick to dry in the sun, or a T-shirt. They were men wanted by the law, for murder more often than not. The state police knew they were out there, and nobody enquired why they were not picked up, but payoffs were inevitably suspected."[8] The strangeness of the landscape sparked Bellow's imagination, helping to produce the strangest of his fictions, *Henderson the Rain King*, a novel mostly set in Africa, a place he'd never been, with a desert landscape very like that of Pyramid Lake.[9]

In many ways Bellow's time in Nevada was just what he needed. "You will be astonished not to hear complaints from me," he wrote to Sam Freifeld in a November 5 letter, "but I haven't any. And now the first six weeks are almost out, and I find myself almost regretting that they've gone so quickly. This sort of life suits me more than I would have thought possible. I fish and ride, and walk and read and write; at moments I even think." Writing to Ralph Ellison on April 2, 1956, he was still high on Nevada. "I hope it's been a good year for you and Fanny; for Sondra and me it's been a remarkable one. You wouldn't have known me, Ralph, with my casting outfit and a new reel pulling in rainbow trout. Sitting a horse, too." Bellow liked the people he met at the lake as well as the life he was leading. Peggy was good company. Forty years earlier she had come to Reno for a divorce and never left. She was lively, warm, casual in manner and appearance, a big woman, hard-drinking and smoking, with a heavy wheeze. Only when she began talking did one realize that she was well-born, from a "good" family in St. Louis but with plenty of wild stories about her past. She also told stories about the Drackerts, the Paiute Indians, most of whom lived at the other end of the lake, twenty miles away, her well-off friends Nora and Pat Pattridge, who lived up in the hills in what Sasha recalls as "a lovely, elegant farmhouse," and whom Bellow also got to know and like, and several "elderly ladies who lived at mountain sides and in lonely canyons."[10] Like Peggy, Joan Drackert was both a talker and a heroic smoker. Liebling describes her as "a blonde with a good figure and an inquiring mind, and her wide gray eyes were slightly keener than a chicken hawk's."[11] The Drackerts had a bar, little more than a shack, and a modest gift shop, the Indian Trading Post, on the main road, selling Paiute arts and crafts; it was here that the telephone was located. The bar was mostly tended by Joan and when there were calls for guest ranch residents or Bellow or Peggy, Harry or an old ranch hand named Red would be summoned to notify one or other of them.

In "Leaving the Yellow House" (1958), one of the most powerful of Bellow's stories, the heroine, Hattie Waggoner, is based on Peggy Marsh. Hattie is admirable in her independence, despite many failings.[12] She is seventy-two, divorced, a heavy drinker, and has lived at Sego Desert Lake for more than twenty years. She comes from money and was well educated but has been poor for some time. Her interest in ideas is "very small."[13] She is lazy and "never made any bones about it: an idle life was all she was good for" (p. 269). A friend and former employer, India, another hard-drinking woman, has left her the yellow house. As her friend Jerry Rolfe—a character based on Pat Pattridge—reminds her, "without it you wouldn't have had a pot of your own" (p. 263). Yet living on the edge only intermittently bothers Hattie: "she was not one to be miserable for long; she had the expression of a perennial survivor" (p. 263). Bellow depicts her with sympathy and from the inside:

> She was weak, she was old, she couldn't follow a train of thought very easily, she felt faint in the head. But she was still here; here with her body, it filled space, a great body. And though she had worries and perplexities, and once in a while her arm felt as though it was about to give her the last stab of all; and though her hair was scrappy and old, like onion roots, and scattered like nothing under the comb, yet she sat and amused herself with visitors; her great grin split her face; her heart warmed with every kind word.

And she thought, people will help me out. It never did me any good to worry. At the last minute something turned up, when I wasn't looking for it (p. 264).

Hattie's existence at Sego Desert Lake is doomed, and her narrow prospects narrow further over the course of the story, but she knows her nature and refuses to heed the reality instructors (partly drawn from the Drackerts and the Pattridges) who advise her to sell up and leave. Looking back on her life she thinks: "*Youth is terrible, frightening. I will wait it out. And men? Men are cruel and strong. They want things I haven't got to give.' There were no kids in me*, thought Hattie. *Not that I wouldn't have loved them, but such my nature was. And who can blame me for having it? My nature?*" (p. 278). There is something indomitable about this "nature," which is depicted with what Daniel Fuchs calls "lyrical personalism," a quality Bellow also brought to the depiction of Henderson.[14] The story ends with Hattie putting off a decision about the house: "I'm drunk and so I need it. And tomorrow, she promised herself, I'll think again. It'll work out, for sure." (p. 281).

It worked out for Peggy Marsh. When she found herself backed into a similar corner at Pyramid Lake, no longer able to live alone in her pink house, she sold it to buyers who guaranteed her life tenancy in the shack. "Now have agreeable companions," she wrote to Bellow on June 6, 1959, "unlimited electricity and water, free gratis for nothing!" The pink house is now white with blue trim, the shack, too, has been painted: "and I don't pay taxes, so I should worry." Peggy had read *Henderson*, which she thought "superb." She especially admired the ending: "The last chapter landing in Newfoundland is perfect. No maudlin meeting or reconciliation with Lily." Though Henderson's imperfections were "terrible," they "endeared him to the reader." Three years later, in a letter of October 10, 1962, Peggy writes from Charlottesville, Virginia, where she is staying with a niece: "I am not very spry these days. Have had gout and 3 heart attacks in '62. But in spite of that, I have a pleasant and quiet life—I love bridge, as you know, and this city is famous for it." Nora and Pat Pattridge reported the same news about the pink house, in a letter dated April 6 (without a year). They added that friends in San Francisco have given them "Leaving the Yellow House" to read. "Never realized you were studying us all so minutely—comparatively, you let *us* off very gently."

In mid-November, before his three months were up, Bellow left

Nevada sub rosa and drove to Malibu, stopping first at San Francisco and Palo Alto. The risk of leaving the state was minimal; as Arthur Miller puts it, "the whole business was a fantasy or formality anyway, patently devised to bring divorce-hungry visitors to the state and fees to the lawyers."[15] To Ruth Miller, in a letter of November 5, Bellow wrote of being "horribly excited" at the prospect of returning to civilization; to Sam Freifeld, on the same day, he admitted to being "in a state of rare excitement" at the prospect of seeing Sasha, "after [her] many weeks alone in L.A." "He was lonely," Sasha remembers, "he missed me, I missed him" (p. 85). Once together, they decided to stay together; she returned with him to Nevada for the remainder of the required three months. At Pyramid Lake, Peggy offered to swap residences: her comfortable pink house had two bedrooms, one of which Bellow could use for writing; she could manage happily in the shack. The items the pink house lacked, Sasha soon discovered, were a vacuum cleaner, a dishwasher, and any other electrical appliance. Housework was challenging. The routine was for Bellow to begin writing immediately after breakfast, while Sasha busied herself with domestic chores. When the chores were finished she walked over to the shack to listen to Peggy's stories, then returned to the house to serve Bellow lunch. After lunch Bellow did more work and Sasha walked down to the bar to gossip with Joan, who spent most of her time there reading or going over paperwork. Several afternoons a week Sasha rode out into the hills with Red, the guest ranch hand; Bellow, too, rode in the afternoons, or went off by himself to fish or to hike in the hills and howl, a Reichian exercise. In Reno, on their weekly visits, they met some of the faculty at the University of Nevada, and developed a social life of sorts.[16] They also gambled. "We'd each have ten dollars," Sasha recalled, "and Saul always blew his ten dollars and I always won."

The reason Bellow stopped in Palo Alto on his way down to see Sasha was that the McCloskys were there. Herb had a year's fellowship at the Center for Advanced Study in Behavioral Sciences at Stanford, described by Bellow as "an Institute like the one at Princeton but for social scientists."[17] In late December, Bellow returned to Palo Alto with Sasha, to see in the New Year with the McCloskys. On New Year's Eve itself, he looked especially gloomy, telling Herb: "Tonight is the eighteenth anniversary of my marriage to Anita."[18] The mood passed quickly. On January 2, 1956, back at the pink house, the writing was going well: he finished the Illinois piece ("It ran to forty pages and was much work"[19]); put the finishing touches to the expanded *Seize the Day*; and, most important, was working "like a miner" on a new novel, the "African Book," *Henderson the Rain King.*[20] Happy at his work he was happy away from it. Sasha was happy as well, reading D. H. Lawrence and Thomas Hardy, writing "little poems, sometimes, in the hills." After they left, Arthur Miller reported in a letter of July 8 that their mailman had been "in love with both of you. He kept me standing there for twenty minutes while he praised you both, saying 'They talk about Western hospitality. I found the Eastern people much better.'" The only difficult moment in the stay occurred when Joan Drackert let slip that Bellow had had a brief fling with a woman guest at the ranch before Sasha's arrival. "More shocked than angry," Sasha confronted him, for what she called the first and only time. "I had never suspected him of being with other women and this badly rattled me." Bellow was contrite: "he had been so 'lonely,' it was a moment of 'weakness,' a need for 'comfort,' I had to forgive him, I was all he ever wanted. I bought it all" (p. 87).

The winter of 1956 at Pyramid Lake was freezing and sometimes Bellow and Sasha huddled together in bed in their overcoats. Once they'd gotten over the revelation of the affair, "Saul and I did very well together. This was undoubtedly the best time of our life together. He was going great guns on Henderson, and this kind of concentrated energy would always help him be more centered, calmer, distracted but reasonable. I typed his manuscript, we talked over his 'dailies.' We had long conversations about whatever we were reading, especially about Hardy and Lawrence; we hiked down along the lake; we drove around a bit and did a little sightseeing" (p. 88). In this productive and harmonious state, Bellow asked Sasha to marry him. "Have you gotten the wedding announcement?" he wrote to Ruth Miller sometime in February. "I shall let a Yiddish word speak for me: *glucklikh* [lucky]." To Sam Freifeld, also in an undated letter, he described himself as Sasha had, employing an image from carpentry or plumbing that recurs in writing of this period. "I am perfectly satisfied with Sondra and marriage, with the house we live in and the work I am doing. In all my life I have never stood so level. The bubble is in the middle of me. Perhaps an uneven landscape like these mountains makes your head sit straight on your shoulders." Bellow's only complaints in the letter are of Anita's demands and of being separated from Greg. "When can I come back? I wish I knew. Anita still wields her wicked power. She wants money,

money, money, money, or failing money, blood. Now she wants to insure my life, too, with a term policy. This is her way of telling me that she is betting I will die soon. . . . Not even my death would improve her. The boy writes to me, and I to him. The separation is a bad business."

Bellow left the wedding arrangements to Sasha, except for the guest list and the actual date, February 1, 1956, chosen to coincide with a visit to California by the Covicis, Reno being only a short drive from San Francisco. Pat Covici was a crucial figure to Bellow in this period. In *To Jerusalem and Back: A Personal Journey* (1976), he describes him as a recognizable type:

> One of those men in broad-brimmed fedoras who took drawing rooms on the Twentieth Century Limited in the John Barrymore days, people who knew headwaiters and appreciated well-turned-out women. There were many Jews of this sort, big butter-and-egg men who made and lost fortunes. My late friend Pascal Covici, the publisher, was one of these. Pat knew how to order a fine dinner, how long to let wine breathe, how to cherish a pretty woman, how to dart into the street and stop a cab by whistling on his fingers, how to negotiate a tough contract—not so tough, perhaps, since he paid out too many advances and lost his shirt (pp. 71–72).

The other outside guests were Jack and Leya Ludwig. Sasha explains Bellow's choices: "I guess it was important to him to have a father and a brother present, and of course he couldn't wait to unveil Henderson." Sasha invited no one. "I didn't even think of it. Where would we put them? Not even my mother was invited because I knew she would have to stay with us for more than a few days and I couldn't imagine it and so, with a thoughtlessness I was to be deeply ashamed of later in life, I told her not to come" (p. 89). Sasha set about the wedding preparations with great energy. She found a rabbi in Reno (an English rabbi, who knew Bellow's novels, and was eager to talk with him about *Commentary* and Jewish American fiction). She scrubbed the pink house till it was "spotlessly clean," cooked and laid out the wedding feast. She accompanied Covici as he drove all over Reno in search of a drinkable brand of champagne ("when it was still a small town with just two biggish hotels and two clubs" [p. 89]). After the Reno ceremony, the party drove back to the pink house for the bridal supper. The local invitees—Peggy, the Pattridges, Harry and Joan Drackert, and Red the ranch hand—came "respectfully to the synagogue and then, rollicking, to the house." After consuming what Sasha describes as "a fine, noisy meal," the locals disappeared and "Saul read Henderson aloud, for a very long time, and then he went to bed; I washed dishes for hours and thus passed my wedding night. I thought it perfect." In the week that followed, Sasha bought engraved wedding announcements ("I had my etiquette lessons firmly in place on that score") and sent them to all their friends. In early spring, Bellow wrote to Sam Goldberg to tell him "I've never seen Sondra so well. You wouldn't know her. I can't congratulate myself enough."

Anita and the lawyers agreed on a settlement not long after the wedding. She was to receive $100 a month in alimony until she remarried and $150 a month in child support. Bellow was to pay all legal fees for both sides, stretching back to October 1955. The plan now was for bride and groom to remain at Pyramid Lake till early summer, returning to New York in time to spend a month with Greg. On March 15, Bellow received a letter from Arthur Miller, who was also published by Covici. He was coming to Nevada "to spend the fated six weeks and [had] no idea where to live." Could Bellow advise him, especially in the light of a problem "of slightly unusual proportions"? This problem concerned the occasional visits of a person "who is very dear to me, but who is unfortunately recognizable by approximately a hundred million people, give or take three or four." It was Marilyn Monroe, who had herself come to Reno ten years earlier to divorce her first husband. "She has all sorts of wigs, can affect a wig, sunglasses, bulky coats, etc., but if it is possible I want to find a place, perhaps a bungalow or something like, where there are not likely to be crowds looking in through the windows. Do you know of any such places?" Bellow did, offering what Miller calls "one of the two cottages facing the lake."[21] Soon Miller was accompanying Bellow, or Bellow and Sasha, on their weekly trips into Reno, walking down to the telephone on the main highway to receive daily calls from "Mrs. Leslie," Monroe's code name, and keeping a keen eye out for reporters. Miller stayed at Pyramid Lake for eight weeks, not six, and was especially struck by Bellow's "emptying his lungs roaring at the stillness," which he called "the day's biggest event." Monroe was shooting *Bus Stop* in Los Angeles, and never got to Nevada; instead Miller flew into L.A. on weekends, staying with her at the Chateau Marmont in Hollywood.[22]

In June, after nine months for Bellow and six for Sasha, the newlyweds said goodbye to the pink house and slowly drove back to the East Coast, a honeymoon of sorts, also a parading of the bride. Sasha, though, was feeling poorly, so much so that she forgot Bellow's birthday, his fortieth. En route they stopped in Boulder, Colorado, where Lillian Blumberg McCall had moved. In Chicago, proofs of *Seize the Day* awaited Bellow. Here, for the first time, Sasha met the Bellow relatives: Sam, Maury, Jane, and their families, as well as the Dworkins. She was not impressed, particularly by Maury, "a big fat pig of a vulgar man" is how she described him to Atlas. "I said to Saul, 'Lose my number: I don't need these people.'"[23] ("I only met them one time," she told me, "heavy-set, gross people. . . . They ignored me completely, they were so full of themselves, in their entirely white apartment . . . and Saul was like the little *pisherkeh* [squirt, bedwetter].") She mentions nothing of Maury's recent troubles, which had gotten his name in the papers again. He and Marge now owned and managed the Shoreland Hotel, in which Jimmy Hoffa, head of the Teamsters Union, had an interest. Whenever Hoffa or his people were in town, they stayed at the Shoreland. In November 1956, in front of the cashier window of his hotel, Maury confronted a Teamster enforcer, Robert "Barney" Baker, to complain that his unpaid bill was too high (it included cash advances of $1,200). Baker took offense and tried to strangle Maury. Maury was fat but Baker weighed 370 pounds, much of it muscle. It took several bystanders to drag him off Maury. When the incident was reported in the press, Marge was quoted as calling Baker "a killer." Later, at a Senate Rackets Committee hearing, Baker conceded that "he might have 'argued' with Bellows."[24]

What Sasha recalls of Sam Bellows is that he was "very neat, very together, quiet but with a good sense of humor." His wife, Nina, however, was "arrogant . . . very proud of herself." Sister Jane was "easy, placid, pleasant" (a view not shared by the rest of the family) and husband Charlie was "a *shlub* [clumsy, graceless, an oaf]." Maury's and Marge's self-absorption notwithstanding, the family "were all perfectly nice to me." She was less harsh about Bellow's friends, Dave Peltz ("I loved Dave"), Sam Freifeld ("a nice jolly guy"), and Isaac Rosenfeld, who'd left New York shortly after she'd arrived on the scene. The Tarcovs no longer lived in Chicago, having moved to New York in the spring of 1955. Freifeld and Rochelle, his wife, were in crisis at the time of the visit. He had moved out of the house, and she had had a breakdown. In an undated letter written just before leaving Pyramid Lake,

Bellow asked Sam if there was "anything I can do for you? You realize that if you were to tell me to fly to Lima Peru tonight, I'd depart without question." Freifeld wrote back that Rochelle thought of Bellow as having taken sides, Sam's side, and Bellow wrote back that she wasn't wrong, but that he should "remind her that far from being her enemy I am very much concerned about her. I should like, if possible, to talk with her."

Isaac Rosenfeld was also in a bad way. After splitting from Vasiliki, he had been turned down for a second Guggenheim. He had failed to get the job at Bard and was teaching in the basic Humanities program of the University of Chicago, a Loop adjunct of the main university, a step down from the university proper. He wrote to Oscar Tarcov to see about a job with the Anti-Defamation League. There was none. He tried and failed to get a job at Brandeis. When Bellow and Sasha met him he was living in the same whitewashed coal cellar on Woodlawn Avenue that he'd lived in as an undergraduate. Later in the summer he moved to a furnished room on the North Side, which an unnamed friend described to Atlas as "the kind of place where you expected to see Raskolnikov sharpening his axe."[25] In the journal entries for this period quoted by his biographer, Steven Zipperstein, Rosenfeld describes himself as both depressed and sickly.[26] Within a month, on July 14, 1956, he was dead of a heart attack, at thirty-eight. When Bellow failed to attend Rosenfeld's funeral in Chicago, Isaac's father, Sam, was furious. Atlas offers several theories for why Bellow stayed away: "he was afraid to confront his own mortality"; "to fully grieve would have been to recognize his dependence on Rosenfeld"; and not to attend fit "a lifelong pattern: to deny and run away from pain."[27] Other explanations are possible. Perhaps he did not attend because he was overcome with grief and/or guilt (at having prospered when his best friend failed). What Sasha remembers of the decision is that Bellow "was too distraught to go to the funeral." What Greg remembers is that he was "inconsolable" (for which he criticizes him in his memoir: "my father was unable to see beyond his own grief"[28]). Perhaps also Bellow was reluctant to leave Greg so soon after returning to New York. He hadn't seen him in nine months and leaving for Chicago would cut into their time together.[29]

In Minneapolis, Bellow and Sasha stayed with John and Ann Berryman. Bellow read portions of *Henderson* to Berryman and Berryman read portions of the *The Dream Songs* to Bellow. Bellow also visited with friends from the English Department and Humanities, including the head of the Humanities program, Ralph Ross, his old boss at

NYU, who offered him a job in the Spring Semester. Sasha, meanwhile, continued to feel unwell, though it was not until they arrived in New York that she discovered why: she was pregnant, a condition "unexpected, unplanned, and, for nine pain-filled, stomach-wrenching months, unwelcome" (p. 91). Once back in New York, they settled in the country rather than the city, renting Andrews Wanning's house in Germantown in Columbia County, just north of Dutchess County. (Wanning, Bellow's colleague at Bard, was away for the summer.) Here Greg could spend time with his father in a rural setting, one from which a more permanent home could be scouted. Bellow was keen on buying a property in the Hudson Valley. Sasha would have preferred Manhattan but was happy enough with the Bard area. Above all she wanted to settle: the pregnancy unnerved her and almost any place would do. "I definitely wasn't ready, I felt like a teenager, still, and I was revolted by the idea of something growing in me, and petrified of pain" (p. 91). What she remembered of Germantown is feeding enormous meals to twelve-year-old Greg, described by Bellow as "5'2" and physically a man," while feeling queasy with morning sickness, and playing many games and sports with him, "when I wasn't in the bathroom."[30] What Greg remembered of his Hudson Valley summers is volleyball and swimming at the Bard pool, shooting baskets with Sasha in the Bard gym, and tennis lessons with Keith Botsford, an excellent player but in Greg's account a hopeless teacher: "'Tennis lessons' consisted of his hitting shots difficult even for a skilled adult to return and me running after tennis balls."[31]

Bellow made clear from the start his feelings about the impending birth. "He was too old to take on the care of a child," he told Sasha, "it was going to be my job, solo" (p. 91), a position she accepted, and one not unusual for the times. Bellow was forty, the sole breadwinner in the family, and while drawn to women of strong character, wholly conventional in his view of gender roles. Sasha neither earned nor possessed any money, so "Saul paid the bills, made the decisions, negotiated contracts, free-lance assignments, and teaching or lecture gigs without ever consulting me." Sasha, however, was used to such dependence, having always lived "from day to day, on very little" (p. 92). In an interview, she adds: "We were just married and we'd survived living alone in the desert for a number of months . . . I was perfectly content with Saul at that time, we were fine." With rare exceptions—she names Mary McCarthy, Hannah Arendt—most women she knew were the same, and those who weren't often found themselves subjected to crude accounts of Freudian theory, "the religion of the intellectuals at the time," with much talk of castrating women and penis envy. Though Sasha eventually went on to live an independent life, when newly married, "I was perfectly happy to cook and clean and bear his young and type his manuscripts and listen to him; it was my job description, to be there to fulfil his needs. That was perfectly reasonable to me." All she knew at this time, the summer of 1956, of Bellow's finances was that he had inherited enough money from his father to buy a house. How much money she only learned when reading Atlas's biography forty-four years later. Bellow himself gave a figure of $16,000, part as a direct legacy, part as stock (the figure Atlas gives is $20,000, the amount Moses Herzog inherits).[32] Whatever the exact amount, that the money came from Abraham gave Bellow another reason to resent divorce payments. "I don't like to hand my father's money over to Anita," he wrote to Ralph Ellison in the letter of April 2, 1956, "since they hated each other, but I tell myself that it does something for Greg."

Bellow was accompanied in his house hunting by Jack Ludwig, a frequent correspondent over the Nevada months (though Sasha remembers "some kind of rift" for a period, "because he [Ludwig] wasn't properly appreciative of something Saul wrote"). The letters from Ludwig are gossipy, ingratiating, and full of feeling. On October 7, he sends the latest Bard news, much of it involving Sam Goldberg, his rival for Bellow's friendship. Goldberg had business of some sort with Bard, which Ludwig distrusted. He refers to Goldberg as "slippery Sam" ("Who profits? Goldberg!"). He also reports on Isaac Rosenfeld's job interview at Bard, which did not go well (though Ludwig himself needed only "one look" to see Rosenfeld as an "ally"). The letter closes with "love and sustaining *schmotchkehs*" (a Ludwig coinage?) from wife Leya and daughter Susie. "From me I send strength and love and joy." Earlier in the letter, in Ludwig's version of "free-style," he enjoins Bellow: "Joy find. Why not? When we weep doesn't the sound of our weeping reach Nevada? Twang here and there a heart string and tell me about the music you hear." On November 16 Ludwig writes of Greg, who had recently spent a weekend with the Hoffmans. "His routine in the city is the same as before (Anita, incidentally, didn't get a woman to come in for the afternoons)." The letter contains no other Anita gossip, as "neither Ted [Hoffman] nor I wanted to pump the kid since we wanted his time here to be a holiday all the way." As for Bard colleagues: "these guys depress the life out of me." In a letter of March 15 Ludwig asks for a reference: "The one blight on our friendship, the yearly appeal for a letter, come round again. . . . You don't know how I hate the intrusion of a note that isn't disinterested." On April 7, after the trip west for the wedding, Ludwig offers advice about teaching posts at Bard and places to rent for the summer (it was Ludwig who arranged rental of Wanning's Germantown house). The letter closes with news of his novel, abbreviated alternately as *Shlomo* or *Solomon*, and of a visit to Bard by Harry Levin, the Harvard English professor: "a nice enough guy, I suppose, but . . . what will it come to, when being a Jew is a quiet closed chapter in your past, reopened only by anti-semitism too blatant to be ignored?"

The determination to please would not have been missed. Sasha, however, discounts the view that Bellow sought an acolyte in Ludwig. Precisely the qualities Bellow lacked were the ones that attracted him to Ludwig. "Their personalities were so different that they were complementary. Ludwig was very expansive, warm, big, big-hearted. . . . He just simply was a larger-than-life character, which was everything Saul was not. Saul was more intellectual, refined, more ascetic, more of a solitary personality. . . . There was always a kind of distance, he always looked at the world sideways" (even with Ludwig, she is implying). "His head was always [slightly] turned away from you . . . he literally did not turn his head straight on . . . like a bird, very bright, observant, like a magpie, going to take something and use it." Ludwig, in contrast, was a tactile person, as were other close friends of Bellow's: Schwartz, Freifeld, Covici, Peltz. "Saul was not one to initiate that sort of thing but he enjoyed it. These were men who were expansive and affectionate." In addition, Ludwig was eccentric and Bellow "always liked eccentric people," not only "because you knew he was going to use it," but because "he was also charmed by it." Sasha's analysis recalls Herzog on his attraction to Gersbach, the Ludwig character: "Herzog had a weakness for grandeur, and even bogus grandeur" (p. 479).

Early after their return from Pyramid Lake, Bellow and Sasha had dinner with Arthur Miller and Marilyn Monroe. Miller had been back from Nevada since the end of May.[33] The dinner was to be preceded by a drink at Miller's place. According to Sasha, when she and Bellow arrived, Monroe was in the bedroom getting ready. By the time they'd finished their drink she still hadn't emerged. Miller went back to check on her and returned to say she'd be out in a minute, offering a second drink. This drink, too, was finished and still Monroe had not emerged. Sasha then asked Miller if he thought Marilyn might need her help. Miller thought this a good idea. When Sasha entered the bedroom she found Monroe sitting naked on the bed surrounded by discarded items of clothing. She had been unable to decide. With Sasha's encouragement an outfit was chosen and the two couples set off for dinner. A table had been booked at Rocco's, a popular Italian restaurant in the Village. It was near a window and visible from the sidewalk. Soon a large crowd of gawkers gathered in front of it, threatening to push it in. The diners were forced to retreat. On July 8, Miller wrote to Bellow to apologize for Monroe's behavior that night. "Marilyn was ill, and much troubled by something which, thank God, got settled next day. She felt badly that she hadn't her energy and hopes you two understand. She is now cooking, waxing floors, and treating me like a pasha."

IT DID NOT TAKE LONG for Bellow and Ludwig to find a house, nor did they have to travel far to find it. It was in Tivoli, a village just north of Bard. Bellow purchased the house for $12,000 (a $6,000 deposit plus a $6,000 mortgage). "'House' is not the word for it," he wrote. "It was, or had once been, a Hudson River mansion. It had a Dutch cellar kitchen of flagstones and a kitchen fireplace. There was a dumb-waiter to the dining room above. The first floor had a ballroom, but according to my informants, Tivoli's townspeople, no one had danced in it for eighty years. Tivoli had been the birthplace of Eleanor Roosevelt. The villagers were the descendants of the servants and groundskeepers of the Dutchess County aristocrats."[34] The house dated from 1824 and had three floors and fourteen rooms, including the ballroom with its elaborately corniced floor to ceiling windows. On the same floor there were two sitting rooms off a central hall and staircase. Upstairs were eight bedrooms, each with its own fireplace, and three bathrooms. In the basement, in addition to the kitchen, now defunct, there was space for a dining room and lavatory. Broad crumbling porches and open fields surrounded the house. The rooms were large and airy, reminding Sasha of the Lincoln house in Springfield, Illinois. To Bellow, the place had a Russian feel, like a dacha, though he also likened it to "an old Faulkner mansion that had drifted north."[35] After a period in which the house was used as an old folks' home and a summer camp, it became a private residence again in the 1940s, the home first of a Hollywood scriptwriter then of a couple of antique dealers.[36] It was from the antique dealers that Bellow bought the house.

Sasha was impressed. "Of course, I knew nothing at all about houses, or what you should pay attention to before you buy one, and to my untutored eye this was one grand manor, and I could easily and happily see myself as the great lady to the manor born" (p. 92). By early August Bellow was addressing letters from Tivoli, though Sasha believed they did not move in until September 3, Labor Day.[37] Only after the sale went through did they realize how much work had to be done on the place. "We needed to drill a well [at the cost of $1,000], the external decorative carvings were dangerously decayed, there was no [working] kitchen, no heating, no furniture, no way to move into this without major work" (p. 93). Did Bellow himself not check on these matters? Or Ludwig? Bellow's explanation, in an undated letter to Ralph Ellison, was that "a couple of beguiling fairies sold us the place and lied about the water, the roof." At the time of writing, he was "not sure I'll have enough to keep things going."

To get them going, at least, he hired a contractor, described by Sasha as "a wiry Scandinavian with three hefty tall sons, whom I called the 'Vikings'" (p. 93). To pay for the Vikings, again according to Sasha, Bellow asked Esther, her mother, for a loan of $5,000, money she'd saved without Tschacbasov knowing (rather as Bellow's own mother had saved money for her brothers in Russia). This money was to become a source of dispute in the marriage, for Bellow believed it had been given as a gift not a loan. As the Vikings hammered away, climbing over the house, ripping off the rotting cornice along its top, the decaying balconies around the sides, installing miles of copper tubing, cutting down blighted elms, and drilling the well ("at 175 ft. the drillers did strike some veins but I don't know yet whether they didn't give enough water," he wrote to Ellison in the undated letter), a stream of late summer visitors arrived from the city, among them Vasiliki Rosenfeld, only recently divorced from Isaac, and "in no condition to be left alone."[38] "All of this cost tons of money," Sasha recalls in the memoir, "and Saul was trying to write amid the noise and confusion of the Vikings. So he handed me the checkbook (I had never had one of my own in my life) and said, 'I'm going to Yaddo, pay the Vikings—but watch them'" (p. 93). Bellow stayed at Yaddo from September 3 to 22. Sasha, meanwhile, got the house in order and by Thanksgiving was able to cook a big turkey dinner for Bard friends as well as several recently arrived refugees from the Soviet invasion of Hungary (they were on campus to learn English). Though more work remained to be done on the house—only part of it was habitable—Sasha was proud of what had been accomplished. At Yaddo, Bellow had also been productive, "doing more and better work [on *Henderson*] than before,"[39] traveling to New York City on Thursdays to teach a course at the New School. At Yaddo he also forged an important friendship with John Cheever, who was finishing *The Wapshot Chronicle* (1957). Once settled at Tivoli, Bellow wrote to John Berryman on December 6 with a report on how things were going. Though distracted by money and house worries, struggling with work ("I put *Henderson* on me like a plumber's level. The bubble is usually in the wrong place, so I sigh and knock off for the day"), and surrounded both by friends low in spirits and by ghosts, "large numbers of highly individualized ghosts," there were important compensations: "Sondra is a beautiful mother-to-be, and Greg gave me much pleasure last month, so my life is far from barren."

IT IS ODD THAT Bellow says nothing of *Seize the Day*, published in book form in November 1956. The novella was born out of important and painful relationships and its publication history was difficult. After *The New Yorker* turned it down in 1955 but before it appeared in the summer 1956 issue of *Partisan Review*, Viking offered to publish it in a volume with six short stories, an offer Bellow suspected was less than enthusiastic. "My friend in Chicago will send Covici his damn stories," he wrote in an undated letter to Volkening. "I'm in no mood for any nonsense from Viking." On November 1, 1955, he had written to Covici to say that he knew that "some of your editorial colleagues" weren't pleased with *Seize the Day*. These colleagues, "indispensable to you, whereas I am not," had been grumbling about his "unpleasant-ness": "I hear the echo from you. . . . And should I be happy when it is necessary to submit my stories, like any lousy beginner, before a contract can be drawn? The stories should have come to me for reworking, and when I was satisfied with them it is my opinion that Viking should have received them and published them without a single damn syllable of protest. If you don't want these stories you needn't take them." He was not going to leave Viking, he reassured Covici, but he wanted to be treated "honorably." The letter ends: "You old bat, if I didn't love you like a parent I'd never get so worked up."

Covici's reply, on November 8, opens: "Before I begin spanking, as a parent I should, belonging to the old school, please bear in mind that my colleagues are no more indispensable to me than I am to them." He then asks: "Who grumbles about you? The firm did a brilliant job with AUGIE MARCH and are proud of it and proud of you. As to complaints of your unpleasantness—I haven't heard of any, and that is no double-talk either. Not that I put it past you being unpleasant when and if you choose." Covici denies that his colleagues disliked the novella: "they both liked it, but agreed with me that it should not be published as a short novel, certainly not by itself." A possible source of Bellow's suspicions, one deduces from the letter, was Henry Volkening, who had met with Covici to discuss terms: "When I asked Henry to gather your short stories," Covici writes, "I made a luncheon date with him. At our meeting we discussed the advance. . . . I am proud to be your editor, your mentor, your conscience. Your function is to make life worth living, and may God help you."[40] Covici promised to read the stories over the weekend and send them to Bellow for final revision. Volkening may have relayed grumbles from Covici's colleagues, though these could equally have been relayed by Lynn Hoffman. Sometime after Covici's letter of November 8, Bellow wrote again: "Please don't fiddle around with me about small sums of money. . . . I'm in no mood to be trifled with. In fact, I'm damned sore about everything, and down on everyone—no exceptions. I've been idiotically timid and meek, and I begin to feel it's time I made a fight."

Six months later, after the marriage to Sasha, the divorce settlement with Anita, and a period of post-wedding harmony and productivity, Bellow's suspicions resurfaced. It was his impression that Covici and others at Viking not only thought *Seize the Day* "depressing" but that they didn't much like the stories either. "I wouldn't dream of asking you to publish something of which you don't approve," Bellow wrote to Covici in a letter in early May. "On that score I want to make myself absolutely clear. If you and Harold [Guinzburg] and Marshall [Best, the editorial director of Viking] don't like these stories of mine then *don't* print them." Covici claimed to have no idea what Bellow was talking about. As he wrote in an answer of May 11: "I thought I made myself clear over the telephone when I told you what a brilliant job of revision you did with 'Seize the Day.' Please tell me why Viking should want to publish it if we do not approve of it?" In reply, Bellow admitted that he had been "a little nutty" in the letter of early May but also reminded Covici that he, the author, had to telephone to learn of his editor's approval, which "naturally grieved me."[41]

In the end, *Seize the Day* was published with three stories not six, plus *The Wrecker*. These stories were "Looking for Mr. Green," "The Gonzaga Manuscripts," and "A Father-to-Be." Adding "A Father-to-Be" and "The Wrecker" to *Seize the Day* gave a certain thematic unity to the volume: three male protagonists with weak characters ("Mr. Bellow's very subject is the transparency of human weakness," declared Kazin in his November 18 review of *Seize the Day* in *The New York Times Book Review*), three failed or rocky relationships.[42] Writing to Covici from Yaddo, in a letter received on September 12, two months before publication, Bellow asked to see a copy of the book jacket. "All the divorced men in America will buy a copy, mark my words, o ye of little faith. I expect Viking to sell it enthusiastically to those weary and surfeited hearts, the book-dealers." Bellow was not alone in sensing uncertainty or insecurity ("o ye of little faith") on the part of his publishers. In *Saturday Review*, Hollis Alpert described *Seize the Day* as falling somewhere between short story and novel length: "It is long enough, and interesting enough, to have been worth publishing between its own hard covers, but the publisher, or perhaps Mr. Bellow, has seen fit to offer three short stories and a one-act play as part of the package."[43]

Seize the Day looks back both thematically and formally to *The Victim* and *Dangling Man*. "That's the way I think of it myself," Bellow told an interviewer, "it really is true that Wilhelm belongs to the victim-group."[44] Its resemblance to *Augie* lies in its awkward length, to Viking at least (both works were too long, *Augie* as a novel, *Seize the Day* as a story). In his later years, Bellow published several novellas (*A Theft, The Actual, The Bellarosa Connection*), perhaps because he lacked the stamina for longer works. His attraction to the form, however, could be said to derive from lifelong habits of composition. In the course of his writing career, Bellow produced a number of novel manuscripts abandoned at novella length ("Memoirs of a Bootlegger's Son," the "Zetland" manuscripts, "Far Out," "Olduvai George," "A Case of Love," "All Marbles Accounted For"). Philip Roth detects novella-length units within longer finished novels as well. "For all Saul's tremendous deep intelligence," he conjectures, "he was a very spontaneous writer. I think these things took shape as he was writing. . . . Usually about half way through the book the original impulse weakens and then he gets a mess in the middle." In the case of *Augie March*, the first third of the novel, the Chicago section, came to Bellow in a rush, with few revisions; then problems developed, improbabilities, false starts, forced transitions. The example Roth cites is *Mr. Sammler's Planet,* "a wonderful book," in which "half way through he gets the moon guy [Professor Lal, author of "The Future of the Moon"]. Half way through it's one kind of book and then in the middle it becomes another kind of book. . . . I don't think Saul cared. I don't know, maybe he suffered over those things. I don't think so. Maybe he just pulled the trigger." Another metaphor is that he just dove in, surfacing at novella length, looking up to see where he was, then trying to figure out where to go next. In an undated letter to Richard Stern, written from Tivoli sometime in autumn 1960 while at work on *Herzog,* he describes a process just like this: "*Herzog* has got me down. As sometimes happens by the hundredth page, my lack of planning, or the subconscious cunning, catch up with me, and so I'm back in Montreal in 1922, trying to get a drunk to bed and I'm not sure what I'll do once he's sleeping. God will provide. Consider the lilies of the field—do they write books?"

There is little evidence that publishing constraints or conventions played much part in Bellow's calculations as a writer. Toward the end of his life he talked openly of his attraction to the novella and the long short story (almost all his short stories are long; as he admitted to Covici in a letter of January 22, 1960, "they always turn into novels, because one thing leads to another"). After answering a question from Norman Manea about *Seize the Day,* he explained: "You know I'm very much attached to my short stories and novellas. I've written some of them at the top of my form, I feel, and sometimes I feel that maybe that's what I should've been doing all the time. I'm freer in those things; in a way they're less ambitious and I feel more liberated when I write them."[45] When the short story collection *Him with His Foot in His Mouth* (1984) was published by Harper, Bellow protested to his editor, Edward Burlingame, about the way it was being marketed. "You're treating it like a book of short stories," Burlingame remembered Bellow complaining. "But it *was* a book of short stories," he wanted to say. Burlingame recounts Bellow's remark by way of illustrating how difficult an author he could be, but at the same time he understood what lay behind the remark, calling the stories in the volume "among the best things Saul Bellow ever wrote, every one a gem."[46]

———

BELLOW'S REVERSION TO a more controlled or restrained style in *Seize the Day* was welcomed by reviewers, though not always in ways likely to please. Leslie Fiedler, in *The Reporter* (December 13, 1956), contrasted the book's "slow solemn beauty" to "the almost hysterical need to assert joy" in *Augie*; Alfred Kazin praised its "plainness of feeling" in contrast to the "keyed-up virtuosity" of *Augie*. The power of the cathartic ending, in which forty-four-year-old Tommy Wilhelm, having lost job, home, family, and the last of his money, is swept into a stranger's funeral and breaks down weeping, was admitted by all, even by those, John Berryman among them, who claimed not to understand it. Bellow himself claimed not to understand the ending, at least not fully. "Thanks for your kind words about the story," he wrote to Berryman on November 26, the day after Sasha's Thanksgiving feast at Tivoli. "It is pitched high, but I am especially fond of it. That the last pages bewilder you I do not wonder, for I'm not ready to swear that I knew what I meant. Quite." He offers a tentative reading:

> Perhaps something like this: in a city like NY a man must adopt an occasion or convert it to the needs of his heart when those needs become irrepressible. Thus the most private things are done, if need be, in public. And perhaps something like this: suffering is not a way of life but must have a culmination, and its highest culmination is in the passionate understanding. This sort of understanding belongs to the heart. . . . I thought I was putting this on the page, but if this is not what you got out of it I am ready to accept the responsibility.

Bellow's stress here on the New York setting is important. The action takes place in a single day on the Upper West Side, with scenes set in a residential hotel, the Gloriana, not far from the Ansonia. The hotel's residents, mostly old Jews, include Tommy's father, Dr. Adler, a retired physician, and Dr. Tamkin, a shyster psychologist and financial advisor, the man who encourages Tommy to speculate on the commodities market with disastrous results.[47] New York does Tommy no good. "There's too much push here for me," he tells his disapproving father. "It works me up too much. I take things too hard" (p. 37). For Bellow, "the loneliness, shabbiness, and depression of the book find a singular match in the uptown Broadway surroundings." Tommy's sense of defeat derives in part from Bellow's experiences in just these surroundings: "I congratulated myself with being able to deal with New York, but I never won any of my struggles there, and I never responded with full human warmth to anything that happened there."[48] He did, however, survive, unlike his friends Isaac Rosenfeld and Delmore Schwartz, models for Tommy. Atlas notes Tommy's physical resemblance to Schwartz, both being "large, shambling insomniacs who popped pills, swilled Coke, and dropped cigarette butts into their coat pockets. Tommy's small teeth and wavy blonde hair clearly belonged to Schwartz in his mid-forties."[49] Tommy's resemblance to Rosenfeld is a matter of openness, gullibility. Rosenfeld "came to take the town and he got took. From his standpoint it proved to be a very dangerous place." New York for Tommy, as for Rosenfeld, was a city where, as Bellow puts it to Roth, "there was nothing you could turn to. I mean, if you turn to somebody for help you'd make the biggest mistake in your life if you chose Dr. Tamkin."[50] Or if you chose Wilhelm Reich, whom Tamkin often sounds like, with his talk of "the real soul and a pretender soul" (p. 58), of living in the "here-and-now" (p. 55), of moneymaking as "aggression" ("That's the whole thing. The functionalistic explanation is the only one. People come to the market to kill" [p. 57]).

Tommy's assessment of Tamkin is not far from Bellow's assessment of Reich: "He spoke of things that mattered, and as very few people did this he could take you by surprise, excite you, move you" (p. 68). To the extent that Bellow chose Reich, he, too, is figured in Tommy. He's also figured in Tommy, and the protagonists of "A Father-to-Be" and *The Wrecker*, in his tendency to complain: "You have an enviable way of referring to your troubles," he writes to Robert Penn Warren on March 27, 1954, "as a youngest child I learned to make the most of mine."[51] When Bellow began *Seize the Day* he was still in Reichian therapy. Though no longer in therapy when the work was completed, he was still practicing Reichian exercises, howling in the hills around Pyramid Lake, the woods around Bard and Tivoli.[52] Authorial self-pity as well as self-criticism underlie the drawing of Tommy, as comparably mixed feelings underlie the creation of Tamkin,[53] even of censorious Dr. Adler, conceived by Bellow in the midst of furious rows with Abraham over money. Eighty-year-old Dr. Adler, who refuses Tommy emotional as well as financial support, "with some justice, wanted to be left in peace" (p. 36) (Moses Herzog comes to a similar conclusion when he thinks of his father having to endure "the smirk of [his] long-suffering son . . . . Those looks were agony to him. He deserved to be spared, in his old age" [p. 669]). When Bellow tells Berryman that "suffering is not a way of life," he is quoting Dr. Adler, who warns Tommy "don't marry suffering. Some people do. They get married to it, and sleep and eat together, just as husband and wife" (p. 82).

Seize the Day was the Bellow novel Bernard Malamud most admired, partly for its handling of point of view. In the copy of the novel he used for teaching, Malamud marked a passage in which Tommy braces himself to confront his father with yet another request for money:

> He had opened the *Tribune*; the fresh pages drooped from his hands; the cigar was smoked out and the hat did not defend him. He was wrong to suppose that he was more capable than the next fellow when it came to concealing his troubles. They were clearly written out upon his face. He wasn't even aware of it (p. 12).

In the margin beside the last three sentences Malamud writes "p. of v.," to mark the moment Bellow moves away from Tommy to see him from the outside.[54] The critic James Wood also discusses Bellow's handling of point of view in *Seize the Day*, singling out a transition he thinks unconvincing. At the uptown Manhattan commodities exchange where Dr. Tamkin lures Tommy into losing his last $700, an old hand named Rappaport is smoking a cigar:

> A long perfect ash formed on the end of the cigar, the white ghost of the leaf with all its veins and its fainter pungency. It was ignored, in its beauty, by the old man. For it was beautiful. Wilhelm he ignored as well (p. 73).

While full of praise for the beauty and precision of the description, Wood detects a "wobble" in Bellow's handling of point of view:

> *Seize the Day* is written in a very close third person narration, a free indirect style that sees most of the action from Tommy's viewpoint. Bellow seems to imply here that Tommy notices the ash, because it was beautiful, and that Tommy, also ignored by the old man, is also in some way beautiful. But the fact that Bellow tells us this is surely a concession to our implied objection: how and why would Tommy notice this ash, and notice it so well, in *these* fine words? To which Bellow replies, anxiously, in effect: "Well you might have thought

Tommy incapable of such finery, but he really did notice this fact of beauty, and that is because he is somewhat beautiful himself."[55]

Bellow may be anxious here, but it is not true, as Wood implies, that Tommy is incapable of finery or wholly unbeautiful. Bellow had little time for *Seize the Day* in later years. "I don't like that book," he told Roth, "I never think about it, I never take it up, I don't touch it" (though writing it, he told another interviewer, had given him "a great deal of satisfaction"[56]). Nor had late Bellow much feeling for Tommy. "I sympathize with Wilhelm but I don't like him," he told Roth, "but my task was to represent him not to recommend him. . . . Many readers assumed that as an enlightened person I would naturally be on Tommy's side. On the contrary I saw him as a misfit wooing his hard-nosed father with the corrupt platitudes of affection, or job-lot, bargain-sale psychological correctness. I thought he was one of those people who make themselves pitiable to extract your support."[57]

"Suffering is not a way of life," Bellow tells Berryman, "but must have a culmination." This culmination, he continues, results in "understanding," in Tommy's case a product not of intellect but of the heart. Here is the novel's oft-quoted final paragraph:

> The flowers and the lights fused ecstatically in Wilhelm's blind, wet eyes; the heavy sea-like music came up to his ears. It poured into him where he had hidden himself in the center of a crowd by the great and happy oblivion of tears. He heard it and sank deeper than sorrow, through torn sobs and cries toward the consummation of his heart's ultimate need (p. 99).

This need is for release, figured in Reichian terms as an orgasmic loss of self. There is also a spiritual dimension to the ending, anticipated in earlier moments of "understanding," when self is lost in kinship with others and the world. In the subway beneath Times Square, Tommy, "all of a sudden, unsought," feels a "general love for all these imperfect and lurid-looking people" (p. 70). His reaction is an equivalent to the "spring of love" that rises "unaware" in the heart of Coleridge's ancient mariner in "The Rime of the Ancient Mariner," allowing him to bless creatures, water snakes, once seen as "a thousand thousand slimy things." Coleridge's poem is almost as important a presence in the novella as Milton's "Lycidas," about the death by shipwreck of his friend Edward King, quoted early in the novel's first chapter ("Sunk though he be beneath the wat'ry floor" [p. 11]) and alluded to at the end, in the "heavy sea-like music" that pours into Tommy at the funeral chapel (p. 99).[58] A similar moment of sympathy or connection occurs when Tommy and his father are joined at breakfast by Mr. Perls, an old man as repellent to Tommy as Tommy is to his father (in an undated letter to Sam Freifeld, probably written sometime in the spring of 1956, Bellow refers to *Seize the Day* as a "comical-terrible thing"). Tommy thinks: "Who is this damn frazzle-faced herring with his dyed hair and his fish teeth and this drippy mustache. . . . What is the stuff on his teeth? I never saw such pointed crowns." As he looks more closely, however, he "relent[s] a little toward Mr. Perls, beginning at the teeth. Each of those crowns represented a tooth ground to the quick, and estimating a man's grief with his teeth . . . it came to a sizable load" (p. 26).

Tommy affords a similar sympathetic attentiveness to Rappaport, old, blind, rich, wholly selfish, refusing Tommy "the merest sign" or bit of advice about the market. Tommy helps Mr. Rappaport across the street to the cigar store and receives no thanks at all. When he listens to Rappaport declare his love for Teddy Roosevelt, however, he begins to feel for him: "Ah, what people are! He is almost not with us, and his life is nearly gone, but T.R. once yelled at him, so he loves him. I guess it is love, too. Wilhelm smiled" (p. 86). To Ellen Pifer, an astute critic of Bellow's novels, it is this human concern that dooms Tommy in a world of "function."[59] While helping Rappaport to get his cigars, Tommy's shares in the commodities market (in lard, appropriately) plummet and he loses his chance to sell. Feeling figures also, Pifer suggests, in Tommy's failures in Hollywood. Tommy is now "mountainous" (p. 35), sallow in complexion, with scruffy hair and a stammer, but in college his youthful good looks elicited an inquiry from a Hollywood talent agent who had seen his photograph in the college yearbook.[60] Dropping out of college was "his first great mistake" (p. 15). He went to Hollywood on spec, changed his name from Wilhelm Adler to Tommy Wilhelm, and never got a part.[61] "Don't be afraid to make faces and be emotional. Shoot the works," the talent agent tells Tommy before his screen test. When the agent sees the results of the test, however, he backs away. As Pifer puts it, "the screen proves drastically inhospitable to the display of Wilhelm's 'emotions.'"[62] Feeling figures as well in Tommy's more recent loss of his job as a salesman, where, as he himself

admits, it "got me in dutch at Rojax. I had the *feeling* that I belonged to
the firm, and my *feelings* were hurt when they put Gerber in over me"
(p. 47). Bellow sees the danger of so feeling a nature, but knows it from
the inside. Tamkin asks Tommy: "You love your old man?"

> Wilhelm grasped at this. "Of course, of course I love him. My
> father. My mother—" As he said this there was a great pull at the
> very center of his soul. When a fish strikes the line you feel the live
> force in your hand. A mysterious being beneath the water, driven by
> hunger, had taken the hook and rushes away and fights, writhing.
> Wilhelm never identified what struck within him. It did not reveal
> itself. It got away (p. 77).

Tommy's capacity for delicacy of perception (Wood's "finery") is
revealed not only in his sympathy for figures as unlikely as Perls and
Rappaport, but in moments of Cheever-like luminosity, intimations of
a renewed world. In the early breakfast scene, Tommy enters the hotel
dining room and spots Dr. Adler "in the sunny bay at the far end."
Bellow does not describe Tommy sitting down nor does he say specifically that it is he who sees his father scatter sugar over his strawber-
ries, but we are to assume that what is described is what Tommy sees,
including the "small hoops of brilliance . . . cast by the water glasses on
the white tablecloth, despite a faint murkiness in the sunshine" (p. 26).
This delicate perception is registered matter-of-factly and all but wiped
from the reader's memory a few pages later when Dr. Adler watches
him eat a boiled egg. "A faint grime was left by his fingers on the white
of the egg after he had picked away the shell. Dr. Adler saw it with silent
repugnance" (p. 30). Toward the end of the novella, however, the image
of reflections as "hoops of brilliance" recurs. As Tommy considers life
in New York, concluding "that everybody is outcast," bewildered, alone,
misunderstood, a "queer look" comes over his face, out of nowhere, as
it were, like the ancient mariner's "spring of love," moving his thought
"several degrees further." What now he understands is that "there is a
larger body from which you cannot be separated" (as the mariner concludes that "the dear God who loveth us, / He made and loveth all"). At
this point the "hoop of brightness" formed by the water glass becomes
"an angel's mouth," suggesting, in a way intelligible to the heart if not
the intellect, that "truth for everybody may be found, and confusion

is only—only temporary" (p. 70). At such moments, Tommy realizes that finding truth is "the business of life, the real business . . . the only important business, the highest business" (p. 46).

For all his slovenliness and childishness, Tommy is both capable of "finery" and "somewhat beautiful himself," in his sensitivity, sympathy, and concern for higher things. There is evidence to counter Wood's reading, evidence that helps to explain the offense Bellow took at Brendan Gill's condescending review of the novella in *The New Yorker* ("Long and Short," January 5, 1957). In the review Gill calls Bellow "one of the three or four most talented writers to come along in this decade," but he also describes *Seize the Day* as "a hell of gross, talkative, ill-dressed nonentities, offensive to look at, offensive to listen to, offensive to touch. But it is a true hell and its denizens are very much alive; against all our wishes, we look at them, listen to them, and reach out and touch them." Gill's distaste for the novella's Upper West Side milieu recalls James on the Lower East Side. The "denizens" he finds so offensive are Jewish. The review ends: "Someday, Mr. Bellow is going to abandon his hell of odious and uninteresting people, and, oh, how willingly we are going to follow him!" Such sentiments recall the sources of Bellow's combativeness and suspicion. "That *New Yorker* outfit is a strange one," he writes to the critic and editor Granville Hicks in an undated letter of early 1957. "First they give me a chance to beat up on A[nthony]. West which, like a gent, I refuse. Then they give my next book to Gill knowing full well (Wm. Maxwell was present) that Gill and I have had a hassle. Strange people. But I tell you this, I have no desire to understand them."[63]

TIVOLI WAS FREE OF Scandinavian builders around the time of the Thanksgiving feast. What followed was the worst winter in years. The Hudson froze, guests who came for meals were unable to get home. To Sasha, "it was a challenge. I had a great deal of fun becoming very expert in the kitchen. . . . I baked my own bread, I baked everything. You couldn't find anything up there." To buy decent provisions involved "a long haul" over treacherous roads, to Rhinebeck or Red Hook, with stops at farms along the way for produce. If Bellow accused Sasha of having extravagant tastes, she accused him of being fussy about food and drink, like Moses Herzog who was "normally particular about food" (p. 417). "Although he liked to bill himself as a man of simple tastes," she writes in the memoir, "he actually was anything but. He enjoyed good wines, he expected the very finest food, he had lived in France, after all, and had developed some high in the instep preferences" (p. 96). He also, for all his need for quiet during the day, liked company at night, and was pleased when visitors came for dinner.

As winter wore on, Sasha's morning sickness persisted. More worrying symptoms appeared. Violent nosebleeds and wrenching cramps landed her in the Rhinebeck Hospital "next to a woman who was torn up from delivering a fourteen pound baby" (p. 94). She was diagnosed with gall bladder disease and thought to be in danger of diabetes. State troopers took to stopping by the house regularly, worried about getting Sasha to the hospital on days when the weather was particularly bad. Though Bellow was frequently away, teaching or having meetings in the city, there were "lots of people around, and I didn't feel neglected." Jack Ludwig frequently dropped by. In late January, however, with the baby due in a month and a half, Sasha began to retain fluids; by the beginning of February she was confined to bed. Finally, on February 19, three weeks overdue, Adam Abraham Bellow was born, weighing under six pounds, healthy and in good voice. Sasha describes herself as "enthralled and awed. And exhausted" (p. 94); Bellow, too, was deeply moved: "He came into the room and he was very excited. There were tears in his eyes: 'He looks like he walked all the way. He looks like he walked all the way'" (because the baby's feet were red and wrinkled at birth). There had been a lengthy wrangle over names: Lisa for a girl, after Bellow's mother, caused no problem, but Sasha vetoed Abraham for a boy. "'I don't want an Abie,' I said. 'How will he bear it growing up in Dutchess County with such a name, not a Jew in sight.'" Bellow gave in, countering that he wouldn't have "one of your Catholic names like Timothy." Only after the birth was "Adam Abraham" agreed to, "while the nurse stood patiently by the bed waiting to write down the name" (p. 94).

TWO WEEKS AFTER the birth Bellow was in Minneapolis to begin teaching. It would be another month before Sasha and Adam could join him, traveling by train not plane, on doctor's orders. Bellow's arrival in Minnesota was announced on March 3 in the *Minneapolis Sunday Tribune* under the heading "Prize Author Returning as 'U' Lecturer." According to the article, he would be holding classes on Nietzsche,

Kierkegaard, Chekhov, and Thomas Mann, and nonstudents could audit his classes for a modest fee.[64] Bellow was happy to be back in Minnesota. He liked Ralph Ross and had a number of good friends at the university. In addition to the McCloskys, John and Ann Berryman (a second wife, married in 1956, a week after his divorce from Eileen) were in residence, John having been appointed in the previous year by Ross. Allen Tate, whom Bellow had known for many years, was a new professor in the English Department. Robert Hivnor, his playwright friend, was there, teaching freshman English. The influence of the older WASP professors had been diluted by figures closer to Bellow's age or background, including Leo Marx, Murray Krieger, and William Van O'Connor, though how much contact he had with English Department types is not clear.

On April 13, 1957, Ralph Ross wrote to Phil Siegelman to say that "Saul and Sasha seem settled, and relatively happy," though Sasha had a recurrence of gall bladder trouble and might need an operation. In her memoir, Sasha says nothing of ill health, describing herself and Bellow as having had a "surprisingly good time" in Minnesota (p. 95). Bellow's close friendship with Berryman was now matched by Sasha's friendship with Berryman's wife, Ann, who had given birth to their son, Paul, just weeks after Adam was born (Ann, too, was a Bennington girl, at the same time as Sasha, though they had not met there). "We drove around together," Sasha recalls, "lulling our boys through colic, soothed by the motion of the vehicle" (p. 95). Social life for both couples revolved around the McCloskys, as it had for Bellow and Anita in 1946–48. After Tivoli, Sasha was grateful for the spring weather and the easy domestic arrangements. The furnished semidetached house Bellow had rented near the campus was "heaven," not least because "it was small, thankfully." In Minneapolis there was a diaper service, milk was delivered to the door, "and I could hop in the car and drive anywhere in a few minutes. There were people to meet and to be entertained by. No major cooking or changing sheets and cleaning up after a stream of visitors" (p. 95).

On April 9, a memorial meeting was held at the University of Minnesota to honor Isaac Rosenfeld and to raise money for his children. Rosenfeld had been brought to the university in 1952 by Ralph Ross and had taught in the Humanities program for two years. Rosenfeld had been a much loved figure, popular with students and faculty alike, and when he left to take a job in the Humanities program at the University of Chicago even his closest friends were surprised. Ross came up with the idea of the memorial and Bellow and Berryman were involved in the planning. "By one count there were 517 people present," Ross wrote on April 13 to the Siegelmans (who were in Cambridge, Massachusetts, Phil on a Ford Fellowship). "People sat in the lobby, in the gallery all around the head of the stairs, completely covered the stairs themselves, and some were standing." Bellow, Berryman, Ross, and Allen Tate spoke on the panel, and Berryman, Ross reported, "was in top form, witty, charming, and pointed."

Bellow was especially close to Berryman at this time. For five months, the two friends shared an office in Temporary North of Mines (TNR), a wooden building north of the School of Mines with a view of "a gully, a parking lot, and many disheartening cars."[65] Their talk, as always, was of literature: "There was little personal conversation. We never discussed money, or wives, and we seldom talked politics" (p. 268). When Berryman broke his leg and his doctor, A. Boyd Thomes, later Bellow's doctor, was called out in the middle of the night, "John said, as the splint was being applied, 'You must hear this new Dream Song!' He recited it as they carried him to the ambulance" (p. 269). Often Bellow and Berryman would stroll "about a pond, through a park, and then up Lake Street, 'where the used cars live!'" They talked of Yeats and read each other's work, in Bellow's case, *Henderson*, and the short story he had recently written, "Leaving the Yellow House." Berryman pronounced the story "delicious" ("a favorite expression"), though also "faulty, inconclusive. (We told each other exactly what we thought [p. 269])."

The friendship between Bellow and Berryman had begun in Princeton after Berryman read a transcript of *Augie March*. According to Eileen Simpson, "after the first chapter, he said 'It's damn good.' When he finished, 'Bellow is *it*. I'm going to have lunch with him and tell him he's a bloody genius and so on." At this lunch, Bellow described his decision to break from the "Flaubertian standard" of *Dangling Man* and *The Victim*, thus, "unwittingly," as Eileen Simpson puts it, giving Berryman "the push he needed to make the final break . . . with his hero-worshipping attitude towards father-figures, Yeats above all."[66] In his foreword to Berryman's posthumously published autobiographical novel, *Recovery* (1973), Bellow quotes from the last letter he received from the poet:

"Let's join forces, large and small, as in the winter beginning of 1953 in Princeton, with the Bradstreet blazing and Augie fleecing away. We're promising." According to Bellow, "what he said was true: we joined forces in 1953 and sustained each other for many years" (p. 267). In an interview with Keith Botsford, Bellow names three figures as having been "great influences" in his life: Isaac Rosenfeld, Delmore Schwartz, and John Berryman.[67] In a note from 1958, Berryman mentions feeling close "w. 4 American poets just now," but closer to Bellow, who alone gives him a "sense of sustaining 'craft,'" a point he underlines with added emphasis: *My friendship w. one magnificent Amer. Novelist gives me more sense of inter-relating artistic life, trial, movement on.*[68]

Berryman was an alcoholic, in and out of hospitals and drying-out clinics. Drink, for him, Bellow conjectures, "replaced the public sanction that poets in the Twin Cities (or in Chicago, in Washington or New York) had to do without. . . . No one minded if you bred poodles. No one objected if you wrote Dream Songs" (p. 270). When, however, this view was invoked as a way of explaining Berryman's suicide—on January 7, 1972, after years of alcoholism and depression, he jumped off the Washington Avenue Bridge in Minneapolis, plunging to his death in the Mississippi—Bellow wrote sardonically to Ralph Ross on August 13, 1973: "There's something culturally gratifying, apparently, about such heroic self-destruction. It's good-old-Berryman-he-knew-how-to-wrap-it-up. It's a combination of America, Murderer of Poets, and This Is the Real Spiritual Condition of Our Times."

That Berryman had few doubts about the heroic nature of the self-destructive artist is suggested in an exchange with Irving Howe. "Don't you feel," Berryman asked, "that Rimbaud's chaos is central to your life?" Howe reports being "guileless enough to say no, I did not. And that, for Berryman, was the end of me: I might be a nice fellow, but I was not one of the haloed victims, not like the Delmore he adored as the suffering poet of the modern city."[69] By the time success came to Berryman, the chaos was ineradicable, as Dream Song 75, which he dedicated to Bellow, suggests. *The Dream Songs*, Berryman explains, "is essentially about an imaginary character (not the poet, not me) named Henry, a white American in early middle age sometimes in blackface, who has suffered an irreversible loss and talks about himself sometimes in the first person, sometimes in the third, sometimes even in the second; he has a friend, never named, who addresses him as Mr. Bones and variants thereof."[70] Dream Song 75 begins: "Turning it over, considering, like a madman / Henry put forth a book." At first this book, likened to a tree, evokes little response, but after "seasons went and came" and "leaves fell" it begins to attract attention. Its success seems to derive from Henry's madness. Its "flashing & bursting" is what makes it "remarkable." That Henry is "thoughtful" and "surviving" as well as "savage" is registered, but it is energy which makes both book and poem stand out.

That energy connects Berryman's poetry to Bellow's fiction. The "chaos" central to Berryman's life, seen in part as a product of modernity, produces art that is exuberant, inclusive, comic. Even when most cast down, Henry's accounts of his condition exhilarate. In stanza one of Dream Song 53, he's in a very bad way, prone on a bed in some hospital or facility, a fallen Achilles (Berryman calls him "Pelides," son of Peleus) pumped full of Sparine (an antipsychotic drug).[71] In stanza two, Henry evokes the attempts of other literary warrior-heroes to ward off or withstand the chaos of modernity, what Wyndham Lewis, in a favorite phrase of Bellow's, called "the moronic inferno."[72] First he quotes "the Honourable Possum" (T. S. Eliot), who says "I seldom *go to films*. They are too exciting," then an unnamed novelist "hot as a firecracker" (Bellow himself, or so Bellow told John Haffenden, Berryman's biographer, in a letter of September 16, 1972), who complains that "it takes me so long to read the 'paper / . . . / because I have to identify myself with everyone in it, / including the corpses, pal." In the poem's third and final stanza (most Dream Songs have only three stanzas) the heavy cost of an artistic vocation is communicated matter-of-factly, in a quotation attributed to Gottfried Benn: "We are using our own skins for wallpaper and cannot win."

Bellow may at times have felt skinned alive but never as often or as intensely as Berryman, whom he loved but was unable to help. In the foreword to *Recovery* he recounts interrupting a conversation with Berryman about Rilke "to ask him whether he had, the other night, somewhere in the Village, pushed a lady down a flight of stairs."

"Whom?"

"Beautiful Catherine [Lindsay, a writer, with whom Bellow had been involved], the big girl I introduced you to."

"Did I do that? I wonder why?"

"Because she wouldn't let you into the apartment."

He took a polite interest in this information. He said, "That I was in the city at all is news to me."

We went back to Rilke. There was only one important topic. We had no small talk.

In the foreword Bellow also recalls a time at Minnesota when Berryman apparently disappeared for several days. Bellow and Ralph Ross went to his home, forced a window, and found him lying facedown diagonally across the bed (like Henry in Dream Song 53, who "lay in the middle of the world, and twitcht"). "From this position he did not stir. But he spoke distinctly. 'These efforts are wasted. We are unregenerate'" (p. 268).

Berryman described the sort of language he evolved for *The Dream Songs* as a "simulation of the (improved) colloquial,"[73] which aptly describes the language Bellow evolved for *Augie*. W. S. Merwin says Berryman "flaunted" the originality of this language, but that it was "saved from affectation by the sheer authority and authenticity of the voice it embodies."

> The verse proceeds with an oddity skating on the edge of comprehensibility and frequently skipping well beyond it. Syntax, tone, diction, and movement—subjects that Berryman pondered fixedly for years—were deliberately arranged, syllable by syllable, cadenzas on carefully tuned strings. But the high artifice was countered by wild liberties taken with grammar, allusion, meter, and every pattern of expectation that the verse suggested.[74]

This passage recalls Martin Amis on the style of *Augie*, which "loves and embraces awkwardness." Berryman lived the language of *The Dream Songs* as he lived Henry's condition. The eccentric emphases in his poems ("I seldom *go* to *films*") became those of his daily speech.[75] This is unlike Bellow, who resembled Augie in a number of respects, but did not talk like him, just as he did not talk like Henderson or write letters like Herzog. Bellow did not have to "dive" for his pearls, in Richard Stern's phrase, as did Berryman. Bellow had more distance from his creations than Berryman.

Though the two men were different in character, they gained

strength from each other, thought themselves "joint labourers" (Wordsworth's description of himself and Coleridge).[76] "Just now in Poetry I read four Dream Songs," Bellow writes to Berryman on November 13, 1962, "and wish to say, this being an hour when strength is low, thank you. We keep each other from the poorhouse. If it hadn't been for you there would have been many a night of porridge and a thin quilt. I will try and return the favor." On August 1, 1963, Berryman writes to Bellow: "After the adrenalin heaved on me by your raving master-works *Augie* & *Henderson*—without which I would be dreaming out an agrarian existence—guess how I feel abt any counter-thrust."

Bellow first showed Berryman drafts of *Henderson* when he and Sasha stopped in Minneapolis on their way back to New York from Nevada. Earlier, he had briefly described it in an undated letter in joke-French: "I have a sort of zany book [*Seize the Day*] coming in November. It isn't exactly worthy of us, perhaps. C'est pour gagner la vie. But in addition I have accomplished something vraiment pas mal. Sans blague, Berrimon. I think you will be pleased." Berryman had been writing individual Dream Songs since August 1955, but sometime after reading the *Henderson* drafts he introduced an unnamed friend of Henry's who addresses him in blackface as "Mr. Bones" and whom, in 1962, Henry begins to answer in blackface, a language inspired at least in part by the language Bellow gives the African characters in *Henderson*. The language of these characters is openly artificial, resembling no real African voice, as other aspects of the novel's Africa resemble no real Africa. In the spring 1959 issue of *Partisan Review*, Elizabeth Hardwick called the novel's setting "a joke Africa with whimsical tribes" ("A Fantastic Voyage," p. 300). The language of characters like Romilayu and Itelo, less so Dahfu, King of the Wariri, is the language of American "Negroes" in minstrel shows, described by Bellow's friend Ralph Ellison in an essay published in *Partisan Review* in spring 1958 ("Change the Joke and Slip the Yoke") as "pseudo-Negro dialect," "a ritual of exorcism." "This blackfaced figure of white fun," Ellison writes of the blackface minstrel, "is for Negroes a symbol of everything they rejected in the white man's thinking about race" (p. 23) (a description that recalls the *schlemiel* of Yiddish literature, in Ruth Wisse's words quoted in Chapter 1 of this book, "the Jew as he is defined by the anti-Semite, but reinterpreted by God's appointee"). The Princeton professor Carlos Baker, in a review of *Henderson* in *The New York Times Book Review* (February 22, 1979), complained that "except for King Dahfu, all the natives talk like a combination of Uncle Remus and the Emperor Jones." But as Catherine Fitzpatrick argues, in a study of the literary friendship of Bellow and Berryman, Bellow's interest in *Henderson* is less with Africa than with "white American primitivist fantasies about Africa," an interest shared by Berryman.[77] In Bellow's case, "that the imaginary Africans of the novel should turn out to talk, not like any real people, but instead in the tones of the imaginary black Americans of minstrelsy, is entirely appropriate."[78]

It is hard to believe that Bellow was unaware of the resonances of the language he gives his Africans ("You no like dat, sah?" asks Romilayu; "Mus' be no ahnimal in drink wattah," explains Itelo).[79] All during his second teaching stint at Minnesota, while the two friends read and discussed each other's work, Bellow was writing *Henderson*. Berryman's first datable use of blackface occurs in Dream Song 26, written in November 1958, some months after this period yet before he'd read Carl Wittke's *Tambo and Bones* (1930), a history of the American minstrel stage. "Given the similarities between the two blackfaces," Fitzpatrick argues, "and given that Berryman's clearly developed later, it seems that *Henderson*, or even Bellow himself, in 'private readings,' was, at the least, a major source of Berryman's blackface." At the same time, "Berryman's adoption of something that was clearly 'minstrel,' even at this early date, provides important confirmation that Bellow, from whom he was adopting it, understood the voice he was using in *Henderson* to be distinctly 'blackface' rather than generically 'black.'"[80]

This interpretation of the language of the African characters in *Henderson* points to a more general feature of Bellow's and Berryman's writing during this period: their determination to treat serious matters comically. For Bellow, Henderson is "the absurd seeker of higher qualities," as Henry for Berryman is Achilles on Sparine.[81] The modern condition becomes a source of laughter (the laughter in *Augie* is different, has less of the absurd about it). As Bellow puts it in "Literature," an essay he wrote for an *Encyclopaedia Britannica* publication entitled *The Great Ideas Today* (1963), "'the inner life,' the 'unhappy consciousness,' the management of personal life, 'alienation'—all sad questions for which the late romantic writer reserved a special tone of disappointment, of bitterness, are turned inside-out by the modern comedian. Deeply subjective self-concern is ridiculed. *My* feelings, *my* early traumas, *my* moral seriousness, *my* progress, *my* sensitivity, *my* fidelity, *my* guilt—the modern reader is easily made to laugh at all of these." Today,

Bellow asserts, comedy is "our only relief from the long prevalent mood of pessimism, discouragement, and low seriousness (the degenerate effect of the ambition for high seriousness)." It is not that comic writing lacks seriousness or that the search for higher qualities is useless, only that accounts of its difficulty ought not to result in what Bellow calls "the popular orgy of wretchedness in modern literature."[82] These views were Berryman's as well; his seriousness, too, is "comical-terrible," inevitably, given the suffering he and Henry shared. As he declared in a note written in late 1955, each of the Dream Songs should have "one stroke of some damned serious humor," "gravity of matter" should combine with "gaiety of manner,"[83] a conjunction that marked Berryman in life as on the page. Here is Bellow on Berryman the man: "He was a husband, a citizen, a father, a householder, he went on the wagon, he fell off, he joined A.A. He knocked himself out to be like everybody else—he liked, he loved, he cared, but he was aware that there was something peculiarly comical in all this."[84]

There were stages in the "inter-relating artistic life" of Bellow and Berryman. *Augie* was an influence in creating the voice of *The Dream Songs*. The voice of *The Dream Songs* was an influence in the creation of Henderson's voice (along with Hemingway's tough-guy talk and the bombast of Chanler Chapman[85]). The speech of the African characters in *Henderson* was an influence on the blackface of Henry as "Mr. Bones" and of his unnamed friend.[86] It could also be argued that Berryman's example encouraged Bellow to draw later novels undisguisedly from painful personal experience. By the end of the 1960s, a decade or so after their time together at Minnesota, Berryman had become a literary celebrity, interviewed in *Life* magazine, much photographed and profiled. *77 Dream Songs*, dedicated to Berryman's third wife, Kate, and to Bellow, had won the Pulitzer Prize for Poetry in 1965 and was followed by *His Toy, His Dream, His Rest*, consisting of a further 306 Dream Songs, which won the National Book Award for Poetry in 1969. In both volumes, as in what he said about them, Berryman maintained the distinction between Henry and himself, as Bellow maintained a distinction between himself and his fictional alter egos. Berryman did so, however, in a voice indistinguishable from Henry's. "Henry does resemble me and I resemble Henry," he told a student interviewer from Harvard, "but on the other hand I am not Henry. You know, I pay income tax; Henry pays no income tax. And bats come over and they stall in my hair—and fuck them, I'm not Henry; Henry doesn't have any bats."[87]

The closeness of the life to the work in *The Dream Songs*, especially when embarrassing or wounding aspects of the life are involved, was hard for readers to ignore. The success of Robert Lowell greatly influenced Berryman in this regard, and critics often linked the two poets, along with Sylvia Plath, Allen Ginsberg, Anne Sexton, Sexton's teacher, W. D. Snodgrass, and other "confessional" poets.[88] That Berryman's example inspired *Herzog*, the novel that follows *Henderson*, is suggested in their correspondence. In the letter of November 13, 1962, in which Bellow thanks Berryman for the four Dream Songs, without which "there would have been many a night of porridge and a thin quilt," it is *Herzog* that he hopes will "return the favor." Berryman's response to *Herzog* was that "Nobody has ever sat down & wallowed to this extent in his own life, *with* full art—I mean novelists. I don't know anything to compare it to, except you."[89]

Berryman's influence on Bellow lived on after his suicide, most obviously in the character of Von Humboldt Fleisher in *Humboldt's Gift*. The depiction of Humboldt grew out of feelings like those Humboldt inspires in Charlie Citrine: of love, affection, helplessness, but also guilt, at coolly observing a friend's troubles, making use of him in one's writing. As Charlie puts it, in words quoted in the introduction to this book, "I did incorporate other people into myself and consume them. When they died I passionately mourned. I said I would continue their work and their lives. But wasn't it a fact that I added their strength to mine? Didn't I have my eye on them in the days of their vigor and glory?" (p. 282). In Bellow's account of Berryman's last visit to Chicago in the foreword to *Recovery* all these feelings are evoked. Berryman was the William Vaughn Moody lecturer at the University of Chicago in 1971. He arrived to give a reading on January 27, a day after receiving a letter from Allen Tate attacking the first part of *Love & Fame* (1970), a recent collection of poems. The attack drove him back to drink after a period of sobriety.

> He came to give a reading—he arrived in Chicago in freezing weather. High-shouldered in his thin coat and big homburg, bearded, he coughed up phlegm. He looked decayed. He had been drinking, and the reading was a disaster. His Princeton mutter, once an affectation, had become a vice. People strained to hear a word. Except when, following some arbitrary system of dynamics, he shouted loudly, we could hear nothing. We left, a disappointed,

bewildered, angry audience. Dignified, he entered a waiting car, sat down, and vomited. He passed out in his room at the Quadrangle Club and slept through the faculty party given in his honor. But in the morning he was full of innocent cheer. He was chirping. It had been a great evening. He recalled an immense success. His cab came, we hugged each other, and he was off for the airport under a frozen sun.[90]

ON MAY 27, 1957, shortly before leaving Minnesota, Bellow wrote to Ralph Ellison with news and plans for the summer. "The new kid" (Adam) was sitting up and taking notice of things: "He seems to have a sense of humor. Having survived the birth trauma he finds life a laughing matter." The time in Minneapolis had been enjoyable: "It was just what we needed. On the farm [in Tivoli] the year round we'd both go nuts. . . . I find the Midwest agrees with me. Here I recognize things. And I'm near Chicago." The plan now was to return to Tivoli for the summer, but to spend the following winter in Chicago. Bellow had accepted a ten-week teaching stint at Northwestern. The Tivoli house would then be free and open to Ellison "for as long a time as you like or need" (Ellison and his wife, Fanny, were in Rome, where for the past two years he'd been a fellow at the American Academy). Once back in Tivoli, Bellow and Sasha entertained a stream of visitors. Sasha returned to a life of household chores, cooking, and wifely duties, and was happy at first. "I typed, grew my own herbs, made jams, canned peaches and plums. Saul grew corn, huge zucchini and lots of tomatoes. . . . It was similar to Pyramid Lake, except with electricity and people" (p. 96). Bellow did chores in the afternoon, or walked in the fields surrounding the house, or drove into town on errands. He did push-ups to keep in shape, made sure Rufus, the cat, was fed, checked on the garden. Herb Gold and Keith Botsford "were there a lot," Sasha remembers, "both somewhat flirtatious, but while Herb flirted with me in a light, harmless way, Keith appreciated me. I mean, he liked my clothes. Keith was one of the few men in our world I found familiar. He, too, did 'dress up' . . . playing 'English Aristocrat,' while I was doing Russian Countess." As the summer wore on, however, cooking and cleaning for houseguests began to exhaust Sasha. Her gall bladder problem resurfaced and she was confined to bed for ten days. "We called a halt to visitors, and I began to regain my health" (pp. 95–96).

The letter to Ellison mentions several visits to Chicago during Bellow's time in Minnesota. In one of these visits, in May, Maury was back in the news, having been threatened with a lawsuit by the city for unlicensed property dealings. "'As one of the largest land holders in the Calumet area,'" he was reported as saying by the *Chicago Tribune*, "he had no intention of jeopardizing his future by operating a disreputable enterprise."[91] Bellow had come to Chicago on this occasion at the invitation of Richard Stern, who taught at the University of Chicago.[92] Stern was a writer not a scholar, the first to be appointed to the English Department at the university (Thornton Wilder, whose lectures Bellow attended as an undergraduate, had been a Hutchins or "college" appointment). In his second year in charge of the department's creative writing courses, Stern obtained funds from the dean to bring well-known novelists and poets to campus. For a stipend of $500 visiting writers were asked to give a talk and sit in on classes. Bellow was the first writer Stern invited: "I thought he was the best writer of his time" (later invitees included Berryman and Robert Lowell). Stern and Bellow had met once before, briefly, at a party given for Bellow by the critic Morton Dauwen Zabel, an older colleague in the English Department. The party was at the Quadrangle Club and Stern remembers being struck by Bellow's gray hair, elegant dress, and large prominent eyes (a feature he claims Bellow was drawn to in others, women in particular). It was not until the May visit, however, that the two writers got to know and like each other. On later visits and during Bellow's time at Northwestern they often met for coffee and doughnuts at Pixley and Ehlers, a cafeteria at Randolph and Michigan, opposite the old location of the Chicago Public Library. Bellow liked the place for its mixed clientele. "He would always have the details [concerning Chicago types]," Stern remembered, including stories of "who had been shot nearby."

The creative writing class Bellow sat in on had approximately fifteen students, several of genuine talent (the poets George Starbuck and David Ray were among their number). When the class failed to provide an appropriate story for Bellow's visit, Stern called upon a friend of his, a young instructor in the college, also a promising writer, and asked if he had a story the class could use. The instructor was Philip Roth, twenty-four at the time, and the story he came up with was "The Conversion of the Jews," published the following March in *The Paris Review* and a year later in Roth's first collection, *Goodbye, Columbus*, which won the National Book Award for Fiction in 1960 (and was favorably reviewed in *Commentary* by Bellow[93]). Roth had dropped out of the PhD program in English at Chicago to write ("I lasted half of a quarter, one eighth of a year"), teaching composition courses in the morning and writing stories in the afternoon. He'd read Bellow's early novels while an undergraduate at Bucknell University in Pennsylvania and in the summer before coming to Chicago read *Augie March*, which excited him greatly. "These were Jews and Jewish families and here was a guy making literature out of them, and that was a great revelation to me," Roth recalled in an interview. "Coincidentally, my going to Chicago made it that much more interesting." Once in Chicago, Roth read and admired *Seize the Day*, which Stern also admired. Roth's memory of how he came to meet Bellow is slightly different from Stern's: "Dick had read in manuscript my story 'The Conversion of the Jews,' and suggested using the story, and I was delighted. I said sure, and can I come to the class? So I came to the class and I just sat in the back and didn't say anything."

Roth didn't say anything partly because writers whose works were discussed in class were meant to remain silent, partly because he was in awe of Bellow. "I hadn't met that many writers in my life. I hadn't met any of his stature." What he remembers of the discussion is that the students criticized the story solemnly "from the points of view that criticism came in in those days," while Bellow laughed a lot when he talked about it. "He found it a comedy. I guess he admired the energy, the spirit in it. It's a primitive story but it's lively. He liked the scene with the kid going up on the roof. I was delighted, and afterwards Dick said do you want to have a cup of coffee and we went over to Reynolds Hall, I think it was called, a coffee place over in the university compound. . . . And we walked across the quadrangle to have a cup of coffee. As I remember it, Saul was very lively and good-natured and laughing and very kind to me." In his novel *The Ghost Writer* (1979) Roth makes comedy of this encounter.[94]

THE FICTIONAL MEETING BETWEEN Zuckerman and Felix Abravanel, the Bellow-like novelist in *The Ghost Writer*, is revealing as much for what it suggests about the effects of celebrity as about Bellow's character. Zuckerman is a "writer-worshipping" college senior at Chicago (p. 57). It is his story that the creative writing professor has chosen for Abravanel to discuss in class. Abravanel was sent the story in advance and read

it on the plane to Chicago (Stern remembers that Bellow arrived in Chicago by plane, the first flight of his life[95]). After class it is Abravanel who
extends Zuckerman the invitation to come for coffee, along with the
creative writing professor, a professor from the Sociology Department
(a figure very much like Edward Shils, who would later maneuver with
Stern to get Bellow a job at Chicago), and Abravanel's "luminous" mistress. "They're a rough bunch, Zuckerman," Abravanel says. "You better come along for a transfusion" (p. 64). Over coffee, Abaravanel "said
not a word," leaning back in his chair "looking smooth and strokable
as a cat in his teaching attire of soft gray flannel slacks, a light mauve
pullover, and a cashmere sports coat. With hands and ankles elegantly
crossed, he left it to his buoyant young companion to do the talking."
The buoyant young companion "was in ecstasy" (p. 64).

Earlier, the mistress had reported that as Abravanel read Zuckerman's story on the plane to Chicago, "he just kept throwing back
his head and laughing." She said she thought of telling him to recommend the story to "Sy" Knebel, "editor for twenty years of the New
York intellectual quarterly that I had been devouring for the past two"
(p. 63). This information she conveyed to Zuckerman at a reception
for Abravanel, who was busy fending off hovering graduate students.[96]
When Abravanel leaves after coffee he says "Good luck" to Zuckerman
but mentions nothing of the editor and the story. The mistress says
"even less" (p. 65). Had she forgotten about Sy? Had she told Abravanel
and he'd forgotten? "Or maybe she'd told him and he answered 'Forget
it.'" "I realized they'd had other things than my story to think about."
Young Zuckerman is left slightly deflated, resentful even, reactions
often inspired by celebrity encounters. "Felix Abravanel was clearly not
in the market for a twenty-three-year-old son" (p. 66), he concludes.
The encounter is described by the adult Zuckerman from the point of
view both of the younger aspiring writer and the older celebrated one.

BELLOW'S TEACHING AT Northwestern was for the Winter Quarter,
from January 6 to March 22, 1958. The appointment, arranged through
his old teacher, Moody Prior, now dean of the College of Liberal Arts,
was part of a program that brought "distinguished non-academic persons" to campus.[97] Dwight Macdonald taught in it the year before and
Sean O'Faolain would follow Bellow in the spring. In addition to pro-

fessors from Bellow's undergraduate days (Edward B. Hungerford, Bergen Evans), the English faculty at Northwestern included noteworthy new appointments (Richard Ellmann in particular, who in 1950 had tried to get Bellow a Briggs-Copeland Fellowship at Harvard). Bellow taught two courses: a creative writing course for seniors and a literature course, "The Hero in the Modern Novel," examining the changing status of fictional heroes from the nineteenth century to the present "as reflected in selected works of continental, English, and American novelists." In addition to teaching, Bellow delivered several lectures, including one in a series on "Religion and Art" at Hillel House. He and Sasha were also treated to a heavy schedule of dinners and receptions. "I cooked no meals, really," Sasha remembers, "because we were dining out almost nightly." Mornings, as usual, were sacrosanct, devoted to writing. "For months I've been absorbed in the remotest bush with Henderson," Bellow wrote to Berryman on February 19. "From Labor Day I started *de nouveau* and have written about five hundred pages since. The last fantasy is taking place in Newfoundland. Crash fire—crash ice. I need to cool things off."

In the first weeks of the Evanston stay, all three Bellows were laid up. First Adam, then Sasha and Bellow "had pneumonia, more or less."[98] In an undated letter from late February, Sasha reported to the McCloskys that "we are barely making it what with relatives and constant colds. We country folk are not used to the big city battle with germs and I expect, like the Eskimos would probably die from chicken pox, measles and the common (all too common) cold." This letter was written from the Evanshire Hotel, on the corner of Main and Hinman in downtown Evanston, which the Bellows moved to after staying briefly with Sasha's relatives in nearby Skokie, a suburb west of Evanston. The Evanshire was a small residential hotel and the apartment they'd rented consisted of two rooms and a kitchenette. "Adam is walking," Bellow reported to Ellison, in a letter of February 14, 1958. "Life is just one long country fair for that kid. He's medicinal to me." Except in the mornings. Then Sasha had to take Adam away for three and a half hours, she complained to Stern. Bellow was like Moses Herzog, who couldn't think when his baby daughter, Junie, was crying and would rush from his room "hollering" (p. 455) (if Northwestern provided Bellow with an office, he seems not to have used it to write). Most days Sasha took Adam to visit relatives in Skokie, in particular Aunt Cookie, her mother's sister, and

Uncle Lester, Cookie's husband, who had put them up upon arrival. Cookie was "generous with her love and admiration, always" (from early on she knew the secret of Sasha's childhood, offering "wholehearted acceptance and protection" [p. 98]). Sasha describes Uncle Lester as "quiet, reserved, street smart, [with] an ethical code of his own, despite being a bookie, a contrast to Cookie who was sparkling, brash, a Zieg-feld type, Chicago style" (p. 97). She recalls Lester laboring through *Augie March* "night after night, sweating it out, cover to cover. 'How would it look,' he said to my aunt, 'if I don't read this book, now he's in the family'" (p. 97). Bellow adored Cookie and Lester, Sasha remembers; they were just the Chicago types he liked, "the real thing" (p. 97).

That Cookie and Lester doted on Adam and were happy to baby-sit allowed Sasha to accompany Bellow to various Northwestern social engagements, "part of the deal." "We were both being courted," Sasha recalls, "Saul because he was the visiting celebrity, and I because I was, by Evanston standards, glamorous. I was certainly young and lively and, as usual, exotic in my wardrobe" (p. 97). At a New Year's Eve party thrown by Richard and Mary Ellmann, Sasha wore a white-fringed flapper dress, while the other women "wore tweed skirts and little sweaters." When not being feted in Evanston or Skokie, they visited Bellow's relatives: sister Jane, her husband, Charlie, and their boys, Larry and Bobby; brother Sam, his wife, Nina, and their children, Lesha and Shael. Presumably they did not visit Maury and Marge and their children, Joel and Lynn, since in the memoir Sasha says she saw Maury only once. To reciprocate all this hospitality, she and Bellow gave a party at Cookie and Lester's, inviting everyone they knew. Stern remembers picking up Edward Shils and then Josephine Herbst to drive them to Skokie; stuffy English Department types mixed happily with Dave Peltz, Sam Freifeld, Lester the bookie. Atlas quotes a guest at the party who claims that Sasha at one point looked at Bellow "with fury in her eyes," an incident she told me she did not remember.[99] She recalled no arguments or coldness between herself and Bellow at the party; it was a great success. But she does admit that in this period "Adam had my whole heart and I gloried—no, wallowed—in mother-hood, astonished I could ever have imagined not having this miraculous child. I felt whole, purposeful, grateful. And, in truth, motherhood and rediscovering family and my place in it, meant that I was not paying much attention to Saul. He didn't seem to mind, then" (p. 98).

ON FEBRUARY 5, 1958, about a month after Bellow arrived in Evanston, he received a telegram electing him as a life member to the National Institute of Arts and Letters, described in a Northwestern press release as "the highest ranking honor society of the arts in the United States."[100] The honor was accompanied by a request that Bellow help the institute determine its fiction awards. A day later, on February 6, Harold Rosenberg wrote inviting him to serve with Alfred Kazin and Marianne Moore on the literary board of the Longview Foundation. Rosenberg was the foundation's program director, responsible for organizing schemes to purchase artworks from promising painters and sculptors, and to give awards to writers. "The way the awards are set up," Rosenberg wrote to Bellow, "you will be able to bestow five of them on your own, besides your votes on ten others." This influence Bellow exercised generously. He was now frequently asked to write Guggenheim letters (by 1959 he had written on behalf of James Baldwin, Bernard Malamud, Leslie Fiedler, Mel Tumin, Herb Gold, and Harvey Swados). Elizabeth Ames asked him to sit on the Yaddo board to select fellows (there were twelve members of the board, which met twice a year). He wrote recommending authors or aspiring authors to Henry Volkening and Pat Covici. Though some Guggenheim letters (he wrote fifty or so over his lifetime) are more effusive than others, none is without praise and none seeks to undermine the applicant.

Bellow also exercised influence in several literary controversies in the period. In October 1956 he received a telegram from Harvey Breit, editor of *The New York Times Book Review*, urging him to attend a meeting of the writers' and publishers' committee of "People to People," a lobbying group set up by the Eisenhower administration to counter Soviet propaganda and promote American values. The meeting was to be held just after Thanksgiving in Breit's apartment in Manhattan. Eisenhower himself had appointed William Faulkner chair of the committee. In a telegram of October 8 Bellow wired that he was "TOTALLY CONFUSED. UNDERSTAND NOTHING OF THIS FAULKNER-EISENHOWER BUSINESS. NEVERTHELESS AM WILLING TO RISE TO EMERGENCY." At the meeting, Faulkner, who had had a lot to drink, so annoyed Bellow in a discussion of Hungarian refugees (the sort Bellow had just shared

Thanksgiving turkey with at Tivoli) that Bellow left in disgust, missing a discussion likely to annoy him even more, in which Faulkner argued in support of a campaign to release Ezra Pound from Saint Elizabeths Hospital in Washington, D.C., where he'd been held for treasonous wartime radio broadcasts. When Faulkner's account of the issues discussed at the meeting was posted to committee members, Bellow wrote back from Tivoli on January 7, 1957. He had no objection to Eastern Europeans being invited to the United States to sample its freedoms "provided they are not harmed by the police of those countries when they return." As for Pound, "if sane he should be tried again as a traitor; if insane he ought not to be released merely because he is a poet." Bellow explained:

> Pound advocated in his poems and in his broadcasts enmity to the Jews and preached hatred and murder. Do you mean to ask me to join you in honoring a man who called for the destruction of my kinsmen? I can take no part in such a thing even if it makes effective propaganda abroad, which I doubt. Europeans will take it instead as a symptom of reaction. In France Pound would have been shot. . . . What staggers me is that you and Mr. Steinbeck who have dealt for so many years in words should fail to understand the import of Ezra Pound's plain and brutal statements about the "kikes" leading the "goy" to slaughter. Is this—from the Pisan Cantos—the stuff of poetry? It is a call to murder. If it were spoken by a farmer or a shoemaker we would call him mad.

Bellow's position on Pound's incarceration was exactly that of his friend Karl Shapiro in an earlier Pound controversy. Shapiro was the only judge to vote against awarding the 1949 Bollingen Prize in Poetry to Pound for the *Pisan Cantos*. The other judges were Robert Lowell, Allen Tate, Conrad Aiken, Louise Bogan, W. H. Auden, T. S. Eliot, and Robert Penn Warren. Bellow was in Paris at the time of the controversy over the award, but would have followed it in the pages of *Partisan Review*. After publishing an attack on the judges' decision by William Barrett in its April issue, *PR* published an article in its defense, by Auden and Tate, in the issue of May–June (the issue in which Bellow's "A Sermon by Dr. Pep" appeared). Shapiro then replied in the November issue (which contained "From the Life of Augie March," an early version of the novel's first chapter). Allen Tate had been the most active of Pound's defenders, aided by John Berryman, who helped to collect seventy-three signatures for a letter defending the award.[101]

Almost as enraging for Bellow as the question of Pound's release was a second literary controversy concerning the supposed death of the novel. Granville Hicks had asked Bellow to contribute an essay on modern fiction for a volume of essays pointedly titled *The Living Novel: A Symposium* (1957). Bellow wrote back on March 16, 1956, from Pyramid Lake commending the idea of the anthology and sketching out his views about "the state of fiction today."

> Of course we are continually aware, while working, that we are under attack, and so perhaps it is wiser not to pretend that we are a species without enemies. I am familiar with Lionel Trilling's attitude, of course. It is one of the historical blessings of Jewish birth that one is used to flourish in the face of hostile opinion. . . . The modern world is full of people who declare that other people are obsolete. Stalin and the Kulaks, Hitler and the Jews and Slavs and gypsies, and Trilling and T. S. Eliot and several others have decided that novels are done for historically.

Stalin, Hitler, Lionel Trilling, T. S. Eliot. In "Distractions of a Fiction Writer," the essay Bellow eventually produced for the anthology, he qualifies but repeats the conjunction. The distractions in question are of several sorts, beginning with those of the reader. "The Ancient Mariner" is invoked by way of example: "The Wedding Guest is distracted when the Ancient Mariner stops him. . . . The Guest can only tear his hair out as he hears the loud bassoon. He is cut off from his beloved distractions by the power of art, and he cannot choose but hear. This is the position we [modern readers] are all in." In place of the loud bassoon and the wedding feast we have the distractions of American materialism, mass communication, and mass cult (the factors Wordsworth singles out in the 1800 preface to the *Lyrical Ballads* as "acting with a combined force to blunt the discriminating powers of the mind, and unfitting it for all voluntary exertion to reduce it to a state of almost savage torpor"). As Bellow puts it, "the giant producers of goods need our defenseless attention. They catch us on the run and through the eyes and ears fill us with the brand names of cars and cigarettes and soaps. And then news and information distracts us. Bad art distracts us."[102]

These distractions act upon authors as well as readers, and it is the role of authors, novelists in particular, to winnow and order them to artistic purpose. "The novelist works more deeply with distractions than any other kind of artist," Bellow argues. "The novelist begins at a great depth of distraction and difficulty. Sometimes, as in James Joyce's *Ulysses*, he risks total immersion in distraction." Today, it is claimed, distraction "has reached its limit. . . . And so we are told by critics that the novel is dead" (p. 6), a message disseminated in universities as well as newspapers and literary periodicals, by now a species of common wisdom. "You go to a party and a psychiatrist tells you that *his* analyst believes literature is dying" (p. 15) (Bellow hated such parties, hated listening to the literary opinions of psychoanalysts, architects, cultured real-estate agents).[103] To Bellow the opinion that literature or the novel was dying was "an act of aggression," bad enough when voiced by non-literary people, worse when voiced by people in the know, "the subtlest of enemies . . . those who get you over to their own side. You read the authoritative words of an eminent critic; they sound reasonable; you half agree, and then you are distracted and stiflingly depressed" (pp. 15–16). Who are these critics who say the novel is finished? "We have heard this from Valéry and from T. S. Eliot, from Ortega and from Oswald Spengler, and most recently from the summit of Morningside Heights" (p. 16).

Morningside Heights was the home not only of Columbia but of Lionel and Diana Trilling, whose approval Bellow distrusted. The year before the Trillings praised *Augie March*, Diana wrote an article in the "Speaking of Books" column of *The New York Times Book Review* (June 15, 1952) lamenting the demise of American fiction in general, the result of what she saw as the nation's "cultural situation." Her view was seconded a week later (June 22) by John Aldridge, again in a "Speaking of Books" column, who identified the novel's demise with a breakdown of class boundaries, the lack of any coherent social order. A related account of the decline of fiction is cited by Bellow in the "Distractions" essay. In J. M. Cohen's 1956 Penguin survey, *A History of Western European Literature*, the order that is lacking is religious or metaphysical rather than social: "The novel has died a victim to an agreed picture of the Universe, which has faded with the stifling of Christianity by non-dogmatic idealism and crude materialism" (p. 17).

It was Lionel Trilling who recommended that Bellow read his

wife's *New York Times* piece and the Aldridge follow-up, and on June 23 Bellow wrote to Trilling to tell him what he thought. It would take no "Swami powers . . . to divine the fact that I disagree most violently." There have always been weak or deficient novels, Bellow wrote, nor is there any proof that proportionately more of them are being written or read today than in the past. "Really, things are now as they always were, and to be disappointed in them is extremely shallow." This is not to say that living in the present is easy for a writer; Bellow would hardly say such a thing, given his views on the influence of American materialism. "We may not be strong enough to live in the present. But to be *disappointed* in it! To identify oneself with a better past! No, no!" The manner in which critics pronounced the novel's death also rankled. "How odd it is that these words 'obsolete' and 'finished' should never be spoken with regret or pain," Bellow notes in the "Distractions" essay. "The accent is rather one of satisfaction" (p. 16).

Three pages later Bellow brings out a sledgehammer, perhaps suspecting that he and others like him were being seen as the unspoken agents of decline:

> A lot of things have been called obsolete. I brooded over Spengler in college. As a Jew, I was, in his vocabulary, a magian and therefore obsolete. Toynbee, unless I am mistaken, has a similar view of Jews, that they are a sort of fossil. Marx and Engels, too, were prophets of obsolescence. For Stalin the kulaks were obsolete; for Hitler, all the "inferior" breeds of men. . . . I don't mean to say that there is no such thing as obsolescence. I merely wish to show that the term "obsolete," derived from evolutionary thought, has a place of some importance in the history of modern persecution. Far, far down in the scale of power, far from Rome and Berlin and Leningrad, in certain academic and critical circles we hear it said that a particular kind of imagination is now obsolete (p. 19).

The personal or autobiographical element at work in Bellow's defense of the novel accounts for its violence. The novel's "enemies" have gone over to the other side, capitulating to American society's measure of its "leading activities." "Sometimes it is the lawgiver who is in the highest place, and sometimes the priest, and sometimes the general. With us it is the businessman, the administrator, the political leader, the military man. These have the power; they are the representative men; in them manhood is mirrored" (p. 8). The novelist refuses this measure, at some cost. "Chances are that he is working, bitterly working, in an effort to meet his brothers of the office and factory satisfactorily. The odds are good that he is literally a brother and comes out of the same mass. And now for some strange reason he is trying to throw a bridge from this same place, from a room in Chicago to, let us say, Ahab, to Cervantes, to the Kings of the old Chronicles, to Genesis. For he says, 'Aren't we still part of the same humanity, children of Adam?'" (p. 10). In their prophecies of cultural decline, the Trillings and T. S. Eliot are linked in Bellow's mind not only to Hitler and Stalin but to his scoffing businessmen father and brothers. Bellow's reaction, as always when threatened, was to attack.

BEFORE BELLOW RETURNED with Adam and Sasha to Tivoli in April 1958, he went to California. From there he wrote a letter to Covici on the morning he'd begun typing the finished longhand version of *Henderson*. He was exhausted, had worn himself out "between Evanston and *Henderson*." He thought the novel needed cutting. "I've got to work it out at leisure, now that I've got all the facts down. Leisure, I said. Not to be confused with idleness." San Francisco—where he gave lectures and visited Alice Adams and other friends—was "all right, I guess, although it makes you feel that after a journey of three thousand miles you might at least have gotten out of America." What he needed back in Tivoli was "a couple of weeks of sleep." Only then would he "be fit to start the final campaign." For this campaign, Covici provided Bellow with a secretary. Bellow read out the handwritten manuscript of his novel to the typist, altering, adding, and cutting as he went along.[104]

Covici was anxious to get *Henderson* in print and Bellow was under pressure. In a letter of January 31, 1959, to Josephine Herbst, a writer he'd gotten to know and like at Yaddo in the summer of 1953, he recalled "working eight, ten, twelve and fourteen hours a day for six weeks. By mid-August, I was near suicide." Exhausted on their return to Tivoli, Bellow grew increasingly moody, impatient of interruption and distraction and hard on Sasha. "He was either distant or lashing out at me," she recalled. "I irritated him mightily, he lost his temper over the house, grabbing me by the shoulder like an unruly child, marching me to the scene of my latest failing (the dust in front of the door, the pot I forgot to clean, the socks in the sink)"—like Henderson's complaints about "kids' diapers under the bed and in the cigar humidor. The sink . . . full of garbage and grease" (p. 216) or Herzog's complaints about "eggshells, chop bones, tin cans under the table, under the sofa" (p. 475). On occasion, Sasha claims, the lashing out was physical, though he was "always contrite afterwards." In addition, his trips to the city were becoming more frequent. Absorbed with household chores, visitors, and Adam, Sasha admits that she "was too exhausted to care, and certainly didn't realize he was seeing other women" (p. 98). She spent a lot of time with the Ludwigs, who "were sympathetic to my problems in the marriage; I unburdened myself—Saul was disapproving, constantly finding fault, selfish beyond belief in every way in bed and out. And Saul, apparently, I learned later, was confiding in Jack about his disappointment with me: I was too demanding, imperious, too centered around the baby, immature, spoiled, a sexual flop" (p. 100).

The Ludwig marriage was also in trouble at this time. Although Leya Ludwig was pregnant with a second daughter, Brina, they had agreed to split up, or so Jack told Sasha. When Leya went into labor in early May, both Bellow and Sasha waited at the hospital. The labor was long and difficult and eventually Bellow returned to Tivoli to get some sleep. Sasha stayed with Jack in the waiting room and sometime that night "with a brotherly and comforting hug," he revealed to her the many complaints Bellow had made about her, including sexual complaints, as well as how disappointed he was in the marriage. Then he told Sasha of Bellow's infidelities, known, he claimed, by all their friends (in Sasha's words: "the Hoffmans, the Botsfords, Ellisons, Dupees, the New York and Princeton pals—you name it" [p. 99)]). In the weeks that followed Sasha brooded over Ludwig's revelations. She said nothing to Bellow of what she had been told, partly out of confusion and shock, partly at Ludwig's urging. Ludwig became her counselor and confidant, "friendship personified, comforting, concerned, caring, with his brotherly hugs, feeding me more gossip, but asking me not to reveal the source of this information to Saul" (p. 100). Ludwig began showing up at Tivoli in late mornings while Bellow was still at work. He and Sasha would talk over coffee and when Bellow emerged from his morning's writing she would serve the two men lunch. Then Bellow and Ludwig would go off together. One day when Bellow was in the city Ludwig showed up at the usual time. "He stood very close to me, staring. I was uneasy. He kissed me. I was still. He said, 'Don't you know what this means?' 'What,' I asked, confused. 'My feelings for you.'" Before this moment, Sasha claims, she had had no interest in Ludwig "as a man." Now, though, "I looked into his eyes, really looked, and somehow fell into them. A coup de foudre" (p. 100).

Another view of the Pyramid (Gus Bundy Collection, courtesy of Special Collections Department, University of Nevada, Reno Library)

13

Betrayal

THE AFFAIR BETWEEN Sasha and Ludwig began soon after his declaration of May 1958, fueled for Sasha by a new set of fantasies. "I was flying in the stratosphere, I was Sleeping Beauty, Snow White, all the fairy tale figures awakening at last."[1] Meanwhile, relations between Bellow and Sasha were deteriorating under the pressure of work on his side and guilt and resentment on hers. In June they had a serious fight, involving the money from Sasha's mother, perhaps heated by recent bad feeling over a photograph the mother had taken of Bellow, one he didn't like and about which Sasha says he was rude.[2] In the memoir, she describes the fight as though it happened the day Ludwig made his declaration. After describing her Sleeping Beauty fantasies, she writes: "We [she and Ludwig] talked about the future. Leya was returning to Winnipeg. I knew I would have to make some plans, but before I was able to think clearly enough to do so, Saul came back and we had a violent quarrel" (p. 100). Sasha's mother had inquired in a letter about the $5,000 they'd received from her for repairs to the house, and when Sasha mentioned the letter to Bellow he got angry. "'That was no loan,' he shouted. 'She gave us that money.'" Sasha was dumbfounded, calling her mother's money "everything she had" (p. 100). Then she lost her composure completely:

> We were in the dining room, he pounded on the table, the dishes rattled and slid around. "I won't be made a fool of by the two of you!" he roared, and in that moment I saw him through a red haze of fury and, in an adrenalin surge, lifted the table at my end and

flung it at him. I ran upstairs, hoisted Adam and grabbed the car keys, downstairs in a flash. I jumped in the car. He stood in the driveway, daring me. "Get out of the way, Saul, now, or I'll run you over," I shrieked, and started up the car—he jumped away, and I went to the Ludwigs (pp. 101–2).

In an interview, Sasha gives the impression that some days at least had intervened between Ludwig's declaration and the quarrel with Bellow. "I started up with him in May," she recalled, though "I couldn't bring myself to be entirely unfaithful. . . . I'm seeing Jack a little bit, a little hugging and kissing in the backroads, and I'm thinking what am I doing." In this period, Ludwig, at times in the presence of his wife, fed Sasha more stories of Bellow's infidelities. He told her about a Japanese lover Bellow had in New York, about how Bellow slept with Elsa, the Bard student, in the marital bed in Tivoli. "He told me some really ugly stories" (p. 101).

By the time of the fight, Sasha was not only furious with Bellow but had fallen for Ludwig. "I gave him no encouragement initially," she recalled, but he was "supportive and sympathetic" and the tales he told her about Bellow left her "wounded and vulnerable and susceptible." She and Ludwig talked about a future together and he opened up "a whole new world for me emotionally which I hadn't experienced." "I did love him," she admitted. "I couldn't eat or sleep." The lovers concealed their feelings from their spouses. When Bellow called at the Ludwigs' after Sasha stormed out, she refused to see him. Some days later, when he was away from Tivoli, she sneaked back into the house and gathered up clothes for herself and Adam. Her friend Anita Maximilian agreed to take the two of them in until Sasha found a place of her own. Before boarding the train for the city, Sasha told Jack that "he needed to be honest with Leya, she deserved the truth, although Saul did not" (p. 101). It seems that in this instance he did as instructed. "Leya had said for years that their marriage was not working out," Sasha said in an interview, "and she said to him I can understand." Leya also understood "how no one could talk to Saul."[3] In Manhattan Sasha found a job standing in at an art gallery for the summer (the gallery belonged to the mother of her roommate from the Ansonia, the one who was having an affair with her father). She then sublet an apartment in Brooklyn from a friend of Anita's who was away for the summer, using a nanny agency to look after Adam during the day. The job at the gallery was undemanding: "Nobody really came in—except Ralph Ellison . . . always on the verge of saying something, but I never knew what he wanted. Of course I knew he really liked me and was probably attracted to me, but I was also sure he was there to report back to Saul. I said not a word to him or anyone about Jack," including her mother, who was "frantic with alarm over the rift with Saul, but didn't really want to know what the problem was" (p. 101). Others had their suspicions. Richard Stern visited New York in the summer of 1958 and when he learned Sasha was working at a gallery in the city, called her up. She invited him and his wife over and "we went out to Brooklyn and who should be there but Jack Ludwig. Obviously something was going on. I don't think Saul knew."

Around the beginning of July 1958, Leya Ludwig and the children left to visit family in Winnipeg. "And that's when I really started having the affair," Sasha recalled. Bellow, meanwhile, was working flat out on *Henderson*. Soon after Sasha left for Brooklyn, fourteen-year-old Greg arrived to spend the summer with his father. When he asked Bellow where Sasha and Adam were, "my father, in a dead-pan tone of voice, announced that she was moving to Brooklyn 'to get away and think.' Meanwhile Jack Ludwig was driving down to Brooklyn on a regular basis, ostensibly to 'mediate' between Saul and Sasha."[4] Jesse Reichek, Bellow's painter friend from Paris, was also staying at Tivoli at this time, while his wife, Laure, visited her family in France. "Jesse drew and Saul wrote all morning," Greg recalls, "but by then I had a rickety bicycle to get me to the local swimming pool." Laure Reichek remembers Jesse telling her of fierce arguments that summer between Bellow and Greg over Greg's interest in the stock market. "Apparently Saul was so distressed about the affinity I expressed for capitalism," Greg writes in his memoir, "that it brought him to tears."[5] Reichek also recalled tensions with Sasha, as well as moments when Bellow expressed pride in her looks. On one occasion when she appeared in a bathing suit he whispered "Doesn't she look beautiful? Isn't she beautiful?" Bellow's account of the summer (his nonfictional account, that is) was reported in an interview of March 16, 1972, in the *Chicago Sun-Times*: "He had written 'Henderson' with the help of a stenographer because it was overdue and he owed the publisher $10,000. 'I dictated it from 8 a.m. to 1 p.m. every day. Then I'd do the dishes, do the shopping and cook supper. After supper I'd dictate again for the rest of the evening. I worked this way for an entire summer during a time of great personal difficulty. The worse things grew for me personally the more amusing I began to think the whole thing was."[6]

Bellow's correspondence from the summer of 1958 is sparse, mostly undated, and unrevealing. On July 15 he wrote to Josephine Herbst, who lived in Pennsylvania, suggesting a visit: "Let's get together at least once before Sasha and I take off for Minnesota." On July 24 he wrote to Berryman: "When may we see you and Ann and Paul? Tivoli stands open." Only in the letter of January 31, 1959, to Herbst, quoted at the end of the last chapter, does he go into detail about the summer. It is not clear whether the unperturbed references to Sasha in the letters of July 15 and 24 signaled a rapprochement; they may have been a way of avoiding having to explain matters. At some point in the summer, Sasha did return to Tivoli. While vacationing in New Hampshire, Oscar Tarcov, whose health had long been a worry, had his first heart attack. Bellow offered to take in the Tarcov children, Nathan and Miriam, for the period before they went off to summer camp. When he asked Sasha if she'd return to Tivoli to help look after them and Greg and then drive them to camp, she agreed, though there seems to have been no talk of returning to Bellow or resuming the marriage.[7] All Greg recalls of this period is that "eventually Sasha moved back to Tivoli, where she and I grew closer in rural isolation."[8]

Before Sasha's flight from Tivoli, Bellow, who was running short of money, had accepted an offer from Ralph Ross to teach Humanities at the University of Minnesota for the coming academic year. Whether he did so before Ludwig's declaration of his feelings for Sasha is not clear. He had a condition before accepting the job: Ludwig, his good friend, must also be offered a post. "I had to understand one very peculiar complication," Ross told Atlas. "Ludwig was so close a friend that they had made a pact: neither one of them could go unless both of them could go." With the exception of an anthology of stories coedited with Richard Poirier, Ludwig had not yet published a book, but he had a PhD, was chair of the Division of Languages and Literature at Bard (which, nevertheless, was unwilling to keep him on), and had references from F. W. Dupee and Ted Weiss. Ross's suspicion was that "Bellow was conned into this arrangement because Ludwig wanted to be where Sondra was."[9] In 1972 on a visit to Bellow in Vermont, Ruth Miller, his old friend and biographer, heard him talk about Ludwig's betrayal and the breakup of his marriage "as if it were a week ago." The impression she received was that it was Sasha who urged Bellow to tell Ross "that he wouldn't go unless they hired Ludwig, too."[10] This impression was shared by Mitzi McClosky, recalling a visit she and Herb paid to Tivoli early in the summer, around the time of the fight and Sasha's flight. "Saul said, 'We're having a lot of trouble. She doesn't really want to come back to Minnesota. . . . We have to bring our friends back, because otherwise Sondra would be unhappy. It would be too much of a change for her.'" Sasha makes no mention, either in her memoir or in our interviews, of how or when Ludwig's appointment was arranged, or of pressuring Bellow to get Ludwig a job. All she says of the end of the summer is that "Leya left for Winnipeg, and [Jack] was getting signed up for Minnesota in September" (p. 101).

Sasha and Ludwig now had a plan, or what passed for one. "I would go to California, and then we would be able to have a life together after his stint in Minneapolis. He'd get another teaching job and we would start fresh" (p. 101). In an interview she remembered Ludwig saying, "Adam's going to have a real father, I'm going to have a real husband." Looking back on the plan in the memoir, Sasha admits its impracticality: "I never thought about money, about divorce proceedings, about Adam and his father. . . . I was in a bubble of love and sexual discovery, in a fantasy world about a happy life to come" (p. 101). If Ludwig and Bellow were to be colleagues at Minnesota, the affair had to be hidden; it made sense for her to live away for the year, to avoid gossip, discovery, confrontation. Why did she choose California? Why not Chicago, where she had relatives and where it would be easier for Bellow to visit Adam and for Ludwig to visit her? The reason she gives in the memoir is that "Cookie had remarried and there was no room in the house for me and Adam" (p. 102). But Lester did not die until September 1960 and Cookie did not remarry until 1968. In an interview Sasha revealed that Cookie "did not like Jack at all," thought him "bad news, he's using you." The decision not to go to Chicago, however, remains puzzling: Sasha had other relatives there and at least a few contacts, and Cookie would still have been a support. She says Bellow accepted the California plan, but it is hard to believe that he did so thinking it was for a whole year. All that is known for certain is that at the end of the summer Bellow left Tivoli and Sasha wrote to her friend Sand Higson to say that she and Adam were coming to California and "would be grateful for a visit with her until I could get myself and Adam settled" (p. 102). Once Bellow left Tivoli, Sasha returned to pack and ship a trunk of clothing to Malibu.

Just before this point, terrible news arrived for Bellow from Chicago. Larry Kauffman, his nephew, the elder of his sister Jane's two sons, had committed suicide in San Francisco. Bellow drove directly to Chicago from Tivoli upon hearing the news.[11] Sam Bellows was dispatched by the family to find out what had happened, but the more details he uncovered, according to Greg in his memoir, the more sordid the story became. So he simply "stopped asking questions."[12] On August 22, 1958, the night before he was scheduled for release, Larry hanged himself in his cell. He was twenty-four. That he had been arrested for stealing came as no surprise to Bellow and Greg. During a visit Larry paid to Tivoli, money began to disappear from handbags, though not, strangely, when left out in the open. Bellow asked Greg what he knew about the missing money, "no doubt hoping to dispel his worst fears about his nephew." Greg, a prickly teenager, was "outraged" at the suggestion that he might be involved (in a letter to Bellow of June 27, on the eve of Greg's visit, Anita described Greg as in good spirits: "He is still plenty fresh, but his overall manner is not so sullen and angry").[13] On August 25 Larry's body was flown back to Chicago for burial. Months later, in a letter of November 13, Richard Stern wrote with information about him. Stern had met the college friend who'd accompanied Larry on his visit to Tivoli. "I asked him about the suicide, and he said that Larry was a kleptomaniac and had tried to kill himself a couple of times, and he'd been in trouble with the Army for stealing fencing equipment and that he'd stolen stuff from the fraternity house where he and friend lived."

Larry's death devastated the whole family, including Bellow. Worn to the bone by the rush to finish *Henderson*, the knowledge that he'd sunk his legacy in a collapsing Hudson Valley mansion, the quarrel and breakup with Sasha, the news of Oscar Tarcov's heart attack, and the grief of his family in Chicago, Bellow was near collapse. In Minneapolis, where he went directly from the funeral, he rented a small apartment at 1408 West 28th Street near Lake Calhoun, about a twenty-minute drive from campus. From there he wrote to Sasha. "Would I come and spend some time with him on my way to California? Just a couple of weeks, to get him through the grief and horror. He would pay for my tickets and give me some money to get settled in California—$300" (p. 102).

Sasha accepted the offer. When she and Adam arrived in Minneapolis they stayed at the McCloskys'. Bellow was "grateful to see Adam" and pleaded with Sasha not to end the marriage. "He was at rock bottom, he said, he understood what he was losing and asked for another chance" (p. 102). Meanwhile, the McCloskys were "pressing me not to take his son away from him." Ludwig was in Winnipeg still and Sasha began to worry. As she put it in an interview, "Jack is being very peculiar now about it. He's not giving me a solution, no guidance. I was thinking maybe he was having second thoughts." Then a letter arrived from Sand Higson. "She was sorry things were falling apart in my marriage, she would be happy to have us stay for a few days, but . . . she and Jim were not willing to have a young child around the house for longer than that" (Adam was eighteen months). Sasha was thrown, having expected to spend several weeks with the Higsons, "long enough to find work, get settled, etc." Her only money was the $300 Bellow had sent her. "How long would $300 last?" Moreover, "Saul was so unbearably and touchingly sad" (p. 102). After a long talk, she gave in:

> I would stay, at least for a while, no guarantees. But I had conditions: he needed to go into therapy, but not some Reichian scream thing. And I was not willing to resume the physical relationship unless we could get past these problems. I was in despair. Jack arrived to a done deal. I told him that Saul needed me, that there was no money for me to leave the marriage, and that I had awakened to the fact that I couldn't so easily take his son away. I could not have a love affair on the side, I told him, and I needed to commit to the marriage, and so we had to end it. I even suggested that he bring his family to Minneapolis and that we should both try to make our marriages work" (pp. 102–3).

Before leaving for Chicago and Minneapolis, Bellow had made arrangements for Tivoli. At his urging, Ralph Ellison had applied for and accepted a teaching job at Bard. For several years now, Ellison had sought Bellow's advice about a range of problems—money, an affair he'd started in Rome that he needed to break off, what he called a "writer's block as big as the Ritz."[14] Bellow's advice was to make a clean break. He pooh-poohed Ellison's fears that teaching would harm his writing and offered free residence at Tivoli in exchange for looking after the house. Ellison was an admirer of Bellow's writing and shared many of his views. In "Society, Morality and the Novel," Ellison's contribution to the 1957 Granville Hicks volume, *The Living Novel*, he questions Trilling's sense of the novel's "classic intention . . . the investigation of the problem of reality beginning in the social field."[15] Trilling's view, according to Ellison, is that "American novelists cannot write French or English novels of manners" (p. 83). Ellison accepts this view, but argues that they can write "the picaresque, many-sided novel, swarming with characters and with varied types and levels of experience," like *The Adventures of Augie March* or *Invisible Man*. "We love the classics," Ellison declares, but "have little interest in what Mr. Trilling calls the 'novel of manners,' and I don't believe that a society hot in the process of defining itself can for long find its image in so limited a form. Surely the novel is more than he would have it be, and if it isn't then we must make it so" (p. 89). In addition to these shared literary beliefs, the two writers were similar as men, refusing to be restricted by or to hide their backgrounds, alternately difficult and charming, good-looking, much concerned with appearance and dress, hard dogs to keep on the porch, to use an expression applied to President Clinton.

Bellow's defense of writers as university teachers was voiced publicly as well as privately. In "The University as Villain," an article of November 16, 1957, in *The Nation*, he begins by rehearsing familiar complaints about the condescension and narrowness of literary academics—"discouraged people who stand dully upon a brilliant plane, in charge of masterpieces but not themselves inspired." He then canvasses the alternatives for writers, calling into question the determining character of any setting or environment. "It is not easy to find the right way," he admits, by which he means the right way to live one's life away from the desk, but whatever the nonwriting existence the writer chooses, "you must learn to govern yourself, you must learn autonomy, you must manage your freedom or drown in it." Some writers put a premium on "experience," others on "culture," but "you can make a fool of yourself anywhere." Encouraged by Bellow's advice, Ellison accepted an offer to teach two related courses on American literature at Bard, one in each semester, leaving plenty of time to write. He settled into the Tivoli mansion and used his skills as a handyman to help with upkeep and repairs.[16] He fixed broken windows, plugged leaks, replaced a garage door when the wind blew it off. "I'm used to cleaning the apartment in the city," he wrote to Bellow, "and have vacuumed and scrubbed and dusted and am quite concerned that the place be and remain shipshape."[17] Chanler Chapman gave him permission to shoot on his land, and he joined the Rod and Gun Club of Red Hook. When teaching began, he was careful to steer clear of Bard coeds, with their "aching blue-jeans, short-shorts, padded bras, and adolescent adventurism."[18] Weekends were spent with Fanny, his wife, who worked in the city, either at Tivoli or at their apartment on Riverside Drive.

Bellow's correspondence with Ellison in the academic year 1958–59 mixes practical and personal matters with literary gossip. On September 5, he described his tumultuous August, beginning with news of Larry's suicide. "It was a considerable trip, and the arrival was considerable, too. My sister is in a state I won't undertake to describe. But then, with Sasha's aunt's help, I've made good progress out of my own difficulties. At least Sasha and Adam and I are together in Minneapolis. We're temporarily at 1408 W. 28th St., which isn't like Chelsea in the least."[19] Before answering questions about the house, Bellow passes along a request from Sasha: that Ellison find and send on to Minneapolis an untied carton of her winter things "near the marble fireplace at the north end of the ballroom." The date of the letter makes clear that Bellow and Sasha were back living together before Ludwig left Winnipeg. When Ludwig arrived in Minneapolis, outwardly he was his usual ebullient self. Mitzi McClosky's first impression was that he was Bellow's "greatest fan, he just adored him, they had such fun together"; "he and Saul had so many jokes together . . . they were just buddies." The McCloskys liked Ludwig, "he was a raucous good fellow and lots of fun, lots of excitement." They thought he was good for Bellow, who arrived in Minneapolis "depressed and down and very worried," also "drinking a lot." Ellen Siegelman thought Ludwig funny and lively, but when she said she found him "crude" in comparison to Ralph Ross (described by Philip Siegelman as "having the great misfortune to look like John Barrymore"), she earned, inexplicably, Sasha's "terrible ill-will." As for Bellow, he not only enjoyed Ludwig's company but, as Mitzi puts it, "thought Jack was on his side. He told us, you know Jack is very helpful in presenting my point of view to Sondra and making my case with her." When Ludwig was alone with Sasha, his ebullience disappeared. As she recalls in the memoir, he "brooded and looked at me with his heart in his eyes, showed up when I was alone in the house, and sorely tested my resolve" (p. 103).

THE THERAPIST BELLOW AGREED to see, as a condition of Sasha's returning to the marriage, was Paul Meehl, the McCloskys' friend, chair of the Department of Psychology at Minnesota. Meehl was a clinician as well as an eminent researcher in social psychology. Although he knew Bellow through the McCloskys, he took him on, in Mitzi's words, because he "was entranced with Saul" (in his defense, Meehl pointed out that Freud also saw patients he knew). On October 2, Bellow wrote to Covici to say he'd had a month of sessions with Meehl and that he'd been pronounced "normal after all. It makes me sorry for the rest of you guys. So this is life? What *I've* got? And normal life, too? How sad for every body!" When Meehl suggested that Sasha also see him, another unorthodox practice, she agreed. In a letter of March 18, 1959, Ellison responded to the question of Bellow's "normality" with a suggestive theory, one that connects to a view, at times entertained by Bellow himself, that he somehow concocted or needed his difficulties. "Surely we, you and I, must be as nutty as Cal Lowell or Berryman or Roethke, we just aren't the type to enjoy exploiting it. Mythomania compels [us] to seek extreme relationships as a means of affirming our reality. Thus we fight and argue and produce wild fictions inhabited by wild men. But perhaps we're hopelessly sane."

With the pressure of *Henderson* off his back, Bellow's spirits began to recover, and Sasha, too, began to enjoy herself. She enrolled as a graduate student in history and found her studies absorbing. "She reads Med. History sixteen hours a day and has little time for anything else," Bellow reported in the letter of October 2 to Covici. "A kind sort of woman looks after Adam from 9 to 3:30 daily. It costs a little, but then I don't know how to enjoy money, anyway." In addition to her studies, Sasha was buoyed by a lively circle of friends. In the memoir, she singles out Ralph Ross and his young pretty wife, Alicia; Joseph Frank and his wife, Giguitte, "whom I liked enormously"; Allen Tate and his second wife, the poet Isabella Gardner (another beauty, in addition to being well-born and wild); the poet Howard Nemerov and his wife, Margaret (Nemerov was a visiting professor both semesters); and, of course, the McCloskys and Berrymans. There was much talk of politics and political personalities, especially at the McCloskys' parties, where the most interesting of the political and social scientists at the university were to be found. Chief among these figures were Arthur Naftalin, chair of the Department of Political Science, later four times mayor of Minneapolis, and Ben Nelson, an acquaintance of Bellow's from Hyde Park days. Nelson, a friend and pupil of Edward Shils's, was an authority on medieval usury and immensely learned. He was Sasha's teacher and figures in *Herzog*, thinly fictionalized as the gluttonous medieval historian Egbert Shapiro. The parties at the McCloskys' were lively, with much drinking and dancing (Nelson, despite his girth, was an agile and enthusiastic dancer). To Ellen Siegelman, who describes herself as "hopelessly monogamous," they were sexually as well as intellectually challenging. "When there wasn't actual sex there was a lot of flirtation."

Paul Meehl and his wife, Alice, were regulars at these parties, even after both Bellows became patients. According to James Atlas, who interviewed Meehl about the Bellows' therapy, "Jack Ludwig was a focal point for both of them—Sondra confessing her divided affections to Meehl while Bellow tried to find out what the doctor knew." In *Herzog*, Bellow turns Meehl into Moses Herzog's therapist, Dr. Edvig, "a fair, mild man," "a calm Protestant Nordic Anglo-Celtic" (Meehl himself was a devout Lutheran). Moses is "encouraged by the kindness of Dr. Edvig's bearded smile," also by his diagnosis of him as "reactive-depressive" (as opposed to depressive for no reason), the sort who "tended to form frantic dependencies and to become hysterical when cut off, when threatened with loss" (pp. 471, 470). Meehl judged Bellow's portrait of him as Dr. Edvig "not bad,"[20] despite the fact that Edvig is later described as falling under the spell of Mady or Madeleine, the Sasha character. When Meehl was drunk, according to Mitzi McClosky, he became affectionate. At one party, she remembers, he kissed every woman in sight, including Sasha, his patient, who was wearing an enticing low-cut dress. Bellow "was enraged" and Sasha stopped seeing him. In an interview Sasha claimed Meehl "did admit to his attraction to me," but judged he would neither act on it nor say anything to Bellow about her feelings for Ludwig; she was anxious not "to demean his professional position." The Bellows' doctor, A. Boyd Thomes, was also often present at the McCloskys' parties. Thomes treated Berryman, the McCloskys, and others in the circle. Like Berryman, he had a highly stylized manner of speaking, described by Phil Siegelman as "sardonic," "witty," "very charming." Siegelman remembers him as "a terrific doctor" though "rather careless about talking about his patients." Sasha thought Thomes, too, came on to her, a revelation Mitzi McClosky found hard to believe. "I think he probably said you're a very beautiful woman, and she interpreted this as a pass. He never did that with patients." Mitzi describes Sasha, here and elsewhere, as "dramatic and hyperbolic." Her "singular fault was dramatic exaggeration." As for Meehl, "I don't think Paul sober would ever make a pass."

Sasha's good spirits lasted through much of the autumn. "We entertained, we were entertained, I studied the Middle Ages with fervor. I finally entered into the marriage fully. Saul was charmed." Partly he was charmed because "I had learned much during the summer in Brooklyn and had a more sophisticated idea of how to please him." If she means in bed—sex being a topic, according to Mitzi, about which "both of them complained . . . something about being too needy and it not working all that well"—what she learned in Brooklyn, she learned from Ludwig. This possibility made a subsequent revelation particularly uncomfortable: "I did not know for many years that he was continuing to discuss our intimate life with Jack" (p. 103). Bellow's assessment of the autumn of 1958 was guardedly optimistic. In the letter of January 31 to Josephine Herbst, he announces that "Sondra and I patched things up. Which means just about as much as it says. Patches, for two or three months, were all we had to bless ourselves with. More recently we've done better. . . . Anyway, life has brightened, if it doesn't glitter, downright. But then there isn't enough glitter in half a lifetime to dunk your toast in." Four days later he offered a similar summary to Keith Botsford, now teaching at the University of Puerto Rico in San Juan.

> Sasha and I stand much better now than we did before. She's erratic, to put it modestly, and I'm a little nuts myself, and the house in Tivoli was just the priceless ingredient, the catalyst to our explosive mixture. So we had an explosion and it blew everything to bits except the essentials. Despite the shock of it it was rather profitable than no. We carry our relations on now in a propositional fashion—that is, each saying exactly what he thinks. No more dragging of the frills in the soup. It works very handsomely, 9/10ths of the conceptual interference having been trimmed away.

Sasha's "erratic" behavior refers to angry and unpredictable outbursts and rages, a product of repressed feeling and frustration with Bellow's own "nuttiness," his impatience, irritability, and "constant" complaining (among the many inexplicable aspects of Jack Ludwig's behavior, Sasha said in an interview, was how he "was able to listen to this man complain about everything"). According to Atlas, the violence of Sasha's anger led her doctor (it is not clear if he means Meehl or Thomes) to order tests "to see if she had a neurological condition." In an undated letter to Covici, Bellow wrote of a diagnosis of "a small lesion of the temporal lobe," suggesting that "she may have to take drugs to control it. Meanwhile she's having treatment from my doctor. He says it's not a dangerous illness but needs to be understood and watched."[21] Bellow said something similar to Herbst in the letter of January 31: "It turned out that Sondra has a nervous disorder, in itself not too serious. It doesn't affect her health but it does account for our marital disorders to a considerable extent."[22] The intensity of Sasha's bouts of frustration and fury, also of "queenliness," bewildered Bellow.[23] That he'd been unfaithful in the marriage she seemed to have gotten over. That he was sometimes selfish, demanding, critical, was hardly new. What was new was the violence of her complaints, a product of circumstances Bellow did not see or allow himself to see: she was in love with Ludwig and trying and failing, after only "a few months," by December at least, to resist resuming their affair.

BELLOW WAS MUCH PREOCCUPIED that autumn with a new venture, one he, Ludwig, and Botsford had been thinking about since Bard days: a literary magazine. Sometime after Bellow arrived in Minneapolis at the end of the summer, a backer was finally found for the magazine, the nonfiction paperback imprint Meridian, whose publisher was Arthur A. Cohen and whose chief editor was Aaron Asher. Asher's background was like Bellow's: he was raised on the northwest side of Chicago, a graduate of Marshall High School and the University of Chicago. He knew the world out of which Bellow's fiction grew and liked and admired its author. According to his wife, Linda, Asher traced the magazine's origins to Bellow's troubled history with *The New Yorker*, in particular to its refusal to publish *Seize the Day*. Meridian agreed to a semiannual paperback publication with a first printing of 25,000 copies. After rejecting a range of titles—"New Orbit," "Now," "The Pinwheel," "Chanticleer"—the editors settled on *The Noble Savage*. The magazine's notepaper listed its contributing editors as John Berryman, Ralph Ellison, Herbert Gold, Arthur Miller, Wright Morris, and Harvey Swados. Bellow had several aims for the publication: to encourage new talent, to get writers out into the world (as when he suggested Harvey Swados write about the Floyd Patterson fight with

Ingemar Johansson, an article which appeared in issue 1),[24] to get himself out into the world, and to get away from the notion "that literature is about itself."[25] "We hoped to break down specialization, let novelists write on politics and politicians on art (if they were literate): in short, to enlarge the scope of all the writers we knew and free them from the suffocating choice between the literary quarterly and the slick."[26]

Bellow's models for the magazine were *The Dial*, *The American Mercury*, and *The American Jitters* (which featured Edmund Wilson's writing "before he became the great blimp of The New Yorker").[27] At an initial organizing meeting at the Algonquin Hotel in New York, putative contributing editors and others were convened to shape the magazine's character and content. In subsequent meetings the three coeditors decided on types of contribution: "Arias" (like "Talk of the Town" pieces), "Poems," "Archives" (out-of-print or forgotten works by eminent authors, including Samuel Butler, D. H. Lawrence, Isaac Babel, Alexander Pushkin), "Investigations," "Lives" (including memoirs of Greenwich Village in the 1940s and 1950s by Seymour Krim and Dan Wakefield), "Texts" (a type hard to characterize, often extracts from longer pieces, as in contributions from Ralph Ellison, Thomas Pynchon, Edward Hoagland). Ideas were to figure in the magazine as well as stories but in a manner accessible to general readers. "I love your review," Bellow wrote to Richard Stern on November 3, 1959, "it's written in the style I approve of (Biedermeier of ideas)." The magazine lasted five issues, from February 1960 to October 1962, and was of high quality. In addition to pieces from the contributing editors and the authors already mentioned, there were contributions from Harold Rosenberg, Philip O'Connor, Louis Simpson, Anthony Hecht, Howard Nemerov, Frederick Seidel, Louis Guilloux, Robert Coover, John Hawkes, S. J. Perelman, Cynthia Ozick, Grace Paley, Jules Feiffer, and Nelson Algren.

Bellow mostly confined himself to "Arias" (a scene of comic rudeness and avarice on the Upper West Side in issue 1, a sardonic meditation on bomb shelters in issue 4), though "Ralph Ellison at Tivoli" in issue 3 was a longer piece. In issue 1 Ludwig contributed a story entitled "Confusions: Thoreau in California," an extract from his first novel, *Confusions* (1963); Botsford contributed a piece entitled "Memoirs of a Russophile" in issue 2, "about my many connections with matters Russian, the language, friends, etc."[28] Botsford recalls only a single rule in the event of editorial disagreement: "each has one absolute right of inclusion and one of exclusion."[29] That so many of Bellow's friends appeared in the magazine, famous ones but also nonfamous ones, including girl-friends and Tuley pals (Hyman Slate, Louie Lasco), can be seen in two ways: as a mark of the caliber of his friends ("I'm not printing Slate's Proof for old times' sake," he wrote to Slate, soliciting further contributions), and as a mark of his editorial sway.[30] "I'm one of the editors," he wrote to Josephine Herbst on February 18, 1959, *"primus inter pares,"* an admission reiterated in a letter of August 15: "authority on the *Savage* is shared by three of us, but I holler most." It was Bellow's name that got the magazine published. Without his participation it would not survive. Though his younger, as yet unpublished, coeditors had strong voices, his prevailed. "I insist upon setting and bettering the editorial style," he wrote to Botsford in an undated letter written late in the magazine's life. "I should have been *primus inter pares* because it is obvious, if only in point of seniority and experience, that I should take the lead. When you surpass me I shall be glad to let you make these decisions on policy, I think you may count on me to draw back as soon as this happens. But until then you should abide without competitive bitterness by my judgment." When Alfred Kazin read a piece in issue 3 by John McCormick, a friend of Bellow's from Paris and Salzburg, he made the following entry in his journal (as much a description of himself as of the magazine's contributors):

I see something by John McCormick in the Noble Savage, and suddenly say to myself, why is it so right for *him* to be in that magazine. Answer: he is a bit of a shipwreck, a storm, an anger. There is a kind of special egotism of suffering and bitterness that I associate with writers for that magazine—Saul's haughty and prophetic loneliness (without his gifts). A sort of snarling independence not so much of thought as of manner. They bristle with anticipatory defiance.[31]

Ludwig and Botsford bristled a fair bit in the course of producing the magazine, while Bellow, in Botsford's words, was its "unwobbling pivot" (a phrase from Confucius). Botsford was teaching in Puerto Rico and felt isolated from his coeditors. He also felt isolated because he wasn't Jewish. It did not help that at times he could be dilatory and unclear. "You condemn the thing almost totally and yet conclude that he ought to publish it," Bellow complains in a letter about a story under consideration.[32] Ludwig was touchy and quarrelsome, more of a stirrer than Botsford. "Dear boychick and chickchick," begins a letter of July 10, 1959, to Bellow and Sasha, a reply to a Bellow letter containing complaints from Botsford about a "faction" against him. "How you like that Botsford and his State Department bananas? We haven't been each in our separate countries [Ludwig was in Winnipeg for the summer] long enough for even cold war and already he's calling us to a Summit Conference! . . . Some spick laundry must have shrunk his double-breasted vest. What else could account for such a tone?" Later in the letter he complains: "Is this my reward for staying up till 5 a.m. listening to his 'Fourteen Reasons for Becoming a Jew'—and me a Jew by birth, that is, for no reason at all? I'm going to withdraw my permission for him to call himself Botsfeld." In a letter of July 25, Ludwig reports that "Keith wrote a very sharp analysis of Mrs. Goffman, pointing out things which are limitations to the story, and which, for the most part, I knew were limitations when I wrote it. . . . I hope he doesn't further mistake things, and assume the criticism I wrote of his novel to be a kind of response in kind. That's all we need. Paranoia on the masthead. I'm anxious to hear what you think of his MS." The letter ends "Kiss Adam for me."

In an article in issue 3 of *The Noble Savage* Bellow recalls the skepticism with which friends and acquaintances greeted the idea of the magazine. "The wise money," he begins, "was not on *The Noble Savage*."[33] There was also concern that editorial work was a waste of Bellow's time. To a dubious Pat Covici he explained, in an undated letter of early 1959: "As for the magazine: The more I do, the more connection I feel with people, causes, the more fluently I write." This argument he reiterates in a letter to Covici of February 19, a week after receiving a two-year $16,000 grant from the Ford Foundation, "the biggest gravy train of them all," according to Ellison, to free him from teaching (it arrived, Ellison adds in the same letter of March 18, "just at the time when you were about to take off on the yakoyak circuit for dough"). "I can't see what objection there is to the magazine. It *excites* me. Isn't that as good as money? And since I won't be teaching it'll be highly beneficial because I need some other kind of interest even when I'm writing." Having a life away from the desk was essential to Bellow, who not only taught throughout his career but for periods took on administrative jobs and committee work, in addition to serving on boards of foundations and prize and fellowship committees. In previous years the Ford money would have freed him for travel; now there were reasons to stay put: Sasha's studies, but also, as he explains in the letter of February 19, "the psychiatry and neurology. . . . They tell me I'm making good speed, and Sondra too is much better." The marriage, he felt, was mending: "All's well in the sack, unusually well, and we're beginning to feel much affection for each other. So it'd be ridiculous to depart for long from this base." As he told the student newspaper, the *Minnesota Daily*, on February 20, "I like Minnesota. I think the place you come from stamps you; I consider myself a mid-westerner."

FEBRUARY 1959 WAS an important month for Bellow. Some ten days after receiving news of the Ford Foundation Fellowship on the 12th, *Henderson the Rain King* was published to mixed reviews. These reviews Sasha filtered for Bellow: "She feels that I shouldn't have to lick any more wounds than I received last summer, and I suppose she's right."[34] "I was much criticized for yielding to anarchic or mad impulses and abandoning urban and Jewish themes," Bellow recalled in his interview with Roth. "But I continue to insist that my subject ultimately was America," a realization that only came to him in the course of writing. "I didn't know what I was doing when I wrote 'The Rain King.' I was looking for my idea to reveal itself as I investigated the phenomena—the primary phenomenon being Henderson himself, and it presently became clear to me that America has no idea—not the remotest—of what America is."[35] That Henderson was meant to personify America in some way was clear even to hostile reviewers. Elizabeth Hardwick in *Partisan Review* criticized the novel not so much for "abandoning urban and Jewish themes"—for Bellow, "America"—as for abandoning his "superb gift for characterization."[36] "*Henderson the Rain King* is a book deliberately without any characters at all. The hero is not a character in the usual sense" (despite all he tells us about his background and temperament). His symbolic identity, however, is clear. "Henderson, then, is not a 'character' but he is an 'American,'" which leads Hardwick to conclude that he is simultaneously "thinly" and "deeply" drawn.

The terms "thinly" and "deeply" allude to an article Bellow published on the front page of *The New York Times Book Review* on February 15, 1959, a week before *Henderson* appeared in print. Its title was "Deep Readers of the World, Beware!" In it Bellow warns reviewers against overly symbolic or "deep" readings, which he parodies. Such readings are often ludicrous, but even when plausible they block or shortcut feeling, which Bellow sees as arising from "the concrete and the particular," "flesh and bone." Asking what Achilles's anger symbolizes can prevent one from realizing that he "*was* angry. To many teachers he would represent much, but he would not *be* anything in particular." Absence of being is just what Hardwick objects to about the character of Henderson, which is why she calls the "Deep Readers" article "part of the joke." "*Henderson* cannot be read except deeply, nor be understood except symbolically." A second criticism is that the deep or symbolic meanings the novel tempts readers into "do not come readily to mind." The reader senses "possible interpretations, perhaps even 'world-wide' implications," but "that they do not jump out at us is a real fault."

This second criticism is puzzling, though Hardwick was not alone in voicing it. In an interview, Roth described the novel as "an uninterpretable allegory. . . . The braille isn't raised above the page. I think Saul was looking for a loose allegory, to write about breaking loose."[37] Henderson as a symbol of America, however, is multiply signaled. His ancestors "stole land from the Indians" (p. 120). The founder of the family fortune, a Dutch sausage maker, became "the most unscrupulous capitalist in America" (p. 82). His great-grandfather was secretary of state. His father was a renowned scholar and friend of Henry Adams and William James. He's as American as Chanler Chapman (and as comical, a shadow of heroic or noble ancestors, like many modern literary heroes, an object of satire). "Alfred Kazin asked what Jews could possibly know about American millionaires," Bellow told Roth in their interview. "For my purposes, I felt that I knew enough. Chanler Chapman, the son of the famous John Jay Chapman, was the original of Eugene Henderson."[38] Henderson is a figure of America in size as well as background: he's big, six foot four, 230 pounds (fourteen pounds at birth), with a twenty-two-inch neck and an enormous head, as big as an entire baby or half the body of a man (pp. 104, 180). Then there's his nature: he's "strong and healthy, rude and aggressive and something of a bully" (p. 121). He's also turbulent, heedless, striving: "When it comes to struggling," he brags, "I am in a special class. From earliest times I have struggled without rest" (p. 164).

What exactly Henderson is struggling for he finds hard to articulate, which is presumably what Hardwick has in mind when she says the novel's symbolic meanings do not jump out at us or Roth when he calls its allegory uninterpretable. "*I want, I want, I want!*" is Henderson's cry. "It happened every afternoon, and when I tried to suppress it it got even stronger." When he asks himself "What do you want?" he gets no answer (pp. 121, 122). Henderson is hardly without assets or advantages. He's an Ivy League graduate, a war hero, a millionaire pig farmer with a large estate outside Danbury, Connecticut, which he shares with a beautiful wife, twenty years his junior, and their two children. Despite this good fortune, Henderson is unhappy, disgusted with himself, a mess (the pig farming recalls not only his sausage-making ancestor but what he thinks of as the piggishness of his own behavior and being). When offered a chance to visit Africa with a friend, he grabs it, "hoping to find a remedy for my situation" (p. 139). Though hard to name, the yearning that drives him is familiar: it is Romantic (the cry "I want, I want" is taken from plate 9 of Blake's small book of engravings, *For Children: The Gates of Paradise*), expressing a need for spiritual well-being, rebirth.[39] In a letter of March 30, 1992, Bellow says as much, in response to a query from a German doctoral student, Barbara Bitzer: "I can't say whether his *Sehnsucht* [longing] has anything to do with Goethe's *zelige Sehnsucht* [holy longing]. Romantic literature is filled with longings and Henderson probably got his *Sehnsucht* from Keats or Shelley or Wordsworth." When Henderson sees a magical pink light on the side of a white hut in Africa he recalls a comparable light from childhood (discussed earlier in Chapter 3). The childhood light produces an epiphany, what Wordsworth calls a "spot of time," a moment when perceived object and perceiving subject come alive and come together. In Henderson's words, "the dumb begins to speak . . . I hear the voices of objects and colors; then the physical universe starts to wrinkle and change and heave and rise and smooth" (p. 192). In Africa, Henderson seeks such experiences, things "which I saw when I was still innocent and have longed for ever since, for all my life—and without which *I could not make it.* My spirit was not sleeping then, I can tell you" (pp. 193–94) (Henderson's desire to "*burst the spirit's sleep*" [p. 171] comes from the Dedication to Shelley's *Laon and Cythna*, originally known as *The Revolt of Islam*).

In addition to being Romantic, the desire for a renewed or awakened life can be thought of as American, though for Henderson, America in its present state is what stands in its way. As Eusebio L. Rodrigues, an English professor at Georgetown University, puts it, the cry "I want, I want" echoes the "promise of hope and rejuvenation that was made when the old world came to the new." In this sense, Henderson is archetypally American, but he is also of his age, both "the embodiment of mid-twentieth century America, bursting with vital energy, victorious in war [he was awarded a Purple Heart in World War II], triumphant in technology, at the very peak of its prosperity,"[40] and unfulfilled, in search of spiritual knowledge, a more than material well-being. "It isn't just me," Henderson tells his African guide, Romilayu:

> millions of Americans have gone forth since the war to redeem the present and discover the future. I can swear to you, Romilayu, there are guys exactly like me in India and in China and South America and all over the place. Just before I left home I saw an interview in the paper with a piano teacher from Muncie who became a Buddhist monk in Burma. You see, that's what I mean. I am a high-spirited kind of guy. And it's the destiny of my generation of Americans to go out in the world and try to find the wisdom of life. It just is (p. 354).

Early on, Henderson confesses of his adult life in America: "By three o'clock I was in despair. Only toward sunset the voice would let up. And sometimes I thought maybe this was my occupation because it would knock off at five o'clock of itself. America is so big, and everybody is working, making, digging, bulldozing, trucking, loading, and so on, and I guess the sufferers suffer at the same rate" (p. 123). Nine-to-five America not only fails to supply Henderson with what he needs but shapes him to its rhythms.

These rhythms are deforming. In addition to restlessness, they produce recklessness or rashness, the sort that leads Henderson, in an effort to help, to blow up the water supply of the Arnewi, the first tribe he meets. The rhythms of Africa, in contrast, are seen by Henderson as natural, accepting, including of death, which modern America fears and flees. "You fled what you were," Dahfu, king of the Wariri, tells Henderson. "You did not believe you had to perish" (p. 339). Dahfu is Henderson's instructor, and his teachings, which take up almost two thirds of the novel, are closely patterned on those of Wilhelm Reich, a point that Bellow's friend Richard Stern claims to have been the first to reveal in print. "I know Bellow, and have talked with him about this novel," he admits in a footnote to his review of *Henderson* in *The Kenyon Review*, "I feel I know what effects were wanted at certain moments; I also feel 'in' on such genetic factors as Bellow's interest in Reich."[41] For evidence of Dahfu's teachings as Reichian, Stern points to the attention he pays to Henderson's rigid posture: "You appear cast in one piece. The midriff dominates. Can you move the different portions? Minus yourself of some of your heavy reluctance of attitude. Why so sad and so earthen? Now you are a lion. Mentally, conceive of the environment. The sky, the sun, the creatures of the bush. You are related to all. The very gnats are your cousins. The sky is your thoughts. The leaves are your insurance, and you need no other" (pp. 343–44) (presumably because they return in spring). Dahfu is also an advocate of roaring, making Henderson get down on his hands and knees and bellow: "And so I was the beast. I gave myself to it, and all my sorrow came out in the roaring. My lungs supplied the air but the note came from my soul" (p. 345). Henderson's suffering, we learn on the novel's first page, is felt as a pressure in the chest, the prime location, Reich claims, of trapped energy; the results are sudden and uncontrolled bursts of repressed feeling.

The Arnewi are presided over by Prince Itelo and his aunt, Queen Willatale. The equanimity of Queen Willatale impresses Henderson deeply. "Good nature emanated from her; it seemed to puff out on her breath as she sat smiling." Henderson is encouraged to place his hand on Willatale's chest, between her breasts, a traditional Arnewi greeting. In contrast to the pressure or congestion within his own breast, he feels "the calm pulsation of her heart participating in the introduction. This was as regular as the rotation of the earth, and it was a surprise to me; my mouth came open and my eyes grew fixed as if I were touching the secrets of life" (p. 166). In later years, Bellow was quite open about the Reichian "factors" in *Henderson*. "All the while I was writing Dahfu I had the ghost of Rosenfeld near at hand, my initiator into the Reichian mysteries."[42]

Henderson's attitude to Dahfu is like Bellow's attitude to Reich. Dahfu has life wisdom, but he's cracked. "It is possible that he lost his head, and that he was carried away by his ideas. This was because he was no mere dreamer but one of those dreamer-doers, a guy with a program. And when I say that he lost his head, what I mean is not that his judgement abandoned him but that his enthusiasms and visions swept him far out" (p. 221). Reich's enthusiasms swept him far out when he claimed that orgone therapy could cure cancer or when he conducted experiments in "cloud-busting." Rodrigues is shrewd as well as dogged in uncovering the Reichian elements in the novel. The Wariri, like the Arnewi, suffer terribly in the drought. At the tribe's rain-making ceremonies, Henderson's strength allows him to win a competition to lift and carry a Wariri cloud totem, the Mummah, at which point the empty sky fills with lowering clouds. As the cloud bursts, Henderson is declared "Sungo" or Rain King. Rodrigues explains: "The rain-making ceremonies seem to belong to a primitive Africa and may appear to have been derived from Bellow's anthropological reading [detailed in Chapter 5 of this book], but they are in fact a vivid and comic drama- tization of the Reichian method of 'cloud-busting' and rain-making." Rodrigues quotes Reich's claim that "one may create clouds in the cloud-free sky in a certain manner, *disturbing the evenness in the distri- bution of the atmospheric OR* [orgone] *energy*; thus clouds appear upon drawing energy from the air." Reich's experiments as a rainmaker took place at Orgonon, his home and research lab in Rangeley, Maine. "He caused long hollow pipes to be aimed at the cloud-free sky in order to draw off OR energy."[43] Henderson describes the rain clouds that appear after he lifts Mummah as "colossal tuberous forms" (p. 285); he sees the sky "filling with hot, gray, long shadows, rain clouds, but to my eyes of an abnormal form, pressed together like organ pipes or like the ocean ammonites of Paleozoic times" (p. 284). The resulting downpour is figured in orgasmic, which is to say Reichian, terms, as is its effect on Henderson (an effect recalling Tommy's sobbing at the end of *Seize the Day*):

> A heated, darkened breeze sprang up. It had a smoky odor. This was something oppressive, insinuating, choky, sultry, icky. Desir- ous the air was, and it felt tumescent, heavy. It was very heavy. It yearned for discharge, like a living thing. . . . I felt like Vesuvius, all the upper part flame and the blood banging upward like the pitch or magma (p. 284).

Though the cloud burst seems to come about through Henderson's efforts, he remains skeptical, just as he never loses his fear of following Dahfu into the den of Atti, the lioness, the final phase of his "therapy" (in one early version of the novel he calls his meetings with Dahfu "ses- sions," of which there are eleven).[44] The scenes with Atti are especially wild and memorable—the novel's version of the Caligula episode in *Augie March*. Henderson's sense of the lunacy of walking into Atti's den is played partly for laughs; though full of suspense and wonderfully observed descriptions of Atti as she moves about, nuzzling the terrified Henderson "upward first at my armpits, and then between my legs," the scenes are also farcical. "Are you afraid?" Dahfu asks. "I can't even bring my hands together to wring them," Henderson answers (p. 340). Though he follows Dahfu into the den, his faith in the king's teachings remains qualified. For Dahfu's sake, he tells us (in a passage quoted earlier in this book, in Chapter 10), "I accepted the discipline of being like a lion. Yes, I thought, I believed I could change; I was willing to overcome my old self; yes, to do that a man had to adopt some new standard; he must even force himself into a part; maybe he must deceive himself a while, until it begins to take. . . . I would never make a lion, I knew that; but I might pick up a small gain here and there in the attempt" (p. 373). This willingness to suspend disbelief, indulging spiritual intimations, is shared both by the protagonists of succeeding Bellow novels and stories and by their creator, as is a reluctance to commit to one view or the other. "*Henderson* is not Reichian confusion, but comedy," Bellow writes in an undated letter to Leslie Fiedler. "I shun doctrine." "I have always had intelligence enough (or the intuition)," Bellow writes in a letter of April 10, 1974, to Daniel Fuchs, "to put humor between myself and final claims"—about the afterlife, for example ("any psychologist will probably tell that it's just childish fantasy," Bellow says in his interview with Manea, "but all the same it's hard to get rid of these feelings"), or "the original soul," or God himself, whose existence Bellow seems only at the end of his life, or so he tells Manea, to have "stopped arguing with myself about."[45]

What tests or challenges Henderson's spiritual intimations is his language. Though partly Chanler Chapman's language, it is also Dr. Pep's or Gooley MacDowell's or Augie's, mixing street slang, Yiddishisms, literary and biblical allusion, philosophical speculation, and arcane learning. The urban world, the world of Bellow's brothers, is heard throughout despite Henderson's WASP upbringing. "These guys are putting the squeeze on her," he tells Dahfu (p. 329). "What do they want?" he asks of Dahfu's enemies. "You should abdicate, like the Duke of Windsor?" (p. 312). Henderson's high cultural references are comparably incongruous, improbable. In a conversation with Willatale's sister, Mtalba, he alludes to T. S. Eliot's "Burnt Norton," "that poem about the nightingale singing that humankind cannot stand too much reality" (p. 196). He talks of "being" and "becoming" ("Becoming was beginning to come out of my ears. Enough! Enough! Time to have become!

Time to be! Burst the spirit's sleep. Wake up, America!" [p. 247]), as if he'd read Heidegger or Sartre; of the "noumenal," as if he'd read Plato or Kant (as in "the physical is all there and it belongs to the world of science. But then there is the noumenal department" [p. 253]). Henderson's literary and musical references range from Eugène-Melchior de Vogüé (1848–1910), the French travel writer (p. 113), to Massenet's opera *Thaïs* (p. 128), to Homer, *The Odyssey* in particular, and the poems of Longfellow, Whitman, Tennyson, Blake, John Clare, and Ovid. Elizabeth Hardwick mocks Henderson's language as "Broadway, hip," "wise-guy," a style "afraid of pretension and yet overflowing with boozy speculations." What she leaves out is Bellow's comic intent, as when Henderson confronts the sinister Bunam, chief priest of the Wariri, imagining what the Bunam sees in him:

> What he was saying I knew. I heard it. The silent speech of the world to which my most secret soul listened continually now came to me with spectacular clarity. Within—within I heard. Oh, what I heard! The first stern word was *Dummy!* I was greatly shaken by this. And yet there was something there. It was true. And I was obliged, it was my bounden duty to hear. *And nevertheless you are a man. Listen! Hearken unto me, you shmohawk! You are blind. The footsteps were accidental and yet the destiny could be no other. So now do not soften, oh no, brother, intensify rather what you are. This is the one and only ticket—intensify* (p. 272).

These words might almost have come from Berryman's Henry, shifting register from line to line. Henderson's voice is openly unreal, like the "noble savage" and blackface voices of the novel's African characters. Its function is partly to debunk (motivated by what Hardwick tendentiously describes as Bellow's "fear of pretension"), a function taken up in later works by the protagonists' girlfriends, Herzog's Ramona, Charlie Citrine's Renata. Here the women serve other functions. Henderson's first wife, Frances, smokes gold-tipped Sobranies, like Sasha, and is an intellectual, not at all afraid of pretension; Lilly, his second wife, "a large, lively woman," (p. 105), is down-to-earth, messy, with "many negligent and also dirty habits" (p. 115). Henderson worries about Lily's truthfulness rather than her lack of sympathy for boozy speculation. "Look at the way she lied about all her fiancés. And I'm not sure that Hazard did punch her in the eye on the way to the wedding" (recalling Bellow's skepticism about Sasha's stories of paternal abuse). Lily's flaws suggest other complaints against Sasha: "she is reckless and a spendthrift and doesn't keep the house clean and is a con artist and exploits me" (p. 324).

Neither of Henderson's wives figures in the main body of the novel, once he arrives in Africa. Nor does Henderson end up in Lily's arms at the novel's close, though he's heading back to her in the final chapter. The women he meets in Africa are objects neither of romantic nor sexual interest. Willatale and her sister, Mtalba, are old, the former a sort of earth mother, the latter enormously fat. The troop of naked amazons who guard King Dahfu press upon Henderson from all sides in "their volupté (only a French word would do the job here)" (p. 240). They are frightening rather than arousing. One of Dahfu's jobs as king is to satisfy what he calls the "prerogatives" of these wives: "You may not think so on first glance, but it is a most complex existence requiring that I husband myself" (p. 242). If Dahfu weakens, he tells Henderson, the wives "will report me and then the Bunam who is chief priest here, with other priests of the association, will convey me out into the bush and there I will be strangled" (p. 244). When the prospect arises of Henderson succeeding Dahfu as king, the wives loom large in his imagination. "I'd break my heart here trying to fill his position," he tells Romilayu, "and anyway, I am no stud. No use kidding, I am fifty-six, or going on it. I'd shake in my boots that the wives might turn me in" (p. 390). The passage calls to mind Bellow's complaints about Sasha's "needs." Yet the depiction of women in the African portion of the novel is as much literary as autobiographical. *Henderson* is a novel of quest and adventure, filled with Odyssean echoes. The Wariri wives function as do the treacherous females Odysseus encounters (Calypso, Circe, the Sirens). They threaten both *nostos* or return and the realization of the hero's quest.

According to Ruth Miller, his friend and biographer, "Bellow has always said *Henderson* was his favorite novel."[46] When asked in 1963 which of his books gave him the greatest satisfaction, he answered "writing *Henderson* stirred me more than writing any of the other books. I felt the sheer pleasure of release from difficulty."[47] A year later when asked which of his characters was most like him, he answered "Henderson—the absurd seeker of high qualities." The resemblance, he explained, derived first from Henderson's unwillingness to endure "continuing anxiety: the indeterminate and indefinite anxiety, which most of us accept as the condition of life" (the source of this anxiety, he reminds the interviewer, is "death"). The second point of resemblance between himself and his hero is the comical nature of Henderson's determination to remedy his anxiety: "All his efforts are a satire on the attempts people make to answer the enigma [of existence] by movement and random action or even by conscious effort. This is why I feel Henderson and I are spiritually close—although there are no superficial likenesses."[48] The novel is thus a form of self-satire, as is its successor, *Herzog*, whose hero seeks "answers to the enigma" through learning and intellect as well as movement, random action, and conscious effort. Late in life, in his interview with Norman Manea, Bellow emphasized the novel's satire, calling it "a very funny book," "the only book I go back to, for amusement."[49] At the time of writing, he also emphasized its inventiveness. As he wrote to Josephine Herbst in a letter of August 15, 1959, "some of it is all right—the language mostly, and the physical imagination." Philip Roth calls *Henderson* "the sport of all the books," a product of "energy and aliveness and confidence" (*Augie* had given Bellow "a tremendous shot of B12.")[50] In his interview with Bellow, Roth describes the novel as a "screwball stunt," though he admits its sincerity and "great screwball authority." Bellow accepts the screwball description but asserts that "its oddities were not accidental but substantive."[51] At the time of publication, however, close on the heels of what Daniel Fuchs calls "the psychological *vayizmir* [woe is me] of *Seize the Day*,"[52] he knew the work would baffle many readers. "I'm aware," he told Herbst in the letter of August 15, "that it gets mixed up between comedy and earnestness, which is another way of saying that I've got literature mixed up with lots of other matters." Hence "Deep Readers of the World, Beware!" published a week before *Henderson*. Don't lose sight of the work as literature, Bellow is saying, let its humor and invention register before running after "other matters." For many readers this advice was hard to follow. That Bellow felt the need to give it signals insecurity. "No amount of assertion will make an ounce of art," he wrote to Stern on November 3, 1959. "I took a chance with *Henderson*. I can tell you what I wished it to be, but I can't say what it *is*." On April 2, 1959, Ted Hoffman wrote teasingly to cheer Bellow up. A review of the novel by Norman Podhoretz had appeared in the *New York Herald Tribune*: "I've been meaning to console you about the review—just because Podhoretz says Henderson is great doesn't mean that it isn't. Don't you forget it—though I smell a Trilling plot to ruin your digestion."[53]

AFTER THE FORD FOUNDATION GRANT came through, Bellow stopped teaching and spent the spring at work on a play, a two-act farce that would eventually, after many drafts, be produced on Broadway in 1964 as *The Last Analysis*. He also did some traveling, lecturing in Chicago, in Urbana-Champaign, in Pittsburgh, where Hoffman was now teaching, and in Purdue, a tour that earned him $700. In Chicago, Bellow had dinner with Marilyn Monroe, in town to promote *Some Like It Hot*. They ate at the Pump Room of the Ambassador East Hotel, where she was staying. She signed the guest book: "Proud to be the guest of the Chicago writer Saul Bellow."[54] "Today the news sleuths are pumping me," Bellow wrote to Covici after the dinner in an undated letter: "Marilyn seemed genuinely glad to see a familiar face. I have yet to see anything in Marilyn that wasn't genuine." In between Chicago and Pittsburgh, Bellow stayed for a few days in New York with the Covicis, "to see Greg and Lillian Hellman," the latter about his play, and to visit Tivoli and Ralph Ellison. His mood was buoyed by praise for *Henderson* from fellow writers, including Bernard Malamud, Henry Miller, and John Cheever.[55] The letter from Cheever, undated, but probably written in February, ends: "For powers of vision, perfect pitch, a fine concern with salvation and a grasp of cast-iron absurdity you have no equal." Through Catherine Lindsay, the "big beauty" whom Berryman couldn't remember pushing down the stairs (and with whom Bellow had had an affair), Bellow began a correspondence with an admiring young writer named Mark Harris, and printed one of Harris's stories in issue 1 of *The Noble Savage*. Harris, as was mentioned earlier, would eventually write a book about Bellow, or about the difficulties of writing a book about him.[56] Bellow also received a letter on February 27 from E. W. McDiarmid, dean of the College of Science, Literature, and the Arts at the University of Minnesota, congratulating him on the Ford Foundation grant—"even though our feelings are mixed, since it means that we may not have the benefit of your presence on the faculty"—and conveying "our great appreciation for your work here and our wholehearted desire to have you back."

Less pleasing was the meeting Dave Peltz arranged with Bellow and Nelson Algren at a tough Polish bar on the northwest side of Chicago. Bellow and Algren had been wary of each other since Writers' Project days. Bellow thought Algren paraded his proletarian roots (unlike

Peltz, who came from a similar background). When Algren arrived at the bar in Army fatigues, as if to say "You weren't in the Army like I was," they quickly got into an argument and Bellow left.[57] There were also difficulties with Greg, who turned fourteen on April 16. Though Greg pleased his father by winning admission to Bronx High School of Science, also by mentioning that he'd seen *Henderson* on the bestseller lists, he was newly assertive. He missed his father and felt out of touch, wondering in a letter of January 7 "why don't you write me?" On January 30, before the novel's publication, he wrote again: "Mommy says 'Please send check early because she had some dental work done and she needs the doe [*sic*].'" In his memoir, Greg describes how his attitude to his father changed in his teenage years: "my childhood sadness turned to adolescent anger . . . usually grounded in my high moralistic sense of right and wrong." There were more arguments now than tears and sulks, and on occasion an accusatory tone in correspondence, to which Bellow responded in kind. Yet "for years Saul told me that he found an angry teenager much easier to deal with than a morose child," a confession Greg attributes to guilt: "No doubt he was relieved to see me put the sadness caused by his departure behind me."[58]

THE BELLOWS RETURNED TO Tivoli early in June 1959. Some months before their return Bellow wrote to Ellison with requests for the garden. Would he go to the farmer's co-op in Red Hook "and buy sweet corn, cucumber and squash seed and plant a few rows, please. . . . You can do all this in a few hours and oblige me greatly. It'll keep us all in produce this summer, and give Sasha and me a good reason to go out in the sun. . . . I'd feel crazy to live in the country without corn and tomatoes. It's bad enough not to have a cow." On May 16 he turned from vegetables to plants and flowers. "The bush at the front of the house near the drive is mock-orange," he wrote to Ellison, "and the three beds at the back are peonies. They flower the last week in May. At this time of year I miss the old place and as the lilacs and tulips appear I ask myself what state Tivoli's in. We should have dug up the bulbs last fall." He also jokes that Ellison will "need to show me how your shotgun loads. I hear by scuttle that Chanler has got it in his mind that he is Henderson and is on the warpath. Or is that one of those mad Annandale rumors? Do I need a switchblade, a judo book, a pistol? Ha, I'll set Rufus [the cat] on him." He was clearly looking forward to the summer.

IT HAD BEEN a year since the start of the affair between Ludwig and Sasha. Bellow still had no idea. Nor had he any idea that, sometime in the spring, Sasha got pregnant and had an abortion. "Yes, I was sleeping with both of them in Minneapolis," she said in one of our interviews. "There was a period when I was running an affair and a marriage at that time. . . . How awful that was." All Sasha says about the pregnancy in the memoir is that "there was no way to know whose child it was. . . . I secretly flew to New York to Anita [Maximilian] who arranged an abortion, and when I came back, revolted by my duplicitous life, horrified by my decision to end the pregnancy, an act that violated every principle I thought I had, I knew I had to end the marriage" (p. 103). Sasha lived with this knowledge through the summer at Tivoli, while Ludwig was in Winnipeg with his family and Bellow worked on his play. Late in the summer, Bellow went to stay with Lillian Hellman on Martha's Vineyard to consult about the play, while Sasha left for Minneapolis with Adam to find a place to live, ostensibly with Bellow. She stayed with the McCloskys and according to Mitzi "after a day or two she announced that Jack Ludwig was going to come and stay with us, too, to find an apartment." Sasha and Ludwig lived with the McCloskys "for at least two and a half weeks," Sasha sleeping in the study, Ludwig on a couch in the living room. "As soon as Jack came," Mitzi recalled, "she said we have to look for an apartment together; would you look after Adam. . . . She dragooned my daughter to take care of him." The McCloskys were busy at this time, getting ready to decamp to Berkeley, where they were to spend the year, Herb on a Rockefeller Fellowship. Mitzi recalls stifling her anger as Sasha went off each morning, "assuming one of us would take care of Adam. She did that every day."

The house Sasha found was at 3139 East Calhoun in Minneapolis, "a very pretty house" with a view of the lake, twenty minutes from campus by car. By the time Bellow arrived in September, she had begun classes. Sometime in early October, she walked into the living room and announced to Bellow that she wanted a divorce. To Covici, in a letter of November 1, Bellow describes her tone as one of "icy control." In other letters (to the Ellisons, Botsford, Richard Stern, as well as Covici), he claims to have been baffled by the announcement, while admitting recent difficulties. "Sasha and I are no longer together," he writes to the Ellisons in an undated letter in October. "Not by my choice. You saw us together all summer, so you probably understand as well as I. She has no complaint to make of me this time. All she has is a decision. She says she likes me, respects me, enjoys going to bed with me—and no longer wants to be my wife. I have no explanations to offer, only the facts. I don't know what she may have to say. I have to say only that I'm in misery, and especially over Adam." What Sasha says in the memoir partly confirms this account. She left Bellow "not because Saul was so difficult—actually he had settled down—but because I was. I knew he was not really happy with me. How could he be? I was a zombie and he was ever sensitive to neglect" (p. 103). Bellow's letter to the Ellisons ends with a plea that they "don't speak of this to anyone." To Botsford, writing on October 15, Bellow reports his difficulties in vague terms, "with the understanding that it remain *entre nous*." He says nothing of divorce, only that "no one here knows that Sash and I have been going through another very bad—a desperate—period." The letter ends: "Yesterday Sash cut her hand so badly with a coffee can that I thought her finger was severed and phoned an ambulance. The gash went to the bone. Five stitches and insanely painful. I'm taking care of Adam now. . . . Please forgive me for this note, and please say nothing to Ann." Bellow's efforts at secrecy were unavailing. Word of the breakup, and not just of the breakup, was soon circulating in Minneapolis. Ellen Siegelman remembers visiting with Ann Berryman on Thanksgiving weekend and being told about the affair with Ludwig, about which she'd already had suspicions.

As the letter of November 1 to Covici makes clear, Sasha acted with dispatch. Her icy announcement was already three weeks old and "the divorce papers are signed. I'm to pay a hundred fifty a month for the baby, and till the end of the year I'll maintain the house, since it was rented for a year." (The word "signed" here must mean by Sasha alone, given that a final agreement would not be reached until May 1960.) Over the past three weeks, Bellow's attitude had hardened. "If she were to change her mind again, I wouldn't change mine. It isn't that I don't love her. I do. But she'd only take the rest of my life and I'm not ready to part with that. Not yet, even though I've lost her, lost the boy, lost almost everything." Two days later he writes to Stern about *Henderson*, ending "on a personal note": "I'm having an ugly time—suffering no end. Sondra and I are both in despair over the course things have taken and I *don't* expect a happy ending. . . . There are no frigidities, impotencies, adulteries, only miseries. Poor little Adam doesn't know he's about to be sentenced. I can't help him because it has nothing at all to do with me. I love Sash and respect her. But she has drawn the sword, and is just *meshuggah* [crazy] enough to swing it." When Bellow says the sentence "has nothing at all to do with me," he is speaking narrowly; he was willing to put up with things as they were. That these things were impossible for Sasha—turning her into a "zombie"—he seems not to have noticed, or so he claimed to Covici. Now, however, he understood: "last summer when things seemed at their best they were really, for her, at their worst."

Bellow accepted Sasha's assurance that no third party was involved in her decision. "No frigidities, no impotencies, no adulteries." In addition to Sasha's adultery with Ludwig, there were Bellow's earlier adulteries, which helped to drive her into Ludwig's arms (gossip about his current adulteries seems not to have figured).[59] In the November 1 letter to Covici, Bellow suggests explanations for Sasha's decision: "She may not have loved me at all. She certainly doesn't love me now, and perhaps even hates me. When I was weaker there was some satisfaction for her in being the strong one. But when I recovered confidence and loved her more than before, even sexually, she couldn't bear it." Bellow makes similar points in a letter of November 5 to Botsford: "No, there's really nothing I can do—no remedy that pride prevents me from applying. Nothing can change Sasha's mind. It's she who's doing this, cutting me off, taking away Adam. I can't say for what failures of mine. Not the ordinary ones like money, sex, rivals or any of that. But maybe *because* there have been no such failures. If I were miserably weak she would pity or protect me. It's what I am that's unbearable to her. The essence of me. . . . Sasha is an absolutist. I think I've loved even *that*, in her. I believe I learned with her to love a woman, and I can't see where or how my heartsickness will end." By November 10, in a second letter to Covici, he tries to rein in rising anger: "I succeed best when I think of her as her father's daughter. For she is Tschacbasov. She has a Tschacbasov heart—an insect heart. But really I love her too much and understand her too well to feel the murderous hatred that would help me (therapeutically). And there's the child."

Looking back, almost fifty years later, Sasha underplays the drama. After a passage in the memoir in which she complains of Bellow's insatiable and exhausting need for reassurance—the passage, oddly, comes right after she says he was no longer "so difficult—actually he had settled down"—she describes how she asked for the divorce:

So one day, finally, I told him we needed to separate. "You're not happy, with me, Saul," I said, "And you deserve better." He agreed, grateful, I think to have it out in the open. "But," he said a little regretfully, "who'll cook for me" (p. 104).

In an interview Sasha repeated this account: "He was fine with it. He wasn't unhappy"; "it really wasn't working for him either." When quizzed about Bellow's question about cooking, Sasha admitted that it may not have been as bad as it sounds (she clearly meant it to sound bad, both in the memoir and initially in the interview). "I think maybe he was being uncomfortable," she allowed, "a little discomfort, irony, humor, but more 'I don't know what else to say.'" Her final judgment of Bellow, as of herself at this time, is forgiving: "he wasn't such a bad guy nor was I such a bad person. . . . He was a very selfish man and he wasn't capable of loving a person. . . . He couldn't maintain a relationship that required him not to be at the center . . . it was his angst, his problems, his needs, his needs. If you're a young woman, just starting out . . . there comes a point when you want something else. This is ordinary stuff." The part that's not ordinary involved Ludwig and the affair with Ludwig, which Bellow at this point knew nothing about. "The tragedies of my life were not over Saul. They were over Ludwig."

Bellow thought Paul Meehl gave Sasha the courage to ask for a divorce. "I don't know why she waited until we settled down in Minneapolis, holding a lease, etc.," he writes in the November 1 letter to Covici. "I guess she leaned somewhat on her psychiatrist. With his support, she was able to tell me she didn't and couldn't love me, and perhaps had never loved anyone except as a child. The psychiatrist doesn't approve of what she's doing, but he's bound to help her and so she's able to make use of him." In *Herzog*, Mady, the Sasha character, kicks Moses out after he has "built shelves, cleared the garden, and repaired the garage door," then "put up the storm windows" (p. 423). "That would be the last thing that I would do," Sasha said, laughing. "It is just such bad manners. I would never do that." She admitted "it might have happened, but I wouldn't have thought of it. Had I thought about it I never would have done it." "That's his suspicion," she added. "He thinks everyone's out to get him." Madeleine might do such a thing, but she was not Madeleine. In a memorable scene in the novel, Moses watches Madeleine put on her makeup and arrange her hair, "with unhesitating speed and efficiency, headlong, but with the confidence of an expert." She is at this time working at a Catholic university:

> First she spread a layer of cream on her cheeks, rubbing it into her straight nose, her childish chin and soft throat. It was gray, pearly bluish stuff. Over this she laid the makeup. She worked with cotton swabs, under the hairline, about the eyes, up the cheeks and on the throat. Despite the soft rings of feminine flesh, there was already something discernibly dictatorial about that extended throat.... She put on a pale powder with her puff, still at the same tilting speed.... Still without pauses or hesitations, she put a touch of black in the outer corner of each eye, and redrew the line of her brows to make it level and earnest.

The full description is two pages long. At one point Madeleine "picks up a large tailor's shears and puts them to her bangs": "She cut as if discharging a gun, and Herzog felt an impulse of alarm, short-circuited. Her decisiveness fascinated him" (p. 527). According to Sasha, Bellow "never saw me put on my makeup." Adam, however, who admires the accuracy of the description, claims to have seen her do so "countless" times.[60]

Banished from the house, Bellow moved in with a lawyer friend, Jonas Schwartz, an early supporter both of civil rights and of Hubert Humphrey, whom he'd met through the McCloskys.[61] Ralph Ross picked Bellow up and drove him to Schwartz's house. There Bellow stayed for a few days before moving to a hotel, where Adam was allowed to visit him once a week, ferried by third parties. Schwartz originally represented both Sasha and Bellow in the divorce, an arrangement Ross warned Bellow against (Schwartz also represented Ann Berryman in her divorce, around about the same time). It was not until February, however, that Bellow took Ross's advice, retaining John Goetz as counsel on Ross's recommendation. "You were absolutely right," he wrote on February 4, "I can't trust Jonas Schwartz, and I don't know what arrangements he will think just" (why he couldn't trust Schwartz he does not say). According to Goetz, as reported by James Atlas, "it wasn't just greed that made Schwartz long for a piece of the action; it was vanity. In the fall of 1959, the Bellows' marital crisis was the best show in town. 'Everyone wanted to get into the act,' said John Goetz,"[62] including Ludwig, who played the loyal and saddened mediator, counseling Bellow, presiding over meetings between Schwartz and Goetz ("I know nothing of this $1,000 loan from Sondra's mother," writes Ross to Bellow on May 12, 1960, "but you can scarcely claim it was anything else because Jack told Goetz it was indeed a loan").[63] Sasha thought Schwartz was motivated by friendship for Bellow as well as herself. In *Herzog*, as discussed in this book's introduction, Schwartz becomes Sandor Himmelstein, Moses and Madeleine's choleric and misshapen lawyer.[64]

It was a terrible time for Bellow. "The best show in town" was not just for friends and acquaintances, but for readers citywide, with Bellow as male lead. "Novelist's Wife Seeks Divorce" read the headline to an article of November 29 in *The Minneapolis Tribune*. Under the circumstances—with no teaching, limited access to Adam, and a hotel room for a home—it made sense for Bellow to leave town, at least for a while. Over the summer, he had been invited by the State Department to travel to Eastern Europe, lecturing in an "Experts and Specialists" program administered by the United States Information Agency. The tour was scheduled to begin on January 1, would last for three months, and on it Bellow would be accompanied by a second speaker, Mary McCarthy. In mid-November he set out for the East Coast, staying briefly at Yaddo, then for a while in Herb Gold's apartment on the Upper West Side while Gold was at Yaddo. On November 26, he flew to London and from London to Paris. On November 27, after Bellow's departure from New York, Covici wrote to him care of Eileen and Stanley Geist, on the rue de Verneuil. "It was nice having you for a bit. Any man who has made the journey through all the circles of Purgatory as you have and can still write farce that shakes me into uncontrollable laughter [*The Last Analysis*], is nothing but a genius." On February 13, well into the trip, Bellow explained its appeal in a letter to Harvey Swados: "I'd never have consented to be a world-tour-bum or cultural functionary without the need to wear myself out so that I could bear the misery of divorce."

NOW BEGAN a period of strenuous womanizing. In Paris he had an affair with a friend of Eileen Geist's named Helen Grisky, an expatriate New Yorker working in the film business. At some point they spent a weekend together in London, not altogether successfully.[65] He seems also to have reconnected with a Frenchwoman named Annie Doubillon, whom he had known from Bard. She, too, worked in the film business. Whether he took up again with Nadine Nimier is not known. In Poland he had a fling with a married sculptor, Alina Slesinska, who spoke no English. In Yugoslavia he had an affair with a writer and translator, Jara Ribnikar, president of the Association of Writers of Serbia, whose letters (she and Bellow corresponded throughout the 1960s) are funny and endearing. "Darling friend brother, brother friend darling and friend darling brother," begins one, "don't lose the smell of my bitter flower. And my king I would not let you fight with a lion, please. . . . Please excuse all my stupidities. I can be reasonable if it is necessary, sure." Another begins: "I kiss your nose." In her own language, Ribnikar could write (as the Polish sculptor could sculpt, with solo exhibitions in Europe and the United States).[66] Issue 3 of *The Noble Savage* contains her story "Copperskin," originally written in Serbian, translated by the author, and revised "by Saul Bellow and Susan Glassman," the latter soon to figure prominently in Bellow's life.

While on tour, Bellow received news from Minneapolis, particularly about Adam, from Schwartz and Paul Meehl. Schwartz, writing on January 4, had seen Adam, "my champion," and would soon see Sasha; mother and son had only just returned from Chicago, where they'd stayed with Cookie over the holidays. Schwartz sent Bellow New Year's greetings and encouraged him "to make an honest effort to stop annoying yourself." A day later Meehl wrote in response to a postcard from Bellow. He hadn't seen Sasha since a week or two before Christmas but "I believe everything is under control." Meehl's letter does not sound like the sort of thing a psychiatrist writes to a patient: "Just past my 40th birthday—whee! Working like a lunatic but not on what I am 'supposed' to be doing. Bad trait, that. Have fun, Paul." On January 13, Bellow wrote to Oscar Tarcov from Frankfurt ("a sort of Chicago"). In Poland he'd visited Auschwitz "and understood that concern with my private life was childish. Before that I had forty nights of insomnia over Sondra; now I'm losing sleep over the camps, and the ghettos of Warsaw and Cracow." From Warsaw Bellow returned to Bonn, from where he would travel to Yugoslavia in a few days. On the 18th he wrote to Covici from Belgrade, where he stayed until the end of the month. He was distraught: no mail awaited him upon arrival. Was everyone all right? None of the four people he'd written to in Minnesota had answered. "The universal silence makes me afraid."

Two days later, in a letter to Ralph Ellison, Bellow pronounced himself "much better. I'm beginning to sit up and take nourishment, and I'd enjoy my convalescence greatly if I didn't have to do this cultural functionary bullshit." He and McCarthy were worked hard on the tour: sometimes they had to deliver several lectures a day, in addition to giving interviews and meeting literary officials and bureaucrats. Partly Bellow felt better because he'd phoned Meehl from Macedonia to find out about Adam, who was fine ("this was Macedonia's first call to Minneapolis"), partly he felt better because he found Eastern Europe interesting. "It has told me a lot about my family—myself, even. It's made a slavophile of me." In a letter of August 18, 1993, to the food critic Mimi Sheraton he recalled visiting "the Polish hinterland." Poznań "was the image of Scranton, Pennsylvania circa 1937. Except that the trolley cars were of an earlier time—say, 1905. I went also to Cracow and wandered through the totally empty ghetto there. My parents often spoke about mud in the old country. I had never really understood why it should have been described in such extraordinary terms. The mud was like a thick, old gray soup, cold of course and pouring into your shoes when you crossed the street. There was nothing in the shops except pages torn from Hebrew and Yiddish books. For the first time in my life I understood why Eastern European Jews drank tea with lemon. They needed it for warmth, and a slice of lemon was important not only for its flavor but also because it resembled the sun they never saw. Lemon played a figurative role here, something like a reminder of the absent cosmic radiance."

On January 22, in a letter to Covici, Bellow gave further evidence of recovered spirits: "I've even begun to sleep again, without drugs. And I met a young lady in Poland [the sculptor]—well, not so young, but lovely—who comforted me well. I thought she had also given me the clap, and I was very proud but the doctor in Warsaw said it was only a trifling infection." He'd also been working—on the play and a story that sounds like the beginnings of *Herzog*: "The story *is* about Sondra, and it may be a trial run, who knows? . . . I'd better come home, I think, and file my taxes and move East and complete the play and start the book. And begin my life." In the week that followed he went to Italy. On February 15, he sailed from Naples to Haifa. On March 3 he was back in Rome and on March 18 in London. He returned home on March 22, trailed by letters not only from Helen, Annie, Jara, and Alina, but from Maryi, Hannah, Daniela, Maude (from Milan, scared off by "your big red dressed romantic girl"), and Iline.[67] "Home," he explained in a letter of March 8 to Ellison, meant "two days to see Greg," then "Washington and Chicago and Mpls. There I expect to stay a month (six weeks!), get divorced, kiss Adam, and towards the end of May join you in Tivoli." In Venice, writing a day or two later (the postmark is illegible), he was greeted by a snowstorm. "God salts my every bite," he wrote to Richard Stern. "Just the same it *is* Italy. Even the irrigation ditches are dug with sensitivity." In a subsequent postcard to Stern he writes: "Israel and Italy sublime and gorgeous respectively," but also exhausting. "I'm down about 20 lbs. and ready to go back to my business," he writes to Covici on March 4 from Tel Aviv, "which is to be fatter and to write books. I've had too much of sights and flights, and girls. Still, I wanted to wear myself out, and I'm well satisfied with the results I've gotten." He adds that he's seen Billy Rose in Tel Aviv, a detail stored for nearly thirty years before put to use in *The Bellarosa Connection*. On March 16, no longer exhausted, he reported to Marshall Best of Viking: "I'm fit again."

In the letter to Best, Bellow defends the tour, which had caused Best embarrassment. This embarrassment was provoked by a Ford Foundation executive who was "distressed" to hear that Bellow was traveling rather than writing. Bellow replied that he *was* writing. "I always manage to keep at it," he assured Best. "You know that I'm not reckless and irresponsible and that I wouldn't go off on a toot abandoning all work and responsibility. An emergency arose and I met it as well as I could." The next day he wrote a second letter to Best, still brooding over the implied rebuke. Far from being on a "gay lark in Europe,"

> I have been dutifully suffering my way from country to country, thinking about Fate and Death. . . . Will that do as an explanation? And if, here and there, I gave a talk in Poland and Yugoslavia, did I violate the by-laws? All jokes aside, what I saw between Auschwitz and Jerusalem made a change in me. To say the least. And that ought not to distress the Ford Foundation. I'm sorry to cause you an embarrassment, but there ought not to be any in my going to Europe and the Middle East for a few months. Now I'm coming back to write a book, and I see nothing wrong anywhere. I might have written a thousand pages in Minneapolis and thrown them away. I know I've done the necessary and proper thing and it annoys me to be criticized for it.

Coming to Israel after Eastern Europe led Bellow to think hard about his identity as a Jew and an American. Several Riga cousins had survived German occupation, immigrating to Israel after the war. In Holon, near Tel Aviv, Bellow visited cousin Lisa and her husband, Baruch Westreich. Lisa's mother, Rachel, adored Bellow's mother, Liza, her sister, after whom she named her daughter. The Westreichs knew all about Bellow and his family, through correspondence with Abraham, who often urged them to come to the United States, offering to pay their way. According to Lisa's daughter, Sabina Mazursky, Abraham described Bellow as a great worry to the family, the only son "not working only writing." Sabina was twelve in 1960. On Bellow's next visit to Israel, in 1967, to report for *Newsday* on the Six Day War, she "fell in love" with him: he was "good looking and full of charm and so clever," also "a little bit sarcastic." Bellow liked the Westreichs, who owned a small grocery store "no bigger than a pantry" and lived a hard life "on their feet ten hours a day."[68] On this trip he must also have met cousin Moshe Gordin, the son of Liza's and Rachel's brother, Hone (or Khanan or Aron). Moshe, according to his nephew, Mikhail Gordin, "was a bulldozer, stubborn—he only went his way," and "like all the men in the Gordin family . . . got angry fast." Moshe served in the Russian army in World War II. Before the war, he had been a welder, but he also drew and made steel sculptures. According to Mikhail, Moshe was the model for the Israeli sculptor Eisen in *Mr. Sammler's Planet* (1970). When Moshe read the novel, he "was insulted about how Saul Bellow depicted him." The Riga cousins Bellow met in Israel led what he calls "plain" lives. These lives they accepted, having known "arrest, deportation, massacre and war" in Europe. As Bellow writes in *To Jerusalem and Back*, "they have, curiously, more rest in their souls than the American side of the family; they are less secure but also less fretful. Observing their temper and their ways [Bellow was writing in 1975, after a number of visits], I wonder about the effects of limitless expectation on the American sense of reality."[69]

Related thoughts about national and cultural identity were prompted by an encounter with S. Y. Agnon, "the dean of Hebrew writers," an encounter described by Bellow in the introduction to *Great Jewish Short Stories* (1963). Agnon received Bellow at his house in Jerusalem, "not far from the barbed wire entanglements that divide the city." As the two writers drank tea, Agnon asked Bellow if any of his books had been translated into Hebrew: "If they had not been, he had better see to it immediately, because, he said, they would survive only in the Holy Tongue." Agnon was teasing but he was also serious. When Bellow mentioned Heine as a Jewish poet "who had done rather well in German," Agnon replied, "we have him beautifully translated into Hebrew, he is safe." Bellow had more patience for Agnon than for other champions of Hebrew—of Israel, ultimately, the only place, it was suggested to him, where a Jew could be fully Jewish. "With less wit and subtlety than Mr. Agnon, other Jewish writers worry about using the languages of the Diaspora," Bellow writes in the introduction to *Great Jewish Short Stories* (and quoted in Chapter 1), but "Jews have been writing in languages other than Hebrew for more than two thousand years."[70] "It cannot be argued that the stories of Isaac Babel are not characteristically Jewish," he argues, though Babel wrote in Russian.[71] Bellow disliked what he saw as a xenophobic strain in Israeli attitudes to the literature and experience of Diasporan Jews, shaming champions of Hebrew by linking them with Oswald Spengler's limiting notions of Judaism. For Spengler, the Jews were permanently identified "with a period in culture which he calls the Magian, and will never belong in spirit to the modern order."[72] The champions of Hebrew, Bellow implies, are Magians. In 1975, in Jerusalem, Bellow met the Israeli novelist Amos Oz, who writes in Hebrew. Bellow peppered him with questions, many of them technical, about how he could possibly write a modern novel in an ancient language. Behind these questions lay a defense of Jewish writers of the Diaspora, as voiced at the end of the introduction to *Great Jewish Short Stories*: "We make what we can of our condition with the means available. We must accept the mixture as we find it."[73]

Bellow's "gay lark in Europe" ended where it began, in London, where he was entertained by his new British publisher, George Weidenfeld. On the advice of Sonia Orwell, Weidenfeld had taken Bellow on as an author when John Lehmann, his previous publisher, went bankrupt in 1953. The first Bellow novel published by Weidenfeld and Nicolson (Nigel Nicolson was the firm's cofounder) was *The Adventures of Augie March*. In London, Weidenfeld hosted a party for Bellow attended by J. B. Priestley, Anthony Powell, Stephen Spender, Louis MacNeice, and Karl Miller, the literary editor of *The Spectator*. As Bellow was now famous, he was largely immune to the slights and offenses, real or imagined, he'd complained of a decade earlier after Lehmann's party. He was also comfortable with Weidenfeld, who was shrewd, convivial, charming, and Jewish. Weidenfeld had escaped from Vienna in 1939, a virtually penniless law student. By 1960 he was rich and well connected in literary, political, and social, including aristocratic, circles. According to Weidenfeld, he and Bellow were politically compatible: "We both belonged to what you might call the NCL, Non-Communist Left." Unlike Bellow, however, Weidenfeld was a passionate Zionist, much influenced in his youth by Ze'ev Jabotinsky, the Zionist activist. Weidenfeld claims that Bellow "was amazed that I had these non-Jewish acquaintances and was totally committed to Israel." "I didn't have hang-ups," he explained, "my mentality towards the English aristocracy was we are better than them. . . . Who are you? Robbers! Fourteenth century? My family are rabbis who came from Barcelona. Who the hell are you? And Saul Bellow was astonished by that." In addition to entertaining Bellow, Weidenfeld put him up in a guest apartment in his house in Hyde Park Gate.[74] Weidenfeld liked and admired Bellow but "had my reservations about some traits of his character. He was enormously self-absorbed." Other factors prevented close friendship. For Weidenfeld, politics and history mattered more than literature; he had comparatively little to do with the firm's fiction list. "I've never cultivated artists, with one exception, Mary McCarthy, a woman interested in affairs, a very intimate close friend. We talked about communism not Proust or James." In addition, Bellow was well taken care of by Weidenfeld's colleague, Barley Alison, who not only looked after his publishing needs but advised him on a range of personal matters. It was Alison who became a close and trusted friend.

Barley Alison played a key role in Bellow's life in Europe. Slight, fragile-looking, elegant, she came from a background very different from Bellow's. She was born in 1920 in Cannes and grew up in France, Australia, and England. She had been a debutante. She joined the Land Army in 1940 and in 1941 she was posted to Algiers, where she worked in intelligence, briefing agents who were about to infiltrate France. In Algiers she befriended Albert Camus, A. J. Ayer, and Duff Cooper, who had her posted to the British embassy in Paris in 1944 when he became ambassador. In Paris she rose to third secretary, one of the first women in the foreign service to hold a full diplomatic post. In 1948 she returned to London, working in the Foreign Office until 1953. Then she traveled the Middle East for eighteen months as a freelance journalist. Weidenfeld met her at a lunch party and lured her into publishing in 1955 as an investor and temporary employee (she was independently wealthy, with money inherited from a grandfather who owned property in Australia). Within a decade she, together with Ed Victor, later a powerful agent, ran the firm's general department, responsible for 150 titles a year. Among the authors Alison took care of were Margaret Drabble and Piers Paul Read, both of whom she discovered, Mickey Spillane, Umberto Eco, and Vladimir Nabokov. To Bellow, as to all her authors, she was fiercely devoted, an indefatigable letter writer (her correspondence in the Regenstein is voluminous), a fund of gossip and anecdote, and sound in judgment, both literary and commercial. She was famously stylish, loved entertaining—Margaret Drabble called her "recklessly hospitable"—and though never married (a *femme seule*, she called herself), had many affairs, often with married or otherwise unsuitable lovers. For Bellow, as for Drabble, she was "a one woman initiation ceremony,"[75] quickly and tactfully taking him under her wing. "I am so glad Paris is being a success" begins a letter to Bellow of December 12, 1960, written only weeks after they'd met. "Will you give Pauline Graham [the actress and poet] a note? According to the English 'Emily Posts' you should write. . . . I could give you an equally unimportant list for France. I think it must be my diplomatic training." Later she vetted Bellow's girlfriends and advised him about the best places to buy handmade shoes and shirts.

Bellow's tour of Europe was just what he needed. It wore him out, distracted him, and deepened his understanding both of the world his parents came from and of the horrors of the war and of recent Jewish history. His complaints were few, mostly having to do with lack of news from home. He got on with Mary McCarthy, whose companionship brought unexpected benefits, particularly at receptions and social functions. "She had such an easy way with top officials," Bellow told one of McCarthy's biographers. "I remember when we were received by the Ambassador in Belgrade . . . she took charge. I was a sort of observer—the cat in the corner—which is my favorite position as a novelist. She marched me around Belgrade several days in a row. It was very cold and I was talking a mile a minute. She wanted to know the story of my life." McCarthy's way of finding out about a person, Bellow recalled, was "inquisitional. There was a battery of questions." Her interest in him was solely intellectual: "I never connected it with any sexual motive she might have." Not that she was without sexual motives. McCarthy, too, had been busy on tour, flirting with a cultural attaché in Warsaw, James West, whom she later turned up with in Paris and eventually married; going off "with some Serb or other in Belgrade." As has previously been mentioned, Bellow admired McCarthy's "enamelled" beauty, but was put off by it as well. "I can imagine what it would be like to go to bed with her," he told her biographer. "She'd put you through your paces. I didn't feel like going through hoops for Mary or anybody else. I'd had that." Intellectually, McCarthy was good company, though she could be rigid in her views. "Once she had developed a line she became inflexible."[76] McCarthy's feelings about Bellow, conveyed at the end of the tour in a letter to Hannah Arendt, were comparably mixed: "Saul and I parted good friends, though he is too wary and raw-nerved to be friends, really, even with people he decides to like. He is in better shape than he was in Poland, yet I felt very sorry for him when I saw him go off yesterday, all alone, on his way to Italy, like Augie with a cocky sad smile disappearing into the distance."[77]

NOTHING IS RECORDED of Bellow's time in New York after he returned from Europe, nor of his debriefing at the State Department in Washington. His stay in Minneapolis lasted eleven days and was horrible. "Adam apart," he wrote to Ralph Ross, in an undated letter, it was "a nightmare. . . . Sandra threatened to call the cops if I came near the house, and I repressed the impulse to kill her so well I didn't even want to see her. Then her lawyer tried to put me over the barrel, breaking every agreement we reached before I left in Nov." Sasha was angry about the continuing legal wrangles with Bellow, especially over her mother's loan.[78] She insisted on keeping the car and most of the furniture and presented him with a bill of $400 from a local department store. Bellow still knew nothing of the affair with Ludwig, though when the two men met he sensed a change in Ludwig's manner. As he wrote to Botsford, "towards me Jack behaved *appropriately* in Mpls. This is an observation rather than a complaint. He did for the most part what a friend should have done, but his compassion is spoken rather than shown. Once he has made his mind up over the issues, he tends to be the King and to speak from a throne. What I needed was good sense, not authority." From Minnesota Bellow fled to Chicago, where he stayed for several weeks, partly to receive an award on April 23 from the Friends of Literature, an Evanston book club, partly to see family. Edward Shils, the sociologist, was in England and lent Bellow his office at the University of Chicago. It may have been at this time that Bellow started an affair with a writer named Roberta "Bobby" Markels, then living in Evanston. This seems also to have been the time when he started, or seriously started, an affair with an ex-girlfriend of Philip Roth's, Susan Glassman.

Once back in Tivoli in May, Bellow entered therapy with Albert Ellis, author of *Sex Without Guilt* (1958). Ellis described the "goal" of Bellow's therapy as "to get him unangry, which wasn't easy with a person like that because he was a novelist, and novelists think that all emotions are good."[79] Not surprisingly, Bellow quit the therapy after a few months. "It was pool-room grad work," he told Atlas, "what to do, how to lay a girl, getting rid of character problems that are an obstacle to pleasure" ("how to lay a girl," presumably, means once in bed, as opposed to getting them to bed, suggesting that sexual dysfunction or dissatisfaction as well as anger figured in their sessions). What helped Bellow most was returning to Tivoli and to work. "The only sure cure is to write a book," he advised a depressed Alice Adams in a letter of September 10, 1960. "I've been so pressed, harried, driven, badgered, bitched, delayed," he wrote to Susan Glassman on May 5, "that I haven't even had time to sit down and cross my legs. Till now, in Tivoli. Good old Tivoli." "I crept back to Tivoli," he wrote the McCloskys around about the same time. "I'm winding up the play, *The Last Analysis*. I am getting ready to write a novel. . . . Greg and Adam are fine, and I'm not too bad."

It was a recuperative summer. Ellison was there with his dog, Tucka, a pedigree black Labrador, bought from John Cheever. Bellow got on well with Ellison but "the important thing was that the gloomy house was no longer empty—no longer gloomy."[80] They would meet for breakfast, Ellison dressed in an exotic Moroccan robe and slippers. Ellison taught Bellow how to brew drip coffee "properly" (an elaborate procedure, which, when tested by myself, was hard to see as worth the effort).[81] After the day's work they would meet for cocktails, to chat about their writing, or Bellow's *Noble Savage* correspondence (Ellison had a contribution in issue 1), or current events, including the coming presidential election (both were Kennedy supporters). In addition, they exchanged literary and artistic views ("about Malraux, about Marxism, or painting or novel writing") and personal histories. Bellow was struck by "the strength and independence" of Ellison's mind. "Ralph, it was clear, had thought things through for himself, and his ideas had little in common with the views of the critics in the literary quarterlies." Neither writer was prepared to accept "the categories prepared for us by literary journalists."[82] If not visiting or being visited—the summer brought many guests and invitations—they prepared supper together in the ground-floor kitchen, kept cool by thick stone walls. After supper there was drinking and more talk late into the evening. Like Bellow, Ellison played the recorder and liked classical music; they often listened to records after supper in Bellow's upstairs study (Bach, Scarlatti, Poulenc). Gossip about the friendship was inevitable. According to Atlas, "one day, around the time Leslie Fiedler published his widely read essay about Mark Twain, 'Come Back to the Raft [Ag'in], Huck Honey,' making the case that Huck Finn and Nigger Jim were homosexual lovers, Herb Gold remarked that he'd heard Ellison was living in the Tivoli house. 'Don't tell Leslie,' Bellow joked."[83]

In June, the divorce finally went through, and as Bellow reported to Berryman on July 4, 1960, he was "the better for it." Sasha had not asked for alimony: Bellow was to pay $150 a month child support, the sum Anita received for Greg, and to set up a trust fund for Adam. That summer, only Tucka, Ellison's dog, caused problems, being less than a year old and not fully housebroken. In addition to pissing on Bellow's Persian rugs, shitting indoors and on the porch, he had a tendency to chew up furniture and books. "Stubborn about his dog's rights," Arnold Rampersad, Ellison's biographer, writes, "Ralph refused to discipline Tucka or even to clean up after him," complaining to John Cheever, as Bellow recalls it, that "with my upbringing, I was incapable of understanding, I had no feeling for pedigrees and breeds, and that I knew only mongrels and had treated his *chien de race* like a mongrel."[84] According to Gore Vidal, when relations were "edgy" between Bellow and Ellison, "Ralph's beautiful wife would come up and smooth things."

THE SOCIAL LIFE AT Tivoli in the summer of 1960 involved Bellow's children, Bard people, associated writers and critics, friends and relations from Manhattan and beyond, and Ellison's beautiful wife, Fanny, who arrived regularly on Friday and returned on Sunday afternoon to her city job. It extended also to a few well-born river types, through Vidal and the Dupees. "Ralph and I in our slummy mansion could not entertain these far more prosperous literary country squires," Bellow recalled in 1996, two years after Ellison's death. "Gore viewed us with a certain ironic pity. Socially, we didn't exist for him." The two writers, however, were unperturbed. "'A campy patrician' said Ralph [of Vidal]. We were as amused by him as he was by us." Bellow mentions Max

Weber's description of Jews as "aristocratic pariahs," adding that "Ralph himself had an aristocratic demeanor." In fact, "no one in our Dutchess County group was altogether free from pride. Gore had genealogical claims, and money as well. Dupee had affinities with Henry James and Marcel Proust. The presence of a Jew or a Negro in any group is apt to promote a sense of superiority in those who—whatever else—are neither Jews nor Negroes."[85]

In the afternoons, visitors might help Bellow tend the plants and vegetables. Ellison showed off the African violets and bonsai trees he cultivated in the ballroom, where he set up his study (Bellow worked at a long writing table upstairs, with a view of the river and classical music pouring from the record player). There were shooting and fishing expeditions. When not weeding, tending the vegetable garden, feeding Rufus, the rust-colored tomcat, entertaining, or doing repairs (roofs, windows, trailing vines), Bellow attended to his correspondence, or read Donne and Blake in the hammock at the front of the house. In May he gave a reading from *The Last Analysis* at a party at Aaron and Linda Asher's house on the Upper West Side. Mike Nichols, Jules Feiffer, and Grace Paley were in attendance, as was Susan Glassman, who was visiting Bellow from Chicago, staying with him at Tivoli. At the reading, parts were assigned. Bellow played the lead, Mike Nichols volunteered to play the lead's business manager, and Linda Asher took all the women's parts. The reading was lively, often interrupted by laughter, from author as well as audience.[86] After the reading, Bellow struck up a conversation with an attractive professor of French from Queens College named Rosette Lamont, who had been brought to the evening by Paolo Milano. "Bellow reads with charm and humor," Milano had told her. "He likes to try out some of his work in progress on people he trusts."[87] Before leaving the party with Susan Glassman, Bellow asked Lamont for her phone number. A few days later, after Glassman's return to Chicago, he invited Lamont to Tivoli. Fred Dupee remembers boating on the Hudson with the two of them: "It was rough, Saul was scared, and Rosette made fun of him. Nonetheless we liked her."[88] At some point during this period, Bellow also slept with the poet Sandra Hochman and the actress Helen Garrie, both in New York.

In mid-August Bellow and Susan drove from New York to Chicago, where Sasha and Adam were staying with Cookie in Skokie. Bellow was allowed a week's visit with Adam (after what he describes, in a letter to Glassman of June 29, 1960, as "the regulation four-bladed duel" with

Sasha). It was better seeing Adam in Chicago than Minneapolis, where, as John Berryman reported, "every academic louse and beetle in those parts [was] slavering over it [the divorce and attendant gossip]."[89] In a letter of August 18 to Ellison, Susan described the time in Chicago as "splendid . . . *tout va bien!* Adam looks marvelous and remembers Rufus and you . . . in that order. He's happy and he and Saul spent a lot of time kissing each other. *C'est belle!* The trip was joyous fun & Saul is feeling great . . . and therefore, so am I."

IT WAS MOST LIKELY in the autumn of 1960, on a visit to see Adam in Minneapolis at the end of November, that Bellow discovered the affair between Sasha and Ludwig. Sasha had taken on a lodger to help with the rent and with baby-sitting. The lodger was a fellow graduate student who supported herself by working a couple of days a week as a dental technician.[90] "We got on well," Sasha writes in the memoir, "we quizzed each other for our exams, and she was a pleasant housemate, fairly reserved." One day, after a visit from Ludwig, the housemate said to Sasha: "'I'm going after him.' Startled and appalled I blurted out the truth about our relationship" (p. 104). The housemate said nothing, returned to her room, and some days later told Sasha she was leaving. She also said that she had called both Leya and Bellow "and told them about Jack and me." According to Atlas, the night Bellow learned of the affair he rushed over to Ralph Ross's house and announced "I'm going to catch that son-of-a-bitch Ludwig and beat him to a pulp." Ross had to restrain Bellow physically, later telling him, "Be a mensch—have an ulcer." In Chicago, again according to Atlas, at the Quadrangle Club, Bellow "talked wildly of getting a gun."[91] Bellow did not confront Sasha about the affair. She is "hazy about the fact" but thinks "I didn't see him for a while and when the semester ended I couldn't afford to continue my graduate studies and I got a job writing copy for a lumber company, and moved out of the house into an apartment nearer to campus" (p. 105).

That Bellow did not learn of the affair until the November visit is suggested by letters he wrote that autumn. On September 24, in a letter to Botsford, he refers to a previous letter he'd written on the back of a letter from Ludwig, "in which [Ludwig] explains—or says, without feeling the need to explain—that a secretary at the University had buried 'some things' (all I had sent him for two months). I've been doing all that I could do under this handicap [he means for issue 3 of *The Noble Savage*]. . . . In the near future we'd better have an understanding the 3 of us, on the meaning of the magazine." It is unlikely that Bellow would have contemplated working with Ludwig if he'd known of the affair. On October 4 Bellow wrote again to Botsford with concerns about the magazine: "It's not just that I've been unreliable, or you, or Jack, but the magazine hasn't come alive." He adds: "I go to Mpls in November to see Adam, and I shall have to have things out with Jack. Our relations are not good" (not good, presumably, since the April visit, when he sensed a change in Ludwig's manner toward him). On October 12 Bellow wrote to Botsford about issue 2, a great improvement on issue 1, and about the material for issue 3, which looked promising. He was editing "a Yugoslav manuscript of great power" (the Ribnikar story). "Meantime my problems with Jack continue. You must understand. I am not at all angry. Rather it begins to be funny. Does Jack think that he's functioning as the ed. of a magazine? I can't persuade him to do a thing—not even to return mss. he's kept since August. I have to write apologetic notes to the authors. Somehow we'll get by, but eventually Jack will have to decide whether he can really carry the editorial burden."

On November 21, in another letter to Botsford, Bellow again expresses irritation at Ludwig's deficiencies as editor. "About Jack, you mustn't think I'm putting you in the middle. I'm capable of dealing with all the difficulties myself, and my feelings about him are not what you have supposed. We can make out. It's only that he's not reliable in the editorial department. He keeps calling for editing continually but offers to do none of it. Every fourth time it happens I find it very funny." In January Bellow took a job, arranged by Botsford, at the University of Puerto Rico, so letters between them stop. The first dated letter to suggest Bellow's knowledge of the affair was written on January 29 to Ralph Ross, whom he addresses as if he knew all about it (something Ross later denied, in a letter of July 10, 1963). Several of Bellow's students from Minnesota had asked Ross to pass on to him their hopes that he'd return to teach at the university, also to express their continuing loyalty. "The scandal on the grapevine from Mpls evidently isn't all contra-Bellow," Bellow responded to Ross. "Well, well—it has its amusing aspect, even. All these senseless old words like *adultery* and *infidelity* and *love honor obey*. Well, you told me I didn't understand the fabric of society and a word to the wise has made a student of me. Not a cynic, but a student." Bellow was writing from Puerto Rico, "a long way from the Jacks and Jills and Jonases. It suits me fine." In a second letter to Ross, this one undated but also from January ("They'll never carve 1960 on my tombstone, come what may"), Bellow wrote that he missed seeing Berryman when he came east in December. Sasha, too, had been east, but he saw neither her "nor Ludwig, our co-editor, who spent a week or more in these parts, but didn't phone or reply to my call." The letter continues:

Honi soit qui mal y pense.

The meek shall inherit the hearse.

Well, I am greatly pleased at the way matters have turned out. My stupidity deserved far worse, but poetic justice has its own way with all us dumb joiks.

Such a mixture of talent, character and *fidelity*—above all, fidelity.[92]

VERY FEW LUDWIG LETTERS TO Bellow survive from the months leading up to late November 1960. Those that do are breezy, confident, full of opinion. On June 20 Ludwig pronounces himself "sorely pissed off at Meridian" for not honoring their contract with the magazine and for what he sees as a patronizing attitude to its editors. He has news of Adam: "terrific, tanning, a sand and water boychik evidently." He also writes that Knopf has bought the contract for his novel, *Confusions*, from Viking, and that he's doing "a five nights a week one hour TV show" (a broadcast version of his undergraduate course "Humanities in the Modern World").[93] On July 7, Ludwig sends Bellow a note saying that his mother died on June 30, and that he's only just returned to Minneapolis from Winnipeg. "I'll write you about all the things I should be writing you about as soon as I can do it." If he did so, the letter has not survived. Nothing of what does survive before February 4, 1961, betrays the slightest unease on Ludwig's part, though he must have been told, by Sasha if not Leya, that Bellow now knew of the affair.

For whatever reason—fury, shame, embarrassment, a mixture of the three—Bellow avoided direct confrontation with Ludwig as well as Sasha. He and Botsford did, however, sometime in January demand Ludwig's resignation, for on February 4 Ludwig wrote a letter in his defense. The letter begins by admitting that he was wrong not to get in touch with Bellow when he was in town in December (though he claims a mix-up explains his not replying to Bellow's telephone message). He had come to New York to hand in the manuscript of *Confusions* to Knopf and feared being distracted from crucial last-minute revisions ("I knew I wouldn't be able to resist an invitation to go up there [to Tivoli]"). What he calls "a turn in the manuscript" meant that he had to spend all of New Year's Day revising the novel, "had an hour at Knopf's the next morning and then took off for Mpls (I had a public lecture to give there)." He's willing to resign if they insist, "but it's one fuck of a way to wind up the effort that went into three issues of stacked-high material which I was involved with steadily (regardless of how long I was forced to hang on to the MSS because of the press of teaching duties here). I of course am saying I behaved like an asshole but realize that if my work on these three issues had been snuffed out by this unintended slight that's how it will have to stand. . . . Just do me a favor, eh, mates or ex-mates? Knock off the bureaucratic horseshit about resignations and the letters that sound like IBM Watson sending a manager's manager's manager down. You want me off the masthead—O.K.? Don't think that my commitment to what we were trying to do in TNS will be one bit lessened by that. I would still want it to work. And I would wish you guys the best of luck." Ludwig signs the letter, "Yours in Coventry, Jack."

Bellow's reply is undated. He begins by saying that he has "tried very hard" to avoid writing the sort of thing he's about to write, but that Ludwig's "phenomenal" letter of February 4 has forced him "to tell you a few of the things I feel about your relations to the magazine and me, personally." Ludwig has neglected his responsibility as editor: "you have done nothing for months but read a few manuscripts. Others you have detained for periods up to half a year. . . . When I asked you to edit things, you said you couldn't, you had TV programs, lectures and other obligations. Still the manuscripts kept coming back from you, when in their own sweet time they did come back, with scrawled notes recommending editing." All through the summer and autumn Bellow had "carried" Ludwig, as correspondence would show, "those unanswered letters which were never without friendly inquiries." It is true that he was absent when on tour in Poland and Yugoslavia. The reasons for his absence, "you understand as well as I do, and perhaps even better. By now I can't be sure that I do know more about them." The rattle in these sentences is audible, as is a reluctance to accept what he's been told ("I can't be sure"). Ludwig says he's looking forward to contributing to issue 4, but "what can you, without hallucination, believe you have to do with *TNS*?" What, after all, did he do for issue 3? "You sent two inept and scarcely readable paragraphs for the arias which I threw out in disgust. I don't think you are a fit editor for the magazine. . . . You are too woolly, self-absorbed, rambling, ill-organized, slovenly, heedless and insensitive to get on with. And you must be in a grotesque mess, to have lost your sense of reality to the last shred. I think you never had much of it to start with, and your last letter reveals that that's gone, too."

Bellow then turns to the "personal" aspect of their relationship, "since we're not only colleagues but 'friends'":

> In all this there is some ugliness, something I don't want explained, though I'm sure that as a disciple of the Hasidim and believer in Dialogue and enthusiast for Heschel, and a man of honor from whom I have heard and endured many lectures and reproaches and whose correction I have accepted, you have a clear and truthful explanation. And all the worse for you if you are not hypocritical. The amount of internal garbage you have not taken cognizance of must be, since you never do things on a small scale, colossal.

Ludwig will never see his behavior for what it is. Bellow wants no "Dialogue" with him, no explanations, no "Hasidic" sincerity. When he writes that "it wouldn't do much good to see matters clearly," "clearly" is meant ironically. It alludes to what he imagines will be Ludwig's "clear and truthful explanation." "With the sharpest eyes in the world I'd see nothing but the stinking fog of falsehood. And I haven't got the sharpest eyes in the world." These bitter sentences raise questions. If the fog of falsehood Bellow faced—from Ludwig, from Sasha—was so thick that even the sharpest eyes could not see through it, how was it that so many of his friends noticed what was going on, while Bellow himself, the great noticer, noticed nothing? One answer is that he wasn't paying attention, or that it wasn't in his interest to pay attention, at least in the short term. That Sasha had been desperately unhappy in the summer of 1959 Bellow failed to notice; that in the preceding spring she'd gotten pregnant and had an abortion he also failed to notice. He was working. He needed Sasha to be all right, as he needed Ludwig to be the friend and ally he presented himself as being. In not seeing or noticing, he was at fault, "not superman but superidiot. Only a giant among idiots would marry Sondra and offer you friendship." Many years later, writing to Ralph Ross on March 22, 1977, Bellow attributed his blindness to "self-absorption":

> Only it was no ordinary form of self-absorption because I *could* understand what I was determined to understand. . . . Evidently I was determined not to understand whatever was deeply threatening— allowed myself to know what conformed to my objectives, and no more. A tall order, to bury so many powers of observation. That sounds immodest; I mean only to be objective. But all the orders have been tall. If you had followed up your shrewd remark you might have saved me some time, but I assume you thought that if I couldn't work out the hint I couldn't be expected to bear a full examination either. I had to go through the whole Sondra–Jack Ludwig business, for instance. I gave them, and others, terrific entertainment.

In the letter to Ludwig, Bellow admits he has faults. "I leave infinities on every side to be desired. But love her as my wife? Love you as my friend? I might as well have gone to work for Ringling Brothers and been shot out of a cannon twice a day. At least they would have let me wear a costume." The letter ends: "Coventry, pal, is not the place."

THAT BELLOW AVOIDED CONFRONTING Sasha and Ludwig about the affair hardly means he couldn't face the reality of their betrayal. By February 1961 he was well along in *Herzog*, whose hero resembles the clownlike figure he imagines himself to be in the letter to Ludwig. In writing *Herzog* he would exact revenge, but he would also seek the truth of what happened, searching out its causes in the widest as well as the most narrowly personal contexts. He would delve into the motives of the betrayers but also of the betrayed. And he would shape his findings to his needs as an artist. Terrible as it was to be so humiliated, he was energized by the effort of turning his humiliation into art. Some years later, as we shall see, Ludwig, ever imitative, wrote his own novel about the affair, or drawing on the affair, the only public account he has given of his part in the betrayal. With characteristic bravado or *chutzpah* he also reviewed *Herzog*, adopting a "man of honor" silence about its real-life origins, praising it dispassionately while including subtle digs. When asked if he would agree to be interviewed for this book, Ludwig politely declined. His children "want an end to this matter, which of course is not possible." He had been traduced by previous biographers; James Atlas had "Swiftboated" him (a reference to the campaign to discredit John Kerry in the 2004 presidential campaign). Kerry had a venue for responding to his "Swiftboating," one that he "stupidly" did not use; "I neither had a venue nor did I want to engage Tar Baby." When, ten years later, such a "venue" was offered him, he several times declined: "Alas, I have no 'side' to offer . . . no 'record' to 'set straight.' Saul was hurt. By his friend. That's it. Tags—'Iago,' 'overbearing,' 'boastful' will be gospelized, *sans* dissent. Tough. Yay Atlas!"[94] Ludwig cannot have wanted the echo here: "Demand me nothing, what you know you know, / From this time forth I never will speak word."[95]

SB and Jack Ludwig, Tivoli, 1957

14

Susan / *Herzog*

B ELLOW ARRIVED AT the University of Puerto Rico at Río Piedras on January 12, 1961, to teach for a term. It was his first university post in more than two years and he took the job because
he needed the money: he owed Viking $10,000, he had to pay Anita
and Sasha more than $5,000 a year in alimony and child support, and
repairs at the Tivoli house continued to be a financial drain.[1] The salary
he received from the university was $6,000 for three months' teaching
(Keith Botsford's yearly salary). His duties were to teach one literature
course, one writing course, and deliver one public lecture, a schedule
that took up three afternoons a week, Wednesday through Friday, leaving plenty of time for *Herzog.*[2] He got the job through Botsford, who
had come to the university in December 1958 from CBS, the television network, where he'd worked after Bard. Botsford is vague about
his position at the university. "I was supposed to 'run' the University's
media, film, television, radio and all their respective bits and pieces."[3]
Within a year Botsford had the ear of the rector of the university, the
"formidable" (p. 329) Jaime Benítez Rexach, as well as that of his assistant, Jorge Enjuto Bernal, described by Botsford in *Fragment VI* of his
memoirs as "a man of the most distinguished manners and bearing"
(p. 334), and persuaded them to fund a trip in the summer of 1959 to
Minneapolis, Chicago, and New York. "Now I had money in my pocket
and a first-class ticket," he writes, "and I had a mission—to bring Saul
to Puerto Rico."[4] That the mission succeeded was due in part to the
University of Minnesota's discovering, prior assurances notwithstanding, that it had no post for Bellow (presumably because of the recent

scandal of his breakup with Sasha, a reason also for suspecting that Bellow would be unlikely to accept such a post). Only after he had agreed to come to Puerto Rico did Bellow realize, as he wrote to Botsford on March 19, 1960, that he couldn't in fact begin teaching until March 1961, when the Ford grant ran out (otherwise "the Fords would be justifiably outraged"). Nevertheless, he arranged to come to the university in January. On the eve of his departure, his feelings were mixed. "I'll leave reluctantly for Puerto Rico," he wrote to Alice Adams in an undated letter. "But who knows? It may do me good."

On the plane to Puerto Rico, first impressions were inauspicious. "Only I had bathed," he reported to Susan Glassman in a letter of January 16. "There were 300 passengers and 600 children. Next to me a priest smoked cigars. He had a dozen in his upper coat pocket and said that'll be just about enough for the trip. Then came cold supper. Ham wrapped around asparagus, roast beef in red something and glazed chicken breast with a first lieutenant's stripe in red pimento. . . . Everybody dying of heat."[5] What struck Bellow upon arrival was the beauty of the island's vegetation, beginning with the "great mahogany tree waving its skirts at my window," and the constant noise, especially at night: "loud trailer-trucks, Sherman tanks, juke boxes. The Puerto Riqueños adore noise. It proves something to them. Ah yes—dog fights, too. At 3 am" (dogs appear in a later, undated letter to Ralph Ellison, where they are described as "Asiatic—wandering tribes of mongrels. They turn up in all the fashionable places, and in the modern university buildings, the cafeterias—there are always a few hounds sleeping in a cool classroom"). "Perhaps the noise means something," Bellow reiterates in the Ellison letter, which is why, at least at the beginning, he "tr[ied] to tune in." Soon, though, Botsford's offer to have him lodge at his place in Cupey Alto, a forty-five-minute drive from the noise of Río Piedras, began to appeal. In the memoir Botsford describes the road to Cupey Alto as flanked by avocado trees, while on the far side of the house "the property declines with prickly pineapples, pink grapefruit, oranges, lemons and limes" (p. 324). Later in Bellow's stay, the Botsfords moved to a second house in San Lorenzo, to the east of Cupey Alto.

Lodging with the Botsfords had its drawbacks. In addition to Botsford and his wife, Annie, whom Bellow describes in the letter of January 16 to Susan as kind and generous, there were "three kids, and maid." The kids were "lovely" but they were noisy. The noise bothered Bellow in the mornings in particular, when he worked in a dark cool room at the back of the house. There was also the matter of transport. Until he got a car of his own he had to be driven everywhere; the buses were unreliable and "I see now that a Vespa is suicidal. The driving makes Rome and Paris look like Wellesley and Vassar" (in the undated letter to Ellison he reports that the "drivers read at the wheel, they sing, they eat and they screw while driving"). The Botsfords, however, were keen. Annie doted on Bellow, calling him "dear . . . like a child you want to cuddle" (p. 471). The children doted as well, when not being yelled at for making noise. Away from his desk, Bellow giggled a lot with the children and talked to them like adults, something he could do, Botsford thought, because they weren't his. The Botsfords lived well in Puerto Rico (Botsford seems always to have lived well, at times with no visible means of support). On January 18 Bellow wrote to Susan from Botsford's tennis club, "two Cuba libres in me," "tropical sunset," "the palm trees doing their job in front. . . . The island is marvelous. You will fall in love with it." On weekends he joined the family and other visitors on expeditions. "Often we drove into town together," Botsford writes in the memoir, "we lollygagged on the beach. Saul was partial to clear water and to the lechoncito on which we lunch. He swam ably and did calisthenics on his beach-towel" (p. 452).[6]

At first Bellow found the heat of the island stupefying. "I feel the tropics. I have bad dreams," he writes to Susan on January 20. "Still, I have been getting up earlier because the cows low and the sun bursts in, and at the same time mildly excited as well as depressed. It's probably a great deal physiological." Three days later he again writes to Susan—they are writing almost daily now—of trying "to wake up from this pressing, beautiful heat, everlasting summer and the depressed sense of having come out of the movies at midday." He has been advised "to rest more and give up the Northern tempo" but he can't. "I adore running and dislike repose. . . . Shall I lie under a tree with eyes shut and mouth open, like a child, and let the lizards chase over me?" (or, to Ellison, in another undated letter, "drift with the stray dogs and the lizards and wonder how many ways a banana leaf can split"). A week later, on January 28, he announces that he has left the Botsfords and taken a room on campus while looking for a place where he and Susan, who was to visit in March, could be on their own. "I begin now to thrive better." On January 30 he reports to Susan that he has a car, the product of "a very elaborate financial arrangement" engineered by Botsford. "I take a loan, Keith buys a station wagon with it, and I have his Volkswagen for the term and it is or should be tax-deductible." The place he eventually found was on the outskirts of Río Piedras, a basement apartment in a house belonging to Jack Delano, a colleague of Botsford's, for a time manager of the island's state-owned television station. Delano, according to Botsford, was "a charmer, a gifted musician, photographer, and idealist agitator" (p. 328), part of a loose circle of leftist exiles and expats from both the New Deal and the Spanish Civil War (p. 334). Jorge Enjuto Bernal, the rector's assistant, was "a remnant of republican pre-war Spain" (p. 334).

Herzog progressed nicely on the island, had "grown big and fat," Bellow wrote to Richard Stern in another undated letter. "The first pages you saw were only throat clearings. I amaze myself. I don't recognize myself. So meek and yet so terrible. As for P.R., it does its stuff: sun, oranges, bananas, fish, incredible noise." To Susan, on February 2, Bellow describes going "a little faster with the book, and a little carelessly because I think it's better just now, invites variety . . . it's necessary now to stick out my neck a bit more." On February 15, again to Susan, he confesses that "I *feel* so much about this story, I can't accept the formal limits, and yet those formal limits were set to protect the book from the desperate feelings themselves." When classes began in March progress on the book was unimpeded. The syllabus for the literature course Bellow taught, "Character in the Novel," was made up of books he knew well (by Stendhal, Flaubert, Dreiser, Tolstoy, Dostoyevsky). According to a fellow instructor in the English Department, Bernard Lockwood, who sat in on the course, Bellow would "stand in front of the classroom, kind of shy, folding his arms over each other, look at the ceiling, and start to talk. . . . If someone had taped those lectures, they could have been published as is, without changing a comma or semicolon."[7] Bellow's creative writing course was enlivened by the presence of at least one strong writer, William Kennedy, at the time managing editor of the *San Juan Star*, later a Pulitzer Prize winner (for *Ironweed*, one of a series of novels set in his native Albany, New York). In 1961, Kennedy, who had not yet published any fiction, sent Bellow a manuscript and was accepted immediately on the course. "You don't need instruction," Bellow remembered telling him. "What you need is a publisher."[8] In class, Kennedy took Bellow's criticisms of his work "very seriously":

He would explain that my writing was "fatty"—I was saying every-thing twice and I had too many adjectives. He said it was also occa-sionally "clotty"—it was imprecision he was talking about. . . . When he pointed that out to me, I would go back through the whole book and slash—it turned me into a real fiction editor of my own copy, and it later helped when *I* became a teacher. . . . Bellow also talked about being prodigal. He said a writer shouldn't be parsimonious with his work, but "prodigal, like nature." . . . I never became that kind of writer, but I think the effusion, the principle was impor-tant. I was never afraid of writing too much, never thought that just because you've written a sentence it means something, or it's a good sentence just because you've written it.[9]

Bellow also stressed the importance of not giving up. One needed tal-ent, certainly, "but after that, it's character." When Kennedy asked what Bellow meant by character, he "smiled at me, and never said any-thing," a silence Kennedy interpreted as meaning "character is equiva-lent to persistence." In addition to giving advice, Bellow played a part in getting Kennedy's earliest fiction published. He was also instrumental in finding a publisher for *Ironweed* (1983). After at least nine publish-ers had turned it down, Bellow wrote to Viking to say that "he didn't think it was proper for his [Bellow means his own] former publisher to let a writer like Kennedy go begging." As Kennedy remembers it, "two days later I got a call from Viking saying they wanted to pub-lish *Ironweed* and what did I think of the possibility of publishing *Legs* [1975] and *Billy Phelan* [1978] again at the same time."[10] Only Bellow's performance as a lecturer disappointed. In Botsford's words, the public address he was required to deliver was "desultory and off-hand." When the rector expressed dismay, Botsford told him to "blame Herzog; his head is full" (p. 453).[11]

BOTSFORD MIGHT ALSO HAVE told Don Jaime to blame Susan Glass-man, with whom Bellow was falling in love, or more deeply in love, while in Puerto Rico. Susan had first met Bellow at Bard in the summer of 1956, but the meeting that led to their affair took place several years later, at the University of Chicago, where Bellow had come to deliver a talk at Hillel House, the Jewish campus organization.[12] Susan had been brought to the talk by Philip Roth, whom she was dating.[13] Roth had met her in a class at the university. "She was very glamorous, certainly for a university classroom and she was very pretty." Like everyone who met her, Roth was immediately struck by Susan's eyes, "startling eyes. She was a beautiful girl. Slender and she dressed very well. She looked 'dressed.' I remember she wore gloves sometimes, long, long gloves."[14]

In addition to being beautiful and glamorous, Susan was smart. After Wellesley College, she did graduate work in English at Harvard, continuing her studies at the University of Chicago. Though she got her MA, she never enrolled in a PhD program. According to her cousin, Stanley Katz, to whom she was close, "she didn't quite know what she wanted to do" and "certainly never had a conventional academic ambition." But she was serious. "She thought of herself as an intellectual, she presented herself as an intellectual." When Bellow met her at Hillel House, she was living at home again, at 3800 Lake Shore Drive, on the North Side of the city. Her father, Dr. Frank Glassman, was a prominent orthopedic surgeon at Michael Reese Hospital, for a time the doctor to both the Chicago Bears football team and the Blackhawks hockey team.[15] He was a big man, over six feet, large-boned, with red hair. Stanley Katz describes him as "hearty, garrulous, overbearing," with a surgeon's self-confidence, "a dominant presence in any room he was in." Dominant and crude: in *More Die of Heartbreak*, a character very much like Glassman, a "medical big shot" (p. 106), takes his new son-in-law, the world-renowned botanist Benn Crader, along on his hospital rounds. "He had done this before and people got a kick out of it, mostly, masquerading as doctors" (p. 213). Benn and his father-in-law enter a ward filled with old women: "He had saved them up for me. They were all hip cases, pinned hips, and they didn't need more than a glance. . . . He was barging in and out of the rooms, pushing away the door and everything else, yanking off the covers. The ladies' hair was dyed and set, they had on lipstick, other makeup, they wore lacy bed jackets, and then there were the stitched scars, and short thighs, and warm, shiny shins, the mound of Venus and the scanty hair—all those bald mounds." Later, in the corridor, the father-in-law says: "I get a pretty girl once in a while. As a patient, don't misunderstand. It's not always old snatch" (pp. 213–14). According to Daniel Bellow, Bellow and Susan's son, Frank Glassman gave Bellow just such a tour at Michael Reese Hospital.

Glassman was handsome, but it was generally agreed that Susan's looks came from her mother, Dolores. According to Katz, all the women on her mother's side of the family, including her aunts and grandmother, were "gorgeous." Daniel Bellow says his grandmother was "drop-dead gorgeous; she'd make you drop dead." Barbara Wiesenfeld, a lifelong friend of Susan's, describes Dolores as "the epitome of style"; Katz remembers her as "very bright and very sophisticated," "culture was very important to her." Both mother and daughter, Katz adds, "cared a lot about social status." Though the Glassmans lived in comfort, they did so on what Frank earned. Frank drove a Cadillac and belonged to the Standard Club (for German Jews, a cut above the Covenant Club, Maury's club, for *ostjuden*). But the Glassmans could not afford a country club, Susan went to a public high school, unlike her friends, who went to private school (as did her younger brother, Philip), and the family did not take expensive vacations.

"I had always heard about Susan when I was growing up," recalls Joan Schwartz (who is in part the model for Katrina Goliger in "What Kind of Day Did You Have?"). Among "the professional Jewish families" of the North Side, she was "legendarily brainy and beautiful." "She was the most beautiful girl in Chicago," Katz says, "everyone knew that. . . . All the college men wanted to take her out." When Schwartz first met Harold Rosenberg, with whom she later had a long affair, it was at a talk he gave in 1964 at the University of Chicago. Susan was there with Bellow. "I was much more interested in meeting Susan and Saul than Rosenberg," Schwartz remembers. When introduced to Susan, "I was dumbstruck, she was blindingly beautiful," also "utterly uninterested in me." Another close friend, Diane Silverman, recalls seeing Susan for the first time at a later talk given by Bellow at the University of Chicago. Silverman was an undergraduate, "one of a host of young female students who had ambitions to write." After the talk she went up to meet Bellow. "There were all these young women sort of wanting to shake his hand, to flirt with him, and I looked around and I saw this incredibly beautiful young woman." It was Susan, standing to one side, watching the women crowd around Bellow. She herself had been such a woman. Roth remembers Bellow at the Hillel talk as "very engaging, tremendously charming," full of "self-delight, in the best sense, generosity." When he finished speaking, Roth recalls, Susan said "I'm just going to go up and say hello to him. I said 'fine.' Turned out to be the best thing that ever happened to me, and the worst thing that ever happened to Saul. I could see that Saul was very animated in talking to her. But I was so young it never even occurred to me that a man of forty [forty-two] would be interested in a woman of twenty-three. How could that be? Now I know about men of seventy-five interested in girls of twenty-three."

The relationship developed over the course of Bellow's visits to Chicago and Susan's to New York and can be traced in correspondence.[16] After the terrible encounter with Sasha in Minnesota in April 1959, Bellow traveled to Chicago where he saw Susan, among others. In late May Susan was in New York for the reading of *The Last Analysis*. In July she came east again to stay at Tivoli, and in August she was with Bellow during his week in Chicago with Adam. Throughout this period Susan was thinking about a move to New York, a move that frightened her but which Bellow encouraged. She didn't like Chicago and was depressed about having to live with her parents. In her letters from the summer of 1960, she admits to worries about Bellow's feelings. "You never speak your mind on a subject at any given moment, do you?" she writes on August 27. In a second letter written the same day, she complains of his volatility: "that grim voice of yours that starts those announcements with 'Now look . . .' Then you call, day rates no less, and say you're nutty about me." She writes a lot about being depressed, and after one gloom-filled letter Bellow gently rebukes her in a letter of September 1. He's sorry she's low, but her being low makes it "all the more important" that he keep his balance (which is to say, that she not bring him down). As for the move east, it is "*not* so hard. . . . Besides, in me you have a friend. I've never refused my friendship, now have I?"

Susan could be self-absorbed as well as somber. Roth found her "difficult," "perhaps the first man or woman I'd met, I was still in my early twenties, who had an air of entitlement about her." Barbara Wiesenfeld had known Susan since grade school and always wondered why she wasn't "happier, more secure, lighter." When she was in a good mood "she was great, but when she was in a dark mood it would spill over . . . there was some sort of heaviness about her." Wiesenfeld thinks a physical condition underlay this heaviness. Susan's paternal grandfather died at a relatively early age of an aneurism, a fact that, according to Stanley Katz, Susan's father was "very aware of." "He took out a large insurance policy on his life because he was convinced he was going to die young." He died in his sixties of an aneurism. Susan, too, died of an aneurism in her sixties. "She always felt she was going to die early," Wiesenfeld recalls. "She didn't feel all that well. She was sweet and she was high-minded but she always had a little pressure on her brain." In *Humboldt's Gift*, Charlie Citrine's wife, Denise, has something of Susan's heaviness: "Her hair was piled on top of her head and gave it too much weight. If she hadn't been beautiful you wouldn't have noticed the disproportion. . . . She was a burdened woman. Getting out of bed to make breakfast was almost more than she could face. Taking a cab to the hairdresser was also very hard. The beautiful head was a burden to the beautiful neck" (p. 219). Like Susan, Denise is interested in politics, that is in electoral politics, Stevenson, the Kennedys. When Citrine is invited to the White House—as Bellow was—Denise corners President Kennedy. Citrine watches her animated conversation with Kennedy and thinks "she'd have made him an excellent Secretary of State, if some way could be found to wake her before 11 a.m." (p. 59).

Denise is not the only character in a Bellow novel to resemble Susan. Matilda Layamon in *More Die of Heartbreak* also has trouble waking: "she hated waking—*hated* it" (p. 136). According to her husband, Benn, "the trouble she had making the transition from sleep to waking suggested a struggle between two natures." When Matilda "reluctantly" wakens, she needs silence: "Sometimes she shut Benn up altogether. She said, 'Oh, for Chrissakes, Benno, don't make heavy conversation before I'm awake. It gives me such a headache'" (p. 137). Matilda makes "a cult of deep sleep" (p. 285), a sleep "devoid of consciousness of any kind" (p. 137). There is a connection here between Denise and Matilda and Bellow's fictional portraits of his brother Maury, especially as Simon in *The Adventures of Augie March* and Julius in *Humboldt's Gift* (both characters are discussed in Chapter 3). When Simon dives into the waters of Lake Michigan, he does so, thinks Augie, "with a thought of never coming back to the surface alive, as if he went to take a blind taste of the benefits of staying down. . . . I knew it made a strong appeal to him to go down and not come up again" (p. 647). Earlier, as quoted in Chapter 3, Augie sees suicidal as well as attacking impulses in "the way [Simon] drove and the way he leaped forward in arguments, hit him who would; he kept a tire tool under the driver's seat for his weapon in traffic arguments, and he cursed everybody in the street, running through lights and scattering pedestrians" (p. 640). Julius in *Humboldt's Gift* is subject to similar impulses, figured, according to brother Charlie, in his search for "a seascape devoid of landmarks" (p. 411); "the inhuman water, the middle of the ocean, the formless deep, the world-enfolding sea" (p. 410) signify to Julius, or so Charlie believes, a "release from the daily way and the horror of tension" (p. 411)—that is, from the life he has chosen, or, as far as he's concerned, from life.

Neither Denise nor Matilda is explicitly linked with a death wish, as are Simon and Julius. Maury's son, Joel, does not believe his father was a man in search of release or secretly despairing, like his fictional alter egos. Susan, however, in letters of August 27 and 28, 1960, writes of times "when I hardly had courage to get through the day, much less to be." Her diary for the years 1955 to 1959, she tells Bellow, is full of despairing entries and "it took the death of Barbara's mother to make me see how I was flirting with my own." For both Julius and Simon, the desire for oblivion is linked to a choice of money and status over love. Matilda and Denise are also much concerned with money and status, as are their fathers. Denise's father, like Frank Glassman, comes from "the West Side Chicago gutters" (p. 43); Matilda's father "was raised near the old produce market" (p. 116) and "belonged to an earlier somatic type, that of immigrants and the first generation of their children" (p. 150). According to Stanley Katz, Frank Glassman was "bitter" about having to live off his salary, about not having as much money as richer friends and relations, "and Susan must have grown up with that." Matilda and Denise have little patience with the spiritual or nonmaterial interests of their husbands, especially when these interests are linked to the intensity of childhood experience. "She doesn't care for that far-away-and-long-ago stuff?" Benn's nephew asks. "'That's it,' said Uncle" (p. 116). In this impatience they are like Simon and Julius, who want only to forget their "gutter" emotions and origins. Susan's letters convey deep feeling, but she, too, had little patience with her husband's attraction to Humboldt Park, and to some of his relations and childhood friends, whom she thought of as crude. Charlie Citrine connects the intensity of his love for his earliest relations—his sense that they are still alive somewhere—to the possibility of an afterlife. "Love is gratitude for being. This love would be hate," he tells Julius, "if the whole thing was nothing but a gyp." Such a speech makes no impact on Julius, "one of the biggest builders of south-east Texas. Such communications were prohibited under the going mental rules," rules sanctioned by "the many practical miracles" of American materialism: "To accept the finality of death was part of his package, however. There was to be no sign of us left" (p. 382). It is possible that Bellow's reserve in the early correspondence with Susan owes something to his sensing in her this complex of thought and feeling.

THROUGHOUT THEIR CORRESPONDENCE in the summer and fall of 1960, Bellow and Susan address each other as "Dolly." "Be my sweet and balanced Dolly" ends Bellow's letter of September 1. But there's distance on his side. Susan is his "friend"; there's not much talk of love until he goes to Puerto Rico. By the end of September, Susan had arrived in New York and was looking for a job and an apartment in Manhattan, writing to Bellow at Tivoli, visiting with him on the weekends. As he bucks her up, she bucks him up. When he worries that he's treated Sasha badly (before he learns of the affair with Ludwig), Susan reassures him, in blunt terms, in a letter of October 3: "With Sondra you were stupid and unrealistic, but you were not seeking evil for her." On October 19 she writes enthusiastically of Norman O. Brown's *Life Against Death: The Psychoanalytical Meaning of History* (1959), an enthusiasm Bellow does not share (a decade later he has Artur Sammler condemn Brown along with the German-born political philosopher Herbert Marcuse, with whom Brown was often linked). Susan now had an apartment on the Upper West Side at 68th Street, and would soon have an unsatisfactory job at *Horizon* magazine (the American *Horizon*, launched in 1958, a magazine of literature and the arts, in its way as high-minded as the British *Horizon*, edited by Cyril Connolly). Susan's letters report dinners with the Covicis, the Ashers, the Tarcovs. There seems not to have been any question of her accompanying Bellow to Puerto Rico in January, another sign of hesitancy on his part, caused, perhaps, by his still carrying on with Rosette Lamont, who knew about Susan and thought of her as a rival.

Like Susan, Rosette claimed to know what was best for Bellow and how to make him happy. She, too, was a serious person, often earnest in manner, and earnest about sex. Her fictional counterpart in *Herzog*, Ramona Donsell, is a student rather than a professor, but a serious student; this is a problem for Moses, since "in principle, he opposed affairs with students, even with students like Ramona Donsell, who were obviously made for them." Though Moses describes himself as "a wild man," he remains "in frightful earnest." "Of course it was just this earnestness," he adds, "that attracted Ramona" (pp. 430, 431). Rosette was assertive and quick to take offense, though Susan, too, could take offense (as when she objects to Bellow writing, in a letter of January 23, 1961, that "I really do miss you—even your earnestness; sometimes it has struck me as funny, but I miss it").[17] Rosette writes on October 1, 1960, that her "blood boiled" when Bellow claimed "that I made you break with your friend Susie" (something he seems to have told her he'd done, though the extant correspondence suggests otherwise). It is hardly surprising that Bellow's complicated love life involved him in deception. The Rosette letter gives a sense of what it was like to be romantically involved with Bellow in this period:

> Please remember that when you asked me to bear with you through July [when Susan was with him at Tivoli] it was I who suggested we stop seeing each other for *two weeks* or more. Then she arrived and you wrote me a frantic note signed The Repentant Sinner and in which you asked me "not to keep my countenance from you." Then we saw each other. You said it was good to come back to me and you suggested that after your return from Chicago [where he was with Susan as well as Adam] we go away together and really try "to make it." You came to spend a week with me *while your friend Susie was still in the city.* This was ample proof of what you wanted. *You* made all the decisions and I simply agreed. Then, when I saw how serious you were I broke with *all* my previous attachments in order to be completely fair to you, to me, to us. You say it's important for you to feel you make the decisions. *You made them all.* The only decision I made was that of stopping our relationship, since it did not seem to *live* and *develop.*

Rosette did not stop the relationship, responding in a letter of November 3 to a "gentle, tender letter" from Bellow, "full of the grief of hesitancy." Bellow was to go to Puerto Rico, she was to go to Greece, then the Soviet Union. But after these trips? "As for 'choosing' I do not want you to make any choice, nor am I choosing either. I have a strange awareness that something has been chosen for us." Later Rosette asks "how can it be weakness to choose someone vital, someone who has warmth and self-respect, someone who comes to you with love and trust. I think it is weakness to reject this vital love, to say it is too good, to suspect and fear it." In describing herself as a woman of "warmth and self-respect," Rosette may be implying a contrast with Susan. But Susan's letters do not lack these qualities. While Bellow was in Puerto Rico, he asked her to run errands for him. Her accounts of meetings with Volkening, Asher, Covici, the man from Laurel-Dell (publisher of *Great Jew-*

ish Stories), are perfectly confident, as are her written responses to the pages of *Herzog* Bellow sent her. In *More Die of Heartbreak*, Matilda lacks warmth but hardly self-respect. "You'll be much happier," she tells Benn toward the end of the novel, "if I feel my standards are being met" (p. 287). In *Humboldt's Gift*, Denise is fierce rather than warm (understandably, since we mostly see her battling with Citrine over the divorce) and hardly lacking in self-respect. Before the divorce, however, according to Citrine, she "would start up in the night and sob and say that she was *nothing*" (p. 302). There is no such note in Susan's letters to Bellow during their separation, unless one counts a persistent strain of longing. Though she was busy at her job and often out with friends, her life in New York seems, from the letters, mostly to have been spent waiting to be summoned to Puerto Rico.

Bellow's letters during this period are briefer than Susan's. When Susan did not immediately respond to the pages of *Herzog* he sent her, he worried that she didn't like them. He kept her abreast of developments with *The Noble Savage*, informing her on January 30, 1961, that "Ludwig hasn't answered Keith's letter. He has two days more and we pull the trapdoor." (When the question arose of whether and how to announce Ludwig's departure from the magazine, Susan offered advice. "I certainly don't think an editorial statement has to be made in the magazine, enclosed in a black-bordered box yet," she writes on February 7. "Why call attention and who is it you have in mind that you feel you have to explain to?") About her work at *Horizon*, Bellow offers encouragement and sympathy, as he does when she complains of problems with her family. Toward the end of January, he, too, begins to chafe under the separation. In an undated letter, probably written at the very end of the month, he writes: "So you'll be here March 1st! A long wait, but it was my idea, so I'll teach myself patience." Later he declares: "Dolly, I love you dearly. Use a typewriter" (Susan's handwriting is maddeningly illegible). She writes back that she misses him so much she can't sleep at night; she finds their separation "more and more pointless every day. . . . I'm tired of building my character. Henderson says 'enough becoming' (more or less he says that)." On February 3 Bellow writes that he "got drunk last night on something that might be called a date, but more awful. I filled up with rum and when I got home I couldn't sleep. . . . I want you to come. Will you come, dolly? I'll find out when Easter holiday is. It's toward the end of March, like. I shall fight off the mañana and inform myself definitely today." The letter ends with news about the University of Chicago, where work is offered for next year. "I wouldn't want to go there without you either," he writes, "be assured. But I'm thinking." On February 6 Bellow offers a confession: "I feel so very sweet towards you, I'd melt your snows for you if I were there, on 68th St. You know it puzzles me not to have feelings for anyone else. I was once ubiquitously rousable and I even worry, I grieve at times, at my lack of interest in these passing chicks. Is it maturity or frost? I ask myself. Perhaps you can tell me."

AS BELLOW WORKED ON *Herzog* and wrote letters to Susan, he worried about the year ahead. Greg was doing well in high school, getting good grades, and had shown an interest in the University of Chicago. "I don't see how I can turn down the U of C—because of him," he writes to Susan. "He's applied for a scholarship. So the money I'm paid there will be the least of it. As for you and me, dolly, I am not supposing that by next winter there'll be such a problem ab't Chicago as you anticipate. . . . I love you very much, Susie." The job at Chicago was one he had been offered earlier but had been forced to turn down because of the Ford grant (Ralph Ellison got it instead, partly at Bellow's suggestion). Richard Stern had arranged the original offer and renewed it now for Winter Quarter 1962, January to March. Bellow would be "Celebrity in Residence" in the English Department, a job title concocted by the university's public relations office. On February 27, 1961, Bellow wrote to Stern from Puerto Rico to say he expected to be in Chicago at the end of May, when he would be "quite willing to talk [about the post, he means]. Even about Susan, if you like. I think by now I know her quite well. I can tell you more about her than most others can tell me. I shrink from marriage still, but not from Susan."

Bellow stayed on in Puerto Rico until mid-May, describing himself in an undated reply to a letter of April 7 from Susan as the only person "in all the island . . . steadily at work." Back in Manhattan, after her March visit, Susan was job hunting, having given up the *Horizon* job to come to Puerto Rico "for *us*, and you wanted me to." On May 6, she writes of a fifth-grade teaching job at the Dalton School, a fashionable private school on the Upper East Side ("not too interested in fifth grade but very interested in Dalton"). In the letter of April 7, Susan is loving but also recalls rocky moments during the visit to Puerto Rico: "your getting irritable, my getting resentful . . . you only spoke your mind in rages . . . and then I was angry, and worse, withdrew." But Bellow was unperturbed, writing on April 8, "first I missed you hungrily, and now I'm more peaceful, and in about ten days I'll have gotten every advantage of solitude and I'll have a head full of ache and a void at heart." Four days later, in "cheerful" mood, he wrote to Ralph Ross to say "I have a very sweet girl, Susan, and one of these days, when I stop trembling at the word, I may get married again." Susan herself "ached" for Bellow's return in the April 7 letter.

Yet in a letter that hasn't survived, Susan announced that she would not be accompanying Bellow to Chicago in January. Bellow describes this letter, in an undated reply, as "downcast," admitting that he "didn't like [it] very much." He wonders if Susan's decision was a product of parental pressure or depression, even suggesting she consider medication ("It can't hurt, I hear, to take this Librium"). He also wonders if the contrast between New York and Chicago, which she seems to have visited shortly after returning from Puerto Rico, may have played a part in the decision, "the normal swing of coming in safe to New York, and being in your own place, and the friends and the glamour after all of the Big Town, to solitude again [in Chicago] and bitter thoughts." There were practical reasons for the decision as well, which may account for the parental pressure. Bellow was going to Chicago for Winter Quarter only and Susan would have to quit whatever job she'd gotten in New York only months after getting it. Then she'd have to find another job when she and Bellow returned from Chicago in early spring. Though Bellow seems on the surface to have accepted Susan's decision, in another undated letter he subtly disparages it. He has had dinner in Puerto Rico with a friend of his brother Maury. This friend, a woman from Washington, who worked as a lobbyist, "told me how a Senator tried to lay her in the Capitol during a roll-call vote. . . . She said, 'Only after the vote.'" The anecdote reminds Bellow of something Susan once said about the role of material advantage in love relations. "You are right about these marriage-business alliances, of course, but I suppose this represents the efforts of people who have given up the love-quest to find a reason for being together." He was not such a person: "my only vote, dolly, I cast for beautiful you." Then, perhaps with Susan's decision about Chicago in mind, he adds, "but people who see God in one another . . . [the ellipsis is his] aren't on the make in NYC." "How gladly I'd have crept into your bed last night," he writes on April 24. "I missed you badly. And today, and daily and especially nightly. . . . My heart is on 68th St. Love, you say? Love." Yet the separation and the solitude served him well. On May 1 he writes of receiving "a raving letter from Pat [Covici, about *Herzog*], foaming with superlatives." On the eve of his departure for New York, Bellow writes that "getting off this island is to me identical in feeling with the finishing of this book—two prongs of the same force."

WHEN BELLOW RETURNED TO Tivoli in May 1961, Ralph Ellison was preparing to leave. He and Fanny had a new apartment overlooking the Hudson, one in which Ellison felt he could write; he would move out when the Bard semester ended in June. Ellison's time at Tivoli, according to his biographer, Arnold Rampersad, had been "often a joy, albeit at times also lonely and melancholy. But he had arrived expecting to polish off his novel. He hadn't."[18] Bellow, meanwhile, had *Herzog* to finish, and another rewrite of his play, which, if he could get it produced, would make him, he told William Phillips, "rich as a pig."[19] Bellow looked forward to the spring at Tivoli—"fall and spring are Tivoli's best seasons," he told the Kazins in a letter of July 26—but almost as soon as he got there he was on the move, "a run at top speed, from my descent at Pan Am."[20] Money was part of the motive. To make ends meet he agreed to teach at a two-week writing conference at Wagner College in Staten Island, to deliver an endowed lecture at the University of Michigan, and to write lots of reviews of books but also of films (for *Horizon*, where Susan had worked).[21] "I have no money coming in and I must hack," he wrote to Botsford in a letter of June 7, "and since I'm not too good at it I hack for a long time at some trifle and spend weeks brooding unhappily over assignments then push them over in a single morning, usually a Sunday when I have a headache and a nightmare beforehand to stir me up."

The title of the Hopwood Lecture at the University of Michigan, delivered on May 25, was "Where Do We Go from Here? The Future of Fiction," a theme rehearsed and returned to in other essays of the period, including the twenty-thousand-word "Literature" chapter for *The Great Ideas Today* (discussed in Chapter 12). As with the essays Bellow produced in the period immediately preceding the publication of *Henderson the Rain King*, these can be seen as attempts to prepare the ground for *Herzog*. The lecture begins by examining the fashionable assertion that the novel is dead and with Bellow's claim that whatever truth there is in this assertion derives from the disappearance of "the person, the character, as we knew him in the plays of Sophocles or Shakespeare, in Cervantes, Fielding, and Balzac."[22] He then identifies a second cause of decline: the fact that in much modern fiction, "drama has passed from external action to internal movement. In Proust and Joyce we are enclosed by and held within a single consciousness" (not a consistent "personality," with reliable qualities like courage, fearfulness, even unreliability, but "a quaintly organized chaos of instinct and spirit"). A third claim is that the novel's future requires a return to character as disclosed in action in the world. This claim, which is implicit in the Hopwood Lecture, is made explicit in a long article Bellow published on February 11, 1962, in *The New York Times Book Review*, "Facts That Put Fancy to Flight," in which he sees the internality or introspection of modern fiction as having provoked a reaction in readers and novelists who overvalue the external world, the world of fact.[23]

After the Hopwood Lecture, Bellow went on to Chicago to visit Adam, now aged four. They went to the zoo and the aquarium and shopped for toys. "I saw Sondra, too, for a moment," he wrote to Botsford on June 7, "and I might have seen Jack, I suppose, if I'd cared to look for him." Sasha's father was suing Sasha over her mother's will, and had let Bellow know (presumably through their mutual friend, Sam Goldberg) "that he would go to court to witness against Jack and his daughter if I wanted to bring suit for custody of the child." This offer did not appeal: "I want nothing to do with any of them. Through the kid, I'm already involved, but I mean to hold relations with the whole bunch to a sanitary minimum." While in Chicago, Bellow also saw Dick Stern about the "Celebrity in Residence" job. In July an early version of the first chapter of *Herzog* was published in *Esquire*, raising expectations. Alfred Kazin wrote to say how much he liked it; Ralph Ross told Bellow he had "the best prose of anyone writing fiction in the country"; Harvey Swados even described Bellow as "the *only one* of my contemporaries in whom I feel the capacity for greatness that I do in myself."[24] Now began the steady stream of invitations, job offers, honors, and awards that was to accompany Bellow until the day he died. Robert Lowell and Elizabeth Hardwick, husband and wife, wrote separately to recruit him as a contributor to the first issue of *The New York Review of Books*. Hardwick put aside her views on *Henderson* and pressed Bellow to join Auden, Kazin, Trilling, and other distinguished recruits: "You are the one we want more than anything, truly. I can't tell you how seriously we feel we need you because of your absolute leadership (it was decided at our meeting) in what is called 'the field of fiction.'"[25] Shortly after the *Herzog* extract appeared, Bellow arrived at Wagner College for the writing conference, which was organized by Rust Hills, the literary editor of *Esquire*. Hills chose three tutors for the conference: Robert Lowell for poetry, Edward Albee for drama, and Bellow for fiction.

The conference worked them hard. Staten Island, Bellow wrote to Botsford, was boiling in July, with "an average heat of 106 degrees, like a stokehold."[26] He describes himself as "sweating over papers and talking 12 hours a day till my mouth was like an ashpit." There were seventeen students in his fiction class, several with talent. Donald Barthelme, described by a fellow student, Susan Dworkin, as "wry—drunk a lot," produced a story which Bellow didn't think much of, but that was later widely anthologized. Barthelme had a good time at the conference and, in Dworkin's words, "didn't care what Saul Bellow thought of his work." The same could not be said for other students, including "Buzz" Farbar, later a close friend of Norman Mailer's and an actor in his movies, Arno Karlen, already published and "said to be the most promising writer among us," and Dworkin herself, nineteen at the time. When Bellow described Dworkin's writing as "just fine," "very good," she "couldn't remember ever being so happy." Then she overheard him at a party confessing "that he always told young writers they were good. He hadn't the heart to do otherwise. They needed encouragement so much, much more than they needed hard criticism." She went to her room in tears and "for weeks after at home, I cried." Something else Bellow said at the party helped to explain the peculiar manner in which he listened when the students read their work: "He sat with his thumb pressed to his temple, like a man rehearsing suicide. Sometimes he gazed into space—and when he was forced to look at us it was with *fear*." What Bellow said at the party was that "he was scared by the need in their faces; he remembered his own need when he was young."[27]

Arno Karlen in particular aroused in Bellow memories of his youth. Karlen was so upset by Bellow's treatment of him at the conference that he wrote to tell him so, though he also described Bellow as "an absolutely brilliant reader of people's fiction, utterly apposite and penetrating— a brilliant teacher."[28] Bellow's response, in a letter of August 17, echoes what Dworkin overheard. He begins with an apology: "I'm sincerely sorry if I offended you at the conference." He understands why Karlen is upset: "I myself have often been indignant with older writers, and I know how you must have felt." That Karlen is talented "was so obvious to me that I fixed at once on the things that were less satisfactory. Among these were tendencies present in me, and superabundantly present, at your age [Karlen was twenty-four in 1961]. In scolding you, was I perhaps correcting myself a long generation ago? 'Perhaps' is just rhetoric. It was positively so." Karlen was right to claim that his writing was on a "parallel track" to Bellow's. "I noted at once in your writing the power to cut through superfluities, the hardness of attack that I favor." That Karlen heard only Bellow's criticisms was easy for Bellow to understand, being similarly quick to take offense. If Bellow was tactless in his criticisms, it was partly because Karlen himself was so tough on his fellow students: "You had it all over most of the people there anyway, and weren't denied publication, and you might therefore have gone a little more softly with them, less gifted and less lucky as they were. An odd tightness or hardness came over you when they criticized you. I saw my own pale face twenty years ago, and I spoke and no doubt said the wrong thing." Bellow also admits to less laudable motives. He was angry with himself for having agreed to go to the conference: "To deal with seventeen people within ten days was not easy. And the financial reward was negligible." Also, "I frankly and willingly admit that to interrupt the writing of *Herzog* irritated me and possibly made me bearish." What he would not admit, however, were "failures of instruction." "I was there to make my own views clear; that's all anyone can do in this enterprise. To the best of my ability I did make them clear." Here and throughout the letter Bellow's tone is matter-of-fact, unembarrassed. "People who write," he tells Karlen, "tend to be despotic in life, as they often are towards their characters." The letter ends with him wishing Karlen luck.

According to Elinor Bergstein, another student at the conference, later author of the screenplay for the film *Dirty Dancing*, Bellow's attitude to the women students was formal and wary.[29] Bette Howland, also in the class, remembers things differently. Bellow took to Howland from the start, "since I'm from Chicago and probably reminded him of his relations, and actually I can write," and she and Bellow became lifelong friends, reading and commenting on each other's writing. Howland was raised in Chicago, in Lawndale, near Humboldt Park. Her father was a factory worker and her mother a "sometime social worker." After Marshall High School, she went to the University of Chicago on scholarship, "mainly to get out of the house." Then she enrolled in law school at the university, dropping out to marry "the first person who asked me," a neurophysiologist with whom she had two sons. The marriage lasted six years. By the time of the conference she was a single mother, had published several stories, but had never read anything by Bellow. Dworkin identifies Howland as the author of a harrowing story about an abortion, but Howland says the story was written by another student in the class. Dworkin describes Bellow as dismissing the story; Howland remembers Bellow praising it, though he did make a crude crack—a "Him with His Foot in His Mouth" crack—about not approving "women writers who wear their ovaries on their sleeves." Bellow the teacher, Howland recalls, "was in general, as I saw it, rather kind . . . liking the people there, mainly the ladies. It was fun." He was charming and the women found him attractive, though whether he made a pass at any of them she does not know. "Many of us heard his line," she recalls, "we were all exchanging it." Later, at a reading Bellow gave at the University of Iowa, where Howland was studying for an MFA, they met up again. "It did start out as it usually started out with women," Howland recalled, but "I soon realized there was no percentage in this, it was quite senseless, and we just became friends. He was a real pain in the neck in another kind of relationship."

Once back in Tivoli, Bellow was overwhelmed with *Noble Savage* tasks. As he wrote to one of the magazine's contributors, Louis Gallo, in a letter of June 15, "Editing has been more than I bargained for. I took it on with the usual good intentions, familiar underfoot en route to hell, and now it has become a full-time unpaid job, with all the troubles and injustices and errors for which executives get high salaries." There were worries about the magazine's future. On June 15 Bellow wrote to Botsford to say that Arthur A. Cohen of Meridian was willing to pay them each $1,500 per issue and "very much wants the magazine to continue" (like Aaron Asher, who was preoccupied at the moment "with an expecting wife"). Meridian was prepared to take a loss ("five or six thousand a year") but Bellow and Botsford had "to convince people that we were worth losing money on," especially since Meridian's funding company, World Books, was undergoing "a new upheaval." Ultimately, unless the magazine came close to selling thirty thousand copies its future would be precarious. The first three issues had gotten nowhere near this figure. On July 24 Bellow wrote again to Botsford. "The world, assailed by crisis, is not fighting over the *Noble Savage* at the bookstores." All he could advise was that they knuckle down, though "we might also attempt to spend less money, both of us." Six months later, on January 19, Bellow confessed to Susan, "I must abandon *The Noble Savage*. Can't handle the mail," and a year later, after sales of issue 4 showed no improvement, Meridian called it quits. On January 22, 1962, Aaron Asher wrote to say that "nothing is coming to you and Keith until 20,000 of an issue are sold, a pipe dream." On February 20, Asher wrote again to say "it's hopeless to continue with it." Issue 5 would go ahead and if it was to be the last issue, "let's really make the 'public' regret its disappearance."

ASHER'S LETTER WAS RECEIVED BY Bellow in Chicago, where he was "Celebrity in Residence." Susan remained in New York, having taken a job at the Dalton School, where she had been teaching all autumn. She was now Mrs. Saul Bellow. They had married in November, the month divorce terms were finally settled between Bellow and Sasha. On December 1, 1961, the *Chicago Tribune* published a brief marriage announcement:

> Dr. and Mrs. Frank Glassman of Lake Shore Drive were in New York recently for the marriage of their daughter, Miss Susan Alexandra Glassman, to Saul Bellow of Tivoli, N.Y. The new Mr. and Mrs. Bellow will make their home in New York City.

Neither the decision to marry nor the wedding is described in correspondence or interviews. In *More Die of Heartbreak*, Kenneth Trachtenberg offers an account of his Uncle Benn's decision to marry Matilda. "I ran through the facts as I then knew them: A beautiful woman unites herself with a world-famous botanist. He may think it will serve *his* needs. No, all the while she has been thinking what she can do with *him*. . . . Benn was a botanist looking for a wife, and he found a wife who wanted just such a botanist to be a host to celebrities. . . . Matilda had quite clear objectives. She knew what she wanted and she got it. He didn't know what he wanted, and he was going to get it" (p. 147). Bellow may have seen his marriage to Susan in this way, but their loving correspondence at the time paints a more complex picture. Benn Crader's motive for marrying is described by his nephew as "longing. *Such* longing! You can't expect longing of such depth to have, or to find, definitive objectives" (p. 107). In the autumn of 1961, while Susan taught and lived in Manhattan, and Bellow spent much of the week writing in Tivoli, they exchanged few letters. The letters he wrote to her from Chicago during Winter Quarter are full of longing, but are playful and affectionate rather than deep. Often they're about sex. "I miss you in the sack," he writes in a newsy letter postmarked January 9, 1962, "and I love you." Two days later: "Herzog is about to enter the final stages, not much else gets done, between teaching and writing and check-signing. When you come, perhaps I can catch up on reading as well as fucking. I begin to have erotic dreams about you." Later in the same letter: "now I'm off to fetch Adam, to take him to Lesha's party, take him home, come south, to lie down and wait for more dreams." On February 26 he writes "I miss you," signing off "Your loving *Husband*."

The University of Chicago made a big deal of its new "Celebrity in Residence." The Development Office sent out a press release describing Bellow as "one of the leading American writers of his generation," winner of "more awards than any prose writer of his time." There were further items about the course he would teach, "The Modern Novel and Its Heroes." It would be held on Mondays and Wednesdays from 3:30 to 5:00, limited to twenty-one third- and fourth-year undergraduates. Over the Winter Quarter, some ten weeks, it would discuss novels by Balzac, Flaubert, Tolstoy, Dostoyevsky, Hardy, Samuel Butler, Joyce, Lawrence, Hemingway, Faulkner, and Thomas Mann. One of the students in the course, Michael C. Kotkin, kept the notes he took in class. In an article about the course, he described Bellow as "simpatico," "charismatic," entering the room "with a twinkle in his eye" and an "engaging smile." Kotkin was struck by how little reference Bellow made to secondary sources. The sole critical work he mentioned was Erich Auerbach's *Mimesis: The Representation of Reality in Western Literature* (1946), a work of great learning, which ends, in a chapter on Virginia Woolf, by subtly disparaging modernist fictions.[30] The course's lone requirement was a five-page paper on the construction of character in one or several novels of the student's choosing. Here, too, Bellow "recommended that we look not at criticism but at essays written by the author or authors in question."[31] Bellow frequently discussed novels in pairs, reading *Père Goriot* with *Madame Bovary*, *Anna Karenina* with *Notes from Underground*. Themes familiar from recent essays—the decline of the hero, the interiority of modern fiction, the need to balance world and self—appear in Kotkin's notes. In discussing D. H.

Lawrence, Bellow claimed, according to Kotkin's notes, that "the novel of the twentieth century becomes more personal—the writer trying to solve in his book the problems he is trying to solve in his life," a claim that clearly applies to *Herzog*.

During the Winter Quarter Bellow stayed at an apartment on Ingleside Avenue, a minute's walk from campus. Shortly after he arrived, he reported in the letter of January 9, 1962, to Susan, he saw his brother Maury and sister, Jane. Maury gave Bellow "a handsome Irish tweed coat, the houndstooth check which seems to fit" (Kotkin describes Bellow as having a "middle-aged man's body, formerly slight and athletic, now spreading"). Relations between the brothers were tricky. "Apparently I insulted him bitterly," Bellow reported to Susan, "when he said he couldn't read any of my books, except a few chapters of *Augie*; the rest was nonsense to him and he couldn't understand how they could be published profitably. I said that after all he was not a trained reader, but devoted himself to business and love. He was offended and said I didn't *respect* him, and that I was a terrible snob. I thought I was being angelically mild and put my arms around him and said I was his loving brother, wasn't that better than heaping up grievances?" Maury had other reasons for being upset. He was soon in the papers again. On February 10 the *Chicago Daily Tribune* ran an article reporting that he and Marge had divorced. Marge was to receive a settlement of $312,000, plus their home in Florida. Maury's assets, she claimed, exceeded $2 million. She also testified that he "struck her on numerous occasions. Once, she said, he 'split my head open,' and she was hospitalized. On another, he blackened an eye." Yet the divorce pained her. Three months later, on May 18, after Bellow's return to Tivoli, she wrote from Florida: "I was divorced legally but not emotionally. But I suppose this too will pass. After all, I'm not broke. I wish money was my only problem, this I could handle." In the letter she invites Bellow and Susan to come to Florida when brother Sam Bellows and Sam's wife, Nina, were there, adding that "friends of mine are friends of the Glassmans and have known Susan for many years. They only say nice things about her and if a bunch of Canasta playing Lake Shore Drive women say nice things she must be nice."

ON MAY 11, 1962, Bellow and Susan were invited to a dinner at the White House in honor of André Malraux, at that time the French minister of culture. Over two hundred of the nation's leading writers, artists, musicians, and painters were invited, among them many old friends and colleagues: Robert Penn Warren and Eleanor Clark, Arthur Miller, Allen Tate and Caroline Gordon (no longer married, though they remained friends), Robert Lowell and Elizabeth Hardwick. Bellow wrote an "Aria" about the dinner for issue 5 of *The Noble Savage*, identifying himself only as "one of the editors" and explaining that he'd been invited "because the magazine has made so important a contribution to American culture." Surveying the other guests, he noted the presence of "several novelists and poets at one time strongly alienated, ex-intransigents, former enemies of society, old grumblers, and lifelong manger dogs, all having a hell of a good time, their faces beaming, their wives in evening gowns (could they afford them?)." Though not much taken with the orchestra, which played "a sort of Catskill-intercourse music," he was impressed by the Marines in braid, the butlers. Everyone was on their best behavior: "Only Adlai Stevenson preserved a shade of intellectual irony. Everybody else seemed absurdly and deeply tickled."[32] At one point the painter Mark Rothko "whispered privately to me that of course this is all a lot of crap and meant nothing to him. 'But my *sister*!' he said." When Bellow asked where she was, Rothko answered, "Home with the kids. But absolutely beside herself with excitement. It's a great day for my sister" (p. 70). The "Aria" ends by reflecting more generally on the relations between politicians and intellectuals, including artists. Malraux in his speech claimed that "America had not sought imperial power," to which Edmund Wilson "exclaimed irascibly, in the tones of Mr. Magoo, 'Hooey!'" (p. 71). Suppose Wilson was right: "What is to be done? How shall we behave toward the mighty in Washington?" (as opposed, one notes, to how shall we challenge the power of the mighty). Historical precedent offers little help: Descartes, Pushkin, Voltaire, Pound all suffered misery or humiliation at the hands of the mighty. The figure to emulate, Bellow decided, was Samuel Johnson, engaged in private conversation with King George in the library at the Queen's House:

> To the king's questions about one Dr. Hill, Johnson answered "that he was an ingenious man, but had no veracity." Urged to say more, he declined to louse up Dr. Hill. "I now began to consider that I was depreciating this man in the estimation of his Sovereign, and

thought it was time for me to say something that might be more favourable" (p. 72).

In *Humboldt's Gift*, Charlie Citrine, in the course of lousing up Denise, recalls her preparations for what sounds very much like the Malraux dinner. At the beauty salon Denise speed-reads *Time* and *Newsweek* and *U.S. News and World Report*. On the flight to Washington, she and Citrine review "the Bay of Pigs and the Missile Crisis and the Diem problem." Watching Denise corner the president after dinner, as Susan had cornered him in real life, Citrine "tittered to myself when I saw them together. But JFK could take care of himself, and he liked pretty women. I suspected that he read *The U.S. News and World Report*, too, and that his information might not be much better than her own" (p. 59) (in real life, Bellow recalled to Atlas, Susan "was sizing him up as an influence for the good; he was sizing her up as a lay"[33]). Citrine was amused by the dinner, remembering "the impressive hauteur of Charles Lindbergh, the complaint of Edmund Wilson that the government had made a pauper of him, the Catskill resort music played by the Marine Corps orchestra, and Mr. Tate keeping time with his fingers on the knee of a lady" (p. 59). In the "Aria," Bellow adopts a similarly amused pose, while entertaining no illusions that artists or intellectuals would be much use or more liberal as politicians or statesmen. When the Han dynasty was governed by men of letters, the state passed into "a long torpor of orthodoxy and dogmatism" (p. 72). The "Aria" accurately reflects Bellow's attitude to politics in this period. There are almost no references to current affairs in his letters from the late 1950s and early 1960s. Politicians who professed a love of culture were no different from operagoing businessmen or bankers. At the Malraux evening, the president was witty and graceful, calling it "the most extraordinary collection of talent, of human knowledge, that has ever been gathered together at the White House, with the possible exception of when Thomas Jefferson dined alone."[34] After the dinner and the speeches and the Schubert recital, however, Kennedy spent most of his time deep in conversation with "Mr. David Rockefeller of the Chase Manhattan bank" (p. 72).[35]

The incompatibility of high culture and political power is seen also in *Herzog*. In the grip of mania, Herzog writes letters to all sorts of figures, including politicians. The poignancy and humor of the letters he writes to General Eisenhower and Governor Stevenson derive in part from their abstract or philosophical idiom, as ill-fitting as the idiom used to address Nietzsche, Spinoza, Heidegger, and God (to Heidegger: *"Dear Doctor Professor, I should like to know what you mean by the expression 'the fall into the quotidian.' When did this fall occur? Where were we standing when it happened?"* [p. 465]; or *"Dear Herr Nietzsche—My dear sir, May I ask a question from the floor?"*; later, *"some of these expressions, I must tell you, have a very Germanic ring"* [p. 740]). After complaining that Eisenhower's Committee on National Aims was composed of *"corporation lawyers, big executives, the group now called the Industrial Statesmen,"* Herzog invokes *"the old proposition of Pascal (1623–1662) that man is a reed but a thinking reed,"* reinterpreting it (not all that clearly) to fit *"the modern citizen of a democracy. He thinks, but he feels like a reed bending before centrally generated winds."* When Moses decides that "Ike would certainly pay no attention to this," he tries again:

> *Tolstoi (1828–1910) said, "Kings are history's slaves." The higher one stands in the scale of power, the more his actions are determined. To Tolstoi freedom is entirely personal. That man is free whose condition is simple, truthful—real. To be free is to be released from historical limitation. On the other hand, GWF Hegel (1770–1831) understood the essence of human life to be derived from history. . . .*

The letter goes on for a few more sentences before Herzog realizes, "not without humor in his despair," that Ike would pay no more attention to Tolstoy and Hegel than to Pascal. "I'm bugging all these people—Nehru, Churchill, and now Ike, whom I apparently want to give a Great Books course" (p. 579). Had President Kennedy survived, Moses thinks, perhaps he "would have been interested," though to no effect, nothing would change. The governments of Eisenhower and Johnson "could not function without intellectuals—physicists, statisticians—but these are whirling lost in the arms of industrial chiefs and billionaire brass. Kennedy was not about to change this situation, either. Only he seemed to have acknowledged, privately, that it existed." Moses therefore turns from men of power to men of intellect, offering an outline of his ideas to Harris Pulver, "who had been his tutor in 1939 and was now the editor of *Atlantic Civilization*" (p. 580). In 1961 Bellow was commissioned to write a profile of Khrushchev for *Esquire*. Like Herzog, he took what might be called a meta-political or antipolitical approach, focusing not on policy but on character, what he saw as Khrushchev's archetypal character. "Other statesmen are satisfied to represent their countries. Not so Khrushchev. He wishes to personify Russia and the communist cause," a point Bellow makes (as we saw in Chapter 1) through comparisons with Dostoyevsky's Father Karamazov. Herzog might well have drawn such parallels, though without Bellow's light touch; he would have been drawn into abstraction, gone on too long. Bellow differs from Herzog in having a sense of audience and of proportion, but he engages with politics and world affairs at Herzog's level.[36]

RICHARD STERN WANTED Bellow to stay on at the University of Chicago. The English Department, however, was reluctant to hire another creative writer ("I think they felt one was enough"). That Stern was on leave during Winter Quarter, in Rome and Venice, made lobbying on Bellow's behalf difficult. It was Edward Shils, a sociologist on the faculty of the Committee on Social Thought, who was, as Stern puts it, "the moving force." Shils had known Bellow since the 1930s. He was aware that Bellow had applied for and failed to get a job at the Committee in 1943, and rightly thought it would be a better fit for him than the English Department, being something of an academic *salon des refusés*, home to scholars and thinkers whose wide interests and independent characters often put them at odds with traditional departments. Committee faculty were drawn from literature, philosophy, history, religion, art, politics, and society, and encouraged to pursue general themes and questions, often of an interdisciplinary nature. The ethos was that of the Humanities programs Bellow had taught in at Minneapolis and NYU, but the student body was quite different, as the Committee admitted only a small number of carefully screened graduate students. In addition to taking seminars from Committee faculty, these students were required to pass a "Fundamentals Examination" before writing a dissertation. As is still the case today, each student was required to draw up a list of a dozen or so classic texts, both ancient and modern, in consultation with faculty. These lists were to include works of imaginative literature, of philosophy, religion, and theology, and of history and social theory, and at least one of the works on the list had to be read in the original language. Each list had to be approved by every member of the faculty and every member of the faculty was invited to provide questions for examination. According to the current Committee website, preparation for the Fundamentals Exam provides "a kind of liberal education on the graduate level."[37] It is "the defining experience for students in the Committee on Social Thought." For a writer like Bellow, drawn to philosophy and theory, teaching in the Committee was a way to renew acquaintance with classic texts from a range of disciplines, and to discuss them with able students and eminent authorities. His responsibilities as a Committee member would be light and largely self-determined. It was common for faculty with similar interests to co-teach seminars. The financial and personal incentives for joining the Committee also drew Bellow: Greg would be able to attend the university tuition-free; Bellow could see Adam regularly, as Sasha was still in Skokie; and Bellow preferred living in Chicago to living in New York. That Susan didn't like living in Chicago was a difficulty, but Susan had friends and family in the city and might like it better when living with Bellow than with her parents.

IN 1962, the Committee on Social Thought consisted of nine faculty members, among them John U. Nef, a historian, the founding chair; Mircea Eliade, a scholar of comparative religion; David Grene, a classicist; Friedrich A. Hayek, the economist; Frank Knight, another economist, a key figure in the creation of the Committee; James Redfield, a classicist, the son of Robert Redfield, the anthropologist, a third key figure in the Committee's creation; and Edward Shils. In founding the Committee, Nef hoped to bring together not only scholars but people "in other creative walks of life than the academic." That no such person was on the Committee in 1962 was a help with Shils's efforts on Bellow's behalf. The man who took persuading was Edward Levi, the provost of the university, later its president (also, from 1975 to 1977, attorney general under Gerald Ford). In an interview with James Atlas, Levi described himself as disapproving of writers in academic posts. Shils knew of this disapproval but was undaunted. He was a skillful academic politician and once confessed to his friend, the writer Joseph Epstein, that he dreamt of being a cardinal in Rome, a job he would have loved. While Levi ran the university, according to Epstein, Shils was something of the figure he dreamt of being, "a powerful and not at all behind the scenes influence."[38] Shils arranged a lunch with Bellow and Levi. After "reluctantly" agreeing to the lunch, Levi told Atlas, "I changed my mind completely. . . . It was quite clear that I was talking to a learned person who was serious about his learning and serious about teaching."[39]

Edward Shils became Bellow's closest friend at the university and was for almost a decade an important influence on his life. He was a polarizing figure: irascible, fierce in his loyalties and enmities, confrontational, learned, charming at times, and bitingly funny. In appearance he was like a bullock: five foot eight, stocky, with a reddish complexion and once red hair. He dressed in heavy tweeds, never went out in public without a tie, and carried a cudgel-like walking stick. He was as formal in manner as in dress. According to Epstein, "he had students, acquaintances, really quite dear friends of several decades whom he continued to call Mr. or Mrs. or Miss; they usually called him Professor Shils" (p. 3). Shils taught half the year at the Committee on Social Thought and half in Britain, first at the London School of Economics, then at King's College, Cambridge, then at Peterhouse, Cambridge. He had what Epstein describes as a mid-Atlantic accent and people often thought he was British or rich or both. "When the man who wrote Edward's obituary for the *Times* of London, a Cambridge don [the political theorist Maurice Cowling] who I believe knew Edward longer than I, called me for information, he said. 'He came from railroad money, didn't he?'" (p. 4). In fact, he came from *ostjuden* immigrants from Philadelphia. His father was a cigar maker in a factory, and Shils went to Philadelphia public schools, acquiring his learning, in the first instance, in public libraries. Like Bellow, Shils made no secret of his Jewishness and loved Yiddish, perhaps because it suited his talent for denigration, or helped to form it. A favorite Yiddish word, Epstein recalls, was *chachem* or *chachema*, meaning greatly learned man or woman, "always used sarcastically" (p. 15). "Joseph," Epstein recalls Shils saying, "pointing to three thuggish-looking youths standing on the opposite corner as we emerged one gray winter afternoon from Bishop's chili parlor on Chicago's light-industrial near West Side, 'note those three *schlumgazim.*'" When Epstein asked for a translation, Shils replied: "'*schlumgazim* are highwaymen who, after stealing your purse, out of sheer malice also slice off your testicles'" (p. 4).

As an undergraduate at the University of Pennsylvania, Shils "deliberately set out to make himself European." Yet he loved America, "with all its philistinism and coarseness" (p. 5). He knew Chicago and its ethnic neighborhoods, especially its ethnic restaurants, better than most native Chicagoans; he had an encyclopedic knowledge of baseball, until he decided baseball no longer interested him. As an undergraduate at Pennsylvania he studied languages and Continental thought, in particular German social thought. As a graduate student and young instructor at the University of Chicago, he was influenced by Frank Knight and by the sociologist Robert Park. He wrote books and papers on a range of topics: tradition, intellectuals, naturalism, civil society, the primordial. He taught Hegel, Hobbes, Tocqueville, and Weber. He read widely in literature as well as the social sciences, taught a course on T. S. Eliot at the Committee, and admired Conrad "above all authors" (p. 7). In the living room of his Hyde Park apartment he kept a bust of Conrad by Jacob Epstein alongside one of Weber. He had no television, didn't drive, type, or use a computer, but he kept up with the modern world and American culture through newspapers and periodicals. He could be extremely generous. Before Richard Stern broke with him he frequently received expensive gifts from Shils: a silver marrow spoon at Christmas, two or three volumes of a collected Heine to complete a set. Shils also found Stern his first British publisher. Epstein reports that Shils once gave a graduate student $10,000 "to help her finish a difficult final year of her studies. He might give another young couple a five thousand dollar Christmas gift, merely because he wanted them to know he loved them" (p. 22). If crossed, however, Shils could be rough. When invited to give a talk at Reed College in Portland (a college known for its progressive views—Bellow had visited it in 1953), he was interrupted by a student who informed him that it was customary at Reed to have dialogue between speaker and audience. "I didn't come two thousand miles," Shils told the student, "to listen to children."

In *Humboldt's Gift* Bellow depicts a character much like Shils. In appearance, Charlie Citrine's friend Richard Durnwald was "reddish, elderly but powerful, thickset and bald, a bachelor of cranky habits but a kind man" (p. 109). Durnwald and George Swiebel, the Dave Peltz character, are Citrine's closest friends during the period of his marriage to Denise; they are also rivals for his affection, with very different notions of what is good for him. George "always came down heavily on Durnwald," Citrine explains, because "he knew how attached I was to Dick Durnwald. In crude Chicago Durnwald, whom I admired and even adored, was the only man with whom I exchanged ideas. But for six months Durnwald had been at the University of Edinburgh, lecturing on Comte, Durkheim, Tönnies, Weber, and so on. 'This abstract stuff is poison to a guy like you,' said George. 'I'm going to introduce you to guys from South Chicago.' He began to shout. 'You're too exclusive, you're going to dry out'" (p. 62). George calls Durnwald "the professor's professor. . . . He's heard it or read it all. When I try to talk to him I feel that I'm playing the ping-pong champion of China. I serve the ball, he smashes it back, and that's the end of that" (pp. 61–62) (later in the novel Citrine describes Durnwald as having "a peremptory blunt butting even bullying manner" [p. 109]). If George shouts at Citrine, Durnwald scolds him. For Durnwald, as for Shils, "the only brave, the only passionate, the only manly life was a life of thought" (p. 183). For a while, but only for a while, Citrine agrees, just as for a period Bellow fell under Shils's influence. What draws Swiebel and Durnwald together is their disapproval of Citrine's interest in Rudolf Steiner and anthroposophy, an interest Bellow began to develop in the mid-1970s. "Durnwald dismissed the subject sharply because he wished to protect his esteem for me" (p. 270).

It was not until July 26, 1963, that Bellow received a formal invitation from John Nef to join the Committee. The appointment was at professorial level, for an initial period of five years, and at a salary of $14,000 a year. Bellow was to have the office of Friedrich Hayek, who was leaving the Committee to go to the University of Freiburg. Bellow's letter of acceptance, dated August 10, has some of the formality of Professors Nef and Shils. "To be invited to join the faculty of the Committee on Social Thought is a great honor," he writes, adding that he hopes "you will have no objection to my honoring some previous commitments. They will take me away from the University very seldom, and for brief periods." Nef's reply on August 14 begins: "Your warm letter accepting our invitation to join the Faculty of the Committee on Social Thought delighted me, and I know my colleagues will share my pleasure." It ends: "Let me add that the whole purpose of the Committee on Social Thought is to facilitate the creative life of its members, and I hope consequently that we can be of use to you. You will be of enormous use to us. Let me say again how grateful I am for your acceptance." On September 12, Shils wrote from King's College, Cambridge: "My dear Saul: First, I must tell you how marvelous it will be for me and for the University to have you with us." Later in the letter he informs Bellow that he will soon hear from "a *very* fine, very intelligent, very lively young friend of mine, Tony Tanner, a Fellow of this college, who is spending a year in the United States and whom I would warmly commend to your attention simply on the grounds of his personal and intellectual merits. In addition to this, however, he is writing a little book about your work. . . . I am sure you will appreciate him as much as I do." Tanner's book, published in 1965, was the first critical study devoted solely to Bellow's writing.

NEF'S LETTER OF August 14, 1962, was received by Bellow on Martha's Vineyard, where he and Susan had taken a house for part of the summer. "The Vineyard is beautiful—we love it," Bellow wrote to Stern on August 22. "*Herzog* in final stages—*TNS* put to bed. Freud should have had such a beach—he wouldn't have had so many theories." On August 31, however, soon after leaving the Vineyard, Bellow's mood was darkened by another terrible fight with Sasha, the worst they'd ever had. The fight took place in Peekskill, New York, in Westchester County, where Sasha and Adam were visiting Ann Berryman. Bellow had gone to pick Adam up for a weekend at Tivoli. Sasha describes the fight in her memoir:

> He was spoiling for it, I could see his tense lip and twitch that always telegraphed a simmering rage. But I was reckless and confronted him about the lateness of the checks, and said it was a problem now, since I was running out of money. He made some remark, about how the money was for Adam not for me. I brought up the money he never paid my mother and should give to me, now that she was dead. He countered with something nasty about not supporting my lover, so I slapped him and he grabbed me by the pony tail and swung me around punching me with his other hand. I was bruised for a week and took out a restraining order. I knew that I had really provoked him, but the extraordinary violence was bubbling inside him, barely controlled, waiting for a trigger (p. 107).

In a letter of September 10 to her lawyer, Jonas Schwartz, Sasha described the fight somewhat differently. The trouble started "after some unpleasant exchanges between us concerning getting my things from Tivoli—he refused to let me pick them up." She says nothing of slapping Bellow nor of refusing to let him take Adam for the weekend, as he later claimed. In a passage underlined for emphasis, she writes "*I did not provoke this attack, nor did I make any physical gesture towards him which could even remotely* [be] *mistaken for an attack,*" adding that "it was only the intervention of Ann Berryman whose houseguest I was for a few weeks, which ended the attack." Bellow, she claims, threatened to cut off divorce payments, so she asks Schwartz to subpoena his income tax records to ensure that he lived up to the terms of the divorce agreement, which stipulates that over a certain income a percentage sum should be set aside in trust for Adam. She elaborates on her injuries: "severe bone bruises behind one ear, cuts on my left temple and left eyelid, and a bad bruise on my left breast. My scalp is a mess of lumps and bruises."

The letter to Schwartz was written from Tarrytown, New York, where Sasha and Adam were now living. "Chicago was not for me," Sasha explains in the memoir, "too parochial" (p. 106). Tarrytown was hardly the big city but it was near Ludwig, who was now teaching at the State University of New York at Stony Brook. After a period of estrangement on Ludwig's part, a product of paranoid suspicions about other men, according to Sasha, and while she and Adam were still living in Skokie, Ludwig had begun calling and writing again, and she found herself "flying to NY for a weekend here and there to see him" (p. 106). The move to Tarrytown came about during a visit to Ann Berryman, perhaps the one that included the fight. Sasha saw an advertisement in the local paper for a post at the Hudson Institute, a research organization in Tarrytown, answered it, and got the job. She was to be an assistant to the head of the institute, Herman Kahn, a military strategist and systems analyst, a model for Stanley Kubrick's Dr. Strangelove. Three or so weeks after the fight, on September 24, Sasha wrote to Bellow about visiting arrangements for Adam. He could see Adam "anytime" but he was "not to call or come for him or return him yourself but to make these arrangements through someone else." Her lawyer and doctor had advised her to take out an injunction against him "should you fail to live up to these arrangements." The police had been given his photograph "in the interests of my personal safety" and they would be called if she saw him anywhere near her apartment. "There are a number of people around here and in Minnesota who remember your threats to beat me up, and others who remember that you did, in fact, do so on two occasions during our marriage. I advise you to remember that."

On September 30, Bellow replied, "On Labor Day you used the child to bargain for some supposed advantage and refused to let him come with me as we had arranged. Adam was greatly disappointed. The violence of that occasion was provoked by you, perhaps deliberately. You tore my clothing, bruised me, and had to be restrained by Ann Berryman from continuing your attack." In a later paragraph he writes: "Your pugnacity is a matter of record. Even before the divorce you struck me with your fists. You tried to run me down with the car. On the day you claim to have been assaulted, I came home with bruises. You have been known to do things which you could not remember later. My 'violence' is probably another one of your hallucinations." When Sasha refused to let Bellow see Adam on a subsequent occasion, she was "simply giving me the runaround." She knew that he would be leaving soon for Chicago and gone for months and that this was one of his few chances to see Adam before departing. Bellow insists that some regular pattern of visits be established. "I shall be coming in periodically during my temporary residence in Chicago. You will have ample notice of my visits. I want to have Adam with me on all holidays—Christmas, Easter and part of every summer. If you do not agree to reasonable arrangements I shall have to go to law to try to obtain my rights." The letter ends: "I plan to come to Tarrytown next Friday to pick him up, and I expect to hear from you that he will be delivered to me by someone other than yourself. I will not ask anyone to go in my place while I wait in a restaurant like a wrongdoer. I won't send anyone for him. I will insist on my rights, and the thing will be done decently and in good order. I expect a reply from you before Friday. I hope you will not compel me to take legal steps."

Both parties were shading the truth. Sasha, Bellow claims, provoked the violence, thus admitting that there was some. By putting violence in quotation marks, however, and calling it "one of your hallucinations," he suggests that it wasn't real violence, wasn't much of anything. In the memoir, Sasha admits that she slapped Bellow and provoked the violence, but in the letter to Schwartz she writes that *"I did not provoke this attack nor did I make any physical gesture towards him which could even remotely* [be] *mistaken for an attack."* Here, too, there is room for equivocation, though only just. A slap might not be thought to constitute an "attack." In a letter of October 11, written after Adam's weekend visit, Bellow informs Sasha that he plans to return to New York from Chicago on the weekend of December 7. "With nearly two months' notice I hope you will not invent any appointments at the last moment. Two weeks ago you told me Adam could not see me because he had to see the dentist. He told me last Saturday that he's never been to the dentist." In the memoir, Sasha remembers a circumstance that may have contributed to Bellow's fury, one she hadn't considered at the time: "Saul later said that he took the job at the University of Chicago to be near Adam, and that I had, instead, deliberately moved away to New York." She defends herself against this accusation by saying that Bellow's decision to move "was news to me when I heard it. He never asked me what my plans were, never told me he was thinking of returning to the Midwest." This may be true, but just as Sasha may not have known of the move, Bellow may not have known she didn't know.

The physical violence of the Labor Day weekend had a symbolic sequel, occasioned by the return of Sasha's belongings from Tivoli. Sasha had hired a trucker to collect these belongings—"an early American sideboard, a coffee table and a Mexican chair that had belonged to my mother, as well as a few paintings" (p. 108)—and to deliver them to Tarrytown. When the trucker arrived and Sasha asked him to unload the things and bring them into her apartment, he hesitated:

> "What is it?" I asked.
>
> "Well, I don't know if you want everything," he said, uncomfortable. "You better look." Saul had sent several barrels of ashes and trash, with a pair of men's shoes on top. "There's some mistake," I said.
>
> "No, the gentleman was very insistent that I take these."
>
> "Why did he send the garbage, Mama?" five-year-old Adam asked. I assured him it was a mistake, and sent the trucker off with the barrels, leaving me with more to fuel my anger. And that was the flavor of the relationship for the next few years (p. 108).

In a letter of October 18, Sasha gives further details. Her mother's clothes, she claims, were jumbled amidst the gravel and broken glass, "and to crown the whole with Jack's shoes, is an evil act. In your blind desire to 'even scores' you are hitting out at a dead woman, a man's infirmity, a little boy, —and by reference to that period in my life during which I experienced some mild form of epilepsy, you have only added to the wickedness." She makes much of Adam's reaction to the incident. If he was looking unhappy on a recent visit, "perhaps it was because he was angry with the trash you sent. Didn't you know he would think you sent it to him as well, since he lives here? If you failed to realize this you were being quite stupid." If Adam was angry, presumably he didn't believe Sasha's excuse about the trash being sent by mistake, or she eventually told him the truth.[40]

In the letter of October 18, Sasha defends herself against Bellow's accusations by accusing him, in turn, of inventing things, not only refusing to face the truth, but not knowing the difference between truth and fiction (an occupational malady for novelists, she suggested in an interview):

> You have often told a story of how I tried to run you down with the car in Tivoli. As you know perfectly well, I was trying to leave, with Adam in the car and you deliberately put yourself in my path knowing, of course, that I would not run you down, but stop. Unfortunately I did stop, for as you know, you dragged me from the car by my hair across the lawn, kicked me and whipped me with your cap. . . .
>
> On another and earlier occasion you report that I "went for a knife." As you know, I was reaching for the telephone to call for help since we had been quarrelling violently. There was no knife about, but you somehow have had to justify these now three separate scenes of your beating or attacking me, with some physical provocation on my part which simply did not occur.
>
> You cannot take a thought that flashes, perhaps in your own mind, like, "I wonder if she will stop the car" or, "Would she like to kill me" and translate that into something that actually happened. These things did *not* happen. What is true is that I was in a car and trying to leave; that I was reaching, but for a phone; that I did not provoke or attack *you* in Peekskill, but that you were carrying out a threat you made in Minneapolis. Do you remember that Ralph Ross told you to "have an ulcer" since a man does not indulge his passions in this way, however hurt he may be?

These accusations and counteraccusations are rehearsed here because they are part of the life Bellow lived as he wrote *Herzog*, in which marriage to Sasha, her adultery with Ludwig, and the mental state of a hero very much like himself are given fictional form. Real life is woven into fiction almost immediately. To look to the novel for what really happened—who did the provoking, how much violence there actually was, who lied or shaded the truth—or even what Bellow thought happened, is futile. The novel offers evidence of what Bellow made of his experience, by which is meant how he turned the thoughts and feelings it raised into art.

CONSIDER THE DEPICTION OF violence in the novel. Sasha claimed to fear for her life; Bellow claimed her rages were so intense she was capable of murder. In early versions of the novel, Herzog uses physical force on Madeleine, who is less murderous than in the published novel.[41] In the published novel, Herzog seriously contemplates murder. "I sometimes think," he tells Harvey Simkin, the Sam Goldberg figure, "if she died I'd get my daughter back. There are times when I know I could look at Madeleine's corpse without pity." The thought that Herzog might murder Madeleine, a thought that excites Simkin, is pondered by Herzog: "Well, it's true. I've tested it in my mind with a gun, a knife, and felt no horror, no guilt. . . . So perhaps I might kill them. But I'll say no such thing to Harvey" (p. 632). Later, as Moses reflects on the injustice done to him, "his right as an Innocent Party," the thought of killing Madeleine and Gersbach returns: "now his rage is so great and deep, so murderous, bloody, positively rapturous, that his arms and fingers ache to strangle them. So much for his boyish purity of heart" (p. 638). Immediately he feels shame. As he looks in the mirror he thinks: *My God! Who is this creature? It considers itself human. But what is it? Not human of itself. But has the longing to be human. And like a troubling dream, a persistent vapor. A desire. Where does it all come from? And what is it? And what can it be! Not immortal longing. No, entirely mortal, but human"* (pp. 638–39). For Moses, to be human, a man or *mensch*, is something one works at, a capacity or potential, as in the capacity to resist murderous impulse. When Moses retrieves Father Herzog's pistol before setting out to confront Madeleine and Gersbach, he is "determined to act without clearly knowing what to do, and even recognizing that he had no power over his impulses" (p. 660). He is *indulging* his impulses, having "determined" to be guided by them. As he drives south toward Madeleine's apartment in Hyde Park he still hasn't decided what he will do. Madeleine "had threatened him with arrest if he so much as showed his face near the house. The police had his picture" (p. 673). He works himself into a fever on the drive: "It's not everyone who gets the opportunity to kill with a clear conscience. They had opened the way to justifiable murder. They deserved to die. He had a right to kill them" (p. 674).

Herzog has this right, he believes, because Madeleine, for whom "hatred . . . is the most powerful element in her life," has acted toward him like a "murderess": "In spirit, she was his murderess, and therefore he was turned loose, could shoot or choke without remorse. He felt in his arms and in his fingers, and to the core of his heart, the sweet exertion of strangling—horrible and sweet, an orgastic rapture of inflicting death. He was sweating violently, his shirt wet and cold under his arms. Into his mouth came a taste of copper, a metabolic poison, a flat but deadly flavor" (p. 674). These physical symptoms signal "human" resistance, like an antibody fighting infection. In cover of darkness Herzog sneaks behind the house on Harper Avenue and peers in at Madeleine, Gersbach, and June, through a back window. He resembles Frankenstein's monster, a wronged "creature," peering in on a human scene from which he is excluded. As Gersbach bathes June, Herzog watches. What he sees and what he makes of what he sees are described in a justly famous passage:

> The man washed her tenderly. His look, perhaps, was false. But he had no *true* expressions, Herzog thought. His face was all heaviness, sexual meat. Looking down his open shirt front, Herzog saw the hair-covered heavy soft flesh of Gersbach's breast. His chin was thick, and like a stone ax, a brutal weapon. And then there were his sentimental eyes, the thick crest of hair, and that hearty voice with its peculiar fraudulence and grossness. The hated traits were all there. But see how he was with June, scooping the water on her playfully, kindly. He let her wear her mother's flowered shower cap, the rubber petals spreading on the child's head. Then Gersbach ordered her to stand, and she stooped slightly to allow him to wash her little cleft. Her father stared at this. A pang went through him, but it was quickly done. She sat again. Gersbach ran fresh water on her, cumbersomely rose and opened the bath towel. Steady and thorough, he dried her, and then with a large puff he powdered her. The child jumped up and down with delight. "Enough of this wild stuff," said Gersbach. "Put on those p-j's now."
>
> She ran out. Herzog still saw faint wisps of powder, that floated over Gersbach's stooping head. His red hair worked up and down.

He was scouring the tub. Moses might have killed him now. His left hand touched the gun, enclosed in the roll of rubles [the gun had been sent from Russia by Herzog's grandfather, along with the rubles]. He might have shot Gersbach as he methodically salted the yellow sponge rectangle with cleansing powder. There were two bullets in the chamber. . . . But they would stay there. Herzog clearly recognized that. Very softly he stepped down from his perch, and passed without sound through the yard again. He saw his child in the kitchen, looking up at Mady, asking for something, and he edged through the gate into the alley. Firing this pistol was nothing but a thought.

The human soul is an amphibian, and I have touched its sides (pp. 676–77).

The fever broken, Herzog reflects on what might have been:

To shoot him!—an absurd thought. As soon as Herzog saw the actual person giving an actual bath, the reality of it, the tenderness of such a buffoon to a little child, his intended violence turned into *theater*, into something ludicrous. He was not ready to make such a complete fool of himself. Only self-hatred could lead him to ruin himself because his heart was "broken." How could it be broken by such a pair? Lingering in the alley awhile, he congratulated himself on his luck. His breath came back to him; and how good it felt to breathe! It was worth the trip (p. 677).

In future, Herzog will only come to Chicago "to do June good, genuine good. No more of this hectic, heart-rent, theatrical window-peering" (p. 724).

Herzog is saved by human particularity, complication, individuality. His intended violence would have made him a figure out of melodrama or theater, the realm of Mady and Gersbach, "those two grotesque love-actors" (p. 677). When Mady "has an audience [she] begins spellbinding" (p. 608); "*Conversation was a theatrical event for Madeleine,*" Herzog writes to Monsignor Hilton, a Bishop Sheen figure, "*Theater—the art of upstarts, opportunists, would-be aristocrats.* Monsignor himself was an actor" (p. 529). As for Gersbach, "it's perfectly plain to me the fellow is an actor," Simkin says, "and I know damn well Madeleine is an actress" (p. 636), a knowledge gained from Simkin's friendship with Madeleine's father, Pontritter, "the American Stan-islavsky" (p. 424). Had Herzog played his part, he would have become the creature in *Frankenstein*, a novel first made famous through theatri-cal adaptation. What stops him is what he sees: the way Gersbach rises "cumbersomely" after drying June, his scooping water over her "play-fully, kindly," the way the washing is "quickly done" (p. 676). With such details the external world breaks through Herzog's interiority, or combines with that interiority, not only to bring him to his senses but to rescue the novel itself from melodrama and theater (the stolen pistol, the fevered drive south, the spying in darkness). In describing his "sharp senses" at this moment, Herzog attributes to them the familiar powers of the artist, as in Wordsworth's description of poetic creativity, "an ennobling interchange / Of action from without and from within; / The excellence, pure function, and best power / Both of the object seen, and eye that sees" (*Prelude*, 1850, 12.376–79). Here is Herzog's descrip-tion of his newly charged perceptive powers:

> In these days of near-delirium and wide-ranging disordered thought, deeper currents of feeling had heightened his perceptions, or made him instill something of his own into his surroundings. As though he painted them with moisture and color taken from his own mouth, his blood, liver, bowels, genitals. In this mingled way, therefore, he was aware of Chicago, familiar ground to him for more than thirty years. And out of its elements, by this peculiar art of his own organs, he created his version of it. . . . Reality. Moses had to see reality. Perhaps he was somewhat spared from it so that he might see it better, not fall asleep in its thick embrace. Aware-ness was his work; extended consciousness was his line, his busi-ness. Vigilance. If he borrowed time to take his tiny daughter to see the fishes he would find a way to make it up to the vigilance-fund (pp. 698–99).

Which he does, as when describing the turtle at the aquarium, quoted in the introduction to this book. Herzog's immediate thoughts upon leaving the yard after spying on Madeleine, Gersbach, and June are genealogical, how much June looks like a Herzog, how genetic traits are passed on from *"You and your children and children's children"* (p. 678). Moses recalls Father Herzog, taunted by scornful Tante Zipporah. *"He could never use a gun on anyone,"* Zipporah says, *"never keep up with team-*

sters, butchers, sluggers, hooligans, razboiniks. *'A gilded little gentleman.'*
Could he hit anyone on the head? Could he shoot?" Agreeing with his aunt,
Moses "could confidently swear that Father Herzog had never—not
once in his life—pulled the trigger of this gun. Only threatened"
(p. 678). In the novel's penultimate section, Moses, with June in the
car, is involved in a traffic accident outside the Museum of Science and
Industry in Hyde Park. No one is hurt. When the police arrive, they
discover Father Herzog's gun and take Herzog and June to the station.
The police call Madeleine and Herzog calls his brother Will, the Sam
figure. When Will arrives he asks Moses what he was doing with the
gun. Moses replies: "You know I'm no more capable of firing it at someone than Papa was. . . . I remembered those old rubles in his drawer and
then I took the revolver too. I shouldn't have. At least I ought to have
emptied it. It was just one of those dumb impulses" (p. 726).

The violence of the novel is verbal as well as physical, and in the
depiction of Madeleine, murderous impulses go unchecked, there are
no softening or humanizing particulars. Madeleine is a bitch goddess,
the sort of woman who really does *"eat green salad and drink human
blood"* (p. 458). To Stanley Edgar Hyman, in a review of the novel in
The New Leader, Madeleine "resembles no real or imaginable person,
but is a vicious madwoman, based on the Poison Damsel of folktale."
To Irving Howe, in *The New Republic,* "Madeleine is drawn with pure
venom, a sentiment capable of generating in writers, as in other men,
great quantities of energy. . . . The portrait is unjust, an utter libel,
but a classic of male retaliation." To Philip Rahv, writing in the *New
York Herald-Tribune,* "Mady, the treacherous wife, does not really come
through except as an object of hostility, though a weirdly interesting
one." To Richard Ellmann, in the *Chicago Sun-Times,* Madeleine's "ultimate malevolence is a mystery that refuses solution," echoing larger
inhumanities "that have been perpetrated during our time."[42] All these
critics knew Sasha, which is partly why they use phrases like "utter
libel" and "unjust"; not because they took her side but because they
knew her as a person, with virtues as well as failings, and legitimate
complaints. At the police station in Chicago, what Herzog sees in Madeleine's face is "a total will that he should die. This was infinitely more
than ordinary hatred. It was a vote for his nonexistence, he thought"
(p. 722), like a vote for the nonexistence of a people.

Madeleine's totalizing hatred is "mysterious" in part because of
Herzog's ultimate benignity. Herzog has flaws: he's fretful, timid,

inattentive, self-absorbed, gloomy, and a philanderer; also, according to Mady, "overbearing, infantile, demanding, sardonic and a psychosomatic bully" (p. 609). What he is not is imperious, mean, in several senses, violent, sometimes physically, vindictive in act, and paranoid, qualities Sasha attributes to Bellow in her memoir and in our interviews, by way of explaining both her adultery and her anger. Wayne Booth, the literary critic, remembered encountering Bellow in Hyde Park shortly before he'd finished the final draft of *Herzog*. He was revising madly, he told Booth, four hours every morning, "going through the manuscript and weeding out parts of myself that I don't like."[43] In making Madeleine's malevolence mysterious, underdetermined, Bellow indulged vindictive feelings toward Sasha, but doing so also served fictional ends, licensing the character's connection to a wider malevolence, comparably totalizing and underdetermined, generating passages of "great energy," bravura demonizing passages, as in the screaming, cursing rages that leave Madeleine with "an odd white grime in the corners of her mouth" (p. 473), the furious glare "so intense that her eyes seemed twisted" (p. 541), a desire "to kick out his brains with a murderous bitch foot" (p. 510). Madeleine is not Sasha, she's a character in a novel, a defense Sasha accepted. Did she ever confront Bellow about *Herzog*? Not at the time, nor in person. She read the excerpt in *Esquire*, when Madeleine was called Juliana, a name that made her laugh, being much too regal for the girl she remembered herself being in her early twenties, insecure, out of her depth. When she read the published novel several years later, "there was a certain resignation: 'Well, what did you expect, you married a writer?'" Sasha's tone in saying this recalled her tone when reminded of the scene in which Madeleine tells Herzog that the marriage is over just after he's put up the storm windows. As was mentioned in Chapter 13, the idea that she would consciously do such a thing made her laugh. "I would never do that. Those are the kinds of things that make sense for the character of Madeleine."

It is not just violence or hatred that degrades or traduces the human. "Potato love" does, too. The term first surfaces in the letter to Adlai Stevenson, whom Moses supported in 1952. *"I am sure the Coriolanus bit was painful,"* he writes, *"kissing the asses of the voters, especially in cold states like New Hampshire. Perhaps you did contribute something useful in the last decade . . . the look of the 'intelligent man' grieving at the loss of his private life, sacrificed to public service. Bah! The general won because he expressed*

low-grade universal potato love" (p. 482). When Moses recoils from the
bleakness of recent historical writing, including that of Mady's tutor,
Egbert Shapiro, with its "vision of mankind as a lot of cannibals, running in packs, gibbering, bewailing its own murders, pressing out the
living world as dead excrement," he forces himself to acknowledge the
truth it points to: "Do not deceive yourself, dear Moses Elkanah, with
childish jingles and Mother Goose. Hearts quaking with cheap and
feeble charity or oozing potato love have not written history. Shapiro's
snarling teeth, his salivating greed, the dagger of an ulcer in his belly
give him true insights, too. Fountains of human blood that squirted
from fresh graves! Limitless massacre! I never understood it!" (p. 493).
When Himmelstein tells Moses "I love you better than my own effing
family," that "You're my boy. My innocent kind-hearted boy," and gives
him a kiss, "Moses felt the potato love. Amorphous, swelling, hungry,
indiscriminate, cowardly potato love." The next line reads: "'Oh, you
sucker,' Moses cried to himself in the train. 'Sucker'" (p. 507). Not all
deep feeling, though, is fraudulent. Moses loves his old tutor, Harris
Pulver, "tiny, nervous Pulver with his timid, whole-souled blue eyes"
in an "immoderate heart-flooded way," but a way distinguished from
potato love. The marvelous Napoleon Street flashbacks, minimally
adapted from "Memoirs of a Bootlegger's Son," are also "heart-flooded,"
but again different from potato love, because rich with complicating, humanizing particulars. Real potato love is gross, a feature of the
hard-headed, the "Reality-Instructor" (p. 446). "Sentiment and brutality," Herzog says of Gersbach, "never one without the other, like fossils
and oil" (p. 697). In addition, potato love is often a tactic, only partly
conscious, using bogus feeling to get people to do what you want or see
things your way.

Herzog sees the rise of potato love as a reaction to the horrors of
modernity. In New York, as he drops his subway token in the slot, he
sees "a whole series of tokens" within the lit and magnified glass:

> Innumerable millions of passengers had polished the wood
> of the turnstile with their hips. From this arose a feeling of
> communion—brotherhood in one of its cheapest forms. This was
> serious, thought Herzog, as he passed through. The more individ-
> uals are destroyed (by processes such as I know) the worse their
> yearning for collectivity. Worse, because they return to the mass

agitated, made fervent by their failure. Not as brethren, but as degenerates. Experiencing a raging consumption of potato love. Thus occurs a second distortion of the divine image, already so blurred, wavering, struggling (p. 594).

The "divine image" is taken from William Blake, who locates divinity in human particulars, human virtues, the human form.[44] Current conditions have distorted this image, replacing it with a degenerate longing for communion with the mass, the folk or *volk*, the proletariat or *comrades*. The falsity of potato love breeds further falsities. "Having discovered that everyone must be indulgent with bungling child-men," Herzog "willingly accepted the necessary quota of consequent lies," which he calls "emotional goodies." The lies in his case are to himself, about his professed devotion to "truth, friendship . . . children (the regular American worship of kids)" (p. 685). When his Chicago friend, the zoologist Luke Asphalter, agrees to give him a bed because "You're an old friend," Herzog to his surprise has difficulty speaking: "A swift rush of feeling, out of nowhere, caught his throat. His eyes filled up. The potato love, he announced to himself. It's here. To advert to his temperament, call things by the correct name, restored his control. Self-correction refreshed him" (p. 687).

By not attending to things as they are, to the reality of his internal world as well as of the world outside, Herzog finds himself in his current fix. In the novel's present, he is determined to see things aright, beginning with his own behavior. His childlike passivity, he now sees, was part of a "deal—a psychic offer—meekness in exchange for preferential treatment," a self-judgment that held no "terror for him; no percentage now in quarreling with what one was" (p. 571). As he later puts it, "weakness, or sickness, with which he had copped a plea all his life (alternating with arrogance), his method of preserving equilibrium—the Herzog gyroscope—had no further utility. He seemed to have come to the end of *that*" (p. 705). When Madeleine leaves him the first time, as Sasha did early in the summer of 1958, they get back together.

And then she and Valentine ran my life for me. I didn't know a thing about it. All the decisions were made by them—where I lived, where I worked, how much rent I paid. Even my mental problems were set by them. They gave me my homework. And when they decided that I had to go, they worked out all the details—property settlement, alimony, child support. I'm sure Valentine thought he acted in my best interests. He must have held Madeleine back. He knows he's a good man. He understands, and when you understand you suffer more. You have higher responsibilities, responsibilities that come with suffering. I couldn't take care of my wife, poor fish. He took care of her. I wasn't fit to bring up my own daughter. He has to do it for me, out of friendship, out of pity, and sheer greatness of soul. He even agrees that Madeleine is a psychopath (p. 612).

At the time this takeover occurred, Herzog was willfully blind, saw advantages in being so (as in the discovery that "everyone must be indulgent with bungling child-men"). Potato love replaces real love. "What the fuck does *he* know what it is to face facts," cries Himmelstein, barely restrained by his wife. "All he wants is everybody should love him. If not, he's going to scream and holler" (p. 500). One recalls the adult Moses sitting at the side of the tub watching, like a child, as Madeleine, who thinks him "mother-bound" (p. 530), applies her makeup, or the way he listens to Himmelstein, "like a child to a tale" (p. 507). He was "used to being a favorite" (p. 528), to getting what he wants, which may account for his adult propensity to pursue every woman who attracts him, "one after another." Why he wants them, however, "I myself didn't understand, didn't have a clue" (p. 584). A related childishness is his susceptibility to fantasy. Madeleine's mother, Tennie, plays on Herzog's weakness for "good deeds," to act the knight in shining armor: "she flattered this weakness, asking him to save this headstrong deluded child of hers. Patience, loving-kindness, and virility would accomplish this. But Tennie flattered him even more subtly. She was telling Moses that he could bring stability into the life of this neurotic girl and cure her by his steadiness," an appeal that "stirred his impure sympathies intensely" (p. 526).

MUCH OF *HERZOG* concerns Moses's attempt to find in "thought" a force that can free him from "the humiliating comedy of heartache" (p. 583). This attempt is traced and dramatized in the unsent letters he writes "to explain, to have it out, to justify, to put in perspective, to clarify, to make amends" (p. 418). To Philip Roth, the novel's "special appeal," a product in large measure of the letters, lies in Bellow's ability "to hoist the weight of [his] thinking up from the depths to the narrative's surface without sinking the narrative's mimetic power."[45] The letters overflow with erudite allusion and reflection, often inspired by the sorts of texts found in Humanities courses and the Fundamentals Lists of Committee students. Since Herzog is an intellectual historian, author of a book entitled *Romanticism and Christianity*, now at work, or meant to be at work, on a second volume, "on the social ideas of the Romantics" (p. 421), his erudition is dramatically appropriate, plausible (though as Stanley Edgar Hyman points outs, he's "somewhat more fussed-over and foundation-granted, somewhat richer and freer, than his circumstances in the novel entitle him to be").[46] Herzog's aim with the blocked second book is to challenge what he calls "post-Renaissance, post-humanistic, post-Cartesian dissolution, next door to the Void" (pp. 509–10), a fashionable pessimism that feeds into Romantic notions of the artist as alienated hero, a figure he parodies in the person of his childhood friend, Nachman, a clichéd Left Bank and Greenwich Village bohemian.

According to Herzog, in the letter to his old tutor, Harris Pulver, the Void or "Wasteland outlook" is found *"in philosophy and literature as well as in sexual experience, or with the aid of narcotics, or in 'philosophical,' 'gratuitous' crime and similar paths of horror. (It never seems to occur to such 'criminals' that to behave with decency to another human being might also be 'gratuitous')"* (p. 581). "The very Himmelsteins, who had never even read a book of metaphysics, were touting the Void as if it were so much salable real estate" (p. 510). Chief among the tenets of the Void is a view of the self or soul as a construction, a view conditioned by Sartre's formulation "existence precedes essence" (Ellmann calls Herzog "the first anti-Existentialist hero"). "According to the latest from Paris and London," says Herzog, in an early draft of the novel, "there is no person. According to Bertrand Russell 'I' is a grammatical expression."[47] For Herzog, in contrast, the self is "a mysterious given as unique as a face,"[48] something with which we are born, no mere product of grammar or historical necessity. "In our greatest confusion," Bellow has written, "there is still an open channel to the soul. It may be difficult to find because by midlife it is overgrown, and some of the wildest thickets that surround it grow out of what we describe as our education. But the channel is always there, and it is our business to keep it open, to have access to the deepest part of ourselves."[49] Truth similarly, for all its elusiveness, is neither inaccessible nor "true only as it brings down more disgrace and dreariness upon human beings, so that if it shows anything except evil it is illusion" (p. 510).

Herzog's views are those of the liberal humanist, of a piece with his championing of freedom (despite a mothlike attraction to bullies, bosses, "Reality-Instructors"), generosity (contra Freud, who, like Calvin, offers *"a lousy, cringing, grudging conception of human nature"* [p. 474]), brotherhood (in defiance of "preachers of dread [who] tell you that others only distract you from metaphysical freedom" [p. 692]), and civic usefulness ("politics in the Aristotelian sense" [p. 511]). Often Herzog writes letters to the thinkers whose ideas he considers (Heidegger, Kierkegaard, Nietzsche, Spengler), though ideas figure in other letters. In earliest versions of the novel there are no letters at all; then Bellow adds letters of a personal nature (for example, to Dr. Edvig, the therapist); only in later versions does he add what Daniel Fuchs calls "idea-letters (along with a heightening of the idea element in the straight dramatic parts)."[50] Far from limiting the novel's appeal, these letters helped to account for its commercial success, sparked by the approving attention they received from reviewers. *Herzog* spent forty-two weeks on the bestseller lists and sold 142,000 in hardback, a success that bred detractors, thought of by Bellow as "out there in the grass."[51]

For all its prominence in the novel, "thought" proves of little assistance to Herzog, failing to explain or heal either his personal state or the state of the world. All it offers is "a second realm of confusion, another more complicated dream, the dream of intellect, the delusion of total *explanations*" (p. 583). Like "theater" it distorts and simplifies. As Bellow put it in an interview with Norman Manea:

> One of the things that bothers Herzog, that eats at him, is the fact that his extensive education doesn't work for him at all. He put his money on the wrong horse, as an American would say. He assumed all along that if he played the game by the going rules that it would work for him, his education would work for him, as it does for others, but the question in *Herzog* is whether it works for anybody. The answer is probably not, because you can't apply the lessons of high culture to the facts of ordinary life. That's where the comedy comes from. Herzog finds no support in the culture that he embraced. . . . He's been a good boy and he'd done all that the teacher told him to do and in a pinch nothing works.[52]

In an interview with Botsford, while talking of his time with Sasha, Bellow describes arriving at exactly this point in his own life:

> I had an additional burden—my "higher education." That counts for a great deal. When that higher education was put to the test, it didn't work. I began to understand the irrelevancy of it, to recoil in disappointment from it. Then one day I saw the comedy of it. Herzog says, "What do you propose to do now that your wife has taken a lover? Pull Spinoza from the shelf and look into what he says about adultery? About human bondage?" You discover, in other words, the inapplicability of your higher learning, the absurdity of the culture it cost you so much to acquire. True devotion to Spinoza, et al. would have left you no time for neurotic attachments and bad marriages. *That* would have been a way out for you.
>
> What the above argues is not that higher education is a bad thing but that our conception of it is ridiculous.[53]

HERZOG EXPRESSES VIEWS like these at several points in the novel. What intellectuals love, he says in the penultimate section, *"is an imaginary human situation invented by their own genius and which they believe is the only true and the only human reality"* (p. 725). "Human life," he elsewhere says, mostly with Heidegger and Nietzsche in mind, "is far subtler than any of its models. . . . Do we need to study *theories* of fear and anguish?" (p. 691) (especially theories used to justify fear and anguish, if not by the theorists themselves then by their followers). *"I can't accept this foolish dreariness,"* Herzog declares. *"We are talking about the whole life of mankind. The subject is too great, too deep for such weakness, cowardice"* (p. 491). Such was to be the message of Herzog's blocked second book, ending "with a new angle on the modern condition, showing how life could be lived by renewing universal connections" (p. 455). It is also the message the letters struggle toward. After all, "what can thoughtful people and humanists do but struggle toward suitable words" (p. 692). As Herzog seeks these words, the novel draws closer to nineteenth-century or realist models. In a 1975 essay on Bellow, John Bayley argued that the "American-Jewish novel has the obvious but enormous advantage of continuity not only with the almost pre-fictional tradition of the *honnête homme*, but with the great humanistic liberal and Victorian novel world of Dickens, Thackeray and George Eliot. . . . A certain kind of

Jewish image today is a product not of the Torah and the Hasidim but of *Little Dorrit* and John Stuart Mill."[54]

At the novel's close, an ineffable calm and resolve settles over Herzog. Intimations of this state occur earlier in the novel. At Woods Hole, on Cape Cod, he waits for a ferry in the late afternoon sun:

> He loved to think about the power of the sun, about light, about the ocean. The purity of the air moved him. There was no stain in the water, where schools of minnows swam. Herzog sighed and said to himself, "Praise God—praise God." His breathing had become freer. His heart was greatly stirred by the open horizon; the deep color; the faint iodine pungency of the Atlantic rising from weeds and mollusks; the white, fine, heavy sand; but principally by the green transparency as he looked down to the stony bottom webbed with golden lines. Never still. If his soul could cast a reflection so brilliant, and so intensely sweet, he might beg God to make such use of him (p. 508).

This wish Herzog immediately checks: "too simple," "too childish," the sun is in fact "not clear like this, but turbulent, angry" (p. 508). Nonetheless, the moment, like Tommy Wilhelm's perception of the luminescent water glasses in *Seize the Day*, lingers, as does a comparable moment in a Western Union office in Hyde Park. Standing in the office, Moses suddenly finds "ground to hope that a Life is something more than such a cloud of particles, mere facticity. Go through what is comprehensible and you conclude that only the incomprehensible gives any light. This was by no means a 'general idea' with him now. It was far more substantial than anything he saw in this intensely lighted telegraph office. It all seemed to him exceptionally clear" (pp. 685–86). A similar clarity, what Richard Ellmann in his review of the novel calls "a state of secular blessedness," is reached by Herzog at the novel's close. He returns to his ramshackle house in Ludeyville in the Berkshires, a thinly fictionalized Tivoli. In the sparkling summer light, the unoccupied house "rose out of weeds, vines, trees and blossoms" (p. 730). Herzog calls it his folly, "Monument to his sincere and loving idiocy, to the unrecognized evils of his character" (p. 730). As he begins to recount these evils, he stops: "But enough of that—here I am. *Hineni!* How marvelously beautiful it is today" (p. 731).

Hineni is Hebrew for "Here I am," the word of acceptance uttered

by Abraham as he prepares to sacrifice Isaac. It signals Herzog's acceptance not only of his situation, but of his faith in the ideals the modern
world would deny, and behind them, of something, a radiance, that
stands in the place of Abraham's God. Herzog surveys the garden,
"a thick mass of thorny canes, roses and berries twisted together. It
looked too hopeless—past regretting" (p. 731). He enters the musty
house. Cans of food are stacked in the kitchen, "fancy goods bought by
Madeleine . . . S.S. Pierce terrapin soup, Indian pudding, truffles, olives"
(p. 731). He starts a fire in the fireplace and as the bark drops away from
an old log, the insects underneath, "grubs, ants, long-legged spiders,"
scramble away. He gives them "every opportunity to escape" (p. 731).
In the toilet bowl he finds "the small beaked skulls and other remains
of birds who had nested there after the water was drained, and then had
been entombed by the falling lid. He looked grimly in, his heart aching
somewhat at this accident" (p. 733). Flat-faced owls perch on the red
valances in the bedroom. "He gave them every opportunity to escape,
and, when they were gone, looked for a nest. He found the young owls in
the large light fixture over the bed where he and Madeleine had known
so much misery and hatred" (pp. 733–34). Not wishing to disturb the
owlets, he lugs the mattress into June's room. He opens windows to
let the clear summer air in and is "surprised to feel contentment . . .
contentment? Whom was he kidding, this was joy! . . . His servitude
was ended, and his heart released from its grisly heaviness and encrus-
tation" (p. 734). Now begins the last series of letters, including a letter
to Madeleine and Gersbach: "*Dear Madeleine—You are a terrific one, you
are! Bless you! What a creature! . . . And you, Gersbach, you're welcome to
Madeleine. Enjoy her—rejoice in her. You will not reach me through her, however. I know you sought me in her flesh. But I am no longer there*" (p. 739).

Forgiveness is offered, but with bite, lending realism to Herzog's
transformation. Also realistic is the shakiness with which he negoti-
ates the visit of his brother Will, who has come to Ludeyville to see
if he's all right. Will is worried that Moses may need to be committed
to some sort of hospital. "He must be very careful with Will," Herzog
thinks, "and talk to him only in the most concrete terms about concrete matters" (p. 747). The dialogue between the two brothers (briefly
discussed in Chapter 4) is touching. Will shows "great politeness"
(p. 751) to Moses, is obviously concerned and obviously loves him;
Moses, in turn, feels great sympathy for Will, for the restraints he has
imposed upon himself. Will, being a Herzog, "had a good deal to hold

down" in maintaining his habitual "poise and quiet humor, part dec-
orousness, part (possibly) slavery" (p. 749), a realization that brings
Moses to the verge of tears. The meeting between the brothers follows
the last of the letters written from Ludeyville, a few brief lines to God:

> *How my mind has struggled to make coherent sense. I have not been too
> good at it. But I have desired to do your unknowable will, taking it, and
> you, without symbols. Everything of intensest significance. Especially if
> divested of me* (p. 747).

At this point Moses lies down under the locust trees outside the house.
He feels "confident, even happy in his excitement, stable" (p. 747). In
the very last pages of the novel Ramona comes to visit and Herzog
treats her with new consideration. She has afforded him, as have his
other lovers, consolation and escape, not only from Madeleine but from
the self-image Madeleine has left him with, as failed lover and husband.
Now he will care for her. He buys candles for the dinner they are to
have, because he knows she likes them. He picks flowers for her, confident "that they couldn't be turned against him" (Ramona is a florist).
Ellen Pifer is good on this moment: "Herzog is for once the assertive
host rather than Ramona's passive guest. Earlier in New York City, she
had been 'emphatic about the wine,' refusing to let him bring a bottle
along for the dinner. At that time Herzog attributed her insistence that
he not bring wine to the 'feeling of protectiveness' he 'produced' in
people. Now it is Herzog's turn to insist on supplying all the provisions
for dinner—and the 'emphatic' tone is his. 'You'll do nothing of the
sort,' he tells Ramona when she offers to bring the wine."[55]

In the novel's final paragraph Herzog declares that he will write no
more letters. "Whatever had come over him during these last months,
the spell, really seemed to be passing, really going" (p. 763). After
returning home with provisions, he lies down again, this time on the
couch. He hears the "steady scratching" of the cleaning lady's broom
and thinks he should tell her to sprinkle the floor with water, so as not
to raise so much dust. "In a few minutes he would call down to her,
'Damp it down, Mrs. Tuttle. There's water in the sink.' But not just
yet. At this time he had no messages for anyone. Nothing. Not a single
word." These are the final words of the novel and their effect, or one of
their effects, is to call to mind and complicate the novel's opening sentence, consistent through all drafts: "If I am out of my mind, it's all right

with me, thought Moses Herzog." This sentence, the ending reminds us, is uttered after the "spell" has broken, and refers not to Moses's fevered letter writing and erratic behavior, but to his newfound calm. In a review of *Herzog* in *The Massachusetts Review*, Rosette Lamont, the model for Ramona, commends the "wonderful sense of peace" at the novel's conclusion, describing as "Buddhist" Herzog's reverence for all forms of life.[56] She also recalls his attraction to the Russian religious philosophers Soloviev (with his theory that for the Jews God is "a subsistent I") and Berdyaev (who claims that religious life, in Lamont's paraphrase, "must pass from the subjective, individualistic phase into a phase of supra-rational, supra-personal spirituality").[57] The Russian she might also have mentioned is Tolstoy. At the end of *Anna Karenina*, a novel Bellow frequently taught while at work on *Herzog*, Levin, like Herzog, returns to his estate in the country and attains a spiritual certainty difficult for him to explain:

> "This new feeling has not changed me, has not made me happy and enlightened me all of a sudden as I had dreamed it would. . . . There was no surprise about it either. But whether it is faith or not—I don't know what it is—but that feeling has entered just as imperceptibly into my soul through suffering and has lodged itself there firmly.
>
> "I shall still get angry with my coachman Ivan, I shall still argue and express my thoughts inopportunely; there will still be a wall between the holy of holies of my soul and other people, even my wife, and I shall still blame her for my own fears and shall regret it; I shall still be unable to understand with my reason why I am praying, and I shall continue to pray—but my life, my whole life, independently of anything that may happen, every moment of it, is no longer meaningless as it was before, but has an incontestable meaning of goodness, with which I have the power to invest it."[58]

NOT ALL CRITICS OF *HERZOG* were persuaded by Moses's comparable transformation, not even those who praised the novel and counted themselves Bellow's friends. Ted Solotaroff found the prose of the concluding section "so naturally luminous and moving that one tends to overlook the fact that it is quietly burying most of the issues that earlier had been raised in connection with Herzog's relations to society. At the end, he rests more firmly and spiritually in his passivity, but it is still passivity." And later: "Isn't he merely availing himself of the solace of faith without committing himself to its substance? . . . God requires more desire than Herzog has to give; so far he hasn't abandoned the old Self but merely found an illusion of having done so."[59] Another critic, Roger Sale, also in a positive notice, described Herzog in the concluding part of the novel as "simply and unhelpfully full of faith."[60] The most forceful and wounding of the objections to Herzog's transformation came from Richard Poirier, who first met Bellow in 1960 at Bard College, "when I was visiting my friends and his, Jack Ludwig and his wife Leah [Leya]."[61] Poirier and Ludwig coedited the volume *Stories, British and Modern* (1953) and during the years Bellow and Ludwig were best friends, the three men met on several occasions, both in New York and in Boston (where Poirier was a professor of English at Harvard from 1953 to 1961). Bellow and Poirier also met for dinner at Lillian Hellman's house in Martha's Vineyard, when Poirier was a houseguest and Hellman was helping Bellow with *The Last Analysis.* Bellow invited Poirier to the launch party for *Herzog* at "21," where, according to Poirier, they "had a brief but pleasant exchange, though not about the book, which I hadn't yet read. He asked, among other things, how I was getting on at *Partisan Review* (where I had been an editor) with William Phillips and Philip Rahv."

That Poirier's review appeared in *Partisan Review* ("Bellows to Herzog," Spring 1965) compounded Bellow's upset and caused a bitter break with William Phillips (Rahv at this time, according to Phillips, "contributed very little to the daily running of the magazine, very little to the editorial side"[62]); many years later, when Poirier and Phillips were admitted as members of the Century Association, Bellow resigned in protest.[63] Poirier's review begins *"Herzog* is an insufferably smug book" and ends by calling its hero's ideas "sophomoric tag-lines" that "don't deserve the status of 'ideas.' Whatever they are they're really as comfortable as old shoes, especially when you can so believe in their 'unbearable intensity' that you can lie down. And it is from this position that the story is told."[64] The letters, Poirier writes, "for all the parroted praise the reviews have given them, are frequently uninventive and tiresome" (p. 267). They are "pseudo-philosophical or sociological or historical expansions" of the hero's parochial or personal dilemmas, lamentable because Bellow takes them straight, having lost "his customary ear for banality of expression or for the fatuity of the expressions thus phrased" (p. 267). Poirier was a formidably well-read and penetrating critic who deserves to be taken seriously. So was Frank Kermode, who reviewed the novel in the *New Statesman* (November 5, 1965). For Kermode, the letters are an ingenious way of showing "an intellectual operating in the world." "They seem to me to have the exceptional merit of turning the technical trick and then, because sparingly used and full of wit, to become delightful in themselves." In a passage of Poirier's review that recalls John Bayley on Bellow's debt to the Victorians, the "thought" or "idea" sections of the novel are said to "read like a lesser *Middlemarch*, the longest of the 'ridiculous' letters offering pretty much what Bellow-Herzog want to say about 'modern' life." "Ridiculous," here, is Herzog's word and points to Poirier's other main objection to the novel: that Herzog's self-criticisms allow Bellow to "operate snugly (and smugly) within the enclosure of his hero's recollections, assured, at least to his own satisfaction, that he has anticipated and therefore forestalled antagonistic intrusions from outside." Herzog's sufferings at the hands of Gersbach and Madeleine (whose versions of the betrayal, which Poirier calls "alleged," never appear) "issue forth less as accusations against others than as self-contempt for his having been cozened by them." As a consequence, according to Poirier, they help to support the hero's "claims to guiltlessness" (p. 267). Poirier's "alleged" I take to be a slip, as it calls to mind the book's real-life origins, high-mindedly ignored elsewhere in the review. The novel itself offers no reason to question the betrayals.

Poirier's criticisms nestle cheek by jowl with praise for the Napoleon Street sections of the novel and what he calls "the world of Herzog," a creation of "an energy marvelously wasteful of detail, dazzling in its plays of style, properly self-delighting in its ingenuities of pace and timing and proportion" (p. 266). Poirier associates energy with excess, transgression, performance, qualities Herzog distrusts and relates to Romantic and modernist notions of the artist as alienated outsider or outlaw. In Poirier's view, the letters and other extended "ideas" passages in *Herzog* are deficient in energy; he sees them, I'd suggest, much as others see the heroes and heroines of Dickens novels (the Esther Summersons and David Copperfields) or Milton's God in comparison to his Satan. "My objection isn't merely that Bellow would replace the 'commonplaces' of alienation with even more obvious commonplaces about 'the longing to be human,'" Poirier writes. "I mean that his works, the truest and sure direction of their energy, suggest to me that imaginatively Bellow does not himself find a source of order in these commonplaces" (p. 268). For Poirier, goodness or "the longing to be human," like Henry de Montherlant's happiness ("Le bonheur"), writes white, as Milton, for William Blake, "was a true Poet and of the Devil's party without knowing it."[65] Poirier admired the writing of Norman Mailer, very much a writer of the Devil's party, author of "The White Negro" (1957), with its praise of the hipster as psychopath. Mailer's latest novel, *An American Dream* (1965), was serialized monthly in *Esquire* in 1964. It opens with the hero, Stephen Rojack, strangling his wife, then walking downstairs to bugger the wife's German maid. Mailer was famous for having stabbed his second wife in 1960 and nearly killing her. Poirier defended the novel against the criticisms of Elizabeth Hardwick, Philip Rahv, and others in a review in the June 1965 issue of *Commentary.*

Mailer at this date was almost as famous for literary pugilism as for wife stabbing, and had been jabbing at Bellow for some time. He called *The Adventures of Augie March* "a travelogue for timid intellectuals," complaining that Bellow's writing "does no obvious harm, but I think one must not be easy on art which tries for less than it can manage."[66] Though he praised *Henderson the Rain King* in a review in *Esquire*—the review begins "Well, one might as well eat crow right here. Henderson is an exceptional character, almost worthy of Gulliver or Huckleberry Finn"—he also pronounced the ending a damp squib and Bellow "too timid to become a great writer."[67] Bellow responded coolly in an interview of 1964. "I'm sure I'm not a great writer in Norman Mailer's light, but then I don't want to be a great writer in Norman Mailer's light. I satisfy neither his idea of greatness nor mine. . . . I sense in Mailer a certain pathos; he senses a rudderless feeling in himself and all the rest. He sees me with a bit of a rudder but sailing in the wrong way."[68] When *Herzog* was published Mailer was asked to comment about both the novel and Bellow's not wanting to be Mailer's sort of great writer. At a publishers' association press conference, Mailer declared that the "moral nihilists" Herzog and Bellow attacked "are responsible for all the real developments in literature. We are the adventurous ones. Conventional morality attacks violence . . . but better to attack an act of violence against one person than to curb that impulse and spend twenty years poisoning the lives of everyone around you." As for *Herzog*, "I admire the novel . . . very much. But it is not a book of ideas. There is nothing intellectually new in it. Bellow is mindless. There is depth of feeling in his novel. His humanity gets to you. But his mind is that of a college professor who had read all the good books and absorbed none of them." Mailer concluded by calling his rival novelist a "hostess of the intellectual canapé table," a remark J. Michael Lennon, Mailer's biographer, describes as "widely quoted."[69] In less public settings, Mailer was harsher, yet also more admiring. In a letter to Bellow of December 23, 1964, Aaron Asher paraphrased an unprompted drunken monologue Mailer treated him to at a party given by Rust Hills:

> He read *Herzog* with his "pistol out." Nothing in it works, the women are no good, Herzog is no good, the ideas are no good—Bellow is shopping around among other men's ideas. The book is scummy. But—he doesn't exactly know why—the scum is only scum, on the surface. Underneath runs something clean and strong. It's an important book, "he's done it, something." Ramona, what's she doing with this slob? She should put a pistol to the back of his neck and pull the trigger, "I would." But there's all that compassion in it. If Hitler had read the book he would have spared half his victims. I asked, "Are you tougher than Hitler?" He said not to take him literally when he spoke of pistols. All this in his staccato, but fuzzy with drink. And then he said, "But why does Bellow always write about people who are dumber than he is? He's smart and he writes about fools. I'm the opposite. There aren't two people in the world less alike than we are."

Though Bellow may have been right in thinking Mailer saw himself as rudderless, to many observers the ultimate course he was steering was clear—toward the counterculture and the New Left. The contents of the spring 1965 issue of *Partisan Review*, containing Poirier's review of *Herzog*, give a sense of the controversy this direction or trend was stirring in intellectual circles and of the way Mailer and Bellow were being positioned in relation to it. The lead article was a debate between Nat Hentoff and Michael Harrington on "The New Radicalism." The next article was by Susan Sontag on "Marat/Sade/Artaud." Poirier's attack on Bellow was balanced by Elizabeth Hardwick's attack on Mailer's *An American Dream*, which she described as "an intellectual and literary disaster, poorly written, morally foolish and intellectually empty" ("Fixes for Fiction," p. 291). Opposite the review was an advertisement for the next issue, listing Jack Ludwig among the contributors. Before the review appeared Philip Rahv wrote to Bellow on April 6, 1965, registering both his disapproval of the decision to publish it and his suspicions of the political as well as personal motives behind the decision:

> Dear Saul,
>
>   I am extremely sorry to tell you that the next issue of PR has a review in it of your novel by Dick Poirier which is negative and hostile. Given my present rather tenuous relationship with the magazine, I could do nothing to stop it. It's a ridiculous review, full of sophistries. What Dick is doing is practicing one-upmanship, trying to differentiate himself from me. It's an attack on my judgment. *Entre nous,* what William and Dick are doing is lining up with the swingers, particularly the camp culturati led by Susan Sontag. Being plainly a heterosexual type, you are typed as a square by those people, just as I am typed in the same manner. In my view, the magazine is done for, especially since I'm going back to Brandeis in the fall and to Europe this summer. It won't be long before I get off it altogether . . .
>
>   Cordially, Philip

In later years, William Phillips regretted the decision to publish Poirier's review. "We did think of him [Bellow] as part of the new alignment of writers, and there was a good deal of affection and respect for him." The decision to publish involved "a conflict between literary sympathy and adverse criticism. I now feel the claims of community and loyalty to the history of the magazine may be more important than an abstract principle of objectivity."[70] This was certainly what Bellow felt. Poirier, in contrast, by the report of friends and supporters as well as enemies, had no such regrets. "One had the impression that he [Poirier] was fearless, at least in professional and social contexts," writes James Barszcz, an ex-student, loyal friend, and colleague at the literary magazine *Raritan*, of which Poirier was founding editor (Poirier was also, with Edmund Wilson, the founder of the Library of America series, the edition used here for many of Bellow's writings). "He was certainly unapologetic; he would not allow himself to be bored and he didn't care what people thought when he showed it. . . . He is said to have fought ferociously in administrative political battles at Rutgers and elsewhere. . . . He was said to have ruined people's professional lives through caustic letters of recommendation, and to have brought opponents to tears during debates in faculty meetings."[71] But Poirier also helped many students, had a wide circle of literary acquaintance, and was a founder with Reuben Brower of the storied Hum 6 course at Harvard, which encouraged students to read "in slow motion," in the manner of New Critical close reading.

That Poirier and Ludwig discussed both *Herzog* and the relative merits of Bellow and Mailer is more than likely. In December 1964, before Poirier's review appeared, Ludwig, now at Stony Brook (Poirier was now at Rutgers), spoke on a panel at the MLA Convention in New York on "Topics in Modern Literature," taking as his title, "Bellow, Mailer, and Ellison." The panel was chaired by Irving Howe, and according to Lewis Nichols in *The New York Times Book Review*, "preliminary rumors hinted that [it] would set off fireworks, and almost 1,000 members turned out to watch them."[72] Bellow's marital difficulties had become an item of intellectual and academic gossip far beyond Minneapolis. Two months after the MLA Convention, with characteristic *chutzpah*, Ludwig wrote a long review of *Herzog* in *Holiday* magazine. Like his MLA talk, the review was fulsome in praise of Bellow, an artist "of enormous gifts." It also anticipated several of the criticisms in Poirier's review. Herzog's spiritual transformation at the end of the novel was snidely dismissed: "Moses on the Berkshire Mountain can contemplate the Promised Land secure in the knowledge that on the flats brother Shura is playing the necessary footsie with the Golden Calf." The review also made much of Herzog's tendency to whine and complain, then to criticize himself for doing so, a move seen, as in the Poirier review, as protective on Bellow's part as well as Herzog's. Ludwig begins by disapproving of readers who "confound the author with his hero," but his own reading is at moments biographical. After warning that Bellow's "superbly intricate novel needs a reader who will not take any of Herzog's wooden nickels," by which he means not take his claims at face value, he describes how the character's perspective is all-controlling:

> He describes a universe in which he is the center and source of light, the universe being a set of revolving, whirling characters—wives, children, family, friends, colleagues—each reflecting as much light as Herzog allows. There is no Eisenhower but Herzog's Eisenhower, no Mady but Herzog's, no Doctor Edvig but *his*. Herzog has woven a web; all who enter are caught. In Herzog's universe the moon has no other side. Those who are brought in come as testi-

monials to a Herzog who smells sweet, tells great stories, loves with fervor. From time to time Herzog's great double perspective, which sees suffering *and* its possible absurdity, reasserts itself, and in so doing makes a novel of great richness.

Why talk here of Mady's "other side" unless you're thinking of a real-life model? Or unless you're the sort of critic who asks how many children Lady Macbeth had, a question no self-respecting literary academic would ask in 1965.[73] Why, elsewhere in the review, complain of Herzog's "mysterious depth of tastelessness" in describing the hunchbacked Himmelstein as a "humped rat"? Herzog is furious with Himmelstein, the description is something he thinks, not says, and Himmelstein *is* a "rat" (professing love for Herzog while siding with Madeleine, as well as acting for her). Jonas Schwartz might not have been a rat, Sandor Himmelstein was. The cruelty of the phrase, it should also be said, is funny, a product of the energy Poirier admires, as is Herzog's description of Ramona's lovesick admirer, George Hoberly, as "that sobbing prick!" (p. 626). A personal or extraliterary note is also struck when Ludwig wonders how "Herzog, with his Japanese girlfriend Sono, differed so radically from his wife, Mady," or "what brought about a divorce between two such obviously 'nice' people as Herzog and his first wife, Daisy." That Herzog was, as he says of himself, "brought up on moral principles," is for Ludwig one of the "wooden nickels" he claims Bellow wants the reader not to buy. The review is clever and when Bellow read it he was impressed as well as appalled. In a letter of January 28, 1965, to Alfred Kazin, he called the review "a masterpiece in its own way—a great virtuoso performance on the high-wire of self-justification. Ingenious, shrewd, supersubtle, shamanistic, Rasputin-like. I'm really proud of the man. His cast-iron effrontery is admirable, somehow."

Three years later, in 1968, Ludwig produced his own fictional account of the real-life incidents out of which *Herzog* grew, in a novel entitled *Above Ground*.[74] The hero of Ludwig's novel is Josh, a literary academic who has a bad leg, the result of a poorly treated fractured hip that never mended. Josh has known excruciating pain, which he bears stoically. He lives life to the full because he knows suffering and because he is afraid of death (his goal is to stay "above ground" for as long as possible). Fear of death also explains Josh's promiscuity, every bit as pronounced as Herzog's. He falls in love frequently and has many serious lovers, both before and after marrying Maggie, with whom he has a daughter. He loves Maggie but he also loves all the other women in his life because he has a big heart. The most dangerous of these women is Mavra, a neighbor married to a neurotic sculptor named Louie. Mavra latches onto Josh and Maggie. She is promiscuous, self-destructive, in therapy (with a Paul Meehl/Edvig figure), a congenital liar and fantasist, self-centered, and contemptuous of Louie. Mavra and Louie live in a "carriagebarn" (p. 245). When Mavra gives birth to Dov, their son, Louie, "a small bugeyed man" (p. 255) later said to have a "hairyknuckle hand" (p. 262), sobs and carries on: "The kid—did you see the kid? His feet! Dusty. He walked all the way. Mavrie, sweet girl. She looks just like Ma. Ma gave birth—hair like that—I can't stand it. Those feet. My kid!" (p. 255). Louie and Mavra don't get on in bed. Louie accuses Mavra of being frigid, partly because she's been sexually abused by her father. There's a fight in which Mavra flees with Dov in the car and Louie accuses her of trying to run him down.

Louie is a secondary character both in Mavra's life and in the novel, as Sasha claimed Bellow was in her life (she and Bellow were only briefly married, she reminded me several times, while her second marriage, according to her son and others, was strong, happy, and lasted more than forty years, until her death in 2012). Brave, loving Josh is the focus, torn between Maggie and Mavra. Maggie is steadfast, true, and long-suffering; Mavra is like Madeleine, only worse, being a nymphomaniac as well as psychotic (there are lengthy extracts from soft-porn letters "concocted" by Mavra, she says, to amuse Josh, which Bellow claimed Ludwig lifted from Sasha's own letters[75]). "Look at her victory!" Maggie cries. "She has you. Louie has the story of his maim" (p. 340) (this story is spoken of as an asset, like the story of Bellow's "maim" at the hands of Sasha and Ludwig, turned to profit in *Herzog*, Ludwig implies). There are connections between Maggie and Gersbach's wife, Phoebe, who accuses Herzog and Madeleine of corrupting Gersbach. The difference is that Maggie's decision not to leave Josh signals love and intelligence, whereas Phoebe's staying with Gersbach is seen mostly as weakness. "With Gersbach she could still be a wife. He came home. She cooked, ironed, shopped, signed checks. Without him, she could not exist, shop, make beds. The trance would break" (p. 683).[76] These and other differences in plot and characterization pale before the gulf in talent and competence between the two novels. Ludwig's novel is terrible, as bad in the sections on Josh's childhood in Winnipeg, pale equivalents of the Napoleon Street scenes in *Herzog*, as in scenes from the narrative present. When Bellow read it, he was disgusted, as he makes clear in an undated letter to Sasha, quoted in part in the introduction to this book. Sasha had written to him to complain about money and about his rudeness to her at a recent meeting. After apologizing for the rudeness, he turns to money and the question of humiliation:

> First of all, then: I wrote a successful book. I owe you nothing for that. You damn near killed me. I've put that behind me, but I haven't forgotten the smallest detail. Nothing, I assure you. I made something of the abuses I suffered at your hands. As for the "humiliations" you speak of, I can match you easily. There is another book, isn't there? It is the product of two minds and two spirits, not one. Kind acquaintances and friends have made sure that I would read it. The letters of the heroine are consciously superior in style, but the book is garbage. It is monstrous to be touched by anything so horribly written. The worst thing about it, to a man who has been faithful to his art for thirty years, is the criminal vulgarity of the thing. I don't worry too much about my reputation, the "image"

An undated photograph of Susan Glassman Bellow (b. 1933)

(I don't think you pay much attention to that, either), but I loathe being even peripherally involved with such shit. Now I've gotten a foot in the cesspool. Enough of that. But suppose the book had been good, successful. Can you see me demanding damages? I don't think you can. So now . . . let the thing stop there. I want you to say nothing more to me about money, and I don't want any hints about damages and indemnities.

The tone of command here would be heard with increasing frequency in the years to come. The letter was written in 1968, by which time Bellow was rich, famous, internationally acclaimed, a figure of power and influence in literary and intellectual circles. The struggle to be recognized as a writer, then as a writer of greatness, had been won, but he remained embattled, at war with his wives, outraged by the excesses of the 1960s. Recognition itself now threatened his freedom; he was hounded by the demands of fame, distracted by its many temptations. Though his personal life was in turmoil, he was writing some of the best things he'd ever written. He would remain in Chicago, his routine for the most part the same, he continued to teach, to travel, to see old friends and family, but his life had changed: he had arrived at the pinnacle of American letters, and he knew it.

Acknowledgments

I am indebted to Andrew Wylie, who first suggested that I write Bellow's biography and who has been a staunch supporter of this book throughout. I am indebted also to the Saul Bellow Literary Estate, to Janis Freedman Bellow and Walter Pozen. Bellow's sons, Gregory, Adam, and Daniel, have been generous with their knowledge and time, granting lengthy interviews and enduring numerous queries. Bellow had five wives. His first and third wives, Anita Goshkin Bellow and Susan Glassman Bellow, died before I began work on the biography. His second wife, Sondra "Sasha" Tschacbasov Bellow; his fourth wife, Alexandra Ionescu Tulcea Bellow; and his fifth wife, Janis Freedman Bellow, generously granted me interviews, as well as helping in innumerable other ways with queries and introductions. Bellow took a keen and loving interest in his larger family and I have been much helped by a number of his relatives, in particular by his nephew Joel Bellows and his niece Lesha Bellows Greengus, together with her husband, Sam Greengus. The children of Bellow's nephews and nieces also granted interviews and answered queries. Other Bellow relatives were generous with their time as well. Soon after I began work on the biography I was put in touch with Benjamin Taylor, who was editing Bellow's letters and is now at work on a volume of Bellow's essays, published to coincide with the centennial of Bellow's birth. Ben has been a friend of this book since its inception. A full list of those who agreed to formal interviews, subsequently helping with inquiries, is provided in the Note on Sources.

For advice and assistance I am grateful to the administration and staff of the Special Collections Research Center at the Joseph Regenstein Library at the University of Chicago, in particular to Dan Meyer, Alice Schreyer, Eileen Ielmini, David Pavlich, Barbara Gilbert, and Julia Gardner. Eileen Ielmini not only helped me to navigate the enormous Bellow collection, with its complicated inventories, but was unfailingly helpful before and after my several stays in Chicago. In Winter Quarter 2008 I was a visiting professor at the Committee on Social Thought, where Bellow taught for more than thirty years. There I conducted a seminar on his novels and stories and learned a great deal from the responses of my students, both those from the Committee and those from other departments. I am especially grateful to Robert Pippin, chair of the Committee, for arranging my visit, to Anne M. Gamboa, the Committee's administrative assistant, for smoothing my way once I'd arrived, and to those Committee members who knew and worked with Bellow, offering me interviews, advice, and assistance, among them Nathan Tarcov, Paul Friedrich, Wendy Doniger, Ralph Lerner, James Redfield, and Leon Kass. David Nirenberg arrived at the Committee after Bellow but was a friendly and informative colleague throughout my stay. The late Richard Stern, Bellow's great friend from the English Department, also welcomed me, as did W. J. T. Mitchell, another English Department member. Finally, I am grateful to Donna Sinopoli of the University of Chicago's Housing Services, who found my wife and me an apartment on the twelfth floor of the Cloisters, the splendid 1920s apartment building where Saul Bellow lived for more than a dozen years. Although wary of the "footsteps" approach to biography, it was inspiring to live in a building Bellow lived in, to share much the same view he had, and to walk each morning to an office at the Committee on Social Thought along the routes he would have taken.

I am grateful to the Guggenheim Foundation for a Fellowship in 2009 to free me from teaching. I am also grateful to the Department of English and Creative Writing at the University of Roehampton for Research Leave in 2014. The first chapter of the biography was written outside Genoa at the Liguria Study Center for the Arts and Humanities, on a monthlong fellowship from the Bogliasco Foundation. At the University of Roehampton I am grateful for the support of my colleagues, in particular Jenny Hartley, Laura Peters, and Jenny Watt, of the Department of English and Creative Writing. At the Wylie Agency

I owe thanks to Jeffrey Posternak and Jessica Henderson in New York and James Pullen in London. At Jonathan Cape I am indebted to the continued support of Dan Franklin and at Knopf to the continued support of Erroll McDonald, both of whom published my biography of Kingsley Amis. Caroline Bleeke and Nicholas Thomson of Knopf were especially helpful in the preparation of the manuscript, but I also owe thanks to Meghan Hauser, Kathleen Fridella, Jessica Purcell, Cassandra Pappas, Lisa Montebello, Fred Chase, George Wen, Bert Yaeger, and to Douglas Matthews, who prepared the index. At Jonathan Cape I owe thanks to Clare Bullock, Kris Potter, and Joe Pickering.

For careful reading of the entire manuscript I am grateful first and foremost to Lindsay Duguid, who improved the book at every stage of its composition. Andrew Gordon also read the entire manuscript, correcting mistakes and offering shrewd advice. For reading portions of the manuscript I am grateful to Karl Miller, Nathan Tarcov, Erik Tarloff, John Lloyd, Philip Roth, Ellen Siegelman, and Janis Freedman Bellow. Much is owed to several researchers: Jonathan Roy Turner, in particular, a resourceful and efficient research student at Roehampton; David Goodstone in London, now San Francisco; Aleksander Feigmanis in Moscow; Angelina Davydova and Andrei Kudryashov in St. Petersburg; Krista Reynan, Laura Alagna, Abby Durnett, and Justin Race in Chicago; and Manny Steinberg, who acted as translator for several interviews with Bellow's non-English-speaking relatives in Israel.

For help in archives, libraries, foundations, and institutions I am grateful to the following: Cheryl Schnirring, Abraham Lincoln Presidential Library, Springfield, Illinois; Donald Davis, Archives, American Friends Service Committee; Helene Tieger, Bard College Library; Anne Garner and Isaac Gewirtz, Berg Collection, New York Public Library; Robert Rothstein, Geddes Language Center, Boston University; Pamela Hopkins and Yu Hua Li, Harvard University Archives; Claudine Klose, Historic Red Hook; Ellen Keith, Matt Krc, and Debbie Vaughan, Chicago History Museum; Susan Art, Sharon Hudak, Jeanine I. Alonso, Heatherlyn Mayer, Rita Vazquez, Office of the Registrar, University of Chicago; Rare Book and Manuscript Library, Butler Library, Columbia University; Laurie Rizzo, Special Collections, University of Delaware Library; Elizabeth B. Dunn and David M. Rubenstein, Rare Book and Manuscript Library, Duke University; André Bernard and Edward Hirsch, Guggenheim Foundation; William Furry, Illinois State Historical Society; Shannon Hodge and Eva Raby, Jewish Public Library Archives, Montreal; Alice Birney, Manuscript Division, Library of Congress; London Library; Barbara Cline and Tina Houston, Lyndon Baines Johnson Library; Erin George and Elizabeth Kaplan, University of Minnesota Archives, Elmer L. Andersen Library; Frank Blalark, Office of the Registrar, University of Minnesota; Liat Cohen, Elie Derman, Ofira Ratsab, Mishkenot Sha'ananim, the Jerusalem Foundation; Maria Molestina, the Morgan Library and Museum; Patrick Quinn and Janet C. Olson, Northwestern University Archives; Tamara Thatcher, Council of the Humanities, Princeton University; Kristen Turner and Rosalba Varella Recchia, Mudd Manuscript Library, Princeton University; Rare Books and Special Collections, Firestone Library, Princeton University; Cheryl Van Emburg, Salzburg Seminars; Wendy Chmielewski and Mary Beth Sigado, Swarthmore Peace Collection; Dean Rogers, Archives and Special Collection, Vassar College Libraries; Georgette Ballweg, Office of the Registrar, University of Wisconsin; Lori B. Bessler and Lee Grady, Wisconsin Historical Society; Leslie L. Leduc, Corporation of Yaddo.

I am grateful to the following individuals for offering information, advice, and hospitality: Victoria Aarons, Gillon Aitken, Martin Amis, Janet Ariad, David Bell, Julie Ann Benson, Judith and Lawrence Besserman, Dina Binstock, Dean Borok, Emily Budick, Shirley Cohen, Jay Corcoran, Gloria L. Cronin, H. M. Daleski, Philip Davis, Carol Denbo, Barbara Dickstein, Morris Dickstein, Jane Dietrich, Peggy Eisenstein, Paul Ekman, Esther Elster, Anne Feibleman, Catherine J. Fitzpatrick, Judith Flanders, Kappy Flanders, June Fox, Liz Frank, Rani Friedlander, Abraham Fuks, David Gooblar, Grey Gowrie, Selina Hastings, the Hellmuths (Mary, John, Alison, Spencer, and Molly), Christopher Hitchens, Jacob Howland, Lewis Hyde, Nicole Jackson, Eric Jacobson, Neil Jarmonville, Leslie Kaplan, Sheila Kay, Shirley Kaufman, Edmund Keeley, Mark Lambert, Scott Latham, Roz Leader, Zoe Leader, Alexandra Lidov, John Lloyd, Peter Manning, Bobby Markels, Anita Maximilian, Carolyn McGrath, Edward Mendelson, Michael Mewshaw, David Mikics, Elèna Mortara, Janet Nippel, Richard O'Brien, Doris Palca, Thomas Passin, Matt Phillips, Arnold Rampersad, Michael Roberts, Mary Rynerson, Rosemarie Sanchez-Fraser, Dr. Rachel Schultz, Sasha Schwartz, Tim Seldes, Adam Shils, Elaine and English Showalter, Margalit Steinberg, Christopher Turner, Patricia Vidgerman, Annie Dubouillon Walter, Ann Weinstein, Jacob Weisberg, Catherine Wells-Cole, Rose Wild, Hana Wirth-Nesher, Nancy Bass Wyden, Steven J. Zipperstein.

Finally, I thank my wife, Alice Leader, the dedicatee of this volume, my sons, Nick and Max Leader, and their partners, Nicole Jackson and Zoe Smith. Like many friends and colleagues, they have heard rather a lot about Saul Bellow in recent years.

A Note on Sources

Unless specified, all unpublished or manuscript material by Saul Bellow, including letters, is to be found among the Saul Bellow Papers in the Special Collections Research Center of the Joseph Regenstein Library at the University of Chicago, cited within the text and notes as Regenstein. I have been given unrestricted access to all 350 boxes of the Bellow Papers, including previously restricted materials contained in some 81 boxes.

The cataloging of the Bellow Papers raises problems for scholars and researchers. From 1960 onward, in a series of gifts and deposits, Bellow sent his papers (including notebooks, galley proofs, unpublished speeches and essays, hand-corrected manuscripts, typewritten drafts, letters, and miscellaneous items pertaining to his life and work, including interviews, profiles, photographs, tax returns, legal and financial documents, and reviews of his novels, stories, essays, and plays) to the Regenstein. Before 1968, writers were eligible to receive a tax deduction for such gifts; when the law involving cultural property changed in reaction to enormous deductions obtained by visual artists, Bellow's gifts became deposits, held but not owned by the library, an arrangement agreed to in the hope that the new law would be reversed and deposits could then become donations. After Bellow's death in 2005, at the age of eighty-nine, the executors of his literary estate decided that his papers should be kept together at the Regenstein. As a result of this decision, roughly 150 boxes of materials joined the two hundred boxes already housed in Special Collections. The Papers are yet to be formally organized or indexed by the University of Chicago Library, in part for financial reasons, in part because the library had been under-standably reluctant to process deposits, which, unlike donations, were owned by the author or the author's estate.

The Regenstein is now in the process of raising money to process the Bellow Papers properly. The present "Scope Note" to the Papers offers guidance to only part of the collection and is organized by deposit or gift. In the case of correspondence, letters from longtime friends and associates are scattered in dozens of deposits or gifts with sepa-rate inventories. In the case of manuscript material there are related problems. Bellow was a demon reviser, he rarely dated manuscripts, and the inventories make only a few shrewd attempts at ordering drafts. Daniel Fuchs, the author of *Saul Bellow: Vision and Revision* (1984), the best study of Bellow's composing process, gives reference names and numbers to the manuscripts he discusses but does so from outdated inventories. Fuchs's study is an invaluable resource for students of Bel-low's writing but it is very difficult, at times impossible, to identify the draft versions he cites, not only for researchers but for the collection's efficient and professional archivists. Given the partial nature of the current inventories, together with the high likelihood of the collection being rationalized and properly processed in the near future, I have decided against providing folder, box, and deposit or gift numbers and names for unpublished correspondence or draft material, though I give dates and estimated dates for individual items.

The Regenstein is the location of almost all letters to Bellow quoted from in the biography. The exceptions are several letters from Barley Alison, in the possession of her niece, Rosie Alison; from Susan Glass-man Bellow, in the possession of Daniel Bellow; and from Ralph Ross, in the possession of Philip Siegelman. Sondra (Sasha) Bellow gave me a copy of her unpublished memoir, "What's in a Name?" Daniel Bellow provided me with access to his mother's unpublished essay, "Mugging the Muse." Richard M. Cook provided me with unpublished entries in Alfred Kazin's journals, located in the Berg Collection in the New York Public Library. Published letters by Saul Bellow are from Benja-min Taylor, ed., *Saul Bellow: Letters* (New York: Viking, 2010), which "includes about two fifths of Saul Bellow's known output of letters" (p. 553). On occasion, passages omitted by Taylor are restored from the original letter. Accents omitted by Bellow in original letters, many written by hand, have been added, and misspelled proper names corrected. Taylor lists the locations for Bellow letters not located in the Regenstein (pp. 553–56). The fullest annotated bibliography of works by and about Bellow remains Gloria L. Cronin and Blaine H. Hall, *Saul Bellow: An Annotated Bibliography*, 2nd ed. (New York: Garland, 1987), available electronically at http://www.saulbellow.org/bibliography. The *Saul Bellow Journal*, eds. Gloria L. Cronin and Victoria Aarons, has been in publication since 1981 and currently appears twice annually. It publishes updated "Selected Annotated Bibliographies," edited by Gloria L. Cronin and Robert Means, and is available electronically on EBSCO. There have been three previous biographical studies of Saul Bellow: *Saul Bellow: Drumlin Woodchuck* (1980) by Mark Harris, *Saul Bellow: A Biography of the Imagination* (1991) by Ruth Miller, and *Bellow: A Biography* (2000) by James Atlas. Harris's book is a memoir, as much about his problems trying to write Bellow's biography as about Bellow himself. Miller's book mostly reads the life through the fiction. Only Atlas's book is a full-scale biography. As is clear from text and notes, I am indebted to the work of all three of my predecessors, but especially to that of James Atlas. Although I do not always agree with Atlas about Bellow's life and works, I wholly share his sense that the "biographical forays" of my predecessors have "paved the way for my own."

Texts of Bellow's works cited in the notes refer to the editions used by the author. A list of Editions Cited, including details of original publication, can be found at the head of the notes. After an initial note, quotations from Bellow's fiction and other sources are cited within the text by page numbers.

Unless otherwise specified in text or notes, the phrase "in an interview" means an interview with Zachary Leader. All unattributed quotations in the biography come from the following interviews:

Ada Aharoni, 23 May 2010 (Nesher, Israel); Rosie Alison, 1 December 2007 (London); Aharon Appelfeld, 21 May 2010 (Jerusalem); Linda Asher, 9 January 2009 (New York); John Barnardo, 2 August 2010 (Boston); Wolf Baronov, 23 July 2008 (Chicago); Adam Bellow, 23, 27 March, 20 May 2008 (New York); Alexandra Bellow, 5 February, 1, 3 April 2008 (Chicago); Daniel Bellow, 11, 15 May 2008 (Great Barrington, MA); Gregory Bellow, 20 August, 30 December 2008 (Redwood City and San Francisco, CA); Janis Freedman Bellow, 5, 6, 7 August 2010 (Brattleboro, VT); Juliet Bellow,

20 December 2008 (San Francisco); Lily Bellow, 27 March 2008 (New York); Rachel Bellow, 7 August 2010 (Cambridge, MA); Sondra "Sasha" Bellow, 30 July 2007, 22, 23 March 2008 (New York); Bambi Bellows, 19 January 2008 (Chicago); Joel Bellows, 19 April, 28 June 2008 (Chicago); Kyle Bellows, 24 April 2008 (Chicago); Keith Botsford, 13, 14, 15 March 2008 (Cahuita, Costa Rica); Nathalie Botsford, 12 May 2008 (Boston); Polly Botsford, 5 November 2009 (London); Leon Botstein, 26 July 2007 (Annandale-on-Hudson, NY); Jack Cella, 8 April 2008 (Chicago); Art and Lynda Copeland, 6 August 2007 (Brattleboro, VT); Esther Corbin, 10 July 2007 (Homewood, IL); Paul Dolan, 18 May 2008 (New York); Wendy Doniger, 1 February 2008 (Chicago); Judith Dunford, 10 January 2009 (New York); Brenda and Monroe Engel, 3 August 2007 (Block Island, RI); Eileen Finletter, 18 May 2008 (New York); Joseph and Marguerite Frank, 19 August 2008 (Stanford, CA); Harvey and Sonia Freedman, 6 August 2010; Wendy Freedman, 7 August 2008 (Pasadena, CA); Susan Freifeld, 13 August 2007, 19 February 2008 (Chicago); Paul Friedrich, 11 February 2008 (Chicago); David and Simon Gameroff, Leonard and Shelley Lewkowict, 18 September 2009 (Montreal); Fran Gendlin, 17 May 2008 (New York); Herbert Gold, 18 August 2008 (San Francisco); Sydney Goldstein, 29 December 2008 (San Francisco); Eugene Goodheart, 2 August 2007 (Cambridge and Watertown, MA); Jana Gordin, 30 May 2008 (telephone); Mikhail Gordin, 30 May 2010 (Holon, Israel); Naum and Jana Gordin, 4 August 2010 (Brookline, MA); Ethel Grene, 4 September 2010 (Wilmette, IL); John Gross, 26 October 2007 (London); Christopher Hitchens, 19 February 2008 (Washington, DC); Doris and Marshall Holleb, 3 March 2008 (Chicago), Bette Howland, 2 July 2008 (Longansport, IN); Chantal and John Hunt, 18 September 2008 (Lyons, France); William Hunt, 3 August 2010 (Westport, MA); Beema Kamlani, 6 January 2009 (New York); Max Kampelman, 23 May 2008 (Washington, DC); Harold Kaplan, 6 May 2008, 28 March 2009 (Paris); Roger Kaplan, 23 May 2008 (Washington, DC); Leon Kass, 25 April 2008 (Chicago); Stanley Katz, 26 March 2008 (Princeton, NJ); Eugene Kennedy, 16 April 2008 (Chicago); Jascha Kessler, 20 July 2007 (Los Angeles); Bettyane and Dan Kevles, 4 August 2010 (Centerville, Cape Cod, MA); Joan and Jonathan Kleinbard, 20 February 2008 (Philadelphia); George Kliger, 26 June 2008 (Minneapolis); Amos Kollek,

29 May 2010 (Jerusalem); Irving Kristol, Gertrude Himmelfarb, 19 February 2008 (Washington, DC); Arlette Landes, 22 May 2008 (Bethesda, MD); Will Lautzenheiser, 12 May 2008 (Brookline, MA); Ralph Lerner, 25 February 2008 (Chicago); Paul Levy, 30 April 2010 (Oxford); Frank Maltese, 7 August 2007 (Brattleboro, VT); Norman Manea, 9 January 2009 (New York); Sabina Mazursky, 25 May 2010 (Tel Aviv); Mitzi McClosky, 17 August 2008 (Berkeley, CA); Susan Missner, 29 July 2009 (Chicago); Vivien Missner, 11 July 2009 (Skokie, IL); John Nathan, 16 September 2014 (telephone); Evelyn Nef, 5 August 2007 (Great Barrington, MA); Amos Oz, 27 May 2010 (Tel Aviv); Jean Passin and Miriam Tarcov, 8 December 2009 (Phoenix); Sid Passin, 25 March 2008 (New York); David Peltz, 9, 15 February 2008 (Chicago); Robert Pippin, 31 January 2008 (Chicago); Norman Podhoretz, 23 March 2008 (New York); Walter Pozen, 22 January 2008, 25, 30 January 2014 (Brattleboro, VT, and New York, telephone); Antoinette Ralian, 29 October 2012 (telephone); James Redfield, 14, 21 January 2008 (Chicago); Laure Reichek, 15 August 2008 (Petaluma, CA); Christopher Ricks, 11 July 2010 (London); Carol Alane Rollings, 29 May 2008 (Chicago); Tom Rosenthal, 3 November 2009 (London); Mark Rotblatt, 14 February 2008 (Chicago); Philip Roth, 20 March 2008 (New York); Floyd Salas, 28 November 2008 (Berkeley, CA); James Salter, 10 August 2010 (Bridgehampton, NY); Joan Schwartz, 25 March 2008 (New York); Ellen and Philip Siegelman, 16 August 2008 (Berkeley, CA); John Silber, 13 May 2008 (Boston); Diane Silverman, 29 January 2008 (Chicago); Eleanor Fox Simmons, 9 July 2007 (Chicago); Maggie Staats Simmons, 20, 21 May 2008 (New York); Herbert Sinaiko, 6 February 2008 (Chicago); Barbara Probst Solomon, 30 July 2007 (New York); Carol and Jay Stern, 8 September 2010 (Chicago); Richard Stern, 8 January, 29 May 2008 (Chicago); Miriam Tarcov, 7, 8 December 2009 (Tucson, AZ); Nathan Tarcov, 24, 31 January and 28 February 2008 (Chicago); Sylvia Tumin, 25 July 2007 (Princeton, NJ); Bella and Mischa Ullman, 30 May 2010 (Hod Hasharon, Israel); Patty Unterman, 18 August 2008 (Berkeley, CA); George and Sarah Walden, 21 November 2009 (London); Chris Walsh, 12 May 2008 (Boston); Judith Freifeld Ward, 19 February 2008 (Washington, DC); Rebecca Warren, 14 September 2010 (New York); Lord Weidenfeld, 14 December 2007 (London); Renée Weiss, 25 July 2007

(Stonebridge, NJ); Leon Wieseltier, 19 February 2008 (Washington, DC); Barbara Wiesenfeld, 7 August 2008 (Santa Monica, CA); George Wislocki, 10 June 2008 (telephone); Ruth Wisse, 1 August 2007 (Cambridge, MA); James Wood, 13 May 2008 (Cambridge, MA); Michael Wu, 5 June 2008 (Chicago); Andrew Wylie, 15 September 2010 (New York); A. B. Yehoshua, 24 May 2010 (Haifa, Israel).

Notes

EDITIONS OF SAUL BELLOW'S WORKS CITED
(INCLUDING FIRST PUBLICATION DETAILS)

Novels

Dangling Man (New York: Vanguard, 1944); Library of America, 2003 (in *Saul Bellow: Novels 1944–1953*).

The Victim (New York: Vanguard, 1947); Library of America, 2003 (in *Saul Bellow: Novels 1944–1953*).

The Adventures of Augie March (New York: Viking, 1953); Library of America, 2003 (in *Saul Bellow: Novels 1944–1953*).

Seize the Day (New York: Viking, 1956); Library of America, 2007 (in *Saul Bellow: Novels 1956–1964*).

Henderson the Rain King (New York: Viking, 1959); Library of America, 2007 (in *Saul Bellow: Novels 1956–1964*).

Herzog (New York: Viking, 1964); Library of America, 2007 (in *Saul Bellow: Novels 1956–1964*).

Mr. Sammler's Planet (New York: Viking, 1970); Penguin, 1972.

Humboldt's Gift (New York: Viking, 1975); Penguin, 1977.

The Dean's December (New York: Harper, 1982); Penguin, 1998.

More Die of Heartbreak (New York: Morrow, 1987); Penguin, 2004.

A Theft (New York: Viking Penguin, 1989); Penguin, 2002 (in Saul Bellow, *Collected Stories*).

The Bellarosa Connection (New York: Viking Penguin, 1989); Penguin, 2002 (in Saul Bellow, *Collected Stories*).

The Actual (New York: Viking Penguin, 1997); Penguin, 1998.

Ravelstein (New York: Viking, 2000).

Collected Stories

Mosby's Memoirs and Other Stories (New York: Viking, 1968); Penguin 1996 (excluding stories reprinted in *Collected Stories*, Penguin, 2002).

Him with His Foot in His Mouth and Other Stories (New York: HarperCollins, 1984); Penguin, 2002 (in *Collected Stories*, which contains all the stories in this volume).

Something to Remember Me By: Three Tales (New York: Penguin, 1990); Penguin, 2002 (in *Collected Stories*, which contains all three stories in this volume).
Collected Stories (New York: Viking, 2001); Penguin, 2002.

Nonfiction

To Jerusalem and Back (New York: Viking, 1976); Penguin, 1998.
It All Adds Up: From the Dim Past to the Uncertain Future: A Nonfiction Collection (New York: Viking Penguin, 1994); Penguin, 1995.
Saul Bellow: Letters, ed. Benjamin Taylor (New York: Viking Penguin, 2010).
There Is Simply Too Much to Think About: Collected Nonfiction, ed. Benjamin Taylor (New York: Viking Penguin, 2015).

Plays

The Wrecker, in *New World Writing*, No. 6 (New York: New American Library, 1954); reprinted in *Seize the Day* (New York: Viking, 1956).
The Last Analysis (New York: Viking, 1965); Viking Compass, 1969.
A Wen, in *Traverse Plays*, ed. Jim Haynes (Harmondsworth: Penguin, 1966). One of three one-act plays performed on Broadway and in London in 1966 as *Under the Weather*.
Orange Soufflé, in *Traverse Plays*, ed. Jim Haynes (Harmondsworth: Penguin, 1966). One of three one-act plays performed on Broadway and in London in 1966 as *Under the Weather*.
Out from Under (unpublished in English). Italian translation, *C'è speranza nel sesso* (Milan: Feltrinelli, 1967); English version cited in manuscript, in Saul Bellow Papers, Special Collections Research Center, Joseph Regenstein Library, University of Chicago.

ABBREVIATIONS USED IN THE NOTES

Atlas, *Biography*   James Atlas, *Bellow: A Biography* (New York: Random House, 2000)
Botsford interview, "A Half Life"   Keith Botsford, "A Half Life," the first of two interviews conducted by Botsford, Bellow's friend and sometimes colleague, orginally printed in *Bostonia* magazine (November–December 1990), reprinted in Saul Bellow, *It All Adds Up: From the Dim Past to the Uncertain Future*
Botsford interview, "A Second Half Life"   Keith Botsford, "A Second Half Life," the second of two interviews conducted by Botsford, originally printed in *Bostonia* magazine (January–February 1991), reprinted in Saul Bellow, *It All Adds Up: From the Dim Past to the Uncertain Future*
Cronin and Siegel, eds., *Conversations with SB*   Gloria L. Cronin and Ben Siegel, eds., *Conversations with Saul Bellow* (Jackson: University of Mississippi Press, 1994)
"I Got a Scheme!"   "'I Got a Scheme!': The Words of Saul Bellow," *The New Yorker* (25 April 2005), an edited and rewritten interview between Saul Bellow and Philip Roth
Koch interview   An eight-hour interview Saul Bellow gave in 1987 to Sigmund Koch, a "University Professor" (as Bellow would himself become) at Boston University, one of seventeen such interviews with writers Koch conducted between 1983 and 1988 as part of the Boston University Aesthetics Research Project. The interviews were videotaped and are held at the Geddes Language Center at Boston University.
Manea, "Conversation"   Norman Manea, "Saul Bellow in Conversation with Nor-

man Manea," *Salmagundi* 2007, 155/156 (Page numbers from the Literature Online version, http://lion.chadwyck.com)

PR   *Partisan Review*

Regenstein   The Special Collections Research Center at the Joseph Regenstein Library, University of Chicago

Roth/SB interview typescript   Typed transcript of conversations between Saul Bellow and Philip Roth out of which came *The New Yorker* article "I Got a Scheme!" The typescript is among the Bellow Papers in the Regenstein. For details, see Chapter 3, note 11.

SB   Saul Bellow

SB, "CB"   Saul Bellow, "Chicago Book," an unfinished manuscript Saul Bellow worked on in the late 1970s, located in the Regenstein. It exists in several parts: a manuscript in eighty-four numbered pages; shorter sections, often just notes, numbered differently or not numbered at all; and sixteen background folders on a range of Chicago topics and personalities. The title comes from the heading of a section dated 5 April 1979: "Notes for Chicago Book."

SB, *IAAU*   Saul Bellow, *It All Adds Up: From the Dim Past to the Distant Future: A Nonfiction Collection* (1994; Harmondsworth: Penguin, 1995)

SB, "Memoirs"   Saul Bellow, "Memoirs of a Bootlegger's Son," an unfinished manuscript among the Bellow Papers in the Special Collections Research Center at the Joseph Regenstein Library, University of Chicago

Taylor, ed., *Letters*   Benjamin Taylor, ed., *Saul Bellow: Letters* (New York: Viking, 2010)

"What's in a Name?"   An unpublished memoir by Sondra "Sasha" Bellow, Saul Bellow's second wife, copies of which she gave to the author and to her son Adam Bellow, Saul Bellow's second son

INTRODUCTION: BELLOW AND BIOGRAPHY

1. See, for example, James Wood, "Give All," review of James Atlas, *Bellow: A Biography*, in *The New Republic*, 13 November 2000, p. 30, where he calls SB "probably the greatest writer of American prose of the twentieth century," a view he characterizes as "relatively uncontroversial."

2. This quotation comes from Norman Manea, "Saul Bellow in Conversation with Norman Manea," in *Salmagundi* 155/156 (2007): 131–211. Here and throughout, my page numbers come from the Literature Online version, http://lion.chadwyck .com, in this case, p. 37 (henceforth cited as Manea, "Conversation"). Eugene Goodheart is an emeritus professor of English at Brandeis University. He and SB became friends in 1960 when Goodheart taught at Bard College in upstate New York. SB lived nearby in a house in Tivoli, the model for the Ludeyville house in *Herzog*, which SB was writing at the time.

3. W. B. Yeats's poem "The Choice" (1932) begins: "The intellect of man is forced to choose / Perfection of the life, or of the work, / And if it take the second must refuse / A heavenly mansion, raging in the dark."

4. SB to Al Ellenburg, a former student of SB's at Bard, undated, quoted in James Atlas, *Bellow: A Biography* (New York: Random House, 2000), p. 314 (henceforth cited as Atlas, *Biography*), p. 314.

5. The SB quotations about Susan Bellow come from her unpublished and undated essay, "Mugging the Muse," p. 7, a copy of which was lent me by Daniel Bellow and which he thinks might have been composed "around 1980." The "lousing up" quotation comes from SB, *Humboldt's Gift* (1976; Harmondsworth, Middlesex: Penguin, 1977), p. 122 (henceforth cited within the text by page numbers).

6. Susan Bellow, "Mugging the Muse," p. 7.

7. These quotations are from an interview I conducted with Joan Ullmann Schwartz, who complained to SB about the resemblance between herself and Katrina in a letter of 26 January 1984, having been alerted by a friend to the forthcoming publication of "What Kind of a Day Did You Have?" in the February issue of *Vanity Fair*. SB wrote back on 26 March, calling Schwartz's letter "intelligent and gentle" and quoting Alexander Pope's letter to Arabella Fermor, the model for Belinda in "The Rape of the Lock": "Pope said: 'The character of Belinda . . . resembles you in nothing but Beauty.' He adds that all the passages in his poem are 'fabulous,' and that 'the Human persons are as fictitious as the Airy ones.' . . . I feel extremely lucky to have found in a great master the total clarification of a diabolically complex problem."

8. For Humboldt on his prospects if Stevenson wins, see *Humboldt's Gift*, pp. 29–30. The Falstaff quotation is from *King Henry IV, Part Two*, V.iii.132–33.

9. Ibid., V.v.46.

10. See SB, *The Adventures of Augie March* (1953), reprinted in *Saul Bellow: Novels 1944–1953* (New York: Library of America, 2003), pp. 792, 805, 843 (henceforth cited within the text by page numbers).

11. For William Hazlitt's description of Bolingbroke, see his *Characters of Shakespeare's Plays* (1817), in P. P. Howe, ed., *The Complete Works of William Hazlitt*, 21 vols. (London: J. M. Dent, 1930–34), 4:275.

12. Robert Penn Warren, SB's friend, reviewed *The Adventures of Augie March* in "The Man with No Commitments," *The New Republic*, 2 November 1953.

13. Philip Roth, *The Ghost Writer* (1979; New York: Vintage, 1995), p. 58. The Roth character in the novel is called Nathan Zuckerman, the SB character is called Felix Abravanel.

14. See Hillel G. Fradkin and Nathan Tarcov, Bloom's executors, authors of the acknowledgments page of Bloom's posthumously published *Love and Friendship* (New York: Simon & Schuster, 1993). SB seems also to have discussed Shakespeare's history plays with David Grene, another colleague from the Committee on Social Thought, a classicist. See an undated letter from Grene among SB's papers in the Special Collections Research Center at the Regenstein Library, University of Chicago: "Dear Saul. This is not all that I have done, but it is all that I found time to revise and type. It's also rather rough—and I haven't got any of the stuff on Hotspur in. However, if you find the time to tell me whether you think it is the proper *sort* of continuation I would be glad." For SB's papers in the Regenstein, see the "Note on Sources." Tim Spiekerman, a student of Bloom and SB, had transcribed *Love and Friendship* from Bloom's dictation. He also wrote a dissertation on Shakespeare's history plays, including a chapter on "Shakespeare and Machiavelli." In the spring of 2000, SB taught a course at Boston University entitled "An Idiosyncratic Survey of Modern Literature." It started with *King Henry IV, Parts One and Two*.

15. Bloom, *Love and Friendship*, pp. 405, 407–8.

16. Ibid., p. 401.

17. SB, *Ravelstein* (New York: Viking, 2000), p. 13 (henceforth cited within the text by page numbers). According to Adam Bellow, on at least three occasions SB told him that Bloom had said he should do a portrait of him in some form or other, because he, Bloom, was a unique personality. As Adam recalls it, his father said: "Bloom had made it clear to me that he expects me to write about him and to tell the truth of it." But Adam remains wary: "You can never be sure—you can never be sure—I wouldn't declare that in court. He was trying to ascertain if I was okay about it" (notes taken after a meeting with Adam Bellow, 9 January 2009).

18. In a letter of 11 August 2000 to Clifford Orwin, SB wrote: "As you are bound to suspect, it was no easy thing to decide whether *Ravelstein* should or should not be written. I can't guess whether Allan would have been for it or against it." The "it" here may refer specifically to the depiction of Ravelstein's death from

AIDS. Bloom may have encouraged SB to "*do* him" before his fatal illness: "There were special considerations also to take into account," SB wrote to Orwin. "One of those considerations was the presence of James Atlas, my self-appointed biographer, on the margins. I did not want to give him a monopoly of the subject. He would have liked nothing better than to break the story of Allan's illness to a public of scandal-consumers."

19. For quoted references to Citrine, or the Citrine figure, and biography, in early versions of *Humboldt's Gift*, see Daniel Fuchs, *Saul Bellow: Vision and Revision* (Durham, NC: Duke University Press, 1984), pp. 235–36.

20. "Charm and Death" exists in a ninety-seven-page typescript in the Regenstein Library at the University of Chicago. Also among SB's papers is a letter of 1 December 1970 from his agent, Henry Volkening: "Alan Williams has had this morning delivered to me the first ninety-one pages of *Charm and Death*. . . . I will, of course, bear in mind that this is a first draft."

21. See SB, *Dangling Man* (1944), reprinted in *Saul Bellow: Novels 1944–1953* (New York: Library of America, 2003), pp. 5, 16 (henceforth cited within the text by page numbers).

22. SB, *Mr. Sammler's Planet* (1970; Harmondsworth: Penguin, 1972), p. 21 (henceforth cited within the text by page numbers); "Mosby's Memoirs," first published in *The New Yorker*, 20 July 1968, reprinted in SB, *Collected Stories* (New York: Penguin, 2001), p. 362 (henceforth cited as SB, *CS*).

23. This quotation comes from notes for a lecture written around the time of *Humboldt's Gift* in which SB discusses Paul Valéry's hostility to novelists. It is quoted in Fuchs, *Saul Bellow: Vision and Revision*, p. 279. When describing SB's sense of mission as a novelist, Alfred Kazin, in *New York Jew* (New York: Alfred A. Knopf, 1978), p. 41, invokes D. H. Lawrence: "Being a novelist, I consider myself superior to the saint, the scientist, the philosopher, and the poet, who are all great masters of different bits of man alive, but never get the whole hog."

24. SB, "The French as Dostoyevsky Saw Them," foreword to Fyodor M. Dostoyevsky, *Winter Notes on Summer Impressions* (New York: Criterion, 1955); first published in *The New Republic*, 23 May 1955; reprinted in SB, *It All Adds Up: From the Dim Past to the Distant Future: A Nonfiction Collection* (New York: Penguin, 1995), pp. 45–46 (henceforth cited as SB, *IAAU*).

25. SB, "Zetland: By a Character Witness," originally published in 1974 in *Modern Occasions* 2, reprinted in SB, *CS*, p. 245 (henceforth cited within the text by page numbers).

26. Manea, "Conversation," pp. 20, 18.

27. This letter, undated, was written sometime in September 1968, while SB was at the Villa Serbelloni in Bellagio, on a monthlong Rockefeller Foundation fellowship.

28. It was Volkening who used the word "crushed" in a letter to SB of 14 September 1967; his other comment comes from a letter of 13 November 1967. Lindley's letter about SB being "at peak form" was written on 8 August 1967.

29. This quotation is from an interview conducted with David Peltz by the journalist D. J. R. Bruckner, who was at work on a television documentary entitled "Saul Bellow's Chicago," aired on Channel 5 in Chicago on 27 March 1981. Bruckner conducted interviews in 1980 and his recordings are in the Regenstein.

30. From SB, "Chicago and American Culture: One Writer's View," a talk delivered on 10 October 1972 at the Centennial Celebration of the Chicago Public Library, a typescript of which is among SB's papers in the Regenstein (the quotation occurs on p. 18 of the typescript). A version of the talk was printed in the *Chicago Sun-Times*.

31. Mark Harris, *Saul Bellow: Drumlin Woodchuck* (Athens: University of Georgia Press, 1980), p. 97.

32. SB, *Herzog* (1964), reprinted in SB, *Novels 1956–1964* (New York: Library of America, 2007), p. 593 (henceforth cited within the text by page numbers).

33. The excerpt appeared in the July 1961 issue of *Esquire*, pp. 116–30.

34. James Wood, "Give All," p. 35. See also Wood's review of Greg Bellow, *Saul Bellow's Heart: A Son's Memoir* (2013), "Sins of the Father: Do Great Novelists Make Bad Parents?," *New Yorker*, 22 July 2013, in which he admits the brutality (to family, to friends) of the "storm of assertion" whereby the writer seeks to justify his or her existence as a writer: "The history of that private destruction is briefly alluring, sometimes appalling. In two or three generations, that story will have faded from memory, outlived by what it enabled."

35. Patrick French, *The World Is What It Is: The Authorized Biography of V. S. Naipaul* (New York: Alfred A. Knopf, 2008), p. xiv. Naipaul on biography could not be more different from SB: "The lives of writers are a legitimate subject of inquiry; and the truth should not be skimped. It may well be, in fact, that a full account of a writer's life might in the end be more a work of literature and more illuminating—of a cultural or historical moment—than the writer's books" (from a speech given in 1994 at Tulsa, Oklahoma, where Naipaul's papers are held, quoted by French, ibid., p. xi.).

36. SB, *More Die of Heartbreak* (1987; Harmondsworth: Penguin, 2004), p. 54 (henceforth cited within the text by page numbers).

37. Manea, "Conversation," p. 45.

38. See Wood, "Give All," p. 36, quoting Atlas: "'While Bellow, the great novelist, went about the serious business of making art'—the phrase pulses with resentment. But Bellow *is* a great novelist, and making art *is* a serious business." Or see Richard Poirier, "How Far Shall I Take This Character?," a review of Atlas's biography in the *London Review of Books*, 2 November 2000, on what he sees as Atlas's damaging hostility to SB: "the development of such hostility over the long haul of a biography is not unfamiliar." See also Atlas's reprinted or reconstructed diary entries in a *New Yorker* article of 26 June and 3 July 1995 entitled "The Shadow in the Garden." The article traces his relations with SB from the time he first broached the idea of a biography in 1987 to August 1994. In an entry of 10 May 1991, SB takes Atlas on a tour of his childhood neighborhood, which makes Atlas think of his own grandparents' home. "In writing this book, I'm not just retrieving Bellow's past," he writes. "I feel a momentary twinge of resentment: why him and not me?" In an entry of 30 August 1992, Atlas "babble[s] something about how it's a wonderful project for me. B, deadpan: 'I'm glad I haven't lived in vain.'" From the same entry: "The person with whom I used to experience a huge paternal transference doesn't exist as powerfully for me anymore; I feel independent of him but also sad. There is no Dad. Certainly not this difficult, prickly character." From 23 August 1993: "so much concentration, combined with the suppression of self." From 23 October 1993: "For the first time, I feel impatience; I want to get on with my story, live *my* life."

39. See SB to Edward Shils, 3 October 1975 (Shils was SB's colleague on the Committee on Social Thought): "James Redfield's new book on the Iliad has brought up the matter of his promotion. I am favorably impressed with it, after two chapters, and I should like you to have a copy of it and to know what you think of James's scholarship and his eligibility for a full professorship. He should have it, I believe. Our collisions have not deprived me of objectivity. He is a young curmudgeon but mingled among his detestable qualities are many good ones. He is one of the few thoroughly thoughtful people around. In his books you can virtually see the thoughts coming through. I am not so besotted by my 12 years at this university that I cannot still recognize a working mind. Of course Redfield is quite perverse in his conclusions, as you will see for yourself, but he is 'quality' nevertheless."

40. In an interview with the author, 14 August 2008.

41. Ellmann's acceptance speech is available at http://www.nationalbook.org/nbaacceptspeech_rellmann.html.

42. Atlas, *Biography*, p. 42.

1. RUSSIA/ABRAHAM

1. These are the words of Joel Bellows, Maurice (Maury) Bellows's son, recounted in an interview. Maurice was the eldest of the three Bellow brothers. His words are from Joel in the same interview. Joel's version of this story was heard also by his cousins, Greg Bellow, SB's oldest son, and Lesha Bellows Greengus, the daughter of Samuel Bellows, the middle of Abraham Bellow's three sons. The cousins heard the story from both Sam and Maury Bellows.

2. This information comes from Louis Dworkin, a cousin of Abraham Bellow's, who reported to his granddaughter, Susan Missner, that the grocer's name was Frumkin. At the start of his career, Abraham also worked in the produce business, perhaps benefiting from his father's contacts and expertise.

3. The quote about red hair and the Bellow men comes from Joel Bellows. Charlie Citrine's reference to his grandfather and the Talmud comes from p. 239 of *Humboldt's Gift*. SB's sons and Lesha Bellows Greengus, unlike their cousin Joel Bellows, remember being told that it was Moses Gordin, SB's maternal grandfather who knew the Talmud by heart, not Berel Bellow.

4. In *Herzog* (1964), the Abraham figure, Father Herzog, comes "from the greatest Hasidic rabbis. Reb Zusya! Herschele Dubrovner! Just remember" (p. 559). The surviving manuscript of "Memoirs of a Bootlegger's Son" is among SB's papers in the Special Collections Research Center at the Regenstein Library, University of Chicago. It is undated but the title page reads: "This is the first part of a rough draft 'Memoirs of a Bootlegger's Son.'" Below these words SB gives his name and an address: "333 Riverside Drive, New York City." He rented an apartment at this address on 30 December 1953, and lived there for almost half a year. On 14 June 1955, in a letter to Leslie Fiedler, he was still at work on "Memoirs." The quotations about "the Berel figure" in the novel (Grandpa Lurie), and his son, "the Abraham character" (Jacob Lurie, or "Pa"), are from page 2 of the manuscript. In "A Talk with Saul Bellow," an interview of 20 September 1953 with Harvey Breit in *The New York Times Book Review*, SB is asked if his father appears in *The Adventures of Augie March*: "'No,' Mr. Bellow said laughingly, 'I've saved him'"—for "Memoirs," presumably. All subsequent quotations from "Memoirs" are cited within the text by page numbers.

5. In 1900 Druya had a Jewish population of 3,006, more than half the total population, according to the "Druya/Druja" page of the database "JewishGen" (http://www.JewishGen.org), the Internet site for Jewish Genealogy, a nonprofit organization affiliated with the Museum of Jewish Heritage in New York, founded in 1987. The phrase "more than half" is an estimate, based on figures for 1939, when Druya had c. 4,000 inhabitants, c. 2,500 of whom were Jews.

6. The age at which Father Herzog is sent away to yeshiva is four.

7. In 1900 the population of Dvinsk was 69,489, of whom 32,639 were Jewish (from the "Dvinsk/Daugavpils" page of the database "JewishGen"); it was thirteen times larger than the population of Druya. When SB's paternal grandfather, Berel Belo, married Shulamith Dworkin, according to her nephew Louis Dworkin, it was considered a good marriage for the grandmother because her new husband had connections in a bigger and more important place than Druya. SB seems sometimes to have described his father as having come from Dvinsk rather than Druya, perhaps because he thought people were more likely to have heard of it. In a letter to SB of 27 November 1976 (among the Bellow Papers in the Regenstein),

Shelley Jacobson recalls his asking her where her parents came from: "I knew only too well that my father was born in Dvinsk, near the Lithuanian border—a little too near for the comfort of my mother, who was apparently well-bred and a snob. . . . My mother did not consider Dvinsk a suitable place to be born in. . . . So when you asked me that question . . . I was back with my mother and her reminiscences. . . . 'He was born in Riga,' I said, blushing. You answered, 'MY father was born in Dvinsk.'"

8. According to James Atlas, *Bellow: A Biography* (Random House: New York, 2000), p. 6 (henceforth cited as Atlas, *Biography*).

9. The granddaughter is Lesha Bellows Greengus, daughter of Samuel Bellows, the middle Bellow brother (email, 25 November 2009).

10. According to Willie Greenberg, a Montreal neighbor, who remembers Abraham, when out of work, visiting his mother in the Greenberg kitchen and entertaining her with stories of life in Russia (Atlas, *Biography*, p. 13); see also Alan Hustak, "St. Dominique St.'s Legacy Recalls '20s Era," *Montreal Gazette*, October 1990, in which Greenberg recalls his mother's comments on SB's own storytelling: "'Oy is dos kind a bluffer'—'Oh boy, is this kid a bullshitter!'" Compare also Ijah Brodsky, the narrator of "Cousins" (1974), reprinted in SB, *CS*, p. 201, on himself and his father: "As usual, I gave more information than my questioner had any use for, using every occasion to transmit my sense of life. My father before me also did this."

11. The 1990 interview, the first of two conducted by SB's friend and sometime colleague Keith Botsford, was originally printed in *Bostonia* magazine, November–December 1990, under the title "A Half Life," reprinted in SB, *IAAU*, p. 291. Abraham Bellow as "feisty" comes from Manea, "Conversation," p. 11.

12. Lesha and her husband, Sam Greengus, remember hearing this story from Maury himself, but about himself, not Abraham.

13. For SB on his father's "adventures," see Manea, "Conversation," p. 17; "A Silver Dish" (1978), reprinted in SB, *CS*, p. 18.

14. *A Theft* (1989), published as a paperback original by Penguin; reprinted in SB, *CS*, p. 124.

15. SB quotations from Manea, "Conversation," pp. 10, 44, 45.

16. SB, *More Die of Heartbreak*, p. 16; *Ravelstein*, p. 30.

17. SB was much taken with the surviving photograph of Moses Gordin (see illustrations) and describes it in *Dangling Man*: "It was a study of my grandfather, my mother's father, made shortly before his death. It showed him supporting his head on a withered fist, his streaming beard yellow, sulphurous, his eyes staring and his clothing shroudlike." To Joseph, the novel's SB-like protagonist, the photograph is "proof of my mortality. . . . Through the years he would reclaim me bit by bit, till my own fists withered and my eyes stared" (p. 53). Though striking, the photograph is misleading. SB's mother, Lescha, had arranged for it to be taken without telling Moses in advance. He was furious. He looks every inch the otherworldly, mystical Jew, though his strand of Judaism was rational, anti-mystical. No photographs of Berel Belo survive.

18. According to Esther Elster, SB's second cousin, who has compiled a family tree and genealogical records, Moses died in 1904. Not all Esther Elster's dates jibe with those of official records, though, and many, as here, are based on word of mouth. According to police files for Vitebsk Province compiled in 1889, for Jews residing in rural areas not towns (see National Historical Archives, Belarus; fond 1416, inventory 3, file 21,591, page 421 ob), Moses was born in 1847; according to the 1897 census he was born in 1843. Esther Elster's records say he was born in 1840. Elster is the daughter of SB's cousin Moshe Gordin (1915–2007), son of Hone (Chana) Gordin (Moshe was named after his deceased grandfather Moses); she lives in Israel and is a research chemist, previously a professor at Bar-Ilan University in Ramat Gan, in the Tel Aviv district.

19. According to Moshe Gordin, Moses was thirteen when he married Sara Gurevich, who was nine at the time. Toward the end of his life, on 13 February 2003, Moshe Gordin published an impressionistic family memoir entitled "Memories" in the Russian-language Israeli periodical *Vesti Negev*. This memoir gets some details of the Russian family wrong, according to Elster, who "trust[s] more the data he gave me about 20 years ago, when his memory was sharp" (email, 8 June 2010), but its account of the marriage of Moses and Sara matches the earlier account. "On the first marriage night," he writes in "Memories," "the bride ran away. It required a lot of brains and tact from the women of the family of the child bride to convince her not to run away again. . . . Bit by bit, the two of them got used to each other and young Sarochka gave her Moshe 13 children" (from a translation by John Lloyd, 19 July 2010).

20. The 1877 date comes from the police files for Vitebsk Province compiled in 1889. The 1879 date comes from p. 805 of the 1897 census, the first census for the Russian Empire based on reliable sources.

21. The number twelve comes from notes taken by Janis Bellow of a conversation between SB and his sister, Jane Bellow Kauffman, in July 1990.

22. According to Moshe Gordin in "Memories," one of the men who ran the farm for his grandfather was envious of his success and set fire to the farm's cattle shed: "The material loss which came from that could be borne. But oh, how terrible! That fire was a black day for grandfather and grandmother. At that time, my uncle's sister was in the cowshed. Her long hair caught fire in an instant. They put out the fire but they didn't manage to save Moshe's daughter, my uncle's sister. The police arrested the guilty party and he was threatened with hard labor. But my grandfather made his own judgment. He was a godly Jew and decided that God himself should condemn the incendiary. He didn't want to hand him over to the Jewish court and he asked the official, who was his good friend, to let the guilty man go. Experiencing a terrible guilty conscience, that man couldn't live in his job with any pride, and one day he came to my uncle . . . [and] offered all his savings, scraped together from years of service to my grandfather, but my uncle refused. Having lost everything, the man who was guilty of that tragedy went off to Palestine. He dreamed of softening the bitter memory of his sins at the Wailing Wall." According to Elster, the episode took place in 1904, the name of the daughter who died in the fire was Gutka, and the name of the envious employee was Shepsl Lipgot.

23. The population of Dagda in 1897 was 1,516, 70 percent of whom were Jewish (according to p. 805 of the 1897 census, from which the description of Moses Gordin's profession and the house he and his family lived in also come). Lipushki was even smaller.

24. Manea, "Conversation," p. 3. There is some dispute about whether Robert's fortune came from South African diamonds or gold. Atlas, *Biography*, p. 7, says diamonds, presumably on the word of SB in an interview; Lesha Bellows Greengus remembers a conversation in 2000 with her Uncle Saul in which he said Robert's money came from "the gold fields." In *Herzog*, Robert's fictional alter ego, Mikhail, is said to have "made money out of those miserable black Kaffirs! Who knows how" (p. 560).

25. Several streets south of Nevsky Prospect, a cluster of adjacent wards made up the city's Jewish district, "jokingly nicknamed Petersburgskii Berdichev" (Benjamin Nathans, *Beyond the Pale: The Jewish Encounter with Late Imperial Russia* [Berkeley: University of California Press, 2002], p. 113). The population of Berdichev, a city in northern Ukraine, was overwhelmingly Jewish. The city was famous as a center of Jewish life and culture. Sholom Aleichem lived there. Joseph Conrad, son of impoverished Polish Christian nobility, was born there.

26. According to interviews with his daughter Vivien Missner and granddaughter Susan Missner.

27. These details from Ruth Miller, *Saul Bellow: A Biography of the Imagination* (New York: St. Martin's, 1991), pp. 3, 297. SB's term, "produce-broker," from Atlas, *Biography*, p. 6.

28. Miller, *Biography of the Imagination*, p. 296.

29. Quoted in Irving Howe, *A Margin of Hope: An Intellectual Autobiography* (New York: Harcourt Brace Jovanovich, 1982), p. 7.

30. Salo Baron, *The Russian Jew Under Tsars and Soviets* (New York: Macmillan, 1964), p. 114. According to Zvi Gitelman, *A Century of Ambivalence: The Jews of Russia and the Soviet Union, 1881 to the Present* (London: Viking, 1988), p. 40, by the time of the 1897 census, all but 300,000 of the 5.2 million Jews in the Russian Empire resided within the fifteen provinces that made up the Pale of Settlement. Within the Pale, Jews accounted for 11 percent of the population, within the Russian Empire as a whole they made up 4 percent. In urban areas within the Pale where they were especially concentrated, Jews made up "more than half the population. . . . By the end of the century more Jews were living in cities than in *shtetlekh*, those largely Jewish hamlets which occupied a position midway between the vast expanses of rural Russia and her growing cities."

31. Quoted in Irving Cutler, *The Jews of Chicago: From Shtetl to Suburb* (Urbana: University of Illinois Press, 1996), p. 51.

32. Details of the story are sketchy and the only dates recorded are those of birth. According to the family tree compiled by Esther Elster, Nota was born in 1800 and his wife, Selda (her surname is not known), was born in 1821. Their first child, again according to Elster, was born in 1838, when Selda was sixteen or seventeen and Nota thirty-seven or thirty-eight.

33. The 1897 census lists a "Moses Notkov Gordin," fifty-four years old, born in Rezekne, identified as literate, a self-employed baker, married to "Sora" (Sara), fifty years old, the daughter of Samuel. "Notkov" means "son of Nota" or "son of Natan," thus indicating Moses's real or birth father. The 1897 census lists no Gordins in the region who identify themselves as sons of Shmuel (Samuel) Gordin. It lists a number of Imenitovs, however. Aleksander Feigmanis, from Riga, a doctoral candidate and researcher for JewishGen, checked the census lists for me and found no Imenitov named Popa or Wulf. But he did find an "Aron Notov Imyanitov," forty-three, living as a merchant in Rezekne, identified as literate, and the owner of a bookstore. The dates fit, and "Notov" is suggestive, but Esther Elster's records of the children of Nota and Selda Imenitov make no mention of a son named Aron. It is possible that her records are wrong or incomplete. SB himself believed that Moses's original family name was Imenitov; Lesha Bellows Greengus, in an email of 25 November 2009, reports his having told her so.

34. See Nathans, *Beyond the Pale*, p. 28.

35. From *The Complete Works of Isaac Babel*, ed. Nathalie Babel, tr. Peter Constantine, intro. Cynthia Ozick (New York: W. W. Norton, 2002), p. 601. "The Story of My Dovecote" is one of two Babel stories selected by SB in his edition of *Great Jewish Short Stories* (London: Valentine, Mitchell, 1971).

36. See Nathans, *Beyond the Pale*, p. 135, on the Russian stereotype of the Jewish merchant: "'Chase the Jew out the door and he'll return through the window,' warned a popular folk-saying. Whether in openly anti-Semitic diatribes such as Dostoyevsky's *Diary of a Writer* and *Novoe Vremia*'s influential article 'Zhid idet!' ('The Kike Is Coming!'), or, more subtly, in the widespread belief among ruling elites that gullible Russian peasants required protection from the Jews' overdeveloped entrepreneurial spirit, the culturally coded contrast between indefatigable Jew and easygoing Russian defined contemporary attitudes toward ethnic difference."

37. According to Gitelman, *A Century of Ambivalence*, p. 34, in the 1905 pogrom in Odessa "over 300" Jews were murdered, "thousands were wounded,

nearly six hundred children were orphaned, and about 40,000 Jews were 'materially wounded.'"

38. See Simon M. Dubnow, *History of the Jews in Russia and Poland from the Earliest Times to the Present Day*, tr. I. Friedlaender (1918; New Jersey: Avoteyna, 2000), pp. 479–80.

39. Vladimir Nabokov, *Strong Opinions* (1973; New York: Vintage, 1993), p. 57.

40. Bely's novel is close in some respects to Joseph Conrad's *Under Western Eyes* (1911), also set in St. Petersburg, with a plot partly based on the assassination of a high government official, Vyacheslav Konstantinovich von Plehve, minister of the interior from 1902 to 1904. Von Plehve's portrait hangs in Apollon Apollonovich's office, and he is presented in Bely's novel as having been Apollon's closest protector in government. He was killed by a bomb planted by assassins.

41. Andrei Bely, *Petersburg*, tr. Robert A. Maguire and John E. Malmstad (Bloomington: University of Indiana Press, 1978), pp. 19, 308n.

42. Manea, "Conversation," p. 3.

43. Nathans, *Beyond the Pale*, p. 105. Population figures for St. Petersburg are provided in the "St. Petersburg" entry in *The Jewish Encyclopedia* (New York: Funk & Wagnalls, 1908) (available online at http://www.jewishencyclopedia.com). In 1905 the city's population was 1,635,100. In 1914 it had risen to 2,217,500. The official Jewish population of the city in 1900 was 20,385 or 1.4 percent.

44. Manea, "Conversation," p. 8. The observations of Rose Dworkin, wife of Abraham Belo's cousin, Louis Dworkin, were recounted to her daughter, Vivian Missner, who in turn told them to Susan Missner, Rose's granddaughter (email, 30 March 2010).

45. Nathans, *Beyond the Pale*, p. 110; see also Gitelman, *A Century of Ambivalence*, p. 41: "In a country where 80 per cent of the population was illiterate as late as the eve of World War I, almost all Jewish boys and most of the girls, learned to read and write their own language. By the twentieth century over 30 per cent of Jewish men and 16 per cent of the women could also read Russian." For SB's parents' reading, see Manea, "Conversation," p. 4, and SB to Oscar Tarcov, 2 October 1937.

46. An odd moment in the "Memoirs" manuscript is perhaps worth noting here. When Pa Lurie upbraids Ma Lurie for putting aside money for her brothers, she says: "And if I do? . . . Think, Jacob. Did they do nothing for you?" To which Jacob replies: "And did they do nothing *to* me?" (p. 33). What Jacob means here is unexplained. It is possible—though at this level of speculation, anything is possible—that Pa Lurie is referring to some connection between the brothers and his arrest. As they were the ones who initially supplied him with forged papers or helped him to bribe officials to live and work in St. Petersburg, perhaps they also put him onto criminal connections, ones who somehow brought about his arrest.

Attempts to uncover the truth of Abraham's arrest, trial, and escape from prison are hindered by the destruction of archives in the first days of the February 1917 Revolution. Archives of police investigations in St. Petersburg were destroyed early in the revolution by fire and riot, leaving virtually no criminal files at all for the period in question. Records from the Court Chamber were also destroyed by fire, as were other state archives, including the archive of the St. Petersburg Fire Brigade. Andrei Kudryashov, a theater historian and film critic from St. Petersburg, conducted research on my behalf in the Russian National Library, Library of the Academy of Sciences, and the Russian State Historical Archives. No mention of Abraham Belo (or Belous or Belousov) appears in the following locations: *St. Petersburg Enquiry Book for Merchants and Other Ranks* (1905–13); St. Petersburg Merchant Council (1906, 1908); legal, court, and police publications for the period 1909–13 (*Civil Legislation Newsletter, Legal Newsletter, Newsletter of Law and Notary, Police Newsletter, Bulletin of Certificates of Convictions, Archive of Judicial and Legal*

Practices, Decisions of the General Assembly of the First and Cassational Departments of the Ruling Senate, Decisions of the Civil Cassational Department of the Ruling Senate, Decisions of the Criminal Cassational Department of the Ruling Senate); Jewish periodicals (*Newsletter of the Jewish Community, Newsletter of Jewish Emigration and Colonization, Speech* [*Rech*], *Jewish Field* [*Evreiskaya Niva*], *New Dawn* [*Novy Voskhod*], *Dawn* [*Rassvet*], *Newsletter of Jewish Education*); St. Petersburg newspapers (*St. Petersburg News, Stock Exchange News, St. Petersburg Sheet*); or Moscow newspapers (*Moscow Governorate News, Early Morning, Moscow Evening News, Voice of Moscow, Moscow Newspaper*).

47. The remarks of Sam Bellows are recounted in an email from his daughter, Lesha Bellows Greengus, 3 March 2010. As for the fate of relatives, according to SB, his uncle Aron Gordin, Lescha's brother, was forced to dig his own grave in Dagda and then murdered by his neighbors. Aron's son, Nota, who had fled Russia with the partisans and eventually served in the Russian army, later found one of the neighbors and had to be restrained from beating him to death by his fellow soldiers. According to SB (as recalled in an email from Janis Bellow, 4 July 2009), three of Abraham's sisters (Brochka, Hassya, and Pesse) also perished in the Holocaust.

48. See Nathans, *Beyond the Pale*, pp. 86ff, for the literature of Jewish criminality in St. Petersburg in the last third of the nineteenth century. Among the works discussed are Gershon Lifshits's autobiographical novel, *Confessions of a Criminal* (1881), Lev Levanda's *Confessions of a Wheeler Dealer* (1880), Victor Nikitin's story "Seeker of Happiness" (1875), and Sholem Asch's novel *Petersburg* (1929), set in the decade before the Russian Revolution.

49. Philip Roth, *The Ghost Writer* (New York: Farrar, Straus & Giroux, 1979), p. 48.

50. SB, ed., *Great Jewish Short Stories*, p. 16. The Sholom Aleichem story SB translated was "Eternal Life," in Irving Howe and Eliezer Greenberg, eds., *A Treasury of Yiddish Stories* (1953; New York: Viking, 1959).

51. Email from Lesha Bellows Greengus, 7 March 2010.

52. SB, *The Bellarosa Connection*, published in 1979 as a Penguin paperback original, reprinted in SB, *CS*, p. 39 (henceforth cited within the text by page numbers).

53. The details of Harry Fonstein's escape fit accounts of the arrest and rescue of Jews in Genoa in 1943–44, in the first three chapters of Alexander Stille, *Benevolence and Betrayal: Five Italian-Jewish Families Under Fascism* (New York: Summit, 1991). Stille's account of how documents were forged, arrests avoided, and escapes engineered shows how ingenious, resourceful, and entrepreneurial, as well as brave, participants were: "Teglio [the heroic head of DELASEM, an underground assistance group for Jews in Genoa] obtained copies of official letterhead from various southern Italian towns. Through friends he found an engraver who would make rubber and metal stamps he could use to prepare documents with official-looking markings. The Archbishop's Office produced stamps for the corresponding church parishes, thus enabling Teglio to create baptismal certificates to go along with the identity cards. Before long he assembled a whole workshop for manufacturing false documents; he kept the various tools hidden in different apartments to minimize chances of betrayal" (p. 250). The opportunities for bribery and inadvertent disclosure in this sort of operation are clear, and as likely to have operated in St. Petersburg in 1913 as in Genoa in 1943.

54. From Janis Bellow's Preface to SB, *CS*, p. vii. See also her journal entry of 24 May 1989, recording a second dinner with the Vermont neighbors: "We had dinner with the Hillmans the night before last. B. told them about Bellarosa and Herb told us so many more details about the real man's life. His name was Karl Schwarz (no 't'). He had 2 children—a son and a daughter. His wife was a teacher—nothing like Sorella in looks: smallish, plain. He did meet her in Cuba. They did live in New Jersey. While in Italy, Schwarz worked his way up to chief

clerk in one of Rome's largest hotels. He did meet Hitler. He was arrested first by the Italians, and released. They had done terrible things to him. . . . When released, he was told by an Italian girlfriend to contact Billy Rose by telegram. She had heard that he had an underground and was helping people. Schwarz did send a telegram. When he was arrested a second time, by the Germans, Rose arranged his release: in the middle of the night someone will come to your cell door. It will be open, keep going. He stayed in Genoa. In two weeks another of Rose's agents contacted him, gave him money and passage. . . . B. wished he had more of the details, but said they weren't important. Wld. have cluttered up the story. You don't want to be forced to follow the facts."

55. "You write, and then you erase," Abraham is reported to have said to his son, early in SB's career as an author: "You call that a profession? *Was meinst du?* 'A writer'?" (Atlas, *Biography*, p. 60). As Joel Bellows remembers: "My grandfather had a wicked, demeaning tongue."

56. This latter interpretation is bolstered, on the one hand, by the description of Father Herzog as not serving his sentence, "Because he was nervy, hasty. Obstinate, rebellious." On the other hand, later in the novel, we are told, "He had a fool's paradise in Petersburg for ten years, on forged papers. Then he sat in prison with common prisoners" (p. 565), though this may refer only to an initial few days after arrest, from which he would be released during the period of his trial.

57. Janis Bellow, email, 6 June 2009.

58. The manifest or passenger list of the *Ascania* can be found in Canadian Passenger Lists, 1865–1935 (Roll T-4751), available from Ancestry.ca, the self-described "largest online collection of genealogical documents anywhere in the world." The names of the Belos and of "Rafael Gordin" are listed on p. 2 of the manifest. The destination listed there is Montreal, but immigrants were required to list their ultimate destination rather than their point of disembarkation. Most got off at Halifax, the main point of entry to Canada. In *Herzog*, Moses Herzog's family is met in Montreal by Pa Herzog's Canadian relatives. Having arrived in Halifax, as the manifest states, they traveled to Montreal by train, which is likely the route traveled by the Bellow family. Details of the crossing, from SB's sister, Jane, were recalled by her niece Lesha Bellows Greengus, email 3 March 2010. The Belos were part of the enormous immigration of Russian and Polish Jews to the United States and Canada at the turn of the century. According to Gitelman, *A Century of Ambivalence*, p. 16, between 1891 and 1910, "nearly one million Jews fled the Russian Empire for the United States," almost a fifth of the number of Jews in the 1897 census. "The anti-Semitic wave of the 1880s and thereafter, coming from both the peasantry 'below' as well as from the tsar and the aristocracy 'above,' engulfed Jews of all political and cultural persuasions."

59. The essay of 1993 was "Writers, Intellectuals, Politics: Mainly Reminiscence," originally published in *The National Interest*, Spring 1993, reprinted in SB, *IAAU*, p. 99. The quote about the Heimat comes from Manea, "Conversation," p. 3. The name Russian Literary Society at Tuley High School comes from Atlas, *Biography*, p. 260.

60. SB, "Zetland: By a Character Witness," reprinted in SB, *CS*, p. 245.

61. For the V. S. Pritchett quote, see Daniel Fuchs, *Saul Bellow: Vision and Revision* (Durham, NC: Duke University Press, 1984), p. 29; for "Flaubertian standard," see Gordon Lloyd Harper's *Paris Review* interview with SB, "The Art of Fiction: Saul Bellow" 9, no. 36 (1966): 48–73, reprinted in Gloria L. Cronin and Ben Siegel, eds., *Conversations with Saul Bellow* (Jackson: University of Mississippi Press, 1994), p. 63 (henceforth cited as Cronin and Siegel, eds., *Conversations with SB*).

62. The remark to Herbert Gold is quoted in Atlas, *Biography*, p. 260; the letter mentioning his and Tolstoy's "method" was to Anita Shreve, 25 March 1980.

63. In addition to other great Russian writers—Pushkin, Turgenev, Gogol, Chekhov—SB was influenced, later in life in particular, by Russian thinkers or philosophers, including Nikolai Fyodorov (1829–1903), Nikolai Berdyaev (1874–1948), and Vasily Rozanov (1856–1919).

64. Kazin's remark is quoted in Carol Brightman, *Writing Dangerously: Mary McCarthy and Her World* (1992; London: Secker & Warburg, 1993), p. 317. Later in the same passage Kazin explains: "One way or another people like [Philip] Rahv, like Mary [McCarthy], people that age, Eleanor Clark, Robert Penn Warren's wife, they're all communists, but the ones who felt it most deeply were Rahv and the others [of Russian Jewish background]." Among other joke salutations between SB and Kazin were "Much-esteemed Damyon Mikarkovitch," "Much-esteemed Ippolit Paschunyakovitch."

65. Alfred Kazin, *A Walker in the City* (New York: Harcourt Brace, 1951), p. 61.

66. The correspondent is addressed only as "Mr. Levinson" and no place of residence is included or alluded to in the letter, which is among SB's papers in the Regenstein. The envelope is missing as well. But there are letters from an Alex Levinson of Moscow, written in 1991; presumably they are the same Levinson.

67. In 1912, sixteen-year-old Louis Dworkin traveled from Druya to Dvinsk, where he spent the night in the house of his great-aunt and -uncle, Berel and Shulamith Belo. For an account of his journey, see Chapter 3.

68. From Manea, "Conversation," p. 9. On p. 3 of the same interview, SB mentions his paternal grandfather's taking refuge in the Winter Palace.

69. Ibid., p. 5; "Literary Notes on Khrushchev," *Esquire*, March 1961, reprinted in SB, *IAAU*, p. 36.

70. See, for example, Prince Myshkin, in Dostoyevsky's, *The Idiot*, tr. Henry and Olga Carlisle (New York: Signet, 1969), pp. 562–63, responding to accusations of "overardency": "It is not just we who are surprised by our strange Russian intensity in such cases, but all Europe. If one of us becomes a Catholic, he is bound to become a Jesuit, and one of the most subterranean. If one of us becomes an atheist he is bound to demand the uprooting of faith in God by force, that is, of course, by the sword." In the introduction to this edition of the novel, SB's friend Harold Rosenberg describes Dostoyevsky's "identification with Russian extremism as both a dangerous weakness and a sacred gift," and also as "the basis of his emotional nationalism. 'Everywhere and in everything,' he wrote to Maikov [the Russian poet], 'I go to the ultimate limit, all my life I have crossed over the frontier'" (p. x).

71. *Saul Bellow: Novels 1944–1953* (New York: Library of America, 2003), p. 3.

72. See Ronald Hingley, *The Russian Mind* (New York: Scribner, 1977), p. 13.

73. In the Khrushchev profile, reprinted in SB, *IAAU*, p. 37, SB calls Father Karamazov "that corrupt and deep old man" and likens Khrushchev's outbursts at the United Nations to those of Karamazov, calling them "corrupt and hypocritical," "he feigns simplicity."

74. Reprinted in SB, *Novels, 1944–1953*, p. 163 (henceforth cited within the text by page numbers).

75. Ruth R. Wisse, *The Schlemiel as Modern American Hero* (Chicago: University of Chicago Press, 1971), p. 6. See also Julian Behrstock to SB, 23 February 1995, in the Regenstein. Behrstock was a friend of SB's from university in the 1930s:

> Somehow your letter triggered reminiscence about episodes and snatches of conversation together.
> I say to you: "A curious thing happens whenever something causes me to hit the depths of despondency. I suddenly and inexplicably find myself *observing* my dilemma—despair gives way to a surge of laughter."

Your comment: "That's Russian. It's the reversal factor that enabled the Jews to survive."

76. SB to Melvin Tumin, 21 April 1948.

77. Philip Davis, *Bernard Malamud: A Writer's Life* (Oxford: Oxford University Press, 2007), p. 49.

78. Irving Howe, *A Margin of Hope*, p. 338.

79. Ibid., p. 339.

80. Atlas, *Biography*, p. 516.

81. The quotation about parents and heroic ancestors comes from the first of the two interviews with Keith Botsford, "A Half Life" (1990), reprinted in SB, *IAAU*, p. 287; the preceding quotation comes from the second interview, "A Second Half Life" (1991), ibid., p. 321; the quotation from "What Kind of a Day Did You Have?," originally published in *Vanity Fair*, February 1984, comes from SB, *CS*, p. 322 (henceforth cited within the text by page numbers). See also *Ravelstein*, p. 96: "God appeared very early to me. His hair was parted down the middle. I understood that we were related because he had made Adam in his own image, breathed life into him. My eldest brother also combed his hair in the same style."

82. Samuel Greengus reports that "malachi," in Wulpy's quote, should be "malechei" (see Genesis 28:12) (email, 14 January 2011).

83. "Something to Remember Me By" was first published in *Esquire*, July 1990, reprinted in SB, *CS*, p. 437 (henceforth cited within the text by page numbers).

84. Janis Bellow, email, 4 July 2009.

85. In *Herzog*, Nahum's fictional alter ego, Mikhail, dies of typhus.

86. In SB, "Memoirs," the Robert figure is called Mordecai. Pa Lurie sees his son Joshua as similar in character: "He had run away to Africa and made a fortune among the Kaffirs and later he sold cattle to the Russians during the Japanese war. When they lost they didn't settle their debt, but he made a fortune nevertheless. He came back to Russia after this, and until the War led the life of a rich man. According to Ma, he was princely, dashing, brave and open-handed. By Pa's account, he drank too much and spent his money on women and neglected his respectable wife. Pa would sometimes frown at me and say that I reminded him of Mordecai" (p. 34).

87. Abraham Bellow's letter is among SB's papers in the Regenstein.

2. CANADA/LIZA

1. Quoted in an edited and rewritten interview between SB and Philip Roth, "'I Got a Scheme!': The Words of Saul Bellow," *New Yorker* (25 April 2005), p. 77.

2. See SB, "By the St. Lawrence," SB, *CS*, p. 3.

3. Two-flats are residential buildings containing two apartments, one on top of the other, with separate entrances. The term is used in Buffalo and Detroit as well as by Chicagoans.

4. Manea, "Conversation," p. 3.

5. From p. 2 of a draft of SB's speech at the ceremony renaming the Lachine Library. The speech was never published but a draft is preserved in the Regenstein. Henceforth cited as Lachine speech.

6. Wordsworth, "The Two-Part Prelude" (1799), ll. 1.12.

7. Women from the Caughnawaga reservation worked in Lachine selling baskets or, like SB's nurse, as domestics. Many Caughnawaga men worked at Dominion Bridge. To return to the reservation they crossed the St. Lawrence over the unprotected Canadian Pacific Bridge; if a train appeared, they had to jump into the river, which was very swift. Many men drowned, "because they got drunk in

Lachine, tried to get back to the reservation, and then jumped in the river when they were overtaken by a train." This information and the quotation come from an eight-hour interview SB gave in 1987 to Sigmund Koch, a "University Professor" (as SB himself would become) at Boston University. Koch, a psychologist, had been funded by the Ford Foundation to conduct a series of videotaped interviews with artists and authors. Between 1983 and 1988, as part of the Boston University Aesthetics Research Project, he conducted seventeen eight- to ten-hour interviews with, among others, Toni Morrison, Arthur Miller, and Richard Wilbur, as well as SB. Ruth Miller, a friend and former student of SB's, who was at work on a book about him, also took part in the Koch interviews. The videotapes of the interviews are held at Boston University. All subsequent quotations from them in this chapter are taken from the first of four two-hour videotapes.

8. For the mother "mute with love," see SB, "By the St. Lawrence," *CS*, p. 2, a memory recounted by SB on several occasions; the other female protectors and Lachine as paradise come from the Lachine speech, p. 5.

9. See *Herzog*, p. 559.

10. Quoted in Atlas, *Biography*, p. 9.

11. There is a discrepancy here between the ship docking at Halifax, according to Library and Archives Canada, which has all ship manifests on microfilm (available on Ancestry.ca), and the Herzog family being described as "getting off the train."

12. According to Atlas, *Biography*, p. 8, this account was questioned by Ruth Gameroff, wife of Sam (Shmuel David) Gameroff, the cousin who was sent to fetch the doctor. She claimed the doctor's name was Dixon and that he was "not a drinking man." The episode took place when Sam was seventeen, though, well before he married Ruth (née Clark), an American from Connecticut. When SB was sent a draft of Ruth Miller's *Saul Bellow: A Biography of the Imagination*, he wrote "wrong" in the margin next to a passage in which he is said to describe the doctor as "the drunken goy" (Regenstein).

13. This letter is in the Regenstein.

14. Maurice Bellows was born on 27 December 1907; Sam Bellows was born on 17 April 1911.

15. This quotation comes from an eight-hour interview SB gave in 1987 to Sigmund Koch, a "University Professor" (as SB himself would become) at Boston University. Koch, a psychologist, had been funded by the Ford Foundation to conduct a series of videotaped interviews with artists and authors. Between 1983 and 1988, as part of the Boston University Aesthetics Research Project, he conducted seventeen eight- to ten-hour interviews with, among other authors, Toni Morrison, Arthur Miller, and Richard Wilbur, as well as SB. Ruth Miller, a friend and former student of SB's, who was at work on a book about him, also took part in the Koch interviews. The videotapes of the interviews are held at Boston University. All subsequent quotations from them in this chapter are taken from the first of four two-hour videotapes (henceforth cited as Koch interview). The detailed memories that follow come from the Lachine speech, p. 5, and the Koch interview.

16. Koch interview. In a letter of 27 March 1987 to Fred Mancuso, son of the landlady at 130 Eighth Avenue, SB remembers the tomatoes that were put out to dry at the end of summer, "upstairs and all around the house," also the cow Aunt Rosa bought for fresh milk. But these memories of Lachine may be from visits after the family had moved to Montreal.

17. "Ode: Intimations of Immortality," ll. 2–4. The "Chicago Book" (henceforth cited as SB, "CB") was intended as a work of reportage and reminisences, along the lines of *To Jerusalem and Back*. It exists in several parts: a manuscript of eighty-four pages, many autobiographical (the "Wordsworthian linkage" comes from this section, on p. 36); shorter sections, often just notes, on such topics as

"American Materialism" or "A Visit to County Jail," numbered separately or not numbered; and sixteen background files or folders containing clippings, notes, ephemeral publications, and correspondence on a range of Chicago topics and personalities. All these materials can be found in the Regenstein. The title "Chicago Book" comes from the heading of a section dated 5 April 1979: "Notes for Chicago Book."

18. Koch interview.

19. Botsford interview, "A Half Life," SB, *IAAU*, p. 298.

20. William Hazlitt, "My First Acquaintance with Poets" (1823), in *"Sketches and Essays" and "Winterslow,"* ed. W. Carew Hazlitt (London: George Bell, 1902), p. 271.

21. The quote beginning "When I was a very small child" is from the Botsford interview, "A Half Life," SB, *IAAU*, p. 298; subsequent quotes are from the Koch interview. SB's faith in physical appearance as a key to character was shared by Sherwood Anderson, a key early influence. *Winesburg, Ohio* (1919), the book that made Anderson's reputation, and a book SB frequently taught, begins with a story called "Hands," about a character who had long been a mystery in Winesburg: "Wing Biddlebaum talked much with his hands. The slender expressive fingers, forever active, forever striving to conceal themselves in his pockets or behind his back, came forth and became the piston rods of his machinery of expression. . . . Their restless activity, like unto the beating of the wings of an imprisoned bird, had given him his name. Some obscure poet of the town had thought of it. . . . They became his distinguishing feature, the source of his fame. Also they made more grotesque an already grotesque and elusive individuality" (*Winesburg, Ohio* [1919; New York: Random House, 2002], pp. 9–10). Tolstoy, too, SB felt, saw character in facial features and gestures. In a letter of 26 January 1966 to Edward Shils, he writes: "I'm convinced that Leo was a somatological moralist. Eyes, lips and noses, the color of the skin, the knuckles and the feet do not lie. The tone of Speransky's laughter [in *War and Peace*] tells you his social ideas are unreliable. It's not a bad system. I seem to have used it myself, most of the time."

22. These quotes come from Manea, "Conversation," p. 42.

23. SB, *The Dean's December* (1982; Harmondsworth: Penguin, 1998), p. 116 (henceforth cited within the text by page numbers).

24. See also SB to Eugene Goodheart, 21 April 1980. Goodheart wanted to stay at Mishkenot Sha'ananim, the guesthouse for artists and scholars in Jerusalem, and SB agreed to write to Kollek on his behalf: "Teddy and I have a payola relationship and I am one-up on him. He won't dream of refusing."

25. "A Conversation with Saul Bellow," by Chirantan Kulshrestha, *Chicago Review* 23.4–24.1 (1972), reprinted in Cronin and Siegel, eds., *Conversations with SB*, p. 92.

26. Atlas, *Biography*, p. 363.

27. Koch interview.

28. Ibid.

29. Max and Annie Cohen had three daughters, as do Uncle Asher and Aunt Taube in SB, "Memoirs," and there are other similarities between real and fictional characters; but there are also differences (for Asher and Taube, see SB, "Memoirs," p. 39).

30. In "Here and Gone," an unfinished and undated autobiographical story, the SB-like central character tells a reporter: "My father devoted his life to business but he wasn't really good at it. His talent was for failure. The big emotions were what he invested in" (p. 27). "Here and Gone" resembles "By the St. Lawrence" in that it recounts the return of an elderly writer, Mr. Immenitov (the birth name of SB's maternal grandfather, Moses Gordin), to Lachine and Montreal. The manuscript can be found among SB's papers in the Regenstein.

31. Koch interview.

32. The houses on St. Dominique Street were renumbered after the Bellows left Montreal in 1924. What was 1092 is now 3902. Today's 1092 is a vacant lot just past Boulevard René-Lévesque, much closer to the harbor and the heart of Chinatown than the old 1092, which was between Roy and Napoleon Streets.

33. In SB, "Memoirs," the Luries' second-floor apartment, also in a row of unprepossessing two-flats, is said to contain a single painting: of Moses holding up the Tablets (p. 57).

34. The description of the back staircase is from the fictional apartment in "Here and Gone," p. 4, rather than from an interview. Since in other respects the fictional apartment conforms to SB's descriptions of the real-life apartment, I include the description of the back staircase here.

35. According to Willie Greenberg, a neighbor and playmate of SB's on St. Dominique Street, interviewed in Alan Hustak, "St. Dominique St.'s Legacy Recalls '20s Era," *Montreal Gazette*, October 1990.

36. Mordecai Richler, *The Apprenticeship of Duddy Kravitz* (1959; Harmondsworth: Penguin, 1964), p. 45.

37. Hustak interview, "St. Dominique St.'s Legacy Recalls." Esplanade is one block farther west than St. Urbain. It is the setting for "Mr. Katz, Mr. Cohen, and Cosmology," one of the earliest of SB's short stories, published in *Retort: A Quarterly of Social Philosophy and the Arts* 1, no. 2 (June 1942): 12–20, and never reprinted. The two title characters walk through the Esplanade to a little wood near Outremont, where they sit and reflect on the formation of mountains and the nature of time. See also note 37 in Chapter 2.

38. The Montreal General Hospital has now merged with the Royal Victoria Hospital, located on Mount Royal, at the corner of Cedar Avenue and Côte-des-Neiges Road.

39. See Pierre Anctil, *Saint-Laurent: Montreal's Main* (Montreal: Septentrion, 2002), p. 40.

40. Aline Gubbay, *A Street Called the Main: The Story of Montreal's Boulevard Saint-Laurent* (Montreal: Meridian, 1989), p. 107.

41. Interview with Keith Botsford, "A Half Life," in SB, *IAAU*, p. 288.

42. Atlas, *Biography*, p. 15.

43. *Herzog*, p. 708. There was a *shochet* or ritual slaughterer who lived near the Bellows on St. Dominique Street, near Roy Street. His name was Mr. Aspler and he was a much honored figure in the neighborhood. See Dusty Vineberg, "Last Vestiges of the Ghetto: Memories of the Rich in Spirit," *Montreal Star*, 24 January 1972.

44. These details about the St. Dominique Street neighborhood come from Willie Greenberg (in the Hustak interview, and the Vineberg article, above), also from "Here and Gone," p. 3.

45. See "I Got a Scheme!," p. 75.

46. Koch interview.

47. Manea, "Conversation," p. 2.

48. Michael Greenstein, "Bellow's Canadian Beginnings," *Saul Bellow Journal* 7, no. 1 (Winter 1988): 33.

49. Santayana's definition of piety is quoted by SB in a speech given to the Anti-Defamation League on 14 November 1976. A month later, on 14 December, the speech was printed in *The New York Times* under the title "I Said That I Was an American, a Jew, a Writer by Trade." The extended passage from the Lachine library speech comes from pp. 4–5.

50. The quotation about not knowing what language he spoke comes from the Lachine speech, p. 2; the quote following is from Manea, "Conversation," p. 2.

That SB began studying Hebrew at three he tells Philip Roth in "I Got a Scheme!," p. 75: "At the age of three, I was sent to Mr. Stein across the way to learn Hebrew."

51. In the interview with Koch, SB speaks of having been enrolled in kindergarten at the Devonshire School at age five and refusing to go.

52. Interview with Eleanor Wachtel, on CBC Radio, broadcast 4 March 2001.

53. Koch interview.

54. *The Forward* was first imported from New York to Montreal in 1902 by Hirsch Hershman, a bookseller on the Main. For an account of Hershman, see Israel Mendes, "The Influence of the Jewish Press on Life in the U.S.A. and Canada," *Canadian Jewish Chronicle*, 19 September, 1952.

55. See Pierre Anctil, ed., *Through the Eyes of the Eagle: The Early Montreal Yiddish Press, 1907–1916* (Montreal: Véhicule Press, 2001), p. 141.

56. Among SB's papers at the Regenstein is a nine-page handwritten document entitled "Memories," written by Fannie Wiener and dated February 1985. In it she recounts how her family moved from Russia to Lachine, where her father went into the bakery business with two partners. He then bought "a very fine farm with a partner in Valleyfield. I remember that on a holiday weekend we had some cousins come in from Lachine, one day it was discovered that their little boy was missing, after looking around for a while the men got on the horses and rode out looking for him—after riding around on the roads, they sighted a man on horseback with a little boy, and happily, it was the missing child, he was three years old then. I mention it now because that little boy grew up to become a famous writer by the name of Saul Bellow." Elsewhere in "Memories" Fannie Wiener mentions that her mother had two brothers in Montreal, and that her father had a brother in New York. Annie Cohen had two brothers in the Montreal area (i.e., Lachine): Abraham and Willie. The Cohens emigrated from Lachine to Georgia, then moved back to Montreal.

57. Atlas, *Biography*, p. 300.

58. "He [SB] was a nice, quiet young boy, studious and polite," recalled Meyer Gameroff, the middle of the three male Gameroff cousins (quoted in Charles Lazarus, "St. Dominique Neighbor Recalls Nobel Winner Bellow's Boyhood," *Montreal Star*, 22 October 1976). But see "Memoirs" (p. 51) and "The Old System" (p. 95), in which SB provides a counterinstance. The narrator, at seven, is staying in the country with relatives very like the Gameroffs. He irritates an older cousin and his girlfriend by refusing to leave them alone, is roughly dismissed, and in fury attacks the cousin with a piece of wood. As punishment the cousin slaps him hard, boots him in the rear, and the child is sent back to Montreal.

59. Rexler uses this phrase to describe his cousin Albert in "By the St. Lawrence," p. 10.

60. Or so he told Janis Bellow.

61. This quotation comes from a tape recording of a speech given by Samuel Bellows at his sixtieth birthday party. The recording is in the possession of his daughter, Lesha Greengus.

62. SB's reference to his draining wound comes in a letter to Stephen Mitchell, 22 June 1991. The detail of the syringe comes from "Here and Gone," p. 17. The diaper pin detail comes from the unfinished novel "Charm and Death," p. 43, a thinly fictionalized account of SB's friend and rival Isaac Rosenfeld. The short story "Zetland: By a Character Witness" (1974), reprinted in SB, *CS*, pp. 240–54, began life as section 2 of "Charm and Death."

63. Interview with Botsford, "A Half Life," in SB, *IAAU*, p. 289.

64. For the absence of chairs, see "Here and Gone," p. 17. It is in the Lachine speech that SB says he spent "four to five" months in the hospital; Atlas, *Biography*, p. 15, says six months. It is impossible to confirm the exact length of SB's stay, or

details of his treatment and of hospital regulations, since all medical records from the Royal Victoria Hospital prior to 1940 were destroyed in a fire (according to the hospital's Medical Record Archivist, Nathalie Andrignon, in a letter to the author, 10 August 2009).

65. Manea, "Conversation," pp. 13, 41.

66. Ibid., pp. 6, 7.

67. SB spoke of his mother's mocking Christmas in the radio interview with Eleanor Wachtel. The tree and stockings are mentioned in SB to Werner Dannhauser, 13 December 1995.

68. Manea, "Conversation," p. 15. Manea asks SB if he felt guilty about eating the pork: "Sure, but I knew enough about Jewish tradition to know that this was permitted—anything was permitted that keeps you alive, right?" (p. 16).

69. Wachtel interview.

70. Manea, "Conversation," p. 40.

71. SB's remarks about his reading come from Manea, "Conversation," p. 16, and the Botsford interview, "A Half Life," SB, *IAAU*, p. 289; see also *Herzog*, where Moses imagines having an embarrassing conversation with "the Christian lady": "'Where do you live, little boy?' 'On Napoleon Street.' Where the Jews live. 'What does your father do?' My father is a bootlegger. He has a still in Point-St. Charles. The spotters are after him. He has no money" (p. 439).

72. Koch interview.

73. This friend was Walter Pozen.

74. Manea, "Conversation," p. 16.

75. Ibid., p. 8.

76. The anecdote about the movie theater comes from Bette Howland, recounted in an interview.

77. For references to Henderson's mother, see pp. 113, 123, 127, 132, in SB, *Henderson the Rain King* (1959).

78. Nothing at all is said of Benn Crader's mother in *More Die of Heartbreak*, though Kenneth Trachtenberg's mother, Benn's sister, is alive and unimpressed by her son: "She was disappointed in me, even angry. She had wanted me to be a big shot. I should have been the *Times*'s number one man in Paris, or *chef de bureau* for *Le Monde* in Washington, or NBC's head for Western Europe with thirty people under me, or *Porte-parole* at the Moscow Embassy" (p. 89). In *The Actual*, all we learn of Harry Trellman's mother is that she was impatient, "had a disease of the joints that sent her from sanitarium to sanitarium" (p. 2) and used to call him "You little gonif," signifying "that I had a masked character" (p. 71).

79. Chick in *Ravelstein* could perhaps be added to this list. He calls himself "a child of the Depression," as SB often did, and many of the events in his fictional life are undisguisedly taken from SB's life. But when Chick tells Rosamond he is convinced "that half a century later I feel I haven't seen the last of my mother" (p. 163), he and Rosamond have already moved to Boston. SB and Janis Freedman Bellow moved to Boston in 1993, when he was seventy-eight. For Chick's mother to have died in his adolescence he would have to be younger than SB when he moved to Boston, which he might or might not be. As for Charlie Citrine in *Humboldt*, he, too, might have been added to this list, though there are only hints of his age at the time his mother died. We know she is long dead. Charlie's older brother Julius can barely remember what she looked like. Menasha Klinger, who boarded with the Citrines during Charlie's adolescence, refers to her as "your kind poor mother" (p. 323), which he would not have done were she still alive when Charlie, early on in his life, became rich and famous. In *Dangling Man*, we are given no clues at all as to Joseph's age at the time his mother dies. In *Henderson* all we know of the death of the hero's mother is that it took place before he was sixteen (p. 132).

80. Charlie's view of the mother-son bond is closer to that of the British psy-

choanalyst D. W. Winnicott, an "object-relations" or "post-Kleinian" psychoanalytic theorist, than to that of Freud. Winnicott's theories of child development and creativity draw upon the writings of the English Romantic poets, especially Coleridge and Wordsworth, as well as upon those of psychoanalytic predecessors. See Leader, *Writer's Block* (Baltimore: Johns Hopkins University Press, 1991), pp. 96–103.

81. Grandma Lausch thinks the marriage ought never to have taken place, only did so because Mama, characteristically, gave away her affections "too easily" (p. 395).

82. For "esprit," see D. J. R. Bruckner, "A Candid Talk with Saul Bellow," *New York Times Magazine*, 15 April 1984: "Although no character in his stories exactly reproduces a real person, anyone who knows many of the people Bellow is interested in can recognize bits and pieces of them, very large bits in some cases. . . . He borrows his motto from Stendhal: 'I take someone from real life and give him more esprit than he has.'"

83. Botsford, "A Half Life," SB, *IAAU*, p. 290. There is a puzzle about dates here. If SB entered the Royal Victoria Hospital in the winter of 1923, sometime before Christmas, and stayed for between four, five, or even six months, he got out of the hospital in April or May 1924. That he did not return to school for the few months before the family removed to Chicago in July fits this dating. But if the dating is correct, it means that when Abraham left for Chicago (in, say, January or February 1924), SB was still in the hospital. There must therefore have been a period of several months in which only the mother and the siblings came for weekly visits. It is odd that SB should have said nothing about this period, either in interviews or to family members.

84. In *The Adventures of Augie March*, during the Depression, Augie's friend Joe Gorman, with whom he's previously been involved in a robbery, offers him money for "running immigrants over the border from Canada, from around Rouse's Point over to Massena Springs, New York. . . . If you want to come along and be my relief on the road as far as Massena Springs I'll give you fifty bucks and all expenses." Augie needs the money and "as for the immigrants, my thought about them was, Hell, why shouldn't they be here with the rest of us if they want to be? There's enough to go around of everything, including hard luck" (p. 567).

85. Manea, "Conversation," p. 10.

86. Bruckner, "A Candid Talk with Saul Bellow."

87. Koch interview.

3. CHICAGO/MAURY

1. Louis Dworkin's history comes from interviews with his daughter, Vivien Missner, and her daughter, Susan Missner. Toward the end of her grandfather's life, Susan Missner took detailed notes of a conversation she had with him about his early years in Chicago. The other major source for these early years is SB's "Chicago Book" (henceforth cited as SB, "CB"), for which, see Chapter 2, note 17. The detail about Abraham wiring Louis from Montreal comes from the autobiographical section of SB, "CB," p. 26, as do all the page references in this chapter, unless otherwise specified.

2. SB, "CB," p. 28.

3. SB, "Cousins," reprinted in SB, *CS*, p. 215 (henceforth cited within the text by page numbers).

4. SB, "CB," p. 28.

5. Quoted from the second of SB's Jefferson Lectures (1977), reprinted in SB, *IAAU*, p. 144; Petrush and the rats but not the finger are mentioned in SB, "CB," p. 27. SB's predecessors as Jefferson lecturers were Lionel Trilling (1972), Erik

Erikson (1973), Robert Penn Warren (1974), Paul A. Freund (1975), and John Hope Franklin (1976). The overall title for SB's lectures was "The Writer and His Country Look Each Other Over."

6. SB, "CB," p. 26.

7. SB, *Henderson the Rain King* (1958), p. 193 (henceforth cited within the text by page numbers).

8. SB, "CB," p. 26.

9. Ibid.

10. SB, *The Adventures of Augie March* (1953), p. 403 (henceforth cited within the text by page numbers).

11. For the Bellows' arrival in Chicago, see SB, "CB," p. 27ff; Roth/SB interview typescript; and "'I Got a Scheme!': The Words of Saul Bellow," *New Yorker* (25 April 2005) (henceforth cited as "I Got a Scheme!"), which draws on the typescript. Both typescript and *New Yorker* article were products of a proposal Roth made to SB in the summer of 1998, when SB was eighty-three—that they conduct "an extensive written interview" about his "life's work." "I would reread the books," Roth explains in the article, p. 72, "then send my thoughts on each, structured as questions, for him to respond to at length however he liked. As it turned out, we never got much beyond a beginning, despite Saul's willingness and my prodding. Every few months, in response to a letter or a phone call from me, some pages would arrive in the mail or through the fax machine, but then months would pass without a word from him, and, despite a weeklong visit I made to his Boston home one December, when he and I sat together for several hours every day talking about the books . . . the project petered out, and, reluctantly, I let him be." Eventually, Roth gathered his thoughts on SB's novels into an essay, "Re-reading Saul Bellow: A Novelist's Notes on Half a Century's Achievement," *New Yorker* (9 October 2000), and shortly after SB's death Roth reread the pages he had been sent and offered them to *The New Yorker*, where they were printed as "I Got a Scheme!" They appear, Roth explains, "as [Bellow] wrote them, without any editorial correction or alteration." Hence the arrival in Chicago of the Bellow family at the Harrison Street Station on p. 78 and at the Dearborn Street Station on p. 80. After the appearance of "Re-reading Saul Bellow," SB wrote to Roth to praise the piece: "no Eng. Lit. Prof. would be capable of doing what you've done with my books. And I too have learned from you" (the letter, written from Brookline, Massachusetts, is undated; see Benjamin Taylor, ed., *Saul Bellow: Letters* (New York: Viking, 2010), p. 550 (henceforth cited as Taylor, ed., *Letters*).

SB's niece Lesha Greengus has unearthed documents that complicate the accounts SB gave of the family's arrival in Chicago. In an email to the author of 6 February 2011 she writes: "I went through Jane's [this is Jane Bellow Kauffman, SB's sister] naturalization file and discovered an affidavit by Louis Dworkin, dated April 14, 1967. In his affidavit Louie states that he was married in December 1923 and that both Grandpa and Jane were present at the wedding. Jane's application states that she and Grandpa entered the U.S.A. (Syracuse, NY) on November 4, 1923. My father (Sam) wrote a notarized letter in the file, stating that he—and evidently Saul, Maury and their mother—arrived in the United States in July 1924." This is the only account of the family's removal from Canada to Chicago in which Jane is said to have accompanied her father, arriving six months before the rest of the family. It seems improbable that no one in the family would have mentioned the fact. Where did she stay? What did she do while Abraham worked at Imperial? She was sixteen at the time. Perhaps she was there only to attend the wedding and returned shortly afterward, presumably illegally, since she had entered the United States illegally. Had she finished her schooling by November 1923? The overworked Liza would have needed her to help out at home with the housework and cooking, particularly as SB was in the hospital at the time.

The date of November 4, 1923, however, fits with existing accounts of his father's arrival in the United States. See note 84 in Chapter 2 for the account of illegal border crossing in Chapter 9 of *The Adventures of Augie March* (p. 567).

12. SB, "CB," p. 27.

13. See the first page of SB, "America and Augie," a five-page typescript in the Regenstein, dated 3 March 2000, probably part of the "extensive written interview" (see note 11 above) on which he and Roth were working.

14. "I Got a Scheme!," p. 80.

15. Ibid., p. 78.

16. Quoted in Atlas, *Biography*, p. 19.

17. See Ijah, the narrator of "Cousins," on "the furious upright growth of Cousin Shana's ruddy hair" (p. 203), and "I Got a Scheme!," p. 78, for Louis Dworkin's red Mohawk stripe.

18. SB, "CB," p. 33.

19. SB, "Jefferson Lectures," *IAAU*, p. 146.

20. "Variations on a Theme from Division Street," the second of SB's two Tanner Lectures, delivered on 25 May 1981 at Brasenose College, Oxford, under the general title "A Writer from Chicago," and printed in *The Tanner Lectures on Human Values*, ed. Sterling M. McMurrin (Salt Lake City: Univerity of Utah Press, 1982), p. 202.

21. See SB, "CB," p. 26, and "Jefferson Lectures," *IAAU*, p. 144.

22. SB, "CB," p. 33.

23. "That was where you really saw it," SB remembered in the Koch interview, speaking of street life. "You didn't see it so much on the back streets. On the back streets you saw immigrant families."

24. SB, "CB," p. 43; also SB's speech given to the Council of Scholars at the Library of Congress on 20 November 1980, p. 1, which lists "Evolutionists, Nietzscheans, Single-Taxers, Anarchists and Wobblies ... Nudists ... Fundamentalists." This speech exists in manuscript and was revised into the second of the Tanner Lectures, where the list of speakers now includes "Nietzscheans, Anarchists, Zionists, followers of Max Nordau, Henry George, Brann the Iconoclast, interpreters of Karl Kautsky or Rosa Luxemburg" (pp. 201–2). In the Koch interview, SB's list of speakers also includes ballet dancers and "Fletcherians," who advocated "chewing every mouthful one hundred times." For details about the Jewish population of Chicago and the city's Jewish neighborhoods, see Irving Cutler, *The Jews of Chicago: From Shtetl to Suburb* (Urbana: University of Illinois Press, 1996).

25. Council of Scholars speech (20 November 1980), p. 2. In the second Tanner Lecture, "Variations on a Theme from Division Street," p. 2, the park bench intellectuals become "garment workers and carpenters read[ing] Ibsen."

26. "I Got a Scheme!," p. 75.

27. Botsford interview, "A Half Life," SB, *IAAU*, p. 297.

28. Ibid., p. 300. To find such a book in front of a Humboldt Park drugstore was, perhaps, unsurprising, given that it was the sort of neighborhood in which the tailor, Finer, subscribed to *The New Republic* (Atlas, *Biography*, p. 25).

29. SB, "CB," p. 39.

30. SB, "A Matter of the Soul," first published in *Opera News*, 11 January 1975, reprinted in SB, *IAAU*, p. 74.

31. SB, "Chicago and American Culture: One Writer's View," a talk delivered at the Centennial Celebration of the Chicago Public Library on 10 October 1972. A version of this talk was later printed under the same title in *Chicago* (May 1973), pp. 82–89. I have quoted from a twenty-one-page typescript of the talk itself, with handwritten corrections, in the Regenstein.

32. SB, "CB," pp. 29–30.

33. Preface, Rebecca West, ed., *Selected Poems of Carl Sandburg* (1926; New York: Harcourt, Brace, 1954), pp. 18–19, 20–21.

34. SB, "CB," p. 36.

35. Rosenfeld is quoted in ibid., p. 30; for the subsequent quotation about "Venetian or Neapolitan possibilities," see p. 31.

36. Koch interview.

37. SB, "CB," p. 32. In the Council of Scholars speech (20 November 1980), p. 14, SB cites Harvey W. Zorbaugh, *The Gold Coast and the Slum* (Chicago: University of Chicago Press, 1929), on the boundaries between rich and poor, not only in the Gold Coast but in the city as a whole.

38. SB, "CB," pp. 31–32.

39. For the cottonwood, see SB, "CB," pp. 33, 42, 48; "Jefferson Lectures," SB, *IAAU*, p. 147; and the Council of Scholars speech (20 November 1980), p. 3, where he talks of the tree's "yellow leather leaves." For "shabby," see *Herzog*, p. 661.

40. SB, "CB," p. 30.

41. SB, "Chicago and American Culture: One Writer's View," p. 4.

42. SB, "CB," p. 41; for "connoisseur of the near-nothing," see p. 15 of the nineteen-page section of "CB" entitled "American Materialism"; for the "catkins," see p. 33 of the main eighty-four-page section.

43. SB, "CB," p. 48.

44. When asked by Keith Botsford if he viewed the world differently on first coming to Chicago, SB answered: "I must have. . . . I certainly made decisions based on my condition. I had to decide, for instance, whether I would accept the role of convalescent sickly child or whether I would beef myself up. I decided on course two." He recalls reading a book written by the football coach Walter Camp entitled *How to Get Fit and How to Stay So* (the actual title was *Keeping Fit All the Way*), which involved "carrying coal scuttles at arms' length, and I did that because we had coal in the shed (this was in Chicago) and one of my jobs, which I was glad to do, was to go up and down the stairs. Up with the coal and down with the ashes. I became quite fanatical about training" (Botsford interview, "A Half Life," SB, *IAAU*, p. 290).

45. All quotes about the Chicago street from SB, "CB," pp. 34, 35, 37, 38–39. SB is mistaken here about George M. Cohan, who was 100 percent Irish, not Jewish.

46. Koch interview, where SB adds of the Polish community in Humboldt Park that it "was very tight, so that the third and fourth generation people still weren't speaking English very well. This was not the way it was with the rest of us."

47. Botsford interview, "A Half Life," SB, *IAAU*, p. 294.

48. Manea, "Conversation," p. 294.

49. Botsford interview, "A Half Life," SB, *IAAU*, p. 294.

50. See "I Got a Scheme!," p. 79: "I discovered that Cahan of the Yiddish *Forward* made a serious effort to educate his immigrant readers. Though he was a socialist he understood that the older Europeans had little use for Marxism."

51. SB, "Jefferson Lectures," *IAAU*, p. 144.

52. Manea, "Conversation," p. 22.

53. Ibid.

54. SB, "A Silver Dish," reprinted in SB, *CS*, p. 17.

55. From the unedited Roth/SB interview typescript, 2 December 1999.

56. SB, "Mr. Sugarman's Pledge of Allegiance," *Chicago Tribune*, 25 August 1996.

57. See Dominic A. Pacyga, *Chicago: A Biography* (Chicago: University of Chicago Press, 2009), p. 155; also James L. Merriner, *Grafters and Goo Goos: Corruption and Reform in Chicago, 1833–2003* (Carbondale: Southern Illinois University Press, 2004). For "verbal swagger," see "I Got a Scheme!," pp. 75–76: "In the papers, you followed the events leading to the killing of Dion O'Bannion [*sic*], of the Northside bootlegging gang, and of the indictment of Al Capone for tax evasion. You knew all the facts about the death of Lingle, the *Tribune*'s gang reporter, who was shot

down in the Illinois Central Randolph Street tunnel. The papers informed you that Big Bill Thompson, the mayor, was in the pocket of Capone. . . . Chicago was big on gab in the twenties and thirties, and under the influence of gab you came to feel yourself an insider. Verbal swagger was a limited art cultivated in the Hearst papers."

58. SB, "Mr. Sugarman's Pledge of Allegiance." See also SB, "CB," p. 79: "In a single year, during Thompson's mayoralty, gang boss Johnny Torrio, who preceded Al Capone, Chicago's most famous gangster, grossed $4,000,000 from his Chicago beer peddling, $3,000,000 from gambling, $3,000,000 from prostitution and another $4,000,000 from similar enterprises in the suburbs. Payoffs to police officials and politicians were high and frequent, but Torrio had no objections as long as he could carry on without too much harassment. Chicago alone had more than 12,000 speakeasies, beerflats and brothels that sold illegal liquor."

59. SB, "Chicago and American Culture: One Writer's View," p. 8.

60. Manea "Conversation," p. 10.

61. SB, "CB," p. 40.

62. Ibid., p. 36.

63. Ibid., p. 45.

64. Ibid., p. 40.

65. SB, "A Talk with the Yellow Kid," first published in *The Reporter* (6 September 1956), reprinted in SB, *IAAU*, p. 47.

66. SB, "Chicago: Once Over Lightly," the first of the Tanner Lectures, p. 192.

67. SB, "A Talk with the Yellow Kid," p. 49.

68. Ibid., pp. 52, 53.

69. SB, "A Cry of Strength: The Unfashionably Uncynical Saul Bellow," interview with Cathleen Medwick, *Vogue* (March 1982), reprinted in Cronin and Siegel, eds., *Conversations with SB*, p. 192.

70. SB, "Chicago and American Culture: One Writer's View," p. 1; Botsford interview, "A Half Life," SB, *IAAU*, p. 291.

71. SB, "Chicago and American Culture: One Writer's View," pp. 1, 5.

72. Botsford interview, "A Half Life," SB, *IAAU*, pp. 291, 292.

73. Atlas, *Biography*, p. 25.

74. There were three main Chicago newspapers at this time: two Hearst papers, the *Herald Examiner* and the *Evening American*, and a McCormick paper, the Republican *Tribune*, the only one of the three to survive. SB does not say which of these he read. In "I Got a Scheme!," the source of the quote about reconciling the Trojan War with Prohibition (p. 78), SB also mentions "the Chicago *Journal*, a paper that did not survive the Depression." The *Journal* was noteworthy for publishing "a weekly literary supplement" (p. 82). The Leopold and Loeb case concerned a famous murder trial, that of two wealthy law students from the University of Chicago motivated by a desire to commit the perfect murder. In 1924 Nathan Leopold, Jr. (1904–71) and Richard Loeb (1905–36) kidnapped and murdered fourteen-year-old Bobby Franks. After their arrest they retained Clarence Darrow as their lawyer. They were sentenced to life imprisonment. Alfred Hitchcock made a movie about the case, *Rope* (1948), based on the play by Patrick Hamilton (1929).

75. Koch interview.

76. Ruth Miller, *Saul Bellow: A Biography of the Imagination* (New York: St. Martin's, 1991), p. 7.

77. Koch interview.

78. Botsford interview, "A Half Life," SB, *IAAU*, p. 305: Botsford: "When did that fundamental idea of all writers, that this is what you are going to do with yourself, write, first strike you? In what form did it come?" SB: "It came early in my high school years, when I began to realize that I thought of myself all along as a writer."

79. From "Saul Bellow—A Boy I Knew," the text of a talk Esther Robbins delivered "a number of times for various organizations." A copy of the talk is included in a letter to SB of 24 July 1989 (Regenstein). All subsequent quotations from Robbins come from this text.

80. Koch interview.

81. SB, "CB," p. 34.

82. "I Got a Scheme!," p. 82.

83. SB, "CB," p. 34 for Mrs. Cox; SB, "In the Days of Mr. Roosevelt," originally printed in *Esquire* (December 1983), reprinted in SB, *IAAU*, p. 17, for Mrs. Davis, who made the remark on the occasion of Lindbergh's flight to Paris on 20–22 May 1927 (when SB was twelve); for the Santayana quote see *Character and Opinion in the United States* (1920; New York: Anchor, 1967), p. 29.

84. Botsford interview, "A Half Life," SB, *IAAU*, p. 293.

85. SB, "The Distracted Public," the Romanes Lecture, Oxford University, 10 May 1990, reprinted in SB, *IAAU*, p. 153.

86. Koch interview.

87. SB, "America and Augie," pp. 4, 2.

88. SB, "CB," p. 36.

89. To David Peltz, for example, what was most notable about SB the adolescent (they met when they were both fifteen) was his sense of self: "He was focused, he was dedicated to becoming what he was, from the beginning. I mean, he never veered. He believed in himself."

90. "Deck the Tisch with Sabbath Cholly" is the example Robbins recalls.

91. In Manea, "Conversation," p. 7, SB says that his sidelocks were cut off at three, that "until late adolescence" he attended synagogue each Saturday, sitting downstairs with his father and the other men, while his mother and sister sat upstairs, and that for the same period he ate only kosher. SB had his Bar Mitzvah at the Spaulding Street synagogue west of the Park.

92. Rebecca West describes looking down at the beach from the dining room "of a magnificent hotel built like an Italian *palazzo*," which, in SB, "CB," p. 31, SB decides must be the Drake Hotel, making the beach the Oak Street Beach.

93. Manea, "Conversation," p. 10.

94. Rockwell Gray, Harry White, and Gerald Nemanic, "Interview with Saul Bellow," *TriQuarterly* 60 (1984): 12–34, reprinted in Cronin and Siegel, eds., *Conversations with SB*, p. 209.

95. In "Starting Out in Chicago," originally a 1974 Brandeis University commencement address, reprinted in the *American Scholar* 44 (Winter 1974–75), SB describes a person that could be the model for Cousin Mendy, the brother of his first wife, Anita: "J.J., my brother-in-law, born Jascha in the old country, practiced law in the Loop" (p. 76). For more on J.J. or Jack Goshkin, see Chapter 6, pp. 216–17.

96. Ibid., pp. 76, 77. Arkady was Anita's cousin, not SB's.

97. SB, "Him with His Foot in His Mouth," originally published in *The Atlantic Monthly* (November 1982), reprinted in SB, *CS*, p. 378.

98. SB, "Mozart: An Overture," *Bostonia* Magazine (Spring 1992), originally a speech delivered at the Mozart Bicentennial, 5 December 1991, in Florence, Italy, reprinted in SB, *IAAU*, p. 2. It is Atlas, *Biography*, p. 24, who locates these lessons in the Fine Arts Building; but on p. 3 of a section of "CB" entitled "Notes on Meeting with Sen. Niestein—April 30, 1979," SB writes that Borushek had a studio "on the second floor of a much-ornamented building on the southeast corner of California and North Avenues."

99. SB, "Mozart: An Overture," pp. 2, 1.

100. When the Bellow family got its first radio is not clear. In "A Half Life," SB, *IAAU*, p. 293, SB says that "in those early days" in Chicago he got his political ideas from the newspapers, since "there was no radio as yet." However, in hand-

written notes in the Regenstein for the 1974 Brandeis commencement address, later printed under the title "Starting Out in Chicago," he writes: "As I make these notes on March 4, 1974, I remember that on March 4, 1928, I had a sore throat and sat at home listening to the inauguration of Herbert Hoover on the Majestic radio." In the Koch interview SB tells this story, adding "we had just bought a radio."

101. SB, "Mozart: An Overture," SB, *IAAU*, p. 2.

102. SB, "A Matter of the Soul," in SB, *IAAU*, pp. 73 (for the music teacher's gramophone selections) and 73–74.

103. SB, "Jefferson Lectures," SB, *IAAU*, p. 121.

104. Even today, it is the largest container port in the Western Hemisphere, the third largest in the world. See Deanna Isaacs, "Fall Books Special: Chicago's Life Story," an interview with Dominic Pacyga, in *Chicago Reader* (5 November 2009); see also Pacyga, *Chicago: A Biography*, pp. 404–9.

105. SB, from the "American Materialism" section of SB, "CB," p. 4.

106. For the Auditorium Theatre, see Pacyga, *Chicago: A Biography*, pp. 133–37. As for the date of SB's unpaid ushering, the theater shut down during the Depression, the Crash occurred in October 1929, and SB did not enter Tuley High School until September 1930.

107. SB, "Jefferson Lectures," SB, *IAAU*, p. 122.

108. "Interview with Saul Bellow," reprinted in Cronin and Siegel, eds., *Conversations with SB*, p. 199.

109. SB, "CB," p. 14; see also SB's Council of Scholars speech (20 November 1980), p. 19: "It is clear . . . that there would be no art if we were governed in all things by the collective state of mind which has given us our visible achievements in the material sphere."

110. Botsford interview, "A Half Life," SB, *IAAU*, p. 293.

111. Koch interview.

112. The "Something Chicago College of Law" is as close as SB could come to the school's name (in the Roth/SB interview transcript). Maury's son, Joel Bellows, never knew the name.

113. This quotation was remembered by Lesha Greengus, Maury's niece (email of 27 February 2011).

114. Roth/SB interview transcript; SB, "Something to Remember Me By," *Esquire* (July 1990), reprinted in SB, *CS*, p. 424.

115. Manea, "Conversation," p. 10.

116. From the last page of a four-page typescript in the Regenstein, mostly about Isaac Rosenfeld, with handwritten corrections. Across the top, in another hand, is the message: "Saul, Sent Roth a copy of this, warning him of its drafty nature." The message is signed, but I cannot make out the signature or hand, nor is there a date on the typescript, clearly part of the "extended written interview" project Roth first proposed in the summer of 1998.

117. Manea, "Conversation," p. 11.

118. The quotation about Americanization comes from the Botsford interview, "A Half Life," SB, *IAAU*, p. 293; for the quotation about family affection, see Roth/SB interview typescript.

119. Manea, "Conversation," p. 9.

120. Kyle Bellows, Joel's son, provides an example of Maury's feeling for family: "When I was a small child I had a very life-threatening surgery where I had to have a kidney removed and he flew in to see if he could be a possible organ-donor match. That really was very, very special." It was also, Kyle adds, "essentially out of character for him." Most of what Kyle learned of Maury came from his maternal grandfather, who knew Maury from the Covenant Club, for affluent Russian Jewish businessmen (it is thinly fictionalized as Simon's club in *The Adventures of Augie*

March): "He [Kyle's maternal grandfather] really thought of him as—how do I put this in a way that's not derogatory—an immoral scumbag. I don't mean to be glib about this. I know he had a very tough, a very punitive upbringing. When put into context, it's understandable how somebody could come out that way. But in the long run, who really cares?"

121. Botsford interview, "A Half Life," SB, *IAAU*, p. 293.

122. Koch interview.

123. Roth/SB interview typescript.

124. Koch interview.

125. The one member of the Dworkin family Maury became close with was Alvin Baron, son of Flora and Isidor. Alvin was the model for the gangster Tanky Metzger in "Cousins." Through Maury, Alvin became close to Jimmy Hoffa and Allen Dorfman, who managed the Teamsters' investments. Dorfman was close to the Chicago and Cleveland syndicates, to Las Vegas gangsters, and to all the varied interests funded by the Teamsters. He was murdered near Vivien Missner's home in Skokie when it was thought he might testify against the mob. Alvin Baron succeeded Dorfman as the union's "Asset Manager." When he, too, was indicted, like Tanky Metzger, he refused to disclose information and was sentenced to prison. Before sentencing, SB wrote a letter to the judge attesting to the good character of Alvin's family, as Ijah writes a letter attesting to the good character of Tanky's family. Alvin remained silent, served his time, moved to Las Vegas, where influential "friends" set him up in business, and lived a prosperous life. See Steven Brill, *The Teamsters* (New York: Simon & Schuster, 1978).

126. Amos, Joseph's older brother in SB's first novel, *Dangling Man* (1944), might join this list, but Amos is more conventional and family-minded than Maury, in this respect more like Sam Bellows.

127. This anecdote recalled by Lesha Bellows Greengus (email, 27 February 2011).

128. For Updike review, see "Draping Radiance with a Worn Veil," *New Yorker* (15 September 1975); for the quotations about Rabbit, see *Rabbit at Rest* (London: André Deutsch, 1990), pp. 164, 90.

129. The Sherry was the first high-rise hotel on the South Side of Chicago. When Marge and Maury bought it, it was an apartment-hotel, which they renovated and turned into a commercial hotel. Other real estate and business ventures followed. In 1955 they sold the Sherry and in 1956 bought the thousand-room Shoreland Hotel, again on the South Side, just north of the Sherry at 5454 South Shore Drive. Al Capone used to conduct business in the Shoreland under previous ownership. Jimmy Hoffa kept a room there during the time the Bellowses owned it, as did the economist Milton Friedman.

130. So, too, with Marge and Maury. According to their grandson, Mark Rotblatt, "they were both crazy people. . . . Tough, tough people." Marge "used to like to say she was Leona Helmsley before Leona Helmsley, and proud of it." When they fought, "they were like throwing the most expensive Steuben bowls, the Baccarat vases. If it didn't have value it wasn't worth throwing . . . and the screaming and the carrying on."

131. Roth/SB interview transcript.

132. Maury's way of driving seems to have been passed on to his daughter, Lynn. Greg Bellow remembers driving with her: "She was cutting in and out of traffic, people were honking at her, she was driving on the edge of the roadway, passing people, weaving. I don't even think we were late. I said, 'You drive like this all the time?' She said, 'Yeah, sure, my father drove like this.'" When Lynn's son, Mark, was learning to drive, "I'd be real aggressive and I'm still pretty aggressive and my grandma [Marge] would say: 'He's Maury Bellows behind the wheel.'"

133. A similar doubleness is expressed about Chicago: "I have had an *odi et amo*

attitude towards Chicago for nearly fifty years. I am greatly attached to it, I am also deeply estranged from it" ("Chicago and American Culture: One Writer's View," p. 3).

134. According to Lesha Bellows Greengus, after she and her family returned from the Nobel ceremonies, Maury expressed interest "in the monetary size of the prize, whether it was tax free, and whether Saul could keep it in an offshore account. He did express genuine affection for Saul and pride in his world-class honor; at the same time he was quite certain that Saul would not be able to hold on to the money. 'He is going to piss it away'" (email, 27 February 2011).

135. Roth/SB interview transcript.

136. "I Got a Scheme!," p. 80.

4 · TULEY

1. Lazer Bailen was the son of the sister of Sara Gurevich Gordin, Moses Gordin's wife. According to Jane Bellow Kauffman, SB's, Sam's, and Maury's sister, as recalled by Lesha Bellows Greengus, Maury was "madly in love" with Mildred Bailen, Lazar's daughter, "who jilted him for a wealthier catch, who turned out to be Jack Dworkin (Louie's younger brother)" (email, 6 February 2011). This episode is fictionalized in Chapter 8 of *The Adventures of Augie March*, when the beautiful Cissy Flexner jilts Simon, who is "powerfully in love" with her, for Five Properties, (p. 552). Lazer Bailen eventually went into the real estate business ("by which we believe he managed some real estate properties"), lost everything in the Depression, moved the family to Philadelphia, then returned the family to Chicago permanently (according to Lesha Bellow Greengus, in the email of 6 February 2011, and Susan Missner, Louis Dworkin's granddaughter, in an email of 12 February 2011).

2. According to Lesha (email, 6 February 2011), Abraham did not break completely with Imperial until 1931; there was a period of several years, therefore, in which he was both selling wood to other bakeries and working for cousin Louis. SB offers a fictional account of the new business in "Far Out," a novel he worked on in the 1970s but never finished. It was sent in installments to Harvey Guinzburg of Harper and Row and exists in its most finished form in a hundred-page typed manuscript (deposited in the Regenstein, along with earlier draft material). The novel is set in the 1950s and on p. 28 of an early draft its hero, Peter Vallis, recalls his father's business in Chicago "selling lumbermill scraps to bakers for their ovens. He had a yard on Cherry Street, near Fulton—'poultry, eggs and fish'—and the wood came in freight cars from mills in the Upper Peninsula and was stacked up in swaying piles. Deliveries were made in a busted Diamond Truck with solid tires. There was a little office with a wagon-scale under the window and a wooden bench from a waiting room where Isidro [Peter's father] took his siesta. . . . He needed Pete to drive the old Willys Knight Whippet to Northern Wisconsin to buy mill-ends or trimmings, and around town to make sales or collections."

3. Manea, "Conversation," pp. 10–11.

4. There is a problem here about addresses. When SB took his wife Janis on a tour of the old neighborhood, he identified the address of his family's apartment on Le Moyne as either 3245 or 3246 Le Moyne, in a building no longer standing. The Chicago phone directories list the address as 3340, the address Atlas gives in *Biography*, p. 31. Nathan Tarcov, the son of SB's friend from Tuley High School Oscar Tarcov, believes Oscar's family lived at 3340. He has envelopes addressed to his father at 3340 Le Moyne. He also has a letter to his father from July 1937 addressed to 3340 but then changed to 3342. The Chicago phone books have no listing for Oscar's father, though there is a listing for Anita Tarcov, Oscar's much older sister, at 3342 Le Moyne. Perhaps the Tarcovs and the Bellows lived in sepa-

rate apartments in the same building on Le Moyne, or the Tarcovs lived there after the Bellows. That no one from either family remembers this being so, however, is puzzling, as are Janis Bellow's notes identifying the street number as 3245 or 3246.

5. Manea, "Conversation," p. 12.

6. These numbers come from Sam's son, Shael Bellows, as relayed to Lesha Bellows Greengus, who includes them in a "Bellow/s Family Chronology 1923–1962" (email, 6 February 2011).

7. Manea, "Conversation," p. 12.

8. Joel Bellows, email, 30 January 2011. Bellows Coal lasted until Maury bought Bunge Coal and Oil in the late 1940s, then the fourth largest coal company in Chicago. Joel thinks that there must have been some arrangement between Maury and his father and Sam about not competing for customers. Lesha Bellows Greengus remembers that Maury's first coal yard was farther west than Carroll Coal.

9. Sam told his son, Shael, according to Lesha Bellows Greengus (email, 6 February 2011), that Abraham had had an accident the first time he tried to drive, and that he never tried again.

10. Rachel Greengus Schultz, email, 31 January 2011.

11. SB's quotation comes from a tape recording played for me by Lesha Bellows Greengus.

12. Manea, "Conversation," p. 11; Stuart Brent, the Chicago bookseller, recalls this description of Sam in a letter to SB, 4 June 1985.

13. "I Got a Scheme!," p. 79. For the genesis of this article, a product of conversations between SB and Philip Roth, see Chapter 3, note 11.

14. Manea, "Conversation," p. 8.

15. On 3 March 1963, the Chicago Jewish Community honored Sam Bellows as its "Man of the Year" at a dinner at the Sheraton-Chicago Hotel on North Michigan Avenue. The program for the evening (a copy is in the Regenstein) lists Sam's charitable activities: chairman of the board of the Chicago Jewish Academy, president of the Academy Associates, president of the Orthodox Congregation Tifereth Zion, member of the board of directors of Associated Talmud Torahs, Hebrew Theological College, and Chicago Jewish Academy, and active supporter of Religious Zionists of Chicago and the Israel Bond Organization of Chicago.

16. Irving Cutler, *The Jews of Chicago: From Shtetl to Suburb* (Urbana: University of Illinois Press, 1996), p. 230.

17. Lesha Greengus, email, 6 February 2011.

18. SB, "Chicago and American Culture: One Writer's View," p. 8, a talk delivered at the Centennial Celebration of the Chicago Public Library on 10 October 1972. A version of this talk was later printed under the same title in *Chicago* (May 1973), pp. 82–89. I have quoted from a twenty-one-page typescript of the talk itself, with handwritten corrections, in the Regenstein. On the same page, SB is, if anything, harder on the conspicuously "cultured": "the fairly low-grade morons and buffoons—that portion of the public which put on cultural airs—did not inspire kindly amusement in the rest." A second typescript of the talk in the Regenstein is titled "Address at the Chicago Public Library."

19. That Adelsky is loosely based on the Chicago billionaire Abram (A. N.) Pritzker, a client of SB's friend Marilyn Mann, an interior decorator, the second wife of Sam Freifeld, was suggested by Mann herself, who resembles Amy Wustrin in some ways. SB's dual attitude toward business success recalls Theodore Dreiser, an early and continuing influence. The scenes in Simon's coal yard in *Augie* are partly drawn from real-life experiences and locations, but they also have something of the atmosphere of the railroad scenes toward the end of *Sister Carrie* (Chapters 43–44), in which George Hurstwood scabs during a strike by motormen and conductors and narrowly escapes serious injury.

20. Koch interview.

21. SB, "The Old System" (1968), in *CS*, p. 101 (henceforth cited within the text by page numbers).

22. Judith Greengus thinks SB, too, was frightened of women, certainly strong women, "with financial independence, a career, and birth control" (a view relayed by her mother, Lesha Greengus, in an email of 2 February 2010). For SB on Sam's view of women, see Manea, "Conversation," p. 8.

23. Ibid., p. 9.

24. According to SB's agent, Harriet Wasserman, in *Handsome Is: Adventures with Saul Bellow: A Memoir* (New York: Fromm International, 1997), p. 130, when she visited him in Vermont in July 1978, and Daniel, his youngest son, was fourteen, SB told her: "'When I was Daniel's age [thus in 1929, the summer of Jane and Charlie's wedding, though presumably before the wedding], my mother was sitting with me outside on a day like this. She took her blouse off because she thought the sun would be healing.' Saul saw the terrible scar of the missing breast, and she said to him, 'You see. This is why your father doesn't come near me anymore.' It struck me, then, that Saul had really been traumatized at an early age." This story was heard also by Joel Bellows.

25. See SB, *Herzog*, p. 668, when Moses quarrels with Father Herzog over money: "'Idiot!' was what the old man had shouted. 'Calf!' Then he saw the angry demand underlying Moses's look of patience. 'Get out! I leave you nothing! Everything to Willie and Helen! You . . . ? Croak in a flophouse.' Moses rising, Father Herzog shouted, 'Go. And don't come to my funeral.'"

26. "She *could* be darling," Rachel Schultz insists, in the same email (22 February 2011) in which she talks of her grandmother's signature dishes, "but she was *never* docile."

27. This quotation and the one that follows come from the "American Materialism" section of SB, "CB," p. 6.

28. Chicago May "used to throw her escorts' clothes out of the window to her accomplice in the alley" (*The Adventures of Augie March,* p. 601). See also the practices of the real-life Mickey Finn, who ran a whorehouse in the Levee district, Chicago's red-light district, just south of the business area of the city. Finn opened the Lone Star Saloon and Palm Garden in 1896. It was here that he developed the knockout drink that bears his name. As the Chicago historian Dominic A. Pacyga, in *Chicago: A Biography* (Chicago: University of Chicago Press, 2009), p. 107, describes it: "After being drugged Finn dragged the victim into a small room at the rear of the Palm Garden . . . stripped him and took his money. Finn often kept the man's clothes and substituted old clothing before throwing the target out into the alley."

29. SB, "CB," p. 6. The Edgewater Beach Hotel was in this neighborhood, so it was easy for Kid Weil to hire his naked prostitutes.

30. SB, "Something to Remember Me By," in SB, *CS*, p. 423 (henceforth cited within the text by page numbers).

31. Relayed in an email from Lesha Greengus, 2 February 2010.

32. Atlas, *Biography*, p. 42. This business of the names is puzzling. Though the Chicago phone books for 1931–32 and 1933 list Abraham's name as Abraham Bellows not Bellow, SB's official records at Tuley High School and Northwestern University list him as Bellow.

33. Koch interview.

34. According to an "Official Record" of SB's years at Tuley supplied by the Chicago Public Schools Department of Compliance.

35. In 1979 it was renamed the Roberto Clemente Community Academy or Clemente High School.

36. From the first of two "Jefferson Lectures" (1977), reprinted in SB, *IAAU*, p. 120. According to SB's friend and classmate Sydney J. Harris, "Tuley was a very

good school in that it was tremendously heterogeneous. I mean you'd have the children of a shoemaker there and one of the Goldblatt kids [of Goldblatts department stores, where SB worked on Saturdays in a branch near Charlie Kauffman's dental practice]. . . . You really had a splendid cross-section of the city and nobody was concerned about who anybody's father was. It was a very pleasant way to grow up, on the whole." This quotation is from an interview conducted with Harris by the journalist D. J. R. Bruckner, who was at work on a television documentary about SB. The program, *Saul Bellow's Chicago*, was aired on Channel 5 in Chicago on 27 March 1981. Bruckner conducted his interviews in 1980 and his recordings are in the Regenstein.

37. Atlas, *Biography*, p. 30.

38. "Chicago and American Culture: One Writer's View," p. 7.

39. Ibid., p. 8. In "Variations on a Theme from Division Street," the second of his two Tanner Lectures, delivered on 25 May 1981 at Brasenose College, Oxford, under the general title "A Writer from Chicago," and printed in *The Tanner Lectures on Human Values*, ed. Sterling M. McMurrin (Salt Lake City: University of Utah Press, 1982), p. 201, SB mentions memorizing "Hence loathed melancholy" and "Sweet Auburn, loveliest village of the plain."

40. SB, "The Distracted Public," originally delivered as the Romanes Lecture, Oxford University, 10 May 1990, reprinted in SB, *IAAU*, pp. 152, 153–54.

41. "I Got a Scheme!," p. 76.

42. Botsford interview, "A Half Life," SB, *IAAU*, p. 296.

43. SB to Danny Godfrey, 16 October 1992.

44. In "Charm and Death," the unpublished novel (the manuscript is in the Regenstein) from which the story "Zetland: By a Character Witness" is drawn, what sounds like "Boys Shop" is recalled. The narrator describes "the stannic fragrance of the metal shop at school in Chicago, years ago . . . the square little table furnace soldering irons gaping fire through the helmet-mouth" (p. 9).

45. "I was a determined athlete, but not outstanding. I was not in a class with Julius Echeles, now a criminal lawyer, who was the school's (Tuley High) basketball star. 'Lucky' was his nickname. I'd been a sickly child and was determined in adolescence not to be a convalescent adolescent. And I drove myself hard. Characteristically, I read a great deal about body building. I studied physical development books like *How to Get Strong and How to Stay So*. From the great Walter Camp I learned to carry scuttles filled with coal, holding them out at arm's length" (interview with Steve Neal, "The Quintessential Chicago Writer," *Chicago Tribune Magazine*, 6 September 1979, reprinted in Cronin and Siegel, eds., *Conversations with SB*, p. 173.

46. The last digit in the handwritten number "254" on the Chicago Public Schools "Official Record" is hard to decipher, written over or above a "2," perhaps. It looks like "4" to me.

47. Dave Schwab's recollection comes from Atlas, *Biography*, p. 26; Arthur Wineberg's from a 1980 interview with D. J. R. Bruckner.

48. Koch interview. Tuley was easygoing about its student radicals. According to Sidney Passin, brother of SB's close friend Herb Passin, the principal of Tuley, Mr. Yebutz, was an "elderly guy, warm-hearted"; the assistant principal, Mr. Jacobson, "Jake," was "a disciplinarian everyone liked." Sydney J. Harris, a year below SB, remembers Jacobson as "a very amusing fellow": "We were very militant, and we'd picket the school and instead of upbraiding us he'd march with us, eating peanuts." Arthur Wineberg recalls this march, at which Jacobson offered him peanuts with the greeting "Nuts for the nuts?" These recollections from Harris and Wineberg come from 1980 interviews with D. J. R. Bruckner.

49. Manea, "Conversation," p. 6.

50. See SB, "In the Days of Mr. Roosevelt," originally printed in *Esquire*,

December 1983, reprinted in SB, *IAAU*, pp. 19–20: "For older citizens it was a grim time—for the educated and professional classes the Depression was grievously humiliating—but for the young this faltering of order and authority made possible an escape from family and routine."

51. This quotation comes from p. 2 of an untitled sixteen-page handwritten manuscript in the Regenstein, dated March 1974, and beginning "How, in the city of Chicago, does a young person become a writer?" Much of it appears in "Starting Out in Chicago, *The American Scholar* 44 (Winter 1974–75), originally delivered as a commencement address at Brandeis University on 22 May 1974.

52. Botsford interview, "A Half Life," SB, *IAAU*, p. 300.

53. SB, "Starting Out in Chicago," p. 73.

54. SB, "Chicago and American Culture: One Writer's View," pp. 10–11.

55. Theodore Dreiser, *Sister Carrie*, ed. James L. W. West III (1981; Harmondsworth: Penguin, 1994), p. 62 (henceforth cited within the text by page numbers).

56. Theodore Dreiser, *Jennie Gerhardt*, ed. James L. W. West III (1992; Philadelphia: University of Pennsylvania Press, 1994), pp. 125–26.

57. SB quoted in Rockwell Gray, Harry White, and Gerald Nemanic, "Interview with Saul Bellow," *TriQuarterly* 60 (1984): 12–34, reprinted in Cronin and Siegel, eds., *Conversations with SB*, p. 205. See also, from the same interview: "Dreiser loves . . . to theorize clumsily about their motives [he is talking about the "money titans" in his novels], the 'chemisms' that drive them. He's crammed himself with T. H. Huxley, Herbert Spencer, Darwin and a heavy diet of 'artistry,' but he's such a passionate materialist that he carries you with him even while you are dismissing his theories, and his clumsy artiness" (p. 206). In the "American Materialism" section of "CB," p. 15, where SB quotes Mencken on Dreiser's "inexorable particularity," he also describes Dreiser as "fact-intoxicated," his novels being "stuffed to surfeit with money, property, deals, interest rates, bookkeeping, bribery, and the bottomless appetite of acquisition," an appetite matched only by his characters' "predatory and almost carnivorous sexuality" (pp. 15–16).

58. Interview with Gordon Lloyd Harper, "The Art of Fiction: Saul Bellow," *Paris Review* 9, no. 36 (1966): 48–73, reprinted in Cronin and Siegel, eds., *Conversations with SB*, pp. 60–61. See also SB, "Chicago and American Culture: One Writer's View," p. 12: "The young novelists and would-be novelists working on the newspapers were charged with a sense of the place. Coming from bleak villages from the sticks, they were overcome by the color and power of Chicago. One sees this most vividly in Theodore Dreiser who so movingly combines great strength of judgement and sympathy with gee whiz—the gee whiz of the dazzled country boy."

59. From p. 3 of a typed manuscript in the Regenstein entitled "Literature and de Tocqueville," the transcript of a talk entitled "Literature in a Democracy: From de Tocqueville to the Present," delivered by SB in Mandel Hall, University of Chicago, 6 December 1995.

60. Terry Teachout, *The Skeptic: A Life of H. L. Mencken* (New York: HarperCollins, 2002), p. 103.

61. From SB to William J. Bennett, 9 July 1984.

62. "I Got a Scheme!," p. 76.

63. Ibid., p. 82, for the Nietzsche quote; for *Herzog* and Nietzsche, see Daniel Fuchs, *Saul Bellow: Vision and Revision* (Durham, NC: Duke University Press, 1984), p. 16. For the Leopold and Loeb case see Chapter 3, Note 74.

64. "I Got a Scheme!," p. 76.

65. From p. 4 of an eight-page "Memorial Speech for Sydney J. Harris," who died on 8 December 1986, a typescript of which is in the Regenstein (henceforth cited within the text by page numbers).

66. Quoted in Atlas, *Biography*, p. 25.

67. Rockwell Gray, Harry White, and Gerald Nemanic, "Interview with Saul Bellow," reprinted in Cronin and Siegel, eds., *Conversations with SB*, p. 220.

68. Quoted in Friedrich Nietzsche, *The Birth of Tragedy and the Case of Wagner*, trans. and ed. Walter Kaufmann (Vintage: New York, 1967), p. 36.

69. Arthur [Artur] Schopenhauer, *The World as Will and Idea*, tr. R. B. Haldane and J. Kemp, 3 vols. (London: 1906), 2.248.

70. SB, *Mr. Sammler's Planet*, p. 172 (henceforth cited within the text by page numbers).

71. Botsford interview, "A Half Life," SB, *IAAU*, p. 300.

72. SB, "Isaac Rosenfeld," originally published in *Partisan Review* 23, no. 4 (Fall 1956): 565–67, and reprinted three times: as the foreword to Isaac Rosenfeld, *An Age of Enormity: Life and Writing in the Forties and Fifties*, ed., Theodore Solotaroff (Cleveland: World, 1962); as the foreword to Mark Shechner, ed. *Preserving the Hunger: An Isaac Rosenfeld Reader* (Detroit: Wayne State University Press, 1988), pp. 17–19; and as "Isaac Rosenfeld," SB, *IAAU*, pp. 264–66. The quoted passage is one of several omitted in the reprints, which offer an edited version of the original *Partisan Review* piece.

73. SB, "Zetland: By a Character Witness" (1974), reprinted in SB, *CS*, p. 244.

74. Isaac Rosenfeld, *Passage from Home* (1946: Cleveland: Meridian, 1965), p. 210 (henceforth cited within the text by page numbers).

75. Steven J. Zipperstein, *Rosenfeld's Lives: Fame, Oblivion, and the Furies of Writing* (New Haven: Yale University Press, 2009), p. 26.

76. From the first page of a four-page typescript in the Regenstein, mostly about Isaac Rosenfeld, with handwritten corrections. For an account of this typescript see Chapter 3, note 116.

77. Zipperstein, *Rosenfeld's Lives*, p. 20.

78. Four-page typescript to Roth, p. 1; see Chapter 3, note 116.

79. Ibid., p. 2. On the same page SB describes what his own father's opinion of the Rosenfelds "as a category" would have been: "Yiddish culture types it was safe to say that he despised. My father's good opinion was not easy to obtain. He would have thought it infra-dig to meddle with the adolescent friendships of your gifted son."

80. Ibid. See also, from the same page: "He had agreed to be the boy wonder, the prodigy and prize-winner who would compensate his father for the death of two wives and the poor moron daughter [born of the second wife] who pounded through the rooms giving harsh cries—an incomprehensible, unreasonable girl."

81. Zipperstein, *Rosenfeld's Lives*, p. 22.

82. Four-page typescript to Roth; see Chapter 3, note 116.

83. SB, "Isaac Rosenfeld," SB, *IAAU*, p. 263.

84. Zipperstein, *Rosenfeld's Lives*, p. 21.

85. Isaac Rosenfeld, "The World of the Ceiling," first printed in *Midstream* 2, no. 1 (1956), reprinted in Shechner, ed., *Preserving the Hunger*, p. 367.

86. Zipperstein, *Rosenfeld's Lives*, p. 26.

87. SB, foreword to Shechner, ed., *Preserving the Hunger*, p. 14; also "Isaac Rosenfeld," SB, *IAAU*, p. 264.

88. Ten counting Jeanne and Anita's son Irving, born in 1933.

89. Manea, "Conversation," p. 30. The quote from Allen Tate comes from the dust jacket of *Bravo, My Monster*, published in 1953 by the Chicago publishing firm Henry Regnery.

90. SB felt bad that the review, entitled "Suicide by Proxy," was brief and not quite as effusive as it might have been. As he wrote to Edith Tarcov on Thanksgiving Day 1953: "The review in *Saturday Review* had to be done as I did it because I was in the position of having asked for the book. I could not have reviewed it in

the tone I would have taken had the book come unsolicited. They would not have accepted from me a review they considered obviously written for a friend. The political problem was a delicate one. I say this only because I have intimations of Oscar's dissatisfaction with the piece I wrote. You have my assurance that I did my utmost."

91. Daniel Bell, "A Parable of Alienation," *Jewish Frontier* 13, no. 11 (November 1946): 12–19; Irving Howe, "The Lost Young Intellectual," *Commentary* 2, no. 4 (October 1946), pp. 361–67.

92. Isaac Rosenfeld, "Kafka and His Critics," first published in *The New Leader* 30, no. 15 (April 12, 1947), as a review of Angel Flores, *The Kafka Problem*; reprinted in Shechner, ed., *Preserving the Hunger*, pp. 170, 171.

93. Zipperstein, *Rosenfeld's Lives*, p. 96.

94. Alfred Kazin, *New York Jew* (New York: Alfred A. Knopf, 1978), pp. 50, 49. That Rosenfeld could "do" manners is clear from *Passage from Home*, as in details describing Bernard's grandparents: the grandmother in the kitchen "doing more than she could successfully manage and therefore getting in the way"; the grandfather, at the table, whom Bernard watches "tear out a deep, doughy chunk, avoiding the crust, chewing with his mouth open and rolling the bread over his gums. He smeared his fingers with his beard, and wiped his hands on his jacket before drawing out a crusty handkerchief with which he dabbed his lips." Bernard recalls: "I hated to see him placed, by his weaknesses, in a position of such obvious inferiority to myself" (p. 86).

95. Botsford interview, "A Half Life," SB, *IAAU*, pp. 298–99; interview with Nina Steers, "Successor to Faulkner?," *Show* 4 (September 1964), pp. 36–38, reprinted in Cronin and Siegel, eds., *Conversations with SB*, p. 35.

96. SB to George Sarant, 9 September 1990. "Sarant" was a shortened version of Rosenfeld's wife's name, Sarantakis, which she readopted shortly after his death. In *A Margin of Hope: An Intellectual Biography* (New York: Harcourt Brace Jovanovich, 1982), Irving Howe describes Rosenfeld as "profligate with his being, his time, his thought, [lacking] only that cunning economy that enables writers to sustain lengthy careers" (p. 134). He also offers this description of Rosenfeld in the late 1940s and early 1950s: "Isaac seemed a literary offspring of Sholem Aleichem but his mind had succumbed to Kafka—not, as it turned out, a happy affair. Still, he was our golden boy, more so than Bellow, for there was an air of Yeshiva purity about Isaac that made one hope wildly for his future" (p. 133). According to Zipperstein, in *Rosenfeld's Lives*, had Rosenfeld lived he might well have redeemed his promise; the myth of inexorable decline is a myth: "Rosenfeld died of a fatal heart attack, not writer's block" (p. 206); at his death at thirty-eight he was writing, had a teaching job, a girlfriend, a new, airy apartment in Chicago, a red convertible, and on the morning of his death "announced that he'd finally made a breakthrough on his novel" (p. 234). What remained after his death, however, was relatively little, given both the promise and ability: *Passage from Home*, published when he was twenty-eight; a book of stories, *Alpha and Omega* (1966), published posthumously; and two collections of reviews and stories: *The Age of Enormity* (1962) and *Preserving the Hunger* (1988).

97. SB to Nathan Tarcov, 22 October 1963. For fuller discussion of this letter and of SB's claim that Tarcov "invested his life in relationships," see Chapter 1 of volume 2 of this biography, forthcoming.

98. According to Susan Freifeld, "the family loved it [*Augie*]. My father thought it was pretty accurate." According to her sister, Judith, "he was very proud that the family appeared as characters in the novel. He felt that some of the portrayals came very much from him and his close association with Saul . . . [though] not every event that happens to Einhorn happened to my father [that is, Ben Freifeld]."

According to Judith Freifeld Ward, "my grandmother is in there, my Uncle Louie is Dingbat."

99. SB, "In the Days of Mr. Roosevelt," SB, *IAAU*, p. 21.

100. The undated letter is reprinted in Taylor, ed., *Letters*, pp. 45–46. Rosenfeld's biographical sketch is quoted in Zipperstein, *Rosenfeld's Lives*, p. 29.

101. "I Got a Scheme!," p. 82.

102. This quotation and the earlier reference to a first meeting are from page one of SB's "Memorial Speech for Sydney J. Harris." All quotations from Harris are from the Bruckner interview.

103. Koch interview.

104. "I Got a Scheme!," p. 82.

105. SB, "Memorial Speech for Sydney J. Harris," p. 2. See also Manea, "Conversation," p. 11, in which SB describes his Tuley circle as "all fairly wild, but of course people seemed a lot wilder to me than they may have been in reality because I came from a family where parental control was so strong. They did things that I envied but I didn't dare do."

106. SB, "Memorial Speech for Sydney J. Harris," p. 2. The stories SB and Harris wrote were submitted to *Argosy* magazine, without success. *Argosy* and *True Confessions* published the stories of the first writer SB ever met, an elderly neighbor in Chicago, "a tool-and-diemaker who turned out pulp stories" (see "Skepticism and the Depth of Life," in J. E. Miller, Jr., and P. D. Herring, eds., *The Arts and the Public* [Chicago: University of Chicago Press, 1967], p. 13).

107. SB, "How, in the city of Chicago, does a young person become a writer?," pp. 3–4 (see note 51 above).

108. SB recounts the story of "Herbert Sanders" in "I Got a Scheme!," pp. 82–83, in Roth/SB interview typescript "Arriving in Chicago and Sydney J. Harris," pp. 3–4, and in the "Memorial Speech for Sydney J. Harris," pp. 5–8. These versions do not contradict each other but add different details. My account draws on all three sources.

109. In the April–May 1937 issue of *Soapbox*, the magazine of the University of Chicago Socialist Club, which contains articles by several Tuleyites, including SB, Tarcov, and Nate Gould, there is a poem by S. G. Fairfield, who might just be Freifeld, since the poem has an Eliot-like epigraph from John Webster, the Jacobean dramatist; but it might also be Harris, posing as a version of his creation, Farefield, now Fairfield.

110. George Reedy to Al Glotzer, 26 September 1996, among SB's papers in the Regenstein, along with "In Memory of Yetta Barshevsky."

111. For Nathan Gould's name I am indebted to his son, Andrew Gould: "'Nathan Goldstein' and 'Nathan Gould' are the same person. . . . My father was born 'Nathan Goldstein' but gave his name as 'Nathan Gould' at the time of an early politically-related arrest (so as to avoid having his mother find out about the arrest). He then adopted this name and legally changed it. I am not sure what name he was using in High School, but I would be surprised if it were 'Gould' since he could not have legally changed it until he was of age, and the high school certainly would have insisted that he use his legal name" (email, 1 June 2011).

112. Pearl's only other appearance in SB's correspondence is in a letter to Oscar Tarcov, postmarked 29 September 1937: "Your elaborate, desperate rakishness was more than I could take. It went back beyond New York, beyond your mother, beyond Pearl too."

113. Atlas, *Biography*, p. 34n.

114. See SB, *Humboldt's Gift*, p. 210.

115. Dolnick's letter to Ruth Miller is dated 22 July 1994; SB's letter to Dolnick is dated 10 October 1995; and Eleanor Fox Simmons's letter to SB is undated. The originals of all three letters are in the possession of Eleanor Fox Simmons.

116. Manea, "Conversation," p. 37.

117. Notes to Roth about Isaac Rosenfeld, p. 2.

5. POLITICS/ANTHROPOLOGY

1. This quotation is from an interview conducted with David Peltz by the journalist D. J. R. Bruckner, who was at work on a television documentary about SB. The program, *Saul Bellow's Chicago*, was aired on Channel 5 in Chicago on 27 March 1981. Bruckner conducted interviews in 1980 and his recordings are in the Regenstein.

2. For this quote and the quote from Glotzer, see Atlas, *Biography*, pp. 35, 37.

3. In SB, *The Adventures of Augie March* (1953), p. 526, SB describes this program as "a city-sponsored introduction to higher notions and an accidental break into Shakespeare and other great masters along with the science and math leveled at the Civil-Service exam."

4. SB, "In the Days of Mr. Roosevelt," originally printed in *Esquire*, December 1983, reprinted in SB, *IAAU*, p. 17.

5. Ibid., p. 17. Details both of the history of Crane Junior College and of educational funding in Chicago in the Depression come from Dominic A. Pacyga, *Chicago: A Biography* (Chicago: University of Chicago Press, 2009), pp. 259–60; the entry for "Colleges, Junior and Community," in *The Electronic Encyclopedia of Chicago* (2005), compiled by the Chicago Historical Society (http://www.encyclopedia .chicagohistory.org/pages/312./html); and the entry for "Crane Junior College," in the "City Colleges of Chicago" website (http://www.ccc.edu/MissionHistory.asp).

6. SB, "In the Days of Mr. Roosevelt," SB, *IAAU*, p. 22.

7. SB, "Writers, Intellectuals, Politics: Mainly Reminiscence," first published in *The National Interest* (Spring 1993), reprinted in *IAAU*, p. 99.

8. Ibid.

9. It is possible that by "the forum" SB meant Bronstein's Friday night forum, mistakenly locating it on California Avenue. In an email of 26 May 2011, Peltz provides more detail: "My uncle, David Bronstein, tailor and Torah scholar, with his wife, my Aunt Esther, as newly arrived immigrants fell in with a wealthy born-again Christian, the wife of the president of the Bowman Dairy Company. Hugely wealthy and zealously born-again, Mrs. Peck spent weeks proselytizing Uncle David, who had a true connection to the biblical story of Jesus. Not as the Messiah but as another in the long line of prophets. Aunt Esther seeing an opportunity . . . dragged her husband into the business of running a community center that became a cover for a mission house to bring Jews to Jesus. They took over an abandoned Lutheran church with high gables and turned it into a basketball court and a debating arena giving full sway to the Stalinists, the Trotskyists, the Norman Thomas Socialists and more, all waiting their turn at the podium, fiercely advocating the overthrow of the failed capitalist system. Aunt Esther pounding her ample breasts just as fiercely answering their solutions as stupidly unworkable. 'Only by changing the hearts of men through Jesus' could any system for the good work. The wealthy 'born againers' were enthralled, slumming Friday nights among the poor and getting turned on by Aunt Esther's passion for Jesus. The mission house was on Washtenaw and Crystal. Not California Avenue."

10. This quotation and the one about being a socialist in high school come from Manea, "Conversation," p. 12. The quotation about being a Trotskyist in college comes from "Writers, Intellectuals, Politics: Mainly Reminiscence," SB, *IAAU*, p. 100. SB's conversion experience was like that of F. W. Dupee, the literary critic, who would become his friend and colleague in the early 1950s. He, too, joined the Trotskyists after reading Trotsky's *History* (see Alan M. Wald, *The New York Intellectuals: The Rise and Decline of the Anti-Stalinist Left from the*

1930s to the 1980s [Chapel Hill: University of North Carolina Press, 1987]), pp. 87–88.

11. Leszek Kolakowski, *Main Currents of Marxism*, tr. P. S. Falla (1978; New York: W. W. Norton, 2005), p. 961 (this is the one-volume paperback, containing the three volumes: *The Founders, The Golden Age,* and *The Breakdown*).

12. Interview with D. J. R. Bruckner.

13. SB, "Writers, Intellectuals, Politics: Mainly Reminiscence," SB, *IAAU,* p. 100.

14. SB, "In the Days of Mr. Roosevelt," SB, *IAAU,* p. 25.

15. Quoted in Joseph Dorman, *Arguing the World: The New York Intellectuals in Their Own Words* (New York: Free Press, 2000), p. 54.

16. SB, "Writers, Intellectuals, Politics: Mainly Reminiscence," SB, *IAAU,* p. 101.

17. Quoted in Paul N. Siegel, *Leon Trotsky on Literature and Art* (New York: Pathfinder, 1970), p. 9.

18. SB, "Writers, Intellectuals, Politics: Mainly Reminiscence," SB, *IAAU,* p. 100.

19. Dorman, *Arguing the World,* p. 60. For how few Trotskyists there were, see Albert Glotzer, *Trotsky: Memoir and Critique* (Buffalo: Prometheus, 1989), p. 310: "I doubt if the total combined world membership ever surpassed a thousand."

20. Irving Howe, *A Margin of Hope: An Intellectual Autobiography* (New York: Harcourt Brace Jovanovich, 1982), p. 33.

21. SB, "Writers, Intellectuals, Politics: Mainly Reminiscence," SB, *IAAU,* p. 100. For the Burnham quote on Trotsky's style, see Wald, *The New York Intellectuals,* p. 177.

22. William Wordsworth, *The Prelude,* 1805 version, Book 9, ll. 41–110.

23. Glotzer belonged to the majority Foster-Cannon faction of the American Communist Party, led by William Z. Foster and James P. Cannon, which was soon suspected of having Trotskyist leanings and ousted from leadership. After Foster and Cannon split, Cannon and his allies, Martin Abern and Max Shachtman, were put on trial by the party. In November 1928, they and their followers, Glotzer included, were expelled.

24. Glotzer's association with the CLA was relatively short-lived. As factionalism engulfed the Trotskyists, with divisions over the Nazi-Soviet Pact, the beginnings of World War II, including the invasion of Finland (defended by Trotsky as progressive on the grounds that it would lead to the nationalization of property) and continued support of the Soviet Union as a workers' state, Glotzer became disillusioned. Eventually, in 1940, he joined Max Shachtman and others in founding the breakaway Workers Party, later named the Independent Socialist League (in 1949).

25. The Harris quotation is from his interview with D. J. R. Bruckner. Jay Lovestone (1897–1990) briefly headed the Communist Party in the United States before being deposed by Stalin in 1929. He and his followers then formed the Communist Party of the United States, later titled the Independent Labor League of America, and were called Lovestoneites. The group disbanded in 1940 and Lovestone turned against Communism, heading the pro-war Committee to Defend America, which sought support for Britain and the other Allies. He later worked for many years in the International Affairs Department of the merged AFL-CIO. Dorman, *Arguing the World,* p. 51.

26. Dorman, *Arguing the World,* p. 51.

27. Lionel Trilling, *The Middle of the Journey* (1947; New York: New York Review Books, 2002), pp. 168, 140.

28. Manea, "Conversation," p. 17.

29. SB, "In the Days of Mr. Roosevelt," SB, *IAAU,* p. 27.

30. For the first and third of the three quotations from SB, see "Writers, Intellectuals, Politics: Mainly Reminiscence," SB, *IAAU*, p. 102; for the second, see "In the Days of Mr. Roosevelt," SB, *IAAU*, p. 23.

31. SB, "In the Days of Mr. Roosevelt," SB, *IAAU*, pp. 28–29.

32. SB, "A Silver Dish" (1978), reprinted in SB, *CS*, p. 23, where Morris Peltz's talk is said to be "about washing under the arms or in the crotch or of drying between your toes or of cooking supper, of baked beans and fried onions, of draw poker or of a certain horse in the fifth race at Arlington."

33. David Peltz, email, 24 March 2011.

34. Peltz is not sure of the year SB made his request. Arendt came to Chicago to deliver a lecture at the University of Chicago in 1956, was a visiting professor at Northwestern University in 1961, and taught at the Committee on Social Thought from 1963 to 1973, so the request is likely to have come sometime in either 1956, 1961, or 1963.

35. This quotation, like the earlier one about Hannah Arendt's "peculiar gift," comes from the Koch interview.

36. In SB, "Problems in American Literature," in *Literary Imagination, Ancient and Modern: Essays in Honor of David Grene*, ed. Todd Breyfogle (Chicago: University of Chicago Press, 1999), p. 375, a revised version of a lecture SB gave at the University of Chicago's Mandel Hall in December 1995, he wrongly says he was seventeen when he entered the University of Chicago.

37. For Abraham's reluctance to pay tuition, see the Koch interview; for SB on classmates, see SB, "Problems in American Literature," pp. 375–76.

38. Koch interview.

39. Manea, "Conversation," p. 12.

40. These and other materials pertaining to SB's years at Northwestern come from the Archives of the Northwestern University Library, either from the Saul Bellow Papers, as in this case; or from the Melville J. Herskovits Papers, which contain letters of reference Herskovits, a professor of anthropology, wrote on SB's behalf; or from the papers of SB's friend Julian Behrstock; or from those of Behrstock's friend Jack Harris.

41. From an interview with Dick Cavett, broadcast on ABC in three half-hour episodes (12–14 May 1982).

42. Edward Shils, *Portraits: A Gallery of Intellectuals* (Chicago: University of Chicago Press, 1997), p. 124. My account of Hutchins and the University of Chicago in the 1930s comes principally from Mary Ann Dzuback, *Robert M. Hutchins: Portrait of an Educator* (Chicago: University of Chicago Press, 1991); Shils's chapter on Hutchins in *Portraits*, pp. 124–54; and William H. McNeill, *Hutchins' University: A Memoir of the University of Chicago, 1929–1950* (Chicago: University of Chicago Press, 1991).

43. In the years immediately prior to Hutchins's arrival, preliminary attempts had been made to reform the largely elective undergraduate program, in which specialized faculty interests determined undergraduate offerings. Hutchins's restructuring built on these attempts.

44. Koch interview.

45. For Hutchins's and his supporters' rationale, see Dzuback, *Robert M. Hutchins*, pp. 105–6. For corroborating accounts of the inadequacy of undergraduate provision in the most prestigious research universities, see Diana Trilling, *The Beginning of the Journey: The Marriage of Diana and Lionel Trilling* (New York: Harcourt Brace, 1994), on her undergraduate education at Radcliffe (1921–25): "The Radcliffe-Harvard education of my day was very much a training in scholarship. It did not encourage the exercise of the critical intelligence" (p. 69); "What we were learning were facts, more facts, and yet more facts, how to gather them, how to memorize them and how to put them together in orderly fashion" (p. 75).

46. The structure of the undergraduate curriculum Hutchins introduced was simple. There were four required General Courses for students at the College, each organized by one of the university's four academic divisions: the Humanities, the Social Sciences, the Biological Sciences, and the Physical Sciences. These large lecture courses were devised and taught by faculty from their respective divisions; weekly discussion groups were led by instructors, who were supervised by the faculty.

47. SB's courses and grades while a student at the University of Chicago come from his Official Academic Record, Office of the University Registrar. According to the record, which provides marks and dates for "Examinations Taken" as well as "Courses," SB twice failed his English "Qualifying Test" (in November 1933 and February 1934) and was given a U (Unsatisfactory) in Winter Quarter 1935 in Biological Sciences.

48. This quotation and the one that precedes it come from the Botsford interview "A Half Life," SB, *IAAU*, p. 305. The General Courses met four days a week and on the fifth day "you actually got to see your quiz instructor for an hour and you would go over the lectures with your master tutors. And they were masters. Very good people gave those general courses. But you never got to know anybody, and nobody ever knew you."

49. Koch interview.

50. Ibid.; "Venus Urania" figures in Shelley's *Adonais* (1821).

51. SB, "Chicago and American Culture: One Writer's View," p. 81, a talk delivered at the Centennial Celebration of the Chicago Public Library on 10 October 1972. A version of this talk was later printed under the same title in *Chicago* (May 1973), pp. 82–89. I have quoted from a twenty-one-page typescript of the talk, with handwritten corrections, in the Regenstein.

52. Koch interview.

53. The anecdote about Professor Scott comes from SB, "Problems in American Literature," p. 375; for Mortimer Adler, see Rockwell Gray, Harry White, and Gerald Nemanic, "Interview with Saul Bellow," *TriQuarterly* 60 (1984): 12–34, reprinted in Cronin and Siegel, eds., *Conversations with SB*, p. 215.

54. SB, "Nobel Lecture" (1976), reprinted in SB, *IAAU*, p. 88. Walter Blair's quotation is from his interview with D. J. R. Bruckner.

55. SB, "Problems in American Literature," p. 357.

56. A version of these lines occurs in the first of the two Jefferson Lectures (1977), reprinted in SB, *IAAU*, p. 124.

57. Among SB's friends, Tarcov and Rosenfeld were still at Tuley, Passin still at Marshall High School. Nate Gould and Herman Slate, among others, could have been the unnamed roommate, though when Gould and SB overcame their political differences (not to mention rivalry over Yetta Barshevsky) is not clear.

58. SB, "Problems in American Literature," pp. 375, 376.

59. SB, "Jefferson Lectures," SB, *IAAU*, p. 120; "Problems in American Literature," p. 376.

60. Koch interview.

61. After Chicago, Barrett went on to teach philosophy at NYU and to serve as an associate editor at *Partisan Review*; Goodman became a prominent figure on the Greenwich Village scene, grouped with SB in Daniel Bell's chart of "New York Jewish Intellectuals" (see Daniel Bell, "The 'Intelligentsia' in American Society," a lecture given in 1976 at the Hebrew Union College in Cincinnati, first published in Samuel Sandmel, ed., *Tomorrow's American: The Weil Lectures of 1976* (Oxford: Oxford University Press, 1976), reprinted in Daniel Bell, *The Winding Passage: Sociological Essays and Journeys* (1980; New Brunswick, NJ: Transaction, 1991), pp. 127–29. SB was included in the chart, along with Leslie Fiedler and Seymour Lipset, with an asterisk: "Outside New York but had status as members";

Roditi worked in the Office of Wartime Information in New York (with Claude Lévi-Strauss, Klaus Mann, André Breton, André Maurois, and Julien Green); as did Kaplan, before joining a special group of French-speakers recruited to work in North Africa, a small branch of what was soon to become "a very big and swollen propaganda services," the CIA. Kaplan would later write the "Paris Letter" for *Partisan Review*, while working in Paris in the U.S. embassy. Wieboldt Hall was to SB's generation of University of Chicago student-intellectuals what Hartley Hall was to Lionel Trilling's comparable generation ten years earlier at Columbia. Along with Trilling, "many of the Hartley Hall group—Meyer Schapiro, Jacques Barzun, Clifton Fadiman, Francis Steegmuller, Edgar Johnson—would be known in one or another sphere of the intellectual activity of the country" (Diana Trilling, *The Beginning of the Journey*, p. 83).

62. SB, "Problems in American Literature," p. 376.

63. Isaac Rosenfeld, "Life in Chicago," reprinted in Mark Shechner, ed., *Preserving the Hunger: An Isaac Rosenfeld Reader* (Detroit: Wayne State University Press, 1988), p. 95.

64. The quotation from Passin is in Atlas, *Biography*, p. 44; SB's quotation is from "In the Days of Mr. Roosevelt," SB, *IAAU*, p. 24.

65. See 1963 interview with Bruce Cook, "Saul Bellow: A Mood of Protest," reprinted in Cronin and Siegel, eds., *Conversations with SB*, p. 14. By "Socialist Club," SB may mean the ASU, American Student Union.

66. This quotation is from an undated letter of SB to Irving Halperin, professor of Humanities at San Francisco State University, written sometime after 1968, when they'd first met.

67. The course was Zoology, and the average was that of his senior year.

68. Botsford interview, "A Half Life," SB, *IAAU*, p. 305.

69. Figures for Jewish undergraduates at Northwestern come from Atlas, *Biography*, p. 47, which cites Harold F. Williamson and Payson S. Wild, *Northwestern University: A History, 1850–1975* (Evanston, IL: Northwestern University Press, 1975). The University of Chicago figures come from Dzuback, *Robert M. Hutchins*, p. 286.

70. Interview with D. J. R. Bruckner.

71. According to Helen Jaffe, in ibid., Jaffe and SB were "very, very good friends," though they were only together for the academic year 1935–36 (in SB's senior year Jaffe went off to work).

72. Cook interview, in Cronin and Siegel, eds., *Conversations with SB*, p. 14: "In the beginning, he continued to live on the south side near the Midway, commuting to classes on the El"; Atlas, *Biography*, p. 53, says SB lived at home when he began at Northwestern.

73. On April Fools' Day 1936 *The Daily Northwestern* published a humorous piece by SB entitled "Pets of the North Shore," which makes gentle fun of Evanston women and their dogs. This is the most notable of SB's contributions to the paper.

74. SB's pseudonym was "John Paul," an Americanized version of "Jean Paul," the pseudonym of Johann Paul Friedrich Richter (1763–1825), the German satirist.

75. In a letter of reference to the Social Sciences Research Council, Melville J. Herskovits, professor of anthropology, praised SB's independence as well as his ambition, the ability "to make his own appraisals of what for him are worthwhile objectives" (Herskovits Papers, Northwestern University Archives).

76. See Cavett interview for Hungerford not handling SB; Koch interview for Hungerford as "loveable."

77. Sinclair Lewis, *It Can't Happen Here* (New York: Doubleday Doran, 1935), pp. 25, 28.

78. Delmore Schwartz, "A Man in His Time," *Partisan Review* 11 (1944): 348.

79. Leon Trotsky, "War and the Fourth International," *Writings of Leon Trotsky*,

1933–34, volume 6 of *Writings of Leon Trotsky*, eds., George Breitman and Sarah Lovell, 14 vols. (New York: Pathfinder, 1947–78), pp. 306–7. See also Trotsky's "The Imperialist War and the Proletarian Revolution," in volume 13 of *Writings, 1929–1933*, p. 183: "Differences undoubtedly exist among the political regimes of bourgeois society, just as there are degrees of comfort in different class railway carriages. But when the whole train is heading for the precipice, the contrast in comfort between the different carriages loses all significance. Capitalist civilization is sliding toward the precipice. Differences between decaying democracy and barbarian fascism disappear in the face of the collapse of the entire capitalist system."

80. See Manea, "Conversation," p. 15, for the quotation's continuation: "Somehow it didn't come through, as it would have for a European, because we had no immediate contact with it. It went into the historical record as a horror but it was not—I didn't recognize it, from my Jewish side, for what it had been. It took a long time for me to get a grip on it. I don't know what that was. It remained the Jewish Question instead of the horror it should have been. I ask myself often nowadays: why were you so slow in picking this up? I don't know why. Maybe because it didn't accord with the main themes of my life."

81. At Northwestern, it was simply assumed that Arthur Behrstock was a Communist. When Julian wrote an admiring profile of him for the student magazine, *The Gadfly*, its editor changed the title from "Portrait of a Rebel" to "Portrait of a Communist." When confronted, Julian recalls, the editor "brushed off my protest, said he had been a friend of Arthur's as an undergraduate and that *his* title was a more accurate description than mine." Details of Arthur Behrstock's life come from p. 2 of a memorial address by Julian Behrstock, among the Bellow Papers at the Regenstein. The address is undated but Arthur Behrstock died in 1985.

82. After the war Harris taught anthropology at the University of Chicago until Ralph Bunche invited him to become part of his staff at the United Nations, working on African issues.

83. Harris, like Arthur Behrstock, lost his job after pleading the Fifth; unlike Arthur, however, his appeal was upheld. He never returned to the UN.

84. The FBI report is among the Harris Papers in the Northwestern University Archives.

85. He also enlisted big names to serve on the magazine's Advisory Board, including Robert Hutchins, Harold Ickes, Philip La Follette (the governor of Wisconsin), and Robert Morss Lovett (an English professor at the University of Chicago and an associate editor of *The New Republic*).

86. Though Farrell's novel is hardly "the finely turned product of a skilled craftsman," SB praises it for its "acute characterization . . . and a feel for the quality of the milieu of the *dramatis personae*." If the crude speech of its characters offends, "that fault is not with Farrell but with stomachs accustomed to more delicate fare."

87. For these and other details, see Jerry Gershenhorn, *Melville J. Herskovits and the Racial Politics of Knowledge* (Lincoln: University of Nebraska Press, 2004); also Joseph H. Greenberg, "Melville Jean Herskovits," in volume 42 of *Biographical Memoirs*, National Academy of Sciences of the United States of America (New York: Columbia University Press, 1971), pp. 65–77.

88. Gershenhorn, *Herskovits*, p. 15.

89. Ibid., p. 17.

90. As Gershenhorn puts it, "by attacking racist science, which concluded that blacks were inferior to whites, Boas was able to mount an indirect challenge to the anti-Semitic belief that Jews were an inferior race" (p. 20). Herskovits's decision to concentrate on the relations between African culture and African American culture was similarly motivated, a product of a shared experience among Jews and blacks of being considered, in his words, "different, or inferior, or something to be disdained" (p. 21).

91. Gershenhorn, *Herskovits*, p. 139.

92. These are the words of Suzanne Blier, professor of Fine Arts and of African and African American Studies at Harvard, in an article entitled "Field Days: Melville J. Herskovits in Dahomey," *History in Africa* 16 (1989): 1. According to Greenberg, "Melville Jean Herskovits," *Biographical Memoirs*, p. 69, "it is not too much to say that . . . Herskovits virtually founded Afroamerican studies as a scientific field in its own right."

93. As SB put it in an undergraduate limerick, "There was a guy named Melville J. / Who does oodles of work every day / To prove that Brer Rabbit / And blues on the Sabbath / Came from Old Dahomey" (Atlas, *Biography*, p. 49).

94. Kevin A. Yelvington, "A Life In and Out of Anthropology: An Interview with Jack Sargent Harris," *Critique of Anthropology* 28, no. 4 (2008): 453.

95. There were problems with Herskovits, particularly after SB abandoned graduate work. See SB to Melvin Tumin, in an undated letter of 1942: "Even *Hersky* has aimed his little boot at me. Last week he called me up at two thirty in the afternoon. It seems I had used him as a reference in connection with the national roster of scientific and specialized personnel. He had phoned to tell me how much trouble it was to fill out the forms. He was a busy man, a busy man! In some detail he insulted me on each of the following: 1. The fact that I am unemployed and at home at 2:30 p.m. 2. My lack of qualification as an applicant for any consideration from the national roster. 3. The fate of my novel. (He had anticipated what would happen, he gave me to understand.) And at last, *in algemein* [in general], my wasted life" (Taylor, ed., *Letters*, pp. 25–26).

96. Koch interview.

97. For accounts of such prejudice among English Departments, see Diana Trilling, *The Beginning of the Journey*, especially pp. 273–80 and 319–22, which contain Lionel Trilling's memorandum of his 1936 dismissal from the Columbia University English Department and reproduce part of Diana Trilling's account of his reinstatement, from her 1979 essay, "Lionel Trilling: A Jew at Columbia," reproduced in *Speaking of Literature and Society* (New York: Harcourt Brace Jovanovich, 1989). Harold Kaplan tells a similar story to that of SB about the University of Chicago. When he applied in 1937 from the University of Illinois to read for a PhD in English at the University of Chicago, he was turned down. Kaplan's father was a carpenter and had just gone into bankruptcy. Without a scholarship, graduate work was out of the question. When he told his professors at Illinois how disappointed he was not to have been awarded a scholarship by the Chicago English Department, those who taught him French, a subject he was also good at, asked friends in the Chicago French Department to consider him for a scholarship. These friends, two professors from the École Normale, invited Kaplan to Hyde Park, interviewed him, and gave him a scholarship. Many years later Kaplan told Lionel Trilling the story: "When I told him I hadn't got a scholarship, he said, 'I know why,' because he was an expert" (from an interview with Philippe Meyer, broadcast on 23 July 2010 on *France Culture*, and published as "Conversations avec le vieil Harold (II)," *Commentaire* 33, no. 130 (Summer 2010) (translation is courtesy of Kaplan's son, Roger).

98. Presumably saving him $200, the fee for nonresident graduate students being $100 per semester.

99. Letters of reference of 10 February 1937 to Professor E. A. Ross, Department of Sociology and Anthropology, University of Wisconsin, and 11 February 1937 to Dean E. B. Fred, the Graduate School, University of Wisconsin, in Herskovits Papers, Northwestern University Archives. Whether SB applied anywhere else aside from Wisconsin is unclear: according to files at Northwestern, a copy of his transcript was sent to New York University, but no letter of reference from Herskovits has survived, nor are there records of a completed application.

100. The address given on SB's graduate admissions form at Wisconsin, dated

22 September 1937, is 112 South Mills Street, which is the address found on SB's letters to Oscar Tarcov, from September through November 1937. In December, however, SB writes to Tarcov from a new address, 1314 St. James Court. This is the address on Isaac Rosenfeld's graduate registration form, though all the letters he wrote to Tarcov, from September through December 1937, are addressed from 11 North Mills Street. According to Atlas, *Biography*, p. 56, "In September 1937, Bellow moved into a boarding house on North Mills Street. . . . They [SB and Rosenfeld] shared a room." If the two friends shared a room, when, where, and for how long is not clear from surviving records and correspondence. Steven J. Zipperstein, *Rosenfeld's Lives: Fame, Oblivion and the Furies of Writing* (New Haven: Yale University Press, 2009), p. 39, says the two friends "roomed at Madison," though "they soon moved into separate apartments close to each other."

101. Information about SB's courses and grades comes from his graduate record, provided by the Office of the Registrar, University of Wisconsin, Madison. Both Vivas and Young would eventually move to Northwestern.

102. Atlas, *Biography*, p. 57.

103. SB to Jean Pool, 3 June 1989.

104. These jobs, according to the university's files, were menial, involving "clipping, dating, and sorting items," work SB was spared when he left for Chicago in December.

105. SB, "Isaac Rosenfeld," *Partisan Review* 23, no. 4 (Fall 1956): 566, and SB's foreword to William Phillips, ed., *Sixty Years of Great Fiction from Partisan Review* (Boston: Partisan Review Press, 1997), p. vi.

106. Zipperstein, *Rosenfeld's Lives*, p. 41.

107. SB calls "Twin Bananas" "a play by Oscar," in "Isaac Rosenfeld," *Partisan Review* 23 no. 4 (Fall 1956): 566, though Zipperstein, *Rosenfeld's Lives*, p. 40, says the three friends wrote it together.

108. For Ruth Wisse's text, translation, and commentary, see "Language as Fate: Reflections on Jewish Literature in America," *Studies in Contemporary Jewry* 12 (1996): 129.

109. Pinsky's praise is cited in Zipperstein, *Rosenfeld's Lives*, p. 43, from Francis X. Clines, "Laureate's Mission Is to Give Voice to a Nation of Poets," *New York Times*, 17 March 1998.

110. Ruth Wisse, *The Modern Jewish Canon: A Journey Through Language and Culture* (New York: Free Press, 2000), p. 298.

111. Zipperstein, *Rosenfeld's Lives*, pp. 42–43.

112. Atlas, *Biography*, p. 56.

113. Rosenfeld to Tarcov, 25 September 1937, in the Tarcov Papers, Regenstein Library.

114. SB, *To Jerusalem and Back*, pp. 94, 130.

115. Botsford interview, "A Half Life," SB, *IAAU*, p. 299.

116. Taylor, ed., *Letters*, p. xix.

117. Tom Fitzpatrick, "Bellow's Books Too Deep?," *Chicago Sun-Times*, 16 March 1972. The "time of great personal difficulty," as we shall see, involved his second wife, Sondra (Sasha) Tschacbasov.

118. Botsford interview, "A Half Life," SB, *IAAU*, pp. 303–4.

119. Nina A. Steers, "Successor to Faulkner?," *Show* 4 (September 1964), p. 36, reprinted in Cronin and Siegel, eds., *Conversations with SB*, p. 28.

120. For this quote and the preceding resemblances, see Eusebio L. Rodrigues, "Bellow's Africa," *American Literature* 43, no. 2 (May 1971): 242–56; the quote itself, about SB's genius, is on p. 249.

121. Sheila Fischman, "Saul Wanders Streets of His Montreal Past," *Montreal Star*, 3 May 1976. What "it" means in SB's quote is not clear. "Arnewi and Wariri custom"? Not "Africa," surely.

122. Koch interview.

123. The first of the reasons given for not continuing with anthropology (having to measure skull sizes) comes from ibid.; the second (SB's and Goldenweiser's, about his being too literary) comes from Atlas, *Biography*, p. 57, and Harvey Breit, "A Talk with Saul Bellow," *New York Times Book Review*, 20 September 1953, reprinted in Cronin and Siegel, eds., *Conversations with SB*, p. 4.

124. Botsford interview, "A Half Life," SB, *IAAU*, p. 304.

6. ANITA/DANGLING

1. According to Greg Bellow, Beatrice "Beebee" Schenk (1914–2000) first met SB when they were "seventeen or eighteen." At the time he met Anita, Beebee was a student at the University of Chicago. She got her MEd in 1941 and eventually became a well-known author of children's picture books, including books illustrated by Maurice Sendak and Edward Gorey.

2. To SB and others, Anita was variously described as pretty, beautiful, attractive. "She was very pretty," remembers Oscar Tarcov's daughter, Miriam, "always very attractive, but if you compare her to Sasha or Susan [SB's second and third wives] there wasn't, maybe, the dramatic flair.... [She was] not particularly exotic, mysterious or fetching in that way.... She was salt of the earth, steady, you couldn't rock her, she understood things, she had her point of view. Your first comment about her wouldn't be 'Oh, she was such a beautiful woman.'"

3. These and other details of Anita's life come from interviews with Greg Bellow and from "Anita Goshkin Bellow Busacca—A Biographic Sketch," a fourteen-page memoir of his mother written by Greg in 2007 and deposited among SB's papers in the Regenstein.

4. Records of Passin's education are unclear. According to an obituary in *The New York Times* (9 March 2003), as well as the headnote to Passin's papers in Special Collections and University Archives, University of Massachusetts, Amherst, he received a PhD in anthropology at Northwestern University in 1941. But Northwestern has no record of his being a student, though it does have a record of his being an instructor in the Anthropology Department, 1941–42, and there is a letter to Melville Herskovits (in the Herskovits Papers at Northwestern) in which Passin mentions, without giving dates, that he attended the University of Chicago as both a graduate student and an undergraduate. According to Rita Vazquez, assistant registrar at the University of Chicago, in an email of 21 December 2011, "It looks as if Mr. Passin began his studies with the University of Chicago by taking College courses during the Autumn 1936 Quarter (10/1/1936) though he chose not to take the undergraduate Bachelor of Arts degree.... He then transferred to the Division of the Social Sciences graduate program in the Winter Quarter 1937 (January) and completed his studies to receive a Master of Arts in Anthropology, awarded 8/28/1941." According to the *Columbia Daily Spectator* obituary, Passin graduated with a BA from the University of Chicago in 1936. The obituary also states that Passin was "one of the only professors ever to receive tenure without having a PhD" (http://columbiaspectator.com/2003/03/14/former-prof-japan-expert-dies-86).

5. Tom Passin, in an email of 29 December 2011: "Although my mother always called it a 'Chinese' restaurant, I see that my father wrote, in his book *Encounter with Japan* (p. 22), that it was actually a Japanese restaurant, which they went to at Saul's suggestion."

6. This quotation and others from Tom Passin come from an email to Jeanne Passin, Herb Passin's niece, 14 December 2009, in answer to questions Jeanne had passed on from me.

7. "I Got a Scheme!," p. 76.

8. SB, "Starting Out in Chicago," *The American Scholar* 44 (Winter 1974–75), p. 73, originally delivered as a commencement address at Brandeis University on 22 May 1974. A nine-page typescript of the Brandeis address is in the Regenstein, as is the typescript's source, a sixteen-page handwritten draft in the form of questions and answers, beginning "How, in the city of Chicago, does a young person become a writer?"

9. "My father has had to give me money, to my shame," SB writes in an undated letter of 1942 to Melvin Tumin. "You know how full of ugly, bastardly pride I am, It really has embittered me."

10. Quotations about SB's routine while living in Ravenswoood come from the typescript of his 1974 Brandeis University commencement address, pp. 4–6, reprinted as "Starting Out in Chicago," in *American Scholar* 44 (Winter 1974–75).

11. From the first of SB's two Jefferson Lectures (1977), reprinted in SB, *IAAU*, p. 127.

12. SB, handwritten draft for Brandeis address, beginning "How, in the city of Chicago, does a young person become a writer?," p. 7, the source of SB's 1974 Brandeis address and "Starting Out in Chicago," in neither of which this sentence appears.

13. SB, "Starting Out in Chicago," p. 74; the negative references to the paralyzing spirit of the house and the need to resist it come from p. 6 of the handwritten draft for the Brandeis address and were excised in the later versions; the trembling hand is from "Starting Out in Chicago," p. 75. In both "Starting Out in Chicago" and the Brandeis address, SB refers to Sonia Goshkin as "Sophie."

14. They do so in five pages (27–31) of draft material separate from the main hundred-page "Far Out" manuscript:

> It was July and the weather was memorable. Anywhere else it would have been glorious, open summer but under the El structure in the Negro slum it was as if you had gone into a coal mine. Hoping for some open air to bring some freshness you waited for the trolley. . . . And there was a young woman waiting, pale skin, green eyes, darkish-blonde, in a seersucker skirt and jacket, fresh and clean. There was something slightly painful in this first impression, something to be sorry for. She was wiping at her eyes with a handkerchief. [H]e stepped up and introduced himself as a medical student, offered to take out the speck. . . . Nettie hesitated, but she smiled, too. He was waiting for the same car, holding a book, he was a student and she allowed him to look at her eye. He lifted the soot from her eyeball with the point of her handkerchief. As he bent over her face, with its Russian cheekbones, her warmth came up together with a clear sort of fragrance. . . . Nettie was on the small side but her figure was full and she was a very beautiful woman (pp. 29–30).

15. SB, in 1974 handwritten source for the Brandeis address, p. 6 (cut from both the address and "Starting Out in Chicago").

16. SB, "Cousins" (1974), reprinted in SB, *CS*, p. 228.

17. SB, "Starting Out in Chicago," p. 76.

18. Ibid., pp. 76–77. In the handwritten source for the Brandeis address, SB writes of Jack: "He made a bid for personal freedom and he was deluded. . . . In his dying days he spoke Yiddish again" (p. 6).

19. SB to Marjorie Janis, 10 April 1994.

20. This quotation, like the one in parentheses, comes from the second of two videotaped interviews SB gave in 1987 to Sigmund Koch, a "University Professor" (as SB himself would become) at Boston University. For details of these interviews, see Chapter 2, note 7. All subsequent quotations from the interview in this chapter are taken from the second videotape.

21. Ibid.

22. Ruth Miller, *Saul Bellow: A Biography of the Imagination* (New York: St. Martin's, 1991), p. xvi.

23. Ibid., p. xvii.

24. SB, first "Jefferson Lecture," in SB, *IAAU*, p. 124.

25. Atlas, *Biography*, p. 62. For SB journalism and fiction were hardly incompatible, especially for a Chicago writer. In "Chicago and American Culture: One Writer's View," a talk delivered at the Centennial Celebration of the Chicago Public Library on 10 October 1972, SB remembered his situation in the 1930s: "Times had changed for, at the turn of the century, young writers could and often did become newspaper reporters. The papers in those days were willing to take them on. Ambrose Bierce was hired by Hearst. Stephen Crane, Theodore Dreiser and Ring Lardner were journalists. The papers, the public and literature itself benefited from this" (p. 11). A version of this talk was later printed under the same title in *Chicago* (May 1973), pp. 82–89. I have quoted from a twenty-one-page typescript of the talk itself, with handwritten corrections, in the Regenstein.

26. SB to the journalist and writer Adam Lisberg, 21 October 1992.

27. SB, "Writers, Intellectuals, Politics: Mainly Reminiscence" (1993), in SB, *IAAU*, p. 103. Algren joined the Writers' Project in September 1936. According to his biographer, Bettina Drew, in *Nelson Algren: A Life on the Wild Side* (1989; London: Bloomsbury, 1990), p. 104, "whatever his official status, Algren worked actively and openly for the Communist Movement, and he definitely considered himself a Communist. . . . Algren sided with the Stalinists, was enthralled by Baudelaire, but was vehement in his distaste for 'decadent' writers such as T. S. Eliot." He got on well with Louis Wright, the Writers' Project's first director, and less well with Frederick, whose political sympathies were closer to those of SB and his fellow Trotskyists than to Algren's or Conroy's.

28. For Morris, see his interview with the journalist D. J. R. Bruckner, who was at work on a television documentary about SB. The program, *Saul Bellow's Chicago*, was aired on Channel 5 in Chicago on 27 March 1981. Bruckner conducted interviews in 1980 and his recordings of the interviews are in the Regenstein.

29. Quoted in Joyce Illig, "An Interview with Saul Bellow," *Publishers Weekly*, 22 October 1973, reprinted in Cronin and Siegel, eds., *Conversations with SB*, p. 104.

30. "Midwestern" in ibid., p. 105; "Illinois" in Botsford interview, "A Half Life," reprinted in SB, *IAAU*, p. 306; "American" authors in Atlas, *Biography*, p. 63.

31. Illig, "An Interview with Saul Bellow," in Cronin and Siegel, eds., *Conversations with SB*, p. 105. The Illinois State Historical Society has a collection of WPA Federal Writers' Project material, including several of SB's profiles for Frederick. Atlas, *Biography*, pp. 63–64, names several of the writers SB wrote about—Dos Passos, Farrell, Anderson—quoting him on Farrell and Anderson.

32. Botsford interview, "A Half Life," in SB, *IAAU*, p. 306. The quote about never having it so good is from the Koch interview.

33. Other close Hyde Park friends from this period are Hyman Slate and his wife, Evelyn (Hyman was a fellow classmate of SB's at Tuley, as well as at the University of Chicago, and would remain a lifelong friend), and Abe Kaufman, also from Tuley, who figures prominently in the early correspondence with Tarcov, went on to do a PhD in philosophy at Harvard, but dropped out of SB's life in the 1960s. When Kaufman died in 1996, SB wrote to Slate on 9 September saying he hadn't heard from him for thirty years. Relations with Slate were warm in the late 1930s and got warmer over the years. Kaufman was a more difficult character. "I frequently offered Kaufman friendship in as many ways as I could think of," SB wrote to Slate in the 9 September 1996 letter, "but he was comically high and mighty with me."

34. In the 1972 "Address at the Chicago Public Library," SB recalls his family's

reactions to him in this period, writing away in Ravenswood or Hyde Park, "while real people were at work": "His existence could not be explained to the neighbors by his family. If he were any good, he would be on the Riviera with E. Phillips Oppenheim or in the South Seas, like Somerset Maugham. Or at least in New York, the center of things" (p. 15).

35. Tarcov graduated from the University of Chicago in August 1939. In December 1939 SB writes to him in New York; three months later, in March 1940, he is writing to him in Urbana-Champaign, where he had enrolled as a graduate student in anthropology. He's still writing to him there in May 1941. Nathan Tarcov says his father went to New York "after graduating in 1939." At the time, in his son's words, he was still "a Trotskyist, and met the City College people, Irving Kristol, Martin Diamond." It seems likely that his stay in New York was brief, for he started doing graduate work in anthropology at the University of Illinois in Urbana-Champaign at midyear, early in 1940.

36. SB's letters to Tarcov are in the Tarcov Papers at the Regenstein.

37. How openly these doubts were expressed is uncertain. "On the University of Chicago campus," Lionel Abel writes of this period in *The Intellectual Follies: A Memoir of the Literary Venture in New York and Paris* (New York: W. W. Norton, 1984), p. 69, "I knew two people who thought the Trotskyist political line on the war ridiculous and said so openly." These were Nathan Leites, a political scientist acquaintance of SB's, the instructor who amused him by crossing the road while reading a book (and who annoyed him by calling him a *romancier*), and Edward Shils, who would for a period become one of SB's closest friends.

38. SB, "Him with His Foot in His Mouth" (1982), reprinted in SB, *CS*, p. 408.

39. "I Got a Scheme!," p. 76.

40. Ibid., p. 76.

41. Ibid., p. 77.

42. SB to Edward Simmen, director, Division of Graduate Studies, Universidad de las Américas, Puebla, Mexico, 13 January 1981, and editor of an anthology of American short stories about Mexico entitled *Gringos in Mexico* (1988).

43. A version of the work Passin did in Chihuahua for the PhD, which he never completed, was published as *The Place of Kinship in Tarahumara Social Organization*, first in 1941, then in an expanded edition in 1943, both editions by the University of Chicago Press.

44. Atlas, *Biography*, p. 68.

45. SB, "I Got a Scheme!," p. 77.

46. Ibid.

47. Atlas, *Biography*, p. 191, puts Mannix's side in the dispute, which claims that SB "lifted" the whole episode of the eagle's training from an article Mannix published in *The Saturday Evening Post* ("Hunting Dragons with an Eagle," 18 January 1941): "The most dramatic scenes in the Mexico chapter—Augie's tense efforts to train the eagle, the sensation their entourage causes in the village squares of dusty Mexican towns, the lizard hunts in the desert—are a detailed rendering of the Mannixes' experience. *Too* detailed, according to Mannix. When Bellow's account appeared . . . Mannix threatened to sue; Bellow was forced to insert a passage obliquely crediting him. Thus the curious sentence in chapter 14 of the book explaining that Thea 'had gotten the idea for this hunt from reading articles by Dan and Julie [*sic*] Mannix, who actually had gone to Taxco some years before with a trained bald eagle and used the bird to catch iguanas.'" Presumably this sentence (p. 627) is what SB refers to as a "footnote" in the interview with Roth. Atlas's account of the borrowings derives in part from "a telephone interview with Daniel Mannix; a letter from Mannix elaborating on our conversation (November 13, 1991); and a letter to me from Keith Jennison" (p. 627). Atlas also cites Eusebio Rodrigues, "Augie March's Mexican Adventures," *Indiana Journal of American*

Studies 8, no. 2 (1978): pp. 39–43, which traces both SB's borrowings and their transformation into fiction in *Augie*. Rodrigues, too, received a letter from Mannix, on 29 July 1977, thirty-seven years after the event (though at least a decade and a half earlier than the one Atlas received). In it, Mannix tells him of one crucial respect in which Aguila resembled Caligula: "After a number of flights, an iguana bit our eagle's toe off. After that, she was afraid of them, so when we made the motion picture, we had to get another eagle. . . . Jack Champion, a 'pulp' writer who was living in Taxco and was showing Bellow around probably told him that our bird was afraid of the lizards but didn't know why" (quoted on p. 42). In defense of SB, Rodrigues points to a number of "concrete visual details" that vivify the Caligula episode, "adding to and enriching his material"; most important, "Bellow changed the Mannix success story into a story of failure to suit his own fictional purposes" (p. 41).

48. "I Got a Scheme!," p. 78.

49. Grandma Lausch had a cousin who used to recite "The Eagle" by Lermontov, in Russian, "which," Augie says, "I didn't dig" (p. 764).

50. Caligula is also said to be "an Attila's horseman" (p. 782, already quoted), to be "gliding like a Satan" (p. 770), and to be "close kin to the [bird] that lit on Prometheus once a day" (p. 762).

51. "I Got a Scheme!," p. 77.

52. SB, "Mosby's Memoirs," first printed in *The New Yorker*, 21 July 1968, reprinted in SB, *CS*, p. 362 (henceforth cited within the text by page numbers).

53. For Aztec and Mayan myth and civilization, their influence on modern Mexico, and SB's use of them in his fiction, see Michael C. Meyer, William L. Sherman, and Susan M. Deeds, *The Course of Mexican History* (New York: Oxford University Press, 2007); Rosemary Gipson, "Los Voladores, The Flyers of Mexico," *Western Folklore* 30, no. 4 (1971): 269–78; D. W. Gunn, *American and British Writers in Mexico, 1556–1973* (Austin: University of Texas Press, 1974); and the Rodrigues article mentioned above (note 47). I am grateful to Ariel Marcus, a graduate student in the Committee on Social Thought at the University of Chicago, for discovering the Gipson article, and for an illuminating paper he wrote on "Bellow in Mexico" in the class on SB's fiction I taught in the Committee in Winter Quarter 2008.

54. D. H. Lawrence, "Corasmin and the Parrots" (1925), reprinted in *Selected Essays* (1950; Harmondsworth: Penguin, 1965), p. 203. The essay was originally published in *Adelphi* (1925), reprinted in *Mornings in Mexico* (1925).

55. Atlas, *Biography*, p. 68.

56. Ibid., p. 68.

57. Manea, "Conversation," p. 20.

58. For Smyth, see "The Press: Jap Agents," *Time*, 14 September 1942.

59. Eventually Passin and Bennett drew these interviews to the attention of Margaret Mead and officials of the U.S. Department of Agriculture, and in the fall they received funds from the Department of Agriculture to return to the Kincaid area and conduct further interviews. For these and other details, see John W. Bennett, "Doing Photography and Social Research in the Allied Occupation of Japan, 1948–1951: A Personal and Professional Memoir" (2008), from the Rare Books and Manuscripts Library, Ohio State University. Passin, who was in Japan with Bennett, contributes footnotes to the memoir. See also Jon Muller, *Archeology of the Lower Ohio River Valley* (Walnut Creek, CA: Left Coast Press, 2009), p. 18.

60. Manea, "Conversation," p. 13.

61. The question of Mercader's name is complex. According to the assassin himself, the name he used when entering Mexico in October 1939 on a false passport was Frank Jacson, the name given to him in Paris by a member of the Fourth International. His real name, he said, was Jacques Mornard-Vandendreschd. He

claimed to be a Belgian citizen, born in Iran. The truth of this claim is called into question, however, by Leandro A. Salazar and Julián Gorkin, *Murder in Mexico: The Assasination of Leon Trotsky* (London: Secker & Warburg, 1950), pp. 105–6; see also Albert Goldman, *The Assassination of Leon Trotsky* (1944; New York: Pioneer, 2007), and Alain Dugrand, *Trotsky in Mexico, 1937–1940* (Manchester: Carcanet Press, 1992).

62. SB, *IAAU*, p. 101. In a letter to Albert Glotzer of 7 August 1990, among the Albert Glotzer Papers in the Hoover Institution, Box 48, SB confirms this passage's assertion that he and Passin had pretended to be newspapermen in order to get in to see Trotsky's body. I owe this reference to Richard O'Brien, whose PhD dissertation, "The Radical Politics of American Fiction: Saul Bellow and *Partisan Review*, 1941–1953" (Leeds Metropolitan University, December 2010) is extremely useful for SB's early writings and political and literary connections.

63. Atlas, *Biography*, p. 69.

64. Since the story's original publication, it has been reprinted only once, in William Phillips and Philip Rahv, eds., *The Partisan Reader: Ten Years of Partisan Review, 1934–1944: An Anthology* (New York: Dial, 1946), from which, cited within the text, my page numbers are taken.

65. SB to Edward Simmen, 13 January 1981. Simmen had written to SB to inquire about "The Mexican General."

66. Julián Gorkin (1901–87), a leader of the Spanish worker's party, POUM (Partido Obrero e Unificacíon Marxista), a splinter group with Trotskyist sympathies, had escaped to Mexico after the Civil War. Like other opponents of the Communist International, he was accused both by the Mexican Communist Party and influential political supporters of the party of being an agent of Hitler. From 1942 onward, *PR* exposed and condemned the wider Stalinist campaign in Mexico against "anti-fascist refugees," with its threats of deportation, internment, even murder.

67. As O'Brien points out in "The Radical Politics of American Fiction: Saul Bellow and *Partisan Review*, 1941–1953," p. 130, the general is also unable to identify the portrait of Vasco de Quiroga (c. 1470/78–1565), first bishop of Michoacán, and defender of the Indians, which hangs in the hotel bedroom occupied by his "nieces." O'Brien quotes Michael C. Meyer, in Meyer, Sherman and Deeds, *The Course of Mexican History*, p. 196: "Quiroga attempted, with considerable success, to create an ideal society in the New World. He formed communities in which the Indians received training . . . in the rudiments of self-government. . . . Under Quiroga's tutelage, the Indians became self-sufficient. . . . With his death the utopian villages declined, but he had established some fine traditions that persisted."

68. These questions, presumably, included Trotsky's defense of the invasion of Finland, the Hitler-Stalin Pact, and the Soviet Union as a workers' state.

69. Manea, "Conversation," pp. 13, 14.

70. SB to Tarcov, postmarked 21 January 1941.

71. It may also allude to, without actually endorsing, Trotskyist policy. Constance Ashton Myers, in *The Prophet's Army: Trotskyists in America, 1928–1941* (Westport, CT: Greenwood, 1977), p. 50, sees this policy as rooted in fear: that entry into the war would lead to tyranny and the suppression of workers' rights. Hence, "rather than support a national war effort, even against reactionary or fascist powers, [Trotskyists] were expected to embrace 'revolutionary defeatism'; they were to sabotage the home government to precipitate revolution in obedience to the slogan, 'Turn the Imperialist War into a Civil War!' 'Defeatism' meant to carry the class struggle to its highest level—civil war—never flinching for patriotic niceties" (I owe this quotation to O'Brien, "The Radical Politics of American Fiction: Saul Bellow and *Partisan Review*, 1941–1953," p. 111).

72. Botsford interview, "A Half Life," in SB, *IAAU*, pp. 307, 308.

73. Ibid., p. 307; the quotation from Hugh Wilford is from *The New York Intellectuals: From Vanguard to Institution* (Manchester: Manchester University Press, 1995), p. 50. For wartime censorship see O'Brien, "The Radical Politics of American Fiction: Saul Bellow and *Partisan Review*, 1941–1953," p. 134: "Non-interventionist newsletters like *Uncensored* were forced to cease publication as contributions began to dry up; the Institute for Propaganda Analysis was forced to shut down, its staff called upon to manufacture rather than debunk items of misinformation. The editor of the *Emporia Gazette* dropped the syndicated 'Washington Merry-Go-Round' column because he was anxious for its 'too enterprising' authors not to 'possibly give aid and comfort to our enemies.' . . . More importantly, a 'friend' of *Partisan Review* informed the magazine that the Post Office News Company (a large books and magazine store, and *PR*'s biggest Chicago outlet) had cancelled with immediate effect its standing order of the magazine following the attack on Pearl Harbor. Indeed, the outlet had purged its shelves of *all* left-wing publications in a sweeping act of unofficial self-censorship."

74. Atlas, *Biography*, p. 79.

75. Though it was a triumph to have "Two Morning Monologues" accepted by *PR*, even the acceptance had its humiliations. Originally, there were four morning monologues: "Macdonald wrote me asking if he could print the first two monologues," SB wrote to Tarcov in the 8 February 1941 letter, "the other two, he said, weakened the whole effect and should be left out."

76. In a letter of 21 May 1941 to Tarcov, SB asks him to "stop in and tell the editors either to publish it or get off the pot. They have no business holding it for two months if they don't intend to use it." The story was returned. One story that was published, in an obscure periodical entitled *Retort: A Quarterly of Social Philosophy and the Arts* 1, no. 2 (June 1942): 14–20, entitled "Mr. Katz, Mr. Cohen and Cosmology," is set in Montreal in 1922. The two title characters, a clothing cutter and a tailor, are friends and board in the same rooming house. Mr. Katz knows many things—about the stars, the movement of the planets, the formation of mountains, the age of the earth; Mr. Cohen, though older, is ignorant, his world is simple, but he is outgoing and content. At the end of the story, ignorant Mr. Cohen says a striking thing, leading Katz to conclude "that Time is a subject on which the simplest cannot help being profound" (p. 19). That night, alone in his room, looking out at the stars, Mr. Katz has a moment of sublime insight:

> He lies still and hears his clock, the tread of the train on the Grand Trunk, hollow whistling on the corner. These too are a part of it [the ever-changing or irrevocable nature of existence], since they can never come again. He sees his life as pieces of cloth fed under the falling and again falling needle of a machine. All of these, he thinks as he sets his alarm for six, are part of one apparatus. The train, the clock returned to the table in the night's center, the whistling, all are stitching shut long seams, drawing in—to close it forever—all of past life" (p. 20).

77. Manea, "Conversation," p. 19.

78. William Barrett, *The Truants: Adventures Among the Intellectuals* (New York: Anchor/Doubleday, 1982), p. 49.

79. In *Dangling Man*, which takes place in the four months between mid-December and mid-April 1942, the induction of Joseph, the protagonist, is delayed first because of his Canadian birth, second "through a new clause affecting married men" (p. 4). "The papers say no husbands have been drafted from Illinois since last summer," he writes in his journal in February 1943. "But now the supply of men is lower, and married men without dependents will soon be called up" (p. 97). The dates of these particular changes in Joseph's status fit those of SB.

80. Henle may have been encouraged to ask to see future works by Farrell, a

supporter of SB's, who had dedicated the *Studs Lonigan* trilogy to Henle and his wife. Some at Vanguard had second thoughts about rejecting the novel: there is an undated memo from "E.S. [Evelyn Shrifte] to Henle: "Re Saul Bellow, I wonder if it would be worth looking at that Negro ms. again—since Saul is going into Merchant Marine and we won't get another ms. soon. What do you think?" Henle's answer on the same memo reads: "I'd say yes if I hadn't read that Kafka story. It's so MUCH like it. But let's discuss." The Vanguard material can be found in the Rare Book and Manuscript Library, Columbia University.

81. Koch interview.

82. That *Dangling Man* is short, less than two hundred pages, fits this hypothesis.

83. In an undated letter to Melvin Tumin, SB announced that "Two weeks ago I stopped work on my novel—it was not direct enough—and have since solaced myself with a book called *The Notebook of a Dangling Man.*"

84. Melvin Tumin (1919–94), a distinguished sociologist at Princeton, wrote on race relations, in part the subject of his PhD; crime and violence; social stratification; and education. He received BA and MA degrees in psychology from the University of Wisconsin (in 1939 and 1940, respectively), and a PhD in anthropology from Northwestern (in 1944). SB and Tumin met in Madison when Tumin was a senior at Wisconsin and SB a graduate student. They were introduced by Tumin's roommate, Leslie Fiedler, a friend from Newark. Fiedler, who would become a well-known critic, was studying for an MA in English and introduced Tumin to several literary friends at the university.

85. This assertion is made by Chambers himself, in *Witness* (New York: Random House, 1952), p. 44.

86. In his memoir, *Good-bye, Union Square* (New York: Quadrangle, 1970), pp. 70–71, Albert Halper claims that Lieber's client list included, at one time or another, Louis Adamic, Erskine Caldwell, Katherine Anne Porter, John Cheever, Josephine Herbst, Albert Maltz, John O'Hara, James Farrell, Nathanael West, Maxim Gorky, Theodore Dreiser, and Langston Hughes. As for SB's reference to the army, on December 10, 1942, Harold Kaplan had written to Mel Tumin reporting that "Sol wrote [to Isaac Rosenfeld] (rather mysteriously) of going off to the army around January first." He would not, in fact, be called up for another year and a half.

87. From the archive of *Story* magazine in the Department of Rare Books and Special Collections, Firestone Library, Princeton University.

88. When SB's friend, the writer and sociologist David T. Bazelon, told him he'd sold a story to *politics* (founded by Dwight Macdonald in 1944, after his split with *PR*), SB reassured him in a letter of 22 March 1944, in terms that make clear his sense of *PR* and its readers as primary audience: "I don't think it makes much difference where a story appears just so it reaches the people you want it to reach, and *politics* is read by pretty much the same people as *PR*."

89. SB to Dwight Macdonald, undated, in Taylor, ed., *Letters*, p. 34.

90. Maggie Simmons, "Free to Feel: Conversation with Saul Bellow," in *Quest*, February 1979, reprinted in Cronin and Siegel, eds., *Conversations with SB*, p. 161.

91. Gordon Lloyd Harper, "The Art of Fiction: Saul Bellow," *Paris Review* 9, no. 36 (1966), reprinted in ibid., p. 63. SB also thought perfectionism had kept him out of print. When proofs of "Two Morning Monologues" arrived, he told Tarcov in a letter of 20 February 1941 he could not "look at them long enough to make the needed corrections. This is no exaggeration. I would much rather have published something else. Maybe I am too demanding and exacting; maybe I lack what is essential: the careless attitude of journalism which teaches you to throw into print anything you scribble off; maybe it is wrong to be so painstakingly careful and perhaps I might have been in print long ago but for that scrupulous observance of

standards." In later life SB would refer to *Dangling Man* and *The Victim* as "formal requirements," like an MA and PhD (see Michiko Kakutani, "A Talk with Saul Bellow: On His Work and Himself," *New York Times Book Review*, 13 December 1981, reprinted in ibid., p. 184). See, in comparison, Philip Roth in *The Facts* (1988; New York: Vintage, 1997), p. 60, on his own earliest stories, which "were intended to be 'touching'; without entirely knowing it, I wanted my fiction to become 'refined,' to be elevated into realms unknown to the lower-middle-class Jews of Leslie Street, with their focus on earning a living and raising a family and trying occasionally to have a good time. To prove in my earliest undergraduate stories that I was a nice Jewish boy would have been bad enough; this was worse—proving that I was a nice boy, period. The Jew was nowhere to be seen; there were no Jews in the stories, no Newark, and not a sign of comedy—the last thing I wanted to do was to hand anybody a laugh in literature."

92. Manea, "Conversation," p. 34. See also the profile by Steve Neal, "The Quintessential Chicago Writer," *Chicago Tribune Magazine*, 16 September 1979, reprinted in Cronin and Siegel, eds., *Conversations with SB*, p. 179: "Since young writers are and should be imitative, in my first book (*Dangling Man*), I imitated Rilke's *Journal of My Other Self* [the novel's title in the 1930 translation by John Linton]." Malte, the protagonist of Rilke's novel, like Joseph, is in his twenties, and at the loosest of loose ends (the following quotations are from a translation by Burton Pike [Champaign, IL: Dalkey Archive Press, 2008]): "I think I should learn to work on something," Malte declares in an early notebook entry, "I am twenty-eight and just about nothing has happened. Let's summarize: I have written a study of Carpaccio, which is bad, a drama called *Marriage* that tries to prove something false by ambiguous means, and poems" (p. 13). "No-one" knows about Malte (p. 15). He wanders Paris aimlessly, or lies in bed all day, "and my day, which nothing interrupts, is like a dial without a hand" (p. 46). His thoughts turn to art and ideas, but he lacks power in both realms. Malte also shares Joseph's complex feelings about modernity. The world he inhabits is Joseph's modern world: "we have no theatre, as little as we have a God: for that you need community. Everyone has his own particular ideas and fears" (p. 171). Like Joseph, Malte is torn between resistance to this world, and a concomitant sense of loss, on the one hand, and a desire to fit his art, or artistic sense, to it, on the other. His isolation or alienation is not just from friends and, especially, family, but from the twentieth century, which he nonetheless feels he must embrace, again like Joseph. In addition to these resemblances, the novel, like *Dangling Man*, is dominated by its narrator's feelings and thoughts rather than his actions and it has hardly any plot.

93. Harold Kaplan to Melvin Tumin, undated, but from autumn 1942. Kaplan's letters are in the possession of Melvin Tumin's widow, Sylvia.

94. See Chapter 1, note 17, for a description of the photograph.

95. Bruce Cook, "Saul Bellow: A Mood of Protest," *Perspectives on Ideas and the Arts*, 12 February 1963, reprinted in Cronin and Siegel, eds., *Conversations with SB*, p. 14.

96. SB, *IAAU*, pp. 61, 61–62.

97. Though the letter to Tumin is undated, it was probably written sometime in the first half of 1943, perhaps as late as April–May, since in it SB predicts "I shall be finished in a month, for certain and perhaps sooner," and Vanguard accepted the novel in early July. But this is also the letter in which SB says he's written "twenty-thousand words already and not come one third of the whole way."

98. The letter from which this quotation comes is also undated. Erich Fromm (1900–1980) was a German Jewish psychoanalytic theorist, educated in Germany and associated with the Frankfurt School of critical theory. After fleeing the Nazis in 1934, he arrived in New York, obtaining a teaching post at Columbia. In *Escape from Freedom* (1941), the first of his books to be published in English, Fromm dis-

tinguishes modern man from medieval man, who, though "not free in the modern sense," was neither alone nor isolated: "In having a distinct, unchangeable, and unquestionable place in the social world from the moment of birth, [medieval] man was rooted in a structuralized whole, and thus life had a meaning which left no place, and no need for doubt" ([New York: Rinehart, 1941], pp. 41–42). As SB paraphrases Fromm in the letter to Tumin, modern man has lost this security, and with it a connection with nature, "inward and outward." He has done so, however, through a hard-won and ennobling battle for freedom, which produces "loneliness and anxiety," feelings often too frightening and painful to bear. Seeking to escape anxious isolation, through what Fromm calls "automaton conformity" (as in Joseph's submission to "regimentation"), results in both psychological conflict and destructiveness, in which one simultaneously hates and seeks to destroy the world in a "desperate attempt to save myself from being destroyed by it" (p. 177).

99. Chief among these questions is how best to respond to fallen modernity, whether to resist it or resign oneself to it (with Flaubertian or Hemingwayesque sangfroid). It is possible that the balance is tipped in resistance's favor by resignation's most eloquent spokesman in the novel, Joseph's alter ego, the Dostoyevskian "Spirit of Alternatives," called also "On the Other Hand" and "*Tu As Raison Aussi*." This "Spirit" is an equivalent of, or nod to, Ivan Karamazov's "Grand Inquisitor." Daniel Fuchs, in *Saul Bellow: Vision and Revision* (Durham, NC: Duke University Press, 1984), p. 42, calls the Inquisitor "a representation of [Ivan's] own worst, his own 'stupidest' ideas and tendencies," implying a similar valuing of Joseph's "Spirit." Dostoyevsky ultimately looks down on Ivan for his ideas, as he looks down on the Underground Man, whom Joseph also resembles, and whom Dostoyevsky treats comically. Whether a similar distance separates SB from Joseph is less certain.

100. Atlas, *Biography*, p. 99. Evidence for Rahv's view comes early in the novel, when Joseph admits that dangling is "only one of the sources of my harassments," only "the backdrop against which I can be seen swinging" (p. 5).

101. Edmund Wilson, "Doubts and Dreams: *Dangling Man* under a Glass Bell," *New Yorker*, 1 April 1944. SB had met Wilson in Hyde Park, sat in on a course he was offering at the University of Chicago on Dickens, and greatly admired him, but they were never close. After the review of *Dangling Man*, SB asked Wilson in 1945 if he'd be a referee on his second application for a Guggenheim Fellowship, and Wilson agreed, but he was never again to write about SB's fiction in public. Wilson's brief reference was for both Randall Jarrell and SB. In it he calls SB "a first-rate candidate. He hasn't yet shown himself to be so remarkable as Jarrell, but he is younger, I believe, and has written one interesting and rather original novel."

102. Compare Schwartz's account of his generation's disillusion, as depicted in *Dangling Man*, with Dwight Macdonald's essay "Reading from Left to Right," *Partisan Review* 8, no. 1 (January–February 1941): 30: "By now, bourgeois democracy is broken down so completely as a social and economic system that increasingly large sections of the population have lost all faith in it. They just don't believe the words any more."

103. According to Atlas, *Biography*, p. 101. Diana Trilling's review appeared in the issue of 15 April 1944, under the heading "Fiction in Review."

104. Botsford interview, "A Half Life," SB, *IAAU*, p. 309.

105. This quotation is from the Koch interview. More fully: "I wasn't called up for the draft until 1943 or so. I meant to take part in the war but I was writing. So I kept saying well all right I'll do it. Then I had the surgery and then I decided to go to the Merchant Marine."

106. Botsford interview, SB, *IAAU*, pp. 309–10. The moment Hitler was recognized for "what he was" was reached at different points by SB's contemporaries. Alfred Kazin, in *New York Jew* (New York: Alfred A. Knopf, 1978), pp. 26–27,

recalls coming to it at an earlier date: "1943. Now began the nightmare that would bring everything else into question. . . . The Nazis had organized the killing of every Jew within their grasp. . . . The systematic killing of Jews had not begun by the time we entered the war. But by the end of 1942 and especially the terrible spring of 1943, when the Warsaw ghetto was destroyed after its last desperate attack on the Nazis it was clear." In contrast, Lionel Abel seems to have come to his realization about Hitler even later than SB. As he explains in *Intellectual Follies*, pp. 270–71, "when a Polish refugee in 1941 told the American Supreme Court Justice, Felix Frankfurter, of having witnessed mass executions of Jews, Frankfurter replied, 'I don't say you're lying, but I don't believe you.' In Trotskyist circles, it was generally assumed that stories of mass executions were allied propaganda. . . . For their position was that there was equal lying on both sides, and this naturally created on the left an additional difficulty in assessing the truth of stories of Nazi mass murder, and when the war was over there were other embarrassments for the left. How was it that the Polish Socialists had not generously provided arms to the Jews fighting the Nazis in the Warsaw ghetto? How was it that the Russian Red Army had remained on the other side of the Vistula—thus giving the Nazi army time in which to put down the Polish resistance movement and execute its leaders—before advancing into Poland? . . . But I had no real revelation of what had occurred until sometime in 1946, more than a year after the German surrender, when I took my mother to a motion picture and we saw in a newsreel some details of the American army going into the concentration camps at Buchenwald."

7. NEW YORK

1. According to Irving Kristol, in an interview. See Chapter 11 of *The Adventures of Augie March* (1953), reprinted in *Saul Bellow: Novels 1944–1953*: "The house where I was living on the South Side was a student house within range of the university chimes and chapel bell when the evenings were still, and it had a crowded medieval fullness, besides, of hosts inside the narrow walls, faces in every window, every inch occupied. I had some student book customers and even several friends here" (p. 613). That house is operated by Owens, an old Welshman, and his spinster sister, not Mrs. Huppeler.

2. Atlas, *Biography*, p. 104.

3. Ibid., p. 92.

4. For the *Syntopicon* and Great Books series, see Herman Kogan, *The Great EB* (Chicago: University of Chicago Press, 1958); Mortimer Adler, *Philosopher at Large: An Intellectual Autobiography, 1902–1976* (New York: Macmillan, 1977); and Mary Ann Dzuback, *Robert M. Hutchins: Portrait of an Educator* (Chicago: University of Chicago Press, 1991); see also Dwight Macdonald's devastating attack, "The Book-of-the-Millennium Club," *New Yorker*, 25 November 1952.

5. Atlas, *Biography*, p. 89. Himmelfarb had hoped also to get a job at the Committee. She was interviewed for a position by Nef but turned down: "he really wanted a medievalist."

6. See "Syntopicon Booklet Draft," Box 4, Special Collections, Regenstein Library, University of Chicago; for rejected topics, see Mortimer J. Adler to Bruce Barton, 22 April 1950, also Special Collections, in the Adler Papers.

7. For the topics SB oversaw, see his annotation to the manuscript of Ruth Miller's *Saul Bellow: A Biography of the Imagination*, among the SB Papers; for the works and authors he indexed, see Atlas, *Biography*, p. 93.

8. First published in *The National Interest*, Spring 1993, reprinted in SB, *IAAU*, p. 105.

9. Steven J. Zipperstein, *Rosenfeld's Lives: Fame, Oblivion and the Furies of Writing* (New Haven: Yale University Press, 2009), p. 55.

10. There are five substantial manuscripts in the Regenstein concerned with the Zetland character. All are undated but seem to come from the late 1960s and the 1970s. The longest, titled "Zetland and Quine," is 117 pages. What seems to be an earlier version of this manuscript, labelled "Z & Q," is one hundred pages long. A third manuscript, titled simply "Zetland," is also one hundred pages. SB has written on the first page of this manuscript: "Harriet—kindly keep this copy. There'll be more." "Harriet" is Harriet Wasserman, who worked in the office of SB's literary agents, Russell and Volkening. By the early 1970s, with the decline of Henry Volkening's health (he died in 1972), she became SB's sole agent. The fourth manuscript, "Charm and Death" (ninety-seven pages), is referred to in a letter to SB of 1 December 1970 from Volkening: "Alan Williams [of Viking] has had this morning delivered to me the first 91 pages of *Charm and Death.* . . . I will, of course, bear in mind that this is a first draft." Finally, there is "An Exalted Madness," a twenty-six-page manuscript. Zetland is basically the same character in all the manuscripts and there is much overlap of material, but there are differences. "Charm and Death" is probably the most finished of the manuscripts. The short story "Zetland: By a Character Witness" is the only portion of the Zetland material to be published in SB's lifetime. In early versions of what would become *Humboldt's Gift*, Zetland material was included; the novel was to be more evenly split between New York and Chicago settings. Atlas conjectures that when in the fall of 1978 Harriet Wasserman had lunch with Erwin Glickes, the editorial director of Harper and Row, and Glickes offered SB a two-book contract for "A Non-Fiction Book About Chicago" and "a Greenwich Village love story," that the latter was "probably the 'Zetland' manuscript" (Atlas, *Biography*, p. 481). The "Bad Housekeeping" reference comes from Chapter 1 of "Zetland and Quine."

11. Alan M. Wald, *The New York Intellectuals: The Rise and Decline of the Anti-Stalinist Left from the 1930s to the 1980s* (Chapel Hill: North Carolina University Press, 1987), p. 51. According to Alfred Kazin, in *Starting Out in the Thirties* (1962; London: Secker & Warburg, 1966), pp. 72–73, Hook was "the most devastating logician the world had ever seen. . . . Humorless but never petty; obstinate but not malicious; domineering but not self-centered."

12. Howe's reference to Rosenfeld as "golden boy" (also "*wunderkind*") comes from *A Margin of Hope: An Intellectual Autobiography* (New York: Harcourt Brace Jovanovich, 1982), p. 133; Bazelon's Yiddishing of "golden boy" comes from *Nothing but a Fine Tooth Comb: Essays in Social Criticism, 1944–1969* (New York: Simon & Schuster, 1969), p. 19.

13. Bazelon, *Nothing but a Fine Tooth Comb*, p. 18.

14. Lionel Trilling, "Four Decades of American Prose," *Nation*, 7 November 1942.

15. Alfred Kazin, *New York Jew* (New York: Alfred A. Knopf, 1978), p. 40.

16. Ibid., pp. 40, 41.

17. Ibid., pp. 41, 42.

18. Ibid., p. 42.

19. Atlas, *Biography*, p. 83.

20. Howe, *Margin of Hope*, p. 169.

21. William Barrett, *The Truants: Adventures Among the Intellectuals* (New York: Anchor/Doubleday, 1982), p. 49.

22. William Phillips, *A Partisan View: Five Decades of the Literary Life* (New York: Stein & Day, 1983), pp. 118, 119.

23. Janet Richards, *Common Soldiers: A Self-Portrait and Other Portraits* (San Francisco: Archer, 1979), p. 119.

24. Eileen Simpson, *Poets in Their Youth: A Memoir* (1982; New York: Vintage, 1983), p. 218.

25. Ann Birstein, *What I Saw at the Fair: An Autobiography* (New York: Welcome Rain Publishers, 2003), p. 121.

26. Atlas, *Biography*, p. 101.

27. Kazin, *New York Jew*, p. 42.

28. In the second Guggenheim application, SB adds Edmund Wilson to his list of referees. His dual reference for SB and Randall Jarrell is discussed in note 101 of the previous chapter. More fulsome praise comes from Kazin and Farrell, though Farrell also puts SB second in comparison with another applicant for whom he is writing. "I consider Mr. Bellow to be the most honest, the most serious, the most gifted of what seems to me to be a group of writers and intellectuals, younger than myself, whose attitudes and values are quite different from my own," Farrell confesses. The "note of disillusionment" SB shares with others of his generation, "for instance, the writer and critic, Mr. Isaac Rosenfeld," is not to Farrell's taste, but is sounded "honestly, and with a real literary gift." For Henle, SB is "of all the young men who in recent years have come under my observation . . . the most gifted, the most intelligent and the most sincere." Kazin calls him "one of the most talented writers of our generation, and one who brings to the novel a background of genuine learning."

29. Atlas, *Biography*, pp. 86–87. These reviews, for which SB received "five bucks apiece" (according to reminiscences recorded in a transcript of remarks made on 15 October 1985 at the Whiting Foundation Writers' Program Ceremony), were unsigned. Among *New York Times Book Review* articles written by SB in the 1940s are "A Revolutionist's Testament," 21 November 1943, a review of Arthur Koestler's novel *Arrival and Departure*; "Irish Egoist and Patriot," a review of Harold Nicholson, *The Desire to Please*, 3 October 1943; and "Belgian Picaroon," a review of Charles De Coster, *The Great Adventures of Tyl Ulenspiegl*, 31 October 1943. Atlas, *Biography*, p. 85, says "one of his first assignments was Maurice Samuel's *The World of Sholom Aleichem* (1943)."

30. SB, foreword to William Phillips, ed., *Sixty Years of Great Fiction from Partisan Review* (Boston: Partisan Review Press, 1997), p. viii.

31. See SB to Victoria Miller, 16 July 1996: "What Eleanor Clark and I had in common before her marriage to Red Warren were our literary interests. We wrote for the Partisan Review and met occasionally at its offices in the Village. I know little or nothing of her personal life at that time. She did put me up for a job at the O.S.S. and I went down to Washington in a train compartment with two Intelligence gentlemen. The trouble then was that I was still a Canadian citizen and therefore ineligible for the job. The gentlemen in the train, smooth and experienced operatives, had nothing to offer me except entertainment. One of them had been in Russia in 1917. There he had known Lenin and Trotsky and numerous lesser Bolsheviks. His impersonations were very funny." SB fictionalizes this encounter in one of the "Zetland" manuscripts, "Zetland and Quine," pp. 38–40.

32. Kaplan's comments come from an undated letter to Mel Tumin, in the possession of Tumin's widow, Sylvia. Allanah Harper (1904–92) founded *Echanges: Revue Trimestrielle de Littérature Anglaise et Française* in 1929 with the express purpose of introducing English writers to the French and vice versa. Among the English authors she published were W. H. Auden, T. S. Eliot, Virginia Woolf, Gertrude Stein, and Ivy Compton-Burnett; among her French authors were André Gide and Henri Michaux.

33. Dana Tasker to Ik Shuman, 13 August 1943, in the New York Public Library, Records, Manuscripts and Archives section, quoted in Atlas, *Biography*, p. 91.

34. SB television interview with Melvin Bragg, reprinted as "Off the Couch by Christmas," in *The Listener*, 20 November 1975.

35. SB interview, "The Quintessential Chicago Writer," in *Chicago Tribune Magazine*, 16 September 1979, reprinted in Cronin and Siegel, eds., *Conversations with SB*, p. 175.

36. Phillips, *A Partisan View*, p. 110. For Agee's reputation, see Morris Dickstein, who knew him, in *Dancing in the Dark: A Cultural History of the Great Depression* (New York: W. W. Norton, 2009), p. 108: "Agee was a legend in his own time: an incandescent, self-consuming personality, a bohemian in the 1920s style, by then *out* of style, a poet trapped at Time, Inc., a hard drinker and luminous talker who could describe a movie lovingly, frame by frame, yet also a Christian gentleman from Tennessee by way of Exeter and Harvard who felt compelled to do penance for his mildly privileged background."

37. Sam Tanenhaus, *Whittaker Chambers: A Biography* (New York: Random House, 1997), p. 196.

38. For SB on Agee, see the "Zetland" manuscript, in which Zetland gets a job at *Time*: "Jim Agee was one of Zetland's Village friends. Chambers valued and trusted Agee and hired Zet on his recommendation but was intensely suspicious of him. Not on political grounds; he knew that Zet was an anti-Stalinist; but Zet was too odd, too kinky for him. . . . Princely Agee, a gentleman (Exeter, Yale [Harvard, in fact]) wooed Chambers for him. . . . Zet granted that Agee was a man of talent, and generous, and amiable, and handsome. . . . He sometimes added that Agee was too High Church for him. Too much T. S. Eliot business. Zet didn't care for the professoriate, for culture heroes, for Wasp humanists and solemnities of tradition which he considered phoney" (pp. 8–9).

39. SB, foreword to Phillips, ed., *Sixty Years of Great Fiction from Partisan Review*, p. vii.

40. Phillips, *A Partisan View*, p. 13. John Reed Clubs, named after the American journalist, poet, and activist John Reed (1887–1920), were literary, artistic, and intellectual clubs encouraging young or unknown writers from the working classes. The first such club was founded in New York in 1929 by staff from *New Masses* magazine. Originally independent organizations, in 1930 they formally affiliated with Moscow, as did *New Masses*.

41. Ibid., p. 36.

42. Alfred Kazin, *Starting Out in the Thirties*, p. 5.

43. Phillips, *A Partisan View*, p. 38.

44. Examples of abhorrent party policies include the defense of the Moscow trials; of Communist attacks on the Spanish workers' party, POUM; of Popular Front alliances with so-called progressive capitalists; of the makers of soppy Hollywood films.

45. Phillips, *A Partisan View*, pp. 47, 48.

46. For Barrett's portrait of Mary McCarthy, see *The Truants*, pp. 65–69. Here is Kazin on McCarthy: "Herself an orphan, with none of the pusillanimous dependence on family love that was the besetting weakness of so many anxious intellectuals, she turned the very outrageousness of her judgments into a social virtue. She operated on her circle, in Provincetown and New York, with open scorn, and impressed them—they who were so solemn—with her power to make them ridiculous" (*Starting Out in the Thirties*, p. 156).

47. Frances Kiernan, *Seeing Mary Plain: A Life of Mary McCarthy* (New York: W. W. Norton, 2000), p. 268.

48. Phillips, *A Partisan View*, p. 48.

49. Barrett, *The Truants*, p. 49.

50. Botsford interview, "A Half Life," reprinted in SB, *IAAU*, p. 308. To Daniel Bell, SB's attitude was uncomplicated: "Saul never liked the New York intellectuals, just really never liked them. Didn't like Phillips or Rahv and others. He thought they were prattlers."

51. SB, "Writers, Intellectuals, Politics: Mainly Reminiscence," in *IAAU*, p. 105.
52. Botsford interview, "A Second Half Life," SB, *IAAU*, p. 326.
53. Howe, *A Margin of Hope*, p. 159.
54. Barrett, *The Truants*, p. 29.
55. Ibid., p. 42.
56. Howe, *A Margin of Hope*, p. 130. In rejected passages from an early draft of *Humboldt's Gift*, a novel originally conceived of, according to Daniel Fuchs, whose work SB commended, as "a fusion of two separate novels, one about Humboldt and New York, one about Swiebel and Cantabile and Chicago," SB offers satirical portraits of Rahv and Phillips, thinly fictionalized as Ablove and Sharfer, editors of *Avantgarde*, a left-wing literary magazine. Citrine, the narrator, praises Ablove, the Rahv character, for publishing important European writers in his magazine. Humboldt, modeled on Delmore Schwartz, cuts him off: "You've missed about ten essentials. What about the social climbing, the craze for upperclass gentile women, the big, declamatory fist, the ideas lifted from Wyndham Lewis, the funny deals with publishers?" Here is Citrine on Sharfer: he's "Miaow Tse Tung, the revolutionary kittycat. Silly, also canny, weakly, hypochondriac, overpsychoanalyzed." According to Citrine, Sharfer thinks "that the GPR is seeking his life because he was one of five hundred signers of a statement about the death of General Krivitsky." (General Walter Krivitsky was a Soviet intelligence officer who revealed plans for the Nazi-Soviet Pact. He defected before World War II began and was found dead in New York in 1941, either having committed suicide or been murdered by Soviet intelligence. The largest Soviet foreign intelligence agency was GRU not GPR.) When Ablove turns down Humboldt's request for a third share in *Avantgarde*, Humboldt accuses him of being in the pay of the State Department, an allusion to the CIA's funding of *Encounter* and other European magazines. "All the anti-Stalinist radicals are being offered funds. Whittaker Chambers is Nixon's pal and he advises him. Jay Lovestone is a big man in Washington now. He's got all the ex-communists into this." Humboldt then threatens Ablove: "Do you want me to tell your wife whom you've been sleeping with?" ("'So you've switched from poetry to blackmail?' said Ablove"). Later Ablove does down Humboldt behind his back, describing him to Citrine as "really a very misanthropic and cynical person who took you in by his kidding, his routines, his wide-ranging mind, his mad sense of fun, his charm, all camouflage for gloom, envy, hatred." These passages, written by SB in the early 1970s, confirm accounts by other acquaintances of Rahv, Phillips, and Schwartz; their harshness, however, may misrepresent SB's feelings in the 1940s, reflecting a later disaffection with left intellectuals, particularly in the 1960s. That SB chose not to include Ablove and Sharfer in *Humboldt* or any other published work ought also to be noted. Fuchs's discussion of the passages is to be found in *Saul Bellow: Vision and Revision* (Durham, NC: Duke University Press, 1984), pp. 234–45 and 252.
   As this episode suggests, there was much internal bickering and jockeying for position at *PR*. "I wasn't very good at it," SB admitted, in the second of two videotaped interviews he gave in 1987 to Sigmund Koch, "mainly because I didn't have any interest in it. I didn't see the point, and if they were going to write then they should be writing," especially if they were good. Delmore Schwartz was more than good: "those early things of his were among the best things in this century by any American, but especially his story 'In Dreams Begin Responsibilities.'" As the Ablove and Sharfer passages suggest, however, Schwartz was among the magazine's chief schemers. "So one was greatly stirred up," SB recalls. "It is true that some of the people had more academic talent or more organizational talent than literary talent and some of them were tremendous promoters in the field of art and much of it was just fun. You just enjoyed watching them in action."
57. Kiernan, *Seeing Mary Plain*, p. 267.

58. Atlas, *Biography*, p. 112.

59. Joseph Dorman, *Arguing the World: The New York Intellectuals in Their Own Words* (New York: Free Press, 2000), p. 102.

60. Ibid., p. 102.

61. Lionel Abel, *The Intellectual Follies: A Memoir of the Literary Venture in New York and Paris* (New York: W. W. Norton, 1984), p. 52. Phillips's account of his relations with Rahv is understandably different: "At first we did get along, at least enough to collaborate, or I thought we did. We were constantly arguing, sometimes violently, but there was sufficient basic agreement for the arguments to be settled by persuasion or compromise, or by a shifting of terms—a tactic at which Rahv was a master" (p. 271); "I did become aware early on that he would claim most of the credit for finding new writers and for other achievements of the magazine, leaving him free to deal with contributors and publishers and thus to be in on the more visible and the more rewarding activities. He was able to do this mostly by preserving his incompetence in the financial and other practical aspects of *Partisan Review*—and by my tolerance of this division of labor. . . . I had a general distaste for his almost reflexive reaching for the limelight and what amounted to a constant push for power" (pp. 271–72).

62. Barrett, *The Truants*, p. 46.

63. These entries from *Alfred Kazin's Journals*, ed. Richard M. Cook (New Haven and London: Yale University Press, 2011), are from 10 January 1942 (p. 28), 30 August 1944 (p. 62), 30 August 1944 (p. 63), 30 September 1948 (p. 121), 3 January 1952 (p. 163), 23 September 1955 (p. 196), 31 January 1949 (p. 126), 3 October 1961 (p. 274), 24 January 1954 (p. 176), and 18 December 1958 (p. 238).

64. Howe, *A Margin of Hope*, p. 140.

65. Birstein, *What I Saw at the Fair*, pp. 106–7.

66. Diana Trilling, *The Beginning of the Journey* (New York: Harcourt Brace, 1993), p. 335.

67. In an untitled and undated manuscript among the Bellow Papers in the Regenstein, recalling a train trip SB took on the Long Island Rail Road with Rosenberg.

68. SB, "Him with His Foot in His Mouth" (1982), reprinted in SB, *CS*, pp. 384–85. In *Abstract Expressionism: A Tribute to Harold Rosenberg: Paintings and Drawings from Chicago Collections*, by Harold Rosenberg, Edward A. Maser, and SB (Chicago: University of Chicago Press and David and Alfred Smart Gallery, 1979), p. 10, SB attributes Kippenberg's remark to Rosenberg, who uttered it "many years ago in Chicago [when] he said he wanted to listen to something I had written. The hour was late, and after I'd read aloud for fifteen or twenty minutes and observed that he was nodding, I said, 'I'm putting you to sleep.' He said, 'On the contrary, you're keeping me awake.'"

69. SB, "What Kind of a Day Did You Have?" (1984), reprinted in SB, *CS*, p. 288 (henceforth cited within the text by page numbers).

70. *Journey to the End of the Night* was much pondered and referred to by SB, as well as frequently chosen for "Fundamentals" or qualifying examinations by graduate students in the Committee on Social Thought, where he taught for over thirty years. For the episode referred to here, in which Robinson is shot dead by his mistress, see SB to the Canadian psychoanalyst and writer Norman Doidge, in a fax transcript of a telephone interview, 26 April 2000: "What got [Allan] Bloom especially about Céline was the conclusion of the *Journey to the End of the Night*, where Robinson's girlfriend, a tramp, insists that he say, 'I love you.' Robinson is a nihilist, and he says, 'No, I won't say that.' She says, 'You do get a hard on as do other men!' But Robinson says, 'I refuse to say the phony thing.' On this matter of love, Robinson had a rigorous principle: he wouldn't say I love you to a tramp who would pump herself up with self-importance. She takes her gun out of her purse,

and says, 'Are you going to say it or not.' 'No,' he says. So she shoots him dead. Bloom takes from this that even nihilists can't sustain nihilism. No matter how much they have abused their lives with ideas, they still have principles. But I would say to him, 'Maybe this nihilist was tired of life, and only too pleased to be shot.'"

71. Richard Kaye, "Art Critic Harold Rosenberg Memorialized," *Chicago Maroon* (University of Chicago student newspaper), 12 October 1979, p. 3.

72. Atlas, *Biography*, pp. 353–54.

73. SB, *IAAU*, p. 105. In Dorman, *Arguing the World*, p. 71, SB distinguishes between two kinds of *PR* critics: "one the professorial type and the other, the free-wheeling type. Harold Rosenberg was a free-wheeling type, whereas Lionel Trilling was a professorial type. And I didn't take too much interest in the professorial ones and I was mad for Harold Rosenberg. On every subject under the sun he has developed a view."

74. From a note by SB entered in a small undated spiral notebook among his papers in the Regenstein. In *A Margin of Hope*, p. 114, Irving Howe describes meeting Rosenberg in 1947, shortly after publishing his first review in *Commentary* (of Rosenfeld's *Passage from Home*): "At a party, I was approached by a giant of a man who looked like a pirate, complete with a game leg. In a rasping voice he said: 'You'll write better ones.' From Harold Rosenberg, encouragement of sorts." Howe recalls Philip Rahv's comparably rough good humor: "In a gesture I later recognized as his way of opening a conversation, Rahv started poking his finger into my chest, establishing a tradition in which mockery served as a token of friendliness" (p. 118), a tradition that recalls Kazin wagging his finger under Philip Roth's nose and telling him "You don't understand a word I say. You don't even understand when I say you don't understand."

75. Manea, "Conversation," p. 44.

76. SB first encountered Rosenberg in person around the same time he encountered him on the page, through Philip Rahv, who "had a sense of responsibility towards the young writers he published in the *Partisan Review*. Fresh from Chicago, I was under his protection, and he said that I must meet Harold Rosenberg. We walked along Second Avenue, the three of us, and stopped for a cup of coffee at the Cafe Royal. There followed a long discussion of some problem in Marxist theory. This did not interest me greatly" (SB, in Rosenberg, Maser, and SB, *Abstract Expressionism—A Tribute*, p. 9).

77. SB, *IAAU*, p. 134.

78. Harold Rosenberg, "The Fall of Paris," *Partisan Review* (November–December 1940), pp. 441, 442.

79. Ibid., p. 448.

80. Botsford interview, "A Half Life," SB, *IAAU*, p. 308.

81. Kazin, *New York Jew*, p. 152.

82. The quotations from Abel and Rosenberg are from Howe, *A Margin of Hope*, pp. 135, 290. The term "action painting" was coined by Rosenberg in the essay "American Action Painters" in the December 1952 issue of *ARTnews*, reprinted in *The Tradition of the New* (1959; New York: Grove, 1961). In this essay Rosenberg describes action paintings as "events" rather than "objects," "processes" rather than "products": action painting "has broken down every distinction between art and life" (p. 28); the meaning of such a painting lies in how "the artist organizes his emotional and intellectual energy as if he were in a living situation" (p. 29). The task for the spectator or critic of abstract painting is "to think in a vocabulary of action: its inception, duration, direction—psychic state, concentration and relaxation of the will, passivity, waiting" (p. 29).

83. Phillips, *A Partisan View*, p. 68.

84. Greenberg's essay is reprinted in *Art and Culture: Criticial Essays* (Boston: Beacon, 1961), where the quotation can be found on p. 208.

85. Barrett, *The Truants*, p. 134.

86. SB, foreword to Phillips, ed., *Sixty Years of Great Fiction from Partisan Review*, pp. viii, ix.

87. T. J. Clark, "Clement Greenberg's Theory of Art," *Critical Inquiry* 9, no. 1 (September 1982): 139.

88. SB, foreword to Phillips, ed., *Sixty Years of Great Fiction from Partisan Review*, p. ix.

89. Quoted in Mark Shechner, ed., *Preserving the Hunger: An Isaac Rosenfeld Reader* (Detroit: Wayne State University Press, 1988), p. 437, from a selection of undated entries from the journals Rosenfeld kept between 1941 and his death in 1956.

90. The narrator of "Charm and Death" can't help "poking fun" at "the little zoo" (p. 47) in the Zetlands' apartment. In the manuscript entitled "Zetland," this zoo consists of Smokey the dog, plus "gerbils, hamsters, Siamese cats, tropical birds and fishes." It was so big because "friends who were moving or divorcing could give their animals to the humane Zetlands" (p. 33).

91. SB, "Zetland," p. 34.

92. Before he turned against Rosenfeld, Alfred Kazin found visiting him exhilarating: "Going down the steps from that Barrow Street tenement," he writes in *New York Jew*, "the sound of Isaac's impeccable phrasing still in my ears, I felt that some promised beauty in my life waited for me" (pp. 52–53).

93. Zipperstein, *Rosenfeld's Lives*, p. 137; Kazin, *New York Jew*, p. 52.

94. Richards, *Common Soldiers*, p. 153.

95. Ibid., p. 155.

96. "The ray that blights" might be Klonsky's inability to work rather than work itself. Though relatively unproductive, that might be because, as he claimed, he suffered from writer's block.

97. In Shechner, ed., *Preserving the Hunger*, p. 443.

98. Wallace Markfield, *To an Early Grave* (New York: Simon & Schuster, 1964), p. 16.

99. Shechner, ed., *Preserving the Hunger*, p. 446. Here is Bazelon, in *Nothing but a Fine Tooth Comb*, p. 36, on women: "I can state this clearly: I always wanted conversation with women, primarily with women, and then to bed. Since women always take conversation as a form of weakness on the man's part—and, this weakness coming from a 'him,' therefore status on their part—I was early in life called upon, painfully, to interrupt my own most desired conversation with women in a brutal manner, in order to get laid at all. . . . This was then held against me as exhibiting excessive carnal appetite and toward disinterest in Them-as-People."

100. Bazelon, *Nothing but a Fine Tooth Comb*, p. 25.

101. A passage inspired by Kazin, who worked at *Fortune*, wrote about the Transcendentalists, and put people off with his intensity and earnestness. Kazin was not the only literary figure to work at *Fortune*: so, too, did John Chamberlain, Ralph Ingersoll, Dwight Macdonald, Archibald MacLeish, Robert Cantwell, Louis Kronenberger, and James Gould Cozzens. Writers who worked at Time, Inc. included not just James Agee but Robert Fitzgerald and John Hersey. According to Kazin, "the possibility of self-betrayal was as much a convention around Time, Inc. as it was in Hollywood" (*Starting Out in the Thirties*, pp. 111–12).

102. SB shared something of Harold Rosenberg's superior attitude to Greenwich Village, which he contrasted with the Tenth Street milieu favored by painters like de Kooning and Kline. As he explains: "In his 'Tenth Street' essay [*Art News Annual*, 1959] Harold shrewdly observes that modern Greenwich Village is a transplant, an imitation of Paris; its little trees, its crooked streets were meant to make painters feel more painterly. 'Greenwich Village was the gate through which American artists entered the twentieth century as semi-Frenchmen,' says

Harold. In reaction to this, American painters 'learned to speak in the modern idiom.' The Village nevertheless had a good effect in a bad example. It was an eye-opener for 'the artist who wished to begin with his own reality.' Nobody could 'mistake Tenth Street for an aesthetic creation.' The artists' block with its liquor shops, its poolroom and metal-stamping factory was identical 'with rotting side streets in Chicago, Detroit and Boston.'" As SB puts it: "the setting chosen by the artist did reflect his conception of art. Simple location was unimportant. In a business society of advanced technology the artist must not expect to draw strength from an 'art-life'" (Rosenberg, Maser, and SB, *Abstract Impressionism—A Tribute*, pp. 10–11).

103. SB, foreword to Shechner, ed., *Preserving the Hunger*, p. 23.

104. Though in a letter of 6 October 1965 SB seems willing to revive it, professing to be "dying to know what your fifth career will be—I'm not in a position to tease you about marriages [there were three], for perfectly obvious reasons." After a period in the Village, Bazelon went to Yale Law School, became a corporate attorney in New York, worked briefly as a writer and interviewer for ABC television, taught law at Rutgers, then English and policy studies at SUNY Buffalo.

105. Manea, "Conversation," p. 37.

106. These statistics come from http://www.usmm.org/casualty.html, which also states, in a revised posting of 26 August 2006, that "mariners suffered the highest rate of casualties of any service in World War II, but unfortunately, the U.S. Merchant Marine has no official historians and researchers, thus casualty statistics vary." The figures supplied by the site are drawn from U.S. Coast Guard records, www.USMM.org; and Arthur R. Moore, *A Careless Word—A Needless Sinking: A History of the Staggering Losses Suffered by the U.S. Merchant Marine, Both in Ships and Personnel, During World War II* (Kings Points, NY: American Merchant Marine Museum, 1998).

107. Botsford interview, "A Half Life," SB, *IAAU*, p. 309.

108. SB, in Atlas, *Biography*, p. 105.

109. SB, in ibid., p. 109.

110. From an undated letter of condolence of 1945 (over the death of Freifeld's father), printed in Taylor, ed., *Letters*, pp. 39–40.

111. Atlas, *Biography*, p. 108.

112. Information about Arthur Lidov and his relations with SB in the 1940s and 1950s comes from Alexandra Lidov in emails to the author (28 August 2010 and 24 September 2010).

113. Richard M. Cook, *Alfred Kazin: A Biography* (New Haven: Yale University Press, 2008), p. 109.

114. Ibid. According to Alexandra Lidov, Kazin lived at 91 Pineapple Street at the time of SB's initial meeting with Lidov, but in a different apartment.

115. Atlas, *Biography*, p. 108.

116. Where SB stayed in New York before the Lidovs' invitation to join them in Patterson is unclear, perhaps with the Rosenfelds, perhaps with David Bazelon. Also unclear is the Lidovs' financial situation at the end of 1945: Atlas describes them at this period as "so poor that whenever Arthur got paid by a magazine, Victoria drove the seventy miles to New York to pick up the check instead of waiting for it to arrive in the mail" (*Biography*, p. 108); Cook describes them as "suddenly in the money" (*Alfred Kazin: A Biography*, p. 109) because of what Alexandra Lidov calls "a quite spectacular entry into illustration."

117. Krueger had been the Socialist Party candidate for vice president under Norman Thomas in 1940.

118. Kazin, *New York Jew*, p. 150; the harsh journal descriptions of Lidov come from an entry in Kazin's Journals of 15 March 1983 (memories occasioned by Kazin's chance meeting with Lidov's first wife, Victoria, in a Chinese restaurant in

New York). This entry is not included in Cook's selection of *Alfred Kazin's Journals* but he kindly supplied me with a transcript. The original can be consulted in the Berg Collection of the New York Public Library.

119. According to Daniel Fuchs, *Saul Bellow: Vision and Revision*, p. 65.

120. Kazin, reporting SB's question and astonishment, in *New York Jew*, p. 65.

121. "The war had just ended," SB recalled in a letter of 5 October 1998 to Steve Hare, who was researching the history of Penguin Books: "I was trying to write *The Victim*, my second novel, and I did all kinds of jobs to feed my sheep and stay alive myself."

122. SB's quotations come from the transcript of remarks made on 15 October 1985 at the Whiting Foundation Writers' Program Ceremony (see note 29 above).

123. See John Barrell, *The Infection of Thomas De Quincey: A Psychopathology of Imperialism* (New Haven: Yale University Press, 1991); and Nigel Leask, *British Romantic Writers and the East: Anxieties of Empire* (Cambridge: Cambridge University Press, 1992).

124. The sickly atmospherics of the city are also picked up in "the blink of the yellow light" of an approaching bus (after which "an eddy of exhaust gas caught him in the face") (p. 262), and in the harbor at night, "the crimson and yellow spots hung from the cranes and hulls swinging between the slip and the incandescent low crust of the shore" (p. 268).

125. Though young Charlie Citrine in *Humboldt* mentions nothing of Schopenhauer when he arrives for the first time in New York in 1938, he does allude to Nietzsche (and Shelley in Platonic mode). Charlie was then "a person keenly aware of painted veils, of Maya, of domes of many-coloured glass staining the white radiance of eternity, quivering in the intense inane and so on. I was a nut about such things" (p. 6).

126. For an early example of such esteem, see SB to Mel Tumin, October 1942 [according to a penciled scrawl at its head, perhaps by SB]: "The East was a good thing for me. I went around receiving my accolades. It was such a relief to come out of the Chicago basin where two or three friends had made me subsist on their estimates and to find in the larger world of New York that I was regarded as an up-and-comer. Bertram D. Wolf said my story ["The Mexican General"] was one of the finest he had ever seen an American writer do on Mexico. Clement Greenberg said . . . I don't want to quote all these testimonials myself, it would seem like such self-gilding. I will simply name the names: Mary McCarthy, Nigel Denis, Alfred Kazin, ad regurgitam."

8. MINNEAPOLIS

1. Shortly after the war ended, Freifeld was sent overseas as a criminal investigator, first in Berlin, then in England, where he was discharged in February 1946. These and other details of his war service come from his daughter, Judith Ward, in an email of 17 March 2012.

2. At the same time, as we shall see, as he treated SB's second wife.

3. SB's objections to McClosky's empirical or "scientific" psychology were related to comparable objections to the findings of anthropology and sociology: "I listen to them [sociologists] here," he writes in a letter of 21 April 1948 to Mel Tumin, himself a sociologist, "with every effort to be fair and understanding but I can't make out their Man. Surely that's not *homo sapiens, mon semblable!* The creature the theologians write about is far closer to me."

4. For McWilliams and anti-Semitism in Minneapolis, see Max Kampelman, *Entering New Worlds: The Memoirs of a Private Man in Public Life* (New York: HarperCollins, 1991), p. 64.

5. See Chapter 6, note 84, on the question of where SB and Tumin first met.

6. A rationale for the Humanities Program is provided by its cofounder, Alburey Castell, in "The Humanities in the Modern World," the first of three lectures delivered to the Machette Foundation, Purdue University, March 1948. The printed version of the first lecture is fifteen pages long, followed by an outline of Humanities I, II, and III. The topics and texts discussed are worth enumerating, since SB would be thinking about and teaching them, at least some of them, while at Minnesota. In Humanities I they were "God and the World" (Voltaire, *Candide*; Paine, *The Age of Reason, Part 1*; Goethe, *Faust, Part I*; Durant, *Story of Philosophy*, Chapters 5–7; "Man in Society" (Rousseau, *The Social Contract*, Parts I and II; Burke, *Reflections on the Revolution in France*; Tolstoy, *War and Peace*; Becker, *Modern History*, Chapters 6–9); "Poetry and Art" (no texts specified). In Humanities II they were "Industrial Revolution" (Carlyle, *Past and Present*; Marx and Engels, *The Communist Manifesto*; Zola, *Germinal*; Becker, *Modern History*, Chapters 16–19); "Liberalism" (Mill, *On Liberty*; Ibsen, *A Doll's House and Other Plays*; Dostoyevsky, *The Brothers Karamazov*); "Poetry and Art" (no texts specified). In Humanities III the topics and texts were "The Impact of Science" (Thomas Huxley, *Agnosticism and Christianity and Other Essays*; Turgenev, *Fathers and Sons*; Arnold, *Literature and Science and Other Essays*; Bury, *History of Freedom of Thought*, Chapters 6–8); "Civilization on Trial" (Nietzsche, *Thus Spake Zarathustra*; Shaw, *Major Barbara* and *Back to Methuselah*; Mann, *The Magic Mountain*; Durant, *Story of Philosophy*, Chapters 8–9); and "Poetry and Art" (no texts specified).

7. For these and other statistics and facts about the University of Minnesota in 1946–48, see Stanford Lehmberg and Ann M. Pflaum, *The University of Minnesota, 1945–2000* (Minneapolis: University of Minnesota Press, 2001), pp. 4–30.

8. Atlas, *Biography*, p. 115. Warren, a professor in the Department of English at Minnesota, was on leave from the university; SB had met him before his appointment.

9. Email, 25 November 2009.

10. Atlas, *Biography*, pp. 115–16.

11. Ibid., p. 115.

12. SB to Robert Penn Warren, 17 November 1947, excerpted in Taylor, ed., *Letters*, p. 45.

13. Atlas, *Biography*, pp. 114–15; Unger's comment is on p. 115.

14. Ibid., p. 116.

15. For Beach and Warren on Beach, see Joseph Blotner, *Robert Penn Warren: A Biography* (New York: Random House, 1997), p. 202.

16. Ibid.

17. See SB to Bazelon, 22 November 1946: "*Gott sei dank, The Victim* is in the penultimate stage. Only the epilogue remains to be written."

18. This second part of Sartre's book—extended essay, really—focuses on the "Jew" rather than the "anti-Semite" and was even more controversial than the first, prompting immediate responses from Sidney Hook and Harold Rosenberg. Both were exercised by Sartre's claim that the Jewish people "have no history. The sole tie that binds them is the hostility and disdain of the societies which surround them" (*Anti-Semite and Jew*, tr. George J. Becker [1948; New York: Schocken, 1965], p. 91). In SB's words, "for Sartre, the Jew exists because he is hated, not because he has a history, not because he has origins of his own—but simply because he is designated, created, in his Jewishness by an outrageous evil" (quoted in Gordon Lloyd Harper, "The Art of Fiction: Saul Bellow," *Paris Review* 9, no. 36 [1966], reprinted in Cronin and Siegel, eds., *Conversations with SB*, p. 74). Excerpts from *Anti-Semite and Jew* appear in *Commentary* in 1948 in the issues of April ("The Situation of the Jew"), May ("Portrait of an Inauthentic Jew"), and June ("Gentile and Jew").

19. Lional Abel, *The Intellectual Follies: A Memoir of the Literary Venture in New York and Paris* (New York: W. W. Norton, 1984), p. 73.

20. Irving Howe, *A Margin of Hope: An Intellectual Autobiography* (New York: Harcourt Brace Jovanovich, 1982), p. 254.

21. Sartre, *Anti-Semite and Jew*, p. 48.

22. Manea, "Conversation," p. 15.

23. SB, "Zetland: By a Character Witness," first printed in Philip Rahv, ed., *Modern Occasions* 2 (1974), reprinted in SB, *CS*, p. 243.

24. Greg Bellow, "Anita Goshkin Bellow Busacca—A Biographic Sketch," a fourteen-page memoir of his mother written in 2007 and deposited among SB's papers in the Regenstein. The quotation from Mitzi McClosky is on p. 5.

25. SB, "A Father-to-Be," first published in *The New Yorker*, 5 February 1955, reprinted in *Mosby's Memoirs and Other Stories* (1968; Harmondsworth: Penguin, 1977), p. 145 (henceforth cited within the text by page numbers).

26. Men and women can also be comic and pathetic at the same time, as in the following exchange in *Humboldt's Gift* between Charlie and Renata:

> I once suggested to her, "A woman like you can be called a dumb broad only if Being and Knowledge are entirely separate. But if Being is also a form of Knowledge, one's own Being is one's own accomplishment in some degree . . ."
> "Then I'm not a dumb broad after all. I can't be, if I'm so beautiful. That's super! You've always been kind to me, Charlie."
> "Because I really love you, kid" (p. 394).

27. For SB on female rather than male offspring, see his letter of 18 December 1948 to J. F. Powers: "Congratulations on the baby. It's an excellent thing to have daughters, once one has accepted fatherhood in principle, and to be spared the Oedipal struggle. Sons don't light your cigar and bring your slippers."

28. SB to David Bazelon, undated letter of 1947.

29. SPAN website: www.minnesotaspan.org/history.

30. According to Atlas, *Biography*, p. 119, presumably recounting memories from SB himself and/or the McCloskys, SB spent much of his time "languishing queasily in a deck chair reading the galleys of his novel. The task bored him so much that he muttered about throwing them overboard." In my interviews with Mitzi McClosky, however, she insisted that SB did not read proofs until the journey home.

31. Atlas, *Biography*, p. 120.

32. Botsford interview, "A Half Life," SB, *IAAU*, p. 311.

33. Ibid.

34. For Atlas's reference to the "blonde, buxom girl," see *Biography*, p. 121; all SB quotations, aside from the one from the "Spanish Letter," are from the Botsford interview, "A Half Life," SB, *IAAU*, p. 311.

35. Botsford interview, "A Half Life," SB, *IAAU*, p. 311.

36. Ibid.

37. Atlas, *Biography*, p. 123.

38. SB, "The Gonzaga Manuscripts," first published in *Discovery 4* (New York: Pocket Books, 1954), reprinted in *Mosby's Memoirs and Other Stories*, p. 122 (henceforth cited within the text by page numbers).

39. Atlas, *Biography*, p. 123.

40. The Trilling quotation about *The Plenipotentiaries* is taken from the dust jacket of *The Spirit and the Bride*.

41. From a transcript of four radio conversations between Kappy and Philippe Meyer broadcast on France Culture on 27, 28, 29, and 30 October 2009 under the title "Un américain peu ordinaire," in a translation by Roger Kaplan, Kappy's son. An edited version of these conversations appeared in the French periodical *Commentaire* nos. 129 and 130 (printemps et été, 2010) under the titles "Conversations

avec le vieil Harold (I) and (II)." When quoting from the interviews I provide page numbers from the Roger Kaplan translation. This particular quotation comes from p. 14; see also p. 429 of part two of the *Commentaire* version.

42. Though SB did not share Siegelman's view of Sam Monk, he did, it seems, share his view of Huntington Brown, Robert Penn Warren's affection for Brown notwithstanding. See SB to David Bazelon, 10 April 1949: "Yah, I'll write to Huntington Brown for you. I hope it does you good, for Huntington and I had difficult times with each other. He's the archetype of the learned idiot. He's a Harvard Ph.d., conservative to the flap of his long underwear, collects pornographic poetry, has a pistol range in his basement, knows how to mend a dog sled in driving snow and is an Admiral Peary *manqué*, is president of the burial society of Minneapolis and takes vitamin B1 all summer long on the belief that mosquitos will not bite a man whose perspiration is saturated with it. And that's not all."

43. After 1948 McGehee returned to the South and published an excerpt from a novel in progress in *Partisan Review* (April 1949). As SB explained in a letter of 30 March 1949 to the novelist J. F. Powers, McGehee "was planning to return to Minnesota [for the academic year 1948–49], but didn't quite fit into the budget, which was unexpectedly cut." He had almost finished his novel and was about to send it to an agent. The excerpt of the novel was titled "The Photograph's If." The novel from which it was taken was called "Face to Face" and seems never to have been published. It was set in the South before the Civil War. In an undated letter to Robert Hivnor, a playwright and professor of theater at Minnesota, written early in 1950, SB says that "McGehee writes occasionally, terribly depressed about Southern (American) mentality. . . . Also he says that Leiper had a sort of heart attack and has been very ill." McGehee and Leiper were in Paris in the autumn of 1948 and the Bellows saw them shortly after arrival. In a letter of 25 October to Henry Volkening, SB praised the manuscript of McGehee's novel as "very unusually good," while also reporting that his interview with Diarmuid Russell had gone badly and that he was "rather angry with Russell." According to Greg Bellow (in an email of 17 July 2012), the Bellows ran into Leiper on the street one day quite unexpectedly. Greg is uncertain whether the meeting occurred at the beginning of the family's stay in Paris or later. Leiper told them that his French was so poor that the only thing he could order in restaurants was "côte de porc." In 1950, Leiper wrote a story called "The Magnolias," which took second prize in the O. Henry Short Story competition and was later published in *The Atlantic Monthly*. According to Robert Penn Warren, in a letter to Paul Engle, 21 July 1950, in Randy Hendricks and James A. Perkins, eds., *Selected Letters of Robert Penn Warren*, 6 vols. (Baton Rouge: Louisiana State University Press, 2006), 3:364, Leiper was in 1950 living in Blauvelt, New York, working on a novel on a Eugene F. Saxton Memorial Fellowship (an award associated with Harper and Row). At some point he abandoned fiction, returned to the South, and became general manager of the Chamber of Commerce in Gatlinburg City, Tennessee, his hometown, later writing a history of the city's Christus Gardens.

44. Greg Bellow, "Biographic Sketch," p. 6.

45. SB to Henry Volkening, in an undated letter, in Taylor, ed., *Letters*, p. 48.

46. Atlas, *Biography*, p. 130. According to Mitzi McClosky, Kampelman's linking of McClosky and SB is misleading: "Herb was a 'culinary' and Jewish-joke-telling Jew, whereas Saul was deeply versed in Jewish history and religion. He taught us both about Judaism, and to me, he came off as the voice of the Prophets themselves. From him I learned to be proud of my heritage."

47. SB to David Bazelon, 8 March 1948.

48. Manea, "Conversation," p. 33.

49. Atlas, *Biography*, p. 131. See also an undated spring 1948 letter from SB to Henry Volkening beginning "Thanks for your note": "I'm teaching, not too

conscientiously, three courses and though I have assistants (two of them) to grade papers I cannot rule from afar. My presence is indispensable." He seems to have been more engaged, or more interested, with the creative writing students (see another, later undated letter to Volkening that begins: "How am I? In the real world walking a sober path with the schizophrenics wheeling round me like pigeons round a breeder. I'm speaking of my students, my clients, my patients, my putative writers, and I mean to say that I'm happy and thriving. . . . I leave here on Saturday and will be in Chicago until August 7th or 8th").

50. In "I Got a Scheme!," p. 72, SB says: "I got a Guggenheim, thanks to Jim Farrell." Farrell wrote on his behalf in two earlier Guggenheim applications, but his name does not appear as a referee on the third application, nor does a third reference survive in the Guggenheim files, nor does SB refer to such a reference in his letters from the period, to Farrell or anyone else.

51. Diana Trilling's review appeared in her "Fiction Review" in *The Nation*, 3 January 1948. I have been unable to trace the *New Leader* article. A second regret SB had about his *New Leader* article concerned R. P. Blackmur, who, he was told by Bazelon, "thinks well of me. . . . I had it in mind to exempt him personally [from the article's negative remarks about critics], for I really learned a great deal from *The Double Agent* and *The Expense of Greatness*" (SB to Tumin, undated letter, in Taylor, ed., *Letters*, p. 53). I have been unable to trace the *New Leader* article.

52. SB to David Bazelon, 1 December 1947; the undated SB letter to James Henle is quoted in Atlas, *Biography*, p. 130; the *New York Times* review was by Charles Poore, "Books of the Times," 22 November 1947; the anonymous *Time* magazine review, "Suffering for Nothing," appeared in the issue of 1 December 1947.

53. In Taylor, ed., *Letters*, p. 50; the letter is said to be undated.

54. These passages, extracted from the unsent letter to Henle, are included in SB to Henry Volkening, received 9 January 1948.

55. This quotation is also from the 9 January 1948 letter. In an earlier, undated letter to Volkening (it begins "Thank the Lord, we're off"), SB reported that Ed McGehee had recently visited Chicago and couldn't find *The Victim* "in *any* Loop bookstore," despite the fact that "Guy Henle had been through less than a month ago on his semiannual selling trip. The distributor for the area didn't have a copy in the warehouse." See also SB to Volkening, in another undated letter, in Taylor, ed., *Letters*, p. 58: "I got a jog today from some friends in Philadelphia who couldn't obtain *The Victim*. They wrote to friends in Passaic, and they couldn't get it. The results in Rochester were no better."

56. SB to Volkening, received 9 January 1948.

57. SB to Henry Volkening, 18 February 1948.

58. This is from the undated letter to Volkening beginning "Thank the Lord, we're off" (see note 55).

59. SB to David Bazelon, 8 March 1948.

60. SB to Henry Volkening, April 1948; in an earlier undated letter to Volkening, SB writes that "in the last two weeks I've had feelers from Random, Whittlesey and Harper's and have replied honorably to all that I am pledged, betrothed. Promised and bound and indentured to Vanguard. It's not, however, a joking matter" (the letter begins, "No, I never again heard from Auerbach").

61. The letter is undated.

62. SB to Henry Volkening, undated; the letter begins "Henle has released me."

63. Ibid. See also SB to Volkening, April 1948: "I know you favor my staying with Vanguard. At least you don't want to be the instrument of divorce. But I can't see why I should stay. I think I'd be better off with another house."

64. Harriet Wasserman, *Handsome Is: Adventures with Saul Bellow: A Memoir* (New York: Fromm International, 1997), p. 17.

65. See Henry Volkening, "Tom Wolfe: Penance No More," *Virginia Quarterly Review* (Spring 1939): 196–215.

66. Michael Kreyling, *Agent and Author: Eudora Welty and Diarmuid Russell* (New York: Farrar, Straus & Giroux, 1992), p. 46. Volkening represented Ellison from 1943 to 1951, shortly after Ellison submitted the manuscript of *Invisible Man*. Ellison's split with Volkening puzzles his biographer, Arnold Rampersad: "Though over the years Ralph had given Volkening very little to sell, Ralph clearly believed that his agent didn't deserve a cut of his royalties. For some reason he was unhappy about the way Volkening had treated him during his years in the wilderness. Volkening . . . settled with Random House, although he knew he could have prevailed over Ralph in almost any court of law. After a pleasant lunch with Albert Erskine [of Random House], he let Ralph know that 'we hereby relinquish all rights and interests' in [*Invisible Man*]. It was an 'amicable release'" (*Ralph Ellison: A Biography* [New York: Alfred A. Knopf, 2007], p. 256).

67. Wasserman, *Handsome Is*, p. 101.

68. See note 62.

69. SB to Henry Volkening, undated. The letter begins "I have your fascinating letter."

70. SB to Frank Taylor, 5 July 1948. Atlas, *Biography*, p. 136, reads what looks to me like "intuitions" (the letter is handwritten) as "instructions," and sees the letter as characteristic in trying to evade responsibility.

71. SB to Melvin Tumin, undated, in Taylor, ed., *Letters*, p. 59.

72. The novella's title comes from the Schiller ballad "The Diver" ("Der Taucher") (1797), "*Es freue sich, / Wer da atmet im rosigten Licht*" (lines 91–92); the English translation is that given in SB to David Bazelon, 5 January 1948. The story is "about the *amor fati*, the vein of enjoyment that runs through our deepest suffering, and it centers about a man who is rotting to death in a hospital room. His stink offends the other patients. The hero of the story defends him because nothing is, for him, more valuable than life or more sacred than the struggle to remain alive."

73. The undated letter to Volkening, with the reference to "25,000 words," begins "Thank the Lord, we're off."

74. For this quotation from *Ecce Homo*, see Walter Kaufmann, ed. and trans., *Basic Writings of Nietzsche* (New York: Modern Library, 1967), p. 714.

75. SB, "The Trip to Galena," *Partisan Review* (November–December 1950), p. 779 (henceforth cited within the text by page numbers). Atlas, *Biography*, p. 143, refers to Scampi as Weyl's "bedridden neighbor," but the story is set, we are told on its first page, "here on the fire escape of the sixth floor of the hospital where this young Weyl had brought him [i.e., Scampi]" (p. 779).

76. "I Got a Scheme!," p. 74.

77. SB to Melvin Tumin, undated letter, in Taylor, ed., *Letters*, p. 59.

78. Atlas, *Biography*, p. 149.

79. Ibid. The letter begins "Dearest Betty—You'll be wondering why I'm writing now and why I haven't written earlier." If SB had simply wanted to drop Betty, felt no "chemistry of the soul," he wouldn't have written at all.

9. PARIS

1. "I Got a Scheme!," p. 72.

2. His fictional equivalent, Ryehurst in *The Adventures of Augie March* (1953), p. 976, an "old crook of a Britisher," has an even more peculiar suit, "like for burial, purple flannel without lapels or buttons or buttonholes."

3. SB, "The French as Dostoyevsky Saw Them," foreword to Fyodor M. Dostoyevsky, *Winter Notes on Summer Impressions* (New York: Criterion, 1955); first published in *The New Republic*, 23 May 1955, SB, *IAAU*, p. 38.

4. See SB to Monroe Engel, 25 October 1948: "I don't get out very often now and when I think of it resent this voluntary encapsulation and damn writing as an occupation."

5. Janet Flanner, *Paris Journal, 1944–1965*, ed. William Shawn (New York: Atheneum, 1965), pp. 95–96.

6. Ibid., entries of 23 June and 26 May, 1948, pp. 91, 86.

7. "I Got a Scheme!," p. 74. In "My Paris," originally printed in *The New York Times Magazine*, Part 2, *The Sophisticated Traveler*, 13 March 1983, reprinted in SB, *IAAU*, p. 234, SB writes of Americans who came to Paris with "schemes for getting rich." One friend, a young man from Minnesota, "came over to open a caramel-corn factory in Florence," the obvious inspiration for a character in an unfinished and undated SB story titled "Nothing Succeeds." The story exists in a typed manuscript of eighteen pages, is set in Paris in 1948, and concerns the narrator's cousin, Sam Hammersmark, from Minnesota, who attempts to enlist a friend, Herbie Shaffer, in "a scheme to go into the caramel-corn business on the Riviera" (p. 7). Herbie, another business schemer, spends his time "with black-market types" (p. 2). He wants the narrator to get him gasoline ration stamps, as they fetch "fancy prices on the black market, bringing the value of your dollar to six hundred plus" (p. 17). Herbie and his wife, Violet, a student of twelve-tone music and Erik Satie, came to Paris in 1947 loaded with "nylons, cigarette lighters, and other marketable items, the tinier the better." These they purchased by liquidating all their assets in the United States except Herbie's Marxist library, "which was in storage" (p. 12). Having been a lifelong reader of Marx and Lenin, Herbie claims, "gave him superior business powers" (p. 14). Herbie is clearly the model for the hapless Lustgarten in "Mosby's Memoirs" (and, more distantly, for Nachman in *Herzog*), archetypal *schlemiels*.

8. SB, "The French as Dostoyevsky Saw Them," SB, *IAAU*, pp. 38–39.

9. SB to Jane Vogel, 25 January 1984.

10. SB, "The French as Dostoyevsky Saw Them," SB, *IAAU*, p. 38.

11. SB, "My Paris," SB, *IAAU*, p. 231.

12. Atlas, *Biography*, p. 139.

13. See SB to Henry Volkening, 25 October 1948: "something tells me my real affinity is for Italy." The remark about having several novels in mind comes from this letter. Rome, SB declared in a letter to David Bazelon of 25 January 1949, was "magnificent," though the spaghetti was better "at Eddie's Aurora of W. 4th St."

14. In "How I Wrote Augie March's Story," *New York Times Book Review*, 31 January 1954, SB recalls that "across the street pneumatic drills were at work on the concrete of a hospital whose construction had been abandoned at the outbreak of the war."

15. This quotation comes from page 12 of "Paris, France: The Autobiography of HJK," a copy of which I was given by Kappy shortly before his death in 2011. The work exists in a typed manuscript of 166 pages and is unfinished (henceforth cited as "Autobiography").

16. Ibid., pp. 131, 4.

17. Or so Kappy claims in ibid., p. 59. Barrett's review dealt with all of Sartre's work, not just *Being and Nothingness*, and was particularly harsh on what he described as Sartre's "naïve" assessment of the role of the Soviet Union and the French Communist Party. If Kappy was a CIA agent, he does not appear in Frances Stonor Saunders's *Who Paid the Piper? The CIA and the Cultural Cold War* (1999; London: Granta, 2000), which devotes several chapters to CIA-funded and -inspired propaganda efforts in postwar Paris, naming not only agents but writers and intellectuals who knew of or suspected CIA involvement.

18. Biographical information about Kappy comes from interviews with the author; also from a transcript of four radio conversations between Kappy and

Philippe Meyer broadcast on France Culture on 27, 28, 29, and 30 October 2009 under the title "Un américain peu ordinaire," in a translation by Roger Kaplan, Kappy's son. An edited version of these conversations appeared in the French periodical *Commentaire* nos. 129 and 130 (printemps et été, 2010), under the titles "Conversations avec le vieil Harold (I) and (II)." When quoting from these interviews I provide page numbers from the Roger Kaplan translation.

19. Kappy interview with Philippe Meyer, pp. 45, 15.

20. Ibid., p. 53.

21. Rousset became a friend of Kappy's and Kappy "watched him, a skeleton, just back from Buchenwald in 1945, become David Rousset, a plethoric jolly fat man" ("Autobiography," p. 98).

22. In an interview, Kappy identified his Jewishness as a major source of his anti-Communism, in terms that recall Rousset on the kapos of Buchenwald: "I was affronted by the fact that so much of the Soviet leadership was Jewish, so much of their leadership in all of Eastern Europe was Jewish, until Stalin himself became anti-Semitic and began to purge all that. . . . There was an element, I realized later, of saying that's sort of the last indignity to be visited upon the Jewish people, to be associated with this hideous, hideous regime. I was a great admirer of Mr. Conquest [Robert Conquest, author of *The Great Terror*, 1964, among other studies of Soviet history and politics] and all the research he did, even before the archives were open."

23. SB, "The French as Dostoyevsky Saw Them," SB, *IAAU*, p. 39. According to Kappy, "Autobiography," p. 7, writing of the late 1940s, "from early November to mid-March you practically never saw the sun."

24. SB, "The French as Dostoyevsky Saw Them," SB, *IAAU*, p. 41.

25. Ibid., p. 39.

26. Ibid., p. 41. SB's friend Herbert Gold in "Notes from La Vie Bohème (Avec Tout Confort)," *Hudson Review* 5, no. 2 (Summer 1952): 262, is good on these matters. He attributes the French reluctance to invite Americans into their homes as in part a matter of money ("almost all families are aware of decline within their lifetimes, and the process of gradual impoverishment has been a condition of bourgeois life"), in part a symptom of the Parisian's traditional "separation of family life from the life connected with his work *en ville*, his impulse to keep his wife unsullied by contact with his friends, his desire to master his family and to guard its purity. . . . Skepticism about the possibility of monogamy associates itself with an assumption all the more stern concerning the sanctity of the home."

27. SB, "The French as Dostoyevsky Saw Them," SB, *IAAU*, pp. 41–42. SB means Etienne Cabet, the philosopher and Utopian sociologist, not Sebastien Cabet.

28. In "My Paris," SB, *IAAU*, p. 238, SB writes: "Paris, which had been a center, still *looked* like a center and could not bring itself to concede that it was a center no longer."

29. Ibid., p. 234. See also SB to Henry Volkening, 13 April 1949, on "The Crab and the Butterfly": "it's certainly full of astonishing things—I mean things that astonish me. I'm hunting for point of view with a long gun and shoot at anything that moves, especially Henry James." Madame Vionnet is the sophisticated French hostess in *The Ambassadors*.

30. Flanner, *Paris Journal*, entry of 23 June 1948, p. 92. In "My Paris," SB, *IAAU*, p. 234, the equivalent of what Flanner calls the "tourist intelligentsia" is described by SB as made up of "travelers, poets, painters, and philosophers . . . students of art history, cathedral lovers, refugees from the South and the Midwest."

31. SB, "My Paris," SB, *IAAU*, p. 235. Lionel Abel makes a similar point in his *Partisan Review* "Paris Letter" of April 1949: "It is often said in New York: Well, all this talk of intellectual life in France is bunk. What have the French produced

after all, that is, in recent years? The best things they have done have been translated, and are not so hot. . . . Here I think my friends in America miss the point, and quite characteristically. What makes for a living intellectual milieu is not the continuous production of masterpieces . . . but the readiness to give expression to a persistent intellectual curiosity" (p. 399).

32. SB, "Writers, Intellectuals, Politics: Mainly Reminiscence," originally printed in *The National Interest*, Spring 1993, reprinted in SB, *IAAU*, p. 106.

33. Ibid., p. 106. SB's view of Sartre's philosophical antecedents, not just Husserl but Heidegger, is like Sidney Hook's, in "Reflections on the Jewish Question," a review of *Anti-Semite and Jew* in the May 1949 issue of *Partisan Review*. In the review Hook argues that the true democrat "only wants to destroy those individuals and social institutions which seek to deprive human beings of their power of uncoerced choice. That is what is perennially valid in the liberating ideas of the French and Anglo-American Enlightenment which Sartre has renounced for a noisome mess of Heideggarian anguish and neo-Marxist historicism" (p. 482).

34. The "Report on the International Day Against Dictatorship and War" begins with an account of the International Day's origins: "The idea of the International Day of Resistance to Dictatorship and War, held in Paris on April 30, 1949 was suggested to David Rousset, its chief initiator, by the meeting conducted in Freedom House in New York City on March 26, by Americans for Intellectual Freedom" (p. 722). See also William Phillips, *A Partisan View: Five Decades of the Literary Life* (New York: Stein & Day, 1983), pp. 147–49, on the origins of two organizations with which SB would become peripherally involved, the American Committee for Cultural Freedom and the Congress for Cultural Freedom: "It all started with the staging of a peace conference of writers and some people from the other arts at the Waldorf in April 1949. The auspices and most of the participants were pro-Communist, with official delegates and speakers from the Soviet Union. . . . There were three thousand delegates, but the meeting was totally controlled by the Communists. . . . To counter this big circus for peace and Communist propaganda, a number of writers, including myself, hastily organized another group, called Americans for Intellectual Freedom [the nucleus for the American Committee for Cultural Freedom], which operated from a suite at the Waldorf, to expose the true character and false claims of the Peace Conference. . . . The leading figure, non-elected but by common consent, was Sidney Hook." For the role played by the CIA in funding and inspiring anti-Communist efforts such as the American Committee for Cultural Freedom, the International Day of Resistance to Dictatorship and War, and the Congress for Cultural Freedom see Frances Stonor Saunders, *Who Paid the Piper?*, in particular Chapters 4 and 5.

35. Janet Flanner, in an 11 January 1950 entry in her *Paris Journal*, quotes an article in *Le Monde* about the evils of Coca-Cola: "What the French criticize is less Coca-Cola than its orchestration, is less the drink itself than the civilization, the style of life of which it is a sign and in a certain sense a symbol. For the implanting of Coca-Cola in a country is generally accompanied by advertising in the American manner, with red delivery trucks promenading publicity, neon lights, and walls covered with signs, placards, and advertisements. . . . It is now a question of the whole panorama and morale of French civilization" (p. 118).

36. Botsford interview, "A Half Life," reprinted in SB, *IAAU*, pp. 309, 308.

37. Phillips, *A Partisan View*, lays out the differences between the American Committee for Cultural Freedom and the Congress for Cultural Freedom. The chief difference was that the American Committee had no CIA funding. In both groups, hard-line anti-Communists predominated; both were critical of Senator McCarthy, contrary to the "various charges that have been made by people who have not been disinterested" (p. 151). It was the secrecy of the funding that mattered most: "the essence of work in culture and the arts is that it must be open and

freewheeling. Hidden financing means hidden control, despite any denials about pressure or censorship" (p. 156). In "The CIA and the Intellectuals," an influential article of 20 April 1967 in *The New York Review of Books*, Jason Epstein elaborates: what the the CIA funding created, through the Ford Foundation and other ostensibly independent funding agencies, was

> An apparatus of intellectuals selected for their correct cold-war positions, as an alternative to what one might call a free intellectual market where ideology was presumed to count for less than individual talent and achievement, and where doubts about established orthodoxies were taken to be the beginning of all inquiry. . . . It was not a matter of buying off and subverting individual writers and scholars, but of setting up an arbitrary and factitious system of values by which academic personnel were advanced, magazine editors appointed, and scholars subsidized and published, not necessarily on their merits, though these were sometimes considerable, but because of their allegiances.

Saunders, *Who Paid the Piper?*, pp. 151, 201–3, discusses the relations of the CIA and its affiliates to the American Congress for Cultural Freedom in terms of supervision or oversight rather than funding.

38. SB. "Writers, Intellectuals, Politics: Mainly Reminiscence," SB, *IAAU*, p. 109.

39. For accounts of the politics surrounding the Europe-America Groups, see Richard M. Cook, *Alfred Kazin: A Biography* (New Haven: Yale University Press, 2007), p. 131; and Carol Brightman, *Writing Dangerously: Mary McCarthy and Her World* (1992; London: Secker & Warburg, 1993), pp. 303–7.

40. Flanner, *Paris Journal*, p. 98.

41. "I Got a Scheme!," p. 74.

42. Kim Wilshire, "Hollande Sorry for Wartime Deportation of Jews," *Guardian*, 22 July 2012, an account of a speech given on 22 July 2012 by French president François Hollande to commemorate the seventieth anniversary of the Vél d'Hiv Rafle. Hollande's speech is reprinted and translated in *The New York Review of Books*, 27 September 2012. The figures given in the speech by President Hollande are different from those reported in the *Guardian* article: "Seventy-six thousand French Jews were deported to the death camps. Only 2,500 returned." Hollande states that "no German soldiers—not a single one—were mobilized at any stage of the operation. The truth is that this crime was committed in France, by France." SB never mentions the Rafle, but in an interview with Rockwell Gray, Harry White, and Gerald Nemanic in *TriQuarterly* 60 (1984), reprinted in Gloria L. Cronin and Ben Siegel, eds., *Conversations with SB*, p. 217, he remembers "in Paris in '48 and '49, being perfectly aware that the Nazis had just left. And I knew that when I took a deep breath I was inhaling the crematorium gases still circulating in the air."

43. SB, "My Paris," SB, *IAAU*, p. 235.

44. "I Got a Scheme!," p. 74. SB shared his gloomy thoughts with his friends. See Herbert Gold to SB, 24 November 1955, recounting a recent meeting with an executive at the publisher Little, Brown: "Meeting Arthur Thornhill, Senior, is an experience which comes closer than your walk with me in Paris to making me wish I had chosen some other life."

45. The reference to "signing up with the blacks" is puzzling, probably metaphorical. In the past, Weyl "sold black-market francs to tourists in front of the American Express in Nice" and "dealt in rationed gas, and I ran with the *voyous* [hoodlums] and Arabs, and so on" (p. 782); elsewhere, he is said to hang out with "Sheridan Road whores" (p. 786). Sister Fanny, before her Simon-like marriage for money, had been with a "black bookie's clerk" (p. 787). Perhaps the phrase means something like "walking on the wild side."

46. Manea "Conversation," p.14; the quotation from SB interview with Botsford, "A Half Life," SB, *IAAU*, occurs on p. 319. William Barrett, in *The Truants: Adventures Among the Intellectuals* (New York: Doubleday, 1982), p. 120, offers a suggestive account of the relation of Sartre's background, as sketched in *The Words* (1964), to his philosophy of personal freedom, including freedom from conventional morality: "His father died while he was an infant and thus remained unknown to him. Sartre therefore grew up, he tells us, without a superego; without that moral conscience that usually comes through the authoritarian figure of the father. And Sartre is exuberant in telling this about himself; he grew up more free and unencumbered than other young men he knew, who had to carry the burden of their fathers on their backs, like Aeneas lugging the aged Anchises from the ruins of Troy. In a sense, his whole philosophy, with its doctrine of unencumbered liberty, is the expression of a man without a superego; it pursues the notion of an absolute liberty not hedged by the ordinary restraints of human nature." Nothing, of course, could be further from SB's background.

47. SB, "My Paris," SB, *IAAU*, pp. 235–36.

48. Daniel Fuchs, *Saul Bellow: Vision and Revision* (Durham, NC: Duke University Press, 1984), p. 287.

49. "I Got a Scheme!," p. 74.

50. SB to Henry Volkening, undated.

51. SB, "My Paris," SB, *IAAU*, pp. 232, 236, 237.

52. In ibid., p. 233, SB unaccountably locates Le Rouquet on rue du Bac.

53. See SB to Oscar Tarcov, undated, in Taylor, ed., *Letters*, p. 90. Sigfried Giedion (1888–1968) was a Swiss historian and critic of architecture. *Mechanization Takes Command: A Contribution to Anonymous History* was published in 1948.

54. Flanner, *Paris Journal*, pp. 91–92.

55. As Laure Reichek remembers it, when the Marxes moved from 33 rue Vaneau, the Bellows took over their apartment. In "How I Wrote Augie March's Story," SB describes the apartment at 33 rue Vaneau as half of Mme Lemelle's apartment, and in an undated letter to Herb and Mitzi McClosky, Anita describes it as "three rooms and a kitchen in someone else's apartment, coal stoves—and a bathtub in the kitchen! We did have a beautiful apartment but we had to move." If Laure Reichek is correct, the Marxes, too, had previously shared the apartment with Mme Lemelle, which is hard to believe, as the Marxes had money. SB gave up his writing room at 33 rue Vaneau and "since I had by this time gotten used to writing away from home I found another room in the vicinity of St. Sulpice, a gloomy region of shops specializing in ecclesiastical goods." The new writing room was no more than five minutes south of the cafés of Saint-Germain.

56. For SB, "Nothing Succeeds," see note 7; this quotation is from pp. 4–5.

57. According to Laure Reichek, in an interview with the author.

58. See SB to Herb and Mitzi McClosky, 21 October 1949: "I've rented a room where my typewriter is less likely to be stolen and have set myself up in business once more." It is not clear where in number 33 this room was; whether it was in someone else's apartment or self-contained.

59. SB, "My Paris," SB, *IAAU*, p. 233. The comments about Mme Lemelle come from "How I Wrote Augie March's Story."

60. Phillips, *A Partisan View*, p. 195.

61. Barrett, *The Truants*, p. 90.

62. See SB to J. F. Powers, 18 December 1948.

63. "I Got a Scheme!," p. 79. These words appear also in SB, "How I Wrote Augie March's Story," where Caffi is called "Scaferlati" ("to protect his privacy") and where he is described when reading as "favoring his left eye" and "engaged in a study of heavy books at close range."

64. Lionel Abel, *The Intellectual Follies: A Memoir of the Literary Venture in New York and Paris* (New York: W. W. Norton, 1984), p. 177.

65. Ibid., p. 166.

66. "I Got a Scheme!," p. 80.

67. When SB and Abel knew Caffi, however, at the very end of the 1940s, he had taken to defending the pro-Communist line of Sartre and Merleau-Ponty in *Les Temps Modernes*, on the grounds that his formerly held views would "lead to nothing," "offered no plan for action or reform" (Abel, *Intellectual Follies*, p. 189).

68. Ibid., p. 183.

69. Ibid., p. 182.

70. "I Got a Scheme!," p. 79.

71. Anita's quotes come from an undated letter to Herbert and Mitzi McClosky; see also SB to Henry Volkening, 13 April 1949; Greg's memory of visiting the orphanage comes from page 7 of Greg Bellow, "Anita Goshkin Bellow Busacca—A Biographic Sketch," a fourteen-page memoir of his mother written by Greg in 2007 and deposited among SB's papers in the Regenstein.

72. Greg Bellow, "Biographic Sketch," p. 7.

73. See SB to John Lehmann, 12 December 1949, in which he writes of his plans for the visit.

74. Phillips, *A Partisan View*, p. 202.

75. Lehmann was also the editor of *Penguin New Writing*, which had recently published, in issue no. 38, SB's monologue "The Thoughts of Sergeant George Flavin."

76. SB to Robert Hivnor, undated, in Taylor, ed., *Letters*, p. 97.

77. See SB to Henry Volkening, 9 October 1949: "Just back from a recuperative visit in Spain." Anita reports in an undated letter to the Tarcovs, written sometime in 1949, having met Capote at a party at the Richard Wrights'.

78. This quotation comes from the undated letter to Hivnor in Taylor, ed., *Letters*, p. 97.

79. Phillips, *A Partisan View*, p. 201.

80. Herbert Gold, *Still Alive! A Temporary Condition: A Memoir* (New York: Arcade, 2008), pp. 204–5.

81. Ibid., 206. See also SB to Monroe Engel, 15 July 1950: "I know Gold well, and like him; some of his things that I've read, the most recent, are very good; the very last thing he sent me was well-nigh perfect. One of a series, he says, I believe he's going to call it *The Economic Life*. You ought to ask him for it."

82. These quotations come from interviews with the author. In an article entitled "Notes from La Vie Bohème (Avec Tout Confort)," in *The Hudson Review* 5, no. 2 (Summer 1952): 264, Gold offers the following portrait of an American expatriate couple: "The litterateur who uses his wife's mother's money to court poets and critics, fancying himself the poor student of Flaubert and Mallarmé but hiring a cook with a high cauliflower hat when he invites his aesthetic friends to dinner. This one, having been an American in Paris for four years, lives in a world of abstractions and gossip, culture and fierce incestuous rivalries with his local compatriots." According to W. J. Weatherby, *James Baldwin: Artist on Fire* (London: Michael Joseph, 1990), p. 78, Baldwin had the impression that SB disliked him: "Bellow was already an established novelist, but Baldwin's essays had established him in the American colony. Otto Friedrich recalled: 'I was touting Jimmy as a great writer in the Latin Quarter and various Jewish writers were touting Bellow. My hero is better than your hero! They were used as rivals.'"

83. For a slightly different print version of this exchange, see Gold, *Still Alive!*, pp. 226–27. When SB was biting about Baldwin it was about his conduct rather than his writing. See SB to David Bazelon, 10 April 1949: "There's Jimmy Bald-

win, for instance, who seems to be down and out and is sponging mercilessly. He hasn't applied his sponge to me yet. He doesn't do a great deal. Whenever I pass the Flore and the Deux Magots he's in company, drinking beer."

84. Greg Bellow, "Biographic Sketch," p. 7.

85. H. J. Kaplan, *The Plenipotentiaries* (New York: Harper Brothers, 1950), p. 19 (henceforth cited within the text by page numbers).

86. Strauss is described as "the most Parisian of foreigners, the prototype and founding father of the American-of-Paris!" (p. 154). He writes "chit-chat" for a magazine catering to expatriates and knows everything that's going on in the city. Although he is nonpolitical, when invited to a party attended by a well-known Communist poet, he refuses to go: "I've got to the point where I can no longer shake his hand. . . . It's a feeling of physical repulsion. . . . Like the feeling I had before the war, when I was invited to dine at the German Embassy. Does one ask a lamb chop to dine with a hyena?" (p. 58).

87. The episode recalls Feiler in SB's story "The Gonzaga Manuscripts," rebuked as if personally responsible for the atom bomb and carbon 14. Toward the end of the novel, Tony not only marvels at the powers the French attribute to him, but begins to see himself as possessed of these powers, by virtue of being seen as representatively American: "Full powers! How conceive a world in which the outsiders become plenipotentiaries, solemn emissaries with portfolios bulging with secrets? Consulates, Embassies, Information Services—these are nothing compared to the activity of our astonished double agents!" (p. 206).

88. The irony and knowingness of the Tarskis is neither approved nor rejected. That Pierre Tarski really has journeyed to the end of the night, having survived Buchenwald, makes his affectless adulteries hard to condemn, for all the pain they occasion. Tarski loves Marie, his wife, but can only admit it "with a purposely underscored insincerity" (p. 108). In *The Spirit and the Bride*, also set in postwar Paris, John Clifford, the protagonist, is as knowing and ironic as Tarski, but determined to free himself from "the world he lived in and the world that lived in him" (p. 233). A middle-aged American professor, he is as much a "realist" as Tarski, but he also believes in the possibility of a better life. Though "at the top of his profession" (p. 85), Clifford is "deeply unhappy," both with work and with his marriage: "Now that his irony had corroded everything, protected him from everything, there was an awesome void at the core of him" (p. 117) (which is how Tarski is presented in *The Plenipotentiaries*). For Clifford, "there was no god in his universe, the old worlds had come to their ends" (p. 236). Though the life he leads is real in the sense of unillusioned, it is unreal in being no life at all.

89. At the end of the novel, the exotic Arab girl whose lovemaking helps him to "*la vraie vie*," returns to her thuggish boyfriend. Clifford does not protest.

90. Kaplan, "Autobiography," p. 131.

91. Atlas, *Biography*, p. 141.

92. All direct quotations from Mme. Nimier come from a letter to the author, 2 September 2014. With the exception of Kappy, the staff at *Rapports* were French; the articles were in French, written by French and American authors. The magazine had a wide circulation, was intellectually respectable, and wrote about the failings as well as the virtues of American society, while being open about its propaganda aims. James Baldwin, for example, wrote on "Le Problème Noir en Amérique." See Brian Angus McKenzie, *Remaking France: Americanization, Public Diplomacy and the Marshall Plan* (New York: Berghahn, 2008), pp. 200–205.

93. Atlas, *Biography*, p. 141.

94. See Gold, *Still Alive!*, p. 208. For SB's reasons for the trip to Spain, see his letter to Herbert and Mitzi McClosky, 21 October 1949: "Things got to be a little too hot for me in September, and I took off for Spain again. I stayed for several weeks on the Catalan coast and in Barcelona and Mallorca."

95. Gold, *Still Alive!*, p. 209. In the quote about dreading the meal, Gold writes "we" about the trip south into Spain. In fact, as he told me in an interview, he and Edith parted company with SB (amicably) in Banyuls-sur-Mer.

96. See Atlas, *Biography*, p. 148, for these discrepancies and quotes. If Edith was in the backseat during the drive south, with the window open—it was summer and there was no air conditioning—she may well have missed SB's complaints.

97. This letter is in the Regenstein. According to Atlas, *Biography*, p. 148, SB "had commandeered Julian Behrstock's beat-up old car, a Deux Chevaux." Behrstock, SB's friend from Northwestern, came to Paris in 1948 to work at UNESCO in its Department of Mass Information.

98. For the date of this morning, see SB to J. F. Powers, 30 March 1949, which suggests that *Augie* must have begun life in April or May, since he describes himself still at work on "The Crab and the Butterfly": "I'm about half done with a book; the subject's a gloomy one but the book is funny, a combination I can trust you to understand. The title I've chosen for it is *The Crab and the Butterfly*, which I think does the tendency justice, and if I don't go anywhere—it isn't likely; the slack has just about been run out of Mr. Guggenheim's bounty—I ought to be done with it in the summer." The date can be further narrowed, to the second half of April, by SB to Henry Volkening, 13 April 1949, which makes no mention of *Augie* and is confident of delivery of "The Crab and the Butterfly": "With a book to show [i.e., the completed "The Crab and the Butterfly"], I can apply in 1950 for a Guggenheim renewal." Corroboration for a late April or early May date is provided in SB to Herbert and Mitzi McClosky, undated, but written sometime in March 1950, in which he explains the difficulty he'll have getting the Guggenheim renewed: "I worked eight months on a book I decided to put aside ["The Crab and the Butterfly"]. Since October [1949], I've finished about two-thirds of *Augie March*." The "eight months" in question must be from the time he arrived in Paris, which would fit the epiphanal moment's being in April or May of 1949. That the trip to Spain was partly motivated by the "jump" to *Augie* is suggested in SB to Henry Volkening, 9 October 1949: "Just back from a recuperative visit to Spain; and the reason recuperation was necessary is that after months of writing a book nearly finished, I read it all through and found it wasn't what I had wanted at all. Much, most of it, in fact, is still good and only needs to be recast in a more satisfactory way. But I haven't got the patience or the perspective necessary and so I have taken to Augie March instead. It goes very fast."

99. It is not clear whether the writing room SB was walking toward was at the Hôtel de l'Académie or the room at 33 rue Vaneau. In "I Got a Scheme!," SB calls the room a "small studio," which suggests rue Vaneau; but in a letter to John Lehmann of 3 October 1949, long after he'd begun work on *Augie*, he says "I don't live in the Académie, I only write there."

100. "I Got a Scheme!," pp. 74, 75; also the Botsford interview, "A Half Life," SB, *IAAU*, p. 318.

101. "I Got a Scheme!," p. 78. SB first used the Warren quote in "How I Wrote Augie March's Story," *New York Times Book Review*, 31 January 1954.

102. For an account of this moment in Wordsworth's life, see Stephen Gill, *William Wordsworth: A Life* (Oxford: Clarendon Press, 1989), p. 161.

103. "I Got a Scheme!," pp. 77, 78.

104. See SB to Henry Volkening, 28 November 1949.

105. On p. 116 of the Guggenheim's records for "1950 Matters re Fellows," dated "March 17, 18, 19, 1950," is an entry for SB. It reads: "Denied. The Secretary [Henry Moe] reported that his Fellowship novel did not mark any advance." SB's worries that this might happen were recalled to him by Julian Behrstock in a letter of 27 December 1979. Something SB said in an interview about how easily *Augie* came to him "brought to mind a moment together over a late afternoon coffee at

the Deux Magots in which you reported that you were supposed to be writing a serious book for Guggenheim but that *another* book kept intruding and that this irrepressible one was disconcertingly sexy and generally rather wild and unstoppable (or words to that effect)."

106. Atlas, *Biography*, p. 147.

107. Heller was later Fernand Braudel's assistant at the Maison des Sciences de l'Homme in Paris.

108. See the obituary for Clemens Heller published in the *Austrian Press and Information Service, Washington, D.C.*, vol. 55, September–October 2002, titled "Clemens Heller—Founder of the 'Marshall Plan of the Mind.'" For a history of the early years of the seminar, see Henry Nash Smith (SB's colleague at Minnesota), "The Salzburg Seminar," *American Quarterly* 1 (1949): 30–37; also Timothy W. Ryback (a former director of the seminar), "The Salzburg Seminar— A Community of Scholars," http://www.salzburgglobal.org/current/history-b .cfm?goto=community.

109. Kingsley Ervin was in charge of the winter program for the Salzburg Seminar.

110. John McCormick would later become a professor of comparative literature at Rutgers and write a scholarly biography of Santayana. In 1952, Hoffman and Baker married and returned to the States: Baker to work as a reader at Viking, a low-paying but prestigious job SB helped her to obtain; Hoffman to undertake graduate work in English at Columbia, then to seek work in the theater and as a lecturer in theater studies. In 1953, he was appointed head of the Theater Department at Bard College, where he helped to get SB a job for the academic year 1953–54, the year *Augie* was published.

111. According to a letter of 2 May 1950 to Henry Volkening.

112. See Atlas, *Biography*, p. 156, for these details; also the Archives of the Salzburg Seminar in American Studies, Schloss Leopoldskron, Salzburg, Austria.

113. Alfred Kazin, *New York Jew* (New York: Alfred A. Knopf, 1978), p. 168. The camp held some fourteen hundred adults and five hundred children.

114. SB to Olivier Schmidt, 7 June 1996, dictated by Chris Walsh.

115. Kazin, *New York Jew*, pp. 169–70.

116. SB, "How I Wrote Augie March's Story." This routine SB gives to Augie at the end of the novel: "I got into the habit of going every afternoon to the Café Valadier in the Borghese Gardens on top of the Pincio, with the whole cumulous Rome underneath, where I sat at a table and declared that I was an American, Chicago born, and all these other events and notions" (p. 975).

117. SB to Robert Hivnor, 18 June 1950.

118. The poem is included in SB to Oscar Tarcov, 26 June 1950, reprinted in Taylor, ed., *Letters*, pp. 105–6. Though jokey, as well as crudely rhymed and end-stopped, it points to SB's creative health and high spirits in the post-Salzburg period:

"SPRING ODE"

Thunder brings the end of winter,
Rinsing the yellow snow from the gutter;
Calico spots flare at the window;
I lie in my bathrobe, eating butter.
Grease on my cheeks—the fat of the season
Now dead and sealed, now dead and waxy.
Foxes yap on the tenement stairs;
Hope arrives in a Checker taxi.
His clever face is now surveying
The hallway with its sooty tatters,
The playing-card banners overhead,

The cymbals, scales and other matters.
My bathrobe sleeves are stiff with yolks,
Speckled with crumbs of my winter's eating;
Bottles and eggshells on the floor
Lie between us at our meeting.
He falls into my arms, we kiss,
We cry like reunited brothers.
He tells me how he searched for me
Among the others.
My cheeks are fat, my eyes are wet,
His hand rests sadly on my shoulder;
We cannot help but see how much
Each has grown older.

119. SB to Henry Volkening, 10 November 1949.

120. SB to Monroe Engel, 30 April 1950. For the Briggs-Copeland job at Harvard, see SB to Robert Hivnor (the undated letter about his trip to London) and SB to Monroe Engel, 12 January 1950.

121. Atlas, *Biography*, p. 166.

122. Botsford interview, "A Half Life," SB, *IAAU*, p. 317.

123. For this and subsequent quotes, see Greg Bellow, "Biographic Sketch," pp. 6–7.

10. PRINCETON/DELMORE

1. Atlas, *Biography*, p. 490. Unless otherwise indicated, all other quotations from Dean Borok are from letters to SB in the Regenstein.

2. Atlas, *Biography*, p. 490.

3. Dean Borok to SB, 1 January 1982. Borok never personally harassed SB or anyone else from the family. As he writes in a letter of 12 December 1997: "Your attitude has been, if I ignore him maybe he'll go away. And I did go away. I wrote some insulting letters to you, but I never tried to call you or see you or interfere with you in any way. I am way too proud for that."

4. The two-year-old was Dean Borok and the seven-month-old was his brother, Robert. According to Dean Borok, in an email of 9 August 2014, Robert was knocked off his bike by a car and killed when he was nine. He was not Maury's son. Immediately after Robert's death, Borok remembers, his mother telegraphed a man in Chicago named Joel, telling him what had happened. Borok has no idea who the man was: "my belief is that Bobby was fathered by the guy and later denied by him, the same pattern she had followed with my father, Morrie Bellow, which was to entrap the guy with pregnancy and then separate him from his money. What she never figured out was that these guys were as mean and desperate as she was." In a subsequent email of 20 October 2014, Borok offers some background on his mother, "who was not just a trashy homeless waif that my father picked up at the bus station on Randolph Street. She had eloped with the scion of one of New Jersey's finest Jewish families, Howard Borok of the Borok furniture company, but she couldn't stand the idea of being a New Jersey housewife so she walked out on him and caught a bus to Chicago. That's how I got the name Borok."

5. The subpoena story also appeared on 30 December in the *Chicago Herald-American*, under the headline "Name Chicagoan in Paternity Suit." Joel recalls another incident, even more dramatic: "Marcie had lain in wait for Maury to come out of the Sherry Hotel [in Chicago, owned by Maury and Marge], and from across the street had fired three or four shots. . . . She had just taken a bunch of shots at him." The date of this incident, which Joel says appeared in all the Chicago papers, is unknown; I could not find any references to it in the Chicago papers.

Dean Borok offers a somewhat different account of this episode, one he heard from his mother, in an email of 12 August 2014 titled "Gun Shy," which is posted in its entirety on his website 200motels.net. Here are the relevant extracts:

> My mother recounted a story to me about how she chased my father with the intent to shoot him down like Frankie shot Johnny. I only know what she told me, and she only told me what she wanted me to know. When Morrie came over to see her, he would leave his pistol lying around to take his clothes off. Like the character of Charles IX of France, as portrayed in *Queen Margot* by Alexandre Dumas, my father, Morrie, kept a little pied-à-terre across town where he could put his feet up in front of the fire and indulge in a few sentimental moments of reflection in the company of his devoted peasant mistress and their tiny lovechild. That was the deal that my father had with my mother, except that he was the King of the Planet of the Apes and my mother was Miss Jersey Shore, with a big Hollywood complex, and she wasn't about to let herself get shoved off to the side. . . .
>
> New Jersey women are known for their ferocity. "Is that what you think you're going to do to me, keep me locked up in a cage?" she screamed violently. When he first met her, my father would take my mother around with him in his Caddy all day and introduced her to his tough-guy mob associates, which she adored. Now she wasn't about to let herself get reduced to the level of a freakin milkmaid, waiting faithfully at the door with papi's pipe and slippers, and the baby sleeping peacefully in the cradle. She wanted some ACTION. She picked up a perfume bottle and threw it at his head, and then a glass. "Morrie, I'll kill you and kill myself." She ran to a table where he had put his pistol while disrobing, grabbed the handgun, and screamed, "Now I'm going to kill you and kill me!" She waved the gun and it went off, shocking herself. She fired again as Morrie ran for his life. She tried to shoot again, but she did something wrong and the gun didn't shoot. Sensing his opportunity, Morrie ran over and took the gun away from her. "When the cops get here, you don't say anything," he told her.
>
> Morrie fixed the cops in five minutes. It cost him a couple of long ones but, hey, that's Saturday Night in Chicago. Nevertheless the beat cops and station cops would sell the item to a reporter for five bucks, and the story got out anyway. After it appeared in the papers, Morrie told my mother, "Well, you wanted to get your name in the papers. Are you happy now?"

6. Atlas, *Biography*, p. 190, makes the five-year claim.

7. This is exactly what Wordsworth does upon his return from France in *The Prelude*, resulting in blockage and breakdown. "Wearied out with contrarieties" (those of political theory, of Burke, Paine, and Godwin), he "yielded up moral questions in despair" (Book 11:304–5, 1805 version).

8. Daniel Fuchs, *Saul Bellow: Vision and Revision* (Durham, NC: Duke University Press, 1984), p. 61. The immediately preceding discussion of excised political material from the final chapter of *Augie*, including Augie's remark about the Germans and politics, is from pp. 60–61.

9. Steven J. Zipperstein, *Rosenfeld's Lives: Fame, Oblivion, and the Furies of Writing* (New Haven: Yale University Press, 2009), p. 100.

10. Ibid., p. 134.

11. Rosenfeld's undated letter to Tarcov is among the Tarcov Papers in the Regenstein.

12. Zipperstein, *Rosenfeld's Lives*, p. 193.

13. Manea, "Conversation," p. 37.

14. There are discrepancies between SB's earlier and later accounts of his expe-

riences with Reichian therapy, as there are in accounts of other aspects of his life. The quotation from Atlas, *Biography*, is from p. 165, where Dr. Raphael comments: "That's a peculiar way to put it. He came because he had problems. He never expressed any of this to me." For the account given to Roth in their interview, see "I Got a Scheme!," p. 84.

15. Wilhelm Reich, *Selected Writings: An Introduction to Orgonomy* (New York: Farrar, Straus & Giroux, 1973), p. 37.

16. Christopher Turner, *Adventures in the Orgasmatron: William Reich and the Invention of Sex* (London: Fourth Estate, 2011), p. 222. The subtitle for the American edition is *How the Sexual Revolution Came to America*.

17. In Chester M. Raphael and Mary Higgins, eds., *Reich Speaks of Freud* (New York: Noonday, 1968), p. 109, quoted in Turner, *Orgasmatron*, p. 93, Reich describes "character armor" as an "artificial mask of self-control, of compulsive, insincere politeness and of artificial sociality."

18. See Turner, *Orgasmatron*, pp. 224, 5, 8, 232.

19. Ibid., pp. 331, 6; see also p. 226, where Turner quotes Reich's letter of 30 December 1940 to Einstein. In it Reich claims to have discovered "a specific, biologically effective energy which in many ways behaves differently from anything that is known about electromagnetic energy. The matter is too complicated and sounds too improbable to be explained clearly in a brief letter. I can only indicate that I have evidence that this energy, which I have called orgone, exists not only in living organisms but also in the soil and the atmosphere; it is visible and can be concentrated and measured, and I am using it with some success in research on cancer therapy." Turner comments: "Einstein, full of good will towards a fellow émigré and attracted to any idea that might help to fight fascism, invited Reich to come to see him in Princeton two weeks later. . . . Reich had mentioned that he'd been the late Sigmund Freud's assistant at the Ambulatorium in Vienna for eight years; this would have recommended him to Einstein, who had met Freud in Berlin in 1926."

20. See ibid., pp. 246–47, 248, 6, 7, for quotations from Baldwin and Rieff and preceding details of Reich's influence among intellectual and bohemian types.

21. SB, foreword to Isaac Rosenfeld, *An Age of Enormity: Life and Writing in the Forties and Fifties*, ed. Theodore Solotaroff (Cleveland: World, 1962), p. 11.

22. Zipperstein, *Rosenfeld's Lives*, p. 191.

23. Atlas, *Biography*, p. 163.

24. From Solotaroff's introduction to Reich, *An Age of Enormity*, pp. 38–39.

25. See Zipperstein, *Rosenfeld's Lives*, pp. 119–20, which quotes the recollections of both SB and Rosenfeld's son, George Sarant.

26. See Turner, *Orgasmatron*, p. 259.

27. Mark Shechner, ed., *Preserving the Hunger: An Isaac Rosenfeld Reader* (Detroit: Wayne State University Press, 1988), p. 27.

28. Zipperstein, *Rosenfeld's Lives*, p. 191. According to SB, in later years Rosenfeld turned against Reichianism and the destructive behavior it seemed to license or encourage. "Isaac ended by believing that therapy had done him great harm," SB wrote to Rosenfeld's son, George Sarant, in a letter of 9 September 1990. "We had a long conversation a month or two before he died and he declared that he had been out of his mind for a decade."

29. Alfred Kazin, *New York Jew* (New York: Alfred A. Knopf, 1978), p. 51.

30. Manea, "Conversation," p. 37, for this and the following quotation about the expressive properties of the face and body.

31. Not in Queens, as the unnamed acquaintance claimed to Atlas.

32. After Reich moved to Maine in 1950, the house became the Orgone Institute Diagnostic Clinic.

33. SB's remarks about Reichianism first appeared in print in 1962, in the foreword to the Rosenfeld anthology, *An Age of Enormity*. When Dr. Raphael read

them he wrote to SB in a letter of 12 October 1962, expressing "surprise and consternation" and asking a series of questions. The series begins: "Do you deny that the genital misery of the human animal is a basic cause of his suffering? Do you deny that the human animal develops a protective apparatus in the form of characterological and muscular defenses against his inner impulses and the threatening outer world and that he is crippled by them?" When the series of questions ends, Raphael concludes: "I am sure that you would give honest answers to these questions. And I am equally sure that those answers would make you a 'Reichian.'" Whether SB answered Raphael's questions is not known.

34. "Fine isolated verisimilitude" is from Keats's definition of "negative capability" in a letter of 21 December 1817 to his brothers, George and Thomas.

35. Later in the "Far Out" manuscript, Vallis declares that "truth itself has a dreamlike character. We've been bullied out of it by hatred and calculation. To get a glimpse of truth you have to go to the zoo" (p. 39).

36. Vallis grew up in such a city and speaks of the coarsening effect it has on sexual attitudes: "Schoolyards, factories, alleys, poolhalls sexually saturated. 'You put the blocks to a broad, as you did with a car to stop it from rolling while you worked on the engine. You gave her a jump, gave her a bang. What else . . . you fry the fat, you tear off a piece, punch her in the pants, you service her. . . . That's a mixture of the farm and the gas station'" (p. 33).

37. In later years, as explained in a letter of 8 January 1991 to George Demetriou, SB admitted a silver lining to the "otherwise somber and threatening cloud" of his years with Dr. Raphael. On nights of terrible insomnia, "when I find that I have almost stopped breathing," he often puts Reich's techniques to work: "my fingers creep toward the points of muscle attachment—the shoulders, the pectorals, and other places where normal people are not aware of having any muscles at all: the forehead, the eyebrows, the cheeks, and jaws and the eyes themselves. I find those ultra-sore places that can be relaxed by hard rubbing with the knuckles. And then one does begin to breathe again."

38. Atlas, *Biography*, p. 171.

39. In a 1953 application for a return visit to Yaddo, from 5–31 July, in answer to the question "What work have you planned for another visit, if it can be arranged?" The application is found among the Yaddo Papers in the Manuscripts and Archives Division of the New York Public Library. The idea for the novella may have come from a letter Ted Hoffman sent him on 5 January 1950, prior to his arrival in Salzburg: "There is one small plum attached to our spring activities. We are now in rather well with the American Hauser in Germany and they have offered to invite any of our faculty on a German lecture tour, including Berlin. Not too many lectures would be asked, the choice of topic would be largely up to you, the same lecture or lectures could be repeated in different cities." This offer SB declined in a letter to Hoffman of 25 January 1950: "I am interested in the Amerika Hauser lectures, but I don't think I can go. I do have to finish a book, and while I haven't been slack about it I haven't made record-time either."

40. Bernage is on a fellowship and at work on a biography of Friedrich von der Trenck (1726–94), a Prussian officer, adventurer, and author who was guillotined in the French Revolution. Von der Trenck is the subject also of the play Charlie Citrine writes in *Humboldt's Gift*, which wins him the Pulitzer Prize.

41. Atlas, *Biography*, p. 170.

42. Karl Shapiro, *The Younger Son* (1990), volume 1 of *Poet: An Autobiography in Three Parts* (1988–90) (Chapel Hill: Algonquin, 1990), p. 89. SB was not the only lecturer to attract female students. An English girl knocked on Shapiro's door to show him her poems and tell him "which girl was pairing off with which man and why." Two nights later, as Shapiro was getting ready for bed, there was a soft knock at his door "and he opened it to find about ten of the girls in their pajamas

who asked to come in" (p. 89), for a pajama party. The English girl was not among them. Later Shapiro went to bed with a German girl, a student from Munich.

43. Lillian Blumberg McCall, a clinical psychologist, had written a dissertation on Freud, parts of which were published as articles in *Commentary* ("Does Psychoanalysis Cure?," November 1950; "The Hidden Springs of Sigmund Freud," April 1954). These articles were critical of Freud and caused a stir. McCall had been a girlfriend of Clement Greenberg, moved in *Partisan Review* circles, and lived in the building where she found SB his apartment. This building she describes as located on Minetta Lane not Minetta Street. See p. 107 of her partial, unpublished, and untitled 1982 memoir, a copy of which, with SB's handwritten annotations, is among his papers in the Regenstein. SB encouraged McCall to write the memoir. "He not only tried to persuade me, he got his editor to write me several letters. The late Pat Covici of Viking, to whom *Herzog*, which I think is Saul's master work, is dedicated, was very persistent. . . . I'm writing the book now because for reasons I cannot comprehend, my daughter's generation seems fascinated by that period of Greenwich Village life and because, finally, I understand what happened" (p. 31)(henceforth cited within the text by page numbers). After her time in New York, she moved to Colorado, divorced, and then moved to Berkeley, where she and Mitzi McClosky became close friends.

44. That Minetta Lane was where SB lived rather than wrote is suggested by the letter to Hivnor of 25 January 1952, written from Salzburg: "If Clark is happy in that room [presumably MacDougal Alley] I think he can stay there. I'd take over Rosenfeld's flat on Hudson St., opposite Carver" (Katie Carver also had a room in the Casbah). In "How I Wrote Augie March's Story," in *The New York Times*, 31 January 1954, SB mentions writing a chapter of the novel in the Hudson Street apartment.

45. The review in *Billboard* appeared on 10 May 1952; the play's opening was on 2 May. The play, in two acts, was adapted by Leonard Lesley and produced by David Hellwell and Robert Winter-Berger. When informed by Volkening of plans to stage an adaptation, SB's response, in an undated letter from Salzburg, was "sure, go ahead, tell them to proceed to make a fortune with it. I took out the most obnoxious things, I think, and it's no longer a bloodbath." The review in *The New York Times* appeared on 3 May 1952.

46. The letter is found in the Manuscripts and Archives Division of the New York Public Library.

47. Two previous excerpts, subsequently revised, appeared in *Partisan Review*: "From the Life of Augie March," appeared in the issue of November 1949, published when SB was in Paris; and "The Einhorns" appeared in the issue of November–December 1951.

48. For SB's dealings with the Rockefeller Foundation, see Atlas, *Biography*, p. 168, which draws on the archives of the Rockefeller Foundation, Pocantico Hills, North Tarrytown, New York. The Trilling episode is discussed on p. 182. Marshall was associate director of the Rockefeller Foundation. He was an admirer of *The Victim* and in January 1951 invited SB to come in for a chat. In the course of the chat SB asked him for a grant. Marshall in turn asked SB to write an essay on "the responsibility of the novelist in society," for which he was given a $75 honorarium. SB's essay focused on the diminishing stature of fictional heroes: "As the external social factor grows larger, more powerful and tyrannical, man appears in the novel reduced in will, strength, freedom and scope." Two weeks later SB met with another foundation director, Edward "Chet" D'Arms (Marshall was away), whose minutes of the meeting record that he "was not greatly impressed at B's intellectual position nor encouraged by his slight but persistent truculence." D'Arms could not square what he called the "narrow focus" of SB's first two novels with his call for heroes of greater stature and was unimpressed with SB's claims for

the unfinished *Augie March*. In early May 1951 the board decided it could not help SB, a decision that involved, in Marshall's words, "a certain regret for all of us."

49. SB's memorial eulogy for Bernard Malamud was delivered in his absence by Howard Nemerov on 5 December 1986 at the annual luncheon of the American Academy of Arts and Letters; it is reprinted in Taylor, ed., *Letters*, p. 435.

50. See, for example, Michiko Kakutani, "A Talk with Saul Bellow: On His Work and Himself," in *New York Times Book Review*, 13 December 1981, reprinted in Cronin and Siegel, eds., *Conversations with SB*, p. 185.

51. That the Rockefeller funded the Gauss Seminars, which Blackmur ran and originated, may help account for their generosity toward him.

52. Atlas, *Biography*, p. 173.

53. Al Alvarez, *Where Did It All Go Right?* (1999; London: Bloomsbury, 2002), p. 167.

54. The passage from *Humboldt's Gift* continues: "And if I later became such a formidable mass of credentials it was because I put such slights to good use. I avenged myself by making progress. So I owed Sewell quite a lot and it was ungrateful of me, years later when I read in the Chicago paper that he was dead, to say, as I sipped my whisky, what I occasionally did say at such moments—death is good for some people." In the Botsford interview, "A Second Half Life," in SB, *IAAU*, p. 316, SB says of Blackmur: "I never got to know him at all well. I observed that he liked to have an entourage sitting on the floor listening to his labyrinthine muttered monologues. I listed him as a brilliant court-holder." In Monroe Engel's words: "I don't think Bellow liked Blackmur at all and I don't think Delmore liked him very much. . . . I didn't like him either, even though he gave me a job for a year."

55. Quoted from a report to the dean of the faculty (now in the Seeley Mudd Library in Princeton).

56. For SB on his Princeton students, see Robert Gutwillig, "Talk with Saul Bellow," *New York Times Book Review*, 20 September 1964, reprinted in Cronin and Siegel, eds., *Conversations with SB*, p. 26; for SB on not assuming a posture of disaffection, see "A Second Half Life," SB, *IAAU*, p. 315.

57. "Berryman, John," in *American National Biography*, vol. 2 (New York: Oxford University Press, 1999), in association with the American Council of Learned Societies, p. 690.

58. Botsford interview, "A Second Half Life," SB, *IAAU*, p. 316.

59. Lewis was at work on what would become *The American Adam: Innocence, Tragedy and Tradition in the Nineteenth Century* (1955), a landmark study of American literature.

60. Edmund Wilson, *The Fifties: From Notebooks and Diaries of the Period*, ed., Leon Edel (New York: Farrar, Straus & Giroux, 1986), p. 46, from Edel's introduction to the section titled "Princeton, 1952–1953."

61. Roethke had on several occasions been committed to mental hospitals during his time at the University of Washington, most recently in the spring of 1950, when Berryman was employed to replace him. For Roethke at Princeton, see Eileen Simpson, *Poets in Their Youth: A Memoir* (1982; New York: Vintage, 1983), pp. 219–22; see also Allan Seager, *The Glass House: The Life of Theodore Roethke* (Ann Arbor: University of Michigan Press, 1991), pp. 206–7. Seager's description of the Wilson party omits any reference to the poet's knocking down Percy Wood. He describes Roethke's behavior at the party as "aggressively sober" and manic, mentioning how he invited one female guest to accompany him "immediately" to the Caribbean. Later in the evening he took Wilson, his host, aside, and suggested: "Let's blow this and go upstairs and I'll show you some of my stuff."

62. SB, "My Paris," *New York Times Magazine*, 13 March 1983, reprinted in SB, *IAAU*, p. 236. A slightly different version of this meeting is given in Manea, "Conversation," p. 34: "We ran into Koestler and he said, 'is this your child?' and I

said, 'yes,' and he said, 'should a writer have children? Isn't it irresponsible of you?' I said, 'what do you want me to do, give him back?'"

63. For the quote about Ellison, see Botsford interview, "A Second Half Life," SB, *IAAU*, p. 316; for SB's review of *Invisible Man*, see "Man Underground," *Commentary*, June 1952.

64. Botsford interview, "A Second Half Life," SB, *IAAU*, p. 318.

65. James Atlas, *Delmore Schwartz: The Life of an American Poet* (1977; New York: Avon, 1978), p. 291.

66. William Phillips, *Partisan Review: Five Decades of the Literary Life* (New York: Stein & Day, 1983), p. 76.

67. William Barrett, *The Truants: Adventures Among the Intellectuals* (New York: Anchor/Doubleday, 1982), p. 27.

68. In 1939 Schwartz wrote an essay in *The Kenyon Review* on Eliot's journal, *Criterion*. In November of that year Eliot wrote back thanking Schwartz. "You are certainly a critic," the letter ended, "but I want to see more poetry from you; I was much impressed by *In Dreams Begin Responsibilities*." Eliot's letter is quoted in Atlas, *Delmore Schwartz*, p. 145.

69. See Simpson, *Poets in Their Youth*, p. 217.

70. According to Atlas, in *Biography*, p. xii, SB had "kind words" to say about the Schwartz biography.

71. Atlas, *Delmore Schwartz*, pp. 261–62.

72. Ibid., p. 285.

73. Ibid., p. 280.

74. Ibid., pp. 280–81.

75. Ibid., pp. 286–87.

76. Simpson, *Poets in Their Youth*, p. 217.

77. Both quotations from Irving Howe, *A Margin of Hope: An Intellectual Autobiography* (New York: Harcourt Brace Jovanovich, 1982), p. 165.

78. Atlas, *Delmore Schwartz*, p. 288.

79. Simpson, *Poets in Their Youth*, p. 222.

80. Atlas, *Biography*, p. 179.

81. Richard J. Kelly, ed., *We Dream of Honour: John Berryman's Letters to His Mother* (New York: W. W. Norton, 1988), p. 244.

82. The Wordsworth quotations are from the concluding lines of *The Prelude*: "deliverance" in the 1850 version was originally "redemption" in the 1805 version; the "savage torpor" quotation is from Wordsworth's 1800 preface to his and Coleridge's *Lyrical Ballads* (1798). The "unacknowledged legislators" quotation is from Shelley's "A Defence of Poetry" (1821).

83. Atlas, *Delmore Schwartz*, p. 285. Randall Jarrell, a visitor to Princeton in 1952–53, who had in the previous year taught in the writing program at Princeton with Berryman, shared Schwartz's Shelleyan view. "Any American poet under a certain age," he writes in *Poetry and the Age* (1953; New York: Ecco, 1980), p. 10, "has inherited a situation in which no one looks at him and in which, consequently, everyone complains that he is invisible."

84. Howe, *A Margin of Hope*, p. 164.

85. "I Got a Scheme!," p. 84.

86. Though Anita-like characters are invariably rigid in SB's fiction they are not incapable of love. In an interview, Mitzi McClosky stressed Anita's toughness but not her lack of love. The closest one can come to the Anita of SB's letter to Freifeld is in an undated letter of Rosenfeld to Tarcov: "The original attraction is gone. Nothing has taken its place, except an increased domesticity which he doesn't want. Anita acts sour and cranky at times" (quoted in Atlas, *Biography*, p. 166).

87. From p. 8 of Greg Bellow, "Anita Goshkin Bellow Busacca—A Biographic

Sketch," a fourteen-page memoir of his mother written in 2007 and deposited among SB's papers in the Regenstein.

88. Presuming the split occurred before 12 December, Anita having been born on that date in 1914.

89. Botsford interview, "A Second Half Life," SB, *IAAU*, p. 316. Monroe Engel tells the story of Riggs's death: "In the summer of 1953 we rented a house for a month in the Adirondacks and Tom was going to come out and visit us and he'd taken up with some Englishwoman who was having affairs with quite some number of people and she was going to come up with him. And they stopped at Blue Mountain Lake and Tom dove into the water and apparently hit his head on a stone and killed himself. We were having dinner and I got a call from the morgue saying that I had to come down and identify the body. And I must say that young Englishwoman had been very gutsy. She looked through Tom's address book and found the names of people to call."

90. Mrs. Riggs's young helper gives her name in the letter as Mrs. Paul Ripley. She writes from Ireland.

91. Botsford interview, "A Second Half Life," SB, *IAAU*, p. 316.

92. Atlas, *Biography*, p. 180, locates the party in Riggs's apartment, though in *Delmore Schwartz*, p. 296, he calls it "one of the Blackmurs' Christmas gatherings." Simpson says it took place in the Blackmur apartment, which SB was renting.

93. Simpson, *Poets in Their Youth*, pp. 218–19.

94. Ibid., p. 219.

95. The description of Schwartz "literally dragging" his wife out of the room comes from p. 67 of Sasha Bellow's unpublished memoir, "What's in a Name?" (henceforth cited within the text by page numbers). The memoir consists of two parts, 121 typed pages written sometime in 2006, and a postscript entitled "The Years Between" written in 2008. The numbering of this postscript, which deals with Sasha's life from twelve to twenty, continues from pp. 122–30, and is followed by a letter to her son, Adam, dated May 2008, in which she explains how difficult it was "to dredge up memories" for what she calls the "dark ages" of her life. The memoir, she tells Adam, "is not an autobiography. In fact, it is fairly fragmented, surprisingly incomplete in many respects and, significantly, does not even touch on the last thirty plus years (my best) at all." The letter is numbered as though part of the memoir (pp. 131–32). My dating of the first two parts of the manuscript is conjectural, based on the May 2008 letter to Adam and the first sentence of the postscript: "I spent nearly two years trying to tackle the years 12–20 that are missing in the memoir." Sasha gave me a copy of the memoir in 2010, the year before she died. The memoir records the difficulties she encountered over her various names when at Bennington. In her second year she needed a birth certificate to travel to Mexico with a roommate: "Because I had no other recent, official record of my legal existence, I had to get signed and notarized affidavits from my mother and my aunt, attesting that Saundra and Sandra Richter, Sondra and Alexandra Tschacbasov were all the same person" (p. 2).

96. The quotation is from p. 65 of "What's in a Name?" According to Ted Hoffman, as quoted in Atlas, *Biography*, p. 180, when Schwartz, in fury, dragged Elizabeth away from the party, SB set out after them; then Hoffman and Monroe Engel set out after SB: "We found Saul on Nassau Street at two o'clock in the morning . . . having coffee with Sondra."

97. Ann Birstein, *What I Saw at the Fair* (New York: Welcome Rain Publishers, 2003), p. 154.

98. From p. 139 of the unpublished, untitled, and unfinished memoir of Lillian Blumberg McCall, a copy of which can be found among SB's papers in the Regenstein.

99. Nina Steers, "Successor to Faulkner?," *Show* 4, September 1964, reprinted in Cronin and Siegel, eds., *Conversations with SB*, p. 35.

100. According to Joel Bellows in an interview: "He would start out early in the morning with a terrycloth towel around his neck and he would sweat, as you would with Indian clubs. And when you saw him at noon or one o'clock—drenched. The concentration was so incredible and he was developing those habits in the year with Anita. So she must have made it very, very convenient."

101. See SB's 1981 interview with Michiko Kakutani, "A Talk with Saul Bellow," reprinted in Cronin and Siegel, eds., *Conversations with SB*, p. 186: "'For many years,' he explains, 'Mozart was a kind of idol to me—this rapturous singing for me that's always on the edge of sadness and melancholy and disappointment and heartbreak, but always ready for an outburst of the most delicious music.'"

102. SB's answers were dictated to a secretary on 16 September 1965, in reply to a questionnaire sent him by A. C. Ohlson, "studying the methods and techniques of contemporary creative writing."

103. Nina Steers, "Successor to Faulkner?," in Cronin and Siegel, eds., *Conversations with SB*, p. 31.

104. SB, "Mozart: An Overture," the first essay in SB, *IAAU*, p. 11, first published in *Bostonia* magazine (Spring 1992), from a speech delivered at the Mozart Bicentennial, 5 December 1991, in Florence, Italy.

105. Berryman, before he grew his beard, could look like a young businessman (to Leon Edel, at least), and Schwartz was full of moneymaking schemes, but neither was likely to be called businesslike.

106. SB, "The Distracted Public," originally delivered as the Romanes Lecture, Oxford University, 10 May 1990, reprinted in SB, *IAAU*, p. 153.

107. Ibid., pp. 168, 169.

108. "An Interview with Myself," originally titled "Some Answers and Questions," *New Review* (1975), pp. 51–61, reprinted in SB, *IAAU*, p. 80. Later in the interview SB says: "In busy America there was no Weimar, there were no cultivated Princes" (p. 87), and again one wonders: no Guggenheims or Morgans or Rockefellers or Mellons or MacArthurs or Fords?

109. The contributors in May–June were Newton Arvin, James Burnham, Allan Dowling, Leslie Fiedler, Norman Mailer, Reinhold Niebuhr, Philip Rahv, David Riesman, Mark Schorer, and Lionel Trilling; in July–August they were William Barrett, Jacques Barzun, Joseph Frank, Horace Gregory, Louis Kronenberger, and C. Wright Mills; in September–October they were Louise Bogan, Richard Chase, Sidney Hook, Irving Howe, Max Lerner, William Phillips, Arthur Schlesinger Jr., and Delmore Schwartz. Louise Bogan was the only woman to contribute.

110. Phillips, *A Partisan View*, p. 79.

111. The Macdonald essays that helped to popularize the concept of mass culture were "A Theory of Popular Culture," which appeared in the first issue of *politics* (February 1944) and a revised and expanded version of the essay, entitled "A Theory of Mass Culture," which appeared in *Diogenes* in 1953. In this second essay Macdonald cited the influence of writers of the Frankfurt School, notably Theodor Adorno, Max Horkheimer, and Leo Löwenthal.

112. Irving Howe, the only other contributor to "Our Country and Our Culture" to take an oppositional stance, was to expand his piece into an essay entitled "The Age of Conformity: Protest and Rejoinder," published by *PR* in the issue of March–April 1954.

113. Joseph Frank, in an essay entitled "Lionel Trilling and the Conservative Imagination," *Sewanee Review* 64, no. 2 (Spring 1955), suggests that the publication of Trilling's *The Liberal Imagination* (1950) played an important part in these trends. For Frank, the book's "disillusionment with politics" is less disturbing than

Trilling's "confining his criticism to the *liberal* imagination, and not extending it to politics in general." To Irving Howe, extrapolating on Frank's view, Trilling "provided a rationale for a dominant trend within the intellectual community," one that helped not only to dissuade people from "a militant politics in behalf of both social reform and a measure of egalitarianism" but helped to hasten or license "the absorption . . . of large numbers of intellectuals into government bureaucracy, the industries of pseudoculture, and the corporations. As advisors helpers, and spokesmen, intellectuals gained power" (pp. 231, 234). One remembers the Trillings praising SB at the dinner table of the Rockefeller Foundation's John Marshall. A similar line to Howe and Frank is taken by Thomas Bender, "Lionel Trilling and American Culture," *American Quarterly* 42, no. 2 (June 1990): 339.

114. Barrett, *Truants*, pp. 189–90.

115. Quoted in Atlas, *Delmore Schwartz*, p. 298.

116. Atlas, *Biography*, p. 176.

11. AUGIE/BARD/SASHA

1. "I Got a Scheme!," p. 76.

2. SB interview with Bernard Kalb, 19 September 1953, *Saturday Review* (previously, until 1952, *The Saturday Review of Literature*). SB uses the identical words in an interview with Bruce Cook, "Saul Bellow: A Mood of Protest," *Perspectives on Ideas and the Arts*, 12 February 1963, reprinted in Cronin and Siegel, eds., *Conversations with SB*, p. 14.

3. Martin Amis, "The American Eagle: *The Adventures of Augie March* by Saul Bellow," originally published in *The Atlantic Monthly*, October 1995, reprinted in *The War Against Cliché: Essays and Reviews, 1971–2000* (London: Jonathan Cape, 2001), p. 466.

4. SB, "The Thoughts of Sergeant George Flavin," in John Lehmann, ed., *Penguin New Writing 38* (London: Penguin, 1949), p. 48 (henceforth cited within the text by page numbers).

5. "I Got a Scheme!," p. 77.

6. Atlas, *Biography*, p. 152.

7. Adam Thirlwell, *Miss Herbert* (London: Jonathan Cape, 2007), p. 267.

8. Daniel Fuchs, *Saul Bellow: Vision and Revision* (Durham, NC: Duke University Press, 1984), p. 58.

9. Thirlwell, *Miss Herbert*, pp. 270–71.

10. See the first page of Randall Jarrell's introduction to the 1965 reprint of Christina Stead's *The Man Who Loved Children* (1940), itself reprinted in the Picador paperback edition (2001).

11. The phrase is from the preface to volume 7 of the New York edition of James's novels, which introduces *The Tragic Muse*. James asks of the novels of Thackeray, Dumas, and Tolstoy, "what do such large loose baggy monsters, with their queer elements of the accidental and the arbitrary, artistically *mean*?" (p. x).

12. In Botsford interview "A Second Half Life," reprinted in SB, *IAAU*, p. 325. On the same page, SB attributes the "small-public"/"great-public" distinction to Wyndham Lewis.

13. From Manea, "Conversation," p. 21.

14. Fuchs, *Saul Bellow: Vision and Revision*, p. 69.

15. Elsewhere Einhorn is likened to Francis Bacon, Hephaestus, Anchises, Sardanapalus, and Socrates. Augie is "Achilles among the maidens" (which should really be Odysseus among the maidens); even Five Properties is seen in heroic terms, though calling him "that Apollo" (p. 408) is clearly ironic.

16. Lionel Trilling makes a similar point at the beginning of his review of *Augie March* in *The Griffin*, a version of which he reprinted as the introduction to

the Modern Library edition of the novel (New York, 1965). He calls *The Victim* "the kind of novel in which the author develops a single controlling idea with skill and precision, calling upon his conscious intelligence to do a considerable amount of the work of creation" (p. vii).

17. Not all the real-life models for characters in *Augie* responded as SB feared. On 18 June 1960, Ben Shapiro, a childhood companion, recognized himself as Jimmy Klein and wrote to say: "I enjoyed Augie March. I appreciate what it is that you did for me, the implied conversion was absolutely painless, from petty thief to store detective. To me it meant only that the old love for each other still existed." In the letter to Freifeld, SB adds, apropos of the depiction of his father: "I feel that I have kept things [from] obscurity which should not sink and for that reason the book is as much intended for you as for myself. The personal identification is altogether warranted. If you didn't make it I'd feel that I had missed the mark."

18. Atlas, *Biography*, p. 188, takes a different view, calling *Augie* "an American bildungsroman—a novel of education" and describing its hero as "the prototypical sensitive young man of modern literature, a variant of Stendhal's Julien Sorel and Flaubert's Frédéric Moreau, Joyce's Stephen Dedalus and D. H. Lawrence's Paul Morel." In support of this view he quotes a terse manuscript note reading: "Doesn't want to be what others want to make of him. Stendhal exceptional champion of this." However, the problem of development remains. Trilling, in his introduction to the Modern Library edition of the novel, p. xi, specifically contrasts SB with Stendhal, calling *Augie* "the inversion or negation of the kind of nineteenth-century novel of which *The Red and the Black* may be taken as the prototype, in which the hero, rising from poor or provincial beginnings, directs his heroic ambitious will upon the world of power and glory. For Augie makes it the great point of his life to reject the power and the glory. . . . He refuses the 'heroic' in favor of what he believes the heroic destroys, a complete humanity. It is in this formulated, programmatic rejection of the heroic will that *Augie March* is most specifically and essentially comic."

19. Trilling, introduction to *The Adventures of Augie March*, pp. xii, xiii.

20. From the previously quoted response, undated, to Malamud's letter of 28 November 1953. Malamud's "baseball" novel, *The Natural*, was published in 1952.

21. For quotes on control in *Augie*, see SB interviews with Nina Steers, "Successor to Faulkner?," originally published in *Show* 4 (September 1964), and Gordon Lloyd Harper, "The Art of Fiction: Saul Bellow," originally published in *Paris Review* 9, no. 36 (1966), both reprinted in Cronin and Siegel, eds., *Conversations with SB*, pp. 34, 63.

22. According to Richard Stern, in an interview.

23. Philip Roth, "Rereading Saul Bellow," originally published in *The New Yorker* (9 October 2000), reprinted in *Shop Talk: A Writer and His Colleagues and Their Work* (New York: Houghton Mifflin, 2001), p. 140.

24. In "A Personal Record," a review of Joyce Cary's novel *Except the Lord*, in *The New Republic* (22 February 1954), SB declares that "a novel cannot matter to us if it fails to inform us about the elementary circumstances of the lives of its characters. The novelist need not flaunt the hero's socks continually at us, but he must be able to exhibit them on demand—the socks of Dmitri Karamazov, the socks even of Lambert Strether in *The Ambassadors*."

25. These profiles, in the form of typed manuscripts, have been preserved, along with all Illinois Federal Writers' Project Records, in the Abraham Lincoln Presidential Library in Springfield, Illinois (formerly the Illinois State Historical Library). Subsequent references are cited within the text by page numbers.

26. Quoted by John Updike in his introduction to the Modern Library edition of *Winesburg, Ohio* (New York: Modern Library, 2002), p. xvi.

27. An extract from Anderson's "Apology" appears after the text in ibid., p. 243; the quoted sentences conclude the original *Dial* article.

28. Ibid., p. 88 (further quotations cited within the text by page numbers).

29. Anderson's attention to bodily features, gestures, and movements also recalls SB. See Chapter 2, note 21.

30. James T. Farrell, "A Note on Sherwood Anderson," in *Reflections at Fifty and Other Essays* (New York: Vanguard, 1966), pp. 166, 164.

31. SB, "Looking for Mr. Green," first published in *Commentary* (March 1951), reprinted in SB, *CS*, p. 174.

32. The novel is dotted with Yiddish phrases and sayings, plus occasional Yiddish-inflected locutions: "I could not find myself in love without it should have some peculiarity" (p. 750); "I don't want you should have anything against me" (Five Properties) (p. 587); "Owgie, the telephone ringt. Hear!" (Anna Coblin) (p. 402).

33. Roth, "Rereading Saul Bellow," *Shop Talk*, pp. 142–43.

34. SB, "Him with His Foot in His Mouth," first published in *The Atlantic Monthly*, November 1982, reprinted in SB, *CS*, p. 383.

35. Irving Howe and Eliezer Greenberg, eds., *A Treasury of Yiddish Stories* (1954; New York: Meridian, 1958). The quotations at the end of the previous paragraph come from pp. 10, 25.

36. Irving Howe, *A Margin of Hope: An Intellectual Autobiography* (New York: Harcourt Brace Jovanovich, 1982), p. 262.

37. Howe and Greenberg, eds., *A Treasury of Yiddish Stories*, p. 46.

38. Examples from SB's translation of Isaac Bashevis Singer, "Gimpel the Fool," in ibid., pp. 402, 410, 406. For a detailed account of SB's translation, see Sidra DeKoven Ezrahi, "State and Real Estate: Territoriality and the Modern Jewish Imagination," in *Terms of Survival: The Jewish World Since 1945* (London: Routledge, 1995), p. 50, in which it is argued that SB's translation was "as much cover-up as exposure [of the lost Old World of the shtetl]". According to Hana Wirth-Nesher, "'Who's He When He's at Home?': Saul Bellow's Translations," in Michael P. Kramer, ed., *New Essays on Seize the Day* (Cambridge: Cambridge University Press, 1998), p. 4: "In translating for a *Partisan Review* readership removed from Judaic texts and sources a story originally intended for an audience well versed in Jewish tradition, SB retained only seven Yiddish words: golem, mezuzah, *challah, kreplach, schnorrer, dybbuk* and *Tisha B'av*. With the exception of the last term, an annual day of mourning and fasting to commemorate the destruction of the second Temple and the resulting two millennia of exile, these terms had already seeped into the American Jewish lexicon. . . . Actual liturgical references, however, no matter how common, were converted into American equivalents. And this is where the cross-cultural plot thickens. For in the English translation of 'Gimpel,' Bellow translated the well-known Hebrew prayer for the dead, 'El molei rachamim' into the Christian 'God 'a mercy,' a shift that transformed Gimpel's Eastern European setting into Southern Baptist terrain." Though SB's dialect translation properly associates the prayer with American folk and regional customs, it sounds incongruous, and as Wirth-Nesher points out, "the linguistic shift from Hebrew ["El molei rachamim" is a Hebrew name] to Yiddish, from the sacred to the profane, is not retained but flattened into one language" (p. 31). See also David Roskies, "Gimpel the Simple and on Reading from Right to Left," in Justin Cammy et al., eds., *Arguing the Modern Jewish Canon: Essays on Literature and Culture in Honor of Ruth R. Wisse* (Cambridge, MA: Harvard University Press, 2008), in which Roskies argues that "in English Gimpel the Fool is less of a male, less of a folk artist, less of a Jew. The cup that Bellow handed the English reader in 1953 was at best half empty. Not so, Gimpel the Simple, who is endowed with the fullness of years, of voice, of human emotion, and of mystical knowledge. In celebration thereof, on the eve of the Passover festival in 1945, Yitshok Bashevis presented the Yiddish reader with an Elijah cup, filled to overflowing" (pp. 339–40).

39. Delmore Schwartz, "Adventure in America," a review of SB, *The Adventures of Augie March*, in *Partisan Review* (January–February 1954). The review opens: "Saul Bellow's new novel is a new kind of book. The only other American novels to which it can be compared with any profit are *Huckleberry Finn* and *U.S.A.*, and it is superior to the first by virtue of the complexity of its subject matter and to the second by virtue of a realized unity of composition" (p. 112).

40. Robert Gorham Davis, "Augie Just Wouldn't Settle Down," and Harvey Breit, "Talk with Bellow," both in *New York Times Book Review*, 20 September 1953.

41. In the first sentence of Harvey Curtis Webster's review of *Augie*, "Quest Through the Modern World," *Saturday Review*, 19 September 1953. Later in the review Webster contrasts the nature of the perplexity occasioned by the two novels: Joyce in *Ulysses* perplexes from the start, whereas "like Rabelais and Cervantes, Mr. Bellow makes easy sense from page to page, yet his total meaning is elusive."

42. Atlas, *Biography*, p. 198.

43. "Have letter here from Librairie Plon claiming first shot at *Augie*, the which claim I wish to acknowledge as Plon has translated my first book," SB writes to Volkening in an undated letter that Volkening answers on 29 September 1953. "Look Henry," SB had earlier written to Volkening, on 25 August 1953, after being informed of an offer from the British publisher André Deutsch: "Would you marry your daughter off to her first suitor. This book, old man, is a child of mine. Let's have not so simply a figure but some notion of the Deutsch intentions. Heavens! *You* should know *this*!!!" *Augie* was published in Britain by Weidenfeld & Nicolson.

44. West's review, "A Crash of Symbols," *New Yorker*, 26 September 1953, made SB out, he complained in the same letter to White, as "a disciple of the New Criticism . . . [but] in writing the book I was aware of no symbolic aims": "'Simon' and 'Simony,' 'eagles' and 'virility,' 'sex' and 'culture'—really, it is simply too much!"

45. The originals of SB's correspondence with Katherine White are deposited in the archives of *The New Yorker* in the New York Public Library; copies, along with White's replies, can be found among SB's papers in the Regenstein.

46. Norman Podhoretz, *Making It* (1967; New York: Bantam, 1969), pp. 116–17.

47. In the undated response to Bernard Malamud's letter of 28 November: "I made many mistakes; I must plead guilty to several of your charges. Yes, Augie is too passive, perhaps. Yes, the episodes do not have enough variety; the pressure of language is too constant and uniform."

48. Norman Podhoretz, "The Adventures of Saul Bellow, 1953–1959," originally appeared in Podhoretz, *Doings and Undoings: The Fifties and After in American Writing* (New York: Farrar, Straus & Giroux, 1964), reprinted in Thomas L. Jeffers, ed., *The Norman Podhoretz Reader: A Selection of His Writings from the 1950s Through the 1990s* (New York: Free Press, 2004), pp. 14, 16.

49. Norman Podhoretz, *Making It*, pp. 114, 118, 119, 120.

50. Atlas, *Biography*, p. 201.

51. Excerpted from *Ex-Friends* (New York: Free Press, 1999), in Jeffers, ed., *The Norman Podhoretz Reader*, p. 382. Berryman's drunken threat to Podhoretz can be paired with Delmore Schwartz's joking offer to threaten Anthony West: "I take it you would like to have Anthony West's head broken in," he writes to SB on 9 October 1953: "I will. Before I'm thru West will be East."

52. Alfred Kazin, *New York Jew* (New York: Alfred A. Knopf, 1978), p. 47, for all quotations.

53. The phrase "the whole American question" comes from Percy Lubbock, James's friend and editor, in "Henry James, O.M.," Lubbock's eulogy in *The Times* (London), 29 February 1916: "Through all his long residence in Europe, his relations with America were closer and more constant than may perhaps have been generally understood; and the whole American question, in whatever aspect, was one in which he was always eager to keep himself instructed." And see Philip Rahv,

"Henry James's America," a review of F. O. Matthiessen, *The American Novels and Stories of Henry James*, in *New York Times Book Review*, 2 March 1947: "for a writer who, as the legend goes, was enamored of old-world privilege and by no means aglow with belligerent fervor in dealing with the national ideals, the work collected in this volume is astonishing, in that it shows us to what an extent James was able to express creatively the meaning and quality of American life."

54. For Henry James on Yiddish speakers, see *The American Scene* (London: Chapman Hall, 1907), pp. 132, 139, 135. To James, the Lower East Side was marked by "a sense of great swarming. . . . There is no swarming like that of Israel when once Israel has got a start . . . multiplication of everything was the dominant note, at the bottom of some vast sallow aquarium in which innumerable fish, of over-developed probiscus, were to bump together" (p. 131). In discussing *The American Scene*, Jonathan Freedman in *The Temple of Culture: Assimilation and Anti-Semitism in Literary Anglo-America* (Oxford: Oxford University Press, 2000), argues that "for all [James's] worrying about the threat posed by Jews to the English language, there is a countervailing and envious sense of the vitality of Yiddish culture" (p. 121). For SB's references to *The American Scene*, see for example the final paragraphs of the second of the "Jefferson Lectures" (1977) or "My Paris" (originally printed in *New York Times Magazine*, 13 March 1983), both reprinted in SB, *IAAU*, pp. 151–52, 234.

55. Leon Edel, *The Life of Henry James, Volume II: 1899–1916* (2 vols.; Harmondsworth: Penguin, 1977), p. 599.

56. This account, including the quote from Edel, is taken from Atlas, *Biography*, p. 210.

57. Diana Trilling, *The Beginning of the Journey* (New York: Harcourt Brace, 1993), p. 87. Diana Trilling may be right that SB was testing Lionel, but if so he seems not to have been pleased at his guest's discomfort. See SB to Susan Glassman, 23 January 1962: "A little discouraging last night. Dave Peltz and I took Trilling out slumming. A cold coming we had of it."

58. This journal entry does not appear in Richard M. Cook, ed., *Alfred Kazin's Journals* (New Haven: Yale University Press, 2012), but Cook provided it to me, along with a sheaf of references to SB not printed in his selection. The journals are to be found among the Alfred Kazin Papers held in the Berg Collection of the New York Public Library. When Kazin's essay collection, *The Inmost Leaf* (1955), was published, Cleanth Brooks, a New Critic and Southern Agrarian, the target also of attacks by Kazin in *On Native Grounds* (1942) and elsewhere, gave it a hostile review in *The New York Times Book Review*. In an undated letter to Kazin, SB denounced Brooks in full battle mode: "I haven't seen your book yet. But I did chance to see the review in the *Times*, which I thought so foul that I wanted to bang Brooks on the head. Eastern white-collar? Why, he might as well have come out flatly with 'Jew.' What vileness! How I detest these 'rooted' southerners among us poor deracinated Hebes of the north. I notice that they teach at Yale, though, or Minnesota. If they are not missionaries from southern culture they are liars and cowards. Christly heavens, what *chutzpah!*"

59. Lynn Hoffman, email to the author, 3 October 2012. Because SB found negative reviews of *Augie* so painful, he sought sustenance and reassurance from friends, colleagues, and family. On 20 September, the day of the *New York Times* review, he wrote to Freifeld to thank him for his friendship: "When I want to know *who* I am I must still turn to you." Nine days later, Isaac Rosenfeld wrote from Minneapolis, where Ralph Ross, now head of Humanities at the University of Minnesota, had gotten him a job. "I may not have been able to get along with you in recent years," Rosenfeld writes, "but I got along famously with *Augie*. I loved it, immensely, most every bit of it, and even the parts I didn't like I liked. . . . I tell you, it's encouraged *me* more than anything I've read in a long time." Herbert

Gold wrote on 24 September in similar vein, pleased to find in *Augie* "so much of you . . . of you *relaxed* and letting go, enjoying yourself." Leslie Fiedler, in a letter of 9 October, wondered admiringly how SB "had managed to write such an American book—such a Huckleberry Finn-ish, Melvillian, go-to-hell ragbag. . . . Your only sin against the American spirit was to make sex so infallibly (the *infallible* part raised your sex to a pastoral level that troubled even me) enjoyable; I'll bet yours is the first 'serious' American book to show a boy's initiation in a whore house as anything but torture!" In a letter of 21 October, Zita Cogan, a friend from Tuley days, reported the complaints of "the young orthodox Jewry of Chicago," for whom *Augie* presents the Jewish people "very, very unfavorably." Her letter ends: "take care of yourself at all those cocktail parties you're probably being guested." On Thanksgiving Day 1953 SB writes to thank Edith Tarcov for her warm praise of *Augie*, commending her "for having observed, as no one else has, Augie's bent for the illicit. I have often felt that the effort to lead a normal American life would make an outlaw out of me." The reaction of SB's family was slow in coming and mixed. For Jane, Sam, and their families, pride mixed with embarrassment (over the Simon/Renée episode); Maury was simply angry. Father Abraham, in the letter quoted in full at the end of Chapter 1, congratulated SB on the book's success, sent money for further copies, and signed off as patriarch: "Still I am The head of all of U." Perhaps the most heartening of the letters of congratulation SB received came from the punch-press operator and would-be opera singer who roomed with the family at 2629 West Augusta Avenue. It was signed "Your old friend, Ezra Davis."

60. Sasha had only recently been fired from *Partisan Review*, edited by Phillips and Rahv. Her description of the launch party comes from p. 73 of her unpublished memoir, "What's in a Name?" (henceforth cited within the text by page numbers). For the origins and nature of the memoir, see Chapter 10, note 95.

61. Languages and Literature was one of four academic divisions into which Bard was organized. The other three were Social Studies; Art, Music, Drama, and Dance; and Natural Sciences. For Ted Hoffman as "Consigliori," see Lynn Hoffman email to the author, 3 October 2012.

62. Botsford interview, "A Second Half Life," SB, *IAAU*, p. 320.

63. See pages 86 and 87 of the *Bard College Bulletin* for 1953–54, also for a description of John Bard, the college's founder, as "a country-squire of wide interests and deep religiosity," and for the "pioneering efforts" referred to two sentences later in the text.

64. Ibid., p. 7. In Mary McCarthy's *The Groves of Academe* (1952; Harcourt/Harvest paperback, 1992), p. 61, "Jocelyn College," the novel's Bard-like setting, has "a ratio of one teacher to every 6.9 students, which made possible the practice of 'individual instruction' as carried on at Bennington (6.4:1), Bard (6.9:1), and St. John's (7.7:1)."

65. SB to Alfred Kazin, 7 January 1954. A high number of Bard students, according to SB, were troubled or in analysis. Atlas, *Biography*, p. 197, reports the complaint of one such student that SB was inadequate as an advisor because he'd not been in analysis (apparently Reichian therapy didn't count). In "Him with His Foot in His Mouth," Herschel Shawmut has a similarly minded student at Ribier College: "A girl I was assigned as an advisor has asked for another one because I haven't been psychoanalyzed and can't even begin to relate to her" (SB, *CS*, p. 377).

66. For SB on Bard, see Botsford interview, "A Second Half Life," SB, *IAAU*, p. 320; Sasha Bellow described Bard as "Bennington with boys" in several places (to me in an interview; to Atlas, *Biography*, p. 197).

67. Mary McCarthy, *The Groves of Academe*, pp. 25–27, 36–37.

68. Michael Rubin, *A Trip into Town* (1961; New York: MacFadden-Bartell, 1964), pp. 76, 75, 78–79, 83.

69. Ibid., pp. 92, 139, 140.

70. Botsford interview, "A Second Half Life," SB, *IAAU*, p. 320.

71. Artine Artinian, who taught French, was on leave, as was Ted Weiss.

72. Keith Botsford, from a draft version of pp. 2–3 of the fifth volume of Botsford's memoir *Fragments*. In finished form, the memoir will appear as *Fragments I–VI*, 2 vols. (Las Vegas and London: Republic of Letters Books, 2014). Volume 2, comprised of *Fragments IV–VI*, will contain material on SB, Bard, Ludwig, et al. "The text of *V* is ok as is," Botsford writes in an email of 26 July 2014, "but it will doubtless be very different by the time your first volume comes out. You should probably say, 'references to *Fragments* in this volume are as of July, 2014'—as are page numbers" (henceforth cited within the text).

73. Gore Vidal, *Palimpsest: A Memoir* (1995; London: Abacus, 1996), pp. 243, 259.

74. See SB, *Henderson the Rain King* (1958), pp. 135–36: "She had remodeled a building on the property, one of the few I didn't take for the pigs because it was old and out of the way. I told her to go ahead, but then I held back on the dough, and instead of wood, wallboard was put in, with other economies on down the line. She made the place over with a new toilet and had it painted inside and out. But it had no insulation. Came November and the tenant began to feel cool. Well, they were bookish people; they didn't move around enough to keep their body heat up."

75. Jim Detjen, "'Rain King' Recalls Nobel Prize Winner's Years in Barrytown," *Poughkeepsie Journal*, 22 October 1976.

76. Aldrich's claim comes from a note of 13 April 2005 by Helene Tieger, the Bard College archivist, in the library's collection of SB's papers. According to Sasha in an interview, "once he'd written that Henderson shot the cat he told the story that Chanler Chapman shot the cat—but he didn't"; "once he found a better story, it was his story and he's sticking to it." The episode in which Henderson shoots the cat is recounted in Chapter 8, pp. 183–85. The cat belonged to the tenants who rented the apartment on Henderson's property remodeled by his wife, Lily. These tenants, a mathematics teacher and his wife, complained because the place was too cold.

77. See SB to Robert Penn Warren, 27 March 1954; see also Atlas, *Biography*, p. 210, for Lynn Hoffman quotation.

78. Detjen, "'Rain King' Recalls Nobel Prize Winner's Years in Barrytown," *Poughkeepsie Journal*. Detjen identifies Wilson as teaching English at Bard, which he did for four decades, though he was not in the Division of Languages and Literature the year SB was there. He had been an undergraduate at Bard (class of '48) and in 1953–54 was a graduate student in English at Columbia.

79. This quotation is from the third page of a five-page speech, undated, written by SB for a 1995 memorial for Ralph Ellison. It is among SB's papers in the Regenstein.

80. Vidal, *Palimpsest*, p. 259.

81. Botsford interview, "A Second Half Life," SB, *IAAU*, p. 321.

82. Vidal, *Palimpsest*, pp. 259, 260.

83. Atlas, *Biography*, p. 208.

84. It is not clear how seriously to take these complaints, recalled by Vidal in an interview. According to Atlas, *Biography*, p. 210, they came at a time when "for once in his life, he had money; Pat Covici sent him a second royalty check for five thousand dollars, and Bellow gave his brother Sam ten thousand dollars to invest for him." See SB to Sam Freifeld in an undated letter of spring 1956: "Sam says he is investing $10,000 for me. I'm grateful for his efforts. He really does seem to have good business instincts. Without pride, I confess I have not."

85. The school was set in four hundred acres of farmland, woods, and streams; it had horses, cows, goats, and chickens; there were "no grades, no scores, no tests, no competitive sports" (p. 40); all the teachers were called by their first names.

Paul Goodman taught at Manumit and in 1951 published a novel about his time there; two of Pete Seeger's children were pupils when Sasha attended, as was Mary Travers of Peter, Paul and Mary, and Sholom Aleichem's grandchildren.

86. On p. 127, Sasha describes how "night after night, he would creep down the stairs from the bedroom he shared with my mother, put his hand over my mouth while I slept, insatiable, sometimes violent (I often had bruises on my upper arms), pinning me down, while the tears leaked from my tightly shut eyes, but I knew to be silent."

87. In the main body of the memoir Sasha describes her mother as "afraid to make the break [from the marriage], and still too tied to her compelling but unstable husband, and seduced, as well, by the fantasy of the glamorous artistic life in New York. She did not want the 'bourgeois' life that a return to Chicago would mean, and the image of her as a failure was insupportable, I think" (p. 25).

88. According to *Time*, 14 April 1952, in an article entitled "Bishop Fulton Sheen: The First 'Televangelist.'"

89. According to Greg Bellow, *Saul Bellow's Heart: A Son's Memoir* (London: Bloomsbury, 2013), p. 79.

90. This quotation is from an interview with the author.

91. On p. 7 of the memoir, Sasha mentions a recent story about her family having Turkish origins: "untrue as it may be . . . I am truly sorry I did not know of this rumor in my younger years. I could have made much of it in creating my own exotic background. After all, in my twenties I wore black all the time and smoked Turkish cigarettes—gold-tipped black Sobranies, in an ivory cigarette holder, no kidding."

92. Vidal's Iago comment comes from an interview with the author; Hecht's from Atlas, *Biography*, p. 258.

93. Atlas, *Biography*, p. 257, where Elsa is identified as Elsa Hester and Ellison's remark is quoted on p. 258. That it was Ludwig who told Sasha that SB was sleeping with a girl named Elsa is recalled in "What's in a Name?," p. 99. Botsford paints a similar picture in *Fragments*, using piscatorial rather than barnyard imagery: "We, the faculty, fished for students; they, the students, fished for faculty. Relations which began as intellectual, as discipleships, often enough became intimate and emotional" (p. 10).

94. Elsewhere Botsford calls Ludwig "the Golem [Saul] had conjured up, the alter ego of his carnal self" (p. 4).

95. Alfred Kazin to SB, 22 February 1965.

96. Greg Bellow, *Saul Bellow's Heart*, p. 103.

97. See SB, *Herzog:* "Moses recognized that under his own rules the man who had suffered more was more special, and he conceded willingly that Gersbach had suffered harder, that his agony under the wheels of the boxcar must have been far deeper than anything Moses had ever suffered" (p. 479).

98. Greg Bellow, *Saul Bellow's Heart*, p. 103.

99. Atlas, *Biography*, p. 257.

100. Ibid.

101. Greg Bellow, *Saul Bellow's Heart*, p. 99.

102. See, for example, Don Morrison, "Popular 'U' Teacher Finds Self Jobless," *Minneapolis Sunday Tribune*, 16 April 1961, or "'U' Humanities Lecturer Takes Post in N.Y.," *Minneapolis Tribune*, 24 April 1961, and letters of 28 April and 4 May, also in the *Tribune*. The student newspaper, the *Minnesota Daily*, ran numerous articles in Ludwig's defense. That the Ludwig "case" involved controversial questions about the status and autonomy of the Humanities Program at Minnesota may partly account for the attention it received, as may Ludwig's appearance on local educational television (which broadcast one of his regular college classes, "Humanities in the Modern World," from 9 to 10 p.m., Monday through Friday).

103. Email, 3 April 2013.

104. Botsford email, 28 July 2014.

105. Greg Bellow, *Saul Bellow's Heart*, p. 75.

106. This judgment of Anita as reserved is based only on the handful of letters and postscripted remarks I have seen among correspondence in the SB and Tarcov Papers in the Regenstein.

107. Greg Bellow, *Saul Bellow's Heart*, p. 75.

108. Ibid., pp. 75, 76.

109. *New World Writing* was published by New American Library's Mentor imprint. *The Wrecker* appears in Number 6. It was reprinted in the first edition of *Seize the Day* (New York: Viking, 1956).

110. In a postcard of 14 June 1954, SB announces to Arabel J. Porter, executive editor of *New World Writing*, that "I have a full length play in process," probably an early version of *The Last Analysis* (1965), parts of which were published as "Scenes from 'Humanitis'—A Farce," in *Partisan Review* in 1962. In addition to *The Last Analysis*, which was first produced on Broadway in 1964, SB produced three one-act plays in this period, *A Wen*, *Orange Soufflé*, and *Out from Under*. The first two of these plays were published in *Esquire* in January and October 1965, and all three were performed in 1966 in London and on Broadway as *Under the Weather*. Citations from *The Wrecker* are given within the text; page numbers refer to the edition printed in *Seize the Day*. SB begins his theater chronicle, "The Pleasures and Pains of Playgoing," *Partisan Review* (May–June 1954), with an experience that put him off Broadway for some time, a production of *Harvey*, "the last play I saw prior to this season": "I have not been able to forget that evening, though I have tried." This negative reaction, he claims, had nothing to do with intellectual snobbery. "To anticipate a criticism, I am not a highbrow, though I do not disclaim intelligence, and I do not go to the theater in quest of ideas but to be diverted, delighted, awed, and in search of opportunities to laugh and to cry" (p. 312). There follows an attack both on symbol mongering and humorlessness. On the surface, T. S. Eliot's *The Confidential Clerk* looks like a simple play, but audiences today "know that everything simple is not *really* simple. . . . Jack and Jill can no more be merely Jack and Jill than Moby Dick can be nothing but a whale. Critics have proved to us that mythological and religious entities inhabit ordinary Midwestern personalities. Passengers descending from street-cars illustrate the *Reisemotiv*. Little boys in Mississippi are really Aeneas" (p. 314). The play's "emotional albinism" also puts SB off. The impressive self-command of its characters "made me wonder whether anything so close to death was really suitable to dramatic representation and, also, why this aridity of the British character should be admired and associated with culture or religion" (p. 314). The pleasures playgoing offers, it turns out, are afforded by SB's friends: Ted Hoffman's off-Broadway production of Sartre's *No Exit* is praised for refusing "to let the philosophical element devour the theatrical." Though not even Sartre's "stubbornnest admirers can read his novels . . . his plays can, as Mr. Hoffman has just shown, be stirring" (p. 315). Also praised are Lionel Abel's *The Death of Odysseus* and Robert Hivnor's comedy *The Ticklish Acrobat*. At Hivnor's play, "everyone looked happy. Later, I am sure, the spectators thought of love and history, ritual and religion, but that was in continuation of their pleasure, and they did not have to suffer the pains of culture-anxiety or agonies of ignorance, wondering which sip of the cocktail represented the eucharist" (p. 317).

111. SB to the McCloskys, undated letter of spring 1954. See "I Got a Scheme!": "I found a nice apartment on Riverside Drive. But somehow it just didn't work. I never knew any real comfort in New York. I always felt challenge and injury around the corner. I had always considered it a very risky place, where one was easily lost. And I think I saw New York through the being of Isaac Rosenfeld. . . . He

came to take the town and he got took. From his standpoint it proved to be a very dangerous place" (pp. 83–84).

112. These quotations from Greg Bellow, *Saul Bellow's Heart*, pp. 72, 77.

113. Ibid., p. 78.

114. According to Botsford, *Fragments V*, p. 32, at the very beginning of the summer, he and SB, "needing extra money," stayed on at Bard "and explained America to Israeli and Pakistani Fulbrights."

115. Entry of 6 August 1962 in Richard M. Cook, *Alfred Kazin's Journals* (New Haven: Yale University Press, 2012), p. 287.

116. Carol Brightman, *Writing Dangerously: Mary McCarthy and Her World* (1992; London: Secker & Warburg, 1993), p. 371. SB was wary rather than unfriendly. As he explained in his interview to Botsford: "Mary was unquestionably a witty writer, but she had a taste for low sadism. She would brutally work over people it wasn't really necessary to attack. . . . You'd run into her on the street, as Nicola Chiaromonte once told me he did. She was blooming, he said, and he asked, 'Why are you looking so well, Mary?' She said, 'I just finished a piece against So-and-so, and now I'm writing another, about such and such. Next I'm going to tear You-know-who to pieces'" (Botsford interview, "A Second Half Life," SB, *IAAU*, pp. 319–20). In Randall Jarrell's novel about a college like Bard, *Pictures from an Institution* (1954; Chicago: University of Chicago Press, 1986), p. 134, which SB thought "much more amusing" than *The Groves of Academe*, the main character, Gertrude Johnson, based on McCarthy, writes books described as "a systematic, detailed, and conclusive condemnation of mankind for being stupid and bad"; as a teacher, "she was always able to fail the clever for being bad, the good for being stupid."

117. Ann Birstein, *What I Saw at the Fair* (New York: Welcome Rain Publishers, 2003), pp. 158–59.

118. Atlas, *Biography*, p. 219.

119. For "potato love," see *Herzog*: "Do not deceive yourself, dear Moses Elkanah, with childish jingles and Mother Goose. Hearts quaking with cheap and feeble charity or oozing potato love have not written history" (p. 493); "He gave Moses a kiss. Moses felt the potato love. Amorphous, swelling, hungry, indiscriminate, cowardly potato love" (p. 507).

120. According to Maury Bellows's daughter, Lynn Rotblatt, as quoted in Atlas, *Biography*, p. 337: "The crescent moon in the doorbell, the chimes that play 'Merrily We Roll Along,' his stepmother's shuffling footsteps in her slippers—I'm reading this and the tears are rolling down my face. He was writing my life. That's when I knew he was a genius."

121. Greg Bellow, *Saul Bellow's Heart*, pp. 83, 84.

122. See Mark Harris, *Saul Bellow: Drumlin Woodchuck* (Athens: University of Georgia Press, 1980), p. 13; for Ruth Miller, see Atlas, *Biography*, p. 222. Harris's book is about his failed attempts to become SB's biographer. The title comes from a Robert Frost poem, "A Drumlin Woodchuck," which characterizes the woodchuck as a peaceful creature who "shrewdly pretends that he and the world are friends." A "drumlin" is a ridge made by a glacier pushing its way through prehistoric land. It serves as an ideal retreat, a sort of rocky burrow, for the woodchuck, or ground hog. In *Seize the Day*, Tommy Wilhelm admits that he "wasn't what I thought I was. And wasn't even careful to take a few precautions, as most people do—like a woodchuck has a few exits to his tunnel" (p. 41).

123. Manea, *Conversation*, p. 9. Here is SB on Father Herzog's funeral: "This day was just like—he braced himself and faced it—like the day of Father Herzog's funeral. Then, too, it was flowering weather—roses, magnolias. Moses, the night before, had cried, slept, the air was wickedly perfumed; he had had luxuri-

ant dreams, painful, evil, and rich, interrupted by the rare ecstasy of nocturnal emission—how death dangles freedom before the enslaved instincts: the pitiful sons of Adam whose minds and bodies must answer strange signals" (p. 699).

124. "I Got a Scheme!," p. 83.

125. Atlas, *Biography*, pp. 214, 215, 216.

12. PYRAMID LAKE

1. SB to Henry Volkening, undated letter, written from Reno, hence after 28 September 1955.

2. SB, "Illinois Journey," reprinted in SB, *IAAU*, p. 196. Subsequent references to "Illinois Journey" cited within the text by page numbers.

3. James Atlas, *Delmore Schwartz: The Life of an American Poet* (1977; New York: Avon, 1978), p. 305.

4. The first quotation about the drive west comes from p. 84 of Sasha's unpublished memoir, "What's in a Name?" (henceforth cited within the text by page numbers). For the origins and nature of the memoir, see Chapter 10, note 95.

5. Mark Lundahl, "A Part of Old Reno Gone," obituary of Harry Drackert in the *Reno Gazette Journal*, 29 December 1990. Liebling published two articles on the Drackerts and their guest ranch entitled "The Mustang Busters" in *The New Yorker* (3 and 10 April 1954) and four articles on Pyramid Lake and the Paiute Indians under the heading "The Lake of the Cui-ui Eaters," also in *The New Yorker* (1, 8, 15, 22 January 1955). The four "Cui-ui" articles are reprinted in A. J. Liebling, *A Reporter at Large: Dateline: Pyramid Lake, Nevada*, ed. Elmer R. Rusco (Reno: University of Nevada Press, 2000).

6. Perhaps the best known of the sci-fi movies shot at Pyramid Lake was *Planet of the Apes* (1968). The lake doubled for the Sea of Galilee in another Charlton Heston movie, *The Greatest Story Ever Told* (1965).

7. Arthur Miller, *Timebends: A Life* (London: Methuen, 1987), p. 378.

8. Ibid., pp. 377–82.

9. See SB, *Henderson the Rain King* (1958), p. 143: "I got clean away from everything, and we came into a region like a floor surrounded by mountains. It was hot, clear, and arid and after several days we saw no human footprints. Nor were there many plants; for that matter there was not much of anything here; it was all simplified and splendid, and I felt I was entering the past—the real past, no history or junk like that. The prehuman past. And I believed that there was something between the stones and me. The mountains were naked, and often snakelike in their forms, without trees, and you could see the clouds being born on the slopes. From this rock came vapor, but it was not like ordinary vapor, it cast a brilliant shadow. Anyway I was in tremendous shape those first long days, hot as they were. At night, after Romilayu had prayed, and we lay on the ground, the face of the air breathed back on us, breath for breath. And then there were the calm stars, turning around and singing, and the birds of the night with heavy bodies, fanning by. I couldn't have asked for anything better." On the way to the Wariri, Henderson notices "jumbled white stones that looked as if they had been combed out by an ignorant hand from the elements that make least sense. . . . I am no geologist but the word calcareous seemed to fit them. They were composed of lime and my guess was that they must have originated in a body of water. Now they were ultra-dry but filled with little caves. . . . The cave mouths were open and there was this coarse and clumsy gnarled white stone" (p. 207)—like the tufa-encrusted stones of Pyramid Lake.

10. SB to Grace Wade, 7 March 1972.

11. A. J. Liebling, "The Mustang Busters," *New Yorker* (3 April 1954).

12. See Noriko M. Lippit, "A Perennial Survivor: Saul Bellow's Heroine in the Desert," *Studies in Short Fiction* 12 (1975).

13. SB, "Leaving the Yellow House," first published in *Esquire*, January 1958, reprinted in SB, *CS*, p. 265 (henceforth cited within the text by page numbers).

14. Daniel Fuchs, *Saul Bellow: Vision and Revision*, p. 295.

15. Miller, *Timebends*, pp. 384–85. Nothing is said of Malibu in SB's correspondence, but Henderson recalls meeting his son Edward there. Edward lived in a cabin beside the Pacific, which is nicely caught, especially in the movement of the surf: "The water was ghostly, lazy, slow, stupefying, with a vast dull shine. Coppery. A womb of white. Pallor; smoke; vacancy; dull gold; vastness; dimness; fulgor; ghostly flashing" (p. 213).

16. In 1990, SB received a letter from Robert M. Gorrell, vice president for academic affairs emeritus at the University of Nevada, in which he relayed the news of Harry Drackert's death, also of the activities of other people SB knew. Though Reno had now "spread all over the valley," "Pyramid remains pretty much unspoiled . . . with the Paiutes resisting the temptation to let developers take it over."

17. SB to Sam Freifeld, 5 November 1955.

18. Atlas, *Biography*, p. 229.

19. SB to Henry Volkening, undated.

20. SB to Pascal Covici, undated.

21. Miller, *Timebends*, p. 377. The identity of the "cottage" Miller stayed in is unclear, as SB and Sasha were in the pink house and Peggy in the shack, at least at the beginning of Miller's stay.

22. Atlas, *Biography*, p. 233.

23. Ibid., p. 242.

24. William Moore, "Reveal Gems in Love Nest of Hoffa Aide," *Chicago Daily Tribune*, 22 August 1958.

25. Atlas, *Biography*, p. 235.

26. Steven J. Zipperstein, *Rosenfeld's Lives: Fame, Oblivion and the Furies of Writing* (New Haven: Yale University Press, 2009), p. 200ff.

27. Atlas, *Biography*, p. 235.

28. Greg Bellow, *Saul Bellow's Heart: A Son's Memoir* (London: Bloomsbury, 2013), p. 90.

29. The depth of SB's feeling for Rosenfeld is clear in his many writings about him, beginning with the *Partisan Review* memorial piece, "Isaac Rosenfeld" (Fall 1956). That he was devastated by the news of his death is clear from his correspondence. See SB to Gertrude Buckman, 2 August 1956: "I had been thrown millions of light years by Isaac Rosenfeld's death"; also 23 August 1956 to Ruth Miller: "I myself have been none too hot, either, since Isaac's death." In a letter postmarked 6 December 1956 to John Berryman he writes: "I think and think about Isaac, and my recollections are endless—twenty-six years, of which I've forgotten very little." SB to Ralph Ellison, 2 April 1956, suggests that August was the month when Greg was going to be with SB, but plans seem to have changed. See Greg Bellow, *Saul Bellow's Heart*, p. 90: "One morning in the summer of 1956 a phone call woke us with news that Isaac Rosenfeld had died in Chicago. Saul was inconsolable." As Rosenfeld died on 14 July, this suggests that Greg and SB reconnected as soon as SB returned from Nevada; attending the funeral would have meant leaving Greg again, almost as soon as they'd gotten together. Returning to Chicago for Isaac's funeral would also have meant leaving Sasha to take care of him—alone in the house in Germantown, while she was suffering from morning sickness.

30. See SB to Ralph Ellison, 2 April 1956, for Greg's height; for Sasha's nausea, see p. 91 of her unpublished memoir.

31. Greg Bellow, *Saul Bellow's Heart*, pp. 88–89.

32. According to Atlas, *Biography*, p. 241, SB received an $8,000 legacy plus stock in Carroll Coal, which was valued at around $12,000. The $16,000 figure comes from SB, "Ralph Ellison in Tivoli," in *News from the Republic of Letters* 3 (January 1998), later reprinted in *Partisan Review* 65:4 (Fall 1998) and the Bard College magazine, *The Bardian* (Spring 1999). For the $20,000 legacy Moses Herzog inherits, see SB, *Herzog* (1964), p. 536.

33. Monroe had been scheduled to visit Miller at Pyramid Lake the week after SB and Sasha left, but the day before she was due to arrive a reporter from the New York *Daily News* showed up. Miller tried to put him off but the next morning, according to a letter he wrote to SB on 2 June 1956, "the front page of the News has us about to be married, and me 'readying' my divorce here. All hell breaks loose. The phones all around never stop ringing. Television trucks—(as I live!)—drive up, cameras grinding, screams, yells, —I say nothing, give them some pictures, retire into the cabin." Two hours before Monroe's flight to Reno, Miller got ahold of her by phone and canceled the visit.

34. SB, "Ralph Ellison in Tivoli."

35. Atlas, *Biography*, p. 241.

36. In 1926, the owner of the house, William B. Ward, of the Ward Baking Company, gave it to a local charity as a site for an old folks' home and for summer camps for underprivileged residents of New York City's Lower East Side. Later it served as a settlement house for young girls from Manhattan.

37. SB to Gertrude Buckman, 2 August 1956; also 23 August 1956 to Ruth Miller: "If the house were in better repair I'd ask you up for Labor Day. But now the well has given out."

38. SB to Ruth Miller, 23 August 1956.

39. SB to Pascal Covici, received on 12 September 1956.

40. Covici's letter describes his discussion with Volkening about the advance: "He would like me to ask, he said, for $2,500. My feeling was, since our option calls for a book of short stories with an advance of only $300, that his asking figure was a little bit 'mishuga [crazy],' and I, therefore, suggested $1,500. When I got back to the office and told Harold [Guinzburg, the publisher] about it there was no hesitation on his part—$1,500 was O.K. And nobody, including myself, had read a single short story before hand."

41. Atlas, *Biography*, p. 231.

42. The title of Kazin's 18 November 1956 review was "In Search of Light."

43. Hollis Alpert, "Uptown Dilemmas," review of SB, *Seize the Day*, *Saturday Review* (24 November 1956).

44. Chirantan Kulshrestha, "A Conversation with Saul Bellow," *Chicago Review* 23.4–24.1 (1972), reprinted in Cronin and Siegel, eds., *Conversations with SB*, p. 89.

45. Manea, "Conversation," p. 38.

46. From a note made of a conversation with the author on 10 January 2009 in New York City. See also Atlas, *Biography*, p. 526.

47. On 24 December 1956 SB received a letter on headed paper from Arthur S. Tamkin, PhD, of Florence, Massachusetts: "Dear Mr. Bellow, I found your novella 'Seize the Day' very entertaining particularly because of the coincidence of the similarities between myself and your fictitious character Dr. Tamkin. It struck me as astounding that we both shared the same name, title, profession, religion, and even interests, viz., financial speculation. How did you ever dream up such a character?"

48. Both SB quotations from "I Got a Scheme!," p. 83.

49. Atlas, *Biography*, p. 236.

50. Dr. Tamkin had a real-life original, SB told Roth in "I Got a Scheme!," p. 84: "He was a friend of two friends. The second friends were a European couple whom I liked very much, and their only child had been killed in an accident and

'Dr. Tamkin' came and took charge, emotional charge, of the family, as he would. And I hated him for it. I saw what he was doing; he had no feeling for these people. He was just a scatterbrain, a poseur. Self-anointed helper of mankind, full of generosity to everybody. That was the real background of this foolish grotesque. She was a Jewish Frenchwoman. He was a German Jew. Their child, about fifteen years old, was knocked down in the street by a truck on his way home from school."

51. For a reading of *Seize the Day* that takes Tommy as an overgrown child, see Judith Oster, "The Reader as Parent in Saul Bellow's *Seize the Day*," in the *Saul Bellow Journal* 24, no 1 (Winter–Spring 2011): "the adult Tommy—himself by contrast a devoted father—is portrayed as a child at the same time that we are reminded of his adult status. No matter how often we are made aware of his full-grown size (given Tommy's self-descriptions as 'hippopotamus' or 'rhino') as well as his very adult concerns, he is called a child by others, talked to as one would talk to a child, cries out—cries—and therefore sees himself as childlike, telling himself, 'It's time I stopped feeling like a kid toward him, a small son'" (p. 20). Greg Bellow, in *Saul Bellow's Heart*, p. 85, describes Abraham's opinion of SB as follows: "an overgrown crybaby who had failed to absorb the lesson life taught him: the necessity of emotional toughness. I think that my father agreed but could do little to control his emotions."

52. According to Greg Bellow, *Saul Bellow's Heart*, p. 70, he and his father would roar together in the subway in New York whenever a train came rattling into the station.

53. There is much in the story to suggest SB's continuing faith in Reichian concepts. It is the narrator (not Tamkin, not Tommy) who employs Reichian terms to describe Tommy's state. For Reich, the chest is the seat of physical and psychic stress. Tommy's chest, we are told, is "congested with anger" (p. 25). When criticized by his father for giving money to his ex-wife, Tommy's lips work in silence before he speaks: a sign that "the congestion was growing" (p. 38). He feels "a great knot of wrong tied tight within his chest" (p. 44). He can't swallow, for "his chest pained him still" (p. 76). As Tommy hardens himself to avoid crying, he feels "a violent, vertical pain go through his chest, like that caused by a pocket of air under the collar bone" (p. 87). In the steam room with his father, "my chest is all up—I feel choked" (p. 91).

54. For Malamud on *Seize the Day*, the source of this anecdote, see Philip Davis, *Bernard Malamud: A Writer's Life* (Oxford: Oxford University Press, 2007), pp. 187–88.

55. James Wood, *How Fiction Works* (2008; London: Vintage, 2009), p. 30. After praising the novel, Monroe Engel had a similar criticism (in an undated letter to SB, now among SB's papers at the Regenstein): "I am shaken by the cry of anguish I know and remember well—which is your own voice. Only this is my trouble with the story too. That the voice is almost always your voice in the crises. That I don't believe it belongs to Tommy Wilhelm. That when he's in the telephone booth, for example, I hear you in there with him, like Cyrano making love for his friend."

56. "I Got a Scheme!," p. 83; the quote in parentheses is from David D. Galloway, "An Interview with Saul Bellow," *Audit-Poetry* 3 (1963), reprinted in Cronin and Siegel, eds., *Conversations with SB*, p. 21.

57. "I Got a Scheme!," p. 83.

58. Here are the relevant stanzas from "The Rime of the Ancient Mariner," in the 1817 version. The mariner, having shot the albatross, is marooned at sea:

> *The many men so beautiful!*
> *And they all dead did lie:*
> *And a thousand thousand slimy things*
> *Lived on; and so did I.* (ll.236–39)

Then comes the moment of breakthrough:

> *Beyond the shadow of the ship,*
> *I watched the water snakes:*
> *They moved in tracks of shining white,*
> *And when they reared, the elfish light*
> *Fell off in hoary flakes.*
>
> *Within the shadow of the ship*
> *I watched their rich attire:*
> *Blue, glossy green, and velvet black,*
> *They coiled and swam; and every track*
> *Was a flash of golden fire.*
>
> *O happy living things!*
> *No tongue their beauty might declare:*
> *A spring of love gushed from my heart,*
> *And I blessed them unaware:*
> *Sure my kind saint took pity on me,*
> *And I blessed them unaware.*
>
> *The selfsame moment I could pray;*
> *And from my neck so free*
> *The albatross fell off and sank*
> *Like lead into the sea.* (ll.272–91)

In *Herzog* Moses experiences "breakthroughs" like Tommy's, of an orgasmic character. But he distrusts them: "What I seem to do, thought Herzog, is to inflame myself with drama, with ridicule, failure, denunciation, distortion, to inflame myself voluptuously, esthetically, until I reach a sexual climax. And that climax looks like a resolution and an answer to many 'higher' problems" (pp. 626–27).

59. I am much indebted to Pifer's reading of the novella in *Saul Bellow Against the Grain* (Philadelphia: University of Pennsylvania Press, 1990), pp. 78–95.

60. Tommy's experience with Hollywood begins in a way that recalls his creator's experience. As was mentioned in Chapter 7, when *Dangling Man* was published in 1944 SB received a telephone call from a studio executive at Metro-Goldwyn-Mayer. The executive had seen the photograph of him from the jacket of *Dangling Man* and thought he could become a movie star. Though Bellow was neither handsome nor tough enough to be the male lead, the executive thought he could have a good career, so SB recalled, as the man "who loses the girl to the George Raft or Errol Flynn type" (Atlas, *Biography*, p. 101). In *Seize the Day* the agent tells Tommy: "I have you placed as the type that loses the girl to the George Raft type or the William Powell type" (p. 18).

61. Hana Wirth-Nesher, "'Who's He When He's at Home?': Saul Bellow's Translations," in Michael P. Kramer, ed., *New Essays on Seize the Day* (Cambridge: Cambridge University Press, 1998), pp. 29–30, makes much of the name change; she also connects "Tommy" and Tommy's story to Isaac Bashevis Singer's story "Gimpel the Fool," in Yiddish, "Gimpel Tam" (pronounced "Tom").

62. Pifer, *Saul Bellow Against the Grain*, p. 84. Though I agree with Pifer's reading here, the passage lists other reasons for Tommy's rejection: "when Venice saw the results of the screen test he did a quick about-face. In those days Wilhelm had a speech difficulty. It was not a true stammer, it was a thickness of speech which the soundtrack exaggerated. The film showed that he had many peculiarities, otherwise unnoticeable. When he shrugged, his hands drew up within his sleeves.

The vault of his chest was huge, but he really didn't look strong under the lights" (p. 19).

63. For the "hassle" with Brendan Gill, see Atlas, *Biography*, p. 247. As Gill told Atlas, it "barely even qualified as a dispute: At a literary conference at Smith College two years earlier, Bellow made a disparaging comment about *The New Yorker*, and Gill had risen to its defense. 'Bellow replied in a way calculated to give further offense,' as William Maxwell remembered the episode. In the ensuing debate, neither one 'ever hesitated for a second before replying, and they had to an equal degree the talent for giving expression to anger, contempt, deliberate insolence, and personal dislike.'" SB's animus toward *The New Yorker* derived not only from the Anthony West review of *Augie* and the decision to turn down *Seize the Day*, but from the rejection of another story SB submitted entitled "Legacies," which sounds at first as though it might be about a character like his sister, Jane (the character is married to a dentist, has two sons, is overly protective, so much so that her son refuses to see her when she turns up at his fraternity house, a detail Katherine White canvassed her fellow *New Yorker* editors about, reporting in a letter of 6 April 1956 to Volkening, "I can find no man in the office who can believe that the son would utterly refuse to see his mother if she arrived with soup and blankets"). The story does not appear among SB's papers in the Regenstein. Interestingly, though White thought it had potential—"it could have, I feel, a good deal of the wonderful crazy quality and the subtle overtones of that last Saul Bellow short story, 'A Father-to-Be'"—it was turned down, ultimately, because of length. "To go so deeply into Annie's family and youth seems more like novel technique than like that of a short story. . . . All I can honestly say is that we like elements of the story very much, but feel that it is a slight one for its forty-six page length."

64. The appointment was only confirmed at the last minute, too late to be listed in the February 1957 Budget for Interdisciplinary Studies (previously General Studies, the department that housed the Humanities Program).

65. SB, "John Berryman," reprinted in SB, *IAAU*, p. 268, a reprinting of SB's foreword to Berryman's novel *Recovery* (1973), also published in the *New York Times Book Review*, 27 May 1973 (henceforth cited within the text by page numbers).

66. Eileen Simpson, *Poets in Their Youth: A Memoir* (1982; New York: Vintage, 1983), p. 267. See also Paul Mariani, *Dream Song: The Life of John Berryman* (New York: William Morrow, 1990), p. 213: "Bellow he met at a friend's house [in Princeton, in the fall of 1952], where he listened to him play Purcell 'very sweetly' on the recorder."

67. In Botsford interview, "A Half Life," reprinted in SB, *IAAU*, p. 310.

68. This note is from the Berryman Papers in the Special Collections of the University Library of the University of Minnesota, Unpublished Prose, Box 1, Folder "Amer. Writer 1958." It is quoted in Catherine Fitzpatrick's PhD thesis, "John Berryman and Saul Bellow: Literary Friendship and Mutual Influence" (University of Sheffield, August 2011), p. 44, which is where I found it, along with much other useful information on SB and Berryman, as well as much shrewd interpretation of their writings.

69. Irving Howe, *A Margin of Hope: An Intellectual Autobiography* (New York: Harcourt Brace Jovanovich, 1982), pp. 163–64.

70. From the author's note to John Berryman, *The Dream Songs* (2007; New York: Farrar, Straus & Giroux, 1969), p. xx. In the author's note Berryman explains the work's titling: "This volume combines 77 *Dream Songs* and *His Toy, His Dream, His Rest*, comprising Books I through VII of a poem whose working title, since 1955, has been *The Dream Songs*."

71. SB visited Berryman in several drying-out facilities: "It's always Pleasant St. Golden Valley Lotos Island" (Atlas, *Biography*, p. 425).

72. The phrase comes from Chapter 31 of Lewis's *Rude Assignment: An Intellectual Autobiography* (1950; Santa Barbara: Black Sparrow Press, 1984), p. 183.

73. John Berryman, *The Freedom of the Poet*, preface by Robert Giroux (New York: Farrar, Straus & Giroux, 1976), p. 13.

74. From Merwin's introduction to Berryman, *The Dream Songs*, p. xxiii.

75. For a sample of Berryman's compellingly eccentric style of reading and speaking, see YouTube versions of him introducing and reciting Dream Song 14, "Life, friends, is boring."

76. See the 1850 version of Wordsworth's *Prelude*, the "poem addressed to Coleridge," Book XIV, lines 437–45.

77. Catherine Fitzpatrick, "John Berryman and Saul Bellow," p. 47 (see note 68). In the summer of 1951 Berryman lectured at the University of Vermont's School of Modern Critical Studies in Burlington. One of Berryman's lectures was "Africa," though it was in fact about the modern American novel. It began by pointing out the number of novels—thirty—published by Americans and Britons during the last two decades that dealt with or were set in Africa. Paul Mariani, in *Dream Song*, p. 238, summarizes the lecture's main point: "America itself had become so complex in the past forty years that even Henry James could not have dealt with what it had become. . . . So, just as Shakespeare and other Elizabethans had been drawn to Italy as to an idealized and exotic place, American novelists had been drawn to Africa."

78. Catherine Fitzpatrick, "John Berryman and Saul Bellow," p. 47.

79. These quotations are from pp. 389 and 155, but similar ones can be found throughout *Henderson*. Atlas, *Biography*, p. 273, offers "Wo, dem be trouble" while also claiming that the African women in the novel are "notable mainly for their big behinds." Presumably it is the Wariri amazons Atlas is referring to: "Corset-like vests were the only garments worn by these large women, which were rather heavy or bunchy in build, and unusally expanded behind" (p. 235).

80. Fitzpatrick, "John Berryman and Saul Bellow," p. 48, where she dates Berryman's reading of Wittke's *Tambo and Bones*.

81. For SB on Henderson, see Nina Steers, "Successor to Faulkner?," *Show* 4, September 1964, reprinted in Cronin and Siegel, eds., *Conversations with SB*, p. 34.

82. SB, "Literature," in *The Great Ideas Today*, ed. W. Benton (Chicago: Encyclopedia Britannica, 1963), pp. 164, 170, 171. See also SB, ed., *Great Jewish Short Stories* (New York: Dell, 1963), p. 12, in which he claims that in Jewish literature "laughter and trembling are so curiously mingled that it is not easy to determine the relations of the two."

83. For the quoted Berryman phrases from the note of 1955, see Mariani, *Dream Song*, p. 301. Uncharacteristically, SB in "The Distracted Public," his Romanes Lecture at Oxford (10 May 1990), reprinted in SB, *IAAU*, pp. 161–64, cites Nabokov as an ally in the matter of seriocomic heroes, describing Humbert in *Lolita* in terms that recall Henry or Henderson. Such views about the changing nature of literary heroes were much in the air in the 1950s, as in Northrop Frye's *Anatomy of Criticism* (1957), an unavoidable topic in this period in university English Departments (and among the literature teachers in Humanities Programs). Frye, it has been suggested, was an indirect spur or stimulus for Ellison's essay on blackface, which responds to an earlier essay by Ellison's friend Stanley Edgar Hyman. According to Arnold Rampersad, in *Ralph Ellison: A Biography* (2007; New York: Vintage, 2008), p. 351, Hyman's essay applied Frye's "archytypal" criticism to black stereotypes. SB's talk of the turning inside out of late-Romantic attitudes recalls Frye's sequencing of genres in *Anatomy of Criticism*. This sequencing ends with a phase of satire in which comedy derives from the humiliation and embarrassment of the antihero.

84. SB, "John Berryman," SB, *IAAU*, p. 272.

85. Here is Chapman, SB's acknowledged starting point for Henderson, in an interview with Robert H. Boyle, "Step in and Enjoy the Tumult," *Sports Illustrated* (13 June 1977): "You can abolish rectitude, you can abolish the laws of gravity, but don't do away with good old American hogwash"; "'Winty' [Aldrich, Chapman's cousin] is the essence of nothing. He has the personality of an unsuccessful undertaker and uses semicolons when he writes. He knits with his toes."

86. See, for example, Dream Song 60: "You may be right, Friend Bones. / Indeed you is. Dey flyin ober de world, / de pilots ober ofays" (etc.).

87. "An Interview with John Berryman," conducted by John Plotz of the *Harvard Advocate*, 27 October 1968, reprinted in *Berryman's Understanding: Reflections on the Poetry of John Berryman*, ed. Harry Thomas (Boston: Northeastern University Press, 1988), p. 7.

88. When Berryman published *Love & Fame* (1970) he dropped the distinction between voice and creator. SB corresponded with Anne Sexton in this period. In a brief undated letter he writes, "At this particular point we seem to have entered each other's minds. A marriage of true minds, or meeting arranged by Agape. (Where has Eros gotten me?) . . . Your poem is genuinely Hendersonian—'breathing in loops like a green hen' is absolutely IT! Yours in true-minded friendship, Saul Bellow."

89. Fitzpatrick, "John Berryman and Saul Bellow," p. 83, dates this letter, found among the SB papers in the Regenstein, "probably June 1 1964"; Fitzpatrick also draws attention to a structural debt *Herzog* owes to *The Dream Songs*. Herzog's letters, she argues, function as do Henry's dreams: "both are inherently self-contained, and allow for the full and forcible expression of an idea or image and at the same time for absolute contingency, or deniability" (p. 109).

90. SB, "John Berryman," SB, *IAAU*, p. 271. In addition to this sequence of "inter-relations" there were specific borrowings, of favorite phrases ("pal," "jerk") and anecdotes. "Let us suppose, valleys & such ago," begins Dream Song 15, which retells an SB anecdote in its first two stanzas, about a Polish girl SB encountered in a bar. "Excusez mon vol," wrote Berryman to SB on 14 August 1962, "but I warned you ten years ago that if by some point you hadn't used this, I would."

91. See Sheila Wolfe, "Seek Industry to Use Site of Trailer Camp," 27 May 1957, also "Trailer Park Suit Trial to Begin," 9 May 1957, in *Chicago Tribune*.

92. Richard Stern was born in New York in 1928 and from the age "of twelve or thirteen" knew he wanted to be a writer. He studied at the University of North Carolina at Chapel Hill, where he befriended the poets Edgar Bowers and Donald Justice, and got to know Justice's sister, Eleanor, who was married to the Tennessee writer Peter Taylor. Through Taylor, he connected with John Crowe Ransom (who would publish his first stories in *The Kenyon Review*) and other Southern writers in and around Vanderbilt. Stern got an MA in English from Harvard, taught in France and Germany for two years on a Fulbright Fellowship, and then returned to the United States to do a PhD at the University of Iowa, the only place in the country where one could get a doctorate for creative writing (in his case for a collection of stories). After teaching for a year at Connecticut College, he got the job at Chicago.

93. SB, "The Swamp of Prosperity," review of Philip Roth, *Goodbye, Columbus*, in *Commentary* (July 1959).

94. In Philip Roth, *The Ghost Writer* (1979; New York: Vintage, 1995), p. 57 (henceforth cited within the text by page numbers), Abravanel's books are described by Zuckerman as "seething with unbuttoned and aggressive innocence. . . . [Abravanel] found irresistible all vital and dubious types, not excluding the swindlers of both sexes who trampled upon the hearts of his optimistic, undone heroes; the writer who could locate the hypnotic core in the most devious American self-seeker and lead him to disclose, in spirited locutions all his own, the depths of

his conniving soul; the writer whose absorption with 'the grand human discord' made every paragraph a little novel in itself, every page packed as tight as Dickens or Dostoyevsky with the latest news of manias, temptations, passions, and dreams, with mankind aflame with feeling."

95. There were commercial airline flights from Minneapolis to Chicago. When Rosenfeld died early in the summer of 1956, Phil Siegelman took one to attend the funeral (according to an email from Ellen Siegelman, 30 June 2013). In class the students criticize Zuckerman's story in ways that explain what Roth means by "the points of view that criticism came in." When Abravanel discusses the story he does so "with oblique admiration, defending it, largely with his laugh, from criticism brought by the orthodox Forsterites that my narrator was 'two-dimensional' instead of being 'round' like the characters he's read about in *Aspects of the Novel*" (p. 63).

96. Zuckerman describes how he felt as he listened to what the mistress was telling him:

> the effect would have been no more stunning if she had said, "After the reception I have to get back to the hotel to interview Marshal Tito in the bar—but while I do, Felix can rise into Heaven from the lobby and discuss your funny little mimeographed story with the author of *The Brothers Karamazov*. We all met in Siberia when Felix and I did the prison tour." Somewhere behind me I heard Abravanel applying himself to another serious question from the graduate division. "Alienation? Oh," he said, with that light laugh, "let the other guy be alienated" (p. 62).

97. The phrase is Moody Prior's, quoted in an article in the *Daily Northwestern* (26 November 1957) entitled "Author on NU Faculty During Next Quarter," the source also of details of SB's teaching.

98. SB to Ralph Ellison, 14 February 1958.

99. Atlas, *Biography*, p. 259. Sasha thought the look likely to have been misinterpreted (it probably meant nothing more than "pick up a glass").

100. The press release is dated 14 February 1958. It is among the SB papers in University Archives, Northwestern University Library. Others elected to the National Institute of Arts and Letters in SB's year were Louise Bogan, Aaron Copland, Malcolm Cowley, and Robert Penn Warren.

101. See Ian Hamilton, *Robert Lowell, A Biography* (New York: Random House, 1982), pp. 142–43.

102. SB, "Distractions of a Fiction Writer," in Granville Hicks, ed., *The Living Novel: A Symposium* (New York, Macmillan, 1957), pp. 3–4 (henceforth cited within the text by page numbers).

103. See Rosette Lamont, "Bellow Observed: A Serial Portrait," *Mosaic: A Journal for the Comparative Study of Literature and Ideas* 8, no. 1 (Fall 1974): 256: "A woman painter who imagined herself to be a *salonnière* was told by Bellow, as she was lionizing him and attempting to discuss with him the American Novel: 'Literature is too serious a topic to waste on those who know nothing about it.'"

104. SB's dictating *Henderson* has been compared to Henry James composing in his head (see Atlas, *Biography*, p. 262), though James was composing in his head and SB reading from a handwritten manuscript, which he corrected, cut, and added to as he went along.

13. BETRAYAL

1. This quotation comes from p. 100 of Sasha's unpublished memoir, "What's in a Name?" (henceforth cited within the text by page numbers). For the origins and nature of the memoir, see Chapter 10, note 95.

2. From an interview with the author. Unless otherwise indicated, all subsequent Sasha quotations or recollections are from interviews with the author.

3. Though Sasha does not specify, there were a number of reasons why "no one could talk to Saul": because of the humiliation it would cause him, or the fury it would provoke, or the fear that he would retaliate "and try to take Adam from me" (p. 102), or the damage his knowing might cause Ludwig's career.

4. Greg Bellow, *Saul Bellow's Heart*, p. 93.

5. Ibid., p. 93 (for the quote about Reichek and the rickety bicycle), p. 94 (for Greg and capitalism).

6. Tom Fitzpatrick, *Chicago Sun-Times*, "Bellow's Books Too Deep," 16 March 1972.

7. Nathan Tarcov was ten and his sister, Miriam, fifteen, at the time of their father's heart attack in early July. Oscar was taken to a hospital in Hanover, New Hampshire, and after a brief stay at a nearby bed-and-breakfast, the children were taken first to Beebee de Regnier's apartment in Manhattan, then to Tivoli. During this time Edith Tarcov stayed in Hanover with Oscar. The children spent several weeks in camp in Cold Spring, New York, by which time Oscar and Edith had returned home. Neither Nathan nor Miriam recalls anything about Saul and Sasha that summer (email from Nathan Tarcov, 17 July 2013).

8. Greg Bellow, *Saul Bellow's Heart*, p. 94.

9. Both Ross quotations from Atlas, *Biography*, p. 263.

10. Ruth Miller, *Saul Bellow: A Biography of the Imagination* (New York: St. Martin's, 1991), pp. 134, 135.

11. Atlas, *Biography*, p. 262, says SB drove from Tivoli, a view supported by SB to Josephine Herbst, 4 January 1959; Sasha's memoir suggests he drove from Minneapolis.

12. SB's description of what happened to Larry, in the letter of 31 January 1959 to Josephine Herbst, was simple and poignant: "being in great trouble, and seeing no way out, he killed himself." Larry had joined the army the previous year, was caught stealing "and perhaps more" (Greg's phrase) and was being held in a stockade in the Presidio, a military base in San Francisco, now a park (*Saul Bellow's Heart*, p. 95, also for Sam's having "stopped asking questions").

13. Greg Bellow, *Saul Bellow's Heart*, p. 95.

14. Arnold Rampersad, *Ralph Ellison: A Biography* (2007; New York: Vintage, 2008), p. 349.

15. Granville Hicks, ed., *The Living Novel: A Symposium* (New York: Macmillan, 1957), pp. 83, 76 (Ellison's essay henceforth cited within the text by page numbers).

16. Ellison's skills as a handyman came from an unhappy stint as a janitor. He had a lifelong interest in technology and electronics. According to his friend David Sarser, "He was always for anything new . . . and he loved gadgets and devices and machines. He would stop his writing in a second if there was something fresh to explore in science or technology" (Rampersad, *Ralph Ellison: A Biography*, p. 252).

17. Ralph Ellison to SB, 21 September 1958, quoted in ibid., p. 362.

18. SB to Albert Murray, 27 June 1959, quoted in ibid., p. 361.

19. The nature of Cookie's help is unspecified by either SB or Sasha.

20. Atlas, *Biography*, p. 264.

21. Ibid., p. 263.

22. The intimacy of this letter to Herbst is explained by SB's long silence in correspondence: "I don't tell you this to have it weigh on your heart . . . but only because it will seem loutish of me not to have answered."

23. For "queenliness," see SB to Ralph Ellison, 10 February 1959: "it's a relief to know that Sasha's behavior has an organic cause in part, and all the queenliness is in the same class as my gray hairs or my freckles."

24. Swados shared the editors' feeling that writers should get out into the world. As he wrote to SB in a letter of 14 April 1959: "Only The Nation wants me to do things . . . that involve seeing and talking to real living human beings. Everybody else wants to know what I think, sitting on my ass in the country, about the beats, the angries, and Jesus Christ Salinger, and it is all such a fucking bore I could scream."

25. SB to Josephine Herbst, 18 February 1959. See also, from same letter: "To some extent it will of course be literary, but we want to avoid overemphasis on literature. There'll be no criticism in it, or very little."

26. See SB, "Great and Not So Great Expectations," *The Noble Savage*, issue 3 (May 1961), reprinted in SB and Keith Botsford, eds. *Editors: The Best from Five Decades* (London: Toby Press, 2001), p. 11.

27. Atlas, *Biography*, p. 279.

28. Keith Botsford, email to the author, 30 July 2013.

29. Keith Botsford, "On the Facts," in SB and Botsford, eds., *Editors*, p. 5.

30. The letter to Slate, presumably undated, is quoted in Atlas, *Biography*, p. 281.

31. Alfred Kazin, 26 May 1961, Journal 47. Kazin's Journals are located in the Berg Collection of the New York Public Library. Unpublished entries involving SB were kindly provided to me by Richard M. Cook, ed. of *Alfred Kazin's Journals* (New Haven: Yale University Press, 2011). Atlas, *Biography*, p. 281, describes the quintessential *Noble Savage* piece as "caustic, irreverent, at once erudite and deflating of pretension."

32. Botsford replied to SB: "Frankly you are too ready to be suspicious of the motives of others," quoted in Atlas, *Biography*, p. 280. In Botsford's *Fragments VI*, he takes issue with Atlas's account: "Pace Jimmy Atlas or next-generation readers like Jim Burns, Saul was no Mother Hen with Jack and myself as quarrelsome chicks. Jack was early out: published once, he never re-surfaced" (p. 40). Ludwig was officially and unwillingly out by February 1961, when most of issue 3 (May 1961) had been assembled, though, as we've seen, according to SB he'd done little work for the issue.

33. SB, "Great and Not So Great Expectations," in SB and Botsford, eds., *Editors*, p. 7.

34. SB to Josephine Herbst, 19 February 1959, in which he also elaborates on his attitude to reviews: "I can't allow myself to brood on any of it, good or bad. I've seen more than one reader stop his work to concern himself for a year or two or three with the fate of a particular book then to discover that he had lost a thread." For reviews, see Miller, *Saul Bellow: A Biography of the Imagination*, p. 132: "Writing for the *New Republic*, a month after *Henderson* appeared, Reed Whittemore reviewed the early reviews and counted four approvals with qualifications, five disapprovals, with qualifications, and then he registered his vote and brought the tally to four and six." The Whittemore review was titled "Safari Among the Wariri," *New Republic*, 16 March 1959. On 6 April 1959, SB wrote to Pat Covici asking about sales: "you said it wouldn't sell a hundred fifty thousand copies. Of course not. But forty? Thirty? Even thirty would be very good. It would pay the mortgage at Tivoli." In the event, the novel failed to earn back his advance, amounting to $15,000. It lasted only three weeks on the bestseller list and in the end, according to Atlas, "just about" sold twenty thousand copies, "respectable sales but hardly a commercial triumph" (*Biography*, pp. 268, 276).

35. SB quotations from "I Got a Scheme!," p. 85.

36. Dwight Macdonald, no longer at *PR*, was so angered by Hardwick's review that he sent a letter of rebuttal to the magazine insisting that they print it in the same issue. SB himself wrote in protest to William Phillips on 13 July 1959: "Every

few months in *PR* your rats gnaw at my toes. It would be unnatural if I did not notice."

37. Orville Prescott voices similar complaints in his 23 February 1959 review in the daily *New York Times*: "many readers will probably conclude that Mr. Bellow has tried to convey it [the book's meaning or message] in an unfortunate form. His African background and his melodramatic adventures are not intended to be realistic. But somehow they can't be accepted as either fantasy or allegory. Too often they just seem silly. And Henderson himself is not an interesting character. It may well be that he actually resembles other wastrels who have tried to escape from themselves on expeditions to far places, but, for all his bluster and ego, all his kindness and humility, all his recondite references to art, literature and history, Henderson remains only a bore cursed with the most embarrassing flow of fancy talk in a library of recent fiction."

38. "I Got a Scheme!," p. 85.

39. Daniel Fuchs, *Saul Bellow: Vision and Revision* (Durham, NC: Duke University Press, 1984), p. 106, points to what he calls the "College Outline Romanticism" of an earlier version of the novel, which is "subdued" in revision: "the final version gives us a more sophisticated Romanticism." According to Atlas, *Biography*, p. 271n., "Bellow carried a copy of *The Portable Blake* around with him for years and told Richard Stern that when he was writing *Henderson* the lion imagery of 'Little Girl Lost' in *Songs of Innocence and [of] Experience* had 'sunk deeply' into his unconscious."

40. Eusebio L. Rodrigues, "Saul Bellow's Henderson as America," *The Centennial Review* 20, no. 2 (1976): 190.

41. Richard Stern, "Henderson's Bellow," *The Kenyon Review* 21, no. 4 (Autumn 1959): p. 66in.

42. Atlas, *Biography*, p. 272. For Daniel Fuchs, *Saul Bellow: Vision and Revision*, p. 112, "it was not Reich but Paul Schilder who was the greater influence. Bellow has explicitly said as much in a letter to the writer and translator Jascha Kessler: 'It was not . . . Reich who got me going in Henderson but a neurophysiologist named Paul Schilder whose book The Image and Idea (sic Appearance) of the Human Body came highly recommended.'" Schilder is explicitly named in manuscript versions but not in the finished novel.

43. Eusebio L. Rodrigues, "Reichianism in 'Henderson the Rain King,'" *Criticism* 15, no. 3 (Summer 1973): 225.

44. According to Fuchs, *Saul Bellow: Vision and Revision*, p. 111.

45. Manea, "Conversation," pp. 31, 18.

46. Miller, *Saul Bellow: A Biography of the Imagination*, p. 122.

47. David D. Galloway, "An Interview with Saul Bellow, *Audit-Poetry 3* (1963), reprinted in Cronin and Siegel, eds., *Conversations with SB*, p. 21.

48. Interview with Nina Steers, "Successor to Faulkner?," *Show* 4 1964, in Cronin and Siegel, eds., *Conversations with SB*, p. 34.

49. Manea, "Conversation," p. 48.

50. From an interview with the author. That the language of *Henderson* was made possible by *Augie*, SB himself suggests in a letter of 29 June 1960 to Susan Glassman: "I made the discovery in it [*Augie*, that is] about language and character from which *Henderson* arose."

51. "I Got a Scheme!," p. 85.

52. Fuchs, *Saul Bellow: Vision and Revision*, p. 100.

53. Podhoretz's review, "Saul Bellow's Power-Filled, Puzzling Novel of a Millionaire in Africa," appeared in the *New York Herald-Tribune* on 22 February 1959.

54. Atlas, *Biography*, p. 277.

55. SB to Covici, 27 February 1959. The letter from Malamud was dated

26 February; from Miller, 21 April 1959. On 18 March, the art historian Meyer Schapiro wrote to SB praising "the strange Africa you've created, which is neither the ethnologists' nor the modern traveller's—it is something more human, more poetic, too."

56. Harris was teaching at San Francisco State University and saw a letter of reference SB had written for Catherine Lindsay, who had applied for a teaching post there, which she got. He was so taken with the reference that he wrote instantly to SB praising both the letter and SB's fiction. In his account of this episode in *Saul Bellow: Drumlin Woodchuck* (Athens: University of Georgia Press, 1980), p. 10, Harris mentions that Lindsay "told me that she was Lily in *Henderson the Rain King*. True, she was one of 'these big beauties,' as Henderson calls her."

57. This anecdote, from Atlas, *Biography*, p. 277, was confirmed in an interview with Peltz, who admitted he had been unwise in trying to bring the two together again.

58. Greg Bellow, *Saul Bellow's Heart*, pp. 105, 106.

59. Atlas, *Biography*, p. 282, claims "Bellow had at least one fling with a student" at Minnesota.

60. Adam Bellow, "When My Parents Were in Love," *Talk Magazine*, October 1999.

61. Schwartz was a specialist in bankruptcy and corporate reorganization. He was a longtime member of the Minneapolis Urban League and the Minneapolis United Negro College Fund and according to an obituary in *The Minneapolis Tribune* (27 June 1966) "was the leader in many civil rights battles including the integration of the armed forces." With Walter Mondale, Schwartz successfully argued in the Supreme Court for the integration of the National Guard. He was also a union organizer and drew up Minnesota's fair employment practices legislation.

62. Atlas, *Biography*, p. 283.

63. Whether this is what is left of the $5,000 loan from Sasha's mother, or is another loan entirely, is not clear.

64. The caricature is cruel, but not wholly inaccurate, judging by the violence and volatility of Schwartz's language, in person and on paper. In a letter of 19 October 1960, SB wrote to Schwartz to say that "I don't want to get into an argument with you; I'm fond of you and I think your heart is in the right place" (he may have changed his mind over the course of the composition of *Herzog*). Toward the end of the letter he adds, "Greet the bourgeoisie of Minneapolis for me. They all come to your cellar to drink your whiskey and enjoy your emotional outbursts." This letter had been written in response to a letter of 14 October from Schwartz: "My one hope is that with the passing of time you will appreciate the unenviable position I have been in during this last year, both with respect to yourself and with respect to your former wife. Each time I think of the trouble we have given each other I feel like kicking myself. . . . At least I, in my own mind, feel that I have maintained my integrity to Adam, for whom as a lawyer, I had a primary responsibility." In an email of 20 September 2014, Schwartz's daughter, Miriam Schwartz Shelomith, writes: "I do remember the screaming bouts between Saul and Father in the living room. They were followed by tears and hugs being shared by the two men."

65. See Helen Grisky to SB, 21 April 1960: "Of course I knew Minneapolis wouldn't be gay for you and from your letter it sounded dreadful. . . . You mentioned London again. Please don't think I've kept a bad memory of our weekend. There was so much warmth in it, for me at least."

66. Jara Ribniker's letters are undated; she and SB stayed in touch into the 1970s. SB tried to get Alina Slesinska a show in the United States. See letter to SB of 18 April 1960 from Peter Selz, a curator at the Museum of Modern Art in New York: "I would be most happy to write her a letter welcoming her to New

York. . . . I could also mention that I will try to find a gallery connection for her in this country."

67. The Maude letter, dated 18 July 1960, gives no last name; she seems to have been an editor or publisher.

68. See SB, *To Jerusalem and Back*, p. 129. Maury and Sam Bellows helped the Westreichs to obtain their apartment and Lisa wrote to SB on 20 April 1960 sending kind regards to all "your noble family" and reiterating her thanks to "your dearest brothers." In a letter to SB of 18 July 1960, Lisa writes of opening a small café in Holon called Café Riga.

69. Ibid.

70. SB, ed. and intro., *Great Jewish Short Stories* (New York: Dell, 1963), pp. 14–15. According to Philip Siegelman, his wife, Ellen, helped SB to choose stories for the anthology.

71. SB adds that Babel could have written in Yiddish, which he knew well, having been in charge of publishing the stories of Sholom Aleichem in Yiddish.

72. SB, ed. and intro., *Great Jewish Short Stories*, p. 16.

73. Ibid.

74. The house was designed by Edwin Lutyens and previously owned by Sir Simon Marks of Marks and Spencer (Weidenfeld's first wife was a Sieff, a granddaughter of the firm's founder).

75. The Drabble quotations come from an obituary in *The Guardian*, 2 June 1989.

76. These quotations were transcribed by McCarthy's biographer, Frances Kiernan, and sent to SB on 28 February 1999 for checking. I have quoted from SB's undated hand-corrected versions, now among his papers in the Regenstein. Kiernan's biography was *Seeing Mary Plain: A Life of Mary McCarthy* (New York: W. W. Norton, 2000).

77. Atlas, *Biography*, p. 287.

78. After her mother's death in February 1961 following a brain operation in Chicago, Sasha eventually received $11,000 in her will. This money she used to move to Skokie, partly to look after her aunt Cookie, devastated by the death of her sister. Her father tried to get his hands on the money, Sasha claims, with the help of Sam Goldberg. Sasha's inheritance suggests that the $5,000 SB received from her mother, over which they fought so bitterly two years earlier, was unlikely to have been "everything she had," as Sasha claims in the memoir (p. 100), though doubtless Sasha did not know this at the time.

79. From an interview with Atlas, who quotes him in *Biography*, p. 296. Paul Meehl may have suggested Ellis as a therapist; he wrote the foreword to Daniel N. Weiner's *Albert Ellis: Passionate Skeptic* (New York: Praeger, 1988).

80. SB, "Ralph Ellison in Tivoli," *The Bardian* (Spring 1999), p. 11. This article is the prime source of further details of the two writers' time together at Tivoli; a second source is Rosette Lamont, "Bellow Observed: A Serial Portrait," *Mosaic: A Journal for the Comparative Study of Literature and Ideas* 8, no. 1 (Fall 1974).

81. According to Rampersad, *Ralph Ellison: A Biography*, p. 252, "Ralph's love of technological precision would extend even to brewing coffee, in which he would be schooled by a friend on the Tuskegee faculty. Saul Bellow remembered that 'he had been taught by a chemist to do it with ordinary laboratory paper filters and water at room temperature. The coffee then was heated in a bain-marie—a pot within a pot. Never allowed to boil. Using a thermometer at every brewing, he precisely kept the water between 195 and 200 degrees fahrenheit."

82. SB, "Ralph Ellison at Tivoli," p. 11.

83. Atlas, *Biography*, p. 301.

84. Rampersad, *Ralph Ellison: A Biography*, p. 376; see also SB, "Ralph Ellison in Tivoli," p. 12.

85. These quotations are from a typescript in the Regenstein of an address or tribute for Ellison written in 1996, different from SB's remarks at the 1998 memorial service for Ellison at the 92nd Street Y in New York.

86. See Richard Stern to SB, 19 May 1960: "The comments on your reading all indicate that it went extremely well, despite your encounter with a couple of the creeps. The one who asked about 'bad taste' really is a sewer."

87. Rosette Lamont, "Bellow Observed: A Serial Portrait," p. 248.

88. Atlas, *Biography*, p. 301.

89. Berryman was reporting to SB in a letter of 10 October 1960 about his visit to Minneapolis in June.

90. In her memoir, Sasha identifies the dental assistant as "Pat." Further identification may be provided in a letter to Ralph Ross, 12 June 1961, in which SB professes himself "surprised by your saying my wounds must be still raw. They seem to me fairly well-healed. . . . [Only] now and then a piece of 'intelligence' reaches me which re-opens old grievances. At Yale, last fall . . . I was accosted by someone who 'knew' from Pat Reeves etc., and that was disagreeable, of course."

91. The details concerning Ross come from Atlas, *Biography*, p. 305. The "Be a mensch" anecdote comes from interviews with Phil Siegelman and Mitzi McClosky; "Be a man" is how Sasha remembers Ross's advice in her memoir (p. 104).

92. As often in SB's correspondence, there is a bravura character to the passage, also some unclarity. The coupling of Ludwig and Sasha is clear, but what does "the meek shall inherit the hearse" mean? *"Fidelity"* is ironic and applies to them both, though to Ludwig in particular; "talent, character and *fidelity*" suggests him rather than her. The "matters" SB refers to in the letter are now clearly personal not editorial. *"Honi soit qui mal y pense"* ("Shame be to him who thinks evil of it" or "Evil be to him who evil thinks") is also ironic; impossible not to think badly of the behavior of Sasha and Ludwig, though the effects of doing so, of giving in to anger and suspicion, can be corrosive, lowering.

93. See Don Morrison, "Educational TV: Work for Unemployed Minds," *Minneapolis Sunday Times*, 3 July 1960.

94. Ludwig's refusal comes in an email of 19 April 2013 to his friend and ex-pupil Carolyn McGrath, who had forwarded an email from me asking if she thought it worth my while trying one more time to contact Ludwig. In my email I mentioned that what I'd written about Ludwig "he wouldn't like—it is all about people accusing him of being like Iago or in love with Bellow or overbearing or boastful. . . . It doesn't seem fair to have only such sources to draw on."

95. *Othello*, V.ii.304–05.

14. SUSAN/HERZOG

1. See undated letter to Gregory Bellow, conjecturally dated February and printed in Taylor, ed., *Letters*, pp. 213–14.

2. SB to Susan Glassman, 16 January 1961.

3. Keith Botsford, *Fragment VI* of his memoirs, *Fragments I–VI*, p. 328 (henceforth cited within the text by page numbers). For details of the memoir's forthcoming publication see Chapter 11, note 73.

4. The sentence is from p. 25 of an earlier draft of *Fragment VI*. See also, from the revised version, "Saul was a pretty big flea to drop in Jaime's ear" (p. 441).

5. Though SB smoked cigars early in his life, he had long given them up by 1961.

6. *Lechoncito* is the diminutive of *lechón*, meaning pig or suckling pig; so SB had not yet given up eating pork.

7. Atlas, *Biography*, p. 304. SB got on well with colleagues at the university,

who were also friends of Botsford's. He stayed in touch with Tom McMahon, who became chair of the English Department at Puerto Rico, and was a friend of Botsford's from Yale, and his wife, Penny; with Robert "Sing" Stephenson, who ran the Humanities program, and his much younger wife, Halle; and with Joseph Summer.

8. SB in testimonial letter, 29 March 1991. The letter is typed on Boston University stationery with "Kennedy, William" written in the top right corner but is without an address line. SB was to recommend Kennedy to Pat Covici.

9. William Kennedy, "The Art of Fiction No. 111," *The Paris Review* (Winter 1989): 5, online version.

10. Ibid., pp. 5, 3 online version.

11. Botsford can't remember the subject of SB's lecture.

12. Atlas, *Biography*, p. 254, says the talk was given "in the fall of 1957," presumably on a visit from Minnesota, where SB was living and teaching. It might also have been delivered in January or February 1958, when SB was living and teaching in Evanston (from 7 January to 22 March). Susan Glassman was born in 1933 and in an interview Roth says she was twenty-three at the time of SB's Hillel talk.

13. Roth thinks he'd seen SB once at a party at Richard Stern's in the period between the Hillel talk and their first meeting in Stern's creative writing class in May 1957. "I remember to this day his saying in response to something said in a jokey way, well Sondra keeps me on my toes, or something like that. And at the time, young stupid kid that I was, I sensed 'bad marriage.'"

14. In Roth's *The Facts: A Novelist's Autobiography* (1988; New York: Vintage, 1997), p. 96, he mentions that Josie, his tempestuous ex-lover, also attended the Hillel House talk: "Later in the evening, when I got back to my apartment, I found a scribbled note in my mailbox, tellingly succinct—and not even signed—to the effect that a rich and spoiled Jewish clotheshorse was exactly what I deserved."

15. Frank Glassman also treated SB's brother Sam and niece Lesha. He was a poker buddy of Sam's doctor.

16. In the course of searching for his mother's correspondence, Daniel Bellow showed me a thick packet of letters from rejected suitors. "All these guys going 'I want to kill myself,' all these tear-stained letters."

17. See Susan Glassman to SB, 29 January 1961: "I will confess that your crack about my earnestness made me sore."

18. Arnold Rampersad, *Ralph Ellison: A Biography* (2007; New York: Vintage, 2008), p. 380.

19. Atlas, *Biography*, p. 310.

20. SB to Botsford, 7 June 1961.

21. These reviews appeared in *The New York Times Book Review*, *The Nation*, the newly founded *New York Review of Books*, and *Saturday Review*. His movie reviews appeared in *Horizon* in the issues of September and November 1962 and January and March 1963. Among the films he reviewed were Buñuel's *Viridiana* (November 1962). For SB on film, see "At the Movies" in SB, *There Is Simply Too Much to Think About: Reflections from Seven Decades*, ed. Benjamin Taylor (New York: Viking, 2015), pp. 131–45.

22. SB, "Where Do We Go from Here? The Future of Fiction," delivered as the Hopwood Lecture at the University of Michigan, reprinted in the *Michigan Quarterly Review* 1, no. 1 (Winter 1962): 27.

23. As SB puts it in the *New York Times* article, on the one hand, "the living heirs of Henry James and Virginia Woolf . . . have receded altogether too far from externals, from observation. . . . They give us very little information. . . . The novel of sensibility has failed to represent society and become totally uninteresting"; on the other hand, "those writers who wish to meet the demands of information have perhaps been successful as social historians, but they have neglected

the higher forms of the imagination." Among SB's papers in the Regenstein is an essay entitled "On Fact and Feeling in the Novel," which makes similar points: "On the one side books like *Advise and Consent* [by Allen Drury, winner of the 1960 Pulitzer Prize; a novel about the workings of the United States Senate]; on the other, *Other Voices, Other Rooms* [an autobiographical novel of 1948 by Truman Capote]," an opposition that leads SB to conclude that "the time may have come for the recombination of information and feeling in the novel. . . . The problem of the novelist in this generation . . . is to discover how to return, after his long absence, to the world." I have been unable to discover if, where, or when this essay was published.

24. Alfred Kazin's letter is undated; Ralph Ross's letter is dated 21 January 1962; Harvey Swados's letter was written on 10 August 1961. After *Esquire* published a second extract from the novel in August 1963, Edward Hoagland wrote on 12 September to say "You're the very best we have, and, not only that, you're my Sherwood Anderson and I will forever be grateful to you." According to Volkening, in a letter to SB of 26 March 1963, SB received more for his extract ($1,000) than comparable extracts *Esquire* printed from Cheever ($750), Nabokov ($350), and Flannery O'Connor ($350).

25. Elizabeth Hardwick to SB, 13 January 1961.

26. SB to Keith Botsford, 24 July 1961.

27. Susan Dworkin's comments on the Wagner State writer's course come from her article in the March 1977 issue of *Ms.* magazine, "The Great Man Syndrome: Saul Bellow and Me," republished in the *Chicago Daily News*, 5 May 1977.

28. Atlas, *Biography*, p. 310.

29. Atlas, *Biography*, p. 312.

30. See, for example, Erich Auerbach, *Mimesis: The Representation of Reality in Western Literature* (1946; Princeton: Princeton University Press, 1968), p. 551, with the novels of Virginia Woolf and James Joyce most immediately in mind: "There is often something confusing, something hazy about them, something hostile to the reality which they represent. We not infrequently find a turning away from the practical will to live, or delight in portraying it under its more brutal forms. There is hatred of culture and civilization, brought out by means of the subtlest stylistic devices which culture and civilization have developed, and often a radical and fanatical urge to destroy. Common to almost all of these novels is haziness, vague indefinability of meaning: precisely the kind of uninterpretable symbolism which is also to be encountered in other forms of art of the same period."

31. Michael C. Kotkin, "Remembering Saul Bellow," *JUF News*, May 2005 (a publication of the Jewish United Fund of Chicago).

32. The "Aria," entitled "White House and Artists," is reprinted in SB, *IAAU*, p. 69.

33. Atlas, *Biography*, p. 317.

34. A remark not mentioned in SB's "Aria." For a recent acount of the remark and the evening, see Mark White, *A Cultural History of an American Icon* (London: Bloomsbury, 2013), p. 44.

35. Atlas, *Biography*, p. 317, quotes SB as saying: "The next day I realized the president had spent the whole evening talking to David Rockefeller about fiscal matters."

36. SB, "Literary Notes on Khrushchev," *Esquire*, March 1961, reprinted in SB, *IAAU.*

37. Among the SB papers in the Regenstein are several Fundamentals lists circulated to Committee faculty, SB included. Here are two lists, the first from 1966, the second from 1967: List 1: Aristophanes, *Clouds, Frogs*; Aristotle, *Ethics, Poetics*; Augustine, *De Ordine*; Herodotus, *History*; Homer, *Odyssey*; Kant, *Critique of Pure Reason*; Paul, *Romans*; Plato, *Apology, Crito, Republic*; Ranke, *History of the Popes*;

Sophocles, *Philoctetes, Oedipus at Colonus*; Tolstoy, *War and Peace*; Whitehead, *Science and the Modern World, Adventures of Ideas*, part one. List 2: Shakespeare, *Richard III, Othello, Macbeth, The Tempest*; Ibsen, *Hedda Gabler, The Master Builder, When We Dead Awaken*; Faulkner, *Light in August*; Melville, *Billy Budd*; Plato, *Apology, Crito, Phaedo*; Aristotle, *Ethics, Poetics*; Spinoza, *Ethics*; Nietzsche, *Genealogy of Morals*; Husserl, *Cartesian Meditations*; Thucydides, *Peloponnesian War*, Marx, *The Eighteenth Brumaire of Louis Bonaparte*.

38. Joseph Epstein, "My Friend Edward," in Edward Shils, *Portraits: A Gallery of Intellectuals*, ed. and intro. Joseph Epstein (Chicago: University of Chicago Press, 1997), pp. 6, 23 (henceforth cited within the text by page numbers).

39. Atlas, *Biography*, p. 316.

40. Adam Bellow's memories of visits with his father during the warring period between his parents are understandably disturbing. What he remembers of relations with his father when he was three is that "I would somehow find myself in the Loop. There'd be a handoff, like a football. He'd take me somewhere. . . . We wouldn't talk very much and he'd ask me questions as though I were a stranger, and then there would always come a point when my mother would come up, as a subject . . . and then he'd become very angry." At this period, "I was very jittery and scared of my father. I would usually wet the bed after I saw him."

41. See Daniel Fuchs, *Saul Bellow: Vision and Revision* (Durham, NC: Duke University Press, 1984), p. 141.

42. Reviews of *Herzog*: Stanley Edgar Hyman, "Saul Bellow's Glittering Eye," *The New Leader*, 28 September 1964; Irving Howe, "Odysseus, Flat on His Back," *The New Republic*, 19 September 1964; Philip Rahv, "Bellow the Brain King," *New York Herald-Tribune*, 20 September 1964; Richard Ellmann, "Search for the Internal Something: Herzog," *Chicago Sun-Times Book Week*, 27 September 1964.

43. Atlas, *Biography*, p. 328.

44. See William Blake, "The Divine Image," *Songs of Innocence and of Experience*. Here are the poem's closing stanzas:

> *For Mercy has a human heart,*
> *Pity a human face,*
> *And Love, the human form divine,*
> *And Peace, the human dress.*
>
> *Then every man, of every clime,*
> *That prays in his distress,*
> *Prays to the human form divine,*
> *Love, Mercy, Pity, Peace.*
>
> *And all must love the human form,*
> *In heathen, turk, or jew;*
> *Where Mercy, Love, & Pity dwell*
> *There God is dwelling too.*

In an early draft of the novel, Herzog calls Blake "the only writer he could bear reading nowadays" (Fuchs, *Saul Bellow: Vision and Revision*, p. 177).

45. Philip Roth, from p. 26 of Roth SB interview transcript, dated 2 December 1999 (in the Regenstein), one of several interviews from which "I Got a Scheme!" is drawn.

46. See Hyman's review of *Herzog*, "Saul Bellow's Glittering Eye."

47. Fuchs, *Saul Bellow: Vision and Revision*, p. 158.

48. This striking phrase is Fuchs's, ibid.

49. SB, "The Civilized Barbarian Reader," *New York Times Book Review*, 8 March 1987.

50. Fuchs, *Saul Bellow: Vision and Revision*, p. 130.

51. This phrase is quoted in an interview by Walter Pozen, SB's friend, a lawyer and an executor of his estate. Sales figures and best-seller figures from Atlas, *Biography*, p. 339.

52. Manea, "Conversation," p. 23. Early in the novel, the zoologist Luke Asphalter expresses naive surprise that Herzog hadn't guessed about Madeleine's affair, because, as he tells him, "your intelligence is so high—well off the continuum" (p. 460).

53. Botsford interview, "A Second Half Life," reprinted in SB, *IAAU*, p. 322.

54. John Bayley, "By Way of Mr. Sammler," *Salmagundi* 30 (Summer 1975), quoted in Fuchs, *Saul Bellow: Vision and Revision*, p. 162.

55. Ellen Pifer, *Saul Bellow Against the Grain* (Philadelphia: University of Pennsylvania Press, 1990), p. 126.

56. Rosette Lamont, "The Confessions of Moses Herzog," *Massachusetts Review* 6, no. 3 (Spring–Summer 1965): 635. Early in the novel, Lamont recalls, Herzog writes to Gandhi's disciple Dr. Vinoba Bhave, leader of the Bhudan Yajna movement. In the letter he describes himself as having always wanted "*to lead a moral, useful, active life*" (p. 464). The letter breaks off mid-thought, but we are told that "what he had vaguely in mind was to offer his house and property in Ludeyville to the Bhave movement," though he then thinks "what could Bhave do with it? Send Hindus to the Berkshires?" (p. 465). Lamont sees Herzog at the novel's close as "divesting himself of personality" rather than property, reaching out "to God, and to all others."

57. Ibid., p. 633. In *Herzog*, pp. 488–89, it is Madeleine, in the role of eager graduate student, who is enthusiastic about Soloviev and Berdyaev.

58. Leo Tolstoy, *Anna Karenina*, tr. David Magarshack (1877; New York: New American Library, 1961), p. 807.

59. Ted Solotaroff, "Napoleon St. and After," review of *Herzog*, in *Commentary*, December 1964.

60. Roger Sale, "Provincial Champions and Grandmasters," review of *Herzog*, in *The Hudson Review* 17, no. 4 (Winter 1964–65): 618.

61. Richard Poirier, "How Far Shall I Take This Character?," review of James Atlas, *Saul Bellow: A Biography*, in *London Review of Books*, 2 November 2000. This is the source of further quotations from Poirier about his relations with SB. Leya is sometimes Leah in correspondence.

62. William Phillips, *A Partisan View: Five Decades of the Literary Life* (New York: Stein & Day, 1983), p. 275.

63. SB resigned from the Century Association on 27 June 1977. His letter of resignation read: "Gentlemen: I am afraid it is time for me with great regret to resign from the Century Club. In recent years people have been elected to membership whom I would avoid in the street, much less wish to greet as fellow Centurions. I have of course many good friends in the Club, but I can arrange to meet these privately on my infrequent visits to the city. Sincerely yours, Saul Bellow." See also SB to Fred Kaplan, 10 February 1978: "I resigned from the Century Club because Poirier and Wm. Phillips were admitted to membership. I *am*, after all, some sort of snob myself. You and I used to discuss snobbism; it was one of our subjects, do you remember? I said in resigning that there were people I simply didn't care to meet in the club rooms. My letter was posted on the bulletin board as evidence of my unbelievable effrontery. All this gave me the greatest pleasure. . . . I am not one of your *resigned* types. One fights on."

64. Richard Poirier, "Bellows to Herzog," *Partisan Review* 2 (Spring 1965): 271 (henceforth cited within the text by page numbers).

65. The Montherlant quotation is a well-known abbreviated form of a line from his play *Don Juan* (1958): "Le Bonheur écrit à l'encre blanche sur des pages

blanches" (2.4.1048); the Blake quotation about Milton is from plate 5 of *The Marriage of Heaven and Hell* (1790–93).

66. Bruce Cook, "Saul Bellow: A Mood of Protest," *Perspectives on Ideas and the Arts*, 12 February 1963, reprinted in Cronin and Siegel, eds., *Conversations with SB*, p. 7. Mailer was somewhat less pugnacious in private, as in a letter to William Styron of 7 October 1954, quoted in J. Michael Lennon, *Norman Mailer: A Double Life* (New York: Simon & Schuster, 2013), p. 174: "I found it impressive but somehow unexciting. Really the damndest book—I have to admire his courage, his ambition, his 'openness' to try anything and everything, but the pieces are more exciting than the whole, and nothing in it really disturbs one."

67. See Norman Mailer, "Norman Mailer Versus Nine Writers: Further Evaluations of the Talent in the Room," *Esquire*, July 1963. The article was accompanied by a full-page photo of Mailer by Diane Arbus. He is shown in suit and tie standing in the corner of a boxing ring with a belligerent expression on his face.

68. Nina Steers, "Successor to Faulkner?," *Show* 4, September 1964, reprinted in Cronin and Siegel, eds., *Conversations with SB*, p. 35.

69. These quotations are from Lennon, *Norman Mailer: A Double Life*, p. 348, drawn from reports of a press conference on 11 March 1965 arranged by the Publishers Publicity Association as part of the National Book Award events. *Herzog* had won the fiction award the day before. The first quote is from a report in *The Kansas City Star* (date not given), the second from the *Boston Herald*, 14 March 1965.

70. Phillips, *A Partisan Review*, pp. 117–18.

71. James Barszcz, "Introduction: The Work of Knowing Richard Poirier," in *College Hill Review* 5 (Winter–Spring 2010), reprinted in http://www.collegehillreview.com/005/print/p0050101.html.

72. Lewis Nichols, "In and Out of Books," *New York Times Book Review*, 10 January 1965, quoted in Atlas, *Biography*, p. 340.

73. L. C. Knights, "How Many Children Had Lady Macbeth? An Essay in the Theory and Practice of Shakespeare Criticism" (1933), reprinted in *Explorations: Essays in Criticism Mainly on the Literature of the Seventeenth Century* (1946; New York: George P. Stewart, 1947).

74. Jack Ludwig, *Above Ground* (1968; Toronto: McClelland & Stewart, 1974) (henceforth cited within the text by page numbers).

75. The letters Mavra sends are about other lovers. In real life, Sasha claims, Ludwig's paranoia took the form of jealous suspicions. In the period just before she moved to Tarrytown, these suspicions were especially intense, she recalled in an interview: "And finally I said I have to do something. . . . So I came east and I lived in Tarrytown and it started to get worse and worse and I saw nobody. Then . . . I made a really critical and stupid decision. I decided to confess. Confess what? I decided—it's so embarrassing . . . [this has] got to be one of the most bizarre things . . . if I could enter into this madness we could work through it. . . . He managed to convince me that all I had to do was confess [to "adulteries," thus showing he wasn't crazy]. . . . It was a kind of brainwashing that I was susceptible to—[he had a] very powerful way about him. . . . And I was extremely vulnerable." Did Sasha's "confessions" of going with other men take the form of letters? When SB described the Mavra letters as written by her, she denied it in an undated response, written sometime after September 4, 1968: "I never saw a word of the manuscript beyond the first third, and my first view of it was an inscribed copy sent from England. I was your friend, truly, when I told you never to read it. . . . I wanted to spare you the shock and horror I experienced. . . . Can you imagine what I must have felt thinking I was loved and respected and honored only to open to a sheer act of murder? I was all alone with that, Saul, and thought I would completely lose

my mind. If there had been a grain of truth in it, if I had deserved it even on a symbolic level, I could have coped with it somehow. . . . But this thing is not merely a distortion, but a vicious crucifixion of the humanity involved. I am surprised you fell into his trap. He is clever enough to hit upon my tone, rather convincingly, and the only quality the book has is in the occasional level set by the various women who all tend to talk in my voice here and there. But you know I don't and never did write letters like that, and that I may be angry and sometimes ugly but not coarse and vulgar."

76. Ruth Miller, SB's friend and ex-pupil, was on the English faculty at Stony Brook at the time, a colleague of Ludwig's and a friend of the family. "In 1965–66," she writes, in *Saul Bellow: A Biography of the Imagination* (New York: St. Martin's, 1991), p. 179, "the Ludwigs rented my house in Roslyn, Long Island, while my family and I went off for a Fulbright year in India; they remained in Roslyn on our return. It was curious to me to listen to Leah [Leya] Ludwig's description of her situation, telling me as she formed the little dough packets for her verenikes, or tossed the crepes for her blintzes, that she really didn't care about Sondra and Jack, or *Herzog* and *Above Ground*; she had a fine house, lovely children—so she did— a good income, and what did Sondra have? Jack." Only Sondra didn't, not for long. Miller remembered Ludwig at this time as "a popular and prestigious member of the English Department, driving a showy Jaguar, sort of moving and shaking students, faculty, and administration alike. Bellow sighed. He had probably paid for the Jaguar."

Index

Works by Saul Bellow (SB) appear directly under title; works by others under author's name. Page numbers in *italic* refer to illustrations in text.

PERMISSIONS ACKNOWLEDGMENTS

Grateful acknowledgment is made to the following for permission to reprint previously unpublished material:

Rosie Alison: Excerpt of letter from Barley Alison to Saul Bellow, December 12, 1960. Reprinted by permission of Rosie Alison.

Linda Asher: Excerpt of letter from Aaron Asher to Saul Bellow, December 23, 1964. Reprinted by permission of Linda Asher.

Monique Behrstock: Excerpt of letter from Julian Behrstock to Saul Bellow, February 23, 1995. Reprinted by permission of Monique Behrstock.

Dean Borok: Excerpts of letters from Dean Borok to Saul Bellow, December 12, 1977, and November 24, 1990. Reprinted by permission of Dean Borok.

Keith Botsford: Excerpt from *Fragments* by Keith Botsford. Reprinted by permission of Keith Botsford.

Joan C. Covici: Excerpt of letter from Pascal Covici to Saul Bellow, November 8, 1955. Reprinted by permission of Joan C. Covici.

Monroe Engel: Excerpt of undated letter from Monroe Engel to Saul Bellow. Reprinted by permission of Monroe Engel.

Joseph Epstein: Excerpt of letter from Edward Shils to Saul Bellow, September 12, 1963. Reprinted by permission of Joseph Epstein.

Lindsay Harris: Excerpt from "I Come to Bury Caesar" by Sydney J. Harris. Reprinted by permission of Lindsay Harris.

William R. Goetz: Excerpt of letter from John Goetz to Saul Bellow, December 6, 1975. Reprinted by permission of William R. Goetz, personal representative of the Estate of John R. Goetz.

Lynn Hoffman: Excerpt of letter from Ted Hoffman to Saul Bellow, January 5, 1950. Reprinted by permission of Lynn Hoffman.

Carol Alane Rollings: Excerpt of undated letter from Richard Stern to Saul Bellow. Reprinted by permission of Carol Alane Rollings, sole literary executor and custodian of Richard Stern's work.

Eleni Sarant Rosenfeld: Excerpt of letter from Isaac Rosenfeld to Saul Bellow, September 29, 1953. Reprinted by permission of Eleni Sarant Rosenfeld.

Andrea Tamkin and Ruth H. Tamkin: Excerpt of letter from Arthur S. Tamkin to Saul Bellow, December 24, 1956. Reprinted by permission of Andrea Tamkin and Ruth H. Tamkin.

The Wylie Agency LLC: Excerpt of journal entry dated May 26, 1961, by Alfred Kazin, copyright © 1961 by Alfred Kazin; excerpts of letters from Arthur Miller to Saul Bellow, June 2, 1956, and July 8, 1956, copyright © 1956 by Arthur Miller. Reprinted by permission of The Wylie Agency LLC.

A NOTE ON THE TYPE

This book was set in Janson, a typeface long thought to have been made by the Dutchman Anton Janson, who was a practicing typefounder in Leipzig during the years 1668–1687. However, it has been conclusively demonstrated that these types are actually the work of Nicholas Kis (1650–1702), a Hungarian, who most probably learned his trade from the master Dutch typefounder Dirk Voskens. The type is an excellent example of the influential and sturdy Dutch types that prevailed in England up to the time William Caslon (1692–1766) developed his own incomparable designs from them.

Composed by North Market Street Graphics,
Lancaster, Pennsylvania

Printed and bound by Berryville Graphics,
Berryville, Virginia

Designed by Cassandra J. Pappas